Less managing. More teaching. Greater learning.

INSTRUCTORS...

Would you like your **students** to show up for class more **prepared**? *(Let's face it, class is much more fun if everyone is engaged and prepared...)*

Want ready-made application-level **interactive assignments,** student progress reporting, and auto-assignment grading? *(Less time grading means more time teaching...)*

Want an **instant view of student or class performance** relative to learning objectives? *(No more wondering if students understand...)*

Need to **collect data and generate reports** required for administration or accreditation? *(Say goodbye to manually tracking student learning outcomes...)*

Want to **record and post your lectures** for students to view online?

With **McGraw-Hill's *Connect*™ Management,**

INSTRUCTORS GET:

- Interactive Applications – **book-specific interactive assignments** that require students to APPLY what they've learned.

- Simple **assignment management,** allowing you to spend more time teaching.

- **Auto-graded** assignments, quizzes, and tests.

- **Detailed Visual Reporting** where student and section results can be viewed and analyzed.

- Sophisticated **online testing** capability.

- A **filtering and reporting** function that allows you to easily assign and report on materials that are correlated to accreditation standards, learning outcomes, and Bloom's taxonomy.

- An easy-to-use **lecture capture** tool.

STUDENTS...

Want an online, **searchable version** of your textbook?

Wish your textbook could be **available online** while you're doing your assignments?

 ### Connect™ Plus Management eBook

If you choose to use *Connect™ Plus Management*, you have an affordable and searchable online version of your book integrated with your other online tools.

Connect™ Plus Management eBook offers features like:

- Topic search
- Direct links from assignments
- Adjustable text size
- Jump to page number
- Print by section

 ## STUDENTS...

Want to get more **value** from your textbook purchase?

Think learning management should be a bit more **interesting**?

 ### Check out the STUDENT RESOURCES section under the *Connect™* Library tab.

Here you'll find a wealth of resources designed to help you achieve your goals in the course. You'll find things like **quizzes, PowerPoints, and Internet activities** to help you study. Every student has different needs, so explore the STUDENT RESOURCES to find the materials best suited to you.

management

A PRACTICAL INTRODUCTION

fifth edition

Angelo Kinicki

Arizona State University

Brian K. Williams

**McGraw-Hill
Irwin**

MANAGEMENT: A PRACTICAL INTRODUCTION

Published by McGraw-Hill/Irwin, a business unit of The McGraw-Hill Companies, Inc., 1221 Avenue of the Americas, New York, NY, 10020. Copyright © 2011, 2009, 2008, 2006, 2003 by The McGraw-Hill Companies, Inc. All rights reserved. No part of this publication may be reproduced or distributed in any form or by any means, or stored in a database or retrieval system, without the prior written consent of The McGraw-Hill Companies, Inc., including, but not limited to, in any network or other electronic storage or transmission, or broadcast for distance learning.

Some ancillaries, including electronic and print components, may not be available to customers outside the United States.

This book is printed on acid-free paper.

1 2 3 4 5 6 7 8 9 0 QDB/QDB 1 0 9 8 7 6 5 4 3 2 1 0

ISBN   978-0-07-811271-3
MHID   0-07-811271-0

Vice president and editor-in-chief: *Brent Gordon*
Editorial director: *Paul Ducham*
Executive editor: *Michael Ablassmeir*
Executive director of development: *Ann Torbert*
Development editor II: *Laura Griffin*
Editorial assistant: *Andrea Heirendt*
Vice president and director of marketing: *Robin J. Zwettler*
Marketing director: *Amee Mosley*
Executive marketing manager: *Anke Braun Weekes*
Marketing coordinator: *Annie Ferro*
Vice president of editing, design, and production: *Sesha Bolisetty*
Lead project manager: *Harvey Yep / Pat Frederickson*
Senior buyer: *Michael R. McCormick*
Interior designer: *Pam Verros*
Senior photo research coordinator: *Jeremy Cheshareck*
Photo researcher: *Judy Mason*
Senior media project manager: *Greg Bates*
Media project manager: *Cathy L. Tepper*
Cover design: *Pam Verros*
Cover image: *© Jon Arnold Images / Masterfile*
Typeface: *10.5/12 Times New Roman*
Compositor: *Aptara®, Inc.*
Printer: *Quad/Graphics*

Library of Congress Cataloging-in-Publication Data

Kinicki, Angelo.
    Management : a practical introduction / Angelo Kinicki, Brian K. Williams.—5th ed.
        p. cm.
    Includes index.
    ISBN-13: 978-0-07-811271-3 (alk. paper)
    ISBN-10: 0-07-811271-0 (alk. paper)
    1. Management. I. Williams, Brian K. II. Title.
HD31.K474 2011
658—dc22
                                                                                    2010030319

brief contents

ABOUT THE

authors

Angelo Kinicki is a professor of management at the W. P. Carey School of Business at Arizona State University. He also was awarded the Weatherup/Overby Chair in Leadership in 2005. He has held his current position since 1982, when he received his doctorate in organizational behavior from Kent State University.

Angelo is recognized for both his teaching and research. As a teacher, Angelo has been the recipient of several awards, including the Outstanding Teaching Award—MBA and Master's Programs (2007–2008) the John W. Teets Outstanding Graduate Teacher Award (2009–2010), Graduate Teaching Excellence Award (1998–1999), Continuing Education Teaching Excellence Award (1991–1992), and Undergraduate Teaching Excellence Award (1987–1988). He also was selected into Wikipedia, Who's Who of American Colleges and Universities, and Beta Gamma Sigma. Angelo is an active researcher. He has published over 80 articles in a variety of leading academic and professional journals and has coauthored six college textbooks (20, counting revisions). His textbooks have been used by hundreds of universities around the world. Angelo's experience as a researcher also resulted in his selection to serve on the editorial review boards for the *Academy of Management Journal, the Journal of Vocational Behavior,* and the *Journal of Management.* He received the "All-Time Best Reviewer Award" from the *Academy of Management Journal* for the period of 1996–1999.

Angelo also is an active international consultant who works with top management teams to create organizational change aimed at increasing organizational effectiveness and profitability. He has worked with many Fortune 500 firms as well as numerous entrepreneurial organizations in diverse industries. His expertise includes facilitating strategic/operational planning sessions, diagnosing the causes of organizational and work-unit problems, implementing performance management systems, designing and implementing performance appraisal systems, developing and administering surveys to assess employee attitudes, and leading management/executive education programs. He developed a 360° leadership feedback instrument called the Performance Management Leadership Survey (PMLS) that is used by companies throughout the United States and Europe.

One of Angelo's strengths is his ability to teach students at all levels within a university. He uses an interactive environment to enhance undergraduates' understanding about management and organizational behavior. He focuses MBAs on applying management concepts to solve complex problems; PhD students learn the art and science of conducting scholarly research.

Angelo and his wife, Joyce, have enjoyed living in the beautiful Arizona desert for 28 years but are natives of Cleveland, Ohio. They enjoy traveling, golfing, and hiking with Nala, their golden retriever.

Brian Williams has been managing editor for college textbook publisher Harper & Row/Canfield Press in San Francisco; editor-in-chief for nonfiction trade-book publisher J. P. Tarcher in Los Angeles; publications and communications manager for the University of California, Systemwide Administration, in Berkeley; and an independent writer and book producer based in the San Francisco and Lake Tahoe areas. He has a B.A. in English and an M.A. in communication from Stanford University. He has coauthored 20 books (52, counting revisions), which include such best-selling college texts as *Using Information Technology* with his wife, Stacey C. Sawyer, being revised in its tenth edition with McGraw-Hill. He has also written a number of other information technology books, college success books, and health and social science texts. In his spare time, he and Stacey enjoy travel, music, cooking, hiking, and exploring the wilds of the American West.

dedication

To Laci Goretcki, for your continued efforts and dedication toward the success of our company and my books. We could not do what we do without you. You are a tremendous member of the team.

—A.K.

To my wife, Stacey, for her 25 years of steadfast, patient support and for her collaboration and shared adventures; and to my beloved children and their families—Sylvia, Scott, and Atticus; and Kirk, Julia, Nicolas, and Lily.

—B.K.W.

A promise: To make learning management easy, efficient, and effective

The fifth edition of *Management: A Practical Introduction*—a concepts book for the introductory course in management—uses a wealth of instructor feedback to identify which features from prior editions worked best and which should be improved and expanded. By blending Angelo's scholarship, teaching, and management-consulting experience with Brian's writing and publishing background, we have again tried to create a research-based yet highly readable, innovative, and practical text.

Our primary goal is simple to state but hard to execute: to make learning principles of management as easy, effective, and efficient as possible. Accordingly, the book integrates writing, illustration, design, and magazine-like layout in **a program of learning that appeals to the visual sensibilities and respects the time constraints and different learning styles of today's students.** In an approach initially tested in our first edition and fine-tuned in the subsequent editions, **we break topics down into easily grasped portions** and incorporate **frequent use of various kinds of reinforcement techniques.** Our hope, of course, is to make a difference in the lives of our readers: to produce a text that students will enjoy reading and that will provide them with practical benefits.

The text covers the principles that most management instructors have come to expect in an introductory text—planning, organizing, leading, and controlling—plus the issues that today's students need to be aware of to succeed: customer focus, globalism, diversity, ethics, information technology, entrepreneurship, work teams, the service economy, and small business.

Beyond these, our book has **four features that make it unique:**

1. A student-centered approach to learning.
2. Imaginative writing for readability and reinforcement.
3. Emphasis on practicality.
4. Resources that work.

> "Kinicki/Williams is an effective principles of management textbook that does an excellent job of conveying the excitement of management and leadership to undergraduates. Engaging and practical, it comes with a comprehensive set of support materials that range from the traditional to exciting new uses of technology that supercharge the teaching of critical concepts. We looked at over ten textbooks before we adopted Kinicki, and we're most certainly glad that we did. Publisher support has been excellent."
>
> —**Gary B. Roberts,**
> *Kennesaw State University*

A Student-Centered Approach to Learning

CHAPTER OPENERS: Designed to help students read with purpose

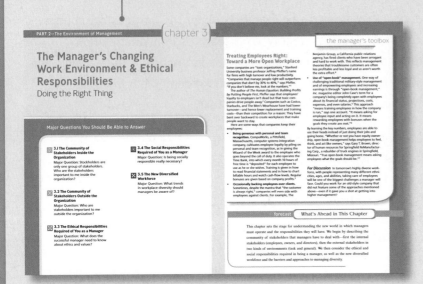

Each chapter begins with four to eight provocative, motivational **Major Questions,** written to appeal to students' concern about "what's in it for me?" and help them read with purpose and focus.

Instead of opening with the conventional case, as most texts do, we open with **The Manager's Toolbox,** a motivational device offering practical nuts-and-bolts advice pertaining to the chapter content students are about to read—and allowing for class discussion.

CHAPTER SECTIONS:

Structured into constituent parts for easier learning

Chapters are organized to cover each major question in turn, giving students bite-sized chunks of information. Each section begins with a recap of the **Major Question** and includes **"The Big Picture,"** which presents students with an overview of how the section they are about to read answers the Major Question.

"This style textbook succeeds in presenting management information with a fresh face. Each chapter is filled with current and useful information for students. The chapters begin by asking major questions of the reader. As the student reads, they are engaged by these questions and by the information that follows. A totally readable text with great illustrations and end of chapter exercises!"

—**Catherine Ruggieri,** *St. John's University, New York*

Chapter tools help students learn how to learn

In focus groups, symposiums, and reviews, instructors told us that many students do not have the skills needed to succeed in college. To support students in acquiring these skills, we offer the following:

---

the manager's toolbo

A One-Minute Guide to Success in This Class

Got one minute to read this section? It could mean the difference between getting an A instead of a B. Or a B instead of a C.

It is our desire to *make this book as practical as possible for you.* One place we do this is in the Manager's Toolbox, like this one, which appears at the beginning of every chapter and which offers practical advice appropriate to the subject matter you are about to explore. Here we show you how to be a success in this course.

Four Rules for Success

The following four rules will help you be successful in this (or any other) course.

- **Rule 1:** Attend every class. No cutting allowed.
- **Rule 2:** Don't postpone studying, then cram the night before a test.
- **Rule 3:** Read or review lectures and readings more than once.
- **Rule 4:** Learn how to use this book.

How to Use This Book Most Effectively

When reading this book, follow the steps below:

- Get an overview of the chapter by reading over the first page, which contains the section headings and Major Questions.
- Read "Forecast: What's Ahead in This Chapter."

"A One-Minute Guide to Success in This Class," found on page 3, lays down four rules for student success in class and suggestions for how to use this book most effectively.

"Getting Control of Your Time: Dealing with the Information Deluge in College & in Your Career," at the end of Chapter I, gives students a crash course in time management skills, solid study habits, memory aids, and learning from lectures.

Practical Action

Getting Control of Your Time: Dealing with the Information Deluge in College & in Your Career

Professionals and managers all have to deal with this central problem: how not to surrender their lives to their jobs. The place to start, however, is in college. If you can learn to manage time while you're still a student, you'll find it will pay off not only in higher grades and more free time but also in more efficient information-handling skills that will serve you well as a manager later on.

Using Your "Prime Study Time"

Each of us has a different energy cycle. The trick is to use it effectively. That way, your hours of best performance will coincide with your heaviest academic demands. For example, if your energy level is high during the evenings, you should plan to do your studying then.

the least effective means of absorbing information. Research shows that it's best to space out your studying of a subject over successive days. A series of study sessions over several days is preferable to trying to do it all during the same number of hours on one day. It is repetition that helps move information into your long-term memory bank.

Review Information Repeatedly—Even "Overlearn It"

By repeatedly reviewing information—what is known as "rehearsing"—you can improve both your retention and your understanding of it. Overlearning is continuing to review material even after you appear to have absorbed it.

Use Memorizing Tricks

The Systems Viewpoint

The 52 bones in the foot. The monarchy of Great Britain. A weather storm front. Each of these is a system. **A *system* is a set of interrelated parts that operate together to achieve a common purpose.** Even though a system may not work very well—as in the inefficient way the Russian government collects taxes, for example—it is nevertheless still a system.

The *systems viewpoint* **regards the organization as a system of interrelated parts.** By adopting this point of view, you can look at your organization both as (1) a collection of *subsystems*—**parts making up the whole system**—and (2) a part of the larger environment. A college, for example, is made up of a collection of academic departments, support staffs, students, and the like. But it also exists as a system within the environment of education, having to be responsive to parents, alumni, legislators, nearby townspeople, and so on.

Key terms are highlighted and terms and definitions are in boldface, to help students build their management vocabulary.

Other devices to help students develop understanding:

- Important **scholar names in boldface** so students remember key contributors to the field of management.
- Frequent use of **advance organizers, bulleted lists, and headings** to help students grasp the main ideas.
- **Illustrations positioned close to relevant text discussion** so students can refer to them more easily and avoid flipping pages.

- A *policy* **is a standing plan that outlines the general response to a designated problem or situation.** Example: "This workplace does not condone swearing." This policy is a broad statement that gives managers a general idea about what is allowable for employees who use bad language, but gives no specifics.

- A *procedure* (or *standard operating procedure*) **is a standing plan that outlines the response to particular problems or circumstances.** Example: White Castle specifies exactly how a hamburger should be dressed, including the order in which the mustard, ketchup, and pickles are applied.

- A *rule* **is a standing plan that designates specific required action.** Example: "No smoking is allowed anywhere in the building." This allows no room for interpretation.

"It's hard enough to try to make the class exciting, and the only way is to incorporate up-to-date, relevant, and interesting examples. This text and McGraw-Hill have done just that. [It] makes my life easier, but more importantly, the students are getting the valuable education that they've paid for by having better materials and instruction."

—Laura L. Alderson, *University of Memphis*

Imaginative Writing for Readability

Research shows that textbooks written in **an imaginative, people-oriented style significantly improve students' ability to retain information.** We employ a number of journalistic devices to make the material as engaging as possible for students.

We **use colorful facts, attention-grabbing quotes, biographical sketches, and lively tag lines** to get students' attention as they read.

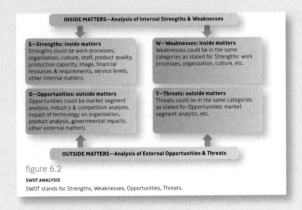

figure 6.2

SWOT ANALYSIS
SWOT stands for Strengths, Weaknesses, Opportunities, Threats.

Example

Crisis Leading to the Strategic-Management Process: JetBlue Weathers an Ice Storm

Founded in 1998, JetBlue started out as a low-fare airline, promising fares up to 65% lower than competitors along with, in one description, "creature comforts like assigned seating, leather upholstery, and satellite TV on individual screens in every seat."[29] The formula was an immediate hit, and by 2007 JetBlue had grown from 6 daily flights and 300 employees to 575 daily flights to 52 destinations and 9,300 employees.

Then in 2005, the founder, David Neeleman, decided to depart from the low-cost model of Southwest Airlines-style carriers and to imitate more traditional airlines. He added different kinds of aircraft, increased routes and airports, and built a $25 million training center in anticipation of expanding the workforce to 30,000 by 2010. "These moves," says one analysis, "increased the airline's costs while drawing it into competition with a greater number of rivals, which in turn made it harder for JetBlue to raise fares."[30] JetBlue lost $20 million in 2005 and $1 million in 2006.

The Valentine's Day Ice Storm. Then the Valentine's Day crisis happened. On February 14, 2007, an ice storm settled on JetBlue's New York hub at John F. Kennedy International Airport, preventing planes from taking off. Having acted on forecasters' prediction that the ice would change to rain, JetBlue had continued to load flights and allowed them to taxi to the runway. The result: planes couldn't take off, and passengers were stuck in their seats for hours—up to 6 hours, in some cases. In fact, only 17 of the airline's 156 scheduled departures left JFK that day, disrupting the entire system and displacing crews and aircraft. "In subsequent days," says one account, "JetBlue management canceled more and more flights, angering thousands of passengers, until finally, on February 20, normal operations resumed."[31]

Our emphasis on practicality and applications extends to the **Example Boxes,** "mini-cases" that use snapshots of real-world institutions to explain text concepts. **"Your Call" invites student critical thinking and class discussion at the end of each example.** Suggestions for how to use the example boxes are found in the Instructor's Manual.

"The Kinicki/Williams text is attractive and well organized. The writing is engaging, and there is much more than my current text in terms of examples, application, summaries, and cases. The graphical quality of the book is much better than the black and white version[s] [of texts]. Overall, I think this book represents an excellent approach to the subject of management from both an instructor and learner perspective."

*—***Jeffrey Anderson,** *Ohio University*

An Emphasis on Practicality

We want this book to be a "keeper" for students, a resource for future courses and for their careers—so we give students **a great deal of practical advice** in addition to covering the fundamental concepts of management. Application points are found not only throughout the text discussion but also in the following specialized features.

Practical Action

How to Achieve Your Important Goals: Don't Keep Every Option Open

We've all been told that "It's important to keep your options open." But should we?

"You don't even know how a camera's burst-mode flash works, but you persuade yourself to pay for the extra feature just in case," writes a journalist about this phenomenon. "You no longer have anything in common with someone who keeps calling you, but you hate to just zap the relationship. Your child is exhausted from after-school soccer, ballet, and Chinese lessons, but you won't let her drop the piano lessons. They could come in handy."[37]

The natural reluctance to close any doors is pointed

and settle on the one with the highest rewards. But when students stayed out of a room, the door would start shrinking and eventually disappear. Researchers found that most students would waste clicks by rushing back to reopen doors, even though they lost money by doing so—and they continued to frantically keep all their doors open even when they were fined for switching.

Were the students just trying to "keep their options open"? Ariely doesn't think so. The real motivation, he suggests, is fear of loss. "Closing a door on an option is experienced as a loss, and people are willing to pay a

Practical Action boxes, appearing one or more times in each chapter, offer students practical and interesting advice on issues students will face in the workplace. Detailed discussions of how to use these sections appear in the Instructor's Manual.

End-of-Chapter Resources that reinforce applications

Each chapter continues our strategy of repetition for learning reinforcement. We include various unique pedagogical features to help students take away the most significant portions of the chapter's content:

Management in Action cases depict how companies students are familiar with respond to situations or issues featured in the text. Discussion questions are included for ease of use in class, as reflection assignments, or over online discussion boards.

Self-Assessment Exercises enable students to personally apply chapter content. These exercises include objectives for ease in assigning, instructions for use, guidelines for interpreting results, and questions for further reflection. They can also be found on the text Web site.

Ethical Dilemmas present cases—often based on real events—that require students to think through how they would handle the situation, helping prepare them for decision making in their careers.

Resources that Work

No matter the course you teach—on campus, hybrid, or online courses—we set out to provide you with the most comprehensive set of resources to enhance your Principles of Management course.

Audio visuals for your visual students: We present the richest and most diverse video program on the market to engage your students in the important management concepts covered in this text:

McGraw-Hill's Expanded Management Asset Gallery! McGraw-Hill/Irwin Management is excited to now provide a one-stop shop for our wealth of assets, making it super quick and easy for instructors to locate specific materials to enhance their courses.

All of the following can be accessed within the Management Asset Gallery:

Manager's Hot Seat! This interactive, video-based application puts students in the manager's hot seat and builds critical thinking and decision making skills and allows students to apply concepts to real managerial challenges. Students watch as 15 real managers apply their years of experience when confronting unscripted issues such as bullying in the workplace, cyber loafing, globalization, inter-generational work conflicts, workplace violence, and leadership vs. management.

Self-Assessment Gallery. Unique among publisher-provided self-assessments, our 23 self-assessments provide students with background information to ensure that students understand the purpose of the assessment. Students test their values, beliefs, skills, and interests in a wide variety of areas allowing them to personally apply chapter content to their own lives and careers.

Every self-assessment is supported with PowerPoints and an instructor manual in the Management Asset Gallery, making it easy for the instructor to create an engaging classroom discussion surrounding the assessments.

Test Your Knowledge. To help reinforce students' understanding of key management concepts, Test Your Knowledge activities provide students a review of the conceptual materials followed by application-based questions to work through. Students can choose practice mode, which provides them with detailed feedback after each question, or test mode, which provides feedback after the entire test has been completed. Every Test Your Knowledge activity is supported by instructor notes in the Management Asset Gallery to make it easy for the instructor to create engaging classroom discussions surrounding the materials students have completed.

Management History Timeline. This web application allows instructors to present and students to learn the history of management in an engaging and interactive way. Management history is presented along an intuitive timeline that can be traveled through sequentially or by selected decade. With the click of a mouse, students learn the important dates, see the people who influenced the field, and understand the general management theories that have molded and shaped management as we know it today.

Principles of Management Video DVD Volumes I & 2— Offers more than 70 video clips from sources such as *BusinessWeek* Online, BBC, CBS, FiftyLessons, NBC, PBS, & McGraw-Hill are provided on three DVD sets. These company videos are organized by the four functions of management and feature companies such as PlayStation, Panera Bread, Patagonia, Mini Cooper, the Greater Chicago Food Depository, Employer-Subsidized Commuting, Grounded: Are U.S. Airlines Safe?, Using Facebook at Work, Adult Bullies, and Encore Careers in 2½- to 15-minute clips. Corresponding video cases and a guide that ties the videos closely to the chapter can be found in the Instructor's Manual and online.

The Instructor's Resource CD includes multiple resources to make your teaching life easier.

- The **Instructors Manual,** authored by Bobbie Knoblauch of Wichita State University, was revised and updated to include thorough coverage of each chapter as well as time-saving features such as an outline on incorporating PowerPoint slides, lecture enhancers that supplement the textbook, video cases and video notes, and answers to all end-of-chapter exercises.

- Also included is a set of **PowerPoint slides** prepared by Brad Cox of Midlands Technical College, improved and streamlined for this edition. In addition to providing comprehensive lecture notes, these slides also include questions for the class as well as company examples not found in the textbook.

- Finally, the **Test Bank** by Tia Quinlan-Wilder from University of Denver, includes more than 100 questions per chapter in a variety of formats; it has been revised for accuracy and expanded to include a greater variety of comprehension and application (scenario-based) questions as well as tagged Bloom's Taxonomy levels and AACSB requirements.

McGraw-Hill's flexible and easy-to-use electronic testing program **EZ Test** (found on the IRCD) allows instructors to create tests from book-specific items. It accommodates a wide range of question types, and instructors may add their own questions. Multiple versions of the test can be created, and any test can be exported for use with course management systems such as WebCT or BlackBoard. And now **EZ Test Online (www.eztestonline.com)** allows you to access the test bank virtually anywhere at any time, without installation, and it's even easier to use. Additionally, it allows you to administer EZ Test–created exams and quizzes online, providing instant feedback for students.

The **Online Learning Center** is located at **www.mhhe.com/kw5e.** At this site, students can take chapter quizzes to review concepts, review chapter PowerPoint slides and watch videos that relate back to concepts covered in this chapter. Students can easily upgrade to a richer set of Premium Online Resources right on this site.

Assurance of Learning–Ready

Many educational institutions are often focused on the notion of *assurance of learning,* an important element of some accreditation standards. *Management: A Practical Introduction,* 5e is designed specifically to support your assurance of learning initiatives with a simple, yet powerful solution.

Each test bank question for *Management: A Practical Introduction,* 5e maps to a specific chapter learning outcome/objective listed in the text. You can use our test bank software, EZ Test and EZ Test Online, or in *Connect Management* to easily query for learning outcomes objectives that directly relate to the learning objectives for your course. You can use the reporting features of EZ Test to aggregate student results in a similar fashion, making the collection and presentation of assurance of learning data simple and easy.

AACSB Statement

The McGraw-Hill Companies is a proud corporate member of AACSB International. Understanding the importance and value of AACSB accreditation, *Management: A Practical Introduction,* 5e recognizes the curricula guidelines detailed in the AACSB standards for business accreditation by connecting selected questions in [the text and/or the test bank] to the six general knowledge and skill guidelines in the AACSB standards.

The statements contained in *Management: A Practical Introduction,* 5e are provided only as a guide for the users of this textbook. The AACSB leaves content coverage and assessment within the purview of individual schools, the mission of the school, and the faculty. While *Management: A Practical Introduction,* 5e and the teaching package make no claim of any specific AACSB qualification or evaluation, we have within *Management: A Practical Introduction,* 5e labeled selected questions according to the six general knowledge and skills areas.

McGraw-Hill *Connect Management*

Less Managing. More Teaching. Greater Learning. McGraw-Hill *Connect Management* is an online assignment and assessment solution that connects students with the tools and resources they'll need to achieve success.

McGraw-Hill *Connect Management* helps prepare students for their future by enabling faster learning, more efficient studying, and higher retention of knowledge.

McGraw-Hill *Connect Management* Features: *Connect Management* offers a number of powerful tools and features to make managing assignments easier, so faculty can spend more time teaching. With *Connect Management,* students can engage with their coursework anytime and anywhere, making the learning process more accessible and efficient. *Connect Management* offers you the features described below.

Diagnostic and Adaptive Learning of Concepts: LearnSmart

Students want to make the best use of their study time. The LearnSmart adaptive self-study technology within *Connect Management* provides students with a seamless combination of practice, assessment, and remediation for every concept in the textbook. LearnSmart's intelligent software adapts to every student response and automatically delivers concepts that advance the student's understanding while reducing time devoted to the concepts already mastered. The result for every student is the fastest path to mastery of the chapter concepts.

- Applies an intelligent concept engine to identify the relationships between concepts and to serve new concepts to each student only when he or she is ready.
- Adapts automatically to each student, so students spend less time on the topics they understand and practice more those they have yet to master.
- Provides continual reinforcement and remediation, but gives only as much guidance as students need.
- Integrates diagnostics as part of the learning experience.
- Enables you to assess which concepts students have efficiently learned on their own, thus freeing class time for more applications and discussion.

Online Interactives: Online Interactives are engaging tools that teach students to apply key concepts in practice. These interactives provide them with immersive, experiential learning opportunities. Students will engage in a variety of interactive scenarios to deepen critical knowledge of key course topics. They receive immediate feedback at intermediate steps throughout each exercise, as well as comprehensive feedback at the end of the assignment. All Interactives are automatically scored and entered into the instructor grade book.

Student Progress Tracking: *Connect Management* keeps instructors informed about how each student, section, and class is performing, allowing for more productive use of lecture and office hours. The progress-tracking function enables you to

- View scored work immediately and track individual or group performance with assignment and grade reports.
- Access an instant view of student or class performance relative to learning objectives.
- Collect data and generate reports required by many accreditation organizations, such as AACSB.

Smart Grading: When it comes to studying, time is precious. *Connect Management* helps students learn more efficiently by providing feedback and practice material when they need it, where they need it. When it comes to teaching, your time also is precious. The grading function enables you to

- Have assignments scored automatically, giving students immediate feedback on their work and side-by-side comparisons with correct answers.
- Access and review each response; manually change grades or leave comments for students to review.
- Reinforce classroom concepts with practice tests and instant quizzes.

Simple Assignment Management: With *Connect Management,* creating assignments is easier than ever, so you can spend more time teaching and less time managing. The assignment management function enables you to

- Create and deliver assignments easily with selectable end-of-chapter questions and test bank items.
- Streamline lesson planning, student progress reporting, and assignment grading to make class-room management more efficient than ever.
- Go paperless with the eBook and online submission and grading of student assignments.

Instructor Library: The *Connect Management* Instructor Library is your repository for additional resources to improve student engagement in and out of class. You can select and use any asset that enhances your lecture. The *Connect Management* Instructor Library includes

- Instructor Manual
- PowerPoint files
- Test Bank
- Management Asset Gallery
- eBook

Student Study Center: The *Connect Management* Student Study Center is the place for students to access additional resources. The Student Study Center

- Offers students quick access to lectures, practice materials, eBooks, and more.
- Provides instant practice material and study questions, easily accessible on the go.
- Give students access to self-assessments, video materials, Manager's Hot Seat, and more.

Lecture Capture Via Tegrity Campus: *Increase the attention* paid to lecture discussion by decreasing the attention paid to note taking. For an additional charge, Lecture Capture offers new ways for students to focus on the in-class discussion, knowing they can revisit important topics later.

McGraw-Hill *Connect Plus Management*: McGraw-Hill reinvents the textbook-learning experience for the modern student with *Connect Plus Management*. A seamless integration of an eBook and *Management, Connect Plus Management* provides all of the *Connect Management* features plus the following:

- An integrated eBook, allowing for anytime, anywhere access to the textbook.
- Dynamic links between the problems or questions you assign to your students and the location in the eBook where that problem or question is covered.
- A powerful search function to pinpoint and connect key concepts in a snap.

In short, *Connect Management* offers you and your students powerful tools and features that optimize your time and energies, enabling you to focus on course content, teaching, and student learning. *Connect Management* also offers a wealth of content resources for both instructors and students. This state-of-the-art, thoroughly tested system supports you in preparing students for the world that awaits.

For more information about *Connect,* go to **www.mcgrawhillconnect.com,** or contact your local McGraw-Hill sales representative.

Tegrity Campus:

Lectures 24/7: Tegrity Campus is a service that makes class time available 24/7 by automatically capturing every lecture in a searchable format for students to review when they study and complete assignments. With a simple one-click start-and-stop process, you capture all computer screens and corresponding audio. Students can replay any part of any class with easy-to-use browser-based viewing on a PC or Mac.

Educators know that the more students can see, hear, and experience class resources, the better they learn. In fact, studies prove it. With Tegrity Campus, students quickly recall key moments by using Tegrity Campus's unique search feature. This search helps students efficiently find what they need, when they need it, across an entire semester of class recordings. Help turn all your students' study time into learning moments immediately supported by your lecture. Lecture Capture enables you to

- Record and distribute your lecture with a click of button.
- Record and index PowerPoint presentations and anything shown on your computer so it is easily searchable, frame by frame.
- Offer access to lectures anytime and anywhere by computer, iPod, or mobile device.
- Increase intent listening and class participation by easing students' concerns about note taking. Lecture Capture will make it more likely you will see students' faces, not the tops of their heads.

To learn more about Tegrity, watch a two-minute Flash demo at **http://tegritycampus.mhhe.com.**

McGraw-Hill Customer Care Contact Information: At McGraw-Hill, we understand that getting the most from new technology can be challenging. That's why our services don't stop after you purchase our products. You can e-mail our product specialists 24 hours a day to get product training online. Or you can search our knowledge bank of Frequently Asked Questions on our support Web site. For customer support, call **800-331-5094,** e-mail **hmsupport@mcgraw-hill.com,** or visit **www.mhhe.com/support.** One of our technical support analysts will be able to assist you in a timely fashion.

eBook Options: eBooks are an innovative way for students to save money and to "go green." McGraw-Hill's eBooks are typically 40% of bookstore price. Students have the choice between a online and a downloadable CourseSmart eBook.

Through *CourseSmart*, students have the flexibility to access an exact replica of their textbook from any computer that has internet service without plug-ins or special software via the version, or create a library of books on their hard drive via the downloadable version. Access to the CourseSmart eBook(s) is for **1 year.**

Features: *CourseSmart* eBook(s) allow students to highlight, take notes, organize notes, and share the notes with other *CourseSmart* users. Students can also search terms across all eBook(s) in their purchased *CourseSmart* library. *CourseSmart* eBook(s) can be printed (5 pages at a time).

More info and purchase: Please visit **www.coursesmart.com** for more information and to purchase access to our eBook(s). *CourseSmart* allows students to try one chapter of the eBook(s), free of charge, before purchase.

Create: Craft your teaching resources to match the way you teach! With McGraw-Hill Create, **www.mcgrawhillcreate.com,** you can easily rearrange chapters, combine material from other content sources, and quickly upload content you have written, like your course syllabus or teaching notes. Find the content you need in Create by searching through thousands of leading McGraw-Hill textbooks. Arrange your book to fit your teaching style. Create even allows you to personalize your book's appearance by selecting the cover and adding your name, school, and course information. Order a Create book and you'll receive a complimentary print review copy in 3-5 business days or a complimentary electronic review copy (eComp) via email in about one hour. Go to **www.mcgrawhillcreate.com** today and register. Experience how McGraw-Hill Create empowers you to teach *your* students *your* way.

acknowledgments

We could not have completed this product without the help of a great many people. The first edition was designed by Karen Mellon, to whom we are very grateful. Sincere thanks and gratitude also go to our former executive editor John Weimeister and to our present executive editor Michael Ablassmeir. Among our first-rate team at McGraw-Hill, we want to acknowledge key contributors Laura Griffin, developmental editor II, and editorial coordinator Andrea Heirendt; Anke Braun Weekes, executive marketing manager, and Annie Ferro, marketing specialist; Harvey Yep, senior project manager; lead production supervisor Michael R. McCormick; designer Pam Verros; senior photo research coordinator Jeremy Cheshareck; photo researcher Judy Mason, senior media project manager Greg Bates. We would also like to thank Bobbie Knoblauch for her work on the Instructor's Manual; Brad Cox for the PowerPoint slides; and Tia Quinlan-Wilder for the test bank.

Warmest thanks and appreciation go to the individuals who provided valuable input during the developmental stages of this edition, as follows:

Laura L. Alderson, *University of Memphis*

Jeffrey Anderson, *Ohio University*

Patricia Bernson, *College County of Morris*

Barbara A. Carlin, *University of Houston*

Julie J. Carwile, *John Tyler Community College*

J. Dana Clark, *Appalachian State University*

Glenda Coleman, *University of South Carolina*

Kate Demarest, *Carroll Community College*

Ken Dunegan, *University of Cincinnati*

Bob Eliason, *James Madison University*

Paul Fadil, *University of North Florida*

Lucy R. Ford, *Saint Joseph's University*

Marie Gould, *Peirce University*

Anne Kelly Hoel, *University of Wisconsin-Stout*

Richard Kimbrough, *University of Nebraska-Lincoln*

Todd Korol, *Monroe Community College*

Sal Kukalis, *California State University-Long Beach*

Chi Lo Lim, *Northwest Missouri State University*

Natasha Lindsey, *University of North Alabama*

Guy Lochiatto, *MassBay Community College*

James Manicki, *Northwestern College*

Daniel W. McAllister, *University of Nevada-Las Vegas*

Zack McNeil, *Longview Community College*

Sheila Petcavage, *Cuyahoga Community College-Western Campus*

Anthony Plunkett, *Harrison College*

Cynthia Preston, *University of Northwestern Ohio*

George Redmond, *Franklin University*

Rosemarie Reynolds, *Embry Riddle Aeronautical University*

Gary B. Roberts, *Kennesaw State University*

Catherine Ruggieri, *St. John's University-New York*

Frederick J. Slack, *Indiana University of Pennsylvania*

Wynn Teasley, *University of West Florida*

Joy Turnheim Smith, *Elizabeth City State University*

Carolyn Waits, *Cincinnati State Technical & Community College*

Tekle O. Wanorie, *Northwest Missouri State University*

Velvet Weems-Landingham, *Kent State University-Geauga*

David A. Wernick, *Florida International University*

Wendy V. Wysocki, *Monroe County Community College*

We would also like to thank the following colleagues who served as manuscript reviewers during the development of previous editions:

G. Stoney Alder, *Western Illinois University*

Phyllis C. Alderdice, *Jefferson Community College*

Scott Anchors, *Maine Business School*

John Anstey, *University of Nebraska at Omaha*

Maria Aria, *Camden County College*

James Bell, *Texas State University-San Marcos*

Victor Berardi, *Kent State University*

David Bess, *University of Hawaii*

Stephen Betts, *William Paterson University*

Danielle Beu, *Louisiana Tech University*

Randy Blass, *Florida State University*

Larry Bohleber, *University of Southern Indiana*

Melanie Bookout, *Greenville Technical College*

Robert S. Boothe, *University of Southern Mississippi*

Susan M. Bosco, *Roger Williams University*

Roger Brown, *Western Illinois University*

Marit Brunsell, *Madison Area Technical College*

Neil Burton, *Clemson University*

Jon Bryan, *Bridgewater State College*

Pamela Carstens, *Coe College*

Glen Chapuis, *St. Charles Community College*

Rod Christian, *Mesa Community College*

Mike Cicero, *Highline Community College*

Jack Cichy, *Davenport University*

Anthony Cioffi, *Lorain County Community College*

Deborah Clark, *Santa Fe Community College*

Sharon Clinebell, *University of Northern Colorado*

Ron Cooley, *South Suburban College*

Gary Corona, *Florida Community College*

Ajay Das, *Baruch College*

Kathleen DeNisco, *Erie Community College*

Pamela A. Dobies, *University of Missouri—Kansas City*

David Dore, *San Francisco City College*

Lon Doty, *San Jose State University*

Ron Dougherty, *Ivy Tech Community College/Columbus Campus*

Scott Droege, *Western Kentucky University*

Steven Dunphy, *University of Akron*

Linda Durkin, *Delaware County Community College*

Subhash Durlabhji, *Northwestern State University*

Jack Dustman, *Northern Arizona University*

Ray Eldridge, *Freed-Hardeman University*

Judy Fitch, *Augusta State University*

David Foote, *Middle Tennessee State University*

Tony Frontera, *Broome Community College*

Michael Garcia, *Liberty University*

Evgeniy Gentchev, *Northwood University*

James Glasgow, *Villanova University*

Kris Gossett, *Ivy Tech State College*

Kevin S. Groves, *California State University, Los Angeles*

Joyce Guillory, *Austin Community College*

Stephen F. Hallam, *The University of Akron*

Charles T. Harrington, *Pasadena City College*

Santhi Harvey, *Central State University*

Samuel Hazen, *Tarleton State University*

Jack Heinsius, *Modesto Junior College*

Kim Hester, *Arkansas State University*

Mary Hogue, *Kent State University*

Edward Johnson, *University of North Florida*

Nancy M. Johnson, *Madison Area Technical College*

Rusty Juban, *Southeastern Louisiana University*

Dmitriy Kalyagin, *Chabot College*

Heesam Kang, *Bacone College*

Marcella Kelly, *Santa Monica College*

Bobbie Knoblauch, *Wichita State University*

Rebecca Legleiter, *Tulsa Community College*

David Leonard, *Chabot College*

David Levy, *United States Air Force Academy*

Beverly Little, *Western Carolina University*

Mary Lou Lockerby, *College of DuPage*

Paul Londrigan, *Charles Stewart Mott Community College*

Tom Loughman, *Columbus State University*

Brenda McAleer, *University of Maine at Augusta*

David McArthur, *University of Nevada Las Vegas*

Tom McFarland, *Mount San Antonio College*

Joe McKenna, *Howard Community College*

Jeanne McNett, *Assumption College*

Spencer Mehl, *Coastal Carolina Community College*

Mary Meredith, *University of Louisiana*

Douglas Micklich, *Illinois State University*

Christine Miller, *Tennessee Tech University*

Val Miskin, *Washington State University*

Gregory Moore, *Middle Tennessee State University*

Rob Moorman, *Creighton University*

Robert Myers, *University of Louisville*

Francine Newth, *Providence College*

Jack Partlow, *Northern Virginia Community College*

Don A. Paxton, *Pasadena City College*

John Paxton, *Wayne State College*

Sheila Petcavage, *Cuyahoga Community College*

Barbara Petzall, *Maryville University*

Leah Ritchie, *Salem State College*

Barbara Rosenthal, *Miami Dade Community College/Wolfson Campus*

Gary Ross, *Barat College of DePaul University*

Cindy Ruszkowski, *Illinois State University*

William Salyer, *Morris College*

Diane R. Scott, *Wichita State University*

Marianne Sebok, *Community College of Southern Nevada*

Randi Sims, *Nova Southeastern University*

Erika E. Small, *Coastal Carolina University*

Gerald F. Smith, *University of Northern Iowa*

Mark Smith, *University of Southwest Louisiana*

Jeff Stauffer, *Ventura College*

Raymond Stoudt, *DeSales University*

Robert Scott Taylor, *Moberly Area Community College*

Virginia Anne Taylor, *William Patterson University*

Jerry Thomas, *Arapahoe Community College*

Joseph Tomkiewicz, *East Carolina University*

Robert Trumble, *Virginia Commonwealth University*

Isaiah Ugboro, *North Carolina Agricultural & Technical State University*

Anthony Uremovic, *Joliet Junior College*

Barry Van Hook, *Arizona State University*

Susan Verhulst, *Des Moines Area Community College*

Annie Viets, *University of Vermont*

Tom Voigt, *Jr., Aurora University*

Bruce C. Walker, *University of Louisiana at Monroe*

Charles Warren, *Salem State College*

Allen Weimer, *University of Tampa*

James Whelan, *Manhattan College*

John Whitelock, *Community College of Baltimore/Catonsville Campus*

Wendy Wysocki, *Monroe County Community College*

The following professors also participated in an early focus group that helped drive the development of this text. We appreciate their suggestions and participation immensely:

Rusty Brooks, *Houston Baptist University*

Kerry Carson, *University of Southwestern Louisiana*

Sam Dumbar, *Delgado Community College*

Subhash Durlabhji, *Northwestern State University*

Robert Mullins, *Delgado Community College*

Carl Phillips, *Southeastern Louisiana University*

Allayne Pizzolatto, *Nicholls State University*

Ellen White, *University of New Orleans*

We would also like to thank the following students for participating in a very important focus group to gather feedback from the student reader's point of view:

Marcy Baasch, *Triton College*

Diana Broeckel, *Triton College*

Lurene Cornejo, *Moraine Valley Community College*

Dave Fell, *Elgin Community College*

Lydia Hendrix, *Moraine Valley Community College*

Kristine Kurpiewski, *Oakton Community College*

Michelle Monaco, *Moraine Valley Community College*

Shannon Ramey, *Elgin Community College*

Arpita Sikand, *Oakton Community College*

Finally, we would like to thank our wives, Joyce and Stacey, for being understanding, patient, and encouraging throughout the process of writing this edition. Your love and support helped us endure the trials of completing this text.

We hope you enjoy reading and applying the book. Best wishes for success in your career.

Angelo Kinicki   **Brian K. Williams**

contents

part 6
Controlling

Chapter Sixteen

Control & Quality Control Improvement: Techniques for Enhancing Organizational Effectiveness 506

Appendix

The Project Planner's Toolkit: Flowcharts, Gantt Charts, & Break-Even Analysis A

management

A PRACTICAL INTRODUCTION

The Exceptional Manager
What You Do, How You Do It

Major Questions You Should Be Able to Answer

1.1 Management: What It Is, What Its Benefits Are

Major Question: What are the rewards of being an exceptional manager?

1.2 Seven Challenges to Being an Exceptional Manager

Major Question: Challenges can make one feel alive. What are seven challenges I could look forward to as a manager?

1.3 What Managers Do: The Four Principal Functions

Major Question: What would I actually *do*—that is, what would be my four principal functions—as a manager?

1.4 Pyramid Power: Levels & Areas of Management

Major Question: What are the levels and areas of management I need to know to move up, down, and sideways?

1.5 Roles Managers Must Play Successfully

Major Question: To be an exceptional manager, what roles must I play successfully?

1.6 The Entrepreneurial Spirit

Major Question: Do I have what it takes to be an entrepreneur?

1.7 The Skills Exceptional Managers Need

Major Question: To be a terrific manager, what skills should I cultivate?

A One-Minute Guide to Success in This Class

Got one minute to read this section? It could mean the difference between getting an A instead of a B. Or a B instead of a C.

It is our desire *to make this book as practical as possible for you*. One place we do this is in the Manager's Toolbox, like this one, which appears at the beginning of every chapter and which offers practical advice appropriate to the subject matter you are about to explore. Here we show you how to be a success in this course.

Four Rules for Success

The following four rules will help you be successful in this (or any other) course.

- **Rule 1:** Attend every class. No cutting allowed.
- **Rule 2:** Don't postpone studying, then cram the night before a test.
- **Rule 3:** Read or review lectures and readings more than once.
- **Rule 4:** Learn how to use this book.

How to Use This Book Most Effectively

When reading this book, follow the steps below:

- Get an overview of the chapter by reading over the first page, which contains the section headings and Major Questions.
- Read "Forecast: What's Ahead in This Chapter."
- Look at the Major Question at the beginning of each section before you read it.
- Read the "The Big Picture," which summarizes the section.
- Read the section itself (which is usually only 2–6 pages), *trying silently to answer the Major Question.* This is important!
- After reading all sections, use the Key Terms and Summary at the end of the chapter to see how well you understand the major concepts. Reread any material you're unsure about.

If you follow these steps consistently, you'll probably absorb the material well enough that you won't have to cram before an exam; you'll need only to lightly review it before the test.

For Discussion Do you sometimes (often?) postpone keeping up with coursework, then pull an "all-nighter" of studying to catch up before an exam? What do you think happens to people in business who do this?

---

forecast | **What's Ahead in This Chapter**

We describe the rewards, benefits, and privileges managers might expect. We also describe the seven challenges to managers in today's world. You'll be introduced to the four principal functions of management—planning, organizing, leading, and controlling—and levels and areas of management. We describe the three roles managers must play. Then we consider the contributions of entrepreneurship. Finally, we describe the three skills required of a manager.

major question?

What are the rewards of being an exceptional manager?

THE BIG PICTURE

Management is defined as the pursuit of organizational goals efficiently and effectively. Organizations, or people who work together to achieve a specific purpose, value managers because of the multiplier effect: Good managers have an influence on the organization far beyond the results that can be achieved by one person acting alone. Managers are well paid, with the CEOs and presidents of even small and midsize businesses earning good salaries and many benefits.

Yahoo! CEO Carol Bartz. While CEO with her previous employer, Autodesk, Bartz promoted the concept of "fail fast-forward," shaping a company to risk failure in some tasks but to move on quickly if failure should occur. Bartz attributes this "just deal with it" approach to growing up on a Midwestern farm that encouraged hard work. "The farm won't wait for a better mood." If you were in her shoes, what would you consider to be the key component of managerial success?

In January 2009, Carol Bartz became chief executive officer (CEO) of Yahoo!, the California-based Internet services company that operates the second- or third-most-visited Web site in the United States (after Google and possibly Facebook). Yahoo! had been in a financial funk for two years and thus, Bartz observed dryly, "frankly, could use a little management." What induced her, an already well-off veteran manager, to take on such a difficult, high-risk job?

Bartz is regarded as a "tough operator" and has great resilience. When she was eight, her mother died, and Bartz was raised by her grandmother. She was one of only two girls in her high school to take physics. She earned a degree in computer science from the University of Wisconsin–Madison while supporting herself as a cocktail waitress. She quit 3M, the manufacturing conglomerate, over blatant gender discrimination. She is a breast cancer survivor. After early jobs with technology companies DEC and Sun Microsystems, she became CEO of design software maker Autodesk, putting down a rebellion of programmers, imposing a management hierarchy, and growing annual revenues over 14 years from $285 million to $1.5 billion.[1] Now, after a short retirement, she was back working as top manager for Yahoo! because, she says, "I love to work. I love to run companies. I love to help people I work with. And I don't let anything get in the way of doing what I love."[2]

Yahoo! faces a host of challenges, including threats from Google and Microsoft, and not everyone believes the new CEO is up to the task. However, Bartz is used to being underestimated. "Failure is not in her vocabulary," says an Autodesk product manager. Actually, her favorite motto is "fail fast-forward." "It's about not being afraid to fail," she says, "and if you do, identify it quickly and move ahead fast so no momentum is lost."[3] She also embraces change. "I like change. Frankly, it's hard for me to understand why more people don't embrace it."

The ability to embrace change and to keep going forward despite failures is important to any manager's survival, and dealing with continuing change—in the world and in the workplace—is a major theme of this book.

The Art of Management Defined

Is being an exceptional manager a gift, like a musician having perfect pitch? Not exactly. But in good part it may be an art. Fortunately, it is one that is teachable.

Management, said one pioneer of management ideas, is "the art of getting things done through people."[4]

Getting things done. Through people. Thus, managers are task oriented, achievement oriented, and people oriented. And they operate within an *organization*—**a group of people who work together to achieve some specific purpose.**

More formally, *management* **is defined as (1) the pursuit of organizational goals efficiently and effectively by (2) integrating the work of people through (3) planning, organizing, leading, and controlling the organization's resources.**

Note the words *efficiently* and *effectively,* which basically mean "doing things right."

- *Efficiency—the means.* Efficiency is the means of attaining the organization's goals. **To be *efficient* means to use resources—people, money, raw materials, and the like—wisely and cost-effectively.**

- *Effectiveness—the ends.* Effectiveness is the organization's ends, the goals. **To be *effective* means to achieve results, to make the right decisions and to successfully carry them out so that they achieve the organization's goals.**

Good managers are concerned with trying to achieve both qualities. Often, however, organizations will erroneously strive for efficiency without being effective.

Example

Efficiency versus Effectiveness: "Let Me Speak with a Person—*Please!*"

We're all now accustomed to having our calls to companies for information and customer support answered not by people but by automated answering systems. Certainly this arrangement is *efficient* for the companies, since they no longer need as many employees to answer the phones. But it's not *effective* if it leaves us, the customers, fuming and less inclined to continue doing business. "Just give me a person to speak with, *please,*" pleads a Nevada resident.[5] Even most online shoppers, 77% to 23%, say they'd prefer to have contact with a real person before they make a purchase.[6]

Still, a lot of companies obviously favor efficiency over effectiveness in their customer service. "The approximate cost of offering a live, American-based customer service agent averages somewhere around $7.50 per phone call," says one researcher. "Outsourcing calls to live agents in another country brings the average cost down to about $2.35 per call. Having customers take care of the problem themselves, through an automated response phone system, averages around 32 cents per call, or contact."[7]

However, the president of one firm that does surveys on customer service says that 90% of consumers say they want nothing to do with an automated telephone system. "They just don't like it," he says. The

Effective? Is this irate customer dealing with a company customer-support system that is more efficient than effective?

most telling finding is that 50% of those surveyed had become so irritated that they were willing to pay an additional charge for customer service that avoids going through an automated phone system.[8] The head of a firm that evaluates the experiences of call-center customers says that companies "create more value through a dialogue with a live agent." A call is an opportunity to build a relationship, to encourage a customer to stay with the brand. There can be a real return on this investment.[9] Recognizing this, Netflix, the DVD-by-mail rental company, in 2007 added 24/7 live operators to deal with customers' problems.[10]

YOUR CALL

The average wait for customer service at Facebook was 99 minutes (rated "Horrible" by users); for Amazon.com it was 1 minute ("Excellent"). These and other company wait times and ratings appeared recently on a Web site called Get Human (**www.gethuman.com),** started by technology officer Paul English to try to "change the face of customer service." Get Human also publishes the unpublicized codes for reaching a company's human operators and cut-through-automation tips.[11] What recent unpleasant customer experience would you want to post on this Web site?

Why Organizations Value Managers: The Multiplier Effect

Some great achievements of history, such as scientific discoveries or works of art, were accomplished by individuals working quietly by themselves. But so much more has been achieved by people who were able to leverage their talents and abilities by being managers. For instance, of the top 10 great architectural wonders of the world named by the American Institute of Architects, none was built by just one person. All were triumphs of management, although some reflected the vision of an individual. (The wonders are the Great Wall of China, the Great Pyramid, Machu Picchu, the Acropolis, the Coliseum, the Taj Mahal, the Eiffel Tower, the Brooklyn Bridge, the Empire State Building, and Frank Lloyd Wright's Fallingwater house in Pennsylvania.)

Good managers create value. The reason is that in being a manager you have a *multiplier effect:* Your influence on the organization is multiplied far beyond the results that can be achieved by just one person acting alone. Thus, while a solo operator such as a salesperson might accomplish many things and incidentally make a very good living, his or her boss could accomplish a great deal more—and could well earn two to seven times the income. And the manager will undoubtedly have a lot more influence.

Exceptional managers are in high demand. "The scarcest, most valuable resource in business is no longer financial capital," says a *Fortune* article. "It's talent. If you doubt that, just watch how hard companies are battling for the best people. . . . Talent of every type is in short supply, but the greatest shortage of all is skilled, effective managers.[12] Even in recessionary times—maybe *especially* in such times—companies reach out for top talent.

Financial Rewards of Being an Exceptional Manager

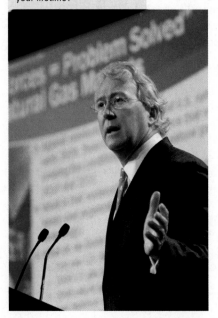

Aubrey McClendon. The CEO of Chesapeake Energy earned $112 million (including a $77 million bonus) in 2008, making him one of the highest-paid managers in the United States that year. What do you think your chances are of making over $100 million in your lifetime?

How well compensated are managers? According to the U.S. Bureau of Labor Statistics, the median weekly wage in 2009 for American workers of all sorts was $748, or $38,896 a year.[13] Education pays: The median 2008 yearly income for full-time workers with a bachelor's degree was $48,097 and with a master's degree was $58,522. (For high-school graduates, it was $27,693.)[14]

The business press frequently reports on the astronomical earnings of top chief executive officers such as Chesapeake Energy's CEO Aubrey McClendon, whose 2008 compensation was $112 million.[15] However, this kind of huge payday isn't common. Median compensation for CEOs in North America in 2008 was $2 million, according to a survey of 3,242 participating CEOs.[16] More usual is the take-home pay for the head of a small business: According to recent research, the median salary for a small business chief executive was $233,500. (A small business was classified as a company with up to 500 full-time employees.) The national median salary for a CEO with 500 to 5,000 employees was $500,000, and $849,375 for those at companies with more than 5,000 employees.[17]

Managers farther down in the organization usually don't make this much, of course; nevertheless, they do fairly well compared with most workers. At the lower rungs, managers may make between $25,000 and $50,000 a year; in the middle levels, between $35,000 and $110,000.

There are also all kinds of fringe benefits and status rewards that go with being a manager, ranging from health insurance to stock options to large offices. And the higher you ascend in the management hierarchy, the more privileges may come your way: personal parking space, better furniture, lunch in the executive dining room, on up to—for those on the top rung of big companies—company car and driver, corporate jet, and even executive sabbaticals (months of paid time off to pursue alternative projects).

What Are the Rewards of Studying & Practicing Management?

Are you studying management but have no plans to be a manager? Or are you trying to learn techniques and concepts that will help you be an exceptional management practitioner? Either way there are considerable rewards.

The Rewards of Studying Management   Students sign up for an introductory management course for all kinds of reasons. Many, of course, are planning business careers, but others are taking it to fulfill a requirement or an elective. Some students are in technical fields, such as accounting, finance, computer science, and engineering, and never expect to have to supervise other people.

Here are just a few of the payoffs of studying management as a discipline:

- **You will understand how to deal with organizations from the outside.** Since we all are in constant interaction with all kinds of organizations, it helps to understand how they work and how the people in them make decisions. Such knowledge may give you some defensive skills that you can use in dealing with organizations from the outside, as a customer or investor, for example.

- **You will understand how to relate to your supervisors.** Since most of us work in organizations and most of us have bosses, studying management will enable you to understand the pressures managers deal with and how they will best respond to you.

- **You will understand how to interact with co-workers.** The kinds of management policies in place can affect how your co-workers behave. Studying management can give you the understanding of teams and teamwork, cultural differences, conflict and stress, and negotiation and communication skills that will help you get along with fellow employees.

- **You will understand how to manage yourself in the workplace.** Management courses in general, and this book in particular, give you the opportunity to realize insights about yourself—your personality, emotions, values, perceptions, needs, and goals. We help you build your skills in areas such as self-management, listening, handling change, managing stress, avoiding groupthink, and coping with organizational politics.

The Rewards of Practicing Management   However you become a management practitioner, there are many rewards—apart from those of money and status—to being a manager:

- **You and your employees can experience a sense of accomplishment.** Every successful goal accomplished provides you not only with personal satisfaction but also with the satisfaction of all those employees you directed who helped you accomplish it.

- **You can stretch your abilities and magnify your range.** Every promotion up the hierarchy of an organization stretches your abilities, challenges your talents and skills, and magnifies the range of your accomplishments.

- **You can build a catalog of successful products or services.** Every product or service you provide—the personal Eiffel Tower or Empire State Building you build, as it were—becomes a monument to your accomplishments. Indeed, studying management may well help you in running your own business.

Finally, productivity-improvement expert Odette Pollar of Oakland, California, concludes that this is an opportunity to counsel, motivate, advise, guide, empower, and influence large groups of people. These important skills can be used in business as well as in personal and volunteer activities. If you truly like people and enjoy mentoring and helping others to grow and thrive, management is a great job."[18] ●

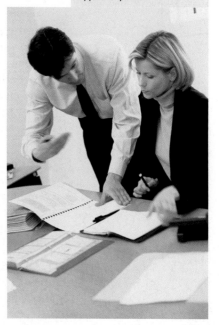

Mentoring. Being a manager is an opportunity "to counsel, motivate, advise, guide, empower, and influence" other people. Does this sense of accomplishment appeal to you?

major question?

Challenges can make one feel alive. What are seven challenges I could look forward to as a manager?

THE BIG PICTURE

Seven challenges face any manager: You need to manage for competitive advantage—to stay ahead of rivals. You need to manage for diversity in race, ethnicity, gender, and so on, because the future won't resemble the past. You need to manage for the effects of globalization and of information technology. You always need to manage to maintain ethical standards. You need to manage for sustainability—to practice sound environmental policies. Finally, you need to manage for the achievement of your own happiness and life goals.

The ideal state that many people seek is an emotional zone somewhere between boredom and anxiety, in the view of psychologist Mihaly Csikzentmihalyi.[19] Boredom, he says, may arise because skills and challenges are mismatched: You are exercising your high level of skill in a job with a low level of challenge, such as licking envelopes. Anxiety arises when one has low levels of skill but a high level of challenge, such as (for many people) suddenly being called upon to give a rousing speech to strangers.

As a manager, could you achieve a balance between these two states—boredom and anxiety, or action and serenity? Certainly managers have enough challenges to keep their lives more than mildly interesting. Let's see what they are.

Challenge #1: Managing for Competitive Advantage— Staying Ahead of Rivals

Competitive advantage **is the ability of an organization to produce goods or services more effectively than competitors do, thereby outperforming them.** This means an organization must stay ahead in four areas: (1) being responsive to customers, (2) innovation, (3) quality, and (4) efficiency.

1. Being Responsive to Customers   The first law of business is: *Take care of the customer*. Without customers—buyers, clients, consumers, shoppers, users, patrons, guests, investors, or whatever they're called—sooner or later there will be no organization. Nonprofit organizations are well advised to be responsive to their "customers," too, whether they're called citizens, members, students, patients, voters, rate-payers, or whatever, since they are the justification for the organizations' existence.

2. Innovation   **Finding ways to deliver new or better goods or services is called** *innovation.* No organization, for-profit or nonprofit, can allow itself to become complacent—especially when rivals are coming up with creative ideas. "Innovate or die" is an important adage for any manager.

We discuss innovation in Chapter 3.

3. Quality   If your organization is the only one of its kind, customers may put up with products or services that are less than stellar (as they have with some airlines whose hub systems give them a near monopoly on flights out of certain cities), but only because they have no choice. But if another organization comes along and offers a better-quality travel experience, TV program, cut of meat, computer software, or whatever, you may find your company falling behind. Making improvements in quality has become an important management idea in recent times, as we shall discuss.

Example

Losing Competitive Advantage: How Did Newspapers Lose Their Way?

American newspapers are more widely read than ever before—72 million unique visitors a month in 2009 versus 60 million two years earlier.[20] The problem: Many people aren't paying for news; they're getting it free online. Indeed, newspaper revenues have dropped steadily for 20 years, and in 2009 fewer papers were sold than at any other time since the 1940s. Lower revenues have forced newsroom layoffs and thus less original news gathering. What happened to bring this long-standing industry to this point?

First: Giving Away the Product. At the beginning of the Internet age, newspaper proprietors, seduced by the new technology, decided to promote their product by giving it away for free to various Web sites. They didn't reckon on more and more readers (especially younger ones) preferring to get their news online, particularly if it was free.

Second: Relying Too Much on Advertising for Revenue. Even before the Web came along, for decades publishers relied for revenues more on advertising than on readers willing to pay, and so were discounting subscriptions, providing premiums, and giving away copies to boost readership figures to attract advertisers. "The new Internet editions," says a veteran newsman, "were merely the ultimate extension of that trend: free news to the consumer, total reliance on the advertiser."[21] But because of search sites and many other new competitors, online ads produced only a fraction of the revenues of print ads. In addition, classified ads, the lifeblood of newspapers, migrated to Craigslist and eBay.

YOUR CALL

Newspapers are protected by the U.S. Constitution because the free flow of news is considered essential

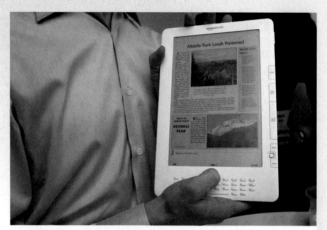

Kindle DX. After the success of its book-size Kindle 2, Amazon.com introduced the Kindle DX, with a 9.7-inch screen, designed to be used for electronic newspapers and magazines.

to citizens participating in their government. However, the disciplined function of gathering and verifying original news is expensive, not something most bloggers and other Web opinion makers can do. Some critics suggest it's too late for newspapers to now begin charging readers for online news, but *The Wall Street Journal,* a specialized business paper, has done it for years, and *The New York Times* plans to do so.[22] Other sites, such as Politico and TMZ, dig for news, but none fulfill the traditional role of traditional newspapers.[23] Some publishers are working on refashioning their brands for a tablet world, such as the Kindle DX or the Apple iPad.[24] What do you think newspaper proprietors should do to exploit their competitive advantage—professional news gathering?

4. Efficiency   A generation ago, organizations rewarded employees for their length of service. Today, however, the emphasis is on efficiency: Companies strive to produce goods or services as quickly as possible using as few employees (and raw materials) as possible. Although a strategy that downgrades the value of employees might ultimately backfire—resulting in the loss of essential experience and skills and even customers—an organization that is overstaffed may not be able to compete with leaner, meaner rivals. This is the reason why, for instance, today many companies rely so much on temp (temporary) workers.[25]

Challenge #2: Managing for Diversity—The Future Won't Resemble the Past

Today nearly one in six American workers is foreign-born, the highest proportion since the 1920s.[26] But greater changes are yet to come. By midcentury, the mix of American racial or ethnic groups will change considerably, with the United States becoming half (54%) racial or ethnic minority. Non-Hispanic whites are projected to decrease from 66% of the population in 2008 to 46% in 2050. African Americans will increase from 14% to 15%, Asians and Pacific Islanders from 5.1% to 9.2%, and Hispanics (who may be of any race) from 15% to 30%. In addition, in the coming years there will be a different mix of women, immigrants, and older people in the general population, as well as in the workforce. For instance, in 2030, nearly one in five U.S. residents is expected to be 65 and older. This age group is projected to increase to 88.5 million in 2050, more than doubling the number in 2008 (38.7 million).[27]

Some scholars think that diversity and variety in staffing produce organizational strength, as we consider elsewhere.[28] Clearly, however, the challenge to the manager of the near future is to maximize the contributions of employees diverse in gender, age, race, and ethnicity. We discuss this matter in more detail in Chapter 3.

Challenge #3: Managing for Globalization—The Expanding Management Universe

"In Japan it is considered rude to look directly in the eye for more than a few seconds," says a report about teaching Americans how to behave abroad, "and in Greece the hand-waving gesture commonly used in America for goodbye is considered an insult."[29]

The point: Gestures and symbols don't have the same meaning to everyone throughout the world. Not understanding such differences can affect how well organizations manage globally.

American firms have been going out into the world in a major way, even as the world has been coming to us—leading to what *New York Times* columnist Thomas Friedman has called, in *The World Is Flat,* a phenomenon in which globalization has leveled (made "flat") the competitive playing fields between industrial and emerging-market countries.[30] Managing for globalization will be a complex, ongoing challenge, as we discuss at length in Chapter 4.

Challenge #4: Managing for Information Technology

The challenge of managing for information technology, not to mention other technologies affecting your business, will require your unflagging attention. Most important is the ***Internet,* the global network of independently operating but interconnected computers, linking hundreds of thousands of smaller networks around the world.**

By 2012, more than a billion consumers are projected to spend $1.2 trillion online, and online commerce between businesses will be 10 times larger, totaling $1.2 trillion, according to IDC Research.[31] This kind of ***e-commerce,* or electronic commerce—the buying and selling of goods or services over computer networks—is**

The famous golden arches. This McDonald's store in Beijing is an example of globalization.

麦当劳

reshaping entire industries and revamping the very notion of what a company is. More important than e-commerce, the information technology has facilitated *e-business*, **using the Internet to facilitate *every* aspect of running a business.** As one article puts it, "at bottom, the Internet is a tool that dramatically lowers the cost of communication. That means it can radically alter any industry or activity that depends heavily on the flow of information."[32]

Some of the implications of e-business that we will discuss throughout the book are as follows:

- **Far-ranging e-management and e-communication.** Using wired and wireless telephones, fax machines, electronic mail, or *e-mail*—**text messages and documents transmitted over a computer network**—as well as *project management software*—**programs for planning and scheduling the people, costs, and resources to complete a project on time**—21st-century managers will find themselves responsible for creating, motivating, and leading teams of specialists all over the world. This will require them to be masters of organizational communication, able to create concise, powerful e-mail and voice-mail messages.

- **Accelerated decision making, conflict, and stress.** The Internet not only speeds everything up, it also, with its huge, interconnected *databases*—**computerized collections of interrelated files**—can overwhelm us with information, much of it useful, much of it not. For example, studies show that employees lose valuable time and productivity when dealing with excessive and unimportant e-mail volume and increasing amounts of cell-phone spam (junk messages).[33] Among the unavoidable by-products are increased conflict and stress, although, as we will show, these can be managed.

- **Changes in organizational structure, jobs, goal setting, and knowledge management.** With computers and telecommunications technology, organizations and teams become "virtual"; they are no longer as bound by time zones and locations. Employees, for instance, may *telecommute,* **or work from home or remote locations using a variety of information technologies.** Meetings may be conducted via *videoconferencing,* **using video and audio links along with computers to let people in different locations see, hear, and talk with one another.** In addition, *collaborative computing,* **using state-of-the-art computer software and hardware, will help people work better together.** Goal setting and feedback will be conducted via Web-based software programs such as eWorkbench, which enables managers to create and track employee goals. All such forms of interaction will require managers and employees to be more flexible, and there will be an increased emphasis on *knowledge management*—**the implementing of systems and practices to increase the sharing of knowledge and information throughout an organization.**

Challenge #5: Managing for Ethical Standards

With the pressure to meet sales, production, and other targets, managers can find themselves confronting ethical dilemmas. What do you do when you learn an employee dropped a gyroscope but put it in the helicopter anyway in order to hold the product's delivery date? How much should you allow your sales reps to knock the competition? How much leeway do you have in giving gifts to prospective clients in a foreign country to try to land a contract? In an era of global warming and rising sea levels, what is your responsibility to "act green"—avoid company policies that are damaging to the environment?

World's biggest fraud. Financier Bernard Madoff got away with the world's biggest fraud for years, and he might still be in business had not his scheme been undermined by the 2007–2008 recession. At age 71, he was sentenced to 150 years in prison. If you're tempted to stretch your ethics in order to pass a college course, do you think you'd do the same in business, where the pressures can be even worse?

Ethical behavior is not just a nicety; it is a very important part of doing business. This was certainly made clear in December 2008, when financier Bernard Madoff confessed that his investments were all "one big lie"—not investments at all, but rather a $50 billion scheme (*Ponzi scheme*), using cash from newer investors to pay off older ones.[34] A few months later, the perpetrator of the world's biggest fraud, then age 71, was sentenced to 150 years in prison.[35] Madoff joins a long list of business scoundrels whose names came to light in the early 21st century. Earlier there were Tyco International CEO Dennis Kozlowski (now serving prison time for grand larceny, securities fraud, and other crimes), WorldCom head Bernard Ebbers (doing 25 years for fraud), Adelphia CEO John Rigas (15 years for conspiracy and bank fraud), and former Enron chief Jeffrey Skilling (24 years for similar white-collar crimes). Not since sociologist Edwin Sutherland invented the term "white-collar crime" in the 1930s were so many top-level executives being hauled into court. We consider ethics in Chapter 3 and elsewhere in the book.

Practical Action

Are Lying & Cheating Required to Succeed?

Today's teenagers and young adults are much more likely than their parents "to believe they're great people, destined for maximum success as workers, spouses, and parents," says an article summarizing a study spanning the years 1975 to 2006.[36] In part, this may be because their parents were much more likely to praise them.

Nothing wrong with self-confidence. But another study suggests a more troubling trend: Teenagers and young adults are more cynical than people over 40 and "are more likely to believe it is necessary to lie or cheat to succeed."[37] The study, by the Los Angeles–based Josephson Institute of Ethics, found that younger generations are more likely to engage in dishonest conduct, including cheating on exams in high school, which meant they were "at least twice as likely to become unethical adults."

Some of the findings include the following:[38]

- Of teenagers 17 and younger in 2008, 64% cheated on an exam, 42% lied to save money, and 30% stole something from a store.

- Teens 17 or under are five times more likely than adults over 50 to believe that lying and cheating are necessary to succeed (51% versus 10%) and four times more likely to deceive their boss (31% versus 8%).

- Young adults (18–24) are more than twice as likely to lie to their boyfriend, girlfriend, spouse, or partner about something significant (48% versus 18%).

- Regardless of age, people who believe that lying and cheating are a necessary part of success are more likely, in fact, to lie and cheat. They are three times more likely to misrepresent themselves on a résumé; three times more likely to lie to a customer; more than twice as likely to conceal or distort information to their boss; and much more likely to illegally copy software, videos, or music.

Your Call

The Josephson Institute suggests that parents can take a TEAM (Teach. Enforce. Advocate. Model.) approach to help children learn the importance of honesty. But perhaps companies can also take steps to create ethical employees and customers—building trust by trusting. One New York doughnut shop owner, for example, began letting customers make their own change from coins left out on the counter. The result: faster service, more loyal customers, and a leg up on his competitors. Do you think companies should trust their employees on how much vacation to take and not require management approval of expense reports? Do you think such companies would generally have loyal employees?[39]

Challenge #6: Managing for Sustainability— The Business of Green

An apparently changing climate, bringing increased damage from hurricanes, floods, and fires throughout the United States and the world, has brought the issue of "being green" to increased prominence. Former U.S. Vice President Al Gore's documentary film *An Inconvenient Truth,* along with his book by the same name, further popularized the concepts of global climate change and the idea of sustainability as a business model.[40]

Our economic system has brought prosperity, but it has also led to unsustainable business practices because it has assumed that natural resources are limitless, which they are not. ***Sustainability* is defined as economic development that meets the needs of the present without compromising the ability of future generations to meet their own needs.**[41] In the United States, the U.S. Chamber of Commerce, which is supposed to represent the views of business, has been resistant to climate change legislation.[42] However, a number of companies, including Apple Inc. and Pacific Gas & Electric, resigned from the Chamber in protest.[43] Perhaps, then, business can begin to take the lead. After years of being slow to address climate change, major corporations—including industrial giants that make products ranging from electricity to chemicals to bulldozers—have begun to call for limits on global warming emissions.[44]

Challenge #7: Managing for Your Own Happiness & Life Goals

Ann Garcia had the view that good managers push decision making down, spread the compliments, and take the blame, but after being given a team to manage at her technology company, she gave it up. "I'm just not a big enough person all the time to want to do that," she said. "Many of us realize that we don't want the career path that corporate America has to offer."[45]

Some employment experts counsel that the lesson of today is that you're working for yourself—that employees should identify themselves with the job, not the company.[46] Regardless of how well paid you are, then, you have to consider whether in meeting the organization's challenges you are also meeting the challenge of realizing your own happiness.

Many people simply don't find being a manager fulfilling.[47] They may complain that they have to go to too many meetings, that they can't do enough for their employees, that they are caught in the middle between bosses and subordinates. They may feel, at a time when Dilbert cartoons have created such an unflattering portrayal of managers, that they lack respect. They may decide that, despite the greater income, money cannot buy happiness, as the adage goes.

In the end, however, recall what Odette Pollar said: "If you truly like people and enjoy mentoring and helping others to grow and thrive, management is a great job." And it helps to know, as she points out, that "one's experience in management is greatly affected by the company's culture."[48] Culture, or style, is indeed an important matter, because it affects your happiness within an organization, and we discuss it in detail in Chapter 8.[49] ●

⧖ I.3 WHAT MANAGERS DO: THE FOUR PRINCIPAL FUNCTIONS

major question?

What would I actually *do*—that is, what would be my four principal functions—as a manager?

THE BIG PICTURE

Management has four functions: *planning, organizing, leading,* and *controlling.*

What do you as a manager do to "get things done"—that is, achieve the stated goals of the organization you work for? You perform what is known as the ***management process,*** **also called the *four management functions:* planning, organizing, leading, and controlling.** (The abbreviation "POLC" may help you to remember them.)

As the diagram below illustrates, all these functions affect one another, are ongoing, and are performed simultaneously. *(See Figure 1.1.)*

figure I.I

THE MANAGEMENT PROCESS

What you as a manager do to "get things done"— to achieve the stated goals of your organization.

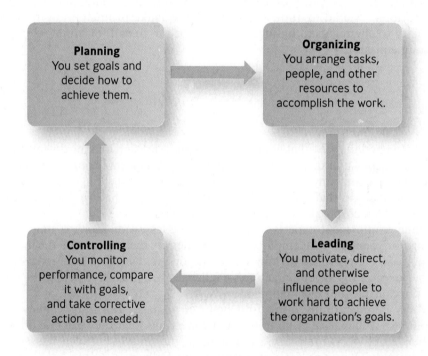

Planning
You set goals and decide how to achieve them.

Organizing
You arrange tasks, people, and other resources to accomplish the work.

Controlling
You monitor performance, compare it with goals, and take corrective action as needed.

Leading
You motivate, direct, and otherwise influence people to work hard to achieve the organization's goals.

Although the process of management can be quite complex, these four functions represent its essential principles. Indeed, as a glance at our text's table of contents shows, they form four of the part divisions of the book. Let's consider what the four functions are, using the management (or "administration," as it is called in nonprofit organizations) of your college to illustrate them.

Planning: Discussed in Part 3 of This Book

***Planning* is defined as setting goals and deciding how to achieve them.** Your college was established for the purpose of educating students, and its present managers, or administrators, now must decide the best way to accomplish this. Which of several possible degree programs should be offered? Should the college be a residential or a commuter campus? What sort of students should be recruited and

Leading. Steve Jobs, cofounder and CEO of Apple Inc. and Pixar Animation, is famous for being an innovative leader. Do you think you have the ability to take the kind of risks he has?

admitted? What kind of faculty should be hired? What kind of buildings and equipment are needed?

Organizing: Discussed in Part 4 of This Book

***Organizing* is defined as arranging tasks, people, and other resources to accomplish the work.** College administrators must determine the tasks to be done, by whom, and what the reporting hierarchy is to be. Should the institution be organized into schools with departments, with department chairpersons reporting to deans who in return report to vice presidents? Should the college hire more full-time instructors than part-time instructors? Should English professors teach just English literature or also composition, developmental English, and "first-year experience" courses?

Leading: Discussed in Part 5 of This Book

***Leading* is defined as motivating, directing, and otherwise influencing people to work hard to achieve the organization's goals.** At your college, leadership begins, of course, with the president (who would be the chief executive officer, or CEO, in a for-profit organization). He or she is the one who must inspire faculty, staff, students, alumni, wealthy donors, and residents of the surrounding community to help realize the college's goals. As you might imagine, these groups often have different needs and wants, so an essential part of leadership is resolving conflicts.

Controlling: Discussed in Part 6 of This Book

***Controlling* is defined as monitoring performance, comparing it with goals, and taking corrective action as needed.** Is the college discovering that fewer students are majoring in nursing than they did five years previously? Is the fault with a change in the job market? with the quality of instruction? with the kinds of courses offered? Are the Nursing Department's student recruitment efforts not going well? Should the department's budget be reduced? Under the management function of controlling, college administrators must deal with these kinds of matters. ●

major question?

What are the levels and areas of management I need to know to move up, down, and sideways?

THE BIG PICTURE

Within an organization, there are managers at three levels: *top, middle,* and *first-line.* Managers may also be *general managers,* or they may be *functional managers,* responsible for just one organizational activity, such as Research & Development, Marketing, Finance, Production, or Human Resources. Managers may work for for-profit, nonprofit, or mutual-benefit organizations.

The workplace of the future may resemble a symphony orchestra, famed management theorist Peter Drucker said.[50] Employees, especially so-called knowledge workers—those who have a great deal of technical skills—can be compared to concert musicians. Their managers can be seen as conductors.

In Drucker's analogy, musicians are used for some pieces of music—that is, work projects—and not others, and they are divided into different sections (teams) based on their instruments. The conductor's role is not to play each instrument better than the musicians but to lead them all through the most effective performance of a particular work.

This model is in sharp contrast to the traditional pyramid-like organizational model, where one leader sits at the top, with layers of managers beneath. We therefore need to take a look at the traditional arrangement first.

The Traditional Management Pyramid: Levels & Areas

A new Silicon Valley technology start-up company staffed by young people in sandals and shorts may be so small and so loosely organized that only one or two members may be said to be a manager. General Motors or the U.S. Army, in contrast, has thousands of managers doing thousands of different things. Is there a picture we can draw that applies to all the different kinds of organizations and describes them in ways that make sense? Yes: by levels and by areas, as the pyramid on the next page shows. *(See Figure 1.2.)*

Three Levels of Management

Not everyone who works in an organization is a manager, of course, but those who are may be classified into three levels—top, middle, and first-line.

Top Managers   Their offices may be equipped with expensive leather chairs and have lofty views. Or, as with one Internet service provider (ISP), they may have plastic lawn chairs in the CEO's office and beat-up furniture in the lobby. Whatever their decor, an organization's top managers tend to have titles such as "chief executive officer (CEO)," "chief operating officer (COO)," "president," and "senior vice president."

Some may be the stars in their fields, the men and women whose pictures appear on the covers of business magazines, people such as MySpace cofounders Tom Anderson and Chris DeWolfe or PepsiCo CEO Indra Nooyi, who appeared on the cover of *Fortune,* or former eBay CEO Meg Whitman or AT&T CEO Ed Whitacre, who were on the cover of *Forbes.* As we've seen, the salaries and

Levels of Management

Top managers

Middle managers

First-line managers

Nonmanagerial personnel

Functional Areas

R&D   Marketing   Finance   Production   Human resources

figure 1.2

THE LEVELS AND AREAS OF MANAGEMENT

Top managers make long-term decisions, middle managers implement those decisions, and first-line managers make short-term decisions.

One kind of top manager. Jeffrey Immelt, chairman and CEO, has worked at General Electric for over 28 years. Known for its consumer appliances, GE also sells aircraft engines, lighting, and medical imaging equipment. Do you see yourself joining a company and staying with it for life, as Immelt did, or is that even possible anymore?

bonuses can average $290,000 a year for CEOs and presidents of small and mid-size companies to far over $10 million for top executives in large companies.

Top managers **make long-term decisions about the overall direction of the organization and establish the objectives, policies, and strategies for it.** They need to pay a lot of attention to the environment outside the organization, being alert for long-run opportunities and problems and devising strategies for dealing with them. Thus, executives at this level must be future oriented, dealing with uncertain, highly competitive conditions.

These people stand at the summit of the management pyramid. But the nature of a pyramid is that the farther you climb, the less space remains at the top. Thus, most pyramid climbers never get to the apex. However, that doesn't mean that you shouldn't try. Indeed, you might end up atop a much smaller pyramid of some other organization than the one you started out in—and happier with the result.

Middle Managers *Middle managers* **implement the policies and plans of the top managers above them and supervise and coordinate the activities of the first-line managers below them.** In the nonprofit world, middle managers may have titles such as "clinic director," "dean of student services," and the like. In the for-profit world, the titles may be "division head," "plant manager," and "branch sales manager." Their salaries may range from under $50,000 up to $110,000 a year.

Sometimes the titles have become more creative, in accordance with the changing face of management. For instance, now there are titles such as chief security officer, chief sales officer, chief revenue officer, and chief investment officer. A company may also have a "chief learning officer" in charge of training, a "chief green (or sustainability)

Top manager of another sort. Mark Zuckerberg, shown at the Palo Alto, California, headquarters of Facebook, has become one of today's most watched techno-entrepreneurs. Zuckerberg founded the well-known social networking site in his dorm room at Harvard during a semester break in 2004. Do you think a top manager is always adventurous?

officer" in charge of environmental concerns, and even a "chief beer officer," a position created by the Sheraton Hotels Four Points chain for a person who selects beers for hotel menus and leads brewery tours.[51]

First-Line Managers The job titles at the bottom of the managerial pyramid tend to be on the order of "department head," "foreman" or "forewoman," "team leader," or "supervisor"—clerical supervisor, production supervisor, research supervisor, and so on. Indeed, *supervisor* is the name often given to first-line managers as a whole. Their salaries may run from $25,000 to $50,000 a year.

Following the plans of middle and top managers, *first-line managers* **make short-term operating decisions, directing the daily tasks of nonmanagerial personnel,** who are, of course, all those people who work directly at their jobs but don't oversee the work of others.

No doubt the job of first-line manager will be the place where you would start your managerial career. This can be a valuable experience because it will be the training and testing ground for your management ideas.

Areas of Management: Functional Managers versus General Managers

We can represent the levels of management by slicing the organizational pyramid horizontally. We can also slice the pyramid vertically to represent the organization's departments or functional areas, as we did in Figure 1.2.

In a for-profit technology company, these might be *Research & Development, Marketing, Finance, Production,* and *Human Resources.* In a nonprofit college, these might be *Faculty, Student Support Staff, Finance, Maintenance,* and *Administration.* Whatever the names of the departments, the organization is run by two types of managers—functional and general. (These are line managers, with authority to direct employees. Staff managers mainly assist line managers).

Functional Managers If your title is Vice President of Production, Director of Finance, or Administrator for Human Resources, you are a functional manager. A *functional manager* **is responsible for just one organizational activity.** Marissa Mayer, who joined Google as the search company's first female engineer, is now Vice President of Search Products & User Experience, responsible for overseeing the development of Web search, Google Earth, Google Desktop, and several other products. Leading this specialized sort of research-and-development activity makes her a functional manager.

General Managers If you are working in a small organization of, say, 100 people and your title is Executive Vice President, you are probably a general manager over several departments, such as Production and Finance and Human Resources. A *general manager* **is responsible for several organizational activities.** At the top of the pyramid, general managers are those who seem to be the subject of news stories in magazines such as *BusinessWeek, Fortune, Forbes, Inc.,* and *Fast Company.* Examples are big-company CEO Jeffrey R. Immelt of General Electric and former CEO Anne Mulcahy of Xerox Corp. It also includes small-company CEOs such as Gayle Martz, who heads Sherpa's Pet Trading Co., a $4 million New York company with 10 employees that sells travel carriers for dogs and cats. But not all general managers are in for-profit organizations.

Dr. Rick Aubry is president of Rubicon Programs, a San Francisco–area nonprofit formed after California state psychiatric hospitals were closed in 1973. The organization funds training, housing, and employment programs that have helped thousands of former patients and disabled, impoverished, and homeless people reenter society. Rubicon funds most of its $18 million annual budget from its rental properties, enterprises, and services, such as the Rubicon Bakery and Rubicon Landscape Services, which also provide job training. Aubrey makes a point of running Rubicon like a business, reflecting the strategic vision of a top-level general manager.[52] Rubicon was a recipient of *Fast Company* magazine's 2008 Social Capitalist awards.[53]

Managers for Three Types of Organizations: For-Profit, Nonprofit, Mutual-Benefit

There are three types of organizations classified according to the three purposes for which they are formed—*for-profit, nonprofit, and mutual-benefit.*[54]

Nonprofit manager. A general manager is responsible for several organizational activities. Rick Aubry oversees a nonprofit organization serving 4,000 people annually with $18 million annual revenues. Do you think managerial skills are different for nonprofit and for-profit organizations?

I. For-Profit Organizations: For Making Money   For-profit, or business, organizations are formed to make money, or profits, by offering products or services. When most people think of "management," they think of business organizations, ranging from Allstate to Zenith, from Amway to Zagat.

2. Nonprofit Organizations: For Offering Services   Managers in nonprofit organizations are often known as "administrators." Nonprofit organizations may be either in the public sector, such as the University of California, or in the private sector, such as Stanford University. Either way, their purpose is to offer services to some clients, not to make a profit. Examples of such organizations are hospitals, colleges, and social-welfare agencies (the Salvation Army, the Red Cross).

One particular type of nonprofit organization is called the *commonweal organization.* Unlike nonprofit service organizations, which offer services to *some* clients, commonweal organizations offer services to *all* clients within their jurisdictions. Examples are the military services, the U.S. Postal Service, and your local fire and police departments.

3. Mutual-Benefit Organizations: For Aiding Members   Mutual-benefit organizations are voluntary collections of members—political parties, farm cooperatives, labor unions, trade associations, and clubs—whose purpose is to advance members' interests.

Do Managers Manage Differently for Different Types of Organizations?

If you become a manager, would you be doing the same types of things regardless of the type of organization? Generally you would be; that is, you would be performing the four management functions—planning, organizing, leading, and controlling—that we described in Section 1.3.

The single biggest difference, however, is that in a for-profit organization, the measure of its success is how much profit (or loss) it generates. In the other two types of organization, although income and expenditures are very important concerns, the measure of success is usually the effectiveness of the services delivered—how many students were graduated, if you're a college administrator, or how many crimes were prevented or solved, if you're a police chief. ●

major question?

To be an exceptional manager, what roles must I play successfully?

THE BIG PICTURE

Managers tend to work long hours at an intense pace; their work is characterized by fragmentation, brevity, and variety; and they rely more on verbal than on written communication. According to management scholar Henry Mintzberg, managers play three roles—*interpersonal, informational,* and *decisional.* Interpersonal roles include figurehead, leader, and liaison activities. Informational roles are monitor, disseminator, and spokesperson. Decisional roles are entrepreneur, disturbance handler, resource allocator, and negotiator.

Clearly, being a successful manager requires playing several different roles and exercising several different skills. What are they?

The Manager's Roles: Mintzberg's Useful Findings

Maybe, you think, it might be interesting to shadow some managers to see what it is, in fact, they actually do. That's exactly what management scholar **Henry Mintzberg** did when, in the late 1960s, he followed five chief executives around for a week and recorded their working lives.[55] And what he found is valuable to know, since it applies not only to top managers but also to managers on all levels.

Consider this portrait of a manager's workweek: "There was no break in the pace of activity during office hours," reported Mintzberg about his subjects. "The mail (average of 36 pieces per day), telephone calls (average of five per day), and meetings (average of eight) accounted for almost every minute from the moment these executives entered their offices in the morning until they departed in the evening."[56]

Multitasking. Multiple activities are characteristic of a manager—which is why so many managers carry a smart phone to keep track of their schedules. Many students already use these. Do you?

Only five phone calls per day? And, of course, this was back in an era before e-mail, texting, and Twitter, which nowadays can shower some executives with 100, even 300, messages a day. Indeed, says Ed Reilly, who heads the American Management Association, all the e-mail, cell-phone calls, text messaging, and so on can lead people to end up "concentrating on the urgent rather than the important."[57]

Obviously, the top manager's life is extraordinarily busy. Here are three of Mintzberg's findings, important for any prospective manager:

I. A Manager Relies More on Verbal Than on Written Communication Writing letters, memos, and reports takes time. Most managers in Mintzberg's research tended to get and transmit information through telephone conversations and meetings. No doubt this is still true, although the technology of e-mail and texting now makes it possible to communicate almost as rapidly in writing as with the spoken word.

2. A Manager Works Long Hours at an Intense Pace "A true break seldom occurred," wrote Mintzberg about his subjects.

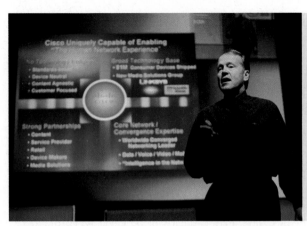

A Mintzberg manager. John T. Chambers, CEO of network gear maker Cisco Systems, relies more on verbal than on written communication, works long hours, and experiences an "interrupt-driven day." Interestingly, Chambers is successful despite having had lifelong dyslexia, the common language-related learning disability. He compensates by leaving 40 or 50 voice mails a day, studies summaries in briefing binders, and tapes videos for employees. What kind of personal adversity have you had to overcome?

"Coffee was taken during meetings, and lunchtime was almost always devoted to formal or informal meetings."

Long hours at work are standard, he found, with 50 hours being typical and up to 90 hours not unheard of. A 1999 survey by John P. Kotter of the Harvard Business School found that the general managers he studied worked just under 60 hours per week.[58]

Are such hours really necessary? Three decades following the Mintzberg research, Linda Stroh, Director of Workplace Studies at Loyola University Chicago, did a study that found that people who work more also earn more. "Those managers who worked 61 hours or more per week had earned, on average, about two promotions over the past five years," she reported.[59] Prior to the 2008 recession, researchers at Purdue and McGill universities found that more companies were allowing managers to reduce their working hours and spend more time with their families yet still advance their high-powered careers.[60] However, during economic hard times, top managers may be more apt to see subordinates' work-life flexibility as a "perk" they can no longer afford.

3. A Manager's Work Is Characterized by Fragmentation, Brevity, & Variety
Only about a tenth of the managerial activities observed by Mintzberg took more than an hour; about half were completed in under 9 minutes. Phone calls averaged 6 minutes, informal meetings 10 minutes, and desk-work sessions 15 minutes. "When free time appeared," wrote Mintzberg, "ever-present subordinates quickly usurped it."

No wonder the executive's work time has been characterized as "the interrupt-driven day" and that many managers—such as the late Mary Kay Ash, head of the Mary Kay Cosmetics company—get up as early as 5 A.M. so that they will have a quiet period in which to work undisturbed.[61] No wonder that finding balance between work and family lives is an ongoing concern and that many managers—such as Dawn Lepore, executive V.P. of discount broker Charles Schwab & Co.—have become "much less tolerant of activities that aren't a good use of my time" and so have become better delegators.[62]

It is clear from Mintzberg's work that *time and task management* are major challenges for every manager. The Practical Action box on the next page, "Executive Functioning: How Good Are You at Focusing Your Thoughts, Controlling Your Impulses, & Avoiding Distractions," examines this challenge further. The box "Getting Control of Your Time: Dealing with the Information Deluge in College & in Your Career" at the end of this chapter also offers some important suggestions.

Executive Functioning: How Good Are You at Focusing Your Thoughts, Controlling Your Impulses, & Avoiding Distractions?

Managers are executives, of course, and good managers have what psychologists call good "executive functioning." This is a psychological, rather than a workplace, term that involves the ability to manage oneself and one's resources in order to achieve a goal. Specifically, this means the ability to focus your thoughts, control your impulses, and avoid distractions.[63]

How good is your executive functioning right now? A recent study found that 8- to 18-year-olds spend more than 7½ hours a day on smart phones, computers, TVs, or other electronic devices. And, because so many of them are multitasking—as in listening to music while surfing the Web—they pack on average nearly 11 hours of media content into those 7½ hours.[64] Today 16- to 18-year-olds multitask by performing seven tasks on average in their free time—such as watching TV while texting on their cell phone, sending instant messages, and checking in with Facebook—according to psychology researcher Larry Rosen.[65] Add to that the fact that U.S. households consumed a mind-boggling average of 33.8 gigabytes of information and 10,845 trillion words

(equivalent to a seven-foot stack of Dan Brown novels) in 2008, and you can see that the challenges to staying focused are overwhelming.[66]

"Life," says Winifred Gallagher, author of *Rapt,* "is the sum of what you focus on."[67] Another writer says, "You can drive yourself crazy trying to multitask and answer every e-mail message instantly. Or you can recognize your brain's finite capacity for processing information."[68] When you read this textbook while listening to music and watching TV, you may think you're simultaneously doing three separate tasks, but you're really not. "It's like playing tennis with three balls," says one expert.[69]

Your Call

Do you procrastinate about getting your work done? Most people do—and in fact the problem has worsened over the years: Today about 26% of Americans think of themselves as chronic procrastinators, up from 5% in 1978. The reason: too many tempting diversions, especially electronic ones.[70] Is this a problem for you? What can you do to improve your "executive functioning"?

Three Types of Managerial Roles

Three Types of Managerial Roles: Interpersonal, Informational, & Decisional   From his observations and other research, Mintzberg concluded that managers play three broad types of roles or "organized sets of behavior": *interpersonal, informational,* and *decisional.*

1. Interpersonal Roles—Figurehead, Leader, and Liaison   In their *interpersonal roles,* managers interact with people inside and outside their work units. The three interpersonal roles include *figurehead, leader,* and *liaison* activities.

2. Informational Roles—Monitor, Disseminator, and Spokesperson   The most important part of a manager's job, Mintzberg believed, is information handling, because accurate information is vital for making intelligent decisions. In their three *informational roles*—as *monitor, disseminator,* and *spokesperson*—managers receive and communicate information with other people inside and outside the organization.

3. Decisional Roles—Entrepreneur, Disturbance Handler, Resource Allocator, and Negotiator   In their *decisional roles,* managers use information to make decisions to solve problems or take advantage of opportunities. The four decision-making roles are *entrepreneur, disturbance handler, resource allocator,* and *negotiator.*

These roles are summarized on the next page. *(See Table 1.1.)*

Did anyone say a manager's job is easy? Certainly it's not for people who want to sit on the sidelines of life. Above all else, managers are *doers.*   ●

table 1.1 THREE TYPES OF MANAGERIAL ROLES: INTERPERSONAL, INFORMATIONAL, AND DECISIONAL

Broad Managerial Roles	Types of Roles	Description
Interpersonal Managerial Roles	**Figurehead role**	In your *figurehead role*, you show visitors around your company, attend employee birthday parties, and present ethical guidelines to your subordinates. In other words, you perform symbolic tasks that represent your organization.
	Leadership role	In your role of *leader*, you are responsible for the actions of your subordinates, since their successes and failures reflect on you. Your leadership is expressed in your decisions about training, motivating, and disciplining people.
	Liaison role	In your *liaison* role, you must act like a politician, working with other people outside your work unit and organization to develop alliances that will help you achieve your organization's goals.
Informational Managerial Roles	**Monitor role**	As a *monitor*, you should be constantly alert for useful information, whether gathered from newspaper stories about the competition or gathered from snippets of conversation with subordinates you meet in the hallway.
	Disseminator role	Workers complain they never know what's going on? That probably means their supervisor failed in the role of *disseminator*. Managers need to constantly disseminate important information to employees, as via e-mail and meetings.
	Spokesperson role	You are expected, of course, to be a diplomat, to put the best face on the activities of your work unit or organization to people outside it. This is the informational role of *spokesperson*.
Decisional Managerial Roles	**Entrepreneur role**	A good manager is expected to be an *entrepreneur*, to initiate and encourage change and innovation.
	Disturbance handler role	Unforeseen problems—from product defects to international currency crises—require you be a *disturbance handler*, fixing problems.
	Resource allocator role	Because you'll never have enough time, money, and so on, you'll need to be a *resource allocator*, setting priorities about use of resources.
	Negotiator role	To be a manager is to be a continual *negotiator*, working with others inside and outside the organization to accomplish your goals.

major question?

Do I have what it takes to be an entrepreneur?

THE BIG PICTURE

Entrepreneurship, a necessary attribute of business, means taking risks to create a new enterprise. It is expressed through two kinds of innovators, the entrepreneur and the intrapreneur.

Yelp is the 2004 brainchild of Jeremy Stoppelman and Russel Simmons, two engineers in their twenties working for PayPal, the online payments firm in California's Silicon Valley, who wanted to make it easier for consumers to find good businesses and avoid bad ones. "What they created," says one account, "was an online yellow pages with attitude. Yelp lets anyone critique any business and grade it, with ratings from one star to five stars."[71] All kinds of businesses are rated, from restaurants to mechanics to dentists. While the idea of rating businesses is not new, Yelp uses a special algorithm (step-by-step problem-solving procedure) that determines which reviews are deleted, which featured prominently, and which displayed inconspicuously. And the company keeps the algorithm a closely guarded secret.

The idea for Yelp came to Stoppelman and Simmons over lunch one fall, when they talked about building a Web site for people to e-mail friends questions such as "Who knows a good auto mechanic in San Francisco?" and then posting the results online. But, as sometimes happens with new enterprises, the core idea—allowing people to publish reviews without being prompted—was an afterthought. Nevertheless, after lunch the pair went back to the office and successfully pitched their boss (who had made tens of millions on PayPal) to invest $1 million.

With this initial help, the Yelp founders were hoping to build momentum and launch a national company, but the idea failed to catch fire. After a few months, without any additional funding, the two decided they had to stay local. "If we just create a cool city guide to San Francisco and it's worth $10 or $20 million, that would be a win," Stoppelman said. To focus on making Yelp famous locally, they selected a few dozen of the most active reviewers on the site and invited them to an open-bar party; 100 people showed up. Yelp threw more parties for

Entrepreneurs. Jeremy Stoppelman and Russel Simmons founded Yelp in San Francisco in 2004. Most people, even young people, prefer the security of a job with a paycheck rather than the risks of starting a business. Which life would you prefer?

prolific reviewers, which gave casual users a reason to use the site more. By mid-2005, Yelp had 12,000 reviewers. With additional funding, it hired more party planners in New York, Chicago, and Boston. As the Yelp influence grew, bars and restaurants became more willing to host (for free) the parties in the hopes that crowds would come back and write favorable reviews. The company also began setting up call centers to sell advertising to businesses that had been reviewed.

Yelp is not without controversy. By encouraging consumers to be unsparing in their critiques, it helps good businesses to thrive, but it also empowers users to be unnecessarily cruel and to hurt small mom-and-pop businesses already struggling with the Great Recession and strong competition. Still, the company seems to have achieved success, earning what is thought to be about $30 million a year in revenue, and may be a candidate to be acquired by a larger company.

Entrepreneurship Defined: Taking Risks in Pursuit of Opportunity

Yelp is one of the many small outfits in the United States that is one of the primary drivers of the nation's economy. Indeed, according to the Small Business Administration, small outfits create some 75% of all new jobs, represent 99.7% of all employers, and employ 50% of the private workforce.[72] (Note, however: Because many small firms fail, "new businesses are important to job creation primarily because they get founded," says entrepreneurial studies professor Scott Shane, "not because most of them tend to grow.")[73] Today women-owned businesses seem to be becoming America's new job-creation machine. One report projects that female-owned small businesses, which now provide only 16% of total U.S. employment, will be responsible for creating one-third of the jobs by 2018. This could transform the workplace by creating opportunities for other people, creating a positive working environment, and being more customer focused.[74]

Most small businesses originate with people like Stoppelman and Simmons. They are the entrepreneurs, the people with the idea, the risk takers. The most successful entrepreneurs become wealthy and make the covers of business magazines: Fred Smith of Federal Express, Debbie Fields of Mrs. Fields Cookies, Anita Roddick of The Body Shop, Michael Dell of Dell Computers. Failed entrepreneurs may benefit from the experience to live to fight another day—as did Henry Ford, twice bankrupt before achieving success with Ford Motor Co.

What Entrepreneurship Is *Entrepreneurship* **is the process of taking risks to try to create a new enterprise.** There are two types of entrepreneurship:

- **The entrepreneur. An *entrepreneur* is someone who sees a new opportunity for a product or service and launches a business to try to realize it.** Most entrepreneurs run small businesses with fewer than 100 employees.

- **The intrapreneur. An *intrapreneur* is someone who works inside an existing organization who sees an opportunity for a product or service and mobilizes the organization's resources to try to realize it.** This person might be a researcher or a scientist but could also be a manager who sees an opportunity to create a new venture that could be profitable.

How Do Entrepreneurs & Managers Differ? While the entrepreneur is not necessarily an inventor, he or she "always searches for change, responds to it, and exploits it as an opportunity," Peter Drucker pointed out.[75] How does this differ from being a manager?

Example of an Intrapreneur: Marissa Mayer Develops a Researcher's Little Personal Program into Google News

Some products developed internally are the results of happy accidents. (This was how Post-it notes came about, the eventual result of an experimental adhesive discovered by 3M employee Art Fry, for which the company at first could find no use.) At Google in 2001, following the terror attacks of 9/11, researcher Krishna Bharat wrote a little program to help him read news better, gathering news from his 15 favorite sources and using artificial intelligence to group them. After using the tool for his personal news reading, he offered it to some colleagues.

"The promise and excitement I felt when I first saw Krishna's tool was immense," says Marissa Mayer, then Google's Vice President of Search Products. "It wasn't impressive in that first form—a plain white page with small groups of five plain blue links per topic and only about 10 topics covered. But I could see immediately how we could make it into a polished online news experience."[76]

Eventually the program went through 64 different iterations before it was launched as Google News as a way to facilitate browsing between different sections such as sports, business, and entertainment, tapping into 4,000 news sources.

YOUR CALL

What companies are you aware of that do their own in-house research and development of products?

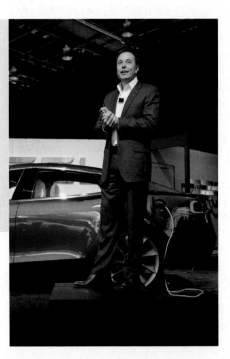

Green entrepreneur. South African-born entrepreneur Elon Musk became a lead investor and later CEO at Tesla Motors in Palo Alto, California, a company incorporated in 2003 to pursue mass production of an electric sports car. The Tesla Roadster runs on a lithium-ion battery, has a range of greater than 200 miles on a single charge, and retails for a base price of $109,000. What passion of yours might you turn into a business?

Being an entrepreneur is what it takes to *start* a business; being a manager is what it takes to *grow* or *maintain* a business. As an entrepreneur/intrapreneur, you initiate new goods or services; as a manager you coordinate the resources to produce the goods or services.

The examples of success we mentioned above—Fred Smith, Debbie Fields, Anita Roddick, Michael Dell—are actually *both* entrepreneurs and effective managers. Some people, however, find they like the start-up part but hate the management part. For example, Stephen Wozniak, entrepreneurial cofounder with Steve Jobs of Apple Computer, abandoned the computer industry completely and went back to college. Jobs, by contrast, went on to launch another business, Pixar, which among other things became the animation factory that made the movies *Toy Story* and *Finding Nemo*.

Entrepreneurial companies have been called "gazelles" for the two attributes that make them successful: *speed and agility*. "Gazelles have mastered the art of the quick," says Alan Webber, founding editor of *Fast Company* magazine. "They have internal approaches and fast decision-making approaches that let them move with maximum agility in a fast-changing business environment."[77]

Is this the kind of smart, innovative world you'd like to be a part of? Most people prefer the security of a job and a paycheck. Entrepreneurs do seem to have psychological characteristics that are different from managers, as follows:[78]

- **Characteristic of both—high need for achievement.** Both entrepreneurs and managers have a high need for achievement. However, entrepreneurs certainly seem to be motivated to pursue moderately difficult goals through their own efforts in order to realize their ideas and, they hope, financial rewards. Managers, by contrast, are more motivated by promotions and organizational rewards of power and perks.

- **Also characteristic of both—belief in personal control of destiny.** If you believe "I am the captain of my fate, the master of my soul," you have what is known as ***internal locus of control,*** **the belief that you control your own destiny,** that external forces will have little influence. (External locus of control means the reverse—you believe you don't control your destiny, that external forces do.) Both entrepreneurs and managers like to think they have personal control over their lives.

- **Characteristic of both, but especially of entrepreneurs—high energy level and action orientation.** Rising to the top in an organization probably requires that a manager put in long hours. For entrepreneurs, however, creating a new enterprise may require an extraordinary investment of time and energy. In addition, while some managers may feel a sense of urgency, entrepreneurs are especially apt to be impatient and to want to get things done as quickly as possible, making them particularly action oriented.

- **Characteristic of both, but especially of entrepreneurs—high tolerance for ambiguity.** Every manager needs to be able to make decisions based on ambiguous—that is, unclear or incomplete—information. However, entrepreneurs must have more tolerance for ambiguity because they are trying to do things they haven't done before.

- **More characteristic of entrepreneurs than managers—self-confidence and tolerance for risk.** Managers must believe in themselves and be willing to make decisions; however, this statement applies even more to entrepreneurs. Precisely because they are willing to take risks in the pursuit of new opportunities—indeed, even risk personal financial failure—entrepreneurs need the confidence to act decisively.

Of course, not all entrepreneurs have this kind of faith in themselves. So-called *necessity* entrepreneurs are people such as laid-off corporate workers, discharged military people, immigrants, and divorced homemakers who suddenly must earn a living and are simply trying to replace lost income and are hoping a job comes along. These make up about 11% of entrepreneurs. However, so-called *opportunity* entrepreneurs—the other 89%—are those who start their own business out of a burning desire rather than because they lost a job. Unlike necessity types, they tend to be more ambitious and to start firms that can lead to high-growth businesses.[79]

Which do you think you would be happier doing—being an entrepreneur or being a manager? ●

PepsiCo's Indra Nooyi. Are entrepreneurs and managers really two different breeds? Indian-born Nooyi, CEO of PepsiCo, has taken the lead in attempting to move the company away from fast food and sodas into more healthy foods.

To be a terrific manager, what skills should I cultivate?

THE BIG PICTURE

Good managers need to work on developing three principal skills. The first is *technical,* the ability to perform a specific job. The second is *conceptual,* the ability to think analytically. The third is *human,* the ability to interact well with people.

A few days before becoming the new CEO at Autodesk, Carol Bartz (currently CEO of Yahoo!) was diagnosed with breast cancer. Yet she took only four weeks off, instead of the doctor-recommended six, for surgery and recovery and worked through the entire seven months of chemotherapy. Is this the kind of beyond-the-call-of-duty activity that's required to have the right management stuff? (Actually, today Bartz says she shouldn't have rushed things.) Let's see what the "right stuff" might be.

In the mid-1970s, researcher **Robert Katz** found that through education and experience managers acquire three principal skills—*technical, conceptual,* and *human.*[80]

1. Technical Skills—The Ability to Perform a Specific Job

Bartz has a B.A. degree in computer science and worked for a number of computer hardware and software companies. Missing from her résumé, however, is much Internet or Web advertising experience, which is critical to Yahoo!.[81] Some analysts would have preferred a "turnaround manager" rather than what they view as a "sustaining manager" to take the lead job. On the other hand, Bartz clearly raised the fortunes of Autodesk and, as one former director said, "She has this enormous [managerial] capability to make things happen." She is also on the boards of several Silicon Valley companies, such as Cisco, Intel, and Network Appliance.

Technical skills **consist of the job-specific knowledge needed to perform well in a specialized field.** Having the requisite technical skills seems to be most important at the lower levels of management—that is, among first-line managers.

2. Conceptual Skills—The Ability to Think Analytically

Bartz also has the "big picture" knowledge to keep up with her job. While she does have a private life—a husband who is a Sun Microsystems vice president, three children, and an interest in gardening—about balancing career with family, she says, "I have belief that life isn't about balance, because balance is perfection. . . . Rather, it's about catching the ball before it hits the floor."[82] Thus, among her first acts at Yahoo! she asked for an organization chart, then proceeded to upend the organizational structure, replacing executives and cutting 5% of the staff, to get some breathing room to figure out what Yahoo! should do. She also negotiated an Internet search partnership with rival Microsoft, resolving a tense relationship that began with her predecessors.[83] Bartz is said to lead with a consumer-based vision. "Who wants innovation for innovation's sake if it doesn't make your life easier, more efficient, more productive?" she says. "So expect us to hear you better and take better care of you."[84]

Conceptual skills **consist of the ability to think analytically, to visualize an organization as a whole and understand how the parts work together.** Conceptual skills are particularly important for top managers, who must deal with problems that are ambiguous but that could have far-reaching consequences.

3. Human Skills—The Ability to Interact Well with People

This may well be the most difficult set of skills to master. *Human skills* **consist of the ability to work well in cooperation with other people to get things done**—especially with people in teams, an important part of today's organizations (as we discuss in Chapter 13). Often these are thought of as "soft skills." These skills—the ability to motivate, to inspire trust, to communicate with others—are necessary for managers of all levels. But because of the range of people, tasks, and problems in an organization, developing your human-interacting skills may turn out to be an ongoing, lifelong effort.

Bartz believes that women manage differently from men and that she is able to get people to open up to her about their personal and professional concerns.[85] One device she used at Autodesk was to have a series of "brown-bag chats" with employees. One observer of these events found her "direct and quick-witted, quick to laugh, and willing to tease her way through tense situations."[86] On the other hand, an Autodesk manager said she often talked like a sailor, famous for profanity-laced phone calls and described as someone who "doesn't spend a lot of time worrying about how people are going to feel. She always wanted to make sure the job got done."[87] But others found her equally comfortable talking to technologists as well as businesspeople such as marketers or Wall Street analysts.

Yahoo! campus. This sprawling office complex, or "campus," in Sunnyvale, California, is headquarters for most of Yahoo!'s enterprises, including CEO Carol Bartz's office. Bartz seems to have the three skills—technical, conceptual, and human—necessary to be a terrific manager for such a complex organization. Which skill do you think you need to work on the most? (Human skills are the most difficult to master.)

The Most Valued Traits in Managers

"In the range of difficulty in turning Yahoo around, from one to ten, this is an eleven," says one analyst about the challenge confronting Bartz.[88] By the time you read this, you may have an idea whether she's had some success or whether the company has met another kind of fate. Still, Bartz embodies the qualities sought in star managers, especially top managers. "The style for running a company is different from what it used to be," says a top executive recruiter of CEOs. "Companies don't want dictators, kings, or emperors."[89] Instead of someone who gives orders, they want executives who ask probing questions and force the people beneath them to think and find the right answers.

Among the chief skills companies seek in top managers are the following:

• The ability to motivate and engage others.

• The ability to communicate.

• Work experience outside the United States (although Bartz actually has never worked overseas).

• High energy levels to meet the demands of global travel and a 24/7 world.[90]

Let's see how you can begin to acquire these and other qualities for success. ●

Getting Control of Your Time: Dealing with the Information Deluge in College & in Your Career

Professionals and managers all have to deal with this central problem: how not to surrender their lives to their jobs. The place to start, however, is in college. If you can learn to manage time while you're still a student, you'll find it will pay off not only in higher grades and more free time but also in more efficient information-handling skills that will serve you well as a manager later on.[91]

Using Your "Prime Study Time"

Each of us has a different energy cycle. The trick is to use it effectively. That way, your hours of best performance will coincide with your heaviest academic demands. For example, if your energy level is high during the evenings, you should plan to do your studying then.

To capitalize on your prime study time, you take the following steps: (1) Make a study schedule for the entire term, and indicate the times each day during which you plan to study. (2) Find some good places to study—places where you can avoid distractions. (3) Avoid time wasters, but give yourself frequent rewards for studying, such as a TV show, a favorite piece of music, or a conversation with a friend.

Improving Your Memory Ability

Memorizing is, of course, one of the principal requirements for succeeding in college. And it's a great help for success in life afterward.

Here are some tips on learning to concentrate:[92]

Choose What to Focus On

"People don't realize that attention is a finite resource, like money," one expert says. "Do you want to invest your cognitive cash on endless Twittering or Net surfing or couch potatoing [watching TV]?" She adds, "Where did the idea come from that anyone who wants to contact you can do so at any time? You need to take charge of what you pay attention to instead of responding to the latest stimuli."[93] For example, to block out noise, you can wear earplugs while reading, to create your own "stimulus shelter."

Devote the First 1½ Hours of Your Day to Your Most Important Task

Studying a hard subject? Make it your first task of the day, and concentrate on it for 90 minutes. After that, your brain will probably need a rest, and you can answer e-mail, return phone calls, and so on. But until that first break, don't do anything else, because it can take the brain 20 minutes to refocus.

Space Your Studying, Rather Than Cramming

Cramming—making a frantic, last-minute attempt to memorize massive amounts of material—is probably the least effective means of absorbing information. Research shows that it's best to space out your studying of a subject over successive days. A series of study sessions over several days is preferable to trying to do it all during the same number of hours on one day. It is repetition that helps move information into your long-term memory bank.

Review Information Repeatedly—Even "Overlearn It"

By repeatedly reviewing information—what is known as "rehearsing"—you can improve both your retention and your understanding of it. Overlearning is continuing to review material even after you appear to have absorbed it.

Use Memorizing Tricks

There are several ways to organize information so that you can retain it better. For example, you can make drawings or diagrams (as of the parts of a computer system). Some methods of establishing associations between items you want to remember are given in the box. *(See Exhibit I.I.)*

- **Mental and physical imagery:** Use your visual and other senses to construct a personal image of what you want to remember. Indeed, it helps to make the image humorous, action-filled, sexual, bizarre, or outrageous in order to establish a personal connection. Example: To remember the name of the 21st president of the United States, Chester Arthur, you might visualize an author writing the number "21" on a wooden chest. This mental image helps you associate chest (Chester), author (Arthur), and 21 (21st president).

- **Acronyms and acrostics:** An acronym is a word created from the first letters of items in a list. For instance, Roy G. Biv helps you remember the colors of the rainbow in order: red, orange, yellow, green, blue, indigo, violet. An acrostic is a phrase or sentence created from the first letters of items in a list. Fox example, *Every Good Boy Does Fine* helps you remember that the order of musical notes on the staff is E-G-B-D-F.

- **Location:** Location memory occurs when you associate a concept with a place or imaginary place. For example, you could learn the parts of a computer system by imagining a walk across campus. Each building you pass could be associated with a part of the computer system.

exhibit I.I   **SOME MEMORIZING TRICKS**

- **Word games:** Jingles and rhymes are devices frequently used by advertisers to get people to remember their products. You may recall the spelling rule "*I* before *E* except after *C* or when sounded like *A* as in *neighbor* or *weigh*." You can also use narrative methods, such as making up a story.

How to Improve Your Reading Ability: The SQ3R Method

SQ3R stands for "survey, question, read, recite, and review."[94] The strategy behind it is to break down a reading assignment into small segments and master each before moving on. The five steps of the SQ3R method are as follows:

1. *Survey the chapter before you read it:* Get an overview of the chapter or other reading assignment before you begin reading it. If you have a sense of what the material is about before you begin reading it, you can predict where it is going. In this text, we offer on the first page of every chapter a list of the main heads and accompanying key questions. At the end of each chapter we offer a Summary, which explains what the chapter's terms and concepts mean and why they are important.

2. *Question the segment in the chapter before you read it:* This step is easy to do, and the point, again, is to get you involved in the material. After surveying the entire chapter, go to the first segment—section, subsection, or even paragraph, depending on the level of difficulty and density of information. Look at the topic heading of that segment. In your mind, restate the heading as a question. In this book, following each section head we present a Key Question. An example in this chapter was "What are three directions of computer development and three directions of communications development?"

    After you have formulated the question, go to steps 3 and 4 (read and recite). Then proceed to the next segment and restate the heading there as a question.

3. *Read the segment about which you asked the question:* Now read the segment you asked the question about. Read with purpose, to answer the question you formulated. Underline or color-mark sentences that you think are important, if they help you answer the question. Read this portion of the text more than once, if necessary, until you can answer the question. In addition, determine whether the segment covers any other significant questions, and formulate answers to these, too. After you have read the segment, proceed to step 4.

(Perhaps you can see where this is all leading. If you read in terms of questions and answers, you will be better prepared when you see exam questions about the material later.)

4. *Recite the main points of the segment:* Recite means "say aloud." Thus, you should speak out loud (or softly) the answer to the principal question or questions about the segment and any other main points.

5. *Review the entire chapter by repeating questions:* After you have read the chapter, go back through it and review the main points. Then, without looking at the book, test your memory by repeating the questions.

Clearly the SQ3R method takes longer than simply reading with a rapidly moving color marker or underlining pencil. However, the technique is far more effective because it requires your involvement and understanding. This is the key to all effective learning.

Learning from Lectures

Does attending lectures really make a difference? Research shows that students with grades of B or above were more apt to have better class attendance than students with grades of C- or below.[95]

Some tips for getting the most out of lectures:

Take Effective Notes by Listening Actively

Research shows that good test performance is related to good note taking.[96] And good note taking requires that you listen actively—that is, participate in the lecture process. Here are some ways to take good lecture notes:

- *Read ahead and anticipate the lecturer:* Try to anticipate what the instructor is going to say, based on your previous reading. Having background knowledge makes learning more efficient.

- *Listen for signal words:* Instructors use key phrases such as "The most important point is . . . ," "There are four reasons for . . . ," "The chief reason . . . ," "Of special importance . . . ," "Consequently . . ." When you hear such signal phrases, mark your notes with a ! or *.

- *Take notes in your own words:* Instead of just being a stenographer, try to restate the lecturer's thoughts in your own words, which will make you pay attention more.

- *Ask questions:* By asking questions during the lecture, you necessarily participate in it and increase your understanding.

Review Your Notes Regularly

Make it a point to review your notes regularly—perhaps on the afternoon after the lecture, or once or twice a week. We cannot emphasize enough the importance of this kind of reviewing.

collaborative computing 11
competitive advantage 8
conceptual skills 29
controlling 15
databases 11
decisional roles 22
e-business 11
e-commerce 10
e-mail 11
effective 5
efficient 5
entrepreneur 25
entrepreneurship 25

first-line managers 18
four management functions 14
functional manager 19
general manager 19
human skills 29
informational roles 22
innovation 8
internal locus of control 27
Internet 10
interpersonal roles 22
intrapreneur 25
knowledge management 11
leading 15

management 5
management process 14
middle managers 17
organization 5
organizing 15
planning 14
project management
  software 11
sustainability 13
technical skills 28
telecommute 11
top managers 17
videoconferencing 11

Summary

 1.1 Management: What It Is, What Its Benefits Are
Management is defined as the pursuit of organizational goals *efficiently,* meaning to use resources wisely and cost-effectively, and *effectively,* meaning to achieve results, to make the right decisions, and to successfully carry them out to achieve the organization's goals.

 1.2 Seven Challenges to Being an Exceptional Manager
The seven challenges are (1) managing for competitive advantage, which means an organization must stay ahead in four areas: being responsive to customers, innovating new products or services, offering better quality, and being more efficient; (2) managing for diversity among different genders, ages, races, and ethnicities; (3) managing for globalization, the expanding universe; (4) managing for computers and telecommunications/information technology; (5) managing for right and wrong, or ethical standards; (6) managing for sustainability; and (7) managing for your own happiness and life goals.

 1.3 What Managers Do: The Four Principal Functions
The four management functions are represented by the abbreviation *POLC:*

(1) *planning*—setting goals and deciding how to achieve them; (2) *organizing*—arranging tasks, people, and other resources to accomplish the work; (3) *leading*—motivating, directing, and otherwise influencing people to work hard to achieve the organization's goals; and (4) *controlling*—monitoring performance, comparing it with goals, and taking corrective action as needed.

 1.4 Pyramid Power: Levels & Areas of Management
Within an organization, there are managers at three levels: (1) *top managers* make long-term decisions about the overall direction of the organization and establish the objectives, policies, and strategies for it; (2) *middle managers* implement the policies and plans of their superiors and supervise and coordinate the activities of the managers below them; and (3) *first-line managers* make short-term operating decisions, directing the daily tasks of nonmanagement personnel. There are three types of organizations: (1) *for-profit*—formed to make money by offering products or services; (2) *nonprofit*—to offer services to some, but not to make a profit; and (3) *mutual-benefit*—voluntary collections of members created to advance members' interests.

I.5 Roles Managers Must Play Successfully

The Mintzberg study shows that, first, a manager relies more on verbal than on written communication; second, managers work long hours at an intense pace; and third, a manager's work is characterized by fragmentation, brevity, and variety. Mintzberg concluded that managers play three broad roles: (1) *interpersonal*—figurehead, leader, and liaison; (2) *informational*—monitor, disseminator, and spokesperson; and (3) *decisional*—entrepreneur, disturbance handler, resource allocator, and negotiator.

I.6 The Entrepreneurial Spirit

Entrepreneurship, a necessary attribute of business, is the process of taking risks to create a new enterprise. Two types are (1) the *entrepreneur,* who sees a new opportunity for a product or service and launches a business to realize it; and (2) the *intrapreneur,* working inside an existing organization, who sees an opportunity for a product or service and mobilizes the organization's resources to realize it. Entrepreneurs start businesses; managers grow or maintain them. Both (but especially entrepreneurs) have a high need for achievement, high energy level and action orientation, and tolerance for ambiguity. Entrepreneurs are more self-confident and have higher tolerance for risk.

I.7 The Skills Exceptional Managers Need

The three skills that exceptional managers cultivate are (1) *technical,* consisting of job-specific knowledge needed to perform well in a specialized field; (2) *conceptual,* consisting of the ability to think analytically, to visualize an organization as a whole, and to understand how the parts work together; and (3) *human,* consisting of the ability to work well in cooperation with other people in order to get things done.

Management in Action

Chrysler Group CEO Sergio Marchionne Faces an Overwhelming Managerial Challenge

A decline in sales isn't the only big problem facing **Chrysler Group** LLC. Another, according to Chief Executive Sergio Marchionne, is the almost in-grained tendency to react to falling sales by slashing prices.

In Detroit, "there's almost a fanatical, maniacal interest in [market] share," Mr. Marchionne told reporters Monday on the opening day of the North American International Auto Show. But rarely, he added, has heavy discounting in pursuit of high volumes helped automakers generate profits in the long term. . . .

For the past seven months, the 57-year-old Italian-born Canadian has been working to shake up Chrysler and move the company away from old ways that forced it into bankruptcy reorganization last year. He has ousted several veteran executives, flattened its bureaucracy, and, according to people who have worked closely with Mr. Marchionne, injected an element of fear into its ranks.

One of the more frustrating problems for Mr. Marchionne has been the use of heavy rebates and other incentives to maintain sales—an issue that has plagued General Motors Co. and Ford Motor Co. over the years.

Last July, for example, when the U.S. government offered as much as $4,500 in "cash for clunkers" rebates, Chrysler's sales chief at the time, Peter Fong, drew up a plan to offer an additional $4,500 from Chrysler, two people familiar with the matter said. . . .

But when Mr. Marchionne found out about it, he was furious, these people said. In an August meeting with Mr. Fong and his sales team, the CEO excoriated them, saying doubling discounts amounted to "giving away margin" at a time when Chrysler was scrambling for profits, one person familiar with the details of the meeting said. "Sergio was ballistic," this person said. . . .

Mr. Marchionne took the helm at Chrysler in June, when the company exited bankruptcy protection and formed an alliance with Italy's Fiat SpA, where he also serves as CEO and which owns about 20% of Chrysler. In November, he laid out a turn-around plan that calls for Chrysler to launch a series of small cars designed by Fiat, and envisions Chrysler breaking even in 2010 and returning to profitability by 2011.

Besides working out ways for the two companies to work together, Mr. Marchionne has tried to shake up Chrysler's plodding corporate culture. . . .

To select his new management team, Mr. Marchionne held dozens of 15-minute interviews with Chrysler executives over several days to evaluate which ones to keep and which to push out, according to people who participated in the process.

When the process was over, Mr. Marchionne had 23 people reporting to him. Some were junior executives who had been moved up a level or two in the organization. . . .

Mr. Marchionne took an office on the fourth floor of the technology center at Chrysler's headquarters in Auburn Hills, Michigan, among Chrysler's engineers, instead of an office in its adjoining executive tower. His management team began meeting weekly in a nearby conference room equipped with video gear so that Fiat executives in Italy could take part.

In these meetings, Mr. Marchionne often spelled out what he saw as Chrysler's many deficiencies: margins and vehicle quality needed to improve and better control over pricing was imperative, according to one person who has been in the sessions. Details of the discussions weren't to leave the room. Security officers even called senior executives over the summer to make sure no one was talking to reporters about the company's plans.

Mr. Marchionne, a notorious workaholic, carries five BlackBerrys and works seven days a week. He spends about one full week a month in Michigan and flies back for weekend meetings when he isn't in town.

For Discussion

1. Which of the seven managerial challenges discussed in this chapter is Sergio Marchionne facing at Chrysler? Discuss.

2. Using Figure 1.1 as a guide, describe which functions of management were displayed by Marchionne.

3. Which of the three types of managerial roles did Marchionne display?

4. To what extent did Marchionne display an entrepreneurial orientation while trying to turn around Chrysler? Explain.

5. How would you evaluate Marchionne's technical, conceptual, and human skills? Discuss your rationale.

Source: Excerpted from Kate Linebaugh and Jeff Bennett, "Marchionne Upends Chrysler's Ways," *The Wall Street Journal*, January 12, 2010, pp. B1, B2. Copyright © 2010 by Dow Jones & Company, Inc. Reproduced with permission of Dow Jones & Company, Inc. via Copyright Clearance Center.

Self-Assessment

To What Extent Do You Possess an Entrepreneurial Spirit?

Objectives

1. To assess whether or not you have motivations, aptitudes, and attitudes possessed by entrepreneurs.

2. To consider whether or not you would like to start your own company.

Introduction

Earlier in the chapter we noted that small businesses are creating the majority of new jobs in the United States. We also discussed a variety of personal characteristics that differentiate managers from entrepreneurs. The overall goal of this exercise is for you to take a self-assessment that allows you to compare your motivations, aptitudes, and attitudes to those found in a sample of entrepreneurs from a variety of industries.

Instructions

Take an entrepreneurial self-assessment at **www.bdc .ca/en/advice_centre/tools/entrepreneurial_self_ assessment/Pages/entrepreneurial_self_assessment .aspx.** The quiz enables you to compare your motivation, aptitudes, and attitudes to a group of entrepreneurs.

Questions for Discussion

1. To what extent are your motives, aptitudes, and attitudes similar to entrepreneurs? Explain.

2. Based on your results, where do you have the biggest gaps with entrepreneurs in terms of the individual motives, aptitudes, and attitudes?

3. What do these gaps suggest about your entrepreneurial spirit? Discuss.

4. Do these results encourage or discourage you from thinking about starting your own business? Explain.

To Delay or Not to Delay?

You have been hired by a vice president of a national company to create an employee attitude survey, to administer it to all employees, and to interpret the results. You have known this vice president for more than 10 years and have worked for her on several occasions. She trusts and likes you, and you trust and like her. You have completed your work and now are ready to present the findings and your interpretations to the vice president's management team. The vice president has told you that she wants your honest interpretation of the results, because she is planning to make changes based on the results. Based on this discussion, your report clearly identifies several strengths and weaknesses that need to be addressed. For example, employees feel that they are working too hard and that management does not care about providing good customer service. At the meeting you will be presenting the results and your interpretations to a group of 15 managers. You also have known most of these managers for at least 5 years.

You show up for the presentation armed with slides, handouts, and specific recommendations. Your slides are loaded on the computer, and most of the participants have arrived. They are drinking coffee and telling you how excited they are about hearing your presentation. You also are excited to share your insights. Ten minutes before the presentation is set to begin, the vice president takes you out of the meeting room and says she wants to talk with you about your presentation. The two of you go to another office, and she closes the door. She then tells you that her boss's boss decided to come to the presentation unannounced. She feels that he is coming to the presentation solely looking for negative information in your report. He does not like the vice president and wants to replace her with one of his friends. If you present your results as planned, it will provide this individual with the information he needs to create serious problems for the vice president. Knowing this, the vice president asks you to find some way to postpone your presentation. You have 10 minutes to decide what to do.

Solving the Dilemma

What would you do?

1. Deliver the presentation as planned.

2. Give the presentation but skip over the negative results.

3. Go back to the meeting room and announce that your spouse has had an accident at home and you must leave immediately. You tell the group that you just received this message and that you will contact the vice president to schedule a new meeting.

4. Invent other options. Discuss.

chapter 2

Management Theory
Essential Background for the Successful Manager

Major Questions You Should Be Able to Answer

2.1 Evolving Viewpoints: How We Got to Today's Management Outlook

Major Question: What's the payoff in studying different management perspectives, both yesterday's and today's?

2.2 Classical Viewpoint: Scientific & Administrative Management

Major Question: If the name of the game is to manage work more efficiently, what can the classical viewpoint teach me?

2.3 Behavioral Viewpoint: Behaviorism, Human Relations, & Behavioral Science

Major Question: To understand how people are motivated to achieve, what can I learn from the behavioral viewpoint?

2.4 Quantitative Viewpoints: Management Science & Operations Research

Major Question: If the manager's job is to solve problems, how might the two quantitative approaches help?

2.5 Systems Viewpoint

Major Question: How can the exceptional manager be helped by the systems viewpoint?

2.6 Contingency Viewpoint

Major Question: In the end, is there one best way to manage in all situations?

2.7 Quality-Management Viewpoint

Major Question: Can the quality-management viewpoint offer guidelines for true managerial success?

2.8 The Learning Organization in an Era of Accelerated Change

Major Question: Organizations must learn or perish. How do I build a learning organization?

Evidence-Based Management: An Attitude of Wisdom

"These days, there aren't any hot, new trends, just a lot of repackaged ones from the past," writes *Wall Street Journal* columnist Carol Hymowitz.[1] "Executives have been treated to an overdose of management guides that mostly haven't delivered what they promised. Many bosses have adopted them all, regardless of their company's business model, balance sheet, competition, employee bench strength, or any other unique qualities. They have become copycat managers, trying to find a one-stop, fix-it-all answer to their various problems."

How will you know whether the next "fix-it-all" book to hit the business bestseller list is simply a recycling of old ideas? The answer is: You have to have studied history—the subject of this chapter.

Management: Art or Science?

Is the practice of management an art or a science? Certainly it *can* be an art. Lots of top executives have no actual training in management—Yahoo! CEO Carol Bartz, discussed in Chapter 1, has a B.S. in computer science, not business. Great managers, like great painters or actors, have the right mix of intuition, judgment, and experience.

But management is also a science. That is, rather than being performed in a seat-of-the-pants, make-it-up-as-you-go-along kind of way—which can lead to big mistakes—management can be approached deliberately, rationally, systematically. That's what the scientific method is, after all—a logical process, embodying four steps: (1) You observe events and gather facts. (2) You pose a possible solution or explanation based on those facts. (3) You make a prediction of future events. (4) You test the prediction under systematic conditions.

Following the Evidence

The process of scientific reasoning underlies what is known as evidence-based management. *Evidence-based management* means translating principles based on best evidence into organizational practice, bringing rationality to the decision-making process.[2] Evidence-based management derives from evidence-based medicine, embracing what Stanford business scholars Jeffrey Pfeffer and Robert Sutton call *an attitude of wisdom*. This is a mind-set that, first, is willing to set aside belief and conventional wisdom and to act on the facts and, second, has an unrelenting commitment to gathering information necessary to make informed decisions and to keeping pace with new evidence to update practices.[3]

"The way a good doctor or a good manager works," Sutton says, "is to act with knowledge while doubting what you know. So if a patient goes to a doctor, you hope the doctor would do two things: first look at the literature and make the best decision given what's available. Then actually track the progress of the treatment and see what unexpected side effects you're having and what things are working."[4]

Three Truths

Evidence-based management is based on three truths:

- **There are few really new ideas:** Most supposedly new ideas are old, wrong, or both.

- **True is better than new:** Effective organizations and managers are more interested in what is true than in what is new.

- **Doing well usually dominates:** Organizations that do simple, obvious, and even seemingly trivial things well will dominate competitors who search for "silver bullets and instant magic."

For Discussion Do you think managers are often driven by fads, by what they've read in the latest book or heard in the latest management seminar? Have you ever heard of a manager taking an experimental approach, as in trying out a new idea with an open mind to see what happens? How could you profit by taking an evidence-based approach to the ideas we will discuss in this chapter?

forecast What's Ahead in This Chapter

This chapter gives you a short overview of the three principal *historical* perspectives or viewpoints on management—*classical, behavioral,* and *quantitative.* It then describes the three principal *contemporary* viewpoints—*systems, contingency,* and *quality-management.* Finally, we consider the concept of *learning organizations.*

What's the payoff in studying different management perspectives, both yesterday's and today's?

THE BIG PICTURE

After studying theory, managers may learn the value of practicing evidence-based management, bringing rationality to the decision-making process. This chapter describes two principal theoretical perspectives—the *historical* and the *contemporary.* Studying management theory provides understanding of the present, a guide to action, a source of new ideas, clues to the meaning of your managers' decisions, and clues to the meaning of outside events.

"The best way to predict the future is to create it," Peter Drucker said. The purpose of this book is, to the extent possible, to give you the tools to create your own future as a manager.

Who is **Peter Drucker**? "He was the creator and inventor of modern management," says management guru Tom Peters (author of *In Search of Excellence*). "In the early 1950s, nobody had a tool kit to manage these incredibly complex organizations that had gone out of control. Drucker was the first person to give us a handbook for that."[5]

An Austrian trained in economics and international law, Drucker came to the United States in 1937, where he worked as a correspondent for British newspapers and later became a college professor. In 1954, he published his famous text, *The Practice of Management,* in which he proposed that management was one of the major social innovations of the 20th century and that it should be treated as a profession, like medicine or law. In this and other books, he introduced several ideas that now underlie the organization and practice of management—that workers should be treated as assets, that the corporation could be considered a human community, that there is "no business without a customer," that institutionalized management practices were preferable to charismatic, cult leaders. Many ideas that you will encounter in this book—decentralization, management by objectives, knowledge workers—are directly traceable to Drucker's pen. "Without his analysis," says one writer, "it's almost impossible to imagine the rise of dispersed, globe-spanning corporations."[6]

Evidence-Based Management: Facing Hard Facts, Rejecting Nonsense

Evidence-based management, described in the Manager's Toolbox, while not invented by Drucker, is very much in the spirit of his rational approach to management. As mentioned, ***evidence-based management*** means **translating principles based on best evidence into organizational practice, bringing rationality to the decision-making process.**

As its two principal proponents, Stanford business scholars **Jeffrey Pfeffer and Robert Sutton,** put it, evidence-based management is based on the belief that "facing the hard facts about what works and what doesn't, understanding the dangerous half-truths that constitute so much conventional wisdom about management, and rejecting the total nonsense that too often passes for sound advice will help organizations perform better."[7] Learning to make managerial decisions based on evidence is the approach we hope you will learn to take after studying many other approaches—the perspectives described in this chapter.

Two Overarching Perspectives about Management: Historical & Contemporary

In this chapter, we describe two overarching perspectives about management:

- **Historical.** The *historical perspective* includes three viewpoints—*classical, behavioral,* and *quantitative.*

- **Contemporary.** The *contemporary perspective* also includes three viewpoints—*systems, contingency,* and *quality-management.*

Five Practical Reasons for Studying This Chapter

"Theory," say business professors Clayton Christensen and Michael Raynor, "often gets a bum rap among managers because it's associated with the word 'theoretical,' which connotes 'impractical.' But it shouldn't."[8] After all, what could be more practical than studying different approaches to see which work best?

Indeed, there are five good reasons for studying theoretical perspectives:

1. **Understanding of the present.** "Sound theories help us interpret the present, to understand what is happening and why," say Christensen and Raynor.[9] Understanding history will help you understand why some practices are still favored, whether for right or wrong reasons.

2. **Guide to action.** Good theories help us make predictions and enable you to develop a set of principles that will guide your actions.

3. **Source of new ideas.** It can also provide new ideas that may be useful to you when you come up against new situations.

4. **Clues to meaning of your managers' decisions.** It can help you understand your firm's focus, where the top managers are "coming from."

5. **Clues to meaning of outside events.** Finally, it may allow you to understand events outside the organization that could affect it or you. ●

Example

Is Cisco's Upsetting of the Traditional Pyramid Hierarchy the Best Way to Organize a Company?

If Management 1.0 is what we're used to now, with its traditional pyramid hierarchy, what would Management 2.0 look like? What if, as management thinker Gary Hamel suggests, Management 2.0 looked a lot like Web 2.0 as represented in Wikipedia, YouTube, and other online communities?[10] Could the traditional hierarchy of boxes with lines actually become a corporate straitjacket?

That's what John Chambers thinks. Chambers is CEO of San Jose, California–based Cisco Systems, $36 billion maker of telecommunications gear. He is concerned that large companies begin to slow down "because they didn't move out of their primary markets" fast enough, as happened with his former employer, Wang Laboratories, bankrupted after missing out on the rise of the PC.[11] As a result, Cisco is attempting an ambitious expansion into 30 different markets simultaneously, from Flip video cameras to multimillion-dollar data centers. Because Chambers needs more managers to oversee these markets, he has established an unusual system of 48 management committees, or "councils." Managers participate in different committees and make decisions collaboratively. Today 70% of Cisco's management decisions are made this way.

YOUR CALL

Will the system of "management councils" work? Some insiders say it adds bureaucracy and dilutes authority and accountability. Chambers argues that the system is the only way a company as large as Cisco can grow fast because it enables it to move as quickly and nimbly as it needs to.[12] What do you think? Could other big organizations—Ford Motor Co., the U.S. Army, United Way—benefit from this arrangement? Do you think studying management theory could help you answer this question?

major question? If the name of the game is to manage work more efficiently, what can the classical viewpoint teach me?

THE BIG PICTURE

The *three historical management viewpoints* we will describe include (1) the classical, described in this section; (2) the behavioral; and (3) the quantitative. The classical viewpoint, which emphasized ways to manage work more efficiently, had two approaches: (a) scientific management and (b) administrative management. *Scientific management,* pioneered by Frederick W. Taylor and Frank and Lillian Gilbreth, emphasized the scientific study of work methods to improve the productivity of individual workers. *Administrative management,* pioneered by Henri Fayol and Max Weber, was concerned with managing the total organization.

Bet you've never heard of a "therblig," although it may describe some physical motions you perform from time to time—perhaps when you have to wash dishes. A made-up word you won't find in most dictionaries, *therblig* was coined by Frank Gilbreth and is, in fact, "Gilbreth" spelled backward, with the "t" and the "h" reversed. It refers to 1 of 17 basic motions. By identifying the therbligs in a job, as in the tasks of a bricklayer (which he had once been), Frank and his wife, Lillian, were able to eliminate motions while simultaneously reducing fatigue.

The Gilbreths were a husband-and-wife team of industrial engineers who were pioneers in one of the classical approaches to management, part of the historical perspective. As we mentioned, there are *three historical management viewpoints* or approaches. *(See Figure 2.1, opposite page.)* They are

- Classical
- Behavioral
- Quantitative

In this section, we describe the classical perspective of management, which originated during the early 1900s. **The *classical viewpoint,* which emphasized finding ways to manage work more efficiently, had two branches—*scientific* and *administrative*—** each of which is identified with particular pioneering theorists. In general, classical management assumes that *people are rational.* Let's compare the two approaches.

Scientific Management: Pioneered by Taylor & the Gilbreths

The problem for which scientific management emerged as a solution was this: In the expansive days of the early 20th century, labor was in such short supply that managers were hard-pressed to raise the productivity of workers. **Scientific management emphasized the scientific study of work methods to improve the productivity of individual workers.** Two of its chief proponents were **Frederick W. Taylor** and the team of **Frank and Lillian Gilbreth.**

Frederick Taylor & the Four Principles of Scientific Management   No doubt there are some days when you haven't studied, or worked, as efficiently as you could. This could be called "underachieving," or "loafing," or what Taylor called it—*soldiering,* deliberately working at less than full capacity. Known as

① **Classical Viewpoint** Emphasis on ways to manage work more efficiently	② **Behavioral Viewpoint** Emphasis on importance of understanding human behavior and motivating and encouraging employees toward achievement	③ **Quantitative Viewpoint** Applies quantitative techniques to management
Scientific management Emphasized scientific study of work methods to improve productivity of individual workers *Proponents*: Frederick W. Taylor Frank and Lillian Gilbreth	**Early behaviorists** *Proponents*: Hugo Munsterberg Mary Parker Follett Elton Mayo	**Management science** Focuses on using mathematics to aid in problem solving and decision making
Administrative management Concerned with managing the total organization *Proponents*: Henri Fayol Max Weber	**Human relations movement** Proposed better human relations could increase worker productivity *Proponents*: Abraham Maslow Douglas McGregor	**Operations management** Focuses on managing the production and delivery of an organization's products or services more effectively
	Behavioral science approach Relies on scientific research for developing theory to provide practical management tools	

figure 2.1

THE HISTORICAL PERSPECTIVE

Three viewpoints are shown.

Frederick W. Taylor. Called the father of scientific management, Taylor published *The Principles of Scientific Management* in 1911.

"the father of scientific management," Taylor was an American engineer from Philadelphia who believed that managers could eliminate soldiering by applying four principles of science:

1. Evaluate a task by scientifically studying each part of the task (not use old rule-of-thumb methods).
2. Carefully select workers with the right abilities for the task.
3. Give workers the training and incentives to do the task with the proper work methods.
4. Use scientific principles to plan the work methods and ease the way for workers to do their jobs.

Taylor based his system on *motion studies,* in which he broke down each worker's job—moving pig iron at a steel company, say—into basic physical motions and then trained workers to use the methods of their best-performing co-workers. In addition, he suggested employers institute a *differential rate system,* in which more efficient workers earned higher wages.

Lillian and Frank Gilbreth. These industrial engineers pioneered time and motion studies. If you're an athlete, you can appreciate how small changes can make you efficient.

Why Taylor Is Important: Although "Taylorism" met considerable resistance from employees fearing that working harder would lead to lost jobs except for the highly productive few, Taylor believed that by raising production both labor and management could increase profits to the point where they no longer would have to quarrel over them. If used correctly, the principles of scientific management can enhance productivity, and such innovations as motion studies and differential pay are still used today.

Frank & Lillian Gilbreth & Industrial Engineering

As mentioned, Frank and Lillian Gilbreth were a husband-and-wife team of industrial engineers who lectured at Purdue University in the early 1900s. Their experiences in raising 12 children—to whom they applied some of their ideas about improving efficiency (such as printing the Morse Code on the back of the bathroom door so that family members could learn it while doing other things)—later were popularized in a book, two movies, and a TV sitcom, *Cheaper by the Dozen.* The Gilbreths expanded on Taylor's motion studies—for instance, by using movie cameras to film workers at work in order to isolate the parts of a job.

Lillian Gilbreth, who received a PhD in psychology, was the first woman to be a major contributor to management science.

Administrative Management: Pioneered by Fayol & Weber

Scientific management is concerned with the jobs of individuals. ***Administrative management* is concerned with managing the total organization.** Among the pioneering theorists were **Henri Fayol** and **Max Weber.**

Henri Fayol & the Functions of Management

Fayol was not the first to investigate management behavior, but he was the first to systematize it. A French engineer and industrialist, he became known to American business when his most important work, *General and Industrial Management,* was translated into English in 1930.

Why Fayol Is Important: Fayol was the first to identify the major functions of management (p. 14)—planning, organizing, leading, and controlling, as well as coordinating—the first four of which you'll recognize as the functions providing the framework for this and most other management books.

Max Weber & the Rationality of Bureaucracy In our time, the word *bureaucracy* has come to have negative associations: impersonality, inflexibility, red tape, a molasseslike response to problems. But to German sociologist Max Weber, a *bureaucracy* was a rational, efficient, ideal organization based on principles of logic. After all, in Weber's Germany in the late 19th century, many people were in positions of authority (particularly in the government) not because of their abilities but because of their social status. The result, Weber wrote, was that they didn't perform effectively.

A better-performing organization, he felt, should have five positive bureaucratic features:

1. A well-defined hierarchy of authority.
2. Formal rules and procedures.
3. A clear division of labor, with parts of a complex job being handled by specialists.
4. Impersonality, without reference or connection to a particular person.
5. Careers based on merit.

Why Weber Is Important: Weber's work was not translated into English until 1947, but it came to have an important influence on the structure of large corporations, such as the Coca-Cola Company.

The Problem with the Classical Viewpoint: Too Mechanistic

A flaw in the classical viewpoint is that it is mechanistic: It tends to view humans as cogs within a machine, not taking into account the importance of human needs. Behavioral theory addressed this problem, as we explain next.

Why the Classical Viewpoint Is Important: The essence of the classical viewpoint was that work activity was amenable to a rational approach, that through the application of scientific methods, time and motion studies, and job specialization it was possible to boost productivity. Indeed, these concepts are still in use today, the results visible to you every time you visit McDonald's or Pizza Hut. The classical viewpoint also led to such innovations as management by objectives and goal setting, as we explain elsewhere. ●

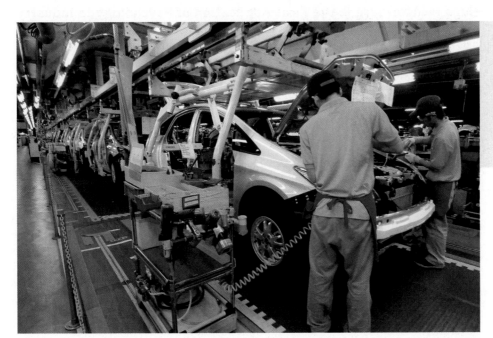

Scientific management. Carmakers have broken down automobile manufacturing into its constituent tasks. This reflects the contributions of the school of scientific management. Is there anything wrong with this approach? How could it be improved?

major question ❓ To understand how people are motivated to achieve, what can I learn from the behavioral viewpoint?

THE BIG PICTURE

The second of the three historical management perspectives was the *behavioral viewpoint*, which emphasized the importance of understanding human behavior and of motivating employees toward achievement. The behavioral viewpoint developed over three phases: (1) *Early behaviorism* was pioneered by Hugo Munsterberg, Mary Parker Follett, and Elton Mayo. (2) The *human relations movement* was pioneered by Abraham Maslow (who proposed a hierarchy of needs) and Douglas McGregor (who proposed a Theory X and Theory Y view to explain managers' attitudes toward workers). (3) The *behavioral science approach* relied on scientific research for developing theories about behavior useful to managers.

The **behavioral viewpoint** emphasized the importance of understanding human behavior and of motivating employees toward achievement. The behavioral viewpoint developed over three phases: (1) early behaviorism, (2) the human relations movement, and (3) behavioral science.

Early Behaviorism: Pioneered by Munsterberg, Follett, & Mayo

The three people who pioneered behavioral theory were **Hugo Munsterberg, Mary Parker Follett,** and **Elton Mayo.**

Mary Parker Follett. She proposed that managers and employees should work together cooperatively.

Hugo Munsterberg & the First Application of Psychology to Industry

Called "the father of industrial psychology," German-born Hugo Munsterberg had a PhD in psychology and a medical degree and joined the faculty at Harvard University in 1892. Munsterberg suggested that psychologists could contribute to industry in three ways. They could:

1. Study jobs and determine which people are best suited to specific jobs.
2. Identify the psychological conditions under which employees do their best work.
3. Devise management strategies to influence employees to follow management's interests.

Why Munsterberg Is Important: His ideas led to the field of *industrial psychology,* the study of human behavior in workplaces, which is still taught in colleges today.

Mary Parker Follett & Power Sharing among Employees & Managers

A Massachusetts social worker and social philosopher, Mary Parker Follett was lauded on her death in 1933 as "one of the most important women America has yet produced in the fields of civics and sociology." Instead of following the usual hierarchical arrangement of managers as order givers and employees as order takers, Follett thought organizations should become more democratic, with managers and employees working cooperatively.

The following ideas were among her most important:

1. Organizations should be operated as "communities," with managers and subordinates working together in harmony.
2. Conflicts should be resolved by having managers and workers talk over differences and find solutions that would satisfy both parties—a process she called *integration*.
3. The work process should be under the control of workers with the relevant knowledge, rather than of managers, who should act as facilitators.

Why Follett Is Important: With these and other ideas, Follett anticipated some of today's concepts of "self-managed teams," "worker empowerment," and "interdepartmental teams"—that is, members of different departments working together on joint projects.

Elton Mayo & the Supposed "Hawthorne Effect"   Do you think workers would be more productive if they thought they were receiving special attention? This was the conclusion drawn by a Harvard research group in the late 1920s.

Conducted by Elton Mayo and his associates at Western Electric's Hawthorne (Chicago) plant, what came to be called the *Hawthorne studies* began with an investigation into whether workplace lighting level affected worker productivity. (This was the type of study that Taylor or the Gilbreths might have done.) In later experiments, other variables were altered, such as wage levels, rest periods, and length of workday. Worker performance varied but tended to increase over time,

Hawthorne effect. Western Electric's Hawthorne plant, where Elton Mayo and his team conducted their studies in the 1920s. Do you think you'd perform better in a robotlike job if you thought your supervisor cared about you and paid more attention to you?

leading Mayo and his colleagues to hypothesize what came to be known as the *Hawthorne effect*—namely, that employees worked harder if they received added attention, if they thought that managers cared about their welfare and that supervisors paid special attention to them. However, later investigators found flaws in the studies, such as variations in ventilation and lighting or inadequate follow-through, that were overlooked by the original researchers. Critics also point out that it's doubtful that workers improved their productivity merely on the basis of receiving more attention rather than because of a particular instructional method or social innovation.[13]

Why the Hawthorne Studies Are Important: Ultimately, the Hawthorne studies were faulted for being poorly designed and not having enough empirical data to support the conclusions. Nevertheless, they succeeded in drawing attention to the importance of "social man" (social beings) and how managers using good human relations could improve worker productivity. This in turn led to the so-called human relations movement in the 1950s and 1960s.

The Human Relations Movement: Pioneered by Maslow & McGregor

The two theorists who contributed most to the **human relations movement—which proposed that better human relations could increase worker productivity**—were Abraham Maslow and Douglas McGregor.

Abraham Maslow & the Hierarchy of Needs

What motivates you to perform: Food? Security? Love? Recognition? Self-fulfillment? Probably all of these, Abraham Maslow would say, although some needs must be satisfied before others. The chairman of the psychology department at Brandeis University and one of the earliest researchers to study motivation, in 1943 Maslow proposed his famous *hierarchy of human needs:* physiological, safety, love, esteem, and self-actualization[14] (as we discuss in detail in Chapter 12, where we explain why Maslow is important).

Douglas McGregor & Theory X versus Theory Y

Having been for a time a college president (at Antioch College in Ohio), Douglas McGregor came to realize that it was not enough for managers to try to be liked; they also needed to be aware of their attitudes toward employees.[15] Basically, McGregor suggested in a 1960 book, these attitudes could be either "X" or "Y."

Theory X represents a pessimistic, negative view of workers. In this view, workers are considered to be irresponsible, to be resistant to change, to lack ambition, to hate work, and to want to be led rather than to lead.

Theory Y represents the outlook of human relations proponents—an optimistic, positive view of workers. In this view, workers are considered to be capable of accepting responsibility, self-direction, and self-control and of being imaginative and creative.

Why Theory X/Theory Y Is Important: The principal contribution offered by the Theory X/Theory Y perspective is that it can help managers avoid falling into the trap of the *self-fulfilling prophecy*. This is the idea that if a manager expects a subordinate to act in a certain way, the worker may, in fact, very well act that way, thereby confirming the manager's expectations: The prophecy that the manager made is fulfilled.

Underlying both Maslow's and McGregor's theories is the notion that more job satisfaction leads to greater worker performance—an idea that is somewhat controversial, as we'll discuss in Chapter 11.

The Behavioral Science Approach

The human relations movement was a necessary correction to the sterile approach used within scientific management, but its optimism came to be considered too simplistic for practical use. More recently, the human relations view has been superseded by the behavioral science approach to management. *Behavioral science* **relies on scientific research for developing theories about human behavior that can be used to provide practical tools for managers.** The disciplines of behavioral science include psychology, sociology, anthropology, and economics. ●

Example

Application of the Behavioral Science Approach: Which Is Better—Competition or Cooperation?

A widely held assumption among American managers is that "competition brings out the best in people." From an economic standpoint, business survival depends on staying ahead of the competition. But from an interpersonal standpoint, critics contend competition has been overemphasized, primarily at the expense of cooperation.[16]

One strong advocate of greater emphasis on cooperation, Alfie Kohn, reviewed the evidence and found two reasons for what he sees as competition's failure:[17]

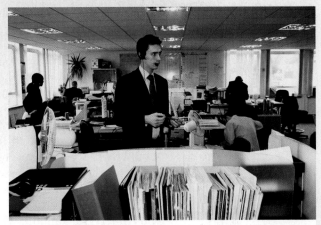

Promoting performance. This open office—no cubicles or partitions— is designed to encourage spontaneous interaction, cooperation, and teamwork, which foster achievement and productivity among employees. The open layout is particularly favored by younger workers. Why do you think that is?

1. **Competition makes people hostile.** Success, he says, "often depends on sharing resources efficiently, and this is nearly impossible when people have to work against one another." Competition makes people suspicious and hostile toward each other. Cooperation, by contrast, "takes advantage of all the skills represented in a group as well as the mysterious process by which that group becomes more than the sum of its parts."

2. **Competition doesn't necessarily promote excellence.** "Trying to do well and trying to beat others simply are two different things," Kohn says. He points out the example of children in class who wave their arms to get the teacher's attention, but when they are finally recognized they then seem befuddled and ask the teacher to repeat the question—because they were more focused on beating their classmates than on the subject matter.

What does the behavioral science research suggest about the question of cooperation versus competition? One team of researchers reviewed 122 studies encompassing a wide variety of subjects and settings and came up with three conclusions: (1) Cooperation is superior to competition in promoting achievement and productivity. (2) Cooperation is superior to individualistic efforts in promoting achievement and productivity. (3) Cooperation without intergroup competition promotes higher achievement and productivity than cooperation with intergroup competition.[18]

YOUR CALL

What kind of office would you prefer to have for yourself—a private office, a shared private office, a partitioned cubicle, or a desk in an area scattered with other desks with no partitions? Which would be most comfortable for you personally? Why does the last one (the open office) best promote superior performance?

major question?

If the manager's job is to solve problems, how might the two quantitative approaches help?

THE BIG PICTURE

The third and last category under historical perspectives consists of *quantitative viewpoints,* which emphasize the application to management of quantitative techniques, such as statistics and computer simulations. Two approaches of quantitative management are *management science* and *operations management.*

During the air war known as the Battle of Britain in World War II, a relative few of England's Royal Air Force fighter pilots and planes were able to successfully resist the overwhelming might of the German military machine. How did they do it? Military planners drew on mathematics and statistics to determine how to most effectively allocate use of their limited aircraft.

When the Americans entered the war in 1941, they used the British model to form *operations research (OR)* teams to determine how to deploy troops, submarines, and other military personnel and equipment most effectively. For example, OR techniques were used to establish the optimum pattern that search planes should fly to try to locate enemy ships.

After the war, businesses also began using these techniques. One group of former officers, who came to be called the Whiz Kids, used statistical techniques at Ford Motor Co. to make better management decisions. Later, Whiz Kid Robert McNamara, who had become Ford's president, was appointed Secretary of Defense and introduced similar statistical techniques and cost-benefit analyses throughout the Department of Defense. Since then, OR techniques have evolved into **quantitative management, the application to management of quantitative techniques, such as statistics and computer simulations. Two branches of quantitative management are *management science* and *operations management.***

FedEx. What management tools do you use to schedule employees and aircraft to deal with wide variations in package volume—such as December 23 versus December 26?

Management Science: Using Mathematics to Solve Management Problems

How would you go about deciding how to assign utility repair crews during a blackout? Or how many package sorters you needed and at which times for an overnight delivery service such as FedEx or UPS? You would probably use the tools of management science.

Management science is not the same as Taylor's scientific management. **Management science focuses on using mathematics to aid in problem solving and decision making.** Sometimes management science is called *operations research.*

Why Management Science Is Important: Management science stresses the use of rational, science-based techniques and mathematical models to improve decision making and strategic planning.

Management Science: Do Calorie Postings in Restaurants Change Eating Habits?

In July 2008, New York City required that restaurant chains post lists of calorie counts for menu items, as a way of fighting obesity and diabetes. How well does the approach work?

Researchers tracked customers at several fast-food chains, such as McDonald's, in high-poverty New York City neighborhoods. They collected receipts two weeks before the calorie-posting law took effect and four weeks afterward (paying customers $2 each for their receipts). About half the customers noticed the posted calorie counts, with 28% of those who noticed saying the information influenced their ordering. But when receipts were examined, it was found that orders had a mean of 846 calories after the labeling law took place, compared with only 825 before.[19] Do calories matter? "I'm looking for the cheapest meal I can," said one customer.[20]

YOUR CALL

If, as a restaurant manager, one of your goals is to discourage obesity, do you think the study is useful? Do low-income people not care about calories? Was the study done too soon and failed to capture behavior change that might occur gradually?

Operations Management: Being More Effective

Operations management focuses on managing the production and delivery of an organization's products or services more effectively. It is concerned with work scheduling, production planning, facilities location and design, and optimum inventory levels.

Why Operations Management Is Important: Through the rational management of resources and distribution of goods and services, operations management helps ensure that business operations are efficient and effective. ●

Operations Management: Was Toyota's "Lean Management" the Right Approach?

Over the years, Toyota Motor Corp. developed a variety of production techniques that drew in part on operations research.[21] First, it emphasized the smoothest possible *flow of work.* To accomplish this, managers performed *value stream mapping,* identifying the many steps in a production process and eliminating unnecessary ones. They also performed *mistake proofing* or *root-cause analysis,* using teamwork to examine problems and fix them as soon as they appeared. In addition, the carmaker helped pioneer the *just-in-time* approach to obtaining supplies from vendors only as they were needed in the factory. These efficient techniques, which all come under the term "lean management," enabled Toyota to sell its cars on the basis of their superior quality.[22]

Then in 1995, the company launched an all-out effort to become the world's largest carmaker. To do so, it opted to use common parts among eight types of cars (Camry, Corolla, Avalon, and others) and to buy them from companies around the globe instead of from its small group of longtime Japanese suppliers. Design engineers may also have cut corners, as by relying on computer simulations rather than building physical prototypes.[23]

Suddenly, beginning in 2004, disturbing reports surfaced about Toyota cars running away because of sudden, unintended acceleration.[24] A research firm documented 2,274 similar incidents, including 18 fatalities.[25] In late 2009, thinking the problem was pedals catching on floor mats, Toyota recalled 4.3 million vehicles. Then, in early 2010, suspecting the problem was in the accelerator mechanism itself, it recalled 2.3 million vehicles and completely stopped new production of eight vehicle lines in North America.

YOUR CALL

In Chapter 1, we described the problem of "efficiency versus effectiveness." Which is lean management mostly about? Can a worldwide car company get back to its roots—reclaim bragging rights to "quality"?

�֎ 2.5 SYSTEMS VIEWPOINT

How can the exceptional manager be helped by the systems viewpoint?

THE BIG PICTURE

Three contemporary management perspectives are (1) the *systems,* (2) the *contingency,* and (3) the *quality-management* viewpoints. The *systems viewpoint* sees organizations as a system, either open or closed, with inputs, outputs, transformation processes, and feedback. The *contingency viewpoint* emphasizes that a manager's approach should vary according to the individual and environmental situation. The *quality-management viewpoint* has two traditional approaches: *quality control,* the strategy for minimizing errors by managing each stage of production, and *quality assurance,* which focuses on the performance of workers, urging employees to strive for zero defects. A third quality approach is the movement of *total quality management (TQM),* a comprehensive approach dedicated to continuous quality improvement, training, and customer satisfaction.

Being of a presumably practical turn of mind, could you run an organization or a department according to the theories you've just learned? Probably not. The reason: People are complicated. To be an exceptional manager, you need to learn to deal with individual differences in a variety of settings.

Thus, to the historical perspective on management (classical, behavioral, and quantitative viewpoints), let us now add the *contemporary perspective,* which consists of three viewpoints. *(See Figure 2.2 below.)* These consist of:

- Systems
- Contingency
- Quality-management

In this section, we discuss the systems viewpoint.

The Systems Viewpoint
Regards the organization as systems of interrelated parts that operate together to achieve a common purpose

The Contingency Viewpoint
Emphasizes that a manager's approach should vary according to—i.e., be contingent on—the individual and environmental situation

The Quality-Management Viewpoint
Three approaches

Quality control
Strategy for minimizing errors by managing each state of production

Proponent:
Walter Shewart

Quality assurance
Focuses on the performance of workers, urging employees to strive for "zero defects"

Total quality management
Comprehensive approach dedicated to continuous quality improvement, training, and customer satisfaction

Proponents:
W. Edwards Deming

Joseph M. Juran

figure 2.2

THE CONTEMPORARY PERSPECTIVE

Three viewpoints

The Systems Viewpoint

The 52 bones in the foot. The monarchy of Great Britain. A weather storm front. Each of these is a system. **A *system* is a set of interrelated parts that operate together to achieve a common purpose.** Even though a system may not work very well—as in the inefficient way the Russian government collects taxes, for example—it is nevertheless still a system.

The *systems viewpoint* regards the organization as a system of interrelated parts. By adopting this point of view, you can look at your organization both as (1) a collection of *subsystems*—**parts making up the whole system**—and (2) a part of the larger environment. A college, for example, is made up of a collection of academic departments, support staffs, students, and the like. But it also exists as a system within the environment of education, having to be responsive to parents, alumni, legislators, nearby townspeople, and so on.

The Four Parts of a System

The vocabulary of the systems perspective is useful because it gives you a way of understanding many different kinds of organizations. The four parts of a system are defined as follows:

1. ***Inputs* are the people, money, information, equipment, and materials required to produce an organization's goods or services.** Whatever goes into a system is an input.

2. ***Outputs* are the products, services, profits, losses, employee satisfaction or discontent, and the like that are produced by the organization.** Whatever comes out of the system is an output.

3. ***Transformation processes* are the organization's capabilities in management and technology that are applied to converting inputs into outputs.** The main activity of the organization is to transform inputs into outputs.

4. ***Feedback* is information about the reaction of the environment to the outputs that affects the inputs.** Are the customers buying or not buying the product? That information is feedback.

The four parts of a system are illustrated below. *(See Figure 2.3.)*

figure 2.3

THE FOUR PARTS OF A SYSTEM

① **Inputs**
The people, money, information, equipment, and materials required to produce an organization's goods or services

Example: For a jewelry designer—design, money, artistic talent, gold and silver, tools, marketing expertise

② **Transformational processes**
The organization's capabilities in management and technology that are applied to converting inputs into outputs

Example: Designer's management skills (planning, organizing, leading, controlling), gold and silver smithing tools and expertise, Web site for marketing

③ **Outputs**
The products, services, profits, losses, employee satisfaction or discontent, etc., produced by the organization

Example: Gold and silver rings, earrings, bracelets, etc.

④ **Feedback**
Information about the reaction of the environment to the outputs, which affects the inputs

Example: Web customers like African-style designs, dislike imitation Old English designs

Closed and open systems. *Top:* The Apple Newton Messagepad, a personal digital assistant released in 1993 and killed in 1998, probably failed because it was developed as a closed system, with inadequate feedback from consumers before launch. It was panned for being too expensive, too large, and having faulty handwriting recognition. *Bottom:* The iPad, Apple's tablet-style device, was released in early 2010 after much secrecy. Could the iPad have benefited from an open system of consumer feedback under such hush-hush conditions? How might this be done?

Open & Closed Systems   Nearly all organizations are, at least to some degree, open systems rather than closed systems. An ***open system*** **continually interacts with its environment. A *closed system* has little interaction with its environment;** that is, it receives very little feedback from the outside. The classical management viewpoint often considered an organization a closed system. So does the management science perspective, which simplifies organizations for purposes of analysis. However, any organization that ignores feedback from the environment opens itself up to possibly spectacular failures.

Why the Systems Viewpoint—Particularly the Concept of Open Systems—Is Important: The history of management is full of accounts of organizations whose services or products failed (such as the 1959 Ford Edsel) because they weren't open enough systems and didn't have sufficient feedback. The concept of open systems, which stresses feedback from multiple environmental factors, both inside and outside the organization, attempts to ensure a continuous learning process in order to correct old mistakes and avoid new ones. ●

Example

Open versus Closed Systems: How Successful Jeans Makers Keep Up

The Baby Boomers (72 million people) were born between 1945 and 1962, and Generation X (17 million) was born 1963 to 1978). Now we have Generation Y, born 1979 to 1994, which at 60 million people is a huge market for denim jeans makers. How can they discover what's cool with this generation?[26]

Open System: The Company That Listened. Internetwise Gen Yers are accustomed to high-speed information, which has made fashions faster changing. For a long time, Tommy Hilfiger stayed ahead of the style curve. "When Hilfiger's distinctive logo-laden shirts and jackets started showing up on urban rappers in the early '90s," says one account, "the company started sending researchers into music clubs to see how this influential group wore the styles." By having constant feedback—an open system—with young consumers, Hilfiger was rewarded: In the late '90s, its jeans became the No. 1 brand in this age group.[27]

Closed System: The Company That Didn't Listen. By contrast, Levi Strauss and Co. was jolted awake in 1997 when the company found the brand was losing popularity among teens, in part because of threats from private-label jeans from Walmart and other big retailers, both low-priced brands and "premium" ($100-plus) jeans.[28] "We all got older, and as a consequence, we lost touch with teenagers," said David Spangler, Levi's director of market research. The jeans maker thereupon opened up its relatively closed system by instituting ongoing teen panels to keep tabs on emerging trends. Generation Y "is a generation that must be reckoned with," said Spangler. "They are going to take over the country."

YOUR CALL

With the onset of the recent recession, the changing denim fashion market took another turn—away from designer and premium jeans.[29] The new hot fad is so-called *workwear,* such as the Levi's 501 jeans that were first manufactured in 1873 for miners and cowboys and now are worn by everyone. "Workwear is coming at a time when the country is saying, 'Let's get back to work' at a very primal level," says one fashion expert.[30] Workwear may dominate for another few fashion seasons, but what would you recommend any jeans maker do to broaden its feedback system and anticipate future changing business conditions?

✳ 2.6 CONTINGENCY VIEWPOINT

In the end, is there one best way to manage in all situations?

major question?

THE BIG PICTURE

The second viewpoint in the contemporary perspective, the contingency viewpoint, emphasizes that a manager's approach should vary according to the individual and environmental situation.

The classical viewpoints advanced by Taylor and Fayol assumed that their approaches had universal applications—that they were "the one best way" to manage organizations. The contingency viewpoint began to develop when managers discovered that under some circumstances better results could be achieved by breaking the one-best-way rule. The *contingency viewpoint* **emphasizes that a manager's approach should vary according to—that is, be contingent on—the individual and the environmental situation.**

Example

The Contingency Viewpoint: What Incentives Work in Lean Times?

Americans of all ages and incomes have grown increasingly unhappy at work, with today only 45% saying they are satisfied with their jobs, according to a recent survey.[31] The reasons: Fewer workers consider their jobs interesting, incomes have not kept up with inflation, and rising health insurance costs have cut into workers' take-home pay. So how, in hard economic times, is a manager to motivate non-overtime-earning workers (those remaining after layoffs) to get them to produce more when raises, bonuses, and promotions are frozen?

At Iowa-based aerospace electronics firm Rockwell Collins, manager Jenny Miller persuaded 20 overworked engineers to come in Thanksgiving weekend to meet a deadline to deliver software to a customer. Her lures? Free lunch and $100 gift cards.

At Ford Motor Co., managers use thank-you notes as rewards. At Ohio drug maker Sanofi-Aventis, one manager "e-mails employees to recognize even small accomplishments, and strategically copies higher-ups," says one account.[32] Another way to increase productivity: screen employees' tasks to remove "discretionary work"—such as internal reports that can be reduced or delayed—in favor of higher-priority work. The mix of approaches represents the contingency viewpoint.

YOUR CALL

What other inexpensive ways of improving productivity can you think of? What theories do the approaches just described seem to represent?

A manager subscribing to the Gilbreth approach might try to get workers to be more productive by simplifying the steps. A manager of the Theory X/Theory Y persuasion might try to use motivational techniques. But the manager following the contingency viewpoint would simply ask, "What method is the best to use under these particular circumstances?"

Management Theory ✳ **CHAPTER 2**   **53**

Contingency approach. Giving employees more money is not the only way to motivate them to be more productive. Sometimes small rewards, such as a free lunch, are equally effective. Would it make a difference to you if your boss showed appreciation of your efforts even in small ways—as by sending you a thank-you note?

Gary Hamel: Management Ideas Are Not Fixed, They're a Process

Discussion of the contingency viewpoint leads us naturally to the thoughts of **Gary Hamel,** cofounder of the Management Innovation Lab and ranked by *The Wall Street Journal* as today's most influential business thinker.[33] "Over time," he says, "every great invention, management included, travels a road that leads from birth to maturity, and occasionally to senescence."[34] Hamel holds that much of management theory is dated and doesn't fit the current realities of organizational life and that management innovation is essential to future organizational success. Indeed, he suggests, what we need to do is look at management as a *process,* and then make improvements and innovation ongoing and systematic. After all, if managers now innovate by creating new products or new business strategies, why can't they be equally innovative in how they manage their companies?

How do you get the ball rolling in management innovation, particularly in a traditional, conventional company? Hamel believes that the answer can be found by identifying core beliefs that people have about the organization, especially those that detract from the pursuit of management innovation. He suggests that these beliefs can be rooted out by repeatedly asking the right questions—namely, the following:

1. Is this a belief worth challenging? Is it debilitating? Does it get in the way of an important organizational attribute that we'd like to strengthen?

2. Is this belief universally valid? Are there counterexamples? If so, what do we learn from those cases?

3. How does this belief serve the interests of its adherents? Are there people who draw reassurance or comfort from this belief?

4. Have our choices and assumptions conspired to make this belief self-fulfilling? Is this belief true simply because we have made it true—and, if so, can we imagine alternatives?[35]

Why the Contingency Viewpoint Is Important: The contingency viewpoint would seem to be the most practical of the viewpoints discussed so far because it addresses problems on a case-by-case basis and varies the solution accordingly. ●

Mindfulness over Mindlessness: Learning to Take a Contingency Point of View

"Be flexible." Isn't that what we're told?

Throughout your career, you will have to constantly make choices about how to solve various problems—which tools to apply, including the theories described in this chapter. However, one barrier to being flexible is *mindlessness*. Instead we need to adopt the frame of mind that Harvard psychology professor Ellen Langer has called *mindfulness,* a form of active engagement.[36]

We've all experienced mindlessness. We misplace our keys. We write checks in January with the previous year's date. Mindlessness is characterized by the three following attributes.

Mindlessness #1: Entrapment in Old Categories

An avid tennis player, Langer says that at a tennis camp she, like all other students, was taught *exactly* how to hold her racquet and toss the ball when making a serve. But later, when watching a top tennis championship, she observed that none of the top players served the way she was taught and all served slightly differently.[37]

The significance: There is no one right way of doing things. In a conditional, or mindful, way of teaching, an instructor doesn't say, "This is THE answer," but rather, "This is ONE answer." Thus, all information—even in the hard sciences and mathematics, where it may seem as though there is just one correct answer—should be regarded with open-mindedness, because there may be exceptions. That is, you should act as though the information is true only for certain uses or under certain circumstances.

Mindlessness #2: Automatic Behavior

Langer tells of the time she used a new credit card in a department store. Noticing that Langer hadn't signed

the card yet, the cashier returned it to her to sign the back. After passing the credit card through the imprinting machine, the clerk handed her the credit card receipt to sign, which Langer did. Then, says Langer, the cashier "held the form next to the newly signed card to see if the signatures matched."[38]

In automatic behavior, we take in and use limited signals from the world around us without letting other signals penetrate as well. By contrast, mindfulness is being open to new information—including that not specifically assigned to you. Mindfulness requires you to engage more fully in whatever it is you're doing.

Mindlessness #3: Acting from a Single Perspective

Most people, says Langer, typically assume that other peoples' motives and intentions are the same as theirs. For example, she says, "If I am out running and see someone walking briskly, I assume she is trying to exercise and would run if only she could," when actually she may only be trying to get her exercise from walking.

For most situations, many interpretations are possible. "Every idea, person, or object is potentially simultaneously many things depending on the perspective from which it is viewed," says Langer.[39] Trying out different perspectives gives you *more choices in how to respond;* a single perspective that produces an automatic reaction reduces your options.

Your Call

Developing mindfulness means consciously adapting: Being open to novelty. Being alert to distinctions. Being sensitive to different contexts. Being aware of multiple perspectives. Being oriented in the present. Picking just one of these characteristics, what would you do to try to become better at it?

Can the quality-management viewpoint offer guidelines for true managerial success?

THE BIG PICTURE

The quality-management viewpoint, the third category under contemporary perspectives, consists of *quality control, quality assurance,* and especially the movement of *total quality management (TQM),* dedicated to continuous quality improvement, training, and customer satisfaction.

At one time in the 20th century, word got around among buyers of American cars that one shouldn't buy a "Monday car" or a "Friday car"—cars built on the days when absenteeism and hangovers were highest among dissatisfied autoworkers. The reason, supposedly, was that, despite the efforts of quantitative management, the cars produced on those days were the most shoddily made of what were coming to look like generally shoddy products.

The energy crisis of the 1970s showed different possibilities, as Americans began to buy more fuel-efficient cars made in Japan. Consumers found they could not only drive farther on a gallon of gas but that the cars were better made and needed repair less often. Eventually American car manufacturers began to adopt Japanese methods, leading to such slogans as "At Ford, Quality Is Job One." Today the average American car lasts much longer than it used to, and some U.S. cars are equal or superior to the best foreign competitors—for example, the Cadillac CTS beats the Mercedes-Benz E350 and Lexus GS 450h, according to *Consumer Reports.*[40]

Although not a "theory" as such, the **quality-management viewpoint, which includes quality control, quality assurance, and total quality management,** deserves to be considered because of the impact of this kind of thinking on contemporary management perspectives.

Quality Control & Quality Assurance

***Quality* refers to the total ability of a product or service to meet customer needs.** Quality is seen as one of the most important ways of adding value to products and services, thereby distinguishing them from those of competitors. Two traditional strategies for ensuring quality are quality control and quality assurance.

Quality Control *Quality control* **is defined as the strategy for minimizing errors by managing each stage of production.** Quality control techniques were developed in the 1930s at Bell Telephone Labs by **Walter Shewart,** who used statistical sampling to locate errors by testing just some (rather than all) of the items in a particular production run.

Quality Assurance Developed in the 1960s, *quality assurance* **focuses on the performance of workers, urging employees to strive for "zero defects."** Quality assurance has been less successful because often employees have no control over the design of the work process.

Total Quality Management: Creating an Organization Dedicated to Continuous Improvement

In the years after World War II, the imprint "Made in Japan" on a product almost guaranteed that it was cheap and flimsy. That began to change with the arrival in Japan of two Americans, **W. Edwards Deming** and **Joseph M. Juran.**

W. Edwards Deming   Desperate to rebuild its war-devastated economy, Japan eagerly received mathematician W. Edwards Deming's lectures on "good management." Deming believed that quality stemmed from "constancy of purpose"—steady focus on an organization's mission—along with statistical measurement and reduction of variations in production processes. However, he also emphasized the human side, saying that managers should stress teamwork, try to be helpful rather than simply give orders, and make employees feel comfortable about asking questions.

In addition, Deming proposed his so-called 85–15 rule—namely, when things go wrong, there is an 85% chance that the system is at fault, only a 15% chance that the individual worker is at fault. (The "system" would include not only machinery and equipment but also management and rules.) Most of the time, Deming thought, managers erroneously blamed individuals when the failure was really in the system.

TQM pioneer. W. Edwards Deming (right), shown with Kenzo Sasaoka, president of Yokogawa Hewlett-Packard, in Japan, 1982.

Joseph M. Juran   Another pioneer with Deming in Japan's quality revolution was Joseph M. Juran, who defined quality as "fitness for use." By this he meant that a product or service should satisfy a customer's real needs. Thus, the best way to focus a company's efforts, Juran suggested, was to concentrate on the real needs of customers.

TQM: What It Is   From the work of Deming and Juran has come the strategic commitment to quality known as total quality management. ***Total quality management (TQM) is a comprehensive approach—led by top management and supported throughout the organization—dedicated to continuous quality improvement, training, and customer satisfaction.***
The four components of TQM are as follows:

1. **Make continuous improvement a priority.** TQM companies are never satisfied. They make small, incremental improvements an everyday priority in all areas of the organization. By improving everything a little bit of the time all the time, the company can achieve long-term quality, efficiency, and customer satisfaction.

2. **Get every employee involved.** To build teamwork and trust, TQM companies see that every employee is involved in the continuous improvement process. This requires that workers must be trained and empowered to find and solve problems. The goal is to build teamwork, trust, and mutual respect.

3. **Listen to and learn from customers and employees.** TQM companies pay attention to their customers, the people who use their products or services. In addition, employees within the companies listen and learn from other employees, those outside their own work areas.

4. **Use accurate standards to identify and eliminate problems.** TQM organizations are always alert to how competitors do things better, then try to improve on them—a process known as benchmarking. Using these standards, they apply statistical measurements to their own processes to identify problems.

Why Total Quality Management Is Important: The total quality management viewpoint emphasizes infusing concepts of quality throughout the total organization in a way that will deliver quality products and services to customers. The adoption of TQM helped American companies deal with global competition. ●

major question? Organizations must learn or perish. How do I build a learning organization?

THE BIG PICTURE

Learning organizations actively create, acquire, and transfer knowledge within themselves and are able to modify their behavior to reflect new knowledge. There are three ways you as a manager can help build a learning organization.

Ultimately, the lesson we need to take from the theories, perspectives, and viewpoints we have described is this: We need to keep on learning. Organizations are the same way: Like people, they must continually learn new things or face obsolescence. A key challenge for managers, therefore, is to establish a culture that will enhance their employees' ability to learn—to build so-called learning organizations.

Learning organizations, says Massachusetts Institute of Technology professor **Peter Senge,** who coined the term, are places "where people continually expand their capacity to create the results they truly desire, where new and expansive patterns of thinking are nurtured, where collective aspiration is set free, and where people are continually learning how to learn together."[41]

The Learning Organization: Handling Knowledge & Modifying Behavior

More formally, a ***learning organization*** **is an organization that actively creates, acquires, and transfers knowledge within itself and is able to modify its behavior to reflect new knowledge.**[42] Note the three parts:

1. **Creating and acquiring knowledge.** In learning organizations, managers try to actively infuse their organizations with new ideas and information, which are the prerequisites for learning. They acquire such knowledge by constantly scanning their external environments, by not being afraid to hire new talent and expertise when needed, and by devoting significant resources to training and developing their employees.

2. **Transferring knowledge.** Managers actively work at transferring knowledge throughout the organization, reducing barriers to sharing information and ideas among employees. Electronic Data Systems (EDS), for instance, practically invented the information-technology services industry, but by 1996 it was slipping behind competitors—missing the onset of the Internet wave, for example. When a new CEO, Dick Brown, took the reins in 1999, he changed the culture from "fix the problem yourself" to sharing information internally.[43]

3. **Modifying behavior.** Learning organizations are nothing if not results oriented. Thus, managers encourage employees to use the new knowledge obtained to change their behavior to help further the organization's goals.[44]

Why Organizations Need to Be Learning Organizations: Living with Accelerated Change

Just as you as an individual will have to confront the challenges we mentioned in Chapter 1—globalization, information technology, diversity, and so on—so will organizations. The challenges posed by competition from a globalized marketplace and from the Internet and e-business revolution have led to unprecedented accelerated change, forcing organizations to be faster and more efficient.

Among some of the consequences of this fast-paced world:

1. **The rise of virtual organizations.** "Strip away the highfalutin' talk," says one industry observer, "and at bottom the Internet is a tool that dramatically lowers the cost of communication. That means it can radically alter any industry or activity that depends heavily on the flow of information."[45] One consequence of this is the ***virtual organization,* an organization whose members are geographically apart, usually working with e-mail, collaborative computing, and other computer connections,** while often appearing to customers and others to be a single, unified organization with a real physical location.[46]

2. **The rise of boundaryless organizations.** Computer connections and virtual organization have given rise to the concept of boundaryless organization. The opposite of a bureaucracy, with its numerous barriers and divisions, a ***boundaryless organization* is a fluid, highly adaptive organization whose members, linked by information technology, come together to collaborate on common tasks; the collaborators may include competitors, suppliers, and customers.** This means that the form of the business is ever-changing, and business relationships are informal.[47]

3. **The imperative for speed and innovation.** "Speed is emerging as the ultimate competitive weapon," says a *BusinessWeek* article. "Some of the world's most successful companies are proving to be expert at spotting new opportunities, marshaling their forces, and bringing to market new products or services in a flash. That goes for launching whole new ventures, too."[48] Speed is being driven by a new innovation imperative. "Competition is more intense than ever," the article continues, "because of the rise of the Asian powerhouses and the spread of disruptive new Internet technologies and business models."

4. **The increasing importance of knowledge workers.** A ***knowledge worker* is someone whose occupation is principally concerned with generating or interpreting information, as opposed to manual labor.** Knowledge workers add value to the organization by using their brains rather than the sweat of their brows, and as such they are the most common type of worker in 21st-century organizations. Because of globalization and information technology, the United States no longer has an advantage in knowledge workers. Indeed, because of the advancement of China, India, Russia, and Brazil; the offshoring of sophisticated jobs; the decrease in math and science skills among today's younger Americans; and other factors, the United States may be in danger of slipping behind.

5. **An appreciation for the importance of human capital.** *Human capital* **is the economic or productive potential of employee knowledge, experience, and actions.**[49] Thinking about people as human capital has an obvious basis: "Attracting, retaining, and developing great people is sometimes the only way our organizations can keep up with the competition across the street or around the globe," says Susan Meisinger, president and CEO of the Society for Human Resource Management. "Research has shown that highly educated, knowledgeable workers—*the most in demand*—are the hardest to find and easiest to lose."[50]

6. **An appreciation for the importance of social capital.** *Social capital* is the economic or productive potential of strong, trusting, and cooperative relationships.[51] Among aspects of social capital are goodwill, mutual respect, cooperation, trust, and teamwork. Relationships within a company are important: In one survey, 77% of the women and 63% of the men rated "good relationship with boss" extremely important, outranking such matters as good equipment, easy commute, and flexible hours.[52]

7. **New emphasis on evidence-based management.** Is it such a radical idea to base decisions on the latest and best knowledge of what actually works? Wouldn't you think this would be the way medicine operates? In fact, say Jeffrey Pfeffer and Robert Sutton, most doctors rely on "obsolete knowledge gained in school, long-standing but never proven traditions, patterns gleaned from experience, the methods they believe in and are most skilled in applying, and information from hordes of vendors with products and services."[53] Business decision makers operate much the same way. Challenging this is a push for the use of evidence-based management in business. We continue the discussion about evidence-based management in Chapter 6.

How to Build a Learning Organization: Three Roles Managers Play

To create a learning organization, managers must perform three key functions or roles: (1) *build a commitment to learning,* (2) *work to generate ideas with impact,* and (3) *work to generalize ideas with impact.*[54]

1. **You can build a commitment to learning.** To instill in your employees an intellectual and emotional commitment to the idea of learning, you as a manager need to lead the way by investing in it, publicly promoting it, creating rewards and symbols of it, and performing other similar activities. For example, Mark Pigott, chairman of PACCAR, Inc., which makes Kenworth and Peterbilt trucks, accomplished this by looking at other kinds of businesses and learning from their success. By focusing intently on how to improve quality, PACCAR can charge up to 10% more than competitors for its trucks.[55]

2. **You can work to generate ideas with impact.** As a manager, you need to try to generate ideas with impact—that is, ideas that add value for customers, employees, and shareholders—by increasing employee competence through training, experimenting with new ideas, and engaging in other leadership activities.

   Soon after Dick Brown became new CEO of EDS, he saw that the company had to be reinvented as a cool brand to make people feel good about working there. His marketing director decided to launch a new campaign at the biggest media event of all: the Super Bowl. EDS ran an ad showing rugged cowboys riding herd on 10,000 cats. The message: "We ride herd on complexity."

3. **You can work to generalize ideas with impact.** Besides generating ideas with impact, you can also generalize them—that is, reduce the barriers to learning among employees and within your organization. You can create a climate that reduces conflict, increases communication, promotes teamwork, rewards risk taking, reduces the fear of failure, and increases cooperation. In other words, you can create a psychologically safe and comforting environment that increases the sharing of successes, failures, and best practices. ●

Key Terms Used in This Chapter

administrative management 42
behavioral science 47
behavioral viewpoint 44
boundaryless organization 59
classical viewpoint 40
closed system 52
contemporary perspective 39
contingency viewpoint 53
evidence-based management 38
feedback 51
historical perspective 39

human capital 59
human relations movement 46
inputs 51
knowledge worker 59
learning organization 58
management science 48
open system 52
operations management 49
outputs 51
quality 56
quality assurance 56

quality control 56
quality-management viewpoint 56
quantitative management 48
scientific management 40
social capital 60
subsystems 51
system 51
systems viewpoint 51
total quality management (TQM) 57
transformation processes 51
virtual organization 59

Summary

 2.1 Evolving Viewpoints: How We Got to Today's Management Outlook
A rational approach to management is evidence-based management, which means translating principles based on best evidence into organizational practice, bringing rationality to the decision-making process. The two overarching perspectives on management are (1) the historical perspective, which includes three viewpoints—classical, behavioral, and quantitative; and (2) the contemporary perspective, which includes three other viewpoints—systems, contingency, and quality-management. There are five practical reasons for studying theoretical perspectives: They provide (1) understanding of the present, (2) a guide to action, (3) a source of new ideas, (4) clues to the meaning of your managers' decisions, and (5) clues to the meaning of outside ideas.

 2.2 Classical Viewpoint: Scientific & Administrative Management
The first of the historical perspectives is the classical viewpoint, which emphasized finding ways to manage work more efficiently. It had two branches: (1) Scientific management emphasized the scientific study of work methods to improve productivity by individual workers. It was pioneered by Frederick W. Taylor, who offered four principles of science that could

be applied to management, and by Frank and Lillian Gilbreth, who refined motion studies that broke job tasks into physical motions. (2) Administrative management was concerned with managing the total organization. Among its pioneers were Henri Fayol, who identified the major functions of management (planning, organizing, leading, controlling), and Max Weber, who identified five positive bureaucratic features in a well-performing organization. The classical viewpoint showed that work activity was amenable to a rational approach, but it has been criticized as being too mechanistic, viewing humans as cogs in a machine.

 2.3 Behavioral Viewpoint: Behavorism, Human Relations, & Behavioral Science
The second of the historical perspectives, the behavioral viewpoint emphasized the importance of understanding human behavior and of motivating employees toward achievement. It developed over three phases: (1) early behaviorism (2) the human relations movement, and (3) the behavioral science approach. Early behaviorism had three pioneers: (a) Hugo Munsterberg suggested that psychologists could contribute to industry by studying jobs, identifying the psychological conditions for employees to do their best work. (b) Mary Parker Follett thought organizations

should be democratic, with employees and managers working together. (c) Elton Mayo hypothesized a so-called Hawthorne effect, suggesting that employees worked harder if they received added attention from managers. The human relations movement suggested that better human relations could increase worker productivity. Among its pioneers were (a) Abraham Maslow, who proposed a hierarchy of human needs, and (b) Douglas McGregor, who proposed a Theory X (managers have pessimistic view of workers) and Theory Y (managers have positive view of workers). The behavioral science approach relied on scientific research for developing theories about human behavior that can be used to provide practical tools for managers.

2.4 Quantitative Viewpoints: Management Science & Operations Research
The third of the historical perspectives, quantitative viewpoints emphasized the application to management of quantitative techniques. Two approaches are (1) management science, which focuses on using mathematics to aid in problem solving and decision making; and (2) operations management, which focuses on managing the production and delivery of an organization's products or services more effectively.

2.5 Systems Viewpoint
We turn from the study of the historical perspective to the contemporary perspective, which includes three viewpoints: (1) systems, (2) contingency, and (3) quality-management. The systems viewpoint regards the organization as a system of interrelated parts or collection of subsystems that operate together to achieve a common purpose. A system has four parts: inputs, outputs, transformational processes, and feedback. A system can be open, continually interacting with the environment, or closed, having little such interaction.

2.6 Contingency Viewpoint
The second viewpoint in the contemporary perspective, the contingency viewpoint emphasizes that a manager's approach should vary according to the individual and the environmental situation.

2.7 Quality-Management Viewpoint
The third category in the contemporary perspective, the quality-management viewpoint is concerned with quality (the total ability of a product or service to meet customer needs) and has three aspects: (1) Quality control is the strategy for minimizing errors by managing each stage of production. (2) Quality assurance focuses on the performance of workers, urging employees to strive for "zero defects." (3) Total quality management (TQM) is a comprehensive approach dedicated to continuous quality improvement, training, and customer satisfaction. TQM has four components: (a) make continuous improvement a priority; (b) get every employee involved; (c) listen to and learn from customers and employees; and (d) use accurate standards to identify and eliminate problems.

2.8 The Learning Organization in an Era of Accelerated Change
A learning organization is one that actively creates, acquires, and transfers knowledge within itself and is able to modify its behavior to reflect new knowledge. Seven reasons why organizations need to become learning organizations are (1) the rise of virtual organizations, with members connected by electronic networks; (2) the rise of fluid, adaptive, boundaryless organizations; (3) the imperative for speed and innovation; (4) the increasing importance of knowledge workers, those principally concerned with generating or interpreting information; (5) an appreciation for the importance of human capital, the economic or productive potential of employees; (6) an appreciation for the importance of social capital, the economic or productive potential of strong and cooperative relationships; and (7) new emphasis on evidence-based management, in which managers face hard facts about what works and what doesn't. Three roles that managers must perform to build a learning organization are to (1) build a commitment to learning, (2) work to generate ideas with impact, and (3) work to generalize ideas with impact.

Providence Regional Medical Center Uses a Variety of Management Theories to Profitably Treat Patients

Walk into most hospitals, and you'll see patients scattered about the halls on gurneys or wheelchairs. They're waiting to be moved from intensive care to a standard ward, or to an X-ray room, or to physical therapy. Each journey adds to the patient's discomfort and increases the risk of infections and other complications. Tally up a single patient's migrations over 24 hours, and they may consume as much as half a day of staff time.

Walk into Providence Regional Medical Center, in Everett, Washington, and you will see a hospital trying something different: It brings the equipment to the patient. In 2003, Providence opened one of the few "single stay" wards in the nation. After heart surgery, cardiac patients remain in one room throughout their recovery; only the gear and staff are in motion. As the patient's condition stabilizes, the beeping machines of intensive care are removed and physical therapy equipment is added. Testing gear is wheeled to the patient, not the other way around. Patient satisfaction with the "single stay" ward has soared, and the average length of hospital stay has dropped by a day or more.

This is just one of many changes—some radical, many quite small—that have enabled Providence Regional to join a special subset of American hospitals: those that do not lose money on Medicare patients.

The crazy world of hospital economics does not offer a lot of incentives to change. Both Medicare and private insurers reimburse on a piecework basis—known as fee-for-service—that encourages hospitals to treat more, prescribe more, and test more. Economists refer to this arrangement as a "value-blind" payment system, since no premium is paid for quality.

Consequently, hospitals have no financial motivation to invest in productivity—enhancing computer technology, management experts, or efficiency research—and by and large, they don't.

Providence took a different path after picketing by workers nine years ago shattered morale. A new administration decided to attack the internal staff divisions and foster collaboration among doctors, nurses, and administrators. Everyone is encouraged to contribute ideas on driving down costs and improving patient outcomes. "I'm eligible for retirement, and under the prior leadership I would have left," says pediatric nurse Kathy Elder, a 34-year veteran of Providence. "They were very hierarchical, very closed. There was a lack of trust all around."

The current CEO, 48-year-old David T. Brooks, a fast-talking Detroit native, took over two years ago. He says the administration is open to suggestions from any and all staffers. "We have scorecards for everything around here, which measures both quality and efficiency. If all we had were great clinical outcomes but costs kept rising, that just wouldn't be good enough."

The staff embraced the challenge to innovate. The nursing team came up with an idea of checking on patients every two hours without waiting for a call button, to see if they need help walking to the bathroom or moving about in their rooms. Ten percent of fatal falls by the elderly in the United States occur in hospitals. This one change at Providence reduced falls by 25%, according to chief nursing officer Kim Williams. "We believe we'll see more improvement over the next six months."

Providence's saving efforts don't stop at the hospital doors. It offers financial training courses to the 800 independent doctors affiliated with the hospital in an effort to get them thinking about cost efficiencies. That's no easy task, however, since savings don't necessarily flow into their pockets. Cutting back on unnecessary services may be better for the bill payer, but it lowers the income of doctors and hospitals.

Providence also seeks to soften contentious encounters among doctors and patients by doing penance for errors. The hospital set up an independent panel to investigate medical mistakes, disclose its findings to the patient, and voluntarily offer a financial award if warranted. As a result, Providence has only two malpractice suits pending, compared with an average of 12 to 14 at other hospitals of similar size.

When Providence can't find standard medical practices, it innovates. That was the case with blood transfusions. Cardiac and orthopedic surgeons realized a few years ago that there was no widely accepted data on the optimal amount of blood to give patients during surgery, despite the $240 cost per bag. Dr. Brevig (director of cardiac surgery at Providence) started looking around and found several studies that correlated greater transfusion volumes with longer patient stays and higher infection rates.

He was particularly surprised that transfusion rates varied greatly from hospital to hospital, regardless of the patient's status. "The variations were related to the culture of the hospital, not the decisions of the doctor," he says. Brevig set out to create a low-transfusion culture at Providence. He got surgeons to slow down because speedy operations cause more blood loss. Settings were changed on heart bypass machines to save blood, and the hospital hired a blood conservation coordinator. In a study of 2,531 operations at Providence, Brevig reported that the incidence of transfusions were reduced to just 18% in 2007, from 43% in 2003, while the average patient stay was reduced by half a day. The changes have saved Providence an estimated $4.5 million.

Brevig has been proselytizing for his plasma practices at medical meetings, but to little avail. Only some 200 U.S. hospitals have a blood conservation program. Since patients are billed the cost of the plasma, doctors aren't motivated to change their habits.

For Discussion

1. To what extent is Providence using evidence-based management? Do you think that this is a good way to run a hospital? Explain your rationale.

2. To what extent are the managerial practices being used at Providence consistent with principles associated with management science and operations management techniques? Discuss.

3. Use Figure 2.3 to analyze the extent to which Providence is using a systems viewpoint.

4. How are the managerial techniques being used at Providence consistent with both a contingency and quality-management viewpoint? Explain your rationale.

5. How can the effective managerial techniques being used at Providence be exported to other hospitals? Discuss.

Source: Excerpted from Catherine Arnst, "Radical Surgery," *Bloomberg BusinessWeek*, January 18, 2010, pp 40–45. Reprinted with permission.

Self-Assessment

What Is Your Level of Self-Esteem?

Objectives
1. To get to know yourself a bit better.
2. To help you assess your self-esteem.

Introduction
Self-esteem, confidence, self-worth, and self-belief are all important aspects of being a manager in any organizational structure. However, the need for strong self-esteem is especially vital today because organizations demand that a manager manage people not as appendages of machines (as in scientific management) but as individuals who possess skills, knowledge, and self-will. Managers used to operate from a very strong position of centralized power and authority. However, in our modern organizational settings power is shared, and knowledge is to some extent "where you find it." To manage effectively in this situation, managers need strong self-esteem.

Instructions
To assess your self-esteem, answer the following questions. For each item, indicate the extent to which you agree or disagree by using the following scale. Remember, there are no right or wrong answers.

1 = strongly disagree
2 = disagree
3 = neither agree nor disagree
4 = agree
5 = strongly agree

Questions

1.	I generally feel as competent as my peers.	1 2 3 4 5
2.	I usually feel I can achieve whatever I want.	1 2 3 4 5
3.	Whatever happens to me is mostly in my control.	1 2 3 4 5
4.	I rarely worry about how things will work out.	1 2 3 4 5
5.	I am confident that I can deal with most situations.	1 2 3 4 5
6.	I rarely doubt my ability to solve problems.	1 2 3 4 5
7.	I rarely feel guilty for asking others to do things.	1 2 3 4 5
8.	I am rarely upset by criticism.	1 2 3 4 5
9.	Even when I fail, I still do not doubt my basic ability.	1 2 3 4 5
10.	I am very optimistic about my future.	1 2 3 4 5
11.	I feel that I have quite a lot to offer an employer.	1 2 3 4 5
12.	I rarely dwell for very long on personal setbacks.	1 2 3 4 5
13.	I am always comfortable in disagreeing with my boss.	1 2 3 4 5
14.	I rarely feel that I would like to be somebody else.	1 2 3 4 5

TOTAL SCORE_____

Arbitrary Norms

High self-esteem = 56–70

Moderate self-esteem = 29–55

Low self-esteem = 14–28

Questions for Discussion

1. Do you agree with the assessment? Why or why not?
2. How might you go about improving your self-esteem?
3. Can you survive today without having relatively good confidence in yourself?

Ethical Dilemma

Should Automotive Business Executives Be Held Liable for Product Defects That Result in Death?

Toyota recalled 2.3 million cars in the United States in early 2010 in response to pressure from federal regulators regarding acceleration problems with its gas pedals. This problem is thought to have caused a number of fatal accidents. In a memorandum to lawmakers on the House Oversight and Government Reform Committee, investigators for the panel pointed to what they called "a growing body of evidence that neither Toyota nor NHTSA (National Highway Traffic Safety Administration) have identified all the causes of sudden unintended acceleration in Toyota vehicles." The memo said that remedies deployed by Toyota, such as redesigning some floor mats and fixing sticky gas pedals, have failed to solve the problem. CTS Corp., the company that makes the gas pedals for Toyota, claims that it is not responsible for the problem.

Toyota officials told Congress that it is "very, very hard to identify" causes of the problem. Some experts contend that the root cause problem is the sophisticated software that is installed in cars to help reduce emissions, control braking, and myriad other tasks. For example, a writer from the *The Wall Street Journal* concluded that "implementing so many virtual and not-so-virtual control features as a network system also creates complexity and multiplies the opportunity for unpredictable software bugs and circuitry mishaps." If this writer is correct, then one must wonder if it is fair to blame executives for defective parts that are being installed as part of an attempt to make cars more efficient, safe, and energy efficient.

Solving the Dilemma

Consider that several Mitsubishi executives were put on trial for manslaughter charges in Japan "for failing diligently to investigate defects in delivery trucks that were subsequently implicated in two deaths." Do you think it is fair to level criminal charges on executives for product defects that can cause death among users?

1. Absolutely not. Individual managers should not be held responsible for the safety of all the parts that go into a car for example.

2. Yes. If we don't hold someone accountable for product defects, then companies will ignore safety in lieu of lower costs and faster delivery.

3. No, but corporations should be held responsible. Individuals can't control or test the safety of all parts used in a car, but organizations can.

4. Invent other options. Discuss.

Source: Material for this case was drawn and extracted from Holman W. Jenkins, Jr., "Toyota and the Curse of Software," *The Wall Street Journal,* February 5, 2010, p. A15; and Kate Linebaugh and Matthew Dolan, "Pedal Maker Says It's Not to Blame," *The Wall Street Journal,* February 9, 2010, p. B3.

(chapter 3)

The Manager's Changing Work Environment & Ethical Responsibilities

Doing the Right Thing

Major Questions You Should Be Able to Answer

 3.I The Community of Stakeholders Inside the Organization

Major Question: Stockholders are only one group of stakeholders. Who are the stakeholders important to me inside the organization?

 3.2 The Community of Stakeholders Outside the Organization

Major Question: Who are stakeholders important to me outside the organization?

 3.3 The Ethical Responsibilities Required of You as a Manager

Major Question: What does the successful manager need to know about ethics and values?

 3.4 The Social Responsibilities Required of You as a Manager

Major Question: Is being socially responsible really necessary?

 3.5 The New Diversified Workforce

Major Question: What trends in workplace diversity should managers be aware of?

Treating Employees Right: Toward a More Open Workplace

Some companies are "toxic organizations," Stanford University business professor Jeffrey Pfeffer's name for firms with high turnover and low productivity. "Companies that manage people right will outperform companies that don't by 30% to 40%," says Pfeffer. "If you don't believe me, look at the numbers."[1]

The author of *The Human Equation: Building Profits by Putting People First*, Pfeffer says that employees' loyalty to employers isn't dead but that toxic companies drive people away.[2] Companies such as Costco, Starbucks, and The Men's Wearhouse have had lower turnover—and hence lower replacement and training costs—than their competitors for a reason: They have bent over backward to create workplaces that make people want to stay.

Here are some ways that companies keep their employees:

- **Being generous with personal and team recognition.** CompuWorks, a Pittsfield, Massachusetts, computer systems-integration company, cultivates employee loyalty by piling on personal and team recognition, as in giving the Wizard of the Week award to the employee who goes beyond the call of duty. It also operates the Time Bank, into which every month 10 hours of free time is "deposited" for each employee to use as he or she wishes. Training is given in how to read financial statements and in how to chart billable hours and watch cash-flow levels. Regular bonuses are given based on company profits.[3]

- **Occasionally backing employees over clients.** Sometimes, despite the mantra that "the customer is always right," companies will even side with employees against clients. For example, The Benjamin Group, a California public relations agency, has fired clients who have been arrogant and hard to work with. This reflects management theories that troublesome customers are often less profitable and less loyal and so aren't worth the extra effort.[4]

- **Use of "open-book" management.** One way of challenging traditional military-style management and of empowering employees and increasing earnings is through "open-book management," *Inc.* magazine editor John Case's term for a company's being completely open with employees about its financial status, projections, costs, expenses, and even salaries.[5] This approach "means training employees in how the company is run," says one account. "It means asking for employee input and acting on it. It means rewarding employees with bonuses when the goals they create are met."[6]

By learning the key numbers, employees are able to use their heads instead of just doing their jobs and going home. "Whether or not you have equity ownership, open-book management helps employees to feel, think, and act like owners," says Gary T. Brown, director of human resources for Springfield ReManufacturing Corp., a rebuilder of truck engines in Springfield, Missouri. "True open-book management means asking employees what the goals should be."[7]

For Discussion In tomorrow's highly diverse workforce, with people representing many different ethnicities, ages, and abilities, taking care of employees will be one of the biggest challenges a manager will face. Could you work for an old-style company that did not feature some of the approaches mentioned above—even if it gave you a shot at getting into higher management?

---

forecast **What's Ahead in This Chapter**

This chapter sets the stage for understanding the new world in which managers must operate and the responsibilities they will have. We begin by describing the community of stakeholders that managers have to deal with—first the internal stakeholders (employees, owners, and directors), then the external stakeholders in two kinds of environments (task and general). We then consider the ethical and social responsibilities required in being a manager, as well as the new diversified workforce and the barriers and approaches to managing diversity.

major question?

Stockholders are only one group of stakeholders. Who are stakeholders important to me inside the organization?

THE BIG PICTURE

Managers operate in two organizational environments—internal and external—both made up of stakeholders, the people whose interests are affected by the organization. The first, or internal, environment consists of employees, owners, and the board of directors.

Costco. In the war of big-box stores, has Costco or Walmart been better for everyone involved?

Which company is better—Walmart Stores (2.1 million employees) or rival warehouse club Costco Wholesale (142,000)? And why?

Fortune named Walmart to the No. 1 or No. 2 spot on its annual "Most Admired Companies" list in the years 2000–2005. (It dropped to No. 11 in 2008 and 2009. Costco was No. 22 in those years.) Is this because Walmart's low prices probably save consumers $20 billion a year? Because it generates 3.5 cents for each dollar on sales compared with Costco's 1.7 cents? Certainly Walmart's "Always low prices" strategy has been hugely successful in bringing in revenues.

But Walmart's strategy also earned it a reputation for being "the most evil company on the planet."[8] That's less of a problem now, as the company has worked hard at improving its relationship with employees and the public, both in word and deed. Walmart also benefited from the recent recession, when low prices became especially important to customers.

In the past, however, the difference in the way Walmart and Costco treated their employees was dramatic, and still is in terms of pay rates: Walmart pays its retail cashiers an average of $8.89 an hour; Costco pays retail cashiers $12.86. At Costco 96% of eligible workers were and are covered by company health insurance (higher than the 80% average at large U.S. companies). Walmart used to claim fewer than 10% of its employees lacked health insurance (it is now less than 5.5%), but the company's system of premiums and deductibles made it difficult for low-wage employees to afford such insurance.[9] Walmart's low-wage policy forced rivals, such as Safeway, to reduce benefits for their workers in order to stay competitive. Costco's wages enabled its employees to buy homes and take vacation trips. Finally, Walmart has reportedly locked out workers overnight, ignored overtime rules, hired illegal immigrants to mop its floors, shut down a store to avoid letting union organizers in, and was slapped with a big discrimination suit.[10]

The differences could be seen in annual employee turnover—at least 50%, perhaps 70%, for Walmart, 24% for Costco.[11] It's been calculated that a 10% reduction in employee turnover can yield a 20% savings on labor costs. Thus, whereas Walmart's labor costs amounted to 12% of its annual sales, Costco's were only 7%. On a per-store basis, Walmart's Sam's Club generated only half the sales of the average Costco store (in part because Costco attracts higher-income shoppers and because it charges a yearly membership fee, spending no money on advertising). Still, the more favorable employee benefits led to a less favorable stock price for Costco compared with Walmart.

Which should a company favor, its employees or its owners (stockholders)? Henry Ford, founder of Ford Motor Co., thought he could serve both. In 1914, he announced workers in his factories would receive $5 a day—a major boost over then-prevailing wages. The reason: He recognized that his promise to build a car affordable to the masses would be hypocritical if he didn't pay his own workers enough to buy it themselves.[12]

Internal & External Stakeholders

Should a company be principally responsible to just its stockholders? Perhaps we need a broader term to indicate all those with a stake in an organization. That term, appropriately, is *stakeholders*—**the people whose interests are affected by an organization's activities.**

Managers operate in two organizational environments, both made up of various stakeholders. *(See Figure 3.1.)* As we describe in the rest of this section, the two environments are these:

- Internal stakeholders
- External stakeholders

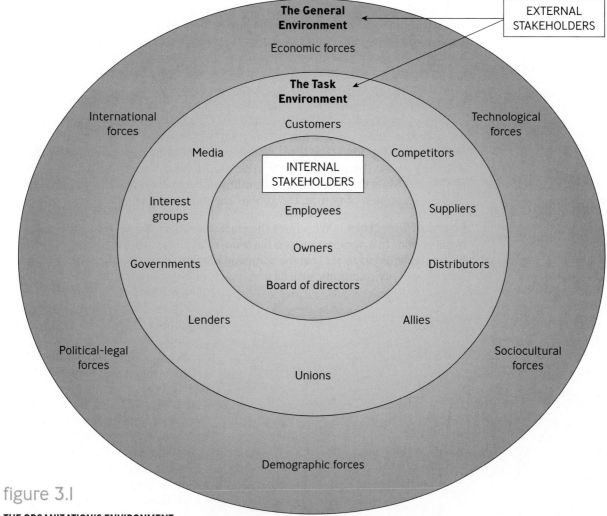

figure 3.1

THE ORGANIZATION'S ENVIRONMENT

The two main groups are internal and external stakeholders.

Source: From Diverse Teams at Work by Lee Gardenswartz. Copyright © 2003 by Society for Human Resource Management (SHRM). Reproduced with permission of Society for Human Resource Management via Copyright Clearance Center.

Internal Stakeholders

Whether small or large, the organization to which you belong has people in it who have an important stake in how it performs. These *internal stakeholders* **consist of employees, owners, and the board of directors, if any.** Let us consider each in turn.

Employees   As a manager, could you run your part of the organization if you and your employees were constantly in conflict? Labor history, of course, is full of accounts of just that. But such conflict may lower the performance of the organization, thereby hurting everyone's stake. In many of today's forward-looking organizations, employees are considered "the talent"—the most important resource.

"My chief assets drive out the gate every day," says Jim Goodnight, CEO of North Carolina–based SAS. "My job is to make sure they come back."[13] SAS is the world's largest privately held software business and No. 1 on *Fortune*'s 2010 list of "100 Best Companies to Work For." Even during the recent Great Recession, when there were six unemployed workers for every available U.S. job opening, SAS continued to treat employees exceptionally well, resulting in a turnover rate of only 2% in 2009, compared with a software industry average of 22%.

Owners   The *owners* **of an organization consist of all those who can claim it as their legal property,** such as Walmart's stockholders. In the for-profit world, if you're running a one-person graphic design firm, the owner is just you—you're what is known as a sole proprietorship. If you're in an Internet start-up with your brother-in-law, you're both owners—you're a partnership. If you're a member of a family running a car dealership, you're all owners—you're investors in a privately owned company. If you work for a company that is more than half owned by its employees (such as Lakeland, Florida-based, Publix Super Markets or W. L. Gore & Associates, maker of Gore-Tex fabric and No. 13 on *Fortune*'s 2010 "Best Companies to Work For" list), you are one of the joint owners—you're part of an Employee Stock Ownership Plan (ESOP).[14] And if you've bought a few shares of stock in a company whose shares are listed for sale on the New York Stock Exchange, such as General Motors, you're one of thousands of owners—you're a stockholder. In all these examples, of course, the goal of the owners is to make a profit.

Board of Directors   Who hires the chief executive of a for-profit or nonprofit organization? In a corporation, it is the *board of directors,* whose members are elected by the stockholders to see that the company is being run according to their interests. In nonprofit organizations, such as universities or hospitals, the board may be called the *board of trustees* or *board of regents.* Board members are very important in setting the organization's overall strategic goals and in approving the major decisions and salaries of top management.

Not all firms have a board of directors. A lawyer, for instance, may operate as a sole proprietor, making all her own decisions. A large corporation might have eight or so members on its board of directors. Some of these directors (inside directors) may be top executives of the firm. The rest (outside directors) are elected from outside the firm. ●

Employee ownership. Zachary's Chicago Pizza, based in Oakland, California, uses a device known as an Employee Stock Ownership Plan, in which employees buy company stock in order to become owners. Although the idea was conceived over 50 years ago, there are only about 11,500 ESOPs today out of hundreds of thousands of businesses. Why do you suppose more companies aren't owned by their employees?

✳ 3.2 THE COMMUNITY OF STAKEHOLDERS OUTSIDE THE ORGANIZATION

Who are stakeholders important to me outside the organization?

major question?

THE BIG PICTURE

The external environment of stakeholders consists of the task environment and the general environment. The task environment consists of customers, competitors, suppliers, distributors, strategic allies, employee associations, local communities, financial institutions, government regulators, special-interest groups, and the mass media. The general environment consists of economic, technological, sociocultural, demographic, political-legal, and international forces.

In the first section we described the environment inside the organization. Here let's consider the environment outside it, which consists of *external stakeholders*—**people or groups in the organization's external environment that are affected by it.** This environment consists of:

- The task environment.
- The general environment.

The Task Environment

The *task environment* **consists of 11 groups that present you with daily tasks to handle: customers, competitors, suppliers, distributors, strategic allies, employee organizations, local communities, financial institutions, government regulators, special-interest groups, and mass media.**

I. Customers The first law of business (and even nonprofits), we've said, is *take care of the customer.* **Customers are those who pay to use an organization's goods or services.** Many customers value service over price, according to a Forrester Research report, with 54% thinking it would be easy to have a customer service issue resolved in clothing and apparel outlets but only 30% thinking the same in health insurance companies.[15]

2. Competitors Is there any line of work you could enter in which there would *not* be *competitors*—**people or organizations that compete for customers or resources,** such as talented employees or raw materials? Every organization has to be actively aware of its competitors. Florist shops and delicatessens must be aware that customers can buy the same products at Safeway or Kroger.

3. Suppliers A *supplier* **is a person or an organization that provides supplies—that is, raw materials, services, equipment, labor, or energy— to other organizations.** Suppliers in turn have their own suppliers: The publisher of this book buys the paper on which it is printed from a paper merchant, who in turn is supplied by several paper mills, which in turn are supplied wood for wood pulp by logging companies with forests in the United States or Canada.

Take care of the customer. Customers have the most faith in the ability of apparel companies, banks, and hotels to handle complaints, less confidence in Internet service providers, computer companies, and health insurers. Do you think this is partly because a piece of clothing, for example, is less complex than a computer or a health insurance policy?

Example

Taking Care of Customers: Amazon.com Obsesses about "the Customer Experience"

What do Wall Street investors care about? Short-term profits. And profits are what Dell Computer tried to deliver when it scrimped on customer service. So did eBay when it saddled its most dedicated sellers with new costs. "Eventually," says *New York Times* business writer Joe Nocera, "those short-sighted decisions caught up with both companies."[16]

By contrast, Amazon.com founder and CEO Jeff Bezos is "obsessed," in his words, with what he calls "the customer experience." Customers "care about having the lowest prices, having vast selection, so they have choice, and getting the products . . . fast," Bezos has said. "And the reason I'm so obsessed with these drivers of the customer experience is that I believe that the success we have had over the past 12 years has been driven exclusively by that customer experience."[17]

Thus, the company has an easy-to-use website, online technology ranked as more bug-free and user-friendly than rivals Walmart.com and Target.com.[18] It also has a money-losing (in Wall Street's view) 2-day free shipping policy on all packages for an annual fee of just $79, and a customer-service phone number that you can actually find. In addition, it has a willingness to correct mistakes that it didn't make, as when it replaced, for free, a $500 PlayStation 3 Christmas present that Nocera had ordered for his son, which disappeared on arriving at his apartment building—and it saw to it that the replacement arrived on Christmas Eve.

YOUR CALL

Spending huge sums of money on "frills" such as free shipping has depressed Amazon's profits from time to time, but in 2009 the company's fourth-quarter earnings skyrocketed 71%, and it did well throughout the year despite the sluggish economy.[19] Other companies also bend over backward to take care of their customers. Can you name examples?

4. Distributors A *distributor* **is a person or an organization that helps another organization sell its goods and services to customers.** Publishers of magazines, for instance, don't sell directly to newsstands; rather, they go through a distributor, or wholesaler. Tickets to the Black Eyed Peas or other artists' performances might be sold to you directly by the concert hall, but they are also sold through such distributors as TicketMaster and Blockbuster Video.

Distributors can be quite important because in some industries (such as movie theaters and magazines) there is not a lot of competition, and the distributor has a lot of power over the ultimate price of the product. However, the rise in popularity of the Internet has allowed manufacturers of personal computers, for example, to cut out the "middleman"—the distributor—and to sell to customers directly.

5. Strategic Allies Companies, and even nonprofit organizations, frequently link up with other organizations (even competing ones) in order to realize strategic advantages. The term *strategic allies* **describes the relationship of two organizations who join forces to achieve advantages neither can perform as well alone.**

With their worldwide reservation systems and slick marketing, big companies—Hilton, Hyatt, Marriott, Starwood, and so on—dominate the high-end business-center hotels. But in many cities, there are still independents—such as The Rittenhouse in Philadelphia, The Hay-Adams in Washington, DC, and The Adolphus in Dallas—that compete with the chains by promoting their prestigious locations, grand architecture, rich history, and personalized service. Recently, however, high-end independents have become affiliated with chains as strategic allies because chains can buy supplies for less and they have more far-reaching sales channels. The 97-year-old U.S. Grant in downtown San Diego, for example, joined Starwood's Luxury Collection in 2005 to gain "worldwide exposure," according to a hotel spokesman.[20]

6. Employee Organizations: Unions & Associations

As a rule of thumb, labor unions (such as the United Auto Workers or the Teamsters Union) tend to represent hourly workers; professional associations (such as the National Education Association or the Newspaper Guild) tend to represent salaried workers. Nevertheless, during a labor dispute, salary-earning teachers in the American Federation of Teachers might well picket in sympathy with the wage-earning janitors in the Service Employees International Union.

In recent years, the percentage of the labor force represented by unions has steadily declined (from 35% in the 1950s to 12.3% in 2009).[21] Indeed, most union members are now government employees, and private-sector unionization, mainly because of recession-related job losses in manufacturing and construction, has fallen off.[22] The composition of the membership has also changed, with 45% of the unionized workforce now female and 38% of union members holding a four-year college degree or more.[23]

7. Local Communities

Local communities are obviously important stakeholders, as becomes evident not only when a big organization arrives but also when it leaves, sending government officials scrambling to find new industry to replace it. Schools and municipal governments rely on the organization for their tax base. Families and merchants depend on its employee payroll for their livelihoods. In addition, everyone from the United Way to the Little League may rely on it for some financial support. If a community gives a company tax breaks in return for the promise of new jobs and the firm fails to do so, does the community have the right to institute *clawbacks*—**rescinding the tax breaks when firms don't deliver promised jobs?**

Example

Local Communities as Stakeholders: What Does a Company Owe Its Community?

Since its founding in 1884 as a cash register company the NCR Corporation, formerly known as National Cash Register and now a maker of automated teller machines and other self-service devices, has been an important company for Dayton, Ohio. But that ended in early 2010 when NCR chief executive Bill Nuti publicly announced the company was relocating its headquarters to Atlanta and posed for photographs with Georgia's governor, whose state had promised a lucrative incentive package.

"The images galled Dayton," reports *The New York Times*, "given Ohio's contention that Mr. Nuti had side-stepped several invitations from its governor since 2007 to discuss NCR's needs and desires."[24] Nuti rejoined that NCR had 22,000 employees around the world, but only 1,200 were in Ohio—fewer than in Georgia. Moreover, he said, Dayton's transportation costs were high and the airport not easy to connect with, and it was difficult to recruit top talent to live and work in the area. Ohioans found these remarks insulting, and in any case didn't 125 years count for something?

Communities & Clawbacks. As mentioned, many communities offer companies inducements to relocate, often trading tax breaks in return for the promise of jobs. But in cash-strapped times, cities that once bent over backward to lure companies are now resorting to "clawbacks"—asserting their right to rescind the tax breaks when the firms fail to deliver. Target Corp., for instance, got tax abatements from DeKalb, Illinois, city, county, and other taxing bodies after promising at least 500 jobs at a local distribution center. "So when the company came up 66 workers short in 2009," says one report, "Target got word its next tax bill would be jumping almost $600,000—more than half of which goes to the local school district, where teachers and programs have been cut as coffers dried up."[25]

YOUR CALL

Should NCR have given Ohio a chance to match Georgia's incentives? Or is the company's loyalty only to its stockholders? What obligations should a community expect of the companies located there?

8. Financial Institutions

Want to launch a small company? Although normally reluctant to make loans to start-ups, financial institutions—banks, savings and loans, and credit unions—may do so if you have a good credit history or can secure the loan with property such as a house. In the recent recession, even good customers found loans hard to get. (Best advice: Get to know some bank loan officers and try to educate them about your business.)[26]

Established companies also often need loans to tide them over when revenues are down or to finance expansion, but they rely for assistance on lenders such as commercial banks, investment banks, and insurance companies.

Government as stakeholder. Lake Tahoe straddles the state lines of California and Nevada. To help preserve the lake's natural beauty and prevent the clarity of its water from being spoiled by development and pollution, the various counties around the lake agreed to submit to being regulated by a bistate agency, the Tahoe Regional Planning Authority (TRPA). People wishing to build, for example, must submit plans not only to their own county but also to TRPA. In what ways do your local government authorities affect business in your area?

9. Government Regulators

The preceding groups are external stakeholders in your organization since they are clearly affected by its activities. But why would *government regulators*—**regulatory agencies that establish ground rules under which organizations may operate**—be considered stakeholders?

We are talking here about an alphabet soup of agencies, boards, and commissions that have the legal authority to prescribe or proscribe the conditions under which you may conduct business. To these may be added local and state regulators on the one hand and foreign governments and international agencies (such as the World Trade Organization, which oversees international trade and standardization efforts) on the other.

Such government regulators can be said to be stakeholders because not only do they affect the activities of your organization, they are in turn affected by it. The Federal Aviation Agency (FAA), for example, specifies how far planes must stay apart to prevent midair collisions. But when the airlines want to add more flights on certain routes, the FAA may have to add more flight controllers and radar equipment, since those are the agency's responsibility.

10. Special-Interest Groups

If the fake fur in the clothes you're wearing is actually made out of dog (specifically, the fur of the raccoon dog, found in Asia), would you know it? Federal law requires clothing manufacturers to identify fur on a clothing item only if its value exceeds $150. In early 2010, California assemblywoman Fiona Ma introduced a bill in the state legislature requiring apparel makers using fur to label their products accordingly regardless of the clothing's value. The political pressure came from the Humane Society of the United States, which for years had been agitating to close the legal loophole.

Special interests. Union members demand bank reform to help families keep their homes and expand lending that creates jobs.

Similar laws already exist in five other states. "All we are saying is, 'Label it,'" said Ma. "This is about a consumer's right to know as well as about animal rights."[27]

Special-interest groups are groups whose members try to influence specific issues, some of which may affect your organization. Examples are Mothers Against Drunk Driving, the National Organization for Women, and the National Rifle Association. Special-interest groups may try to exert political influence, as in contributing funds to lawmakers' election campaigns or in launching letter-writing efforts to officials. Or they may organize picketing and *boycotts*—holding back their patronage—of certain companies, as some African American groups did in recent years to protest reports of racism at Texaco and at Denny's restaurants.[28]

II. Mass Media What is a company supposed to do when it has a crisis? The gold standard in brand crisis management, says one account, is the path followed by health products company Johnson & Johnson in 1982, when several consumers died after taking tainted Tylenol pills. The company's reaction dictated what has become the preferred strategy taught in business schools: "Communicate clearly with the public about a crisis, cooperate with government officials, swiftly begin its own investigation of a problem, and, if necessary, quickly institute a product recall."[29] A big part of the strategy was communicating honestly and frequently through the media. However, a quarter century later, Johnson & Johnson unaccountably abandoned its own model. In January 2010, a J&J division, McNeil Consumer Healthcare, announced the recall—20 months after the initial alarm—of several hundred lots of popular over-the-counter medicines (Benadryl, Rolaids, Tylenol, others) because of customer complaints about temporary digestive problems. The company did not conduct an immediate investigation and did not notify authorities in a timely fashion, resulting in prolonged consumer exposure to the products. The result: a big media black eye for one of the most trusted brands in America. (The same kind of "Tylenol moment" was also a problem for Toyota when it was recalling cars for sticking accelerators.)[30]

J&J's troubles were not the fault of the press. But no manager can afford to ignore the power of the mass media—print, radio, TV, and the Internet—to rapidly and widely disseminate news both bad and good. Thus, most companies, universities, hospitals, and even government agencies have a public-relations person or department to communicate effectively with the press. In addition, top-level executives often receive special instruction on how to best deal with the media.

The General Environment

Beyond the task environment is the ***general environment,*** or ***macroenvironment,*** **which includes six forces: economic, technological, sociocultural, demographic, political-legal, and international.**

You may be able to control some forces in the task environment, but you can't control those in the general environment. Nevertheless, they can profoundly affect your organization's task environment without your knowing it, springing nasty surprises on you. Clearly, then, as a manager you need to keep your eye on the far horizon because these forces of the general environment can affect long-term plans and decisions.

I. Economic Forces *Economic forces* **consist of the general economic conditions and trends—unemployment, inflation, interest rates, economic growth—that may affect an organization's performance.** These are forces in your nation and region and even the world over which you and your organization probably have no control.

Are banks' interest rates going up in the United States? Then it will cost you more to borrow money to open new stores or build new plants. Is your region's unemployment rate rising? Then maybe you'll have more job applicants to hire from, yet you'll also have fewer customers with money to spend. Are natural resources getting scarce in an important area of supply? Then your company will need to pay more for them or switch to alternative sources.

One indicator that managers often pay attention to is productivity growth. Rising productivity leads to rising profits, lower inflation, and higher stock prices. In recent times, companies have been using information technology to cut costs, resulting in productivity growing at an annual rate of 2.7% from 2001 to 2007, slumping to 1.2% in the recession year 2008, then rebounding at an impressive 6.2% rate in 2009.[31]

2. Technological Forces   *Technological forces* **are new developments in methods for transforming resources into goods or services.** For example, think what the United States would have been like if the elevator, air-conditioning, the combustion engine, and the airplane had not been invented. No doubt changes in computer and communications technology—especially the influence of the Internet—will continue to be powerful technological forces during your managerial career. But other technological currents may affect you as well.

For example, biotechnology may well turn health and medicine upside down in the coming decades. Researchers can already clone animals, and some reports say they are close to doing the same with humans.

3. Sociocultural Forces   Long an American rite of passage, the act of getting a driver's license at age 16 is no longer as popular as it was, "on the wane among the digital generation," says one report, "which no longer sees the family car as the end-all of social life."[32] In other words, Facebook, MySpace, Twitter, and other social media are altering long-standing patterns.

Some day, of course, our descendants may well view the craze to have a driver's license as old-fogyish and quaint. That's how it is with sociocultural changes. *Sociocultural forces* **are influences and trends originating in a country's, a society's, or a culture's human relationships and values that may affect an organization.**

Entire industries have been rocked when the culture underwent a lifestyle change that affected their product or service. The interest in health and fitness, for instance, led to a decline in sales of cigarettes, whiskey, red meat, and eggs. And it led to a boost in sales of athletic shoes, spandex clothing, and Nautilus and other exercise machines. Low-carbohydrate, high-protein diets like the Atkins and the South Beach diets triggered a rise in chicken, pork, and beef sales, but then led to an oversupply and consequent dip in prices as consumers turned to a more balanced eating approach.[33] More recently, with more attention focused on the American epidemic of obesity—the rate of obesity among U.S. youths has nearly

Sociocultural forces. The U.S. obesity rate is one of those sociocultural forces capable of altering entire industries. Which ones do you think would be most affected?

tripled in some age groups since the 1970s—many restaurants are touting healthier foods.[34]

4. Demographic Forces *Demographics* derives from the ancient Greek word for "people"—*demos*—and deals with statistics relating to human populations. Age, gender, race, sexual orientation, occupation, income, family size, and the like are known as demographic characteristics when they are used to express measurements of certain groups. ***Demographic forces* are influences on an organization arising from changes in the characteristics of a population, such as age, gender, or ethnic origin.**

During the next 40 years, the United States is expected to undergo some great demographic changes. For instance, more babies are currently being born, the largest number of children born in 45 years—and dramatically exceeding birthrates in Europe. The birthrate is up for all racial and ethnic groups, but the increase for Hispanics is the largest.[35] By 2050, it's predicted, the U.S. population will soar to between 399 million and 458 million (from 308 million today), and minorities are expected to reach 50% of the population by around 2042.[36] By midcentury, the proportion of children and elderly who depend on others will rise to 72 per 100 from 59 per 100 in 2005. The foreign-born share of the workforce will increase to 23%, up from 16% in 2009.[37]

5. Political-Legal Forces *Political-legal forces* **are changes in the way politics shape laws and laws shape the opportunities for and threats to an organization.** In the United States, whatever political view tends to be dominant at the moment may be reflected in how the government handles antitrust issues, in which one company tends to monopolize a particular industry. Should Google, for instance, be allowed to dominate the market for Internet search?

As for legal forces, some countries have more fully developed legal systems than others. And some countries have more lawyers per capita. (The United States has an estimated 25% of the world's lawyers, according to University of Wisconsin law professor Marc Galanter—not the 70% figure repeated for years by some conservative political figures.)[38] American companies may be more willing to use the legal system to advance their interests, as in suing competitors to gain competitive advantage. But they must also watch that others don't do the same to them.

6. International Forces *International forces* **are changes in the economic, political, legal, and technological global system that may affect an organization.**

This category represents a huge grab bag of influences. How does the economic integration of the European Union create threats and opportunities for American companies? U.S. companies that do significant business in Europe are subject to regulation by the European Union. For instance, in a 3-year antitrust case, the EU ruled that Microsoft Corp. had abusively wielded its Windows and Office software monopoly, fined it the equivalent of $735 million, and ordered it to reduce practices that gave Microsoft an advantage in hooking up its products to Windows, limiting competition.[39] We consider global concerns in Chapter 4.

How well Americans can handle international forces depends a lot on their training. The American Council on Education says there is a "dangerous" shortage of experts in non-European cultures and languages. The council urges that schools teach a wider variety of languages and that instruction begin as early as kindergarten, since waiting until students are in college to begin instruction in more obscure languages hinders their ability to become fluent speakers.[40] ●

THE BIG PICTURE

Managers need to be aware of what constitutes ethics, values, the four approaches to ethical dilemmas, and how organizations can promote ethics.

"It's a tough issue, choosing between being a law-abiding person and losing your job," says lawyer Gloria Allred, who represented a woman fired for complaining about running her boss's office football pool.[41] Imagine having to choose between *economic performance* and *social performance,* which in business is what most ethical conflicts are about.[42] This is known as an **ethical dilemma, a situation in which you have to decide whether to pursue a course of action that may benefit you or your organization but that is unethical or even illegal.**

Defining Ethics & Values

Seventy-three percent of American employees working full time say they have observed ethical misconduct at work, and 36% have been "distracted" by it.[43] Most of us assume we know what "ethics" and "values" mean, but do we? Let's consider them.

Ethics *Ethics* **are the standards of right and wrong that influence behavior.** These standards may vary among countries and among cultures. *Ethical behavior* **is behavior that is accepted as "right" as opposed to "wrong" according to those standards.**

What are the differences among a tip, a gratuity, a gift, a donation, a commission, a consulting fee, a kickback, a bribe? Regardless of the amount of money involved, each one may be intended to reward the recipient for providing you with better service, either anticipated or performed. What should be the

Higher self. If you worked for a drug company, would you think it's acceptable to give a medical society several thousand dollars to use on dinner lectures to inform doctors about high blood pressure and how your company's products can treat the condition? Would your perspective change if you were a patient with high blood pressure?

expectations of a medical society that accepts $700,000 from three pharmaceutical companies to be used for dinner lectures to brief doctors on the latest news about high blood pressure? What if the main point of these briefings is to expand the concept of high blood pressure, increasing the pool of people taking blood-pressure medications?[44]

Values Ethical dilemmas often take place because of an organization's ***value system*, the pattern of values within an organization.** *Values* **are the relatively permanent and deeply held underlying beliefs and attitudes that help determine a person's behavior,** such as the belief that "Fairness means hiring according to ability, not family background." Values and value systems are the underpinnings for ethics and ethical behavior.

Organizations may have two important value systems that can conflict: (1) the value system stressing financial performance versus (2) the value system stressing cohesion and solidarity in employee relationships.[45]

Four Approaches to Deciding Ethical Dilemmas

How do alternative values guide people's decisions about ethical behavior? Here are four approaches, which may be taken as guidelines:

1. The Utilitarian Approach: For the Greatest Good Ethical behavior in the ***utilitarian approach* is guided by what will result in the greatest good for the greatest number of people.** Managers often take the utilitarian approach, using financial performance—such as efficiency and profit—as the best definition of what constitutes "the greatest good for the greatest number."[46]

Thus, a utilitarian "cost-benefit" analysis might show that in the short run the firing of thousands of employees may improve a company's bottom line and provide immediate benefits for the stockholders. The drawback of this approach, however, is that it may result in damage to workforce morale and the loss of employees with experience and skills—actions not so readily measurable in dollars.

2. The Individual Approach: For Your Greatest Self-Interest Long Term, Which Will Help Others Ethical behavior in the ***individual approach* is guided by what will result in the individual's best *long-term* interests, which ultimately are in everyone's self-interest.** The assumption here is that you will act ethically in the short run to avoid others harming you in the long run.

The flaw here, however, is that one person's short-term self-gain may *not,* in fact, be good for everyone in the long term. After all, the manager of an agribusiness that puts chemical fertilizers on the crops every year will always benefit, but the fishing industries downstream could ultimately suffer if chemical runoff reduces the number of fish. Indeed, this is one reason why Puget Sound Chinook, or king salmon, are now threatened with extinction in the Pacific Northwest.[47]

3. The Moral-Rights Approach: Respecting Fundamental Rights Shared by Everyone Ethical behavior in the ***moral-rights approach* is guided by respect for the fundamental rights of human beings,** such as those expressed in the U.S. Constitution's Bill of Rights. We would all tend to agree that denying people the right to life, liberty, privacy, health and safety, and due process is unethical. Thus, most of us would have no difficulty condemning the situation of immigrants illegally brought into the United States and then effectively enslaved—as when made to work 7 days a week as maids.

The difficulty, however, is when rights are in conflict, such as employer and employee rights. Should employees on the job have a guarantee of privacy? Actually, it is legal for employers to listen to business phone calls and monitor all nonspoken personal communications.[48]

4. The Justice Approach: Respecting Impartial Standards of Fairness
Ethical behavior in the *justice approach* **is guided by respect for impartial standards of fairness and equity.** One consideration here is whether an organization's policies—such as those governing promotions or sexual harassment cases—are administered impartially and fairly regardless of gender, age, sexual orientation, and the like.

Fairness can often be a hot issue. For instance, many employees are loudly resentful when a corporation's CEO is paid a salary and bonuses worth hundreds of times more than what they receive—even when the company performs poorly—and when fired is then given a "golden parachute," or extravagant package of separation pay and benefits.

White-Collar Crime, SarbOx, & Ethical Training

At the beginning of the 21st century, U.S. business erupted in an array of scandals represented in such names as Enron, WorldCom, Tyco, and Adelphia, and their chief executives—Jeffrey Skilling, Bernard Ebbers, Dennis Kozlowski, and John Rigas—went to prison on various fraud convictions.[49] Executives' deceits generated a great deal of public outrage, as a result of which Congress passed the Sarbanes–Oxley Act, as we'll describe. Did that stop the raft of business scandals? Not quite.

Next to hit the headlines were cases of *insider trading,* **the illegal trading of a company's stock by people using confidential company information.** In 2004, Sam Waksal, CEO of ImClone, a biotechnology company, sold his shares of stock when he learned—before the news was made public—that the U.S. government was blocking ImClone's new cancer drug. For this act of insider trading, he ultimately was sentenced to 87 months in prison and fined $3 million. (This was the case that affected lifestyle guru Martha Stewart as well.) In 2009, authorities arrested billionaire hedge-fund manager Raj Rajaratnam for trading on tips from persons at companies who slipped him advance word on inside information.[50]

Also in that year came the shocking news of financier Bernard Madoff, who confessed that his investments were all "one big lie"—not investments at all, but

Phony financier. Bernard Madoff pleaded guilty to 11 federal crimes connected with his massive Ponzi scheme, which for more than 25 years defrauded investors of between $12 billion and $20 billion. The charges against him included securities fraud, investment advisor fraud, mail fraud, wire fraud, money laundering, false statements, and perjury, among other allegations. Now age 72, his projected release date from federal prison is November 14, 2159.

a $50 billion *Ponzi scheme,* **using cash from newer investors to pay off older ones.**[51] He was later sentenced to 150 years in prison.[52] Others charged in 2009 with building Ponzi schemes included Texas financier R. Allen Stanford, who built a flashy offshore $7 billion financial empire.[53]

The Sarbanes–Oxley Reform Act   The *Sarbanes–Oxley Act of 2002,* **often shortened to** *SarbOx* **or** *SOX,* **established requirements for proper financial record keeping for public companies and penalties of as much as 25 years in prison for noncompliance.**[54] Administered by the Securities and Exchange Commission, SarbOx requires a company's chief executive officer and chief financial officer to personally certify the organization's financial reports, prohibits them from taking personal loans or lines of credit, and makes them reimburse the organization for bonuses and stock options when required by restatement of corporate profits. It also requires the company to have established procedures and guidelines for audit committees.[55]

How Do People Learn Ethics? Kohlberg's Theories   American business history is permeated with occasional malfeasance, from railroad tycoons trying to corner the gold market (the 1872 Credit Mobilier scandal) to 25-year-old bank customer service representatives swindling elderly customers out of their finances.[56] Legislation such as SarbOx can't head off all such behavior. No wonder that now many colleges and universities have required more education in ethics.

"Schools bear some responsibility for the behavior of executives," says Fred J. Evans, dean of the College of Business and Economics at California State University at Northridge. "If you're making systematic errors in the [business] world, you have to go back to the schools and ask, 'What are you teaching?'"[57] The good news is that more graduate business schools are changing their curriculums to teach ethics.[58] The bad news, however, is that a 2006 survey of 50,000 undergraduates found that 26% of business majors admitted to serious cheating on exams, and 54% admitted to cheating on written assignments.[59]

Of course, most students' levels of moral development are established by personalities and upbringing long before they get to college, with some being more advanced than others. One psychologist, **Laurence Kohlberg,** has proposed three levels of personal moral development—preconventional, conventional, and postconventional.[60]

- **Level 1, preconventional—follows rules.** People who have achieved this level tend to follow rules and to obey authority to avoid unpleasant consequences. Managers of the Level 1 sort tend to be autocratic or coercive, expecting employees to be obedient for obedience's sake.

- **Level 2, conventional—follows expectations of others.** People whose moral development has reached this level are conformist but not slavish, generally adhering to the expectations of others in their lives. Level 2 managers lead by encouragement and cooperation and are more group and team oriented. Most managers are at this level.

- **Level 3, postconventional—guided by internal values.** The farthest along in moral development, Level 3 managers are independent souls who follow their own values and standards, focusing on the needs of their employees and trying to lead by empowering those working for them. Only about a fifth of American managers reach this level.

What level of development do you think you've reached?

How Organizations Can Promote Ethics

Ethics needs to be an everyday affair, not a onetime thing. This is why many large U.S. companies now have a chief ethics officer, whose job is to make ethical conduct a priority issue.

There are several ways an organization may promote high ethical standards on the job, as follows.[61]

1. Creating a Strong Ethical Climate   An *ethical climate* **represents employees' perceptions about the extent to which work environments support ethical behavior.** It is important for managers to foster ethical climates because they significantly affect the frequency of ethical behavior. For example, a recent study of 228 project team members revealed that positive ethical climates reduced the amount of misreporting of project status to project managers. Managers can promote ethical climates through the polices, procedures, and practices that are used on a daily basis.

2. Screening Prospective Employees   Companies try to screen out dishonest, irresponsible employees by checking applicants' résumés and references. Some firms, for example, run employee applications through E-Verify, a federal program that allows employers to check for illegal immigrants.[62] Some also use personality tests and integrity testing to identify potentially dishonest people.

3. Instituting Ethics Codes & Training Programs   A *code of ethics* **consists of a formal written set of ethical standards guiding an organization's actions.** Most codes offer guidance on how to treat customers, suppliers, competitors, and other stakeholders. The purpose is to clearly state top management's expectations for all employees. As you might expect, most codes prohibit bribes, kickbacks, misappropriation of corporate assets, conflicts of interest, and "cooking the books"— making false accounting statements and other records. Other areas frequently covered in ethics codes are political contributions, workforce diversity, and confidentiality of corporate information.[63]

In addition, according to a Society for Human Resource Management Weekly Survey, 32% of human resources professionals indicated that their organizations offered ethics training.[64] The approaches vary, but one way is to use a case approach to present employees with ethical dilemmas. By clarifying expectations, this kind of training may reduce unethical behavior.[65]

4. Rewarding Ethical Behavior: Protecting Whistle-Blowers   It's not enough to simply punish bad behavior; managers must also reward good ethical behavior, as in encouraging (or at least not discouraging) whistle-blowers.

A *whistle-blower* **is an employee who reports organizational misconduct to the public,** such as health and safety matters, waste, corruption, or overcharging of customers. For instance, the law that created the Occupational Safety and Health Administration allows workers to report unsafe conditions, such as "exposure to toxic chemicals; the use of dangerous machines, which can crush fingers; the use of contaminated needles, which expose workers to the AIDS virus; and the strain of repetitive hand motion, whether at a computer keyboard or in a meatpacking plant."[66]

In some cases, whistle-blowers may receive a reward; the IRS, for instance, is authorized to pay tipsters rewards as high as 30% in cases involving large amounts of money.[67] Between 1996 and 2005, whistle-blowers helped authorities recover at least $9.3 billion from health care providers who defrauded the government, over $1 billion of which was given to the whistle-blowers themselves.[68] ●

3.4 THE SOCIAL RESPONSIBILITIES REQUIRED OF YOU AS A MANAGER

Is being socially responsible really necessary?

major question?

THE BIG PICTURE

Managers need to be aware of the viewpoints supporting and opposing social responsibility and whether being and doing good pays off financially for the organization.

The 2009 recession had a powerful impact on the year's college freshmen, with 78% declaring that being well off was "very important" or "essential" to them, according to one annual survey.[69] But is money the be-all and end-all in business?

"We tend to categorize value as economic or social," says one observer. "You either work for a nonprofit that creates social value or you work for a for-profit that creates economic value."[70] But what if we did not judge business organizations on profits alone?

If ethical responsibility is about being a good individual citizen, social responsibility is about being a good organizational citizen. More formally, *social responsibility* **is a manager's duty to take actions that will benefit the interests of society as well as of the organization.** When generalized beyond the individual to the organization, social responsibility is called *corporate social responsibility (CSR),* **the notion that corporations are expected to go above and beyond following the law and making a profit.**

Example

Corporate Social Responsibility: Office-Furniture Maker Herman Miller Competes on Sustainability

There are all kinds of ways by which corporate social responsibility is expressed, such as fighting poverty, dealing with water scarcity, or stepping up to the problems of climate change. A big challenge for manufacturing companies is sustainability—meeting the needs of the present without compromising the ability of future generations to meet their own needs.[71]

Herman Miller, maker of office furniture, wants "to make sure we set our sights on sustainability goals so audacious that they drag us kicking and screaming toward them," says CEO Brian Walker.[72] Herman Miller has vowed not to produce landfill waste, hazardous waste, or manufacturing emissions and to rely completely on "green energy" by 2020. Thus, they have directed their suppliers on which materials, chemicals, and compounds are and are not allowable. At first customers were willing to pay a premium, but now they expect companies to have a sustainability focus, and won't pay a premium for it.

YOUR CALL

Does corporate social responsibility really have benefits beyond the acts of selflessness themselves? Can you think of any highly profitable and legal businesses that *do not* practice any kind of social responsibility?

Is Social Responsibility Worthwhile? Opposing & Supporting Viewpoints

In the old days of cutthroat capitalism, social responsibility was hardly thought of. A company's most important goal was to make money pretty much any way it could, and the consequences be damned. Today for-profit enterprises generally make a point of "putting something back" into society as well as taking something out.

Not everyone, however, agrees with these new priorities. Let's consider the two viewpoints.

Against Social Responsibility   "Few trends could so thoroughly undermine the very foundations of our free society," argued the late free-market economist Milton Friedman, "as the acceptance by corporate officials of social responsibility other than to make as much money for their stockholders as possible."[73]

Friedman represents the view that, as he said, "The social responsibility of business is to make profits." That is, unless a company focuses on maximizing profits, it will become distracted and fail to provide goods and services, benefit the stockholders, create jobs, and expand economic growth—the real social justification for the firm's existence.

This view would presumably support the efforts of companies to set up headquarters in name only in offshore Caribbean tax havens (while keeping their actual headquarters in the United States) in order to minimize their tax burden.

For Social Responsibility   "A large corporation these days not only may engage in social responsibility," said famed economist Paul Samuelson, who passed away in 2009, "it had damned well better to try to do so."[74] That is, a company must be concerned for society's welfare as well as for corporate profits.

Beyond the fact of ethical obligation, the rationale for this view is that since businesses create problems (environmental pollution, for example), they should help solve them. Moreover, they often have the resources to solve problems in ways that the nonprofit sector does not. Finally, being socially responsible gives businesses a favorable public image that can help head off government regulation.

Corporate Social Responsibility: The Top of the Pyramid

According to University of Georgia business scholar **Archie B. Carroll**, corporate social responsibility rests at the top of a pyramid of a corporation's obligations, right up there with economic, legal, and ethical obligations. That is, while some people might hold that a company's first duty is to make a profit, Carroll suggests the responsibilities of an organization in the global economy should take the following priorities:[75]

- *Be a good global corporate citizen,* as defined by the host country's expectations.
- *Be ethical in its practices,* taking host-country and global standards into consideration.
- *Obey the law* of host countries as well as international law.
- *Make a profit* consistent with expectations for international business.

These priorities are illustrated in the pyramid opposite. *(See Figure 3.2.)*

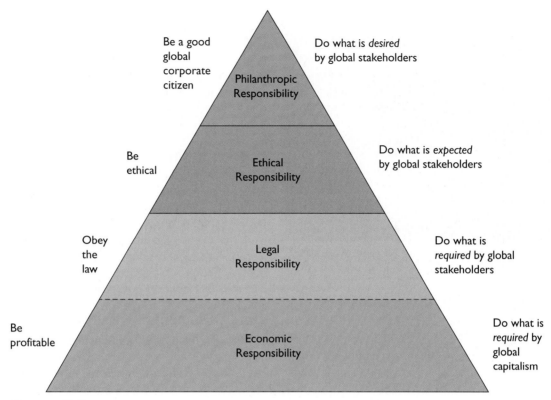

Be a good global corporate citizen

Do what is *desired* by global stakeholders

Philanthropic Responsibility

Be ethical

Do what is *expected* by global stakeholders

Ethical Responsibility

Obey the law

Do what is *required* by global stakeholders

Legal Responsibility

Be profitable

Do what is *required* by global capitalism

Economic Responsibility

figure 3.2

CARROLL'S GLOBAL CORPORATE SOCIAL RESPONSIBILITY PYRAMID

Source: From *Academy of Management Executive: The Thinking Manager's Source* by A. B. Carroll, 2004. Copyright © 2004 by Academy of Management, NY. Reproduced with permission of Academy of Management NY via Copyright Clearance Center.

Practical Action

Going Green: How Businesses & Individuals Can Fight Global Warming

Going green has all kinds of payoffs. Insurance companies are offering lower rates for people who drive less, own hybrid cars, or build energy-efficient homes.[76] Office buildings with increased natural light, eco-friendly carpeting, and better ventilation result in employees taking few sick days and a rise in productivity.[77] Hotels that induce guests to reuse towels and skip having carpets vacuumed and bed linens replaced every day save on water and electricity use.[78]

Global warming is "unequivocal" and will bring "irreversible changes" without immediate action, climate scientists believe, arguing that we can save the planet by investing heavily in alternative energy technology that already exists.[79] A report by energy experts at McKinsey & Company, a consulting firm, says that as much as a 28% reduction in greenhouse gases can be accomplished from steps that would more than pay for themselves in lower energy bills.[80] Small businesses,

for instance, report savings of 20%–30% by making energy-saving moves.[81]

Individuals and businesses can do a number of things to attempt to fight global warming, although the problem is complicated and intractable and needs a great deal more research.[82]

Increase Recycling

Increasing the recycle rate in the United States from 30% to 60% would save the equivalent of 315 million barrels of oil each year. (See **www.earth9ll.org** for tips on recycling.) Old computers and other electronics can be recycled or donated. (See **www.eiae.org**.)[83]

Install Energy-Saving Lightbulbs

Compact fluorescent bulbs (CFLs) cost more than regular incandescent bulbs, but they last up to 10 times

Buy Energy Star Products

Energy Star appliances meet strict energy-efficiency guidelines. (See **www.energystar.gov.**) If every home replaced its TVs, DVD players, VCRs, and telephones with these models, it would be the equivalent of taking 3 million cars off the road.[85]

Convert to Green Energy

More than half of all retail power customers in the United States can now run their homes on renewable energy—electricity produced by wind, solar, and geothermal power; hydropower; and various plant materials—simply by asking their local utility. The cost is about $5 a month more for a typical residential user.[86] Wind energy, incidentally, now generates more than 1% of U.S. electricity.[87] (See **www.eere.energy.gov/greenpower.**)

Store Documents Digitally

Encouraging employees and customers to save documents digitally and not print out millions of paper copies can reduce waste and reduce operating budgets.[88] (See **www.greenbiz.com** and **www.greenerworldmedia.com.**)

Green power. Many electricity users can run their homes on renewable energy simply by asking their local utility.

longer, produce 90% less heat, and also produce fewer emissions. They are also cheaper over the long term: Replacing 30 incandescent bulbs with CFLs can save more than $1,000 over the life of the bulbs.[84]

One Type of Social Responsibility: Philanthropy, "Not Dying Rich"

"He who dies rich dies thus disgraced," 19th-century steel magnate Andrew Carnegie is supposed to have said, after he turned his interests from making money to *philanthropy,* **making charitable donations to benefit humankind.** Carnegie became well known as a supporter of free libraries.

More recently, Bill Gates of Microsoft, the richest person in the world, made headlines when he announced that he would step down from day-to-day oversight of the company he cofounded in order to focus on his $29 billion philanthropy, the Bill and Melinda Gates Foundation, which pledged to spend billions on health, education, and overcoming poverty.[89] This news was closely followed by the announcement of the second-richest man in the world, investor Warren Buffet, chairman of Berkshire Hathaway, that he would channel $31 billion to the Gates Foundation to help in finding cures for the globe's most fatal diseases.[90]

Companies practice philanthropy, too. For example, Google made a pledge to investors when it went public to reserve 1% of its profit and equity to "make the world a better place." Its philanthropic organization benefits groups ranging from those fighting disease to those developing a commercial plug-in, electricity-powered car.[91] But even ordinary individuals can become philanthropists of a sort. Mona Purdy, an Illinois hairdresser, noticed while vacationing in Guatemala that many children coated their feet with tar in order to be able to run in a local race. So she went home and established the nonprofit Share Your Shoes, which collects shoes and sends them around the world. "I always thought I was too busy to help others," she says. "Then I started this and found myself wondering where I'd been all my life."[92]

How Does Being Good Pay Off?

From a hardheaded manager's point of view, do ethical behavior and high social responsibility pay off financially? Here's what some of the research shows.[93]

Effect on Customers According to one survey, 88% of the respondents said they were more apt to buy from companies that are socially responsible than from companies that are not.[94] Another survey of 2,037 adults found that 72% would prefer to purchase products and services from a company with ethical business practices and higher prices compared with 18% who would prefer to purchase from a company with questionable business practices and lower prices.[95]

Effect on Employees' Work Effort Workers are more efficient, loyal, and creative when they feel a sense of purpose—when their work has meaning, says Daniel H. Pink.[96] When employers make profits their primary focus, employees develop negative feelings toward the organization. "They tend to perceive the CEO as autocratic and focused on the short term," says one report, "and they report being less willing to sacrifice for the company."[97] When employees observe the CEO balancing the concerns of customers, employees, and the community, plus being watchful of environmental effects, they report being more willing to exert extra effort—and corporate results improve!

Effect on Job Applicants & Employee Retention Ethics can also affect the quality of people who apply to work in an organization. One online survey of 1,020 people indicated that 83% rated a company's record of business ethics as "very important" when deciding whether to accept a job offer; only 2% rated it as "unimportant."[98] A National Business Ethics Survey found that 79% of employees said their firms' concern for ethics was a key reason they remained.[99]

Effect on Sales Growth The announcement of a company's conviction for illegal activity has been shown to diminish sales growth for several years.[100] One survey found that 80% of people said they decide to buy a firm's goods or services partly on their perception of its ethics.[101]

Effect on Company Efficiency One survey found that 71% of employees who saw honesty applied rarely or never in their organization had seen misconduct in the past year, compared with 52% who saw honesty applied only occasionally and 25% who saw it frequently.[102]

Effect on Company Revenue Unethical behavior in the form of employee fraud costs U.S. organizations around $652 billion a year, according to the Association of Certified Fraud Examiners.[103] Employee fraud, which is twice as common as consumer fraud (such as credit card fraud and identity theft), costs employers about 20% of every dollar earned.[104]

Effect on Stock Price One survey found that 74% of people polled said their perception of a firm's honesty directly affected their decision about whether to buy its stock.[105] Earlier research found that investments in unethical firms earn abnormally negative returns for long periods of time.[106]

Effect on Profits Studies suggest that profitability is enhanced by a reputation for honesty and corporate citizenship.[107]

   Ethical behavior and social responsibility are more than just admirable ways of operating. They give an organization a clear competitive advantage. ●

❉ 3.5 THE NEW DIVERSIFIED WORKFORCE

major question?

What trends in workplace diversity should managers be aware of?

THE BIG PICTURE
One of today's most important management challenges is working with stakeholders of all sorts who vary widely in diversity—in age, gender, race, religion, ethnicity, sexual orientation, capabilities, and socioeconomic background. Managers should also be aware of the differences between internal and external dimensions of diversity and barriers to diversity.

Might you hold a few preconceptions that are worth examining? Here's a reality check:

- **Assumption: Illegal immigrants dramatically impact the U.S. economy.** No, says a study by the Migration Policy Institute. Undocumented immigrants represent only about 5% of the workforce and contribute just 0.03% of the U.S. gross domestic product.[108]

- **Assumption: Customer bias favoring white men has just about disappeared.** Unfortunately not, suggests a study of college students, which found that people give higher ratings for customer satisfaction to white men than to women and members of minorities.[109]

- **Assumption: Young workers are more at risk for being laid off than older workers.** Yes, evidently. In April 2009, the unemployment rate for those ages 25–34 was 9.6% (up from 4.9% a year earlier), compared to 6.2% for workers 55 and older (up from 3.2% a year earlier).[110] It's true, however, that jobless rates for older people were at record highs.[111]

The United States is becoming more diverse in its ethnic, racial, gender, and age makeup—more nonwhite, more single, more working parents, and so on—and the consequences are not always what you would expect.

In the view of Scott E. Page, professor of complex systems, political science, and economics at the University of Michigan, diversity and variety in staffing produces organizational strength.[112] "Diverse groups of people bring to organizations more and different ways of seeing a problem," he told an interviewer, "and, thus, faster/better ways of solving it. . . . There's certainly a lot of evidence that people's identity groups—ethnic, racial, sexual, age—matter when it comes to diversity in thinking."[113]

Diversity may have its benefits, but it can also be an important management challenge. Let's consider this.

How to Think about Diversity: Which Differences Are Important?

***Diversity* represents all the ways people are unlike and alike—the differences and similarities in age, gender, race, religion, ethnicity, sexual orientation, capabilities, and socioeconomic background.** Note here that diversity is not synonymous with differences. Rather, it encompasses both differences and similarities. This means that as a manager you need to manage both simultaneously.

To help distinguish the important ways in which people differ, diversity experts Lee Gardenswartz and Anita Rowe have identified a "diversity wheel" consisting

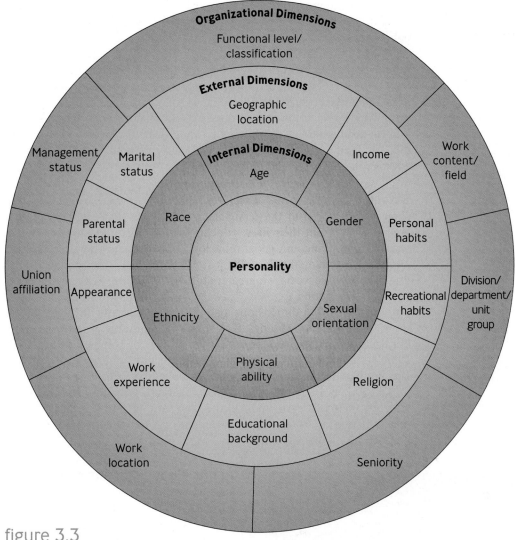

figure 3.3

THE DIVERSITY WHEEL

Four layers of diversity

Source: From L. Gardenswartz and A. Rowe, *Diverse Teams at Work: Capitalizing on the Power of Diversity,* 1994, p. 33. Reprinted with permission of The McGraw-Hill Companies.

of four layers of diversity: (1) personality, (2) internal dimensions, (3) external dimensions, and (4) organizational dimensions. *(See Figure 3.3.)*

Let's consider these four layers:

Personality   At the center of the diversity wheel is personality. It is at the center because *personality* **is defined as the stable physical and mental characteristics responsible for a person's identity.** We cover the dimension of personality in Chapter 11.

Internal Dimensions   *Internal dimensions of diversity* **are those human differences that exert a powerful, sustained effect throughout every stage of our lives:** gender, age, ethnicity, race, sexual orientation, physical abilities.[114] These are referred to as the *primary* dimensions of diversity because they are not within our control for the most part. Yet they strongly influence our attitudes and expectations and assumptions about other people, which in turn influence our own behavior.

What characterizes internal dimensions of diversity is that they are visible and salient in people. And precisely because these characteristics are so visible, they may be associated with certain stereotypes—for example, that black people work in menial jobs. For instance, an African American female middle manager reports that, while on vacation and sitting by the pool at a resort, she was approached by a 50ish white male who "demanded that I get him extra towels. I said, 'Excuse me?' He then said, 'Oh, you don't work here,' with no shred of embarrassment or apology in his voice."[115]

External Dimensions *External dimensions of diversity* **include an element of choice; they consist of the personal characteristics that people acquire, discard, or modify throughout their lives:** educational background, marital status, parental status, religion, income, geographic location, work experience, recreational habits, appearance, personal habits. They are referred to as the *secondary* dimensions of diversity because we have a greater ability to influence or control them than we do internal dimensions.

These external dimensions also exert a significant influence on our perceptions, behavior, and attitudes. If you are not a follower of the Muslim religion, for example, you may not perceive the importance of some of its practices—as with some managers at Atlanta-based Argenbright Security Inc., who sent seven Muslim female employees home for wearing Islamic head scarves at their security jobs at Dulles International Airport. Because wearing head scarves in no way affected their job performance, the company had to reimburse the women for back pay and other relief in a settlement negotiated with the Equal Employment Opportunity Commission.[116]

Diversity enriches. A diverse population in a company can provide ideas, experience, and points of view that strengthen the business culture. What has been your experience, if any, with a diverse workplace?

Organizational Dimensions Organizational dimensions include management status, union affiliation, work location, seniority, work content, and division or department.

Trends in Workforce Diversity

How is the U.S. workforce apt to become more diverse in the 21st century? Let's examine five categories on the internal dimension—*age, gender, race/ethnicity, sexual orientation,* and *physical/mental abilities*—and one category on the external dimension, *educational level.*

Age: More Older People in the Workforce The most significant demographic event, management philosopher Peter Drucker suggested, "is that in the developed countries the number and proportion of younger people is rapidly shrinking. . . . Those shrinking numbers of younger people will have to both drive their economies and help support much larger numbers of older people."[117] In Europe and Japan, births are not keeping pace with deaths. By 2050, the European Union will have 52 million fewer people of working age, despite immigration.[118] Even China is faced with a nationwide aging gap, which means the country is now facing a shortage of cheap labor in some locations.[119]

The United States, suggested Drucker, is the only developed economy to have enough young people, and that is only because immigrants to the United States still have large families. Even so, the median age of the American worker is predicted to reach 41.4 by 2012, up from 34.3 in 1980.[120]

Gender: More Women Working   Since the 1960s women have been flooding into the workplace in great numbers, with about 75% of women ages 25–54 in the workforce, up from about 40% in the late 1950s.[121] During the recent recession, the influx accelerated, and for the first time, women held almost half the nation's jobs, as a higher percentage of men lost their jobs.[122] In addition, more and more businesses are now owned by women—about 28% of all U.S. businesses.[123] Finally, women are gaining ground in the top rungs of business, with more women in managerial and administrative positions (a 24% increase from 1972 to 2006).[124] Indeed, in 2009, 15 Fortune 500 companies were run by women (up from 12 the year before) and 28 Fortune 1000 firms were headed by women (up from 24).[125]

Traditionally, however, women have earned roughly the same pay as men only in jobs paying $25,000–$30,000 a year. The farther up the pay scale and the higher the education level, the wider the earnings gap. Thus, for every dollar a man earns, a woman cashier earns 93 cents, an administrative assistant 93 cents, and a registered nurse 88 cents. But for a woman physician or surgeon, it is 59 cents, a woman lawyer or judge 69 cents, a woman college professor 75 cents, and a woman psychologist 83 cents.[126] The obstacles to women's progress are known as the *glass ceiling*—**the metaphor for an invisible barrier preventing women and minorities from being promoted to top executive jobs.** For instance, according to the Association of Executive Search Consultants, 56% of 357 global senior executives report their companies have one or no women among their top executives.[127] At Fortune 500 companies in 2009, females accounted for only 15.6% of corporate-officer positions.[128]

What factors are holding women back? Three that are mentioned are negative stereotypes, lack of mentors, and limited experience in line or general management.[129] For women who have become vice president or higher in Fortune 1000 companies, four strategies were identified as critical to their success: consistently exceeding performance expectations, developing a style with which male managers are comfortable, seeking out difficult or challenging assignments, and having influential mentors.[130]

Interestingly, however, several studies have suggested that female managers outshine their male counterparts on almost every measure, from motivating others to fostering communication to producing high-quality work to goal-setting to mentoring employees.[131] Indeed, one study, by Catalyst, an advocacy group for women in business, found that companies with more women executives have better financial performance.[132] We discuss this further in a later chapter.

Race & Ethnicity: More People of Color in the Workforce   By 2050, racial and ethnic minorities are expected to make up more than half (54%) of the population, with whites projected to change from two-thirds to 46%, African Americans from 14% to 15%, Asians and Pacific Islanders from 5.1% to 9.2%, and Hispanics or Latinos from 15% to 30%.[133] Unfortunately, three trends show that American businesses need to do a lot better by minority populations.

First, people of color, too, have hit the glass ceiling. For example, whereas in 2008 whites held 36.3% of managerial and professional jobs and Asians 48.2%, blacks held only 27.4% and Hispanics or Latinos only 18.3%.[134]

Second, minorities tend to earn less than whites. Median household income in 2008 was $33,916 for African Americans and $38,679 for

African American success. Police chief Annetta Nunn, the first woman African American police chief of Birmingham, Alabama, at a press conference. Nunn broke through a glass ceiling of a different sort, taking over the police operations in 2003 for a city known for its racial discrimination only a few decades earlier.

Hispanics. It was $54,920 for non-Hispanic whites. (Asians had the highest median income, at $66,103.)[135]

Third, a number of studies have shown that minorities experienced more perceived discrimination, racism-related stress, and less psychological support than whites did.[136]

Sexual Orientation: Gays & Lesbians Become More Visible

Gays and lesbians make up, by some estimates, up to 6% of the U.S. population. Between a quarter and two-thirds report being discriminated against at work (with negative attitudes directed toward them held more by men than by women).[137] One study found that 41% of gay employees said they had been harassed, pressured to quit, or denied a promotion because of their sexual orientation.[138] Homosexual workers report higher levels of stress compared with heterosexual workers, and one source of this may be the fact that in many states homosexuality is still a legitimate legal basis for firing an employee. Finally, gay and bisexual male workers were found to earn 11%–27% less than equally qualified heterosexual counterparts.[139]

How important is the issue of sexual preference? Once again, if managers are concerned about hiring and keeping workplace talent, they shouldn't ignore the motivation and productivity of 6% of the workforce. Many employers are recognizing this: 430 of the top 500 U.S. companies now offer policies prohibiting discrimination based on sexual preference, and more than half offer domestic partner benefits for same-sex couples.[140]

People with Differing Physical & Mental Abilities

One out of six Americans has a physical or mental disability, according to the U.S. Department of Labor. Since 1992 we have had the ***Americans with Disabilities Act,*** **which prohibits discrimination against the disabled** and requires organizations to reasonably accommodate an individual's disabilities.

Even so, disabled people have difficulty finding work. Although two-thirds of people with disabilities want to work, roughly two-thirds are unemployed. (Among blind adults, for example, about 70% are out of work.)[141] Here, too, is a talent pool that managers will no doubt find themselves using in the coming years.

Educational Levels: Mismatches between Education & Workforce Needs

Two important mismatches between education and workplace are these:

- **College graduates may be in jobs for which they are overqualified.** About 27% of people working have a college degree. But some are ***underemployed—*** **working at jobs that require less education than they have**—such as tending bar, managing video stores, or other jobs that someone with less education could do.

- **High-school dropouts and others may not have the literacy skills needed for many jobs.** A 2009 study found that 16% of all people in the United States between the ages of 16 and 24 had dropped out of high school in 2007—nearly 6.2 million students.[142] More than one in five U.S. men were dropouts. In addition, literacy has dropped at every level of education.[143] If, as has been alleged, more than two-thirds of the American workforce reads below ninth-grade level, that is a real problem for employers, because about 70% of the on-the-job reading materials are written at or above that level.[144]

Disability. Everyone recognizes the wheelchair as signifying that a person is disabled, but other disabilities are not easily identified—and may not invite understanding. Do you think that mental disabilities, for example, should be accommodated in employment? If you were subject to mood swings, would you think that would prevent you from doing your job effectively?

Barriers to Diversity

Some barriers are erected by diverse people themselves. In the main, however, most barriers are put in their paths by organizations.[145] When we speak of "the organization's barriers," we are, of course, referring to the *people* in the organization—especially those who may have been there for a while—who are resistant to making it more diverse.

Resistance to change in general is an attitude that all managers come up against from time to time, and resistance to diversity is simply one variation. It may be expressed in the following six ways:

I. Stereotypes & Prejudices *Ethnocentrism* **is the belief that one's native country, culture, language, abilities, or behavior is superior to that of another culture.** (An example is embodied in the title of the Wesley Snipes/Woody Harrelson movie about urban basketball hustlers: *White Men Can't Jump.*) When differences are viewed as being weaknesses—which is what many stereotypes and prejudices ultimately come down to—this may be expressed as a concern that diversity hiring will lead to a sacrifice in competence and quality.

2. Fear of Reverse Discrimination Some employees are afraid that attempts to achieve greater diversity in their organization will result in reverse discrimination—that more black or Asian employees will be promoted to fire captain or police lieutenant, for example, over the heads of supposedly more qualified whites.

3. Resistance to Diversity Program Priorities Some companies, such as 3M, offer special classes teaching tolerance for diversity, seminars in how to get along.[146] Some employees may see diversity programs as distracting them from the organization's "real work." In addition, they may be resentful of diversity-promoting policies that are reinforced through special criteria in the organization's performance appraisals and reward systems.

4. Unsupportive Social Atmosphere Diverse employees may be excluded from office camaraderie and social events.

5. Lack of Support for Family Demands In 2008, there were over 2.5 million married couples with children under 18 in the United States. In 65.9% of such families, both parents worked; in 28.7%, only the father worked; and in 3.6%, only the mother worked.[147] But more and more women are moving back and forth between being at-home mothers and in the workforce, as economic circumstances dictate.[148] Yet in a great many households, it is still women who primarily take care of children, as well as other domestic chores. When organizations aren't supportive in offering flexibility in hours and job responsibilities, these women may find it difficult to work evenings and weekends or to take overnight business trips.

6. Lack of Support for Career-Building Steps Organizations may not provide diverse employees with the types of work assignments that will help qualify them for positions in senior management. In addition, organizations may fail to provide the kind of informal training or mentoring that will help them learn the political savvy to do networking and other activities required to get ahead. ●

Woman manager. On the job she might be a high-powered manager of scores of people, but at home she may still be expected to be the principal manager of an important few—the children.

Key Terms Used in This Chapter

Americans with Disabilities
  Act 94

clawbacks 75

code of ethics 84

competitors 73

corporate social responsibility
  (CSR) 85

customers 73

demographic forces 79

distributor 74

diversity 90

ethnocentrism 95

economic forces 77

ethical behavior 80

ethical climate 84

ethical dilemma 80

ethics 80

external dimensions of
  diversity 92

external stakeholders 73

general environment 77

glass ceiling 93

government regulators 76

individual approach 81

insider trading 82

internal dimensions of
  diversity 91

internal stakeholders 72

international forces 79

justice approach 82

macroenvironment 77

moral-rights approach 81

owners 72

personality 91

philanthropy 88

political-legal forces 79

Ponzi scheme 83

Sarbanes–Oxley Act of 2002 83

social responsibility 85

sociocultural forces 78

special-interest groups 76

stakeholders 71

strategic allies 74

supplier 73

task environment 73

technological forces 78

underemployed 94

utilitarian approach 81

value system 81

values 81

whistle-blower 84

Summary

3.1 The Community of Stakeholders Inside the Organization

Managers operate in two organizational environments—internal and external—both made up of stakeholders, the people whose interests are affected by the organization's activities. The first, or internal, environment includes employees, owners, and the board of directors.

3.2 The Community of Stakeholders Outside the Organization

The external environment of stakeholders consists of the task environment and the general environment.

The task environment consists of 11 groups that present the manager with daily tasks to deal with. (1) Customers pay to use an organization's goods and services. (2) Competitors compete for customers or resources. (3) Suppliers provide supplies—raw materials, services, equipment, labor, or energy—to other organizations. (4) Distributors help another organization sell its goods and services to customers. (5) Strategic allies join forces to

achieve advantages neither organization can perform as well alone. (6) Employee organizations are labor unions and employee associations. (7) Local communities are residents, companies, governments, and nonprofit entities that depend on the organization's taxes, payroll, and charitable contributions. (8) Financial institutions are commercial banks, investment banks, and insurance companies that deal with the organization. (9) Government regulators are regulatory agencies that establish the ground rules under which the organization operates. (10) Special-interest groups are groups whose members try to influence specific issues that may affect the organization. (11) The mass media are print, radio, TV, and Internet sources that affect the organization's public relations.

The general environment includes six forces. (1) Economic forces consist of general economic conditions and trends—unemployment, inflation, interest rates, economic growth—that may affect an organization's performance. (2) Technological forces are new developments in methods for transforming resources into goods and services. (3) Sociocultural forces are influences and trends originating in a country, society, or culture's human relationships and values that may affect an organization. (4) Demographic forces are influences on an organization arising from changes in the characteristics of a population, such as age, gender, and ethnic origin. (5) Political-legal forces are changes in the way politics shapes laws and laws shape the opportunities for and threats to an organization. (6) International forces are changes in the economic, political, legal, and technological global system that may affect an organization.

3.3 The Ethical Responsibilities Required of You as a Manager

Ethics are the standards of right and wrong that influence behavior. Ethical behavior is behavior that is accepted as "right" as opposed to "wrong" according to those standards.

Ethical dilemmas often take place because of an organization's value system. Values are the relatively permanent and deeply held underlying beliefs and attitudes that help determine a person's behavior.

There are four approaches to deciding ethical dilemmas. (1) Utilitarian—ethical behavior is guided by what will result in the greatest good for the greatest number of people. (2) Individual—ethical behavior is guided by what will result in the individual's best long-term interests, which ultimately is in everyone's self-interest. (3) Moral-rights—ethical behavior is guided by respect for the fundamental rights of human beings, such as those expressed in the U.S. Constitution's Bill of Rights. (4) Justice—ethical behavior is guided by respect for the impartial standards of fairness and equity.

Public outrage over white-collar crime (Enron, Tyco) led to the creation of the Sarbanes–Oxley Act of 2002 (SarbOx), which established requirements for proper financial record keeping for public companies and penalties for noncompliance.

Laurence Kohlberg proposed three levels of personal moral development: (1) preconventional level of moral development—people tend to follow rules and to obey authority; (2) conventional level—people are conformist, generally adhering to the expectations of others; and (3) postconventional level—people are guided by internal values.

There are three ways an organization may foster high ethical standards. (1) Top managers must support a strong ethical climate. (2) The organization may have a code of ethics, which consists of a formal written set of ethical standards. (3) An organization must reward ethical behavior, as in not discouraging whistle-blowers, employees who report organizational misconduct to the public.

3.4 The Social Responsibilities Required of You as a Manager

Social responsibility is a manager's duty to take actions that will benefit the interests of society as well as of the organization.

The idea of social responsibility has opposing and supporting viewpoints. The opposing viewpoint is that the social responsibility of business is to make profits. The supporting viewpoint is that since business creates some problems (such as pollution) it should help solve them.

One scholar, Archie Carroll, suggests the responsibilities of an organization in the global economy should take the following priorities: (1) Be a good global corporate citizen; (2) be ethical in its practices; (3) obey the law; and (4) make a profit—in that order.

One type of social responsibility is philanthropy, making charitable donations to benefit humankind.

Positive ethical behavior and social responsibility can pay off in the form of customer goodwill, more efficient and loyal employees, better quality of job applicants and retained employees, enhanced sales growth, less employee misconduct and fraud, better stock price, and enhanced profits.

3.5 The New Diversified Workforce

Diversity represents all the ways people are alike and unlike—the differences and similarities in age, gender, race, religion, ethnicity, sexual orientation, capabilities, and socioeconomic background.

There are two dimensions of diversity: (1) Internal dimensions of diversity are those human differences that exert a powerful, sustained effect throughout every stage of our lives: gender, ethnicity, race, physical abilities, age, and sexual orientation. (2) External dimensions of diversity consist of the personal characteristics that people acquire, discard, or modify throughout their lives: personal habits, educational background, religion, income, marital status, and the like.

There are five categories in the internal dimension and one category in the external dimension in which the U.S. workforce is becoming more diverse: (1) age, (2) gender, (3) race and ethnicity, (4) sexual orientation, (5) disabilities, and (6) educational level.

There are six ways in which employees and managers may express resistance to diversity: (1) Some express stereotypes and prejudices based on ethnocentrism, the belief that one's native country, culture, language, abilities, or behavior is superior to that of another country. (2) Some employees are afraid of reverse discrimination. (3) Some employees see diversity programs as distracting them from the organization's supposed "real work." (4) Diverse employees may experience an unsupportive social atmosphere. (5) Organizations may not be supportive of flexible hours and other matters that can help employees cope with family demands. (6) Organizations may show lack of support for career-building steps for diverse employees.

Management in Action

Google's Values Conflict with Demands from the Chinese Government

Isaac Mao saw this coming. In early 2007, a year after Google launched a China-based version of its search engine that adhered to Beijing's strict censorship rules, the prominent Chinese blogger posted an open letter to founders Larry Page and Sergey Brin. Mao described the frustration he and other Chinese Google fans felt as a company with the informal motto "Don't be evil" obeyed policies forbidding access to sites deemed taboo by China's government. Google's self-censorship "hurts those loyal users a lot," wrote Mao, who said it was "high time to change (Google policy) back to the right track."

Now the 37-year-old Mao seems to be getting his wish. After Google's January 12, 2010, announcement that it would stop censoring search results on Google.cn—in response to what the company called "highly sophisticated" hacking from China of its computer systems and the infiltration of Gmail accounts of human rights activists—Internet users in China had new hope they might gain access to information on the 1989 Tiananmen Square crackdown, the Dalai Lama, and other banned topics. The company says it will quit China if it can't run a permanently unfiltered search engine. It's hard, though, to imagine the Chinese giving Google, or anyone else, that kind of autonomy.

An exit from the mainland would uphold the right of free expression and acquit Google in the eyes of those who protested its initial complicity with Chinese restrictions. "It's a smart move," says Mao. But before heaping too much praise on Page and Brin, it's worth noting that a pullout would also end a bruising commercial battle. In the United States Google has over 60% of the search market. In China its share of search profits is 35.6%, a distant No. 2 to local champion Baidu's 58.4%, according to China data tracker Analysys International. No wonder, says David Wolf, CEO of Beijing-based advisory firm Wolf Group Asia, "Google appears to be more interested in winning hearts and minds than in sustaining its business in China.". . .

Google struggled from the get-go. Despite its submission to censorship, its YouTube business was regularly blocked, and censors still occasionally restricted access to the entire search engine, not just results to offending queries. After Google announced that it would alert Chinese users every time it provided them with a censored result, the government-run media attacked the company for allegedly operating without a license. Chinese Net users even mocked Google's Chinese name, a transliteration of the word *Google* that was rendered inelegantly as "Valley Song." Google also had to wage a bitter court battle in 2005 before winning permission to hire a brilliant Microsoft executive, Kai-Fu Lee, to head its China business. Lee quit in September.

Google says financial considerations have nothing to do with its challenge to the Beijing censors. Outsiders disagree. "Google is in a really tough spot," says Bill Bishop, a Beijing-based angel investor in Chinese start-ups. "There is no long-term potential." By citing the hacking and censorship issues as reasons for leaving, Google can end its agony and "get this incredible lift in brand equity," he says. Google won't lose much financially: Its Chinese business was on target for 2010 sales of $600 million, according to JPMorgan Chase. That's a fraction of Google's estimated overall sales this year of $26 billion.

For Discussion

1. Which internal and external stakeholders are positively and negatively affected by Google's decision to oppose censorship of its search engine?

2. Which of the six general environmental forces influenced Google's decision about censorship in China? Discuss.

3. Use the four approaches to deciding ethical dilemmas to evaluate whether Google made an ethical decision regarding its position about censorship.

4. To what extent did Google respond to the Chinese government in a socially responsible manner? Explain.

5. Do you think Google is making a good decision to fight censorship? Why not just accommodate the Chinese government and continue to make inroads into the lucrative Asian market?

Source: Excerpted from Bruce Einhorn, "Google and China: A Win for Liberty—and Strategy," *Bloomberg BusinessWeek,* January 25, 2010, p. 35.

Self-Assessment

What Is Your Guiding Ethical Principle?

Objectives

1. To understand your ethical approach.
2. To understand that there are different ways to perceive ethics in the workplace.

Introduction

Over the centuries human beings have grappled with defining ethics and behaving ethically. Many different principles have evolved to deal with ethics from different perspectives. None is better or worse than the other—they are simply perspectives. You may choose one to be your guiding principle while your friend follows another. This is also true of companies and their employees. For example, Johnson & Johnson has a valued reputation for being very ethical and socially responsible, whereas actions by companies like Ford and Arthur Andersen have placed a large question mark on their ethical conduct and social responsibility.

Instructions

Rank each of the following principles in order from 1 (my most important guiding principle) to 3 (least relevant to my ethical principles).

1. *Utilitarianism:* The greatest good for the greatest number, or any view that holds that actions and policies should be evaluated on the basis of benefits and costs they will impose on society.

   Violation? The Ford Motor Company knew of the problems with its tires 6 years before they became known in the United States, but this was information from Europe, and U.S. law did not require that the company report it if it did not happen here.

2. *Rights Theory:* A right is an individual's entitlement or claim to something. A person has a right when he or she is entitled to act in a certain way or is entitled to have others act in a certain way toward him or her. It can be a legal right, a moral right, or a human right.

   Violation? Many stockholders at Microsoft want the company to adopt the "U.S. Business Principles for Human Rights of Workers in China," a statement supported by other companies such as Levi Strauss and Reebok. Microsoft management did not agree, arguing that its own principles and code of ethics covered the important points and that the statement principles were too broad and vague. Other companies also thought that American companies should not promote human rights in China because they would be abandoning a position of political neutrality.

3. *Justice as Fairness:* A principle that aims to protect those least able to protect themselves.

Examples: Companies should establish strong affirmative action plans to redress the wrongs of discrimination; or, if a company introduces pay cuts, the workers paid the least should receive the smallest pay cut and those who are paid the most should get the largest pay cut.

Questions for Discussion

1. What are the pros and cons of your primary ethical principle in terms of advancing up the corporate ladder? Discuss.

2. Why do you think ethical principles are important in the workplace? Explain.

3. Which of the previous three principles would you want the company that you work for to adopt? Why?

4. In such a competitive world, how ethical can any company really be?

Developed by Anne C. Cowden, PhD, Laura P. Hartman, and Joseph R. DesJardins, *Business Ethics: Decision-Making for Personal Integrity and Social Responsibility* (Burr Ridge, IL: McGraw-Hill, 2008). See Chapter 3 for a detailed discussion for each approach.

Ethical Dilemma

Should Job Applicants Reveal Their Chronic Illnesses to Potential Employers?

You've just graduated from college and are excited to begin job hunting. You have many exciting prospects, but there is one thing holding you back—you were recently diagnosed with scleroderma. This chronic connective tissue disease is progressive and typically kills patients within 10 years. Your doctor is positive about your prognosis; however, you have already experienced some of the effects, such as swelling and stiffening in your fingers. Federal disability laws bar employers from asking about an applicant's health. However, the U.S. Supreme Court ruled that a company can refuse to hire an applicant whose medical condition might adversely affect the performance of a specific job function.

Solving the Dilemma

Knowing a company might be reluctant to hire you based on your condition, what would you do?

1. Don't immediately mention your disease during the interview. Instead, play up your abilities, experience, and enthusiasm for the job. If you get hired, you can explain your illness and make up for missed work owing to medical appointments and flare-ups by working on weekends.

2. Bring up your disease right away. You don't have to provide vivid details about your symptoms, but it is important for your employer to know you have a chronic disease and how it will affect you.

3. Don't mention your disease at all. If you get the job and have a flare-up and need to take sick days, it is your business.

4. Invent other options. Discuss.

Source: Based on Joann S. Lublin, "Should Job Hunters Reveal Chronic Illness? The Pros and Cons," *The Wall Street Journal*, January 13, 2004, p. B1.

Global Management
Managing across Borders

Learning to Be a Success Abroad: How Do You Become a World Citizen?

Whether you travel abroad on your own or on a work assignment for your company, there are several ways to make your experience enhance your career success.

- **Learn how not to be an "ugly American":** Americans "are seen throughout the world as an arrogant people, totally self-absorbed and loud," says Keith Reinhard, former head of advertising conglomerate DDB Worldwide, who is leading an effort to reverse that through a nonprofit group called Business for Diplomatic Action (BDA), from which many suggestions here are drawn.[1] A survey conducted by DDB in more than 100 countries found that respondents repeatedly mentioned "arrogant," "loud," and "uninterested in the world" when asked their perceptions of Americans.[2] Some sample advice for Americans traveling abroad is: Be patient, be quiet, listen at least as much as you talk, don't use slang, and don't talk about wealth and status.[3]

- **Be global in your focus, but think local:** Study up on your host country's local customs and try to meet new people who might help you in the future. For example, Bill Roedy, President of MTV Networks International, spent time hanging out with Arab rappers and meeting the mayor of Mecca before trying to sign a contract that would launch MTV Arabia.[4] His efforts helped seal the deal.

- **Learn what's appropriate behavior:** Before you go, spend some time learning about patterns of interpersonal communication. In Japan, for instance, it is considered rude to look directly into the eye for more than a few seconds. In Greece the hand-waving gesture commonly used in America is considered an insult. In Afghanistan, a man does not ask another man about his wife.[5]

   Learn rituals of respect, including exchange of business cards. Understand that shaking hands is always permissible, but social kissing may not be. Dress professionally. For women, this means no heavy makeup, no flashy jewelry, no short skirts or sleeveless blouses (particularly in Islamic countries). In some countries, casual dressing is a sign of disrespect. Don't use first names and nicknames with fellow employees overseas, especially in countries with strict social strata.[6]

- **Know your field:** If you know your field and behave with courtesy and assurance, you will be well received around the world. Indra Nooyi successfully uses this advice in her role as CEO of PepsiCo. She's cosmopolitan and well educated and is respected by people around the globe.[7]

- **Become at least minimally skilled in the language:** Whatever foreign country you're in, at the very least you should learn a few key phrases, such as "hello," "please," and "thank you," in your host country's language. Successful international managers have learned there is no adequate substitute for knowing the local language.[8]

For Discussion Have you done much traveling? What tricks have you discovered to make it more satisfying?

---

forecast **What's Ahead in This Chapter**

This chapter covers the importance of globalization—the rise of the global village, of one big market, of both worldwide megafirms and minifirms. We also describe the characteristics of the successful international manager and why and how companies expand internationally. We describe the barriers to free trade and the major organizations promoting trade. Finally, we discuss some of the cultural differences you may encounter if you become an international manager.

major question?

What three important developments of globalization will probably affect me?

THE BIG PICTURE

Globalization, the trend of the world economy toward becoming a more interdependent system, is reflected in three developments: the rise of the "global village" and e-commerce, the trend of the world's becoming one big market, and the rise of both megafirms and Internet-enabled minifirms worldwide.

"You don't have to be big to be global," says Sonia Seye, who runs Hair Universal, a busy Los Angeles salon that specializes in braiding hair and turning multicolored hair extensions into fashionable coifs. With dreams of expanding her business, she launched a search in India for a supplier of human-hair extensions (which come from Hindu temples, where women shave their heads in offerings to the gods).

Seye spent 6 months researching suppliers online, peppering prospects by e-mail and checking them out with the Indian consulate, and then flew to India, where she met her final candidates. By buying direct, instead of going through middlemen, she halved her hair-extension costs and thus is able to undercut the prices of rival salons. The trip to India has more than paid for itself.[9]

Can you visualize yourself operating like this? Like Seye, you are living in a world being rapidly changed by *globalization*—**the trend of the world economy toward becoming a more interdependent system.** Time and distance, which have been under assault for 150 years, have now virtually collapsed, as reflected in three important developments we shall discuss.[10]

1. The rise of the "global village" and electronic commerce.
2. The world's becoming one market instead of many national ones.
3. The rise of both megafirms and Internet-enabled minifirms worldwide.

The Rise of the "Global Village" & Electronic Commerce

The hallmark of great civilizations has been their great systems of communications. In the beginning, communications was based on transportation: the Roman Empire had its network of roads, as did other ancient civilizations, such as the Incas. Later, the great European powers had their far-flung navies. In the 19th century, the United States and Canada unified North America by building transcontinental railroads. Later, the airplane reduced travel time between continents.

From Transportation to Communication   Transportation began to yield to the electronic exchange of information. Beginning in 1844, the telegraph ended the short existence of the Pony Express and, beginning in 1876, found itself in competition with the telephone. The amplifying vacuum tube, invented in 1906, led to commercial radio. Television came into being in England in 1925. During the 1950s and 1960s, as television exploded throughout the world, communications philosopher Marshall McLuhan posed the notion of a "global village," where we all share our hopes, dreams, and fears in a "worldpool" of information. **The *global village* refers to the "shrinking" of time and space as air travel and the electronic media have made it easier for the people of the globe to communicate with one another.**

Then the world became even faster and smaller. Fifteen years ago, cell phones, pagers, fax, and voice-mail links barely existed. When AT&T launched the first cellular communications system in 1983, it predicted fewer than a million users by 2000. By the end of 1993, however, there were more than 16 million cellular phone subscribers in the United States.[11] By mid-2010, it was expected there would be 6.8 billion humans on the planet, and there would be 5 billion cell-phone subscriptions.[12]

The Net, the Web, & the World   Then came the Internet, the worldwide computer-linked "network of networks," of which there were an estimated 1.7 billion users throughout the world in late 2000.[13] The Net might have remained the province of academicians had it not been for the contributions of Tim Berners-Lee, who came up with the coding system, linkages, and addressing scheme that debuted in 1991 as the World Wide Web. "He took a powerful communications system [the Internet] that only the elite could use," says one writer, "and turned it into a mass medium."[14]

The arrival of the Web quickly led to *e-commerce,* **or electronic commerce, the buying and selling of products and services through computer networks.** U.S. retail e-commerce sales were expected to total $36.6 billion in the first quarter of 2010.[15]

Example

E-Commerce: Resolers to the World

Perhaps the most well-known story of e-commerce companies is that of Amazon.com, which was started in 1994 by Jeffrey Bezos as an online bookstore, and later expanded into nonbook areas. In 2010, it reported 2009 net sales of $24.51 billion, up 28% from a year earlier.[16] Now e-commerce has spread well beyond books, CDs, and electronics to embrace even the most mundane of goods and services. Shoe repair, for example.

In the 1930s, there were more than 120,000 shoe-repair businesses in the United States. Now there are about 7,000, the result of increased affordability in new shoes. Still, many people (some with special orthopedic needs) want to hang on to favorite footwear. Into the gap vacated by vanished mainstreet cobblers have stepped several online shoe refurbishment and repair services. Examples: American Heelers, Great Lakes Shoe & Orthopedic Services, NuShoe, Resole America.

Wall Street Journal reporter Sarah Needleman, trying out these four companies' services, went to the Web site of American Heelers, launched in 2007 by Ilya Romanov to augment his father's Woodmere, Ohio, repair shop. There she found service descriptions, prices, and instructions on how to request shipping materials. After placing the order online, she received a quote and shoe mailing envelope. Later she received billing and payment information (final cost: $44.99). Sent back within the five to seven days the company promised, the repaired shoes, "were vastly improved," Needleman writes, "with a new set of full heels and soles, plus they'd been shined, cleaned, waterproofed, and conditioned."[17]

YOUR CALL

Can you think of any other specialized medium-sized or small business, domestic or worldwide, that the Internet has made possible? Could you see yourself launching a similar venture? What would it be?

One Big World Market: The Global Economy

"We are seeing the results of things started in 1988 and 1989," said Rosabeth Moss Kantor of the Harvard Business School a decade later.[18] It was in the late 1980s when the Berlin Wall came down, signaling the beginning of the end of communism in Eastern Europe. It was also when Asian countries began to open their economies to foreign investors. Finally, the trend toward governments deregulating their economies began sweeping the globe. These three events set up conditions by which goods, people, and money could move more freely throughout the world—a

"Oh, same old thing." The cell phone represents a boon to less-developed countries because this kind of telephone infrastructure does not entail the costly process of installing miles of telephone poles and landlines.

global economy. **The *global economy* refers to the increasing tendency of the economies of the world to interact with one another as one market instead of many national markets.**

The economies of the world have never been more entangled. As Kevin Maney writes in *USA Today,* "They're tied together by instantaneous information arriving via everything from currency trading databases to Web sites to CNN broadcasts. Capital—the money used to build businesses—moves globally and moves in a matter of keystrokes."[19]

Positive Effects   Is a global economy really good for the United States? "Ultimately, the medium- to long-term benefits of globalization are positive for everybody," says the CEO of Infosys Technologies in India. "Let me give you an example. As our industry has increased economic activity in India, it's becoming a bigger market for American exports . . . Today you can't find any soft drinks in India except Coke or Pepsi."[20]

In addition, foreign firms are building plants in the United States, revitalizing parts of industrial America.[21] Indeed, foreign direct investment makes up 15% of the country's gross domestic product (total value of all goods and services). Companies based overseas provide jobs for approximately 10% of the U.S. workforce.[22] When the recession ends, suggests Gregg Easterbrook, author of *Sonic Boom: Globalization at Mach Speed,* worldwide economic growth will pick up, "creating rising prosperity and higher living standards. . . . The world will be far more interconnected, leading to better and more affordable products, as well as ever better communication among nations."[23]

Negative Effects   However, global economic interdependency can also be dangerous. Financial crises throughout the world resulted in vast surplus funds from global investments flowing into the United States and being invested badly in a housing-and-credit bubble that burst (the so-called subprime mortgages meltdown), leading to the 2008–2009 Great Recession that hurt so many people.[24]

Another negative effect is the movement, or outsourcing, of formerly well-paying jobs overseas as companies seek cheaper labor costs, particularly in manufacturing. Soaring new U.S. skyscrapers, for example, are more apt to have windows made in China than in Ohio, a glassmaking state.[25] Some economists fear that many jobs lost through the recession and offshoring may simply never come back.[26]

Indeed, while "the horizon has never been brighter," says Easterbrook, "we may not feel particularly happy about it." The reasons: "Job instability, economic insecurity, a sense of turmoil, the fear that even when things seem good a hammer is about to fall—these are also part of the larger trend. As world economies become ever more linked by computers, job stress will become a 24/7 affair. Frequent shakeups in industries will cause increasing uncertainty."[27] But the global economy isn't going to go away just because we don't like some of its destabilizing aspects.

Cross-Border Business: The Rise of Both Megamergers & Minifirms Worldwide

The global market driven by electronic information "forces things to get bigger and smaller at the same time," suggests technology philosopher Nicholas Negroponte. "And that's so ironic, when things want to do both but not stay in the middle. There will be an increasing absence of things that aren't either very local or very global."[28]

If Negroponte is correct, this means we will see more and more of two opposite kinds of businesses: mergers of huge companies into even larger companies, and small, fast-moving start-up companies.

Megamergers Operating Worldwide

Walt Disney + Pixar. Kmart + Sears. Union Pacific + Southern Pacific. Whole Foods + Wild Oats. Bank of America + Merrill Lynch. Chrysler + Fiat. Roche + Genentech. Ticketmaster + Live Nation. Kraft + Cadbury. Comcast + NBC Universal.

The last 20 years have seen a surge in mergers. Certain industries—oil, telecommunications, automobiles, financial services, and pharmaceuticals, for instance—aren't suited to being midsize, let alone

Megamerger? A Porsche + Volkswagen merger is planned for 2011. Do you think we will see more auto company mergers?

small and local, so companies in these industries are trying to become bigger and cross-border. The means for doing so is to merge with other big companies. In automobiles, for instance, Porsche targeted Volkswagen, a much larger company, to ensure that rivals did not get their hands on it; however, after a few years, Porsche gave up the fight and agreed to be acquired by its former prey VW.[29] Oil companies, already behemoths from earlier mergers (Exxon + Mobil, Conoco + Phillips), are expected to begin another wave of acquisitions in the near future.[30]

Minifirms Operating Worldwide

The Internet and the World Wide Web allow almost anyone to be global, which Kevin Maney points out has two important results:

1. **Small companies can get started more easily.** Because anyone can put goods or services on a Web site and sell worldwide, this wipes out the former competitive advantages of distribution and scope that large companies used to have.

2. **Small companies can maneuver faster.** Little companies can change direction faster, which gives them an advantage in terms of time and distance over large companies. ●

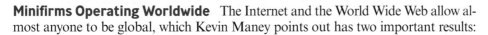

Example 🔍

Small Companies That Get Started More Easily & Can Maneuver Faster: Bay-Traders

Many small firms have come from nowhere to collapse time and distance. For instance, so-called Bay-traders make a living selling things on eBay, the online auction company. Bay-traders find they get higher prices at Internet auctions than at swap meets or collectibles shows because bidding generates excitement and because the Internet's worldwide reach makes multiple bids more likely.

Judi Henderson-Townsand's Oakland, California, company, Mannequin Madness, began when, while working in marketing for a failing dot-com firm, she saw an online ad from a window dresser offering

50 mannequins. After purchasing the entire inventory, she started renting mannequins and later, after buying more from department stores, started selling them to special-event planners, retail stores, and artists.

Henderson-Townsand claims that the Internet, including eBay, has been by far her greatest marketing resource because it allows the firm to reach customers who could never be reached otherwise.[31]

YOUR CALL

Do you have an idea for some uncommon products you might sell on eBay? What would they be?

major question?

Why learn about international management, and what characterizes the successful international manager?

THE BIG PICTURE

Studying international management prepares you to work with foreign customers or suppliers, for a foreign firm in the United States or for a U.S. firm overseas. Successful international managers aren't ethnocentric or polycentric, but geocentric.

Can you see yourself working overseas? It can definitely be an advantage to your career. "There are fewer borders," says Paul McDonald, executive director of recruitment firm Robert Half Management Resources. "Anyone with international experience will have a leg up, higher salary, and be more marketable."[32] The recent brutal U.S. job market has also spurred more Americans to hunt for jobs overseas (and impelled foreign-born professionals who used to work in the United States to return home).[33]

Example

Americans Working Overseas

When Charles Wang, an industrial engineering major, completed his junior year at Georgia Institute of Technology in 2008, he joined United Parcel Service as a project manager. His assignment: Go to Dubai for 10 months and develop a delivery system for the Arab country's first-ever network of streets and addresses. Following graduation, he planned to return to Dubai for a permanent job "because of . . . my inability to find good jobs in the U.S."[34]

Julie Androshick spent 2 years teaching in Samoa, and then worked as a journalist and as an analyst for consulting company McKinsey & Company. Now based in New York, she says working abroad expanded her worldview, gave her the courage to pursue long-shot jobs, and made her a more loyal

employee.[35] After graduating from Northwestern University, Nate Linkon found a job in marketing with InfoSys Technologies, the Indian software giant, in Bangalore.[36] Scott Stapleton, formerly of Oakland, California, also took a marketing job with InfoSys in India. "The job blends practical work experience with life in a developing country," says Stapleton, adding that it's "a rare opportunity to actually witness globalization."[37]

YOUR CALL

How do you feel about following these intrepid travelers? How can you begin to prepare yourself for working overseas?

Foreign experience demonstrates independence, resourcefulness, and entrepreneurship, according to management recruiters. "You are interested in that person who can move quickly and is nimble and has an inquiring mind," says one. People who have worked and supported themselves overseas, she says, tend to be adaptive and inquisitive—valuable skills in today's workplace.[38]

Why Learn about International Management?

International management is management that oversees the conduct of operations in or with organizations in foreign countries, whether it's through a multinational corporation or a multinational organization.

Part of the action. If "all of the action in business is international," as one expert says, what role do you think you might play in it? Do you think cultural bias against women in some foreign countries contributes to the low percentage of U.S. female executives working abroad?

- **A *multinational corporation,* or multinational enterprise, is a business firm with operations in several countries.** Our publisher, McGraw-Hill, is one such "multinational" (see the 17 foreign cities listed on our book's title page). In terms of sales revenue, the real behemoths in multinational corporations include the American firms ExxonMobil, Walmart, Chevron, ConocoPhillips, General Electric, General Motors, and Ford Motor Co. The largest foreign companies are Royal Dutch/Shell (Netherlands/Britain), BP (Britain), Toyota (Japan), Total (oil and gas, France), and ING Group (insurance, Netherlands).[39]

- **A *multinational organization* is a nonprofit organization with operations in several countries.** Examples are the World Health Organization, the International Red Cross, and the Church of Jesus Christ of Latter-day Saints.

Even if in the coming years you never travel to the wider world outside North America—an unlikely proposition, we think—the world will assuredly come to you. That, in a nutshell, is why you need to learn about international management.

Practical Action

Being an Effective Road Warrior

Since business travelers who fly 100,000-plus miles a year are no longer a rare breed, should you prepare for the possibility of joining them?

Business travel can have its rewards. Many people enjoy going to different cities, meeting new people, encountering new cultures. In one survey, people who took business trips of five nights or more said that being on the road provided certain escapes, as from their everyday workplace (35% of those polled), putting out work "fires" (20%), frequent meetings (12%), and co-worker distractions (11%).[40]

Business travelers have learned the following three lessons.

Lesson I: Frequent Travel May Be Needed Because Personal Encounters Are Essential

"There is no substitute for face time," says a *Business-Week* article.[41] Yes, technologies such as smart phones, e-mail, and videoconferencing make it easier to connect with others—superficially, at least. "But," says an investment banker, "in a global world you have to get in front of your employees, spend time with your clients, and show commitment when it comes to joint ventures, mergers, and alliances. The key is thoughtful travel—traveling when necessary."[42] Adds another top executive, "If you are going to disagree with somebody, you certainly don't want to do it by email, and if possible you don't even want to do it by phone. You want to do it face to face."[43]

Lesson 2: Travel May Be Global, but Understanding Must Be Local

Being a road warrior is all about making bets with one's time, calculating the strategy of where to be when. Thus, world-traveling executives must do their homework to know cultures, organizations, and holders of power.

"Cull information on the individuals and companies you're visiting," says one expert. "Follow the news relating to the region. If possible try to read a few books about the history and culture of the lands you will visit. . . . Learn a few words too."[44] Because in Asia and the Middle East personal relationships are crucial to getting things done, you need to engage in small talk and avoid business talk during after-hours outings. Says Ted Dale, president of international business consulting firm Aperian Global, "You need to spend out-of-office time in social settings." In Asia, the Middle East, and Latin America, it's important to understand organizational hierarchy, as represented by professional titles and age.[45]

Lesson 3: Frequent Travel Requires Frequent Adjustments

How do you cope if you travel all the time? Some people pack their own bags. Others keep complete wardrobes in major cities. Lisa Bergson has a detailed packing list that "comprises everything, from voltage adaptors to herbal teas to foot spray." She has also developed a "day-by-day wardrobe chart for every trip of a week or more, attempting to leverage every item and still look chic."[46]

Your Call

As we discussed, managers must be prepared to work for organizations that operate not only countrywide but worldwide. To stay connected with colleagues, employees, clients, and suppliers, you may have to travel a lot. Does this give you cause for concern? What do you think you should do about it?

More specifically, consider yourself in the following situations:

You May Deal with Foreign Customers or Partners While working for a U.S. company you may have to deal with foreign customers. Or you may have to work with a foreign company in some sort of joint venture. The people you're dealing with may be outside the United States or visitors to it. Either way you would hate to blow a deal—and maybe all future deals—because you were ignorant of some cultural aspects you could have known about.

Examples are legion.[47] One American executive inadvertently insulted or embarrassed Thai businessmen by starting gatherings talking about business. "That's a no-no," he says. "I quickly figured out that I was creating problems by talking business before eating lunch and by initiating the talks."

Working for a foreign firm. If you thought you might work for a foreign firm, either at home or overseas, what should you be doing now to prepare for it?

You May Deal with Foreign Suppliers While working for an American company you may have to purchase important components, raw materials, or services from a foreign supplier. And you never know where foreign practices may diverge from what you're accustomed to.

Many software developer jobs, for instance, have been moved outside the United States—to places such as India, New Zealand, and Eastern Europe. A lot of U.S. software companies—Microsoft, IBM, Oracle, Motorola, Novell, Hewlett-Packard, and Texas Instruments—have opened offices in India to take advantage of high-quality labor.[48]

You May Work for a Foreign Firm in the United States You may sometime take a job with a foreign firm doing business in the United States, such as an electronics, pharmaceutical, or car company. And you'll have to deal with managers above and below you whose outlook is different from yours. For instance, Japanese companies, with their emphasis on correctness and face saving, operate in significantly different ways from American companies.

Sometimes it is even hard to know that an ostensibly U.S. company actually has foreign ownership. For example, many American book publishers (though not McGraw-Hill) are British- or German-owned.

You May Work for an American Firm Outside the United States—or for a Foreign One You might easily find yourself working abroad in the foreign operation of a U.S. company. Most big American corporations have overseas subsidiaries or divisions. On the other hand, you might also well work for a foreign firm in a foreign country, such as a big Indian company in Bangalore or Mumbai.

The Successful International Manager: Geocentric, Not Ethnocentric or Polycentric

Maybe you don't really care that you don't have much understanding of the foreign culture you're dealing with. "What's the point?" you may think. "The main thing is to get the job done." Certainly there are international firms with managers who have this perspective. They are called *ethnocentric,* one of three primary attitudes among international managers, the other two being *polycentric* and *geocentric.*[49]

Ethnocentric Managers—"We Know Best" What do foreign executives fluent in English think when they hear Americans using an endless array of baseball, basketball, and football phrases (such as "out of left field" or "Hail Mary pass").[50] *Ethnocentric managers* **believe that their native country, culture, language, and behavior are superior to all others.** Ethnocentric managers tend to believe that they can export the managers and practices of their home countries to anywhere in the world and that they will be more capable and reliable. Often the ethnocentric viewpoint is less attributable to prejudice than it is to ignorance, since such managers obviously know more about their home environment than the foreign environment. Ethnocentrism might also be called *parochialism*—**that is, a narrow view in which people see things solely through their own perspective.**

Is ethnocentrism bad for business? It seems so. A survey of 918 companies with home offices in the United States, Japan, and Europe found that ethnocentric policies were linked to such problems as recruiting difficulties, high turnover rates, and lawsuits over personnel policies.[51]

Polycentric Managers—"They Know Best" *Polycentric managers* **take the view that native managers in the foreign offices best understand native personnel and practices, and so the home office should leave them alone.** Thus, the attitude of polycentric managers is nearly the opposite of that of ethnocentric managers.

Geocentric Managers—"What's Best Is What's Effective, Regardless of Origin" *Geocentric managers* **accept that there are differences and similarities between home and foreign personnel and practices and that they should use whatever techniques are most effective.** Clearly, being an ethno- or polycentric manager takes less work. But the payoff for being a geocentric manager can be far greater. The Manager's Toolbox (page 103) gives some tips on being geocentric. ●

major question ❓ Why do companies expand internationally, and how do they do it?

THE BIG PICTURE

Multinationals expand to take advantage of availability of supplies, new markets, lower labor costs, access to finance capital, or avoidance of tariffs and import quotas. Five ways they do so are by global outsourcing; importing, exporting, and countertrading; licensing and franchising; joint ventures; and wholly-owned subsidiaries.

Who makes Apple's iPod, with its 451 parts? Not Apple, but a number of Asian companies. The hard drive, for instance, is made by a Japanese company, which in turn outsources to the Philippines and China; the chips are made in Taiwan.[52] Who makes the furniture sold by Ethan Allen, that most American of names, evoking Ethan Allen and the Green Mountain Boys of the American Revolution? About half is made overseas, by suppliers in China, the Philippines, Indonesia, and Vietnam.[53] With a goal of boosting sales by 5%–7%, where is consumer-products giant Procter & Gamble going to seek additional consumers? The company operates in 80 countries, one being Mexico, where poor consumers at small, rudimentary markets will buy a single-use P&G shampoo packet for the rock-bottom price of about 19 cents.[54] There are many reasons why American companies are going global. Let us consider why and how they are expanding beyond U.S. borders.

Why Companies Expand Internationally

Many a company has made the deliberate decision to restrict selling its product or service to just its own country. Is anything wrong with that?

The answer is: It depends. It would probably have been a serious mistake for NEC, Sony, or Hitachi to have limited their markets solely to Japan during the 1990s, a time when the country was in an economic slump and Japanese consumers weren't consuming. During that same period, however, some American banks might have been better off not making loans abroad, when the U.S. economy was booming but foreign economies were not. Going international or not going international—it can be risky either way.

Why, then, do companies expand internationally? There are at least five reasons, all of which have to do with making or saving money.

1. Availability of Supplies Antique and art dealers, mining companies, banana growers, sellers of hardwoods—all have to go where their basic supplies or raw materials are located. For years oil companies, for example, have expanded their activities outside the United States in seeking cheaper or more plentiful sources of oil.

2. New Markets Sometimes a company will find, as cigarette makers have, that the demand for their product has declined domestically but that they can still make money overseas. Or sometimes a company will steal a march on its competitors by

U.S. export. Popular entertainment is a major U.S. export, as was the film *Avatar* to Asian countries. Are there any negatives to sending American popular culture overseas?

aggressively expanding into foreign markets, as did Coca-Cola over PepsiCo under the leadership of legendary CEO Robert Goizueta. From 2000 to 2010, exports of American goods jumped 66%; the export of services increased even more—84%.[55]

3. Lower Labor Costs   The decline in manufacturing jobs in the United States is directly attributable to the fact that American companies have found it cheaper to do their manufacturing outside the States. For example, the rationale for using *maquiladoras*—**manufacturing plants allowed to operate in Mexico with special privileges in return for employing Mexican citizens**—is that they provide less expensive labor for assembling everything from appliances to cars. Even professional or service kinds of jobs, such as computer programming, may be shipped overseas. (However, a countertrend, called "deglobalization," is that some companies are moving production back home, because long supply chains can be easily affected by the whims of geopolitics and energy prices.)[56]

4. Access to Finance Capital   Companies may be enticed into going abroad by the prospects of capital being put up by foreign companies. Or sometimes a foreign government will offer a subsidy in hopes of attracting a company that will create jobs, as Ireland did in the 1970s for Lotus sports-car maker John DeLorean.

5. Avoidance of Tariffs & Import Quotas   Countries place tariffs (fees) on imported goods or impose import quotas—limitations on the numbers of products allowed in—for the purpose of protecting their own domestic industries. For example, Japan imposes tariffs on agricultural products, such as rice, imported from the United States. To avoid these penalties, a company might create a subsidiary to produce the product in the foreign country. General Electric and Whirlpool, for example, have foreign subsidiaries to produce appliances overseas.

How Companies Expand Internationally

Most companies don't start out to be multinationals. Generally, they edge their way into international business, making minimal investments and taking minimal risks, as shown in the drawing below. *(See Figure 4.1.)*

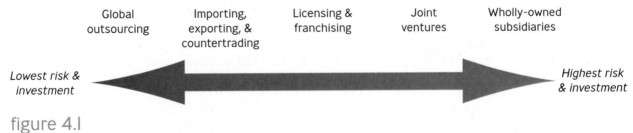

figure 4.1

FIVE WAYS OF EXPANDING INTERNATIONALLY

These range from lowest risk and investment *(left)* to highest risk and investment *(right)*.

Let's consider these five ways.

1. Global Outsourcing   A common practice of many companies, *outsourcing* is **defined as using suppliers outside the company to provide goods and services.** For example, airlines are increasingly farming out aircraft maintenance to other companies.[57] Management philosopher Peter Drucker believed that in the near future organizations might be outsourcing all work that is "support"—such as information systems—rather than revenue-producing.

Global outsourcing (or simply *global sourcing* or *offshoring*) extends this technique outside the United States. **Global outsourcing is defined as using suppliers outside the United States to provide labor, goods, or services.** The reason may be that the foreign supplier has resources not available in the United States, such as Italian marble. Or the supplier may have special expertise, as do Pakistani weavers. Or—more likely these days—the supplier's labor is cheaper than American labor. As a manager, your first business trip outside the United States might be to inspect the production lines of one of your outsourcing suppliers.

2. Importing, Exporting, & Countertrading   When *importing,* **a company buys goods outside the country and resells them domestically.** Nothing might seem to be more American than Jeep Wranglers, but they are made not only in the United States but also in Canada, from which they are imported and made available for sale in the United States. Many of the products we use are imported, ranging from Heineken beer (Netherlands) to Texaco gasoline (Saudi Arabia) to Honda snowblowers (Japan).

Practical Action

Global Outsourcing: Which Jobs Are Likely to Fall Victim to Offshoring?

Will there be any good jobs left for new college graduates?

Americans are rightly concerned about the changing jobs picture, brought about not only by the Great Recession but also earlier in part by offshoring of work to low-wage countries such as China, India, and the Philippines. Although U.S. manufacturing began a post-recession expansion in early 2010, few of the millions of factory jobs that have been lost during the last 10 years have been replaced. This has forced many workers—when they were able to work at all—to accept lower-paying alternatives, such as jobs in retail and health care, which pay on average 21% less than manufacturing jobs.[58] More recently, the same trend—global outsourcing—has been happening with white-collar jobs. Forrester Research estimates that 3.4 million service jobs will have moved offshore between 2000 and 2015.[59] Among them are jobs in office support, computer, business operations, architecture, legal, sales, and art and design.[60]

How Can You Prepare for an Offshored World?

"I believe [companies] should outsource everything for which there is no career track that could lead into senior management," said management philosopher Peter Drucker. An example, he said, is the job of total-quality-control specialist, work that can be done overseas.[61]

"As soon as a job becomes routine enough to describe in a spec sheet, it becomes vulnerable to outsourcing," says another writer. "Jobs like data entry, which are routine by nature, were the first among obvious candidates for outsourcing." But even "design and financial-analysis skills can, with time, become well-enough understood to be spelled out in a contract and signed away."[62] Says Fred Levy, a Massachusetts Institute of Technology economist, "If you can describe a job precisely, or write rules for doing it, it's unlikely to survive. Either we'll program a computer to do it, or we'll teach a foreigner to do it."[63]

Which Jobs Will Remain in the United States?

It is difficult to predict which jobs will remain at home, since even the Bureau of Labor Statistics often can't get it right. However, jobs that endure may share certain traits, listed below, regardless of the industry they serve:[64]

- **Face-to-face.** Some involve *face-to-face contact,* such as being a salesperson with a specific territory or an emergency room doctor.

- **Physical contact.** Other jobs involve *physical contact,* such as those of dentists, nurses, massage therapists, gardeners, and nursing-home aides.

- **Recognizing complex patterns.** Others involve the human ability to *recognize complex patterns,* which are hard to computerize, such as a physician's ability to diagnose an unusual disease (even if the X-rays are read by a radiologist in India). This also describes such high-end jobs as teaching first grade or selling a mansion to a millionaire or jobs that demand an intimate knowledge of the United States, such as marketing to American teenagers or lobbying Congress.[65]

Survival Rules

For you, as a prospective manager, there are perhaps three ideas to take away from all this:

- **Teamwork and creativity.** "Jobs that persist are dynamic and creative and require the ability to team with others," says Jim Spohrer of the IBM Almaden Research Center in San Jose, California, which studies the business operations of IBM's corporate clients. "At its heart, a company is simply a group of teams that come together to create" products and services.[66]

- **Flexibility.** "Jobs used to change very little or not at all over the course of several generations," says Spohrer. "Now, they might change three or four times in a single lifetime." Flexibility—as in being willing to undergo retraining—thus becomes important. Fortunately, as Drucker pointed out, the United States is "the only country that has a very significant continuing education system. This doesn't exist anywhere else." The United States is also the only country, he said, in which it is easy for younger people to move from one area at work to another.[67]

- **Education.** The more education one has, the more one is apt to prevail during times of economic change. Men and women with 4 years of college, for instance, earn nearly 45% more on average than those with only a high school diploma.[68]

Your Call

What kind of job or jobs are you interested in that would seem to provide you with some hopes of prevailing in a fast-changing world?

When *exporting,* **a company produces goods domestically and sells them outside the country.** The United States was ranked the number 3 exporter in the world in 2009, down from number 1 a decade earlier. *(See Table 4.1.)* One of the greatest U.S. exports is American pop culture, in the form of movies, music, and fashion. The United States is also a leader in exporting computers and other information technology.

Rank in 1999	Rank in 2009
1. U.S	China
2. Germany	Germany
3. Japan	U.S.
4. France	Japan
5. Britain	France
6. Canada	Netherlands
7. Italy	Italy
8. Netherlands	Belgium
9. China	South Korea
10. Belgium	Britain
11. Hong Kong	Canada
12. South Korea	Hong Kong

table 4.1

TOP 12 EXPORTING COUNTRIES, 1999 AND 2009

Source: Adapted from graphic in F. Norris, "A Shift in the Export Powerhouses," *The New York Times,* February 20, 2010, p. B3. Exports are measured in U.S. dollars.

Sometimes other countries may wish to import American goods but lack the currency to pay for them. In that case, the exporting U.S. company may resort to *countertrading*—**that is, bartering goods for goods.** When the Russian ruble plunged in value in 1998, some goods became a better medium of exchange than currency.

3. Licensing & Franchising   Licensing and franchising are two aspects of the same thing, although licensing is used by manufacturing companies and franchising is used more frequently by service companies.

In *licensing,* **a company allows a foreign company to pay it a fee to make or distribute the first company's product or service.** For example, the DuPont chemical company might license a company in Brazil to make Teflon, the nonstick substance that is found on some frying pans. Thus, DuPont, the licensor, can make money without having to invest large sums to conduct business directly in a foreign company. Moreover, the Brazilian firm, the licensee, knows the local market better than DuPont probably would.

Franchising **is a form of licensing in which a company allows a foreign company to pay it a fee and a share of the profit in return for using the first company's brand name and a package of materials and services.** For example, Burger King, Hertz, and Hilton Hotels, which are all well-known brands, might provide the use of their names plus their operating know-how (facility design, equipment, recipes, management systems) to companies in the Philippines in return for an up-front fee plus a percentage of the profits.

By now Americans traveling throughout the world have become accustomed to seeing so-called U.S. franchises everywhere: Popeye's Chicken & Biscuits in China, DKNY and The GAP stores in Turkey, Coca-Cola in Mexico, Intercontinental hotels in Hungary.

4. Joint Ventures   *Strategic allies* (described in Chapter 3) are two organizations that have joined forces to realize strategic advantages that neither would have if operating alone. A U.S. firm may form a *joint venture,* **also known as a** *strategic alliance,* **with a foreign company to share the risks and rewards of starting a new enterprise together in a foreign country.** For instance, General Motors operates a joint venture with Shanghai Automotive Industry Group to build Buicks in China.[69]

Sometimes a joint venture is the only way an American company can have a presence in a certain country, whose laws may forbid foreigners from ownership. Indeed, in China, this is the only way foreign cars may be sold in that country.

Jaguar. A number of formerly British-owned carmakers have gone over to foreign ownership. Jaguar and Land Rover became subsidiaries of Ford Motor Co., but then in 2008 were sold to Tata of India. Do you think the American companies General Motors and Ford could ever wind up under foreign ownership?

5. Wholly-Owned Subsidiaries   A *wholly-owned subsidiary* **is a foreign subsidiary that is totally owned and controlled by an organization.** The foreign subsidiary may be an existing company that is purchased outright. A *greenfield venture* **is a foreign subsidiary that the owning organization has built from scratch.**

General Motors owns majority stakes in Adam Opel AG in Germany and Vauxhall Motor Cars Ltd. in the United Kingdom. In early 2010, it announced its intention to sell its half ownership of Saab Automobile AB in Sweden. ●

4.4 THE WORLD OF FREE TRADE: REGIONAL ECONOMIC COOPERATION

What are barriers to free trade, and what major organizations and trading blocs promote trade?

major question?

THE BIG PICTURE
Barriers to free trade are tariffs, import quotas, and embargoes. Organizations promoting international trade are the World Trade Organization, the World Bank, and the International Monetary Fund. Major trading blocs are NAFTA, the EU, APEC, ASEAN, Mercosur, and CAFTA.

If you live in the United States, you see foreign products on a daily basis—cars, appliances, clothes, foods, beers, wines, and so on. Based on what you see every day, which countries would you think are our most important trading partners? China? Japan? Germany? England? South Korea?

These five countries do indeed appear among the top leading U.S. trading partners. Interestingly, however, our foremost trading partners are our immediate neighbors—Canada and Mexico, whose products may not be quite so visible. (*See Table 4.2.*)

table 4.2

TOP 10 U.S. TRADING PARTNERS IN GOODS, DECEMBER 2009

Source: U.S. Census Bureau, "Top Trading Partners," February 10, 2010, http://www.census.gov/foreign-trade/statistics/highlights/topcurmon.html#exports (accessed February 21, 2010).

Top 10 Nations for U.S. Exports	Top 10 Nations U.S. Imports From
1. Canada	China
2. Mexico	Canada
3. China	Mexico
4. Japan	Japan
5. Germany	Germany
6. United Kingdom	United Kingdom
7. South Korea	South Korea
8. Netherlands	France
9. Brazil	Venezuela
10. Hong Kong	Taiwan

Let's begin to consider *free trade,* **the movement of goods and services among nations without political or economic obstruction.**

Barriers to International Trade

Countries often use *trade protectionism*—**the use of government regulations to limit the import of goods and services**—to protect their domestic industries against foreign competition. The justification they often use is that this saves jobs. Actually, protectionism is not considered beneficial, mainly because of what it does to the overall trading atmosphere.

The three devices by which countries try to exert protectionism consist of *tariffs, import quotas,* and *embargoes.*

I. Tariffs   A *tariff* **is a trade barrier in the form of a customs duty, or tax, levied mainly on imports.** At one time, for instance, to protect the American shoe industry, the United States imposed a tariff on Italian shoes.

Actually, there are two types of tariffs: One is designed simply to raise money for the government (revenue tariff). The other, which concerns us more, is to raise the price of imported goods to make the prices of domestic products more competitive (protective tariff). In 2009, following several years of job losses in U.S. tire plants amid a flood of imported tires, the Obama administration imposed a 35% protective tariff on imported Chinese tires. China threatened to retaliate by imposing tariffs on American exports of automotive products and chicken meat, increasing tensions between the two nations.[70]

2. Import Quotas   An *import quota* **is a trade barrier in the form of a limit on the numbers of a product that can be imported.** Its intent is to protect domestic industry by restricting the availability of foreign products.

As a condition of being allowed into the World Trade Organization, China agreed, starting in 2005, to cancel car import quotas, which it had used to protect its domestic car manufacturing industry against imported vehicles from the United States, Japan, and Germany.[71]

Quotas are designed to prevent *dumping,* **the practice of a foreign company's exporting products abroad at a lower price than the price in the home market—or even below the costs of production—in order to drive down the price of the domestic product.** In 2009, the U.S. International Trade Commission imposed antidumping duties of 10%–16% more on Chinese government-subsidized steel imported into the United States that damaged the American steel industry.[72]

3. Embargoes   Ever seen a real Cuban cigar? They're difficult for Americans to get, since they're embargoed. **An *embargo* is a complete ban on the import or export of certain products.** It has been years since anyone was allowed to import Cuban cigars and sugar into the United States or for an American firm to do business in Cuba. The U.S. government also tries to embargo the export of certain supercomputers and other high-tech equipment with possible military uses to countries such as China.

Organizations Promoting International Trade

In the 1920s, the institution of tariff barriers did not so much protect jobs as depress the demand for goods and services, thereby leading to the loss of jobs anyway—and the massive unemployment of the Great Depression of the 1930s.[73] As a result of this lesson, after World War II the advanced nations of the world began to realize that if all countries could freely exchange the products that each could produce most efficiently, this would lead to lower prices all around. Thus began the removal of barriers to free trade.

The three principal organizations designed to facilitate international trade are the *World Trade Organization,* the *World Bank,* and the *International Monetary Fund.*

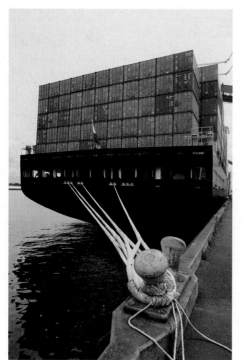

Quite contained. Container ships full of imports from China have benefited the American poor disproportionately, with cheap goods in discount stores, for instance, offsetting recent increased disparities in U.S. income. Could Americans' objections to globalization be misplaced?

I. The World Trade Organization (WTO) Consisting of 153 member countries, the ***World Trade Organization (WTO) is designed to monitor and enforce trade agreements.*** The agreements are based on the *General Agreement on Tariffs and Trade (GATT),* an international accord first signed by 23 nations in 1947, which helped to reduce worldwide tariffs and other barriers. Out of GATT came a series of "rounds," or negotiations, that resulted in the lowering of barriers; for instance, the Uruguay Round, implemented in 1996, cut tariffs by one-third. The current round of negotiations, the Doha Round, which began in Doha, Qatar, is aimed at helping the world's poor by, among other things, reducing trade barriers.

Founded in 1995 and headquartered in Geneva, Switzerland, WTO succeeded GATT as the world forum for trade negotiations and has the formal legal structure for deciding trade disputes. WTO also encompasses areas not previously covered by GATT, such as services and intellectual property rights. A particularly interesting area of responsibility covers telecommunications—cell phones, pagers, data transmission, satellite communications, and the like—with half of the WTO members agreeing in 1998 to open their markets to foreign telecommunications companies.[74]

2. The World Bank The World Bank was founded after World War II to help European countries rebuild. Today the purpose of the ***World Bank* is to provide low-interest loans to developing nations for improving transportation, education, health, and telecommunications.** The bank has 184 member nations, with most contributions coming from Britain, the United States, Japan, and Germany.[75]

In recent years, the World Bank has been the target of demonstrations in Seattle; Washington, DC; Ottawa; and elsewhere. Some protesters believe it finances projects that could damage the ecosystem, such as the Three Gorges Dam on China's Yangtze River. Others complain it supports countries that permit low-paying sweatshops or that suppress religious freedom. Still others think it has dragged its feet on getting affordable AIDS drugs to less-developed countries in Africa. Many of the same protests were leveled against the International Monetary Fund, discussed next. The World Bank has responded by trying to support projects that are not harmful to the environment and that are aimed at helping lift people out of poverty.

3. The International Monetary Fund Founded in 1945 and now affiliated with the United Nations, the International Monetary Fund is the second pillar supporting the international financial community. Consisting of 185 member nations, **the *International Monetary Fund (IMF)* is designed to assist in smoothing the flow of money between nations.** The IMF operates as a last-resort lender that makes short-term loans to countries suffering from unfavorable balance of payments (roughly the difference between money coming into a country and money leaving the country, because of imports, exports, and other matters).

For example, during the late 1990s' "Asian crisis," the value of Thailand's currency dropped until at the end of 1997 it was worth half what it was at the start of the year. This affected Thailand's ***exchange rate,* the rate at which one country's currency can be exchanged for another country's currency.** Because Thailand owed other countries, they, too, were affected: Indonesia's currency dropped 70% and South Korea's 45%. In response to pleas for help, the IMF loaned Asian countries billions of dollars—$57 billion to South Korea alone in 1997.

Major Trading Blocs: NAFTA, EU, APEC, ASEAN, Mercosur, & CAFTA

A *trading bloc,* also known as an *economic community,* is a group of nations within a geographical region that have agreed to remove trade barriers with one another. The six major trading blocs are the *NAFTA nations,* the *European Union,* the *APEC countries,* the *ASEAN countries,* the *Mercosur,* and *CAFTA.*

I. NAFTA—the Three Countries of the North American Free Trade Agreement

Formed in 1994, **the *North American Free Trade Agreement (NAFTA)* is a trading bloc consisting of the United States, Canada, and Mexico,** encompassing 435 million people. The agreement is supposed to eliminate 99% of the tariffs and quotas among these countries, allowing for freer flow of goods, services, and capital in North America. Trade with Canada and Mexico now accounts for one-third of the U.S. total, up from one-quarter in 1989.

Is NAFTA a job killer, as some have complained? In Mexico, it has failed to generate substantial job growth and has hurt hundreds of thousands of subsistence farmers, so that illegal immigration to the United States remains a problem. As for the United States, nearly 525,000 workers, mostly in manufacturing, have been certified by the U.S. government as having lost their jobs or had their hours or wages reduced because of NAFTA's shifting of jobs south of the border. It also spurred a U.S. trade deficit—$74 billion with Mexico and $65 billion with Canada in 2007.[76] However, supporters insist NAFTA ultimately will result in more jobs and a higher standard of living among all trading partners.

2. The EU—the 27 Countries of the European Union

Formed in 1957, **the *European Union (EU)* consists of 27 trading partners in Europe,** covering 455 million consumers.

Nearly all internal trade barriers have been eliminated (including movement of labor between countries), making the EU a union of borderless neighbors and the world's largest free market.

By 2002, such national symbols as the franc, the mark, the lira, the peseta, and the guilder had been replaced with the EU currency, the euro. There has even been speculation that someday the euro could replace the U.S. dollar as the dominant world currency.[77] However, for a period in 2010, Greece's shaky finances revealed an inherent weakness of the union—that both weak and strong economies were expected to coexist. Perhaps, says one writer, "just as the Great Depression forced the U.S. to impose a tighter federalism, today's economic crisis will likely force Europe into a closer political union."[78]

3. APEC—21 Countries of the Pacific Rim

The *Asia-Pacific Economic Cooperation (APEC)* **is a group of 21 Pacific Rim countries whose purpose is to improve economic and political ties.** Most countries with a coastline on the Pacific Ocean are members of the organization, although there are a number of exceptions. Among the 21 members are the United States, Canada, and China. Since the founding in 1989, APEC members have worked to reduce tariffs and other trade barriers across the Asia-Pacific region. APEC member countries are highlighted below.

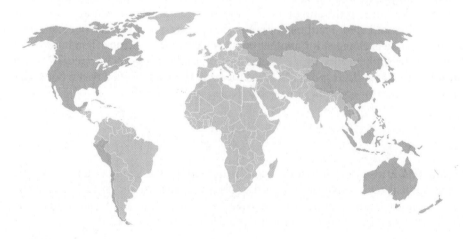

4. ASEAN—11 Countries of the Association of Southeast Asian Nations

The *Association of Southeast Asian Nations (ASEAN)* **is a trading bloc consisting of 11 countries in Asia:** Brunei, Cambodia, China, Indonesia, Laos, Malaysia, Myanmar (Burma), the Philippines, Singapore, Thailand, and Vietnam. Like other trading blocs, ASEAN is working on reducing trade barriers among member countries. When China was admitted at the beginning of 2010, ASEAN became one of the largest free-trade zones, encompassing 1.9 billion people.[79]

5. Mercosur—10 Countries of Latin America

The *Mercosur* **is the largest trade bloc in Latin America and has four core members—Argentina, Brazil, Paraguay, and Uruguay, with Venezuela scheduled to become a full member upon ratification by other countries—and five associate members: Bolivia, Chile, Colombia, Ecuador, and Peru.** Besides reducing tariffs by 75%, Mercosur nations are striving for full economic integration, and the alliance is also negotiating trade agreements with NAFTA, the EU, and Japan.

6. CAFTA-DR—Seven Countries of Central America

The *Central America Free Trade Agreement (CAFTA-DR),* **which involves the United States and Costa Rica, the Dominican Republic, El Salvador, Guatemala, Honduras, and Nicaragua— is intended to reduce tariffs and other barriers to free trade.**[80]

Most Favored Nation Trading Status

Besides joining together in trade blocs, countries will also extend special, "most favored nation" trading privileges to one another. *Most favored nation* **trading status describes a condition in which a country grants other countries favorable trading treatment such as the reduction of import duties.** The purpose is to promote stronger and more stable ties between companies in the two countries. ●

major question ?

What are the principal areas of cultural differences?

THE BIG PICTURE

Managers trying to understand other cultures need to understand the importance of national culture and cultural dimensions and basic cultural perceptions embodied in language, interpersonal space, communication, time orientation, and religion.

Friendship. In the Arab world, not touching another man in greeting may be taken as a sign of disdain. Do you have a problem with men touching or holding hands?

When President George W. Bush and Crown Prince Abdullah of Saudi Arabia met in Crawford, Texas, in the president's second term, they did something not usually done in the United States: They walked hand in hand. Men holding hands may raise eyebrows among most Americans, but it is common in the Middle East and does not carry any sexual connotation. "Holding hands is the warmest expression of affection between men," says one Lebanese sociologist. "It's a sign of solidarity and kinship."[81]

In Hong Kong, an American journalist riding in an elevator said hi to a Chinese colleague. She responded, "You've gained weight." Three other Chinese co-workers told him the same thing, a remark that in the United States would be regarded as tactless and offensive. "In China, such an intimate observation from a colleague isn't necessarily an insult," the journalist wrote. "It's probably just friendliness."[82]

Such are the kinds of cultural differences American managers are going to have to get used to. In the Arab world, which has historically been segregated by sex, men spend a lot of time together, and so holding hands, kissing cheeks, and long handshakes are meant to express devotion and equality in status. In China, people draw different lines between personal and work spaces, so that, for example, it is permissible for office colleagues to inquire about the size of your apartment and your salary and to give assessments of your wardrobe and your muscle tone.

The Importance of National Culture

A nation's **_culture_ is the shared set of beliefs, values, knowledge, and patterns of behavior common to a group of people.** We begin learning our culture starting at an early age through everyday interaction with people around us. This is why, from the outside looking in, a nation's culture can seem so intangible and perplexing. As cultural anthropologist Edward T. Hall puts it, "Since much of culture operates outside our awareness, frequently we don't even know what we know. . . . We unconsciously learn what to notice and what not to notice, how to divide time and space, how to walk and talk and use our bodies, how to behave as men or women, how to relate to other people, how to handle responsibility. . . ."[83] Indeed, says Hall, what we think of as "mind" is really internalized culture.

And because a culture is made up of so many nuances, this is why visitors to another culture may experience culture shock—the feelings of discomfort and disorientation associated with being in an unfamiliar culture. According to anthropologists, culture shock involves anxiety and doubt caused by an overload of unfamiliar expectations and social cues.[84]

Cultural Dimensions: The Hofstede & GLOBE Project Models

Misunderstandings and miscommunications often arise in international business relationships because people don't understand the expectations of the other side. A person from North America, Great Britain, Scandinavia, Germany, or Switzerland, for example, comes from a ***low-context culture*** **in which shared meanings are primarily derived from written and spoken words.** Someone from China, Korea, Japan, Vietnam, Mexico, or many Arab cultures, on the other hand, comes from a ***high-context culture*** **in which people rely heavily on situational cues for meaning when communicating with others,** relying on nonverbal cues as to another person's official position, status, or family connections.

One way to avoid cultural collisions is to have an understanding of various cultural dimensions, as expressed in the Hofstede model and the GLOBE project.

Hofstede's Model of Four Cultural Dimensions   Thirty years ago Dutch researcher and IBM psychologist **Geert Hofstede** collected data from 116,000 IBM employees in 53 countries and proposed his ***Hofstede model of four cultural dimensions,*** **which identified four dimensions along which national cultures can be placed: (1) individualism/collectivism, (2) power distance, (3) uncertainty avoidance, and (4) masculinity/femininity.**[85]

- **Individualism/collectivism—how loosely or tightly are people socially bonded?** The United States, Australia, Sweden, France, Canada, and Great Britain have high individualistic values. *Individualism* indicates a preference for a loosely knit social framework in which people are expected to take care of themselves. Costa Rica, Thailand, Mexico, China, Guatemala, and Ecuador have high collectivist values. *Collectivism* indicates a preference for a tightly knit social framework in which people and organizations are expected to look after each other.

- **Power distance—how much do people accept inequality in power?** *Power distance* refers to the degree to which people accept inequality in social situations. *High power distance,* such as occurs in Mexico, India, Thailand, Panama, and the Philippines, means that people accept inequality in power among people, institutions, and organizations. *Low power distance,* such as occurs in Sweden, Germany, Israel, and Australia, means that people expect equality in power.

- **Uncertainty avoidance—how strongly do people desire certainty?** This dimension is about being comfortable with risk and uncertainty. Countries such as Japan, France, Greece, Portugal, and Costa Rica are very high in *uncertainty avoidance,* which expresses people's intolerance for uncertainty and risk. *High uncertainty avoidance* means people feel uncomfortable with uncertainty and support beliefs that promise certainty and conformity. Countries such as Sweden, India, the United States, Singapore, and Jamaica are very low on this dimension. *Low uncertainty avoidance* means that people have high tolerance for the uncertain and ambiguous.

- **Masculinity/femininity—how much do people embrace stereotypical male or female traits?** *Masculinity* expresses how much people value performance-oriented masculine traits, such as achievement, assertiveness, and material success. Countries with strong masculine preferences are Japan, Mexico,

Austria, and Germany. *Femininity* expresses how much people embrace relationship-oriented feminine traits, such as cooperation and group decision making. Sweden, Norway, Thailand, Denmark, Costa Rica, and France are high on this cultural dimension.

In general, the United States ranked very high on individualism, relatively low on power distance, low on uncertainty avoidance, and moderately high on masculinity.

The GLOBE Project's Nine Cultural Dimensions   Started in 1993 by University of Pennsylvania professor **Robert J. House, the *GLOBE project* is a massive and ongoing cross-cultural investigation of nine cultural dimensions involved in leadership and organizational processes.**[86] (GLOBE stands for Global Leadership and Organizational Behavior Effectiveness.) GLOBE has evolved into a network of more than 150 scholars from 62 societies, and most of the researchers are native to the particular cultures they study. The nine cultural dimensions are as follows:

- **Power distance—how much unequal distribution of power should there be in organizations and society?** *Power distance* expresses the degree to which a society's members expect power to be unequally shared.

- **Uncertainty avoidance—how much should people rely on social norms and rules to avoid uncertainty?** *Uncertainty avoidance* expresses the extent to which a society relies on social norms and procedures to alleviate the unpredictability of future events.

- **Institutional collectivism—how much should leaders encourage and reward loyalty to the social unit?** *Institutional collectivism* expresses the extent to which individuals are encouraged and rewarded for loyalty to the group as opposed to pursuing of individual goals.

- **In-group collectivism—how much pride and loyalty should people have for their family or organization?** In contrast to individualism, *in-group collectivism* expresses the extent to which people should take pride in being members of their family, circle of close friends, and their work organization.

- **Gender egalitarianism—how much should society maximize gender role differences?** *Gender egalitarianism* expresses the extent to which a society should minimize gender discrimination and role inequalities.

- **Assertiveness—how confrontational and dominant should individuals be in social relationships?** *Assertiveness* represents the extent to which a society expects people to be confrontational and competitive as opposed to tender and modest.

- **Future orientation—how much should people delay gratification by planning and saving for the future?** *Future orientation* expresses the extent to which a society encourages investment in the future, as by planning and saving.

- **Performance orientation—how much should individuals be rewarded for improvement and excellence?** *Performance orientation* expresses the extent to which society encourages and rewards its members for performance improvement and excellence.

- **Humane orientation—how much should society encourage and reward people for being kind, fair, friendly, and generous?** *Humane orientation* represents the degree to which individuals are encouraged to be altruistic, caring, kind, generous, and fair.

Data from 18,000 managers yielded the country profiles shown on the next page. *(See Table 4.3.)*

table 4.3 COUNTRIES RANKING HIGHEST AND LOWEST ON THE GLOBE CULTURAL DIMENSIONS

Dimension	Highest	Lowest
Power distance	Morocco, Argentina, Thailand, Spain, Russia	Denmark, Netherlands, South Africa (black sample), Israel, Costa Rica
Uncertainty avoidance	Switzerland, Sweden, Germany (former West), Denmark, Austria	Russia, Hungary, Bolivia, Greece, Venezuela
Institutional collectivism	Sweden, South Korea, Japan, Singapore, Denmark	Greece, Hungary, Germany (former East), Argentina, Italy
In-group collectivism	Iran, India, Morocco, China, Egypt	Denmark, Sweden, New Zealand, Netherlands, Finland
Gender egalitarianism	Hungary, Poland, Slovenia, Denmark, Sweden	South Korea, Egypt, Morocco, India, China
Assertiveness	Germany (former East), Austria, Greece, United States, Spain	Sweden, New Zealand, Switzerland, Japan, Kuwait
Future orientation	Singapore, Switzerland, Netherlands, Canada (English speaking), Denmark	Russia, Argentina, Poland, Italy, Kuwait
Performance orientation	Singapore, Hong Kong, New Zealand, Taiwan, United States	Russia, Argentina, Greece, Venezuela, Italy
Human orientation	Philippines, Ireland, Malaysia, Egypt, Indonesia	Germany (former West), Spain, France, Singapore, Brazil

Source: Adapted from M. Javidan and R. J. House, "Cultural Acumen for the Global Manager: Lessons from Project GLOBE," *Organizational Dynamics,* Spring 2001, pp. 289–305.

The GLOBE dimensions show a great deal of cultural diversity around the world, but they also show how cultural patterns vary. For example, the U.S. managerial sample scored high on assertiveness and performance orientation—which is why Americans are widely perceived as being pushy and hardworking. Switzerland's high scores on uncertainty avoidance and future orientation help explain its centuries of political neutrality and world-renowned banking industry. Singapore is known as a great place to do business because it is clean and safe and its people are well educated and hardworking—no surprise, considering the country's high scores on social collectivism, future orientation, and performance orientation. By contrast, Russia's low scores on future orientation and performance orientation could foreshadow a slower-than-hoped-for transition from a centrally planned economy to free-enterprise capitalism. The practical lesson to draw from all this: *Knowing the cultural tendencies of foreign business partners and competitors can give you a strategic competitive advantage.*

GLOBE researchers also set out to find which, if any, attributes of leadership were universally liked or disliked, the results of which are shown on the next page. *(See Table 4.4.)* Throughout the world, visionary and inspirational leaders who are good team builders generally do the best; self-centered leaders seen as loners or face-savers received a poor reception.

table 4.4   LEADERSHIP ATTRIBUTES UNIVERSALLY LIKED AND DISLIKED ACROSS 62 NATIONS

Universally Positive Leader Attributes	Universally Negative Leader Attributes
Trustworthy	Loner
Just	Asocial
Honest	Noncooperative
Foresight	Irritable
Plans ahead	Nonexplicit
Encouraging	Egocentric
Positive	Ruthless
Dynamic	Dictatorial
Motive arouser	
Confidence builder	
Motivational	
Dependable	
Intelligent	
Decisive	
Effective bargainer	
Win-win problem solver	
Administrative skilled	
Communicative	
Informed	
Coordinator	
Team builder	
Excellence oriented	

Source: Excerpted and adapted from P. W. Dorfman, P. J. Hanges, and F. C. Brodbeck, "Leadership and Cultural Variation: The Identification of Culturally Endorsed Leadership Profiles," in R. J. House, P. J. Hanges, M. Javidan, P. W. Dorfman, and V. Gupta, eds. *Culture, Leadership, and Organizations: The GLOBE Study of 62 Societies,* (Thousand Oaks, CA: Sage, 2004), Tables 21.2 and 21.3, pp. 677–678.

Other Cultural Variations: Language, Interpersonal Space, Communication, Time Orientation, & Religion

How do you go about bridging cross-cultural gaps? It begins with understanding. Let's consider variations in five basic culture areas: (1) *language,* (2) *interpersonal space,* (3) *communication,* (4) *time orientation,* and (5) *religion.*

Note, however, that such cultural differences are to be viewed as *tendencies* rather than absolutes. We all need to be aware that the *individuals* we are dealing with may be exceptions to the cultural rules. After all, there *are* talkative and aggressive Japanese, just as there are quiet and deferential Americans, stereotypes notwithstanding.[87]

I. Language   More than 3,000 different languages are spoken throughout the world. However, even if you are operating in the English language, there are nuances between cultures that can lead to misperceptions. For instance, in Asia, a "yes" answer to a question "simply means the question is understood," says one well-traveled writer. "It's the beginning of negotiations."[88]

In communicating across cultures you have three options: (a) You can speak your own language. (The average American believes that about half the world can speak English, when actually it's about 20%.)[89] (b) You can use a translator. (If you do, try to get one who will be loyal to you rather than to your overseas host.) (c) You can learn the local language—by far the best option (as reflected in the *USA Today* headline: "U.S. Firms Becoming Tongue-Tied. Global Trade Requires Foreign Language Skills").[90] Although 93% of U.S. public middle and high schools with language programs offer Spanish, certainly a widely spoken international language, and 46% offer French, unfortunately only 4% offer Chinese (Mandarin), today one of the world's most important languages.[91]

2. Interpersonal Space   People of different cultures have different ideas about what is acceptable interpersonal space—that is, how close or far away one should be when communicating with another person. For instance, the people of North America and northern Europe tend to conduct business conversations at a range of 3–4 feet. For people in Latin American and Asian cultures, the range is about 1 foot. For Arabs, it is even closer.

This can lead to cross-cultural misunderstandings. "Arabs tend to get very close and breathe on you," says anthropologist Hall. "The American on the receiving end can't identify all the sources of his discomfort but feels that the Arab is pushy. The Arab comes close, the American backs up. The Arab follows, because he can only interact at certain distances."[92] However, once the American understands that Arabs handle interpersonal space differently and that "breathing on people is a form of communication," says Hall, the situation can sometimes be redefined so that the American feels more comfortable.

3. Communication   For small companies doing business abroad, "the important thing to remember is that you don't know what you don't know," says the head of a U.S. firm that advises clients on cross-cultural matters.[93] For instance, an American angling to make a deal in China gave four antique clocks wrapped in white paper to a prospective client. "What the man did not realize," says one account, "was that the words in Mandarin for clock and the number four are similar to the word for death, and white is a funeral color in China."[94] The American did not close the deal.

Even single words and sounds can pose difficulties: Promoters of Apple's "iPad," it's been pointed out, might encounter difficulties in Ireland, where the sound is indistinguishable from "iPod," or in Japan, where the language doesn't even have a sound for the "a" in iPad.[95]

If you, like a growing number of young Americans, head to China for employment, you need to recall that you were brought up in a commercial environment, but younger Chinese were raised at a time when China was evolving from a government-regulated economy to a more free-market system, and so they may have less understanding of business concepts and client services. "In the West, there is such a premium on getting things done quickly," says an American manager, "but when you come to work in China, you need to work on listening and being more patient and understanding of local ways of doing business."[96] In particular, Americans have to be careful about giving criticism directly, which the Chinese consider rude and inconsiderate.

We consider communication matters in more detail in Chapter 15.

4. Time Orientation   Time orientation is different in many cultures. For example, Americans are accustomed to calling ahead for appointments, but South Koreans believe in spontaneity. Thus, when Seoul erupted in protests over tainted American beef, Korean legislators simply hopped on a plane to the United States, saying they would negotiate with the U.S. government. "But since they failed to inform the Americans ahead of time," says one report, "they were unable to meet with anyone of importance."[97]

Anthropologist Hall makes a useful distinction between monochronic time and polychronic time:

- **Monochronic time.** This kind of time is standard American business practice—at least until recently. That is, *monochronic time* **is a preference for doing one thing at a time.** In this perception, time is viewed as being limited, precisely segmented, and schedule driven. This perception of time prevails, for example, when you schedule a meeting with someone and then give the visitor your undivided attention during the allotted time.[98]

  Indeed, you probably practice monochronic time when you're in a job interview. You work hard at listening to what the interviewer says. You may well take careful notes. You certainly don't answer your cell phone or gaze repeatedly out the window.

- **Polychronic time.** This outlook on time is the kind that prevails in Mediterranean, Latin American, and especially Arab cultures. *Polychronic time* **is a preference for doing more than one thing at a time.** Here time is viewed as being flexible and multidimensional.

  This perception of time prevails when you visit a Latin American client, find yourself sitting in the waiting room for 45 minutes, and then learn in the meeting that the client is dealing with three other people at the same time.

Example

Cultural Differences in Time: Peru Strives for Punctuality

Hora peruana, or Peruvian time, which usually means being an hour late, is considered by most citizens of Peru to be an endearing national trait. Students, for instance, are accustomed to professors showing up for class an hour after it has officially begun.

However, Peruvian officials believe that constant lateness reflects a negative attitude toward work and hurts national productivity. It's a "horrible, dreadful, harmful custom," President Alan Garcia said in a nationally televised event to kick off *La Hora sin*

Demora—Time without Delay. The campaign, launched in March 2007, aims at asking schools, businesses, and government institutions to stop tolerating tardiness. A technology consultant from London applauded the campaign, saying that "a lot of Latin American countries lose business" owing to lateness. Although the new effort offers no penalties for being late or rewards for compliance, it hopes to shame latecomers into mending their ways.[99]

"There is a general tendency toward a different way of timekeeping that dominates in most of Latin America," says Robert Levine, a professor of psychology at California State University in Fresno. The author of *A Geography of Time*, Levine theorizes that different cultures mark time in varying "tempos"—some define events by the clock and others allow events to run their natural courses. Peruvian officials are "taking people who have been living on what we might call 'event time,' and asking them to switch to 'clock time,'" Levine says.[100]

Garcia's campaign did not get off to a good start. An invitation to the 11:00 A.M. kickoff ceremony was delivered by messenger to the Associated Press at 1:30 P.M.—after the event had ended.

YOUR CALL

An Associated Press poll found the United States to be an impatient nation, with Americans getting antsy after 5 minutes on hold on the phone and 15 minutes maximum in a Department of Motor Vehicles line.[101] If you were trying to start a manufacturing business in Peru, what would you do to adjust?

5. Religion   Trying to get wealthy Muslim investors in Dubai to buy some of your bank's financial products? Then you need to know that any investment vehicle needs to "conform to the spirit of the Koran, which forbids any investments that pay interest," as one writer puts it. "No mortgages. No bonds."[102] Are you a Protestant doing business in a predominantly Catholic country? Or a Muslim in a Buddhist country? How, then, does religion influence the work-related values of the people you're dealing with?

A study of 484 international students at a midwestern university uncovered wide variations in the work-related values for different religious affiliations.[103] For example, among Catholics, the primary work-related value was found to be consideration. For Protestants, it was employer effectiveness; for Buddhists, social responsibility; for Muslims, continuity. There was, in fact, virtually *no agreement* among religions as to what is the most important work-related value. This led the researchers to conclude: "Employers might be wise to consider the impact that religious differences (and more broadly, cultural factors) appear to have on the values of employee groups."

Current Followers of the Major World Religions	
Christianity	2.1 billion
Islam	1.5 billion
Hinduism	900 million
Chinese traditional religions	394 million
Buddhism	376 million
Judaism	14 million

U.S. Managers on Foreign Assignments: Why Do They Fail?

There are about 300,000 U.S. managers known as *expatriates*—**people living or working in a foreign country**—who are working outside American borders. This number is expected to grow. Supporting expatriate businesspeople and their families overseas is not cheap. "The tab for sending an executive who earns $160,000 in the U.S., plus a spouse and two children, to India for two years is about $900,000," says one expert.[104] Are the employers getting their money's worth? Probably not.

One study of about 750 companies (U.S., European, and Japanese) asked expatriates and their managers to evaluate their experiences. They found that 10%–20% of all U.S. managers sent abroad returned early because of job dissatisfaction or adjustment difficulties. Of those who stayed for the length of their assignments, about one-third did not perform to their superiors' expectations and one-fourth left the company, often to join a competitor—a turnover rate double that of managers who did not go abroad.[105]

Unfortunately, problems continue when expatriates return home, according to a recent study by Pricewaterhouse Coopers. Results indicated that 25% of repatriated employees quit their jobs within 1 year. Organizations can help reduce this turnover by communicating with employees throughout the international assignment and by providing at least 6 months' notice of when employees will return home.[106]

If you were to go abroad as a manager, what are the survival skills or outlook you will need? Perhaps the bottom line is revealed in a study of 72 human resource managers who were asked to identify the most important success factors in a foreign assignment: Nearly 35% said the secret was *cultural adaptability:* patience, flexibility, and tolerance for others' beliefs.[107] ●

Who made this car? Could you become an American manager in Japan but drive a Japanese car made in the United States? Unlikely, but possible. Still, Japanese carmakers build cars in the United States, such as this Toyota Camry, just as Buick builds cars in China. Both plants are located close to their markets.

Key Terms Used in This Chapter

Asia-Pacific Economic Cooperation (APEC) 121

Association of Southeast Asian Nations (ASEAN) 121

Central America Free Trade Agreement (CAFTA) 121

countertrading 116

culture 122

dumping 118

e-commerce 105

economic community 119

embargo 118

ethnocentric managers 111

European Union (EU) 120

exchange rate 119

expatriates 130

exporting 115

franchising 116

free trade 117

geocentric managers 111

global economy 106

global outsourcing 114

global village 104

globalization 104

GLOBE project 124

greenfield venture 116

high-context culture 123

Hofstede model of four cultural dimensions 123

import quota 118

importing 114

International Monetary Fund (IMF) 119

joint venture 116

licensing 116

low-context culture 123

maquiladoras 113

Mercosur 121

monochronic time 128

most favored nation 121

multinational corporation 109

multinational organization 109

North American Free Trade Agreement (NAFTA) 120

outsourcing 113

parochialism 111

polycentric managers 111

polychronic time 128

strategic alliance 116

tariff 118

trade protectionism 117

trading bloc 119

wholly-owned subsidiary 116

World Bank 119

World Trade Organization (WTO) 119

Summary

4.1 Globalization: The Collapse of Time & Distance

Globalization is the trend of the world economy toward becoming more interdependent. Globalization is reflected in three developments: (1) the rise of the global village and e-commerce; (2) the trend of the world's becoming one big market; and (3) the rise of both megafirms and Internet-enabled minifirms.

The rise of the "global village" refers to the "shrinking" of time and space as air travel and the electronic media have made global communication easier. The Internet and the Web have led to e-commerce, the buying and selling of products through computer networks.

The global economy is the increasing tendency of the economies of nations to interact with one another as one market.

The rise of cross-border business has led to megamergers, as giant firms have joined forces, and of minifirms, small companies in which managers can use the Internet and other technologies to get enterprises started more easily and to maneuver faster.

4.2 You & International Management

Studying international management prepares you to work with foreign customers or partners, with foreign suppliers, for a foreign firm in the United States, or for a U.S. firm overseas. International management is management that oversees the conduct of operations in or with organizations in foreign countries.

The successful international manager is not ethnocentric or polycentric but geocentric. Ethnocentric managers believe that their native country, culture, language, and behavior are superior to all others. Polycentric managers take the view that native managers in the foreign offices best understand native personnel and practices. Geocentric managers accept that there are differences and similarities between home and foreign personnel and practices, and they should use whatever techniques are most effective.

4.3 Why & How Companies Expand Internationally

Companies expand internationally for at least five reasons. They seek (1) cheaper or more plentiful supplies, (2) new markets, (3) lower labor costs, (4) access to finance capital, and (5) avoidance of tariffs on imported goods or import quotas.

There are five ways in which companies expand internationally. (1) They engage in global outsourcing, using suppliers outside the company and the United States to provide goods and services. (2) They engage in importing, exporting, and countertrading (bartering for goods). (3) They engage in licensing (allow a foreign company to pay a fee to make or distribute the company's product) and franchising (allow a foreign company to pay a fee and a share of the profit in return for using the first company's brand name). (4) They engage in joint ventures, a strategic alliance to share the risks and rewards of starting a new enterprise together in a foreign country. (5) They become wholly-owned subsidiaries, or foreign subsidiaries that are totally owned and controlled by an organization.

4.4 The World of Free Trade: Regional Economic Cooperation

Free trade is the movement of goods and services among nations without political or economic obstructions.

Countries often use trade protectionism—the use of government regulations to limit the import of goods and services—to protect their domestic industries against foreign competition. Three barriers to free trade are tariffs, import quotas, and embargoes. (1) A tariff is a trade barrier in the form of a customs duty, or tax, levied mainly on imports. (2) An import quota is a trade barrier in the form of a limit on the numbers of a product that can be imported. (3) An embargo is a complete ban on the import or export of certain products.

Three principal organizations exist that are designed to facilitate international trade. (1) The World Trade Organization is designed to monitor and enforce trade agreements. (2) The World Bank is designed to provide low-interest loans to developing nations for improving transportation,

education, health, and telecommunications. (3) The International Monetary Fund is designed to assist in smoothing the flow of money between nations.

A trading bloc is a group of nations within a geographical region that have agreed to remove trade barriers. There are six major trading blocs: (1) North American Free Trade Agreement (NAFTA; U.S., Canada, and Mexico); (2) European Union (EU; 27 trading partners in Europe); (3) the Association of Southeast Asian Nations (ASEAN; 11 countries in Asia); (4) Asia-Pacific Economic Cooperation (APEC; 21 Pacific Rim countries); (5) Mercosur (Argentina, Brazil, Paraguay, and Uruguay; and (6) the Central America Free Trade Agreement (CAFTA-DR; the United States, five Central American Countries, and the Dominican Republic).

Besides joining together in trade blocs, countries also extend special, "most favored nation" trading privileges—that is, grant other countries favorable trading treatment such as the reduction of import duties.

4.5 The Importance of Understanding Cultural Differences

Misunderstandings and miscommunications often arise because one person doesn't understand the expectations of a person from another culture. In low-context cultures, shared meanings are primarily derived from written and spoken words. In high-context cultures, people rely heavily on situational cues for meaning when communicating with others.

Geert Hofstede proposed the Hofstede model of four cultural dimensions, which identified four dimensions along which national cultures can be placed: (1) individualism/collectivism, (2) power distance, (3) uncertainty avoidance, and (4) masculinity/femininity.

Robert House and others created the GLOBE (for Global Leadership and Organizational Behavior Effectiveness) Project, a massive and ongoing cross-cultural investigation of nine cultural dimensions involved in leadership and organizational processes: (1) power distance, (2) uncertainty avoidance, (3) institutional collectivism, (4) in-group collectivism,

(5) gender egalitarianism, (6) assertiveness, (7) future orientation, (8) performance orientation, and (9) humane orientation.

A nation's culture is the shared set of beliefs, values, knowledge, and patterns of behavior common to a group of people. Visitors to another culture may experience culture shock—feelings of discomfort and disorientation. Managers trying to understand other cultures need to understand four basic cultural perceptions embodied in (1) language, (2) interpersonal space, (3) time orientation, and (4) religion.

Regarding language, when you are trying to communicate across cultures you have three options: Speak your own language (if others can understand you), use a translator, or learn the local language.

Interpersonal space involves how close or far away one should be when communicating with another person, with Americans being comfortable at 3–4 feet but people in other countries often wanting to be closer.

Time orientation of a culture may be either monochronic (preference for doing one thing at a time) or polychronic (preference for doing more than one thing at a time).

Managers need to consider the effect of religious differences. In order of size (number of followers), the major world religions are Christianity, Islam, Hinduism, Chinese traditional religion, Buddhism, and Judaism.

Management in Action

Avoiding Cultural Blunders Abroad

Most small companies seeking to tap overseas markets know they'll have to navigate foreign laws, taxes, and regulations. But they also need to figure out how to avoid cultural blunders.

Tom Bonkenburg, director of European operations for St. Onge Company Inc., a small supply-chain consulting firm in York, Pennsylvania, headed to Moscow in 2008 to develop a partnership with a large firm there.

But when he met the company's Russian branch director, "I gave my best smile, handshake, and friendly joke . . . only to be met with a dreary and unhappy look," says Mr. Bonkenburg.

Later, however, Mr. Bonkenburg received an e-mail from the Russian, thanking him for a great meeting. Mr. Bonkenburg later learned that Russian culture fosters smiling in private settings and seriousness in business settings.

"He was working as hard to impress me as I was to impress him," Mr. Bonkenburg says. . . .

According to the U.S. Commercial Service, overseas expansion among small businesses has held steady despite the recession. . . .

For small companies looking to do business abroad, "the important thing to remember is that you don't know what you don't know," says Kari Heistad, CEO of Culture Coach International Inc., a Newton, Massachusetts firm that advises clients on cross-cultural issues. Even subtle cultural insensitivities can have a profound impact, she says.

In the spring of 2009, Dakar Sushi owner George Ajjan wrote to a Senegalese government official—using the French language but in an American English tone—to request a business license for the restaurant. "I'm direct and I shoot to kill," Mr. Ajjan says of his usual correspondence.

To proofread his French grammar, Mr. Ajjan gave the letter to a Senegal native, who noticed the tone was too jarring. If not rewritten in a more deferential voice, the request would most likely get denied, his friend explained. "It wasn't just about translating, but about adapting phrasing to make sure you are in line with what people expect," says Mr. Ajjan.

Similarly, after Ron Gonen expanded his New York–based company, RecycleBank, into England last year, he encountered an unexpected language barrier. The company, which sets up rewards programs for individuals based on the amount they recycle, was offended when the press called the program a "scheme." . . .

Because the press coverage was otherwise positive, Mr. Gonen soon pinpointed the miscommunication: the word *scheme* holds no connotation of deceit in Britain, as it does in America.

For those businesses that commit a cultural blunder, fixing the situation can be costly. The price tag hit seven figures at Toronto-based AlertDriving, a firm that provides online driving training courses to companies with vehicle fleets.

Between 2005 and 2007 AlertDriving, incorporated as Sonic e-Learning Inc., expanded into more than 20 countries before realizing that the product had cultural flaws. The dialogue in the lessons had been poorly translated, and the driving instruction failed to address geographic nuances. For example, AlertDriving teaches that the center lane is the safest on a multilane highway, but that is untrue in Dubai, where the center lane is used exclusively for passing.

According to Gerry Martin, AlertDriving's chief executive, it took years to realize that the foreign clients were unsatisfied because "in some cultures, like Japan, criticism is considered disrespectful." Once the company got the negative feedback, it "had to redo what already was in the market," says Matthew Latreille, AlertDriving's director of global content development.

The company spent about $1 million revamping its existing product line, honing language dialects and local driving habits.

"Now we are 100% localized because we are immersed in the culture," Mr. Latreille says.

For Discussion

1. Which of the recommendations listed in the Manager's Toolbox were used by Toronto-based AlertDriving? Explain.

2. Based on material contained in this chapter, why do you believe small businesses are trying to expand into international markets? Discuss.

3. To what extent did Tom Bonkenburg, George Ajjan, and Ron Gonen follow an ethnocentric, a polycentric, or a geocentric approach? Provide examples to support your conclusions.

4. What differences in cultural variations were ignored by Tom Bonkenburg, George Ajjan, Ron Gonen, and Gerry Martin? Explain.

5. What are the most important lessons to be learned about global management from this case? Discuss.

Source: Excerpted from Emily Maltby, "Expanding Abroad? Avoid Cultural Gaffes," *The Wall Street Journal,* January 19, 2010, p. B5. Copyright © 2010 by Dow Jones & Company, Inc. Reproduced with permission of Dow Jones & Company, Inc, via Copyright Clearance Center.

Self-Assessment

How Well Are You Suited to Becoming a Global Manager?

Objectives

1. To see if you are ready to be a global manager.

2. To help you assess your comfort level with other cultures.

Introduction

As our business world becomes increasingly globalized, U.S. companies need more managers to work in other countries. This usually means vast adjustments for the manager and her or his family during this job assignment. Flexibility is critical as is the ability to adjust to new ways, new people, new foods, different nonverbal communication, a new language, and a host of other new things.

Before agreeing to such an assignment, you need to know more about yourself and how you function in such situations.

Instructions

Are you prepared to be a global manager? Rate the extent to which you agree with each of the following 14 items by circling your response on the rating scale shown below. If you do not have direct experience with a particular situation (for example, working with people from other cultures), respond by circling how you *think* you would feel.

1 = Very strongly disagree
2 = Strongly disagree
3 = Disagree
4 = Neither agree nor disagree
5 = Agree
6 = Strongly agree
7 = Very strongly agree

1. When working with people from other cultures, I work hard to understand their perspectives.	1	2	3	4	5	6	7
2. I have a solid understanding of my organization's products and services.	1	2	3	4	5	6	7
3. I am willing to take a stand on issues.	1	2	3	4	5	6	7
4. I have a special talent for dealing with people.	1	2	3	4	5	6	7
5. I can be depended on to tell the truth regardless of circumstances.	1	2	3	4	5	6	7
6. I am good at identifying the most important part of a complex problem or issue.	1	2	3	4	5	6	7
7. I clearly demonstrate commitment to seeing the organization succeed.	1	2	3	4	5	6	7
8. I take personal as well as business risks.	1	2	3	4	5	6	7
9. I have changed as a result of feedback from others.	1	2	3	4	5	6	7
10. I enjoy the challenge of working in countries other than my own.	1	2	3	4	5	6	7
11. I take advantage of opportunities to do new things.	1	2	3	4	5	6	7
12. I find criticism hard to take.	1	2	3	4	5	6	7
13. I seek feedback even when others are reluctant to give it.	1	2	3	4	5	6	7
14. I don't get so invested in things that I cannot change when something doesn't work.	1	2	3	4	5	6	7

Interpretation

This exercise assesses factors associated with being a successful global manager. These factors include general intelligence, business knowledge, interpersonal skills, commitment, courage, cross-cultural competencies, and the ability to learn from experience.

Total your scores, which will fall between 14 and 98. The higher your score, the greater your potential for success as an international manager.

Arbitrary Norms

High Potential for Success	70–98
Moderate Potential for Success	40–69
Low Potential for Success	39 and below

Questions for Discussion

1. What do the results suggest about your preparedness to be a global manager? Do you agree with these results?

2. How comfortable would you be going to another country at this time in your life?

3. How have your experiences as a citizen of a very diverse nation helped you to understand the other cultures of the world?

4. How might you improve your preparedness to one day assume an international position? Explain.

Sources: Modified and adapted from G. M. Spreitzer, M. W. McCall Jr., and J. D. Mahoney, "Early Identification of International Executive Potential," *Journal of Applied Psychology*, February 1997, pp. 6–29.

Chiquita Brands International Discloses Payments to Colombian Terrorists

Assume that you are on a grand jury in the United States and you are debating whether to file charges against Roderick Hills, former head of Chiquita Brands International Inc.'s audit committee and former chairman of the Securities and Exchange Commission.

The case involves payments that the company made to a violent Colombian group that has been determined by the U.S. government to be a terrorist group. Mr. Hills was in charge of the company's audit committee during the time of the payments. The facts of the case indicate that "a paramilitary organization had threatened to kidnap or kill employees on the banana farms of Chiquita's Colombian subsidiary, Banadex, and Chiquita was concerned that its employees could be harmed if it cut the payments immediately." Mr. Hills and other executives viewed the expense payments as "security payments" that were saving employees' lives. "Lawyers familiar with the case say Mr. Hills and Mr. Olson [former general counsel] believe senior Justice Department officials understood this and were deferring any demand to stop the payments to the United Self-Defense Forces, known by its Spanish abbreviation AUC. Chiquita ultimately paid $1.7 million over seven years." Chiquita never hid the payments from its accountants or Ernst & Young, its auditor.

Solving the Dilemma

What would you do given the current situation?

1. Charge Mr. Hills. He knew that it was against U.S. policy to have dealings with terrorist organizations.

2. Fine the company $25 million. The company should have folded its operations in Colombia rather than make payments to a terrorist organization.

3. Don't charge Mr. Hills. He was trying to protect his employees' lives and he fully disclosed the company's actions to U.S. authorities.

4. Invent other options.

Source: Based on L. P. Cohen, "Chiquita Under the Gun," *The Wall Street Journal*, August 2, 2007, pp. A1, A9.

(chapter 5)

Planning
The Foundation of Successful Management

Major Questions You Should Be Able to Answer

5.1 Planning & Uncertainty
Major Question: How do I tend to deal with uncertainty, and how can planning help?

5.2 Fundamentals of Planning
Major Question: What are mission and vision statements, and what are three types of planning and goals?

5.3 Promoting Goal Setting: Management by Objectives
Major Question: What is MBO and how can it be implemented?

5.4 The Planning/Control Cycle
Major Question: How does the planning/control cycle help keep a manager's plans headed in the right direction?

Planning Different Career Paths: "It's a Career, Not a Job"

The purpose of planning is to help deal with uncertainty, both for the organization and for your individual career. In this chapter, we discuss planning from an organizational point of view, but of course you also need to do personal planning for a career. Today, experts say, success requires coupling an in-demand degree with expertise in emerging trends, such as mastery of social media.[1]

Do you have a sense of where you're going? No doubt what you're looking for is something about which you can say, "It's not just a job, it's a career." Your *career path* is the sequence of jobs and occupations you follow during your career.

Michael J. Driver has suggested there are different possible career paths, among them the *linear career,* the *steady-state career,* and the *spiral career.*[2]

- **The linear career: climbing the stairs.** The *linear career* resembles the traditional view of climbing the stairs in an organization's hierarchy. That is, you move up the organization in a series of jobs—generally in just one functional area, such as finance—each of which entails more responsibility and requires more skills.

  Of course, it's possible that a linear career will *plateau.* That is, you'll rise to a certain level and then remain there; there will be no further promotions. Career plateaus actually happen a lot and need not signify disgrace; they happen even to very successful managers.

  Another possibility, of course, is the *declining career,* in which a person reaches a certain level and then after a time begins descending back to the lower levels. This could come about, for instance, because technology changes the industry you're in.

- **The steady-state career: staying put.** The *steady-state career* is almost the opposite of a linear career: You discover early in life that you're comfortable with a certain occupation and you stay with it. Or you accept a promotion for a while, decide you don't like the responsibility, and take a step down.

  This kind of career is actually fairly commonplace: Sales representatives, computer programmers, or physicians, for example, may decide they are happy being "hands-on" professionals rather than managers.

- **The spiral career: holding different jobs that build on one another.** The *spiral career* is, like the linear career, upwardly mobile. However, on this career path, you would have a number of jobs that are fundamentally different yet still build on one another, giving you more general experience and the skills to advance in rank and status.

  Of course, it's possible that you might (like some salespeople, actors, chefs, or construction workers) favor a variant called the *transitory career.* That is, you're the kind of person who doesn't want the responsibility that comes with promotion. You're a free spirit who likes the variety of experience that comes with continually shifting sideways from job to job or place to place (or you're afraid of making the commitment to doing any one thing).

  A variant is what is known as "portfolio careers" or "slash careers," in which a person puts together a portfolio of careers comprising multiple part-time jobs that, when combined, are equivalent to a full-time position, such as Pilates instructor/art dealer, attorney/minister, teacher/dancer/puppeteer.[3] And then, of course, there are those who change their professions entirely, perhaps by switching departments within their companies or by going back to school and retraining for something else.[4]

For Discussion What kind of career path do you think you're apt to follow? How are you planning for it?

---

forecast | **What's Ahead in This Chapter**

In this chapter, we describe planning, the first of the four management functions. We consider the benefits of planning and how it helps you deal with uncertainty. We deal with the fundamentals of planning, including the mission and vision statements and the three types of planning—strategic, tactical, and operational. We consider goals and action plans, management by objectives (MBO), SMART goals, and the planning/control cycle.

major question? How do I tend to deal with uncertainty, and how can planning help?

THE BIG PICTURE

Planning, the first of four functions in the management process, involves setting goals and deciding how to achieve them. Planning helps you check your progress, coordinate activities, think ahead, and cope with uncertainty. Uncertainty is of three types—state, effect, and response. Organizations respond to uncertainty in various ways.

What is known as the *management process,* you'll recall (from Chapter 1, p. 14), involves the four management functions of *planning, organizing, leading,* and *controlling,* which form four of the part divisions of this book. In this and the next two chapters we discuss *planning,* **which we previously defined as setting goals and deciding how to achieve them.** Another definition: ***Planning* is coping with uncertainty by formulating future courses of action to achieve specified results.**[5] When you make a plan, you make a blueprint for action that describes what you need to do to realize your goals.

Planning & Strategic Management

Planning, which we discuss in this chapter, is used in conjunction with strategic management, as we describe in Chapter 6. As we will see, strategic management is a process that involves managers from all parts of the organization—top managers, middle managers, and first-line managers—in the formulation, implementation, and execution of strategies and strategic goals to advance the purposes of the organization. Thus, planning covers not only strategic planning (done by top managers) but also tactical planning (done by middle managers) and operational planning (done by first-line managers). Planning and strategic management derive from an organization's mission and vision about itself, as we describe in the next few pages. *(See Figure 5.1.)*

figure 5.I

PLANNING AND STRATEGIC MANAGEMENT
The details of planning and strategic management are explained in Chapters 5 and 6.

Why Not Plan?

On the face of it, planning would seem to be a good idea—otherwise we would not be devoting three chapters to the subject. But there are two cautions to be aware of:

1. Planning Requires You to Set Aside the Time to Do It   Time-starved managers may be quite resentful when superiors order them to prepare a 5-year plan for their work unit.

"What?" they may grouse. "They expect me to do that and *still* find time to meet this year's goals?" Somehow, though, that time for planning must be found. Otherwise, managers are mainly just reacting to events.

Planning means that you must involve the subordinates you manage to determine resources, opportunities, and goals. During the process, you may need to go outside the work unit for information about products, competitors, markets, and the like.

2. You May Have to Make Some Decisions without a Lot of Time to Plan   In our time of Internet connections and speedy-access computer databases, can't nearly anyone lay hands on facts quickly to make an intelligent decision? Not always. A competitor may quickly enter your market with a highly desirable product. A change in buying habits may occur. A consumer boycott may suddenly surface. An important supplier may let you down. The caliber of employees you need may not be immediately available at the salary level you're willing to pay. And in any one of these you won't have the time to plan a decision based on all the facts.

Nevertheless, a plan need not be perfect to be executable. While you shouldn't shoot from the hip in making decisions, often you may have to "go with what you've got" and make a decision based on a plan that is perhaps only three-quarters complete.

How Planning Helps You: Four Benefits

You can always hope you'll luck out or muddle through the next time a hurricane, earthquake, tornado, or other natural disaster strikes your area. Or you can plan for it by stocking up on flashlight batteries and canned food. Which is better? The same consideration applies when you're a manager. Some day, after you've dealt with some crisis, you will be very happy that you had a plan for handling it. The benefits of planning are fourfold:

1. Planning Helps You Check on Your Progress   The preprinted score card that golfers use when playing 18 holes of golf isn't blank. For each hole, the card lists the standard number of strokes ("par"), such as three or five, that a good player should take to hit the ball from the tee to the cup. The score card is the plan for the game, with objectives for each hole. After you play the hole, you write your own score in a blank space. At the end of the 18 holes, you add all your scores to see how you performed compared with the standard for the course.

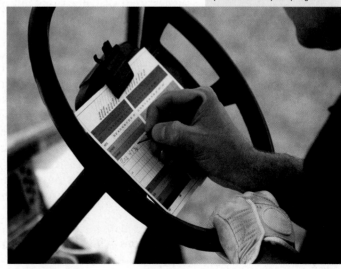

What's the score? Like a golf score card, planning helps you check on your progress.

How well is your work going in an organization? You won't know unless you have some way of checking your progress. That's why, like a golfer, you need to have some expectations of what you're supposed to do—in other words, a plan.

2. Planning Helps You Coordinate Activities   "The right hand doesn't know what the left hand is doing!"

We may hear that expression used, for example, when a crisis occurs and an organization's public relations department, legal department, and CEO's office all give the press separate, contradictory statements. Obviously, such an embarrassment can be avoided if the organization has a plan for dealing with the media during emergencies. A plan defines the responsibilities of various departments and coordinates their activities for the achievement of common goals—such as, at minimum, making an organization not look confused and disorganized.

3. Planning Helps You Think Ahead   Alan R. Mulally, CEO of Ford Motor Company, has big plans to restore Ford to its position as a leader in the global auto industry. Those plans are embodied in the Ford Focus, described as "Ford's first truly global car—a single vehicle designed and engineered for customers in every region of the world and sold under one name."[6] The small, fuel-efficient car is loaded with technology and safety features that Mulally thinks will appeal to consumers in Europe, Asia, and the Americas. His management principles, instilled in the slogan "One Ford . . . One Team . . . One Plan . . . One Goal," have already been demonstrated, first, in Ford's shift away from trucks and sport utility vehicles to cars and, second, in dumping luxury brands (Land Rover, Jaguar, Aston-Martin) that were distracting management.

Similarly, the service or product with which you're engaged will probably at some point reach maturity, and sales will begin to falter. Thus, you need to look ahead, beyond your present phase of work, to try to be sure you'll be one of the quick rather than one of the dead.

4. Above All, Planning Helps You Cope with Uncertainty   You don't care for unpleasant surprises? Most people don't. (Pleasant surprises, of course, are invariably welcome.) That's why trying to plan for unpleasant contingencies is necessary (as we'll describe in Chapter 6). Planning helps you deal with uncertainty.

How Organizations Respond to Uncertainty

How do you personally respond to uncertainty? Do you react slowly? conservatively? proactively? Do you watch to see what others do? Organizations act in similar ways.

Four Basic Strategy Types   Scholars **Raymond E. Miles** and **Charles C. Snow** suggest that organizations adopt one of four approaches when responding to uncertainty in their environment. They become *Defenders, Prospectors, Analyzers,* or *Reactors.*[7]

Defenders—"Let's Stick with What We Do Best, Avoid Other Involvements" Whenever you hear an organization's leader say that "We're sticking with the basics" or "We're getting back to our core business," that's the hallmark of a Defender organization. **Defenders are expert at producing and selling narrowly defined products or services.** Often they are old-line successful enterprises, such as Macy's and JCPenney, which in the 2010 era of consumer frugality found themselves losing customers to discounters like Walmart.[8] They do not tend to seek opportunities outside their present markets. They devote most of their attention to making refinements in their existing operations, such as slashing prices.

Prospectors—"Let's Create Our Own Opportunities, Not Wait for Them to Happen" A company described as "aggressive" is often a Prospector organization.

Prospectors **focus on developing new products or services and in seeking out new markets, rather than waiting for things to happen.** Like 19th-century gold miners, these companies are "prospecting" for new ways of doing things. The continual product and market innovation has a price: Such companies may suffer a loss of efficiency. Nevertheless, their focus on change can put fear in the hearts of competitors. An example of a Prospector company is Gap, which announced it would look for new sales by expanding abroad.[9] Another such company is Apple.

Analyzers—"Let Others Take the Risks of Innovating, and We'll Imitate What Works Best" Analyzers take a "me too" response to the world. By and large, you won't find them called "trendsetters." Rather, *Analyzers* **let other organizations take the risks of product development and marketing and then imitate (or perhaps slightly improve on) what seems to work best.** For years, Microsoft has been accused of taking this approach.[10]

Red Bull. Austrian energy drink maker Red Bull, which was released into the United States in 1997, believes in making unorthodox marketing moves, such as creating a festival for homemade flying machines and building a half-pipe for Olympic snowboarder Shaun White. In 2010, the company opened a $220 million soccer stadium in Harrison, New Jersey, as home for its recently acquired Major League Soccer team, the New York Red Bulls. What strategy type is being followed here?

Reactors—"Let's Wait Until There's a Crisis, Then We'll React" Whereas the Prospector is aggressive and proactive, the Reactor is the opposite— passive and reactive. *Reactors* **make adjustments only when finally forced to by environmental pressures.** In the worst cases, they are so incapable of responding fast enough that they suffer massive sales losses and are even driven out of business. Kmart, for instance, failed to respond to Walmart's development of its distribution and inventory management competencies, resulting in stalled growth and a significant reduction in market share. Kmart's core business never recovered from this reactive strategy.[11] Now Sears, the shrinking retailer with which Kmart merged, is trying to reconfigure itself in an age of iPhone apps and Twitter.[12]

The Adaptive Cycle Miles and Snow also introduced the idea of the *adaptive cycle,* which portrays businesses as continuously cycling through decisions about three kinds of business problems: (1) *entrepreneurial* (selecting and making adjustments of products and markets), (2) *engineering* (producing and delivering the products), and (3) *administrative* (establishing roles, relationships, and organizational processes).

Thus, a business that makes decisions in the entrepreneurial area that take it in the direction of being a Prospector will in a short time also begin making Prospector-oriented decisions in the engineering area, then the administrative area, and then even more so in the entrepreneurial area, and so on. Thus, as one scholar points out, "With enough cycles and insight, a given business becomes a very good, comprehensively aligned Prospector, Analyzer, or Defender. If a business lacks insight, or if it fails to take advantage of alignment opportunities afforded by the adaptive cycle, it will be an incongruent, poorly performing Reactor."[13] ●

<table>
<tr><td>major
question</td><td>What are mission and vision statements, and what are
three types of planning and goals?</td></tr>
</table>

THE BIG PICTURE

Planning consists of translating an organization's mission into objectives. The organization's purpose is expressed as a mission statement, and what it becomes is expressed as a vision statement. From these are derived strategic planning, then tactical planning, then operational planning. The section also discusses SMART goals—goals that are Specific, Measurable, Attainable, Results-oriented, and have Target dates.

"Everyone wants a clear reason to get up in the morning," writes journalist Dick Leider. "As humans we hunger for meaning and purpose in our lives."[14]

And what is that purpose? "Life never lacks purpose," says Leider. "Purpose is innate—but it is up to each of us individually to discover or rediscover it."

An organization has a purpose, too—a mission. And managers must have an idea of where they want the organization to go—a vision. The approach to planning can be summarized in the following diagram, which shows how an organization's mission becomes translated into objectives. *(See Figure 5.2.)*

figure 5.2

MAKING PLANS

An organization's reason for being is expressed in a *mission statement*. What the organization wishes to become is expressed in a *vision statement*. From these are derived *strategic planning,* then *tactical planning,* and finally *operational planning.* The purpose of each kind of planning is to specify *goals* and *action plans* that ultimately pave the way toward achieving an organization's vision.

Mission & Vision Statements

The planning process begins with two attributes: a mission statement (which answers the question "What is our reason for being?") and a vision statement (which answers the question "What do we want to become?").

The Mission Statement—"What Is Our Reason for Being?" An organization's *mission* is its purpose or reason for being. Determining the mission is the responsibility of top management and the board of directors. It is up to them to formulate a *mission statement,* **which expresses the purpose of the organization.**

"Only a clear definition of the mission and purpose of the organization makes possible clear and realistic . . . objectives," said Peter Drucker.[15] Whether the organization is for-profit or nonprofit, the mission statement identifies the goods or services the organization provides and will provide. Sometimes it also gives the reasons for providing them (to make a profit or to achieve humanitarian goals, for example).

Example

Mission Statements for Three Different Companies: Marriott, Patagonia, & Etsy

Mission statements answer the question, "What is our reason for being?" or "Why are we here?"

Here are the mission statements for three companies, drawn from their Web sites. The mission statement for Marriott Hotels, a large company, reads: "Our commitment is that every guest leaves satisfied."

Clothing maker Patagonia's mission statement is to "Build the best product, cause no unnecessary harm, [and] use business to inspire and implement solutions to the environmental crisis."

Etsy, a Web site for promoting the wares of artisans and handicrafters, has as its mission statement: "To enable people to make a living making things, and to reconnect makers with buyers."

YOUR CALL

Do you think any of these mission statements could be adapted to different companies offering different products or services? Give an example.

The Vision Statement—"What Do We Want to Become?" A *vision* is a long-term goal describing *what* an organization wants to become. It is a clear sense of the future and the actions needed to get there. "[A] vision should describe what's happening to the world you compete in and what you want to do about it," says one *Fortune* article. "It should guide decisions."[16]

After formulating a mission statement, top managers need to develop a *vision statement,* **which expresses what the organization should become, where it wants to go strategically.**[17]

Example

Vision Statements for Three Different Companies: Marriott, Patagonia, & Etsy

Vision statements answer the question, "What do we want to become?" or "Where do we want to go?"

Here is Marriott Hotels' statement: "Our vision is to be the world's leading provider of hospitality services."

Patagonia's vision statement: "We prefer the human scale to the corporate, vagabonding to tourism, and the quirky to the toned-down and flattened out."

Etsy's statement: "Our vision is to build a new economy and present a better choice."

YOUR CALL

Do these vision statements work? Do they meet *Fortune*'s criterion of describing "what's happening in the world you compete in and what you want to do about it. It should guide decisions"?

Three Types of Planning for Three Levels of Management: Strategic, Tactical, & Operational

Inspiring, clearly stated mission statements and vision statements provide the focal point of the entire planning process. Then three things happen:

- *Strategic planning by top management.* Using their mission and vision statements, top managers do *strategic planning*—**they determine what the organization's long-term goals should be for the next 1–5 years with the resources they expect to have available.** "Strategic planning requires visionary and directional thinking," says one authority.[18] It should communicate not only general goals about growth and profits but also ways to achieve them.

- *Tactical planning by middle management.* The strategic priorities and policies are then passed down to middle managers, who must do *tactical planning*—**that is, they determine what contributions their departments or similar work units can make with their given resources during the next 6–24 months.**

- *Operational planning by first-line management.* Middle managers then pass these plans along to first-line managers to do *operational planning*—**that is, they determine how to accomplish specific tasks with available resources within the next 1–52 weeks.**

The kinds of managers are described further in the figure below. *(See Figure 5.3.)*

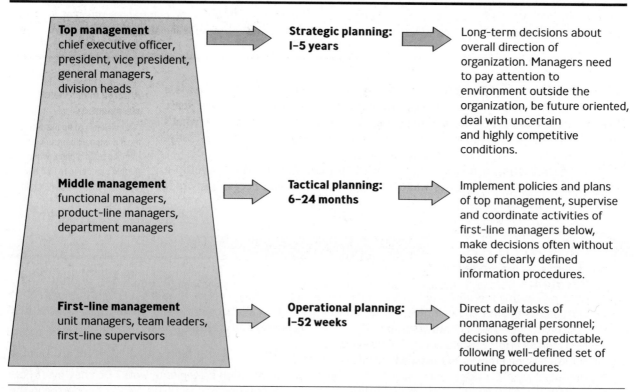

figure 5.3

THREE LEVELS OF MANAGEMENT, THREE TYPES OF PLANNING

Each type of planning has different time horizons, although the times overlap because the plans are somewhat elastic.

It is one thing to formulate a vision statement, however, and another to find concrete methods to manage and measure the performance that makes the vision a reality. One survey found that 73% of organizations said they had a clearly articulated strategic direction, but only 44% of them said they were able to communicate it well to the employees who must implement it.[19]

Goals & SMART Goals, Action Plans & Operating Plans

Whatever its type—strategic, tactical, or operational—the purpose of planning is to set a *goal* and then to formulate an *action plan.*

Goals   A *goal,* also known as an *objective,* is a specific commitment to achieve a measurable result within a stated period of time.

As with planning, goals are of the same three types—strategic, tactical, and operational. Also, like planning, goals are arranged in a hierarchy known as a *means-end chain* because in the chain of management (operational, tactical, strategic) the accomplishment of low-level goals is the means leading to the accomplishment of high-level goals or ends.

- *Strategic goals* are set by and for top management and focus on objectives for the organization as a whole.

- *Tactical goals* are set by and for middle managers and focus on the actions needed to achieve strategic goals.

- *Operational goals* are set by and for first-line managers and are concerned with short-term matters associated with realizing tactical goals.

SMART Goals   Anyone can define goals. But the five characteristics of a good goal are represented by the acronym SMART. A *SMART goal* is one that is *S*pecific, *M*easurable, *A*ttainable, *R*esults-oriented, and has *T*arget dates.

- *Specific:* Goals should be stated in *specific* rather than vague terms. The goal that "As many planes as possible should arrive on time" is too general. The goal that "Ninety percent of planes should arrive within 15 minutes of the scheduled arrival time" is specific.

- *Measurable:* Whenever possible, goals should be *measurable,* or quantifiable (as in "90% of planes should arrive within 15 minutes . . ."). That is, there should be some way to measure the degree to which a goal has been reached.

    Of course, some goals—such as those concerned with improving quality—are not precisely quantifiable. In that case, something on the order of "Improve the quality of customer relations by instituting 10 follow-up telephone calls every week" will do. You can certainly quantify how many follow-up phone calls were made.

- *Attainable:* Goals should be challenging, of course, but above all they should be realistic and *attainable.* It may be best to set goals that are quite ambitious so as to challenge people to meet high standards. Always, however, the goals should be achievable within the scope of the time, equipment, and financial support available. *(See Figure 5.4.)*

figure 5.4

RELATIONSHIP BETWEEN GOAL DIFFICULTY AND PERFORMANCE

Source: Adapted from E. A. Locke and G. P. Latham, *A Theory of Goal Setting and Task Performance* (Englewood Cliffs, NJ: Prentice Hall, 1990).

Performance
A Committed individuals with adequate ability
B Committed individuals who are working at capacity
C Individuals who lack commitment to high goals

If too easy (as in "half the flights should arrive on time"), goals won't impel people to make much effort. If impossible ("all flights must arrive on time, regardless of weather"), employees won't even bother trying. Or they will try and continually fail, which will end up hurting morale.

- *Results-oriented:* Only a few goals should be chosen—say, five for any work unit. And they should be *results-oriented*—they should support the organization's vision.

    In writing out the goals, start with the word "To" and follow it with action-oriented verbs—"complete," "acquire," "increase" ("to decrease by 10% the time to get passengers settled in their seats before departure").

    Some verbs should not be used in your goal statement because they imply activities—the tactics used to accomplish goals (such as having baggage handlers waiting). For example, you should not use "to develop," "to conduct," "to implement."

- *Target dates:* Goals should specify the *target dates* or deadline dates when they are to be attained. For example, it's unrealistic to expect an airline to improve its on-time arrivals by 10% overnight. However, you could set a target date—3 to 6 months away, say—by which this goal is to be achieved. That allows enough time for lower-level managers and employees to revamp their systems and work habits and gives them a clear time frame in which they know what they are expected to do.

The Action Plan & the Operating Plan The goal should be followed by an *action plan,* **which defines the course of action needed to achieve the stated goal,** such as a marketing plan or sales plan. **The *operating plan,* which is typically designed for a 1-year period, defines how you will conduct your business based on the action plan; it identifies clear targets such as revenues, cash flow, and market share.**

Strategic, Tactical, & Operational Goals: Southwest Airlines

Strategic Goals. The goal of top managers of Dallas-based Southwest Airlines is to ensure that the airline is highly profitable, following the general strategy of (a) keeping costs and fares down and (b) offering a superior on-time arrival record. One of the most important strategic decisions Southwest made was to fly just one type of airplane—Boeing 737s. (The fleet has 537 jets.) Thus, it is able to hold down training, maintenance, and operating expenses.[20]

Although the airline had a tough time financially in the 2008–2009 recession (as did its competitors), so far it is achieving its strategic goals: Indeed, by 2010, it had made money for 37 consecutive years. It has continually lowered its costs and is a constant industry leader in on-time performance.[21] (It was second in 2009, after Hawaiian Airlines.)[22]

Another strategic decision was to create a strong corporate culture that, according to one former CEO, allows people to "feel like they're using their brains, they're using their creativity, they're allowed to be themselves and have a sense of humor, and they understand what the mission of the company is."[23]

Tactical Goals. Cutting costs and keeping fares low is a key tactical goal for Southwest's middle managers. For example, the organization cut costs in its maintenance program by doing more work on a plane when it's in for a check instead of bringing it in three different times. In addition, it gets more use out of its planes every day by limiting the turnaround time between flights to 20 minutes, compared to up to an hour for other airlines.

Southwest also usually flies to less-congested airports, thus saving time and money by avoiding traffic. There is just one class of seating, doing away with the distinction between coach and first class. Even the boarding passes are reusable, being made of plastic. Finally, the airline saves by not feeding passengers: it serves mostly peanuts, no in-flight meals.

How do you make arrival times more reliable? To achieve this second tactical goal, middle managers did away with guaranteed seat reservations before ticketing, so that no-shows won't complicate (and therefore delay) the boarding process. (It changed that policy in 2007 to ensure that passengers paying extra for "business select" fares would be placed at the front of the line.)[24]

In addition, as mentioned, the airline is religious about turning planes around in exactly 20 minutes, so that on-time departures are more apt to produce on-time arrivals. Although the airline is about 83% unionized, turnaround is helped by looser work rules, so that workers can pitch in to do tasks outside their normal jobs. "If you saw something that needed to be done," said one former employee, "and you thought you could do it, you did."[25]

Operational Goals. Consider how Southwest's first-line managers can enhance productivity in the unloading, refueling, and cleaning of arriving planes. "One example [of productivity] customers mention all the time," said former chairman Herb Kelleher, "is if you look out the window when the airplane is taxiing toward the jetway, you see our ground crews charging before the airplane has even come to rest. Customers tell me that with other airlines nobody moves until the airplane has turned off its engines."[26]

First-line managers also make sure that seat assignments (boarding passes) are not given out until an hour before the plane is due to leave to make sure that the maximum number of passengers will be on hand to fill the seats available. Recently, Southwest has thrived on being the only U.S. airline that lets passengers check two pieces of luggage for free, a policy that also helps lines move more briskly.[27]

YOUR CALL

Ranking No. 12 on *Fortune's* 2010 Most Admired Companies list, Southwest has inspired a host of low-fare imitators—big ones like JetBlue and AirTran and small ones like Frontier, Spirit, Virgin America, and Allegiant—which have grown rapidly in the last 10 years compared to mainline carriers such as United, Delta, American, Continental, and US Airways.[28]

Although Southwest has stuck to its original keep-it-simple plan—no in-flight meals, first-come/first-served seating, and so on—in mid-2009 it started charging a $75 fee for flying dogs and cats in the passenger cabin, a $25 fee for children ages 5–11 traveling without an adult, and $25–$50 for a third checked bag.[29] Do you think these extra fees for extra services will affect the airline's strategic, tactical, and operational goals?

Types of Plans: Standing Plans & Single-Use Plans

Plans are of two types—*standing plans* and *single-use plans*. *(See Table 5.1.)*

table 5.1

STANDING PLANS AND SINGLE-USE PLANS

There are three types of standing plans and two types of single-use plans.

Plan	Description
Standing plan	For activities that occur repeatedly over a period of time
• Policy	Outlines general response to a designated problem or situation
• Procedure	Outlines response to particular problems or circumstances
• Rule	Designates specific required action
Single-use plan	For activities not likely to be repeated in the future
• Program	Encompasses a range of projects or activities
• Project	Has less scope and complexity than a program

Standing Plans: Policies, Procedures, & Rules *Standing plans* **are plans developed for activities that occur repeatedly over a period of time.** Standing plans consist of policies, procedures, and rules.

- **A** *policy* **is a standing plan that outlines the general response to a designated problem or situation.** Example: "This workplace does not condone swearing." This policy is a broad statement that gives managers a general idea about what is allowable for employees who use bad language, but gives no specifics.

- **A** *procedure* **(or** *standard operating procedure***) is a standing plan that outlines the response to particular problems or circumstances.** Example: White Castle specifies exactly how a hamburger should be dressed, including the order in which the mustard, ketchup, and pickles are applied.

- **A** *rule* **is a standing plan that designates specific required action.** Example: "No smoking is allowed anywhere in the building." This allows no room for interpretation.

Single-Use Plans: Programs & Projects *Single-use plans* **are plans developed for activities that are not likely to be repeated in the future.** Such plans can be programs or projects.

- **A** *program* **is a single-use plan encompassing a range of projects or activities.** Example: The U.S. government space *program* (which was to be closed by the end of 2010) had several projects, including the *Challenger* project and the Hubble Telescope project.

- **A** *project* **is a single-use plan of less scope and complexity than a program.** Example: The space shuttle *Discovery* was one project in the government's space program. ●

THE BIG PICTURE

A technique for setting goals, management by objectives (MBO) is a four-step process for motivating employees.

Do you perform better when you set goals or when you don't? What about when you set difficult goals rather than easy ones?

Research shows that if goals are made more difficult ("Increase study time 30%"), people may achieve them less often than they would easy goals ("Increase study time 5%"), but they nevertheless perform at a higher level. People also do better when the objectives are specific ("Increase study time 10 hours a week") rather than general ("Do more studying this semester").[30]

These are the kinds of matters addressed in the activity known as *management by objectives.* First suggested by **Peter Drucker** in 1954, MBO has spread largely because of the appeal of its emphasis on converting general objectives into specific ones for all members of an organization.[31]

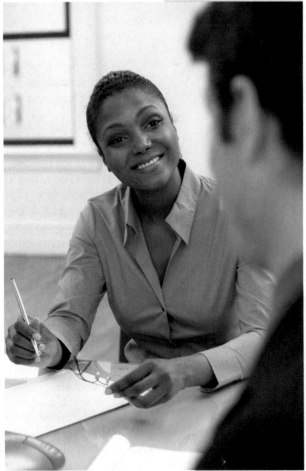

Jointly setting objectives. An important part of MBO is joint manager/subordinate participation in setting objectives. Have you ever held a job that featured this kind of process?

What Is MBO? The Four-Step Process for Motivating Employees

Management by objectives (MBO) **is a four-step process in which (1) managers and employees jointly set objectives for the employee, (2) managers develop action plans, (3) managers and employees periodically review the employee's performance, and (4) the manager makes a performance appraisal and rewards the employee according to results.** The purpose of MBO is to *motivate* rather than control subordinates. Let's consider the four steps.

I. Jointly Set Objectives   You sit down with your manager and the two of you jointly set objectives for you to attain. Later you do the same with each of your own subordinates. Joint manager/subordinate participation is important to the program. It's probably best if the objectives aren't simply imposed from above ("Here are the objectives I want you to meet"). Managers also should not simply approve the employee's objectives ("Whatever you aim for is okay with me"). It's necessary to have back-and-forth negotiation to make the objectives practicable.

One result of joint participation, research shows, is that it impels people to set more difficult goals—to raise the level of their aspirations—which may have a positive effect on their performance.[32] The objectives should be expressed in writing and should be SMART. There are three types of objectives, shown below. *(See Table 5.2.)*

table 5.2

THREE TYPES OF OBJECTIVES USED IN MBO

Improvement Objectives
Purpose Express performance to be accomplished in a specific way for a specific area **Examples** "Increase sport-utility sales by 10%." "Reduce food spoilage by 15%."
Personal Development Objectives
Purpose Express personal goals to be realized **Examples** "Attend 5 days of leadership training." "Learn basics of Microsoft Office software by June I."
Maintenance Objectives
Purpose Express the intention to maintain performance at previously established levels **Examples** "Continue to meet the increased sales goals specified last quarter." "Produce another 60,000 cases of wine this month."

2. Develop Action Plan Once objectives are set, managers at each level should prepare an action plan for attaining them. Action plans may be prepared for both individuals and for work units, such as departments.

3. Periodically Review Performance You and your manager should meet reasonably often—either informally as needed or formally every 3 months—to review progress, as should you and your subordinates. Indeed, frequent communication is necessary so that everyone will know how well he or she is doing in meeting the objectives.

During each meeting, managers should give employees feedback, and objectives should be updated or revised as necessary to reflect new realities. If you were managing a painting or landscaping business, for example, changes in the weather, loss of key employees, or a financial downturn affecting customer spending could force you to reconsider your objectives.

4. Give Performance Appraisal & Rewards, If Any At the end of 6 or 12 months, you and your subordinate should meet to discuss results, comparing performance with initial objectives. *Deal with results,* not personalities, emotional issues, or excuses.

Because the purpose of MBO is to *motivate* employees, performance that meets the objectives should be rewarded—with compliments, raises, bonuses, promotions, or other suitable benefits. Failure can be addressed by redefining the objectives for the next 6- or 12-month period, or even by taking stronger measures, such as demotion. Basically, however, MBO is viewed as being a learning process. After step 4, the MBO cycle begins anew.[33]

Cascading Objectives: MBO from the Top Down

For MBO to be successful, three things have to happen:

I. Top Management Must Be Committed "When top-management commitment [to MBO] was high," said one review, "the average gain in productivity was 56%. When commitment was low, the average gain in productivity was only 6%."[34]

2. It Must Be Applied Organizationwide The program has to be put in place throughout the entire organization. That is, it cannot be applied in just some divisions and departments; it has to be done in all of them.

3. Objectives Must "Cascade" MBO works by *cascading* objectives down **through the organization; that is, objectives are structured in a *unified hierarchy*, becoming more specific at lower levels of the organization.** Top managers set general *organizational* objectives, which are translated into *divisional* objectives, which are translated into *departmental* objectives. The hierarchy ends in *individual* objectives set by each employee.

Example

Setting Objectives: Walmart's CEO Lays Out an Agenda for Change

Tired of criticism of Walmart's business practices, in a 2008 speech, its former CEO H. Lee Scott Jr. laid out new environmental, health, and ethical goals.[35] Besides continuing to promote energy-saving products at low prices in its stores, such as fluorescent lightbulbs, Scott said the company would focus on additional products that use a large amount of energy, like air conditioners, microwave ovens, and televisions, working with suppliers to make such products 25% more energy efficient within 3 years.

On health care, Scott said Walmart would apply its legendary cost-cutting skills to helping other companies deliver health care for their employees. By working with major American employers to help them manage and pay prescription drug claims (an expensive task now handled by companies called pharmacy benefit managers), Walmart hoped to save companies $100 million in that year alone.

Scott also said Walmart was committed to creating a more socially and environmentally conscious network of suppliers around the world, pressing suppliers in China, for instance, to comply with that country's environmental regulations. He also urged other major retailers to join a global network of retailers and consumer goods companies that is developing socially conscious manufacturing standards. Later Walmart

Environmental objective: Walmart aims at saving energy by selling fluorescent light bulbs.

joined with the Environmental Defense Fund to eliminate 20 million tons of carbon emissions from its global supply chain by 2015.[36]

YOUR CALL

How do the objectives outlined by CEO Scott reflect the criteria for SMART goals?

The Importance of Deadlines

There's no question that college is a pressure cooker for many students. The reason, of course, is the seemingly never-ending deadlines. But consider: Would you do all the course work you're doing—and realize the education you're getting—if you *didn't* have deadlines?

As we saw under the "T" (for "has Target dates") in SMART goals, deadlines are as essential to goal setting in business as they are to your college career. Because the whole purpose of planning and goals is to deliver to a client specified results within a specified period of time, deadlines become a great motivator, both for you and for the people working for you.

It's possible, of course, to let deadlines mislead you into focusing too much on immediate results and thereby ignore overall planning—just as students will focus too much on preparing for a test in one course while neglecting others. In general, however, deadlines can help you keep your eye on the "big picture" while simultaneously paying attention to the details that will help you realize the big picture. Deadlines can help concentrate the mind, so that you make quick decisions rather than put them off.

Deadlines help you ignore extraneous matters (such as cleaning up a messy desk) in favor of focusing on what's important—realizing the goals on time and on budget. Deadlines provide a mechanism for giving ourselves feedback. ●

Practical Action

How to Achieve Your Important Goals: Don't Keep Every Option Open

We've all been told that "It's important to keep your options open." But should we?

"You don't even know how a camera's burst-mode flash works, but you persuade yourself to pay for the extra feature just in case," writes a journalist about this phenomenon. "You no longer have anything in common with someone who keeps calling you, but you hate to just zap the relationship. Your child is exhausted from after-school soccer, ballet, and Chinese lessons, but you won't let her drop the piano lessons. They could come in handy."[37]

The natural reluctance to close any door is pointed out by Dan Ariely, a behavioral economist at Duke University and author of *Predictably Irrational: The Hidden Forces That Shape Our Decisions*.[38] In that book, he describes experiments involving hundreds of MIT students who showed that they could not bear to let go of their options—even though it was bad strategy. The experiments involved playing a computer game in which students had 100 mouse clicks to look for money behind three doors on the screen and were paid real cash each time they found it. To earn the most money, a student would quickly find out that the best strategy was to check out the three doors

and settle on the one with the highest rewards. But when students stayed out of a room, the door would start shrinking and eventually disappear. Researchers found that most students would waste clicks by rushing back to reopen doors, even though they lost money by doing so—and they continued to frantically keep all their doors open even when they were fined for switching.

Were the students just trying to "keep their options open"? Ariely doesn't think so. The real motivation, he suggests, is fear of loss. "Closing a door on an option is experienced as a loss, and people are willing to pay a price to avoid the emotion of loss," he says.

Your Call

Obviously, this lesson has some practical payoffs for all of us who are overscheduled and overworked and need all the help we can get to stay focused on our important goals. Are you presently considering adding a class, switching majors, or pursuing another career? Are you wondering whether to continue a personal relationship that no longer benefits you? What would be the advantages of . . . just saying no?

5.4 THE PLANNING/CONTROL CYCLE

How does the planning/control cycle help keep a manager's plans headed in the right direction?

THE BIG PICTURE
The four-step planning/control cycle helps you keep in control, to make sure you're headed in the right direction.

Once you've made plans, how do you stay in control to make sure you're headed in the right direction? Actually, there is a continuous feedback loop known as the planning/control cycle. (The "organizing" and "leading" steps within the Planning-Organizing-Leading-Controlling sequence are implied here.) **The** *planning/control cycle* **has two planning steps (1 and 2) and two control steps (3 and 4), as follows: (1) Make the plan. (2) Carry out the plan. (3) Control the direction by comparing results with the plan. (4) Control the direction by taking corrective action in two ways—namely, (a) by correcting deviations in the plan being carried out, or (b) by improving future plans.** *(See Figure 5.5.)*

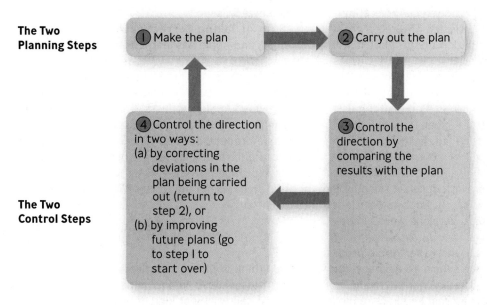

The Two Planning Steps

① Make the plan
② Carry out the plan

The Two Control Steps

④ Control the direction in two ways:
(a) by correcting deviations in the plan being carried out (return to step 2), or
(b) by improving future plans (go to step I to start over)

③ Control the direction by comparing the results with the plan

figure 5.5

THE PLANNING/CONTROL CYCLE

This describes a constant feedback loop designed to ensure plans stay headed in the right direction.

Source: From Robert Kreitner, *Management* 8th edition, Copyright © 2001 South-Western, a part of Cengage Learning, Inc. Reproduced with permission. www.cengage.com/permissions.

The planning/control cycle loop exists for each level of planning—strategic, tactical, and operational. The corrective action in step 4 of the cycle (a) can get a project back on track before it's too late or (b) if it's too late, can provide data for improving future plans. ●

The Planning/Control Cycle: Apple Keeps Its Products Secret to Generate Buzz[39]

Most electronics and computer makers talk about their products well in advance of releasing them in order to give big customers and users a chance to prepare for them. Not Apple Inc., maker of the iPhone, iPod Touch, and iPad and *Fortune*'s No. I Most Admired Company for the years 2008–2010. In 2008, it was also ranked No. I among *Fortune* 500 companies for total return to shareholders over the preceding 10 years.

Secrecy is a big part of the company's marketing strategy. (Even when founder and CEO Steve Jobs was operated on for cancer, it was kept secret.) And the planning/control cycle figures closely in how well it is accomplished.

Step I: The Plan. About 60% of all personal computers are bought by corporate customers and other big technology purchasers. Because of the hefty investment involved, these customers favor suppliers that let them see major product plans a year in advance. However, Steve Jobs has determined that he favors selling technology directly to consumers rather than to corporate buyers and chief technology officers.

By keeping a new product secret, Apple stimulates a great deal of public curiosity. "There's a great deal of mystery and speculation about what it will be," says one seasoned marketing executive. "That's created a marketing aura for them." Such was the plan, for example, when Apple and Hewlett-Packard made a deal to repackage Apple's iPod digital music player and sell it under the H-P label.

Step 2: Carrying Out the Plan. Following its plan to keep new products secret to generate marketing buzz, Apple often didn't tell H-P about new iPod models until the day before they were introduced to the public. It also insisted that H-P work on iPods under tight security, even though Apple's versions were already displayed on store shelves.

The same has been true with other Apple products, with employees being sworn to secrecy for years. When, for example, the company decided to open its own chain of retail stores, an exact replica of a 6,000-square-foot store was built entirely inside a sealed-off warehouse away from Apple's main Cupertino, California, headquarters. When Apple decided to switch to Intel microprocessors, engineers worked on the project for 5 years under hush-hush conditions to adapt the Macintosh operating system to Intel chips.

Step 3: Comparing Results. The use of mystery "helps Apple attract crowds at its retail stores and generally garner much more visibility than its relatively modest advertising budget would suggest," says a *Wall Street Journal* story. "While new wares from Dell Inc. or H-P rarely get front-page treatment, Mr. Jobs has repeatedly appeared on the covers of *Time, Newsweek,* and *Fortune* showing off a new iPod or Macintosh computer."

The same was true in 2010, when Apple announced its electronic tablet, the iPad.[40] Secrecy was a particular boon to Apple's fast-growing iPod product line. Consumers showed their willingness to abandon their old iPods in favor of newer ones that Apple unveiled with great publicity and fanfare. (On the negative side, Hewlett-Packard decided to terminate its iPod partnership with Apple, in part because of the secrecy issue.)

Step 4: Taking Corrective Action. Leaks have occurred, and Apple has learned that secrecy requires strong measures. Thus, Apple has fired and later sued employees who leaked news about unannounced products. It has even sued Web sites that have published gossip about Apple products. The company also assigns different departments dissimilar code names for the same product, so it can more easily track where leaks come from. Employees are outfitted with special electronic badges that grant them access only to specific areas within the fortress-like Apple corporate headquarters.

YOUR CALL

Can you think of a more effective way to generate consumer interest in a forthcoming product than just keeping it secret? What kind of planning/control cycle issues would it raise?

Key Terms Used in This Chapter

action plan 148
Analyzers 143
cascading 153
Defenders 142
goal 147
management by objectives (MBO) 151
means-end chain 147
mission 145
mission statement 145
objective 147

operating plan 148
operational goals 147
operational planning 146
planning 140
planning/control cycle 155
policy 150
procedure 150
program 150
project 150
Prospectors 143
Reactors 143

rule 150
single-use plan 150
SMART goal 147
standing plan 150
strategic goals 147
strategic planning 146
tactical goals 147
tactical planning 146
vision 145
vision statement 145

Summary

5.1 Planning & Uncertainty

Planning is defined as setting goals and deciding how to achieve them. It is also defined as coping with uncertainty by formulating future courses of action to achieve specified results.

Planning has four benefits. It helps you (1) check your progress, (2) coordinate activities, (3) think ahead, and (4) cope with uncertainty.

Organizations respond to uncertainty in one of four ways. (1) Defenders are expert at producing and selling narrowly defined products or services. (2) Prospectors focus on developing new products or services and in seeking out new markets, rather than waiting for things to happen. (3) Analyzers let other organizations take the risks of product development and marketing and then imitate what seems to work best. (4) Reactors make adjustments only when finally forced to by environmental pressures.

5.2 Fundamentals of Planning

An organization's reason for being is expressed in a mission statement. What the organization wishes to become—and the actions needed to get there—are expressed in a vision statement.

From these are derived strategic planning, then tactical planning, then operational planning. In strategic planning, managers determine what the organization's long-term goals should be for the next 1–5 years. In tactical planning, managers determine what contributions their work units can make during the next 6–24 months. In operational planning, they determine how to accomplish specific tasks within the next 1–52 weeks.

Whatever its type, the purpose of planning is to achieve a goal or objective, a specific commitment to achieve a measurable result within a stated period of time.

Strategic goals are set by and for top management and focus on objectives for the organization as a whole. Tactical goals are set by and for middle managers and focus on the actions needed to achieve strategic goals. Operational goals are set by and for first-line managers and are concerned with short-term matters associated with realizing tactical goals.

The five characteristics of a good goal are represented by the acronym SMART. A SMART goal is one that is Specific, Measurable, Attainable, Results oriented, and has Target dates.

The goal should be followed by an action plan, which defines the course of action needed to achieve the stated goal. The operating plan, which is typically designed for a 1-year period, defines how you will conduct your business based on the action plan; it identifies clear targets such as revenues, cash flow, and market share.

Plans may be either standing plans, developed for activities that occur repeatedly over a period of time, or single-use plans, developed for activities that are not likely to be repeated in the future. There are three types of standing plans: (1) A policy is a standing plan that outlines the general response to a designated problem or situation. (2) A procedure outlines the response to particular problems or circumstances. (3) A rule designates specific required action. There are two types of single-use plans: (1) A program encompasses a range of projects or activities. (2) A project is a single-use plan of less scope and complexity.

 5.3 Promoting Goal Setting: Management by Objectives
Management by objectives (MBO) is a four-step process in which (1) managers and employees jointly set objectives for the employee, (2) managers develop action plans, (3) managers and employees periodically review the employee's

performance, and (4) the manager makes a performance appraisal and rewards the employee according to results. The purpose of MBO is to motivate rather than control subordinates.

For MBO to be successful three things have to happen. (1) The commitment of top management is essential. (2) The program must be applied organizationwide. (3) Objectives must cascade—becoming more specific at lower levels of the organization.

Deadlines are essential to planning because they become great motivators both for the manager and for subordinates.

 5.4 The Planning/Control Cycle
Once plans are made, managers must stay in control using the planning/control cycle, which has two planning steps (1 and 2) and two control steps (3 and 4), as follows: (1) Make the plan. (2) Carry out the plan. (3) Control the direction by comparing results with the plan. (4) Control the direction by taking corrective action in two ways—namely, (a) by correcting deviations in the plan being carried out, or (b) by improving future plans.

Management in Action

VW Establishes an Aggressive Vision

When Volkswagen CEO Martin Winterkorn said two years ago that he was determined to zoom past Toyota to become the world's biggest automaker, the notion seemed laughable. At the time, the German automaker sold 3 million fewer vehicles than Toyota, was losing ground in the United States, and had a reputation for iffy quality. . . .

Winterkorn sees a historic opportunity. And with the backing of his formidable boss and mentor, VW Chairman Ferdinand Piëch, he's seizing it. By 2018, Winterkorn vows, VW will pass Toyota. . . .

All over the globe, Winterkorn, 62, is punching the accelerator. VW has agreed to buy a 20% stake in Suzuki Motors to gear up for an assault on the rapidly growing markets of Southeast Asia and India. Winterkorn is going after BMW and Mercedes, committing $11 billion over the next three years to Audi, VW's luxury brand. . . .

Winterkorn's most ambitious plans are in the United States, where he aims to double sales by 2012. It was only five years ago that VW tried and failed to move upmarket in the United States. Remember the Phaeton, the VW with a sticker price of $85,000? Now Winterkorn is reversing course. He's betting that Volkswagen can steal customers from Toyota, Honda, Ford, and others by selling Americans on German engineering and style at affordable prices. . . .

Beating Toyota won't be easy. For starters, VW sells fewer vehicles in the United States than Subaru or Kia and still has a reputation for making unreliable, overpriced cars. In Southeast Asia—a Toyota stronghold—the VW brand is practically unknown. Ditto for India. . . .

Still, VW is a formidable competitor; it earned $975 million in the first three quarters of 2009, despite the global collapse of car sales, and it has $33.3 billion in cash. "We want to make VW the economic, ecological, and technological leader by 2018," Winterkorn wrote in an e-mail. "Our goal is not just about size—we are aiming for quality-driven growth." . . .

In the summer of 2007, Winterkorn and the board met to brainstorm ways to become the world's biggest automaker, say VW's U.S. chief, Stefan Jacoby. High on the agenda was fixing VW's America problem. That year, VW expected to sell 200,000 cars in the United States, a 40% drop from 2000 and a third of what VW sold in 1970 when the Bug and Bus were hippie icons. Jacoby says executives at the meeting saw three choices: They could continue to lose buckets of money selling cars that were too small and too expensive; they could wave the white flag; or they could go on the offensive. They chose Door No. 3.

Jacoby says he persuaded the board to build VW's first U.S. plant. He recalls arguing that doing so would help VW overcome resistance in the American heartland to imported vehicles. If VW built the plant, Jacoby recalls saying, he would sell 150,000 cars from that factory alone each year. The board approved the plan and allocated $1 billion for the facility, which is scheduled to open [in 2011] in Chattanooga, Tennessee. VW's decision to build cars in the United States has not gone unnoticed by its main rival. . . .

According to a source briefed on VW's plans for the United States, the company plans to expand its lineup from 10 cars today to 14 in five years. VW will have new compact and midsized sedans priced for the American market, plus a small SUV. . . .

VW will have to convince Americans its cars are worth buying. In J.D. Powers & Associates Initial Quality Study, which ranks cars in the first three months of ownership, VW came in 15th out of 37 [in 2009]. The company's ranking improved from 24th in 2008. . . .

Winterkorn and Piëch have put in place the pieces of their global strategy. Now that VW's two main rivals, Toyota and GM, are retrenching, they're speeding up their plans. The big question is whether size for size's sake generates real benefits for a car company. Automakers like to get big so they can spread the huge costs of developing new models over mass volume. Of course, car companies have a tendency to get so big that they become unmanageable.

For Discussion

1. Which of the four basic strategy types were used by VW? Explain your rationale.
2. Based on the case, what is VW's vision? Do you think it is realistic? Explain.
3. State two SMART goals for VW based on the case. Are these goals attainable? Discuss.
4. Using Figure 5.5, describe the extent to which VW is using the planning/control cycle.
5. What did you learn about planning based on this case? Explain.

Source: Excerpted from David Welch, "The Transformer: Why VW Is the Car Giant to Watch," *Bloomberg Businessweek,* January 25, 2010, pp. 44, 46–48. Reprinted with permission.

Self-Assessment

Holland Personality Types & You: Matching Your Personality to the Right Work Environment & Occupation

Objectives

1. To understand the need to plan for your career.
2. To try to match your personality with an occupation.

Introduction

What do you want to be when you grow up? Some people seem to know early in life. Others come to a realization in college. Still others may be forced to such awareness by a crisis in later life, such as being dismissed from a job. Of course, most of us make some sort of plans for our careers. But in doing so we may not always be knowledgeable about how to match our personalities with the choices available.

Instructions

There are four parts to this exercise.

First, select a number from the list of six personality types.

Second, match that choice with the personality you think that type would have.

Third, select the work environment you think would be best for that personality type and personality.

Fourth, based on the preceding three choices, select which occupation would fit best. (For example, if you selected #1, C, and f, the best fit for an occupation would be artist, musical conductor, and other related occupations.)

Try to connect each of the four parts and then check the key to see if your pairings are correct. After that, go through the list again, identifying what you think your personality type is, what your personality is, the work environment you like or think you would like best, and then the occupation that you would or do like best. See if there is an alignment by using the scoring guidelines and interpretation shown below; if there is such an alignment, this suggests you may be on your way to a successful career.

Personality Type

1. Artistic
2. Conventional
3. Realistic
4. Enterprising
5. Social
6. Investigative

Personality

A. Prefers to work with things; is present-oriented, athletic, and mechanical.
B. Is analytical, a problem solver, scientific, and original.
C. Relies on feelings and imagination, is expressive, is intuitive, and values esthetics.
D. Sensitive to needs of others, enjoys interpersonal gatherings, and values educational and social issues.
E. Adventurous, has leadership qualities, persuasive, and values political and economic matters.
F. Structured, accurate, detail-oriented, and loyal follower.

Work Environments

a. Technical/mechanical and industrial.
b. Traditional and rewards conformity and dependability.
c. Cooperative and rewards personal growth.
d. Managerial role in organizations and rewards monetary gains and achievements.
e. Rewards high academic achievement and uses technical abilities to complete tasks.
f. Unstructured and allows nonconformity and rewards creativity.

Occupations

7. Chemist/biological scientist, computer analyst, and emergency medical technician.
8. Lawyer, flight attendant, sales representative, reporter.
9. Accountant, bank teller, medical record technician.
10. Cook, drywall installer, auto mechanic.
11. Artist/commercial artist, musical director, architect, writer/editor.
12. Teacher, clergy, nurse, counselor, librarian.

Scoring Guidelines & Interpretation

Scoring is as follows:

1-C-f-11
2-F-b-9
3-A-a-10
4-E-d-8
5-D-c-12
6-B-e-7

The purpose of this type of exercise is to see how personality type, personality, work environment, and occupation can best fit together. When the elements mesh, you will usually feel more competent and more satisfied with your work conditions and occupation. When these elements or factors are mismatched, one can be very frustrated, feel incompetent, or not be good at one's job.

If you wish to know more about career planning, you can avail yourself of a much more in-depth planning process at **www.soice.state.nc.us/sociss/planning/jh-types.htm.**

Questions for Discussion

1. Does your assessment suggest that your career choice is best for your personality type? How do you feel about this assessment?
2. What do you think the management challenges are for those who are mismatched in their work? Explain.
3. Can you see and describe yourself more clearly in terms of personality type, personality, work environment, and occupation given the results of your scoring? Explain.

Developed by Anne C. Cowden, PhD, based on the information provided by the Web site **www.soice.state.nc.us/sociss/planning/jh-types.htm.**

Should Surgical-Device Firms Be Allowed to Market Products for Off-Label Uses That Are Not Approved by the U.S. Government?

Some 250,000 people last year underwent an operation in which tiny bits of heart tissue were burned into a maze pattern to reroute the heart's electrical system. This is done to fix the most common type of faulty heartbeat, atrial fibrillation.

The devices widely used for this operation haven't been approved by the U.S. government to treat that condition. Yet today these products, which have sales of about $100 million a year, are used almost exclusively to treat atrial fibrillation, according to executives, doctors, and others familiar with the industry.

These devices were approved for "ablation," or the destruction of tissue, which historically has often meant sealing a wound to stop bleeding. But the devices aren't specifically approved by the Food and Drug Administration for atrial fibrillation treatment, a more complex procedure. To get approval for treating "A-fib," as it's known, would require companies to conduct expensive clinical testing.

The Justice Department is investigating whether companies that make these surgical-ablation devices have been violating the law by actively marketing them for non-FDA-approved uses, such as treating atrial fibrillation. Although doctors may use drugs or devices for off-label treatments, companies are allowed to market them only for the uses for which they have been FDA-approved. The idea behind this restriction is to limit the number of U.S. patients exposed to experimental, relatively untested treatments.

Solving the Dilemma

As a member of the Justice Department investigating the marketing and use of non-FDA-approved devices, what would you recommend?

1. Device companies should be financially punished for marketing products for non-FDA-approved uses. These practices are against the law.

2. Let's be practical and forget the law in this case. These devices represent "off-label" treatments that are helping people, and the goal of medicine is to help people.

3. It's unfair to allow doctors to use drugs or devices for off-label treatments, but then punish device firms for essentially doing the same thing. Decisions like this should be done on a case-by-case basis and this is a case where device firms should be left alone.

4. Wait a minute. These laws are meant to protect consumers or patients. The Justice Department should attempt to stop device firms from marketing products for off-label treatments.

5. Invent other options.

Source: Excerpted from Thomas Burton, "Surgical-Device Firms Walk Fine Line," *The Wall Street Journal*, March 11, 2010, p. A1. Copyright © 2010 by Dow Jones & Company, Inc. Reproduced with permission of Dow Jones & Company, Inc. via Copyright Clearance Center.

chapter 6

Strategic Management
How Exceptional Managers Realize a Grand Design

How Successful Managers Stay Successful: Seeing Beyond the Latest Management Fads

"How can we build organizations that are as nimble as change itself—not only operationally, but strategically?" asks famed management professor Gary Hamel.[1]

Unfortunately, the way many people deal with the uncertainty of change is by succumbing to fads, or short-lived enthusiasms, suggests University of Delaware sociologist Joel Best, author of *Flavor of the Month: Why Smart People Fall for Fads.*[2] A fad, he says, "is seen as the way of the future, a genuine innovation that will help solve a big problem. . . . A lot of the attraction of a fad is that if you embrace it early, then you feel that you're ahead of other people, that you're hipper and maybe smarter than they are."[3]

That the field of management has its fads is evident in the constant production of business books touting the newest cure-all. Still, some ideas that started out as management fads survive. Why? Because they've been found to actually work. And one of those that has been found to work is *strategic planning,* as we describe in this chapter.

Two lessons of successful managers:

- **Lesson 1—In an era of management fads, strategic planning is still tops.** Every year, Bain & Company, a global business consulting firm, prepares a "Management Tools and Trends" survey of the use of and satisfaction with the most popular management tools. The 2009 survey found that the second most widely used management tool in 2008 (after benchmarking, which vaulted to first place and which we describe in Chapter 10) was a familiar tool from 8 and

even 10 years earlier—namely, *strategic planning,* favored by 67% of the senior managers surveyed. The use of *mission and vision statements* also continued to be popular, favored by 65%.[4] Strategic planning is concerned with developing a comprehensive program for long-term success. Mission statements describe the organization's purpose and vision statements describe its intended long-term goal. Successful managers know how to use all of these.

- **Lesson 2—Managers must be willing to make large, painful decisions to suddenly alter strategy.** Another lesson is that in a world of rapid and discontinuous change, managers must always be prepared to make large, painful decisions and radically alter their business design—the very basis of how the company makes money. Because of fast-spreading world conditions, such as the threat of products becoming commodities, rapidly increasing productivity, and global overcapacity, managers must be able to make difficult decisions: "exiting businesses, firing people, admitting you were wrong (or at least not omniscient)," as writer Geoffrey Colvin puts it. "So the future will demand ever more people with the golden trait, the fortitude to accept and even seek psychic pain."[5]

For Discussion Earlier we described the importance of practicing *evidence-based management,* with managers "seeing the truth as a moving target, always facing the hard facts, avoiding falling prey to half-truths, and being willing to admit when they're wrong and change their ways."[6] Do you think you would have this mind-set when thinking about the overall direction of your organization or work unit?

---

forecast | **What's Ahead in This Chapter**

We describe strategic management and strategic planning and why they're important. We go through the five steps in the strategic-management process. Then we consider competitive intelligence and show how grand strategy is developed, using two strategic-planning tools—SWOT analysis and forecasting. Next we show how strategy is formulated, using such techniques as Porter's four competitive strategies and single-product versus diversification strategies. Finally, we show how strategy is carried out and controlled.

Am I really managing if I don't have a strategy?

THE BIG PICTURE

This section distinguishes among strategy, strategic management, and strategic planning. We describe three reasons why strategic management and strategic planning are important and how they may work for both large and small firms.

Brian Allman, 17, saw a simple vending machine for sale at Sam's Club and bought it for $425. With that he started a small vending-machine business, Bear Snax Vending, stocking the machine and four others he added later with popular candy such as Skittles, M&Ms, and Snickers. His route includes small to midsize businesses, such as banks.[7]

Did Allman have a big-picture vision for his business, incorporating it in a ***business plan,* a document that outlines a proposed firm's goals, the strategy for achieving them, and the standards for measuring success?** Apparently not. But that's often the case with entrepreneurs, even those far older than 17. One study found that 41% of *Inc.* magazine's 1989 list of fastest-growing private firms didn't have a business plan and 26% had only rudimentary plans.[8] A follow-up study by *Inc.* in 2002 found the percentage without a plan remained much the same. However, other evidence suggests that firms with formal business plans are more apt to survive. For instance, Scott Shane of Case Western Reserve University examined research of 396 entrepreneurs in Sweden and found that a greater number of firms that failed never had a formal business plan.[9]

Strategic planning. In 1997, brewer Anheuser Busch, maker of Budweiser and Busch, developed a strategic plan, called "100% Share of Mind," that offered beer distributors financial incentives if they did not distribute rival brands. Anheuser benefited; its share of the U.S. beer market grew. But no strategic plan lasts forever. In the fast-changing alcoholic-beverage industry, distributors with flattening sales began to chafe at carrying only Anheuser products. Some decided to begin selling rival beers, such as Pennsylvania's Yuengling Black & Tan lager. Anheuser's market share was reduced. What kind of strategic plan should it adopt now?

Business plans embody a firm's strategy. In this section, we do the following:

- Define strategy and strategic management.
- Explain why strategic planning is important.
- Describe the three key principles that underlie strategic positioning.
- Discuss strategic management in large versus small firms.

Strategy, Strategic Management, & Strategic Planning

Every organization needs to have a "big picture" about where it's going and how to get there. These are matters of strategy, strategic management, and strategic planning.

Strategy   A *strategy* **is a large-scale action plan that sets the direction for an organization.** It represents an "educated guess" about what must be done in the long term for the survival or the prosperity of the organization or its principal parts. We hear the word expressed in terms like "Budweiser's ultimate strategy . . ." or "Visa's overseas strategy . . ." or *financial strategy, marketing strategy,* and *human resource strategy.*

An example of a strategy is "Find out what customers want, then provide it to them as cheaply and quickly as possible" (the strategy of Walmart). However, strategy is not something that can be decided on just once. Because of fast-changing conditions, it needs to be revisited from time to time, whether every year or every 5 years.

Strategic Management   In the late 1940s, most large U.S. companies were organized around a single idea or product line. By the 1970s, Fortune 500 companies were operating in more than one industry and had expanded overseas. It became apparent that to stay focused and efficient, companies had to begin taking a strategic-management approach.

Strategic management **is a process that involves managers from all parts of the organization in the formulation and the implementation of strategies and strategic goals.** This definition doesn't mean that managers at the top dictate ideas to be followed by people lower down. Indeed, precisely because middle managers are the ones who will be asked to understand and implement the strategies, they should also help to formulate them. The steps in this process are covered in Section 6.2.

Strategic Planning   *Strategic planning,* as we stated in Chapter 5, determines not only the organization's long-term goals for the next 1–5 years regarding growth and profits but also the ways the organization should achieve them.

As one consultant put it, "Simply put, strategic planning determines where an organization is going over the next year or more, how it's going to get there and how it'll know if it got there or not."[10]

Why Strategic Management & Strategic Planning Are Important

An organization should adopt strategic management and strategic planning for three reasons: They can (1) *provide direction and momentum,* (2) *encourage new ideas,* and above all (3) *develop a sustainable competitive advantage.*[11] Let's consider these three matters.

I. Providing Direction & Momentum   Some executives are unable even to articulate what their strategy is.[12] Others are so preoccupied with day-to-day pressures that their organizations can lose momentum. But strategic planning can help people focus on the most critical problems, choices, and opportunities. If everyone is involved in the process, that can also help create teamwork, promote learning, and build commitment across the organization.

Unless a strategic plan is in place, managers may well focus on just whatever is in front of them, the usual run-of-the-mill problems—until they get an unpleasant jolt when a competitor moves out in front because it has been able to take a long-range view of things and act more quickly. In recent times, this surprise has been happening over and over as companies have been confronted by some digital or Internet trend that emerged as a threat—as Amazon.com was to Barnes & Noble; as digital cameras were to Kodak's film business; as Google News, blogs, and citizen media were to newspapers.[13]

But there are many other instances in which a big company didn't take competitors seriously (as Sears didn't Walmart, IBM didn't Microsoft, and GM didn't Toyota). "We were five years late in recognizing that [microbreweries] were going to take as much market as they did," says August Busch III, CEO of massive brewer Anheuser-Busch, "and five years late in recognizing we should have joined them."[14]

Of course, a poor plan can send an organization in the wrong direction. Bad planning usually results from faulty assumptions about the future, poor assessment of an organization's capabilities, ineffective group dynamics, and information overload.[15]

2. Encouraging New Ideas   Some people object that planning can foster rigidity, that it creates blinders that block out peripheral vision and reduces creative thinking and action. "Setting oneself on a predetermined course in unknown waters," says one critic, "is the perfect way to sail straight into an iceberg."[16]

Actually, far from being a straitjacket for new ideas, strategic planning can help encourage them by stressing the importance of innovation in achieving long-range success. Gary Hamel says that companies such as Apple have been successful because they have been able to unleash the spirit of "strategy innovation." Strategy innovation, he says, is the ability to reinvent the basis of competition within existing industries—"bold new business models that put incumbents on the defensive."[17]

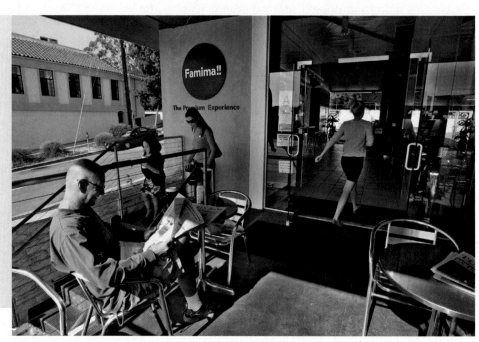

Upscale convenience. Most U.S. convenience stores carry basic necessities, along with candy and slushy drinks. Famima!! represents a different idea, one already successful in Japan—stores catering to people ages 21–41 whose household incomes top $80,000. The stores offer not only diapers and dog food but also such luxuries as French stationery, artisanal teas, and organic oatmeal. Beginning in 2004, the first 30 stores opened in the Los Angeles area, but 9 of them had closed by January 2010. In recessionary times, do you think the concept is still workable?

Some successful innovators are companies creating new wealth in the grocery business, where Starbucks Coffee, Trader Joe's, Petco, ConAgra, and Walmart, for example, have developed entirely new product categories and retailing concepts. For instance, Starbucks (No. 26 on the 2010 Fortune "World's Most Admired Companies"), after going through a period of overambitious growth and an economic meltdown that shut down hundreds of stores, has launched Via as an instant coffee brand that will evolve into "multiple formats and new form factors" for worldwide distribution. It's also becoming the top consumer brand on Facebook and the top coffee brand on Twitter.[18]

3. Developing a Sustainable Competitive Advantage   Strategic management provides a sustainable *competitive advantage,* which, you'll recall (from Chapter 1), is the ability of an organization to produce goods or services more effectively than its competitors do, thereby outperforming them. Sustainable competitive advantage occurs when an organization is able to get and stay ahead in four areas: (1) in being responsive to customers, (2) in innovating, (3) in quality, and (4) in effectiveness.

Example

Developing Competitive Advantage: Is Apple's App Store a Model for Ford?

"Ford is transforming the car into a powerful smartphone," reports one writer, "one that lets you carry your digital world along with you and then customizes it."[19] The basis for this is Ford's new Sync in-dash communications platform, introduced in partnership with Microsoft in 2007, which allows you "to move seamlessly from the connected world contained in your phone to an equally connected world inside your car—without touching a single button." As of mid-2010, there were a million and a half Sync-enabled cars on the road.

Sync also opens the door for an App Store kind of experience, Apple's spectacularly successful program in which customers can download all kinds of applications ("apps" or "aps") for use on their iPhones and which many companies see as the future model for software distribution.[20] Mindful that no new applications should be introduced unless they keep the driver's eyes on the road and hands on the wheel, Ford is introducing voice-activated apps such as one that enables users to make phone calls with one verbal command ("Call Paul at home"). Or drivers could say

"I'm hungry" and benefit from some spoken advice about restaurants, along with navigation-system directions. Or they could verbally activate Pandora, a popular Internet-radio application. "Right now," says an automotive analyst, "Ford has redefined this market, and it has made it very difficult for anybody to enter the space and compete."[21] In other words, Sync is a distinct competitive advantage for the car company.

YOUR CALL

An app store allows a company such as Apple or Ford to tap into ideas from third-party software developers while retaining control over its brand. But in Apple's case, heavy-handed management has irritated developers, causing many to quit building apps for the iPhone, opting instead for "the open, developer-friendly Web," in one description, which allows apps to be run on the iPhone's Web browser.[22] Will Ford jeopardize its competitive advantage if it tries too hard to control its third-party app developers for Sync? But could there be safety issues if it opens Sync to all comers?

What Is an Effective Strategy? Three Principles

Harvard Business School professor **Michael Porter** "is the single most important strategist working today, and maybe of all time," raved Kevin Coyne of consulting firm McKinsey & Co.[23]

Is this high praise deserved? Certainly Porter's status as a leading authority on competitive strategy is unchallenged. The Strategic Management Society, for instance, voted him the most influential living strategist. We will refer to him repeatedly in this chapter.

According to Porter, *strategic positioning* **attempts to achieve sustainable competitive advantage by preserving what is distinctive about a company.** "It means," he says, "performing *different* activities from rivals, or performing *similar* activities in different ways."[24]

Three key principles underlie strategic positioning:[25]

1. Strategy Is the Creation of a Unique & Valuable Position Strategic position emerges from three sources:

- **Few needs, many customers.** Strategic position can be derived from serving the few needs of many customers. Example: Jiffy Lube provides only lubricants, but it provides them to all kinds of people with all kinds of motor vehicles.

- **Broad needs, few customers.** A strategic position may be based on serving the broad needs of just a few customers. Example: Bessemer Trust targets only very high wealth clients.

- **Broad needs, many customers.** Strategy may be oriented toward serving the broad needs of many customers. Example: Carmike Cinemas operates only in cities with populations of fewer than 200,000 people.

2. Strategy Requires Trade-offs in Competing As a glance at the preceding choices shows, some strategies are incompatible. Thus, a company has to choose not only what strategy to follow but what strategy *not* to follow. Example: Neutrogena soap, points out Porter, is positioned more as a medicinal product than as a cleansing agent. In achieving this narrow positioning, the company gives up sales based on deodorizing, gives up large volume, and accordingly gives up some manufacturing efficiencies.

3. Strategy Involves Creating a "Fit" among Activities "Fit" has to do with the ways a company's activities interact and reinforce one another. Example: A mutual fund such as Vanguard Group follows a low-cost strategy and aligns all its activities accordingly, distributing funds directly to consumers and minimizing portfolio turnover. However, when Continental Lite tried to match some but not all of Southwest Airlines' activities, it was not successful because it didn't apply Southwest's whole interlocking system.

Does Strategic Management Work for Small as Well as Large Firms?

You would expect that a large organization, with its thousands of employees and even larger realm of "stakeholders," would benefit from strategic management and planning. After all, how can a huge company such as General Motors run without some sort of grand design?

But what about smaller companies, which account for more than half of total employment and the bulk of employment growth in recent years? One analysis of several studies found that strategic planning was appropriate not just for large firms—companies with fewer than 100 employees could benefit as well, although the improvement in financial performance was small. Nevertheless, the researchers concluded, "it may be that the small improvement in performance is not worth the effort involved in strategic planning unless a firm is in a very competitive industry where small differences in performance may affect the firm's survival potential."[26] ●

✳ 6.2 THE STRATEGIC-MANAGEMENT PROCESS

What's the five-step recipe for the strategic-management process?	major question?

THE BIG PICTURE

The strategic-management process has five steps: Establish the mission and the vision, establish the grand strategy, formulate the strategic plans, carry out those plans, and maintain strategic control. In addition, all the steps may be affected by feedback that enables the taking of constructive action.

When is a good time to begin the strategic-management process? Often it's touched off by some crisis.

Toyota was compelled to do serious soul searching in 2010, when it encountered severe quality problems involving uncontrollable acceleration in its automobiles. Toyota Motor Corporation's President Akio Toyoda concluded that these problems were partly due to the company's "excessive focus on market share and profits." He believes the company needs to reorient its strategy toward quality and innovation.[27] For Edward Lampert, who in 2005 merged Kmart and Sears into megaretailer Sears Holdings, the pressure was being felt in 2010 after years of underperforming returns despite cost cutting and store closures.[28]

Example

Crisis Leading to the Strategic-Management Process: JetBlue Weathers an Ice Storm

Founded in 1998, JetBlue started out as a low-fare airline, promising fares up to 65% lower than competitors along with, in one description, "creature comforts like assigned seating, leather upholstery, and satellite TV on individual screens in every seat."[29] The formula was an immediate hit, and by 2007 JetBlue had grown from 6 daily flights and 300 employees to 575 daily flights to 52 destinations and 9,300 employees.

Then in 2005, the founder, David Neeleman, decided to depart from the low-cost model of Southwest Airlines–style carriers and to imitate more traditional airlines. He added different kinds of aircraft, increased routes and airports, and built a $25 million training center in anticipation of expanding the workforce to 30,000 by 2010. "These moves," says one analysis, "increased the airline's costs while drawing it into competition with a greater number of rivals, which in turn made it harder for JetBlue to raise

fares."[30] JetBlue lost $20 million in 2005 and $1 million in 2006.

The Valentine's Day Ice Storm. Then the Valentine's Day crisis happened. On February 14, 2007, an ice storm settled on JetBlue's New York hub at John F. Kennedy International Airport, preventing planes from taking off. Having acted on forecasters' prediction that the ice would change to rain, JetBlue had continued to load flights and allowed them to taxi to the runway. The result: planes couldn't take off, and passengers were stuck in their seats for hours—up to 6 hours, in some cases. In fact, only 17 of the airline's 156 scheduled departures left JFK that day, disrupting the entire system and displacing crews and aircraft. "In subsequent days," says one account, "JetBlue management canceled more and more flights, angering thousands of passengers, until finally, on February 20, normal operations resumed."[31]

The storm incident cost the carrier around $30 million, according to Neeleman.[32] In addition, he apologized publicly to more than 131,000 customers affected by the cancellations and delays and offered different levels of compensation (such as a full refund and voucher for a free round-trip flight to passengers stuck on a plane for more than 3 hours). He also announced a Customer Bill of Rights, which offered specific kinds of compensation for various types of delays and overbooking resulting in passengers getting bumped. None of these efforts protected his job: Neeleman was replaced as CEO in 2007 and as chairman of the board in 2008.

Lessons from the Crisis. What did the incident show? Principally that the airline had grown too fast and didn't have enough people to handle all the passengers trying to rebook flights or to schedule crews during the disruptions. For instance, JetBlue's reservations system relied on a dispersed workforce that included many agents working flexible hours from home—"a low-cost solution that works well until thousands of passengers need to rebook at once," points out one author.[33] The company set a goal of doubling the number of agents who could access the company's reservations system. It also created a database to track crew locations and contact information, and initiated cross-training so that 900 employees working near JFK would be available during any future operational crisis.

YOUR CALL

Despite its near collapse after the ice storm, JetBlue bounced back, and has been profitable in years when other airlines have not been. Since its start-up, says one analyst, "not a single competitor has matched its effort to provide actual comfort in coach class."[34] Moreover, JetBlue has topped all airlines in J.D. Power's annual customer-service survey for five years in a row.[35] Do you think the airline will be able to continue to expand and still keep its fares low, its comforts relatively high, and have enough staff and arrangements to avoid another Valentine's Day massacre?

The Five Steps of the Strategic-Management Process

The strategic-management process has five steps, plus a feedback loop, as shown below. *(See Figure 6.1.)* Let's consider these five steps.

Feedback: Revise actions, if necessary, based on feedback

figure 6.1

THE STRATEGIC-MANAGEMENT PROCESS

The process has five steps.

Step 1: Establish the Mission & the Vision   We discussed mission and vision in Chapter 5. If you were called on to write a mission statement and a vision statement, how would you go about it?

Characteristics of a Good Mission Statement   The *mission,* you'll recall, is the organization's purpose or reason for being, and it is expressed in a *mission statement.*

For example, the mission statement of McGraw-Hill, publisher of this book, is as follows:

> *To serve the worldwide need for knowledge at a fair profit by gathering, evaluating, producing, and distributing valuable information in a way that benefits our customers, employees, authors, investors, and our society.*

Characteristics of a Good Vision Statement An organization's vision, you'll recall, is its long-term goal describing what it wants to become. It is expressed in a *vision statement,* which describes its long-term direction and strategic intent. For example, Walt Disney's original vision for Disneyland went in part like this:

> *Disneyland will be something of a fair, an exhibition, a playground, a community center, a museum of living facts, and a showplace of beauty and magic. It will be filled with the accomplishments, the joys and hopes of the world we live in. And it will remind us and show us how to make those wonders part of our own lives.[36]*

Although a vision statement can be short, it should be positive and inspiring, and it should stretch the organization and its employees to achieve a desired future state that appears beyond its reach. Consider Google, for example. Google's vision is "to organize the world's information and make it universally accessible and useful." Google CEO Eric Schmidt estimated that it may take 300 years to achieve the company's vision. Doing so will require Google to have strategic patience and to develop a grand strategy that is broad in focus.[37]

Guidelines for constructing powerful mission statements and vision statements are shown below. *(See Table 6.1.)* "Visions that have these properties challenge and inspire people in the organization and help align their energies in a common direction," says Burt Nanus of the University of Southern California's School of Business Administration. "They prevent people from being overwhelmed by immediate problems because they help distinguish what is truly important from what is merely interesting."[38]

Family business. Do small, family-owned businesses need a vision statement? If no, why not?

table 6.1 MISSION STATEMENTS AND VISION STATEMENTS

Mission statements: Does your company's mission statement answer these questions?

1. Who are our customers?	5. What is our commitment to economic objectives?	8. What are our public responsibilities, and what image do we wish to project?
2. What are our major products or services?	6. What are our basic beliefs, values, aspirations, and philosophical priorities?	9. What is our attitude toward our employees?
3. In what geographical areas do we compete?	7. What are our major strengths and competitive advantages?	
4. What is our basic technology?		

Vision statements: Does your company's vision statement answer "yes" to these questions?

1. Is it appropriate for the organization and for the times?	3. Does it clarify purpose and direction?	6. Does it reflect the uniqueness of the organization, its distinctive competence, what it stands for, what it's able to achieve?
2. Does it set standards of excellence and reflect high ideals?	4. Does it inspire enthusiasm and encourage commitment?	7. Is it ambitious?
	5. Is it well articulated and easily understood?	

Sources: F. R. David, "How Companies Define Their Mission," *Long Range Planning,* February 1989, pp. 90–97; and B. Nanus, *Visionary Leadership: Creating a Compelling Sense of Direction for Your Organization* (San Francisco: Jossey-Bass, 1992), pp. 28–29.

Step 2: Establish the Grand Strategy The next step is to translate the broad mission and vision statements into a ***grand strategy,*** which, after an assessment of current organizational performance, then explains how the organization's mission is to be accomplished.[39] Three common grand strategies are growth, stability, and defensive.

The first part of the process of developing a grand strategy, then, is to make a rigorous analysis of the organization's present situation to determine *where it is presently headed.* The second part is to determine where it *should be headed in the future.*

Let's consider the three common grand strategies.

1. The Growth Strategy A *growth strategy* **is a grand strategy that involves expansion—as in sales revenues, market share, number of employees, or number of customers or (for nonprofits) clients served.** Example: PepsiCo, which makes Lay's potato chips, is experimenting with making a new "designer salt" that will reduce the amount of sodium (which can contribute to high blood pressure) consumers ingest, a move calculated to expand Lay's customer base.[40]

2. The Stability Strategy A *stability strategy* **is a grand strategy that involves little or no significant change.** Example: Best Buy, which had strong revenues in 2009, plans to continue the same strategy in the near future, such as keeping prices low and revamping selling space to better show off the latest electronic gadgets.[41]

3. The Defensive Strategy A *defensive strategy* **or a** *retrenchment strategy,* **is a grand strategy that involves reduction in the organization's efforts.** Example: When the 2009 recession caused a falloff in bookings for pleasure travel, cruise-ship operator Carnival Corp. dramatically slashed prices (to as low as $199 a person for a seven-night Caribbean cruise), resulting in only a 10% drop in revenues.[42]

Variations of the three strategies are shown in the table below. *(See Table 6.2.)*

table 6.2

HOW COMPANIES CAN IMPLEMENT GRAND STRATEGIES

Growth strategy

- It can improve an existing product or service to attract more buyers.
- It can increase its promotion and marketing efforts to try to expand its market share.
- It can expand its operations, as in taking over distribution or manufacturing previously handled by someone else.
- It can expand into new products or services.
- It can acquire similar or complementary businesses.
- It can merge with another company to form a larger company.

Stability strategy

- It can go for a no-change strategy (if, for example, it has found that too-fast growth leads to foul-ups with orders and customer complaints).
- It can go for a little-change strategy (if, for example, the company has been growing at breakneck speed and feels it needs a period of consolidation).

Defensive strategy

- It can reduce costs, as by freezing hiring or tightening expenses.
- It can sell off (liquidate) assets—land, buildings, inventories, and the like.
- It can gradually phase out product lines or services.
- It can divest part of its business, as in selling off entire divisions or subsidiaries.
- It can declare bankruptcy.
- It can attempt a turnaround—do some retrenching, with a view toward restoring profitability.

How do you establish a grand strategy? Among the strategic-planning tools and techniques used are (1) *SWOT analysis* and (2) *forecasting*, as we describe in Section 6.3.

Step 3: Formulate Strategic Plans   The grand strategy must then be translated into more specific *strategic plans*, which determine what the organization's long-term goals should be for the next 1–5 years. These should communicate not only the organization's general goals about growth and profits but also information about how these goals will be achieved. Moreover, like all goals, they should be SMART— Specific, Measurable, Attainable, Results-oriented, and specifying Target dates (Chapter 5).

Strategy formulation is the process of choosing among different strategies and altering them to best fit the organization's needs. Because the process is so important, formulating strategic plans is a time-consuming process. Among the techniques used to formulate strategy is *Porter's competitive forces and strategies,* which we describe in Section 6.4.

Honest growth strategy. One growth strategy that Coca-Cola is employing is scouting for small, entrepreneurial beverage brands to add to its lineup. In 2008, Coke invested $40 million for a 40% interest in the trendy tea company Honest Tea, which makes low-calorie, organic teas and juices, such as Honest Ade. Do you think Coke's strategy of expanding into better-for-you and noncarbonated products is on the right track?

Step 4: Carry Out the Strategic Plans   Putting strategic plans into effect is *strategy implementation.* Strategic planning isn't effective, of course, unless it can be translated into lower-level plans. This means that top managers need to check on possible roadblocks within the organization's structure and culture and see if the right people and control systems are available to execute the plans.[43]

Often implementation means overcoming resistance by people who feel the plans threaten their influence or livelihood. This is particularly the case when the plans must be implemented rapidly, since delay is the easiest kind of resistance there is (all kinds of excuses are usually available to justify delays). Thus, top managers can't just announce the plans; they have to actively sell them to middle and supervisory managers.

Step 5: Maintain Strategic Control: The Feedback Loop   *Strategic control* consists of monitoring the execution of strategy and making adjustments, if necessary. To keep strategic plans on track, managers need control systems to monitor progress and take corrective action—early and rapidly—when things start to go awry. Corrective action constitutes a feedback loop in which a problem requires that managers return to an earlier step to rethink policies, redo budgets, or revise personnel arrangements. To keep a strategic plan on track, suggests Bryan Barry, you need to do the following:[44]

- **Engage people.**   You need to actively engage people in clarifying what your group hopes to accomplish and how you will accomplish it.
- **Keep it simple.**   Keep your planning simple, unless there's a good reason to make it more complex.
- **Stay focused.**   Stay focused on the important things.
- **Keep moving.**   Keep moving toward your vision of the future, adjusting your plans as you learn what works.

To see how good you think you'd be, see the Self-Assessment, "Core Skills Required in Strategic Planning," at the end of this chapter.

Now, in Section 6.3, let us consider some of the tools used for Step 2, establishing a grand strategy—competitive intelligence, SWOT, and forecasting. ●

major question? How can competitive intelligence, SWOT, and forecasting help me establish my strategy?

THE BIG PICTURE

To develop a grand strategy, you need to gather data and make projections, using the tools of competitive intelligence, SWOT analysis, and forecasting.

The first part in developing a grand strategy, Step 2 of the five-step strategic-management process, is intelligence gathering—internally and externally. The next part is to make some projections.

Three kinds of strategic-planning tools and techniques are (1) *competitive intelligence,* (2) *SWOT analysis,* and (3) *forecasting*—trend analysis and contingency planning.

Competitive Intelligence

Practicing *competitive intelligence* **means gaining information about one's competitors' activities so that you can anticipate their moves and react appropriately.** If you are a manager, one of your worst nightmares is that a competitor will surprise you with a service or product—as boutique beers did major brewers and mountain bikes did major bicycle makers—that will revolutionize the market and force you to try to play catch-up. Successful companies make it a point to conduct competitive intelligence.

Gaining competitive intelligence isn't always easy, but there are several avenues—and, surprisingly, most of them are public sources—including the following:

- **The public prints and advertising.** A product may be worked on in secret for several years, but at some point it becomes subject to announcement—through a press release, advertising piece, news leak, or the like. Much of this is available free through the Internet or by subscription to certain specialized databases, such as Nexus, which contains hundreds of thousands of news stories.

- **Investor information.** Information about new products and services may also be available through the reports filed with the Securities and Exchange Commission and through corporate annual reports.

- **Informal sources.** People in the consumer electronics industry every year look forward to major trade shows, such as the International Consumer Electronics Show in Las Vegas, when companies roll out their new products. At such times, people also engage in industry-gossip conversation to find out about future directions. Finally, salespeople and marketers, who are out calling on corporate clients, may return with tidbits of information about what competitors are doing.

SWOT Analysis

After competitive intelligence, the next point in establishing a grand strategy is *environmental scanning,* **careful monitoring of an organization's internal and external environments to detect early signs of opportunities and threats that may influence the firm's plans.** The process for doing such scanning is *SWOT analysis*—also known as *a situational analysis*—which is a search for the Strengths, Weaknesses, Opportunities, and Threats affecting the organization. A SWOT analysis should provide you with a realistic understanding of your organization in relation to its internal and external environments so you can better formulate strategy in pursuit of its mission. *(See Figure 6.2.)*

INSIDE MATTERS—Analysis of Internal Strengths & Weaknesses

S—Strengths: inside matters
Strengths could be work processes, organization, culture, staff, product quality, production capacity, image, financial resources & requirements, service levels, other internal matters.

W—Weaknesses: inside matters
Weaknesses could be in the same categories as stated for Strengths: work processes, organization, culture, etc.

O—Opportunities: outside matters
Opportunities could be market segment analysis, industry & competition analysis, impact of technology on organization, product analysis, governmental impacts, other external matters.

T—Threats: outside matters
Threats could be in the same categories as stated for Opportunities: market segment analysis, etc.

OUTSIDE MATTERS—Analysis of External Opportunities & Threats

figure 6.2

SWOT ANALYSIS

SWOT stands for Strengths, Weaknesses, Opportunities, Threats.

The SWOT analysis is divided into two parts: inside matters and outside matters—that is, an analysis of *internal strengths and weaknesses* and an analysis of *external opportunities and threats.* The following table gives examples of SWOT characteristics that might apply to a college. *(See Table. 6.3.)*

table 6.3

SWOT CHARACTERISTICS THAT MIGHT APPLY TO A COLLEGE

S—Strengths (internal strengths)	W—Weaknesses (internal weaknesses)
• Faculty teaching and research abilities	• Limited programs in business
• High-ability students	• High teaching loads
• Loyal alumni	• Insufficient racial diversity
• Strong interdisciplinary programs	• Lack of high-technology infrastructure
O—Opportunities (external opportunities)	**T—Threats (external threats)**
• Growth in many local skilled jobs	• Depressed state and national economy
• Many firms give equipment to college	• High schools enrollments in decline
• Local minority population increasing	• Increased competition from other colleges
• High school students take college classes	• Funding from all sources at risk

Inside Matters: Analysis of Internal Strengths & Weaknesses Does your organization have a skilled workforce? a superior reputation? strong financing? These are examples of *organizational strengths*—the skills and capabilities that give the organization special competencies and competitive advantages in executing strategies in pursuit of its mission.

Or does your organization have obsolete technology? outdated facilities? a shaky marketing operation? These are examples of *organizational weaknesses*—the drawbacks that hinder an organization in executing strategies in pursuit of its mission.

Outside Matters: Analysis of External Opportunities & Threats Is your organization fortunate to have weak rivals? emerging markets? a booming economy? These are instances of *organizational opportunities*—environmental factors that the organization may exploit for competitive advantage.

Alternatively, is your organization having to deal with new regulations? a shortage of resources? substitute products? These are some possible *organizational threats*—environmental factors that hinder an organization's achieving a competitive advantage.

Example

SWOT Analysis: How Would You Analyze Toyota?

"I fear the pace at which we have grown may have been too quick," said the grandson of Toyota Motor Corporation's founder in February 2010 testimony before a U.S. congressional committee looking into sudden acceleration problems. "Priorities became confused, and we were not able to stop, think, and make improvements as much as we were able to before."[45]

Toyota's U.S. sales fell 9% that month because of safety-related recalls of millions of vehicles. Yet they surged 41% in March, as buyers responded to incentives such as 0% financing.[46] Did this mean the car company was back on track to success? If you were a top Toyota manager, what would be the kinds of things you would identify at that point in a SWOT analysis?

The Internal Strengths. Originally the "Toyota Way," as practiced from assembly line to boardroom, stressed the values of continuous improvement ("kaizen") and eliminating waste ("muda"). The Toyota Way, says one report, "mandates planning for the long term; highlighting problems instead of hiding them; encouraging teamwork with colleagues and suppliers; and, perhaps most important, instilling a self-critical culture that fosters continuous and unrelenting improvement."[47] Developed in the 1950s, these precepts later became the basis for such concepts as lean manufacturing and just-in-time inventory management (discussed in Chapter 2). "At their core," says one analysis, "was an attention to detail and a noble frugality that shunned waste of every kind."[48]

The Internal Weaknesses. The company began to change in the 1990s, when it launched an effort to become the world's largest automaker, embarking on aggressive overseas expansion and doubling its plants

in North America, Asia, and Europe. During this time, the focus on cost reduction intensified to the point that the virtue became a vice. Suppliers were continually pushed to design parts that were 10% cheaper and 10% lighter. Common parts were used in most Toyota models, acquired from outside companies instead of trusted traditional suppliers.[49]

From 2000 to 2010, however, driver complaints to the National Highway Traffic and Safety Administration about "vehicle speed control" issues soared, with 11.7% of faulty vehicle components identified as Toyota's. (Ford was second, with 4.8%.)[50] Then came the widely publicized problems with sticking accelerators, prompting two huge recalls and suspension of the sales and production of eight models in the American market.[51] The blow to Toyota's vaunted reputation for quality was severe. "When your whole deal was quality, every mistake is a big deal," said a manufacturing expert.[52]

The External Opportunities. Although slow to awaken to its quality problems, the company went into full PR battle mode, moving to discredit critics who blamed accelerator problems on faulty electronics.[53] It also launched print and TV ads, as well as leveraged social media, to stress its commitment to the United States and reaching out to its millions of customers.[54] In a move to reverse its secretive culture, it also began to publicize the existence of vehicle onboard electronic data recorders, "black boxes" that could determine crash-related data, including whether the fault was the driver's rather than a car defect.[55] Finally, of course, despite all its self-inflicted wounds, Toyota leads most other car companies in quality rankings.

The External Threats. For Ford, GM, and even Chrysler, Toyota's troubles were almost too good to be true, news to overshadow the articles about bankruptcies and government bailouts. Aided by a U.S. government investigation into whether Toyota should have moved more quickly to correct its mechanical problems,

the Big Three had an unprecedent opportunity to grab Toyota's customers—if they could do so without appearing predatory. Ford in particular offers a further threat to Toyota because of its emphasis on aggressive styling, emphasis on quality, and technological innovations (such as the voice-activated Sync system). For GM, the electric Chevy Volt is four times more fuel-efficient than Toyota's Prius, and even Chrysler's Jeep can give Toyota a run for its money.[56]

YOUR CALL

"Comfortably preoccupied with rooting out internal weakness," says one writer, "the Toyota Way is lost when it comes to contending with outside threats. . . . If a flaw does get through, the company as a whole is loath to admit that the system broke down."[57] Do you agree? What would you advise Toyota to do?

Forecasting: Predicting the Future

Once they've analyzed their organization's Strengths, Weaknesses, Opportunities, and Threats, planners need to do forecasting for making long-term strategy. **A *forecast* is a vision or projection of the future.**

Lots of people make predictions, of course—and often they are wrong. In the 1950s, the head of IBM, Thomas J. Watson, estimated that the demand for computers would never exceed more than five for the entire world. In the late 1990s, many computer experts predicted power outages, water problems, transportation disruptions, bank shutdowns, and far worse because of computer glitches (the "Y2K bug") associated with the change from year 1999 to 2000.

Of course, the farther into the future one makes a prediction, the more difficult it is to be accurate, especially in matters of technology. Yet forecasting is a necessary part of planning.

Two types of forecasting are *trend analysis* and *contingency planning.*

Trend Analysis A *trend analysis* **is a hypothetical extension of a past series of events into the future.** The basic assumption is that the picture of the present can be projected into the future. This is not a bad assumption, if you have enough historical data, but it is always subject to surprises. And if your data are unreliable, they will produce erroneous trend projections.

An example of trend analysis is a time-series forecast, which predicts future data based on patterns of historical data. Time-series forecasts are used to predict long-term trends, cyclic patterns (as in the up-and-down nature of the business cycle), and seasonal variations (as in Christmas sales versus summer sales).

Contingency Planning: Predicting Alternative Futures *Contingency planning*—also known as *scenario planning* and *scenario analysis*—**is the creation of alternative hypothetical but equally likely future conditions.** The scenarios present alternative combinations of different factors—different economic pictures, different strategies by competitors, different budgets, and so on.

Fuel proof. Locking in the price of jet fuel with long-term contracts with suppliers, a form of contingency planning, has put low-cost airlines such as Southwest in a competitive position with rivals in controlling costs.

Example

Contingency Planning: Southwest Airlines Uses Hedging to Hold Down Price of Aviation Fuel

In early 2008, when the price of crude oil hit all-time highs ($100 a barrel), the cost of jet fuel threatened to take a big bite out of airline profits. Aviation fuel makes up as much as 15% of an airline's operating costs, the second biggest expense after labor.[58]

Locking in Contracts on Future Prices. Most airlines use a technique known as *hedging* to hold down the price of jet fuel, but Southwest Airlines is particularly good at it, having decided to enter fuel hedge transactions "back when oil prices were so low that oil was cheaper than water," as one observer whimsically put it.[59] In this form of contingency planning, airlines hedge the rise of fuel prices in the futures market by locking in contracts that allow them to buy fuel at a fixed price. Compared with traditional carriers, Southwest has been in a better position to buy favorable futures contracts because of its financial strengths: It avoids expensive labor contracts, operates only one type of aircraft, and flies high-traffic routes.[60]

$51-a-Barrel Oil. In the 2008 world of $100-plus-a-barrel oil, for instance, Southwest had 70% of its fuel hedged at $51 a barrel. For 2010, it had 30% of its fuel hedged at $63 a barrel. These prices are way below what other major airlines get. (United Airlines, for instance, had only 15% of its fuel hedged, and at between $91 and $101 per barrel.)

YOUR CALL

Is hedging like playing poker—like being a riverboat gambler? "You have to have foresight, wisdom, and some courage to hedge," says Tammy Romo, Southwest's treasurer.[61] But if oil consumption will grow by more than 40% over the next quarter century and fuel prices stay high, what do you think airlines will have to do? (*Hint:* increase revenues, decrease costs, consolidate or liquidate assets.)[62]

Because the scenarios try to peer far into the future—perhaps 5 or more years—they are necessarily written in rather general terms. Nevertheless, the great value of contingency planning is that it not only equips an organization to prepare for emergencies and uncertainty, it also gets managers thinking strategically. ●

How can four techniques—Porter's competitive forces, competitive strategies, diversification and synergy, and the BCG matrix—help me formulate strategy?

major question?

THE BIG PICTURE

Strategy formulation makes use of several concepts. Here we discuss Porter's five competitive forces, four competitive strategies, diversification and synergy, and the BCG matrix.

After the grand strategy has been determined (Step 2 in the strategic-management process), it's time to turn to strategy formulation (Step 3). Examples of techniques that can be used to formulate strategy are *Porter's five competitive forces, Porter's four competitive strategies, diversification and synergy,* and the *BCG matrix.*

Porter's Five Competitive Forces

What determines competitiveness within a particular industry? After studying several kinds of businesses, strategic-management expert Michael Porter suggested in his **Porter's model for industry analysis** that business-level strategies originate in **five primary competitive forces in the firm's environment: (1) threats of new entrants, (2) bargaining power of suppliers, (3) bargaining power of buyers, (4) threats of substitute products or services, and (5) rivalry among competitors.**[63]

I. Threats of New Entrants New competitors can affect an industry almost overnight, taking away customers from existing organizations. Example: Kraft Macaroni & Cheese is a venerable, well-known brand but is threatened from the low end by store brands, such as Walmart's brand, and from the high end by Annie's Creamy Macaroni and Cheese with Real Aged Wisconsin Cheddar.[64]

2. Bargaining Power of Suppliers Some companies are readily able to switch suppliers in order to get components or services, but others are not. Example: Clark Foam of Laguna Niguel, California, supplied nearly 90% of the foam cores used domestically to make custom surfboards. When it suddenly closed shop in late 2005, blaming government agencies for trying to shut it down, many independent board shapers and small retailers found they couldn't afford to get foam from outside the country. On the other hand, Surftech in Santa Cruz, California, was one of the few board manufacturers to use resin instead of foam, and so it saw a spike in sales.[65]

3. Bargaining Power of Buyers Customers who buy a lot of products or services from an organization have more bargaining power than those who don't. Customers who use the Internet to shop around are also better able to negotiate a better price. Example: Buying a car used to be pretty much a local activity, but now potential car buyers can use the Internet to scout a range of offerings within a 100-mile or larger radius, giving them the power to force down the asking price of any one particular seller. (Amazon.com's TextBuyIt program lets shoppers compare prices and buy things simply by making a few quick taps on their cell phones.)[66]

4. Threats of Substitute Products or Services   Again, particularly because of the Internet, an organization is in a better position to switch to other products or services when circumstances threaten their usual channels. Example: Oil companies might worry that Brazil is close to becoming energy self-sufficient because it is able to meet its growing demand for vehicle fuel by substituting ethanol derived from sugar cane for petroleum.[67]

5. Rivalry among Competitors   The preceding four forces influence the fifth force, rivalry among competitors. Think of the wild competition among makers and sellers of portable electronics, ranging from cell phones to MP3 audio players to video-game systems. Once again, the Internet has intensified rivalries among all kinds of organizations.

An organization should do a good SWOT analysis that examines these five competitive forces, Porter felt. Then it was in a position to formulate effective strategy, using what he identified as four competitive strategies, as we discuss next.

Porter's Four Competitive Strategies

Porter's four competitive strategies (also called *four generic strategies*) are (1) cost-leadership, (2) differentiation, (3) cost-focus, and (4) focused-differentiation.[68] The first two strategies focus on *wide* markets, the last two on *narrow* markets. *(See Figure 6.3.)* Time Warner, which produces lots of media and publications, serves wide markets around the world. Your neighborhood video store serves a narrow market of just local customers.

figure 6.3

PORTER'S FOUR COMPETITIVE STRATEGIES

	Type of market targeted	
Strategy	Wide	Narrow
I. Cost-leadership	✓	
2. Differentiation	✓	
3. Cost-focus		✓
4. Focused-differentiation		✓

Let's look at these four strategies.

I. Cost-Leadership Strategy: Keeping Costs & Prices Low for a Wide Market   The *cost-leadership strategy* is to keep the costs, and hence prices, of a product or service below those of competitors and to target a wide market.

This puts the pressure on R&D managers to develop products or services that can be created cheaply, production managers to reduce production costs, and marketing managers to reach a wide variety of customers as inexpensively as possible.

Firms implementing the cost-leadership strategy include computer maker Dell, watch maker Timex, hardware retailer Home Depot, and pen maker Bic.

2. Differentiation Strategy: Offering Unique & Superior Value for a Wide Market

The *differentiation strategy* is to offer products or services that are of unique and superior value compared with those of competitors but to target a wide market.

Because products are expensive, managers may have to spend more on R&D, marketing, and customer service. This is the strategy followed by Ritz-Carlton hotels and the makers of Lexus automobiles.

The strategy is also pursued by companies trying to create *brands* to differentiate themselves from competitors. Although Pepsi may cost only cents more than a supermarket's own house brand of cola, PepsiCo spends millions on ads.

3. Cost-Focus Strategy: Keeping Costs & Prices Low for a Narrow Market

The *cost-focus strategy* is to keep the costs, and hence prices, of a product or service below those of competitors and to target a narrow market.

This is a strategy you often see executed with low-end products sold in discount stores, such as low-cost beer or cigarettes, or with regional gas stations, such as the Terrible Herbst or Rotten Robbie chains in parts of the West.

Needless to say, the pressure on managers to keep costs down is even more intense than it is with those in cost-leadership companies.

4. Focused-Differentiation Strategy: Offering Unique & Superior Value for a Narrow Market

The *focused-differentiation strategy* is to offer products or services that are of unique and superior value compared to those of competitors and to target a narrow market.

Some luxury cars are so expensive—Rolls-Royce, Ferrari, Lamborghini—that only a few car buyers can afford them. Other companies following the strategy are jeweler Cartier and shirtmaker Turnbull & Asser. Yet focused-differentiation products need not be expensive. The publisher Chelsea Green has found success with niche books, such as *The Straw Bale House.*

Focused differentiation. The world's largest cruise ship, the 1,112-foot-long, 15-deck *Freedom of the Seas,* features such amenities as a skating rink, rock-climbing facilities, basketball, a surfing pool, a miniature golf course, a three-story-high dining room, and lavish lodging quarters. Clearly, there's something here for everyone—if you can afford it.

Single-Product Strategy versus Diversification Strategy

A company also needs to think about whether to have a *single-product strategy* or a *diversification strategy.* After all, if you have only one product to sell, what do you do if that product fails?

The Single-Product Strategy: Focused but Vulnerable In a *single-product strategy,* a company makes and sells only one product within its market. This is the kind of strategy you see all the time as you drive past the small retail businesses in a small town: There may be one shop that sells only flowers, one that sells only security systems, and so on.

The single-product strategy has both positives and negatives:

* **The benefit—focus.** Making just one product allows you to focus your manufacturing and marketing efforts just on that product. This means that your company can become savvy about repairing defects, upgrading production lines, scouting the competition, and doing highly focused advertising and sales.

    A small-business example: San Francisco's Green Toys makes all its toddler tea sets, toy trucks, and building blocks out of plastic recycled from milk jugs and, in a strategy called "reverse globalization," carries out all its operations in California, a push back against offshoring and outsourcing. (Sales have grown 70% a year since the founding in 2007.)[69] Another example: See's Candies, a chain of 200 stores throughout the West, specializes in making boxed chocolates—something it does so well that when See's was acquired by Berkshire Hathaway, its corporate owner chose not to tamper with success and runs it with a "hands-off" policy.

- **The risk—vulnerability.** The risk, of course, is that if you do *not* focus on all aspects of the business, if a rival gets the jump on you, or if an act of God intervenes (for a florist, roses suffer a blight right before Mother's Day), your entire business may go under.

   Example: Small specialty animal farms trying to capitalize on the popularity with consumers of locally grown foods, such as the one in East Montpelier, Vermont, where Erica Zimmerman and her husband produce pasture-raised pigs, have proved vulnerable to a shortage of slaughterhouses, which has led to backlogs and lengthy waits.[70] Another example: Indian Motorcycle Company, once a worthy rival to Harley-Davidson, sold only motorcycles. It went bankrupt twice, the second time because of quality problems, notably an overheating engine. (It was launched again in 2009.)[71]

The Diversification Strategy: Operating Different Businesses to Spread the Risk   The obvious answer to the risks of a single-product strategy is *diversification,* **operating several businesses in order to spread the risk.** You see this at the small retailer level when you drive past a store that sells gas *and* food *and* souvenirs *and* rents DVD movies.

There are two kinds of diversification—*unrelated* and *related.*

Unrelated Diversification: Independent Business Lines   If you operate a small shop that sells flowers on one side and computers on the other, you are exercising a strategy of *unrelated diversification*—**operating several businesses under one ownership that are not related to one another.** This has been a common big-company strategy. General Electric, for instance, which began by making lighting products, diversified into such unrelated areas as plastics, broadcasting, and financial services. Disney, Time Warner, and Sony run different divisions specializing in television, music, publishing, and the like.

Related Diversification: Related Business Lines   In some parts of the world you have to do all your grocery shopping in separate stores—the butcher, the baker, the greengrocer, and so on. In most U.S. grocery stores, all these businesses appear under the same roof, an example of the strategy of *related diversification,* **in which an organization under one ownership operates separate businesses that are related to one another.** A big-company example: The famous British raincoat maker Burberry started by making and marketing outerwear clothing but since then has expanded into related business lines, including accessories such as umbrellas, children's clothing, and even fragrances, which it sells in its own stores.

Related diversification has three advantages:

- **Reduced risk—because of more than one product.** If one product is weak, others may take up the slack. Example: When rainwear sales are slow, Burberry's economic risk is reduced by sales of its other product lines, such as children's clothes.

- **Management efficiencies—administration spread over several businesses.** Whatever the business, it usually has certain obligatory administrative costs—accounting, legal, taxes, and so on. Example: Burberry need not have separate versions of these for each business line. Rather, it can actually save money by using the same administrative services for all its businesses.

- **Synergy—the sum is greater than the parts.** When a company has special strengths in one business, it can apply those to its other related businesses. Example: PepsiCo can apply its marketing muscle not only to Pepsi Cola but also to 7-Up and Mountain Dew, which it also owns. This is an example of *synergy*—**the economic value of separate, related businesses under one ownership and management is greater together than the businesses are worth separately.**

An example of a company that went from a single-product strategy to a diversification strategy is Skilled Manufacturing Inc. of Detroit, which used to supply power-train components to the auto industry, but shuttered one of its two Michigan plants in 2005 after one of its automotive clients moved the work to Mexico. Now it is reopening the factory because it has branched out to other sectors, such as aerospace, in addition to continuing to serve the auto industry.[72]

The BCG Matrix

Developed by the Boston Consulting Group, the *BCG matrix* **is a means of evaluating strategic business units on the basis of (1) their business growth rates and (2) their share of the market.** Business growth rate is concerned with how fast the entire industry is increasing. Market share is concerned with the business unit's share of the market in relation to competitors.

In general, the BCG matrix suggests that an organization will do better in fast-growing markets in which it has a high market share rather than in slow-growing markets in which it has a low market share. These concepts are illustrated below. *(See Figure 6.4.)* ●

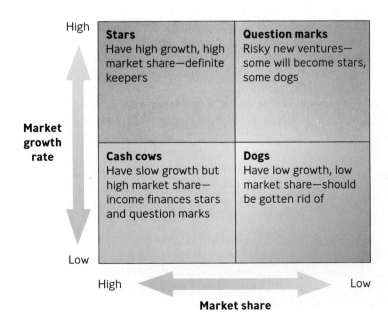

figure 6.4

THE BCG MATRIX

Market growth is divided into two categories, low and high. Market share is also divided into low and high. Thus, in this matrix, "Stars" are business units that are highly desirable (high growth, high market share), compared to "Dogs," which are not so desirable (low growth, low market share).

major question?

How does effective execution help managers during the strategic-management process?

THE BIG PICTURE

Strategic implementation is closely aligned with strategic control. Execution is a process that helps align these two phases of the strategic-management process.

Stage 1 of the strategic-management process was establishing the mission and the vision. Stage 2 was establishing the grand strategy. Stage 3 was formulating the strategic plans. Now we come to the last two stages—4, strategic implementation, and 5, strategic control.

Execution: Getting Things Done

Larry Bossidy, former CEO of AlliedSignal (later Honeywell), and **Ram Charan,** a business adviser to senior executives, are authors of *Execution: The Discipline of Getting Things Done.*[73] **Execution, they say, is not simply tactics, it is a central part of any company's strategy. It consists of using questioning, analysis, and follow-through to mesh strategy with reality, align people with goals, and achieve results promised.**

How important is execution to organizational success in today's global economy? A survey of 769 global CEOs from 40 countries revealed that "excellence in execution" was their most important concern—more important than "profit growth," "customer loyalty," "stimulating innovation," and "finding qualified employees."[74]

Bossidy and Charan outline how organizations and managers can improve the ability to execute. Effective execution requires managers to build a foundation for execution within three core processes found in any business: people, strategy, and operations.[75]

The Three Core Processes of Business: People, Strategy, & Operations

A company's overall ability to execute is a function of effectively executing according to three processes: *people, strategy,* and *operations.* Because all work ultimately entails some human interaction, effort, or involvement, Bossidy and Charan believe that the *people* process is the most important.

Execution. Occupying a sprawling campus in Cary, North Carolina, software maker SAS was No. 1 on Fortune's 2010 list of "100 Best Companies to Work For." Its ability to execute effectively has also made it highly profitable and the world's largest privately owned software company.

The First Core Process—People: "You Need to Consider *Who* Will Benefit You in the Future." "If you don't get the people process right," say Bossidy and Charan, "you will never fulfill the potential of your business." But today most organizations focus on evaluating the jobs people are doing at present, rather than considering which individuals can handle the jobs of the future. An effective leader tries to evaluate talent by linking people to particular strategic milestones, developing future leaders, dealing with nonperformers, and transforming the mission and operations of the human resource department.

The Second Core Process—Strategy: "You Need to Consider *How* Success Will Be Accomplished." In most organizations, the strategies developed fail to consider the "how" of execution. According to the authors, a good strategic plan addresses nine questions. *(See Table 6.4.)* In considering whether the organization can execute the strategy, a leader must take a realistic and critical view of its capabilities and competencies. If it does not have the talent in finance, sales, and manufacturing to accomplish the vision, the chances of success are drastically reduced.

table 6.4

NECESSARY ANSWERS: WHAT QUESTIONS SHOULD A STRONG STRATEGIC PLAN ADDRESS?

1. What is the assessment of the external environment?
2. How well do you understand the existing customers and markets?
3. What is the best way to grow the business profitably, and what are the obstacles to growth?
4. Who is the competition?
5. Can the business execute the strategy?
6. Are the short term and long term balanced?
7. What are the important milestones for executing the plan?
8. What are the critical issues facing the business?
9. How will the business make money on a sustainable basis?

Source: From *Execution* by Larry Bossidy and Ram Charan, Copyright © 2002 by Larry Bossidy and Ram Charan. Used by permission of Crown Business, a division of Random House, Inc.

The Third Core Process—Operations: "You Need to Consider *What Path* Will Be Followed." The strategy process defines where an organization wants to go, and the people process defines who's going to get it done. The third core process, operations, or the operating plan, provides the path for people to follow. The operating plan, as we described in Chapter 5, should address all the major activities in which the company will engage—marketing, production, sales, revenue, and so on—and then define short-term objectives for these activities, to provide targets for people at which to aim.

Building a Foundation of Execution

The foundation of execution is based on leadership (as we discuss in Chapter 14) and organizational culture (discussed in Chapter 8). Bossidy and Charan suggest that there are seven essential types of leader behaviors that are needed to fuel the engine of execution. Managers are advised to engage in seven kinds of behaviors, as follows:

Know Your People & Your Business: "Engage Intensely with Your Employees." In companies that don't execute, leaders are usually out of touch with the day-to-day realities. Bossidy and Charan insist leaders must engage intensely and personally with their organization's people and its businesses. They cannot rely on secondhand knowledge through other people's observations, assessments, and recommendations.

Insist on Realism: "Don't Let Others Avoid Reality." Many people want to avoid or shade reality, hiding mistakes or avoiding confrontations. Making realism a priority begins with the leaders being realistic themselves, and making sure realism is the goal of all dialogues in the organization.

Set Clear Priorities: "Focus on a Few Rather Than Many Goals." Leaders who execute focus on a very few clear priorities that everyone can grasp.

Follow Through: "Establish Accountability & Check on Results." Failing to follow through is a major cause of poor execution. "How many meetings have you attended where people left without firm conclusions about who would do what and when?" Bossidy and Charan ask. Accountability and follow-up are important.

Reward the Doers: "Show Top Performers That They Matter." If people are to produce specific results, they must be rewarded accordingly, making sure that top performers are rewarded far better than ordinary performers.

Expand People's Capabilities: "Develop the Talent." Coaching is an important part of the executive's job, providing useful and specific feedback that can improve performance.

Know Yourself: "Do the Hard Work of Understanding Who You Are." Leaders must develop "emotional fortitude" based on honest self-assessments. Four core qualities are authenticity, self-awareness, self-mastery, and humility.

Organizational culture is a system of shared beliefs and values within an organization that guides the behavior of its members. In this context, effective execution will not occur unless the culture supports an emphasis on getting quality work done in a timely manner. Chapter 8 presents 11 ways managers can attempt to create an execution-oriented culture.[76]

How Execution Helps Implement & Control Strategy

Many executives appear to have an aversion to execution, which they associate with boring tactics—with the tedium of doing, as opposed to the excitement of visioning—and which they hand off to subordinates. But, Bossidy and Charan point out, this notion can be a fatal flaw. "There's an enormous difference between leading an organization and presiding over it," they write. "The leader who boasts of her hands-off style or puts her faith in empowerment is not dealing with the issues of the day. . . . Leading for execution is not about micromanaging. . . . Leaders who excel at execution immerse themselves in the substance of execution and even some of the key details. They use their knowledge of the business to constantly probe and question. They bring weaknesses to light and rally their people to correct them."[77]

By linking people, strategy, and operating plans, execution allows executives to direct and control the three core processes that will advance their strategic vision. ●

Mentoring: The New Rules

Who's going to help you learn the ropes in a new organization? Maybe you need a mentor.

If you can find an experienced employee to mentor you—to be your sponsor and help you understand organizational strategy and navigate your way around—it can be a great asset to your career. Indeed, mentoring may be especially useful for female and minority managers, for whom there may be fewer role models within their particular organizations. One survey of 4,561 respondents from 42 countries found that 46% felt that coaching or mentoring had a great impact and 45% a moderate impact on their career success.[78]

What's the best advice about acquiring a mentor? Here are some of the new rules.[79]

Choose Anyone You Can Learn From, Not Just Someone Higher Up

It used to be thought that a mentor should be a seasoned manager higher up in the organization. But a mentor can also be a peer—someone at your own level inside the organization.

Choose More Than One Mentor

It might be nice to have a single mentor who can give you lots of one-on-one attention. But everyone's busy, so look around and see if there are two or three people who might be helpful to you. "Diversify your mentor portfolio," goes one piece of advice.

Pick Your Mentors, Don't Wait to Be Picked

Don't wait for organizational veterans to select you to be their protégé. It's up to you to make the first move, to be assertive in a nice way.

Do a Self-Assessment

Before you begin contacting people to be mentors, assess where you want to go and what skills and knowledge you need to get there, so that you'll know the kind of help you need.

Look for Someone Different from You

It used to be thought the mentor and mentee should have a lot in common, as in personal chemistry or personal style. But someone who is different from you will challenge you and help you be more objective.

Mentoring. Think you could succeed in a new job with a new organization without the help of mentors? Did mentors help you find your way in college?

Investigate Your Prospects

Before approaching prospective mentors, call their administrative assistants, explain your plans, and ask what their bosses are like to work with. Find out the best time to approach them.

Show Your Prospective Mentor How You Can Be Helpful

"Mentoring is a two-way street," says Anne Hayden, senior vice president of Metropolitan Life insurance company. "The person being mentored gets help, advice, and coaching, and the person doing the mentoring generally gets extra effort—someone very committed to working on special projects or on assignments that maybe don't fall within the boxes on the organizational chart."[80]

Agree on How Your Mentoring Relationship Will Work

In your first meeting, set the ground rules for how frequently you will meet and the type of contact, such as whether it will be in the office, over lunch, or at the gym. A minimum of one meeting a month is recommended, and in between the two of you should keep in touch by phone and e-mail.

BCG matrix 183
business plan 164
competitive intelligence 174
contingency planning 177
cost-focus strategy 181
cost-leadership strategy 180
defensive strategy 172
differentiation strategy 181
diversification 182
environmental scanning 174
execution 184
focused-differentiation
  strategy 181

forecast 177
grand strategy 171
growth strategy 172
organizational opportunities 176
organizational strengths 175
organizational threats 176
organizational weaknesses 176
Porter's four competitive
  strategies 180
Porter's model for industry
  analysis 179
related diversification 182
scenario analysis 177

scenario planning 177
single-product strategy 181
stability strategy 172
strategic control 173
strategic management 165
strategic positioning 168
strategy 165
strategy formulation 173
strategy implementation 173
SWOT analysis 174
synergy 183
trend analysis 177
unrelated diversification 182

Summary

6.1 The Dynamics of Strategic Planning
Every organization needs to have a "big picture" about where it's going and how to get there, which involves strategy, strategic management, and strategic planning. A strategy is a large-scale action plan that sets the direction for an organization. Strategic management involves managers from all parts of the organization in the formulation and implementation of strategies and strategic goals. Strategic planning determines the organization's long-term goals and ways to achieve them.

Three reasons why an organization should adopt strategic management and strategic planning: They can (1) provide direction and momentum, (2) encourage new ideas, and (3) develop a sustainable competitive advantage. Sustainable competitive advantage occurs when an organization is able to get and stay ahead in four areas: (1) in being responsive to customers, (2) in innovating, (3) in quality, and (4) in effectiveness.

Strategic positioning attempts to achieve sustainable competitive advantage by preserving what is distinctive about a company. Three key principles underlie strategic positioning: (1) Strategy is the creation of a unique and valuable position. (2) Strategy requires trade-offs in competing. (3) Strategy involves creating a "fit" among a company's activities.

6.2 The Strategic-Management Process
The strategic-management process has five steps plus a feedback loop.

Step 1 is to establish the mission statement and the vision statement. The mission statement expresses the organization's purpose. The vision statement describes the organization's long-term direction and strategic intent.

Step 2 is to translate the broad mission and vision statements into a grand strategy that explains how the organization's mission is to be accomplished. Three common grand strategies are (1) a growth strategy, which involves expansion—as in sales revenues; (2) a stability strategy, which involves little or no significant change; and (3) a defensive strategy, which involves reduction in the organization's efforts.

Step 3 is strategy formulation, the translation of the grand strategy into more specific strategic plans, choosing among different strategies and altering them to best fit the organization's needs.

Step 4 is strategy implementation—putting strategic plans into effect. Step 5 is strategic control, monitoring the execution of strategy and making adjustments.

Corrective action constitutes a feedback loop in which a problem requires that managers return to an earlier step to rethink policies, budgets, or personnel arrangements.

6.3 Establishing the Grand Strategy

To develop a grand strategy (Step 2 above), you need to gather data and make projections. This starts with competitive intelligence, gathering information about one's competitors' activities so that you can anticipate their moves and react appropriately. Three public sources of competitive intelligence are the public prints and advertising, investor information, and informal sources such as trade shows.

The next point in establishing a grand strategy is environmental scanning, careful monitoring of an organization's internal and external environments to detect early signs of opportunities and threats that may influence the firm's plans. The process for doing such scanning is called SWOT analysis, a search for the Strengths, Weaknesses, Opportunities, and Threats affecting the organization. Organizational strengths are the skills and capabilities that give the organization special competencies and competitive advantages. Organizational weaknesses are the drawbacks that hinder an organization in executing strategies. Organizational opportunities are environmental factors that the organization may exploit for competitive advantage. Organizational threats are environmental factors that hinder an organization's achieving a competitive advantage.

Another tool for developing a grand strategy is forecasting—creating a vision or projection of the future. Two types of forecasting are (1) trend analysis, a hypothetical extension of a past series of events into the future; and (2) contingency planning, the creation of alternative hypothetical but equally likely future conditions.

6.4 Formulating Strategy

Strategy formulation (Step 3 in the strategic-management process) makes use of several concepts, including (1) Porter's five competitive forces, (2) Porter's four competitive strategies, (3) diversification and synergy, and (4) the BCG matrix.

Porter's model for industry analysis suggests that business-level strategies originate in five primary competitive forces in the firm's environment: (1) threats of new entrants, (2) bargaining power of suppliers, (3) bargaining power of buyers, (4) threats of substitute products or services, and (5) rivalry among competitors.

Porter's four competitive strategies are as follows: (1) The cost-leadership strategy is to keep the costs, and hence the prices, of a product or service below those of competitors and to target a wide market. (2) The differentiation strategy is to offer products or services that are of unique and superior value compared with those of competitors but to target a wide market. (3) The cost-focus strategy is to keep the costs and hence prices of a product or service below those of competitors and to target a narrow market. (4) The focused-differentiation strategy is to offer products or services that are of unique and superior value compared with those of competitors and to target a narrow market.

Companies need to choose whether to have a single-product strategy, making and selling only one product within their market, or a diversification strategy, operating several businesses to spread the risk. There are two kinds of diversification: unrelated diversification consists of operating several businesses that are not related to each other; related diversification consists of operating separate businesses that are related to each other, which may reduce risk, produce management efficiencies, and produce synergy, or the sum being greater than the parts.

The BCG matrix is a means of evaluating strategic business units on the basis of (1) their business growth rates and (2) their share of the market. In general, organizations do better in fast-growing markets in which they have a high market share rather than slow-growing markets in which they have low market shares.

6.5 Implementing & Controlling Strategy: Execution

The last two stages of the strategic-management process are 4, strategic implementation, and 5, strategic control.

Execution, say Larry Bossidy and Ram Charan, is not simply tactics; it is a central part of any company's strategy; it consists of using questioning, analysis, and follow-through to mesh strategy with reality, align people with goals, and achieve results promised.

Three core processes of execution are people, strategy, and operations. (1) You have to evaluate talent by linking people to particular strategic milestones, developing future leaders, dealing with nonperformers, and transforming the mission and operations of the human resource department. (2) In considering whether the organization can execute the strategy, a leader must take a realistic and critical view of its capabilities and competencies. (3) The third core process, operations, or the operating plan, provides the path for people to follow. The operating plan should address all the major activities in which the company will engage and then define short-term objectives for these activities, to provide targets for people at which to aim.

By linking people, strategy, and operating plans, execution allows executives to direct and control the three core processes that will advance their strategic vision.

Management in Action

Getting Over the Jet Blues

David Neeleman is in a good mood. Fresh off a flight from São Paulo and gearing up for a round of TV interviews, Neeleman, 50, agrees to meet over lunch at a Così sandwich outlet in Greenwich, Connecticut, near his home in New Canaan. . . . Neeleman has a happy story to tell: Investment firm TPG has just bought a $30 million stake in his Brazilian airline Azul Linhas Aéreas Brasileiras, and Azul has set an industry record, carrying 2.2 million customers in its first year.

Azul's early success is all the more sweet for Neeleman given the bitterness he felt after his ouster from JetBlue Airways. . . . After dabbling with the idea of starting an ethanol company in California, Neeleman went to check out a Brazilian airline called BRA Transportes Aéros as a favor to some investor friends. "It was the furthest thing from an airline I've ever seen," says Neeleman. "I thought, 'If these guys will invest $150 million in this, it must be worth looking around.'" (BRA suspended operations in late 2007.) Neeleman quickly raised $150 million to launch his own start-up airline. Then, just as he was finalizing route plans and securing government clearance to fly, the global economy crashed. With its financing and plane orders locked in, he pushed ahead with his launch in December 2008. Remarkably, Azul—"blue" in Portuguese—is on track to make a profit on 2010. Neeleman, the chairman, owns about 15% and controls the voting shares.

Azul's long-term success will depend in part on how well Neeleman has learned from his mistakes. One challenge, says Vaughn Cordle, managing partner of Washington-based research firm Airline-Forecasts, will be curbing his ambition. "The greatest threat is if they let Azul grow above a sustainable rate," says Cordle. "That's what happened at JetBlue." Neeleman acknowledges the Brazilian market's many challenges, from taxes to infrastructure, and insists he's keeping his expectations in check. But in the same breath he talks about the opportunity. He wants to revolutionize the Brazilian market by bringing air travel to the masses. And he wants redemption.

Brazil was a logical place for Neeleman to go. He spent his first five years there, the son of a reporter for United Press International who had first visited the country as a Mormon missionary. At 19, Neeleman returned to the country of his birth to do his own two-year missionary stint. . . .

His time in Brazil left him with two distinctive advantages: fluency in Portuguese and dual citizenship, which allowed him to get around Brazil's 20% cap on foreign ownership of airlines. Neeleman's instincts told him Brazil was ripe for a new aviation venture. Only a fraction of its 192 million people currently fly; per capita, Americans fly about eight times more, according to Airports Council International. "We're not even close to the level of air travel in mature economies," says Libano Miranda Barroso,

CEO of Tam, Brazil's largest airline, with a 46% market share. "Even our projection for 2027 is equivalent to what the U.S. used to have in the 1970s."

Neeleman is determined to change that by creating a new market of fliers. His target is the 52% of Brazilian households that earn between 1,064 and 4,591 reais a month (about $594 to $2,565) making up Brazil's middle class. They are a fast-growing group that traditionally travels by bus. Many carriers have tried to tap this population, only to be thwarted by strained airports and high costs. As Renato Pascowitch, executive director of domestic Brazilian carrier OceanAir, puts it, fliers "often can't afford to take a taxi to the airport. So how do you get these passengers to board your plane, even if you are offering dirt-cheap tickets?"

Neeleman's reply: "We give them a free ride to the airport." Complementary transportation is all the more crucial because Azul, like Southwest and Ryanair, flies nonstop between secondary airports. Its main hub is Viracopos/Campinas International Airport in Campinas, an attractive and well-run city about 50 miles north of São Paulo. Campinas has about 2.6 million people, and some 30 million live within a 120-mile radius. Azul offers bus service from pickup points in seven cities, with about 50 bus trips a day.

But the real draw is the low fares. Tickets, if purchased in advance, run about the same as a bus trip. Traveling from São Paulo to Salvador by bus, for example, costs about $150 each way and takes 23 hours; on Azul, the lowest one-way fare is just over $100. Christina Maisonnette of Rio de Janeiro had been planning to drive to Natal, a coastal town, before opting to fly. "I hope they survive," she says of Azul. "I want to be able to fly more often."

Like JetBlue in its early days, Azul now has the benefit of a brand-new fleet of planes and a young staff, which means low maintenance costs and cheap labor. Profit margins could come under pressure as costs rise over time and as competitors come in with lower fares to steal business. Even before the ice storm, JetBlue's profitability had been eroding for those very reasons.

For Discussion

1. Based on Michael Porter's discussion of the characteristics of an effective strategy, does Azul Linhas Aéreas Brasileiras have a good growth strategy? Explain.

2. To what extent is Azul Linhas Aéreas Brasileiras following the five steps of the strategic-management process?

3. Conduct an environmental scan or SWOT analysis of Azul Linhas Aéreas Brasileiras's current reality and recommend whether the company's current strategy is poised to succeed.

4. To what extent will Porter's five competitive forces help or hurt Azul Linhas Aéreas Brasileiras's growth strategy? Discuss.

5. What is the greatest takeaway from this case in terms of strategic management?

Source: Excerpted from Diane Brady and Adriana Brasileiro, "Getting Over the JetBlues," *Bloomberg Businessweek*, February 15, 2010, pp. 52, 54. Reprinted with permission.

Self-Assessment

Core Skills Required in Strategic Planning

Objectives
1. To assess if you have the skills to be in strategic planning.
2. To see what you think are the important core skill areas in strategic planning.

Introduction
Strategic planning became important as a method of managing the increasing velocity of change. The business environment no longer evolves at a manageable pace but increasingly through a process Charles Handy calls "discontinuous change"—change that radically alters how we think, work, and often behave. The computer, for instance, has completely changed how we communicate, research, write, and work. To meet this challenge, companies have strategic planners and others knowledgeable about their organizations, culture, and environment to shape strategy. Individuals must develop knowledge about their own abilities so that they formulate their own kind of strategic planning.

Instructions
To see whether you have the required skills needed to be a strategic planner, truthfully and thoughtfully assess your ability level for the following list of 12 skills. Rate each skill by using a five-point scale in which 1 = exceptional, 2 = very high, 3 = high, 4 = low, and 5 = very low.

I. Ability to synthesize	I	2	3	4	5
2. Analytical skills	I	2	3	4	5
3. Computer skills	I	2	3	4	5
4. Decisiveness	I	2	3	4	5
5. Interpersonal skills	I	2	3	4	5
6. Listening skills	I	2	3	4	5
7. Persuasiveness	I	2	3	4	5
8. Problem-solving skills	I	2	3	4	5
9. Research skills	I	2	3	4	5
I0. Team skills	I	2	3	4	5
II. Verbal skills	I	2	3	4	5
I2. Written skills	I	2	3	4	5

Scoring & Interpretation

According to research conducted at the Ohio State University College of Business, the core required skills for the 12 skills above rate as follows:

Ability to synthesize:	2
Analytical skills:	1
Computer skills:	3
Decisiveness:	3
Interpersonal skills:	1
Listening skills:	2
Persuasiveness:	2
Problem-solving skills:	3
Research skills:	3
Team skills:	2
Verbal skills:	2
Written skills:	3

If you scored mostly 4s and 5s, strategic planning is probably not for you.

If you scored near the "perfect" score, it may be a possible career path.

If you scored all 1s and 2s, you might do extremely well at this type of work and might want to look into it more.

Questions for Discussion

1. Based on your results, do you think you would like to make a career out of strategic planning? Why or why not?

2. What appeals or does not appeal to you about this career? Explain.

3. How might you enhance your strategic skills? Discuss.

Developed by Anne C. Cowden, PhD.

Should Companies Be Allowed to Ask Employees about Family Health History?

Companies generally consider the costs and benefits associated with their strategies in order to be successful. This dilemma involves the conflict between a company's desire to decrease health-care costs by encouraging employees to attend wellness classes and an employee's desire for privacy.

"Many employers offer workers cash incentives to fill out health surveys and some use that information to offer health advice or direct at-risk employees to disease-management programs," says a *Wall Street Journal* story. "But the Genetic Information Nondiscrimination Act, which took effect [in 2009], restricts employers' and health insurers' ability to collect and disclose genetic information. That includes not only genetic-test results, but family medical history, too.

"Some employers say the law is stymieing their efforts to promote employee wellness because it bars them from offering worker financial incentives to complete health surveys that ask about family history. Generally, the law prohibits insurers and employers from using genetic information for coverage and employment decisions, such as hiring, firing, and promotion.

"Employers say financial incentives are needed to boost participation in wellness programs, which can reduce overall health-care costs. . . .

"Some supporters of the law say the financial incentives improperly encourage employees to disclose genetic details. 'People should not have to choose between their pocketbooks and participating in a wellness program or a health-risk assessment, particularly in this economy,' says Jeremy Gruber, executive director of the Council of Responsible Genetics."

Solving the Dilemma

How would you resolve this dilemma?

1. In today's economy it is very important to contain or reduce the cost of health care. I would revise the Genetic Information Nondiscrimination Act so that employers are allowed to ask about family health history.

2. If we allow companies to ask about family medical history, they will use that information to discriminate against people. I would reinforce the Genetic Information Nondiscrimination Act and punish companies that ask questions about family medical history.

3. We cannot allow health-care costs to skyrocket; something must be done. That said, we should not allow discrimination based on one's family history. I would keep the law but exempt wellness programs from any regulations about collecting information about family medical history.

4. Invent other options. Discuss.

Source: Excerpted from Cari Tuna, "Wellness Efforts Face Hurdle," *The Wall Street Journal*, February 1, 2010, p. B2.

chapter 7

Individual & Group Decision Making

How Managers Make Things Happen

How Exceptional Managers Check to See If Their Decisions Might Be Biased

The biggest part of a manager's job is making decisions—and quite often they are wrong. Some questions you might ask next time you're poised to make a decision:

- **"Am I being too cocky?" The overconfidence bias.** If you're making a decision in an area in which you have considerable experience or expertise, you're less likely to be overconfident. Interestingly, however, you're more apt to be overconfident when dealing with questions on subjects you're unfamiliar with or questions with moderate to extreme difficulty.[1]

   Recommendation: When dealing with unfamiliar or difficult matters, think how your impending decision might go wrong. Afterward pay close attention to the consequences of your decision.

- **"Am I considering the actual evidence, or am I wedded to my prior beliefs?" The prior-hypothesis bias.** Do you tend to have strong beliefs? When confronted with a choice, decision makers with strong prior beliefs tend to make their decision based on their beliefs—even if evidence shows those beliefs are wrong. This is known as the *prior-hypothesis bias.*[2]

   Recommendation: Although it's always more comforting to look for evidence to support your prior beliefs, you need to be tough-minded and weigh the evidence.

- **"Are events really connected, or are they just chance?" The ignoring-randomness bias.** Is a rise in sales in athletic shoes because of your company's advertising campaign or because it's the start of the school year? Many managers don't understand the laws of randomness.

   Recommendation: Don't attribute trends or connections to a single, random event.

- **"Is there enough data on which to make a decision?" The unrepresentative sample bias.** If all the secretaries in your office say they prefer dairy creamer to real cream in their coffee, is that enough data on which to launch an ad campaign trumpeting the superiority of dairy creamer? It might if you polled 3,000 secretaries, but 3 or even 30 is too small a sample.

   Recommendation: You need to be attuned to the importance of sample size.

- **"Looking back, did I (or others) really know enough then to have made a better decision?" The 20-20 hindsight bias.** Once managers know what the consequences of a decision are, they may begin to think they could have predicted it. They may remember the facts as being a lot clearer than they actually were.[3]

   Recommendation: Try to keep in mind that hindsight does not equal foresight.

For Discussion Facing the hard facts about what works and what doesn't, how able do you think you are to make the tough decisions that effective managers have to make?

---

forecast | What's Ahead in This Chapter

We begin by distinguishing between rational and nonrational decision making, and we describe three nonrational models. We then consider evidence-based decision making and the use of analytics. Next we describe general decision-making styles. We next discuss ethical decision making. We follow by considering how individuals respond to decision situations and four common decision-making biases. We conclude with a discussion of group decision making, including participative management and group problem-solving techniques.

✳ 7.I TWO KINDS OF DECISION MAKING: RATIONAL & NONRATIONAL

major question ?

How do people know when they're being logical or illogical?

THE BIG PICTURE

Decision making, the process of identifying and choosing alternative courses of action, may be rational, but often it is nonrational. Four steps in making a rational decision are (1) identify the problem or opportunity, (2) think up alternative solutions, (3) evaluate alternatives and select a solution, and (4) implement and evaluate the solution chosen. Three examples of nonrational models of decision making are (1) satisficing, (2) incremental, and (3) intuition.

The subject of decisions and decision making is a fascinating subject that is at the heart of what managers do.

A *decision* is a choice made from among available alternatives. *Decision making is the process of identifying and choosing alternative courses of action.*

Example

Which Is Better—Fast or Slow Delivery? Maersk Shipping Line Managers Decide among Alternatives

Managers of the Danish shipping giant Maersk had a decision to make—a choice between two available alternatives: "Fast is better" versus "Slow is better." That is, in a global marketplace dominated by speed, they could choose to order their container ships to continue to sail as fast as possible from port to port. Or they could halve the ships' speed and greatly reduce fuel-consumption costs.

The focus of the 1990s and early 2000s for Maersk and other shippers had been on speed—"How fast can we get it there?"—because, it was believed, speed was indispensable to serving their clients. Yet the "need it now" strategy also meant that ships traveled at speeds far above maximum fuel efficiency.

Fuel Efficiency & the Carbon Footprint. Then in 2008, oil prices shot up and there also arose more environmental concerns about carbon emissions—the "CO_2 footprint"—and talk of levying a carbon tax. Between 1985 and 2007, container ship trade grew eightfold, but transport emissions also accelerated.

Maersk found that by halving its ships' top cruising speeds, which reduced drag and friction on the hulls, fuel consumption on major routes was reduced by as much as 30%—and there was an equal cut in the emission of greenhouse gases. Slowing the ships

also enabled Maersk to cut prices in an ever more competitive market.

Weighing the Alternatives. Before it could invoke the new policy, Maersk had to "prove that slow speeds would not damage ship engines in order to maintain engine warranties that did not cover such slow travel," reports *The New York Times*.[4] The company also had to reckon on absorbing the higher labor costs of having crews at sea for longer periods and adding two ships on the Germany-to-China run to maintain scheduled deliveries. Finally, Maersk had to determine that customers, especially those involved with time-sensitive products such as fashion apparel and electronics, could factor in extra time for shipping. All such concerns, it turned out, were canceled out by the decreased costs made possible by slow shipping.

YOUR CALL

American drivers on open stretches of interstate highway tend to drive at about 70 miles per hour, regardless of what the legal speed limit is.[5] If you drive 55 miles per hour instead of 65, you can reduce carbon dioxide emissions by 20% and save on gas. Do you care? What alternatives are you weighing in deciding whether to drive faster rather than slower?

Decision Making in the Real World

The Maersk example sounds like a model for thoughtful decision making, making rational choices among well-defined alternatives. But that is not always the way it works in the real world. "Our brains do not contain a single, general-purpose decision-making unit," writes psychologist Christopher Chabris. "Instead, we have two systems: one that is rational, analytical, and slow to act, and another that is emotional, impulsive, and prone to form and follow habits." Thus, for example, politicians "have long known that appeals to emotion are more effective than appeals to logic—not because people are stupid but because the mind is designed to use logic as a tool for supporting our beliefs rather than for changing them."[6]

Why do some engineers design electronic products (such as DVD remote controls) with as many as 52 buttons, devices ultimately useful only to other engineers? Why do some professional investors and bankers turn out to be so prone to taking excess risks?[7] Why are some employees so reluctant to adopt new processes? The answer may be what's known as *the curse of knowledge*. As one writer put it about engineers, for example, "People who design products are experts cursed by their knowledge, and they can't imagine what it's like to be as ignorant as the rest of us."[8] In other words, as our knowledge and expertise grow, we may be less and less able to see things from an outsider's perspective—hence, we are often apt to make irrational decisions.

Let us look at the two approaches managers may take to making decisions: They may follow a *rational model* or various kinds of *nonrational models*.

Rational Decision Making: Managers Should Make Logical & Optimal Decisions

The *rational model of decision making*, also called the *classical model*, explains how managers *should* make decisions; it assumes managers will make logical decisions that will be the optimum in furthering the organization's best interests.

Typically there are four stages associated with rational decision making. *(See Figure 7.1.)*

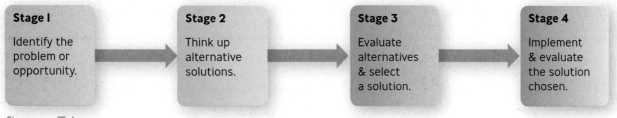

Stage 1

Identify the problem or opportunity.

Stage 2

Think up alternative solutions.

Stage 3

Evaluate alternatives & select a solution.

Stage 4

Implement & evaluate the solution chosen.

figure 7.1

THE FOUR STEPS IN RATIONAL DECISION MAKING

Stage 1: Identify the Problem or Opportunity—Determining the Actual versus the Desirable

As a manager, you'll probably find no shortage of **problems, or difficulties that inhibit the achievement of goals.** Customer complaints. Supplier breakdowns. Staff turnover. Sales shortfalls. Competitor innovations.

However, you'll also often find **opportunities—situations that present possibilities for exceeding existing goals.** It's the farsighted manager, however, who can look past the steady stream of daily problems and seize the moment to actually do *better* than the goals he or she is expected to achieve. When a competitor's top salesperson unexpectedly quits, that creates an opportunity for your company to hire that person away to promote your product more vigorously in that sales territory.

Whether you're confronted with a problem or an opportunity, the decision you're called on to make is how to make *improvements*—how to change conditions from the present to the desirable. This is a matter of ***diagnosis*—analyzing the underlying causes.**

Example

What Do Billionaire Warren Buffett & Female Investors Have in Common? Making a Correct Diagnosis

"Warren Buffett Invests Like a Girl," reads the headline over an article by LouAnn DiCosmo.[9] Is that a good thing? Buffett is the renowned billionaire investor (worth $47 billion in 2010) known as the "Oracle of Omaha" who heads the financial juggernaut Berkshire Hathaway. His investment decisions are so successful that $1,000 invested with him in 1956 was worth $27.6 million at the end of 2006.[10] So, does he really invest like a girl?

Who's the Frazzled One? As it turns out, Buffett and female investors have something in common: "Women trade much less often than men, do a lot more research, and tend to base their investment decisions on considerations other than just numbers," according to one account.[11] Men, says DiCosmo, tend to be "frazzled, frenetic day traders, with their ties askew, hair on end, and eyes bleary. Patience and good decision making help set women apart here." As a result, according to a study cited by DiCosmo, women's portfolios on average gain 1.4% more than men's, and single women's portfolios do 2.3% better than single men's.[12]

(Interestingly, however, the percentage of women drawn to careers in finance is actually shrinking, because they worry their paths to success in that industry are limited.)[13]

The Buffet Approach. As for the fabled Buffett, his approach is to use basic arithmetic to analyze several file-cabinet drawers of annual reports and other readily available company financial documents and to look for a record of "high returns on equity capital, low debt, and a consistent, predictable business with sustainable advantages—like Coca-Cola's soft-drink franchise."[14] In other words, Buffett—whose personal fortune gained $10 billion in the recession year 2009—takes pains to make a correct diagnosis before making a decision.[15]

YOUR CALL

When preparing to make decisions—especially financial decisions—do you spend a lot of time trying to make a correct diagnosis, doing deep research (as women investors are said to do), or do you chase "hot" tips and make snap judgments (as men reportedly do)?

Stage 2: Think Up Alternative Solutions—Both the Obvious & the Creative

Employees burning with bright ideas are an employer's greatest competitive resource. "Creativity precedes innovation, which is its physical expression," says *Fortune* magazine writer Alan Farnham. "It's the source of all intellectual property."[16]

After you've identified the problem or opportunity and diagnosed its causes, you need to come up with alternative solutions.

Stage 3: Evaluate Alternatives & Select a Solution—Ethics, Feasibility, & Effectiveness

In this stage, you need to evaluate each alternative not only according to cost and quality but also according to the following questions: (1) Is it *ethical*? (If it isn't, don't give it a second look.) (2) Is it *feasible*? (If time is short, costs are high, technology unavailable, or customers resistant, for example, it is not.) (3) Is it ultimately *effective*? (If the decision is merely "good enough" but not optimal in the long run, you might reconsider.)

Stage 4: Implement & Evaluate the Solution Chosen

With some decisions, implementation is usually straightforward (though not necessarily easy—firing employees who steal may be an obvious decision, but it can still be emotionally draining). With other decisions, implementation can be quite difficult; when one company acquires another, for instance, it may take months to consolidate the departments, accounting systems, inventories, and so on.

Successful Implementation   For implementation to be successful, you need to do two things:

- **Plan carefully.** Especially if reversing an action will be difficult, you need to make careful plans for implementation. Some decisions may require written plans.

- **Be sensitive to those affected.** You need to consider how the people affected may feel about the change—inconvenienced, insecure, even fearful, all of which can trigger resistance. This is why it helps to give employees and customers latitude during a changeover in business practices or working arrangements.

Example

Faulty Implementation: Customer Service Is Often "Just Talk"

"My claim to fame, the only thing I've ever been really good at, is returning people's phone calls every single day," says Mark Powers. No doubt it is that kind of customer service that is the reason why Excelsior Roofing of San Francisco, founded by Powers's grandfather over 100 years ago, is still in business.[17]

Just Talk. "Executives talk about the importance of responding to customers' needs with top-notch customer service," writes *Wall Street Journal* columnist Carol Hymowitz. "But often it's just talk."[18]

The problem with faulty customer service, however, is that sometimes the company may be the last to hear about it, but a great many other potential customers may hear of it by word of mouth. One study found that only 6% of shoppers who experienced a problem with a retailer contacted the company. However, 31% went on to tell friends, family, and colleagues what had happened. Indeed, if 100 people have a bad experience, a retailer stands to lose between 32 and 36 current or potential customers, according to the study.[19]

In the Shoes of Customers. Consultants working for one large telecommunications company encourage customer service reps at one call center to share their problems and successes with each other and bring in customers to report their positive and negative experiences with the call center. To encourage customer reps

to "step inside the shoes of customers," the consultants also presented a weekly award of a pair of baby shoes to the employee who solved the most customer problems.[20]

YOUR CALL

We're all accustomed to pumping our own gas and doing our own banking through ATMs. Now retailers are moving toward self-service checkout lanes, as is done by some Home Depot stores, and airlines toward self-check-in kiosks.[21]

What do you think the self-serve trend means for customer service?

Evaluation   One "law" in economics is the Law of Unintended Consequences—things happen that weren't foreseen. For this reason, you need to follow up and evaluate the results of the decision.

What should you do if the action is not working? Some possibilities:

- **Give it more time.** You need to make sure employees, customers, and so on have had enough time to get used to the new action.

- **Change it slightly.** Maybe the action was correct, but it just needs "tweaking"—a small change of some sort.

- **Try another alternative.** If Plan A doesn't seem to be working, maybe you want to scrap it for another alternative.

- **Start over.** If no alternative seems workable, you need to go back to the drawing board—to Stage 1 of the decision-making process.

What's Wrong with the Rational Model?

The rational model is *prescriptive,* describing how managers ought to make decisions. It doesn't describe how managers *actually* make decisions. Indeed, the rational model makes some highly desirable assumptions—that managers have complete information, are able to make an unemotional analysis, and are able to make the best decision for the organization. *(See Table 7.1.)*

table 7.1

ASSUMPTIONS OF THE RATIONAL MODEL

- **Complete information, no uncertainty:** You should obtain complete, error-free information about all alternative courses of action and the consequences that would follow from each choice.

- **Logical, unemotional analysis:** Having no prejudices or emotional blind spots, you are able to logically evaluate the alternatives, ranking them from best to worst according to your personal preferences.

- **Best decision for the organization:** Confident of the best future course of action, you coolly choose the alternative that you believe will most benefit the organization.

Example 🔍

Evaluation: The Boeing 787 Dreamliner, a Bet-the-Company Decision

The airline industry is one of the most volatile around, and Boeing Co., the Chicago-headquartered aerospace giant, has been through some rough boom-and-bust cycles. In 1997, for instance, production problems shut down two assembly lines and cost the company $2.5 billion.

A Bold New Strategy for Building Airplanes. Then, at a time when Boeing was losing business to its European rival Airbus, the company was wracked by scandals involving Pentagon contracts, and rising fuel costs were dramatically impacting the commercial airline industry, Boeing management made a bold

decision: It would build a new medium-sized commercial jet, the 787 Dreamliner, its first new aircraft in 10 years, that would fly faster than the competition and would consume 20% less fuel than similar-sized planes. To achieve this, the 787 would feature more fuel-efficient engines and the fuselage would be built from plastic composite materials instead of aluminum. This would cut down on structural fatigue and corrosion, thereby reducing the number of inspections necessary and increasing the number of flights possible. "A light, strong plane is the big payoff for the huge technical risk Boeing is taking in crafting parts out of composites," said aerospace reporter Stanley Holmes.[22]

A Bumpy Ride. First planned for a summer 2007 launch, the date was revised for 2008. Then, in mid-2006, the company began encountering the first of many stories of bad news. The fuselage section had failed in testing, and engineers had discovered worrisome bubbles in its skin. The carbon-fiber wing was too heavy, adding to the plane's overall weight. To hold costs down, Boeing had outsourced about 70% of the production to major suppliers acting as risk-sharing partners and playing a greater role in design and manufacturing. In return for investing more up front and taking on a share of the development costs, suppliers were given major sections of the airplane to build.[23] By late 2007, however, it was apparent that suppliers were struggling to meet the exacting technological demands and deadlines, and their software programs were having trouble communicating with each other. In October, Boeing announced it would no longer meet its May 2008 target date and was postponing its first delivery to late fall of that year.[24]

Changing Dates. In early 2008, the company said the poor quality of outsourced work and the unprecedented amount of coordination among suppliers caused Boeing to shift much of the work back to its Everett, Washington, assembly plant,

adding to delays. It said it was working to try to begin deliveries of the 787 to customers not in late 2008 but in the first quarter of 2009.[25] In April, it changed the scheduled delivery date once again—to the third quarter of 2009.[26] Then in 2009, stress testing revealed new flaws around bolts inside the wings.[27]

Finally, after six delays and nearly 10 years of anticipation, the Dreamliner had its first flight, on December 15, 2009.[28] There then began a months-long flight-test program phase to meet crucial government certification, but as of March 2010 lags in the testing schedule were threatening the year-end delivery of the first planes.[29] All the constant problems, noted a *Newsweek* writer, were "siphoning cash and overlapping with the redesign of the 747-8 jumbo jet, delaying both."[30]

YOUR CALL

By now you, the reader, may be in a position to know whether Boeing made its 2010 delivery deadline and how much it had to pay in financial penalties to the customers it had lined up. Did the company's huge bet on the Dreamliner pay off? Was the strategy of reinventing the approach to building airplanes—using carbon composite rather than aluminum and outsourcing so much of the engineering, design, and manufacturing—a faulty one? How would you evaluate Boeing's decisions?

Nonrational Decision Making: Managers Find It Difficult to Make Optimal Decisions

***Nonrational models of decision making* explain how managers make decisions; they assume that decision making is nearly always uncertain and risky, making it difficult for managers to make optimal decisions.** The nonrational models are *descriptive* rather than prescriptive: They describe how managers *actually* make decisions rather than how they should. Three nonrational models are (1) *satisficing*, (2) *incremental*, and (3) *intuition*.

1. Bounded Rationality & the Satisficing Model: "Satisfactory Is Good Enough."   During the 1950s, economist **Herbert Simon**—who later received the Nobel Prize—began to study how managers actually make decisions. From his research he proposed that managers could not act truly logically because their rationality was bounded by so many restrictions.[31] Called ***bounded rationality,* the concept suggests that the ability of decision makers to be rational is limited by numerous constraints,** such as complexity, time and

figure 7.2

SOME HINDRANCES TO PERFECTLY RATIONAL DECISION MAKING

money, and their cognitive capacity, values, skills, habits, and unconscious reflexes. *(See Figure 7.2.)*

Because of such constraints, managers don't make an exhaustive search for the best alternative. Instead, they follow what Simon calls the *satisficing model—* **that is, managers seek alternatives until they find one that is satisfactory, not optimal.** Once a Motorola-led consortium called Irridium developed a clunky satellite-linked mobile phone that weighed 1 pound, could not be used inside buildings or moving cars, and cost $3,000. Instead of waiting to improve the technology, Irridium tried to market the mobile phone, a clear and costly example of satisficing.

While looking for a solution that is merely "satisficing" might seem to be a weakness, it may well outweigh any advantages gained from delaying making a decision until all information is in and all alternatives weighed. However, making snap decisions can also backfire.

2. The Incremental Model: "The Least That Will Solve the Problem."
Another nonrational decision-making model is the *incremental model,* **in which managers take small, short-term steps to alleviate a problem,** rather than steps that will accomplish a long-term solution. Of course, over time a series of short-term steps may move toward a long-term solution. However, the temporary steps may also impede a beneficial long-term solution.

3. The Intuition Model: "It Just Feels Right."
Despite the lack of supporting marketing research, Bob Lutz, then president of Chrysler Corporation, ordered the development of the Dodge Viper, a "muscle car" that became very

Nonrational decision making?
This renovated McDonald's in Hacienda Heights, California, with its ever-expanding Asian population, was designed with the help of experts in feng shui, the Chinese art of creating harmonious surroundings. Walls are curved, ceiling and floor tiles are placed at distinctive angles, and doors swing open and shut in opposite directions, all in the name of keeping luck within the restaurant. Are these good nonrational decisions?

popular. "It was this subconscious, visceral feeling," he said about his decision later. "And it just felt right."[32]

"Going with your gut," or ***intuition,*** **is making a choice without the use of conscious thought or logical inference.** Intuition that stems from *expertise*—a person's explicit and tacit knowledge about a person, situation, object, or decision opportunity—is known as a *holistic hunch*. Intuition based on feelings—the involuntary emotional response to those same matters—is known as *automated experience*. It is important to try to develop your intuitive skills because they are as important as rational analysis in many decisions. Some suggestions appear below. *(See Table 7.2.)*

table 7.2

GUIDELINES FOR DEVELOPING INTUITIVE AWARENESS

Recommendation	Description
1. Open up the closet.	To what extent do you experience intuition, trust your feelings, count on intuitive judgments, suppress hunches, covertly rely upon gut feel?
2. Don't mix up your I's.	Instinct, Insight, and Intuition are not synonymous; practice distinguishing between your instincts, your insights, and your intuitions.
3. Elicit good feedback.	Seek feedback on your intuitive judgments; build confidence in your gut feel; create a learning environment in which you can develop better intuitive awareness.
4. Get a feel for your batting average.	Benchmark your intuitions; get a sense of how reliable hunches are; ask yourself how your intuitive judgment might be improved.
5. Use imagery.	Use imagery rather than words; literally visualize potential future scenarios that take your gut feelings into account.
6. Play devil's advocate.	Test out intuitive judgments; raise objections to them; generate counterarguments; probe how robust gut feel is when challenged.
7. Capture and validate your intuitions.	Create the inner state to give your intuitive mind the freedom to roam; capture your creative intuitions; log them before they are censored by rational analysis.

Source: E. Sadler-Smith and E. Shefy, "The Intuitive Executive: Understanding and Applying Gut Feel in Decision Making," *Academy of Management Executive,* November 2004, p. 88. Copyright © 2004 by Academy of Management, NY. Reproduced with permission of Academy of Management NY via Copyright Clearance Center.

As a model for making decisions, intuition has at least two benefits. (1) It can speed up decision making, useful when deadlines are tight.[33] (2) It can be helpful to managers when resources are limited. A drawback, however, is that it can be difficult to convince others that your hunch makes sense. In addition, intuition is subject to the same biases as those that affect rational decision making, as we discuss in Section 7.5.[34] Still, we believe that intuition and rationality are complementary and that managers should develop the courage to use intuition when making decisions.[35] ●

THE BIG PICTURE

Evidence-based decision making, which depends on an "attitude of wisdom," rests on three truths. This section describes seven principles for implementing evidence-based management. We also describe why it is hard to bring this approach to bear on one's decision making. Finally, we describe analytics and its three key attributes.

It was the jet that Boeing *didn't* build that avoided what could have been possibly the worst disaster in the company's history and gave the aircraft builder the opportunity to go in a new direction.

In late 2002, Boeing was desperately trying to figure out what kind of passenger airliner to build that would allow the company to effectively compete with its European rival Airbus. In October, Boeing executives met with several global airline representatives in Seattle. A Boeing manager drew a graph on a whiteboard, with axes representing cruising range and passenger numbers. Then he asked airline representatives to locate their ideal position on the graph. "The distribution of the data," reports *Time,* "favored efficiency over speed—the exact opposite of what Boeing was thinking. Two months later, Boeing ditched plans for a high-speed, high-cost jetliner to embark on a new program"—what became the massive attempt to build the 787 Dreamliner.[36]

Evidence-Based Decision Making

"Too many companies and too many leaders are more interested in just copying others, doing what they've always done, and making decisions based on beliefs in what ought to work rather than what actually works," say Stanford professors **Jeffrey Pfeffer** and **Robert Sutton.** "They fail to face the hard facts and use the best evidence to help navigate the competitive environment."[37] This is what Boeing narrowly averted in that Seattle conference, when it was getting ready to spend billions of dollars trying to outcompete Airbus by building a faster aircraft. Companies that use *evidence-based management*—the translation of principles based on best evidence into organizational practice, bringing rationality to the decision-making process, as we defined it in Chapter 2—routinely trump the competition, Pfeffer and Sutton suggest.[38]

Seven Implementation Principles Pfeffer and Sutton identify seven implementation principles to help companies that are committed to doing what it takes to profit from evidence-based management:[39]

- **Treat your organization as an unfinished prototype.** Leaders need to think and act as if their organization is an unfinished prototype that won't be ruined by dangerous new ideas or impossible to change because of employee or management resistance. Example: The products home-shopping network QVC sells are selected through a process of constant experimentation, punctuated by evidence-based analysis as to why some sell and some don't.

Evidence-based decisions. The staff at DaVita kidney dialysis centers try to evaluate evidence before making patient decisions. Would you expect a "just-the-facts" approach to be normal in business (and medical) organizations or unusual?

- **No brag, just facts.** This slogan is an antidote for assertions made with complete disregard for whether they correspond to facts. Example: Hewlett-Packard CEO Carly Fiorina bragged to the press about HP's merger with Compaq but failed to consider facts about consumer dissatisfaction with Compaq products until after the merger. Other companies, such as DaVita, which operates dialysis centers, take pains to evaluate data before making decisions.

- **See yourself and your organization as outsiders do.** Most managers are afflicted with "rampant optimism," with inflated views of their own talents and prospects for success, which causes them to downplay risks and continue on a path despite evidence things are not working. "Having a blunt friend, mentor, or counselor," Pfeffer and Sutton suggest, "can help you see and act on better evidence."

- **Evidence-based management is not just for senior executives.** The best organizations are those in which everyone, not just the top managers, is guided by the responsibility to gather and act on quantitative and qualitative data and share results with others.

- **Like everything else, you still need to sell it.** "Unfortunately, new and exciting ideas grab attention even when they are vastly inferior to old ideas," the Stanford authors say. "Vivid, juicy stories and case studies sell better than detailed, rigorous, and admittedly dull data—no matter how wrong the stories or how right the data." To sell an evidence-based approach, you may have to identify a preferred practice based on solid if unexciting evidence, then use vivid stories to grab management attention.

- **If all else fails, slow the spread of bad practice.** Because many managers and employees face pressures to do things that are known to be ineffective, it may be necessary for you to practice "evidence-based misbehavior"—that is, ignore orders you know to be wrong or delay their implementation.

- **The best diagnostic question: What happens when people fail?** "Failure hurts, it is embarrassing, and we would rather live without it," the authors write. "Yet there is no learning without failure. . . . If you look at how the most effective systems in the world are managed, a hallmark is that when something goes wrong, people face the hard facts, learn what happened and why, and keep using those facts to make the system better." From the U.S. civil aviation system, which rigorously examines airplane accidents, near misses, and equipment problems, to Intel's former CEO Andy Grove's willingness to learn from mistakes, evidence-based management makes the point that failure is a great teacher. This means, however, that the organization must "forgive and remember" people who make mistakes, not be trapped by preconceived notions, and confront the best evidence and hard facts.

What Makes It Hard to Be Evidence Based   Despite your best intentions, it's hard to bring the best evidence to bear on your decisions. Among the reasons:[40] (1) There's too much evidence. (2) There's not enough *good* evidence. (3) The evidence doesn't quite apply. (4) People are trying to mislead you. (5) *You* are trying to mislead you. (6) The side effects outweigh the cure. (Example: Despite the belief that social promotion in school is a bad idea—that is, that schools shouldn't advance children to the next grade when they haven't mastered the material—the side effect is skyrocketing costs because it crowds schools with older students, and angrier students, demanding more resources.) (7) Stories are more persuasive, anyway.

Example

Evidence-Based Decision Making: "If People Are Your Most Important Assets, Why Would You Get Rid of Them?"

It's an axiom of many managers that it's often necessary to cut back on workers during economic downturns—or even in good times—because it helps to increase profitability or drive the company's stock price higher. But in a 2010 cover story for *Newsweek*, Stanford professor Jeffrey Pfeffer, advocate for evidence-based management, took issue with this assumption. "There is a growing body of academic research suggesting that firms incur big costs when they cut workers," he writes.[41]

What Are the Costs of Layoffs? While agreeing that there are circumstances in which layoffs are necessary for a firm to survive (as when an industry is shrinking or competitors are resorting to cheaper overseas labor), Pfeffer suggests companies incur big costs when they cut their labor forces. He cites the direct and indirect costs of layoffs listed by University of Colorado professor Wayne Cascio in his book *Responsible Restructuring:* "severance pay; paying out accrued vacation and sick pay; outplacement costs; higher unemployment-insurance taxes; the cost of rehiring employees when business improves; low morale and risk-averse survivors; potential lawsuits, sabotage, or even workplace violence from aggrieved employees or former employees; loss of institutional memory and knowledge; diminished trust in management; and reduced productivity."

Looking at the evidence, Pfeffer finds that firms that announce layoffs actually *do not* enjoy higher stock prices than their peers, either immediately or over time. Layoffs also don't increase individual company productivity and, in fact, don't even reliably cut costs (because companies often lose the best people first; there is lower morale among survivors, resulting in reduced customer service, innovation, and productivity; and remaining employees are spurred to look for other jobs once things improve).

The Most Successful Airline. Following the 9/11 tragedy in 2001, which coincided with the start of a recession, all U.S. airlines except one announced tens of thousands of layoffs. The exception was Southwest, which has never had an involuntary layoff in its 40-year history. Southwest, Pfeffer points out, is now the largest domestic U.S. airline, and its market worth (capitalization) is greater than that of all its domestic competitors combined. "If people are your most important assets," Pfeffer quotes a former head of the airline's human resources department, "why would you get rid of them?"

YOUR CALL

Can you think of any instances of people being laid off unnecessarily? What is your evidence that it was not necessary?

In Praise of Analytics

Perhaps the purest application of evidence-based management is the use of *analytics,* or *business analytics,* **the term used for sophisticated forms of business data analysis.** One example of analytics is portfolio analysis, in which an investment adviser evaluates the risks of various stocks. Another example is the time-series forecast, which predicts future data based on patterns of historical data.

Some leaders and firms have become exceptional practitioners of analytics. Gary Loveman, CEO of the Harrah's gambling empire, wrote a famous paper and book, *Diamonds in the Data Mine,* in which he explained how data-mining software was used to analyze vast amounts of casino customer data to target profitable patrons.[42] Marriott International, through its Total Hotel Optimization program, has used quantitative data to establish the optimal price for hotel rooms, evaluate use of conference facilities and catering, and develop systems to optimize offerings to frequent customers.[43] To aid in recruitment, Microsoft studies correlations between its successful workers and the schools and companies they arrived from.[44]

Example

Use of Analytics: Could an NBA Star Who Doesn't Rank High in Scoring, Rebounds, Assists, & Steals Actually Be His Team's Most Valuable Player?

One of the poorest teams in Major League Baseball, the Oakland Athletics, managed to become a perennial playoff team against better-financed contenders by avoiding the use of traditional baseball statistics and finding better indicators of player success in on-base percentage, slugging percentage, and the like. Since the 1990s, this creative use of analytics, as described by Michael Lewis in *Moneyball: The Art of Winning an Unfair Game,* enabled managers of the California club to concentrate their limited payroll resources on draft picks who are primarily talented college players rather than veteran professionals.[45]

Analytics in the NBA. Since then, the use of new statistics and unusual analytics to find better ways to value players and strategies has found its way into football, basketball, and other sports. In basketball, for instance, managers of the Houston Rockets found they had allocated such a huge part of the payroll to superstars (Tracy McGrady, Yao Ming) that they couldn't afford more stars. "So we went looking for nonsuperstars that we thought were undervalued," says Daryl Morey, who was hired to rethink basketball for the Rockets.[46] Looking at midlevel NBA players, he came up with a list of 15, near the top of which was forward Shane Battier.

The "Unimpressive" Shane Battier. In many ways, Battier is unimpressive. "He doesn't score many points, snag many rebounds, block many shots, steal many balls, or dish out many assists," says Michael Lewis. However, he observes, these measurements are what are easy rather than important to measure. What analytics show is that when Battier is on the court, "his teammates get better—often a lot better—and his opponents get worse—often a lot worse." He significantly reduces the shooting performance of the Kobe Bryants and other prolific scorers he plays against, and he helps out his teammates in all kinds of subtle ways, as by passing to them. His most distinctive characteristic, in sum, is that he applies a superior intelligence to an overview of the game that helps his teams produce winning records.

YOUR CALL

Executives and personnel people in other lines of work are often like the old sports traditionalists, relying on résumé, degree, years of experience, and even looks in evaluating job applicants. What other, more quantifiable measures might be used instead?

Thomas H. Davenport and others at Babson College's Working Knowledge Research Center studied 32 organizations that made a commitment to quantitative, fact-based analysis and found three key attributes among analytics competitors.[47]

I. Use of Modeling: Going beyond Simple Descriptive Statistics

Companies such as Capital One look well beyond basic statistics, using data mining and predictive modeling to identify potential and most profitable customers. *Predictive modeling* **is a data-mining technique used to predict future behavior and anticipate the consequences of change.** Thus, Capital One conducts more than 30,000 experiments a year, with different interest rates, incentives, direct-mail packaging, and other variables to evaluate which customers are most apt to sign up for credit cards and will pay back their debt.

2. Having Multiple Applications, Not Just One

UPS (formerly United Parcel Service) applies analytics not only to tracking the movement of packages but also to examining usage patterns to try to identify potential customer defections so that salespeople can make contact and solve problems. More recently, as the recession reduced package delivery demand, it began testing whether UPS could be in the business of delivering direct mail, to serve as an alternative to marketing mail delivered by the U.S. Post Service.[48] Analytics competitors "don't gain advantage from one killer app [application], but rather from multiple applications supporting many parts of the business," says Davenport.

3. Support from the Top

"A companywide embrace of analytics impels changes in culture, processes, behavior, and skills for many employees," says Davenport. "And so, like any major transition, it requires leadership from executives at the very top who have a passion for the quantitative approach." ●

Are the customers browned off? Big Brown, or UPS, uses analytics for more than one application—not only to track package deliveries but also to determine if customers are defecting.

| How do I decide to decide? | major question? |

THE BIG PICTURE

Your decision-making style reflects how you perceive and respond to information. It could be directive, analytical, conceptual, or behavioral.

Do men and women differ in the way they make decisions? Do they, for example, differ in risk propensity? *Risk propensity* **is the willingness to gamble or to undertake risk for the possibility of gaining an increased payoff.**

Perhaps another name for this is competitiveness. And research does seem to show that, as one scholar summarized it, "Even in tasks where they do well, women seem to shy away from competition, whereas men seem to enjoy it too much."[49] In an experiment involving winning small amounts of money in number-memorizing tournaments, men were avid competitors and were eager to continue, partly from overconfidence regardless of their success in earlier rounds, and they rated their abilities more highly than the women rated theirs. Most women declined to compete, even when they had done the best in earlier rounds.[50]

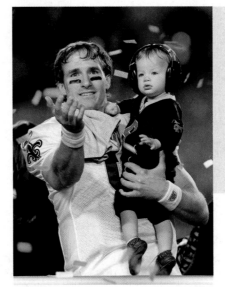

Success. Drew Brees, quarterback for the New Orleans Saints, led his team to victory in the 2010 Super Bowl. As the leader of his team, a quarterback must make many decisions about what is the right way to success. If you were a quarterback, which of the four general decision-making styles do you think you would embody?

This brings us to the subject of decision-making style. **A *decision-making style* reflects the combination of how an individual perceives and responds to information.** A team of researchers developed a model of decision-making styles based on the idea that styles vary along two different dimensions: value orientation and tolerance for ambiguity.[51]

Value Orientation & Tolerance for Ambiguity

Value orientation reflects the extent to which a person focuses on either task and technical concerns or people and social concerns when making decisions. Some people, for instance, are very task focused at work and do not pay much attention to people issues, whereas others are just the opposite.

The second dimension pertains to a person's *tolerance for ambiguity*. This individual difference indicates the extent to which a person has a high need for structure or control in his or her life. Some people desire a lot of structure in their lives (a low tolerance for ambiguity) and find ambiguous situations stressful and psychologically uncomfortable. In contrast, others do not have a high need for structure and can thrive in uncertain situations (a high tolerance for ambiguity). Ambiguous situations can energize people with a high tolerance for ambiguity.

When the dimensions of value orientation and tolerance for ambiguity are combined, they form four styles of decision making: *directive, analytical, conceptual,* and *behavioral. (See Figure 7.3, next page.)*

figure 7.3

DECISION-MAKING STYLES

	High		
Tolerance for ambiguity	Analytical	Conceptual
	Directive	Behavioral
	Low		

Task & technical concerns

People & social concerns

Value orientation

I. The Directive Style: Action-Oriented Decision Makers Who Focus on Facts

People with a directive style have a low tolerance for ambiguity and are oriented toward task and technical concerns in making decisions. They are efficient, logical, practical, and systematic in their approach to solving problems.

People with this style are action oriented and decisive and like to focus on facts. In their pursuit of speed and results, however, these individuals tend to be autocratic, to exercise power and control, and to focus on the short run.

These, er, guys are CEOs? Herb Kelleher, left, in surgical garb and Gary Kelley, dressed as Edna Turnblad, the mom from *Hairspray,* at a staff Halloween party. They are the former and present CEOs of Southwest Airlines, which was founded in 1971 on the premise of getting passengers to their destinations on time at the lowest possible fares and making sure they had a good time doing it. What kind of decision-making styles would you expect these executives to have?

2. The Analytical Style: Careful Decision Makers Who Like Lots of Information & Alternative Choices

Managers with an analytical style have a much higher tolerance for ambiguity and are characterized by the tendency to overanalyze a situation. People with this style like to consider more information and alternatives than those following the directive style.

Analytic individuals are careful decision makers who take longer to make decisions but who also respond well to new or uncertain situations.

3. The Conceptual Style: Decision Makers Who Rely on Intuition & Have a Long-Term Perspective

People with a conceptual style have a high tolerance for ambiguity and tend to focus on the people or social aspects of a work situation. They take a broad perspective to problem solving and like to consider many options and future possibilities.

Conceptual types adopt a long-term perspective and rely on intuition and discussions with others to acquire information. They also are willing to take risks and are good at finding creative solutions to problems. However, a conceptual style can foster an indecisive approach to decision making.

4. The Behavioral Style: The Most People-Oriented Decision Makers

The behavioral style is the most people-oriented of the four styles. People with this style work well with others and enjoy social interactions in which opinions are openly exchanged. Behavioral types are supportive, receptive to suggestions, show warmth, and prefer verbal to written information.

Although they like to hold meetings, people with this style have a tendency to avoid conflict and to be concerned about others. This can lead behavioral types to adopt a wishy-washy approach to decision making and to have a hard time saying no.

Which Style Do You Have?

Research shows that very few people have only one dominant decision-making style. Rather, most managers have characteristics that fall into two or three styles. Studies also show that decision-making styles vary across occupations, job level, and countries.[52] There is not a best decision-making style that applies to all situations.

You can use knowledge of decision-making styles in three ways:

Know Thyself   Knowledge of styles helps you to understand yourself. Awareness of your style assists you in identifying your strengths and weaknesses as a decision maker and facilitates the potential for self-improvement.

Influence Others   You can increase your ability to influence others by being aware of styles. For example, if you are dealing with an analytical person, you should provide as much information as possible to support your ideas.

Deal with Conflict   Knowledge of styles gives you an awareness of how people can take the same information and yet arrive at different decisions by using a variety of decision-making strategies. Different decision-making styles represent one likely source of interpersonal conflict at work.

To get a sense of your own decision-making style, see the Self-Assessment at the end of this chapter. ●

What guidelines can I follow to be sure that decisions I make are not just lawful but ethical?

THE BIG PICTURE

A graph known as a decision tree can help one make ethical decisions. In addition, one should be aware of "the magnificent seven" general moral principles for managers.

The ethical behavior of businesspeople has become of increasing concern in recent years, brought about by a number of events.

First were the business scandals of the early 2000s, from Enron to WorldCom, producing photos of handcuffed executives. "The supposedly 'independent' auditors, directors, accountants, and stock market advisers and accountants were all tarnished," wrote Mortimer Zuckerman, editor-in-chief of *U.S. News & World Report,* "the engine of the people's involvement, the mutual fund industry, was shown to be permeated by rip-off artists rigging the system for the benefit of insiders and the rich."[53] Then, as the Iraq war wore on, reports came back of sweetheart deals and gross abuses by civilian contractors working in Iraq war zones. In 2007, it became apparent that banks and others in the financial industry had forsaken sound business judgment—including ethical judgments—by making mortgage loans (subprime loans) to essentially unqualified buyers, which led to a wave of housing foreclosures and helped push the country into a recession.

Can We Have "Kinder Capitalism"?

Through it all, voices were being raised that American capitalism was not doing enough to help the poorer nations in the world. "We have to find a way to make the aspects of capitalism that serve wealthier people serve poorer people as well," Microsoft's Bill Gates has said. Companies in wealthier countries, he urged, should focus on "a twin mission: making profits and also improving lives for those who don't fully benefit from market forces."[54]

All these concerns have forced the subject of right-minded decision making to the top of the agenda in many organizations. Indeed, many companies now have an ***ethics officer,* someone trained about matters of ethics in the workplace, particularly about resolving ethical dilemmas.** More and more companies are also creating values statements to guide employees as to what constitutes desirable business behavior.[55] As a result of this raised consciousness, managers now must try to make sure their decisions are not just lawful but also ethical, a subject discussed in detail in Chapter 3.

For kinder capitalism. Bill Gates, former chairman of Microsoft, has called for "creative capitalism" that uses market forces to address poor-country needs. Would you agree with him that the rate of improvement in technology, health care, and education for the bottom third of the world's people has been unsatisfactory?

Road Map to Ethical Decision Making: A Decision Tree

One of the greatest pressures—if not *the* greatest pressure—on top executives is to maximize shareholder value, to deliver the greatest return on investment to the owners of their company. But is a decision that is beneficial to shareholders yet harmful to employees—such as forcing them to contribute more to their health benefits, as IBM has done—unethical? Harvard Business School professor

Constance Bagley suggests that what is needed is a decision tree to help with ethical decisions.[56] **A *decision tree* is a graph of decisions and their possible consequences; it is used to create a plan to reach a goal.** Bagley's ethical decision tree is shown above. *(See Figure 7.4.)*

figure 7.4

THE ETHICAL DECISION TREE: WHAT'S THE RIGHT THING TO DO?

When confronted with any proposed action for which a decision is required, a manager should ask the following questions:

1. **Is the Proposed Action Legal?** This may seem an obvious question. But, Bagley observes, "recent [2002–2003] corporate shenanigans suggest that some managers need to be reminded: If the action isn't legal, don't do it."

2. **If "Yes," Does the Proposed Action Maximize Shareholder Value?** If the action is legal, one must next ask whether it will profit the shareholders. If the answer is "yes," should you do it? Not necessarily.

3. **If "Yes," Is the Proposed Action Ethical?** As Bagley points out, though directors and top managers may believe they are bound by corporate law to always maximize shareholder value, the courts and many state legislatures have held they are not. Rather, their main obligation is to manage "for the best interests of the corporation," which includes the interests of the larger community.

    Thus, says Bagley, building a profitable-but-polluting plant in a country overseas may benefit the shareholders but be bad for that country—and for the corporation's relations with that nation. Ethically, then, managers should add pollution-control equipment.

4. **If "No," Would It Be Ethical *Not* to Take the Proposed Action?** If the action would not directly benefit shareholders, might it still be ethical to go ahead with it?

    Not building the overseas plant might be harmful to other stakeholders, such as employees or customers. Thus, the ethical conclusion might be to build the plant with pollution-control equipment but to disclose the effects of the decision to shareholders.

As a basic guideline to making good ethical decisions on behalf of a corporation, Bagley suggests that directors, managers, and employees need to follow their own individual ideas about right and wrong.[57] There is a lesson, she suggests, in the response of the pension fund manager who, when asked whether she would invest in a company doing business in a country that permits slavery, responded, "Do you mean me, personally, or as a fund manager?" When people feel entitled or compelled to compromise their own personal ethics to advance the interests of a business, "it is an invitation to mischief."[58]

Kent Hodgson suggests there are no absolute ethical answers for managerial decision makers. Rather, the goal for managers should be to rely on moral principles so that their decisions are *principled, appropriate,* and *defensible*.[59] Accordingly, Hodgson has put forth what he calls "the magnificent seven" general moral principles for managers. *(See Table 7.3.)* ●

table 7.3 THE MAGNIFICENT SEVEN: GENERAL MORAL PRINCIPLES FOR MANAGERS

1. **Dignity of human life: The lives of people are to be respected.** Human beings, by the fact of their existence, have value and dignity. We may not act in ways that directly intend to harm or kill an innocent person. Human beings have a right to live; we have an obligation to respect that right to life. Human life is to be preserved and treated as sacred.

2. **Autonomy: All persons are intrinsically valuable and have the right to self-determination.** We should act in ways that demonstrate each person's worth, dignity, and right to free choice. We have a right to act in ways that assert our own worth and legitimate needs. We should not use others as mere "things" or only as means to an end. Each person has an equal right to basic human liberty, compatible with a similar liberty for others.

3. **Honesty: The truth should be told to those who have a right to know it.** Honesty is also known as integrity, truth telling, and honor. One should speak and act so as to reflect the reality of the situation. Speaking and acting should mirror the way things really are. There are times when others have the right to hear the truth from us; there are times when they do not.

4. **Loyalty: Promises, contracts, and commitments should be honored.** Loyalty includes fidelity, promise keeping, keeping the public trust, good citizenship, excellence in quality of work, reliability, commitment, and honoring just laws and policies.

5. **Fairness: People should be treated justly.** One has the right to be treated fairly, impartially, and equitably. One has the obligation to treat others fairly and justly. All have the right to the necessities of life—especially those in deep need and the helpless. Justice includes equal, impartial, unbiased treatment. Fairness tolerates diversity and accepts differences in people and their ideas.

6. **Humaneness.** There are two parts: (1) **Our actions ought to accomplish good,** and (2) **we should avoid doing evil.** We should do good to others and to ourselves. We should have concern for the well-being of others; usually, we show this concern in the form of compassion, giving, kindness, serving, and caring.

7. **The common good: Actions should accomplish the "greatest good for the greatest number" of people.** One should act and speak in ways that benefit the welfare of the largest number of people, while trying to protect the rights of individuals.

Source: From Kent Hodgson, *A Rock and a Hard Place: How to Make Ethical Business Decisions When the Choices Are Tough,* AMACOM, 1992, pp. 69–73. Reprinted with permission of the author.

✴ 7.5 HOW TO OVERCOME BARRIERS TO DECISION MAKING

Trying to be rational isn't always easy. What are the barriers?

major question?

THE BIG PICTURE
Responses to a decision situation may take the form of four ineffective reactions or three effective reactions. Managers should be aware of four common decision-making biases.

Do your moods influence your decisions? Do you, for instance, spend more when you're sad and self-absorbed? That's what one experiment found: When researchers exposed student participants to a sadness-inducing video clip about the death of a boy's mentor, the students were inclined to offer more money for a product (a sporty-looking water bottle) than were other subjects who had watched a neutral clip.[60]

Decision Making & Expectations about Happiness

Not just the moods themselves but your expectations about how happy or unhappy you think future outcomes will make you perhaps also can influence your decisions. It seems that people expect certain life events to have a much greater emotional effect than in fact they do, according to Harvard University psychologist Daniel Gilbert, who has studied individual emotional barometers in decision making. College professors, for example, expect to be quite happy if they are given tenure and quite unhappy if they aren't. However, Gilbert found those who received tenure were happy but not as happy as they themselves had predicted, whereas those denied tenure did not become very unhappy.

The expectation about the level of euphoria or disappointment was also found to be true of big-jackpot lottery winners and of people being tested for HIV infection. That is, people are often right when they describe what outcome will make them feel good or bad, but they are often wrong when asked to predict how strongly they will feel that way and how long the feeling will last. Even severe life events have a negative impact on people's sense of well-being and satisfaction for no more than three months, after which their feelings at least go back to normal.[61]

Perhaps knowing that you have this "immune system" of the mind, which blunts bad feelings and smoothes out euphoric ones, can help make it easier for you to make difficult decisions.

How Do Individuals Respond to a Decision Situation? Ineffective & Effective Responses

What is your typical response when you're suddenly confronted with a challenge in the form of a problem or an opportunity? There are perhaps four ineffective reactions and three effective ones.[62]

Four Ineffective Reactions　There are four defective problem-recognition and problem-solving approaches that act as barriers when you must make an important decision in a situation of conflict:

1. Relaxed Avoidance—"There's no point in doing anything; nothing bad's going to happen."　In *relaxed avoidance,* a manager decides to take no action in the belief that there will be no great negative consequences. This condition, then, is a form of complacency: You either don't see or you disregard the signs of danger (or of opportunity).

Example: Relaxed avoidance was vividly demonstrated in the months before the subprime mortgage meltdown, when banks made cheap housing loans to a lot of unqualified buyers, precipitating a huge financial crisis and drying up of credit. During that time, a lot of smart people in denial said not to worry, that the mortgage mess would be "contained." They included many bank presidents and even Ben Bernanke, chairman of the Federal Reserve.[63]

2. Relaxed Change—"Why not just take the easiest way out?" In *relaxed change,* **a manager realizes that complete inaction will have negative consequences but opts for the first available alternative that involves low risk.** This is, of course, a form of "satisficing"; the manager avoids exploring a variety of alternatives in order to make the best decision.

Example: Perhaps people really don't like a lot of choices. In one experiment, 40% of customers stopped by a large assortment of jam jars (24) and only 30% by a small assortment (6)—but only 3% made a purchase in the first case versus 30% in the second.[64]

3. Defensive Avoidance—"There's no reason for me to explore other solution alternatives." In *defensive avoidance,* **a manager can't find a good solution and follows by (a) procrastinating, (b) passing the buck, or (c) denying the risk of any negative consequences.** This is a posture of resignation and a denial of responsibility for taking action. By procrastinating, you put off making a decision ("I'll get to this later").[65] In passing the buck, you let someone else take the consequences of making the decision ("Let George do it"). In denying the risk that there will be any negative consequences, you are engaging in rationalizing ("How bad could it be?").

Example: Defensive avoidance often occurs in firms with high turnover. Although some executives try to stop high performers from exiting by offering raises or promotions, others react defensively, telling themselves that the person leaving is not a big loss. "It's psychologically threatening to those who are staying to acknowledge there's a reason some people are leaving," says the CEO of a corporate-psychology consulting company, "so executives often dismiss them as untalented or even deny that an exodus is occurring."[66] He mentions one financial-services company whose executives insisted turnover was low when in fact 50% of hundreds of new employees quit within years.

4. Panic—"This is so stressful, I've got to do something—anything—to get rid of the problem!" This reaction is especially apt to occur in crisis situations. In *panic,* **a manager is so frantic to get rid of the problem that he or she can't deal with the situation realistically.** This is the kind of situation in which the manager has completely forgotten the idea of behaving with "grace under pressure," of staying cool and calm. Troubled by anxiety, irritability, sleeplessness, and even physical illness, if you're experiencing this reaction, your judgment may be so clouded that you won't be able to accept help in dealing with the problem or to realistically evaluate the alternatives.

Example: Panic can even be life-threatening. When a jetliner skidded off the runway at Little Rock National Airport, passenger Clark Brewster and a flight attendant tried repeatedly to open an exit door that would not budge. "About that time I hear someone say the word 'Fire!'" Brewster said. "The flight attendant bends down and says, 'Please pray with me.'" Fortunately, cooler, quicker-thinking individuals were able to find another way out.[67]

Three Effective Reactions: Deciding to Decide In *deciding to decide,* **a manager agrees that he or she must decide what to do about a problem or opportunity and**

take effective decision-making steps. Three ways to help you decide whether to decide are to evaluate the following:[68]

1. Importance—"How high priority is this situation?" You need to determine how much priority to give the decision situation. If it's a threat, how extensive might prospective losses or damage be? If it's an opportunity, how beneficial might the possible gains be?

2. Credibility—"How believable is the information about the situation?" You need to evaluate how much is known about the possible threat or opportunity. Is the source of the information trustworthy? Is there credible evidence?

3. Urgency—"How quickly must I act on the information about the situation?" Is the threat immediate? Will the window of opportunity stay open long? Can actions to address the situation be done gradually?

Example

Deciding to Decide: How Should MTV Networks React to Broadband Internet?

By the summer of 2006, old-media companies had become aware of the staggering implications of the arrival of broadband Internet. Disney's ABC Network, for instance, had agreed to provide hit shows for downloading to Apple's iTunes, Facebook had jumped to 5.5 million users, and YouTube was launched. However, MTV Networks, owned by Viacom and its cantankerous founder, Sumner Redstone, found itself lagging. "MTV Networks, which for years had been the arbiter of youth culture, seemed to be squandering its birthright," wrote *Newsweek*. "Even as its core audience was embracing the Internet as the next entertainment medium, MTV could not shake its old-media image."[69] How does Redstone decide how to decide?

Is This High-Priority? The first decision—*Should this be considered a high-priority matter?*—became apparent when Redstone observed the aggressive moves being made by his competition. And indeed Viacom went on a buying spree itself to bolster MTV Networks' digital presence, making $200 million in acquisitions, including Atom Entertainment, with its AtomFilms.com and the gaming sites Shockwave.com and AddictingGames.com.

Is the Data Believable? The second decision—*How believable is the information?*—was reinforced when one important deal eluded MTV's grasp, the hot brand known as MySpace, described as the "it" site of social networking, was snatched away by rival Rupert Murdoch's News Corp. Redstone blamed the loss on his longtime lieutenant, Viacom CEO Tom Freston.

How Fast Do We Need to Act? The answer to the final decision—*How quickly should this information be acted on?*—became obvious when Redstone fired Freston and hired a new CEO, Philippe Dauman, with the simple mandate: Make MTV digitally cool, but don't do it by making any extravagant acquisitions (which could repeat the mistake made by old-media company Time Warner when it merged with AOL, a colossal failure). A principal result was that MTV Networks promoted a digital impresario named Mika Salmi, who became a key proponent of Viacom's "thousand front doors" strategy—creating Web presences for properties such as "The Daily Show" and expanding Viacom's social networking efforts. MTV and its related brands now have more than 300 Internet sites, including some 30 media-rich broadband sites featuring video, music, and lots of interactivity (examples: Pimp My Ride, AddictingGames.com).

YOUR CALL

After deciding that the threat to MTV Networks is serious, real, and immediate, how would you have tried to reshape MTV's business strategy, if you were in charge?

Six Common Decision-Making Biases: Rules of Thumb, or "Heuristics"

If someone asked you to explain the basis on which you make decisions, could you even say? Perhaps, after some thought, you might come up with some "rules of thumb." Scholars call them ***heuristics*** (pronounced "hyur-*ris*-tiks")—**strategies that simplify the process of making decisions.**

Despite the fact that people use such rules of thumb all the time, that doesn't mean they're reliable. Indeed, some are real barriers to high-quality decision making. Among those that tend to bias how decision makers process information are (1) *availability,* (2) *confirmation,* (3) *representativeness,* (4) *sunk cost,* (5) *anchoring and adjustment,* and (6) *escalation of commitment.*[70]

I. The Availability Bias: Using Only the Information Available

If you had a perfect on-time work attendance record for 9 months but then were late for work 4 days during the last 2 months because of traffic, shouldn't your boss take into account your entire attendance history when considering you for a raise? Yet managers tend to give more weight to more recent behavior. This is because of the ***availability bias***—**managers use information readily available from memory to make judgments.**

The bias, of course, is that readily available information may not present a complete picture of a situation. The availability bias may be stoked by the news media, which tends to favor news that is unusual or dramatic. Thus, for example, because of the efforts of interest groups or celebrities, more news coverage may be given to AIDS or to breast cancer than to heart disease, leading people to think the former are the bigger killers when in fact the latter is.

2. The Confirmation Bias: Seeking Information to Support One's Point of View

The *confirmation bias* **is when people seek information to support their point of view and discount data that do not.** Though this bias would seem obvious, people practice it all the time.

3. The Representativeness Bias: Faulty Generalizing from a Small Sample or a Single Event

As a form of financial planning, playing state lotteries leaves something to be desired. When, for instance, in one year the New York jackpot reached $70 million, a New Yorker's chance of winning was 1 in 12,913,588.[71] (A person would have a greater chance of being struck by lightning.) Nevertheless, millions of people buy lottery tickets because they read or hear about a handful of fellow citizens who have been the fortunate recipients of enormous winnings. This is an example of the ***representativeness bias,*** **the tendency to generalize from a small sample or a single event.**

The bias here is that just because something happens once, that doesn't mean it is representative—that it will happen again or will happen to you. For example, just because you hired an extraordinary sales representative from a particular university, that doesn't mean that same university will provide an equally qualified candidate next time. Yet managers make this kind of hiring decision all the time.

4. The Sunk-Cost Bias: Money Already Spent Seems to Justify Continuing

The *sunk-cost bias,* or *sunk-cost fallacy,* **is when managers add up all the money already spent on a project and conclude it is too costly to simply abandon it.**

Most people have an aversion to "wasting" money. Especially if large sums have already been spent, they may continue to push on with an iffy-looking project to justify the money already sunk into it. The sunk-cost bias is sometimes called the "Concorde" effect, referring to the fact that the French and British governments continued to invest in the Concorde supersonic jetliner even when it was evident there was no economic justification for the aircraft.

5. The Anchoring & Adjustment Bias: Being Influenced by an Initial Figure

Managers will often give their employees a standard percentage raise in salary, basing the decision on whatever the workers made the preceding year. They may do this even though the raise may be completely out of alignment with what other companies are paying for the same skills. This is an instance of the ***anchoring and adjustment bias,*** **the tendency to make decisions based on an initial figure.**

The bias is that the initial figure may be irrelevant to market realities. This phenomenon is sometimes seen in real estate sales. Before the crash in the real estate markets, many homeowners might have been inclined at first to list their houses at an extremely high (but perhaps randomly chosen) selling price. These sellers were then unwilling later to come down substantially to match the kind of buying offers that reflected what the marketplace thought the house was really worth.

6. The Escalation of Commitment Bias: Feeling Overly Invested in a Decision
If you really hate to admit you're wrong, you need to be aware of the *escalation of commitment bias,* **whereby decision makers increase their commitment to a project despite negative information about it.** History is full of examples of heads of state (presidents Lyndon Johnson in Vietnam and George W. Bush in Iraq) who escalated their commitment to an original decision in the face of overwhelming evidence that it was producing detrimental consequences. A Web site called Swoopo.com capitalizes on this bias by offering a penny auction in which, say, a $1,500 laptop is offered for bidding starting at a penny and going up one cent at a time—but it costs bidders 60 cents to make a bid. "Once people are trapped into playing," suggests one account about this form of bias, "they have a hard time stopping."[72]

The bias is that what was originally made as perhaps a rational decision may continue to be supported for irrational reasons—pride, ego, the spending of enormous sums of money, and being "loss averse." Indeed, scholars have advanced what is known as the *prospect theory,* which suggests that decision makers find the notion of an actual loss more painful than giving up the possibility of a gain.[73] We see a variant of this in the tendency of investors to hold on to their losers but cash in their winners. ●

Example

Avoiding Escalation of Commitment: L.L. Bean CEO Is Glad to Reverse Big Decision, Even at a Cost of $500,000

Most executives, like most people, tend to stick with their initial decisions because they hate to admit they were wrong, or simply because it is the path of least resistance, according to management experts. Indeed, they say, top executives are even less likely to reverse themselves because their position seems to require projecting self-assurance. This is the kind of mind-set that can lead to escalation of commitment.

Is Avoiding Looking "Wishy-Washy" Really Important? Thus, Christopher McCormick, chief executive of outdoor-clothing retailer L.L. Bean, is unusual for being more concerned about making the best decision rather than being bothered about appearing wishy-washy. This makes him very much in the spirit of evidence-based decision making.

In the fall of 2004, L.L. Bean began building a call center near Waterville, Maine. A few months later, mobile-phone carrier T-Mobile USA said it would build its own call center next door, one that would house 700 or more employees. McCormick immediately ordered construction on the Bean center halted, even though

$500,000 beyond the land cost had already been spent on it. A few weeks later, the company announced it would abandon the Waterville site entirely and would open a new call center about 55 miles away.

The Rational Outcome. What circumstances led to this evaluation? McCormick worried that Waterville, population 16,000, didn't have enough workers to supply both companies or that employees would prefer year-round employment with T-Mobile to seasonal employment with Bean.

YOUR CALL

Even though thousands of dollars had already been spent on the Waterville center, McCormick says he had no reservations about his decision. He said he also wanted to send a signal to other Bean executives. "I want my people to consider all the options," he said. "I don't want them to be a champion of one point of view."[74] Do you think you're capable of making such a momentous decision?

How do I work with others to make things happen?

THE BIG PICTURE

Group decision making has five potential advantages and four potential disadvantages. There are a number of characteristics of groups that a manager should be aware of, as well as participative management and group problem-solving techniques.

The movies celebrate the lone heroes who, like Clint Eastwood, make their own moves, call their own shots. Most managers, however, work with groups and teams (as we discuss in Chapter 13). Although groups don't make as high-quality decisions as the best individual acting alone, research suggests that groups make better decisions than *most* individuals acting alone.[75] Thus, to be an effective manager, you need to learn about decision making in groups.

Advantages & Disadvantages of Group Decision Making

Because you may often have a choice as to whether to make a decision by yourself or to consult with others, you need to understand the advantages and disadvantages of group-aided decision making.

Advantages   Using a group to make a decision offers five possible advantages.[76] For these benefits to happen, however, the group must be made up of diverse participants, not just people who all think the same way.

- **Greater pool of knowledge.** When several people are making the decision, there is a greater pool of information from which to draw. If one person doesn't have the pertinent knowledge and experience, someone else might.

- **Different perspectives.** Because different people have different perspectives—marketing, production, legal, and so on—they see the problem from different angles.

- **Intellectual stimulation.** A group of people can brainstorm or otherwise bring greater intellectual stimulation and creativity to the decision-making process than is usually possible with one person acting alone.

- **Better understanding of decision rationale.** If you participate in making a decision, you are more apt to understand the reasoning behind the decision, including the pros and cons leading up to the final step.

- **Deeper commitment to the decision.** If you've been part of the group that has bought into the final decision, you're more apt to be committed to seeing that the course of action is successfully implemented.

Disadvantages   The disadvantages of group-aided decision making spring from problems in how members interact.[77]

- **A few people dominate or intimidate.** Sometimes a handful of people will talk the longest and the loudest, and the rest of the group will simply give in. Or one individual, such as a strong leader, will exert disproportional influence, sometimes by intimidation. This cuts down on the variety of ideas.

- **Groupthink.** *Groupthink* occurs when group members strive to agree for the sake of unanimity and thus avoid accurately assessing the decision situation. Here the positive team spirit of the group actually works against sound judgment.[78]

- **Satisficing.** Because most people would just as soon cut short a meeting, the tendency is to seek a decision that is "good enough" rather than to push on in pursuit of other possible solutions. Satisficing can occur because groups have limited time, lack the right kind of information, or are unable to handle large amounts of information.[79]

- **Goal displacement.** Although the primary task of the meeting may be to solve a particular problem, other considerations may rise to the fore, such as rivals trying to win an argument. *Goal displacement* **occurs when the primary goal is subsumed by a secondary goal.**

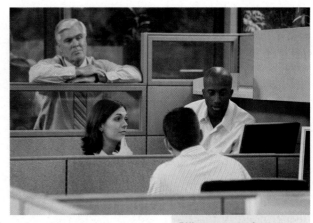

Different perspectives or groupthink? A diversified team can offer differing points of view, as well as a greater pool of knowledge and intellectual stimulation. Or it can offer groupthink and satisficing. What has been your experience as to the value of decision making in the groups you've been in?

What Managers Need to Know about Groups & Decision Making

If you're a manager deliberating whether to call a meeting for group input, there are four characteristics of groups you need to be aware of:

1. They Are Less Efficient Groups take longer to make decisions. Thus, if time is of the essence, you may want to make the decision by yourself. Faced with time pressures or the serious effect of a decision, groups use less information and fewer communication channels, which increases the probability of a bad decision.[80]

2. Their Size Affects Decision Quality The larger the group, the lower the quality of the decision.[81]

3. They May Be Too Confident Groups are more confident about their judgments and choices than individuals are. This, of course, can be a liability because it can lead to groupthink.

4. Knowledge Counts Decision-making accuracy is higher when group members know a good deal about the relevant issues. It is also higher when a group leader has the ability to weight members' opinions.[82] Depending on whether group members know or don't know one another, the kind of knowledge each group member has also counts. For example, people who are familiar with one another tend to make better decisions when members have a lot of unique information. However, people who aren't familiar with one another tend to make better decisions when the members have common knowledge.[83]

Remember that individual decisions are not *necessarily* better than group decisions. As we said at the outset, although groups don't make as high-quality decisions as the *best* individual acting alone, groups generally make better decisions than *most* individuals acting alone. Some guidelines to using groups are presented on the next page. *(See Table 7.4.)*

table 7.4

WHEN A GROUP CAN HELP IN DECISION MAKING: THREE PRACTICAL GUIDELINES

The guidelines may help you as a manager decide whether to include people in a decision-making process and, if so, which people.

I. **When it can increase quality:** If additional information would increase the quality of the decision, managers should involve those people who can provide the needed information. Thus, if a type of decision occurs frequently, such as deciding on promotions or who qualifes for a loan, groups should be used because they tend to produce more consistent decisions than individuals do.

2. **When it can increase acceptance:** If acceptance within the organization is important, managers need to involve those individuals whose acceptance and commitment are important.

3. **When it can increase development:** If people can be developed through their participation, managers may want to involve those whose development is most important.

Source: Derived from George P. Huber, *Managerial Decision Making* (Glenview, IL: Scott Foresman, 1980), p. 149.

Participative Management: Involving Employees in Decision Making

"Only the most productive companies are going to win," says former General Electric CEO Jack Welch about competition in the world economy. "If you can't sell a top-quality product at the world's lowest price, you're going to be out of the game. In that environment, 6% annual improvement may not be good enough anymore; you may need 8% to 9%."[84]

What Is PM?   One technique that has been touted for meeting this productivity challenge is *participative management (PM),* **the process of involving employees in (a) setting goals, (b) making decisions, (c) solving problems, and (d) making changes in the organization.**[85] Employees themselves seem to want to participate more in management: In one nationwide survey of 2,408 workers, two-thirds expressed the desire for more influence or decision-making power in their jobs.[86] Thus, PM is predicted to increase motivation, innovation, and performance because it helps employees fulfill three basic needs: autonomy, meaningfulness of work, and interpersonal contact.[87]

Is PM Really Effective?   Does participative management really work? Certainly it can increase employee job involvement, organizational commitment, and creativity, and it can lower role conflict and ambiguity.[88] Yet it has been shown that, although participation has a significant effect on job performance and job satisfaction, that effect is small—a finding that calls into question the practicality of using PM at all.[89]

So what's a manager to do? In our opinion, PM is not a quick-fix solution for low productivity and motivation. Yet it can probably be effective in certain situations, assuming that managers and employees interact constructively—that is, have the kind of relationship that fosters cooperation and respect rather than competition and defensiveness.[90]

Although participative management doesn't work in all situations, it can be effective if certain factors are present, such as supportive managers and employee trust. *(See Table 7.5.)*

Group Problem-Solving Techniques: Reaching for Consensus

Using groups to make decisions generally requires that they reach a *consensus,* **which occurs when members are able to express their opinions and reach agreement to support the final decision.** More specifically, consensus is reached "when all members can say they either agree with the decision or have had their 'day in court' and were unable to

table 7.5

FACTORS THAT CAN HELP MAKE PARTICIPATIVE MANAGEMENT WORK

- **Top management is continually involved:** Implementing PM must be monitored and managed by top management.

- **Middle and supervisory managers are supportive:** These managers tend to resist PM because it reduces their authority. Thus, it's important to gain the support and commitment of managers in these ranks.

- **Employees trust managers:** PM is unlikely to succeed when employees don't trust management.

- **Employees are ready:** PM is more effective when employees are properly trained, prepared, and interested in participating.

- **Employees don't work in interdependent jobs:** Interdependent employees generally don't have a broad understanding of the entire production process, so their PM contribution may actually be counterproductive.

- **PM is implemented with TQM:** A study of Fortune 1000 firms during three different years found employee involvement was more effective when it was implemented as part of a broader total quality management (TQM) program.

Sources: P. E. Tesluk, J. L. Farr, J. E. Matheieu, and R. J. Vance, "Generalization of Employee Involvement Training to the Job Setting: Individual and Situational Effects," *Personnel Psychology,* Autumn 1995, pp. 607–632; R. Rodgers, J. E. Hunter, and D. L. Rogers, "Influence of Top Management Commitment on Management Program Success," *Journal of Applied Psychology,* February 1993, pp. 151–155; and S. A. Mohrman, E. E. Lawler III, and G. E. Ledford Jr., "Organizational Effectiveness and the Impact of Employee Involvement and TQM Programs: Do Employee Involvement and TQM Programs Work?" *Journal for Quality and Participation,* January/February 1996, pp. 6–10.

convince the others of their viewpoint," says one expert in decision making. "In the final analysis, everyone agrees to support the outcome."[91] This does not mean, however, that group members agree with the decision, only that they are willing to work toward its success.

One management expert offers the following dos and don'ts for achieving consensus.[92]

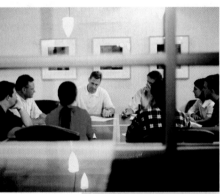

- **Dos:** Use active listening skills. Involve as many members as possible. Seek out the reasons behind arguments. Dig for the facts.

- **Don'ts:** Avoid log rolling and horse trading ("I'll support your pet project if you'll support mine"). Avoid making an agreement simply to keep relations amicable and not rock the boat. Finally, don't try to achieve consensus by putting questions to a vote; this will only split the group into winners and losers, perhaps creating bad feelings among the latter.

Toward consensus. Working to achieve cooperation in a group can tell you a lot about yourself. How well do you handle the negotiation process? What do you do when you're disappointed in a result achieved by consensus?

More Group Problem-Solving Techniques

Decision-making experts have developed several group problem-solving techniques to aid in problem solving. Three we will discuss here are (1) *brainstorming,* (2) the *Delphi technique,* and (3) *computer-aided decision making.*

1. Brainstorming: For Increasing Creativity   *Brainstorming* **is a technique used to help groups generate multiple ideas and alternatives for solving problems.**[93] Developed by advertising executive A. F. Osborn, the technique consists in having members of a group meet and review a problem to be solved. Individual members are then asked to silently generate ideas or solutions, which are then collected (preferably without identifying their contributors) and written on a board or flip

chart. A second session is then used to critique and evaluate the alternatives. A modern-day variation is ***electronic brainstorming,*** **sometimes called** *brainwriting,* **in which members of a group come together over a computer network to generate ideas and alternatives.**[94]

Some rules for brainstorming suggested by IDEO, a product design company, are shown below. *(See Table 7.6.)*

table 7.6

SEVEN RULES FOR BRAINSTORMING

1.	**Defer judgment.** Don't criticize during the initial stage of idea generation. Phrases such as "we've never done it that way," "it won't work," "it's too expensive," and "our manager will never agree" should not be used.
2.	**Build on the ideas of others.** Encourage participants to extend others' ideas by avoiding "buts" and using "ands."
3.	**Encourage wild ideas.** Encourage out-of-the-box thinking. The wilder and more outrageous the ideas, the better.
4.	**Go for quantity over quality.** Participants should try to generate and write down as many new ideas as possible. Focusing on quantity encourages people to think beyond their favorite ideas.
5.	**Be visual.** Use different colored pens (for example, red, purple, blue) to write on big sheets of flip-chart paper, whiteboards, or poster boards that are put on the wall.
6.	**Stay focused on the topic.** A facilitator should be used for keeping the discussion on target.
7.	**One conversation at a time.** The ground rules are that no one interrupts another person, no dismissing of someone's ideas, no disrespect, and no rudeness.

Source: These recommendations and descriptions were derived from B. Nussbaum, "The Power of Design," *BusinessWeek,* May 17, 2004, pp. 86–94. Reprinted with permission.

The benefit of brainstorming is that it is an effective technique for encouraging the expression of as many useful new ideas or alternatives as possible. For example, Mark Hurd, CEO of Hewlett-Packard, engages in brainstorming with his top nine executives to generate ideas for how to increase sales in emerging markets.[95] That said, brainstorming also can waste time generating a lot of unproductive ideas, and it is not appropriate for evaluating alternatives or selecting solutions.

2. The Delphi Technique: For Consensus of Experts The Delphi technique was originally designed for technological forecasting but now is used as a multipurpose planning tool. **The** ***Delphi technique*** **is a group process that uses physically dispersed experts who fill out questionnaires to anonymously generate ideas; the judgments are combined and in effect averaged to achieve a consensus of expert opinion.**

The Delphi technique is useful when face-to-face discussions are impractical. It's also practical when disagreement and conflicts are likely to impair communication, when certain individuals might try to dominate group discussions, and when there is a high risk of groupthink.[96]

3. Computer-Aided Decision Making As in nearly every other aspect of business life, computers have entered the area of decision making, where they are useful not only in collecting information more quickly but also in reducing roadblocks to group consensus.

The two types of computer-aided decision-making systems are *chauffeur driven* and *group driven,* as follows:[97]

- **Chauffeur-driven systems—for push-button consensus.** *Chauffeur-driven computer-aided decision-making systems* ask participants to answer predetermined questions on electronic keypads or dials. These have been used as polling devices, for instance, with audiences on live television shows such as *Who Wants to Be a Millionaire,* allowing responses to be computer-tabulated almost instantly.

- **Group-driven systems—for anonymous networking.** A *group-driven computer-aided decision system* involves a meeting within a room of participants who express their ideas anonymously on a computer network. Instead of talking with one another, participants type their comments, reactions, or evaluations on their individual computer keyboards. The input is projected on a large screen at the front of the room for all to see. Because participation is anonymous and no one person is able to dominate the meeting on the basis of status or personality, everyone feels free to participate, and the roadblocks to consensus are accordingly reduced.

Compared to traditional brainstorming, group-driven systems have been shown to produce greater quality and quantity of ideas for large groups of people, although there is no advantage with groups of 4–6 people.[98] The technique also produces more ideas as group size increases from 5 to 10 members.

Computer-aided decision making has been found to produce greater quality and quantity of ideas than traditional brainstorming for both small and large groups of people.[99] However, other research reveals that the use of online chat groups led to decreased group effectiveness and member satisfaction and increased time to complete tasks compared with face-to-face groups.[100] ●

Traditional group work. This photo shows the kind of traditional arrangement we expect of groups—colleagues are seated close together in clusters to better focus on their particular projects. Do you think you'd rather work in this type of arrangement than in one that is more individually based? Why or why not?

How Exceptional Managers Make Decisions

"Failure is a great teacher." That was one of the life lessons expressed by one CEO who has had to make thousands of decisions during his career.[101] Failure is always a possibility, but that possibility can't stop you from making decisions. And you can probably always learn from the result.

"When Should I Make a Decision & When Should I Delay?"

Often you want to stay open-minded before making a decision. But sometimes that can just be a cover for procrastination. (After all, *not* making a decision is in itself a kind of decision.) How do you know when you're keeping an open mind or are procrastinating? Here are some questions to consider:[102]

Understanding: "Do I have a reasonable grasp of the problem?"

Comfort level about outcome: "Would I be satisfied if I chose one of the existing alternatives?"

Future possible alternatives: "Would it be unlikely that I could come up with a better alternative if I had more time?"

Seizing the opportunity: "Could the best alternatives disappear if I wait?"

If you can answer "yes" to those questions, you almost certainly should decide now, not wait.

"Are There Guidelines for Making Tough Choices?"

"On a daily and weekly basis we can be faced with making hundreds of decisions," says management consultant Odette Pollar. "Most of them are small, but the larger ones where more is at stake can be truly painful." Here are some ways she suggests making decision making easier:[103]

Decide in a timely fashion: "Rarely does waiting significantly improve the quality of the decision," says Pollar. In fact, delay can result in greater unpleasantness in loss of money, time, and peace of mind.

Don't agonize over minor decisions: Postponing decisions about small problems can mean that they simply turn into large ones later.

Separate outcome from process: Does a bad outcome mean you made a bad decision? Not necessarily. The main thing is to go through a well-reasoned process of choosing among alternatives, which increases the chances of success. But even then you can't be sure there will always be a positive outcome.

Learn when to stop gathering facts: "Gather enough information to make a sound decision," suggests Pollar, "but not all the possible information." Taking extra time may mean you'll miss a window of opportunity.

When overwhelmed, narrow your choices: Sometimes there are many good alternatives, and you need to simplify decision making by eliminating some options.

Your Call

Some experts suggest that to help make good decisions you should "be visual," using more pictures and diagrams, and "walk and point" to stimulate areas of the brain that control memory, emotion, and problem solving.[104] What have you found aids you in making decisions?

Key Terms Used in This Chapter

Summary

7.1 Two Kinds of Decision Making: Rational & Nonrational

A decision is a choice made from among available alternatives. Decision making is the process of identifying and choosing alternative courses of action.

Two models managers follow in making decisions are rational and nonrational.

In the rational model, there are four steps in making a decision: Stage 1 is identifying the problem or opportunity. A problem is a difficulty that inhibits the achievement of goals. An opportunity is a situation that presents possibilities for exceeding existing goals. This is a matter of diagnosis—analyzing the underlying causes. Stage 2 is thinking up alternative solutions. Stage 3 is evaluating the alternatives and selecting a solution. Alternatives should be evaluated according to cost, quality, ethics, feasibility, and effectiveness. Stage 4 is implementing and evaluating the solution chosen.

The rational model of decision making assumes managers will make logical decisions that will be the optimum in furthering the organization's best interests. The rational model is prescriptive, describing how managers ought to make decisions.

Nonrational models of decision making assume that decision making is nearly always uncertain and risky, making it difficult for managers to make optimum decisions. Three nonrational models are satisficing, incremental, and intuition. (1) Satisficing falls under the concept of bounded rationality—that is, that the ability of decision makers to be rational is limited by enormous constraints, such as time and money. These constraints force managers to make decisions according to the satisficing model—that is, managers seek alternatives until they find one that is satisfactory, not optimal. (2) In the incremental model, managers take small, short-term steps to alleviate a problem rather than steps that will accomplish a long-term solution. (3) Intuition is making choices without the use of conscious thought or logical inference. The sources of intuition are expertise and feelings.

7.2 Evidence-Based Decision Making & Analytics

Evidence-based management means translating principles based on best evidence into organizational practice. It is intended to bring rationality to the decision-making process.

Scholars Jeffrey Pfeffer and Robert Sutton identify seven implementation principles to help companies that are committed to doing what it takes to profit from evidence-based management: (1) treat your organization as an unfinished prototype; (2) "no brag, just facts"; (3) see yourself and your organization as outsiders do; (4) have everyone, not just top executives, be guided by the responsibility to gather and act on quantitative and qualitative data; (5) you may need to use vivid stories to sell unexciting evidence to others in the company; (6) at the very least, you should slow the spread of bad practices; and (7) you should learn from failure by using the facts to make things better.

Applying the best evidence to your decisions is difficult, for seven reasons: (1) There's too much evidence. (2) There's not enough *good* evidence. (3) The evidence doesn't quite apply. (4) People are trying to mislead you. (5) *You* are trying to mislead you. (6) The side effects outweigh the cure. (7) Stories are more persuasive, anyway.

Perhaps the purest application of evidence-based management is the use of analytics, or business analytics, the term used for sophisticated forms of business data analysis. Among organizations that have made a commitment to quantitative, fact-based analysis, scholars have found three key attributes: (1) They go beyond simple descriptive statistics and use data mining and predictive modeling to identify potential and most profitable customers. (2) Analytics competitors don't gain advantage from one principal application but rather from multiple applications supporting many parts of the business. (3) A companywide embrace of analytics impels changes in culture, processes, behavior, and skills for many employees, and so requires the support of top executives.

7.3 Four General Decision-Making Styles

A decision-making style reflects the combination of how an individual perceives and responds to information. Decision-making styles may tend to have a value orientation, which reflects the extent to which a person focuses on either task or technical concerns versus people and social concerns when making decisions. Decision-making styles may also reflect a person's tolerance for ambiguity, the extent to which a person has a high or low need for structure or control in his or her life. When the dimensions of value orientation and tolerance for ambiguity are combined, they form four styles of decision making: directive, analytical, conceptual, and behavioral.

7.4 Making Ethical Decisions

Corporate corruption has made ethics in decision making once again important. Many companies have an ethics officer to resolve ethical dilemmas, and more companies are creating values statements to guide employees as to desirable business behavior.

To help make ethical decisions, a decision tree—a graph of decisions and their possible consequences—may be helpful. Managers should ask whether a proposed action is legal and, if it is intended to maximize shareholder value, whether it is ethical—and whether it would be ethical *not* to take the proposed action.

A goal for managers should be to rely on moral principles so that their decisions are principled, appropriate, and defensible, in accordance with "the magnificent seven" general moral principles for managers.

7.5 How to Overcome Barriers to Decision Making

When confronted with a challenge in the form of a problem or an opportunity, individuals may respond in perhaps four ineffective ways and three effective ones.

The ineffective reactions are as follows: (1) In relaxed avoidance, a manager decides to take no action in the belief that there will be no great negative consequences. (2) In relaxed change, a manager realizes that complete inaction will have negative consequences but opts for the first available alternative that involves low risk. (3) In defensive avoidance, a manager can't find a good solution and follows by procrastinating, passing the buck, or denying the risk of any negative consequences. (4) In panic, a manager is so frantic to get rid of the problem that he or she can't deal with the situation realistically.

The effective reactions consist of deciding to decide—that is, a manager agrees that he or she must decide what to do about a problem or opportunity and take effective decision-making steps. Three ways to help a manager decide whether to decide are to evaluate (1) importance—how high priority the situation is; (2) credibility—how believable the information about the situation is; and (3) urgency—how quickly the manager must act on the information about the situation.

Heuristics are rules of thumb or strategies that simplify the process of making decisions. Some heuristics or barriers that tend to bias how decision makers process information are availability, confirmation representativeness, sunk-cost anchoring and adjustment, and escalation of commitment. (1) The availability bias means that managers use information readily available from memory to make judgments. (2) The confirmation bias means people seek information to support their own point of view and discount data that do not. (3) The representativeness bias is the tendency to generalize from a small sample or a single event. (4) The sunk-cost bias is when managers add up all the money already spent on a project and conclude that it is too costly to simply abandon it. (5) The anchoring and adjustment bias is the tendency to make decisions based on an initial figure or number. (6) The escalation of commitment bias describes when decision makers increase their commitment to a project despite negative information about it. An example is the prospect theory, which suggests that decision makers find the notion of an actual loss more painful than giving up the possibility of a gain.

7.6 Group Decision Making: How to Work with Others

Groups make better decisions than most individuals acting alone, though not as good as the best individual acting alone.

Using a group to make a decision offers five possible advantages: (1) a greater pool of knowledge; (2) different perspectives; (3) intellectual stimulation; (4) better understanding of the reasoning behind the decision; and (5) deeper commitment to the decision. It also has four disadvantages: (1) a few people may dominate or intimidate; (2) it will produce groupthink, when group members strive for agreement among themselves for the sake of unanimity and so avoid accurately assessing the decision situation; (3) satisficing; and (4) goal displacement, when the primary goal is subsumed to a secondary goal.

Some characteristics of groups to be aware of are (1) groups are less efficient, (2) their size affects decision quality, (3) they may be too confident, and (4) knowledge counts—decision-making accuracy is higher when group members know a lot about the issues.

Participative management (PM) is the process of involving employees in setting goals, making decisions, solving problems, and making changes in the organization. PM can increase employee job involvement, organizational commitment, and creativity and can lower role conflict and ambiguity.

Using groups to make decisions generally requires that they reach a consensus, which occurs when members are able to express their opinions and reach agreement to support the final decision.

Three problem-solving techniques aid in problem solving. (1) Brainstorming is a technique used to help groups generate multiple ideas and alternatives for solving problems. A variant is electronic brainstorming, in which group members use a computer network to generate ideas. (2) The Delphi technique is a group process that uses physically dispersed experts who fill out questionnaires to anonymously generate ideas; the judgments are combined and in effect averaged to achieve a consensus of expert opinion. (3) In computer-aided decision making, chauffeur-driven systems may be used, which ask participants to answer predetermined questions on electronic keypads or dials, or group-driven systems may be used, in which participants in a room express their ideas anonymously on a computer network.

Management in Action

Did Faulty Decision Making Lead to the Death of Luge Racer Nodar Kumaritashvili?

Years before a young luge racer from the Republic of Georgia flew to his death at the Olympics here last week, officials made a series of decisions designed to make the icy track a commercial success after the games but that left it faster—and ultimately more dangerous—than any competitive track before.

Driven in part by the desire to locate the luge and bobsled track from the 2010 Vancouver Games in a high-traffic tourist area, planners chose a valley at a Whistler resort that was steeper and narrower than sites chosen for previous Olympics. . .

Officials say Nodar Kumaritashvili's death had nothing to do with these new speeds and challenges, and maintain that the track was safe. Instead, they say it was because he failed to control his sled.

A reconstruction of the events leading up to Mr. Kumaritashvili's death show that the track was, from its inception, inherently difficult and was the result of decisions that were related to commerce, not sport.

Before Vancouver bid for the 2010 Winter Games, the city's organizing committee members consulted closely with the two international federations that set standards for tracks used by bobsledding and luge: The International Luge Federation and International Federation of Bobsleigh and Tobogganing.

The federations and organizing committee members first looked at Grouse Mountain in North Vancouver, which they considered a top choice for the track, say people involved in the course's early planning.

But soon, the Vancouver bid committee agreed to move the location up into the Canadian Rockies to the mountain ski resort town of Whistler, where the alpine ski events would be taking place.

Tim Gayda, the vice president of sport for the Vancouver organizing committee [Vanoc], told the *Vancouver Sun* in October 2002 that the decision would make the track financially viable after the games.

"In order to make this thing financially sustainable, we want it someplace where people will pay top dollar to go whipping down this thing in both summer and winter," he told the newspaper. The luge and bobsledding federations, he added, were "pushing us to look at options at Whistler.". . .

Bob Storey, the bobsled federation's president and a former bobsledder, said it would be jumping to conclusions to blame Mr. Kumaritashvili's crash on speed. "The Royal Canadian Mounted Police did not attribute it to design flaws and did not attribute it to speed," he said. "The reason they call it an accident is that nobody can define the cause."

Weather was one factor in locating the run in Whistler, according to Terry Gudzowsky, a technical delegate for the bobsled federation who, as then part of Canada's bobsled federation, participated in the initial planning. Grouse Mountain often has warmish, wet winters that could lead to mushier, slower ice. Whistler is at a much higher, alpine elevation, making it more appealing to the sport.

"That was not an engineering decision," says Mr. Storey of the bobsled federation. "That was a commercial decision.". . .

Mr. Gudzowsky says his sketch was sent to German luge-course designer Udo Gurgel. The 71-year-old Mr. Gurgel had built most of the major new luge runs in the world, including six Olympic tracks, over four-plus decades of course design.

He says the Whistler terrain was one of the steepest and narrowest possible. Its 100-yard wide valley compares with Calgary's 300 yards and Salt Lake City's 500 yards.

That meant the site was too narrow to build in typical speed-slowing long curves, called "kreisel" curves, Mr. Gurgel said. Whistler's had to be short and tight, which meant high gravitational forces against the driver in the curves and, toward the end, because the G-forces would be too much to bear, almost no curves, allowing sleds to break through past top speeds.

The course's dangers became part of its marketing.

"Vivid, violent, and rough—the Whistler Sliding Center is not for the faint of heart," the Web site of the center, operated by Vanoc, said in promotional material. . . . "The track has a rhythm that every slider must try to capture. Sliders must find it early in their run. If they lose it, it will be hard to get back on the beat.". . .

"It was crazy fast," recalls Polish luger Maciej Kurowski, who tried out the track when it opened. "The problem is everyone wants to go faster and faster in this sport.". . .

As often happens during Olympic controversies, numerous committees and federations are involved and it is often unclear who bears ultimate responsibility.

The IOC and Vanoc have both said they aren't responsible for the tracks because they essentially subcontract technical specifications out to the luge and bobsleigh federations.

Within a few hours of the accident, those two groups declared their work flawless and blamed the Georgian athlete.

For Discussion

1. Does the decision-making process used to select the site for the luge track resemble more of a rational or nonrational process? Explain.

2. Which of the seven evidence-based decision-making implementation principles were used by Olympic officials? Provide examples to support your conclusions.

3. How could the site selection committee have used analytics to a greater extent than evidenced in the case? Provide specific recommendations.

4. Use the ethical decision-making tree to determine if the site location decision was ethical.

5. Which of the common decision-making biases were evident in this case? Provide examples.

What Is Your Decision-Making Style?

Objectives

1. To assess your decision-making style.

2. To consider the implications of your decision-making style.

Introduction

This chapter discussed a model of decision-making styles. Decision-making styles are thought to vary according to a person's tolerance for ambiguity and value orientation. In turn, the combination of these two dimensions results in four different decision-making styles (see Figure 7.3). This exercise gives you the opportunity to assess your decision-making style.

Instructions

Following are nine items that pertain to decision making. Read each statement and select the option that best represents your feelings about the issue. Remember, there are no right or wrong answers.

1. I enjoy jobs that
   a. are technical and well defined.
   b. have considerable variety.
   c. allow independent action.
   d. involve people.

2. In my job, I look for
   a. practical results.
   b. the best solutions.
   c. new approaches or ideas.
   d. a good working environment.

3. When faced with solving a problem, I
   a. rely on proven approaches.
   b. apply careful analysis.
   c. look for creative approaches.
   d. rely on my feelings.

4. When using information, I prefer
   a. specific facts.
   b. accurate and complete data.
   c. broad coverage of many options.
   d. limited data that are easily understood.

5. I am especially good at
   a. remembering dates and facts.
   b. solving difficult problems.
   c. seeing many possibilities.
   d. interacting with others.

6. When time is important, I
   a. decide and act quickly.
   b. follow plans and priorities.
   c. refuse to be pressured.
   d. seek guidance and support.

7. I work well with those who are
   a. energetic and ambitious.
   b. self-confident.
   c. open-minded.
   d. polite and trusting.

8. Others consider me
   a. aggressive.
   b. disciplined.
   c. imaginative.
   d. supportive.

9. My decisions typically are
   a. realistic and direct.
   b. systematic or abstract.
   c. broad and flexible.
   d. sensitive to the needs of others.

Scoring & Interpretation

Score the exercise by giving yourself one point for every time you selected an A, one point for every B, and so on. Add up your scores for each letter. Your highest score represents your dominant decision-making style. If your highest score was A, you have a directive style; B = analytical; C = conceptual; and D = behavioral. See the related material in this chapter for a thorough description of these four styles.

Questions

1. What are your highest- and lowest-rated styles?

2. Do the results accurately reflect your self-perceptions? Explain.

3. What are the advantages and disadvantages of your style? Discuss.

4. Which of the other decision-making styles is least consistent with your style? How might you work more effectively with someone who has this style? Discuss.

Adapted from A. J. Rowe, J. D. Boulgarides, and M. R. McGrath, *Managerial Decision Making* (Chicago: SRA, 1984).

Should the Principal of Westwood High Allow an Exception to the Graduation Dress Code?

This dilemma involves a situation faced by Helen Riddle, the principal of Westwood High School in Mesa, Arizona. Westwood High has 225 Native American students, including 112 from the Salt River Pima-Maricopa Indian Community, most of which lies within the boundaries of the Mesa Unified School District. Districtwide there are 452 Native American high school students, 149 of whom are from the Salt River Reservation.

Here is the situation: Native American students asked the principal if they could be allowed to wear eagle feathers during their graduation ceremony. Although this may seem like a reasonable request given these students' customs and traditions, Westwood High had a rule stating that, according to a newspaper report, "students were only allowed to wear a traditional cap and gown for graduation, with no other adornments or clothing, including military uniforms. The rules were based on past practice and tradition at schools, not school board policy."

Advocates for the Native American students argued that students should be allowed to wear the eagle feathers because they represent a significant achievement in the lives of those individuals. In contrast, one school board member opposed the exception to the rule because "it would open the door for other students wanting to display symbols of their own culture or background."

Solving the Dilemma

What would you do if you were the principal of Westwood High?

1. Allow the Native American students to wear the eagle feathers now and in the future. This shows an appreciation for diversity.

2. Do not allow the Native American students to wear the eagle feathers because it violates an existing rule. Allowing an exception opens the door for additional requests about changing the dress code. How will you defend one exception over another?

3. Allow the students to wear the eagle feathers only in this year's ceremony, then form a committee to review the dress code requirements.

4. Invent other options. Discuss.

Source: Excerpted from J. Kelley, "Westwood Students Get OK for Eagle Feathers," *The Mesa Republic*, May 25, 2006, p. 15.

Organizational Culture, Structure, & Design
Building Blocks of the Organization

Major Questions You Should Be Able to Answer

8.1 What Kind of Organizational Culture Will You Be Operating In?

Major Question: How do I find out about an organization's "social glue," its normal way of doing business?

8.2 Developing High-Performance Cultures

Major Question: What can be done to an organization's culture to increase its economic performance?

8.3 Organizational Structure

Major Question: How are for-profit, nonprofit, and mutual-benefit organizations structured?

8.4 The Major Elements of an Organization

Major Question: When I join an organization, what seven elements should I look for?

8.5 Basic Types of Organizational Structures

Major Question: How would one describe the seven organizational structures?

8.6 Contingency Design: Factors in Creating the Best Structure

Major Question: What factors affect the design of an organization's structure?

When Should You Delegate & When Not? How Managers Get More Done

All managers must learn how to delegate—to assign management authority and responsibilities to people lower in the company hierarchy. But failure to delegate can happen even with high-powered executives, including those you might least suspect—such as the president of Harvard University. Dr. Neil L. Rudenstine, who became president of Harvard in 1991, initially became so exhausted from overwork that he had to stay home for 2 weeks to recover. The incident sent a message that his future survival would depend on his ability to set priorities and delegate responsibility.[1]

"To do more in a day, you must do less—not do everything faster," says Oakland, California, productivity expert Odette Pollar.[2] If as a manager you find yourself often behind, always taking work home, doing your subordinates' work for them, and constantly having employees seeking your approval before they can act, you're clearly not delegating well. How do you decide when to delegate and when not to? Here are some guidelines:[3]

- **Delegate routine and technical matters:** Always try to delegate routine tasks and routine paperwork. When there are technical matters, let the experts handle them.

- **Delegate tasks that help your subordinates grow:** Let your employees solve their own problems whenever possible. Let them try new things so they will grow in their jobs.

- **Don't delegate confidential and personnel matters:** Any tasks that are confidential or that involve the evaluation, discipline, or counseling of subordinates should never be handed off to someone else.

- **Don't delegate emergencies:** By definition, an emergency is a crisis for which there is little time for solution, and you should handle this yourself.

- **Don't delegate special tasks that your boss asked you to do—unless you have his or her permission:** If your supervisor entrusts you with a special assignment, such as attending a particular meeting, don't delegate it unless you have permission to do so.

- **Match the tasks delegated to your subordinates' skills and abilities:** While recognizing that delegation involves some risk, make your assignments appropriate to the training, talent, skills, and motivation of your employees.

For Discussion Managers fail to delegate for many reasons.[4] An excessive need for perfection. A belief that only they should handle "special," "difficult," or "unusual" problems or clients. A wish to keep the parts of a job that are fun. A fear that others will think them lazy. A reluctance to let employees lower down in the hierarchy take risks. A worry that subordinates won't deliver. A concern that the subordinates will do a better job and show them up. Are any of these reasons why you might not be very good at delegating? What are some others?

forecast | What's Ahead in This Chapter

We consider organizational cultures and organizational structures, and how they should be aligned to help coordinate employees in the pursuit of organization's strategic goals. We then consider the three types of organizations and seven basic characteristics of an organization. We next discuss seven types of organizational structures. Finally, we look at five factors that should be considered when one is designing the structure of an organization.

<table>
<tr><td>

major question?

</td><td>

How do I find out about an organization's "social glue," its normal way of doing business?

</td></tr>
</table>

THE BIG PICTURE

The study of organizing, the second of the four functions in the management process, begins with a study of organizational culture, which exists on three levels. An organizational culture has four functions.

Want to get ahead in the workplace but hate the idea of "office politics"?

Probably you can't achieve the first without mastering the second. Although hard work and talent can take you a long way, "there is a point in everyone's career where politics becomes more important," says management professor Kathleen Kelley Reardon. You have to know the political climate of the company you work for, says Reardon, who is author of *The Secret Handshake* and *It's All Politics.*[5] "Don't be the last person to understand how people get promoted, how they get noticed, how certain projects come to attention. Don't be quick to trust. If you don't understand the political machinations, you're going to fail much more often."[6]

A great part of learning to negotiate the politics—that is, the different behavioral and psychological characteristics—of a particular office means learning to understand the organization's *culture.* The culture consists not only of the slightly quirky personalities you encounter but also all of an organization's normal way of doing business, as we'll explain.

How an Organization's Culture & Structure Are Used to Implement Strategy

Chapter 6 described strategy—the large-scale action plans that reflect the organization's vision and are used to set the direction for the organization. To implement a particular strategy, managers must determine the right kind of (1) *organizational culture* and (2) *organizational structure.* Let's consider these terms.

Organizational Culture: The System of Shared Beliefs & Values   According to scholar **Edgar Schein, *organizational culture,* sometimes called *corporate culture,* is a system of shared beliefs and values that develops within an organization and guides the behavior of its members.**[7] This is the "social glue" that binds members of the organization together. Just as a human being has a personality—fun-loving, warm, uptight, competitive, or whatever—so an organization has a "personality," too, and that is its culture.

Culture can vary considerably, with different organizations having differing emphases on risk taking, treatment of employees, teamwork, rules and regulations, conflict and criticism, and rewards. And the sources of these characteristics also vary. They may represent the strong views of the founders, of the reward systems that have been instituted, of the effects of competitors, and so on.[8] We discuss organizational culture in this section and in Section 8.2.

Culture of risk. At Pfizer, a Connecticut pharmaceutical company, drug discovery is a high-risk, costly endeavor in which hundreds of scientists screen thousands of chemicals against specific disease targets, but 96% of these compounds are ultimately found to be unworkable. The culture, then, is one of managing failure and disappointment, of helping drug researchers live for small victories.

Organizational Structure: Who Reports to Whom & Who Does What

***Organizational structure* is a formal system of task and reporting relationships that coordinate and motivates an organization's members so that they can work together to achieve the organization's goals.** As we describe in Sections 8.3–8.5, organizational structure is concerned with who reports to whom and who specializes in what work.

Whether an organization is for-profit or nonprofit, the challenge for top managers is to create a culture and structure that will motivate its members to work together and coordinate their actions to achieve the organization's goals. *(See Figure 8.1.)* A major point is that there must be *consistency* among all these elements.

figure 8.1

CULTURE PLUS STRUCTURE

Once a strategy has been created that reflects an organization's vision, managers must design the kind of culture and structure that will motivate and coordinate employees in achieving the organization's goals.

Four Types of Organizational Culture: Clan, Adhocracy, Market, & Hierarchy

According to one common methodology known as the *competing values framework,* organizational cultures can be classified into four types: (1) *clan,* (2) *adhocracy,* (3) *market,* and (4) *hierarchy.*[9] *(See Figure 8.2.)*

figure 8.2

COMPETING VALUES FRAMEWORK

Flexibility and discretion

Internal focus and integration / **External focus and differentiation**

Stability and control

Clan	Adhocracy
Thrust: Collaborate	**Thrust:** Create
Means: Cohesion, participation, communication, empowerment	**Means:** Adaptability, creativity, agility
Ends: Morale, people development, commitment	**Ends:** Innovation, growth, cutting-edge output

Hierarchy	Market
Thrust: Control	**Thrust:** Compete
Means: Capable processes, consistency, process control, measurement	**Means:** Customer focus, productivity, enhancing competitiveness
Ends: Efficiency, timeliness, smooth, functioning	**Ends:** Market share, profitability, goal achievement

Adapted from K. S. Cameron, R. E. Quinn, J. Degraff, and A. V. Thakor, *Competing Values Leadership* (Northampton, MA: Edward Elgar, 2006), p. 32.

I. Clan Culture: An Employee-Focused Culture Valuing Flexibility, Not Stability
A ***clan culture*** **has an internal focus and values flexibility rather than stability and control.** Like a family-type organization, it encourages collaboration among employees, striving to encourage cohesion through consensus and job

satisfaction and to increase commitment through employee involvement. Clan organizations devote considerable resources to hiring and developing their employees, and they view customers as partners. Southwest Airlines is a good example of a company with a clan culture. So is online shoe seller Zappos, which encourages managers to spend 10%–20% of their off-work hours with employees.[10]

2. Adhocracy Culture: A Risk-Taking Culture Valuing Flexibility

An *adhocracy culture* **has an external focus and values flexibility.** This type of culture attempts to create innovative products by being adaptable, creative, and quick to respond to changes in the marketplace. Employees are encouraged to take risks and experiment with new ways of getting things done. Adhocracy cultures are well suited for start-up companies, those in industries undergoing constant change, and those in mature industries that are in need of innovation to enhance growth. W. L. Gore is an example of a company with an adhocracy culture. So is Google, which urges engineers to spend 20% of their time on personal projects.[11] Cisco Systems, with its recently introduced unusual system of 48 management "councils," is also trying to become this kind of culture.[12]

3. Market Culture: A Competitive Culture Valuing Profits Over Employee Satisfaction

A *market culture* **has a strong external focus and values stability and control.** Because market cultures are focused on the external environment and driven by competition and a strong desire to deliver results, customers, productivity, and profits take precedence over employee development and satisfaction. Employees are expected to work hard, react fast, and deliver quality work on time; those who deliver results are rewarded. Kia Motors, which fires executives who don't meet their sales goals, is an example of a company with a very aggressive and competitive market culture.[13]

4. Hierarchy Culture: A Structured Culture Valuing Stability & Effectiveness

A *hierarchy culture* **has an internal focus and values stability and control over flexibility.** Companies with this kind of culture are apt to have a formalized, structured work environment aimed at achieving effectiveness through a variety of control mechanisms that measure efficiency, timeliness, and reliability in the creation and delivery of products. General Motors has been an example of a company with a hierarchical structure. So also is UPS, the delivery company.[14]

Example

The Corporate Cultures of Pfizer Pharmaceuticals: The Different "Personalities" Within an Organization

Organizational cultures are nearly as varied as human personalities. And often cultures may vary within the same company—or may vary over time—with, say, the cultural values of the sales and marketing department being quite different from those of the research and development department. Do you recognize the types of organizational cultures in the following?

$2.3 Billion in Fines. Connecticut-based Pfizer Pharmaceuticals was fined $2.3 billion in 2009 for improperly marketing drugs to doctors. "The whole culture of Pfizer is driven by sales," said a former sales representative whose complaint helped the government's case, "and if you didn't sell drugs illegally, you were not seen as a team player."[15] Almost every major drug company has in recent years been accused of giving kickbacks to doctors or shortchanging federal programs.

Free Prescription Drugs to Unemployed. But also in that year, as unemployment hovered around 10% in the United States, Pfizer launched a program in which it offered to supply 70 of its name-brand drugs, such as Lipitor and Viagra, free of charge for up to a year to customers who had lost their jobs and lacked prescription coverage. "We did it because it was the right thing to do," said Pfizer CEO Jeffrey Kindler. "But it was motivational for our employees and got a great response from customers. In the long run, it will help our business."[16]

Ongoing Experimentation. At Pfizer, drug discovery is a high-risk, costly endeavor in which hundreds of scientists screen thousands of chemicals against specific disease targets, but 96% of these compounds are ultimately found to be unworkable. The culture, then, is one of managing failure and disappointment, of helping drug researchers live for the small victories. Thus, says one account, "when a researcher publishes a paper, or when a lab gets some positive results on a new therapy, it's trumpeted throughout the organization."[17] Another example of experimentation, aimed at helping remaining employees to be productive after heavy job cuts, is PfizerWorks, in which 4,000 employees pass off tedious and time-consuming parts of their jobs, such as creating PowerPoint slides and riffling through spreadsheets to outsiders in India.[18]

The preceding are examples of market, clan, and adhocracy cultures, in that order.

YOUR CALL

Not all cultures work well. For instance, some Wall Street firms, such as Citigroup Inc., are reported to have such a strong perform-or-die culture—in which executives are pushed to maximize profits and are quickly fired if they fail to deliver—that it is difficult to find talent to promote from within when chief executives leave.[19] Sometimes a company will do a corporate overhaul in an attempt to improve its performance, but the actual results may turn out otherwise. This reportedly happened with Intel, the Santa Clara, California, computer chip giant, which cut its workforce in 2006, letting go many managers skilled at people development. In the aftermath, employees complained that Intel lost what made it such a celebrated place to work, including being "a place that prizes fresh ideas, frank talk, and employee engagement."[20] What kinds of cultures would these seem to be?

The Three Levels of Organizational Culture

Organizational culture appears as three layers: (1) *observable artifacts,* (2) *espoused values,* and (3) *basic assumptions.*[21] Each level varies in terms of outward visibility and resistance to change, and each level influences another level.

Level 1: Observable Artifacts—Physical Manifestations of Culture

At the most visible level, organizational culture is expressed in *observable artifacts*—physical manifestations such as manner of dress, awards, myths and stories about the company, rituals and ceremonies, and decorations, as well as visible behavior exhibited by managers and employees. Department store retailer JCPenney Co. is trying to revamp itself from a traditional, hierarchical culture into one that is more informal and flexible by, for example, allowing such observable artifacts as business-casual dress on weekdays and jeans on Fridays.[22]

Level 2: Espoused Values—Explicitly Stated Values & Norms

Espoused values **are the explicitly stated values and norms preferred by an organization,** as may be put forth by the firm's founder or top managers. For example, the founders of technology company Hewlett-Packard stressed the "HP Way," a collegial, egalitarian culture that gave as much authority and job security to employees as possible. Although managers may hope the values they espouse will directly influence employee behavior, employees don't always "walk the talk," frequently being more influenced by *enacted values,* **which represent the values and norms actually exhibited in the organization.** Thus, for example, an international corporation hung signs throughout the hallways of its headquarters proclaiming that "trust" was one of its driving principles (espoused value), yet had a policy of searching employees' belongings each time they entered or exited the building (enacted value).[23]

Level 3: Basic Assumptions—Core Values of the Organization

Basic assumptions, which are not observable, represent the core values of an organization's culture—those that are taken for granted and, as a result, are difficult to change. Example: At insurance giant AIG, people worked so hard that the joke around the offices was "Thank heavens it's Friday, because that means there are only two more

HP founders. David Packard (left) and William Hewlett created a close-knit organizational culture that gave a lot of responsibility to employees and fostered innovation within the company. What kind of culture is that?

working days until Monday."[24] Another example: When Peter Swinburn took over in 2008 as CEO of Molson Coors, headquartered jointly in Denver and Montreal, the company had grown into one of the world's largest breweries through a process of 10 acquisitions and joint ventures during the preceding decade. "The challenge was getting a staff of 15,000 workers on three continents to think as one," says one account. "There were different languages and work practices."[25] Swinburn came up with an unofficial motto—"Challenge the expected"—that he hoped would motivate employees to think outside their roles. One survey found that 87% of employees said the company had a "clear vision for the future" in 2009, up from 73% in 2008.

How Employees Learn Culture: Symbols, Stories, Heroes, & Rites & Rituals

Culture is transmitted to employees in several ways, most often through such devices as (1) *symbols,* (2) *stories,* (3) *heroes,* and (4) *rites and rituals.*[26]

1. Symbols A *symbol* **is an object, act, quality, or event that conveys meaning to others.** In an organization, symbols convey its most important values. Example: 3M has a trophy known as the Gold Step award, which is presented every year to employees whose new products achieve significant revenue levels.

2. Stories A *story* **is a narrative based on true events, which is repeated—and sometimes embellished upon—to emphasize a particular value.** Stories are oral histories that are told and retold by members about incidents in the organization's history.

Example: A story told at Ritz-Carlton hotels concerns a beach attendant busily stacking chairs for an evening event, who was asked by a guest to leave out two chairs, because the guest wanted to return to the beach that evening with his girlfriend and propose marriage. "Although the beach attendant was going off duty," according to one account of the story, "he didn't just leave two chairs on the beach; he put on a tuxedo and brought flowers, champagne, and candles. He met the couple when they arrived at the beach later that evening. He escorted them to the chairs, presented the flowers, lit the candles, and served the champagne." The point: The story of the beach attendant's above-and-beyond-the-call-of-duty efforts expresses the Ritz-Carlton dedication to bending over backward to serve customer needs.[27]

3. Heroes A *hero* **is a person whose accomplishments embody the values of the organization.** The accomplishments of heroes, past and present, are put forth to motivate other employees to do the right thing. The Ritz-Carlton beach attendant is an example of one such hero.

4. Rites & Rituals *Rites and rituals* **are the activities and ceremonies, planned and unplanned, that celebrate important occasions and accomplishments in the organization's life.** Military units and sports teams have long known the value of ceremonies handing out decorations and awards, but many companies have rites and rituals as well.

Example: Mary Kay, Inc., annually hosts five back-to-back conventions attended by 50,000 independent beauty consultants to recognize and reward its top producers for outstanding achievements in sales and recruiting. The founder, the late Mary Kay Ash, would personally present the best salespeople with jewelry, trips, and pink Cadillacs—items still awarded today.[28]

The Importance of Culture

Culture can powerfully shape an organization's long-term success. For example, a recent study summarized 25 years of research on the relationship between organizational culture and various measures of organizational effectiveness. Results revealed that companies with clan, adhocracy, and market cultures had significantly higher levels of employee job satisfaction, innovation, and quality of products and services. Organizations with market cultures also reported higher profits and financial growth.[29]

Let us consider the four functions of organizational culture.[30] *(See Figure 8.3.)*

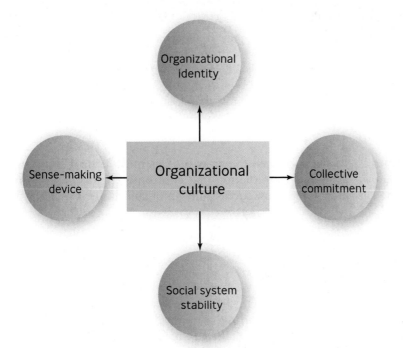

figure 8.3

FOUR FUNCTIONS OF ORGANIZATIONAL CULTURE

Source: Adapted from discussion and reprinted with permission from L. Smircich, "Concepts of Culture and Organizational Analysis," *Administrative Science Quarterly,* September 1983, pp. 339–358. Copyright © Johnson Graduate School of Management, Cornell University.

I. It Gives Members an Organizational Identity At Southwest Airlines, for instance, top executives constantly reinforce the company's message that workers should be treated like customers, and they continually celebrate employees whose contributions go beyond the call of duty.[31]

2. It Facilitates Collective Commitment Consider 3M, one of whose corporate values is to be "a company that employees are proud to be part of." This collective commitment results in a turnover rate of less than 3% among salaried personnel. "I'm a 27-year 3Mer because, quite frankly, there's no reason to leave," says one manager. "I've had great opportunities to do different jobs and to grow a career. It's just a great company."[32]

3. It Promotes Social-System Stability The more effectively conflict and change are managed within an organization and the more that employees perceive the work environment to be positive and reinforcing, the more stable the social system within the organization. At 3M, social stability is encouraged by promoting from within, by hiring capable college graduates in a timely manner, and by providing displaced workers 6 months to find new jobs.

4. It Shapes Behavior by Helping Employees Make Sense of Their Surroundings The culture helps employees understand why the organization does what it does and how it intends to accomplish its long-term goals. 3M sets expectations for innovation, for example, by having an internship and co-op program, which provides 30% of the company's new college hires.

Sometimes culture can be strong enough to take the place of structure; that is, the expectations of the culture replace formal rules and regulations. In these cases, the sense of orderliness and predictability that employees look to for guidance are provided by the culture rather than by a rule book. ●

✳ 8.2 DEVELOPING HIGH-PERFORMANCE CULTURES

major question

What can be done to an organization's culture to increase its economic performance?

THE BIG PICTURE

Three perspectives have been suggested to explain why an organization's culture can enhance the firm's economic performance: strength, fit, and adaptive. A particular culture can become embedded in an organization in many ways, 11 of which are described here.

What does a company do when the growth of its most successful product starts slowing down? This was the situation that confronted financial software maker Intuit Inc., as we shall see. How successfully an organization reacts depends on its culture.

Cultures for Enhancing Economic Performance: Three Perspectives

What types of organizational culture can increase an organization's economic performance in terms of increasing competitiveness and profitability? Three perspectives have been proposed: (1) strength, (2) fit, and (3) adaptive.

I. The Strength Perspective: Success Results When a Firm Has a Strong Culture   The *strength perspective* **assumes that the strength of a corporate culture is related to a firm's long-term financial performance.** A culture is said to be "strong" when employees adhere to the organization's values because they believe in its purpose. A culture is said to be "weak" when employees are forced to adhere to the organization's values through extensive procedures and bureaucracies. The strength perspective embraces the point of view that strong cultures create goal alignment, employee motivation, and the appropriate structure and controls needed to improve organizational performance.[33]

The downside of a strong culture, critics believe, is that such financial success can so reinforce cultural norms that managers and employees become arrogant, inwardly focused, and resistant to change, with top managers becoming blinded to the need for new strategic plans. Example: A case could be made that the strong cultures of American automakers for many years made them resistant to the need to make radical adjustments.

2. The Fit Perspective: Success Results When Culture Fits with the Firm's Business Context   The *fit perspective* **assumes that an organization's culture must align, or fit, with its business or strategic context.** A "correct" fit is expected to foster higher financial performance.

Example: Prior to the arrival of Carleton Fiorina, Hewlett-Packard's "HP Way" culture from 1957 to the early 1990s pushed authority as far down as possible in the organization and created an environment that emphasized integrity, respect for individuals, teamwork, innovation, and an emphasis on customers and community improvement. This fit perspective was a key contributor to HP's success—until the high-technology industry began to change in the late 1990s.[34]

3. The Adaptive Perspective: Success Results When Culture Helps the Firm Adapt

The *adaptive perspective* assumes that the most effective cultures help organizations anticipate and adapt to environmental changes.

Which Perspective Is Accurate? An investigation of 207 companies from 22 industries during the years 1977–1988 partly supported the strength and fit perspectives. However, findings were completely consistent with the adaptive perspective. Long-term financial performance was highest for organizations with an adaptive culture.[35]

Example

The Grateful Dead Demonstrates an Adaptive Culture

You could understand that a successful rock band might be a subject for study by ethnomusicologists or sociologists, but as a topic of interest to business scholars and management theorists? Yet that's the point of view of Joshua Green, author of "Management Secrets of the Grateful Dead" in *The Atlantic*.[36]

Masters of Customer Value. Led by Jerry Garcia, the Grateful Dead became one of the most profitable bands of all time. "The Dead were masters of creating and delivering superior customer value," says Barry Barnes, a business professor at Nova Southeastern University in Florida.[37] How did this come about? "Without intending to—while intending, in fact, to do just the opposite—the band pioneered ideas and practices that were subsequently embraced by corporate America," writes Green.

The band lavished special attention on its most loyal fans, known as the Deadheads. It set up a telephone hotline to alert them to its tour dates ahead of any public announcement. It reserved some of the best seats for some of them, which it distributed through its own mail-order house. "Treating customers well may sound like common sense," says Green. "But it represented a break from the top-down ethos of many organizations of the 1960s and '70s." It was not until the 1980s that competition from Japan compelled American CEOs to adopt a customer-first orientation.

Solid Business Practices. The Dead also incorporated early on and established a board of directors consisting of members of the organization. It created a lucrative merchandising division and sued copyright violators, while at the same time permitting fans to record their shows, shrewdly recognizing that a ban would not only be unenforceable but tape sharing would widen their audience.

YOUR CALL

The kind of adaptability demonstrated by the Dead is what scholar Barnes thinks holds one of the greatest lessons for business—what he calls "strategic improvisation." Do you see evidence of this attribute among other bands you know? What does it take to implant a culture of adaptability within an organization?

Eleven Ways Cultures Become Embedded in Organizations

Those who found a business, and the managers who follow them, essentially use a teaching process to embed the values, beliefs, expectations, behaviors, and business philosophy that constitute the organization's culture. Among the mechanisms used are the following.[38]

1. Formal Statements The first way to embed preferred culture is through the use of formal statements of organizational philosophy, mission, vision, and values, as well as materials used for recruiting, selecting, and socializing employees. Example: Walmart founder Sam Walton stated that three basic values represented the core of the retailer's culture: (1) respect for the individual, (2) service to customers, and (3) striving for excellence.[39]

2. Slogans & Sayings The desirable corporate culture can be expressed in language, slogans, sayings, and acronyms. Example: Robert Mittelstaedt, Dean of the W.P. Carey School of Business at Arizona State University, promotes his goal of having a world-class university through the slogan "top-of-mind business school." This slogan encourages instructors to engage in activities that promote quality education and research.

3. Stories, Legends, & Myths Until a decade ago, major drug companies treated third world countries as not worth the trouble of marketing to. But Andrew Witty, who in 2008 at age 43 became the youngest CEO of GlaxoSmith-Kline, the world's second-largest pharmaceutical company, is making a name for himself by doing more for the poor people of the world than any other big drug company leader. While working in poor countries Witty found "just unbelievable energy to self-improve, to lift themselves up." He has promised to keep prices of drugs sold in poor countries to no more than 25% of what is charged in rich ones and to donate one-fifth of all profits made in such countries toward building their health systems. Now Glaxo is ranked No. 1 on the Access to Medicine index, which rates pharmaceutical companies on their stances toward the poor.[40]

4. Leader Reactions to Crises How top managers respond to critical incidents and organizational crises sends a clear cultural message. Example: Canadian Dov Charney got into the clothing business as a college student, when he would buy thousands of T-shirts at Kmart, then import them via a U-Haul truck into Canada. Then he dropped out of college, borrowed $10,000 from his father, and moved to South Carolina to manufacture clothes—just at a time when the rest of the garment industry found it was cheaper to make clothing overseas. Charney filed for bankruptcy but then moved his company to California, determined to make it work. "I knew I could do it differently, and I knew I could turn it around," he said. "Passion" is the key to success. "When you believe in what you're doing, that's the first thing. And you have to be resilient, because people are going to try to knock you down." Today his company, American Apparel, has over 6,700 employees. And it does something other garment makers have abandoned: it makes all its clothing in the United States.[41]

5. Role Modeling, Training, & Coaching Triage Consulting Group, a health-care financial consulting firm in California, places a high value on superior performance at achieving measurable goals. New employees are immediately prepared for this culture with a 4-day orientation in Triage's culture and methods, followed by 15 training modules scheduled in 6-week intervals. After less than a year, the best performers are ready to begin managing their own projects, furthering their career development. Performance evaluations take place four times a year, further reinforcing the drive for results.[42]

6. Physical Design Intel originally had all its people work in uniform cubicles, consistent with the value it placed on equality. (Top managers don't have reserved parking spaces either.) However, the cubicle arrangement conflicted with the value Intel places on innovation, so the company is experimenting with open-seating arrangements combined with small conference rooms. Not only are open-seating arrangements thought to encourage collaboration, they also can reduce noise because employees can see when their activities are annoying to people nearby. Intel hopes that this environment will better support creative thinking.[43]

7. Rewards, Titles, Promotions, & Bonuses At Triage Consulting Group, employees at the same level of their career earn the same pay, but employees are eligible for merit bonuses, again reinforcing the culture of achievement. The awarding of merit bonuses is partly based on co-workers' votes for who contributed most to the company's success, and the employees who received the most votes are recognized each year at the company's "State of Triage" meeting.[44]

8. Organizational Goals & Performance Criteria Many organizations establish organizational goals and criteria for recruiting, selecting, developing, promoting, dismissing, and retiring people, all of which reinforce the desired organizational culture. Example: PepsiCo sets challenging goals that reinforce a culture aimed at high performance.

9. Measurable & Controllable Activities An organization's leaders can pay attention to, measure, and control a number of activities, processes, or outcomes that can foster a certain culture. Example: ExxonMobil's credo is "efficiency in everything we do," so that managers make a concerted effort to measure, control, and reward cost efficiency. As a result, the company is famous for delivering consistent returns, regardless of whether the price of oil is up or down.[45]

I0. Organizational Structure The hierarchical structure found in most traditional organizations is more likely to reinforce a culture oriented toward control and authority, compared with the flatter organization that eliminates management layers in favor of giving employees more power. Example: The hierarchical structure of a railroad provides a much different culture from that of the "spaghetti organization" formerly employed by Danish hearing-aid maker Oticon, in which employees worked at mobile desks on wheels and were always subject to reorganization.

II. Organizational Systems & Procedures Companies are increasingly using electronic networks to increase collaboration among employees, to increase innovation, quality, and efficiency. For example, Molson Coors CEO Peter Swinburn, mentioned previously, in knitting together employees of several former companies made sure they had better tools to interact with each other. One technology he introduced was Yammer, a Web site for short messages similar to Twitter, on which some 2,000 employees now provide updates and collaborate on projects.[46] ●

major question ?

How are for-profit, nonprofit, and mutual-benefit organizations structured?

THE BIG PICTURE

The organizational structure of the three types of organizations—for-profit, nonprofit, and mutual-benefit—may be expressed vertically or horizontally on an organization chart.

Once an organization's vision and strategy have been determined, as we stated at the beginning of this chapter, the challenge for top managers is, first, to create a culture that will motivate its members to work together and, second, a structure that will coordinate their actions to achieve the organization's strategic goals. Here let us begin to consider the second part—an organization's structure.

According to **Chester I. Barnard's** classic definition, **an *organization* is a system of consciously coordinated activities or forces of two or more people.**[47] By this definition, a crew of two coordinating their activities to operate a commercial tuna fishing boat is just as much an organization as the entire StarKist Tuna Co.

The Organization: Three Types

As we stated in Chapter 1, there are three types of organizations classified according to the three different purposes for which they are formed:[48]

- **For-profit organizations.** These are formed to make money, or profits, by offering products or services.

- **Nonprofit organizations.** These are formed to offer services to some clients, not to make a profit (examples: hospitals, colleges).

- **Mutual-benefit organizations.** These are voluntary collectives whose purpose is to advance members' interests (examples: unions, trade associations).

Clearly, you might have an occupation (such as auditor or police officer) that is equally employable in any one of these three sectors. As a manager, however, you would be principally required to focus on different goals—making profits, delivering public services, or satisfying member needs—depending on the type of organization.

Hybrid. By 2030, some experts say, 72% of fleet vehicles and 85% of new cars will be hybrid electric vehicles. This 2010 Ford Fusion hybrid is the most fuel-efficient car sold in the United States. Are some types of organizations better able to respond to change than others? Why didn't American automakers foresee changes in the price of gasoline?

The Organization Chart

Whatever the size or type of organization, it can be represented in an organization chart. **An *organization chart* is a box-and-lines illustration showing the formal lines of authority and the organization's official positions or work specializations.** This is the family-tree-like pattern of boxes and lines posted on workplace walls and given to new hires. *(See Figure 8.4.)*

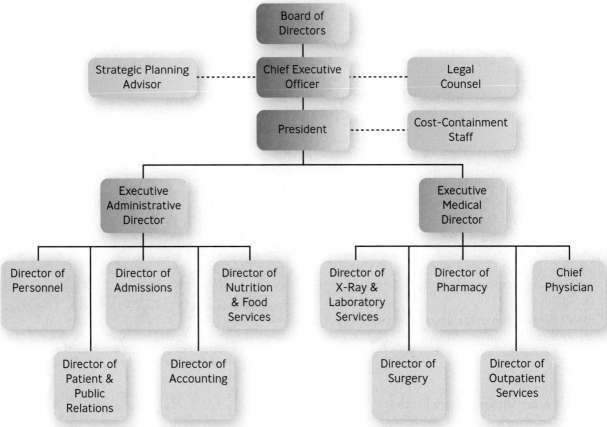

figure 8.4

ORGANIZATION CHART

Example for a hospital

Two kinds of information that organization charts reveal about organizational structure are (1) the *vertical hierarchy of authority*—who reports to whom, and (2) the *horizontal specialization*—who specializes in what work.

The Vertical Hierarchy of Authority: Who Reports to Whom A glance up and down an organization chart shows the *vertical hierarchy,* the chain of command. A formal vertical hierarchy also shows the official communication network—who talks to whom. In a simple two-person organization, the owner might communicate with just a secretary or an assistant. In a complex organization, the president talks principally to the vice presidents, who in turn talk to the assistant vice presidents, and so on.

The Horizontal Specialization: Who Specializes in What Work A glance to the left and right on the line of an organization chart shows the *horizontal specialization,* the different jobs or work specialization. The husband-and-wife partners in a two-person desktop-publishing firm might agree that one is the "outside person," handling sales, client relations, and finances, and the other is the "inside person," handling production and research. A large firm might have vice presidents for each task—marketing, finance, and so on. ●

Practical Action

Transition Problems on Your Way Up: How to Avoid the Pitfalls

Although corporations and managements may make noises about training and support, newly promoted managers may not see any of this and may simply be expected to know what to do. And, as managers move up the ladder, they may encounter other problems that they have not anticipated. How can you avoid some pitfalls as you make your ascent? Some suggestions:[49]

- **Have realistic expectations.** New managers often focus on the rights and privileges of their new jobs and underestimate the duties and obligations.

- **Don't forget to manage upward and sideways as well as downward.** You not only need to manage your subordinates but also the perceptions of your peers and your own managers above you.

- **Stay in touch with managers in other departments.** In addition, you need to have good relationships with managers in other departments—and be perceptive about their needs and priorities—since they have resources you need to get your job done. Don't make the mistake of thinking your own department is the center of the universe.

- **Think about what kind of manager or leader you want to be.** Make a list of all your previous bosses and their good and bad attributes. This may produce a list of dos and don'ts that can serve you well.

- **Get guidance from other managers.** You may not get advice on how to manage from your own manager, who may have promoted you to help reduce his or her workload, not add to it by expecting some coaching. If this is the case, don't be shy

Managing. Being a manager requires a lot of interaction with others—as in "town meetings" with staffers. Do you think you'll need to resist a tendency toward isolation?

about consulting other managers as well as people in professional organizations.

- **Resist isolation.** If you're promoted beyond supervisor of a small team and you have to manage hundreds rather than dozens, or thousands rather than hundreds, you may find the biggest surprise is isolation. The way to stay in touch is to talk daily with your senior managers, perhaps have "town meetings" with staffers several times a year, and employ "management by walking around"—bringing teams together to talk.

Your Call

How would you try to manage the perceptions not only of subordinates but of your peers?

When I join an organization, what seven elements should I look for?

major question?

THE BIG PICTURE

Seven basic elements or features of an organization are described in this section.

Whether for-profit, nonprofit, or mutual-benefit, organizations have a number of elements in common. We discuss four proposed by an organizational psychologist, and then describe three others that most authorities agree on.

Common Elements of Organizations: Four Proposed by Edgar Schein

Organizational psychologist **Edgar Schein** proposed the four common elements of (1) *common purpose,* (2) *coordinated effort,* (3) *division of labor,* and (4) *hierarchy of authority.*[50] Let's consider these.

I. Common Purpose: The Means for Unifying Members   An organization without purpose soon begins to drift and become disorganized. **The *common purpose* unifies employees or members and gives everyone an understanding of the organization's reason for being.**

2. Coordinated Effort: Working Together for Common Purpose   The common purpose is realized through ***coordinated effort,* the coordination of individual efforts into a group or organization-wide effort.** Although it's true that individuals can make a difference, they cannot do everything by themselves.

3. Division of Labor: Work Specialization for Greater Efficiency   ***Division of labor,* also known as *work specialization,* is the arrangement of having discrete parts of a task done by different people.** Even a two-person crew operating a fishing boat probably has some work specialization—one steers the boat, the other works the nets. With division of labor, an organization can parcel out the entire complex work effort to be performed by specialists, resulting in greater efficiency.

4. Hierarchy of Authority: The Chain of Command   The ***hierarchy of authority,* or *chain of command,* is a control mechanism for making sure the right people do the right things at the right time.** If coordinated effort is to be achieved, some people—namely, managers—need to have more authority, or the right to direct the work of others. Even in member-owned organizations, some people have more authority than others, although their peers may have granted it to them.

In addition, authority is most effective when arranged in a hierarchy. Without tiers or ranks of authority, a lone manager would have to confer with everyone in his or her domain, making it difficult to get things done. Even in newer organizations that flatten the hierarchy, there still exists more than one level of management.

Finally, a principle stressed by early management scholars was that of ***unity of command,* in which an employee should report to no more than one manager** in order to avoid conflicting priorities and demands. Today, however, with advances in computer technology and networks, there are circumstances in which it makes sense for a person to communicate with more than one manager (as is true, for instance, with the organizational structure known as the matrix structure, as we'll describe).

Common Elements of Organizations: Three More That Most Authorities Agree On

To Schein's four common elements we may add three others that most authorities agree on: (5) *span of control,* (6) *authority, responsibility, and delegation,* and (7) *centralization versus decentralization of authority.*

5. Span of Control: Narrow (or Tall) versus Wide (or Flat) The *span of control, or span of management,* **refers to the number of people reporting directly to a given manager.**[51] There are two kinds of spans of control, narrow (or tall) and wide (or flat).

Narrow Span of Control This means a manager has a limited number of people reporting—three vice presidents reporting to a president, for example, instead of nine vice presidents. An organization is said to be *tall* when there are many levels with narrow spans of control.

Wide Span of Control This means a manager has several people reporting—a first-line supervisor may have 40 or more subordinates, if little hands-on supervision is required, as is the case in some assembly-line workplaces. An organization is said to be *flat* when there are only a few levels with wide spans of control.

Historically, spans of about 7 to 10 subordinates were considered best, but there is no consensus as to what is ideal. In general, when managers must be closely involved with their subordinates, as when the management duties are complex, they are advised to have a narrow span of control. This is why presidents tend to have only a handful of vice presidents reporting to them. By contrast, first-line supervisors directing subordinates with similar work tasks may have a wide span of control.

The recent emphasis on lean management staffs and more efficiency has meant that spans of control need to be as wide as possible while still providing adequate supervision. Wider spans also fit in with the trend toward allowing workers greater autonomy in decision making. Research in Europe suggests that a manager can oversee 30 or more employees when aided by technology to communicate and help monitor performance.[52]

6. Authority, Responsibility, & Delegation: Line versus Staff Positions
Male sea lions have to battle other males to attain authority over the herd. In human organizations, however, authority is related to the management authority in the organization; it has nothing to do with the manager's fighting ability or personal characteristics. With authority goes *accountability, responsibility,* and the ability to *delegate* one's authority.

Accountability *Authority* **refers to the rights inherent in a managerial position to make decisions, give orders, and utilize resources.** (Authority is distinguished from *power,* which, as we discuss in Chapter 14, is the extent to which a person is able to influence others so they respond to orders.) In the military, of course, orders are given with the expectation that they will be obeyed, disobedience making one liable to a dishonorable discharge or imprisonment. In civilian organizations, disobeying orders may lead to less dire consequences (demotion or firing), but subordinates are still expected to accept that a higher-level manager has a legitimate right to issue orders.

Authority means *accountability*—**managers must report and justify work results to the managers above them.** Being accountable means you have the responsibility for performing assigned tasks.

Responsibility With more authority comes more responsibility. ***Responsibility* is the obligation you have to perform the tasks assigned to you.** A car assembly-line worker has little authority but also little responsibility: just install those windshields over and over. A manager, however, has greater responsibilities.

It is a sign of faulty job design when managers are given too much authority and not enough responsibility, in which case they may become abusive to subordinates and capricious in exerting authority.[53] Conversely, managers may not be given enough authority, so the job becomes difficult.

Delegation ***Delegation*** **is the process of assigning managerial authority and responsibility to managers and employees lower in the hierarchy.** To be more efficient, most managers are expected to delegate as much of their work as possible. However, a business entrepreneur may fall into the common trap of perfection, believing, as one writer puts it, that "you are the only person who can handle a given situation, work with a special client, design a program."[54] But a surprising number of managers fail to realize that delegation is an important part of their job.

Regarding authority and responsibility, the organization chart distinguishes between two positions, *line* and *staff.* (See Figure 8.5.)

figure 8.5

LINE AND STAFF

Line have solid lines, staff have dotted lines.

Line Position ***Line managers*** **have authority to make decisions and usually have people reporting to them.** Examples: the president, the vice presidents, the director of personnel, and the head of accounting. Line positions are indicated on the organization chart by a *solid line* (usually a vertical line).

Staff Position ***Staff personnel*** **have authority functions; they provide advice, recommendations, and research to line managers.** Examples: specialists such as legal counsels and special advisers for mergers and acquisitions or strategic planning. Staff positions are indicated on the organization chart by a *dotted line* (usually a horizontal line).

7. Centralization versus Decentralization of Authority

Who makes the important decisions in an organization? That is what the question of centralization versus decentralization of authority is concerned with.

Centralized Authority **With** *centralized authority,* **important decisions are made by higher-level managers.** Very small companies tend to be the most centralized, although nearly all organizations have at least some authority concentrated at the top of the hierarchy. Kmart and McDonald's are examples of companies using this kind of authority.

An advantage in using centralized authority is that there is less duplication of work, because fewer employees perform the same task; rather, the task is often performed by a department of specialists. Another advantage of centralization is that procedures are uniform and thus easier to control; all purchasing, for example, may have to be put out to competitive bids.

Decentralized Authority **With** *decentralized authority,* **important decisions are made by middle-level and supervisory-level managers.** Here, obviously, power has been delegated throughout the organization. Among the companies using decentralized authority are General Motors and Harley-Davidson.

An advantage in having decentralized authority is that managers are encouraged to solve their own problems rather than to buck the decision to a higher level. In addition, decisions are made more quickly, which increases the organization's flexibility and efficiency. ●

How would one describe the seven organizational structures?

THE BIG PICTURE

Seven types of organizational structures are simple, functional, divisional, matrix, team-based, network, and modular.

Small firm. What type of organizational structure is best suited to a local music shop? Should the number of employees influence the decision?

Culture and structure are often intertwined. Several years ago, the Federal Railroad Administration (FRA) sent inspectors to Union Pacific's headquarters in Omaha, Nebraska, to examine why the railroad had had a series of fatal accidents. There they learned that the company had a top-down, military-style hierarchy and culture that seemed to discourage teamwork and communication. The antiquated style of management had its roots in the days when railroads' executive ranks were filled with combat-hardened former Civil War officers. "When something happened," said a railroad vice president explaining the attitude of leading by fear, "you pulled out your gun and shot the guy in charge of the territory." Said the head of the FRA of Union Pacific's dysfunctional working arrangements, "They were separated from each other in a way that almost guaranteed problems."[55]

We may categorize the arrangements of organizations into seven types of structures: (1) *simple*, (2) *functional*, (3) *divisional*, (4) *matrix*, (5) *team-based*, (6) *network*, and (7) *modular*.

1. The Simple Structure: For the Small Firm

The first organizational form is the simple structure. This is the form often found in a firm's very early, entrepreneurial stages, when the organization is apt to reflect the desires and personality of the owner or founder. **An organization with a *simple structure* has authority centralized in a single person, a flat hierarchy, few rules, and low work specialization.** *(See Figure 8.6.)*

Hundreds of thousands of organizations are arranged according to a simple structure—for instance, small mom-and-pop firms running landscaping, construction, insurance sales, and similar businesses. Examples: Both Hewlett-Packard and Apple Computer began as two-man garage start-ups that later became large.

2. The Functional Structure: Grouping by Similar Work Specialties

The second organizational form is the functional structure. **In a *functional structure*, people with similar occupational specialties are put together in formal groups.** This is a quite commonplace structure, seen in all kinds of organizations, for-profit and nonprofit. *(See Figure 8.7.)*

Examples: A manufacturing firm will often group people with similar work skills in a Marketing Department, others in a Production Department, others in Finance, and so on. A nonprofit educational institution might group employees according to work specialty under Faculty, Admissions, Maintenance, and so forth.

figure 8.6

SIMPLE STRUCTURE: AN EXAMPLE

There is only one hierarchical level of management beneath the owner.

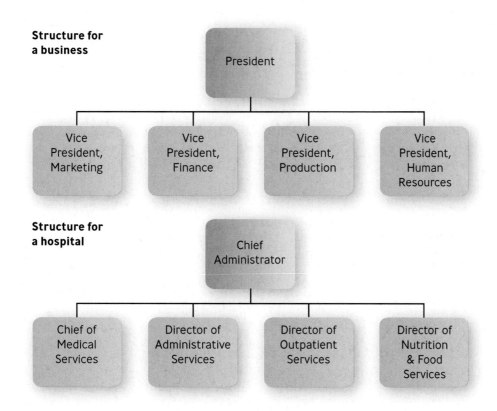

Structure for a business

figure 8.7

FUNCTIONAL STRUCTURE: TWO EXAMPLES

This shows the functional structure for a business and for a hospital.

President

- Vice President, Marketing
- Vice President, Finance
- Vice President, Production
- Vice President, Human Resources

Structure for a hospital

Chief Administrator

- Chief of Medical Services
- Director of Administrative Services
- Director of Outpatient Services
- Director of Nutrition & Food Services

3. The Divisional Structure: Grouping by Similarity of Purpose

The third organizational form is the divisional structure. **In a *divisional structure,* people with diverse occupational specialties are put together in formal groups by similar products or services, customers or clients, or geographic regions.** *(See Figure 8.8, next page.)*

Product Divisions: Grouping by Similar Products or Services *Product divisions* **group activities around similar products or services.** Examples: The media giant Time Warner has different divisions for magazines, movies, recordings, cable television, and so on. The Warner Bros. part of the empire alone has divisions spanning movies and television, a broadcast network, retail stores, theaters, amusement parks, and music.

Customer Divisions: Grouping by Common Customers or Clients *Customer divisions* **tend to group activities around common customers or clients.** Examples: Ford Motor Co. has separate divisions for passenger-car dealers, for large trucking customers, and for farm products customers. A savings and loan might be structured with divisions for making consumer loans, mortgage loans, business loans, and agricultural loans.

Geographic Divisions: Grouping by Regional Location *Geographic divisions* **group activities around defined regional locations.** Example: This arrangement is frequently used by government agencies. The Federal Reserve Bank, for instance, has 12 separate districts around the United States. The Internal Revenue Service also has several districts.

figure 8.8

DIVISIONAL STRUCTURE: THREE EXAMPLES

This shows product, customer, and geographic divisions.

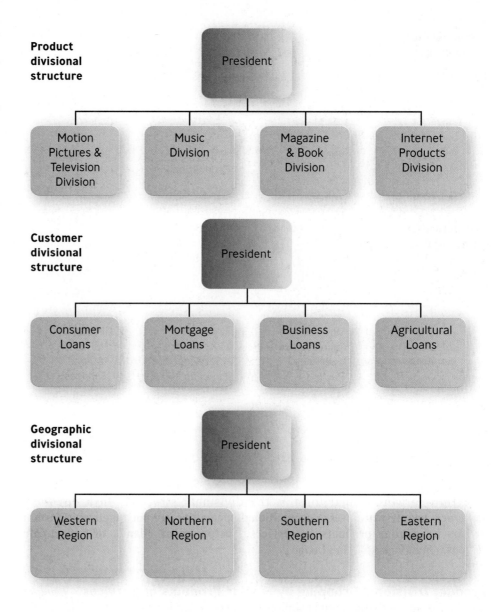

Product divisional structure

President

Motion Pictures & Television Division | Music Division | Magazine & Book Division | Internet Products Division

Customer divisional structure

President

Consumer Loans | Mortgage Loans | Business Loans | Agricultural Loans

Geographic divisional structure

President

Western Region | Northern Region | Southern Region | Eastern Region

4. The Matrix Structure: A Grid of Functional & Divisional for Two Chains of Command

The fourth organizational form is the matrix structure. **In a *matrix structure,* an organization combines functional and divisional chains of command in a grid so that there are two command structures—vertical and horizontal.** The functional structure usually doesn't change—it is the organization's normal departments or divisions, such as Finance, Marketing, Production, and Research & Development. The divisional structure may vary—as by product, brand, customer, or geographic region. *(See Figure 8.9.)*

A hypothetical example, using Ford Motor Co.: The functional structure might be the departments of Engineering, Finance, Production, and Marketing, each headed by a vice president. Thus, the reporting arrangement is vertical. The divisional structure might be by product (the new models of Taurus, Mustang, Explorer, and Expedition, for example), each headed by a project manager. This reporting arrangement is horizontal. Thus, a marketing person, say, would report to *both* the Vice President of Marketing *and* to the Project Manager for the Ford Mustang. Indeed, Ford Motor Co. used the matrix approach to create the Taurus and a newer version of the Mustang.

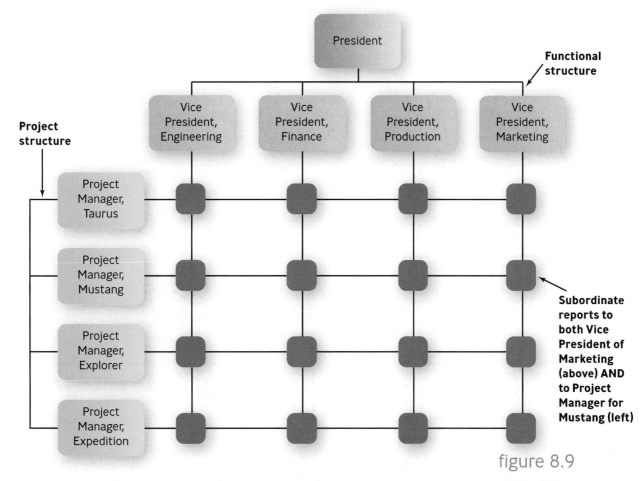

Functional structure

Project structure

President

Vice President, Engineering | Vice President, Finance | Vice President, Production | Vice President, Marketing

Project Manager, Taurus

Project Manager, Mustang

Project Manager, Explorer

Project Manager, Expedition

Subordinate reports to both Vice President of Marketing (above) AND to Project Manager for Mustang (left)

figure 8.9

MATRIX STRUCTURE

An example of an arrangement that Ford might use.

5. The Team-Based Structure: Eliminating Functional Barriers to Solve Problems

The fifth organizational form is the team-based structure. **In a *team-based structure*, teams or workgroups, either temporary or permanent, are used to improve horizontal relations and solve problems throughout the organization.**[56] When managers from different functional divisions are brought together in teams—known as cross-functional teams—to solve particular problems, the barriers between the divisions break down. The focus on narrow divisional interests yields to a common interest in solving the problems that brought them together. Yet team members still have their full-time functional work responsibilities and still formally report to their own managers above them in the functional-division hierarchy. *(See Figure 8.10, next page.)*

Example 🔍

Use of a Team-Based Structure: Motorola Designs a Cell Phone

The mood was grim at Motorola, which had watched rival cell-phone maker Nokia leap to No. I worldwide in market share on the basis of its "candy bar" phone designs. But engineers in Motorola's concept-phone unit had a vision for something different, having produced a mock-up of what was described as "an impossibly thin phone—at ten millimeters . . . half the girth of a typical flip-flop" cell phone.[57] Engineer Roger Jellicoe was told to pull a team together and produce the thinnest phone ever released—and to do it within a year in order to make a splash by handing it out as a high-end niche product to celebrities at the February Academy Awards.

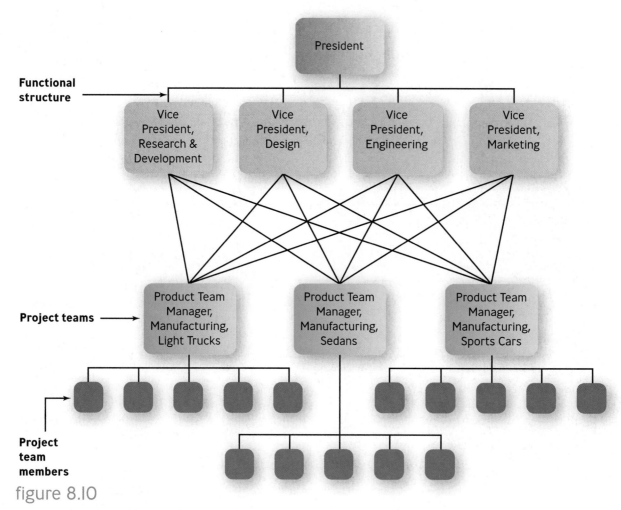

Functional structure

Project teams

Project team members

figure 8.10

TEAM-BASED STRUCTURE

This shows a mix of functional and team arrangements.

The Skunkworks. Eventually the team grew to as many as 20 engineers, who met daily in a conference room in Motorola's Libertyville, Illinois office, to deliberate over how to cram a checklist of components—antenna, speaker, keypad, camera, display, light source, and so on—into minimal space. Operating as a "skunkworks"—a project team whose members are separated from normal company operations—that kept the project secret even from their colleagues, the team members used materials and techniques that Motorola had never tried before. They also threw out accepted models of what a cell phone was supposed to look and feel like. "In short," says a *Fortune* account, "the team that created the RAZR broke the mold, and in the process rejuvenated the company."

As engineers worked on the components, industrial designer Chris Arnholt worked on the look, rendering designs onto a page and then letting another designer translate them into three-dimensional computer graphics, which model makers could use to craft plastic mock-ups. Nearly every activity came down to a trade-off of functionality versus thinness, which eventually led to two compromises: the phone exceeded the original targeted size by about an eighth of an inch and the team missed the original February deadline.

The RAZR Unveiled. When the RAZR was finally unveiled in a splashy presentation in July, it became an instant hit. And the company realized that the product it had designed to be a high-priced, high-end jewel had mass market appeal.

YOUR CALL

The team approach, known as *concurrent engineering* or *integrated product development,* has been found to speed up the design of new products because all the specialists meet at once, instead of separately doing their own thing, then handing off the result to the next group of specialists. Can you think of circumstances in which the old-fashioned nonteam approach would probably work better?

6. The Network Structure: Connecting a Central Core to Outside Firms by Computer Connections

In the sixth organizational form, ***network structure,*** **the organization has a central core that is linked to outside independent firms by computer connections, which are used to operate as if all were a single organization.** *(See Figure 8.11.)* Corporations using this structure are sometimes called *virtual corporations* or *virtual organizations,* as we mentioned in Chapter 2.[58] Another term used is the *hollow corporation* or *hollow organization,* in which the company retains important core processes critical to its performance (such as design or marketing) and outsources most other processes (such as human resources, warehousing, or distribution), thereby seeming to "hollow out" the organization.[59]

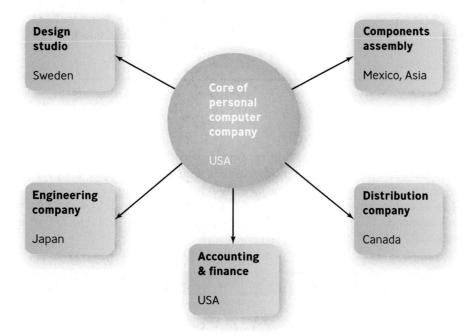

figure 8.11

NETWORK STRUCTURE

This is an example of a personal computer company.

With a network structure, an organization can become a *boundaryless organization,* as we described in Chapter 2, operating with extensive, even worldwide operations, yet its basic core can remain small, thus keeping payrolls and overhead down. The glue that holds everything together is information technology, along with strategic alliances and contractual arrangements with supplier companies.

Example 🔍

Network Structure: EndoStim, a Medical Device Start-up, Operates Virtually

Nowadays a firm can be completely international. An example is the medical device start-up EndoStim, nominally based in St. Louis but operating everywhere.

The Internationalists. Cuban immigrant Raul Perez, MD, came to St. Louis, where he met Dan Burkhardt, a local investor, with whom he began making medical investments. Perez also suffered from acid reflux,

reports *New York Times* columnist Thomas Friedman, and went to Arizona for treatment to an Indian-American physician, V. K. Sharma, who proposed an idea for a pacemaker-like device to control the muscle that would choke off acid reflux. Perez, Burkhardt, and Sharma joined South Africa–born Bevil Hogg, a founder of Trek Bicycle Corporation, who became the CEO of the company named

EndoStim and helped to raise initial development funds. Two Israelis, a medical engineer and a gastroenterologist, joined a Seattle engineering team to help with the design, and a company in Uruguay specializing in pacemakers was lined up to build the prototype. The clinical trials for the device are being conducted in India and Chile.

Continues Friedman, "This kind of very lean start-up, where the principals are rarely in the same office at the same time, and which takes advantage of all the [technological communication tools]—teleconferencing, e-mail, the Internet, and faxes—to access the best expertise and low-cost, high-quality manufacturing anywhere, is the latest in venture investing."[60]

Operating Differently. A virtual, boundaryless company like EndoStim operates differently from a traditional company. For instance, at MySQL, a virtual software maker employing 320 workers in 25 countries, managers have had to learn to evaluate people and give feedback differently. "Productivity is measured strictly by output; mushy factors like charisma don't pertain in cyberspace," says one observer. As might be expected, MySQL hires strictly for skill, not "the ability to play nicely with others."[61]

YOUR CALL

Many people like the social interaction that comes with working in a physical office with other people. Others, however, are turned off by the "office politics" and time-wasting activities that seem to be a necessary concomitant and welcome the opportunity to do task-oriented work in a makeshift home office, occasionally having to cope with loneliness and restlessness. Which would you favor?

7. The Modular Structure: Outsourcing Pieces of a Product to Outside Firms

The seventh organizational form differs from the sixth in that it is oriented around outsourcing certain *pieces of a product* rather than outsourcing certain *processes* (such as human resources or warehousing) of an organization. In a **_modular structure,_ a firm assembles product chunks, or modules, provided by outside contractors.** One article compares this form of organization to "a collection of Lego bricks that can snap together."[62] ●

Example

Modular Structure: Bombardier Builds a Snap-Together Business Jet[63]

Bombardier (pronounced "bom-*bar*-dee-ay"), whose main factory is located in Wichita, Kansas, makes an eight-passenger business jet called the Continental, so named because it can fly across the United States without refueling. The aircraft is designed into a dozen large modules, which are manufactured by a mix of both internal Bombardier divisions and outside contractors around the world.

The cockpit and forward fuselage, for instance, are built by Bombardier Montreal. The center section is built in Belfast, the wing by Mitsubishi in Japan, the stabilizers and rear fuselage by Aerospace Industrial Development in Taiwan, the landing gear by Messier-Dowty in Canada, and the tailcone by Hawker de Havilland in Australia. The engines are provided by General Electric and the avionics gear by Rockwell Collins, both companies in the United States. The 12 modules are shipped to Wichita, where the parts are snapped together in just 4 days.

Bombardier. A regional vice president of sales for Bombardier, David Dixon, poses in front of a Bombardier luxury aircraft, built using the modular structure of organization.

YOUR CALL

Could you envision building automobiles, bicycles, and computers using a modular approach? What other products?

✻ 8.6 CONTINGENCY DESIGN: FACTORS IN CREATING THE BEST STRUCTURE

What factors affect the design of an organization's structure?

major question?

THE BIG PICTURE
Three factors that should be considered when determining the best organizational culture involve whether an organization's environment is mechanistic or organic, whether its environment stresses differentiation or integration, and where the organization is in its four-stage life cycle.

What is the optimal size for an organization? How big is too big?

Medical records company gloStream, which sells software to doctors' offices, was founded in 2005 as a virtual organization, and for four years the approach worked well, with costs kept low and salespeople having no choice but to be out in the field. But in 2009, CEO Mike Sappington decided it was time to "take the company physical." "We've gotten too big to be a virtual company," he told *Inc.* magazine. By the end of 2010, he said, "we'll have 100 employees in the U.S. and another 100 in India. Setting up a conference call or arranging everyone's schedules for a meeting started to take an enormous amount of time."[64]

When managers are considering what organizational arrangements to choose from, stage of development is among the factors, or *contingencies,* they must consider. Recall from Chapter 2 that the *contingency approach* to management emphasizes that a manager's approach should vary according to—that is, be contingent on—the individual and environmental situation. Thus, the manager following the contingency approach simply asks, "What method is the best to use under these particular circumstances?" **The process of fitting the organization to its environment is called** *contingency design.*

Managers taking a contingency approach must consider the following factors (among others) in designing the best kind of structure for their particular organization at that particular time:

1. *Environment—mechanistic versus organic*
2. *Environment—differentiation versus integration*
3. *Life cycle*

I. The Environment: Mechanistic versus Organic Organizations—the Burns & Stalker Model

"Here every job is broken down into the smallest of steps, and the whole process is automated," wrote *BusinessWeek* correspondent Kathleen Deveny, reporting about a day she spent working in a McDonald's restaurant. "Anyone could do this, I think."[65]

Actually, Deveny found that she fell behind in, say, bagging French fries, but it was certainly the intention of McDonald's guiding genius Ray Kroc that, in fact, nearly anyone *should* be able to do this—and that a Big Mac should taste the same anywhere. Thus, for example, procedure dictates that a hamburger is always dressed the same way: first the mustard, then the ketchup, then two pickles.

Could anyone do this? McDonald's follows the model of a mechanistic organization.

table 8.1

MECHANISTIC VERSUS
ORGANIC ORGANIZATIONS

Mechanistic Organizations	Organic Organizations
Centralized hierarchy of authority	Decentralized hierarchy of authority
Many rules and procedures	Few rules and procedures
Specialized tasks	Shared tasks
Formalized communication	Informal communication
Few teams or task forces	Many teams or task forces
Narrow span of control, taller structures	Wider span of control, flatter structures

McDonald's is a hugely successful example of what British behavioral scientists **Tom Burns** and **G. M. Stalker** call a *mechanistic organization,* as opposed to an *organic organization.*[66] *(See Table 8.1.)*

Mechanistic Organizations: When Rigidity & Uniformity Work Best   In a *mechanistic organization,* **authority is centralized, tasks and rules are clearly specified, and employees are closely supervised.** Mechanistic organizations, then, are bureaucratic, with rigid rules and top-down communication. This kind of structure is effective at McDonald's because the market demands uniform product quality, cleanliness, and fast service.

In general, mechanistic design works best when an organization is operating in a stable environment. Yet new companies that have gone through a rough-and-tumble start-up period may decide to change their structures so that they are more mechanistic, with clear lines of authority.

Organic Organizations: When Looseness & Flexibility Work Best   In an *organic organization,* **authority is decentralized, there are fewer rules and procedures, and networks of employees are encouraged to cooperate and respond quickly to unexpected tasks.** Tom Peters and Robert Waterman called this kind of organization a "loose" structure.[67]

Organic organizations are sometimes termed "adhocracies" because they operate on an ad hoc basis, improvising as they go along. As you might expect, information-technology companies such as Motorola favor the organic arrangement because they constantly have to adjust to technological change—yet so do companies that need to respond to fast-changing consumer tastes, such as clothing retailer The Worth Collection, which operates as a virtual company offering high-end women's clothing through direct selling in people's homes.[68]

2. The Environment: Differentiation versus Integration— the Lawrence & Lorsch Model

Burns and Stalker's ideas were extended in the United States by Harvard University researchers **Paul R. Lawrence** and **Jay W. Lorsch.**[69] Instead of a *mechanistic-organic dimension,* however, they proposed a *differentiation-integration* dimension—forces that impelled the parts of an organization to move apart or to come together. The stability of the environment confronting the parts of the organization, according to Lawrence and Lorsch, determines the degree of differentiation or integration that is appropriate.

Differentiation: When Forces Push the Organization Apart   *Differentiation* **is the tendency of the parts of an organization to disperse and fragment.** The more sub-units into which an organization breaks down, the more highly differentiated it is.

This impulse toward dispersal arises because of technical specialization and division of labor. As a result, specialists behave in specific, delimited ways, without coordinating with other parts of the organization. For example, a company producing dental floss, deodorants, and other personal-care products might have different product divisions, each with its own production facility and sales staff— a quite differentiated organization.

Integration: When Forces Pull the Organization Together   *Integration* is the **tendency of the parts of an organization to draw together to achieve a common purpose.** In a highly integrated organization, the specialists work together to achieve a common goal. The means for achieving this are a formal chain of command, standardization of rules and procedures, and use of cross-functional teams and computer networks so that there is frequent communication and coordination of the parts.

3. Life Cycle: Four Stages in the Life of an Organization

Like living things, organizations go through a life cycle. **The four-stage *organizational life cycle* has a natural sequence of stages: birth, youth, midlife, and maturity.** In general, as an organization moves through these stages, it becomes not only larger but also more mechanistic, specialized, decentralized, and bureaucratic. Each stage offers different managerial challenges and different organizational design issues.[70]

Stage I. The Birth Stage—Nonbureaucratic   The *birth stage* is the non-**bureaucratic stage, the stage in which the organization is created.** Here there are no written rules and little if any supporting staff beyond perhaps a secretary.

The founder may be a lone entrepreneur, such as Michael Dell, who began Dell Computers by selling microcomputers out of his University of Texas college dorm room. Or the founders may be pals who got together, as did Apple Computer founders Steven Jobs and Stephen Wozniak, who built the first computer in Wozniak's parents' Palo Alto, California garage, using the proceeds from the sale of an old Volkswagen.

Stage 2. The Youth Stage—Prebureaucratic   In the *youth stage,* the organi-**zation is in a prebureaucratic stage, a stage of growth and expansion.**

Now the company has a product that is making headway in the marketplace, people are being added to the payroll (most clerical rather than professional), and some division of labor and setting of rules are being instituted.

For Apple Computer, this stage occurred during the years 1978–1981, with the establishment of the Apple II product line.

Stage 3. The Midlife Stage—Bureaucratic   In the *midlife stage,* the organiza-**tion becomes bureaucratic, a period of growth evolving into stability.**

Now the organization has a formalized bureaucratic structure, staffs of specialists, decentralization of functional divisions, and many rules.

In the 1980s, Apple Computer became a large company with many of these attributes. In 1983, Pepsi-Cola marketer John Scully was hired as a professional top manager. Jobs became chairman; Wozniak left.

Stage 4. The Maturity Stage—Very Bureaucratic   In the *maturity stage,* the **organization becomes very bureaucratic, large, and mechanistic.** The danger at this point is lack of flexibility and innovation.

After Jobs was fired in a boardroom struggle in 1985, Apple entered a period in which it seemed to lose its way, having trouble developing successful products and getting them to market. Scully, who emphasized the wrong technology (a "personal data assistant" called Newton, which failed to establish a following), was followed by two more CEOs who were unable to arrest the company's declining market share.

In 1997, Jobs was brought back as a "temporary" chairman, and Apple began an unprecedented era of innovation and profitability.

Employees who were present during birth and youth stages may long for the good old days of informality and fewer rules as the organization moves toward more formalized and bureaucratic structures. Whereas clearly some organizations jump the gun and institute such structures before they are appropriate, some expanding companies in effect never grow up, holding on to the prebureaucratic way of life for too long, hindering their ability to deliver goods or services efficiently in relation to their size.

Getting the Right Fit: What Form of Organizational Structure Works Best?[71]

All the organizational structures described in this chapter are used today because each structure has advantages that make it appropriate for some cases and disadvantages that make it not useful for others. For example, the clear roles and strict hierarchy of an extremely mechanistic organization are clearly suitable in a system valuing careful routines and checks and balances, such as a nuclear power plant. A fast-moving start-up drawing on sources of expertise throughout the world may benefit from a more organic structure that lowers boundaries between functions and organizations.

As for the types of organizational structures described in Section 8.5, all have their uses. Functional structures save money by grouping together people who need similar materials and equipment. Divisional structures increase employees' focus on customers and products. A matrix structure tries to combine the advances of functional and divisional, but it can also slow decision making. Teams can arrive at creative solutions and develop new products faster than workers in more traditional structures. Finally, network and modular structures can tap people in particular specialties.

Key Terms Used in This Chapter

accountability 250
adaptive perspective 243
adhocracy culture 238
authority 250
birth stage 261
centralized authority 251
clan culture 237
common purpose 249
contingency design 259
coordinated effort 249
customer divisions 253
decentralized authority 251
delegation 251
differentiation 260
division of labor 249
divisional structure 253
enacted values 239

espoused values 239
fit perspective 242
functional structure 252
geographic divisions 253
hero 240
hierarchy culture 238
hierarchy of authority 249
integration 261
line managers 251
market culture 238
matrix structure 254
maturity stage 261
mechanistic organization 260
midlife stage 261
modular structure 258
network structure 255
organic organization 260

organization 246
organization chart 247
organizational culture 236
organizational life cycle 261
organizational structure 237
product divisions 253
responsibility 250
rites and rituals 240
simple structure 252
span of control (management) 250
staff personnel 251
story 240
strength perspective 242
symbol 240
team-based structure 255
unity of command 249
youth stage 261

8.1 What Kind of Organizational Culture Will You Be Operating In?

Organizational culture is a system of shared beliefs and values that develops within an organization and guides the behavior of its members. Four types of culture are (1) clan, which has an internal focus and values flexibility; (2) adhocracy, which has an external focus and values flexibility; (3) market, which has a strong external focus and values stability and control; and (4) hierarchy, which has an internal focus and values stability and control.

Organizational culture appears as three layers. Level 1 is observable artifacts, the physical manifestations of culture. Level 2 is espoused values, explicitly stated values and norms preferred by an organization, although employees are frequently influenced by enacted values, which represent the values and norms actually exhibited in the organization. Level 3 consists of basic assumptions, the core values of the organization.

Culture is transmitted to employees in symbols, stories, heroes, and rites and rituals. A symbol is an object, act, quality, or event that conveys meaning to others. A story is a narrative based on true events, which is repeated—and sometimes embellished on—to emphasize a particular value. A hero is a person whose accomplishments embody the values of the organization. Rites and rituals are the activities and ceremonies, planned and unplanned, that celebrate important occasions and accomplishments in the organization's life.

Culture, which can powerfully shape an organization's success over the long term, has four functions. (1) It gives members an organizational identity. (2) It facilitates collective commitment. (3) It promotes social-system stability. (4) It shapes behavior by helping employees make sense of their surroundings.

8.2 Developing High-Performance Cultures

What types of organizational culture can increase an organization's competitiveness and profitability? Three perspectives have been proposed: (1) The strength perspective assumes that the strength of a corporate culture is related to a firm's long-term financial performance; (2) the fit perspective assumes that an organization's culture must align, or fit, with its business or strategic context; and (3) the adaptive perspective assumes that the most effective cultures help organizations anticipate and adapt to environmental changes.

Among the mechanisms managers use to embed a culture in an organization are: (1) formal statements; (2) slogans and sayings; (3) stories, legends, and myths; (4) leader reactions to crises; (5) role modeling, training, and coaching; (6) physical design; (7) rewards, titles, promotions, and bonuses; (8) organizational goals and performance criteria; (9) measurable and controllable activities; (10) organizational structure; and (11) organizational systems and procedures.

8.3 Organizational Structure

An organization is a system of consciously coordinated activities or forces of two or more people. There are three types of organizations classified according to the three different purposes for which they are formed: for-profit, nonprofit, and mutual-benefit.

Whatever the size of organization, it can be represented in an organization chart, a boxes-and-lines illustration showing the formal lines of authority and the organization's official positions or division of labor. Two kinds of information that organizations reveal about organizational structure are (1) the vertical hierarchy of authority—who reports to whom, and (2) the horizontal specialization—who specializes in what work.

8.4 The Major Elements of an Organization

Organizations have seven elements: (1) common purpose, which unifies employees or members and gives everyone an understanding of the organization's reason for being; (2) coordinated effort, the coordination of individual efforts into a group or organization-wide effort; (3) division of labor, having discrete parts of a task done by different people; (4) hierarchy of authority, a control mechanism for making sure the right people do the right things at the right time; (5) span of control, which refers to the number of people reporting directly to a given manager. (6) Authority and accountability, responsibility, and delegation: Authority refers to the rights inherent in a managerial position to make decisions, give orders, and utilize resources. Accountability means that managers must report and justify work results to the managers above them. Responsibility is the obligation you have to perform the tasks assigned to you. Delegation is the process of assigning managerial authority and responsibility to managers and employees lower in the hierarchy. Regarding authority and responsibility, the organization chart distinguishes between two positions, line and staff. Line managers have authority to make decisions and usually have people reporting to them. Staff personnel have advisory functions; they provide advice, recommendations, and research to line managers. (7) Centralization versus decentralization of authority: With centralized authority, important decisions are made by higher-level managers. With decentralized authority, important decisions are made by middle-level and supervisory-level managers.

8.5 Basic Types of Organizational Structures

Organizations may be arranged into seven types of structures. (1) In a simple structure, authority is centralized in a single person; this structure has a flat hierarchy, few rules, and low work specialization. (2) In a functional structure, people with similar occupational specialties are put together in formal groups. (3) In a divisional structure, people with diverse occupational specialties are put together in formal groups by similar products or services, customers or clients, or geographic regions. (4) In a matrix structure, an organization combines functional and divisional chains of command in grids so that there are two

command structures—vertical and horizontal. (5) In a team-based structure, teams or workgroups are used to improve horizontal relations and solve problems throughout the organization. (6) In a network structure, the organization has a central core that is linked to outside independent firms by computer connections, which are used to operate as if all were a single organization. (7) In a modular structure, a firm assembles product chunks, or modules, provided by outside contractors.

8.6 Contingency Design: Factors in Creating the Best Structure

The process of fitting the organization to its environment is called contingency design. Managers taking a contingency approach must consider at least three factors in designing the best kind of structure for their organization at that particular time.

1. An organization may be either mechanistic or organic. In a mechanistic organization, authority is centralized, tasks and rules are clearly specified, and employees are closely supervised. In an organic organization, authority is decentralized, there are fewer rules and procedures, and networks of employees are encouraged to cooperate and respond quickly to unexpected tasks.

2. An organization may also be characterized by differentiation or integration. Differentiation is the tendency of the parts of an organization to disperse and fragment. Integration is the tendency of the parts of an organization to draw together to achieve a common purpose.

3. The four-stage organizational life cycle has a natural sequence of stages: birth, youth, midlife, and maturity. The birth stage is the nonbureaucratic stage, the stage in which the organization is created. The youth stage is the prebureaucratic stage, a stage of growth and expansion. In the midlife stage, the organization becomes bureaucratic, a period of growth evolving into stability. In the maturity stage, the organization becomes very bureaucratic, large, and mechanistic. The danger at this point is lack of flexibility and innovation.

SAS's People-Focused Culture Drives Financial Success

Employees at SAS certainly feel kneaded. Every week, several dozen of them get massages at the on-site 66,000-square-foot recreation and fitness center. You have to pay, but it's only $55 for an hour, and that's with pretax dollars. And the convenience is priceless: right up the stairs from the gymnasium, weight room, billiards hall, sauna, hair salon, manicurist, and aqua kickboxing in the Olympic-size pool. (Posted etiquette rules: "A bathing suit is required" and "No cellphones in class.") There's classic massage, Swedish massage, orthopedic massage, and myofascial release—all designed to make workers "more aware of their bodies, move with greater ease and freedom," and "have increased energy, reduced feelings of pain, and feelings of relaxation and well-being." . . .

Though companies in Silicon Valley get lots of press about perk-friendly workplaces, it's here in the less go-go South that employees reign supreme. SAS is not only the world's largest privately held software business—with revenues of $2.3 billion, it's about the size of public Intuit—but also the paragon of perks. In fact when Google, a SAS customer, was putting together its own campus freebies some years ago, it used SAS as a model. SAS (pronounced *sass*) has been on *Fortune*'s list of Best Companies to Work For every one of the 13 years we've been keeping score. But this is the first time SAS is in the No. 1 slot. While its pampering of employees might give corporate scrooges a coronary, CEO Jim Goodnight says the policies make estimable business sense. "My chief assets drive out of the gate every day," Goodnight likes to say. "My job is to make sure they come back." His motives aren't charitable but entirely utilitarian, even a bit Machiavellian. The average tenure at SAS is 10 years; 300 employees have worked for 25 or more. Annual turnover was 2% in 2009, compared with the average in the software industry of about 22%. Women make up 45% of its U.S. workforce, which has an average age of 45. . . .

The notion of easy living frustrates those on the inside. "Some may think that because SAS is family-friendly and has great benefits that we don't work hard," says Bev Brown, who's in external communications. "But people do work hard here, because they're motivated to take care of a company that takes care of them."

For SAS's 4,200 employees at its hilly North Carolina headquarters (there are roughly another 7,000 employees elsewhere, mostly in other countries), the work environment is preternaturally civilized. The typical week is 35 hours; no human resources troll monitors sick days (the average taken annually is two); and many employees can set their own schedule. "What we don't do is treat our employees like they're all, you know, criminals," says Jenn Mann, vice president of human resources. Unless you work at the front gate or in maintenance, nobody much cares whether you show up at 9 or 11. Once you're there, you're not likely to leave for the day—which is much the point.

SAS, as some have put it, is a "golden cage"; there's a very old cemetery on one corner of the property, so the joke goes that you really never have to depart. There are two subsidized day-care centers for 600 children, and then summer camp. Plus there's dry cleaning, car detailing, a UPS depot, a book exchange, a meditation garden, an in-season tax-prep vendor, and an orthotics store. There are also three subsidized cafeterias, which serve 500 breakfasts and 2,300 lunches a day—and provide takeout to bring home for the family; one cafeteria has a piano player, and he takes requests. If you have a child in day care, it's fine to bring him or her to lunch. Hungry later? In kitchens throughout the 20 nondescript buildings around campus, there are free snacks galore, including Krispy Kremes on Fridays and M&M's on Wednesdays. To help work off the sweets, there are extensive on-site workday sports leagues.

The best perk for many employees is the centrally located health-care center, which, like other SAS buildings, is set back from the giant, colorful outside sculptures. Operating 8 a.m. to 6 p.m. most days, it has a staff of 56, including 4 physicians, 10 nurse practitioners, nutritionists, lab technicians, physical therapists, and a psychologist (who will do short-term therapy for such conditions as depression or sexual addiction). . . .

Last year 90% of SAS employees and their families—Goodnight included—made 40,000 visits. SAS says the center, with a budget of $4.5 million still saves the company $5 million annually because employees don't kill time in waiting rooms and are more apt to seek care when they should, and SAS's medical care is cheaper than outside the gates anyway. . . .

Off-campus are SAS family nights at the rodeo, circus, and Monster Jam Trucks. Work/life programs also venture into family issues, providing seminars on such topics as adoption, divorce, special-needs children, raising teenagers, and picking a magnet school. SAS has a "caring closet" that supplies wheelchairs and walkers, and even gets consultants to guide families on long-term elder-care issues. Soon—oh, boy—is the Valentine's swim! Seventy percent of SAS employees take part in at least one of these activities. The challenge, of course, is actually managing to get your work done amid all this. . . .

With a "billion dollars in the bank" and another big building going up on campus, Goodnight is continuing to invest. In a company of elite quantitative analysts, he devotes more than a fifth of revenue to R&D. For 33 straight years, SAS's revenues have gone up—reaching $2.3 billion in 2009. . . .

It may be that such stability and success allows Goodnight to be so free with the goodies, particularly when there are no shareholders to carp. Yet the SAS egg came before the chicken. In its inaugural year, the company established flexible 35-hour workweeks and profit-sharing, as well as fresh fruit on Mondays and other employee perks. Company-sponsored child care started four years later, prompted by an employee who planned to become a stay-at-home mom after her maternity leave. And when SAS had revenue of barely $50 million in 1984, it began creating the infrastructure of the current culture, with the recreation-and-fitness center and the first café. "Very early on, it just made sense," Goodnight recalls. Or as he once told someone, "Contented cows give more milk." He also liked the idea of pumping would-be profits back into the company. "I'd rather spend the money on my employees than send it to Washington as taxes." . . .

But he says that individual peculiarities hardly make SAS the prototype of Silicon Valley East. For one thing, his talent is populated with statisticians rather than engineers or MBAs. They're in offices rather than cube farms. More important, he says, he runs a sane shop that disdains dormlike all-nighters. While folks check their BlackBerrys at home and analysts stay late to meet a deadline, most are home by dinner or tuck-in time. If they've grown bored with their job, they have great freedom to move horizontally instead of having to hunt for another employer.

Most critically, Goodnight says his values produce constancy and continuity and commitment; the boom-and-bust cycle is a foreign concept at SAS. Whereas people in Silicon Valley are so often on the make—ready to join the hottest, coolest start-up around the corner, and preferably if it's yet to go public—SAS employees, gloriously isolated, are typically in it for the long haul.

For Discussion

1. Using the competing values framework as a point of reference, how would you describe the current organizational culture? Provide examples to support your conclusions.

2. What type of culture is desired by Mr. Goodnight to meet his goals? Discuss.

3. Which of the 11 ways to embed organizational culture has SAS used to create its current culture? Provide examples to support your conclusions.

4. Does Mr. Goodnight want to create more of a mechanistic or organic organization? Explain.

5. What is the most important lesson from this case? Discuss.

Source: Excerpted from David Kaplan, "The Best Company to Work For," *Fortune*, February 8, 2010, pp. 57–64.

Self-Assessment

Is Your Organization a Learning Organization?

Objectives

1. To gain familiarity with the characteristics of learning organizations.

2. To identify whether your organization is a learning organization.

Introduction

As we learned in Chapter 2, a learning organization is one that actively creates, acquires, and transfers new knowledge. Learning organizations are places in which new ideas and patterns of thinking are nurtured and in which people are allowed to continually expand their abilities to achieve desired results. Most important, a learning organization is a place in which the organization and individuals in it are continually learning in order to achieve its goals. The purpose of this exercise is to identify whether the organization in which you work is a learning organization.

Instructions

The following survey was created to assess the extent to which an organization follows the principles of a learning organization. If you are currently working, you should answer the questions in regard to this organization. If you are not currently working but have worked in the past, use a past job in completing the survey. If you have never had a job, you can use your school as a reference or use an organization you might be familiar with. For example, you might interview your parents to determine the extent to which the organization they work for follows the principles of a learning organization. Read each statement and use the following scale to indicate which answer most closely matches your response: 1 = strongly disagree; 2 = disagree; 3 = neither agree nor disagree; 4 = agree; 5 = strongly agree.

1. Management uses rewards, praise, and recognition to get what they want done.	1	2	3	4	5
2. The company promotes teamwork.	1	2	3	4	5
3. People are recognized and rewarded on the basis of what they do rather than *who* they know.	1	2	3	4	5
4. I see more examples of optimistic attitudes/behaviors rather than negative and cynical ones.	1	2	3	4	5
5. I have a clear picture of the organization's vision and my role in helping to accomplish it.	1	2	3	4	5
6. This organization relies more on team-based solutions than individual ones.	1	2	3	4	5
7. This organization tends to look at the big picture rather than analyzing problems from a narrow perspective.	1	2	3	4	5
8. People have an open mind when working with others.	1	2	3	4	5
9. This company looks for the root cause of a problem rather than a "quick fix."	1	2	3	4	5
10. I have the skills and knowledge to continuously improve the way I do my job.	1	2	3	4	5

Total _____

Scoring

To get your score, add up the numbers that correspond to your responses. The range will be from 10 to 50. Comparative norms for learning organizations are as follows:

Total score of 10–23 = low learning organization

Total score of 24–36 = moderate learning organization

Total score of 37–50 = high learning organization

When Your Brother-in-Law Is Bending the Rules

Assume you are the purchasing manager for a small, family-run homebuilding firm. Your brother-in-law works in the framing department and your sister is the company's chief financial officer (CFO). The firm has a policy that employees can do small homebuilding jobs (projects valued at less than $2,000) on the side and can purchase their building supplies for these projects through the company. This policy allows employees to make some extra cash while purchasing materials at much discounted rates.

Because of your role, you are aware of all side projects taking place and the dollar amount of materials purchased through the company for these projects. You recently noticed that your brother-in-law has been purchasing raw materials that you suspect will exceed the $2,000 threshold—he purchased $3,000 worth of materials for one project and $1,500 for another.

You approved both of the purchases even though you suspect that he is doing projects that are valued at around $5,000–$8,000. These types of projects are not permitted as side jobs because the company itself does work in this price range. You sense that your brother-in-law's behavior is OK because your sister also knows about these purchases, given her role as CFO.

Solving the Dilemma

Your brother-in-law just submitted a purchase request for materials valued at $10,000 for side jobs. What should you do?

1. Approve the purchase. It's not your job to police your brother-in-law, and your sister is aware of what he's doing.

2. Call your sister and express your concern about what your brother-in-law is doing. Let her deal with any potential ethical breaches.

3. Contact your brother-in-law and ask him if he is abiding by the company policy of not doing side jobs valued at over $2,000. If he says yes, approve the purchases.

4. Go to the CEO and let him know about the details of your brother-in-law's purchases. The CEO can then do whatever he thinks is best.

5. Invent other options.

chapter 9

Human Resource Management
Getting the Right People for Managerial Success

Major Questions You Should Be Able to Answer

9.1 Strategic Human Resource Management

Major Question: How do effective managers view the role of people in their organization's success?

9.2 The Legal Requirements of Human Resource Management

Major Question: To avoid exposure to legal liabilities, what areas of the law do I need to be aware of?

9.3 Recruitment & Selection: Putting the Right People into the Right Jobs

Major Question: How can I reduce mistakes in hiring and find great people who might work for me?

9.4 Orientation, Training, & Development

Major Question: Once people are hired, what's the best way to see that they do what they're supposed to do?

9.5 Performance Appraisal

Major Question: How can I assess employees' performance more accurately and give more effective feedback?

9.6 Managing an Effective Workforce: Compensation & Benefits

Major Question: What are the various forms of compensation?

9.7 Managing Promotions, Transfers, Disciplining, & Dismissals

Major Question: What are some guidelines for handling promotions, transfers, disciplining, and dismissals?

How to Stand Out in a New Job: Fitting into an Organization in the First 60 Days

"Once you are in the real world—and it doesn't make any difference if you are 22 or 62, starting your first job or your fifth," say *BusinessWeek* columnists Jack and Suzy Welch, "the way to look great and get ahead is to overdeliver."[1]

Overdelivering means doing more than what is asked of you—not just doing the report your boss requests, for example, but doing the extra research to provide him or her with something truly impressive.

Among things you should do in the first 60 days:[2]

- **Come in 30 minutes early and stay a little late to see how people behave.** "Many aspects of a company's culture can be subtle and easy to overlook," writes one expert. "Instead, observe everything." Thus, try coming in early and staying a little late just to observe how people operate—where they take their lunches, for example.

- **Get to know some people and listen to what they have to say.** "You've got to realize that networking inside a company is just as important as when you were networking on the outside trying to get in," says one business consultant.[3] During the first 2 weeks, get to know a few people and try to have lunch with them. Find out how the organization works, how people interact with the boss, what the corporate culture encourages and discourages. Walk the halls and get to know receptionists, mail room clerks, and office managers, who can help you learn the ropes. Your role here is to listen, rather than to slather on the charm. Realize that you have a lot to learn.

- **Be aware of the power of first impressions.** Within 3 minutes of meeting someone new, people form an opinion about where the future of the relationship is headed, according to one study.[4] "When meeting someone for the first time, concentrate on one thing: your energy level," says Roger Ailes, CEO of Fox News, who thinks that 7 seconds is all the time people need to start making up their minds about you. Amp it up, he advises. "If you don't demonstrate energetic attitude on your first day, you're already screwing up."[5] (Note: Don't be too upset if you feel you've blown it with someone on the first meeting. What's key, research shows, is to make sure you have other chances to meet that person again so that you can show different sides of yourself.)[6]

- **Make it easy for others to give you feedback.** Ask your boss, co-workers, and subordinates to give you feedback about how you're doing. Be prepared to take unpleasant news gracefully.[7] At the end of 30 days, have a "How am I doing?" meeting with your boss.

- **Overdeliver.** Because performance reviews for new hires generally take place at 60 to 90 days, you need to have accomplished enough—and preferably something big—to show your boss your potential. In other words, do as the Welches suggest: overdeliver.

For Discussion How does the foregoing advice square with your past experiences in starting a new job? Are there things you wish you could have done differently?

---

forecast **What's Ahead in This Chapter**

This chapter considers human resource (HR) management—planning for, attracting, developing, and retaining an effective workforce. We consider how this subject fits in with the overall company strategy, how to evaluate current and future employee needs, and how to recruit and select qualified people. We discuss orientation, training, and development; how to assess employee performance and give feedback; and what HR laws managers should be aware of. Finally, we consider how to manage compensation and benefits, promotions and discipline, and workplace performance problems.

How do effective managers view the role of people in their organization's success?

THE BIG PICTURE

Human resource management consists of the activities managers perform to plan for, attract, develop, and retain an effective workforce. Planning the human resources needed consists of understanding current employee needs and predicting future employee needs.

How do you get hired by one of the companies on *Fortune* magazine's annual "100 Best Companies to Work For" list—companies such as Wegmans Food Markets, Google, Boston Consulting Group, and Genentech on the 2010 list?[8] You try to get to know someone in the company, suggests one guide; you play up volunteer work on your résumé, you get ready to interview and interview and interview, and you do extensive research on the company (far more than just online research, as by talking to customers).[9]

And what kinds of things does an employee of a *Fortune* "Best" company get? At Google, the Mountain View, California search engine company (ranked number 1 in 2007 and 2008, and number 4 in 2009 and 2010), you're entitled to eat in 1 of 11 free gourmet cafeterias, as well as to visit free snack rooms that contain various cereals, candy, nuts, fresh fruit, and other snacks. You can bring your dog to work, get haircuts on-site, work out at the gym, attend subsidized exercise classes, study Mandarin or other languages, have your laundry done free, or consult five on-site doctors for a checkup, free of charge. The company has also launched numerous compensation incentives, special bonuses, and founders' awards that can run into millions of dollars.[10]

The reason for this exceptional treatment? "Happy people are more productive," says CEO Eric Schmidt.[11] That productivity has made Google an earnings powerhouse; in early 2010, for example, it reported a 37% jump in net income for its first quarter over the same quarter a year earlier.[12] Google has discovered, in other words, that its biggest competitive advantage lies in its human resources— its *people*.

Human Resource Management: Managing an Organization's Most Important Resource

Human resource (HR) management **consists of the activities managers perform to plan for, attract, develop, and retain an effective workforce.** Whether it's McKenzie looking for entry-level business consultants, the U.S. Navy trying to fill its ranks, or churches trying to reverse the declining number of priests and ministers, all organizations must deal with staffing.

The fact that the old Personnel Department is now called the Human Resources Department is not just a cosmetic change. It is intended to suggest the importance of staffing to a company's success. Although talking about people as "resources" might seem to downgrade them to the same level as financial resources and material resources, in fact people are an organization's most important resource. Indeed, companies ranked number 1 on *Fortune* magazine's Best Companies list, such as software developer SAS (2010), data storage company NetApp (2009), biotechnology firm Genentech (2006), supermarket chain Wegmans Food Markets (2005), jam maker J. M. Smucker (2004), stockbroker Edward Jones (2003 and 2002), and box retailer The Container Store (2001 and 2000), have discovered that putting employees first has been the foundation for their success. "If you're not thinking all the time about making every person valuable, you don't have a chance," says former General Electric head Jack Welch. "What's the alternative? Wasted minds? Uninvolved people? A labor force that's angry or bored? That doesn't make sense!"[13]

Human Resources as Part of Strategic Planning At many companies, human resources has become part of the strategic-planning process. Thus, HR departments deal not only with employee paperwork and legal accountability—a very important area, as we describe in Section 9.2—but also with helping to support the organization's overall strategy.

For example, is it important, as Wegmans' owners think, to have loyal, innovative, smart, passionate employees who will give their best to promote customer satisfaction (the grocery chain's mission)? Who, then, should be recruited? How should they be trained? What's the best way to evaluate and reward their performance? The answers to these questions should be consistent with the firm's strategic mission. The purpose of the strategic human resource process, then—shown in the yellow-orange shaded boxes at right—is to get the optimal work performance that will help the company's mission and goals.[14] *(See Figure 9.1.)*

Two concepts important in this view of human resource management, which we mentioned in Chapter 2, are *human capital* and *social capital*.

Human Capital: Potential of Employee Knowledge & Actions *Human capital,* you'll recall, is the economic or productive potential of employee knowledge and actions.[15] A present or future employee with the right combination of knowledge, skills, and motivation to excel represents human capital with the potential to give the organization a competitive advantage. Why is human capital important? "We are living in a time," says one team of human resource management authors, "when a new economic paradigm—characterized by speed, innovation, short cycle times, quality, and customer satisfaction—is highlighting the importance of intangible assets, such as brand recognition, knowledge, innovation, and particularly human capital."[16]

Social Capital: Potential of Strong & Cooperative Relationships *Social capital,* we said, is the economic or productive potential of strong, trusting, and cooperative relationships.[17] Relationships do matter. For instance, the brothers running family-owned J. M. Smucker follow a simple code of conduct set forth by their father: "Listen with your full attention, look for the good in others, have a sense of humor, and say thank you for a job well done."[18] (The company's voluntary employee turnover rate is a mere 3%.)

Planning the Human Resources Needed

When a building contractor, looking to hire someone for a few hours to dig ditches, drives by a group of idle day laborers standing on a street corner, is that a form of HR planning? Certainly it shows the contractor's awareness that a pool of laborers usually can be found in that spot. But what if the builder needs a lot of people with specialized training—to give him or her the competitive advantage that the strategic planning process demands?

figure 9.1

THE STRATEGIC HUMAN RESOURCE MANAGEMENT PROCESS

Establish the mission & the vision

Establish the grand strategy

Formulate the strategic plans

Plan human resources needed

Recruit & select people

Orient, train, & develop

Perform appraisals of people

Purpose:
Get optimal work performance to help realize company's mission & vision

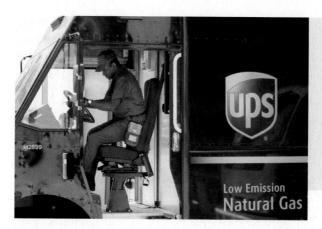

Big Brown. A UPS driver's problems of driving in a big city—traffic, double parking, addressees not at home—are different from those of driving in rural areas, where there may be long stretches of boredom. Specialists in job analysis can interview drivers about their problems in order to write job descriptions that allow for varying circumstances.

Here we are concerned with something more than simply hiring people on an "as needed" basis. ***Strategic human resource planning* consists of developing a systematic, comprehensive strategy for (a) understanding current employee needs and (b) predicting future employee needs.** Let's consider these two parts.

Understanding Current Employee Needs   To plan for the future, you must understand the present—what today's staffing picture looks like. This requires that you (or a trained specialist) do, first, a *job analysis* and from that write a *job description* and a *job specification*.[19]

- **Job analysis.** The purpose of ***job analysis* is to determine, by observation and analysis, the basic elements of a job.** Specialists who do this interview job occupants about what they do, observe the flow of work, and learn how results are accomplished. For example, United Parcel Service has specialists who ride with the couriers and time how long it takes to deliver a load of packages and note what problems are encountered (traffic jams, vicious dogs, recipients not home, and so on).

- **Job description and job specification.** Once the fundamentals of a job are understood, then you can write a ***job description,* which summarizes what the holder of the job does and how and why he or she does it.** Next you can write a ***job specification,* which describes the minimum qualifications a person must have to perform the job successfully.**

This process can produce some surprises. Jobs that might seem to require a college degree, for example, might not after all. Thus, the process of writing job analyses, descriptions, and specifications can help you avoid hiring people who are overqualified (and presumably more expensive) or underqualified (and thus not as productive) for a particular job.

In addition, by entering a job description and specification with their attendant characteristics into a database, an organization can do computer searching for candidates by matching keywords (nouns) on their résumés with the keywords describing the job. A position in desktop publishing, for instance, might be described by the kinds of software programs with which applicants should be familiar: *Adobe FrameMaker, Adobe InDesign, Adobe PageMaker, Corel Ventura, QuarkXPress,* and so on.

Predicting Future Employee Needs   Job descriptions change, of course: auto mechanics, for instance, now have to know how computer chips work in cars. (A C-class Mercedes may have 153 processors on board.) And new jobs are created: Who could have visualized the position of "e-commerce accountant" 10 years ago, for example?

As you might expect, predicting future employee needs means you have to become knowledgeable about the *staffing the organization might need* and the *likely sources for that staffing:*

- **The staffing the organization might need.**   You could assume your organization won't change much. In that case, you can fairly easily predict that jobs will periodically become unoccupied (because of retirement, resignations, and so on) and that you'll need to pay the same salaries and meet the same criteria about minority hiring to fill them.

  Better, however, to assume the organization will change. Thus, you need to understand the organization's vision and strategic plan so that the proper people can be hired to meet the future strategies and work.

- **The likely sources for staffing.**   You can recruit employees from either inside or outside the organization. In looking at those inside, you need to consider which employees are motivated, trainable, and promotable and what kind of training your organization might have to do. A device for organizing this kind of information is a ***human resource inventory,* a report listing your organization's employees by name, education, training, languages, and other important information.**

  In looking outside, you need to consider the availability of talent in your industry's and geographical area's labor pool, the training of people graduating from various schools, and such factors as what kind of people are moving into your area. The U.S. Bureau of Labor Statistics and the U.S. Census Bureau issue reports on such matters. ●

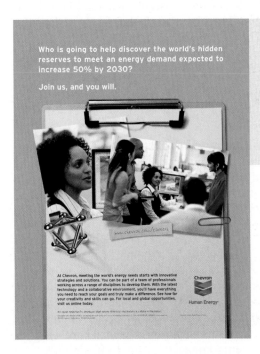

One way to attract potential employees. This Chevron ad serves two purposes: encouraging people to get involved in the energy crisis discussion and appealing to socially responsible engineers, scientists, and strategists looking to work for a company with an active social conscience. A Web site included in the ad shows additional close-ups of each component of the ad collage and a link to Chevron's careers portal.

✳ 9.2 THE LEGAL REQUIREMENTS OF HUMAN RESOURCE MANAGEMENT

major question?

To avoid exposure to legal liabilities, what areas of the law do I need to be aware of?

THE BIG PICTURE

Four areas of human resource law any manager needs to be aware of are labor relations, compensation and benefits, health and safety, and equal employment opportunity.

Whatever your organization's human resource strategy, in the United States (and in U.S. divisions overseas) it has to operate within the environment of American law. Four areas you need to be aware of are as follows. Some important laws are summarized in the table opposite. *(See Table 9.1.)*

I. Labor Relations

The earliest laws affecting employee welfare had to do with unions, and they can still have important effects. Legislation passed in 1935 (the Wagner Act) resulted in the **National Labor Relations Board, which enforces procedures whereby employees may vote to have a union and for collective bargaining.** *Collective bargaining* **consists of negotiations between management and employees about disputes over compensation, benefits, working conditions, and job security.**

A 1947 law (the Taft-Hartley Act) allows the President of the United States to prevent or end a strike that threatens national security.

2. Compensation & Benefits

The Social Security Act in 1935 established the U.S. retirement system. The passage of the *Fair Labor Standards Act* **of 1938 established minimum living standards for workers engaged in interstate commerce, including provision of a federal minimum wage** (currently $7.25 an hour) and a maximum workweek (now 40 hours, after which overtime must be paid), along with banning products from child labor.[20] Salaried executive, administrative, and professional employees are exempt from overtime rules.

3. Health & Safety

From miners risking tunnel cave-ins to cotton mill workers breathing lint, industry has always had dirty, dangerous jobs. Beginning with the Occupational Safety and Health Act (OSHA) of 1970, a body of law has grown that requires organizations to provide employees with nonhazardous working conditions. Later laws extended health coverage, including 2010 health care reform legislation, which requires employees with more than 50 employees to provide health insurance.[21]

4. Equal Employment Opportunity

The effort to reduce discrimination in employment based on racial, ethnic, and religious bigotry and gender stereotypes began with Title VII of the Civil Rights Act of 1964. This established the *Equal Employment Opportunity (EEO) Commission,* **whose job it is to enforce antidiscrimination and other employment-related laws.** Title VII applies to all organizations or their agents engaged in an industry affecting

table 9.1

Year	Law or regulation	Provisions
Labor relations		
1974	Privacy Act	Gives employees legal right to examine letters of reference concerning them
1986	Immigration Reform & Control Act	Requires employers to verify the eligibility for employment of all their new hires (including U.S. citizens)
1988	Polygraph Protection Act	Limits employer's ability to use lie detectors
1988	Worker Adjustment & Retraining Notification Act	Requires organizations with 100 or more employees to give 60 days' notice for mass layoffs or plant closings
2003	Sarbanes-Oxley Act	Prohibits employers from demoting or firing employees who raise accusations of fraud to a federal agency
Compensation and benefits		
1974	Employee Retirement Income Security Act (ERISA)	Sets rules for managing pension plans; provides federal insurance to cover bankrupt plans
1993	Family & Medical Leave Act	Requires employers to provide 12 weeks of unpaid leave for medical and family reasons, including for childbirth, adoption, or family emergency
1996	Health Insurance Portability & Accountability Act (HIPAA)	Allows employees to switch health insurance plans when changing jobs and receive new coverage regardless of preexisting health conditions; prohibits group plans from dropping ill employees
2007	Fair Minimum Wage Act	Increased federal minimum wage to $7.25 per hour on July 24, 2009
Health and safety		
1970	Occupational Safety & Health Act (OSHA)	Establishes minimum health and safety standards in organizations
1985	Consolidated Omnibus Budget Reconciliation Act (COBRA)	Requires an extension of health insurance benefits after termination
2010	Patient Protection & Affordable Care Act	Employers with more than 50 employees must provide health insurance
Equal employment opportunity		
1963	Equal Pay Act	Requires men and women be paid equally for performing equal work
1964, amended 1972	Civil Rights Act, Title VII	Prohibits discrimination on basis of race, color, religion, national origin, or sex
1967, amended 1978 and 1986	Age Discrimination in Employment Act (ADEA)	Prohibits discrimination in employees over 40 years old; restricts mandatory retirement
1978	Pregnancy Discrimination Act	Broadens discrimination to cover pregnancy, childbirth, and related medical conditions; protects job security during maternity leave

table 9.1 *(Continued)*

Year	Law or regulation	Provisions
1990	Americans with Disabilities Act (ADA)	Prohibits discrimination against essentially qualified employees with physical or mental disabilities or chronic illness; requires "reasonable accommodation" be provided so they can perform duties
1991	Civil Rights Act	Amends and clarifies Title VII, ADA, and other laws; permits suits against employers for punitive damages in cases of intentional discrimination

interstate commerce that employs 15 or more employees. Contractors who wish to do business with the U.S. government (such as most colleges and universities, which receive federal funds) must be in compliance with various executive orders issued by the president covering antidiscrimination. Later laws prevented discrimination against older workers and people with physical and mental disabilities.[22]

Three important concepts covered by EEO laws are *discrimination, affirmative action,* and *sexual harassment.*

Discrimination A large gap exists in perceptions between the sexes as to whether men or women have more opportunities for advancement. In a survey of 1,834 business professionals worldwide, 66% of men said opportunities to move to top management were gender neutral, compared with 30% of women.[23] (In actuality, only 3% of CEOs and 13.5% of executive-officer positions in Fortune 500 companies are occupied by women.)

Discrimination **occurs when people are hired or promoted—or denied hiring or promotion—for reasons not relevant to the job,** such as skin color or eye shape, gender, religion, national origin, and the like. (Recently, employment discrimination based on gender identity was also banned in federal jobs.)[24] A fine point to be made here is that, although the law prohibits discrimination in all aspects of employment, it does not require an employer to extend *preferential treatment* because of race, color, religion, and so on.

When an organization is found to have been practicing discrimination, the people discriminated against may sue for back pay and punitive damages. In 2009, the number of workers claiming job discrimination based on disability, religion, or national origin surged to new highs; in particular, charges of disability discrimination rose about 10% (coinciding with changes that made it easier for people with epilepsy, diabetes, and other treatable conditions to claim they are disabled).[25] Charges to the Equal Employment Opportunity Commission (EEOC) of discrimination based on national origin (filed most often by Hispanics and Asians) rose about 5% in that year.[26] Allegations of age discrimination were also at a record high in 2009, up 29% from 2007.[27] Pregnancy bias complaints to the EEOC increased 14% in 2007, up 40% from a decade ago.[28] Between 1988 and 2007, pay discrepancies between women and men improved slightly, but women overall still earned only 80% of men's wages.[29]

Affirmative Action *Affirmative action* **focuses on achieving equality of opportunity within an organization.** It tries to make up for past discrimination in employment by actively finding, hiring, and developing the talents of people from groups traditionally discriminated against. Steps include active recruitment, elimination of prejudicial questions in interviews, and establishment of minority hiring goals. It's important to note that EEO laws *do not* allow use of hiring quotas.[30]

Affirmative action has created tremendous opportunities for women and minorities, but it has been resisted more by some white males who see it as working against their interests.[31] Affirmative action plans are more successful when employees view them as being fair and equitable and when whites are not prejudiced against people of color.[32] In addition, research shows that women and minorities hired on the basis of affirmative action felt stigmatized as unqualified and incompetent and experienced lower job satisfaction and more stress than employees supposedly selected on the basis of merit.[33]

Sexual harassment. If this woman is unaware of the men ogling her legs, does that make their behavior acceptable? Or does it still contribute to an offensive work environment?

Sexual Harassment *Sexual harassment* **consists of unwanted sexual attention that creates an adverse work environment.** This means obscene gestures, sex-stereotyped jokes, sexually oriented posters and graffiti, suggestive remarks, unwanted dating pressure, physical nonsexual contact, unwanted touching, sexual propositions, threatening punishment unless sexual favors are given, obscene phone calls, and similar verbal or physical actions of a sexual nature.[34] The harassment may be by a member of the opposite sex or a member of the same sex, by a manager, by a co-worker, or by an outsider.[35] If the harasser is a manager or an agent of the organization, the organization itself can be sued, even if it had no knowledge of the situation.[36] According to the EEOC, the percentage of sexual harassment claims made by men has doubled from 8% of all claims in 1990 to 16% in 2009.[37]

There are two types of sexual harassment:

- *Quid pro quo—tangible economic injury.* In the *quid pro quo* type, the person to whom the unwanted sexual attention is directed is put in the position of jeopardizing being hired for a job or obtaining job benefits or opportunities unless he or she implicitly or explicitly acquiesces.

- *Hostile environment—offensive work environment.* In the *hostile environment* type, the person being sexually harassed doesn't risk economic harm but experiences an offensive or intimidating work environment. According to one survey, 38% of women said they heard sexual innuendo, wisecracks, or taunts at the office, up from 22% the year before.[38] Another growing problem is bullying on the job, experienced by 37% of workers, male as well as female.[39]

The table below shows some guidelines for preventing sexual harassment. *(See Table 9.2.)* ●

table 9.2

GUIDELINES FOR PREVENTING SEXUAL HARASSMENT

- Don't request or suggest sexual favors for rewards related to work or promotion.

- Don't do uninvited touching, patting, or hugging of someone's body—especially if they wince, frown, or pull away.

- Don't make suggestive jokes of a sexual nature, demeaning remarks, slurs, or obscene gestures or sounds.

- Don't display sexual pictures on the wall or on your computer or write notes of a sexual nature.

- Don't laugh at others' sexually harassing words or behaviors.

Source: Adapted from E. Bernstein, "Touching Me, Touching You—at Work," *The Wall Street Journal,* June 29, 2009, p. D6; "Sexual Harassment: A Fine Line," *The Week,* October 30, 2009, p. II; U.S. Equal Employment Opportunity Commission, "Sexual Harassment," http://www.eeoc.gov/laws/types/sexual_harassment.cfm (accessed April 25, 2010); and Business Owners Toolkit, "Sample Workplace Sexual Harassment Policies," © 1995–2010 Toolkit Media Group, http://www.toolkit.com/tools/bt.aspx?tid=sxhrst_m (accessed April 25, 2010).

✖ 9.3 RECRUITMENT & SELECTION: PUTTING THE RIGHT PEOPLE INTO THE RIGHT JOBS

major question ?
How can I reduce mistakes in hiring and find great people who might work for me?

THE BIG PICTURE
Qualified applicants for jobs may be recruited from inside or outside the organization. The task of choosing the best person is enhanced by such tools as reviewing candidates' application forms, résumés, and references; doing interviews, either structured or unstructured; and screening with ability, personality, performance, and other kinds of employment tests.

"Hiring great people is brutally hard," write *Business Week* columnists Jack (former General Electric CEO) and Suzy Welch. "New managers are lucky to get it right half the time. And even executives with decades of experience will tell you that they make the right calls 75% of the time at best."[40]

However difficult it may be, it's important to try to get hiring right. "We're essentially in an innovation economy where good people come up with really good ideas," says one CEO. "Companies want to hit home runs with the next greatest product, and the imperative is making sure you have great people to do that."[41]

Recruitment: How to Attract Qualified Applicants

At some time nearly every organization has to think about how to find the right kind of people. **Recruiting is the process of locating and attracting qualified applicants for jobs open in the organization.** The word *qualified* is important: You want to find people whose skills, abilities, and characteristics are best suited to your organization. Recruiting is of two types: *internal* and *external*.

1. Internal Recruiting: Hiring from the Inside *Internal recruiting* means **making people already employed by the organization aware of job openings.** Indeed, most vacant positions in organizations are filled through internal recruitment, mainly through *job posting,* **placing information about job vacancies and qualifications on bulletin boards, in newsletters, and on the organization's intranet.** (Companies looking to make strategic changes do better hiring CEOs from within the ranks rather than from outside, according to a recent study.)[42]

2. External Recruiting: Hiring from the Outside *External recruiting* means **attracting job applicants from outside the organization.** Notices of job vacancies are placed through newspapers, employment agencies, executive recruiting firms, union hiring halls, college job-placement offices, technical training schools, and word of mouth through professional associations. Many organizations—and not just high-technology companies—are advertising job openings on the Internet. (However, job hunters who are referred by employees are apt to be given more attention, speeding them to the interview stage.)[43]

Both methods have advantages and disadvantages. *(See Table 9.3.)*

Which External Recruiting Methods Work Best? In general, the most effective sources are employee referrals, say human resource professionals, because, to protect their own reputations, employees are fairly careful about whom they recommend, and they know the qualifications of both the job and the prospective employee."[44] Other effective ways of finding good job candidates are

Internal recruiting

Advantages

1. Employees tend to be inspired to greater effort and loyalty. Morale is enhanced because they realize that working hard and staying put can result in more opportunities.

2. The whole process of advertising, interviewing, and so on is cheaper.

3. There are fewer risks. Internal candidates are already known and are familiar with the organization.

Disadvantages

1. Internal recruitment restricts the competition for positions and limits the pool of fresh talent and fresh viewpoints.

2. It may encourage employees to assume that longevity and seniority will automatically result in promotion.

3. Whenever a job is filled, it creates a vacancy elsewhere in the organization.

External recruiting

Advantages

1. Applicants may have specialized knowledge and experience.

2. Applicants may have fresh viewpoints.

Disadvantages

1. The recruitment process is more expensive and takes longer.

2. The risks are higher because the persons hired are less well known.

---

e-recruitment tools, such as "dot-jobs" Web sites; membership directories for associations and trade groups; social networking sites; and industry-specific blogs, forums, newsgroups, or listservs.[45]

Realistic Job Previews   Often an organization will put on its best face to try to attract the best outside candidates—and then wonder why the new hires leave when the job doesn't turn out to be as rosy as promised.

A better approach is to present what's known as a ***realistic job preview,* which gives a candidate a picture of both positive and negative features of the job and the organization before he or she is hired.**[46] People with realistic expectations tend to quit less frequently and be more satisfied than those with unrealistic expectations.

Selection: How to Choose the Best Person for the Job

Whether the recruitment process turns up a handful of job applicants or thousands, now you turn to the ***selection process,* the screening of job applicants to hire the best candidate.** Essentially this becomes an exercise in *prediction:* How well will the candidate perform the job and how long will he or she stay?

Three types of selection tools are *background information, interviewing,* and *employment tests.*

I. Background Information: Application Forms, Résumés, & Reference Checks   Application forms and résumés provide basic background information about job applicants, such as citizenship, education, work history, and certifications.

Unfortunately, a lot of résumé information consists of mild puffery and even outrageous fairy tales. InfoLink Screening Services, which does background checks, reported that 14% of the tens of thousands of applicants it had screened had lied about their education.[47] Vermont-based ResumeDoctor.com, a résumé-writing service, surveyed 1,133 résumés that had been uploaded to its site and found that nearly 42.7% had at least one inaccuracy and 12.6% had two or more factual errors.[48] A 2003 survey by the Society of Human Resource Management found that 44% of 2.6 million respondents said they had misstated their work experience on their résumés.[49] And Background Information Services, a pre-employment screening company in Cleveland, found 56% of résumés contained falsehoods of some kind.[50] It is risky to lie about your background information because it can be used as a reason for terminating your employment.

Practical Action

Would You Lie Like This on Your Résumé?

What kind of lies do people put on their résumés? Consider the following examples.

Lying about Education. Lying about education is the most prevalent distortion (such as pretending to hold a degree or an advanced degree). A few years ago, RadioShack CEO David Edmondson achieved some notoriety and had to resign after a newspaper discovered he had falsely claimed on his résumé to hold degrees in psychology and theology.[51] Automatic Data Processing of Roseland, New Jersey, which has studied employee background verification, reported that 41% of education records showed a difference between the information provided by an applicant and that provided by the educational institution.[52]

Lying about Employment Histories, Ages, Salaries, & Job Titles. Another common fabrication includes creative attempts to cover gaps in employment history (although there are straightforward ways an applicant can deal with this, such as highlighting length of service instead of employment dates).[53] People also lie about their ages for fear of seeming to be too experienced (hence expensive) or too old.[54] As you might expect, people also embellish their salary histories, job titles, and achievements on projects.[55]

Lying about Criminal Background or Immigration Status. In 2007, it came out that the foundation that runs online encyclopedia Wikipedia had neglected to do a basic background check before hiring Carolyn Doran as its chief operating officer; she had been convicted of drunken driving and fleeing a car accident.[56] Now, more and more job seekers are seeking to legally clear their criminal records—to have their arrests or convictions expunged, when possible.[57]

In addition, as the numbers of illegal (undocumented) workers has risen, it has become incumbent on human resource officers to also verify U.S. citizenship.[58] Use of E-Verify, the federal program that allows employers to quickly check the legal status of potential employees, has taken a big jump.[59] Still, perhaps half of illegal workers slip by the system.[60]

Your Call

What past events are you most worried potential employers will find out about you? What can you do to put them in a better light?

Another difficulty for HR departments is applicants' increasing use of video résumés, which could expose the organization to a possible failure-to-hire claim on grounds of discrimination if the applicant belongs to a "protected class"—a minority individual or older person, for example.[61]

References are also a problem. Many employers don't give honest assessments of former employees, for two reasons: (1) They fear that if they say anything negative, they can be sued by the former employee. (2) They fear if they say anything positive, and the job candidate doesn't pan out, they can be sued by the new employer.[62]

Many employers also like to check applicants' credit references, although there is no evidence that people with weak credit scores are apt to be unqualified or dishonest employees.[63] (Note: Prospective employers need to get written consent to run credit checks on job applicants.)[64]

Applying for a Job? Here Are Some Mistakes to Avoid

There are several mistakes that job candidates often make in initial interviews. Here are some tips.[65]

Be Prepared—Very Prepared

Can you pronounce the name of the company you're interviewing with? Of the person/people interviewing you? Do you understand the company and the position you're interviewing for? Do you know the company's competition? What new products or services are being offered? How about your own job strengths? Your weaknesses? What do you need to improve on to move ahead?

Go online and read the company's Web site. Search for any news articles written about the firm. Call the company and ask about pronunciation. Determine how your strengths fit directly into the context of what the prospective employer does. Also, when asked about your weaknesses, state how you recognized a weakness, overcame a dilemma, and were improved by it. Take time to practice questions and answers so you'll sound confident.

Dress Right & Pay Attention to Your Attitude

Is the company dress code "business casual"? That doesn't mean you should dress that way (or the way you dress on campus) for the interview.

Dress professionally for the interview. Be aware of your attitude as soon as you enter the building. Be on time. (Time your commute by doing a test run a day or so before the interview, and make sure you know the exact location of the interview.) If unforeseeable circumstances arise and cause you to be late, call to inform your interviewer. Be polite to the receptionist, and greet everyone who greets you. Turn off your cell-phone ringer.

Don't Get Too Personal with the Interviewer

Don't be overfriendly and share too much, especially in the initial interview. Although the interviewer will try to make you feel comfortable, you should focus on the position. Rehearse questions to ask the interviewer, such as the challenges for the position in the future. Don't make negative comments about your old company or boss. Rather, figure out the positives and convey what you learned and gained from your experience. If asked an inappropriate question (about age, marital status, whether you have children or plan to), politely state you don't believe the question is relevant to your qualifications. Be enthusiastic; enthusiasm is contagious.

Be Aware That Your Background Will Be Checked

Because it seems to be getting harder to distinguish honest job applicants from dishonest ones, companies now routinely check résumés or hire companies that do so. Ninety-six percent of employers conduct background checks, according to one study.[66] And here's something to think about if you are a MySpace, Facebook, YouTube, or Twitter enthusiast or blogger: employers now frequently use search engines such as Google or Yahoo! as a way to do continuous and stealthy background checks on prospective employees to see if they've posted any racy content. "Many job hunters," says one report, "are . . . continuing to overlook the dangers of posting provocative photos and other dubious content on social-media sites."[67] Checking your Facebook page is also a way employers can make an end run around discrimination laws.[68]

2. Interviewing: Unstructured, Situational, & Behavioral-Description

Interviewing, the most commonly used employee-selection technique, may take place face-to-face, by videoconferencing, or—as is increasingly the case—via the Internet.[69] (In-depth phone interviews of an hour or more may be on the rise, perhaps for cost reasons.[70] However, face-to-face interviews have been found to be perceived as more fair and to lead to higher job acceptance intentions than were videoconferencing and telephone interviews.)[71] To help eliminate bias, interviews can be designed, conducted, and evaluated by a committee of three or more people. The most commonly used employee-selection technique, interviewing, takes three forms.[72]

- **Unstructured interview.** Like an ordinary conversation, an *unstructured interview* involves asking probing questions to find out what the applicant is like. There is no fixed set of questions asked of all applicants and no systematic scoring procedure. As a result, the unstructured interview has been criticized as being overly subjective and apt to be influenced by the biases of the interviewer. Equally important, nowadays it is susceptible to legal attack, because some questions may infringe on non-job-related matters such as privacy, diversity, or disability.[73] However, compared with the structured interview method, the unstructured interview has been found to provide a more accurate assessment of an applicant's job-related personality traits.[74]

- **Structured interview type 1—the situational interview. The *structured interview* involves asking each applicant the same questions and comparing their responses to a standardized set of answers.**

  In one type of structured interview, the *situational interview,* the interviewer focuses on hypothetical situations. Example: "What would you do if you saw two of your people arguing loudly in the work area?" The idea here is to find out if the applicant can handle difficult situations that may arise on the job.

- **Structured interview type 2—the behavioral-description interview.** In the second type of structured interview, the *behavioral-description interview,* the interviewer explores what applicants have actually done in the past. Example: "What was the best idea you ever sold to a supervisor, teacher, peer, or subordinate?" This question (asked by the U.S. Army of college students applying for its officer training program) is designed to assess the applicant's ability to influence others.

Practical Action

The Right Way to Conduct an Interview

Because hiring people who later have to be let go is such an expensive proposition, companies are now putting a great deal of emphasis on effective interviewing. Although this is a subject worth exploring further, following are some minimal suggestions.[75]

Before the Interview: Define Your Needs & Review Applicant's Résumé

Write out what skills, traits, and qualities the job requires. "Looking to hire somebody is like going to the supermarket," says one HR manager. "You need to have a list and know what you need."[76]

Look at the applicant's résumé or application form to determine relevant experience, gaps, and discrepancies.

Write Out Interview Questions

You should ask each candidate the same set of questions, so that you can compare their answers. (This helps keep you out of legal trouble, too.) In general, the questions should be designed to elicit the following types of information.

- **Does the applicant have the knowledge to do the job?** Examples: "Give an example where you came

up with a creative solution." "How would you distinguish our product from competitors'?"

- **Can the applicant handle difficult situations?** Examples: "Tell me about a time when you dealt with an irate customer. How did you handle the situation and what was the outcome?"

- **Is the applicant willing to cope with the job's demands?** Examples: "How do you feel about making unpopular decisions?" "Are you willing to travel 30% of the time?"

- **Will the applicant fit in with the organization's culture?** Examples: "How would your last supervisor describe you?" "How much leeway did they give you in your previous job in charging travel expenses?"

Follow a Three-Scene Interview Scenario

The interview itself may follow a three-scene script.

- **Scene I: The first 3 minutes—small talk and "compatibility" test.** The first scene is really a "compatibility test." It takes about 3 minutes and consists of exchanging small talk, giving you a chance to establish rapport and judge how well the candidate makes a first impression.

Note: As many as four out of five hiring decisions are made within the first 10 minutes of an interview, according to some research. Thus, be aware that if you are immediately impressed with a candidate, you may spend more time talking than listening—perhaps trying to sell the candidate on the job rather than screen his or her qualifications.[77]

- **Scene 2: The next 15–60 minutes—asking questions and listening to the applicant's "story."** In the next scene, you ask the questions you wrote out (and answer those the candidate directs to you). Allow the interviewee to do 70%–80% of the talking.

Take notes to remember important points. Don't ignore your "gut feelings." Intuition plays a role in hiring decisions. (But be careful you don't react to people as stereotypes.)

- **Scene 3: The final 1–2 minutes—closing the interview and setting up the next steps.** In the final minute, you listen to see whether the candidate expresses interest in taking the job.

After the Interview

Write a short report making some sort of quantitative score of the candidate's qualifications. Indicate your reasons for your decision.

Check the applicant's references before inviting him or her to a second interview.

3. Employment Tests: Ability, Personality, Performance, & Others   It used to be that employment selection tests consisted of paper-and-pencil, performance, and physical-ability tests. Now, however, *employment tests* are legally considered to consist of any procedure used in the employment selection decision process, even application forms, interviews, and educational requirements.[78] Indeed, today applicants should expect just about anything, such as spending hours on simulated work tasks, performing role-playing exercises, or tackling a business case study.[79]

Probably the three most common employment tests are the following.

- **Ability tests.** *Ability tests* measure physical abilities, strength and stamina, mechanical ability, mental abilities, and clerical abilities. Telephone operators, for instance, need to be tested for hearing, and assembly-line workers for manual dexterity. Intelligence tests are also catching on as ways to predict future executive performance.[80] Corporate-event company Windy City Fieldhouse uses a test that measures attention to detail, asking takers to do such things as "do a count of the letter 'l' in a three-sentence paragraph to measure how carefully a respondent works," according to one account.[81]

- **Performance tests.** *Performance tests* or *skills tests* measure performance on actual job tasks, as when computer programmers take a test on a particular programming language such as C++ or middle managers work on a small project. Some companies have an *assessment center,* in which management candidates participate in activities for a few days while being assessed by evaluators.[82]

- **Personality tests.** *Personality tests* measure such personality traits as adjustment, energy, sociability, independence, and need for achievement. Career-assessment tests that help workers identify suitable jobs tend to be of this type.[83] One of the most famous personality tests, in existence for 65-plus years, is the 93-question Myers-Briggs Type Indicator, with about 2.5 million tests given each year throughout the world. Myers-Briggs endures, observers say, "because it does a good job of pointing up differences between people, offers individuals a revealing glimpse of themselves, and is a valuable asset in team-building, improving communication, and resolving personality-conflict."[84] However, this and other personality tests need to be interpreted with caution because of the difficulty of measuring personality characteristics and of making a legal defense if the results are challenged.[85]

Personality Tests: How a Sporting-Goods Chain Screens Job Applicants Online

More than 80% of midsize and large companies use personality and ability assessments for entry and mid-level jobs these days, according to one executive at a global human-resources consulting firm.[86]

Southwest Airlines, for instance, has found Myers-Briggs helps build trust in developing teams.[87] Hewlett-Packard uses a personality test to see if employees are temperamentally suited to working alone at home—that is, telecommuting—and can handle limited supervision.[88] At Children's Healthcare of Atlanta, personality tests are used to find employees who will be "nice people"—those with "the qualities of being nurturing, kind, and warm-hearted," in the words of a human resources vice president.[89]

Online Personality Tests. At Finish Line, a nationwide chain of sporting-goods stores, store managers use the results of Web-based personality tests developed by Unicru, of Beaverton, Oregon, to screen applicants for jobs as retail sales clerks. Candidates may apply through Unicru's kiosks or computer phones, which are installed in the stores. One Finish Line store in Chicago screens as many as 70 applicants a week during the store's preholiday season.

Unicru's computer scores test takers according to how strongly they agree or disagree (on a four-point scale) with statements such as "You do not fake being polite" and "You love to listen to people talk about themselves." High scores on attributes such as sociability and initiative reward applicants with a "green" rating that allows them to move on to an interview with a human manager. Scores in the middle earn a "yellow," and a lesser chance of landing a job; low-scoring "reds" are out of luck.

Measurable Results. "The kinds of people who do well," says Unicru psychologist David Scarborough, ". . . obviously have to have good self-control. They have to be patient. They have to enjoy helping people. All those characteristics are quite measurable."[90] Finish Line says that Unicru's system has reduced turnover by 24%.

YOUR CALL

There are, by some estimates, around 2,500 cognitive and personality employment tests on the market, and it's important that employers match the right test for the right purpose.[91] Moreover, tests aren't supposed to have a disparate impact on a protected class of people, such as certain racial or ethnic groups.[92] What questions would you want to ask about a personality test before you submitted yourself to it? (Note: Don't try to psych the test. You might wind up being miserable in a job that doesn't suit you.)

Other Tests   The list of employment testing techniques has grown to include—in appropriate cases—drug testing, polygraph (lie detectors), genetic screening, and even (a questionable technique) handwriting analysis.[93] Human resource professionals need to be aware, incidentally, that there are a variety of products available on the Internet to help employees beat many kinds of drug tests.[94] Recently, however, the hair test has begun to find favor, since it's said to be able to detect a pattern of repetitive drug use over a period of up to 90 days.[95]

Lie detectors. Defense contractors and other security-minded companies are apt to require polygraph testing. Would you object to taking such a test?

With any kind of test, an important legal consideration is the test's *reliability*—**the degree to which a test measures the same thing consistently**—so that an individual's score remains about the same over time, assuming the characteristics being measured also remain the same.

Another legal consideration is the test's *validity*—**the test measures what it purports to measure and is free of bias.** If a test is supposed to predict performance, then the individual's actual performance should reflect his or her score on the test. Using an invalid test to hire people can lead to poor selection decisions. It can also create legal problems if the test is ever challenged in a court of law. ●

9.4 ORIENTATION, TRAINING, & DEVELOPMENT

Once people are hired, what's the best way to see that they do what they're supposed to do?

major question?

THE BIG PICTURE

Three ways newcomers are helped to perform their jobs are through *orientation,* to fit them into the job and organization; *training,* to upgrade the skills of technical and operational employees; and *development,* to upgrade the skills of professionals and managers.

In muckraker Upton Sinclair's 1906 novel *The Jungle,* "employers barely paused when a worker swooned from overwork or fell into a rendering tank," writes columnist Sue Shellenbarger. "They just got another warm body to replace him."[96]

That's hardly the case anymore. Before the 2008–2009 Great Recession, at least, when a hire was made, companies often resorted to what is known as "onboarding," rolling out a welcome by assigning "buddies," providing detailed orientations, even sending goody baskets, so as to bring rookies up to speed quickly and give them a fast introduction to company culture.[97]

Then and now, this is because, as we said, the emphasis is on "human capital." Only a third to half of most companies' stock-market value is accounted for by hard assets such as property, plant, and equipment, according to a Brookings Institution report. Most of a firm's value is in such attributes as patents, processes, and— important to this discussion—employee or customer satisfaction.[98] The means for helping employees perform their jobs are *orientation, training,* and *development.*

Orientation: Helping Newcomers Learn the Ropes

The finalist candidate is offered the job, has accepted it, and has started work. Now he or she must begin, in that old sailor's phrase, to "learn the ropes." This is the start of **orientation, helping the newcomer fit smoothly into the job and the organization.**

Helping New Employees Get Comfortable: The First 6 Months   "How well will I get along with other employees?" "What if I screw up on a project?" Coming into a new job can produce a lot of uncertainty and anxiety. In part this is because, depending on the job, a new hire can accomplish only 60% as much in the first 3 months as an experienced worker, according to MCI Communications.[99]

The first 6 months on a job can be critical to how one performs over the long haul, because that's when the psychological patterns are established. Thus, employers have discovered that it's far better to give newcomers a helping hand than to let them learn possibly inappropriate behavior that will be hard to undo later.[100]

The Desirable Characteristics of Orientation
Like Orientation Week for new college students, the initial socialization period is designed to give new employees the information they need to be effective. In a large organization, orientation may be a formal, established process. In a small organization, it may be so informal that employees find themselves having to make most of the effort themselves.

Group training. In large companies, orientation and ongoing training are often conducted in group sessions led by a presenter while the employees follow along. Do you see any problems with this approach?

Following orientation, the employee should emerge with information about three matters (much of which he or she may have acquired during the job-application process):

- **The job routine.** At minimum, the new employee needs to have learned what is required in the job for which he or she was hired, how the work will be evaluated, and who the immediate co-workers and managers are. This is basic.

- **The organization's mission and operations.** Certainly all managers need to know what the organization is about—its purpose, products or services, operations, and history. And it's now understood that low-level employees perform better if they, too, have this knowledge.

- **The organization's work rules and employee benefits.** A public utility's HR department may have a brochure explaining formalized work rules, overtime requirements, grievance procedures, and elaborate employee benefits. A technology start-up may be so fluid that many of these matters will have not been established yet. Even so, there are matters of law (such as those pertaining to sexual harassment) affecting work operations that every employee should be made aware of.

Training & Development: Helping People Perform Better

Which business strategy offers the highest returns: (1) downsizing; (2) total quality management, which focuses on work methods and process control; or (3) employee involvement, which focuses on upgrading workers' skills and knowledge? According to a study of 216 big firms, the winner is *employee involvement,* which had an average return on investment of 19.1% (versus 15.4% for downsizing and 15% for TQM).[101]

In hiring, you always try to get people whose qualifications match the requirements of the job. Quite often, however, there are gaps in what new employees need to know. These gaps are filled by training. The training process involves five steps, as shown below. *(See Figure 9.2.)*

figure 9.2

FIVE STEPS IN THE TRAINING PROCESS

HR professionals distinguish between *training* and *development.*

- **Training—upgrading skills of technical and operational employees.** Electronics technicians, data processors, computer network administrators, and X-ray technicians, among many others, need to be schooled in new knowledge as the requirements of their fields change. *Training,* then, refers to educating technical and operational employees in how to better do their current jobs.

- **Development—upgrading skills of professionals and managers.** Accountants, nurses, lawyers, and managers of all levels need to be continually educated in how to do their jobs better not just today but also tomorrow. *Development* refers to educating professionals and managers in the skills they need to do their jobs in the future.

Typical areas for which employee training and development are given are customer service, safety, leadership, computer skills, quality initiatives, communications, human relations, ethics, diversity, and sexual harassment.[102]

The Different Types of Training or Development There are all kinds of training and development methods, and their effectiveness depends on whether what is being taught are facts or skills. If people are to learn *facts*—such as work rules or legal matters—lectures, videotapes, and workbooks are effective. If people are to learn *skills*—such as improving interpersonal relations or using new tools—then techniques such as discussion, role playing, and practice work better.

Another way to categorize training methods is to distinguish on-the-job from off-the-job methods.

- **On-the-job training.** This training takes place in the work setting while employees are performing job-related tasks. Four major training methods are coaching, training positions, job rotation, and planned work activities.

- **Off-the-job training.** This training consists of classroom programs, videotapes, workbooks, and the like. Lots of off-the-job training consists of *computer-assisted instruction (CAI),* **in which computers are used to provide additional help or to reduce instructional time.**

Example

Off-the-Job Training: Getting Ahead through E-Learning

College students, of course, have already discovered e-learning (electronic learning). Several million other people are also taking short-term, practical courses related to their careers, mostly at business schools and continuing-education institutions around the country.

The Surge in Virtual Learning. Outside of education, in other U.S. organizations, e-learning has also become a well-established fact. Although instructor-led classrooms are still the dominant training method, at 65% of total student hours, online self-study e-learning and virtual classrooms made up 30%.[103] The benefits of e-learning, of course, are that no transportation is needed and you can follow a flexible schedule and often work at your own pace.

However, there are some drawbacks. "The one thing e-learning boosters don't want to talk about is the simple fact that very few people ever actually finish an e-learning course when it involves a technically

Off-the-job training. How does receiving feedback from an instructor affect your retention of knowledge?

complex or lengthy subject such as software training or programming," says corporate trainer Roland Van Liew. "People perform the complex process of assimilating information best in socially interactive environments."[104]

What about Student-Teacher Interaction? Because of the lack of classroom interaction between students and teachers in online education, both must assume more responsibility. "If students do not receive adequate teacher feedback and reinforcement," points out one writer, "they will not always know whether they possess an accurate knowledge of the subject matter."[105]

YOUR CALL

Neuroscientists are finding out that the human brain is a "social animal" that needs interaction with others.[106] How do you think this fact relates to e-learning? Do you think you learn better in a classroom rather than online?

What If No One Shows Up? Many employers offer employee training, whether internal or external, or funding to attend seminars. But research has shown that a surprisingly high percentage of employees simply don't know about it. For instance, while 92% of employers in one survey offered funding to attend seminars and trade shows, only 28% of employees were aware the funding existed.[107] Clearly, then, employers need to find out whether the training offered fits with the majority of employee development goals. ●

major question? How can I assess employees' performance more accurately and give more effective feedback?

THE BIG PICTURE
Performance appraisal, assessing employee performance and providing them feedback, may be objective or subjective. Appraisals may be by peers, subordinates, customers, or oneself. Feedback may be formal or informal.

If you're a member of Gen Y (born after 1980), you tend to want "frequent and candid performance feedback," according to one survey, and having your managers provide "detailed guidance in daily work" is very important to you.[108] Feedback about how you're doing at work is part of *performance appraisal,* **which consists of (1) assessing an employee's performance and (2) providing him or her with feedback.**

Many performance reviews are worthless, says UCLA management professor Samuel Culbert, coauthor of *Get Rid of the Performance Review!*[109] This is because evaluations are often dictated by a date on the calendar rather than need and are "one-sided, boss-dominated" assessments that come down to whether your superior "likes" you.[110] Stanford business scholar Jeffrey Pfeffer, champion of evidence-based management, also believes most workplace appraisals aren't working. Among the many flaws, "gender and race affect reviews," he writes, "with evaluations more positive for underlings whose managers share their social demographic." Political skill also "helps individuals put a gloss on their performance that ensures a higher rating."[111]

Two Kinds of Performance Appraisal: Objective & Subjective

Clearly, performance appraisals need to be fair and accurate not just because it's right but also because it's essential to effective *performance management,* **the continuous cycle of improving job performance through goal setting, feedback and coaching, and rewards and positive reinforcement.** The purpose of performance management is to focus employees on attaining goals that are tied to the organization's strategic goals and vision, and to evaluate how successful they were in accomplishing those goals.

Appraisals are of two general types—objective and subjective.

I. Objective Appraisals *Objective appraisals,* **also called** *results appraisals,* **are based on facts and are often numerical.** In these kinds of appraisals, you would keep track of such matters as the numbers of products the employee sold in a month, customer complaints filed against an employee, miles of freight hauled, and the like.

There are two good reasons for having objective appraisals:

- **They measure results.** It doesn't matter if two appliance salespeople have completely different personal traits (one is formal, reserved, and patient; the other informal, gregarious, and impatient) if each sells the same number of washers and dryers. Human resource professionals point out that, just as in business we measure sales, profits, shareholder value, and other so-called metrics, so it's important to measure employee performance, benefit costs, and the like as an aid to strategy.[112]

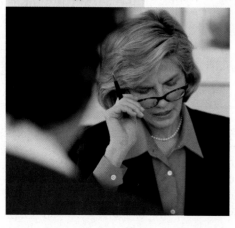

How'm I doing? One of the most important tasks of being a manager is giving employees accurate information about their work performance. Which would you be more comfortable giving—objective appraisals or subjective appraisals?

- **They are harder to challenge legally.** Not being as subject to personal bias, objective appraisals are harder for employees to challenge on legal grounds, such as for age, gender, or racial discrimination.

We discussed an objective approach in Chapter 5 under *management by objectives,* which can encourage employees to feel empowered to adopt behavior that will produce specific results. MBO, you'll recall, is a four-step process in which (1) managers and employees jointly set objectives for the employee, (2) managers develop action plans, (3) managers and employees periodically review the employee's performance, and (4) the manager makes a performance appraisal and rewards the employee according to results. For example, an objective for a copier service technician might be to increase the number of service calls 15% during the next 3 months.

2. Subjective Appraisals Few employees can be adequately measured just by objective appraisals—hence the need for **subjective appraisals, which are based on a manager's perceptions of an employee's (1) traits or (2) behaviors.**

- **Trait appraisals.** *Trait appraisals* are ratings of such subjective attributes as "attitude," "initiative," and "leadership." Trait evaluations may be easy to create and use, but their validity is questionable because the evaluator's personal bias can affect the ratings.

- **Behavioral appraisals.** Behavioral appraisals measure specific, observable aspects of performance—being on time for work, for instance—although making the evaluation is still somewhat subjective. An example is the **behaviorally anchored rating scale (BARS), which rates employee gradations in performance according to scales of specific behaviors.** For example, a five-point BARS rating scale about attendance might go from "Always early for work and has equipment ready to fully assume duties" to "Frequently late and often does not have equipment ready for going to work," with gradations in between.

Who Should Make Performance Appraisals?

If one of your employees was putting on a good show of solving problems that, it turned out, she had actually *created* herself so that she could be an "office hero" and look good, how would you know about it? (This phenomenon has been dubbed "Munchausen at work" because it resembles the rare psychological disorder in which sufferers seek attention by making up an illness.)[113] Most performance appraisals are done by managers; however, to add different perspectives, sometimes appraisal information is provided by other people knowledgeable about particular employees.

Peers, Subordinates, Customers, & Self Among additional sources of information are co-workers and subordinates, customers and clients, and the employees themselves.

- **Peers and subordinates.** Co-workers, colleagues, and subordinates may well see different aspects of your performance. Such information can be useful for development, although it probably shouldn't be used for evaluation. (Many managers will resist soliciting such information about themselves, of course, fearing negative appraisals.)

- **Customers and clients.** Some organizations, such as restaurants and hotels, ask customers and clients for their appraisals of employees. Publishers ask authors to judge how well they are doing in handling the editing, production, and marketing of their books. Automobile dealerships may send follow-up questionnaires to car buyers.

- **Self-appraisals.** How would you rate your own performance in a job, knowing that it would go into your personnel file? Probably the bias would be toward the favorable. Nevertheless, *self-appraisals* help employees become involved in the whole evaluation process and may make them more receptive to feedback about areas needing improvement.

360-Degree Assessment: Appraisal by Everybody   We said that performance appraisals may be done by peers, subordinates, customers, and oneself. Sometimes all these may be used in a technique called 360-degree assessment.

In a "theater in the round," the actors in a dramatic play are watched by an audience on all sides of them—360 degrees. Similarly, as a worker, you have many people watching you from all sides. Thus has arisen the idea of the ***360-degree assessment,*** or ***360-degree feedback appraisal, in which employees are appraised not only by their managerial superiors but also by peers, subordinates, and sometimes clients,*** thus providing several perspectives.

Typically, an employee chooses between 6 and 12 other people to make evaluations, who then fill out anonymous forms, the results of which are tabulated by computer. Or, using a Facebook-style program such as Performance Multiplier or Twitter-like software called Rypple, employees can solicit evaluations through social networking–style systems.[114] The employee then goes over the results with his or her manager and together they put into place a long-term plan for performance goals.

Incorporating 360-degree feedback into the performance appraisal process has advantages and disadvantages. Recent research found that "improvement is most likely to occur when feedback indicates that change is necessary, recipients have a positive feedback orientation, perceive a need to change their behavior, react positively to feedback, believe change is feasible, set appropriate goals to regulate their behavior, and take actions that lead to skill and performance improvement."[115] At the heart of the process is the matter of *trust.* "Trust determines how much an individual is willing to contribute for an employer," says one expert. "Using 360 confidentially, for developmental purposes, builds trust; using it to trigger pay and personnel decisions puts trust at risk."[116]

Example

The 360-Degree Assessment: How Can It Be Compromised?

The 360-degree assessment can be very effective for performance improvement, career development, and even training. Texas computer maker Dell Inc., for instance, realized that it needed to nurture its talent in order to achieve better performance. Accordingly, it designed an in-house training program taught primarily by Dell's own top executives, chairman Michael Dell and then-CEO Kevin Rollins (no longer at the company), who submitted to 360-degree assessments in the hope of inspiring the executives beneath them to do the same. "Pay," says one report, "is now determined in part by how well a manager does at nurturing people."[117]

There are many ways, however, in which 360-degree assessments can become disasters. In one health care organization, the vice president of human resources was rated by his staff as being a strong, positive, effective leader, but his boss, the corporate senior vice president, did not rate him as being very effective. At a meeting to review the 360-degree assessment, the HR manager

asked to discuss the differences in perceptions, but his boss said, "Obviously, everyone else is right and I am wrong. So, we'll just go along with what others have said"—thereby destroying the opportunity to give constructive feedback or coaching to the HR VP.

In another case, a manager confronted specific employees about their 360-degree assessments, effectively compromising the integrity of the process. In a third case, a sales organization executed an effective assessment and feedback, but, as one writer says, "there was no accountability for development plans, there was no follow-up after the initial feedback meetings, and no training was offered or provided for clearly identified weaknesses in a majority of the sales people."[118]

YOUR CALL

If you were the recipient of a 360-degree assessment, what kind of steps would you like to see taken to ensure that you could trust the process?

Forced Ranking: Grading on a Curve   To increase performance, as many as a quarter of Fortune 500 companies (such as General Electric, Ford, Cisco, and Intel) have instituted performance review systems known as forced ranking (or "rank and yank") systems.[119] In *forced ranking performance review systems,* **all employees within a business unit are ranked against one another and grades are distributed along some sort of bell curve**—just like students being graded in a college course. Top performers (such as the top 20%) are rewarded with bonuses and promotions, the worst performers (such as the bottom 20%) are rehabilitated or dismissed. For instance, every year 10% of GE's managers are assigned the bottom grade, and if they don't improve, they are asked to leave the company.

Proponents of forced ranking say it encourages managers to identify and remove poor performers and also structures a predetermined compensation curve, which enables them to reward top performers. If, however, the system is imposed on an organization overnight without preparation, by pitting employees against one another, it can produce shocks to morale, productivity, and loyalty. There may also be legal ramifications, as when employees filed class-action lawsuits alleging that the forced ranking methods had a disparate effect on particular groups of employees.[120]

Effective Performance Feedback

The whole point of performance appraisal, of course, is to stimulate better job performance. But, says Lawrence Bossidy, former CEO of AlliedSignal, the typical appraisal is often three pages long and filled with vague, uncommunicative language and is useless to ensure that improvement happens.[121] Bossidy recommends an appraisal take up half a page and cover just three topics: what the boss likes about your performance, what you can improve, and how you and your boss are going to make sure that improvement happens.

To help increase employee performance, a manager can use two kinds of appraisals—formal and informal.

I. Formal Appraisals   *Formal appraisals* **are conducted at specific times throughout the year and are based on performance measures that have been established in advance.** An emergency medical technician might be evaluated twice a year by his or her manager, using objective performance measures such as work attendance time sheets and more subjective measures such as a behaviorally anchored rating scales (BARS) to indicate the employee's willingness to follow emergency procedures and doctors' and nurses' orders.

As part of the appraisal, the manager should give the employee feedback, describing how he or she is performing well and not so well and giving examples. Managers are sometimes advised to keep diaries about specific incidents so they won't have to rely on their memories (and so that their evaluations will be more lawsuit-resistant). Facts should always be used rather than impressions.

2. Informal Appraisals   Formal appraisals are the equivalent of a student receiving a grade on a midterm test and a grade on a final test—weeks may go by in which you are unaware of how well you're doing in the course. Informal appraisals are the equivalent of occasional unscheduled pop quizzes and short papers or drop-in visits to the professor's office to talk about your work—you have more frequent feedback about your performance. *Informal appraisals* **are conducted on an unscheduled basis and consist of less rigorous indications of employee performance.**

You may not feel comfortable about critiquing your employees' performance, especially when you have to convey criticism rather than praise. Nevertheless, giving performance feedback is one of the most important parts of the manager's job.

Some suggestions for improvement appear at right. *(See Table 9.4.)* ●

table 9.4

HOW TO GIVE PERFORMANCE FEEDBACK TO EMPLOYEES

Think of yourself as a coach, as though you were managing a team of athletes.

- *Take a problem-solving approach, avoid criticism, and treat employees with respect.* Recall the worst boss you ever worked for. How did you react to his or her method of giving feedback? Avoid criticism that might be taken personally.

   Example: Don't say "You're picking up that bag of cement wrong" (which criticizes by using the word *wrong*). Say "Instead of bending at the waist, a good way to pick up something heavy is to bend your knees. That'll help save your back."

- *Be specific in describing the employee's present performance and in the improvement you desire.* Describe your subordinate's current performance in specific terms and concentrate on outcomes that are within his or her ability to improve.

   Example: Don't say "You're always late turning in your sales reports." Say "Instead of making calls on Thursday afternoon, why don't you take some of the time to do your sales reports so they'll be ready on Friday along with those of the other sales reps."

- *Get the employee's input.* In determining causes for a problem, listen to the employee and get his or her help in crafting a solution.

   Example: Don't say "You've got to learn to get here at 9:00 every day." Say "What changes do you think could be made so that your station is covered when people start calling at 9:00?"

✳ 9.6 MANAGING AN EFFECTIVE WORKFORCE: COMPENSATION & BENEFITS

What are the various forms of compensation?

THE BIG PICTURE

Managers must manage for compensation—which includes wages or salaries, incentives, and benefits.

Do we work only for a paycheck? Many people do, of course. But money is only one form of compensation.

Compensation **has three parts: (1) wages or salaries, (2) incentives, and (3) benefits.** In different organizations one part may take on more importance than another. For instance, in some nonprofit organizations (education, government), salaries may not be large, but health and retirement benefits may outweigh that fact. In a high-technology start-up, the salary and benefits may actually be somewhat humble, but the promise of a large payoff in incentives, such as stock options or bonuses, may be quite attractive. Let's consider these three parts briefly. (We expand on them in Chapter 12 when we discuss ways to motivate employees.)

Wages or Salaries

Base pay **consists of the basic wage or salary paid employees in exchange for doing their jobs.** The basic compensation is determined by all kinds of economic factors: the prevailing pay levels in a particular industry and location, what competitors are paying, whether the jobs are unionized, if the jobs are hazardous, what the individual's level is in the organization, and how much experience he or she has. (In 2008, for occupations that exist in both the private and public sectors, average annual pay was $60,046 for the private sector and $67,691 for the federal government.)[122]

Incentives

To induce employees to be more productive or to attract and retain top performers, many organizations offer incentives, such as commissions, bonuses, profit-sharing plans, and stock options. We discuss these in detail in Chapter 12.

Stock options. Companies like to offer favored employees stock options rather than higher salaries as benefits. Not only do employees place a high value on options, but companies can issue as many as they want without hurting corporate profits because, under present accounting rules, they don't have to count the options' value as an expense.

How to Make Incentive Pay Plans Meet Company Goals: Communicate Them to Employees[123]

There are many incentive compensation plans, ranging from cash awards and gifts to profit sharing and stock ownership, as we discuss in detail in Chapter 12.

Here let's ask the question: Do they work?

A survey of 139 companies, more than a third of them in the Fortune 500, found that 72% had variable pay plans. But only 22% said their plans had helped them achieve all their business objectives, and 28% said their plans had achieved none of them.

What explains the difference? Good plan design is important, but so is good communication and oversight.

According to Ken Abosch, a consultant at Chicago-based Hewett Associates, which conducted the survey, often plans fail to deliver on their intended goals because employees aren't told enough about them and aren't kept up to date on the progress of the plans. Eighty-nine percent of companies that regularly communicated with their employees said their incentive plans met their goals, compared with only 57% of companies that did not discuss them with their employees.

Five keys to a successful incentive-pay plan are the following, according to Abosch:

- **Simplicity.** Does the plan pass the simplicity test? As Abosch puts it, "Can you explain it on an elevator ride?"

- **Clear goals.** Are the goals clear? Are the goals fully supported by management?

- **Realistic goals.** Are the goals realistic—that is, neither too difficult nor too easy to achieve?

- **Consistency with present goals.** Is the plan in line with the organization's present goals? Company goals change. "There are very few organizations that have the same business objective for five to seven years," points out Abosch.

- **Regular communication.** Do managers regularly communicate with employees about the plan? "People want a scorecard," Abosch says.

Benefits

Benefits, or *fringe benefits,* **are additional nonmonetary forms of compensation** designed to enrich the lives of all employees in the organization, which are paid all or in part by the organization. Examples are many: health insurance, dental insurance, life insurance, disability protection, retirement plans, holidays off, accumulated sick days and vacation days, recreation options, country club or health club memberships, family leave, discounts on company merchandise, counseling, credit unions, legal advice, and education reimbursement. For top executives, there may be "golden parachutes," generous severance pay for those who might be let go in the event the company is taken over by another company.

Benefits are no small part of an organization's costs. According to the U.S. Chamber of Commerce, employee benefit costs were 42.7% of payroll costs in 2007, with medical benefit costs (at 12.7%) constituting the largest part.[124] (Annual health, pension, and other benefits averaged $9,882 for occupations in the private sector in 2008 versus $40,785 per federal employee.)[125] ●

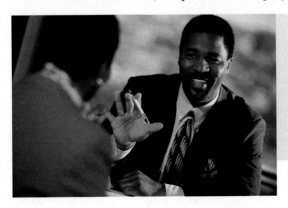

Communication is everything. The questions human resource managers need to keep in mind are: What good does it do a company to have attractive incentive plans if employees don't understand them? Will an employee exert the extra effort in pursuit of rewards if he or she doesn't know what the rewards are?

major question?

What are some guidelines for handling promotions, transfers, disciplining, and dismissals?

THE BIG PICTURE

As a manager, you'll have to manage employee replacement actions, as by promoting, transferring, demoting, laying off, or firing.

"The unemployment rate is an abstraction, an aggregation of bodiless data," writes journalist/novelist Walter Kirn, "but losing a job is a lived experience, written on the nerves. . . . Some blame themselves and some blame everybody. Still others, not knowing whom to blame, explode."[126]

Among the major—and most difficult—decisions you will make as a manager are those about employee movement within an organization: Whom should you let go? promote? transfer? discipline? All these matters go under the heading of *employee replacement.* And, incidentally, any time you need to deal with replacing an employee in a job, that's a time to reconsider the job description to see how it might be made more effective for the next person to occupy it.

You'll have to deal with replacement whenever an employee quits, retires, becomes seriously ill, or dies. Or you may initiate the replacement action by promoting, transferring, demoting, laying off, or firing.[127]

Promotion: Moving Upward

Promotion—moving an employee to a higher-level position—is the most obvious way to recognize that person's superior performance (apart from giving raises and bonuses). Three concerns are these:

Fairness It's important that promotion be *fair.* The step upward must be deserved. It shouldn't be for reasons of nepotism, cronyism, or other kind of favoritism.

Nondiscrimination The promotion cannot discriminate on the basis of race, ethnicity, gender, age, or physical ability.

Others' Resentments If someone is promoted, someone else may be resentful about being passed over. As a manager, you may need to counsel the people left behind about their performance and their opportunities in the future. In fact, if you are passed over yourself, it is important not to let your anger build. Instead, you should gather your thoughts, then go in and talk to your boss and find out what qualities were lacking, suggests one report. You should also create a career action plan and look for ways to improve your knowledge, skills, and abilities.[128]

Transfer: Moving Sideways

Transfer is movement of an employee to a different job with *similar responsibility.* It may or may not mean a change in geographical location (which might be part of a promotion as well).

Employees might be transferred for four principal reasons: (1) to solve organizational problems by using their skills at another location; (2) to broaden their experience in being assigned to a different position; (3) to retain their interest and motivation by being presented with a new challenge; or (4) to solve some employee problems, such as personal differences with their bosses.

Disciplining & Demotion: The Threat of Moving Downward

Poorly performing employees may be given a warning or a reprimand and then disciplined. That is, they may be temporarily removed from their jobs, as when a police officer is placed on suspension or administrative leave—removed from his or her regular job in the field and perhaps given a paperwork job or told to stay away from work.

Alternatively, an employee may be demoted—that is, have his or her current responsibilities, pay, and perquisites taken away, as when a middle manager is demoted to a first-line manager. (Sometimes this may occur when a company is downsized, resulting in fewer higher-level management positions.)

Dismissal: Moving Out of the Organization

Dismissals are of three sorts:

Layoffs   The phrase being *laid off* tends to suggest that a person has been dismissed *temporarily*—as when a carmaker doesn't have enough orders to justify keeping its production employees—and may be recalled later when economic conditions improve.

Downsizings   A *downsizing* is a *permanent* dismissal; there is no rehiring later. An automaker discontinuing a line of cars or on the path to bankruptcy might permanently let go of its production employees.

Firings   The phrase being *fired*, with all its euphemisms and synonyms—being "terminated," "separated," "let go," "canned"—tends to mean that a person was dismissed *permanently "for cause"*: absenteeism, sloppy work habits, failure to perform satisfactorily, breaking the law, and the like.

It used to be that managers could use their discretion about dismissals. Today, however, because of the changing legal climate, steps must be taken to avoid employees suing for "wrongful termination." That is, an employer has to carefully *document* the reasons for dismissals. You also need to take into account the fact that survivors in the company can suffer just as much as, if not more than, their colleagues who were laid off.[129]

Incidentally, in terms of your own career, be aware that layoffs rarely come as a surprise. Most bosses are conflict-averse and you may see the handwriting on the wall when your own manager begins to interact with you less.[130]

The Practical Action box on the next page offers some suggestions for handling dismissals. ●

Practical Action

The Right Way to Handle a Dismissal

"Employment at will" is the governing principle of employment in the great majority of states, which means that anyone can be dismissed at any time for any reason at all—or for no reason. Exceptions are whistle-blowers and people with employment contracts. Civil-rights laws also prohibit organizations' dismissing people for their gender, skin color, or physical or mental disability.[131]

Four suggestions for handling a dismissal follow.

Give the Employee a Chance First

If you're dealing with someone who has a problem with absenteeism, alcohol/drug dependency, or the like, articulate to that employee what's wrong with his or her performance, then set up a plan for improvement (which might include counseling). Or if you're dealing with an employee who has a bad cultural or personality fit with the company—a buttoned-down, by-the-book style, say, that's at odds with your flexible, fast-moving organization—have a conversation and give the employee time to find a job elsewhere.[132]

Don't Delay the Dismissal, & Make Sure It's Completely Defensible

If improvements aren't forthcoming, don't carry the employee along because you feel sorry for him or her. Your first duty is to the performance of the organization. Make sure, however, that you've *documented* all the steps taken in advance of the dismissal. Also be sure that they follow the law and all important organizational policies.[133]

Be Aware How Devastating a Dismissal Can Be—Both to the Individual & to Those Remaining

To the person being let go, the event can be as much of a blow as a divorce or a death in the family. Dismissals can also adversely affect those remaining with the company. This is what psychiatrist Manfred Kets de Vries calls *layoff survivor sickness*, which is characterized by anger, depression, fear, guilt, risk aversion, distrust, vulnerability, powerlessness, and loss of motivation. Indeed, a 5-year study by Cigna and the American Management Association found an enormous increase in medical claims, particularly for stress-related illnesses, not only among those dismissed but among continuing employees as well.[134]

Offer Assistance in Finding Another Job

Dismissing a long-standing employee with only a few weeks of severance pay not only hurts the person let go but will also hurt the organization itself, as word gets back to the employees who remain, as well as to outsiders who might be prospective employees. Knowledgeable employers offer assistance in finding another job.

"The best demonstration that a company's values are real," says management scholar Rosabeth Moss Kanter, "is to act on them today even for people who will not be around tomorrow. A company, like a society, can be judged by how it treats its most vulnerable. . . . Bad treatment of departing employees can destroy the commitment of those who stay."[135]

Key Terms Used in This Chapter

Summary

 9.1 Strategic Human Resource Management
Human resource management consists of the activities managers perform to plan for, attract, develop, and retain an effective workforce. The purpose of the strategic human resource management process is to get the optimal work performance that will help realize the company's mission and vision.

Two concepts important to human resource management are (1) human capital, the economic or productive potential of employee knowledge, and (2) social capital, the economic or productive potential of strong, trusting, and cooperative relationships.

Strategic human resource planning consists of developing a systematic, comprehensive strategy for (a) understanding current employee needs and (b) predicting future employee needs.

Understanding current employee needs requires first doing a job analysis to determine, by observation and analysis, the basic elements of a job. Then a job description can be written, which summarizes what the holder of the job does and how and why he or she does it. Next comes the job specification, which describes the minimum qualifications a person must have to perform the job successfully.

Predicting employee needs means a manager needs to become knowledgeable about the staffing an organization might need and the likely sources of staffing, perhaps using a human resource inventory to organize this information.

 9.2 The Legal Requirements of Human Resource Management
Four areas of human resource law that any manager needs to be aware of are as

follows: (1) Labor relations are dictated in part by the National Labor Relations Board, which enforces procedures whereby employees may vote to have a union and for collective bargaining. Collective bargaining consists of negotiations between management and employees about disputes over compensation, benefits, working conditions, and job security. (2) Compensation and benefits are covered by the Social Security Act of 1935 and the Fair Labor Standards Act, which established minimum wage and overtime pay regulations. (3) Health and safety are covered by the Occupational Safety and Health Act of 1970, among other laws. (4) Equal employment opportunity is covered by the Equal Employment Opportunity (EEO) Commission, whose job it is to enforce antidiscrimination and other employment-related laws. Three important concepts covered by EEO are (a) discrimination, which occurs when people are hired or promoted—or denied hiring or promotion—for reasons not relevant to the job, such as skin color or national origin; (b) affirmative action, which focuses on achieving equality of opportunity within an organization; and (c) sexual harassment, which consists of unwanted sexual attention that creates an adverse work environment and which may be of two types—the *quid pro quo* type, which may cause direct economic injury, and the hostile environment type, in which the person being harassed experiences an offensive work environment.

 9.3 Recruitment & Selection: Putting the Right People into the Right Jobs
Recruiting is the process of locating and attracting qualified applicants for jobs

open in the organization. (1) Internal recruiting means making people already employed by the organization aware of job openings. (2) External recruiting means attracting job applicants from outside the organization. A useful approach with external recruitment is the realistic job preview, which gives a candidate a picture of both positive and negative features of the job and organization before he or she is hired.

The selection process is the screening of job applicants to hire the best candidates. Three types of selection tools are background information, interviewing, and employment tests. (1) Background information is ascertained through application forms, résumés, and reference checks. (2) Interviewing takes three forms. (a) The unstructured interview involves asking probing questions to find out what the applicant is like. (b) The structured interview involves asking each applicant the same questions and comparing their responses to a standardized set of answers. The first type of structured interview is the situational interview, in which the interview focuses on hypothetical situations. (c) The second type of structured interview is the behavioral-description interview, in which the interviewer explores what applicants have actually done in the past. (3) Employment tests are legally considered to consist of any procedure used in the employment selection decision process, but the three most common tests are ability tests, personality tests, and performance tests. Some companies have assessment centers, in which management candidates participate in activities for a few days while being assessed in performance tests by evaluators. Other tests include drug testing, polygraphs, and genetic screening. With any kind of test, an important legal consideration is the test's reliability, the degree to which a test measures the same thing consistently, and validity, whether the test measures what it purports to measure and is free of bias.

9.4 Orientation, Training, & Development
Three ways in which newcomers are helped to perform their jobs are through orientation, training, and development.

(1) Orientation consists of helping the newcomer fit smoothly into the job and organization. Following orientation, the employee should emerge with information about the job routine, the organization's mission and operations, and the organization's work rules and employee benefits. (2) Training must be distinguished from development. Training refers to educating technical and operational employees in how to better do their current jobs. (3) Development is the term describing educating professionals and managers in the skills they need to do their jobs in the future. Both training and development may be effected through on-the-job training methods and off-the-job training methods.

9.5 Performance Appraisal
Performance appraisal consists of assessing an employee's performance and providing him or her with feedback. Appraisals are of two general types—objective and subjective. Two good reasons for having objective appraisals are that they measure results and they are harder to challenge legally. (1) Objective appraisals are based on facts and are often numerical. An example is management by objectives. (2) Subjective appraisals are based on a manager's perceptions of an employee's traits or behaviors. Trait appraisals are ratings of subjective attributes such as attitude and leadership. Behavioral appraisals measure specific, observable aspects of performance. An example is the behaviorally anchored rating scale (BARS), which rates employee gradations in performance according to scales of specific behaviors.

Most performance appraisals are made by managers, but they may also be made by co-workers and subordinates, customers and clients, and employees themselves (self-appraisals). Sometimes all of these may be used, in a technique called the 360-degree assessment, in which employees are appraised not only by their managerial superiors but also by their peers, subordinates, and sometimes clients. In another evaluation technique, forced ranking performance review systems, all employees within a business unit are ranked against one another, and grades are distributed along some sort of bell curve.

Effective performance feedback can be effected in two ways: (1) Formal appraisals are conducted at specific times throughout the year and are based on performance measures that have been established in advance. (2) Informal appraisals are conducted on an unscheduled basis and consist of less rigorous indications of employee performance.

9.6 Managing an Effective Workforce: Compensation & Benefits

Compensation has three parts: wages or salaries, incentives, and benefits. (1) In the category of wages or salaries, the concept of base pay consists of the basic wage or salary paid employees in exchange for doing their jobs. (2) Incentives include commissions, bonuses, profit-sharing plans, and stock options. (3) Benefits are additional nonmonetary forms of compensation, such as health insurance, retirement plans, and family leave.

9.7 Managing Promotions, Transfers, Disciplining, & Dismissals

Managers must manage promotions, transfers, disciplining, and dismissals. (1) In considering promotions, managers must be concerned about fairness, nondiscrimination, and other employees' resentment. (2) Transfers, or moving employees to a different job with similar responsibility, may take place in order to solve organizational problems, broaden managers' experience, retain managers' interest and motivation, and solve some employee problems. (3) Poor-performing employees may need to be disciplined or demoted. (4) Dismissals may consist of layoffs, downsizings, or firings.

Management in Action

Netflix's Human Resource Practices Enhance Employee Retention

[In the summer of 2009], an internal Netflix file found its way onto the Internet. The 128 Power-Point slides set out the company's culture and talent management strategy. Observers speculated how leaders at the usually guarded Netflix had let such a document leak.

As the commentary—pro and con—continues to flow, Reed Hastings, Netflix's chief executive officer, concedes that corporate leaders leaked the document intentionally "to allow job candidates to self-select."

Netflix has a controversial tough love approach to human capital management. It features a culture governed by few rules and zero tolerance for poor or average performers. Workers can earn top-of-market pay but no bonuses or long-term incentives, and they are responsible for their own development. "It's not the Bible, it's just our documentation of what's working for us," Patricia J. McCord, chief talent officer and one of the architects of the company, says of the approach. . . .

Today the company delivers movies by mail and video streaming. At the end of 2009, it had 12.2 million subscribers, and revenue for the year reached $1.67 billion, up 22% from the previous year. Netflix recruiters have added staff at a rate of more than 20% annually. The company has 1,644 employees, about 500 of whom are salaried professionals. . . .

At Netflix, HR professionals serve on the top management team, and McCord and Allison Hopkins, vice president for human resources set the tone. . . .

Software engineers, who make up the majority of the professional staff, are the creative lifeline of the organization, and McCord is obsessive about attracting and recruiting the best. Engineers, she observes, have little patience for bureaucracy. . . .

Hastings and McCord recognized that elite talent in the Silicon Valley could pick and choose where they worked; many other employers also pay top dollar. What else could Netflix do to recruit? The key to differentiation, they concluded, was to deliver a culture that attracted people who identified with and understood the business, who yearned for a flexible work environment with few constraints, and who—more than anything—wanted to be rubbing elbows with the best talent.

At Netflix's modern headquarters in Los Gatos, California, there are no badges or security checkpoints. There is also no dress code. People, most of whom are casually dressed, come and go continuously. . . .

The "creative employee we compete for thrives on freedom," Hastings says. "We're more focused on the absence of procedure—managing through talented people rather than a rule book." But the dearth of rules does not mean that it's a free-for-all environment: the few rules are reviewed by counsel and are "in compliance of federal laws," Hastings says. "We try to manage by strong ethics; we're strong on fairness and equity."

You won't see Netflix recruiters on college campuses or at entry-level career fairs. "We get a different kind of person than other software companies," McCord says. . . .

In contrast, new hires at Netflix typically have 7 to 15 years of experience. "They're accomplished deliverers," McCord says. "You need to know your craft so you can make a contribution when you walk in. You need to be mature, with enough experience to be able to make independent decisions."

And you need to be drawn to the business; Netflix's ranks overflow with film aficionados. People who are not interested in "the context" of the business need not apply. . . .

In other companies, Hopkins says, "policies are written for the lowest common denominator. Here, we don't have to do that. You don't have to write things down. When someone does something wrong, we tell them it was wrong. After that, either they get it or they're out." Hopkins contrasts Netflix with Hewlett-Packard, where, she says, "Everything was done by policy." . . .

"We are a performance culture based on intellectual prowess," Hastings says. "We try to be fair, but [the length of an employee's Netflix career] is not our primary concern. If someone is not extraordinary, we let them go." Based on personal observations, he says the payoff from an extraordinary performer vs. an average one in creative fields is tenfold.

Here then, is perhaps the characteristic that distinguishes Netflix from others recruiting top talent: Leaders are unwavering in their quest for quality and results. If even one person is assessed as mediocre or average during the annual review process but permitted to continue working for Netflix, the elite aura surrounding the workforce will be compromised. Loyalty to people not producing or facing minor setbacks or personal distractions is tolerated, but not for long.

"Keeping the house clean is essential to who we are," Hopkins says. "Too often, really good workers are frustrated at having to work with others who they perceive as average or worse performers. When we ask people why they chose us, they tell us it's not for the money. It's the other stuff. [It's] 'the places

we worked didn't fire people they should have fired.'" . . .

Voluntary employee turnover at Netflix is low. The top six executives have been with the company from the beginning. When it comes to terminations, managers follow two rules:

No surprises. Employees must know where they stand. Annual 360-degree reviews provide "direct and honest feedback," Stokes says. "It's tough to get used to doing them, but when they're done right, they're better than top-down evaluations." . . .

No-fault divorces. Wherever possible, an amicable departure is engineered. "We want them to keep their dignity," McCord says. "In many companies, once I want you to leave, my job is to prove you're incompetent. I have to give you all the documentation and fire you for poor performance. It can take months. Here, I write a check. We exchange severance for a release. To make Netflix a great company, people have to be able to leverage it when they leave" by subsequently getting good jobs.

The line manager delivers the news with coaching from HR professionals. "We don't coddle, it's not about asking how does someone feel," Hopkins says. "Usually, people find new jobs quickly." To date, no one who has been terminated has sued. . . .

"There's no road map that plots out your career," Stokes adds. "I've been here three years, and so far my job and responsibilities have changed every six months."

Hastings says people should manage their own career paths and not rely on the company. "The way you develop yourself is to be surrounded by stunning colleagues. We surround people and let them develop themselves," he explains.

Formal training, except where mandated by law, is not offered. Hastings and HR leaders conclude that most training materials are not useful. "I used to worry that we didn't do training and developing, but then we previewed some training videos and supporting materials," McCord recalls. "It was awful. Reed said, 'This stuff is nauseating and a waste of time.'" . . .

Netflix salaries are based on market conditions but not on company performance—a practice shareholders could find vexing if the company experiences a downturn. For now, the rationale—comparing top talent to major-league pitchers who receive star-level pay whether the team wins or loses—prevails. To be promoted, a person has to be a superstar in his or her current role and often be willing to take a reduction in pay to take on the new assignment. Executives want people to move up for the challenge, with the expectation that they will earn more once they have proved themselves.

1. How would you describe Netflix's organizational culture? Explain.

2. If you were hiring people at Netflix, what questions would you ask applicants to determine if they would fit into the corporate culture? Generate three to five questions.

3. What are the specific human resource practices that Netflix is using to recruit and retain high-quality employees? Explain why they are effective in this context.

4. What is your evaluation of Netflix's approach to training and performance appraisal? Discuss your rationale.

5. Do you like Netflix's approach to firing employees? Explain.

6. Would you like to work at Netflix? Provide your rationale.

Source: Excerpted from Robert J. Grossman, "Tough Love at Netflix," *HR Magazine,* April 2010, pp. 36–41. Copyright © 2010 by Society for Human Resource Management (SHRM). Reproduced with permission of Society for Human Resource Management (SHRM) via Copyright Clearance Center.

Self-Assessment

HR 101: An Overview

Objectives

1. To learn that there is more to HR than recruitment and hiring.

2. To assess your skills and determine if a career in HR is right for you.

Introduction

Your chosen career should optimally be based on your interests. The HR field, for example, offers many different career paths that require many different skills. The purpose of this exercise is to help you become familiar with the different career paths available to an HR professional and to see which path best fits your interests. This experience may help you decide if an HR career is right for you.

Among the professionals in the HR field are the following:

The HR generalist: HR generalists take on many different roles, whether negotiating a company's employee benefits package or interviewing a candidate for a director-level position. An HR generalist is supposed to be flexible and able to change gears at a moment's notice.

Compensation professional: Compensation professionals, who are very much in demand, design reward systems that attract, retain, and motivate employees. The job requires not only good technical skills but good people skills as well, a rare combination. It also requires a great deal of number crunching, creativity, and ingenuity, because a compensation package that might work for one employee might not work for another.

HRIS professional: HRIS stands for Human Resource Information Systems. With technology now such a key part of human resources, HRIS products help companies manage their personnel. Because the information systems are now so sophisticated, there is great demand for experienced HRIS professionals, who must be very detail oriented and, of course, enjoy working with computers. Such professionals are involved in product selection, systems customization, implementation, and ongoing administration.

Benefits professional: This individual is responsible for designing and implementing benefits plans. The job requires strong technical and communication skills.

Training and development professional: This individual is responsible for building environments that foster learning and management and leadership development. People in this field may be involved in distance learning programs as well as on-site, computer-based training programs.

Organizational development professional: Organizational development professionals work with top management to make sure that the organizational design sticks to the company's mission, vision, and goals. Besides doing some training and development, an OD professional must be able to embrace change and work long hours.

Instructions

Ask yourself the following questions and circle whether the statement applies to you. Once you have answered all of the questions, use the interpretation guidelines to analyze your responses and determine if a career in HR is right for you.

1.	Do I enjoy changing gears on a moment's notice?	Yes	No
2.	Am I open to learning about areas in which I currently have no expertise?	Yes	No
3.	Am I comfortable leaving a project unfinished to handle emergency situations?	Yes	No
4.	Do I consider myself fairly flexible?	Yes	No
5.	Am I good at creatively solving problems when resources and instructions are scarce?	Yes	No
6.	Do I have an aptitude for numbers?	Yes	No
7.	Am I comfortable seeing other people's salaries?	Yes	No
8.	Do I have strong communication skills?	Yes	No
9.	Do I have strong computer skills?	Yes	No
10.	Am I comfortable working at a computer all day?	Yes	No
11.	Am I well organized?	Yes	No
12.	Am I detail oriented?	Yes	No
13.	Am I comfortable constantly reworking projects I thought were already done?	Yes	No
14.	Am I willing to pay for and donate my free time to professional certifications?	Yes	No
15.	Am I good at taking complex ideas and making them understandable to the average person?	Yes	No
16.	Am I good at expressing my ideas and getting people to go along with them?	Yes	No
17.	Am I a creative person with strong computer skills?	Yes	No
18.	Am I comfortable in front of an audience?	Yes	No
19.	Am I comfortable working one very long project instead of lots of small projects?	Yes	No
20.	Am I passionate about learning and about teaching others?	Yes	No
21.	Can I handle change? Can I handle it well?	Yes	No
22.	Do I enjoy pulling together pieces of a puzzle?	Yes	No
23.	Do I perform well in times of stress?	Yes	No
24.	Am I a big-picture person?	Yes	No

Interpretation

If you answered yes to three or more of questions 1–4 (which apply to the HR generalist), three or more of questions 5–8 (compensation professional), three or more of questions 9–12 (HRIS professional), three or more of questions 13–16 (benefits professional), three or more of questions 17–20 (training and development professional), and three or more of questions 21–24 (organizational development professional), then you are well suited for the field of HR.

If you answered no to most of the previous 24 questions, the field of HR may not be right for you. (However, since this is only a small sampling of the many aspects of this field, there may still be a place for you in HR.)

Questions for Discussion

1. To what extent did the results fit your interests? Explain.

2. Look at the top two areas of HR for which you tested as being best suited. Look over the descriptions of these fields. What skills do you need to have to be successful? Describe.

3. Even if you do not pursue a career in HR, which skills do you feel you should continue to develop? Explain.

Adapted from R.C. Matuson, "HR 101: An Overview, Parts I and II," *Monster HR*, **www.monster.com**, June 2002.

Ethical Dilemma

Should Goldman Sachs Force Executives to Donate Some of Their Pay to Charity?

Preparing for the negative publicity that's certain to fall on Wall Street when the first 2009 bonus checks are cut, Goldman Sachs is pondering the expansion of a program requiring top staff to donate a percentage of their earnings to charity. *The New York Times* reported on January 11 [2010] that the firm may adopt a scheme like one at failed investment bank Bear Stearns, which compelled more than 1,000 employees to donate 4% of their pay each year. Were Goldman to impose something similar, hundreds of millions of dollars would flow into philanthropic causes. Goldman already has a program under which its 400-plus partners must donate an undisclosed amount to charity.

Solving the Dilemma

How do you feel about forcing employees to donate part of the pay to charity?

1. Goldman should not adopt this policy. Charitable donations are a personal decision and an employer should stay out of an individual's personal decisions.

2. Goldman should adopt this policy. Employees at Goldman make a lot of money and the company has received bad press over its compensation practices. This policy would create positive images in the marketplace.

3. Goldman should encourage employees to donate, but the company should not make it mandatory.

4. Invent other options. Explain.

Source: Excerpted from Timothy Fenton, "Finance: Do-Gooders at Goldman?" *Bloomberg BusinessWeek*, January 25, 2010, p. 13. Reprinted with permission.

chapter 10

Organizational Change & Innovation
Lifelong Challenges for the Exceptional Manager

Major Questions You Should Be Able to Answer

10.1 The Nature of Change in Organizations

Major Question: Since change is always with us, what should I understand about it?

10.2 Organizational Development: What It Is, What It Can Do

Major Question: What are the uses of OD, and how effective is it?

10.3 Promoting Innovation within the Organization

Major Question: What do I need to know to encourage innovation?

10.4 The Threat of Change: Managing Employee Fear & Resistance

Major Question: How are employees threatened by change, and how can I help them adjust?

Managing for Innovation & Change Takes a Careful Hand

"What I try to do is go out and grab lightning every day."

That's the way Terry Fadem, head of business development at DuPont Co., describes the company's never-ending search for tomorrow's breakthroughs.[1]

Managing for innovation and change takes a careful hand. "Even when their jobs depend on adopting and inventing new maneuvers," says columnist Carol Hymowitz, "most workers hold fast to old ones. The majority either are overwhelmed when asked to do things differently or become entrenched, clinging harder to the past."[2]

Because the revolution in technology is inflicting what Tom Peters calls Discontinuous Times, or "a brawl with no rules," dealing with change is an ongoing challenge for every manager.[3] "The one constant factor in business today is we live in a perpetual hurricane season," says Mellon Bank Corp. vice chairman Martin McGuinn. "A leader's job is less about getting through the current storm and more about enabling people to navigate the ongoing series of storms."[4]

Some ways to deal with change and innovation include the following:[5]

- **Allow room for failure.** "If somebody has an idea, don't stomp on it," says a psychologist and developer of ideas at Intuit, the software company famous for TurboTax and QuickBooks. "It's more important to get the stupidest idea out there and build on it than not to have it in the first place."[6] At Intuit, failure is very much an option as long as one learns from it.

- **Give one consistent explanation for the change.** When a company is undergoing change, myriad rumors will fly and employees will be uneasy; you and the managers who report to you need to give one consistent explanation. In McGuinn's case, the explanation for overhauling Mellon Bank's retail division was "We want to be the best retailer in financial services."

- **Look for opportunities in unconventional ways.** Most "new" products and services are really knockoffs or marginal variations of the things already on the market and hence are doomed to failure, says Robert Cooper, professor of marketing at Ontario's McMaster University. This doesn't mean, of course, that there isn't room for leveraging existing products with utterly unoriginal ideas. But most people are blinded by the limits of conventional wisdom and their own experience and fail to see huge potential markets in unconventional concepts. Try this advice from a Yale entrepreneurship instructor: Write down every hassle you encounter during the day. "At the end of the month, you will have 20 business ideas," he says, "and some of them will work."[7]

- **Have the courage to follow your ideas.** This may be the hardest job of all—trying to convince others that your ideas for change are feasible, especially if the ideas are radical. This may mean working to gain allies within the organization, standing up to intimidating competitors inside and out, and perhaps being prepared to follow a lonely course for a long time.[8]

- **Allow grieving, then move on.** Managers overseeing change need to give long-term employees a chance to grieve over the loss of the old ways, says McGuinn, who found that staffers were more willing to change after they had a chance to vent their fears.

For Discussion If you were going to instill a climate of innovation in a company you worked for, what kinds of things would you do?

forecast **What's Ahead in This Chapter**

In this chapter, we consider the nature of change in organizations, including the two types of change—reactive and proactive—and the forces for change originating outside and inside the organization. We describe the four areas in which change is often needed: people, technology, structure, and strategy. We then discuss organizational development, a set of techniques for implementing planned change. We next discuss how to promote innovation within an organization. Finally, we explore the threat of change and how you can manage employee fear and resistance.

major question? Since change is always with us, what should I understand about it?

THE BIG PICTURE

Two types of change are reactive and proactive. Forces for change may consist of forces outside the organization—demographic characteristics, market changes, technological advancements, and social and political pressures. Or they may be forces inside the organization—employee problems and managers' behavior. Four areas in which change is often needed are people, technology, structure, and strategy.

People are generally uncomfortable about change, even change in apparently minor matters. Philosopher Eric Hoffer told how as a younger man he spent a good part of one year as an agricultural worker picking peas, starting in Southern California in January and working his way northward. He picked the last of the peas in June, then moved to another area where, for the first time, he was required to pick string beans. "I still remember," he wrote, "how hesitant I was that first morning as I was about to address myself to the string bean vines. Would I be able to pick string beans? Even the change from peas to string beans had in it elements of fear."[9]

If small changes can cause uneasiness, large changes can cause considerable stress. And as a manager, you will no doubt have to deal with both.

Fundamental Change: What Will You Be Called On to Deal With?

"It is hard to predict, especially the future," physicist Niels Bohr is supposed to have quipped.

But it is possible to identify and prepare for *the future that has already happened,* in the words of management theorist Peter Drucker, by looking at some of the fundamental changes that are happening now.[10] Declining population in developed countries. More diversity in the workforce. China becoming the second-largest economic power. The ascent of knowledge work. Increased globalization. Awareness of global warming and need for sustainability. The rise of business-to-business (B2B) technology. Digital long-distance networks. The increase in data storage. On-demand media. The capturing of customer-specific information. The customization of mass goods. Instant-gratification shopping. Sales in the form of auctions instead of fixed prices.[11]

Beyond these overarching trends there are also some supertrends shaping the future of business:[12]

1. The Marketplace Is Becoming More Segmented & Moving Toward More Niche Products In the recent past, managers could think in terms of mass markets—mass communication, mass behavior, and mass values. Now we have "demassification," with customer groups becoming segmented into smaller and more specialized groups responding to more narrowly targeted commercial messages. "Our culture and economy are increasingly shifting away from a focus on a relatively small number of hits (mainstream products and markets) . . . and moving toward a huge number of niches," says Chris Anderson in *The Long Tail.* "In an era without the constraints of physical shelf space and other bottlenecks of distribution, narrowly targeted goods and services can be as economically attractive as mainstream fare."[13] Or, as the book's subtitle states, "the future of business is selling less of more."

Example: In the Internet Age, retailers like Amazon.com and Apple Computer are not constrained by physical shelf space and can offer consumers a much wider variety of products, yet small sales, one or two rather than millions of items at a time, can produce big profits.

2. More Competitors Are Offering Targeted Products, Requiring Faster Speed-to-Market

Companies offering a broad range of products or services are now experiencing intense pressure from competitors offering specialized solutions—and beating them to the punch by devising novel speed-to-market strategies. Indeed, "Speed is emerging as the ultimate competitive weapon," says one report. "Some of the world's most successful companies are proving to be expert at spotting new opportunities, marshaling their forces, and bringing to market new products or services in a flash."[14]

Example: Virgin Group Ltd., headed by Sir Richard Branson, is known mainly for its music and airline businesses, but it has entered several new businesses one after the other—mobile phones, credit cards, hotels, games, trains, even space travel—and very quickly. Virgin Comics, aimed at India's multibillion-dollar comics market, went from idea to public announcement in less than 11 months.

3. Some Traditional Companies May Not Survive Radically Innovative Change

In *The Innovator's Dilemma: When New Technologies Cause Great Firms to Fail,* Clayton M. Christensen, a Harvard Business School professor, argues that when successful companies are confronted with a giant technological leap that transforms their markets, all choices are bad ones. Indeed, he thinks, it's very difficult for an existing successful company to take full advantage of a technological breakthrough such as digitalization— what he calls "disruptive innovation." Instead, he argues that such a company should set up an entirely separate organization that can operate much like a start-up.[15]

Rising to the challenge.
"Faster times demand faster technology," says Kodak's electronic billboard on the New York Marriott Marquis hotel, indicating that the company is inventing innovative solutions to the digital revolution. Do you think this once-traditional company can survive radically innovative change?

Example: Eastman Kodak found its sales topped out at $14 billion in 1999, then dropped to $13.3 billion in 2003 as digital cameras began to take their toll on the chemical-based film business. This company, however, has survived so far by stopping its big investments in film and shifting resources to digital cameras and accessories, digital health-imaging technologies, and inkjet printing and liquid displays. As it waited for the technological transition to pay off, it also launched a short-term strategy of litigation against other companies (Samsung Electronics, LG Electronics) for violating Kodak patents. Excluding income from such suits, Kodak's profitability improved by more than $100 million in the 2009 fourth quarter compared with a year earlier.[16]

4. China, India, & Other Offshore Suppliers Are Changing the Way We Work

As we said in Chapter 2, globalization and outsourcing are transforming whole industries and changing the way we work. China, India, Mexico, the Philippines, and other countries offer workers and even professionals willing to work twice as hard for half the pay, giving American businesses substantial labor savings. These developing nations also, says *BusinessWeek,* offer "enormous gains in efficiency, productivity, quality, and revenues that can be achieved by fully leveraging offshore talent."[17] While unquestionably some American jobs are lost, others become more productive, with some engineers and salespeople, for example, being liberated from routine tasks so that they can spend more time innovating and dealing with customers.

Example: Querétaro is not a place you would probably go for spring break, but it is rapidly becoming known for something not normally associated with Mexico: aircraft construction. American aircraft makers from Bombardier to Cessna Aircraft to Hawker Beechcraft have various kinds of subassembly work here, where wages are lower but skill levels are not.[18] But if some manufacturing jobs have moved cross-border, so have many customers for American products. Houston-based SolArt, which offers energy management software and services to U.S. airlines, now has new clients such as Singapore Airlines.[19] IBM now makes two-thirds of its revenue abroad.[20] As often as not, however, overseas firms now look to the United States for talented workers, especially in technology and finance. As China, for instance, develops a high-tech economy, it is drawing on the United Sates for researchers.[21]

5. Knowledge, Not Information, Is Becoming the New Competitive Advantage "Information is rapidly becoming a profitless commodity, and knowledge is becoming the new competitive advantage," says San Diego management consultant Karl Albrecht.[22] That is, as information technology does more of the work formerly done by humans, even in high-tech areas (such as sorting data for relevance), many low-level employees previously thought of as knowledge workers are now being recognized as "data workers," who contribute very little added value to the processing of information. Unlike routine information handling, knowledge work is analytic and involves problem solving and abstract reasoning—exactly the kind of thing required of skillful managers, professionals, salespeople, and financial analysts. As futurists Alvin and Heidi Toffler suggest, knowledge work drives the future and creates wealth.[23]

Example: Many *back-office* systems and functions—those the customer does not see, such as inventory management and accounts payable—are rapidly being outsourced. Indeed, even some tasks of software engineers and other technical experts are also being sent overseas.

Clearly, we are all in for an interesting ride.

Two Types of Change: Reactive versus Proactive

As a manager, you will typically have to deal with two types of change: *reactive* and *proactive*.

1. Reactive Change: Responding to Unanticipated Problems & Opportunities When managers talk about "putting out fires," they are talking about **reactive change, making changes in response to problems or opportunities as they arise.** When you have to respond to surprises, there is usually less time to get all the information and resources you need to adequately manage the change, and serious mistakes may be made. Nevertheless, some of the best stories in business concern the intelligent management of unanticipated calamities.

Example

Reactive Change: BP Takes a Chance—& Loses Big-Time[24]

Crises can happen quickly and without warning, and many companies have shown they don't deal with them well, as happened with Coca-Cola's reactions to the 1999 illness in Europe attributed to bottlers in Belgium and France, Bausch & Lomb's delay in 2006 in withdrawing a contaminated contact lens cleaner, and Toyota's slow reaction in 2010 to dealing with its cars' accelerator problems. (You can find out about these mishaps through an online search.)

Crisis in the Gulf of Mexico. For oil giant BP (formerly British Petroleum), the crisis was far bigger than any of these. In April 2010, an explosion on the BP drilling platform Deepwater Horizon in the Gulf of Mexico led to sinking of the rig, loss of 11 lives, and the largest oil spill ever to happen in U.S. waters. Oil wells have emergency shutoff valves called blowout preventers, which can be triggered from the rig. The Deepwater Horizon, which floated 5,000 feet above the ocean floor, was equipped with this device, which nearly always works when wells surge out of control, however, it failed to operate on the day of the Gulf accident.

And what the rig did not have was a *backup* shutoff switch, a remote-control device that carries an acoustic signal through the water that can be activated as a last resort. Such acoustic backup triggers, which cost about $500,000, are not mandated by U.S. regulators, but they also haven't been tested under real-world conditions, because major offshore oil-well blowouts are so rare. (Two other major oil-producing countries, Norway and Brazil, do require them, and some major oil companies, such as Royal Dutch Shell, use them even when regulators don't mandate them.)

BP Reacts. As a total of 2.5 million gallons of oil leaked from the open wellhead, the question was asked: Why wasn't BP prepared for such an accident?

"We will stop the leaks," said one consultant, "but it's not like the technology is just lying around."[25]

YOUR CALL

Twenty-one years after the *Exxon Valdez*'s famous 1989 oil spill in the Gulf of Alaska, the effects of which are still being felt, do you think oil companies have been shortsighted in planning for major accidents? What should BP have been doing?

2. Proactive Change: Managing Anticipated Problems & Opportunities

In contrast to reactive change, ***proactive change,*** or planned change, involves making carefully thought-out changes in anticipation of possible or expected problems or opportunities.[26]

Example

Proactive Change: Being Ahead of the Curve with Natural Beef

The high-desert cattle ranch, 180 miles southeast of Denver in Colorado's San Luis Valley, is the home of Coleman Natural Foods, founded by Mel Coleman Sr. in 1979 on the ranch settled by his ancestors in 1875. Coleman sold "natural" beef back when most shoppers were unaware of the term. On a sales trip in the 1980s, Coleman would pitch grocers that his cows were not given antibiotics and growth hormones like those of the big producers but were fed a vegetarian diet.

The Cultural Shift in Meat. It took Coleman years to win converts, says a *New York Times* story, "not only among retailers but also among consumers and government regulators. Now, paradoxically, natural and organic meats have become so popular that even the big conventional meat producers are getting into the business, and Coleman is left in the unexpected position of scrambling for shelf space."[27]

"Natural" versus "Organic." The word *natural* can signify many things—that the animals were not given hormones or antibiotics, not fed rendered animal by-products, or were raised entirely out of doors—or it can mean nothing at all. *Organic,* however, means the meat adheres to more stringent standards—no use of

antibiotics, growth hormones, or parasite-killing chemicals, and animals were given feed grown without pesticides or chemical fertilizers.[28] Regardless, shoppers have learned to pay a premium, as much as 50% more, particularly for organic beef. Indeed, organic meat is now the fastest-growing segment of the organic food business. The Coleman ranch is now run by Mel Coleman Jr., but his father's legacy lives on. "Mel Sr. was one of the pioneers to develop a truly natural meat company," says an admirer.

YOUR CALL

Most instances of proactive change involve technology companies, symbolized by Apple's willingness to make sharp turns in direction—to be a "cross-boundary disrupter," in one observer's phrase.[29] In 2007, Apple dropped "Computer" from its name, signaling a move beyond computers—the Apple I, Apple II, Macintosh, and so on—into products intended for what it calls "the digital lifestyle," as represented by the iPod, the iPhone, and the iPad. Can you think of other examples of proactive change?

The Forces for Change: Outside & Inside the Organization

How do managers know when their organizations need to change? The answers aren't clear-cut, but you can get clues by monitoring the forces for change—both outside and inside the organization. *(See Figure 10.1, next page.)*

Outside Forces

Demographic characteristics
- Age
- Education
- Skill level
- Gender
- Immigration

Market changes
- Mergers & acquisitions
- Domestic & international competition
- Recession

Technological advancements
- Manufacturing automation
- Office automation

Social & political pressures
- Leadership
- Values

Inside Forces

Employee problems
- Unmet needs
- Job dissatisfaction
- Absenteeism & turnover
- Productivity
- Participation/suggestions

Managers' behavior
- Conflict
- Leadership
- Reward systems
- Structural reorganization

THE NEED FOR CHANGE

figure 10.1

FORCES FOR CHANGE OUTSIDE AND INSIDE THE ORGANIZATION

Forces Originating Outside the Organization   External forces consist of four types, as follows.

1. Demographic Characteristics   Earlier we discussed the demographic changes occurring in the U.S. workforce, with the workforce becoming more diverse. Example: So-called millennials (those born after 1980) are vastly different from their parents in their views on everything from technology to politics to marriage to tattoos.[30]

2. Market Changes   Certainly the global economy has forced U.S. companies to change the way they do business, with Walmart, for example, stepping up its expansion into overseas markets.[31] The recent Great Recession has also drastically affected many organizations. Example: Secondhand shops have suffered from a recession-induced decline in thrift store donations, even as consumer demand for used goods has gone through the roof.[32]

3. Technological Advancements   Technology may be one of the greatest forces for productivity in our lifetime, but it can also create real headaches for somebody. Example: Technology has made it easy for all kinds of illegal copycats in China and elsewhere to make pirated versions of American products—such as DVDs of U.S. movies still in theaters.[33] Another example: The invention of a machine to make plastic corks for wine bottles is severely affecting Portugal, which produces some 52% of the world's natural cork.[34]

4. Social & Political Pressures   Social events can create great pressures. Example: Changing eating habits have led to such a surge in weight gain that by 2015 two out of five Americans may be obese.[35] Another example: Pressures on companies to make their products and services "earth friendly" have made it hard for some consumers to tell the difference between green and *greenwashing*—making unsubstantiated or misleading claims about the environmental benefits of such products.[36]

Forces Originating Inside the Organization Internal forces affecting organizations may be subtle, such as low job satisfaction, or more dramatic, such as constant labor-management conflict. Internal forces may be of the two following types.

1. Employee Problems Is there a gap between the employees' needs and desires and the organization's needs and desires? Job dissatisfaction—as expressed through high absenteeism and turnover—can be a major signal of the need for change. Organizations may respond by addressing job design, reducing employees' role conflicts, and dealing with work overload, to mention a few matters.

Example: As the recent recession lingered on, employees in many organizations became stressed out from months of dealing with layoff concerns, wage cuts, or scaled-back hours, requiring managers to hold meetings and change hiring practices to alleviate their worries.[37]

2. Managers' Behavior Excessive conflict between managers and employees may be another indicator that change is needed. Perhaps there is a personality conflict, so that an employee transfer may be needed. Or perhaps some interpersonal training is required.

Example: "New managers tend to struggle when dealing with regular, day-to-day issues, like people on the team who don't meet deadlines," says Vicki Foley, a director of a career consulting firm.[38] One solution is to become a "servant leader" (discussed in Chapter 14), seeing yourself as someone who helps others do their jobs, fixing problems and giving employees the tools they need.

Areas in Which Change Is Often Needed: People, Technology, Structure, & Strategy

Change can involve any part of the organization. Models of change, however, reveal four targeted areas in which change is most apt to be needed: *people, technology, structure,* and *strategy.*

I. Changing People Even in a two-person organization, people changes may be required. The changes may take the following forms:

- **Perceptions.** Employees might feel they are underpaid for what they do. Managers might be able to show that pay and benefits are comparable or superior to those offered by competitors.

- **Attitudes.** In old-line manufacturing industries, employees may feel that it is the nature of things that they should be in an adversarial relationship with their managers. It may be up to management to try to change the culture and the attitudes by using educational techniques to show why the old labor wars should become a thing of the past.

- **Performance.** Should an organization pay the people who contract to wash its windows by the hour? by the window? or by the total job? Will one method cause them to work fast and sloppily but cost less? Will one cause them to do pristine windows but cost too much? It's often a major challenge to find incentives to improve people's performance.

- **Skills.** Altering or improving skill levels is often an ongoing challenge, particularly these days, when new forms of technology can change an organization's way of doing business, as we describe next.

2. Changing Technology Technology is a major area of change for many organizations. *Technology* **is not just computer technology; it is any machine or process that enables an organization to gain a competitive advantage in changing materials used to produce a finished product.**

Cell-phone power. Camera phones have become commonplace, but the cell phone is still evolving—and rapidly. In South Korea, where cell phones operate at broadband speeds, young commuters on the subway are forsaking print matter and occupying themselves with cell-phone news services, videos, and music downloads, as well as e-mail and phone calls. Cell phones there can double as credit cards: a consumer can point his or her phone at an infrared terminal on a store counter, which sends credit card information straight to the card company. In the future, cell phones might also take the place of ID cards such as driver's licenses. When cell phones and accompanying text-messaging features are joined to advanced search engines and huge databases, the technology will no doubt stand several industries on their heads. Which ones do you think these might be?

Example 🔍

Changing Technology: Web 2.0 Is Radically Altering How Business Is Done

Futurist Paul Saffo, director of the Institute for the Future in Menlo Park, California, says that new technologies lead to new products. The invention of television, for example, led to TV dinners and TV trays. The invention of the iPod led to the selling of music singles—something that hadn't happened since the 45 rpm record. "Each time it gets cheaper to do something," says Saffo, "you get more players. It's irreversibly more complex."[39]

Second-Generation Internet Services. Thus, the original World Wide Web has led to Web 2.0, a second generation of Internet-based services that lets people collaborate and share information online in a new way.[40] Among the results are social networking sites (MySpace, Facebook), photo-sharing sites (Flickr), and wikis (group-editable Web pages, such as the reference source Wikipedia), which all demand active participation and social interaction.

Web 2.0 services have also come into the business world, with wikis, for example, being used by the Walt Disney Co. and other firms to enhance collaboration. Other companies are using social networking services such as LinkedIn Corp to gain sales leads and hiring prospects. The "mobile Web," involving wireless communication and mobile gadgets (BlackBerrys, digital-music players), is changing commerce, allowing wireless shopping, for instance.[41] "In essence," says a *BusinessWeek* article, "these services are coalescing into one giant computer that anyone with access to an Internet-connected PC can use, from anywhere in the world."[42]

Flattened Lines of Authority. A significant structural result of Web 2.0 is further assault on conventional reporting arrangements, already being transformed by globalization and outsourcing. That is, the new free-form technologies help to further flatten clear lines of authority between managers and employees and to reduce organizational boundaries between the company and its partners and customers.

YOUR CALL

What possibilities do you see for applying social networking services, photo-sharing sites, blogs, and wikis to business uses? (Be aware that this area is still sort of the Wild West, with lots of consultants peddling such "measures" as blog mentions, YouTube hits, and number of Twitter followers as gospel, when these catchphrases may not distinguish between what works and what doesn't.)[43]

3. Changing Structure   Changes in strategy frequently require changes in structure. One of our clients, for example, changed from a product-based structure to a matrix structure in order to find new avenues for growing its business. Overall, recent trends are toward "flattening the hierarchy," eliminating several middle layers of management, and to using work teams linked by electronic networks.

4. Changing Strategy   Shifts in the marketplace often may lead organizations to have to change their strategy. Example: Surveys by the Pew Internet Project show that 75% of respondents aged 12–17 agree that music "file-sharing is so easy to do, it's unrealistic to expect people not to do it." "They are Generation Free," comments one writer, "and they just might kill the goose that lays the golden egg"—namely, the very record industry that makes music available.[44] The record industry has tried to shift to a digital strategy, but because illegal downloading is so easy, revenues have steadily plummeted for the past 10 years despite digital sales. ●

✳ 10.2 ORGANIZATIONAL DEVELOPMENT: WHAT IT IS, WHAT IT CAN DO

What are the uses of OD, and how effective is it?

major question?

THE BIG PICTURE

Organizational development (OD) is a set of techniques for implementing change, such as managing conflict, revitalizing organizations, and adapting to mergers. OD has three steps: diagnosis, intervention, and evaluation. Four factors have been found to make OD programs effective.

Organizational development (OD) **is a set of techniques for implementing planned change to make people and organizations more effective.** Note the inclusion of people in this definition. OD focuses specifically on people in the change process. Often OD is put into practice by a person known as a *change agent,* **a consultant with a background in behavioral sciences who can be a catalyst in helping organizations deal with old problems in new ways.**

What Can OD Be Used For?

OD can be used to address the following three matters:

1. Managing Conflict Conflict is inherent in most organizations. Sometimes an OD expert in the guise of an executive coach will be brought in to help advise an executive on how to improve relationships with others in the organization. Example: The two cofounders of Network Appliance, a data-storage firm in Sunnyvale, California, were feuding with each other because one founder couldn't stick to his decisions, which drove the other founder crazy. An organizational behavior specialist began working with the warring executives in separate sessions to solve the problem.

2. Revitalizing Organizations Information technology is wreaking such change that nearly all organizations these days are placed in the position of having to adopt new behaviors in order to resist decline. OD can help by opening communication, fostering innovation, and dealing with stress. Example: Family doctors are paid relatively modestly compared with other physicians and also do a lot of work outside office visits (making phone calls, writing prescriptions, reading lab reports) for which they are not compensated. They will be affected even more heavily by the preventive-medicine orientation of 2010 health care legislation. By getting expert help in adopting electronic records and trying out pilot projects that compensate them for preventive and disease-management work (not just office visits), such physicians can reduce their costs and increase their revenue significantly.[45]

3. Adapting to Mergers Mergers and acquisitions are associated with increased anxiety, stress, absenteeism, turnover, and decreased productivity.[46] What is the organizational fit between two disparate organizations, such as United Airlines and Continental Airlines, which announced a merger in 2010?[47] OD experts can help integrate two firms with varying cultures, products, and procedures.

How OD Works

Like physicians, OD managers and consultants follow a medical-like model. (Or, to use our more current formulation, they follow the rules of evidence-based management.) They approach the organization as if it were a sick patient, using *diagnosis, intervention,* and *evaluation*—"diagnosing" its ills, "prescribing" treatment

Organizational Change & Innovation ✳ CHAPTER 10 **315**

or intervention, and "monitoring" or evaluating progress. If the evaluation shows that the procedure is not working effectively, the conclusions drawn are then applied (see feedback loop) to refining the diagnosis, and the process starts again. *(See Figure 10.2.)*

figure 10.2

THE OD PROCESS

Sources: Adapted from W. L. French and C. H. Bell Jr., *Organization Development: Behavioral Interventions for Organizational Improvement* (Englewood Cliffs, NJ: Prentice-Hall, 1978); and E. G. Huse and T. G. Cummings, *Organizational Development and Change,* 3rd ed. (St. Paul: West, 1985).

1. Diagnosis: What Is the Problem?   To carry out the diagnosis, OD consultants or managers use some combination of questionnaires, surveys, interviews, meetings, records, and direct observation to ascertain people's attitudes and to identify problem areas.

2. Intervention: What Shall We Do about It?   "Treatment" or *intervention* **is the attempt to correct the diagnosed problems.** Often this is done using the services of an OD consultant who works in conjunction with management teams. Some OD activities for implementing planned change are communicating survey results to employees to engage them in constructive problem solving, observing employee communication patterns and teaching them skills to improve them, helping group members learn to function as a team, stimulating better cohesiveness among several work groups, and improving work technology or organizational design.

3. Evaluation: How Well Has the Intervention Worked?   An OD program needs objective evaluation to see if it has done any good. Answers may lie in hard data about absenteeism, turnover, grievances, and profitability, which should be compared with earlier statistics. The change agent can use questionnaires, surveys, interviews, and the like to assess changes in employee attitudes.

Example

Organizational Development: Patagonia Tries to Become Greener[48]

Founded by an environmentalist in 1979, apparel company Patagonia sells outdoor clothing and gear and has long been a strong supporter of the environmental movement. In fact, its mission statement is "Build the best product, cause no unnecessary harm, use business to inspire and implement solutions to the environmental crisis." However, as customers have become more eco-aware, the company has been getting more questions about how "green" the origins and handling

of its products are. The approach Patagonia took resembles the steps in organizational development.

Diagnosis: "What Is the Problem?" Forced to examine how green it actually is, Patagonia sent employees in May 2007 to track the "environmental footprint" of five products, from design studio to raw-materials stage to U.S. distribution center. The investigators visited yarn spinners in Thailand, a footwear factory in China, and a fiber manufacturer in North Carolina. The good news: they learned that transporting products took surprisingly little energy, because most were shipped by sea, which represented less than 1% of the total energy use in the supply chain. The bad news: manufacturing took more energy than was expected and sometimes produced ecologically unfriendly by-products, such as possibly toxic PFOA (perfluorooctanoic acid), found in Patagonia parkas.

Intervention: "What Shall We Do about It?" The company believed that using PFOA-free materials might sacrifice performance, so it continued to use PFOA-containing water-repellant membranes and coatings while searching for alternatives. By fall 2008, it had replaced membranes with polyester and polyurethane. However, no satisfactory substitute was found for the existing coatings.

Evaluation: "How Well Has the Intervention Worked?" Not finding a PFOA substitute for the coatings is not ecologically satisfying, but the company insists on maintaining quality. "We don't want to sacrifice quality for environmental reasons," says Jill Dumain, Patagonia's director of environmental analysis. "If a garment is thrown away sooner due to a lack of durability, we haven't solved any environmental problem." In addition, the findings are of limited value, because only the primary materials were traced, and no packaging was evaluated. Patagonia has posted the results of its investigation of 10 products online under the heading "the Footprint Chronicles" at *http://www.patagonia.com/web/us/footprint/index.jsp.*

YOUR CALL

Do you think every company should take an organizational development approach to the environmental quality of its products and services? Do you feel putting production information in the public domain and available to competitors is risky? Or do the benefits of openness outweigh the costs, because it could spur others to action?

The Effectiveness of OD

Among organizations that have practiced organizational development are American Airlines, B.F. Goodrich, General Electric, Honeywell, ITT, Polaroid, Procter & Gamble, Prudential, Texas Instruments, and Westinghouse Canada—companies covering a variety of industries.

Research has found that OD is most apt to be successful under the following circumstances.

1. Multiple Interventions OD success stories tend to use multiple interventions. Goal setting, feedback, recognition and rewards, training, participation, and challenging job design have had good results in improving performance and satisfaction.[49] Combined interventions have been found to work better than single interventions.[50]

2. Management Support OD is more likely to succeed when top managers give the OD program their support and are truly committed to the change process and the desired goals of the change program.[51] Also, the expectations for change were not unrealistic.[52]

3. Goals Geared to Both Short- & Long-Term Results Change programs are more successful when they are oriented toward achieving both short-term and long-term results. Managers should not engage in organizational change for the sake of change. Change efforts should produce positive results.[53]

4. OD Is Affected by Culture OD effectiveness is affected by cross-cultural considerations. Thus, an OD intervention that worked in one country should not be blindly applied to a similar situation in another country.[54] ●

Team building. One technique for implementing change is team building. Teams are often diverse in gender, age, ethnicity, and educational background and experience. Would you prefer to work with a highly diverse team of people?

What do I need to know to encourage innovation?

THE BIG PICTURE

Innovation may be a product innovation or a process innovation, an incremental innovation or a radical innovation. Two myths about innovation are that it happens in a "Eureka!" moment and it can be systematized. Ways to encourage innovation are by providing the organizational culture, the resources, and the reward system. To make innovation happen, you need to recognize problems and opportunities, gain allies, overcome employee resistance, and execute well.

Innovation, as we've said earlier in the book, is the activity of creating new ideas and converting them into useful applications—specifically new goods and services. Innovation is more likely to occur when organizations have the proper culture, resources, and reward systems to support it. We now take a closer look into innovation and how it can be encouraged within organizations.

Innovation is different from *invention,* which entails the creation of something new. It is also different from **creativity, which is the process of developing something new or unique.** "You need creativity and invention," says Procter & Gamble CEO A. G. Lafley, "but until you can connect the creativity to the customer in the form of a product or service that meaningfully changes their lives, I would argue you don't have innovation."[55] The spirit of innovation is essential to keeping an organization vital and in maintaining a competitive advantage. Otherwise, the innovation will come from your competitors, forcing you to scramble to catch up—if you can.

How Good Are U.S. Firms at Innovating?

American companies constantly put forth ads touting the spirit of innovation. But how well are they actually doing?

Ironically, a survey of 4,559 corporate managers in 36 industries found that U.S. executives thought their own companies gave innovation or creativity short shrift—only 4% felt their organizations could be respected for their leadership in this area.[56] In another survey, 81% of Chinese believed the United States is staying ahead of China on innovation, but only 41% of Americans agreed.[57] The 2010 Bloomberg BusinessWeek annual rankings of Most Innovative Companies found that the majority of corporations in the top 25 are based outside the United States.[58]

Scholars Larry Selden and Ian MacMillan argue that many firms are focusing their innovation efforts in the wrong way: "Companies are pouring money into their insular R&D [research and development] labs, instead of working to understand what the customer wants and then using the understanding to drive innovation."[59]

Cynthia Barton Rabe, a former innovation strategist for Intel, suggests that too much knowledge and experience can actually kill innovation. "When we become expert," she says, "we often trade our 'what if' flights of fancy for the grounded reality of 'what is,'" thereby limiting our approaches to challenges.[60] (This may be the "curse of knowledge" effect we mentioned in Chapter 7.)[61] Other scholars agree, suggesting that when companies try to come up with new ideas, they too often only look where they always look, when most breakthrough ideas "are typically at the edge of a company's radar screen."[62]

Two Myths about Innovation

Two myths about innovation that need to be dispelled are the following:

Myth No. I: Innovation Happens in a "Eureka!" Moment   Many people think that innovation often happens in a bolt-from-the-blue moment of discovery. In this view, innovation happens as a "Eureka!" or "Aha!" epiphany, like the instant revelation about the law of gravity supposedly experienced by Sir Isaac Newton under a tree when an apple fell on his head. Most of the time, however, innovation is the product of hard work and dedication, "forged by a mixed bag of coworkers from up, down, and across an organization, sitting and wrangling it out in the trenches," in the words of Jack and Suzy Welch.[63]

Myth No. 2: Innovation Can Be Systematized   Lots of people also believe that innovation can be systematized—made a codified and standardized process that can be designed to always yield fruitful results. Obviously, if this could be done, many companies would be doing it. The problem with innovation, however, is that there are too many challenges associated with it, which makes success unpredictable, although it's possible to establish cultural and other conditions (as discussed next) that increase the likelihood of a payoff.

The Seeds of Innovation: Starting Point for Experimentation & Inventiveness

Former Microsoft employee Scott Berkun, author of *The Myths of Innovation,* has identified six *seeds of innovation,* **the starting point for organizational innovation.** They are as follows:[64]

I. Hard Work in a Specific Direction   Most innovations come from dedicated people diligently working to solve a well-defined problem, hard work that can span many years.

2. Hard Work with Direction Change   Innovations frequently occur when people change their approach to solving a problem. In other words, hard work closes some doors and opens others.

3. Curiosity   Innovations can begin when people are curious about something of interest to them, which leads to experimentation and inventiveness.

4. Wealth & Money   Innovations frequently occur because an organization or an individual simply wants to make money. Being near bankruptcy, for instance, drove Fiat, the Italian auto company, to look for innovative ways to cut costs and grow its market share in the United States. This is why Fiat took a stake in Chrysler in return for imparting its knowledge of small-car technology.[65]

5. Necessity   Many innovations grow from the desire to achieve something or to complete a task that is needed to accomplish a broader goal. For example, Xerox Corporation hired a pair of researchers as "innovation managers" to hunt for inventions and products from start-ups in India that Xerox might adapt for uses in North America.[66]

6. Combination of Seeds   Many innovations occur as a result of multiple factors.

Types of Innovation: Product or Process, Incremental or Radical

Innovations may be of the following two types.

Product versus Process Innovations   As a manager, you may need to improve your organization's product or service itself; this is generally a technological innovation. Or you may need to improve the process by which the product or service is created, manufactured, or distributed; this is generally a managerial innovation.

More formally, a **_product innovation_ is a change in the appearance or the performance of a product or a service or the creation of a new one. A _process innovation_ is a change in the way a product or service is conceived, manufactured, or disseminated.**

Today, says an article about the world's most innovative companies, "innovation is about much more than new products. It is about reinventing business processes and building entirely new markets that meet untapped customer needs."[67]

Incremental versus Radical Innovations   An innovation may be small or large. The difference is in modifying versus replacing existing products or services. That is, you might have **_incremental innovations_—the creation of products, services, or technologies that modify existing ones.** Or you might have **_radical innovations_—the creation of products, services, or technologies that replace existing ones.**

Practical Action

What Makes a Successful Start-up?

According to the Ewing Marion Kauffman Foundation, which works to further understanding of entrepreneurship, the vast majority of entrepreneurs (called _replicative entrepreneurs_) are those with small businesses that replicate or duplicate products and services already in existence, such as restaurants and dry cleaners. Less common are those entrepreneurs (_innovative entrepreneurs_) who pioneer never-seen-before products and services or production methods, such as eBay.[68]

Entrepreneurship: Exploiting Niche Opportunities. Some replicative entrepreneurs, however, simply do things better and faster. Amar V. Bhidé, author of _The Origin and Evolution of New Businesses,_ suggests that many successful entrepreneurs start out not by having radical ideas but by making "a small modification in what somebody else is doing."[69] Examples would be a doctor offering a drive-through component for flu shots or a lawyer offering the same for legal services (a feature already available for banks and fast food, of course).

That is, they see a small niche opportunity—one in which the company they are currently working for is already involved, or a supplier or customer is involved. "And the person jumps in [to a new business] with very little preparation and analysis," says Bhidé, "but with direct firsthand knowledge of the profitability of that opportunity—and pretty much does what somebody else is already doing, but does it better and faster."

And "better and faster" seems to be the main difference. Usually, such entrepreneurs don't have anything in the way of technology or concept that differentiates them from other businesses. "They just work harder, hustle for customers, and know that the opportunity may not last for more than six or eight months," says Bhidé. "But they expect to make a reasonable return on those six to eight months. And along the way they'll figure out something else that will keep the business going."

Tolerance for Ambiguity. Another quality of entrepreneurs is "a tolerance for ambiguity," Bhidé says. They are willing to jump into things when it's hard to even imagine what the possible outcomes will be, going ahead in the absence of information, of very much capital—or of even a very novel idea.

An example of a start-up that fit these criteria was Netflix, which rents DVD movies by mail to customers ordering online. This concept does not seem very innovative. The wrinkle, however, which struck founder Reed Hastings when he was charged $40 for returning a movie late to a video rental outfit, is that for a $16.99 monthly subscription customers can keep three films out at a time. "If you rent five or six a month," says one California retired engineer, "you're ahead compared to what you pay at Blockbuster." (Blockbuster has since developed a similar subscription model.) Another differentiating feature: when you rate the movie you rented, Netflix will recommend other movies you might enjoy that you might not have heard of.[70]

The Illusions of Entrepreneurship. Think you'd like to create a start-up yourself and make yourself rich? Before you do, you might want to read *The Illusions of Entrepreneurship* by Case Western Reserve University professor Scott Shane.[71] Shane says that the average new venture will fail within 5 years and that even successful founders earn less than they would as employees—35% less over 10 years. The biggest myth, he says, is that entrepreneurs believe "the growth and performance of their startups depends more on their entrepreneurial talent than on the businesses they choose."

Over the past 20 years, he found, about 4% of all the start-ups in the computer and office equipment industry made *Inc.* magazine's Inc. 500 list of America's fastest-growing companies. But only about 0.005% of start-ups in the hotel and motel industries made that list, and 0.007% of start-ups in eating and drinking establishments. "So that means the odds that you make the Inc. 500 are 840 times higher if you start a computer company than if you start a hotel or motel."[72] (As regards information technology companies, despite the famous example of young entrepreneur Mark Zuckerberg, who created Facebook as a student, the average age of tech company founders is 38.)[73]

Your Call

Suppose you want to be your own boss. What "better and faster" niche opportunity do you see? Assuming it's not a computer company that you're starting, what do you think your chances are of being successful?

Celebrating Failure: Cultural & Other Factors Encouraging Innovation

Innovation doesn't happen as a matter of course. Organizations have to develop ways to make it happen—over and over. Three ways to do so are by providing (1) the right organizational *culture,* (2) the appropriate *resources,* and (3) the correct *reward system.*

I. Culture: Is Innovation Viewed as a Benefit or a Boondoggle?

Unlike most Europeans, who abhor "precariousness," or the absence of security, Americans as a whole seem to be more comfortable with taking risks. As one writer puts it, "Risk, movement, and personal ambition are fundamental. . . . The United States is about the endless possibility of self-invention through hard work. It is inseparable from change."[74]

An organizational culture, as we said in Chapter 8, is the "social glue," or system of shared beliefs and values, that binds members together. An organizational culture that doesn't just allow but *celebrates* failure is vital toward fostering innovation. Most new ideas will fail. Only a few will be successful. But if an organization doesn't encourage this kind of risk taking—if people tend to view experimentation as a boondoggle—that organization won't become a superstar in innovation. Says Procter & Gamble's A. G. Lafley, "You learn more from failure than you do from success, but the key is to fail early, fail cheaply, and don't make the same mistake twice."[75]

The top 15 companies in 2010 with cultures that strongly encourage innovation, according to *Bloomberg BusinessWeek,* are Apple, Google, Microsoft, IBM, Toyota Motor (Japan), Amazon.com, LG Electronics (South Korea), BYD (China), General Electric, Sony (Japan), Samsung Electronics (South Korea), Intel, Ford Motor, Research In Motion (Canada), and Volkswagen (Germany).[76]

Open source innovator. In 1991, computer programmer Linus Torvalds, then a graduate student in Finland, posted his free Linux operating system on the Internet. Linux is a free version of Unix, and its continual improvements result from the efforts of tens of thousands of volunteer programmers. Some companies have extended the "open source" idea by taking a Linux-style approach to innovation that taps thousands of people for inspiration. Indeed, because of the Internet, companies can test new ideas at speeds that were unimaginable even a decade ago. Can you think of any innovations that evolved from masses of people?

2. Resources: Do Managers Put Money Where Their Mouths Are? An
organization's managers may say they encourage innovation, but if they balk at the expense, they aren't putting their money where their mouths are. Innovation doesn't come cheap. Its costs can be measured in all kinds of ways: dollars, time, energy, and focus. For instance, an organization's research and development (R&D) department may need to hire top scientists, whose salaries may be high.

Of course, because there is always competition within an organization for resources, innovation may simply be given short shrift because other concerns seem so urgent—even within a company with a culture encouraging experimentation. But the risk of downgrading innovation in favor of more immediate concerns is that a company may "miss the next wave"—the next big trend, whatever that is.

3. Rewards: Is Experimentation Reinforced in Ways That Matter? Top-
performing salespeople are often rewarded with all kinds of incentives, such as commissions, bonuses, and perks. Are R&D people rewarded the same way? Every year Monsanto Corp., for instance, presents a $50,000 award to the scientist or scientists who developed the largest commercial breakthrough.

The converse is also important: People should not be punished when their attempts to innovate don't work out, or else they won't attempt new things in the future. By the nature of experimentation, the end result can't be foreseen. Top managers at 3M, for instance, recognize that three-fifths of the new ideas suggested each year fail in the marketplace. Only when people attempting an innovation are acting halfheartedly, sloppily, or otherwise incompetently should sanctions such as the withholding of raises and promotions be used.

Example

Achieving Success by Celebrating Failure: 3M's On-Again Off-Again On-Again Culture of Innovation

Courtesy of 3M Company.

The year 2010 marked the 30th anniversary of the Post-it Note, invented by 3M employee Art Fry when he found an experimental adhesive helped him hold bits of paper as bookmarks in his church Sunday services hymnbook.[77] 3M is famous for having a culture of innovation that celebrates taking chances—which means achieving success by celebrating failure.

No Failure, No Success. Only with 20–20 hindsight can people see that a policy of celebrating failure can lead to success. No one can know, when setting out on a new course, whether the effort will yield positive results, and usually, in fact, most such experiments *are* failures. But the *attempts* must be encouraged, or innovation will never happen.

For many years, 3M built innovation into its culture. Mistakes were allowed, destructive criticism was forbidden, experimentation was encouraged, and divisions and individuals were allowed to operate with a good deal of autonomy. 3M set goals decreeing that 25%–30% of annual sales must come from products that were only 5 years old or newer. Investment in

research and development was almost double the rate of that of the average American company.

In addition, 3M employees were permitted to spend 15% of their time pursuing personal research interests that were not related to current company projects, knowing that if their ideas weren't successful, they would be encouraged to pursue other paths. The result was a culture that produced a string of hit products: masking tape, Scotchgard, optical films for coating liquid-crystal display screens.[78]

The Culture Change. That culture changed when a former General Electric executive, James McNerney, took over in 2001 as 3M's CEO and instituted a system known as Six Sigma (discussed in Chapter 16). "Efficiency programs such as Six Sigma are designed to identify problems in work processes—and then use rigorous measurement to reduce variation and eliminate defects," says one account. "When these types of initiatives become ingrained in a company's culture, as they did at 3M, creativity can easily get squelched. After all, a breakthrough innovation is something that challenges existing procedures and norms."[79]

Back to Innovating. By 2007, McNerney was gone, and his successor, George Buckley, was struggling to balance efficiency with innovation, which had declined. During the recent recession, Buckley asked employees to improve products with "tweaks and snips" rather than with a few grandiose inventions.[80] By early 2010, 3M had climbed back to No. 17 on *Fortune's* "Most Admired Companies" list.[81]

YOUR CALL

Oxford University organizational behavior scholar Jerker Denrell believes that there is too much study of successes and not enough of failures, although it's very likely that firms pursuing risky strategies tend to achieve either a very high or very low performance whereas firms pursuing conservative strategies always achieve an average performance.[82]

But while risk taking can lead to either spectacular success or disastrous failure, looking only at successes will show a positive correlation between success and risk taking. Do you think this is true?

How You Can Foster Innovation: Four Steps

If you're going to not just survive but *prevail* as a manager, you need to know how to make innovation happen within an organization. Here we offer four steps for doing so. *(See Figure 10.3.)*

figure 10.3

FOUR STEPS FOR FOSTERING INNOVATION

Source: Adapted from eight steps in K. M. Bartol and D. C. Martin, *Management,* 3rd ed., McGraw-Hill/Irwin, 1998, pp. 360–363. Reprinted with permission of The McGraw-Hill Companies.

1. Recognize Problems & Opportunities & Devise Solutions Change may be needed because you recognize a *problem* or recognize an *opportunity*.

- **Recognizing a problem—find a "better way."** Problems, whether competitive threat, employee turnover, or whatever, tend to seize our attention—and sometimes these problems suggest solutions, such as new business ideas. Example: When Nevada real estate agents Barbara and Marshall Zucker watched the Las Vegas foreclosure rate skyrocket 169% from 2006 to 2007, they also noticed that 40% of all home sales were foreclosed properties. So in 2008 they bought a 24-seat Ford bus, named it the Vegas Foreclosure Express, and began offering prospective buyers tours of repossessed homes, offering 10-minute views of each property.[83]

- **Recognizing an opportunity.** Recognition of opportunities may come from long-term employees who regularly expose themselves to new ideas ("technological gate-keepers" in one phrase).[84] Ideas originating at the grassroots level of an organization may be a particularly fruitful source of innovation.

2. Gain Allies by Communicating Your Vision   Once you've decided how you're going to handle the problem or opportunity, you need to start developing and communicating your vision. You need to create a picture of the future and paint in broad strokes how your innovation will be of benefit. That is, you need to start persuading others inside—and perhaps outside—the organization to support you. Having hard data helps. Others will be more persuaded, for example, if you can demonstrate that a similar idea has been successful in another industry. Or if you can take current trends (such as sales or demographics) and project them into the future.

Among the details you'll need to communicate to gain support are the following:

- **Showing how the product or service will be made.** You must figure out how to profitably make the new product or deliver the new service.

- **Showing how potential customers will be reached.** Innovations may fail because a company can't figure out how to get its new product or service into customers' hands. Thus, you might consider breaking down the task of what the customer wants into discrete steps (a task called *job mapping*), to determine the points at which customers might need help.[85]

- **Demonstrating how you'll beat your competitors.** Other companies may be pursuing the same breakthroughs. Thus, it's better to focus on a smaller number of innovations.

- **Explaining when the innovation will take place.** Timing is important. You'll need to think about when employees will be prepared to make the product and customers primed to buy it.

3. Overcome Employee Resistance, & Empower & Reward Them to Achieve Progress   Once you've persuaded and gotten the blessing of your managerial superiors, then you need to do the same with the people reporting to you. It's possible, of course, that the idea for innovation came from them and that you already have their support.

Alternatively, you may have to overcome their resistance. Then you'll need to remove obstacles that limit them in executing the vision, such as having to get management to sign off on all aspects of a project. Finally, you'll need to hand out periodic rewards—recognition, celebrations, bonuses—for tasks accomplished. And the rewards should not be withheld until the end of the project, which may be many months away, but given out for the successful accomplishment of short-term phases in order to provide constant encouragement.

4. Execute Well   What finally will make or break an organization's attempts at bringing new products and services to market is *execution*—the process, as we stated back in Chapter 6 (Section 6.5), of discussing hows and whats, of using questioning, analysis, and follow-through to achieve the results promised and ensure accountability.[86] Execution requires organizations to effectively manage people, groups, and organizational processes and systems in the pursuit of innovation.

In the end, then, the innovation process must be *managed*. This is precisely what is done at Apple, Google, Microsoft, IBM, Amazon.com, General Electric, Intel, Ford Motor, Research In Motion, and other firms rated tops in the world's innovative companies.[87] ●

10.4 THE THREAT OF CHANGE: MANAGING EMPLOYEE FEAR & RESISTANCE

How are employees threatened by change, and how can I help them adjust?

major question?

THE BIG PICTURE

This section discusses the causes of resistance to change and the degree to which employees fear change, from least threatening to most threatening. It also describes Lewin's three-stage change model: unfreezing, changing, and refreezing. Finally, it describes Kotter's eight steps for leading organizational change, which can be linked to Lewin's three stages.

As a manager, particularly one working for an American organization, you may be pressured to provide short-term, quick-fix solutions. But when applied to organizational problems, this approach usually doesn't work: Quick-fix solutions have little staying power.

What, then, are effective ways to manage organizational change and employees' fear and resistance to it? In this section, we discuss the following:

- The causes of resistance to change.
- The extent to which employees fear change and reasons why employees resist change.
- Lewin's change model.
- Kotter's eight stages for leading organizational change.

The Causes of Resistance to Change[88]

***Resistance to change* is an emotional/behavioral response to real or imagined threats to an established work routine.** Resistance can be as subtle as passive resignation and as overt as deliberate sabotage.

Resistance can be considered to be the interaction of three causes: (1) employee characteristics, (2) change agent characteristics, and (3) the change agent–employee relationship. *(See Figure 10.4.)* For example, an employee's resistance is partly based on his or her perception of change, which is influenced by the attitudes and behaviors exhibited by the change agent and the level of trust between change agent and the employee.

Let us consider these three sources.

figure 10.4

A MODEL OF RESISTANCE TO CHANGE

Source: Adapted from R. Kreitner and A. Kinicki, *Organizational Behavior,* 9th ed., McGraw-Hill/Irwin, 2010, p. 549. Reprinted with permission of The McGraw-Hill Companies.

I. Employee Characteristics   The characteristics of a given employee consist of his or her individual differences (discussed in the next chapter), actions and inactions, and perceptions of change. We describe some of these characteristics in the upcoming subsection "Ten Reasons Employees Resist Change."

2. Change-Agent Characteristics   The characteristics of the change agent—the individual who is a catalyst in helping organizations change—also consist of his or her individual differences, actions and inactions, and perceptions of change. Such characteristics that might contribute to employee resistance to change might include leadership style, personality, tactfulness, sense of timing, awareness of cultural traditions or group relationships, and ability to empathize with the employee's perspective.

3. Change Agent–Employee Relationship   As you might expect, resistance to change is reduced when change agents and employees have a trusting relationship—faith in each other's intentions. Mistrust, on the other hand, encourages secrecy, which begets deeper mistrust, and can doom an otherwise well-conceived change.

The Degree to Which Employees Fear Change: From Least Threatening to Most Threatening

Whether organizational change is administrative or technological, the degree to which employees feel threatened by it in general depends on whether the change is *adaptive, innovative,* or *radically innovative.*[89]

Least Threatening: Adaptive Change   *Adaptive change* **is reintroduction of a familiar practice**—the implementation of a kind of change that has already been experienced within the same organization. This form of change is lowest in complexity, cost, and uncertainty. Because it is familiar, it is the least threatening to employees and thus will create the least resistance.

For example, during annual inventory week, a department store may ask its employees to work 12 hours a day instead of the usual 8. During tax-preparation time, the store's accounting department may imitate this same change in work hours. Although accounting employees are in a different department from stockroom and sales employees, it's expected they wouldn't be terribly upset by the temporary change in hours since they've seen it in effect elsewhere in the store.

Somewhat Threatening: Innovative Change   *Innovative change* **is the introduction of a practice that is new to the organization.** This form of change involves moderate complexity, cost, and uncertainty. It is therefore apt to trigger some fear and resistance among employees.

For example, should a department store decide to adopt a new practice of competitors by staying open 24 hours a day, requiring employees to work flexible schedules, it may be felt as moderately threatening.

Very Threatening: Radically Innovative Change   *Radically innovative change* **involves introducing a practice that is new to the industry.** Because it is the most complex, costly, and uncertain, it will be felt as extremely threatening to managers' confidence and employees' job security and may well tear at the fabric of the organization.[90]

For example, a department store converting some of its operations to e-commerce—selling its goods on the Internet—may encounter anxiety among its staff, especially those fearing being left behind.

Ten Reasons Employees Resist Change Whether changes are adaptive, innovative, or radically innovative, employees may resist them for all kinds of reasons. Ten of the leading ones are as follows.[91]

- **Individual's predisposition toward change.** How people react to change depends a lot on how they learned to handle change and ambiguity as children. One person's parents may have been patient, flexible, and understanding, and from the time the child was weaned she may have learned there were positive compensations for the loss of immediate gratification. Thus, she will associate making changes with love and approval. Another person's parents may have been unreasonable and unyielding, forcing him to do things (piano lessons, for example) that he didn't want to do. Thus, he will be distrustful of making changes because he will associate them with demands for compliance.[92]

- **Surprise and fear of the unknown.** When radically different changes are introduced without warning—for example, without any official announcements—the office rumor mill will go into high gear, and affected employees will become fearful of the implications of the changes. Harvard business scholar Rosabeth Moss Kanter recommends that in such cases a transition manager should be appointed who is charged with keeping all relevant parties adequately informed.[93]

- **Climate of mistrust.** Trust involves reciprocal faith in others' intentions and behavior. Mistrust encourages secrecy, which causes deeper mistrust, putting even well-conceived changes at risk of failure. Managers who trust their employees make the change process an open, honest, and participative affair. Employees who trust their managers are more apt to expend extra effort and take chances with something different.

- **Fear of failure.** Intimidating changes on the job can cause employees to doubt their capabilities. Self-doubt erodes self-confidence and cripples personal growth and development.

- **Loss of status or job security.** Administrative and technological changes that threaten to alter power bases or eliminate jobs—as often happens during corporate restructurings that threaten middle-management jobs—generally trigger strong resistance.

- **Peer pressure.** Even people who are not themselves directly affected by impending changes may actively resist in order to protect the interests of their friends and co-workers.

- **Disruption of cultural traditions or group relationships.** Whenever individuals are transferred, promoted, or reassigned, it can disrupt existing cultural and group relationships. Example: Traditionally Sony Corp. promoted insiders to new positions. When an outsider, Howard Stringer, was named as the next chairman and CEO and six corporate officers were asked to resign, creating a majority board of foreigners, the former CEO, Nobuyuki Idei, worried the moves might engender strong employee resistance.[94]

- **Personality conflicts.** Just as a friend can get away with telling us something we would resent hearing from an adversary, the personalities of change agents can breed resistance.

- **Lack of tact or poor timing.** Introducing changes in an insensitive manner or at an awkward time can create employee resistance. Employees are more apt to accept changes when managers effectively explain their value, as, for example, in demonstrating their strategic purpose to the organization.

- **Nonreinforcing reward systems.** Employees are likely to resist when they can't see any positive rewards from proposed changes, as, for example, when one is asked to work longer hours without additional compensation.

To gauge how adaptable you're apt to be to organizational change, try the Self-Assessment at the end of this chapter.

Lewin's Change Model: Unfreezing, Changing, & Refreezing

Most theories of organizational change originated with the landmark work of social psychologist **Kurt Lewin.** Lewin developed a model with three stages—*unfreezing, changing,* and *refreezing*—to explain how to initiate, manage, and stabilize planned change.[95]

I. "Unfreezing": Creating the Motivation to Change
In the *unfreezing stage,* managers try to instill in employees the motivation to change, encouraging them to let go of attitudes and behaviors that are resistant to innovation. For this "unfreezing" to take place, employees need to become dissatisfied with the old way of doing things. Managers also need to reduce the barriers to change during this stage.

2. "Changing": Learning New Ways of Doing Things
In the *changing stage,* employees need to be given the tools for change: new information, new perspectives, new models of behavior. Managers can help here by providing benchmarking results, role models, mentors, experts, and training. It's advisable, experts say, to convey the idea that change is a continuous learning process, not just a onetime event.[96]

3. "Refreezing": Making the New Ways Normal
In the *refreezing stage,* employees need to be helped to integrate the changed attitudes and behavior into their normal ways of doing things. Managers can assist by encouraging employees to exhibit the new change and then, through additional coaching and modeling, by reinforcing the employees in the desired change. *(See Table 10.1.)*

One technique used in Stage 1, to help unfreeze organizations, is **benchmarking, a process by which a company compares its performance with that of high-performing organizations.**[97] Professional sports teams do this all the time, but so do other kinds of organizations, including nonprofit ones.

For example, one company discovered that its costs to develop a computer system were twice those of competitors and that the time to get a new product to market was four times longer. These data were ultimately used to unfreeze employees' attitudes and motivate people to change the organization's internal processes in order to remain competitive.[98]

Kotter's Eight Steps for Leading Organizational Change

An expert in leadership and change management, **John Kotter** believes that, to be successful, organizational change needs to follow eight steps to avoid the eight common errors senior management usually commits.[99] *(See Table 10.2.)* These correspond with Lewin's unfreezing-changing-refreezing steps.

Steps 1–4 represent unfreezing: establish a sense of urgency, create the guiding coalition, develop a vision and strategy, and communicate the change vision.

Steps 5–7 represent the changing stage: empower broad-based action, generate short-term wins, and consolidate gains and produce more change.

---

table 10.1

SIX METHODS FOR MANAGING EMPLOYEE RESISTANCE TO CHANGE

I. Education and communication
2. Participation and involvement
3. Facilitation and support
4. Negotiation and rewards
5. Manipulation and cooptation
6. Explicit and implicit coercion

Source: Adapted from J. P. Kotter and L. A. Schlesinger, "Choosing Strategies for Change," *Harvard Business Review,* March–April 1979, pp. 106–114.

table 10.2

**STEPS TO LEADING
ORGANIZATIONAL CHANGE**

Step	Description
1. Establish a sense of urgency.	Unfreeze the organization by creating a compelling reason for why change is needed.
2. Create the guiding coalition.	Create a cross-functional, cross-level group of people with enough power to lead the change.
3. Develop a vision and a strategy.	Create a vision and a strategic plan to guide the change process.
4. Communicate the change vision.	Create and implement a communication strategy that consistently communicates the new vision and strategic plan.
5. Empower broad-based action.	Eliminate barriers to change, and use target elements of change to transform the organization. Encourage risk taking and creative problem solving.
6. Generate short-term wins.	Plan for and create short-term "wins" or improvements. Recognize and reward people who contribute to the wins.
7. Consolidate gains and produce more change.	The guiding coalition uses credibility from short-term wins to create more change. Additional people are brought into the change process as change cascades throughout the organization. Attempts are made to reinvigorate the change process.
8. Anchor new approaches in the culture.	Reinforce the changes by highlighting connections between new behaviors and processes and organizational success. Develop methods to ensure leadership development and succession.

Source: Reprinted by permission of Harvard Business School Press. From *Leading Change* by J. P. Kotter. Copyright © 1996 by the Harvard Business School Publishing Corporation; all rights reserved.

Step 8, corresponding to refreezing, is to anchor new approaches in the organization's culture.

The value of Kotter's steps is that they provide specific recommendations about behaviors that managers need to exhibit to successfully lead organizational change. It is important to remember that Kotter's research reveals that it is ineffective to skip steps and that successful organizational change is 70%–90% leadership and only 10%–30% management. Senior managers are thus advised to focus on leading rather than on managing change.[100] ●

Lookalikes. One key to the success of Southwest Airlines is that all the planes in its fleet have been the same type, Boeing 737s, which saves on maintenance and training costs. As Southwest expands from being a short-haul, low-fare carrier to running long-haul flights as well, it has needed to add new-generation 737s, which can travel longer distances than the older planes did. Southwest still offers no-frills service—no seat assignments and snacks instead of meals—and competes principally on fare price. In evolving from short routes to long ones, should the company expect to have to undergo any of the steps in Lewin's change model—unfreezing, changing, and refreezing?

adaptive change 326
benchmarking 328
change agent 315
creativity 318
incremental innovations 320
innovative change 326

intervention 316
organizational development (OD) 315
proactive change 311
process innovation 320
product innovation 320

radical innovations 320
radically innovative change 326
reactive change 310
resistance to change 325
seeds of innovation 319
technology 313

Summary

 IO.I The Nature of Change in Organizations
Among supertrends shaping the future of business: (1) The marketplace is becoming more segmented and moving toward more niche products. (2) There are more competitors offering targeted products, requiring faster speed-to-market. (3) Some traditional companies may not survive radically innovative change. (4) China, India, and other offshore suppliers are changing the way we work. (5) Knowledge, not information, is becoming the new competitive advantage.

Two types of change are reactive and proactive. Reactive change is making changes in response to problems or opportunities as they arise. Proactive change involves making carefully thought-out changes in anticipation of possible or expected problems or opportunities.

Forces for change may consist of forces outside the organization or inside it. (1) External forces consist of four types: demographic characteristics, market changes, technological advancements, and social and political pressures. (2) Internal forces may be of two types: employee problems and managers' behavior.

Four areas in which change is most apt to be needed are people, technology, structure, and strategy. (1) People changes may require changes in perceptions, attitudes, performance, or skills. (2) Technology is any machine or process that enables an organization to gain a competitive advantage in changing materials used to produce a finished product. (3) Changing structure may happen when one organization acquires

another. (4) Changing strategy may occur because of changes in the marketplace.

 IO.2 Organizational Development: What It Is, What It Can Do
Organizational development (OD) is a set of techniques for implementing planned change to make people and organizations more effective. Often OD is put into practice by a change agent, a consultant with a background in behavioral sciences who can be a catalyst in helping organizations deal with old problems in new ways. OD can be used to manage conflict, revitalize organizations, and adapt to mergers.

The OD process follows a three-step process: (1) Diagnosis attempts to ascertain the problem. (2) Intervention is the attempt to correct the diagnosed problems. (3) Evaluation attempts to find out how well the intervention worked.

Four factors that make OD work successfully are (1) multiple interventions are used; (2) top managers give the OD program their support; (3) goals are geared to both short- and long-term results; and (4) OD is affected by culture.

 IO.3 Promoting Innovation within the Organization
Innovation is different from invention, which entails the creation of something new. It is also different from creativity, which is the process of developing something new or unique. Two myths about innovation are (1) innovation happens in a "Eureka!" moment and (2) innovation can be systematized.

The starting point for organizational innovation involves the six seeds of innovation: (1) innovation comes from dedicated people working to solve a well defined problem; (2) innovations often occur when people change their approach to solving a problem; (3) innovations can begin when people are curious about something of interest to them; (4) innovation happens because an organization wants to make money; (5) many innovations grow from the desire to achieve something; and (6) many innovations occur as a result of multiple factors.

Innovations may be a product innovation or a process innovation. A product innovation is a change in the appearance or performance of a product or service or the creation of a new one. A process innovation is a change in the way a product or service is conceived, manufactured, or disseminated. Innovations may also be an incremental innovation or a radical innovation. An incremental innovation is the creation of a product, service, or technology that modifies an existing one. A radical innovation is the creation of a product, service, or technology that replaces an existing one.

Innovation doesn't happen as a matter of course. Three ways to make it happen are to provide the right organizational culture, so that it is viewed as a benefit rather than as a boondoggle; to provide the resources; and to provide the rewards, so that experimentation is reinforced in ways that matter. Four steps for fostering innovation are as follows. (1) Recognize problems and opportunities and devise solutions. (2) Gain allies by communicating your vision. (3) Overcome employee resistance and empower and reward them to achieve progress. (4) Execute well by effectively managing people, groups, and organizational processes and systems in the pursuit of innovation.

 ### 10.4 The Threat of Change: Managing Employee Fear & Resistance

Resistance to change is an emotional/behavioral response to real or imagined threats to an established work routine. Resistance can be considered to be the interaction of three causes: (1) employee characteristics, (2) change agent characteristics, and (3) the change agent–employee relationship.

The degree to which employees feel threatened by change depends on whether the change is adaptive, innovative, or radically innovative. Adaptive change, the least threatening, is reintroduction of a familiar practice. Innovative change is the introduction of a practice that is new to the organization. Radically innovative change, the most threatening, involves introducing a practice that is new to the industry.

Ten reasons employees resist change are as follows: (1) individuals' predisposition toward change; (2) surprise and fear of the unknown; (3) climate of mistrust; (4) fear of failure; (5) loss of status or job security; (6) peer pressure; (7) disruption of cultural traditions or group relationships; (8) personality conflicts; (9) lack of tact or poor timing; and (10) nonreinforcing reward systems.

Kurt Lewin's change model has three stages—unfreezing, changing, and refreezing—to explain how to initiate, manage, and stabilize planned change. (1) In the unfreezing stage, managers try to instill in employees the motivation to change. One technique used is benchmarking, a process by which a company compares its performance with that of high-performing organizations. (2) In the changing stage, employees need to be given the tools for change, such as new information. (3) In the refreezing stage, employees need to be helped to integrate the changed attitudes and behavior into their normal behavior.

In a model corresponding with Lewin's, John Kotter suggests an organization needs to follow eight steps to avoid the eight common errors senior management usually commits. The first four represent unfreezing: establish a sense of urgency, create the guiding coalition, develop a vision and strategy, and communicate the change vision. The next three steps represent the changing stage: empower broad-based action, generate short-term wins, and consolidate gains and produce more change. The last step, corresponding to refreezing, is to anchor new approaches in the organization's culture.

General Motors Undergoes Major Organizational Change to Survive

The 15 General Motors dealers who flew to Detroit [in September 2009] for a dinner with GM management were not an easily rattled bunch. They had endured the worst auto sales slide in 25 years, as well as the bankruptcy of the iconic carmaker on which they had built their businesses. Only three months had passed since GM accepted a $50 billion federal bailout, announcing the retirement of four of its eight brands and the shutting down of 1,900 dealers—a third of its domestic retail network. These dealers were the survivors, some of the more prosperous people in their towns, and they wanted a little reassurance.

CEO Fritz Henderson gathered the group in a private conference room at the Westin Detroit Metro Airport and tried to demonstrate that he had a plan, according to an executive in the room who asked not to be named because he was not authorized to describe the dinner. Henderson announced that GM was going on the offensive with better models, new marketing, and a plan to remake its sclerotic corporate culture. Then he introduced the other GM boss in the room, the one the government had sent to keep an eye on the company.

Edward E. Whitacre Jr., a laconic, squinty-eyed, six-foot-four-inch Texan, had been GM's non-executive chairman for barely two months. He was typically blunt. "We're going to get this turned around," Whitacre promised. And if the current leadership can't fix the company, he said, "we'll find someone who can.". . .

Not Henderson, as it turns out. Whitacre and the board fired him on December 1, ending his tryout on day 143. The board, reconstituted in July with Whitacre and seven other new members joining five others from the old guard, had been skeptical that Henderson, a GM lifer, was radical enough to change the company. Whitacre—the former telecom executive who turned a broken Baby Bell into the resurgent AT&T—decided he was the man to fix GM. "Fritz was moving to change things," says an executive with direct knowledge of the decision who was not authorized to speak about it. "But a lot more needed to be done.". . .

Within three months of Henderson's ouster, he had eased out four other executives, reassigned 20 more, and brought in seven outsiders to fill top jobs—a shock to an insular company that had long been famous for paving over failure while compensating it

handsomely. The tide also swept out solid performers allied with the old regime, such as Vice-Chairman Bob Lutz, who had overseen the development of the Chevy Malibu, the Cadillac CTS, and eight other vehicles that were beginning to sell well. Lutz was marginalized by Whitacre and announced his retirement, effective May 1. "In the past," says Lutz, "GM was accused of not enough change. You have to find the balance between the pace of change and trauma to the organization."

People close to Whitacre say he would rather cope with trauma than accept the status quo at a company that lost $84.3 million a day in 2008. Three days after taking over, he reorganized sales and marketing, and then, after just three months, let his deputy reorganize the departments again—a restructuring of the restructuring that caused middle managers to fear for their jobs and even question whether Whitacre had the right disposition for his. Some say the fear has made them more cautious when Whitacre wants them to take more risk. . . .

Former CEO Rick Wagoner, who lost $88 billion between 2005 and 2009, used a dozen metrics to evaluate his executives. Whitacre, who holds just one meeting per week with his 13-member management team, has boiled it down to six: market share, revenue, operating profit, cash flow, quality, and customer satisfaction. He wants nimble managers who decide fast and correct mistakes faster. . . .

The two people tasked with remaking GM's image with consumers, North American President Mark L. Reuss and Marketing Vice-President Susan Docherty, are in their 40s and taking on massive responsibility for the first time in their careers. "He realizes the biggest change GM needs is cultural," says Jim Kahan, who was senior vice-president for corporate strategy under Whitacre at AT&T. . . .

Now Whitacre is rushing to take the company public and recoup most or all of the Treasury Department's $40 billion equity stake in GM. On April 21 [2010], Whitacre announced that GM had finished paying off $8.4 billion to the Governments of the U.S., Canada, and Ontario five years ahead of schedule. . . .

The U.S. still owns $2 billion in preferred shares, which GM will buy back, and 61% of the company. Canada owns 11.7%, while the United Auto Workers' retiree health-care fund holds 17.5%, and bondholders 10%. . . .

Whitacre wants GM to take big risks, too. After the company launches its Chevrolet Volt electric car in November, it hopes to sell 45,000 globally in 2011, a huge number for a $40,000 compact car that needs to be plugged in at night. Demand for electric cars in unproven; less expensive hybrids have grabbed only 2% of the total market in a decade. Whitacre told GM staff that he thinks the Volt will be a hit and wants them to boost production. If he's wrong, the Volt (which is already unlikely to make money because of its steep development costs and $8,000 battery) will generate even more red ink. . . .

In Whitacre's first months on the job he merged marketing and sales—easing out the 78-year-old Lutz, putting Susan Docherty, 47, in charge of both, and handing the North American organization to Reuss. It took Reuss three months to conclude that Whitacre's new structure was a flop. Docherty, a stylish hard-charger who raced up GM's ranks while working for Hummer and GMC trucks, often told her staff that the new GM would demand long hours. If anyone didn't like it, they should go, she told *BusinessWeek* last year. Yet the job proved too much even for her. After several meetings with Whitacre, Reuss split sales and marketing again on March 2. Docherty went from head of sales to vice-president for marketing.

Whitacre realized that all of the change had rattled the workforce, so on March 31 he sent a companywide e-mail, obtained by *Bloomberg Businessweek*. "A smart company changes and adapts to the needs of the business. So, while there will always be individual moves within GM, I want to reassure you that the major leadership changes are behind us."

It will take more than e-mails to prove GM is stable. Few believed Whitacre's letter, says a senior GM product developer who requested anonymity because he doesn't want to anger the boss. Everyone is on pins and needles, he says. . . .

Whitacre wants to roll out the cars faster, but some product developers say he's naïve about how long it takes to bring a product to market. After nine months inside GM, he will still stroll up to a clay model and ask why it can't be in showrooms in a year, griped one designer, who asked not to be named. It typically takes three. Whitacre can't change that—and he knows better than to micromanage the car guys. He doesn't attend Vice-Chairman Tom Stephens' Thursday morning product development meetings; he lets Stephens and chief designer Ed Welburn come up with the models, then approves funding.

In his race to get GM ready for an IPO, Whitacre has delegated a lot to Reuss. His mission is to build sales without pumping up profit-eating incentives.

For years, says Duane Paddock, a Buffalo, New York Chevy dealer, GM built as many cars as it hoped to sell and strong-armed the dealers into taking the inventory. If that didn't work, GM would lay on heavy rebates and give away profit to get the sales volume.

At the same time, dealers complained that they had to subscribe to an outside service to track the incentives GM is offering on various models. GM gives the dealers that information, but in reports so complex that many dealers have trouble deciphering them.

On Whitacre's orders, Reuss is trying to demystify the process. In March, embattled Toyota spent a company record amount on incentives to lure back wary consumers, offering 0% financing and other discounts. Reuss refused to get pulled in, dropping GM's average incentive from last year by $1,200 a car, to $3,500. GM's market share tumbled to 17.6% in March from 19.4% during January and February. But Reuss kept prices up and beat his sales goals. As March was coming to a close, Whitacre looked at the numbers and said: "This looks like we're headed toward growth in a positive way," Reuss recalls. "That's good.". . .

Whitacre had his prairie charm working in March, when he paid his first visit to a GM assembly plant. At the Malibu factory in Fairfax, Kansas, he walked the assembly line in jeans and a plain black sweatshirt, stopping to shake hands with workers and ask them what they did. He even tried to hang a body panel on a Malibu. "They nearly threw me out of the building," he joked later to workers and reporters. One worker said that in 25 years on the line he had never seen a GM CEO.

Whitacre then held a series of "diagonal slice meetings" with employees from all levels of the factory. Some liked that he didn't come at them with edicts about boosting production. Instead, says Dave Robertson, a 29-year line worker who attended one of the meetings, he just said GM needed to "sell more cars." He told the workers they could help by building quality vehicles, and if they needed anything, they should say so. "We're all in this together," he said, promising to come back in a month to talk about "the future of the plant."

For Discussion

1. Which of the forces for change are causing GM to undertake major organizational change? Explain.

2. Which of the four targeted areas of change is GM focusing on? Provide examples.

3. How can Whitacre increase innovation within GM? Provide specific recommendations.

4. Why are some GM employees resisting change? Explain.

5. How might GM use Lewin's and Kotter's models of change to increase the probability of achieving positive organizational change? Provide specific recommendations.

Source: Excerpted from David Welch, "Ed Whitacre's Battle to Save GM from Itself," *Bloomberg BusinessWeek*, May 3–9, 2010, pp. 48–54. Reprinted with permission.

Self-Assessment

How Adaptable Are You?

Objectives
1. To assess your adaptability.
2. To examine how being adaptable can help you cope with organizational change.

Introduction
Ultimately all organizational change passes through an organization's people. People who adapt more easily are better suited to cope with organizational changes, and so they clearly are important assets to any organization. The purpose of this exercise is to determine your adaptability.

Instructions
Read the following statements. Using the scale provided, circle the number that indicates the extent to which you agree or disagree with each statement:

1 = strongly disagree
2 = disagree
3 = neither agree nor disagree
4 = agree
5 = strongly agree

1. In emergency situations, I react with clear, focused thinking and maintain emotional control in order to step up to the necessary actions.	1 2 3 4 5	
2. In stressful circumstances, I don't overreact to unexpected news. I keep calm, focused, and manage frustration well.	1 2 3 4 5	
3. I solve problems creatively by turning them inside out and upside down looking for new approaches to solving them that others may have missed.	1 2 3 4 5	
4. I easily change gears in response to uncertain or unexpected events, effectively adjusting my priorities, plans, goals, and actions.	1 2 3 4 5	
5. I enjoy learning new ways to do my work and I do what is necessary to keep my knowledge and skills current.	1 2 3 4 5	
6. I adjust easily to changes in my workplace by participating in assignments or training that prepare me for these changes.	1 2 3 4 5	
7. I am flexible and open-minded with others. I listen and consider others' viewpoints, adjusting my own when necessary.	1 2 3 4 5	
8. I am open to both negative and positive feedback. I work well in teams.	1 2 3 4 5	

9. I take action to learn and understand the values of other groups, organizations, or cultures. I adjust my own behavior to show respect for different customs.	1	2	3	4	5
10. I adjust easily to differing environmental states such as extreme heat, humidity, cold, or dirtiness.	1	2	3	4	5
11. I frequently push myself to complete strenuous or demanding tasks.	1	2	3	4	5
Total					_____

Interpretation

When you are done, add up your responses to get your total score to see how adaptable you are. Arbitrary norms for adaptability:

11–24 = Low adaptability

25–39 = Moderate adaptability

40–55 = High adaptability

Questions for Discussion

1. Were you surprised by your results? Why or why not?

2. Look at the areas where your score was the lowest. What are some skills you can work on or gain to increase your adaptability? Describe and explain.

3. What are some ways being adaptable can improve the way you handle change? Discuss.

Adapted from S. Arad, M. A. Donovan, K. E. Plamondon, and E. D. Pulakos, "Adaptability in the Workplace: Development of Taxonomy of Adaptive Performance," *Journal of Applied Psychology*, August 2000, pp. 612–624.

Ethical Dilemma

Is It Ethical to Target the Homeless for Admittance into For-Profit Universities?

Benson Rollins wants a college degree. The unemployed high school dropout who attends Alcoholics Anonymous and has been homeless for 10 months is being courted by the University of Phoenix. Two of its recruiters got themselves invited to a Cleveland shelter last October and pitched the advantages of going to the country's largest for-profit college to 70 destitute men.

Their visit spurred the 23-year-old Rollins to fill out an online form expressing interest. Phoenix salespeople then barraged him with phone calls and e-mails, urging a tour of its Cleveland campus. "If higher education is important to you for professional growth, and to achieve your academic goals, why wait any longer? Classes start soon and space is limited," one Phoenix employee e-mailed him on April 15. "I'll be happy to walk you through the entire application process.". . .

Rollins' experience is increasingly common. The boom in for-profit education, driven by a political consensus that all Americans need more than a high school diploma, has intensified efforts to recruit the homeless. Such disadvantaged students are desirable because they qualify for federal grants and loans, which are largely responsible for the prosperity of for-profit colleges. Federal aid to students at for-profit colleges jumped from $4.6 billion in 2000 to $26.5 billion in 2009. Publicly traded higher education companies derive three-fourths of their revenue from federal funds, with Phoenix at 86%, up from just 48% in 2001 and approaching the 90% limit set by federal law.

The privately held Drake College of Business, which trains people to be medical and dental assistants, relied on taxpayers for 87% of its revenue in 2007. Almost 5% of the student body at its Newark (New Jersey) branch is homeless, says Jean Aoun, director of admissions and student services there. Late in 2008 it began offering a $350 biweekly stipend to students who show up for 80% of classes and maintain a "C" average. . . "It would put money in my pocket, help me buy a car," adds Jerome Nickens, 45, who lived at the mission when he talked to a Drake representative but decided not to enroll. . . .

While many caseworkers for the homeless are gratified by the attention, some see only exploitation. The companies "are preying upon people who are already vulnerable and can't make it through a university," says Sara Cohen, a case manager at Shelter Now in Meriden, Connecticut. "It's evil.". . .

Because they don't have to repay their educational loans until they leave school, some homeless students spend beyond their means. Kim Rose, a recovering crack cocaine addict and ex-offender in Raleigh, North Carolina, began pursuing an online bachelor's degree in business last November at Capella Education's Capella University, based in Minneapolis. At the time she was staying in a drug-free program with Internet access. Rose, 38, receives almost $4,000 each academic quarter in federal grants and loans for tuition and living expenses. She splurged last Christmas, spending $700 of her financial aid on presents for her seven-year-old son, who has lived with his grandmother. "I got him everything he wanted," Rose said in a telephone interview. "Games, toys. He's a guitar freak, I got him a guitar. To make up for me not being there."

In February, Rose moved into a shelter where the only computer was broken. As a result, she has struggled to keep up, dropping an English composition course. . . .

In the end Benson Rollins didn't succumb to Phoenix's hard sell. He is taking a class for his high school equivalency degree and hopes to study law enforcement in college. For now, he would like a job so he can pay child support for his one-year-old daughter, whom he rarely sees.

The Phoenix recruiters, he says, failed to mention a critical point: He would have to take out a government loan at 5% to 7% interest to pay the $10,000-plus annual tuition. "I'm in a homeless shelter, and money is hard to come by," Rollins says. "It's not worth going to school to end up in debt."

Solving the Dilemma

What is your feeling about for-profit universities targeting the homeless?

1. There is nothing wrong with this practice. The homeless should be given equal opportunity to attend a university.

2. This practice should be stopped because it drives up our federal expenses. The taxpayer ultimately pays these bills because many of these individuals default on their loans.

3. This practice should be stopped because many of these individuals are not prepared or academically qualified to attend a university.

4. Invent other options.

Source: Excerpted from Daniel Golden, "Hardselling the Homeless," *Bloomberg BusinessWeek*, May 3–9, 2010, pp. 64–68. Reprinted with permission.

Managing Individual Differences & Behavior

Supervising People as People

Major Questions You Should Be Able to Answer

11.1 Personality & Individual Behavior

Major Question: In the hiring process, do employers care about one's personality and individual traits?

11.2 Values, Attitudes, & Behavior

Major Question: How do the hidden aspects of individuals—their values and attitudes—affect employee behavior?

11.3 Work-Related Attitudes & Behaviors Managers Need to Deal With

Major Question: Is it important for managers to pay attention to employee attitudes?

11.4 Perception & Individual Behavior

Major Question: What are the distortions in perception that can cloud one's judgment?

11.5 Understanding Stress & Individual Behavior

Major Question: What causes workplace stress, and how can it be reduced?

Managing Gen Y: What's Different about Today's Generation of Younger Workers

Are the Gen Yers (the 75 million so-called Millennials, born between 1977 and 1994) really so different from earlier generations (the 78 million Baby Boomers, born 1946–1964, and 49 million Gen Xers, 1965–1976)? Does this new crop of twentysomethings—perhaps you're in this group—that is now the largest bloc of employees in the workforce (followed by Boomers) need to be managed in different ways? Experts say the answer to both questions is yes.[1]

Some major characteristics of Gen Yers are as follows: (1) They are extremely independent, because many were raised as day care or latchkey kids by two working parents or by a divorced, single parent, and so they have been left alone to make their own decisions. (2) They are tech-savvy, used to cell phones and the Internet as means of communication and accustomed to a faster pace of life. (3) They are racially and ethnically diverse. (4) They are probably the most educated in American history. (5) While in general they are confident, they are financially anxious and worry that they can't meet their educational, housing, and health care needs.

In the workplace, these translate into a skepticism about rules, policies, and procedures; a requirement for more autonomy; and a need for constant stimulation. What Gen Yers are looking for in the workplace is not only a good income and good relationships with their bosses and co-workers but also challenging daily work, the opportunity for growth, the chance to show off skills and be recognized for their accomplishments, casual dress environment, and flexible schedules for social and personal time.

What should leaders do in managing this group? Here are some suggestions:

- **Allow them independent decision making and expression:** Gen Yers are impatient, skeptical, and blunt and expressive, but they are used to adapting and making decisions. Show appreciation for their individuality and let them participate in decision making.

- **Train them and mentor them:** As the most education-oriented generation in history, Millennials are strongly attracted to education and training, the best kind not being classroom training but forms of independent learning. At the same time, they should be given the chance to create long-term bonds with mentors.

- **Give them constant feedback and recognition:** Gen Yers need to know they are making an impact and need to be recognized for their workplace contributions. Thus, supervisors should show them how their work contributes to the bottom line. This generation revels in, even craves, constant praise, so managers should provide rewards in the form of praise, flextime, and extra responsibility.

- **Provide them with access to technology:** To attract and retain Generation Y employees, companies need to provide the newest and best technology.

- **Create customized career paths:** Gen Yers would most like to be self-employed, but few are able to do it because of high start-up costs. Employers can reinforce the sense of control that this generation desires by providing them with a realistic account of their progress and their future within the organization.

For Discussion As a worker, you might hope to be led by someone who would follow the preceding suggestions. But suppose your boss is of the old "tough guy" school and doesn't manage this way. In a difficult job market, would you stick it out? How would you try to let your supervisor know how you would prefer to be managed?

forecast · What's Ahead in This Chapter

This first of five chapters on leadership discusses how to manage for individual differences and behaviors. We describe personality and individual behavior; values, attitudes, and behavior; and specific work-related attitudes and behaviors managers need to be aware of. We next discuss distortions in perception, which can affect managerial judgment. Finally, we consider what stress does to individuals.

major question ?

In the hiring process, do employers care about one's personality and individual traits?

THE BIG PICTURE

Personality consists of stable psychological and behavioral attributes that give you your identity. We describe five personality dimensions and five personality traits that managers need to be aware of to understand workplace behavior.

In this and the next four chapters we discuss the third management function (after planning and organizing)—namely, leading. *Leading,* as we said in Chapter 1, is defined as *motivating, directing, and otherwise influencing people to work hard to achieve the organization's goals.*

How would you describe yourself? Are you outgoing? aggressive? sociable? tense? passive? lazy? quiet? Whatever the combination of traits, which result from the interaction of your genes and your environment, they constitute your personality. More formally, **personality consists of the stable psychological traits and behavioral attributes that give a person his or her identity.**[2] As a manager, you need to understand personality attributes because they affect how people perceive and act within the organization.

The Big Five Personality Dimensions

In recent years, the many personality dimensions have been distilled into a list of factors known as the Big Five.[3] **The *Big Five personality dimensions* are (1) extroversion, (2) agreeableness, (3) conscientiousness, (4) emotional stability, and (5) openness to experience.**

- **Extroversion.** How outgoing, talkative, sociable, and assertive a person is.
- **Agreeableness.** How trusting, good-natured, cooperative, and soft-hearted one is.
- **Conscientiousness.** How dependable, responsible, achievement-oriented, and persistent one is.
- **Emotional stability.** How relaxed, secure, and unworried one is.
- **Openness to experience.** How intellectual, imaginative, curious, and broad-minded one is.

Assertive and sociable. Does it take a certain kind of personality to be a good salesperson? Have you ever known people who were quiet, unassuming, even shy but who were nevertheless very persistent and persuasive—that is, good salespeople?

Standardized personality tests are used to score people on each dimension to draw a person's personality profile that is supposedly as unique as his or her fingerprints. For example, if you scored low on the first trait, extroversion, you would presumably be prone to shy and withdrawn behavior. If you scored low on emotional stability, you supposedly would be nervous, tense, angry, and worried.

Do Personality Tests Work for the Workplace?

As a manager, you would want to know if personality testing in general and the Big Five model in particular can help predict behavior in the workplace. Is a personality test helpful in predicting a match between personality and job performance? Two findings:

- **Extroversion—the outgoing personality.** As might be expected, extroversion (an outgoing personality) has been associated with success for managers and salespeople. Also, extroversion is a stronger predictor of job performance than agreeableness, across all professions, according to researchers. "It appears that being courteous, trusting, straightforward, and soft-hearted [that is, agreeableness] has a smaller impact on job performance," conclude the researchers, "than being talkative, active, and assertive [that is, extroversion]."[4]

- **Conscientiousness—the dependable personality.** Conscientiousness (strong work ethic) has been found to have the strongest positive correlation with job performance and training performance. According to researchers, "those individuals who exhibit traits associated with a strong sense of purpose, obligation, and persistence generally perform better than those who do not."[5]

The table below presents tips to help managers avoid abuses and discrimination lawsuits when using personality and psychological testing for employment decisions.[6] *(See Table 11.1.)*

table 11.1   CAUTIONS ABOUT USING PERSONALITY TESTS IN THE WORKPLACE

• *Use professionals.* Rely on reputable, licensed psychologists for selecting and overseeing the administration, scoring, and interpretation of personality and psychological tests. This is particularly important, since not every psychologist is expert at these kinds of tests.	• *Don't hire on the basis of personality test results alone.* Supplement any personality test data with information from reference checks, personal interviews, ability tests, and job performance records. Also avoid hiring people on the basis of specified personality profiles. As a case in point, there is no distinct "managerial personality."	• *Be alert for gender, racial, and ethnic bias.* Regularly assess any possible adverse impact of personality tests on the hiring of women and minorities. This is truly a matter of great importance, since you don't want to find your company (or yourself) embroiled in a lawsuit at some point downstream.	• *Graphology tests don't work, but integrity tests do.* Personality traits and aptitudes cannot be inferred from samples of people's penmanship, as proponents of graphology tests claim. However, dishonest job applicants can often be screened by integrity tests, since dishonest people are reportedly unable to fake conscientiousness, even on a paper-and-pencil test.

The Proactive Personality A person who scores well on the Big Five dimension of conscientiousness is probably a good worker. He or she may also be a *proactive personality,* **someone who is more apt to take initiative and persevere to influence the environment.**[7] People of this sort identify opportunities and act on them, which makes them associated not only with success—individual, team, and organizational—but also with entrepreneurship.

Five Traits Important in Organizations

Five of the most important personality traits that managers need to be aware of to understand workplace behavior are (1) *locus of control,* (2) *self-efficacy,* (3) *self-esteem,* (4) *self-monitoring,* and (5) *emotional intelligence.*

I. Locus of Control: "I Am/Am Not the Captain of My Fate"   As we discussed briefly in Chapter 1, *locus of control* **indicates how much people believe they control their fate through their own efforts.** If you have an *internal locus of control,* you believe you control your own destiny. If you have an *external locus of control,* you believe external forces control you.

Research shows internals and externals have important workplace differences. Internals exhibit less anxiety, greater work motivation, and stronger expectations that effort leads to performance. They also obtain higher salaries.[8]

These findings have two important implications for managers:

- **Expect different degrees of structure and compliance for each type.** Employees with internal locus of control will probably resist close managerial supervision. Hence, they should probably be placed in jobs requiring high initiative and lower compliance. By contrast, employees with external locus of control might do better in highly structured jobs requiring greater compliance.

- **Employ different reward systems for each type.**   Since internals seem to have a greater belief that their actions have a direct effect on the consequences of that action, internals likely would prefer and respond more productively to incentives such as merit pay or sales commissions. (We discuss incentive compensation systems in Chapter 12.)

2. Self-Efficacy: "I Can/Can't Do This Task"   A related trait is *self-efficacy,* **belief in one's personal ability to do a task.** Unlike locus of control, this characteristic isn't about how much fate controls events (as in believing whether getting a high grade in a course is determined by you or by outside factors, such as the grade curve or trick questions). Rather, it's about your personal belief that you have what it takes to succeed. (Erik Weihenmayer, 35, is blind but also a self-described "unrealistic optimist," who was the first blind climber to scale Mt. Everest.)[9]

Have you noticed that those who are confident about their ability tend to succeed, whereas those preoccupied with failure tend not to? Indeed, high expectations of self-efficacy have been linked with all kinds of positives: not only success in varied physical and mental tasks but also reduced anxiety and increased tolerance for pain.[10] One study found that the sales performance of life-insurance agents was much better among those with high self-efficacy.[11] A meta-analysis involving 21,616 people also found significant positive correlation between self-efficacy and job performance.[12] Low self-efficacy is associated with *learned helplessness,* **the debilitating lack of faith in one's ability to control one's environment.**[13]

Among the implications for managers:

- **Assign jobs accordingly.**   Complex, challenging, and autonomous jobs tend to enhance people's perceptions of their self-efficacy. Boring, tedious jobs generally do the opposite.

- **Develop self-efficacy.**   Self-efficacy is a quality that can be nurtured. Employees with low self-efficacy need lots of constructive pointers and positive feedback.[14] Goal difficulty needs to match individuals' perceived self-efficacy, but goals can be made more challenging as performance improves.[15] Small successes need to be rewarded. Employees' expectations can be improved through guided experiences, mentoring, and role modeling.[16]

3. Self-Esteem: "I Like/Dislike Myself"   How worthwhile, capable, and acceptable do you think you are? The answer to this question is an indicator of your *self-esteem,* **the extent to which people like or dislike themselves, their overall**

self-evaluation.[17] Research offers some interesting insights about how high or low self-esteem can affect people and organizations.

- **People with high self-esteem.** Compared with people with low self-esteem, people with high self-esteem are more apt to handle failure better, to emphasize the positive, to take more risks, and to choose more unconventional jobs.[18] However, when faced with pressure situations, high-self-esteem people have been found to become egotistical and boastful.[19] Some have even been associated with aggressive and violent behavior.

- **People with low self-esteem.** Conversely, low-self-esteem people confronted with failure have been found to have focused on their weaknesses and to have had primarily negative thoughts.[20] Moreover, they are more dependent on others and are more apt to be influenced by them and to be less likely to take independent positions.

Can self-esteem be improved? According to one study, "low self-esteem can be raised more by having the person think of *desirable* characteristics *possessed* rather than of undesirable characteristics from which he or she is free."[21] Some ways in which managers can build employee self-esteem are shown below. *(See Table 11.2.)*

• Reinforce employees' positive attributes and skills.
• Provide positive feedback whenever possible.
• Break larger projects into smaller tasks and projects.
• Express confidence in employees' abilities to complete their tasks.
• Provide coaching whenever employees are seen to be struggling to complete tasks.

table 11.2

SOME WAYS THAT MANAGERS CAN BOOST EMPLOYEE SELF-ESTEEM

4. Self-Monitoring: "I'm Fairly Able/Unable to Adapt My Behavior to Others" As you're rushing to an important meeting, you are stopped by a co-worker, who starts to discuss a personal problem. You need to break away, so you glance at your watch.

(a) Does your co-worker Get It? Seeing you look at your watch, he says, "Sorry, I see you're busy. Catch you later." Or (b) does he Not Get It? He keeps talking, until you say "Excuse me, I'm late for a big meeting" and start walking away.

The two scenarios show the difference between a high self-monitor and a low self-monitor. ***Self-monitoring* is the extent to which people are able to observe their own behavior and adapt it to external situations.** Of course, we would all like to think we are high in self-monitoring—able to regulate our "expressive self-presentation for the sake of desired public appearances," as some experts write, "and thus be highly responsive to social and interpersonal cues" of others.[22] But whereas some high self-monitors are criticized for being chameleons, always able to adapt their self-presentation to their surroundings, low self-monitors are often criticized for being on their own planet and insensitive to others. Instead, their behavior may reflect their own inner states, including their attitudes and feelings.

It might be expected that people in top management are more apt to be high self-monitors able to play different roles—even contradictory roles—to suit different situations. Research shows a positive relationship between high self-monitoring and career success. Among 139 MBA graduates who were tracked for 5 years, high self-monitors enjoyed more internal and external promotions than did their low self-monitoring classmates.[23] Other research has found that managerial success (in terms of speed of promotions) was tied to political savvy (knowing how to socialize, network, and engage in organizational politics).[24]

5. Emotional Intelligence: "I'm Pretty Good/Not Good at Understanding My Emotions & the Emotions of Others"

Emotional intelligence (EI) has been defined as "the ability to carry out accurate reasoning about emotions and the ability to use emotions and emotional knowledge to enhance thought."[25] Said another way, *emotional intelligence* **is the ability to cope, to empathize with others, and to be self-motivated.**

The trait of emotional intelligence was first introduced in 1909. Since that time much research has examined the components of EI and its consequences.

Recent research underscores the importance of developing higher EI. It was associated with (1) better social relations for children and adults, (2) better family and intimate relationships, (3) being perceived more positively by others, (4) better academic achievement, (5) higher task performance, and (6) better psychological well-being. **Daniel Goleman,** a psychologist who popularized the trait of EI, concluded that EI is composed of four key components: self-awareness, self-management, social awareness, and relationship management.[26] *(See Table 11.3.)*

table 11.3

THE TRAITS OF EMOTIONAL INTELLIGENCE

1. *Self-awareness.* The most essential trait. This is the ability to read your own emotions and gauge your moods accurately, so you know how you're affecting others.

2. *Self-management.* This is the ability to control your emotions and act with honesty and integrity in reliable and adaptable ways. You can leave occasional bad moods outside the office.

3. *Social awareness.* This includes empathy, allowing you to show others that you care, and organizational intuition, so you keenly understand how your emotions and actions affect others.

4. *Relationship management.* This is the ability to communicate clearly and convincingly, disarm conflicts, and build strong personal bonds.

Sources: Adapted from D. Goleman, R. Boyatzis, and A. McKee, "Primal Leadership: The Hidden Driver of Great Performance," *Harvard Business Review,* December 2001, p. 49; and *Primal Leadership: Realizing the Power of Emotional Intelligence,* Boston: Harvard Business School Press, 2002, p. 39.

Is there any way to raise your own emotional intelligence, to sharpen your social skills? Although parts of EI represent stable traits that are not readily changed, other aspects, such as using empathy, can be developed. Two suggestions for improvement are as follows:

- **Develop awareness of your EI level.** Becoming aware of your level of emotional intelligence is the first step. The Self-Assessment at the end of this chapter can be used for this purpose. (Some companies use the Personal Profile Analysis during the hiring process to provide insights into a person's EI.)[27]

- **Learn about areas needing improvement.** The next step is to learn more about those EI aspects in which improvement is needed. For example, to improve your skills at using empathy, find articles on the topic and try to implement their recommendations. One such article suggests that empathy in communications is enhanced by trying to (1) understand how others feel about what they are communicating and (2) gaining appreciation of what people want from an exchange.[28]

Preliminary evidence suggests that emotional intelligence can land you a job. A simulated interview process indicated that interviewers' assessments of an applicant's emotional intelligence were positively associated with their impression of the applicant.[29] However, given the difficulty of measuring emotional intelligence, further research is needed on this new leadership trait.[30] ●

✳ II.2 VALUES, ATTITUDES, & BEHAVIOR

How do the hidden aspects of individuals—their values and attitudes—affect employee behavior?

major question?

THE BIG PICTURE
Organizational behavior (OB) considers how to better understand and manage people at work. In this section, we discuss individual values and attitudes and how they affect people's actions and judgments.

If you look at a company's annual report or at a brochure from its corporate communications department, you are apt to be given a picture of its *formal aspects:* Goals. Policies. Hierarchy. Structure.

Could you exert effective leadership if the formal aspects were all you knew about the company? What about the *informal aspects?* Values. Attitudes. Personalities. Perceptions. Conflicts. Culture. Clearly, you need to know about these hidden, "messy" characteristics as well. *(See Figure 11.1.)*

Organizational Behavior: Trying to Explain & Predict Workplace Behavior

The informal aspects are the focus of the interdisciplinary field known as **organizational behavior (OB), which is dedicated to better understanding and management of people at work.** In particular, OB tries to help managers not only *explain* workplace behavior but also to *predict* it, so that they can better lead and motivate their employees to perform productively. OB looks at two areas:

- **Individual behavior.** This is the subject of this chapter. We discuss such individual attributes as values, attitudes, personality, perception, and learning.

- **Group behavior.** This is the subject of later chapters, particularly Chapter 13, where we discuss norms, roles, and teams.

Let us begin by considering individual values, attitudes, and behavior.

Values: What Are Your Consistent Beliefs & Feelings about *All* Things?

Values **are abstract ideals that guide one's thinking and behavior across all situations.**[31] Lifelong behavior patterns are dictated by values that are fairly well set by the time people are in their early teens. After that, however, one's values can be reshaped by significant life-altering events, such as having a child, undergoing a business failure, or surviving the death of a loved one, a war, or a serious health threat.

From a manager's point of view, it's helpful to know that values are those concepts, principles, things, people, or activities for which a person is willing to work hard—even make sacrifices for. Compensation, recognition, and status are common values in the workplace.[32] However, according to a survey by the Society for Human Resource Management, employees are more interested in striking a balance between work and family life rather than just earning a paycheck.[33] For instance, 60% of working mothers say part-time work would be their ideal work situation.[34] (During the recession, however, women outnumbered men in the workplace—50.3% in nonfarm jobs in 2009—as more men than women lost jobs.)[35]

Formal
Goals
Policies
Hierarchy
Structure

The Organization

Informal
Values
Attitudes
Personalities
Perceptions
Conflicts
Culture

figure II.I

FORMAL AND INFORMAL ASPECTS OF AN ORGANIZATION

Attitudes: What Are Your Consistent Beliefs & Feelings about *Specific* Things?

Values are abstract ideals—global beliefs and feelings—that are directed toward all objects, people, or events. Values tend to be consistent both over time and over related situations. By contrast, attitudes are beliefs and feelings that are directed toward *specific* objects, people, or events. More formally, an **attitude is defined as a learned predisposition toward a given object.**[36] It is important for you to understand the components of attitudes because attitudes directly influence our behavior.[37]

Example: If you dislike your present job, will you be happier if you change to a different job? Not necessarily. It depends on your attitude. In one study, researchers found that the attitudes of 5,000 middle-aged male employees toward their jobs were very stable over a 5-year period. Men with positive attitudes tended to stay positive, those with negative attitudes tended to stay negative. More revealingly, even those who changed jobs or occupations generally expressed the same attitudes they had previously.[38]

The Three Components of Attitudes: Affective, Cognitive, & Behavioral

Attitudes have three components.[39] *(See Table 11.4.)*

table 11.4

EXAMPLES OF THE THREE COMPONENTS OF ATTITUDES

Affective	"I hate people who talk on cell phones in restaurants." "I hate putting on a suit for work." "I really like working from home." "I like commuting by train because I have time to myself." "I don't like working in office cubicles because they don't have doors and so there's no privacy."
Cognitive	"I can't appoint Herschel because creative people don't make good administrators." "The tallest building in the world is in Chicago." (Actually, it's in Dubai—the 2,717-foot Burj Khalifa.)
Behavioral	"I intend to fill out my expense report tomorrow." "I'm going to turn over a new leaf at New Year's and stop eating junk food." "I'm going to try to avoid Sheryl because she's a Democrat." "I'm never going to talk to Mike because he's a Republican."

- **The affective component—"I feel." The** *affective component of an attitude* **consists of the feelings or emotions one has about a situation.**
- **The cognitive component—"I believe." The** *cognitive component of an attitude* **consists of the beliefs and knowledge one has about a situation.**
- **The behavioral component—"I intend." The** *behavioral component of an attitude,* **also known as the** *intentional component,* **refers to how one intends or expects to behave toward a situation.**

All three components are often manifested at any given time. For example, if you call a corporation and get one of those telephone-tree menus ("For customer service, press 1 . . .") that never seems to connect you to a human being, you might be so irritated that you would say:

- "I hate being given the runaround." [*affective component—your feelings*]
- "That company doesn't know how to take care of customers." [*cognitive component—your perceptions*]
- "I'll never call them again." [*behavioral component—your intentions*]

When Attitudes & Reality Collide: Consistency & Cognitive Dissonance

One of the last things you want, probably, is to be accused of hypocrisy—to be criticized for saying one thing and doing another. Like most people, you no doubt want to maintain consistency between your attitudes and your behavior.

But what if a strongly held attitude bumps up against a harsh reality that contradicts it? Suppose you're extremely concerned about getting AIDS, which you believe you might get from contact with body fluids, including blood. Then you're in a life-threatening auto accident in a third-world country and require surgery and blood transfusions—including transfusions of blood from (possibly AIDS-infected) strangers in a blood bank. Do you reject the blood to remain consistent with your beliefs about getting AIDS?

In 1957, social psychologist **Leon Festinger** proposed the term *cognitive dissonance* **to describe the psychological discomfort a person experiences between his or her cognitive attitude and incompatible behavior.**[40] Because people are uncomfortable with inconsistency, Festinger theorized, they will seek to reduce the "dissonance" or tension of the inconsistency. How they deal with the discomfort, he suggested, depends on three factors:

- **Importance.** How important are the elements creating the dissonance? Most people can put up with some ambiguities in life. For example, many drivers don't think obeying speed limits is very important, even though they profess to be law-abiding citizens. People eat greasy foods even though they know that ultimately they may contribute to heart disease.

- **Control.** How much control does one have over the matters that create dissonance? A juror may not like the idea of voting the death penalty but believe that he or she has no choice but to follow the law in the case. A taxpayer may object to his taxes being spent on, say, special-interest corporate welfare for a particular company but not feel that he or she can withhold taxes.

- **Rewards.** What rewards are at stake in the dissonance? You're apt to cling to old ideas in the face of new evidence if you have a lot invested emotionally or financially in those ideas. If you're a police officer who worked 20 years to prove a particular suspect guilty of murder, you're not apt to be very accepting of contradictory evidence after all that time.

Among the main ways to reduce cognitive dissonance are the following. *(See Table 11.5, next page.)*

- **Change your attitude and/or behavior.** This would seem to be the most obvious, even rational, response to take when confronted with cognitive dissonance.

- **Belittle the importance of the inconsistent behavior.** This happens all the time.

- **Find consonant elements that outweigh the dissonant ones.** This kind of rationalizing goes on quite often, as when employees are confronted with ethical dilemmas but fear losing their jobs.

Leon Festinger. In 1957, the psychologist and his associates penetrated a cult whose members predicted that most people on earth would perish in a cataclysmic event except for a handful that would be rescued by aliens in a flying saucer. Festinger found himself standing with cult members on a hilltop awaiting the event, which, of course, did not happen. Later he proposed the term *cognitive dissonance* to explain how they rationalized the failure of their prophecy. Have you observed people employing this mechanism when the surefire thing they predicted did not occur?

Behavior: How Values & Attitudes Affect People's Actions & Judgments

Values (global) and attitudes (specific) are generally in harmony, but not always. For example, a manager may put a positive *value* on helpful behavior (global) yet may have a negative *attitude* toward helping an unethical co-worker (specific). Together, however, values and attitudes influence people's workplace ***behavior—their actions and judgments.*** ●

table 11.5 EXAMPLES OF WAYS TO REDUCE COGNITIVE DISSONANCE

Technique	Examples
Change attitude and/or behavior	Gregory Withow once belonged to the White Aryan Resistance and other racist groups. He preached hatred and bashed Japanese tourists in San Francisco. Then he met Sylvia, who rejected his white-supremacist ideas. As he grew to love her, he found himself caught between his ideas and her disapproval. To decrease this cognitive dissonance, he renounced his old racist beliefs and changed his behavior, even becoming a spokesperson for the antiracist Anti-Defamation League.
Belittle importance of the inconsistent behavior	All cigarette smokers are repeatedly exposed to information that smoking is hazardous to health. But many belittle the habit as not being as risky as the antismoking messages suggest. ("My grandmother smokes, and she's in her 80s.")
Find consonant elements that outweigh dissonant ones	Ethics professor Sissela Bok says students may justify cheating on an exam by saying "I don't usually do this, but here I really have to do it." As one MIT graduate student said, students see cheating take place and "feel they have to. People get used to it, even though they know it's not right."

Sources: R. Plotnik, *Introduction to Psychology,* 3rd ed. (Pacific Grove, CA: Brooks/Cole, 1993), p. 602; S. Bok, cited in E. Venant, "A Nation of Cheaters," *San Francisco Chronicle,* January 7, 1992, p. D3, reprinted from *Los Angeles Times;* A. Dobrzeniecki, quoted in D. Butler, "MIT Students Guilty of Cheating," *Boston Globe,* March 2, 1991, p. 25.

Example

How Values & Attitudes Affect Behavior: IBM Uses an "Innovation Jam" to Move beyond Incremental Improvements to Catalytic Innovations

As a manager, would you think most employees would agree that innovation is beneficial—that the original Silicon Valley firms prospered because they were constantly creating new products and services? Employees may have the *value,* then, that innovation is good—that it leads to productivity and profitability.

However, for a particularly successful product within your company, your employees might have the *attitude* that radical innovation is unnecessary. If the product is so successful, they may feel, why mess with it? Why not just make incremental improvements?

A Hundred Thousand Minds. IBM found that the company's current reputation for constant incremental innovation hadn't inspired investors, resulting in its stock price remaining flat for 3 years. Recent earnings had come through cost-cutting, not the leaps in growth propelled by new business. Accordingly, CEO Samuel J. Palmisano decided to create what he called an "Innovation Jam," pulling together thousands of people—clients, consultants, and employees' family members, as well as IBM workers— in the online equivalent of a town meeting. His hope, according to one account, is that "The opinions of some 100,000 minds will lead to catalytic innovations so powerful they

will transform industries, alter human behavior, and lead to new businesses for IBM."[41] IBM wouldn't own any ideas emerging from the two 72-hour "open source" sessions; they could be used by anyone.

More Jams. IBM's 2006 Innovation Jam brought together more than 150,000 people from 104 countries and 67 companies. As a result, 10 new IBM businesses were launched with seed investment totaling $100 million.[42] In 2009, for the seventeenth consecutive year, IBM racked up more U.S. patents than any other company in the world—4,914, in all, or 94 patents a week.[43] In 2009, IBM held a Smarter Planet University Jam, involving nearly 2,000 students and faculty from more 200 universities from 40 countries. Among the Jam highlights: Showing that the current generation is definitely going green, participants contributed over 100 examples and ideas of how their universities are or could be "going green."[44]

YOUR CALL

The Innovation Jam certainly provides new ideas and furthers IBM's image as a forward-thinking global competitor. Do you think this kind of transformative event could be adapted to a different kind of company (such as Sears), to change employee values and attitudes?

Is it important for managers to pay attention to employee attitudes?

major question?

THE BIG PICTURE

Attitudes are important because they affect behavior. Managers need to be alert to work-related attitudes having to do with job involvement, including job engagement, job satisfaction, and organizational commitment. Among the types of employee behavior they should attend to are their on-the-job performance and productivity, absenteeism and turnover, organizational citizenship behaviors, and counterproductive work behaviors.

"Keep the employees happy."

It's true that attitudes are important, the reason being that *attitudes affect behavior.* But is keeping employees happy all that managers need to know to get results? We discuss motivation for performance in the next chapter. Here let us consider what managers need to know about work-related attitudes and behaviors, particularly as they relate to job involvement.

Job Involvement: Being Immersed in One's Job

"At the end of the day, you've never been so tired—or had so much fun!" says Doug Aberle, an animator/director at Vinton Studios in Los Angeles, which makes the television series *The PJs.* "There's a lot of variety in working on a TV show. There's something different every day."[45]

Aberle clearly expresses a deep sense of *job involvement,* **defined as the extent to which an individual is immersed in his or her present job.** A meta-analysis involving thousands of people suggests that job involvement is positively associated with job satisfaction, organizational commitment, and intrinsic motivation and is negatively associated with intentions to quit.[46]

Work-Related Attitudes: Employee Engagement, Job Satisfaction, & Organizational Commitment

Would finding quiet time at the office, taking small breaks for coffee, listening to music, creating a list of good things that have happened, and thinking about your work as a "calling" (not as just a job) reduce your stress level and boost your happiness at work?[47] How about having an employer-sponsored vegetable garden?[48] All have been tried in attempts to raise employee morale—that is, job involvement.

Three types of attitudes managers are particularly interested in are (1) *employee engagement,* (2) *job satisfaction,* and (3) *organizational commitment.*

1. Employee Engagement: How Connected Are You to Your Work?

Research on job involvement has evolved into the study of an individual difference called *employee engagement,* **defined as an individual's involvement, satisfaction, and enthusiasm for work.**[49]

Engaged employees are expected to be more committed to their employer and to put more effort into their jobs, although there is little scientific research to support this view. Still, some consulting firms have collected data to support the practical value of employee engagement.[50] For example, when an employee is engaged, it can take 10 times as much money to lure him or her away as a disengaged employee, according to data from Watson Wyatt.[51] Case studies from Hay Group further suggest that employee performance increases 10% when employees are highly engaged and increase 50% when they have both high engagement and high enablement (such as a supportive environment).[52]

2. Job Satisfaction: How Much Do You Like or Dislike Your Job? *Job satisfaction* **is the extent to which you feel positive or negative about various aspects of your work.** Most people don't like everything about their jobs. Their overall satisfaction depends on how they feel about several components, such as *work, pay, promotions, co-workers, and supervision.*[53] Among the key correlates of job satisfaction are stronger motivation, job involvement, organizational commitment, and life satisfaction and less absenteeism, tardiness, turnover, and perceived stress.[54]

Reportedly only 45% of U.S. workers were satisfied with their jobs in 2009, down from 52% in 2005 and 61% in 1987, according to a study of 5,000 households.[55] Many such employees indicated they were apt to jump ship once the recession ended.

But what is the relationship between job satisfaction and job performance—does more satisfaction cause better performance or does better performance cause more satisfaction? This is a subject of much debate among management scholars.[56] One comprehensive study found that (1) job satisfaction and performance are moderately related, meaning that employee job satisfaction is a key work attitude managers should consider when trying to increase performance; but (2) the relationship between satisfaction and performance is complex and it seems that both variables influence each other through a host of individual differences and work-environment characteristics.[57]

3. Organizational Commitment *Organizational commitment* **reflects the extent to which an employee identifies with an organization and is committed to its goals.** For instance, some managers question whether mothers with children can be fully committed to their jobs, although one survey found that only 4% of more than 2,612 women said that their bosses think that they are not as committed to their jobs because they have children.[58] Research shows a strong positive relationship between organizational commitment and job satisfaction and a moderate association with job performance.[59] Thus, managers are advised to increase job satisfaction to elicit higher levels of commitment. In turn, higher commitment can facilitate higher performance.[60]

Performance monitors. These British Airways customer service reps are being monitored by software that keeps track not only of ticket sales and customer-complaint resolutions but also of the amount of time spent on breaks and personal phone calls. In tracking employee effectiveness, the technology can count incentive dollars tied to performance and immediately direct them into employee paychecks. Do you think these incentive calculators are justified or do you think they intrude too much on employee privacy?

Important Workplace Behaviors

Why, as a manager, do you need to learn how to manage individual differences? The answer, as you might expect, is so that you can influence employees to do their best work. Among the types of behavior are (1) performance and productivity, (2) absenteeism and turnover, (3) organizational citizenship behaviors, and (4) counterproductive work behaviors.

1. Evaluating Behavior When Employees Are Working: Performance & Productivity Every job has certain expectations, but in some jobs performance and productivity are easier to define than in others. How many contacts should a telemarketing sales rep make in a day? How many sales should he or she close? Often a job of this nature will have a history of accomplishments (from what previous job holders have attained) so that it is possible to quantify performance behavior.

However, an advertising agency account executive handling major clients such as a carmaker or a beverage manufacturer may go months before landing this kind of big account. Or a researcher in a pharmaceutical company may take years to develop a promising new prescription drug.

In short, the method of evaluating performance must match the job being done.

2. Evaluating Behavior When Employees Are Not Working: Absenteeism & Turnover Should you be suspicious of every instance of *absenteeism*—when an employee doesn't show up for work? Of course, some absences—illness, death in the family, or jury duty, for example—are legitimate. However, a lot of no-show behavior is related to job dissatisfaction.[61] One study of 700 managers found 20% called in sick simply because they didn't feel like going to work that day. The top three reasons for employees taking bogus sick days are for doing personal errands, catching up on sleep, and relaxing.[62]

Absenteeism may be a precursor to *turnover,* when employees leave their jobs. Every organization experiences some turnover, as employees leave for reasons of family, better job prospects, or retirement. However, except in low-skill industries, a continual revolving door of new employees is usually not a good sign, since replacement and training is expensive.[63] For instance, one study found the direct and indirect costs of recruiting and training a new midlevel manager—along with lost business to competitors, lost technical knowledge, decreased morale among remaining employees, and the like—came to $64,000.[64] For an hourly employee, experts estimate the cost of turnover is about 30% of annual salary and for professional employees it is up to 150%.[65]

3. Evaluating Behavior That Exceeds Work Roles: Organizational Citizenship Behaviors *Organizational citizenship behaviors* are those employee behaviors that are not directly part of employees' job descriptions—that exceed their work-role requirements. Examples, according to one description, include "such gestures as constructive statements about the department, expression of personal interest in the work of others, suggestions for improvement, training new people, respect for the spirit as well as the letter of housekeeping rules, care for organizational property, and punctuality and attendance well beyond standard or enforceable levels."[66] Research demonstrates a significant and moderately positive correlation between organizational citizenship behaviors and job satisfaction, productivity, efficiency, and customer satisfaction.[67]

4. Evaluating Behavior That Harms the Organization: Counterproductive Work Behaviors The flip side of organizational citizenship behaviors would seem to be what are called *counterproductive work behaviors (CWB)*, **types of behavior that harm employees and the organization as a whole.** Such behaviors may include absenteeism and tardiness, drug and alcohol abuse, and disciplinary problems but also extend beyond them to more serious acts such as accidents, sabotage, sexual harassment, violence, theft, and white-collar crime.[68]

Clearly, if an employee engages in some kind of CWB, the organization needs to respond quickly and appropriately, defining the specific behaviors that are unacceptable and the requirements for acceptable behavior.[69] It is more desirable, however, to take preventive measures. One way is to screen for CWB during the hiring process. For instance, it's been found that applicants scoring higher on cognitive ability (intelligence) tests are less likely to be involved in violence and property damage after they are hired.[70] Employees are also less likely to engage in CWB if they have satisfying jobs that offer autonomy or that don't require them to supervise too many people.[71] ●

Example

Extreme Counterproductive Work Behaviors: Violence in the Workplace

A fairly common kind of CWB is the bullying, harassment, or unfair treatment of subordinates, co-workers, and even customers. Indeed, in one survey of U.S. employees, 45% said they had had a boss who was abusive.[72] Such behavior is especially toxic to the organization because when employees are intimidated, humiliated, or undermined by an abusive manager, they say they are more likely to quit their jobs or to retaliate with CWB aimed at that manager or their fellow workers.[73]

Post Office Massacres. In *Murder by Proxy: How America Went Postal* (2010), filmmaker Emil Chiaberi takes a look at how hostile work environments, along with societal changes and economic downturns, have contributed to shooting sprees in post offices, businesses, and schools in the last quarter century. A focus of the documentary is Royal Oak, Michigan, letter carrier Thomas McIlvane, who was written up for taking lunch at inappropriate locations, ordered to have his vehicle inspected for a brake-light problem everyone could see didn't exist, and then eventually dismissed for swearing at a supervisor. McIlvane later fired 100 rounds at postal employees, killing four and injuring four before turning the gun on himself. A congressional committee determined McIlvane "was a powder keg ready to blow because of petty, intimidating, even 'reprehensible' managers at the Royal Oak Post Office," according to one account.[74]

Recognizing Potential Violence. "Violence rarely begins with someone walking in and shooting others," says psychiatrist Roger Brunswick. "Violence usually builds slowly and starts with bullying, intimidation, and threats."[75] Newspaper stories about mass shootings by disgruntled or mentally ill employees (or students, as at Virginia Tech and Northern Illinois University) have made organizations more aware that erratic behavior has to be spotted and dealt with early. Pitney Bowes, for instance, set up a hotline that employees may call anonymously to report any such concerns, and it has trained managers in identifying signs of troubling behavior.[76]

YOUR CALL

If a co-worker of yours said something like, "I could do what that McIlvane guy did," what would you do?

□ II.4 PERCEPTION & INDIVIDUAL BEHAVIOR

What are the distortions in perception that can cloud one's judgment?

THE BIG PICTURE
Perception, a four-step process, can be skewed by four types of distortion: selective perception, stereotyping, the halo effect, and causal attribution. We also consider the self-fulfilling prophecy, which can affect our judgment as well.

If you were a smoker, which warning on a cigarette pack would make you think more about quitting? "Smoking seriously harms you and others around you." A blunt "Smoking kills." Or a stark graphic image showing decaying teeth.

This is the kind of decision public health authorities in various countries are wrestling with. (And a Canadian Cancer Society study in 2000 found that 58% of smokers who saw graphic images thought twice about the health effects of smoking.)[77] These officials, in other words, are trying to decide how *perception* might influence behavior.

The Four Steps in the Perceptual Process

Perception **is the process of interpreting and understanding one's environment.** The process of perception is complex, but it can be boiled down to four steps. *(See Figure 11.2.)*

figure II.2

THE FOUR STEPS IN THE PERCEPTUAL PROCESS

I. Selective attention	2. Interpretation & evaluation	3. Storing in memory	4. Retrieving from memory to make judgments & decisions
"Did I notice something?"	"What was it I noticed & what does it mean?"	"Remember it as an event, concept, person, or all three?"	"What do I recall about that?"

In this book, we are less concerned about the theoretical steps in perception than in how perception is distorted, since this has considerable bearing on the manager's judgment and job. In any one of the four stages of the perception process misunderstandings or errors in judgment can occur. Perceptual errors can lead to mistakes that can be damaging to yourself, other people, and your organization.

Four Distortions in Perception

Although there are other types of distortion in perception, we will describe the following: (1) *selective perception*, (2) *stereotyping*, (3) the *halo effect*, and (4) *causal attribution.*

I. Selective Perception: "I Don't Want to Hear about That"   Are there topics that you find especially uncomfortable—your own death, say, or child molestation, or cheating in college—so that you tune out these subjects when people bring them up? For example, many people avoid making a will because they find it too awful to think about their future earthly nonexistence. ***Selective perception* is the tendency to filter out information that is discomforting, that seems irrelevant, or that contradicts one's beliefs.**

One classic study found that when executives were asked to determine the key problem in a complex business case, they identified the problem as falling within their particular functional areas of work—they evidently filtered out information about other areas. That is, human resource managers said the principal problem was a people issue, marketing executives said it was a sales issue, and production people said it was a manufacturing issue.[78] This shows how managers can distort problem solving through selective perception.

2. Stereotyping: "Those Sorts of People Are Pretty Much the Same" If you're a tall African American man, do people make remarks about basketball players? If you're of Irish descent, do people believe you drink a lot? If you're Jewish, do people think you're money-oriented? If you're a woman, do people think you're automatically nurturing? All these are stereotypes. ***Stereotyping* is the tendency to attribute to an individual the characteristics one believes are typical of the group to which that individual belongs.**[79]

Principal areas of stereotyping that should be of concern to you as a manager are (1) *sex-role stereotypes,* (2) *age stereotypes,* and (3) *race/ethnicity stereotypes.*

- **Sex-role stereotypes.** A *sex-role stereotype* is the belief that differing traits and abilities make males and females particularly well suited to different roles.

  A study of over 61,647 people—half female, half male—found that in the United States women were labeled as moody, gossip prone, emotional, and catty, but no comparable kinds of negative stereotypes were described of men. When asked who would be more effective leaders, males were preferred over females by a 2-to-1 margin—by both men and women.[80]

  Although research shows that men and women do not differ in stereotypical manners, the stereotypes still persist.[81] And, unfortunately, promotional decisions may still be affected by sex-role stereotyping. A study of a multinational Fortune 500 company, for example, revealed that men received more favorable evaluations than women in spite of controlling for age, education, organizational tenure, salary grade, and type of job.[82]

- **Age stereotypes.** *Age stereotypes* tend to depict older workers as less involved in their work, less satisfied, less motivated, and less committed than younger workers, which may be why workers over age 55 found it harder to get jobs than younger colleagues during the 2009 recession year.[83] But in fact research shows that as employees' age increases, so does their job involvement and satisfaction, work motivation, and organizational commitment.[84]

  Stereotypes also depict older workers as being less creative and more accident prone; however, this is not borne out.[85] Finally, the stereotype that older workers have higher absenteeism is not supported by the research; if anything, managers should focus more attention on absenteeism among younger rather than older workers.[86]

  Because the median age of Americans is currently 36.7 years—the oldest in our history—it seems clear that managers will probably be dealing with an older workforce.[87] Moreover, by 2030, about one-fifth of the population will be over age 65, but many, whether by choice or by necessity, will continue working.[88] World-famous heart surgeon Michael DeBakey, for instance, who was born in 1908, continued to work into his late nineties.[89]

- **Race/ethnicity stereotypes.** *Race/ethnicity stereotypes* don't bear repeating here, but it is noteworthy that there are not a lot of Hispanic and

African American managers in the United States. For example, Hispanics and Latinos held only 17% of managerial and professional jobs and blacks only 27%, compared with 35.5% for whites and 47.3% for Asians.[90] An encouraging sign, incidentally, is that analysis of census data found that in 14 of the 25 largest metropolitan areas, including Boston, New York, and San Francisco, more immigrants (who can be of any race, of course, but are often stereotyped as racial minorities) were employed in white-collar occupations than in lower-wage work, such as construction or cleaning.[91]

3. The Halo Effect: "One Trait Tells Me All I Need to Know" Do you think physically attractive people have more desirable traits than unattractive people—that they are happier, kinder, more successful, more socially skilled, more sensitive, more interesting, independent, exciting, sexually warm, even smarter and nicer? All of these traits have been attributed to attractive people.[92] This situation is an example of the ***halo effect, in which we form an impression of an individual based on a single trait.*** (The phenomenon is also called the *horn-and-halo effect,* because not only can a single positive trait be generalized into an array of positive traits but the same generalization may be made for a negative trait.)

Example

The Halo Effect: Are Attractive Men & Women Paid More Than Ordinary People?

Are attractive employees paid more than ordinary (or unattractive) people for the same work? Two economists, Markus Mobius of Harvard and Tanya Rosenblat of Wesleyan University, decided to look into that question.[93]

Rating on a Beauty Scale. Students were recruited to play the roles of both applicants and employers for a job that involved solving mazes. To determine how attractive applicants were, a separate panel of students was shown their photographs and asked to rate them on a beauty scale. After applicants solved mazes, employers considered the prospective employees under different circumstances. They examined (1) only an applicant's résumé, which listed age, sex, university, graduation date, job experience, and activities and hobbies; (2) the résumé and a photograph; (3) the résumé and a telephone interview; (4) the résumé, a telephone interview, and a photograph; and (5) the résumé, a telephone interview, and a face-to-face interview. The employers used the interview information to form their own estimates of the number of mazes the subjects would solve during their 15-minute jobs, and the subjects then solved the mazes as best they could.

Good Looks = Confident Communicators? The economists found three interesting results:

- Although beautiful people are no better than ordinary people at solving mazes, they are more self-confident about their abilities. "Being good

looking," says one article about the study, "seems to be strongly associated with self-confidence, a trait that is apparently attractive to employers."[94]

- When employers looked only at résumés, physical appearance had no effect on their judgments, as you might expect. With all of the other treatments, employers showed higher estimates for beautiful people's productivity—especially when they had face-to-face interviews but even with telephone-only interviews, the result, apparently, of the effect of self-confidence that came across on the phone.

- Good-looking people are good communicators, which also contributes to employers' positive perceptions.

The Halo Misperception. In sum, "Employers (wrongly) expect good-looking workers to perform better than their less-attractive counterparts under both visual and oral interaction," said the researchers, "even after controlling for individual worker characteristics and worker confidence."

YOUR CALL

Are you yourself influenced in your judgment of people by how attractive they are? Do you think as a manager you could look beyond people's physical appearances to be a good judge of their competence? Why?

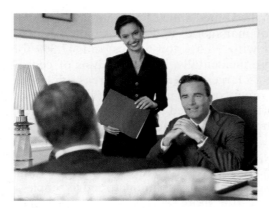

Handsomely compensated. Attractive employees are generally paid better than unattractive ones are. Why do you think that is? Do you think it's inevitable?

As if we needed additional proof that life is unfair, it has been shown that attractive people generally are treated better than unattractive people. Teachers have higher expectations of them in terms of academic achievement.[95] Potential employers are more apt to view them favorably.[96] Attractive employees are generally paid higher salaries than unattractive ones are.[97] Clearly, however, if a manager fails to look at *all* an individual's traits, he or she has no right to complain if that employee doesn't work out.

4. Causal Attributions   *Causal attribution* **is the activity of inferring causes for observed behavior.** Rightly or wrongly, we constantly formulate cause-and-effect explanations for our own and others' behavior. Attributional statements such as the following are common: "Joe drinks too much because he has no willpower; but I need a couple of drinks after work because I'm under a lot of pressure."

Even though our causal attributions tend to be self-serving and are often invalid, it's important to understand how people formulate attributions because they profoundly affect organizational behavior. For example, a supervisor who attributes an employee's poor performance to a lack of effort might reprimand that person. However, training might be deemed necessary if the supervisor attributes the poor performance to a lack of ability.

As a manager, you need to be alert to two attributional tendencies that can distort one's interpretation of observed behavior—the *fundamental attribution bias* and the *self-serving bias*.

- **Fundamental attribution bias.** In the ***fundamental attribution bias*, people attribute another person's behavior to his or her personal characteristics rather than to situational factors.**

    Example: A study of manufacturing employees found that top managers attributed the cause of industrial back pain to individuals, whereas workers attributed it to the environment.[98]

- **Self-serving bias.** In the *self-serving bias*, **people tend to take more personal responsibility for success than for failure.**

    Example: The way students typically analyze their performance on exams shows self-serving bias, with "A" students likely to attribute their grade to high ability or hard work and "D" students blaming factors such as bad luck, unclear lectures, and unfair testing.[99] Another example: Europeans are blaming Wall Street for the 2010 economic collapse in Greece. This is completely wrong according to writers for the *Wall Street Journal*. They note that a close look at Greece's finances "over the nearly

10 years since it adopted the euro shows not only that Greece was the principal author of its debt problems, but also that fellow European governments repeatedly turned a blind eye to its flouting of rules."[100]

The Self-Fulfilling Prophecy, or Pygmalion Effect

The *self-fulfilling prophecy,* also known as the *Pygmalion* ("pig-*mail*-yun") *effect,* describes the phenomenon in which people's expectations of themselves or others lead them to behave in ways that make those expectations come true.

Expectations are important. An example is a waiter who expects some poorly dressed customers to be stingy tippers, who therefore gives them poor service and so gets the result he or she expected—a much lower tip than usual. Research has shown that by raising managers' expectations for individuals performing a wide variety of tasks, higher levels of achievement and productivity can be achieved.[101]

The lesson for you as a manager is that when you expect employees to perform badly, they probably will, and when you expect them to perform well, they probably will. (In the G. B. Shaw play *Pygmalion,* a speech coach bets he can get a lower-class girl to change her accent and her demeanor so that she can pass herself off as a duchess. In 6 months, she successfully "passes" in high society, having become a woman of sensitivity and taste.) ●

Practical Action

How Can Managers Harness the Pygmalion Effect to Lead Employees?

Luke Iorio, president of The Institute for Professional Excellence in Coaching, says that employees want to use their knowledge and experience to contribute to the value of the organization. "Employees have many answers [managers] haven't thought of," he says. "The main thing is to see people as they can be, and to expect great things of them."[102] And more often than not, they'll deliver.

Research in a variety of industries and occupations shows that the effect of the self-fulfilling prophecy can be quite strong.[103] That is, managerial expectations powerfully influence employee behavior and performance. Managers can harness this effect by building a hierarchical framework that reinforces positive performance expectations throughout the organization. The foundation of this framework is employee self-expectations. In turn, positive self-expectations improve interpersonal expectations by encouraging people to work toward common goals. This cooperation enhances group-level productivity and promotes positive performance expectations within the work group.

How to Create a Pygmalion Effect

Because positive self-expectations are the foundation for creating an organizationwide Pygmalion effect, let

us consider how managers can create positive performance expectations. This task may be accomplished using various combinations of the following:

1. Recognize that everyone has the potential to increase his or her performance.
2. Instill confidence in your staff.
3. Set high performance goals.
4. Positively reinforce employees for a job well done.
5. Provide constructive feedback when necessary.
6. Help employees advance through the organization.
7. Introduce new employees as if they have outstanding potential.
8. Become aware of your personal prejudices and nonverbal messages that may discourage others.
9. Encourage employees to visualize the successful execution of tasks.
10. Help employees master key skills and tasks.[104]

Your Call

How can you put the Pygmalion effect to use in college organizational life?

<table>
<tr><td>

major question?

</td><td>

What causes workplace stress, and how can it be reduced?

</td></tr>
</table>

THE BIG PICTURE

Stress is what people feel when enduring extraordinary demands or opportunities and are not sure how to handle them. There are six sources of stress: individual differences, individual task, individual role, group, organizational, and nonwork demands. We describe some consequences of stress and three ways to reduce it in the organization.

Stress **is the tension people feel when they are facing or enduring extraordinary demands, constraints, or opportunities and are uncertain about their ability to handle them effectively.**[105] Stress is the feeling of tension and pressure; **the source of stress is called a** *stressor.*

There's no question that work is stressful. Indeed, a 2009 study found that 67% of people in the general population are stressed by their work.[106]

The Toll of Workplace Stress

The American Institute of Stress estimates that workplace stress costs the U.S. economy over $300 billion a year in health care, missed work, and stress-reduction treatment.[107] Stress can cause conflicts at work, make you fatigued all the time, and generate problems like insomnia, backaches, headaches, and chest pain.[108]

Work stress can also, as you might guess, put managers at risk. Researchers who interviewed 800 hospital heart-attack patients over a 5-year period found that managers run twice the normal risk of heart attack the week after they have had to fire someone or face a high-pressure deadline.[109] Men who suppress anger at work are particularly at risk—two to five times more likely to suffer heart attacks or die from heart disease as those who express their "desk rage."[110] Losing one's job is, as you might imagine, a very stressful event, being associated with decreased psychological and physical well-being.[111] A Yale study found that layoffs more than doubled the risk of heart attack and stroke among older workers.[112]

Workplace stress is negatively related to positive emotions, job satisfaction, organizational commitment, and job performance and positively associated with alcohol and illicit drug use, overeating, and turnover.[113] Indeed, historically researchers have generally believed that there is an *inverted U-shaped relationship* between stress and performance. That is, low levels of stress lead to low performance (because people are not "charged up" to perform), but high levels of stress also lead to an energy-sapping fight-or-flight response that produces low performance. Optimal performance, according to this hypothesis, results when people are subjected to moderate levels of stress.

How Does Stress Work?

Stress has both physical and emotional components. Physically, according to Canadian researcher Hans Selye, considered the father of the modern concept of stress, stress is "the nonspecific response of the body to any demand made upon it."[114] Emotionally, stress has been defined as the feeling of being

Trading frenzy. Many jobs are stressful, but some are more stressful than others, such as those of traders on the floor of the New York Stock Exchange. What occupations do you think are the most stress-inducing?

overwhelmed, "the perception that events or circumstances have challenged, or exceeded, a person's ability to cope."[115]

Stressors can be *hassles,* or simple irritants, such as misplacing or losing things, concerns about one's physical appearance, and having too many things to do.[116] Or they can be *crises,* such as sudden occasions of overwhelming terror—a horrible auto accident, an incident of childhood abuse. Or they can be *strong stressors,* which can dramatically strain a person's ability to adapt—extreme physical discomfort, such as chronic severe back pain.

Stressors can be both *negative* and *positive.* That is, one can understand that being fired or being divorced can be a great source of stress but so can being promoted or getting married. As Selye writes, "It is immaterial whether the agent or the situation we face is pleasant or unpleasant; all that counts is the intensity of the demand for adjustment and adaptation."[117] In addition, Selye distinguished between bad stress (what he called "distress"), in which the result of the stressor can be anxiety and illness, and good stress ("eustress"), which can stimulate a person to better coping and adaptation, such as performing well on a test. In this discussion, however, we are mainly concerned with how stress negatively affects people and their performance.

The Sources of Job-Related Stress

There are six sources of stress on the job: (1) *demands created by individual differences,* (2) *individual task demands,* (3) *individual role demands,* (4) *group demands,* (5) *organizational demands,* and (6) *nonwork demands.*

I. Demands Created by Individual Differences: The Stress Created by Genetic or Personality Characteristics Some people are born worriers, those with a gene mutation (known as BDNF) that Yale researchers identify with people who chronically obsess over negative thoughts.[118] Others are impatient, hurried, deadline-ridden, competitive types with the personality characteristic known as **Type A behavior pattern, meaning they are involved in a chronic, determined struggle to accomplish more in less time.**[119] Type A behavior has been associated with increased performance in the work of professors, students, and life insurance brokers.[120] However, it also has been associated with greater cardiovascular activity and higher blood pressure, as well as to heart disease, especially for individuals who showed strong feelings of anger, hostility, and aggression.[121]

2. Individual Task Demands: The Stress Created by the Job Itself Some occupations are more stressful than others. Being a retail store manager, for instance, can be quite stressful for some people.[122] But being a home-based blogger, paid on a piecework basis to generate news and comment, may mean working long hours to the point of exhaustion.[123]

Low-level jobs can be more stressful than high-level jobs because employees often have less control over their lives and thus have less work satisfaction. Being a high-speed data processor or doing telemarketing sales, for instance, can be quite stressful.

There is also considerable stress caused by worries over the prospective loss of a job. Recent surveys indicate that employees frequently worry about being laid off.[124] Job security is an important stressor to manage because it can result in reduced job satisfaction, organizational commitment, and performance.[125]

3. Individual Role Demands: The Stress Created by Others' Expectations of You *Roles* are sets of behaviors that people expect of occupants of a position.[126] Stress may come about because of *role overload, role conflict,* and *role ambiguity.*

- **Role overload.** Role overload occurs when others' expectations exceed one's ability. Example: If you as a student are carrying a full course load plus working two-thirds time plus trying to have a social life, you know what role overload is—and what stress is. Similar things happen to managers and workers.
- **Role conflict.** Role conflict occurs when one feels torn by the different expectations of important people in one's life. Example: Your supervisor says the company needs you to stay late to meet an important deadline, but your family expects you to be present for your child's birthday party.
- **Role ambiguity.** Role ambiguity occurs when others' expectations are unknown. Example: You find your job description and the criteria for promotion vague, a complaint often voiced by newcomers to an organization.

4. Group Demands: The Stress Created by Co-workers & Managers   Even if you don't particularly care for the work you do but like the people you work with, that can be a great source of satisfaction and prevent stress. When people don't get along, that can be a great stressor. Alternatively, even if you have stress under control, a co-worker's stress might bother you, diminishing productivity.[127]

In addition, managers can create stress for employees in a number of ways. These include: exhibiting inconsistent behaviors; failing to provide support; showing lack of concern; providing inadequate direction; creating a demanding, high-productivity environment; and focusing on negatives while ignoring good performance.[128] People who have bad managers are five times more likely to have stress-induced headaches, upset stomachs, and loss of sleep.[129]

5. Organizational Demands: The Stress Created by the Environment & Culture   The physical environments of some jobs are great sources of stress: poultry processing, asbestos removal, coal mining, fire fighting, police work, ambulance driving, and so on. Even white-collar work can take place in a stressful environment, with poor lighting, too much noise, improper placement of furniture, and no privacy.[130]

An organizational culture that promotes high-pressure work demands on employees will fuel the stress response.[131] The pace of information technology certainly adds to the stress. "For example," says Michael Patsalos-Fox, chairman of the Americas region for consulting firm McKinsey & Company, "you used to have media companies and you used to have telecom [telecommunications] companies, right? . . . The problem is that they are encroaching on each other. The onset of a lot of technologies is blurring the boundary between industries that were quite separate, creating opportunities for industries to attack each other."[132] Such rapidly changing technologies and financial pressures are what keep top executives up at night.

Research shows preliminary support for the idea that organizational stress can be reduced by participatory management.[133]

6. Nonwork Demands: The Stresses Created by Forces Outside the Organization   As anyone knows who has had to cope with money problems, divorce, support of elderly relatives, or other serious nonwork concerns, the stresses outside one's work life can have a significant effect on work. And people with lower incomes, education level, and work status are particularly apt to have higher stress.[134] But even people with ordinary lives can find the stress of coping with family life rugged going.

The Consequences of Stress

Positive stress is constructive and can energize you, increasing your effort, creativity, and performance. Negative stress is destructive, resulting in poorer-quality work, dissatisfaction, errors, absenteeism, and turnover.

Symptoms of Stress   Negative stress reveals itself in three kinds of symptoms:

- **Physiological signs.** Lesser physiological signs are sweaty palms, restlessness, backaches, headaches, upset stomach, and nausea. More serious signs are hypertension and heart attacks.

- **Psychological signs.** Psychological symptoms include boredom, irritability, nervousness, anger, anxiety, hostility, and depression.

- **Behavioral signs.** Behavioral symptoms include sleeplessness, changes in eating habits, and increased smoking/alcohol/drug abuse. Stress may be revealed through reduced performance and job satisfaction.

De-stressing. Experts say that exercise can be a tremendous stress reliever. Many companies maintain physical-fitness centers not only as an employee perk but also because they realize that exercise helps to improve stamina and endurance while reducing tension.

Burnout   "When you keep investing more energy and the return remains low, that's when you burn out," suggests Michael Staver, founder of an executive training company.[135]

    Burnout **is a state of emotional, mental, and even physical exhaustion,** expressed as listlessness, indifference, or frustration. Clearly, the greatest consequence of negative stress for the organization is reduced productivity. Overstressed employees are apt to call in sick, miss deadlines, take longer lunch breaks, and show indifference to performance. However, some may put in great numbers of hours at work without getting as much accomplished as previously.[136]

    Mental health experts estimate that 10% of the workforce suffers from depression or high levels of stress that may ultimately affect job performance. In addition, researchers estimate that in a recent year stress caused 11% of employee absenteeism.[137]

Alcohol & Other Drug Abuse   Have an employee who's often late? Who frequently calls in sick on Mondays? Who is somewhat sloppy? Maybe he or she is afflicted with *alcoholism,* a chronic, progressive, and potentially fatal disease characterized by a growing compulsion to drink. Alcoholics come from every social class, from students to college professors to priests to airline pilots. Alcoholism may not interfere with a person's job in an obvious way until it shows up in absenteeism, accidents, slipshod work, or significant use of a company's medical benefits.

    Alcohol is the most common drug of abuse, but the misuse of others may also affect a person's productivity—legal drugs such as tranquilizers or illegal drugs such as marijuana, Ecstasy, cocaine, or heroin. If you as a manager think you might be dealing with an employee with a substance-abuse problem, it's suggested you not try to make accusations but firmly point out that productivity is suffering and that it's up to the subordinate to do something about it. While not doing any counseling yourself, you can try steering the employee to the Human Resources Department, which may have an employee assistance program that may help employees overcome personal problems affecting their job performance.

    Incidentally, although many people swear by 12-step programs, such as that offered by Alcoholics Anonymous, an examination of several studies found that such programs were no more and no less successful than any other interventions in reducing alcohol dependence and alcohol-related problems.[138]

Reducing Stressors in the Organization

There are all kinds of *buffers,* **or administrative changes, that managers can make to reduce the stressors that lead to employee burnout.** Examples: Extra staff or equipment at peak periods. Increased freedom to make decisions. Recognition for accomplishments. Time off for rest or personal development. Assignment to a new position.[139] Three- to 5-day employee retreats at off-site locations for relaxation and team-building activities. Sabbatical leave programs to replenish employees' energy and desire to work.[140]

Some general organizational strategies for reducing unhealthy stressors are the following:[141]

- **Roll out employee assistance programs.** *Employee assistance programs (EAPs)* **include a host of programs aimed at helping employees to cope with stress, burnout, substance abuse, health-related problems, family and marital issues, and any general problem that negatively influences job performance.**

- **Recommend a holistic wellness approach.** A *holistic wellness program* **focuses on self-responsibility, nutritional awareness, relaxation techniques, physical fitness, and environmental awareness.** This approach goes beyond stress reduction by encouraging employees to strive, in one definition, for "a harmonious and productive balance of physical, mental, and social well-being brought about by the acceptance of one's personal responsibility for developing and adhering to a health promotion program."[142]

- **Create a supportive environment.** Job stress often results because employees work under poor supervision and lack freedom. Wherever possible, it's better to keep the organizational environment less formal, more personal, and more supportive of employees.[143]

- **Make jobs interesting.** Stress also results when jobs are routinized and boring. Better to try to structure jobs so that they allow employees some freedom.

- **Make career counseling available.** Companies such as IBM make career planning available, which reduces the stress that comes when employees don't know what their career options are and where they're headed.

Key Terms Used in This Chapter

II.1 Personality & Individual Behavior
Personality consists of the stable psychological traits and behavioral attributes that give a person his or her identity. There are five personality dimensions and five personality traits that managers need to be aware of to understand workplace behavior.

The Big Five personality dimensions are extroversion, agreeableness, conscientiousness, emotional stability, and openness to experience. Extroversion, an outgoing personality, is associated with success for managers and salespeople. Conscientiousness, or a dependable personality, is correlated with successful job performance. A person who scores well on conscientiousness may be a proactive personality, someone who is more apt to take initiative and persevere to influence the environment.

There are five personality traits that managers need to be aware of in order to understand workplace behavior. (1) Locus of control indicates how much people believe they control their fate through their own efforts. (2) Self-efficacy is the belief in one's personal ability to do a task. Low self-efficacy is associated with learned helplessness, the debilitating lack of faith in one's ability to control one's environment. (3) Self-esteem is the extent to which people like or dislike themselves. (4) Self-monitoring is the extent to which people are able to observe their own behavior and adapt it to external situations. (5) Emotional intelligence is defined as the ability to carry out accurate reasoning about emotions and the ability to use emotions and emotional knowledge to enhance thought.

 II.2 Values, Attitudes, & Behavior
Organizational behavior (OB) is dedicated to better understanding and managing people at work. OB looks at two areas: individual behavior (discussed in this chapter) and group behavior (discussed in later chapters).

Values must be distinguished from attitudes and from behavior. (1) Values are abstract ideals that guide one's thinking and behavior across all situations. (2) Attitudes are defined as learned predispositions toward a given object. Attitudes have three components. The affective component consists of the feelings or emotions one has about a situation. The cognitive component consists of the beliefs and knowledge one has about a situation. The behavioral component refers to how one intends or expects to behave toward a situation. When attitudes and reality collide, the result may be cognitive dissonance, the psychological discomfort a person experiences between his or her cognitive attitude and incompatible behavior. Cognitive dissonance depends on three factors: importance, control, and rewards. The ways to reduce cognitive dissonance are to change your attitude and/or your behavior, belittle the importance of the inconsistent behavior, or find consonant elements that outweigh the dissonant ones. (3) Together, values and attitudes influence people's workplace behavior—their actions and judgments.

 II.3 Work-Related Attitudes & Behaviors Managers Need to Deal With
Managers need to be alert to work-related attitudes having to do with (1) job satisfaction, the extent to which you feel positively or negatively about various aspects of your work; (2) job involvement, the extent to which you identify or are personally involved with your job; and (3) organizational commitment, reflecting the extent to which an employee identifies with an organization and is committed to its goals.

Among the types of behavior that managers need to influence are (1) performance and productivity; (2) absenteeism, when an employee doesn't show up for work, and turnover, when employees leave their jobs; (3) organizational citizenship behaviors, those employee behaviors that are not directly part of employees' job descriptions—that exceed their work-role requirements; and (4) counterproductive work behaviors, behaviors that harm employees and the organization as a whole.

 II.4 Perception & Individual Behavior
Perception is the process of interpreting and understanding one's environment. The process can be boiled down to four

steps: selective attention, interpretation and evaluation, storing in memory, and retrieving from memory to make judgments and decisions. Perceptual errors can lead to mistakes that affect management.

Four types of distortion in perception are (1) selective perception, the tendency to filter out information that is discomforting, that seems irrelevant, or that contradicts one's beliefs; (2) stereotyping, the tendency to attribute to an individual the characteristics one believes are typical of the group to which that individual belongs; (3) the halo effect, the forming of an impression of an individual based on a single trait; and (4) causal attribution, the activity of inferring causes for observed behavior. Two attributional tendencies that can distort one's interpretation of observed behavior are the fundamental attribution bias, in which people attribute another person's behavior to his or her personal characteristics rather than to situational factors, and the self-serving bias, in which people tend to take more personal responsibility for success than for failure.

The self-fulfilling prophecy (Pygmalion effect) describes the phenomenon in which people's expectations of themselves or others leads them to behave in ways that make those expectations come true.

 II.5 Understanding Stress & Individual Behavior
Stress is the tension people feel when they are facing or enduring extraordinary demands, constraints, or opportunities and are uncertain about their ability to handle them effectively. Stress is the feeling of tension and pressure; the source of stress is called a stressor.

There are six sources of stress on the job: (1) Demands created by individual differences may arise from a Type A behavior pattern, meaning people have the personality characteristic that involves them in a chronic, determined struggle to accomplish more in less time. (2) Individual task demands are the stresses created by the job itself. (3) Individual role demands are the stresses created by other people's expectations of you. Roles are sets of behaviors that people expect of occupants of a position. Stress may come about because of role overload, role conflict, or role ambiguity. (4) Group demands are the stresses created by co-workers and managers. (5) Organizational demands are the stresses created by the environment and culture of the organization. (6) Nonwork demands are the stresses created by forces outside the organization, such as money problems or divorce.

Positive stress can be constructive. Negative stress can result in poor-quality work; such stress is revealed through physiological, psychological, or behavioral signs. One sign is burnout, a state of emotional, mental, and even physical exhaustion. Stress can lead to alcohol and other drug abuse.

There are buffers, or administrative changes, that managers can make to reduce the stressors that lead to employee burnout, such as adding extra staff or giving employees more power to make decisions. Some general organizational strategies for reducing unhealthy stressors are to roll out employee assistance programs, recommend a holistic wellness approach, create a supportive environment, make jobs interesting, and make career counseling available.

Management in Action

James Cameron's Personality & Attitudes Drive His Success

Reasonable people can debate the artistic merits of James Cameron's work. . . . What's indisputable, however, is that the *Avatar* director's influence extends far beyond his movie credits. More than George Lucas or Steven Spielberg, Michael Bay, or Pixar, Cameron is the most important commercial force in modern film, and his vision for the future of the movie business is rapidly demolishing anything that gets in its way.

There are 1.64 billion reasons that Cameron is Hollywood's director of the moment—that figure being the mid-January [2010] worldwide gross of *Avatar,* the blue-aliened, 3D extravaganza that earned Golden Globes for best director and best dramatic picture. By the time you read this, *Avatar* may have passed the $1.84 billion mark set by 1997's *Titanic,* Cameron's previous feature and current holder of the title Highest-Grossing Film of All Time. . . .

At 55, the man who declared himself king of the world at the 1998 Oscars has mellowed some. Cameron accepted his 2010 Golden Globes with a mix of humility and amazement. No one knows better than he how close *Avatar* came to not being made. Despite Cameron's track record for delivering large profits on big budgets, Twentieth Century Fox, which co-financed *Titanic,* hesitated to make an even riskier film that required the creation of a three-dimensional alien world. "I knew that if this failed my name would be dirt, but that's the nature of this business," says Cameron. "Every director knows that you can flame and burn like the Hindenburg, and do it very publicly."

With the studio balking, Cameron had to turn himself into an inventor-entrepreneur. Using his own funds, he developed the technology to bring *Avatar* to the screen, betting that what he saw in his head would be so visually persuasive that, ultimately, he could sell his souped-up camera rigs back to Hollywood at a potentially considerable profit. . . .

Cameron wrote the original script for *Avatar* in the mid-1990's. . . . Even 15 years ago, Cameron had a fully formed vision of Pandora—right down to the blue aliens, six-legged mammalian predators, and floating mountains. But he put any plans to film his *Avatar* script on indefinite hold, knowing that the existing technology could not do justice to his ambitions.

By 2000 he was growing impatient. So Cameron contacted Vincent Pace, an entrepreneur who helped design and manufacture the underwater lighting system for Cameron's 1989 movie, *The Abyss.* Through his eponymous company, which develops and rents cameras for use in hazardous conditions, Pace agreed to work with Cameron on a camera rig that could capture 2D and 3D images simultaneously. Cameron says the project cost about $12 million, much of it his money.

It's a rule as old as Hollywood: Never sink your own money into a movie. Ultimately, Cameron felt his investment would be justified not only because it would allow him to make *Avatar* but also because the new technology would accelerate the rollout of 3D, giving theater chains an incentive to upgrade their projectors and screens and moviegoers an incentive to leave their increasingly well-equipped living rooms.

Developing the technology was one massive project. Cameron also had to persuade Fox to finance *Avatar.* Although the studio had backed and distributed several Cameron films, the *Titanic* experience had made Fox executives cautious. Originally budgeted at $110 million, the film's production costs famously ballooned to $200 million when special effects and the cost of constructing the ship delayed filming. There were also months of rumors preceding the film's release that it would prove to be one of the worst business decisions in the history of the movies. Given all that scary background, says Twentieth Century Fox Co-Chairman Tom Rothman, "*Avatar* couldn't be rushed." In 2005 the studio decided to place a small wager on Cameron—$10 million so he could show proof of concept.

With the Fox money, Cameron repaired to the 280,000-square-foot hangar he leases in Playa Vista, California—where in the 1940s Howard Hughes built the *Spruce Goose*—and began working on a 3D film clip that he could use to persuade Fox brass to make the movie. Jeffrey Katzenberg, CEO of DreamWorks Animation, says he and Cameron were in touch frequently during the experimentation phase and that Cameron visited the DreamWorks facility in Glendale, California, to learn more about animation software. "We create our own world in animation," Katzenberg says. "But this was the first time a director could take real characters and put them into a world he created, in real time." . . .

In October 2005, Cameron screened his 3D segment for four Fox executives at the offices of his production company, LightStorm Entertainment, in Santa Monica, California. "Their eyes kind of lit up," Cameron says. "They could see what I had been talking about for months." But *Avatar* producer and Cameron business partner Jon Landau says Fox still wanted a shorter script and a more reasonable budget. In response, says Landau, Cameron combined several characters to trim expenses. Cameron says he also agreed to cut his usual fee in half and take a lower percentage of the film's revenues if *Avatar* wasn't profitable. "Luckily," says Cameron, "We're at such a stratospheric level now that we're not worried about that."

By mid-2006, according to someone involved in the negotiations, Fox was still concerned that making *Avatar* would cost too much money. "They told us in no uncertain terms that they were passing on this film," Cameron says. Cameron decided the best way forward was to try to persuade another studio to get involved. Walt Disney had produced two of the director's underwater documentaries, so Cameron invited Dick Cook, then Disney's studio chief, to watch the clip. "We loved Jim and would have liked to work with him," says Cook. "He has an infectious love of 3D that impressed us. Unfortunately, we never got that far." The reason: Fox had the right of first refusal. "We were never going to let this one get away," says Fox Co-Chairman Jim Gianopoulos.

To get the deal done, the studio decided to bring in partners to share the financial burden. Fox already had a deal with Dune Entertainment, part of a New York private equity fund that since 2006 has contributed financing for Fox movies. To further reduce its risk, Fox began talking to London-based Ingenious Media. . . .

"We consider all filmmaking a dangerous game," says [Rupert Murdoch, chairman and CEO of News Corp., which owns Fox] "and we always lay off [risk] to the film funds when we can. This time we laid off more than usual. But we own much of the distribution and other rights. In the end, we will make much more money than them." In October 2006, Fox agreed to make *Avatar*. Cameron says he still isn't quite sure why Fox finally jumped aboard but recalls studio executives saying: "We don't get the giant blue guys with the tails, but we believe in you." . . .

Production began, and word soon leaked out that something extraordinary was going on in Cameron's airplane hangar. The director had rigged the ceiling of the cavernous space with cameras that tracked his actors, who were wearing versions of the motion-capture suits made famous by the character Gollum in Peter Jackson's *Lord of the Rings* trilogy. Headsets rigged with tiny cameras captured actors' facial expressions and eye movement, a jolt of reality that Cameron deemed crucial if he was going to make the film. Using software developed in-house, the crew imported the actors into Pandora's digital world while Cameron was shooting.

For Discussion

1. How would you evaluate Cameron in terms of the Big Five personality dimensions?

2. How would you evaluate Cameron in terms of the five traits important to organizational behavior? Explain.

3. What were Twentieth Century Fox's attitudes toward producing the film at the start of the case—use the three components of attitudes—and why did they change over time?

4. Do you believe that Cameron's personality and attitudes affected the workplace attitudes and behaviors of the film's actors? Explain your rationale.

5. Did the management at Twentieth Century Fox display any of the four distortions in perceptions? Explain.

6. What factors were causing stress for Cameron? Explain.

Source: Excerpted from R. Grover, T. Lowry, and M. White, "King of the World (Again)," *Bloomberg Businessweek*, February 1 & 8, 2010, pp. 48–53. Reprinted with permission.

Self-Assessment

What Is Your Emotional Intelligence Score?

Objectives

1. To help you assess your emotional intelligence.
2. To expand your knowledge of the new interpretations of intelligence.

Introduction

Employers have long been guided by one dimension of our personality, our intelligence quotient (IQ). However, a number of researchers and observers of human behavior have been examining components of intelligence that include emotions. Your emotional intelligence (EI) includes your abilities to motivate yourself and persist even when you are frustrated, to control your impulses and delay gratification, to regulate your mood and keep distress from overwhelming your thinking ability, to empathize with others, and to hope. The recognition of the emotional dimension to intelligence is vital today in a world of constant change and increased stress. Having a sense of your own EI is fundamental to being successful. The purpose of this exercise is to determine your own EI.

Instructions

Use this scale to indicate the extent to which you agree or disagree with each statement below.

1 = strongly disagree

2 = disagree

3 = neither agree nor disagree

4 = agree

5 = strongly agree

1. I am usually aware—from moment to moment—of my feelings as they change.	1 2 3 4 5
2. I think before I act.	1 2 3 4 5
3. I am impatient when I want something.	1 2 3 4 5
4. I bounce back quickly from life's setbacks.	1 2 3 4 5
5. I can pick up subtle social cues that indicate others' needs or wants.	1 2 3 4 5
6. I'm very good at handling myself in social situations.	1 2 3 4 5
7. I'm persistent in going after the things I want.	1 2 3 4 5
8. When people share their problems with me, I'm good at putting myself in their shoes.	1 2 3 4 5
9. When I'm in a bad mood, I make a strong effort to get out of it.	1 2 3 4 5
10. I can find common ground and build rapport with people from all walks of life.	1 2 3 4 5

Scoring & Interpretation

This questionnaire taps the five basic dimensions of EI: self-awareness (items 1 and 9), self-management (2, 4), self-motivation (3, 7), empathy (5, 8), and social skills (6, 10). Compute your total EI score by adding your responses to all 10 statements. Your total score will fall between 10 and 50. While no definite cutoff scores are available, scores of 40 or higher indicate a high EI. Scores of 20 or less suggest a relatively low EI.

Emotional intelligence is a collection of abilities and competencies that have an effect on a person's capacity to succeed in dealing with demands and pressures. People with high EI have the capacity to correctly perceive, evaluate, articulate, and manage emotions and feelings.

EI may be most predictive of performance in jobs such as sales or management, in which achievement is based as much on interpersonal skills as on technical ability. People with low EI are likely to have trouble managing others, making successful sales presentations, and functioning on teams.

Questions for Discussion

1. Did the results surprise you? Why or why not?

2. Look at the three items on which your score was lowest. What are some skills or attitudes you can work on to improve your EI? Explain.

3. Do you think your EI would help or hinder you when working in a team?

Based on D. Goleman, *Emotional Intelligence: Why It Can Matter More Than IQ* (New York: Bantam, 1995).

Ethical Dilemma

Should the "Fake Bad Scale" Be Used in Injury Lawsuits?

A test designed to expose fakers is roiling the field of personal-injury law, distressing plaintiffs and strengthening the hand of employers and insurers.

Proponents hail the true-or-false test as a valid way to identify people feigning pain, psychological symptoms, or other ills to collect a payout. In hundreds of cases, expert witnesses have testified that the test provided evidence that plaintiffs were lying about their injuries, just as suggested by the test's colorful name: the Fake Bad Scale.

Use of the scale surged last year after publishers of one of the world's most venerable personality tests, the Minnesota Multiphasic Personality Inventory, endorsed the Fake Bad Scale and made it an official subset of the MMPI. The Fake Bad Scale has been used by 75% of neuropsychologists, who regularly appear in court as expert witnesses, according to a survey by St. Louis University.

But now some psychologists say the test is branding as liars too many people who have genuine symptoms. Some say it discriminates against women, too. In May [2008], an American Psychological Association panel said there appeared to be a lack of good research supporting the test.

In two Florida court cases [in 2007], state judges, before allowing the test to be cited, held special hearings on whether it was valid enough to be used as courtroom evidence. Both judges ended up barring it.

"Virtually everyone is a malingerer according to this scale," says a leading critic, James Butcher, a retired University of Minnesota psychologist who has published research faulting the Fake Bad Scale. "This is great for insurance companies, but not great for people."

The test asks a person to answer true or false to 43 statements, such as "My sleep is fitful and disturbed" and "I have nightmares every few nights." Someone who suffers from, say, posttraumatic stress disorder might legitimately answer "true" to these questions. But doing so would earn the test taker two points toward the total of 23 or so that marks a person as a possible malingerer.

Other test statements are "I have very few headaches" and "I have few or no pains." These are false, someone who has chronic headaches would say. Again, those replies would incur two more points toward a possible assessment as a malingerer. About a third of the questions relate to physical symptoms; there are questions about stress, sleep disturbance, and low energy. There is also a batch of questions related to denial of bad behavior. For instance, those who answer false to "I do not always tell the truth" get a point toward malingering. . . .

[The test] recently figured in the case of Steven Thompson, a onetime truck driver in Iraq for the KBR unit of Halliburton Inc. He said he hadn't been able to hold a job since returning to the United States in 2004. Two doctors concluded Mr. Thompson had "chronic" and "fairly severe" posttraumatic stress disorder. He filed a disability claim that was denied by the insurer of Halliburton's since-sold KBR unit.

Mr. Thompson appealed to the U.S. Labor Department, which has jurisdiction in such cases. He testified that memories of attacks on his convoys, seeing dead bodies, and smelling burning flesh led to nightmares and sleeping problems that left him too irritable and difficult to work with to hold a job.

A psychiatrist hired by the defense, John D. Griffith of Houston, concluded Mr. Thompson was exaggerating his symptoms, and cited his score of 32 on the Fake Bad Scale. A Labor Department administrative law judge denied Mr. Thompson's claim, citing the test results along with inconsistencies in his testimony. Mr. Thompson is appealing. . . .

Solving the Dilemma

How would you have ruled if you were the administrative law judge in Mr. Thompson's case?

1. I would deny the claim. The test results show that Mr. Thompson is a malingerer who is most likely lying about his condition. He just wants to be paid for doing nothing.

2. I would grant the claim based on conclusions reached by the American Psychological Association (APA). The APA questioned the validity of the survey and it thus should not be used to determine whether someone is lying.

3. I don't believe that you can determine whether someone is lying based on answers to questions about physical symptoms. Approve the claim.

4. Although more research is needed to support the accuracy of the test, I would deny the claim because Mr. Thompson scored 32 and there were inconsistencies in his testimony.

5. Invent other options.

Source: Excerpted from David Armstrong, "Malingerer Test Roils Personal-Injury Law," *The Wall Street Journal*, March 5, 2008, p. A1, A13. Copyright © 2008 Dow Jones & Company, Inc. Reproduced with permission of Dow Jones & Company, Inc. via Copyright Clearance Center.

chapter 12

Motivating Employees
Achieving Superior Performance in the Workplace

Major Questions You Should Be Able to Answer

12.1 Motivating for Performance
Major Question: What's the motivation for studying motivation?

12.2 Content Perspectives on Employee Motivation
Major Question: What kinds of needs motivate employees?

12.3 Process Perspectives on Employee Motivation
Major Question: Is a good reward good enough? How do other factors affect motivation?

12.4 Job Design Perspectives on Motivation
Major Question: What's the best way to design jobs—adapt people to work or work to people?

12.5 Reinforcement Perspectives on Motivation
Major Question: What are the types of incentives I might use to influence employee behavior?

12.6 Using Compensation & Other Rewards to Motivate
Major Question: How can I use compensation and other rewards to motivate people?

Managing for Motivation: Keeping Employees Invested in Their Jobs

"Get a life!" everyone says. But what, exactly, is a "life," anyway?

As more and more people have begun asking this question, it has spilled over into organizational life. The result has been a new category of work rewards and incentives called *work-life benefits.*

As one definition has it, work-life benefits are programs "used by employers to increase productivity and commitment by removing certain barriers that make it hard for people to strike a balance between their work and personal lives."[1] Examples are nonsalary incentives such as flexible work arrangements, tuition assistance, and paid time off for education and community service.

In managing for motivation, the subject of this chapter, you need to be thinking about employees not as "human capital" or "capital assets" but as people who are *investors:* they are investing their time, energy, and intelligence—their lives—in your organization, for which they deserve a return that makes sense to them.

To keep your employees invested in their jobs and performing well for the company, it helps for you to know what the Gallup Organization discovered in surveying 80,000 managers and 1 million workers over 25 years.[2] Gallup found that in the best workplaces employees gave strong "yes" answers to the following 12 questions:

- Do I know what's expected of me?
- Do I have the right materials and equipment I need to do my work right?
- Do I have the opportunity to do what I do best every day?
- In the last 7 days, have I received recognition or praise for good work?
- Does my supervisor, or someone at work, seem to care about me as a person?
- Is there someone at work who encourages my development?
- Does my opinion seem to count?
- Does the mission of my company make me feel like my work is important?
- Are my co-workers committed to doing quality work?
- Do I have a best friend at work?
- In the last 6 months, have I talked with someone about my progress?
- Have I had opportunities to learn and grow?

The best managers, Gallup says, meet with workers individually at least every 3 months, not just once or twice a year. In doing so, they not only discuss performance but also try to find out what employees want to accomplish and how the manager can help. In addition, good managers focus on strengths, rather than weaknesses, allowing employees to devote time to what they do best.

Even before *Fortune* magazine began publishing its annual list of "The 100 Best Companies to Work For," managers had been concerned about trying to motivate their employees. The best organizations, according to a project leader who helps with the *Fortune* list, keep their employees an average of 6 years, as opposed to the nationwide average of 3.6 years. They accomplish this by pushing for employees at all levels to feel involved in the company's success.[3]

For Discussion Which 3 of the 12 questions listed above are most important to you? Which do you think are most important to most employees?

This chapter discusses how to motivate people to perform well. We consider motivation from four perspectives: content (covering theories by Maslow, Alderfer, McClelland, and Herzberg); process (covering equity, expectancy, and goal-setting theories); job design; and reinforcement. Finally, we apply these perspectives to compensation and other rewards for motivating performance.

What's the motivation for studying motivation?

THE BIG PICTURE

Motivation is defined as the psychological processes that arouse and direct people's goal-directed behavior. The model of how it works is that people have certain needs that motivate them to perform specific behaviors for which they receive rewards, both extrinsic and intrinsic, that feed back and satisfy the original need. The three major perspectives on motivation are need-based, process, and reinforcement.

What would make you rise a half hour earlier than usual to ensure you got to work on time—and to perform your best once there? Among the possible inducements we mentioned earlier (such as those offered by SAS and Google) are the following: free snacks, on-site laundry, child care assistance, scholarships for employees' children, having your dog at work.[4]

But what happens during a recession, when companies get more frugal? Then you would probably lose some of the more exotic boom-time benefits, such as sabbaticals or child-adoption assistance.[5] On the other hand, as managers realize they have to boost employee spirits after staff cutbacks and reward them for doing additional work, remaining workers might well *gain* some benefits: free massages, concierge services, office sports team sponsorships, or whatever.[6] "The cost is so small in comparison with the lift we get in employee morale," says one vice-president at USAA, a Texas financial-services provider.[7] Colorado's New Belgium Brewery, maker of Fat Tire ale, celebrates employees' first-year anniversaries by giving them custom bicycles. "It's a couple of hundred dollars for the bike," says a company officer. "But it means so much more."[8]

Whether employment rates are high or low, there are always companies, industries, and occupations in which employers feel they need to bend over backward to retain their human capital.

Motivation: What It Is, Why It's Important

Why do people do the things they do? The answer is this: they are mainly motivated to fulfill their wants, their needs.

What Is Motivation & How Does It Work?   *Motivation* **may be defined as the psychological processes that arouse and direct goal-directed behavior.**[9] Motivation is difficult to understand because you can't actually see it or know it in another person; it must be *inferred* from one's behavior. Nevertheless, it's imperative that you as a manager understand the process of motivation if you are to guide employees in accomplishing your organization's objectives.

The way motivation works actually is complex. However, in a simple model of motivation, people have certain *needs* that *motivate* them to perform specific *behaviors* for which they receive *rewards* that *feed back* and satisfy the original need. *(See Figure 12.1.)*

For example, as an hourly worker you desire more money (need), which impels you (motivates you) to work more hours (behavior), which provides you with more money (reward) and informs you (feedback loop) that working more hours will fulfill your need for more money in the future.

Rewards (as well as motivation itself) are of two types—*extrinsic* and *intrinsic.*[10] Managers can use both to encourage better work performance.

Feedback Reward informs you whether behavior worked and should be used again.

figure 12.1

A SIMPLE MODEL OF
MOTIVATION

- **Extrinsic rewards—satisfaction in the payoff from others. An *extrinsic reward* is the payoff, such as money, a person receives from others for performing a particular task.** An extrinsic reward is an external reward; the payoff comes from pleasing others.

     Example: An experiment by General Electric found that paying employees who were smokers up to $750—an extrinsic reward—to quit and stay off cigarettes was three times as successful as a comparison group that got no paid incentives.[11] (Other research finds that such extrinsic rewards have little lasting effect on making workers healthier.)[12]

- **Intrinsic rewards—satisfaction in performing the task itself. An *intrinsic reward* is the satisfaction, such as a feeling of accomplishment, a person receives from performing the particular task itself.** An intrinsic reward is an internal reward; the payoff comes from pleasing yourself.

     Example: Jenny Balaze left her post in Ernst & Young LLC's Washington, DC, office to spend 12 weeks in Buenos Aires as a volunteer providing free accounting services to a small publishing firm. It was among "the best three months of my life," says the 27-year-old business advisory services manager.[13]

Why Is Motivation Important?   It seems obvious that organizations would want to motivate their employees to be more productive. Actually, though, as a manager you will find knowledge of motivation important for five reasons.[14] In order of importance, you want to motivate people to . . .

1. *Join your organization.* You need to instill in talented prospective workers the desire to come to work for you.

2. *Stay with your organization.* Whether you are in good economic times or bad, you always want to be able to retain good people.

3. *Show up for work at your organization.* In many organizations, absenteeism and lateness are tremendous problems.[15]

4. *Be engaged while at your organization.* Engaged employees produce higher-quality work and better customer service.

5. *Do extra for your organization.* You hope your employees will perform extra tasks above and beyond the call of duty (be organizational "good citizens").

The Four Major Perspectives on Motivation: Overview

There is no theory accepted by everyone as to what motivates people. In this chapter, therefore, we present the four principal perspectives. From these, you may be able to select what ideas seem most workable to you. The four perspectives on motivation are (1) *content,* (2) *process,* (3) *job design,* and (4) *reinforcement,* as described in the following four main sections. ●

major question? What kinds of needs motivate employees?

THE BIG PICTURE

Content perspectives are theories emphasizing the needs that motivate people. Needs are defined as physiological or psychological deficiencies that arouse behavior. The content perspective includes four theories: Maslow's hierarchy of needs, Alderfer's ERG theory, McClelland's acquired needs theory, and Herzberg's two-factor theory.

Content perspectives, **also known as** *need-based perspectives,* **are theories that emphasize the needs that motivate people.** Content theorists ask, "What kind of needs motivate employees in the workplace?" *Needs* **are defined as physiological or psychological deficiencies that arouse behavior.** They can be strong or weak, and, because they are influenced by environmental factors, they can vary over time and from place to place.

In addition to McGregor's Theory X/Theory Y (see Chapter 2), content perspectives include four theories:

- Maslow's hierarchy of needs theory
- Alderfer's ERG Theory
- McClelland's acquired needs theory
- Herzberg's two-factor theory

Maslow's Hierarchy of Needs Theory: Five Levels

In 1943, Brandeis University psychology professor **Abraham Maslow,** one of the first researchers to study motivation, put forth his *hierarchy of needs theory,* **which proposes that people are motivated by five levels of needs: (1) physiological, (2) safety, (3) love, (4) esteem, and (5) self-actualization.**[16]

Self-actualization. No one has to engage in volunteerism, as this woman is doing by teaching reading to a young girl. But for some people, according to Maslow's theory, it represents the kind of realization of the best life has to offer—after other needs are satisfied. What activity or experience within your lifetime would represent self-fulfillment for you, the best that would realize your potential?

The Five Levels of Needs   In proposing this hierarchy of five needs, ranging from basic to highest level, Maslow suggested that needs are never completely satisfied. That is, our actions are aimed at fulfilling the "deprived" needs, the needs that remain unsatisfied at any point in time. Thus, for example, once you have achieved safety (security), which is the second most basic need, you will then seek to fulfill the third most basic need—love (belongingness).

In order of ascendance, from bottom to top, the five levels of needs are as follows. *(See Figure 12.2.)*

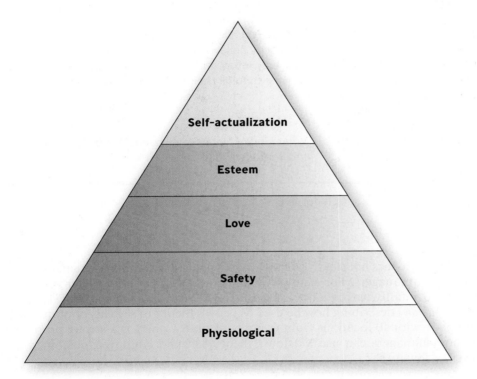

figure 12.2

MASLOW'S HIERARCHY OF NEEDS

1. Physiological Needs   These are the most basic human physical needs, in which one is concerned with having food, clothing, shelter, and comfort and with self-preservation.

2. Safety Needs   These needs are concerned with physical safety and emotional security, so that a person is concerned with avoiding violence and threats.

3. Love Needs   Once basic needs and security are taken care of, people look for love, friendship, and affection.

4. Esteem Needs   After they meet their social needs, people focus on such matters as self-respect, status, reputation, recognition, and self-confidence.

5. Self-Actualization Needs   The highest level of need, self-actualization is self-fulfillment—the need to develop one's fullest potential, to become the best one is capable of being.

Higher-Level Needs: One Man Finds a Way to Measure Integrity

Software engineer Firinn Taisdeal of Walnut Creek, California, designed a social event database, now called LinkUp Central, that offers its 19,000 San Francisco Bay–area members 12,000 events per year, from rock climbing to theater, for $5 a month. But he discovered early on that events were being ruined and hosts disappointed by people who didn't show up. "Flakes," he calls them.

Raising Integrity. Taisdeal's solution was to modify the database to chart patterns of flakiness—an accountability system. Thus, if a person RSVPs for events but doesn't show up 50% of the time, his or her "reliability threshold" goes down. With some events, such as restaurant dinners, guests can sign up only if they have a reliability index of 50% or more. "By changing their behavior over time," says one report, "people can improve their ratings."[17]

Cultural Creatives. Driven to raise the level of integrity in the culture, Taisdeal is an example of a "cultural creative," a term coined by sociologists Paul Ray and Sherry Ruth Anderson to describe people who long to create deep and meaningful change in their lives and in the world.[18] Another name for people like Taisdeal is "tempered radical," the term that Stanford organizational behavior professor Debra Meyerson uses to describe people who work to strike a balance between what they believe in and what the system expects.[19] In this way, they fulfill their safety needs while also striving to fulfill their self-actualization needs.

YOUR CALL

What kind of higher-level needs do you think you could fulfill through your work?

Research does not clearly support Maslow's theory, although it remains popular among managers. For example, Chip Conley, CEO and founder of Joie de Vivre Hospitality, wrote a book (*Peak: How Great Companies Get Their Mojo from Maslow*) describing how he used Maslow's theory to save his boutique hotel company with 40 locations from going bankrupt. Conley is a strong proponent of how managers can use Maslow's theory to build employee, customer, and investor loyalty.[20]

Using the Hierarchy of Needs Theory to Motivate Employees For managers, the importance of Maslow's contribution is that he showed that workers have needs beyond that of just earning a paycheck. To the extent the organization permits, managers should first try to meet employees' level 1 and level 2 needs, of course, so that employees won't be preoccupied with them. Then, however, they need to give employees a chance to fulfill their higher-level needs in ways that also advance the goals of the organization.

Alderfer's ERG Theory: Existence, Relatedness, & Growth

Developed by **Clayton Alderfer** in the late 1960s, *ERG theory* **assumes that three basic needs influence behavior—existence, relatedness, and growth,** represented by the letters E, R, and G.

The Three Kinds of Needs Unlike Maslow's theory, ERG theory suggests that behavior is motivated by three needs, not five, and that more than one need may be activated at a time rather than activated in a stair-step hierarchy. From lowest to highest level, the three needs are as follows:

1. E—Existence Needs   Existence needs are the desire for physiological and material well-being.

2. R—Relatedness Needs   Relatedness needs are the desire to have meaningful relationships with people who are significant to us.

3. G—Growth Needs   Growth needs are the desire to grow as human beings and to use our abilities to their fullest potential.

Alderfer also held that if our higher-level needs (such as growth needs) are frustrated, we will then seek more intensely to fulfill our lower-level needs (such as existence needs). This is called the *frustration-regression component*.[21]

Using the ERG Theory to Motivate Employees   The frustration-regression component of ERG theory certainly has some applicability to the workplace. For example, if you work as a bill collector making difficult phone calls and having no contact with co-workers, you might lobby your boss for better pay and benefits. Also ERG theory is consistent with the finding that individual and cultural differences influence our need states. It's clear, for instance, that people are motivated by different needs at different times in their lives, which suggests that managers should customize their reward and recognition programs to meet employees' varying needs.

McClelland's Acquired Needs Theory: Achievement, Affiliation, & Power

David McClelland, a well-known psychologist, investigated the needs for affiliation and power and as a consequence proposed the ***acquired needs theory,*** **which states that three needs—achievement, affiliation, and power—are major motives determining people's behavior in the workplace.**[22] McClelland believes that we are not born with our needs; rather we learn them from the culture—from our life experiences.

The Three Needs   Managers are encouraged to recognize three needs in themselves and others and to attempt to create work environments that are responsive to them. The three needs, one of which tends to be dominant in each of us, are as follows. *(See Figure 12.3.)*

- **Need for achievement—"I need to excel at tasks."**   This is the desire to excel, to do something better or more efficiently, to solve problems, to achieve excellence in challenging tasks.
- **Need for affiliation—"I need close relationships."**   This is the desire for friendly and warm relations with other people.
- **Need for power—"I need to control others."**   This is the desire to be responsible for other people, to influence their behavior or to control them.[23]

McClelland identifies two forms of the need for power.

The negative kind is the need for *personal power,* as expressed in the desire to dominate others, and involves manipulating people for one's own gratification.

The positive kind, characteristic of top managers and leaders, is the desire for *institutional power,* as expressed in the need to solve problems that further organizational goals.

figure 12.3

McCLELLAND'S THREE NEEDS

A "well-balanced" individual: achievement, affiliation, and power are of equal size.

A "control freak" individual: achievement is normal, but affiliation is small and power is large.

Using Acquired Needs Theory to Motivate Employees McClelland associates the three needs with different sets of work preferences, as follows:[24]

- **Need for achievement.** If you (or an employee) are happy with accomplishment of a task being its own reward, don't mind or even prefer working alone, and are willing to take moderate risks, then you probably have a *high need for achievement.* That being the case, you (or your employee) would probably prefer doing the kind of work that offers feedback on performance, challenging but achievable goals, and individual responsibility for results. People high in need for achievement tend to advance in technical fields requiring creativity and individual skills.[25]

- **Need for power.** If you, like most effective managers, have a *high need for power,* that means you enjoy being in control of people and events and being recognized for this responsibility. Accordingly, your preference would probably be for work that allows you to control or have an effect on people and be publicly recognized for your accomplishments.

- **Need for affiliation.** If you tend to seek social approval and satisfying personal relationships, you may have a *high need for affiliation.* In that case, you may not be the most efficient manager because at times you will have to make decisions that will make people resent you. Instead, you will tend to prefer work, such as sales, that provides for personal relationships and social approval.

Example

Acquired Needs Theory: The Need for Power of an Ad Agency CEO

In their book *The 100-Mile Walk: A Father and Son on a Quest to Find the Essence of Leadership,* Sander A. Flaum and his son, Jonathan, describe the generational values that divide them.[26] Sander, 69, became CEO of health care ad agency Robert A. Becker Euro RSCG in New York, a $1.7 billion business with 975 employees. Jonathan, 38, started his own public/corporate relations firm, WriteMind Communications, in Asheville, North Carolina, and hires people by the project. Sander learned to be diligent and loyal and to put work ahead of family, which led to his divorce. Jonathan grew up to be self-reliant, skeptical, and determined to balance work and family.

Unlike Father, Unlike Son. When the two decided to coauthor a book on leadership, they arranged to walk a combined total of 100 miles together in various places, from New York City to pre–Hurricane Katrina New Orleans, during which they talked about their views of the workplace. The book offers a comparison of their outlooks.

Different Views. Sander's view: "Show company loyalty." Jonathan's view: "Move on if recognition and growth opportunities are absent." Sander: "Young people in India and China are not talking about work/life balance or . . . worrying about how to spend more time at home." Jonathan: "Work without adequate time for intimate connection and personal time has long-term degenerative effects." Sander: "I think you should be attuned to the knowledge that, at any time, every competitor of yours is out to recruit your best people, steal your ideas, take over your customers, and reinvent and improve your products." Jonathan: "Paranoia works . . . sometimes. But it robs us of fully enjoying those times when everything is just fine."

YOUR CALL

In acquired needs theory, Sander would seem to embody the need for power. What needs do you think Jonathan embodies?

Herzberg's Two-Factor Theory: From Dissatisfying Factors to Satisfying Factors

Frederick Herzberg arrived at his needs-based theory as a result of a landmark study of 203 accountants and engineers, who were interviewed to determine the factors responsible for job satisfaction and dissatisfaction.[27] Job satisfaction was more frequently associated with achievement, recognition, characteristics of the work, responsibility, and advancement. Job dissatisfaction was more often associated with working conditions, pay and security, company policies, supervisors, and interpersonal relationships. The result was Herzberg's ***two-factor theory,*** **which proposed that work satisfaction and dissatisfaction arise from two different factors— work satisfaction from *motivating factors* and work dissatisfaction from *hygiene factors.***

Hygiene Factors versus Motivating Factors   In Herzberg's theory, the hygiene factors are the lower-level needs, the motivating factors are the higher-level needs. The two areas are separated by a zone in which employees are neither satisfied nor dissatisfied. *(See Figure 12.4.)*

figure 12.4

HERZBERG'S TWO-FACTOR THEORY: SATISFACTION VERSUS DISSATISFACTION

Motivating factors:
"What will make my people *satisfied*?"
Achievement
Recognition
The work itself
Responsibility
Advancement & growth

No satisfaction   Satisfaction

Neutral area: neither satisfied nor dissatisfied

Dissatisfaction   No dissatisfaction

Hygiene factors:
"What will make my people *dissatisfied*?"
Pay & security
Working conditions
Interpersonal relationships
Company policy
Supervisors

- **Hygiene factors—"Why are my people dissatisfied?"** The lower–level needs, *hygiene factors,* are factors associated with job *dissatisfaction*—such as salary, working conditions, interpersonal relationships, and company policy—all of which affect the job *context* in which people work.

    An example of a hygiene factor is the temperature in a factory that's not air-conditioned during the summer. Installing air-conditioning will remove a cause of job dissatisfaction. It will not, however, spur factory workers' motivation and make them greatly satisfied in their work. Because motivating factors are absent, workers become, in Herzberg's view, merely neutral in their attitudes toward work—neither dissatisfied nor satisfied.

- **Motivating factors—"What will make my people satisfied?"** The higher-level needs, *motivating factors,* or simply *motivators,* are factors associated with job *satisfaction*—such as achievement, recognition, responsibility, and advancement—all of which affect the job content or the rewards of work performance. Motivating factors—challenges, opportunities, recognition—must be instituted, Herzberg believed, to spur superior work performance.

    An example of a motivating factor would be to give factory workers more control over their work. For example, instead of repeating a single task over and over, a worker might join with other workers on a team in which each one does several tasks. This is the approach that Swedish automaker Volvo took in building cars.

Using Two-Factor Theory to Motivate Employees During the recent recession, with fewer jobs available, more people were stuck in jobs they disliked (61% in 2009, compared with 45% in 1987).[28] If you were managing such employees, the basic lesson of Herzberg's research is that you should first eliminate dissatisfaction, making sure that working conditions, pay levels, and company policies are reasonable. You should then concentrate on spurring motivation by providing opportunities for achievement, recognition, responsibility, and personal growth. All these relate to job design and enrichment—creating jobs that include motivating factors—topics we take up in Section 12.4.

The four needs theories are compared below. *(See Figure 12.5.)* ●

figure 12.5

A COMPARISON OF NEEDS THEORIES: MASLOW, ALDERFER, McCLELLAND, AND HERZBERG
McClelland has no classification for lower-level needs.

�҉ 12.3 PROCESS PERSPECTIVES ON EMPLOYEE MOTIVATION

Is a good reward good enough? How do other factors affect motivation?

major
question?

THE BIG PICTURE
Process perspectives, which are concerned with the thought processes by which people decide how to act, have three viewpoints: equity theory, expectancy theory, and goal-setting theory.

Process perspectives **are concerned with the thought processes by which people decide how to act**—how employees choose behavior to meet their needs. Whereas need-based perspectives simply try to understand employee needs, process perspectives go further and try to understand why employees have different needs, what behaviors they select to satisfy them, and how they decide if their choices were successful.

In this section we discuss three process perspectives on motivation:

- Equity theory
- Expectancy theory
- Goal-setting theory

Equity Theory: How Fairly Do You Think You're Being Treated in Relation to Others?

Fairness—or, perhaps equally important, the *perception* of fairness—can be a big issue in organizations. For example, if, as a salesperson for Best Buy, you received a 10% bonus for doubling your sales, would that be enough? What if other Best Buy salespeople received 15%?

Equity theory **focuses on employee perceptions as to how fairly they think they are being treated compared with others.** Developed by psychologist **J. Stacy Adams,** equity theory is based on the idea that employees are motivated to see fairness in the rewards they expect for task performance.[29] Employees are motivated to resolve feelings of injustice. How, for example, might employees respond to knowing that the average pay for CEOs is greater than 180 times the average worker's pay? How about the fact that women make about 20% less than men for comparable work?[30] Some experts suggest that this imbalance is partly responsible for the more than $50 billion a year in employee theft.[31] (In France in 2009, workers about to be laid off at Caterpillar were so angry that they took their managers hostage.)[32]

The Elements of Equity Theory: Comparing Your Inputs & Outputs with Those of Others   The key elements in equity theory are *inputs, outputs (rewards),* and *comparisons. (See Figure 12.6, next page.)*

- **Inputs—"What do you think you're putting into the job?"** The inputs that people perceive they give to an organization are their time, effort, training, experience, intelligence, creativity, seniority, status, and so on.
- **Outputs or rewards—"What do you think you're getting out of the job?"** The outputs are the rewards that people receive from an organization:

figure 12.6

EQUITY THEORY

How people perceive they are being fairly or unfairly rewarded

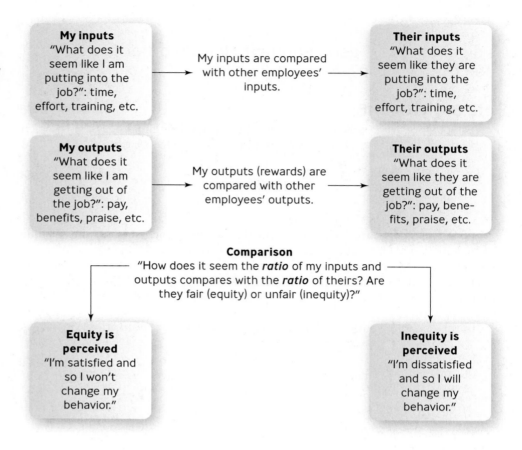

My inputs
"What does it seem like I am putting into the job?": time, effort, training, etc.

My inputs are compared with other employees' inputs.

Their inputs
"What does it seem like they are putting into the job?": time, effort, training, etc.

My outputs
"What does it seem like I am getting out of the job?": pay, benefits, praise, etc.

My outputs (rewards) are compared with other employees' outputs.

Their outputs
"What does it seem like they are getting out of the job?": pay, benefits, praise, etc.

Comparison
"How does it seem the *ratio* of my inputs and outputs compares with the *ratio* of theirs? Are they fair (equity) or unfair (inequity)?"

Equity is perceived
"I'm satisfied and so I won't change my behavior."

Inequity is perceived
"I'm dissatisfied and so I will change my behavior."

pay, benefits, praise, recognition, bonuses, promotions, status perquisites (corner office with a view, say, or private parking space), and so on.

* **Comparison—"How do you think your ratio of inputs and rewards compares with those of others?"** Equity theory suggests that people compare the *ratio* of their own outcomes to inputs against the *ratio* of someone else's outcomes to inputs. When employees compare the ratio of their inputs and outputs (rewards) with those of others—whether co-workers within the organization or even other people in similar jobs outside it—they then make a judgment about fairness. Either they perceive there is *equity*—they are satisfied with the ratio and so they don't change their behavior. Or they perceive there is *inequity*—they feel resentful and act to change the inequity.

To get a sense of your own reaction to equity differences, see the Self-Assessment at the end of this chapter.

Using Equity Theory to Motivate Employees   Adams suggests that employees who feel they are being underrewarded will respond to the perceived inequity in one or more negative ways, as by reducing their inputs, trying to change the outputs or rewards they receive, distorting the inequity, changing the object of comparison, or leaving the situation. *(See Table 12.1, opposite page.)*

By contrast, employees who think they are treated fairly are more likely to support organizational change, more apt to cooperate in group settings, and less apt to turn to arbitration and the courts to remedy real or imagined wrongs.

table 12.1

SOME WAYS EMPLOYEES TRY
TO REDUCE INEQUITY

- **They will reduce their inputs:** They will do less work, take long breaks, call in "sick" on Mondays, leave early on Fridays, and so on.

- **They will try to change the outputs or rewards they receive:** They will lobby the boss for a raise, or they will pilfer company equipment.

- **They will distort the inequity:** They will exaggerate how hard they work so they can complain they're not paid what they're worth.

- **They will change the object of comparison:** They may compare themselves with another person instead of the original one.

- **They will leave the situation:** They will quit, transfer, or shift to another

Three practical lessons that can be drawn from equity theory are as follows.

1. Employee Perceptions Are What Count   Probably the most important result of research on equity theory is this: no matter how fair managers think the organization's policies, procedures, and reward system are, each employee's *perception* of those factors is what counts.

2. Employee Participation Helps   Managers benefit by allowing employees to participate in important decisions. For example, a recent study showed that employees were more satisfied with changes to their jobs when they participated in creating the changes.[33]

3. Having an Appeal Process Helps   When employees are able to appeal decisions affecting their welfare, it promotes the belief that management treats them fairly. Perceptions of fair treatment promote job satisfaction, commitment, and citizenship behavior and reduce absenteeism and turnover.[34]

Expectancy Theory: How Much Do You Want & How Likely Are You to Get It?

Introduced by **Victor Vroom,** *expectancy theory* **suggests that people are motivated by two things: (1) how much they want something and (2) how likely they think they are to get it.**[35] In other words, assuming they have choices, people will make the choice that promises them the greatest reward if they think they can get it.

The Three Elements: Expectancy, Instrumentality, Valence   What determines how willing you (or an employee) are to work hard at tasks important to the success of the organization? The answer, says Vroom, is: You will do what you *can* do when you *want* to.

Your motivation, according to expectancy theory, involves the relationship between your *effort,* your *performance,* and the desirability of the *outcomes* (such as pay or recognition) of your performance. These relationships,

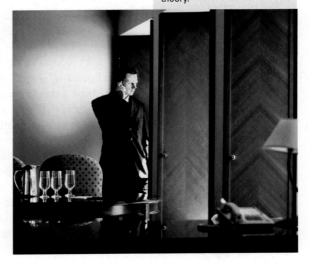

How much do you want? Would a well-appointed office represent the tangible realization of managerial success for you? How likely do you think you are to get it? The answers to these questions represent your important motivations, according to expectancy theory.

which are shown in the following chart, are affected by the three elements of *expectancy, instrumentality,* and *valence. (See Figure 12.7.)*

figure 12.7

EXPECTANCY THEORY: THE
MAJOR ELEMENTS

1. Expectancy—"Will I be able to perform at the desired level on a task?" **Expectancy** **is the belief that a particular level of effort will lead to a particular level of performance.** This is called the *effort-to-performance expectancy.*

Example: If you believe that putting in more hours working at Best Buy selling video-game machines will result in higher sales, then you have high effort-to-performance expectancy. That is, you believe that your efforts will matter. You think you have the ability, the product knowledge, and so on, so that putting in extra hours of selling can probably raise your sales of video-game machines.

2. Instrumentality—"What outcome will I receive if I perform at this level?" **Instrumentality** **is the expectation that successful performance of the task will lead to the outcome desired.** This is called the *performance-to-reward expectancy.*

Example: If you believe that making higher sales will cause Best Buy to give you a bonus, then you have high performance-to-reward expectancy. You believe *if* you can achieve your goals, the outcome will be worthwhile. This element is independent of the previous one—you might decide you don't have the ability to make the extra sales, but if you did, you'll be rewarded. (Lately, because of the public's concern about the quality of the educational system in the United States, school boards and politicians are implementing programs that tie teachers' pay to performance.)[36]

3. Valence—"How much do I want the outcome?" **Valence** **is value, the importance a worker assigns to the possible outcome or reward.**

Example: If you assign a lot of importance or a high value to Best Buy's prospective bonus or pay raise, then your valence is said to be high.

For your motivation to be high, you must have high levels of all three elements—expectancy, instrumentality, and valence. If any element is low, you will not be motivated. Your effort-to-performance expectancy might be low, for instance, because you doubt making an effort will make a difference (because retail selling has too much competition from Internet sellers). Or your performance-to-reward expectancy might be low because you don't think Best Buy is going to give you a bonus for being a star at selling. Or your valence might be low because you don't think the bonus or raise is going to be high enough to justify working evenings and weekends.

Using Expectancy Theory to Motivate Employees The principal problem with the expectancy theory is that it is complex. Even so, the underlying logic is understandable, and research seems to show that managers are not following its principles.[37]

When attempting to motivate employees, managers should ask the following questions:

- **What rewards do your employees value?** As a manager, you need to get to know your employees and determine what rewards (outcomes) they value, such as pay raises or recognition.

- **What are the job objectives and the performance level you desire?** You need to clearly define the performance objectives and determine what performance level or behavior you want so that you can tell your employees what they need to do to attain the rewards.

- **Are the rewards linked to performance?** You want to reward high performance, of course. Thus, employees must be aware that X level of performance within Y period of time will result in Z kinds of rewards. In a team context, however, research shows that it is best to use a combination of individual and team-based rewards.[38]

- **Do employees believe you will deliver the right rewards for the right performance?** Your credibility is on the line here. Your employees must believe that you have the power, the ability, and the will to give them the rewards you promise for the performance you are requesting.

Champions. For athletes, such as these Duke University basketball team members, winners of the 2010 NCAA tournament, performance seems easily measured by a simple outcome—whether or not you win. Do you think performance can be as clearly measured in the business world?

Example

Use of Expectancy Theory: A Drug Company Ties CEO Pay to Performance

Would it surprise you to learn that bankers would not pay for a study on their industry concerning how bonuses affect performance—probably because they were being richly rewarded regardless of results?[39]

While most ordinary workers are paid well if they perform well (and shown the door if they do poorly), this has frequently not been true in the top ranks of management, where bonuses and grants of stock are given outright even when achievement is lacking. Thus, critics applauded a new system of compensation devised for CEO J. Michael Pearson of midsize drug maker Valeant Pharmaceuticals International.

Bigger Bang for the Buck? Arranged by the board of directors' compensation committee, the deal requires Pearson to buy lots of stock with his own money (not given to him by the company) and to hold many shares for years without selling them. It also ties annual equity grants (giving him ownership of additional

stock in the company) to how well the company performs for investors.

"Pay experts say the deal gives Mr. Pearson incentives to boost long-term value for investors," says a *Wall Street Journal* story. "For example, the 49-year-old CEO only gets to keep certain restricted shares if Valeant's share price increased at least 15% a year" through the next two years.

Other Shareholder-Friendly Pay Ideas. G. Mason Morfit, head of Valeant's compensation committee, who devised the plan, also has some other suggestions for shareholder-friendly pay packages for top managers: Be generous on the upside, but tough on the downside—meaning pay executives well at the start, but don't pay them more if they fail. "Don't backslide," he says. "No bonuses if executives miss targets." Another recommendation: "Scrap 'entitlement' perks like car allowances and club dues."[40]

YOUR CALL

In 2009, Pearson received over $24 million in compensation, including bonuses and stock, as the price of Valeant's stock rose steadily, rewarding both investors and himself. Clearly, a pay-for-performance plan may work for CEOs. Why do you suppose, then, that a New York City pilot project that gave parents of poor children payments for things like going to the dentist ($100), holding down a full-time job ($150 per month), and getting children to school regularly ($25–$50 per month) produced no educational or attendance gains, at least for elementary and middle-school students?[41]

Goal-Setting Theory: Objectives Should Be Specific & Challenging but Achievable

Goal-setting theory suggests that employees can be motivated by goals that are specific and challenging but achievable. According to psychologists **Edwin Locke** and **Gary Latham,** who developed the theory, it is natural for people to set and strive for goals; however, the goal-setting process is useful only if people *understand* and *accept* the goals.[42]

Four Elements of Goal-Setting Theory   A *goal* is defined as an objective that a person is trying to accomplish through his or her efforts. To result in high motivation and performance, according to goal-setting theory, goals must be *specific, challenging, achievable,* and *linked to action plans.*

1. Goals Should Be Specific   Goals such as "Sell as many cars as you can" or "Be nicer to customers" are too vague and therefore have no effect on motivation. Instead, goals need to be specific—usually meaning *quantitative.* As a manager, for example, you may be asked to boost the revenues of your unit by 25% and to cut absenteeism by 10%, all specific targets.

2. Goals Should Be Challenging   Goal theory suggests you not set goals that a lot of people can reach, since this is not very motivational. Managers should set goals that are challenging. Remember, people have different levels of abilities, necessitating that each individual should have a unique set of challenging goals.

3. Goals Should Be Achievable   People give up when they feel that goal achievement is impossible. You might ask data-entry clerks to enter 25% more names and addresses an hour into a database, but if they don't have touch-typing skills, that goal won't be attainable. Thus, managers need to make sure employees have additional training, if necessary, to achieve difficult goals.

4. Goals Should Be Linked to Action Plans   An action plan outlines the activities or tasks that need to be accomplished in order to obtain a goal. For example, if your goal is to find a great job after graduation, the action plan would specify all the things you must do to graduate with good grades, work experience, and employment contacts. Research shows that both individuals and organizations are more likely to achieve their goals when they develop detailed action plans.[43]

Small business. Do employees in small businesses, such as these two men who have just closed an important sale, need the same kind of motivational goals as employees in large corporations? Is setting goals in small businesses, where there's apt to be less specialization, more or less difficult than in large organizations?

Using Goal-Setting Theory to Motivate Employees   In addition, when developing employee goals, you need to follow the recommendation made in Chapter 5 that goals should be SMART—that is, Specific, Measurable, Attainable, Results-oriented, and have Target dates. It is also important to make sure that employees have the abilities and resources to accomplish their goals.

Finally, make sure that you give feedback so that employees know of their progress—and don't forget to reward people for doing what they set out to do. ●

THE BIG PICTURE

Job design, the division of an organization's work among employees, applies motivational theories to jobs to increase performance and satisfaction. The traditional approach to job design is to fit people to the jobs; the modern way is to fit the jobs to the people, using job enrichment and approaches that are based on Herzberg's landmark two-factor theory, discussed earlier in this chapter. The job characteristics model offers five job attributes for better work outcomes.

About half of workers reported in 2009 that their current job was stagnant.[44] Is there anything that can be done about this?

Job design is (1) the division of an organization's work among its employees and (2) the application of motivational theories to jobs to increase satisfaction and performance. There are two different approaches to job design, one traditional, one modern, that can be taken in deciding how to design jobs. The traditional way is *fitting people to jobs;* the modern way is *fitting jobs to people.*[45]

Fitting people to jobs is based on the assumption that people will gradually adapt to any work situation. Even so, jobs must still be tailored so that nearly anyone can do them. This is the approach often taken with assembly-line jobs and jobs involving routine tasks. For managers the main challenge becomes *"How can we make the worker most compatible with the work?"*

One technique is *job simplification,* **the process of reducing the number of tasks a worker performs.** When a job is stripped down to its simplest elements, it enables a worker to focus on doing more of the same task, thus increasing employee efficiency and productivity. This may be especially useful, for instance, in designing jobs for mentally disadvantaged workers, such as those run by Goodwill Industries. However, research shows that simplified, repetitive jobs lead to job dissatisfaction, poor mental health, and a low sense of accomplishment and personal growth.[46]

Fitting Jobs to People

Fitting jobs to people is based on the assumption that people are underutilized at work and that they want more variety, challenges, and responsibility. This philosophy, an outgrowth of Herzberg's theory, is one of the reasons for the popularity of work teams in the United States. The main challenge for managers is *"How can we make the work most compatible with the worker so as to produce both high performance and high job satisfaction?"* Two techniques for this type of job design include (1) *job enlargement* and (2) *job enrichment.*

Job Enlargement: Putting More Variety into a Job   The opposite of job simplification, *job enlargement* **consists of increasing the number of tasks in a job to increase variety and motivation.** For instance, the job of installing flat screens in television sets could be enlarged to include installation of the circuit boards as well.

Although proponents claim job enlargement can improve employee satisfaction, motivation, and quality of production, research suggests job enlargement by itself won't have a significant and lasting positive effect on job performance. After all, working at two boring tasks instead of one doesn't add up to a challenging job. Instead, job enlargement is just one tool of many that should be considered in job design.[47]

Job Enrichment: Putting More Responsibility & Other Motivating Factors into a Job

Job enrichment is the practical application of Frederick Herzberg's two-factor motivator-hygiene theory of job satisfaction.[48] Specifically, *job enrichment* **consists of building into a job such motivating factors as responsibility, achievement, recognition, stimulating work, and advancement.**

However, instead of the job-enlargement technique of simply giving employees additional tasks of similar difficulty (known as *horizontal loading*), with job enrichment employees are given more responsibility (known as *vertical loading*). Thus, employees take on chores that would normally be performed by their supervisors. For example, one department store authorized thousands of its sales clerks to handle functions normally reserved for store managers, such as handling merchandise-return problems and approving customers' checks.

The Job Characteristics Model: Five Job Attributes for Better Work Outcomes

Developed by researchers **J. Richard Hackman** and **Greg Oldham,** the job characteristics model of design is an outgrowth of job enrichment.[49] **The *job characteristics model* consists of (a) five core job characteristics that affect (b) three critical psychological states of an employee that in turn affect (c) work outcomes—the employee's motivation, performance, and satisfaction.** The model is illustrated below. *(See Figure 12.8.)*

figure 12.8

THE JOB CHARACTERISTICS MODEL

Source: From J. Richard Hackman and Greg R. Oldham, *Work Redesign,* 1st edition © 1980. Reproduced by permission of Pearson Education, Inc., Upper Saddle River, New Jersey.

Five Job Characteristics   The five core job characteristics are as follows.

1. Skill Variety—"How Many Different Skills Does Your Job Require?"   *Skill variety* describes the extent to which a job requires a person to use a wide range of different skills and abilities.

    Example: The skill variety required by a rocket scientist is higher than that for a short-order cook.

2. Task Identity—"How Many Different Tasks Are Required to Complete the Work?"   *Task identity* describes the extent to which a job requires a worker to perform all the tasks needed to complete the job from beginning to end.

    Example: The task identity for a craftsperson who goes through all the steps to build a handmade acoustic guitar is higher than it is for an assembly-line worker who just installs windshields on cars.

3. Task Significance—"How Many Other People Are Affected by Your Job?"   *Task significance* describes the extent to which a job affects the lives of other people, whether inside or outside the organization.

    Example: A technician who is responsible for keeping a hospital's electronic equipment in working order has higher task significance than does a person wiping down cars in a carwash.

4. Autonomy—"How Much Discretion Does Your Job Give You?"   *Autonomy* describes the extent to which a job allows an employee to make choices about scheduling different tasks and deciding how to perform them.

    Example: College-textbook salespeople have lots of leeway in planning which campuses and professors to call on. Thus, they have higher autonomy than do toll-takers on a bridge, whose actions are determined by the flow of vehicles.

Skill variety. Being an airline pilot—or a jewelry designer, a building contractor, a physician, or an orchestra conductor—requires a greater number of skills than, say, driving a truck. Do highly skilled employees typically make good managers? What skills do airline pilots have that would make them effective managers in other kinds of work?

5. Feedback—"How Much Do You Find Out How Well You're Doing?"

Feedback describes the extent to which workers receive clear, direct information about how well they are performing the job.

Example: Professional basketball players receive immediate feedback on how many of their shots are going into the basket. Engineers working on new weapons systems may go years before learning how effective their performance has been.

How the Model Works According to the job characteristics model, these five core characteristics affect a worker's motivation because they affect three critical psychological states: *meaningfulness of work, responsibility for results,* and *knowledge of results.* (Refer to Figure 12.8 again.) In turn, these positive psychological states fuel *high motivation, high performance, high satisfaction,* and *low absenteeism and turnover.*

One other element—shown at the bottom of Figure 12.8—needs to be discussed: *contingency factors.* This refers to the degree to which a person wants personal and psychological development. Job design works when employees are motivated; to be so, they must have three attributes: (1) necessary knowledge and skill, (2) desire for personal growth, and (3) context satisfactions—that is, the right physical working conditions, pay, and supervision.

Job design works. A meta-analysis of 259 studies involving 219,625 people showed that job design was positively associated with employee performance, job satisfaction, organizational commitment, and physical and psychological well-being. Job design also was associated with lower absenteeism and intentions to quit.[50]

Applying the Job Characteristics Model There are three major steps to follow when applying the model.

- **Diagnose the work environment to see whether a problem exists.** Hackman and Oldham developed a self-report instrument for managers to use called the *job diagnostic survey.* This will indicate whether an individual's so-called motivating potential score (MPS)—the amount of internal work motivation associated with a specific job—is high or low.
- **Determine whether job redesign is appropriate.** If a person's MPS score is low, an attempt should be made to determine which of the core job characteristics is causing the problem. You should next decide whether job redesign is appropriate for a given group of employees. Job design is most likely to work in a participative environment in which employees have the necessary knowledge and skills.
- **Consider how to redesign the job.** Here you try to increase those core job characteristics that are lower than national norms.

Example: Employers want to save on health costs by helping employees with diabetes, heart disease, and similar chronic conditions avoid emergency room visits and hospital admissions. However, since primary care doctors, who could help patients manage their conditions (as by reminding diabetics to monitor their blood-glucose levels daily), are paid less than physicians in other specialties, the system has turned such doctors "into little chipmunks on a wheel, pumping out patients every five minutes," as one observer described it.[51] The solution? Redesign the job by rewarding primary care doctors for spending more time with patients. ●

✕ 12.5 REINFORCEMENT PERSPECTIVES ON MOTIVATION

What are the types of incentives I might use to influence employee behavior?

major question?

THE BIG PICTURE
Reinforcement theory suggests behavior will be repeated if it has positive consequences and won't be if it has negative consequences. There are four types of reinforcement: positive reinforcement, negative reinforcement, extinction, and punishment. This section also describes how to use some reinforcement techniques to modify employee behavior.

Reinforcement evades the issue of people's needs and thinking processes in relation to motivation, as we described under the need-based and process perspectives. Instead, the reinforcement perspective, which was pioneered by **Edward L. Thorndike** and **B. F. Skinner,** is concerned with how the consequences of a certain behavior affect that behavior in the future.[52]

Skinner was the father of *operant conditioning,* the process of controlling behavior by manipulating its consequences. Operant conditioning rests on Thorndike's *law of effect,* which states that behavior that results in a pleasant outcome is likely to be repeated and behavior that results in unpleasant outcomes is not likely to be repeated.

From these underpinnings has come *reinforcement theory,* **which attempts to explain behavior change by suggesting that behavior with positive consequences tends to be repeated, whereas behavior with negative consequences tends not to be repeated.** The use of reinforcement theory to change human behavior is called *behavior modification.*

The Four Types of Reinforcement: Positive, Negative, Extinction, & Punishment

Reinforcement **is anything that causes a given behavior to be repeated or inhibited,** whether praising a child for cleaning his or her room or scolding a child for leaving a tricycle in the driveway. There are four types of reinforcement: (1) *positive reinforcement,* (2) *negative reinforcement,* (3) *extinction,* and (4) *punishment. (See Figure 12.9, next page.)*

Positive Reinforcement: Giving Rewards   *Positive reinforcement* **is the use of positive consequences to encourage desirable behavior.**

Example: A supervisor who's asked an insurance salesperson to sell more policies might reward successful performance by saying, "It's great that you exceeded your quota, and you'll get a bonus for it. Maybe next time you'll sell even more and will become a member of the Circle of 100 Top Sellers and win a trip to Paris as well." Note the rewards: praise, more money, recognition, awards. Presumably this will *strengthen* the behavior and the sales rep will work even harder in the coming months.

Negative Reinforcement: Avoiding Unpleasantness   *Negative reinforcement* **is the removal of unpleasant consequences following a desired behavior.**

Example: A supervisor who has been nagging a salesperson might say, "Well, so you exceeded your quota" and stop the nagging. Note the neutral statement; there is no praise but also no longer any negative statements. This could cause the sales rep to *maintain* his or her existing behavior.

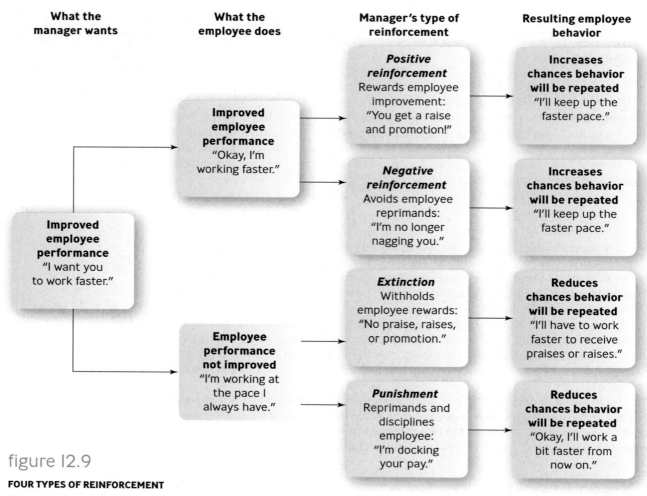

What the manager wants	What the employee does	Manager's type of reinforcement	Resulting employee behavior

Improved employee performance "I want you to work faster."

Improved employee performance "Okay, I'm working faster."

Positive reinforcement Rewards employee improvement: "You get a raise and promotion!"

Increases chances behavior will be repeated "I'll keep up the faster pace."

Negative reinforcement Avoids employee reprimands: "I'm no longer nagging you."

Increases chances behavior will be repeated "I'll keep up the faster pace."

Employee performance not improved "I'm working at the pace I always have."

Extinction Withholds employee rewards: "No praise, raises, or promotion."

Reduces chances behavior will be repeated "I'll have to work faster to receive praises or raises."

Punishment Reprimands and disciplines employee: "I'm docking your pay."

Reduces chances behavior will be repeated "Okay, I'll work a bit faster from now on."

figure 12.9

FOUR TYPES OF REINFORCEMENT

These are different ways of changing employee behavior.

Extinction: Withholding Rewards   *Extinction* is the withholding or withdrawal of positive rewards for desirable behavior, so that the behavior is less likely to occur in the future.

Example: A supervisor might tell a successful salesperson, "I know you exceeded your quota, but now that our company has been taken over by another firm, we're not giving out bonuses anymore." Presumably this will *weaken* the salesperson's efforts to perform better in the future.

Punishment: Applying Negative Consequences   *Punishment* is the application of negative consequences to stop or change undesirable behavior.

Example: A supervisor might tell an unsuccessful salesperson who's been lazy about making calls to clients and so didn't make quota, "Well, if this keeps up, you'll probably be let go." This could *inhibit* the salesperson from being so lackadaisical about making calls to clients.

Using Reinforcement to Motivate Employees

The following are some guidelines for using two types of reinforcement—positive reinforcement and punishment.

Positive Reinforcement There are several aspects of positive reinforcement, which should definitely be part of your toolkit of managerial skills:

Punishment. Does getting a wallet-busting speeding ticket change your behavior? What if it happens several times? Yet consider also other, presumably stronger forms of governmental punishment that are supposed to act as deterrents to bad behavior. Does the possibility of the death punishment really deter homicides? Why or why not?

- **Reward only desirable behavior.** You should give rewards to your employees only when they show *desirable* behavior. Thus, for example, you should give praise to employees not for showing up for work on time (an expected part of any job) but for showing up early.

- **Give rewards as soon as possible.** You should give a reward as soon as possible after the desirable behavior appears. Thus, you should give praise to an early-arriving employee as soon as he or she arrives, not later in the week.

- **Be clear about what behavior is desired.** Clear communication is everything. You should tell employees exactly what kinds of work behaviors are desirable and you should tell everyone exactly what they must do to earn rewards.

- **Have different rewards and recognize individual differences.** Recognizing that different people respond to different kinds of rewards, you should have different rewards available. Thus, you might give a word of praise verbally to one person, shoot a line or two by e-mail to another person, or send a hand-scrawled note to another.

Punishment Unquestionably, there will be times when you'll need to threaten or administer an unpleasant consequence to stop an employee's undesirable behavior. Sometimes it's best to address a problem by combining punishment with positive reinforcement. Some suggestions for using punishment are as follows.

- **Punish only undesirable behavior.** You should give punishment only when employees show frequent *undesirable* behavior. Otherwise, employees may come to view you negatively as a tyrannical boss. Thus, for example, you should reprimand employees who show up, say, a half hour late for work but not 5 or 10 minutes late.

- **Give reprimands or disciplinary actions as soon as possible.** You should mete out punishment as soon as possible after the undesirable behavior occurs. Thus, you should give a reprimand to a late-arriving employee as soon as he or she arrives.

- **Be clear about what behavior is undesirable.** Tell employees exactly what kinds of work behaviors are undesirable and make any disciplinary action or reprimand match the behavior. A manager should not, for example, dock an hourly employee's pay if he or she is only 5 or 10 minutes late for work.

- **Administer punishment in private.** You would hate to have your boss chew you out in front of your subordinates, and the people who report to you also shouldn't be reprimanded in public, which would lead only to resentments that may have nothing to do with an employee's infractions.

- **Combine punishment and positive reinforcement.** If you're reprimanding an employee, be sure to also say what he or she is doing right and state what rewards the employee might be eligible for. For example, while reprimanding someone for being late, say that a perfect attendance record over the next few months will put that employee in line for a raise or promotion. ●

major question?

How can I use compensation and other rewards to motivate people?

THE BIG PICTURE

Compensation, the main motivator of performance, includes pay for performance, bonuses, profit sharing, gainsharing, stock options, and pay for knowledge. Other nonmonetary incentives address needs that aren't being met, such as work-life balance, growth in skills, and commitment.

"In the past, people could see the fruits of their labor immediately: a chair made or a ball bearing produced," writes *Wall Street Journal* columnist Jared Sandberg. However, in the information age, when so much of a person's time is spent looking into a computer screen and working on partial tasks seemingly unconnected to something whole, "it can be hard to find gratification from work that is largely invisible."[53] As work becomes more invisible and intangible, more team-based rather than individual-based, it also becomes harder to measure, harder to define its successful accomplishment—and harder to motivate employees to perform well at it.

Perhaps the first thing that comes to mind when you think about motivating performance is compensation—how much money you or your employees can make. But consider how motivation worked for software engineer Firinn Taisdeal, mentioned previously. In 2003, he walked away from a job just before a historic public offering that probably would have made him rich. Why? Because the people he worked with repelled him. "They were not just greedy," he says. "They had no integrity."[54] Or consider Mary Morse, another software engineer, who turned down several offers from other Silicon Valley firms, at least one of which would have made her wealthy, in order to stay with the computer-aided design firm Autodesk. The reason? She liked her bosses.[55]

Morse in particular demonstrates the truth of a Gallup Organization poll that found that most workers rate having a caring boss higher than they value monetary benefits.[56] Clearly, then, motivating doesn't just involve dollars.

Motivation & Compensation

Most people are paid an hourly wage or a weekly or monthly salary. Both of these are easy for organizations to administer, of course. But by itself a wage or a salary gives an employee little incentive to work hard. Incentive compensation plans try to do so, although no single plan will boost the performance of all employees.

Characteristics of the Best Incentive Compensation Plans In accordance with most of the theories of motivation we described earlier, for incentive plans to work, certain criteria are advisable, as follows. (1) Rewards must be linked to performance and be measurable. (2) The rewards must satisfy individual needs. (3) The rewards must be agreed on by manager and employees. (4) The rewards must be believable, and achievable by employees.

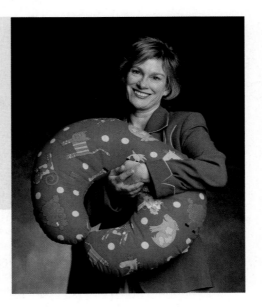

Motivation as a small business owner. Susan Brown of Golden, Colorado, had dreamed of opening her own business since she was a child. However, she invented the Boppy, a simple pillow stuffed with foam, almost accidentally, when her daughter's day care center asked parents to bring in pillows to prop up infants who couldn't sit up on their own. Today the Boppy Co. has annual sales of $15 million to $25 million. For some people, like Brown, the only way to merge motivation and compensation is to own and manage their own business. What factors or incentives motivate you to work hard?

Popular Incentive Compensation Plans How would you like to be rewarded for your efforts? Some of the most well-known incentive compensation plans are *pay for performance, bonuses, profit sharing, gainsharing, stock options,* and *pay for knowledge.*

- **Pay for performance.** Also known as *merit pay,* ***pay for performance* bases pay on one's results.** Thus, different salaried employees might get different pay raises and other rewards (such as promotions) depending on their overall job performance.[57]

  Examples: One standard pay-for-performance plan, already mentioned, is payment according to a ***piece rate,* in which employees are paid according to how much output they produce,** as is often used with farmworkers picking fruit and vegetables. Another is the ***sales commission,* in which sales representatives are paid a percentage of the earnings the company made from their sales,** so that the more they sell, the more they are paid.

  A good deal of the criticism of excessive executive pay is that it has not been tied to company performance.[58]

- **Bonuses.** ***Bonuses* are cash awards given to employees who achieve specific performance objectives.**

  Example: Neiman Marcus, the department store, pays its salespeople a percentage of the earnings from the goods they sell.

  Unfortunately, the documents that most companies file (proxy documents to the Securities and Exchange Commission) to explain what specific targets executives had to meet to earn their bonuses are not very clear, being couched mainly in legalese.[59] (Bonuses for bankers in particular became a hot-button political issue after banks received a $700 billion rescue from taxpayers in 2008, then surging financial markets caused a rebound that allowed such companies to set aside billions of dollars for year-end bonuses.)[60]

- **Profit sharing.** ***Profit sharing* is the distribution to employees of a percentage of the company's profits.**

  Example: In one T-shirt and sweatshirt manufacturing company, 10% of pretax profits are distributed to employees every month, and more is given out at the end of the year. Distributions are apportioned according to such criteria as performance, attendance, and lateness for individual employees.

- **Gainsharing.** *Gainsharing* **is the distribution of savings or "gains" to groups of employees who reduced costs and increased measurable productivity.**

    Example: There are different types of gainsharing plans, but in one known as the *Scanlon plan,* developed in the 1920s by a steel-industry union leader named Joseph Scanlon, a portion of any cost savings, usually 75%, is distributed back to employees; the company keeps the other 25%.[61]

- **Stock options.** With *stock options,* **certain employees are given the right to buy stock at a future date for a discounted price.** The motivator here is that employees holding stock options will supposedly work hard to make the company's stock rise so that they can obtain it at a cheaper price. By giving stock options to all employees who work 20 or more hours a week, Starbucks Corp. was able, prior to the recession, to hold its annual turnover rate to 60%—in an industry (fast food and restaurants) in which 300% is not unheard of.[62] (The use of stock options has been criticized recently because many companies allowed "backdating"—permitting their executives to buy company stock at low purchase prices from previous days or weeks. As one writer points out, this is sort of like being able to make a fortune by betting on a Kentucky Derby whose outcome you've known for some time.)[63]

- **Pay for knowledge.** Also known as *skill-based pay,* *pay for knowledge* **ties employee pay to the number of job-relevant skills or academic degrees they earn.**

    Example: The teaching profession is a time-honored instance of this incentive, in which elementary and secondary teachers are encouraged to increase their salaries by earning further college credit. However, firms such as FedEx also have pay-for-knowledge plans.

Nonmonetary Ways of Motivating Employees

Employees who can behave autonomously, solve problems, and take the initiative are apt to be the very ones who will leave if they find their own needs aren't being met—namely:

- **The need for work-life balance.** A PricewaterhouseCoopers survey of 2,500 university students in 11 countries found that 57% named as their primary career goal "attaining a balance between personal life and career."[64] A 25-year study of values in the United States found that "employees have become less convinced that work should be an important part of one's life or that working hard makes me a better person."[65] Gen Yers in particular are apt to say the most important things in life are "being a good parent" (52%) and "having a successful marriage" (30%) rather than "having a high-paying career" (15%).[66]

- **The need to expand skills.** Having watched their parents undergo downsizing, younger workers in particular are apt to view a job as a way of gaining skills that will enable them to earn a decent living in the future.

- **The need to matter.** Workers now want to be with an organization that allows them to feel they matter. They want to commit to their profession or fellow team members rather than have to profess a blind loyalty to the corporation.

There is a whole class of nonmonetary incentives to attract, retain, and motivate employees. The foremost example is the *flexible workplace*—including part-time work, flextime, compressed workweek, job sharing, and telecommuting, as described in the Practical Action box.

The Flexible Workplace[67]

With so many two-paycheck families, single parents, and other diverse kinds of employees in the workforce, many employers now recognize the idea of a *flexible workplace* as a way of recruiting, retaining, and motivating employees. Among the types of alternative work schedules available are the following.

Part-Time Work—Less Than 40 hours

Part-time work is any work done on a schedule less than the standard 40-hour workweek. Some part-time workers—so-called temporary workers or contingency workers—actually want to work 40 hours or more, but can't find full-time jobs.[68] Others, however, work part time by choice. Today an organization can hire not only part-time clerical help, for instance, but also part-time programmers, market researchers, lawyers, even part-time top executives.

Flextime—Flexible Working Hours

Flextime, or flexible time, consists of flexible working hours, or any schedule that gives one some choices in working hours. If, for example, an organization's normal working hours are 9 A.M. to 5 P.M., a flextime worker might be allowed to start and finish an hour earlier or an hour later—for instance, to work from 8 A.M. to 4 P.M. The main requirement is that the employee be at work during certain core hours, to be available for meetings, consultations, and so on. By offering flextime hours, organizations can attract and keep employees with special requirements such as the need to take care for children or elderly parents. It also benefits employees who wish to avoid commuting during rush hour.

Compressed Workweek—40 Hours in Four Days

In a compressed workweek, employees perform a full-time job in less than 5 days of standard 8- (or 9-) hour shifts. The most common variation is a 40-hour week performed in 4 days of 10 hours each, which gives employees three (instead of two) consecutive days off. The benefits are that organizations can offer employees more leisure time and reduced wear and tear and expense from commuting. The disadvantages are possible scheduling problems, unavailability of an employee to co-workers and customers, and fatigue from long workdays.

Job Sharing—Two People Split the Same Job

In job sharing, two people divide one full-time job. Usually, each person works a half day, although there can be other arrangements (working alternate days or alternate weeks, for example). As with a compressed workweek, job sharing provides employees with more personal or leisure time. The disadvantage is that it can result in communication problems with co-workers or customers.

Telecommuting & Other Work-at-Home Schedules

There have always been some employees who have had special full-time or part-time arrangements whereby they are allowed to work at home, keeping in touch with their employers and co-workers by email and phone. The fax machine, the personal computer, the Internet, and overnight-delivery services have now made work-at-home arrangements much more feasible.

Working at home with telecommunications between office and home is called telecommuting. The advantages to employers are increased productivity because telecommuters experience less distraction at home and can work flexible hours.

Your Call

For what you're doing right now at this point in your life, which of these possibilities would suit you best, and why? Would it be workable for your employer if all your co-workers did it as well?

Other incentives can be expressed simply as *treat employees well,* some examples of which follow.

Thoughtfulness: The Value of Being Nice   A study by Walker Information, an Indianapolis-based research firm, found that employers spend too little time showing workers they matter, as manifested in lack of communication and lack of interest in new ideas and contributions.[69] A majority of employees feel under-appreciated, according to a 1999 survey. Forty percent of employees who rated their boss's performance as poor said they were likely to look for a new job; only

11% of those who rated it excellent said they would.[70] "Being nice" to employees means, for example, reducing criticism, becoming more effusive in your praise, and writing thank-you notes to employees for exceptional performance.[71]

The number one reason people quit their jobs, it's believed, is their dissatisfaction with their supervisors, not their paychecks. Thus, industrial psychologist B. Lynn Ware suggests that if you learn valued employees are disgruntled, you should discuss it with them.[72] Employers can promote personal relationships, which most employees are concerned about on the job, by offering breaks or other opportunities in which people can mix and socialize.

Work-Life Benefits Work-life benefits, according to Kathie Lingle, are programs "used by employers to increase productivity and commitment by removing certain barriers that make it hard for people to strike a balance between their work and personal lives."[73]

Lingle, who is national work-life director for KPMG, an accounting and consulting firm, emphasizes that work-life benefits "are not a reward, but a way of getting work done." After all, some employees are low performers simply because of a lack of life-work balance, with great demands at home. "If you only give these 'rewards' to existing high performers," says Lingle, "you're cutting people off who could, with some support, be high performers." Nevertheless, handing out extra time off can be used to reward performance and prevent burnout.[74]

Besides alternative scheduling, work-life benefits include helping employees with day care costs or even establishing on-site centers; domestic-partner benefits; job-protected leave for new parents; and provision of technology such as mobile phones and laptops to enable parents to work at home.[75]

Surroundings The cubicle, according to new research, is stifling the creativity and morale of many workers, and the bias of modern-day office designers for open spaces and neutral colors is leading to employee complaints that their workplaces are too noisy or too bland. Some businesses, such as advertising giant Grey Group in New York, have even moved beyond cubicles to completely open offices, which has required a business psychologist to hold "space therapy" sessions to ease employee concerns.[76]

"There is no such thing as something that works for everybody," says Alan Hedge, a professor of environmental analysis at Cornell University.[77] An 8-foot-by-8-foot cubicle may not be a good visual trigger for human brains, and companies wanting to improve creativity and productivity may need to think about giving office employees better things to look at.[78]

Skill-Building & Educational Opportunities Learning opportunities can take two forms. Managers can see that workers are matched with co-workers from whom they can learn, allowing them, for instance, to "shadow" (watch and imitate) workers in other jobs or be in interdepartmental task forces. There can also be tuition reimbursement for part-time study at a college or university.[79]

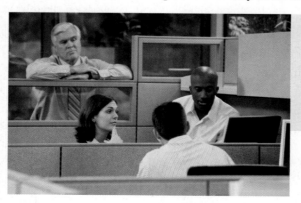

Cubicle culture. It might be too difficult to design a setup in which everyone has an office with a view. But would it be possible to design a layout in which everyone has a private office? Do you think it would better motivate employees?

Sabbaticals   Intel and Apple understand that in a climate of 80-hour weeks people need to recharge themselves. But even McDonald's offers sabbaticals to longtime employees, giving a month to a year of paid time off in which to travel, learn, and pursue personal projects. The aim, of course, is to enable employees to recharge themselves but also, it is hoped, to cement their loyalty to the organization.[80]   ●

Key Terms Used in This Chapter

acquired needs theory 377
bonuses 395
content perspectives 374
equity theory 381
ERG theory 376
expectancy 384
expectancy theory 383
extinction 392
extrinsic reward 373
gainsharing 396
goal-setting theory 386
hierarchy of needs
  theory 374

hygiene factors 380
instrumentality 384
intrinsic reward 373
job characteristics
  model 388
job design 387
job enlargement 387
job enrichment 388
job simplification 387
motivating factors 380
motivation 372
needs 374
negative reinforcement 391

pay for knowledge 396
pay for performance 395
piece rate 395
positive reinforcement 391
process perspectives 381
profit sharing 395
punishment 392
reinforcement 391
reinforcement theory 391
sales commission 395
stock options 396
two-factor theory 379
valence 384

Summary

12.1 Motivating for Performance
Motivation is defined as the psychological processes that arouse and direct goal-directed behavior. In a simple model of motivation, people have certain needs that motivate them to perform specific behaviors for which they receive rewards that feed back and satisfy the original need. Rewards are of two types: (1) An extrinsic reward is the payoff, such as money, a person receives from others for performing a particular task. (2) An intrinsic reward is the satisfaction, such as a feeling of accomplishment, that a person receives from performing the particular task itself.

As a manager, you want to motivate people to do things that will benefit your organization—join it, stay with it, show up for work at it, perform better for it, and do extra for it.

Four major perspectives on motivation are (1) content, (2) process, (3) job design, and (4) reinforcement.

12.2 Content Perspectives on Employee Motivation
Content perspectives or need-based perspectives emphasize the needs that motivate people. Needs are defined as physiological or psychological deficiencies that arouse behavior. Besides the McGregor Theory X/Theory Y (Chapter 1), need-based perspectives include (1) the hierarchy of needs theory, (2) the ERG theory, (3) the acquired needs theory, and (4) the two-factor theory.

The hierarchy of needs theory proposes that people are motivated by five levels of need: physiological, safety, love, esteem, and self-actualization needs.

ERG theory assumes that three basic needs influence behavior—existence, relatedness, and growth.

The acquired needs theory states that three needs—achievement, affiliation, and power—are major motives determining people's behavior in the workplace.

The two-factor theory proposes that work satisfaction and dissatisfaction arise from two different factors—work satisfaction from so-called motivating factors, and work dissatisfaction from so-called hygiene factors. Hygiene factors, the lower-level needs, are factors associated with job dissatisfaction—such as salary and working conditions—which affect the environment in which people work. Motivating factors, the higher-level needs, are factors associated with job satisfaction—such as achievement and advancement—which affect the rewards of work performance.

 ### 12.3 Process Perspectives on Employee Motivation

Process perspectives are concerned with the thought processes by which people decide how to act. Three process perspectives on motivation are (1) equity theory, (2) expectancy theory, and (3) goal-setting theory.

Equity theory focuses on employee perceptions as to how fairly they think they are being treated compared with others. The key elements in equity theory are inputs, outputs (rewards), and comparisons. (1) With inputs, employees consider what they are putting into the job in time, effort, and so on. (2) With outputs or rewards, employees consider what they think they're getting out of the job in terms of pay, praise, and so on. (3) With comparison, employees compare the ratio of their own outcomes to inputs against the ratio of someone else's outcomes to inputs. Three practical lessons of equity theory are that employee perceptions are what count, employee participation helps, and having an appeal process helps.

Expectancy theory suggests that people are motivated by how much they want something and how likely they think they are to get it. The three elements affecting motivation are expectancy, instrumentality, and valence. (1) Expectancy is the belief that a particular level of effort will lead to a particular level of performance. (2) Instrumentality is the expectation that successful performance of the task will lead to the outcome desired. (3) Valence is the value, the importance a worker assigns to the possible outcome or reward. When

attempting to motivate employees, according to the logic of expectancy theory, managers should ascertain what rewards employees value, what job objectives and performance level they desire, whether there are rewards linked to performance, and whether employees believe managers will deliver the right rewards for the right performance.

Goal-setting theory suggests that employees can be motivated by goals that are specific and challenging but achievable and linked to action plans. In addition, the theory suggests that goals should be set jointly with the employee, be measurable, and have a target date for accomplishment and that employees should receive feedback and rewards.

 ### 12.4 Job Design Perspectives on Motivation

Job design is, first, the division of an organization's work among its employees and, second, the application of motivational theories to jobs to increase satisfaction and performance. Two approaches to job design are fitting people to jobs (the traditional approach) and fitting jobs to people.

Fitting jobs to people assumes people are underutilized and want more variety. Two techniques for this type of job design include (1) job enlargement, increasing the number of tasks in a job to increase variety and motivation, and (2) job enrichment, building into a job such motivating factors as responsibility, achievement, recognition, stimulating work, and advancement.

An outgrowth of job enrichment is the job characteristics model, which consists of (a) five core job characteristics that affect (b) three critical psychological states of an employee that in turn affect (c) work outcomes—the employee's motivation, performance, and satisfaction. The five core job characteristics are (1) skill variety—how many different skills a job requires; (2) task identity—how many different tasks are required to complete the work; (3) task significance—how many other people are affected by the job; (4) autonomy—how much discretion the job allows the worker; and (5) feedback—how much employees find out how well they're doing. These five characteristics affect three critical psychological states:

meaningfulness of work, responsibility for results, and knowledge of results. Three major steps to follow when applying the job characteristics model are (1) diagnose the work environment to see if a problem exists, (2) determine whether job redesign is appropriate, and (3) consider how to redesign the job.

12.5 Reinforcement Perspectives on Motivation

Reinforcement theory attempts to explain behavior change by suggesting that behavior with positive consequences tends to be repeated whereas behavior with negative consequences tends not to be repeated. Reinforcement is anything that causes a given behavior to be repeated or inhibited.

There are four types of reinforcement. (1) Positive reinforcement is the use of positive consequences to encourage desirable behavior. (2) Negative reinforcement is the removal of unpleasant consequences followed by a desired behavior. (3) Extinction is the withholding or withdrawal of positive rewards for desirable behavior, so that the behavior is less likely to occur in the future. (4) Punishment is the application of negative consequences to stop or change undesirable behavior.

In using positive reinforcement to motivate employees, managers should reward only desirable behavior, give rewards as soon as possible, be clear about what behavior is desired, and have different rewards and recognize individual differences. In using punishment, managers should punish only undesirable behavior, give reprimands or disciplinary actions as soon as possible, be clear about what behavior is undesirable, administer punishment in private, and combine punishment and positive reinforcement.

12.6 Using Compensation & Other Rewards to Motivate

Compensation is only one form of motivator. For incentive compensation plans for work, rewards must be linked to performance and be measurable; they must satisfy individual needs; they must be agreed on by manager and employee; and they must be perceived as being equitable, believable, and achievable by employees.

Popular incentive compensation plans are the following. (1) Pay for performance bases pay on one's results. One kind is payment according to piece rate, in which employees are paid according to how much output they produce. Another is the sales commission, in which sales representatives are paid a percentage of the earnings the company made from their sales. (2) Bonuses are cash awards given to employees who achieve specific performance objectives. (3) Profit sharing is the distribution to employees of a percentage of the company's profits. (4) Gainsharing is the distribution of savings or "gains" to groups of employees who reduced costs and increased measurable productivity. (5) Stock options allow certain employees to buy stock at a future date for a discounted price. (6) Pay for knowledge ties employee pay to the number of job-relevant skills or academic degrees they earn.

There are also nonmonetary ways of compensating employees. Some employees will leave because they feel the need for work-life balance, the need to expand their skills, and the need to matter. To retain such employees, nonmonetary incentives have been introduced, such as the flexible workplace. Other incentives that keep employees from leaving are thoughtfulness by employees' managers, work-life benefits such as day care, attractive surroundings, skill-building and educational opportunities, and work sabbaticals.

Management in Action

Motivating Temporary Workers Is a Growing Managerial Challenge

You know American workers are in bad shape when a low-paying, no-benefits job is considered a sweet deal. Their situation isn't likely to improve soon; some economists predict it will be years, not months, before employees regain any semblance of bargaining power. That's because this [2008–2009] recession's unusual ferocity has accelerated trends—including offshoring, automation, the decline of labor unions' influence, new management techniques, and regulatory changes—that already had been eroding worker's economic standing.

The forecast for the next 5 to 10 years: more of the same, with paltry pay gains, worsening working conditions, and little job security. Right on up to the C-suite, more jobs will be freelance and temporary, and even seemingly permanent positions will be at greater risk. . . .

Peter Cappelli, director of the Center for Human Resources at the University of Pennsylvania's Wharton School, says the brutal recession has prompted more companies to create just-in-time labor forces that can be turned on and off like a spigot. "Employers are trying to get rid of all fixed costs," Cappelli says. "First they did it with employee benefits. Now they're doing it with the jobs themselves. Everything is variable." . . .

Diminishing job security is also widening the gap between the highest- and lowest-paid workers. At the top, people with sought-after skills can earn more by jumping from assignment to assignment than they can by sticking with one company. But for the least educated, who have no special skills to sell, the new deal for labor offers nothing but downside.

Employers prize flexibility, of course. But if they aren't careful they can wind up with an alienated, dispirited workforce. A Conference Board survey released January 5 [2010] found that only 45% of workers surveyed were satisfied with their jobs, the lowest in 22 years of polling. Poor morale can devastate performance. . . .

The trend toward a perma-temp world had been developing for years. Bosses are no longer rewarded based on how many people they supervise, so they have less incentive to hang on to staff. Instead the increasing use of bonuses tied to short-term profit performance gives managers and incentive to slash labor costs. The Iowa Policy Project, a nonpartisan think tank, estimates that 26% of the U.S. workforce had jobs in 2005 that were in one way or another "nonstandard." That includes independent contractors, temps, part-timers, and freelancers. Of those, 73% had no access to a retirement plan from their employer, and 61% had no health insurance from their employer, the Iowa group said.

Temp employment in the U.S. fluctuates wildly, by design. The whole purpose of bringing on workers who are employed by temporary staffing firms such as Manpower, Adecco, and Kelly Services is that they're easy to shuck off when unneeded. While the number of temps fell sharply during the recent recession, the ranks of involuntary part-timers soared. The tally of Americans working part-time for economic reasons—that is, because full-time work is unavailable—has doubled since the recession began, to 9.2 million. . . .

Boeing typifies the companies that are taking advantage of flexibility. In 2009, it cut 1,500 contingent workers from its commercial division. Says spokesman Jim Proulx: "The first imperative was to reduce all of the contract and contingent labor that we possibly could to shield our regular employees from those layoffs." Boeing says less than 3% of its workforce is contingent. It has also reduced its dependence on costly permanent staff in the U.S. by making new hires abroad. Last March [2009] it announced a research and development center in Bangalore, that will "coordinate the work of more than 1,500 technologists, including 100 advanced technology researchers, from across India." Bill Dugovich, a spokesman for Boeing's white-collar union in the U.S., the SPEEA, complains that the Indian workers "are basically contract labor."

For years Microsoft has been an avid user of temporary-staffing firms such as Volt Information Sciences for a variety of short-term projects, including writing chunks of software, say Microsoft spokesman Lou Gellos. "Our contingent workforce fluctuates wildly depending on the different projects that are going on," Gellos says. "Somebody does just part of a project. They're experts in it. Boom, boom, they're finished." Temps are especially appealing to companies in cyclical industries. "We have been able to get really good talent. Off the charts," says Jeff Barrett, CEO of Eggrock, a manufacturer of pre-built bathrooms based in Littleton, Massachusetts. It has brought on dozens of plumbers, electricians, and administrative workers through Manpower to handle a spike in orders. . . .

The world of temporary work used to be the domain of sneaker-footed admins. No longer. Last year, Kelly Services placed more than 100 people—including lawyers and scientists—in interim stints that paid more than $250,000 a year. At the forefront of the "leadership on demand" movement in the U.S. is the Business Talent Group, whose roster of 1,000 executives has done jobs at companies like mobile-phone content provider Fox Mobile, healthcare company Healthways, and private equity firm Carlyle Group. BTG says its client demand rose 50% in 2009.

Sydney Reiner, of Southern California, has had five assignments in five years as interim chief marketing officer at companies like Coffee Bean & Tea Leaf and Godiva Chocolatier. "I got a call from Godiva on a Wednesday asking if I could be on a plane to Japan on Saturday," says Reiner. "I was." For the past two months, she's been the interim chief marketing officer at beverage maker POM Wonderful. Reiner prefers the challenge of working in short, adrenaline-packed chunks. But . . . the University of Chicago MBA has no access to employer-sponsored health insurance and other benefits. Says Reiner: "To some extent I end up working as hard as a permanent employee, without a lot of the benefits." . . .

At the bottom of the ladder, workers are so powerless that simply getting the minimum wage they're entitled to can be a struggle. A study released in September [2009] and financed by the Ford, Joyce, Haynes, and Russell Sage Foundations found that low-wage workers are routinely denied proper overtime pay and are often paid less than the minimum wage. It followed a Government Accountability Office report from March 2009 that found that poor oversight by the Labor Dept.'s Wage and Hour Div. leaves low-wage workers "vulnerable to wage theft." Some companies have been fined for misclassifying employees as freelancers and then denying them benefits. Meanwhile, the George W. Bush Administration made it easier for people earning as little as $23,600 a year not to be covered by overtime-pay rules.

Workers hired for temporary or contract work face a higher risk of developing mental health problems like depression, according to research presented in 2009 by Amélie Quesnel-Vallée of McGill University. A lack of job security and health-care benefits, as well as social ties to the rest of the workforce, increase stress levels for temps and contractors. . . .

The situation is especially difficult for young people, many of whom haven't been able to get a first foot on the career ladder. The percentage of people 16 to 24 who have jobs has plummeted by 13 percentage points since the beginning of 2000, while the share of workers 55 and over who have jobs has edged up over that period, despite the recession. Some young people are so desperate to get a start, they're working for free as semi-permanent interns. . . .

When employment in the U.S. eventually recovers, it's likely to be because American workers swallow hard and accept lower pay. That has been the pattern for decades now: Shockingly, pay for production and nonsupervisory workers—80% of the private workforce—is 9% lower than it was in 1973, adjusted for inflation. . . .

Look far enough into the future and it's possible to see better times ahead for labor. A decade from now the retirement on the baby boom generation could cause labor shortages and hand some bargaining power back to younger workers, says Robert Mellman, a senior economist at JPMorgan Chase Bank. If that happens, woe unto employers. A survey in 2009 by the benefits consultant now known as Towers Watson found that top-performing employees will be ready to jump ship as soon as a better offer comes along. Says Wharton's Cappelli: "The idea of loyalty—'I will stick with you and you will reward me'—that is effectively gone."

For Discussion

1. How can managers use recommendations derived from need theories to motivate temporary employees? Discuss.

2. To what extent can managers use Herzberg's two-factor theory to motivate temporary workers? Explain your ideas for applying this theory.

3. To what extent is the growing use of temporary workers consistent with both equity and expectancy theory? Explain.

4. What are the pros and cons of using temporary workers? Would you accept a job as a temporary worker after graduation from college?

5. What are the key lessons learned from this case? Discuss.

Source: Excerpted from Peter Coy, Michelle Conlin, and Moria Herbst, "The Disposable Worker," *Bloomberg Businessweek,* January 18, 2010, pp. 33–39. Reprinted with permission.

Self-Assessment

What Is Your Reaction to Equity Differences?

Objectives

1. Assess your reaction to equity differences.

2. Gain more insight into yourself.

Introduction

Have you ever noticed that certain people scream "No fair!" whenever they perceive something as unequal? Have you also noticed that other people don't seem bothered by inequity at all? According to researchers, when given the same amount of inequity, people respond differently depending on their individual equity sensitivity. There are varying degrees of equity sensitivity:

Benevolents are individuals who prefer their outcome/input ratios to be less than the others being compared. These are people who don't mind being underrewarded.

Equity Sensitives are individuals who prefer outcome/input ratios to be equal. These people are concerned with obtaining rewards that they perceive to be fair in relation to what others are receiving.

Entitleds are individuals who prefer that their outcome/input ratios go above those of the others being compared. These people aren't worried by inequities and actually prefer situations in which they see themselves as overrewarded.

The purpose of this exercise is to assess your equity sensitivity.

Instructions

The five statements below ask what you would like your relationship to be within any organization. For each question, *divide* 10 points between the two answers (A and B) *by giving the most points to the answer that is most like you and the fewest points to the answer least like you.* You can give an equal number of points to A and B. You can make use of zeros if you like. Just be sure to use all 10 points on each question. (For instance, if statement A is completely appropriate and B is not at all appropriate, give A 10 points and B zero points. If A is somewhat appropriate and B is not completely appropriate, give A 7 points and B 3 points.) Place your points next to each letter.

In any organization where I might work . . .

I. It would be more important for me to:
   A. Get from the organization _____
   B. Give to the organization _____

2. It would be more important for me to:
   A. Help others _____
   B. Watch out for my own good _____

3. I would be more concerned about:
   A. What I received from the organization _____
   B. What I contributed to the organization _____

4. The hard work I would do should:
   A. Benefit the organization _____
   B. Benefit me _____

5. My personal philosophy in dealing with the organization would be:
   A. If you don't look out for yourself, nobody else will _____
   B. It's better to give than to receive _____

Calculate your total score by adding the points you allocated to the following items: 1B, 2A, 3B, 4A, and 5B. Total score = _____

Analysis & Interpretation

Your total will be between 0 and 50. If you scored less than 29, you are an Entitled; if your score was between 29 and 32, you are an Equity Sensitive; and if your score was above 32, you are a Benevolent.

Questions for Discussion

1. To what extent are the results consistent with your self-perception? Explain.

2. Using the survey items as a foundation, how should managers try to motivate Benevolents, Equity Sensitives, and Entitleds? Discuss in detail.

From R. C. Huseman, J. D. Hatfield, and E. W. Miles, "Test for Individual Perceptions of Job Equity: Some Preliminary Findings," *Perceptual and Motor Skills,* Vol. 62, 1985, pp. 1055–1064. Copyright © Perceptual and Motor Skills 1985.

Ethical Dilemma

How Would You Handle a Confrontation between an Employee & a Customer?

Mala Amarsingh, a JetBlue Airways Corp. attendant, was standing in the Las Vegas airport in June [2007], waiting to hitch a ride to New York to start her shift. An intoxicated female passenger approached her, started cursing, threatened to beat her up, and then spit in her face. The flight attendant says she lost her cool, cursed back at the passenger, and later was terminated by the airline for "inappropriate behavior." JetBlue won't comment about personnel matters, but says "customers traveling today are more frustrated by delays and perceived service lapses."

Ms. Amarsingh thinks "uniformed flight attendants are walking targets for passenger frustrations," which "absolutely" have gotten worse in her more than 6 years in the job.

Assume that you are the vice president of JetBlue and that you just became aware of the situation involving Ms. Amarsingh. What would you do?

1. Do nothing. Ms. Amarsingh's behavior violated corporate policy about the treatment of customers and she deserved to be fired. Changing the decision would set a bad precedent for other employees.

2. Acknowledge that the employee's behavior violates corporate policy, but hire her back given the extenuating circumstances. Provide Ms. Amarsingh with back pay for any lost time.

3. The customer committed assault and battery by purposely spitting in Ms. Amarsingh's face. Hire the employee back and use company resources to sue the customer. This would send a clear message that you care about your employees and that JetBlue will not allow its employees to be assaulted.

4. Invent other options.

Source: Excerpted from Susan Carey, "Cranky Skies: Fliers Behave Badly Again As 9/11 Era Fades," *The Wall Street Journal*, September 12, 2007, p. A16. Copyright © 2007 by Dow Jones & Company, Inc. Reproduced with permission of Dow Jones & Company, Inc. via Copyright Clearance Center.

chapter 13

Groups & Teams
Increasing Cooperation, Reducing Conflict

Major Questions You Should Be Able to Answer

13.1 Groups versus Teams
Major Question: How is one collection of workers different from any other?

13.2 Stages of Group & Team Development
Major Question: How does a group evolve into a team?

13.3 Building Effective Teams
Major Question: How can I, as a manager, build an effective team?

13.4 Managing Conflict
Major Question: Since conflict is a part of life, what should a manager know about it in order to deal successfully with it?

Reaching Across Time & Space: The Challenge of Managing Virtual Teams

Once upon a time, managers subscribed to the so-called Fifty-Foot Rule—namely, "If people are more than 50 feet apart, they are not likely to collaborate." That is no longer true in today's era of virtual teams. Virtual teams (also known as geographically dispersed teams) are groups of people who use information technology—computers and telecommunications—to collaborate across space, time, and organizational boundaries.[1]

As technology has made it easier for workers to function from remote places, it has posed challenges for managers. Following are some suggestions for managing virtual workers, whether they are working a few miles away at home or on the other side of the world:[2]

- **Take baby steps and manage by results.** When trying out virtual arrangements with new employees, take it slow. Let them show they can handle the challenge. Focus on what's accomplished, not whether an employee is working from her patio or at 10 P.M. Set interim deadlines on projects and stick to them.

- **State expectations.** Nip problems in the bud by letting virtual workers know what you expect from them. With home-based workers, for example, go over the terms of your virtual arrangement—whether, for example, you want them to carry an office cell phone—and tell them if there are specific ways you want the job done.

- **Write it down.** Record directions, project changes, and updates in writing, by sending an e-mail or by using Web-based services that allow

for sharing calendars and tracking projects. Keep all communications in a shared database, so that a historical document of the group's work is available for new team members to study.

- **Communicate, but be considerate.** Team members should know what times are appropriate to call one another (think time zones here) and what days (considering cultural, family, or work schedules) are off-limits. Make sure everyone is reachable during normal business hours, as via phone, e-mail, fax, or chat.

- **Be aware of cultural differences.** Even if everyone on a global team speaks English, be aware that others may not understand slang, culturally narrow expressions, and American humor. Encourage everyone to slow down their speech. Realize that team members from China and India, say, may have difficulty saying no or may fall silent in order to save face. At bottom, building global and virtual teams is all about building trust—being respectful and doing what you say you're going to do. Handle serious conflicts face-to-face whenever possible.

- **Meet regularly.** Human contact still matters. If possible, launch the team with a face-to-face meeting. When possible, schedule periodic and regular meetings where all team members can discuss current projects and telecommuters can catch up on office gossip. Fly out-of-towners in at least quarterly, so they can develop working friendships with your in-office staff.

For Discussion What do you feel might be the greatest difficulties of always working online with numerous people that you never see? How would you try to avoid or solve these difficulties?

forecast What's Ahead in This Chapter

In this chapter, we consider groups versus teams and discuss different kinds of teams. We describe how groups evolve into teams and discuss how managers can build effective teams. We also consider the nature of conflict, both good and bad.

major question

How is one collection of workers different from any other?

THE BIG PICTURE

Teamwork promises to be a cornerstone of future management. A team is different from a group. A group typically is management-directed, a team self-directed. Groups may be formal, created to do productive work, or informal, created for friendship. Work teams, which engage in collective work requiring coordinated effort, may be organized according to four basic purposes: advice, production, project, and action. Two types of teams are continuous improvement and self-managed teams.

More than 20 years ago, management philosopher Peter Drucker predicted that future organizations would not only be flatter and information-based but also organized around teamwork—and that has certainly come to pass.[3]

"You lead today by building teams and placing others first," says General Electric CEO Jeffrey Immelt. "It's not about you."[4] "We have this mythology in America about the lone genius," says Tom Kelley, general manager of Ideo, a Palo Alto, California, multidisciplinary industrial design company that helped create the Apple mouse, first laptop computer, and soft-handled Gripper toothbrush for Oral-B. "We love to personify things. But Michelangelo didn't paint the Sistine Chapel alone, and Edison didn't invent the light bulb alone."[5]

The argument for promoting diversity suggested by scholar Scott E. Page (see Chapter 3)—namely, that different kinds of people "bring to organizations more and different ways of seeing a problem and, thus, faster/better ways of solving it"—is also a principal strength of teams.[6] However, teamwork is now the cornerstone of progressive management for many other reasons, as the table below shows. *(See Table 13.1.)* Regardless, when you take a job in an organization, the chances are you won't be working as a lone genius or even as a lone wolf. You'll be working with others in situations demanding teamwork.

table 13.1

WHY TEAMWORK IS IMPORTANT

The Improvements	Example
Increased productivity	At one GE factory, teamwork resulted in a workforce that was 20% more productive than comparable GE workforces elsewhere.
Increased speed	Guidant Corp., maker of lifesaving medical devices, halved the time it took to get products to market.
Reduced costs	Boeing used teamwork to develop the 777 at costs far less than normal.
Improved quality	Westinghouse used teamwork to improve quality performance in its truck and trailer division and within its electronic components division.
Reduced destructive internal competition	Men's Wearhouse fired a salesman who wasn't sharing walk-in customer traffic, and total clothing sales volume among all salespeople increased significantly.
Improved workplace cohesiveness	Cisco Systems told executives they would gain or lose 30% of their bonuses based on how well they worked with peers and in 3 years had record profits.

Groups & Teams: How Do They Differ?

Aren't a group of people and a team of people the same thing? By and large, no. One is a collection of people, the other a powerful unit of collective performance. One is typically management-directed, the other self-directed.

Consider the differences.

What a Group Is: Collection of People Performing as Individuals   A *group* is defined as two or more freely interacting individuals who share collective norms, share collective goals, and have a common identity.[7] A group is different from a crowd, a transitory collection of people who don't interact with one another, such as a crowd gathering on a sidewalk to watch a fire. And it is different from an organization, such as a labor union, which is so large that members also don't interact.[8]

An example of a work group would be a collection of, say, 10 employees meeting to exchange information about various companies' policies on wages and hours.

What a Team Is: Collection of People with Common Commitment   McKinsey & Company management consultants Jon R. Katzenbach and Douglas K. Smith say it is a mistake to use the terms *group* and *team* interchangeably. Successful teams, they say, tend to take on a life of their own. Thus, a *team* **is defined as a small group of people with complementary skills who are committed to a common purpose, performance goals, and approach for which they hold themselves mutually accountable.**[9] "The essence of a team is common commitment," say Katzenbach and Smith. "Without it, groups perform as individuals; with it, they become a powerful unit of collective performance."[10]

An example of a team would be a collection of 2–10 employees who are studying industry pay scales, with the goal of making recommendations for adjusting pay grades within their own company.

Formal versus Informal Groups

Groups may be either formal or informal.

- **Formal groups—created to do productive work. A *formal group* is a group established to do something productive for the organization and is headed by a leader.** A formal group may be a division, a department, a work group, or a committee. It may be permanent or temporary. In general, people are assigned to them according to their skills and the organization's requirements.

- **Informal groups—created for friendship. An *informal group* is a group formed by people seeking friendship and has no officially appointed leader, although a leader may emerge from the membership.** An informal group may be simply a collection of friends who hang out with one another, such as those who take coffee breaks together, or it may be as organized as a prayer breakfast, a bowling team, a service club, or other voluntary organization.

What's important for you as a manager to know is that informal groups can advance or undercut the plans of formal groups. The formal organization may make efforts, say, to speed up the plant assembly line or to institute workplace reforms. But these attempts may be sabotaged through the informal networks of workers who meet and gossip over lunch pails and after-work beers.[11]

However, interestingly, informal groups can also be highly productive—even more so than formal groups.

Example

Informal Groups & Informal Learning: Sharing Knowledge in the Lunchroom & on Social Media

As a manager, what would you think if you saw employees making brief conversation near the lunchroom coffeepot? "The assumption was made that this was chitchat, talking about their golf game," said a training director at the Siemens Power Transmission and Distribution plant in Wendell, North Carolina, where managers worried about workers gathering so often in the cafeteria. "But there was a whole lot of work activity."[12]

Workplace Learning: Mostly Informal. And indeed a 2-year study by the Center for Workplace Development found that 70% of workplace learning is informal.[13] As a result of the study conclusions, Siemens managers alerted supervisors about the informal meetings and even placed overhead projectors and empty pads of paper in the lunchroom to facilitate the exchange of information. Technology firm Qualcomm uses employees' storytelling tendencies as a way to communicate information, as well as to reinforce the company's culture and values.[14]

The Peer-to-Peer Web. What about when employees are in far-flung places and can't gather in a cafeteria? "Sales reps are out in the field and they're kind of on islands," pointed out an executive at ExactTarget, an Indianapolis-based software firm. "It's a challenge to keep everyone connected."[15] So what was the company to do when the 75 reps started overwhelming the sales-support staff with questions about product details and client information? To ease the strain, ExactTarget leveraged the knowledge of its sales force by creating a Web site on which the reps could post and

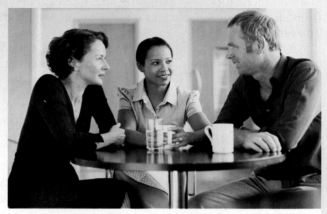

Talking it out. Ever worked in a job in which you got a lot of informal training through conversations over coffee? Could this be done with social networking?

answer questions in an informal peer-to-peer learning setting.

YOUR CALL

Ever heard of Second Life, the multiplayer online role-playing game that is also described as a "3-D Internet" and a "virtual social world"? Could games or other "social media" be used to foster informal workplace collaboration? How would this work? (Hint: Companies such as IBM and PA Consulting Group are already using Second Life for collaboration with employees and customers and for hiring real-life employees.)[16]

Work Teams for Four Purposes: Advice, Production, Project, & Action

The names given to different kinds of teams can be bewildering. We have identified some important ones the opposite page. *(See Table 13.2.)*

You will probably benefit most by understanding the various types of work teams distinguished according to their purpose. Work teams, which engage in collective work requiring coordinated effort, are of four types, which may be identified according to their basic purpose: *advice, production, project,* or *action.*[17]

table 13.2

VARIOUS TYPES OF TEAMS

These teams are not mutually exclusive. Work teams, for instance, may also be self-managed, cross-functional, or virtual.

Continuous improvement team	Volunteers of workers and supervisors who meet intermittently to discuss workplace and quality-related problems; formerly called quality circle.
Cross-functional team	Members composed of people from different departments, such as sales and production, pursuing a common objective.
Problem-solving team	Knowledgeable workers who meet as a temporary team to solve a specific problem and then disband.
Self-managed team	Workers are trained to do all or most of the jobs in a work unit, have no direct supervisor, and do their own day-to-day supervision.
Top-management team	Members consist of the CEO, president, and top department heads and work to help the organization achieve its mission and goals.
Virtual team	Members interact by computer network to collaborate on projects.
Work team	Members engage in collective work requiring coordinated effort; purpose of team is advice, production, project, or action *(see text discussion).*

1. Advice Teams   *Advice teams* are created to broaden the information base for managerial decisions. Examples are committees, review panels, advisory councils, employee involvement groups, and continuous improvement teams (as we'll discuss).

2. Production Teams   *Production teams* are responsible for performing day-to-day operations. Examples are mining teams, flight-attendant crews, maintenance crews, assembly teams, data processing groups, and manufacturing crews.

3. Project Teams   *Project teams* work to do creative problem solving, often by applying the specialized knowledge of members of a **cross-functional team, which is staffed with specialists pursuing a common objective.** Examples are task forces, research groups, planning teams, architect teams, engineering teams, and development teams.

4. Action Teams   *Action teams* work to accomplish tasks that require people with (1) specialized training and (2) a high degree of coordination, as on a baseball team, with specialized athletes acting in coordination. Examples are hospital surgery teams, airline cockpit crews, mountain-climbing expeditions, police SWAT teams, and labor contract negotiating teams.

Self-Managed Teams: Workers with Own Administrative Oversight

To give you an idea of how teams work, consider self-managed teams. These kinds of teams have emerged out of what were called quality circles, now known as ***continuous improvement teams,* which consist of small groups of volunteers or**

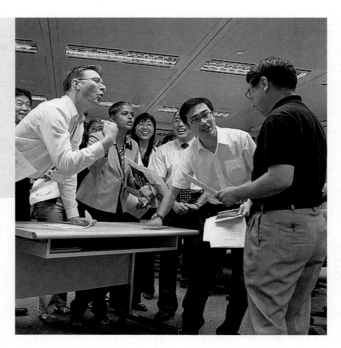

Team building. The team ethic at Hong Kong–based Cathay Pacific has helped the multinational airline provide excellent service that pleases both passengers and shareholders. Here Cathay trainees get practice handling unruly passengers and putting on their best face. Do you think there are better ways to get this training?

workers and supervisors who meet intermittently to discuss workplace- and quality-related problems. Typically a group of 10–12 people will meet for 60–90 minutes once or twice a month, with management listening to presentations and the important payoff for members usually being the chance for meaningful participation and skills training.[18]

From Continuous Improvement Teams to Self-Managed Teams

In many places, such as the Texas Instruments electronics factory in Malaysia, the continuous improvement teams have evolved into a system made up almost entirely of self-managed teams, with routine activities formerly performed by supervisors now performed by team members. "Self-managed" does not, however, mean simply turning workers loose to do their own thing. *Self-managed teams* **are defined as groups of workers who are given administrative oversight for their task domains.** Administrative oversight involves delegated activities such as planning, scheduling, monitoring, and staffing. Nearly 70% of *Fortune* 1000 companies have created self-managed work teams.[19]

Self-managed teams are an outgrowth of a blend of behavioral science and management practice.[20] The goal has been to increase productivity and employee quality of work life. The traditional clear-cut distinction between manager and managed is being blurred as nonmanagerial employees are delegated greater authority and granted increased autonomy.

Technical & Organizational Redesign In creating self-managed teams, both technical and organizational redesign are necessary.

- **New technology.** Self-managed teams may require special technology. Volvo's team-based auto assembly plant, for example, relies on portable assembly platforms rather than traditional assembly lines.
- **New organization.** Structural redesign of the organization must take place because self-managed teams are an integral part of the organization, not patched onto it, as is the case with continuous improvement teams.

Personnel and reward systems need to be adapted to encourage teamwork. Staffing decisions may shift from management to team members who hire their own co-workers. Individual bonuses must give way to team bonuses. Supervisory development workshops are needed to teach managers to be facilitators rather than order givers.[21] Finally, extensive team training is required to help team members learn more about technical details, the business as a whole, and how to be team players.[22] ●

✳ I3.2 STAGES OF GROUP & TEAM DEVELOPMENT

How does a group evolve into a team?	major question?

THE BIG PICTURE
Groups may evolve into teams by going through five stages of development: forming, storming, norming, performing, and adjourning.

Managers often talk of products and organizations going through stages of development, from birth to maturity to decline. Groups and teams go through the same thing. One theory proposes five stages of development: *forming, storming, norming, performing, adjourning.*[23] *(See Figure 13.1.)* Let us consider these stages in which groups may evolve into teams—bearing in mind that the stages aren't necessarily of the same duration or intensity.

figure I3.I

FIVE STAGES OF GROUP AND TEAM DEVELOPMENT

| **Forming** Getting oriented & getting acquainted | → | **Storming** Individual personalities & roles emerge | → | **Norming** Conflicts resolved, relationships develop, unity emerges | → | **Performing** Solving problems & completing the assigned task | → | **Adjourning** Preparing for disbandment |

Stage I: Forming—"Why Are We Here?"

The first stage, *forming,* **is the process of getting oriented and getting acquainted.** This stage is characterized by a high degree of uncertainty as members try to break the ice and figure out who is in charge and what the group's goals are. For example, if you were to become part of a team that is to work on a class project, the question for you as an individual would be "How do I fit in here?" For the group, the question is "Why are we here?"[24]

At this point, mutual trust is low, and there is a good deal of holding back to see who takes charge and how. If the formal leader (such as the class instructor or a supervisor) does not assert his or her authority, an emergent leader will eventually step in to fill the group's need for leadership and direction.

What the Leader Should Do Leaders typically mistake this honeymoon period as a mandate for permanent control, but later problems may force a leadership change. During this stage, leaders should allow time for people to become acquainted and to socialize.

Stage 2: Storming—"Why Are We Fighting Over Who Does What & Who's in Charge?"

The second stage, *storming,* **is characterized by the emergence of individual personalities and roles and conflicts within the group.** For you as an individual, the question is "What's my role here?" For the group, the issue is "Why are we fighting over who does what and who's in charge?" This stage may be of short duration or painfully long, depending on the goal clarity and the commitment and maturity of the members.

This is a time of testing. Individuals test the leader's policies and assumptions as they try to determine how they fit into the power structure.[25] Subgroups take shape, and subtle forms of rebellion, such as procrastination, occur. Many groups stall in stage 2 because power politics may erupt into open rebellion.

What the Leader Should Do   In this stage, the leader should encourage members to suggest ideas, voice disagreements, and work through their conflicts about tasks and goals.

Stage 3: Norming—"Can We Agree on Roles & Work as a Team?"

In the third stage, *norming,* **conflicts are resolved, close relationships develop, and unity and harmony emerge.** For individuals, the main issue is "What do the others expect me to do?" For the group, the issue is "Can we agree on roles and work as a team?" Note, then, that the *group* may now evolve into a *team.*

Teams set guidelines related to what members will do together and how they will do it. The teams consider such matters as attendance at meetings, being late, and missing assignments as well as how members treat one another.

Groups that make it through stage 2 generally do so because a respected member other than the leader challenges the group to resolve its power struggles so something can be accomplished. Questions about authority are resolved through unemotional, matter-of-fact group discussion. A feeling of team spirit is experienced because members believe they have found their proper roles. **Group cohesiveness, a "we" feeling binding group members together,** is the principal by-product of stage 3. (We discuss cohesiveness next, in Section 13.3.)

What the Leader Should Do   This stage generally does not last long. Here the leader should emphasize unity and help identify team goals and values.

Stage 4: Performing—"Can We Do the Job Properly?"

In *performing,* **members concentrate on solving problems and completing the assigned task.** For individuals, the question here is "How can I best perform my role?" For the group/team, the issue is "Can we do the job properly?"

What the Leader Should Do   During this stage, the leader should allow members the empowerment they need to work on tasks.

Stage 5: Adjourning—"Can We Help Members Transition Out?"

In the final stage, *adjourning,* **members prepare for disbandment.** Having worked so hard to get along and get something done, many members feel a compelling sense of loss. For the individual, the question now is "What's next?" For the team, the issue is "Can we help members transition out?"

What the Leader Should Do   The leader can help ease the transition by rituals celebrating "the end" and "new beginnings." Parties, award ceremonies, graduations, or mock funerals can provide the needed punctuation at the end of a significant teamwork project. The leader can emphasize valuable lessons learned in group dynamics to prepare everyone for future group and team efforts. ●

✕ 13.3 BUILDING EFFECTIVE TEAMS

How can I, as a manager, build an effective team?

THE BIG PICTURE

Two types of change are reactive and proactive. Forces for change may consist of forces outside the organization—demographic characteristics, market changes, technological advancements, and social and political pressures. Or they may be forces inside the organization—employee problems and managers' behavior.

Within an organization, you may hear managers loosely (and incorrectly) use the word *team* to describe any collection of people who have been pulled together. But because traditional managers are often reluctant to give up control, no thought is given to providing the "team" (really just a group) with training and support. That is, no attempt is made to sharpen communication skills, reward innovation, or encourage independence without group members running away and losing control.[26]

Thus, as a manager, the first thing you have to realize is that building a high-performance team is going to require some work. But the payoff will be a stronger, better-performing work unit.

The considerations in building a group into an effective team are (1) *performance goals and feedback,* (2) *motivation through mutual accountability,* (3) *size,* (4) *roles,* (5) *norms,* (6) *cohesiveness,* and (7) *groupthink.*

1. Performance Goals & Feedback

As an individual, you no doubt prefer to have measurable goals and to have feedback about your performance. The same is true with teams. Teams are not just collections of individuals. They are individuals organized for a collective purpose. That purpose needs to be defined in terms of specific, measurable performance goals with continual feedback to tell team members how well they are doing.

An obvious example are the teams you see on television at Indianapolis or Daytona Beach during automobile racing. When the driver guides the race car off the track to make a pit stop, a team of people quickly jack up the car to change tires, refuel the tank, and clean the windshield—all operating in a matter of seconds. The performance goals are to have the car back on the track as quickly as possible. The number of seconds of elapsed time—and the driver's place among competitors once back in the race—tells them how well they are doing.

2. Motivation through Mutual Accountability

Do you work harder when you're alone or when you're in a group? When clear performance goals exist, when the work is considered meaningful, when members believe their efforts matter, and when they don't feel they are being exploited by others—this kind of culture supports teamwork.[27] Being mutually accountable to other members of the team rather than to a supervisor makes members feel mutual trust and commitment—a key part in motivating members for team effort. To bring about this team culture, managers often allow teams to do the hiring of new members.

Cooperation and collaboration. Army of Two represents a trend in cooperative video games in which people are invited to play collaboratively, allowing them to make individual moves but also work together to reach common goals. Is this a valuable teamwork business tool?

3. Size: Small Teams or Large Teams?

Size, which is often determined by the team's purpose, can be important in affecting members' commitment and performance. Whereas in some flat-organization structures groups may consist of 30 or more employees, teams seem to range in size from 2 to 16 people, with those of 5–12 generally being the most workable and 5 to 6 considered optimal.[28] A survey of 400 workplace team members in the United States found that the average team consisted of 10 members, with 8 being the most common size.[29]

Small and large teams have different characteristics, although the number of members is, to be sure, somewhat arbitrary.[30]

Small Teams: 2–9 Members for Better Interaction & Morale Teams with 9 or fewer members have two advantages:

- **Better interaction.** Members are better able to interact, share information, ask questions of one another, and coordinate activities than are those in larger teams. In particular, teams with five or fewer members offer more opportunity for personal discussion and participation.
- **Better morale.** They are better able to see the worth of their individual contributions and thus are more highly committed and satisfied. Members are less apt to feel inhibited in participating. Team leaders are subject to fewer demands and are able to be more informal.[31]

However, small teams also have some disadvantages:

- **Fewer resources.** With fewer hands, there will be fewer resources—less knowledge, experience, skills, and abilities to apply to the team's tasks.
- **Possibly less innovation.** A group that's too small may show less creativity and boldness because of the effect of peer pressure.
- **Unfair work distribution.** Because of fewer resources and less specialization, there may be an uneven distribution of the work among members.

Large Teams: 10–16 Members for More Resources & Division of Labor
Teams with 10–16 members have different advantages over small teams. (Again, the numbers are somewhat arbitrary.)

- **More resources.** Larger teams have more resources to draw on: more knowledge, experience, skills, abilities, and perhaps time. These will give them more leverage to help them realize the team's goals.
- **Division of labor.** In addition, a large team can take advantage of *division of labor,* **in which the work is divided into particular tasks that are assigned to particular workers.**

Yet bigness has its disadvantages:

- **Less interaction.** With more members, there is less interaction, sharing of information, and coordinating of activities. Leaders may be more formal and autocratic, since members in teams this size are apt to be more tolerant of autocratic leadership. The larger size may also lead to the formation of cliques.
- **Lower morale.** Because people are less able to see the worth of their individual contributions, they show less commitment and satisfaction and more turnover and absenteeism. They also express more disagreements and turf struggles and make more demands on leaders.

- **Social loafing.** The larger the size, the more likely performance is to drop, owing to the phenomenon known as *social loafing,* **the tendency of people to exert less effort when working in groups than when working alone.**[32] (Today, social loafers are more apt to be known as *sliders*—high achievers who have "checked out," in the words of former *Business Week* columnists Jack and Suzy Welch, and who have to be dealt with "before they begin to suck the team into their negative energy field and drag it down.")[33]

Example

Team Size: And the Magic Number Is . . .

The subject of team size has become a topic of fascination, according to two scholars, because "in the past decade, research on team effectiveness has burgeoned as teams have become increasingly common in organizations of all kinds."[34] What's the right number of people for a team?

The "Two-Pizza Rule." Various companies have various rules. At Amazon.com, there is a "two-pizza rule"—namely, if a team can't be fed by two pizzas, it's too large.[35] Other companies have their own ideal sizes: Titeflex, 6–10 people; EDS, 8–12; Johnsonville Foods, 12; Volvo, 20. Microsoft Corp. felt the optimal size for a software-development team was 8.[36]

J. Richard Hackman, Harvard professor of social and organizational psychology, thinks there should be no more than 6—the maximum he will allow for students forming project groups.[37] In 1970, Hackman and colleague Neil Vidmar set out to discover the perfect size, asking various teams large and small whether their number was too large or too small for the task.[38]

The optimal number: 4.6.

Task Is Key. Size is not the only consideration, however. For instance, says Wharton management professor Katherine J. Klein, the nature of the team's task is key because it defines the type of skills you are looking for and the type of coordination necessary.[39]

YOUR CALL

What's been your experience, if any, with team size? At what point does adding members begin to hurt a team's performance as people become less motivated and group coordination becomes more difficult?

4. Roles: How Team Members Are Expected to Behave

Roles **are socially determined expectations of how individuals should behave in a specific position.** As a team member, your role is to play a part in helping the team reach its goals. Members develop their roles based on the expectations of the team, of the organization, and of themselves, and they may do different things. You, for instance, might be a team leader. Others might do some of the work tasks. Still others might communicate with other teams.

Two types of team roles are task and maintenance.[40]

Task Roles: Getting the Work Done A *task role,* or *task-oriented role,* **consists of behavior that concentrates on getting the team's tasks done.** Task roles keep the team on track and get the work done. If you stand up in a team meeting and say, "What is the real issue here? We don't seem to be getting anywhere," you are performing a task role.

Examples: Coordinators, who pull together ideas and suggestions; orienters, who keep teams headed toward their stated goals; initiators, who suggest new goals or ideas; and energizers, who prod people to move along or accomplish more are all playing task roles.

Maintenance Roles: Keeping the Team Together A *maintenance role,* or *relationship-oriented role,* consists of behavior that fosters constructive relationships among team members. Maintenance roles focus on keeping team members. If someone at a team meeting says, "Let's hear from those who oppose this plan," he or she is playing a maintenance role.

Examples: Encouragers, who foster group solidarity by praising various viewpoints; standard setters, who evaluate the quality of group processes; harmonizers, who mediate conflict through reconciliation or humor; and compromisers, who help resolve conflict by meeting others "halfway."

5. Norms: Unwritten Rules for Team Members

Norms are more encompassing than roles. *Norms* are general guidelines or rules of behavior that most group or team members follow. Norms point up the boundaries between acceptable and unacceptable behavior.[41] Although norms are typically unwritten and seldom discussed openly, they have a powerful influence on group and organizational behavior.[42]

Example

Team Norms: A Steelmaker Treats Workers Like Owners

When the electrical grid at Nucor Corp.'s steelmaking plant in Hickman, Arkansas, failed, electricians drove or flew in from other Nucor plants as far away as Alabama and North Carolina. No supervisor asked them to do so, nor was there any direct financial incentive for them to blow off their weekends to help out. The electricians were following team norms. They came because, as a *BusinessWeek* article states, "Nucor's flattened hierarchy and emphasis on pushing power to the front line lead its employees to adopt the mindset of owner-operators."[43]

A Close-Knit Culture. Nucor's close-knit culture is the outgrowth of former CEO F. Kenneth Iverson's insight that employees would make extraordinary efforts if they were treated with respect, given real power, and rewarded richly. Instead of following the command-and-control model typical of most American businesses in recent decades, Nucor executives motivate their front-line people by "talking to them, listening to them, taking a risk on their ideas, and accepting the occasional failure," says *BusinessWeek.* During the 2008 economic downturn, when rivals let go thousands of employees, Nucor chose to avoid layoffs and

even managed to pay $1,000–$2,000 bonuses to its workers.[44]

Tying Pay to Production. Good work is rewarded—production of defect-free steel can triple a worker's pay—but bad work is penalized, with employees losing bonuses they normally would have made. Executive pay is tied to team building, with bonuses based not just on the performance of a particular plant but on how well the entire corporation does. There is not only healthy competition among facilities and shifts but also cooperation and idea sharing. The result: Nucor was named the top steel manufacturer in 2008 by American Metal Market for producing the most steel in the United States.[45] It has appeared on *BusinessWeek*'s annual list of top-performing companies four times, ranging from number 25 (2008) to number 1 (2005).[46]

YOUR CALL

Can you think of any kind of businesses in which Nucor's model for strengthening team norms would not work very well? Could American manufacturing companies, automakers, and certain airlines make a comeback if their work and pay rules copied Nucor's?

Why Norms Are Enforced: Four Reasons Norms tend to be enforced by group or team members for four reasons:[47]

- **To help the group survive—"Don't do anything that will hurt us."** Norms are enforced to help the group, team, or organization survive.

Special norms. For nearly 100 years, L.L. Bean, the Freeport, Maine mail-order seller of clothing and outdoor gear, has had an unconditional guarantee that it will give a replacement, refund, or charge credit on a Bean product if a customer is dissatisfied with it, no matter when it was bought. As a result, the company has scored in the top position four years running in the National Retail Federation/American Express Customer Choice survey.

Example: The manager of your team or group might compliment you because you've made sure it has the right emergency equipment.

- **To clarify role expectations—"You have to go along to get along."** Norms are also enforced to help clarify or simplify role expectations.

    Example: At one time, new members of Congress wanting to buck the system by which important committee appointments were given to those with the most seniority were advised to "go along to get along"— go along with the rules in order to get along in their congressional careers.

- **To help individuals avoid embarrassing situations—"Don't call attention to yourself."** Norms are enforced to help group or team members avoid embarrassing themselves.

    Examples: You might be ridiculed by fellow team members for dominating the discussion during a report to top management ("Be a team player, not a show-off"). Or you might be told not to discuss religion or politics with customers, whose views might differ from yours.

- **To emphasize the group's important values and identity—"We're known for being special."** Finally, norms are enforced to emphasize the group, team, or organization's central values or to enhance its unique identity.

    Examples: Nordstrom's department store chain emphasizes the great lengths to which it goes in customer service. Every year a college gives an award to the instructor whom students vote best teacher.

6. Cohesiveness: The Importance of Togetherness

Another important characteristic of teams is *cohesiveness,* **the tendency of a group or team to stick together.** This is the familiar sense of togetherness or "we-ness" you feel, for example, when you're a member of a volleyball team, a fraternity or a sorority, or a company's sales force.[48]

Managers can stimulate cohesiveness by allowing people on work teams to pick their own teammates, allowing off-the-job social events, and urging team members to recognize and appreciate each other's contributions to the team goal.[49] Cohesiveness is also achieved by keeping teams small, making sure performance standards are clear and accepted, and following the tips in the following table. *(See Table 13.3, next page.)*

table 13.3

WAYS TO BUILD COLLABORATIVE TEAMS: EIGHT FACTORS THAT LEAD TO SUCCESS

1. Investing in signature relationship practices. Executives can encourage collaborative behavior by making highly visible investments—in facilities with open floor plans to foster communication, for example—that demonstrate their commitment to collaboration.

2. Modeling collaborative behavior. At companies where the senior executives demonstrate highly collaborative behavior themselves, teams collaborate well.

3. Creating a "gift culture." Mentoring and coaching—especially on an informal basis—help people build the networks they need to work across corporate boundaries.

4. Ensuring the requisite skills. Human resources departments that teach employees how to build relationships, communicate well, and resolve conflicts creatively can have a major impact on team collaboration.

5. Supporting a strong sense of community. When people feel a sense of community, they are more comfortable reaching out to others and more likely to share knowledge.

6. Assigning team leaders that are both task- and relationship-oriented. The debate has traditionally focused on whether a task or a relationship orientation creates better leadership, but in fact both are key to successfully leading a team. Typically, leaning more heavily on a task orientation at the outset of a project and shifting toward a relationship orientation once the work is in full swing works best.

7. Building on heritage relationships. When too many team members are strangers, people may be reluctant to share knowledge. The best practice is to put at least a few people who know one another on the team.

8. Understanding role clarity and task ambiguity. Cooperation increases when the roles of individual team members are sharply defined yet the team is given latitude on how to achieve the task.

Source: Reprinted by permission of *Harvard Business Review*. Exhibit from "Eight Ways to Build Collaborative Teams," by L. Gratton and T. J. Erickson, November 2007. Copyright © 2007 by the Harvard Business School Publishing Corporation; all rights reserved.

7. Groupthink: When Peer Pressure Discourages "Thinking Outside the Box"

On a hot day, as the family is comfortably playing dominoes on a porch in Coleman, Texas, the father-in-law suggests taking a 53-mile trip to Abilene for dinner. Though the rest of the family—wife, husband, and mother-in-law—would rather not make the long, hot drive, they keep their preferences to themselves and agree to the trip. Later, back home after suffering a good deal of discomfort (including bad food), the mother-in-law says she would rather have stayed home. The husband and wife chime in that they agreed only to keep the others happy; the father-in-law then announces he only suggested it because he thought the others might be bored. This, says scholar James Harvey, is what he calls the *Abilene paradox*—the tendency of people to go along with others for the sake of avoiding conflict.[50]

The Abilene paradox shows that cohesiveness isn't always good. An undesirable by-product that may occur, according to psychologist **Irvin Janis**, is *groupthink*—**a cohesive group's blind unwillingness to consider alternatives.** In this phenomenon, group or team members are friendly and tight-knit, but they are unable to think "outside the box." Their "strivings for unanimity override their motivation to realistically appraise alternative courses of action," said Janis.[51]

Example: The Senate Intelligence Committee said groupthink was a major factor in the U.S. invasion of Iraq because too many people in the government had tended to think alike and therefore failed to challenge basic assumptions about Iraq's weapons capability.[52]

It cannot be said, however, that group opinion is always risky. Indeed, financial writer James Surowiecki, author of *The Wisdom of Crowds,* argues that "Under the right circumstances, groups are remarkably intelligent, and are often smarter than the smartest people in them."[53] As evidence, he cites how groups have been used to predict the election of the president of the United States, find lost submarines, and correct the spread on a sporting event.

Symptoms of Groupthink   How do you know that you're in a group or team that is suffering from groupthink? Some symptoms include the following:[54]

- **Invulnerability, inherent morality, and stereotyping of opposition.** Because of feelings of invulnerability, group members have the illusion that nothing can go wrong, breeding excessive optimism and risk taking. Members may also be so assured of the rightness of their actions that they ignore the ethical implications of their decisions. These beliefs are helped along by stereotyped views of the opposition, which leads the group to underestimate its opponents.

- **Rationalization and self-censorship.** Rationalizing protects the pet assumptions underlying the group's decisions from critical questions. Self-censorship also stifles critical debate. It is especially hard to argue with success, of course. But if enough key people, such as outside analysts, had challenged Lehman Brothers, the fourth-largest U.S. investment bank, when it seemed to be flying high, it might not have led to the largest bankruptcy filing in corporate history.

- **Illusion of unanimity, peer pressure, and mindguards.** The illusion of unanimity is another way of saying that silence by a member is interpreted to mean consent. But if people do disagree, peer pressure leads other members to question the loyalty of the dissenters. In addition, in a groupthink situation there may exist people who might be called *mindguards*— self-appointed protectors against adverse information.

- **Groupthink versus "the wisdom of crowds."** Groupthink is characterized by a pressure to conform that often leads members with different ideas to censor themselves—the opposite of collective wisdom, says James Surowiecki, in which "each person in the group is offering his or her best independent forecast. It's not at all about compromise or consensus."[55]

The Results of Groupthink: Decision-Making Defects   Groups with a moderate amount of cohesiveness tend to produce better decisions than groups with low or high cohesiveness. Members of highly cohesive groups victimized by groupthink make the poorest decisions—even though they show they express great confidence in those decisions.[56]

Among the decision-making defects that can arise from groupthink are the following:

- **Reduction in alternative ideas.** The principal casualty of groupthink is a shrinking universe of ideas. Decisions are made based on few alternatives. Once preferred alternatives are decided on, they are not reexamined, and, of course, rejected alternatives are not reexamined.

- **Limiting of other information.** When a groupthink group has made its decision, others' opinions, even those of experts, are rejected. If new information is considered at all, it is biased toward ideas that fit the group's preconceptions. Thus, no contingency plans are made in case the decision turns out to be faulty.

Groupthink: Is Nokia Losing Out in Cell Phones?

Nokia makes about a third of all cell phones; however, in 2010 it took in less than 30% of all money spent on these gadgets, down from nearly 50% in 2008. Has the Finnish company focused too much on making basic wireless telephones so that it is risking loss of leadership in handsets?

The Changing Handset. "Handsets are quickly becoming all about instant messaging, Web access, and applications that let you do nifty things like find a free parking space," says one writer. "Voice is becoming an afterthought."[57] Mobile phones are also being put to such uses as movie watching, video conferencing, exchanging money via text message, and "computer visioning"—snapping a picture of an object such as a painting and then looking up information about it online.[58] These conditions may favor computer companies like Apple (iPhone) and Google (Android platform) rather than traditional phone makers such as Nokia and Motorola.[59]

A strategy long used by companies such as Sony, Dell, and General Motors is to make products for the vast middle range of consumers. Now, however, firms targeting the Big Middle are being squeezed at the high end by quality products charging premium prices, such as Apple's iPod, iPhone, and iPad, and at the low end by reasonably well made products that are cheap, such as Acer's laptops. "The products made by mid-range companies are neither exceptional enough to justify premium prices nor cheap enough to win over value-conscious consumers," says financial writer James Surowiecki.[60]

Going for High-End Products. Now, after posting weak earnings in early 2010, Nokia has created a new unit that focuses on smartphones and mobile computers and that is designed to speed up execution and accelerate innovation.[61] But as low-end basic phones become cheap and commoditized, the high-end market will only become hotter, and Nokia will be playing catch-up.

YOUR CALL

If you were CEO of a company that had as much as 30% or 40% of its product category's market share, do you think this success would lead to a culture of groupthink? Why? And how would you change it?

Preventing Groupthink: Making Criticism & Other Perspectives Permissible
Janis believes it is easier to prevent groupthink than to cure it. As preventive measures, he suggests the following:

Fighting groupthink. For a long time, the Coca-Cola Co. had a culture of politeness and consensus that kept it from developing new products, at a time when consumers were flocking to a new breed of coffees, juices, and teas. Now the company is developing new beverages, such as the Full Throttle. Do you think Coke can move beyond groupthink and "me-too" products to become cutting edge?

- **Allow criticism.** Each member of a team or group should be told to be a critical evaluator, able to actively voice objections and doubts. Subgroups within the group should be allowed to discuss and debate ideas. Once a consensus has been reached, everyone should be encouraged to rethink his or her position to check for flaws.

- **Allow other perspectives.** Outside experts should be used to introduce fresh perspectives. Different groups with different leaders should explore the same policy questions. Top-level executives should not use policy committees to rubber-stamp decisions that have already been made. When major alternatives are discussed, someone should be made devil's advocate to try to uncover all negative factors. ●

◉ 13.4 MANAGING CONFLICT

Since conflict is a part of life, what should a manager know about it in order to deal successfully with it?

major question?

THE BIG PICTURE
Conflict, an enduring feature of the workplace, is a process in which one party perceives that its interests are being opposed or negatively affected by another party. Conflict can be negative (bad) or functional (good). Indeed, either too much or too little conflict can affect performance. This section identifies seven sources of conflict in organizations and also describes four ways to stimulate constructive conflict.

You make a mistake that causes problems for your co-workers. You contribute to your team missing a deadline. A co-worker makes a mistake, and you have to deal with an upset customer. You're under pressure and lose your temper with a colleague.[62]

All of these—mistakes, pressure-cooker deadlines, increased workloads, demands for higher productivity, and other kinds of stress—are among the sources of that enduring feature of the workplace: conflict.

The Nature of Conflict: Disagreement Is Normal

Mention the term *conflict* and many people envision shouting and fighting. But as a manager during a typical workday, you will encounter more subtle, non-violent types of conflict: opposition, criticism, arguments. Thus, a definition of conflict seems fairly mild: **Conflict is a process in which one party perceives that its interests are being opposed or negatively affected by another party.**[63] Conflict is simply disagreement, a perfectly normal state of affairs. Conflicts may take many forms: between individuals, between an individual and a group, between groups, within a group, and between an organization and its environment. (To see what your own conflict-management style is, see the Self-Assessment at the end of this chapter.)

Although all of us might wish to live lives free of conflict, it is now recognized that certain kinds of conflict can actually be beneficial.[64] Let us therefore distinguish between *negative conflict* (bad) and *constructive conflict* (good).

- **Negative conflict—bad for organizations.** From the standpoint of the organization, **negative conflict is conflict that hinders the organization's performance or threatens its interests.** As a manager, you need to do what you can to remove negative conflict, sometimes called *dysfunctional conflict.*

- **Constructive conflict—good for organizations.** The good kind of conflict is **constructive conflict, which benefits the main purposes of the organization and serves its interests.**[65] There are some situations in which this kind of conflict—also called *functional conflict* or *cooperative conflict*—is considered advantageous.

Negative & Positive Conflict: Do Nasty Bosses Get Better Performance?

In the film *The Devil Wears Prada,* Meryl Streep stars as a fear-inspiring fashion-magazine editor who keeps her new assistant quivering with dread. Is the portrait real? Says Liz Lange, a maternity-clothes designer, who was herself an editorial assistant, "If you happen to be working for the wrong editor, you could find yourself doing their kid's homework or being yelled at, or crying in the bathroom."[66]

Unfortunately, this kind of tyranny is very common, with 37% of American workers reporting they had been bullied at work, according to a Zogby International survey.[67]

Abuse Flows Downhill. Does such negative conflict get results? Surprisingly, often it does. One study of 373 randomly chosen employees found that, although some reacted to abusive bosses by doing little or nothing, others performed better—in part, it's speculated, to make themselves look good and others look worse.[68]

Yet other research shows that abuse flows downhill, and when supervisors feel they have been unjustly treated, they may vent their resentment by abusing those who report to them. Subordinates generally cope either through avoidance or, less commonly, through confrontation and are in any case less inclined to feel committed to their organizations, to speak unfavorably about their companies to outsiders, and to seek jobs elsewhere.[69]

The "No-Jerk Rule." When Stanford organizational psychologist Robert Sutton published a short essay in which he urged more civility in organizations by steady application of what he calls "the no-jerk rule" (although he used a far stronger word than "jerk"), he elicited more e-mails than he had received on any other subject, showing the topic had touched a nerve.[70]

Jerks may be everywhere, he says, but "the key is to make explicit to everyone involved in hiring decisions that candidates who have strong skills but who show signs they will belittle and disrespect others cannot be hired under any circumstances." In addition, "Insults, put-downs, nasty teasing, and rude interruptions [should be] dealt with as soon as possible, preferably by the most respected and powerful members" of the company.[71]

YOUR CALL

Have you ever worked for jerks (otherwise known, as Sutton puts it, as "tyrants, bullies, boors, destructive narcissists, and psychologically abusive people")? How did you respond to them?

Can Too Little or Too Much Conflict Affect Performance?

It's tempting to think that a conflict-free work group is a happy work group, as indeed it may be. But is it a productive group? In the 1970s, social scientists specializing in organizational behavior introduced the revolutionary idea that organizations could suffer from *too little* conflict.

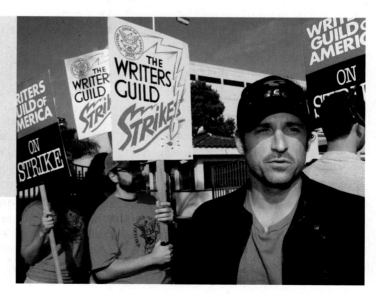

On Strike. *Grey's Anatomy* actor Patrick Dempsey pickets in support of TV and film writers on strike in 2007 over revenue sharing from Internet reuse of their material. What principal issues do you think lead to too much conflict in the workplace?

- **Too little conflict—indolence.** Work groups, departments, or organizations that experience too little conflict tend to be plagued by apathy, lack of creativity, indecision, and missed deadlines. The result is that organizational performance suffers.

- **Too much conflict—warfare.** Excessive conflict, on the other hand, can erode organizational performance because of political infighting, dissatisfaction, lack of teamwork, and turnover. Workplace aggression and violence are manifestations of excessive conflict.[72]

Thus, it seems that a moderate level of conflict can induce creativity and initiative, thereby raising performance, as shown in the diagram below. *(See Figure 13.2.)* As might be expected, however, the idea as to what constitutes "moderate" will vary among managers.

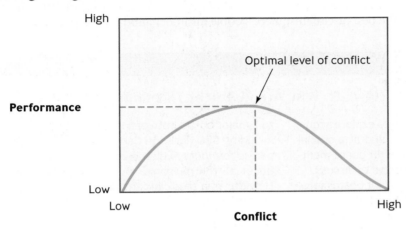

figure 13.2

THE RELATIONSHIP BETWEEN LEVEL OF CONFLICT AND LEVEL OF PERFORMANCE

Too little conflict or too much conflict causes performance to suffer.

Three Kinds of Conflict: Personality, Intergroup, & Cross-Cultural

There are a variety of sources of conflict—so-called *conflict triggers*. Three of the principal ones are (1) between personalities, (2) between groups, and (3) between cultures. By understanding these, you'll be better able to take charge and manage the conflicts rather than letting the conflicts take you by surprise and manage you.

I. Personality Conflicts: Clashes Because of Personal Dislikes or Disagreements We've all had confrontations, weak or strong, with people because we disagreed with them or disliked their personalities, such as their opinions, their behavior, their looks, whatever. ***Personality conflict* is defined as interpersonal opposition based on personal dislike, disagreement, or differing styles.** Some particular kinds of personality conflicts are the following:

- **Personality clashes—when individual differences can't be resolved.** Personality, values, attitudes, and experience can be so disparate that sometimes the only way to resolve individual differences—personality clashes—is to separate two people.

    Example: Are you easygoing, but she's tense and driven? Does he always shade the facts, while you're a stickler for the truth? If you're basically Ms. Straight Arrow and he's Mr. Slippery, do you think you could adapt your personality to fit his? Maybe you should ask for a transfer.

- **Competition for scarce resources—when two parties need the same things.** Within organizations there is often a scarcity of needed resources—for example, funds, office space, equipment, employees, and money for raises. When resources are scarce, being a manager becomes more difficult and conflict more likely.[73]

Example: There are lots of computer glitches but not enough on-site technicians to fix them.

- **Time pressure—when people believe there aren't enough hours to do the work.** Setting a deadline is a useful way of inducing people to perform. Or it can be a source of resentment, rage, and conflict if employees think their manager has unrealistic expectations.

  Example: If you're in the business of marketing Christmas items to department stores and gift shops, it's imperative that you have your product ready for those important trade shows at which store buyers will appear. But the product-ready deadline for Marketing may be completely unworkable for your company's Production Department, leading to angry conflict.

- **Communication failures—when people misperceive and misunderstand.** The need for clear communication is a never-ending, ongoing process. Even under the best of circumstances, people misunderstand others, leading to conflict.

Example

Communication Problem: "Mr. Hewlett, Why Aren't You at This Important Meeting?"

Hewlett-Packard hired a consulting firm to explore acquisition of the computer maker Compaq, and at a crucial directors' meeting the consultant gave HP board members a document about the two companies to discuss.

The Cello Fellow. However, an important board member, Walter Hewlett, son of one of the founders, wasn't there. He was playing his cello somewhere—at an annual event he had appeared in for the past 3 years—and had assumed the board would accommodate him, as it had in the past. But the board plowed ahead, believing Hewlett wouldn't miss such an important session.

Management Misstep. The board's decision to bypass Hewlett turned out to be a crucial misstep for HP management.[74] The miscommunication ultimately led

to a major battle between Hewlett and top HP officers, including CEO Carleton Carly Fiorina. Heirs of the company's founders, which owned 18% of the stock, were upset at the personal tone Fiorina took in painting Hewlett as a musician and academic who flip-flopped over board decisions.

YOUR CALL

Miscommunication happens all the time, much as we might try to avoid it. The real concern is: What should we do once we realize we've not had the same understanding and someone's feelings got hurt? If you were HP's CEO, what should you have done after you found out Hewlett was upset?

2. Intergroup Conflicts: Clashes Between Work Groups, Teams, & Departments The downside of cohesiveness, the "we" feeling discussed earlier, is that it can translate into "we versus them." This produces conflict among work groups, teams, and departments within an organization.

Some ways in which intergroup conflicts are expressed are as follows:

- **Inconsistent goals or reward systems—when people pursue different objectives.** It's natural for people in functional organizations to be pursuing different objectives and to be rewarded accordingly, but this means that conflict is practically built into the system.

  Example: The sales manager for a college textbook publisher may be rewarded for achieving exceptional sales of newly introduced titles. But individual salespeople are rewarded for how many books they sell overall, which means they may promote the old tried and true books they know.

- **Ambiguous jurisdictions—when job boundaries are unclear.** "That's not my job and those aren't my responsibilities." "Those resources belong to me because I need them as part of my job." When task responsibilities are unclear, that can often lead to conflict.

Examples: Is the bartender or the waiter supposed to put the lime in the gin and tonic and the celery in the Bloody Mary? Is management or the union in charge of certain work rules? Is Marketing or Research & Development supposed to be setting up focus groups to explore ideas for new products?

- **Status differences—when there are inconsistencies in power and influence.** It can happen that people who are lower in status according to the organizational chart actually have disproportionate power over those theoretically above them, which can lead to conflicts.

  Examples: If a restaurant patron complains his or her steak is not rare enough, the chef is the one who cooked it, but the waiter—who is usually lower in status—is the one who gave the chef the order. Airlines could not hold their schedules without flight crews and ground crews working a certain amount of overtime. But during labor disputes, pilots, flight attendants, and mechanics may simply refuse managers' requests to work the extra hours.

3. Multicultural Conflicts: Clashes between Cultures With cross-border mergers, joint ventures, and international alliances common features of the global economy, there are frequent opportunities for clashes between cultures. Often success or failure, when business is being conducted across cultures, arises from dealing with differing assumptions about how to think and act.

Example: When in early 2010, drivers of Toyota automobiles were losing control because of sudden acceleration problems, resulting in the manufacturer recalling thousands of vehicles, Toyota failed to recognize differences in the way that Japanese and Americans perceive recalls and safety. For the Japanese, conflicts are all about personal honor. "Japanese consumers are horrified by recalls," says one account, "while Japanese companies avoid them at all costs in order to protect their image. But for U.S. consumers, knowing that any flaw will trigger a recall gives them greater confidence in their cars." By delaying recall, Toyota erred in making a "typically Japanese judgment" for an American market.[75]

Practical Action

Dealing with Disagreements: Five Conflict-Handling Styles

Even if you're at the top of your game as a manager, working with groups and teams of people will now and then put you in the middle of disagreements, sometimes even destructive conflict. How can you deal with it?

There are five conflict-handling styles, or techniques, a manager can use for handling disagreements with individuals, as follows.[76]

Avoiding—"Maybe the Problem Will Go Away"

Avoiding involves ignoring or suppressing a conflict. Avoidance is appropriate for trivial issues, when emotions are high and a cooling-off period is needed, or when the cost of confrontation outweighs the benefits of resolving the conflict. It is not appropriate for difficult or worsening problems.

The benefit of this approach is that it buys time in unfolding or ambiguous situations. The weakness is that it provides only a temporary fix and sidesteps the underlying problem.

Accommodating—"Let's Do It Your Way"

An accommodating manager is also known as a "smoothing" or "obliging" manager. *Accommodating* is allowing the desires of the other party to prevail. As one writer describes it, "An obliging [accommodating] person neglects his or her own concern to satisfy the concern of the other party."[77] Accommodating may be an appropriate conflict-handling strategy when it's possible to eventually get something in return or when the issue isn't important to you. It's not appropriate for complex or worsening problems.

The advantage of accommodating is that it encourages cooperation. The weakness is that once again it's only a temporary fix that fails to confront the underlying problem.

Forcing—"You Have to Do It My Way"

Also known as "dominating," *forcing* is simply ordering an outcome, when a manager relies on his or her formal authority and power to resolve a conflict. Forcing is appropriate when an unpopular solution must be implemented and when it's not important that others be committed to your viewpoint.

The advantage of forcing is speed: It can get results quickly. The disadvantage is that in the end it doesn't resolve personal conflict—if anything, it aggravates it by breeding hurt feelings and resentment.

Compromising—"Let's Split the Difference"

In *compromising,* both parties give up something in order to gain something. Compromise is appropriate when both sides have opposite goals or possess equal power. But compromise isn't workable when it is used so often that it doesn't achieve results—for example, continual failure to meet production deadlines.

The benefit of compromise is that it is a democratic process that seems to have no losers. However, since so many people approach compromise situations with a win-lose attitude, they may be disappointed and feel cheated.

Collaborating—"Let's Cooperate to Reach a Win-Win Solution That Benefits Both of Us"

Collaborating strives to devise solutions that benefit both parties. Collaboration is appropriate for complex issues plagued by misunderstanding. It is inappropriate for resolving conflicts rooted in opposing value systems.

The strength of collaborating is its longer-lasting impact because it deals with the underlying problem, not just its symptoms. Its weakness is that it's very time-consuming. Nevertheless, collaboration is usually the best approach for dealing with groups and teams of people.

Your Call

Which style are you most likely to use, based on your experience?

How to Stimulate Constructive Conflict

Top employee. Companies frequently stimulate constructive competition among employees to produce better performance. Top salespeople, for instance, may be rewarded with a trip to a Mexican resort. Do you think you would do well in a company that makes you compete with others to produce higher results?

As a manager you are being paid not just to manage conflict but even to create some, where it's constructive and appropriate, in order to stimulate performance. Constructive conflict, if carefully monitored, can be very productive under a number of circumstances: when your work group seems afflicted with inertia and apathy, resulting in low performance; when there's a lack of new ideas and resistance to change; when there seem to be a lot of yes-men and yes-women (expressing groupthink) in the work unit; when there's high employee turnover; or when managers seem unduly concerned with peace, cooperation, compromise, consensus, and their own popularity rather than in achieving work objectives.

The following four devices are used to stimulate constructive conflict:

1. Spur Competition among Employees Competition is, of course, a form of conflict, but competition is often healthy in spurring people to produce higher results. Thus, a company will often put its salespeople in competition with one another by offering bonuses and awards for achievement—a trip to a Mexican resort, say, for the top performer of the year.

2. Change the Organization's Culture & Procedures Competition may also be established by making deliberate and highly publicized moves to change the corporate culture—by announcing to employees that the organization is now going to be more innovative and reward original thinking and unorthodox ideas. Procedures, such as paperwork sign-off processes, can also be revamped. Results can be reinforced in visible ways through announcements of bonuses, raises, and promotions.

3. Bring in Outsiders for New Perspectives   Without "new blood," organizations can become inbred and resistant to change. This is why managers often bring in outsiders—people from a different unit of the organization, new hires from competing companies, or consultants. With their different backgrounds, attitudes, or management styles, these outsiders can bring a new perspective and can shake things up.

4. Use Programmed Conflict: Devil's Advocacy & the Dialectic Method
Programmed conflict **is designed to elicit different opinions without inciting people's personal feelings.**[78]

Sometimes decision-making groups become so bogged down in details and procedures that nothing of substance gets done. The idea here is to get people, through role playing, to defend or criticize ideas based on relevant facts rather than on personal feelings and preferences.

The method for getting people to engage in this debate of ideas is to do disciplined role playing, for which two proven methods are available: *devil's advocacy* and the *dialectic method.*

These two methods work as follows:

- **Devil's advocacy—role-playing criticism to test whether a proposal is workable.** *Devil's advocacy* **is the process of assigning someone to play the role of critic** to voice possible objections to a proposal and thereby generate critical thinking and reality testing.[79]

  Periodically role-playing devil's advocate has a beneficial side effect in that it is good training for developing analytical and communicative skills. However, it's a good idea to rotate the job so no one person develops a negative reputation.

- **The dialectic method—role-playing two sides of a proposal to test whether it is workable.** Requiring a bit more skill training than devil's advocacy does, the *dialectic method* **is the process of having two people or groups play opposing roles in a debate in order to better understand a proposal.** After the structured debate, managers are better able to make a decision.[80]

Whatever kind of organization you work for, you'll always benefit from knowing how to manage conflict.   ●

Example

Use of the Dialectic Method: How Anheuser-Busch Debates Important Moves

When the corporate policy committee of Anheuser-Busch is considering a major move—such as whether to make a big capital expenditure or get into or out of a business—it sometimes assigns two, even three, groups of people to make the case for each side of the question. Each team is knowledgeable about the subject, and each has the same information. Sometimes an opponent is asked to play proponent—and vice versa.

The exercise may produce a final decision that represents a synthesis of the opposing views. "We end up with decisions and alternatives we hadn't thought of," says Pat Stokes, who heads the company's beer empire. "You become a lot more anticipatory, better able to see what might happen, because you have thought through the process."[81]

YOUR CALL

What kind of specific business move can you think of in which it would be helpful to apply the dialectic method?

adjourning 414
cohesiveness 419
conflict 423
constructive conflict 423
continuous improvement teams 411
cross-functional team 411
devil's advocacy 429
dialectic method 429
division of labor 416

formal group 409
forming 413
group 409
group cohesiveness 414
groupthink 420
informal group 409
maintenance role 418
negative conflict 423
norming 414
norms 418

performing 414
personality conflict 425
programmed conflict 429
roles 417
self-managed teams 412
social loafing 417
storming 413
task role 417
team 409

Summary

 13.1 Groups versus Teams
Groups and teams are different—a group is typically management-directed, a team self-directed. A group is defined as two or more freely interacting individuals who share collective norms, share collective goals, and have a common identity. A team is defined as a small group of people with complementary skills who are committed to a common purpose, performance goals, and approach for which they hold themselves mutually accountable.

Groups may be either formal, established to do something productive for the organization and headed by a leader, or informal, formed by people seeking friendship with no officially appointed leader.

Teams are of various types, but one of the most important is the work team, which engages in collective work requiring coordinated effort. Work teams may be of four types, identified according to their basic purpose: advice, production, project, and action. A project team may also be a cross-functional team, staffed with specialists pursuing a common objective.

Two types of teams worth knowing about are continuous improvement teams, consisting of small groups of volunteers or workers and supervisors who meet intermittently to discuss workplace and quality-related problems, and self-managed

teams, defined as groups of workers given administrative oversight for their task domains.

 13.2 Stages of Group & Team Development
A group may evolve into a team through five stages. (1) Forming is the process of getting oriented and getting acquainted. (2) Storming is characterized by the emergence of individual personalities and roles and conflicts within the group. (3) In norming, conflicts are resolved, close relationships develop, and unity and harmony emerge. (4) In performing, members concentrate on solving problems and completing the assigned task. (5) In adjourning, members prepare for disbandment.

 13.3 Building Effective Teams
There are seven considerations managers must take into account in building a group into an effective team. (1) They must establish measurable goals and have feedback about members' performance. (2) They must motivate members by making them mutually accountable to one another. (3) They must consider what size is optimal. Teams with nine or fewer members have better interaction and morale, yet they also have fewer resources, are possibly less innovative, and may have work unevenly distributed among members. Teams of 10–16 members

have more resources and can take advantage of division of labor, yet they may be characterized by less interaction, lower morale, and social loafing. (4) They must consider the role each team member must play. A role is defined as the socially determined expectation of how an individual should behave in a specific position. Two types of team roles are task and maintenance. A task role consists of behavior that concentrates on getting the team's tasks done. A maintenance role consists of behavior that fosters constructive relationships among team members. (5) They must consider team norms, the general guidelines or rules of behavior that most group or team members follow. Norms tend to be enforced by group or team members for four reasons: to help the group survive, to clarify role expectations, to help individuals avoid embarrassing situations, and to emphasize the group's important values and identity. (6) They must consider the team's cohesiveness, the tendency of a group or team to stick together. (7) They must be aware of groupthink, a cohesive group's blind unwillingness to consider alternatives. Symptoms of groupthink are feelings of invulnerability, certainty of the rightness of their actions, and stereotyped views of the opposition; rationalization and self-censorship; and illusion of unanimity, peer pressure, and the appearance of self-appointed protectors against adverse information.

The results of groupthink can be reduction in alternative ideas and limiting of other information. Two ways to prevent groupthink are to allow criticism and to allow other perspectives.

13.4 Managing Conflict
Conflict is a process in which one party perceives that its interests are being opposed or negatively affected by another party. Conflict can be negative. However, constructive, or functional, conflict benefits the main purposes of the organization and serves its interests. Too little conflict can lead to indolence; too much conflict can lead to warfare.

Three types of conflict are clashes between personalities, intergroup conflict, and cross-cultural conflict.

Four devices for stimulating constructive conflict are (1) spurring competition among employees, (2) changing the organization's culture and procedures, (3) bringing in outsiders for new perspectives, and (4) using programmed conflict to elicit different opinions without inciting people's personal feelings. Two methods used in programmed conflict are (1) devil's advocacy, in which someone is assigned to play the role of critic to voice possible objections to a proposal, and (2) the dialectic method, in which two people or groups play opposing roles in a debate in order to better understand a proposal.

Management in Action

Teams Are the Foundation of Financial Growth for ICU Medical Inc.

American corporations love teamwork. But few companies are as smitten as ICU Medical Inc.

At the San Clemente, California, maker of medical devices, any worker can form a team to tackle any project. Team members set meetings, assign tasks, and create deadlines themselves. Chief Executive George Lopez says he's never vetoed a team decision, even when he disagreed with it. These teams have altered production

processes and set up a 401(k) plan, among other changes. . . .

Most big companies assign teams for projects. ICU, which has around 1,480 employees, is unusual in that it allows workers to initiate the teams. . . .

Dr. Lopez, an internist, founded ICU in 1984. By the early 1990s, the company had about $10 million in annual revenue and was preparing for a public offering. Demand for the company's Clave product, used in connecting a patient's IV systems, was skyrocketing; Dr. Lopez needed to figure out how to ramp up production.

ICU had fewer than 100 employees but was expanding rapidly. Handling the booming growth and demand "was an overwhelming task for one entrepreneur CEO," says Dr. Lopez, 59 years old. He was still making most decisions himself, often sleeping at the office.

Then, he had an epiphany watching his son play hockey. The opposing team had a star, but his son's team ganged up on him and won. "The team was better than one player," says Dr. Lopez. He decided to delegate power by letting employees form teams, hoping it would help him spread out the decision-making and encourage input from people closest to the problems.

Some executives hated the idea; his chief financial officer quit. Putting the new system in place, Dr. Lopez told employees to form teams to come up with ways to boost production. It didn't work. With no leaders, and no rules, "nothing was getting done, except people were spending a lot of time talking," he says.

After about a year and a half, he decided teams should elect leaders, which brought a vast improvement. In 1995 he hired Jim Reitz, now the human-resources director, who helped him create a structure with a minimum of bureaucracy. They developed core values—"take risks"—and so-called rules of engagement—"challenge the issue, not the person." At the same time, ICU started paying teams rewards based on a percentage of the cumulative salaries of their members.

It worked. Employees embraced teams. Today 12 to 15 teams finish projects each quarter, often meeting once a week or so. The typical team has five to seven members, and the company allots $75,000 quarterly to reward those that succeed.

Teams have propelled changes over the objections of top executives. Dr. Lopez, worried about the cost, didn't want to institute a 401(k) plan, but acquiesced after a team recommended one. He now concedes the plan has helped in retaining employees.

Dr. Lopez can veto team decisions but says he hasn't yet. For teams to work, employees need to feel they have authority, he says. A veto would "really have to be worth it," Dr. Lopez says. The team would have to be putting the company "on a pathway to destruction."

So far, that hasn't happened. ICU's revenue grew 28% last year [2006] to $201.6 million, though the company projects that revenue will decline this year. Its stock has climbed more than sixfold in the past decade. . . .

At ICU, team members don't get a break from their regular jobs. Serving on teams is technically voluntary but some employees with special expertise are "requested" to join. "It's above and beyond your job," says business-applications manager Colleen Wilder, who has served on many teams in the 10 years at ICU. "You still have to get your job done."

The rewards can create tension. Ms. Wilder once balked at sharing a reward with co-workers she thought had joined a team solely for the money. She proposed dividing the money based on what tasks team members performed. "I said, 'You did nothing, and I propose you get nothing,'" she says. The team agreed.

The payment system has been changed to peg the size of the reward to the importance of the project. "People started thinking, 'We created a whole new product for the company and these guys painted the lunch room, and they're getting the same amount of money that we are?'" Mr. Reitz says. He encourages employees to question whether teams really met their goals, or whether a project is significant enough to merit high reward levels.

Over the years, ICU has instituted more rules to help teams function smoothly. A group of employees created a 25-page handbook that concretely spells out team operations—for instance, listing eight items for "What should we do at the first meeting?"—and addresses frequently asked questions. Teams must post notes of each meeting to the company intranet, where any employee can offer feedback. . . .

For Discussion

1. What type of team is being used at ICU? Explain.

2. To what extent are the teams self-managing?

3. Which of the seven techniques for building effective teams have been instituted at ICU Medical? Provide supporting evidence.

4. Rewards have created tensions at ICU Medical. What is your evaluation of how the company has handled the rewarding of teams and team members?

5. Which of the five conflict handling styles were used to resolve conflict about team rewards?

Source: Excerpted from Erin White, "How a Company Made Everyone a Team Player," *The Wall Street Journal,* August 13, 2007. Copyright © 2007 by Dow Jones & Company, Inc. Reproduced with permission of Dow Jones & Company, Inc. via Copyright Clearance Center.

What Is Your Conflict-Management Style?

Objectives
1. To assess your conflict-management style.
2. To gain insight on how you manage conflict.

Introduction
Have you ever had a professor whose viewpoints were in conflict with your own? Have you worked in a group with someone who seems to disagree just to cause conflict? How did you react in that situation? In this chapter, you learned that there are five different ways of handling conflict: (1) *avoiding*—this approach is seen in people who wish to suppress conflict or back down from it altogether; (2) *accommodating*—this approach is seen in people who place the other party's interests above their own; (3) *forcing*—this approach is seen when people rely on their authority to solve conflict; (4) *compromising*—this approach is seen in people who are willing to give up something in order to reach a solution; and (5) *collaborating*—this approach is seen in people who desire a win-win situation, striving to address concerns and desires of all the parties involved in the conflict. The purpose of this exercise is to determine your conflict handling style.

Instructions
Read each of the statements below and use the following scale to indicate how often you rely on each tactic.

1 = very rarely
2 = rarely
3 = sometimes
4 = fairly often
5 = very often

1. I work to come out victorious no matter what.	1 2 3 4 5	
2. I try to put the needs of others above my own.	1 2 3 4 5	
3. I look for a mutually satisfactory solution.	1 2 3 4 5	
4. I try to get involved in conflicts.	1 2 3 4 5	
5. I strive to investigate and understand the issues involved in the conflict.	1 2 3 4 5	
6. I never back away from a good argument.	1 2 3 4 5	
7. I strive to foster harmony.	1 2 3 4 5	
8. I negotiate to get a portion of what I propose.	1 2 3 4 5	
9. I avoid open discussion of controversial subjects.	1 2 3 4 5	
10. When I am trying to resolve disagreements, I openly share information.	1 2 3 4 5	
11. I would rather win than compromise.	1 2 3 4 5	
12. I work through conflict by accepting suggestions of others.	1 2 3 4 5	
13. I look for a middle ground to resolve disagreements.	1 2 3 4 5	
14. I keep my true opinions to myself to avoid hard feelings.	1 2 3 4 5	

15.	I encourage the open sharing of concerns and issues.	1 2 3 4 5
16.	I am reluctant to admit I am wrong.	1 2 3 4 5
17.	I try to save others from embarrassment in a disagreement.	1 2 3 4 5
18.	I stress the advantages of give and take.	1 2 3 4 5
19.	I give in early on rather than argue about a point.	1 2 3 4 5
20.	I state my position and stress that it is the only correct point of view.	1 2 3 4 5

Scoring & Interpretation

Enter your responses, item by item, in the five categories below. Add your responses to get your total for each of the five conflict handling styles. Your primary conflict-handling style will be the area where you scored the highest. Your backup conflict-handling style will be your second-highest score.

Avoiding		Accommodating		Forcing		Compromising		Collaborating	
Item	Score	Item	Score	Item	Score	Item	Score	Item	Score
4.	____	2.	____	1.	____	3.	____	5.	____
9.	____	7.	____	6.	____	8.	____	10.	____
14.	____	12.	____	11.	____	13.	____	15.	____
19.	____	17.	____	16.	____	18.	____	20.	____
Total = ____		Total = ____		Total = ____		Total = ____		Total = ____	

Questions for Discussion

1. Were you surprised by the results? Why or why not? Explain.

2. Were the scores for your primary and backup conflict-handling styles relatively similar, or was there a large gap? What does this imply? Discuss.

3. Is your conflict-handling style one that can be used in many different conflict scenarios? Explain.

4. What are some skills you can work on to become more effective at handling conflict? Describe and explain.

The survey was developed using conflict-handling styles defined by K. W. Thomas, "Conflict and Conflict Management," in M. Dunnette, ed., *Handbook of Industrial and Organizational Psychology* (Chicago: Rand McNally, 1976), pp. 889–935.

When Employees Smoke Marijuana Socially: A Manager's Quandary

You are a supervisor at a telephone call center and have very positive relationships with members of your work team and your manager. A friend of yours, Christina, is also a supervisor, and her younger brother, Blake, is a member of her work team.

Christina invites you to her birthday party at her home, and you happily agree to attend. During the party, you walk out to the backyard to get some fresh air and notice that Blake and several other employees of your company are smoking marijuana. You have been told on several occasions by members of your own work team that these same individuals have used marijuana at other social events.

Blake and his friends are not part of your work team, and you never noticed any of them being impaired at work.

Solving the Dilemma

As a supervisor, what would you do?

1. Report the drug users and the incident to the company's human resources department.

2. Mind your own business. The employees are not on your team and don't appear to be impaired at work.

3. Talk to your boss and get her opinion about what should be done.

4. Invent other options. Discuss.

chapter 14

Power, Influence, & Leadership
From Becoming a Manager to Becoming a Leader

Major Questions You Should Be Able to Answer

14.1 The Nature of Leadership: Wielding Influence

Major Question: I don't want to be just a manager; I want to be a leader. What's the difference between the two?

14.2 Trait Approaches: Do Leaders Have Distinctive Personality Characteristics?

Major Question: What does it take to be a successful leader?

14.3 Behavioral Approaches: Do Leaders Show Distinctive Patterns of Behavior?

Major Question: Do effective leaders behave in similar ways?

14.4 Contingency Approaches: Does Leadership Vary with the Situation?

Major Question: How might effective leadership vary according to the situation at hand?

14.5 The Full-Range Model: Uses of Transactional & Transformational Leadership

Major Question: What does it take to truly inspire people to perform beyond their normal levels?

14.6 Four Additional Perspectives

Major Question: If there are many ways to be a leader, which one would describe me best?

Advancing Your Career: Staying Ahead in the Workplace of Tomorrow

Someday maybe you can afford to have a *personal career coach*—the kind long used by sports and entertainment figures and now adopted in the upper ranks of business. These individuals "combine executive coaching and career consulting with marketing and negotiations," says one account. "They plot career strategy, help build networks of business contacts, . . . and shape their clients' images."[1]

One such career coach is Richard L. Knowdell, president of Career Research and Testing in San Jose, California. He offers the following strategies for staying ahead in the workplace of tomorrow.[2]

- **Take charge of your career, and avoid misconceptions:** Because you, not others, are in charge of your career, and it's an ongoing process, you should develop a career plan and base your choices on that plan. When considering a new job or industry, find out how that world *really* works, not what it's reputed to be. When considering a company you might want to work for, find out its corporate "style" or culture by talking to its employees.

- **Develop new capacities:** "Being good at several things will be more advantageous in the long run than being excellent at one narrow specialty," says Knowdell. "A complex world will not only demand *specialized knowledge* but also *general and flexible skills*."

- **Anticipate and adapt to, even embrace, changes:** Learn to analyze, anticipate, and adapt to new circumstances in the world and in your own life. For instance, as technology changes the rules, *embrace* the new rules.

- **Keep learning:** "You can take a one- or two-day course in a new subject," says Knowdell, "just to get an idea of whether you want to use those specific skills and to see if you would be good at it. Then, if there is a match, you could seek out an extended course."

- **Develop your people and communications skills:** No matter how much communication technology takes over the workplace, there will always be a strong need for effectiveness in interpersonal relationships. In particular, learn to listen well.

For Discussion Which of these five rules do you think is most important—and why?

---

forecast | **What's Ahead in This Chapter**

Are there differences between managers and leaders? This chapter considers this question. We discuss the sources of a leader's power and how leaders use persuasion to influence people. We then consider the following approaches to leadership: trait, behavioral, contingency, full-range, and four additional perspectives.

major question? I don't want to be just a manager; I want to be a leader. What's the difference between the two?

THE BIG PICTURE

Being a manager and being a leader are not the same. A leader is able to influence employees to voluntarily pursue the organization's goals. Leadership is needed for organizational change. We describe five sources of power leaders may draw on. Leaders use the power of persuasion or influence to get others to follow them. Five approaches to leadership are described in the next five sections.

Leadership. What is it? Is it a skill anyone can develop?

Leadership is the ability to influence employees to voluntarily pursue organizational goals.[3] In an effective organization, leadership is present at all levels, say Tom Peters and Nancy Austin in *A Passion for Excellence,* and it represents the sum of many things. Leadership, they say, "means vision, cheerleading, enthusiasm, love, trust, verve, passion, obsession, consistency, the use of symbols, paying attention as illustrated by the content of one's calendar, out-and-out drama (and the management thereof), creating heroes at all levels, coaching, effectively wandering around, and numerous other things."[4]

Managers & Leaders: Not Always the Same

You see the words *manager* and *leader* used interchangeably all the time. However, as one leadership expert has said, "leaders manage and managers lead, but the two activities are not synonymous."[5]

Retired Harvard Business School professor **John Kotter** suggests that one is not better than the other, that in fact they are complementary systems of action. The difference is that . . .

- *Management* is about coping with *complexity,*
- *Leadership* is about coping with *change.*[6]

Let's consider these differences.

Being a Manager: Coping with Complexity Management is necessary because complex organizations, especially the large ones that so much dominate the economic landscape, tend to become chaotic unless there is good management. (We got a good description of a manager's busy day in Chapter 1, as analyzed by Henry Mintzberg.)

According to Kotter, companies manage complexity in three ways:

- **Determining what needs to be done—planning and budgeting.** Companies manage complexity first by *planning and budgeting*—setting targets or goals for the future, establishing steps for achieving them, and allocating resources to accomplish them.

- **Creating arrangements of people to accomplish an agenda—organizing and staffing.** Management achieves its plan by *organizing and staffing,* Kotter says—creating the organizational structure and hiring qualified individuals to fill the necessary jobs, then devising systems of implementation.

- **Ensuring people do their jobs—controlling and problem solving.** Management ensures the plan is accomplished by *controlling and problem solving,* says Kotter. That is, managers monitor results versus the plan in some detail by means of reports, meetings, and other tools. They then plan and organize to solve problems as they arise.

Being a Leader: Coping with Change   As the business world has become more competitive and volatile, doing things the same way as last year (or doing it 5% better) is no longer a formula for success. More changes are required for survival—hence the need for leadership.

Leadership copes with change in three ways:

- **Determining what needs to be done—setting a direction.** Instead of dealing with complexity through planning and budgeting, leaders strive for constructive change by *setting a direction.* That is, they develop a vision for the future, along with strategies for realizing the changes.

- **Creating arrangements of people to accomplish an agenda—aligning people.** Instead of organizing and staffing, leaders are concerned with *aligning people,* Kotter says. That is, they communicate the new direction to people in the company who can understand the vision and build coalitions that will realize it.

- **Ensuring people do their jobs—motivating and inspiring.** Instead of controlling and problem solving, leaders try to achieve their vision by *motivating and inspiring.* That is, they appeal to "basic but often untapped human needs, values, and emotions," says Kotter, to keep people moving in the right direction, despite obstacles to change.

Do Kotter's ideas describe real leaders in the real business world? Certainly many participants in a seminar convened by *Harvard Business Review* appeared to agree. "The primary task of leadership is to communicate the vision and the values of an organization," Frederick Smith, chairman and CEO of FedEx, told the group. "Second, leaders must win support for the vision and values they articulate. And third, leaders have to reinforce the vision and the values."[7]

Do You Have What It Takes to Be a Leader?   Managers have legitimate power (as we'll describe) that derives from the formal authority of the positions to which they have been appointed. This power allows managers to hire and fire, reward and punish. Managers plan, organize, and control, but they don't necessarily have the characteristics to be leaders.

Whereas management is a process that lots of people are able to learn, leadership is more visionary. As we've said, leaders inspire others, provide emotional support, and try to get employees to rally around a common goal. Leaders also play a role in creating a vision and strategic plan for an organization, which managers are then charged with implementing.

Do you have what it takes to be a leader? To learn more about the skills required and to assess your own leadership ability, try the Self-Assessment at the end of this chapter.

Five Sources of Power

To really understand leadership, we need to understand the concept of power and authority. *Authority* is the right to perform or command; it comes with the job. In contrast, *power* is the extent to which a person is able to influence others so they respond to orders.

Amazing Amazon. Jeffrey Bezos, founder and CEO of online retailer Amazon.com, has done nearly everything Kotter suggests. For instance, Bezos's "culture of divine discontent" permits employees to plunge ahead with new ideas even though they know that most will probably fail.

People who pursue *personalized power*—**power directed at helping oneself**—as a way of enhancing their own selfish ends may give the word *power* a bad name. However, there is another kind of power, *socialized power*—**power directed at helping others.**[8] This is the kind of power you hear in expressions such as "My goal is to have a powerful impact on my community."

Within organizations there are typically five sources of power leaders may draw on: *legitimate, reward, coercive, expert,* and *referent.*

1. Legitimate Power: Influencing Behavior Because of One's Formal Position

Legitimate power, **which all managers have, is power that results from managers' formal positions within the organization.** All managers have legitimate power over their employees, deriving from their position, whether it's a construction supervisor, ad account supervisor, sales manager, or CEO. This power may be exerted both positively or negatively—as praise or as criticism, for example.

2. Reward Power: Influencing Behavior by Promising or Giving Rewards

Reward power, **which all managers have, is power that results from managers' authority to reward their subordinates.** Rewards can range from praise to pay raises, from recognition to promotions.

Example: "Talking to people effectively is all about being encouraging," says Andrea Wong, president and CEO of Lifetime Network and Entertainment Services. She tries to use praise to reward positive behavior. "When I have something bad to say to someone, it's always hard because I'm always thinking of the best way to say it."[9]

3. Coercive Power: Influencing Behavior by Threatening or Giving Punishment

Coercive power, **which all managers have, results from managers' authority to punish their subordinates.** Punishment can range from verbal or written reprimands to demotions to terminations. In some lines of work, fines and suspensions may be used. Coercive power has to be used judiciously, of course, since a manager who is seen as being constantly negative will produce a lot of resentment among employees. But there have been many leaders who have risen to the top of major corporations—such as Disney's Michael Eisner, Miramax's Harvey Weinstein, and Apple's Steve Jobs—who have been abrasive and intimidating.[10]

4. Expert Power: Influencing Behavior Because of One's Expertise

Expert power **is power resulting from one's specialized information or expertise.** Expertise, or special knowledge, can be mundane, such as knowing the work schedules and assignments of the people who report to you. Or it can be sophisticated, such as having computer or medical knowledge. Secretaries may have expert power because, for example, they have been in a job a long time and know all the necessary contacts. CEOs may have expert power because they have strategic knowledge not shared by many others.

5. Referent Power: Influencing Behavior Because of One's Personal Attraction

Referent power **is power deriving from one's personal attraction.** As we will see later in this chapter (under the discussion of transformational leadership), this kind of power characterizes strong, visionary leaders who are able to persuade their followers by dint of their personality, attitudes, or background. Referent power may be associated with managers, but it is more likely to be characteristic of leaders.

Example

Cult Leader: Apple's Steve Jobs, "CEO of the Decade"

In May 2010, a landmark moment occurred when California-based Apple Inc.—maker of Macintosh computers, iPods, iPhones, and iPads—overtook its famous rival Microsoft, whose stock was valued at $219 billion, to become the world's most valuable technology company, valued at $222 billion. This was up from a mere $5 billion in 2000, just before Apple launched its "digital lifestyle" strategy. (The only American company worth more today is Exxon Mobil, worth $278 billion in 2009.)[11]

"This changing of the guard," declared the *New York Times,* "caps one of the most stunning turnarounds in business history for Apple, which had been given up for dead only a decade earlier, and its co-founder and visionary chief executive, Steven P. Jobs."[12]

From Apple to Apple. In 1976, the 21-year-old Jobs, then a computer hobbyist and college dropout, along with his friend Steve Wozniak, 26, developed and marketed one of the first commercially successful personal computers, the Apple II. This was followed in the 1980s by the Macintosh, the first successful PC with a graphical user interface. Then, in 1985, following an internal power struggle, Jobs was fired from the very company he had created.

Jobs went on to found NeXT Computer, which developed a system that was not only technologically advanced, with the ability to send e-mail with embedded graphics and audio, but also featured a magnesium case, representing Jobs's passion for aesthetics and design. Jobs also acquired a computer graphics enterprise, which he renamed Pixar and which later produced the profitable and acclaimed film *Toy Story* in collaboration with Disney.

In 1996, Apple announced it would buy NeXT, which brought Jobs back into the company he had helped to start. At the time, Apple was "90 days away from bankruptcy," he admitted later. A few months later, Apple ousted its

existing chief executive and named Jobs interim CEO. Much of NeXT's technology found its way into Apple products, and the company began branching out beyond computers, making forays into consumer electronics (the iPod), music distribution (iTunes), and smartphones (the iPhone).

Managing "the Biggest Startup on the Planet." In late 2009, Jobs received the rare accolade of being named *Fortune*'s "CEO of the Decade" for 10 years of achievements in the fields of music, movies, and mobile phones, not to mention computing. "Remaking any one business is a career-defining achievement," wrote *Fortune* editor Adam Lashinsky; "four is unheard of."[13]

What is it about his leadership that makes Jobs different? "It's often noted that he's a showman, a born salesman, a magician who creates a famed reality distortion field, a tyrannical perfectionist," says Lashinsky. But he's also all business. "He may not pay attention to customer research, but he works slavishly to make products customers will buy." While lauded as a visionary, he's also grounded in reality, "closely monitoring Apple's various operational and market metrics."

Indeed, he continues to manage Apple the giant as he would a start-up—"the biggest startup on the planet," as he calls it, meeting frequently with teams (there are no "committees") with distinct lines of responsibility, creating an environment where ideas rather than rank dominate. "Jobs is one of the most hardcore, relentless bosses in the universe," says writer Patricia Sellers. "But he sure knows how to inspire. And he knows the key to building a great business and a stellar brand: serving, above all, your ultimate customer."[14]

YOUR CALL

Which of the five sources of leadership power do you think Jobs represents? Do you think you could follow his example?

Leadership & Influence: Using Persuasion to Get Your Way at Work

Steve Harrison, CEO of a career management firm, was escorting Ray, his newly hired chief operating officer, to meet people at a branch office. After greeting the receptionist and starting to lead Ray past her into the interior offices, Harrison felt himself being pulled back. He watched as Ray stuck out his hand, smiled, and said, "Good morning, Melissa, I'm Ray. I'm new here. It's so great to meet you!" He then launched into a dialogue with Melissa, to her obvious delight.

Afterward, Harrison asked Ray, "What was that all about?" "It's called the two-minute schmooze," Ray replied. "Our receptionists meet or talk by phone to more people critical to our company in one day than you or I will ever meet in the course of a year."[15]

Ray would probably be considered a leader because of his ability to *influence* others—to get them to follow his wishes. There are nine tactics for trying to influence others, but some work better than others. In one pair of studies, employees were asked in effect, "How do you get your boss, coworker, or subordinate to do something you want?" The nine answers—ranked from most used to least used tactics—were as follows.[16]

1. *Rational Persuasion* Trying to convince someone by using reason, logic, or facts.
Example: "You know, all the cutting-edge companies use this approach."

2. *Inspirational Appeals* Trying to build enthusiasm or confidence by appealing to others' emotions, ideals, or values.
Example: "If we do this as a goodwill gesture, customers will love us."

3. *Consultation* Getting others to participate in a decision or change.
Example: "Wonder if I could get your thoughts about this matter."

4. *Ingratiating Tactics* Acting humble or friendly or making someone feel good or feel important before making a request.
Example: "I hate to impose on your time, knowing how busy you are, but you're the only one who can help me."

5. *Personal Appeals* Referring to friendship and loyalty when making a request.
Example: "We've known each other a long time, and I'm sure I can count on you."

6. *Exchange Tactics* Reminding someone of past favors or offering to trade favors.
Example: "Since I backed you at last month's meeting, maybe you could help me this time around."

7. *Coalition Tactics* Getting others to support your effort to persuade someone.
Example: "Everyone in the department thinks this is a great idea."

8. *Pressure Tactics* Using demands, threats, or intimidation to gain compliance.
Example: "If this doesn't happen, you'd better think about cleaning out your desk."

9. *Legitimating Tactics* Basing a request on one's authority or right, organizational rules or policies, or express or implied support from superiors.
Example: "This has been green-lighted at the highest levels."

These influence tactics are considered *generic* because they are applied in all directions—up, down, and sideways within the organization. The first five influence tactics are considered "soft" tactics because they are considered friendlier than the last four "hard," or pressure, tactics. As it happens, research shows that of the three possible responses to an influence tactic—enthusiastic commitment, grudging compliance, and outright resistance—commitment is most apt to result when the tactics used are consultation, strong rational persuasion, and inspirational appeals.[17]

Knowing this, do you think you have what it takes to be a leader? To answer this, you need to understand what factors produce people of leadership character. We consider these in the rest of the chapter.

Five Approaches to Leadership

The next five sections describe five principal approaches or perspectives on leadership, which have been refined by research. They are (1) *trait,* (2) *behavioral,* (3) *contingency,* (4) *full-range,* and (5) *four additional. (See Table 14.1.)* ●

table 14.1   FIVE APPROACHES TO LEADERSHIP

1. Trait approaches
- *Kouzes & Posner's five traits*—honest, competent, forward-looking, inspiring, intelligent
- *Gender studies*—motivating others, fostering communication, producing high-quality work, and so on
- *Leadership lessons from the GLOBE project*—visionary and inspirational charismatic leaders who are good team builders are best worldwide

2. Behavioral approaches
- *Michigan model*—two leadership styles: job-centered and employee-centered
- *Ohio State model*—two dimensions: initiating-structure behavior and consideration behavior

3. Contingency approaches
- *Fiedler's contingency model*—task-oriented style and relationship-oriented style—*and three dimensions of control:* leader-member, task structure, position power
- *House's path-goal revised leadership model*—clarifying paths for subordinates' goals, and employee characteristics and environmental factors that affect leadership behaviors
- *Hersey's situational leadership® model*—adjusting leadership style to employee readiness

4. Full-range approach
- *Transactional leadership*—clarify employee roles and tasks, and provide rewards and punishments
- *Transformational leadership*—transform employees to pursue organizational goals over self-interests, using inspirational motivation, idealized influence, individualized consideration, intellectual stimulation

5. Four additional perspectives
- *Leader-member exchange (LMX) model*—leaders have different sorts of relationships with different subordinates
- *Shared leadership*—mutual influence process in which people share responsibility for leading
- *Greenleaf's servant leadership model*—providing service to others, not oneself
- *E-Leadership*—using information technology for one-to-one, one-to-many, and between group and collective interactions

✳ 14.2 TRAIT APPROACHES: DO LEADERS HAVE DISTINCTIVE PERSONALITY CHARACTERISTICS?

major question?

What does it take to be a successful leader?

THE BIG PICTURE

Trait approaches attempt to identify distinctive characteristics that account for the effectiveness of leaders. We describe (1) the trait perspective expressed by Kouzes and Posner, (2) some results of gender studies, and (3) leadership lessons from the GLOBE project.

Consider two high-powered leaders of the late 20th century. Each "personifies the word 'stubborn,'" says a *Fortune* magazine account. Both "are piercingly analytical thinkers who combine hands-on technical smarts with take-no-prisoners business savvy. Both absolutely hate to lose."[18]

Who are they? They are two of the most successful former CEOs in American business—Bill Gates of Microsoft and Andy Grove of Intel. Do they have distinctive personality traits that might teach us something about leadership? Perhaps they do. They would seem to embody the traits of (1) dominance, (2) intelligence, (3) self-confidence, (4) high energy, and (5) task-relevant knowledge.

These are the five traits that researcher **Ralph Stogdill** in 1948 concluded were typical of successful leaders.[19] Stogdill is one of many contributors to *trait approaches to leadership,* **which attempt to identify distinctive characteristics that account for the effectiveness of leaders.**[20]

Is Trait Theory Useful?

Traits play a central role in how we perceive leaders, and they ultimately affect leadership effectiveness. On the basis of past studies, we can suggest a list of positive traits that are important for leaders to have, as shown below.[21] *(See Table 14.2.)* If assuming a leadership role interests you, you might wish to cultivate these traits for your future success, using personality tests to evaluate your strengths and weaknesses in preparing (perhaps with the aid of an executive coach) a personal development plan.[22]

table 14.2

KEY POSITIVE LEADERSHIP TRAITS

General trait	Specific characteristics
Task competence	Intelligence, knowledge, problem-solving skills
Interpersonal competence	Ability to communicate and ability to demonstrate caring and empathy
Intuition	
Traits of character	Conscientiousness, discipline, moral reasoning, integrity, honesty
Biophysical traits	Physical fitness, hardiness, energy level
Personal traits	Self-confidence, sociability, self-monitoring, extraversion, self-regulating, self-efficacy

Source: Adapted from R. Kreitner and A. Kinicki, *Organizational Behavior,* 9th ed. (New York: McGraw-Hill/Irwin, 2010), p. 474. These traits were identified in B. M. Bass and R. Bass, *The Bass Handbook of Leadership* (New York: The Free Press, 2008), p. 135.

Two ways in which organizations may apply trait theory are as follows:

Use Personality & Trait Assessments   Organizations may incorporate personality and trait assessments into their selection and promotion processes (being careful to use valid measures of leadership traits).

Use Management Development Programs   To enhance employee leadership traits, organizations may send targeted employees to management development programs that include management classes, coaching sessions, trait assessments, and the like.[23]

Kouzes & Posner's Research: Is Honesty the Top Leadership Trait?

During the 1980s, **James Kouzes** and **Barry Posner** surveyed more than 7,500 managers throughout the United States as to what personal traits they looked for and admired in their superiors.[24] The respondents suggested that a credible leader should have five traits. He or she should be (1) honest, (2) competent, (3) forward-looking, (4) inspiring, and (5) intelligent. The first trait, honesty, was considered particularly important, being selected by 87% of the respondents, suggesting that people want their leaders to be ethical. (We discuss ethical leadership in Section 14.5.)

Although this research does reveal the traits preferred by employees, it has not, however, been able to predict which people might be successful leaders.

Gender Studies: Do Women Have Traits That Make Them Better Leaders?

"Women Aspire to Be Chief As Much As Men Do," declared the headline in *The Wall Street Journal.* A study by a New York research firm found that 55% of women and 57% of men aspire to be CEO, challenging the notion that more women aren't at the top because they don't want to be there.[25] Indeed, women have been found to be as equally assertive as men.[26] In fact, it's possible that women may have traits that make them better managers—indeed, better leaders—than men.

The Evidence on Women Executives   A number of management studies conducted in the United States for companies ranging from high-tech to manufacturing to consumer services were reviewed by *BusinessWeek.*[27] By and large, the magazine reports, the studies showed that "women executives, when rated by their peers, underlings, and bosses, score higher than their male counterparts on a wide variety of measures—from producing high-quality work to goal-setting to mentoring employees." Researchers accidentally stumbled on these findings about gender differences while compiling hundreds of routine performance evaluations and analyzing the results. In one study of 425 high-level executives, women won higher ratings on 42 of the 52 skills measured.[28] In addition, women executives, when rated by their peers, managers, and direct reports, scored higher than their male counterparts on a variety of effectiveness criteria.[29]

What are the desirable traits in which women excel? Among those traits mentioned are teamwork and partnering, being more collaborative, seeking less personal glory, being motivated less by self-interest than in what they can do for the company, being more stable, and being less turf-conscious. Women were also found to be better at producing quality work, recognizing trends, and generating new ideas and acting on them. Women used a more democratic or participative style than men, who were apt to use a more autocratic and directive style than women.[30] Finally, women were seen as displaying more social leadership, whereas men were seen as displaying more task leadership.[31]

A gender comparison of skills is summarized on the next page. *(See Table 14.3.)*

table 14.3

This table summarizes the results of five different management studies. The check mark denotes which group scored higher on each of the respective studies. The asterisk indicates that in one study women's and men's scores in these categories were statistically even.

Skill	Men	Women
Motivating others		✓✓✓✓✓
Fostering communication		✓✓✓✓*
Producing high-quality work		✓✓✓✓✓
Strategic planning	✓✓	✓✓*
Listening to others		✓✓✓✓
Analyzing issues	✓✓	✓✓*

Source: Data from Hagberg Consulting Group, Management Research Group, Lawrence A. Pfaff, Personnel Decisions International Inc., and Advanced Teamware Inc., in table in R. Sharpe, "As Leaders, Women Rule," *BusinessWeek*, November 20, 2000, p. 75.

The Lack of Women at the Top   Why, then, aren't more women in positions of leadership? Males and females disagree about this issue. A team of researchers asked this question of 461 executive women holding titles of vice president or higher in Fortune 100 companies and all the male Fortune 100 CEOs. Men believed that women are not in senior leadership positions because (1) they lack significant general management experience and (2) women have not been in the executive talent pool long enough to get selected. Women, by contrast, believed that (1) male stereotyping and (2) exclusion from important informal networks are the biggest barriers to promotability.[32]

There are additional possible explanations. First, as suggested earlier in the book, many women, though hardworking, simply aren't willing to compete as hard as most men are or are not willing to make the required personal sacrifices.[33] (As Jamie Gorelick, former vice chair of Fannie Mae but also mother of two children ages 10 and 15, said when declining to be considered for CEO: "I just don't want that pace in my life.")[34] Second, women have a tendency to be overly modest and to give credit to others rather than taking it for themselves, which can undermine opportunities for promotions and raises.[35] Third, women are less likely than their male counterparts to have access to a supportive mentor.[36] Fourth—and perhaps most important—early-career success is pivotal; women MBAs start out at lower levels than men do in their first jobs, putting them at a disadvantage that is hard to overcome.[37]

Things may be gradually changing, though not as fast as they should. In 2010, it was reported that 16 female CEOs heading companies in the Standard & Poor's 500 index averaged earnings of $14.2 million in their latest fiscal years, 43% more than the male average. The women who were also CEOs in 2008 got a 19% raise in 2009—compared with a 5% cut for their male counterparts.[38] Moreover, with more than half of college students being women and with women making up half the workforce, it's possible that the new group rising through middle management could well lead to more than 100 Fortune 500 CEOs in the next 10 years, some believe, up from 38 today.[39]

Leadership Lessons from the GLOBE Project

Project GLOBE (Global Leadership and Organizational Behavior Effectiveness), you'll recall from Chapter 4, is a massive and ongoing attempt to develop an empirically based theory to "describe, understand, and predict the impact of specific cultural variables on leadership and organizational processes and the effectiveness of these processes."[40] Surveying 17,000 middle managers working for 951 organizations across 62 countries, the researchers determined that certain attributes of leadership were universally liked or disliked. *(See Table 14.4.)* Visionary and inspirational *charismatic leaders* who are good team builders generally do the best. *Self-centered leaders* seen as loners or face-savers generally receive a poor reception worldwide. ●

table 14.4

LESSONS FROM GLOBE: LEADERSHIP ATTRIBUTES UNIVERSALLY LIKED AND DISLIKED ACROSS 62 NATIONS

Universally positive leader attributes	Universally negative leader attributes
Trustworthy	Loner
Just	Asocial
Honest	Noncooperative
Foresight	Irritable
Plans ahead	Nonexplicit
Encouraging	Egocentric
Positive	Ruthless
Dynamic	Dictatorial
Motive arouser	
Confidence builder	
Motivational	
Dependable	
Intelligent	
Decisive	
Effective bargainer	
Win-win problem solver	
Administrative skilled	
Communicative	
Informed	
Coordinator	
Team builder	
Excellence oriented	

Source: Excerpted and adapted from P. W. Dorfman, P. J. Hanges, and F. C. Brodbeck, "Leadership and Cultural Variation: The Identification of Culturally Endorsed Leadership Profiles," in R. J. House, P. J. Hanges, M. Javidan, P. W. Dorfman, and V. Gupta eds., *Culture, Leadership and Organizations: The GLOBE Study of 62 Societies* (Thousand Oaks, CA: Sage, 2004), Tables 21.2 and 21.3 , pp. 677–678.

✖ 14.3 BEHAVIORAL APPROACHES: DO LEADERS SHOW DISTINCTIVE PATTERNS OF BEHAVIOR?

major question?

Do effective leaders behave in similar ways?

THE BIG PICTURE
Behavioral leadership approaches try to determine the distinctive styles used by effective leaders. Two models we describe are the University of Michigan model and the Ohio State model.

Working on the railroad. What kind of leadership behavior is appropriate for directing these kinds of workers?

Maybe what's important to know about leaders is not their *personality traits* but rather their *patterns of behavior* or *leadership styles.* This is the line of thought pursued by those interested in **behavioral leadership approaches, which attempt to determine the distinctive styles used by effective leaders.** By *leadership styles,* we mean the combination of traits, skills, and behaviors that leaders use when interacting with others.

What all models of leadership behavior have in common is the consideration of *task orientation versus people orientation.* Two classic studies came out of the universities of Michigan and Ohio State.

The University of Michigan Leadership Model

In the late 1940s, researchers at the University of Michigan came up with what came to be known as the **University of Michigan Leadership Model.** A team led by **Rensis Likert** began studying the effects of leader behavior on job performance, interviewing numerous managers and subordinates.[41] The investigators identified two forms of leadership styles: *job-centered* and *employee-centered.*

Job-Centered Behavior—"I'm Concerned More with the Needs of the Job" In *job-centered behavior,* managers paid more attention to the job and work procedures. Thus, their principal concerns were with achieving production efficiency, keeping costs down, and meeting schedules.

Employee-Centered Behavior—"I'm Concerned More with the Needs of Employees" In *employee-centered behavior,* managers paid more attention to employee satisfaction and making work groups cohesive. By concentrating on subordinates' needs they hoped to build effective work groups with high-performance goals.

The Ohio State Leadership Model

A second approach to leadership research was begun in 1945 at Ohio State University under **Ralph Stogdill** (mentioned in the last section). Hundreds of dimensions of leadership behavior were studied, resulting in what came to be known as the **Ohio State Leadership Model.**[42] From surveys of leadership behavior, two major dimensions of leader behavior were identified, as follows.

Initiating Structure—"What Do I Do to Get the Job Done?" *Initiating structure* is leadership behavior that organizes and defines what group members should be doing. It consists of the efforts the leader makes to get things organized and get the job done. This is much the same as Likert's "job-centered behavior."

Consideration—"What Do I Do to Show Consideration for My Employees?"
Consideration is leadership behavior that expresses concern for employees by establishing a warm, friendly, supportive climate. This behavior, which resembles Likert's "employee-centered behavior," is sensitive to subordinates' ideas and feelings and establishes mutual trust.

All in all, one management expert concluded from the Michigan and Ohio studies that effective leaders (1) tend to have supportive or employee-centered relationships with employees, (2) use group rather than individual methods of supervision, and (3) set high-performance goals.[43]

The late Peter Drucker, the famed management expert, recommended a set of nine behaviors that managers can focus on to improve their leadership behaviors. These are shown below. *(See Table 14.5.)* ●

table 14.5 PETER DRUCKER'S TIPS FOR IMPROVING LEADERSHIP EFFECTIVENESS

Drucker believed practices 1 and 2 provide the knowledge leaders need, 3–6 help leaders convert knowledge into effective action, 7–8 ensure that the whole organization feels responsible and accountable, and 9 should be a managerial rule.

1.	Determine what needs to be done.
2.	Determine the right thing to do for the welfare of the entire enterprise or organization.
3.	Develop action plans that specify desired results, probable restraints, future revisions, check-in points, and implications for how one should spend his or her time.
4.	Take responsibility for decisions.
5.	Take responsibility for communication action plans and give people the information they need to get the job done.
6.	Focus on opportunities rather than problems. Do not sweep problems under the rug, and treat change as an opportunity rather than a threat.
7.	Run productive meetings. Different types of meetings require different forms of preparation and different results. Prepare accordingly.
8.	Think and say "we" rather than "I." Consider the needs and opportunities of the organization before thinking of your own opportunities and needs.
9.	Listen first, speak last.

Source: Reprinted by permission of *Harvard Business Review*. Recommendations were derived from "What Makes an Effective Executive," by P. F. Drucker, June 2004. Copyright 2004 by the Harvard Business School Publishing Corporation; all rights reserved.

How might effective leadership vary according to the situation at hand?

THE BIG PICTURE
Effective leadership behavior depends on the situation at hand, say believers in the three contingency approaches: Fiedler's contingency leadership model, House's path–goal leadership model, and Hersey's situational leadership® model.

Perhaps leadership is not characterized by universally important traits or behaviors. Perhaps there is no one best style that will work in all situations. This is the point of view of proponents of the ***contingency approach* to leadership, who believe that effective leadership behavior depends on the situation at hand.** That is, as situations change, different styles become appropriate.

Let's consider three contingency approaches: (1) the *contingency leadership model* by Fiedler, (2) the *path–goal leadership model* by House, and (3) the *situational leadership® model* by Hersey.

I. The Contingency Leadership Model: Fiedler's Approach

The oldest model of the contingency approach to leadership was developed by **Fred Fiedler** and his associates in 1951.[44] **The *contingency leadership model* determines if a leader's style is (1) task-oriented or (2) relationship-oriented and if that style is effective for the situation at hand.** Fiedler's work was based on 80 studies conducted over 30 years.

Two Leadership Orientations: Tasks versus Relationships Are you task-oriented or relationship-oriented? That is, are you more concerned with task accomplishment or with people?

To find out, you or your employees would fill out a questionnaire (known as the least preferred co-worker, or LPC, scale), in which you think of the co-worker you least enjoyed working with and rate him or her according to an eight-point scale of 16 pairs of opposite characteristics (such as friendly/unfriendly, tense/relaxed, efficient/inefficient). The higher the score, the more the relationship-oriented the respondent; the lower the score, the more task-oriented.

The Three Dimensions of Situational Control Once the leadership orientation is known, then you determine *situational control*—how much control and influence a leader has in the immediate work environment.

There are three dimensions of situational control: *leader-member relations, task structure,* and *position power.*

- **Leader-member relations—"Do my subordinates accept me as a leader?"** This dimension, the most important component of situational control, reflects the extent to which a leader has or doesn't have the support, loyalty, and trust of the work group.
- **Task structure—"Do my subordinates perform unambiguous, easily understood tasks?"** This dimension refers to the extent to which tasks

Cone head. Do successful entrepreneurs or small-business managers need to be task-oriented, relationship-oriented, or both? What style of leadership model would best suit a small ice cream store in which employees work without the owner always being present?

are routine, unambiguous, and easily understood. The more structured the jobs, the more influence a leader has.

- **Position power—"Do I have power to reward and punish?"** This dimension refers to how much power a leader has to make work assignments and reward and punish. More power equals more control and influence.

For each dimension, the amount of control can be *high*—the leader's decisions will produce predictable results because he or she has the ability to influence work outcomes. Or it can be *low*—he or she doesn't have that kind of predictability or influence. By combining the three different dimensions with different high/low ratings, we have eight different leadership situations. These are represented in the diagram below. *(See Figure 14.1.)*

figure 14.1

REPRESENTATION OF FIEDLER'S CONTINGENCY MODEL

Situational Control	High-Control Situations			Moderate-Control Situations				Low-Control Situations
Leader-member relations	Good	Good	Good	Good	Poor	Poor	Poor	Poor
Task structure	High	High	Low	Low	High	High	Low	Low
Position power	Strong	Weak	Strong	Weak	Strong	Weak	Strong	Weak
Situation	I	II	III	IV	V	VI	VII	VIII
Optimal Leadership Style	**Task-Motivated Leadership**			**Relationship-Motivated Leadership**				**Task-Motivated Leadership**

Source: Adapted from F. E. Fiedler, "Situational Control and a Dynamic Theory of Leadership," in *Managerial Control and Organizational Democracy,* ed. B. King, S. Streufert, and F. E. Fiedler (New York: John Wiley & Sons, 1978), p. 114. This figure is reprinted from R. Kreitner and A. Kinicki, *Organizational Behavior,* 9th ed. (New York: McGraw-Hill/Irwin, 2010), p. 478.

Which Style Is Most Effective?   Neither leadership style is effective all the time, Fiedler's research concludes, although each is right in certain situations.

- **When task-oriented style is best.** The task-oriented style works best in either *high-control* or *low-control* situations.

   Example of *high-control* situation (leader decisions produce predictable results because he or she can influence work outcomes): Suppose you were supervising parking-control officers ticketing cars parked illegally in expired meter zones, bus zones, and the like. You have (1) high leader-member relations because your subordinates are highly supportive of you and (2) high task structure because their jobs are clearly defined. (3) You have high position control because you have complete authority to evaluate their performance and dole out punishment and rewards. Thus, a task-oriented style would be best.

   Example of *low-control* situation (leader decisions can't produce predictable results because he or she can't really influence outcomes): Suppose you were a high school principal trying to clean up graffiti on your private-school campus, helped only by students you can find after school. You might have (1) low leader-member relations because many people might not see the need for the goal. (2) The task structure might also be low because people might see many different ways to achieve the goal. And (3) your position power would be low because the committee is voluntary and people are free to leave. In this low-control situation, a task-oriented style would also be best.

- **When relationship-oriented style is best.** The relationship-oriented style works best in situations of *moderate control.*

    Example: Suppose you were working in a government job supervising a group of firefighters fighting wildfires. You might have (1) low leader-member relations if you were promoted over others in the group but (2) high task structure, because the job is fairly well defined. (3) You might have low position power, because the rigidity of the civil-service job prohibits you from doing much in the way of rewarding and punishing. Thus, in this moderate-control situation, relationship-oriented leadership would be most effective.

What do you do if your leadership orientation does not match the situation? Then, says Fiedler, it's better to try to move leaders into suitable situations rather than try to alter their personalities to fit the situations.[45]

2. The Path–Goal Leadership Model: House's Approach

A second contingency approach, advanced by **Robert House** in the 1970s and revised by him in 1996, is the *path–goal leadership model,* **which holds that the effective leader makes available to followers desirable rewards in the workplace and increases their motivation by clarifying the *paths,* or behavior, that will help them achieve those *goals* and providing them with support.** A successful leader thus helps followers by tying meaningful rewards to goal accomplishment, reducing barriers, and providing support, so as to increase "the number and kinds of personal payoffs to subordinates for work-goal attainment."[46]

Numerous studies testing various predictions from House's original path–goal theory provided mixed results.[47] As a consequence, he proposed a new model, a graphical version, shown below. *(See Figure 14.2.)*

figure 14.2

GENERAL REPRESENTATION OF HOUSE'S REVISED PATH–GOAL THEORY

① Leader behaviors are . . .

. . . influenced by the two contingency factors of ② employee characteristics and ③ environmental factors . . .

. . . in determining ④ the most effective leadership.

① **Leader behaviors**
- Path–goal clarifying
- Achievement-oriented
- Work facilitation
- Supportive
- Interaction facilitation
- Group-oriented decision making
- Representation & networking
- Value-based

② **Employee characteristics**
- Locus of control
- Task ability
- Need for achievement
- Experience
- Need for path–goal clarity

③ **Environmental factors**
- Task structure
- Work group dynamics

④ **Leadership effectiveness**
- Employee motivation
- Employee satisfaction
- Employee performance
- Leader acceptance
- Interaction facilitation
- Work-unit performance

What Determines Leadership Effectiveness: Employee Characteristics & Environmental Factors Affect Leader Behavior As the drawing indicates, two contingency factors, or variables—*employee characteristics* and *environmental factors*—cause some *leadership behaviors* to be more effective than others.

- **Employee characteristics.** Five employee characteristics are locus of control (described in Chapter 11), task ability, need for achievement, experience, and need for path–goal clarity.

- **Environmental factors.** Two environmental factors are task structure (independent versus interdependent tasks) and work group dynamics.

- **Leader behaviors.** Originally House proposed that there were four leader behaviors, or leadership styles—*directive* ("Here's what's expected of you and here's how to do it"), *supportive* ("I want things to be pleasant, since everyone's about equal here"), *participative* ("I want your suggestions in order to help me make decisions"), and *achievement-oriented* ("I'm confident you can accomplish the following great things"). The revised theory expands the number of leader behaviors from four to eight. *(See Table 14.6.)*

table 14.6

EIGHT LEADERSHIP STYLES OF THE REVISED PATH–GOAL THEORY

Style of leader behaviors	Description of behavior toward employees
1. Path–goal clarifying ("Here's what's expected of you and here's how to do it.")	Clarify performance goals. Provide guidance on how employees can complete tasks. Clarify performance standards and expectations. Use positive and negative rewards contingent on performance.
2. Achievement-oriented ("I'm confident you can accomplish the following great things.")	Set challenging goals. Emphasize excellence. Demonstrate confidence in employee abilities.
3. Work facilitation ("Here's the goal, and here's what I can do to help you achieve it.")	Plan, schedule, organize, and coordinate work. Provide mentoring, coaching, counseling, and feedback to assist employees in developing their skills. Eliminate roadblocks. Provide resources. Empower employees to take actions and make decisions.
4. Supportive ("I want things to be pleasant, since everyone's about equal here.")	Treat as equals. Show concern for well-being and needs. Be friendly and approachable.
5. Interaction facilitation ("Let's see how we can all work together to accomplish our goals.")	Emphasize collaboration and teamwork. Encourage close employee relationships and sharing of minority opinions. Facilitate communication, resolve disputes.
6. Group-oriented decision making ("I want your suggestions in order to help me make decisions.")	Pose problems rather than solutions to work group. Encourage members to participate in decision making. Provide necessary information to the group for analysis. Involve knowledgeable employees in decision making.
7. Representation & networking ("I've got a great bunch of people working for me whom you'll probably want to meet.")	Present work group in positive light to others. Maintain positive relationships with influential others. Participate in organization-wide social functions and ceremonies. Do unconditional favors for others.
8. Value-based ("We're destined to accomplish great things.")	Establish a vision, display passion for it, and support its accomplishment. Communicate high performance expectations and confidence in others' abilities to meet their goals. Give frequent positive feedback. Demonstrate self-confidence.

Source: Adapted from R. J. House, "Path–Goal Theory of Leadership: Lessons, Legacy, and a Reformulated Theory," *Leadership Quarterly,* Autumn 1996, pp. 323–352.

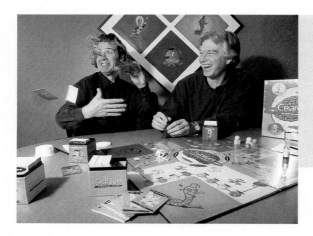

Cranium's grand poo-bah and chief noodler. Richard Tait (left), responsible for business operations and marketing for the 14-person, Seattle-based game company Cranium, takes the unorthodox title of grand poo-bah. Whit Alexander, who focuses on product development, editorial content, and manufacturing, is called chief noodler. In devising the board game Cranium, the two entrepreneurs decided to adopt the acronym CHIFF—for "clever, high quality, innovative, friendly, and fun"—as the criterion by which all decisions would be guided. "Our survival and success will come from optimizing fun, focus, passion, and profits," says Tait. Which one of the eight path–goal leadership styles would you expect to find dominating this organization?

Thus, for example, employees with an internal locus of control are more likely to prefer achievement-oriented leadership or group-oriented decision making (formerly participative) leadership because they believe they have control over the work environment. The same is true for employees with high task ability and experience.

Employees with an external locus of control, however, tend to view the environment as uncontrollable, so they prefer the structure provided by supportive or path–goal clarifying (formerly directive) leadership. The same is probably true of inexperienced employees.

Besides expanding the styles of leader behavior from four to eight, House's revision of his theory also puts more emphasis on the need for leaders to foster intrinsic motivation through empowerment. Finally, his revised theory stresses the concept of shared leadership, the idea that employees do not have to be supervisors or managers to engage in leader behavior but rather may share leadership among all employees of the organization.

Does the Revised Path–Goal Theory Work? There have not been enough direct tests of House's revised path–goal theory using appropriate research methods and statistical procedures to draw overall conclusions. Research on transformational leadership, however, which is discussed in Section 14.5, is supportive of the revised model.[48]

Although further research is needed on the new model, it offers two important implications for managers:

- *Use more than one leadership style.* Effective leaders possess and use more than one style of leadership. Thus, you are encouraged to study the eight styles offered in path–goal theory so that you can try new leader behaviors when a situation calls for them.

- *Modify leadership style to fit employee and task characteristics.* A small set of employee characteristics (ability, experience, and need for independence) and environmental factors (task characteristics of autonomy, variety, and significance) are relevant contingency factors, and managers should modify their leadership style to fit them.[49]

3. The Situational Leadership® Theory Model: Hersey's Approach

A third contingency approach has been proposed by management writers **Paul Hersey** and **Kenneth Blanchard.**[50] **It evolved in 1980 into Hersey's** *situational leadership® theory,* **leadership behavior reflects how leaders should adjust their leadership style according to the readiness of the followers.** The model suggests that managers should be flexible in choosing a leadership behavior style and be sensitive to the readiness level of their employees. *Readiness* **is defined as the extent to which a follower possesses the ability and willingness to complete a task.** Subordinates with high readiness (with high ability, skills, and willingness to work) require a different leadership style than do those with low readiness (low ability, training, and willingness).

The appropriate leadership style is found by cross-referencing follower readiness (low–high) with one of four leaderships styles. *(See Figure 14.3.)*

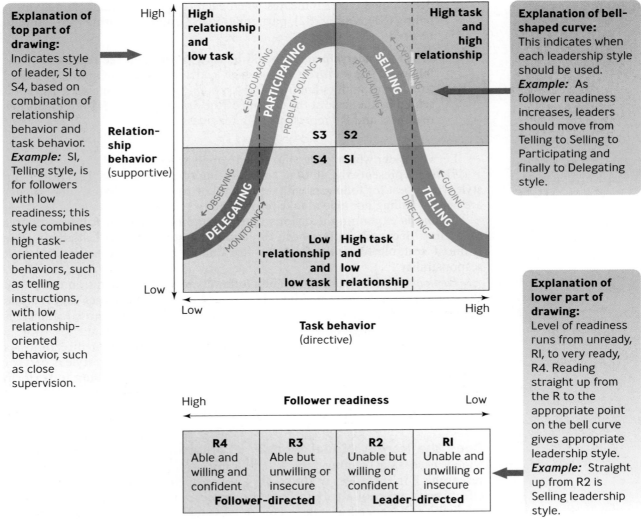

Explanation of top part of drawing: Indicates style of leader, SI to S4, based on combination of relationship behavior and task behavior. *Example:* SI, Telling style, is for followers with low readiness; this style combines high task-oriented leader behaviors, such as telling instructions, with low relationship-oriented behavior, such as close supervision.

Explanation of bell-shaped curve: This indicates when each leadership style should be used. *Example:* As follower readiness increases, leaders should move from Telling to Selling to Participating and finally to Delegating style.

Explanation of lower part of drawing: Level of readiness runs from unready, RI, to very ready, R4. Reading straight up from the R to the appropriate point on the bell curve gives appropriate leadership style. *Example:* Straight up from R2 is Selling leadership style.

R4	R3	R2	RI
Able and willing and confident	Able but unwilling or insecure	Unable but willing or confident	Unable and unwilling or insecure
Follower-directed		**Leader-directed**	

figure I4.3

HERSEY'S SITUATIONAL LEADERSHIP® MODEL

Source: From P. Hersey, K. H. Blanchard, and D. E. Johnson, *Management of Organizational Behavior: Leading Human Resources,* 8e. Copyright © 2006 Reprinted with permission of the Center for Leadership Studies, Inc. Escondido, CA 92025. All rights reserved. Situational Leadership® is a registered trademark of Leadership Studies, Inc. Used herein with permission.

How the Situational Leadership® Model Works   Let's see what the illustration means. (Refer back to the figure on the previous page as you read this.)

- **Leadership styles—relationship behavior plus task behavior.** The upper part of the drawing shows the leadership style, which is based on the combination of relationship behavior (vertical axis) and task behavior (horizontal axis).

   Relationship behavior is the extent to which leaders maintain personal relationships with their followers, as in providing support and keeping communication open.

   Task behavior is the extent to which leaders organize and explain the role of their followers, which is achieved by explaining what subordinates are to do and how tasks are to be accomplished.

- **Four leadership styles—telling, selling, participating, delegating.** The bell-shaped curve indicates when each of the four leadership styles— telling (S1), selling (S2), participating (S3), and delegating (S4)—should be used.

- **When a leadership style should be used depends on the readiness of the followers.** How do you know which leadership style to employ? You need to have an understanding of the *readiness* of your followers, as represented by the scale at the bottom of the drawing, where R1 represents low readiness and R4 represents high readiness.

Let's consider which leadership style to apply when.

Telling represents the guiding and directing of performance. This leadership style works best for followers with a low level of readiness—that is, subordinates are neither willing nor able to take responsibility.

Selling is explaining decisions and persuading others to follow a course of action. Because it offers both direction and support, this leadership style is most suitable for followers who are unable but willing to assume task responsibility.

Participating involves encouraging followers to solve problems on their own. Because it shares decision making, this leadership style encourages subordinates in performing tasks. Thus, it is most appropriate for followers whose readiness is in the moderate to high range.

Delegating is providing subordinates with little support or direction. As such, the leader's role is to observe and monitor. This leadership style is best for followers who have a high level of readiness, both able and willing to perform tasks.

Does the Hersey Model Work?   The situational leadership® model is widely used as a training tool, but it is not strongly supported by scientific research. For instance, a study of 459 salespeople found that leadership effectiveness was not attributable to the predicted interaction between follower readiness and leadership style.[51] This is consistent with another study, in which 57 chief nurse executives were found not to delegate in accordance with situational leadership® theory.[52] Researchers also have concluded that the self-assessment instrument used to measure leadership style and follower readiness is inaccurate.[53] In sum, managers should exercise discretion when using prescriptions from this model.

Applying Situational Theories: Five Steps

Is there a general strategy that managers can use to apply situational theories across many situations? One team of researchers thinks so. Their approach contains five steps, as follows.[54]

Step 1: Identify Important Outcomes: "What Goals Am I Trying to Achieve?"

First, the manager must determine the goals he or she is trying to achieve for a specific point in time.

Examples: For a coach, the goals might be "To win" or "Avoid injury to key players." For a sales manager, they might be "Increase sales 10%" or "Decrease customer complaints."

Step 2: Identify Relevant Employee Leadership Behaviors: "What Management Characteristics Are Best?"

Next managers need to identify which specific behaviors may be appropriate for the situation.

Examples: Relying on the list in Table 14.6 on p. 453, a coach might prefer to emphasize achievement-oriented behaviors, which emphasize challenging goals and excellence. A sales manager might consider work-facilitation and supportive behaviors from that list best for his or her sales team.

Step 3: Identify Situational Conditions: "What Particular Events Are Altering the Situation?"

Fiedler and House both identify potential contingency factors to be considered, but there may also be other practical considerations.

Examples: An injured star quarterback may force a coach to alter the strategy for a game; a virtual sales force spread around the world may affect the kind of leadership required of a sales manager.

Step 4: Match Leadership to the Conditions at Hand: "How Should I Manage When There Are Multiple Conditions?"

If there are too many possible situational conditions, the research may not be able to provide conclusive recommendations. Thus, managers will need to rely on their knowledge of organizational behavior to determine which leadership behavior is best for the situation at hand.

Examples: Referring to Table 14.6, a coach with an injured star quarterback might decide to boost team confidence by drawing on supportive and values-based behavior. A sales manager in charge of a virtual sales force might decide to avoid directive leadership and use empowering leadership plus work-facilitation behaviors.

Step 5: Determine How to Make the Match: "Change the Manager or Change the Manager's Behavior?"

Implementing the decisions reached in Step 4, a manager can take either a contingency theory approach or a House path–goal theory approach. That is, the person in the leadership role can be changed or the manager can change his or her behavior.

Examples: It is not possible for the coach to be changed for a championship game, so the coach will have to change his or her behavior. If the sales manager is considered too directive and doesn't like to empower others, he or she might be replaced or, alternatively, change his or her behavior. ●

✖ 14.5 THE FULL-RANGE MODEL: USES OF TRANSACTIONAL & TRANSFORMATIONAL LEADERSHIP

major question? What does it take to truly inspire people to perform beyond their normal levels?

THE BIG PICTURE

Full-range leadership describes leadership along a range of styles, with the most effective being transactional/transformational leaders. Four key behaviors of transformational leaders in affecting employees are that they inspire motivation, inspire trust, encourage excellence, and stimulate them intellectually.

We have considered the major traditional approaches to understanding leadership—the trait, behavioral, and contingency approaches. But newer approaches seem to offer something more by trying to determine what factors inspire and motivate people to perform beyond their normal levels.

One recent approach proposed by **Bernard Bass and Bruce Avolio,** known as *full-range leadership,* **suggests that leadership behavior varies along a full range of leadership styles, from take-no-responsibility (*laissez-faire*) "leadership" at one extreme, through transactional leadership, to transformational leadership at the other extreme.**[55] Not taking responsibility can hardly be considered leadership (although it often seems to be manifested by CEOs whose companies got in trouble, as when they say "I had no idea about the criminal behavior of my subordinates"). Transactional and transformational leadership behaviors, however, are both positive aspects of being a good leader.

Transactional versus Transformational Leaders

India-born Indra Nooyi, chairman and CEO of PepsiCo Inc., is able to be both a transactional and a transformational leader. Let us consider the differences.

Transactional Leadership As a manager, your power stems from your ability to provide rewards (and threaten reprimands) in exchange for your subordinates' doing the work. When you do this, you are performing ***transactional leadership,*** **focusing on clarifying employees' roles and task requirements and providing rewards and punishments contingent on performance.** Transactional leadership also encompasses the fundamental managerial activities of setting goals and monitoring progress toward their achievement.[56]

Plans, budgets, schedules. Would you expect management in the construction field to focus more on the nonpeople aspects of work?

"You give the team of people a set of objectives and goals and get them all to buy into it, and they can move mountains," says Nooyi, who was ranked No. 1 on *Fortune*'s 2009 list of the Most Powerful Women in Business.[57] Under her leadership, PepsiCo has turned in impressive earnings despite rising costs "through a combination of new products, productivity improvements, higher prices, and packaging tweaks," says one article.[58]

We shouldn't think of a transactional leader as being a mediocre leader—indeed, competent transactional leaders are badly needed. But transactional leaders are best in stable situations. What's needed in rapidly changing situations, as is often the case in many organizations today, is a transformational leader.

Transformational Leadership *Transformational leadership* transforms employees to pursue organizational goals over self-interests. Transformational leaders, in one description, "engender trust, seek to develop leadership in others, exhibit self-sacrifice, and serve as moral agents, focusing themselves and followers on objectives that transcend the more immediate needs of the work group."[59] Whereas transactional leaders try to get people to do *ordinary* things, transformational leaders encourage their people to do *exceptional* things—significantly higher levels of intrinsic motivation, trust, commitment, and loyalty—that can produce significant organizational change and results.

Transformational leaders are influenced by two factors:

- **Individual characteristics.** The personalities of such leaders tend to be more extroverted, agreeable, and proactive than nontransformational leaders. (Female leaders tend to use transformational leadership more than male leaders do.)[60]
- **Organizational culture.** Adaptive, flexible organizational cultures are more likely than are rigid, bureaucratic cultures to foster transformational leadership.

The Best Leaders Are Both Transactional & Transformational

It's important to note that transactional leadership is an essential *prerequisite* to effective leadership, and the best leaders learn to display both transactional and transformational styles of leadership to some degree. Indeed, research suggests that transformational leadership leads to superior performance when it "augments" or adds to transactional leadership.[61]

Example

The Superior Performance of Both a Transactional & Transformational Leader: PepsiCo's CEO Indra Nooyi

For PepsiCo CEO Nooyi, one of her "most stunning talents is the art of suasion," says one writer. "She can rouse an audience and rally them around something as mind-numbing as a new companywide software installation. Her new motto, 'Performance With Purpose,' is both a means of 'herding the organization' and of presenting PepsiCo globally."[62]

The Nooyi Vision. Most important is her vision for moving the company beyond what it calls "fun for you foods" (soda pop and salty snacks) and into "better for you" foods, and into tackling issues like obesity and sustainability.[63]

Healthier Food. Nooyi, says Howard Schultz, CEO of Starbucks, which has a joint-venture partnership with PepsiCo, was "way ahead of her competitors in moving the company toward healthier products. She pushed for PepsiCo to buy Quaker Oats and Tropicana, and . . . PepsiCo removed trans fats from its products well before most other companies did."[64]

YOUR CALL

Do you think you might have what it takes to be both a transactional and transformational leader? What's the evidence?

Four Key Behaviors of Transformational Leaders

Whereas transactional leaders are dispassionate, transformational leaders excite passion, inspiring and empowering people to look beyond their own interests to the interests of the organization. They appeal to their followers' self-concepts—their values and personal identity—to create changes in their goals, values, needs, beliefs, and aspirations.

Sir Richard Branson. One of today's most flamboyant businessmen, Britain's Richard Branson is shown here announcing new service for his Virgin Atlantic airline. Branson left school at 16 to start a 1960s counterculture magazine. By 2006, he was heading a $5 billion-plus empire—the Virgin Group—that includes airlines, entertainment companies, car dealerships, railroads, bridal gowns, soft drinks, financial services, and a space tourism company. Knighted in 2000—which entitles him to be called "Sir"—Branson, who is dyslexic, says he is not for scrutinizing spreadsheets and plotting strategies based on estimates of market share. "In the end," he says, "it is your own gut and your own experience of running businesses." Do you think charismatic business leaders like Sir Richard are able to be more successful than more conventional and conservative managers?

Transformational leaders have four key kinds of behavior that affect followers.[65]

I. Inspirational Motivation: "Let Me Share a Vision That Transcends Us All"

Transformational leaders have *charisma* ("kar-*riz*-muh"), a form of interpersonal attraction that inspires acceptance and support. At one time, *charismatic leadership*—which was assumed to be an individual inspirational and motivational characteristic of particular leaders, much like other trait-theory characteristics—was viewed as a category of its own, but now it is considered part of transformational leadership.[66] Someone with charisma, then, is presumed to be more able to persuade and influence people than someone without charisma.

A transformational leader inspires motivation by offering an agenda, a grand design, an ultimate goal—in short, a *vision,* "a realistic, credible, attractive future" for the organization, as leadership expert Burt Nanus calls it. The right vision unleashes human potential, says Nanus, because it serves as a beacon of hope and common purpose. It does so by attracting commitment, energizing workers, creating meaning in their lives, establishing a standard of excellence, promoting high ideals, and bridging the divide between the organization's problems and its goals and aspirations.[67]

Examples: Civil rights leader Martin Luther King Jr. had a vision—a "dream," as he put it—of racial equality. United Farm Workers leader Cesar Chavez had a vision of better working conditions and pay for agricultural workers. Candy Lightner, founder of Mothers Against Drunk Driving, had a vision of getting rid of alcohol-related car crashes. Apple Computer's Steve Jobs had a vision of developing an "insanely great" desktop computer. Martin Winterkorn, CEO of Volkswagen, established the vision of becoming the world's largest automaker by 2018. [68]

2. Idealized Influence: "We Are Here to Do the Right Thing"

Transformational leaders are able to inspire trust in their followers because they express their integrity by being consistent, single-minded, and persistent in pursuit of their goal. Not only do they display high ethical standards and act as models of desirable values, but they are also able to make sacrifices for the good of the group.[69]

Example: T. Rowe Price's James A. C. Kennedy "prides himself on balancing the demands of office and home," says one account. But over the second weekend of September 2008, as Lehman Brothers was crumbling to dust, he worked the phones from his Baltimore headquarters, trying to ease investor concerns about his own firm. Family, church, and gym all had to wait. 'I think God might forgive me for missing Mass that one day,' says Kennedy."[70]

3. Individualized Consideration: "You Have the Opportunity Here to Grow & Excel"

Transformational leaders don't just express concern for subordinates' well-being. They actively encourage them to grow and to excel by giving them challenging work, more responsibility, empowerment, and one-on-one mentoring.

Example: When Indra Nooyi was chosen over her friend Mike White to lead PepsiCo, she went to great lengths to keep him on. "I treat Mike as my partner," she says. "He could easily have been CEO." At meetings, she always makes sure he is seated at her right.[71]

4. Intellectual Stimulation: "Let Me Describe the Great Challenges We Can Conquer Together"

These leaders are gifted at communicating the organization's strengths, weaknesses, opportunities, and threats so that subordinates develop a new sense of purpose. Employees become less apt to view problems as insurmountable or "that's not my department." Instead they learn to view them as personal challenges that they are responsible for overcoming, to question the status quo, and to seek creative solutions.

Example: Nooyi is intent on balancing profit motive with making healthier foods, having minimal negative impact on the environment, and taking care of PepsiCo's workforce. "Companies today are bigger than many economies," she says. "We are little republics. . . . If companies don't do [responsible] things, who is going to?"

Implications of Transformational Leadership for Managers

The research shows that transformational leadership yields several positive results. For example, it is positively associated with (1) measures of organizational effectiveness;[72] (2) measures of leadership effectiveness and employee job satisfaction;[73] (3) more employee identification with their leaders and with their immediate work groups;[74] and (4) higher levels of intrinsic motivation, group cohesion, work engagement, and setting of goals consistent with those of the leader.[75]

Besides the fact that, as we mentioned, the best leaders are *both* transactional and transformational, there are three important implications of transformational leadership for managers, as follows.

1. It Can Improve Results for Both Individuals & Groups You can use the four types of transformational behavior just described to improve results for individuals—such as job satisfaction, organizational commitment, and performance. You can also use them to improve outcomes for groups—an important matter in today's organization, where people tend not to work in isolation but in collaboration with others.

2. It Can Be Used to Train Employees at Any Level Not just top managers but employees at any level can be trained to be more transactional and transformational.[76] This kind of leadership training among employees should be based on an overall corporate philosophy that constitutes the foundation of leadership development.

3. It Requires Ethical Leaders For a long time, top managers were assumed to be ethical. But in recent years, that notion has been disabused by news stories about scurrilous leaders ranging from the CEOs of Enron to pyramid schemer Bernard Madoff to failed commercial bankers paying themselves huge bonuses even as they accepted taxpayer bailouts and resisted regulation.[77] With such high-profile revelations, the need for ethical leadership has become more apparent. Without honesty and trust, even transformational leaders lose credibility—not only with employees but also with investors, customers, and the public.[78]

To better ensure positive results from transformational leadership, top managers should follow the practices shown below. *(See Table 14.7.)* ●

● **Employ a code of ethics.** The company should create and enforce a clearly stated code of ethics.
● **Choose the right people.** Recruit, select, and promote people who display ethical behavior.
● **Make performance expectations reflect employee treatment.** Develop performance expectations around the treatment of employees; these expectations can be assessed in the performance-appraisal process.
● **Emphasize value of diversity.** Train employees to value diversity.
● **Reward high moral conduct.** Identify, reward, and publicly praise employees who exemplify high moral conduct.

table 14.7

THE ETHICAL THINGS TOP MANAGERS SHOULD DO TO BE EFFECTIVE TRANSFORMATIONAL LEADERS

Source: These recommendations were derived from J. M. Howell and B. J. Avolio, "The Ethics of Charismatic Leadership: Submission or Liberation?" *The Executive,* May 1992, pp. 43–54.

If there are many ways to be a leader, which one would describe me best?

THE BIG PICTURE

We consider four other kinds of leadership. The *leader–member exchange model* emphasizes that leaders have different sorts of relationships with different subordinates. In *shared leadership,* people share responsibility for leading with others. In *servant leadership,* leaders provide service to employees and the organization. *E-leadership* involves leader interactions with others via information technology.

Four additional kinds of leadership deserve discussion: (1) *leader–member exchange (LMX) model of leadership,* (2) *shared leadership,* (3) *servant leadership,* and (4) *e-leadership.*

Leader–Member Exchange (LMX) Leadership: Having Different Relationships with Different Subordinates

Proposed by **George Graen and Fred Dansereau, the *leader–member exchange (LMX) model of leadership* emphasizes that leaders have different sorts of relationships with different subordinates.**[79] Unlike other models we've described, which focus on the behaviors or traits of leaders or followers, the LMX model looks at the quality of relationships between managers and subordinates. Also, unlike other models, which presuppose stable relationships between leaders and followers, the LMX model assumes each manager-subordinate relationship is unique (what behavioral scientists call a "vertical dyad").

In-Group Exchange versus Out-Group Exchange   The unique relationship, which supposedly results from the leader's attempt to delegate and assign work roles, can produce two types of leader–member exchange interactions.[80]

- **In-group exchange.** In the *in-group exchange,* the relationship between leader and follower becomes a partnership characterized by mutual trust, respect and liking, and a sense of common fates. Subordinates may receive special assignments and may also receive special privileges.

- **Out-group exchange.** In the *out-group exchange,* leaders are characterized as overseers who fail to create a sense of mutual trust, respect, or common fate. Subordinates receive less of the manager's time and attention than those in in-group exchange relationships.

Is the LMX Model Useful?   It is not clear why a leader selects particular subordinates to be part of the in-group, but presumably the choice is made for reasons of compatibility and competence. Certainly, however, a positive (that is, in-group) leader–member exchange is positively associated with goal commitment, trust between managers and employees, work climate, satisfaction with leadership, and— important to any employer—job performance and job satisfaction.[81] The type of leader–member exchange also was found to predict not only turnover among nurses and computer analysts but also career outcomes, such as promotability, salary level, and receipt of bonuses, over a 7-year period.[82]

Shared Leadership: Dividing Responsibility for Leading among Two or More Managers

Which is better—leadership in a single chain of command or shared leadership responsibility among two or more individuals? Perhaps, it's suggested, shared leadership is more optimal.[83] ***Shared leadership* is a simultaneous, ongoing, mutual influence process in which people share responsibility for leading.** It is based on the idea that people need to share information and collaborate to get things done. This kind of leadership is most likely to be needed when people work in teams, are involved in complex projects, or are doing knowledge work—work requiring voluntary contributions of intellectual capital by skilled professionals.[84] Researchers are beginning to explore the process of shared leadership, and the results are promising. For example, shared leadership in teams has been found to be positively associated with group cohesion, group citizenship, and group effectiveness.[85]

Example

Shared Leadership: Tech Companies Spread the Power

All kinds of organizations are run with shared leadership. The famed Mayo Clinic, for example, which employs more than 42,000 employees in various hospitals and clinics, relies on shared leadership to provide high-quality health care and customer service.[86] For a while, Ford Motor Company was run by three individuals at the top.[87]

Tech Heads. Some famous technical companies are headed by leaders who share power. At Google, co-founders Sergey Brin, President, Technology, and Larry Page, President, Products, are part of a triumvirate with Eric Schmidt, Chief Executive Officer.[88] One of the fastest-growing Web sites on the planet, with 125 million users, is MySpace.com. The founders, Tom Anderson and Chris DeWolfe, who live in Los Angeles, created the site, according to *Fortune,* "to promote local acts and connect fans and friends . . . who connected friends . . .

who connected friends. . . . The two had a friendship based on business, then they—quite literally—founded a business based on friendship."

Brain & Soul. When News Corp. CEO Rupert Murdoch offered $580 million for MySpace's parent company, they accepted the deal but remained on as the top executives, with DeWolfe as CEO and Anderson as president. (DeWolfe has since stepped down as CEO.) DeWolfe was considered the business brain, the smart person with the compelling vision; Anderson was considered the "soul" of the enterprise, the one who understands the users.[89]

YOUR CALL

If you were leading a business with a friend of yours, which role do you think would suit you best—the "business brain" or the "soul"?

Servant Leadership: Meeting the Goals of Followers & the Organization, Not of Oneself

The term *servant leadership,* coined in 1970 by **Robert Greenleaf,** reflects not only his onetime background as a management researcher for AT&T but also his views as a lifelong philosopher and devout Quaker.[90] ***Servant leaders* focus on providing increased service to others—meeting the goals of both followers and the organization—rather than to themselves.**

Servant leadership is not a quick-fix approach to leadership. Rather, it is a long-term, transformational approach to life and work. Ten characteristics of the servant leader are shown on the next page. *(See Table 14.8.)* One can hardly go wrong by trying to adopt these characteristics.

table 14.8

TEN CHARACTERISTICS OF THE SERVANT LEADER

1. Focus on listening.
2. Ability to empathize with others' feelings.
3. Focus on healing suffering.
4. Self-awareness of strengths and weaknesses.
5. Use of persuasion rather than positional authority to influence others.
6. Broad-based conceptual thinking.
7. Ability to foresee future outcomes.
8. Belief they are stewards of their employees and resources.
9. Commitment to the growth of people.
10. Drive to build community within and outside the organization.

Source: From L. C. Spears, "Introduction: Servant-Leadership and the Greenleaf Legacy," in L. C. Spears, ed., *Reflections on Leadership: How Robert K. Greenleaf's Theory of Servant-Leadership Influenced Today's Top Management,* 1994, pp. 1–14. Reprinted with permission of John Wiley & Sons, Inc.

Example

Servant Leadership: Leaders Who Work for the Led

Who are some famous servant leaders?

A Covenant with Customers. John Donahoe, CEO of eBay, thinks of customers first, and employees second. He tries his best to deliver what customers want. For example, reports one article, "on trips around the world he takes along a Flip video camera and films interviews with eBay sellers to share their opinions with his staff. He has even tied managers' compensation to customer loyalty, measured through regular surveys.[91]

A Covenant with Employees. Starbucks CEO Howard Schultz is also cited as being one of the foremost practitioners of servant-style leadership. Schultz has made sure his employees have health insurance and work in a positive environment, and as a result Starbucks has a strong brand following.[92] Max De Pree, former chairman of furniture maker Herman Miller Inc., promoted a "covenant" with his employees. Leaders, he wrote, should give employees "space so that we can both give and receive such beautiful things as ideas, openness, dignity, joy, healing, and inclusion."[93]

YOUR CALL

Understandably, servant leadership is popular with employees. Can you think of situations in which this kind of leadership role would *not* be appropriate?

E-Leadership: Managing for Global Networks

The Internet and other forms of advanced information technology have led to new possible ways for interacting within and between organizations (e-business) and with customers and suppliers (e-commerce). Leadership within the context of this electronic technology, called *e-leadership,* **can involve one-to-one, one-to-many, within-group and between-group and collective interactions via information technology.**[94] E-leadership means having to deal with quite a number of responsibilities, such as developing business opportunities through cooperative relationships, restructuring a company into global networks, decentralizing the company's organization, and energizing the staff.[95]

E-leaders, says one writer, "have a global mind-set that recognizes that the Internet is opening new markets and recharging existing ones. They don't bother fighting mere battles with competitors because they're too busy creating businesses that will surround and destroy them."[96] Harvard Business School professor D. Quinn Mills, author of *E-Leadership,* suggests that individual companies will be replaced by much broader global networks that a single CEO will not be able to manage. Thus, while 20th-century management emphasized competition, he says, future organizations will run on knowledge sharing and open exchange.[97] ●

Practical Action

Ten Tips on Being an E-Leader

Imagine you are a middle-management e-leader pulling together a virtual global team. How will you make it all work? Some tips on e-leadership offered by Dan McCarthy, Manager of Leadership and Management Development for a Fortune 500 company, at his blog "Great Leadership," are as follows:[98]

1. **Have a live kickoff meeting, if possible.** Although perhaps expensive, this method is the best way to build a strong foundation for the team.

2. **Pay attention to basic mechanics of good meeting and project management.** Agendas, role clarification, action items, and documentation all magnify when you're leading a virtual team.

3. **Be sensitive to time zones.** With a global team, there's no time that's good for everyone, so it's best to take turns being inconvenienced.

4. **Spend a lot of time "off-line" with individual team members.** Schedule some one-on-one meeting time, either in person or on the phone, with each team member for coaching, feedback, reinforcement, and relationship building.

5. **Do formal and informal team building.** After the kickoff meeting, get to know your team members as people by sharing photos and personal information, in order to build trust, cooperation, and commitment.

6. **Study up on cultures.** Learn a few phrases—at least "hello" and "thank you"—of your global team members, which they will appreciate as a show of respect.

7. **Use technology but don't get too caught up in it.** Even with Web conferences, videoconferences, and blogs, the best technology for virtual teamwork may still be the telephone.

8. **Use global English.** Keep your language free of buzzwords, local acronyms, and sports metaphors. Ask global team members to stop you and ask for clarification.

9. **Send material ahead of time.** To give your global team members time to translate or at least read materials ahead of time, send them early. It's challenging to read and understand complex information in a second language.

10. **Have all team members call in on their own phone.** Don't allow team members in the same location to gather in a conference room during team conference calls. People in the same room will have side conversations that you can't hear, and you may not be able to get a word in edgewise. This rule allows individual team members to emerge as stronger contributors.

Your Call

What's the eleventh tip that you would add to this list?

Key Terms Used in This Chapter

14.1 The Nature of Leadership: Wielding Influence

Leadership is the ability to influence employees to voluntarily pursue organizational goals. Being a manager and being a leader are not the same. Management is about coping with complexity, whereas leadership is about coping with change. Companies manage complexity by planning and budgeting, organizing and staffing, and controlling and problem solving. Leadership copes with change by setting a direction, aligning people to accomplish an agenda, and motivating and inspiring people.

To understand leadership, we must understand authority and power. Authority is the right to perform or command; it comes with the manager's job. Power is the extent to which a person is able to influence others so they respond to orders. People may pursue personalized power, power directed at helping oneself, or, better, they may pursue socialized power, power directed at helping others.

Within an organization there are typically five sources of power leaders may draw on; all managers have the first three. (1) Legitimate power is power that results from managers' formal positions within the organization. (2) Reward power is power that results from managers' authority to reward their subordinates. (3) Coercive power results from managers' authority to punish their subordinates. (4) Expert power is power resulting from one's specialized information or expertise. (5) Referent power is power deriving from one's personal attraction.

There are nine influence tactics for trying to get others to do something you want, ranging from most used to least used tactics as follows: rational persuasion, inspirational appeals, consultation, ingratiating tactics, personal appeals, exchange tactics, coalition tactics, pressure tactics, and legitimating tactics.

Four principal approaches or perspectives on leadership, as discussed in the rest of the chapter, are (1) trait, (2) behavioral, (3) contingency, and (4) emerging.

 14.2 Trait Approaches: Do Leaders Have Distinctive Personality Characteristics?

Trait approaches to leadership attempt to identify distinctive characteristics that account for the effectiveness of leaders. Representatives of this approach are Kouzes and Posner, gender studies, and leadership lessons from the GLOBE project. (1) Kouzes and Posner identified five traits of leaders. A leader should be honest, competent, forward-looking, inspiring, and intelligent. (2) Women may rate higher than men do on producing high-quality work, goal setting, mentoring employees, and other measures. Women excel in such traits as teamwork and partnering, being more collaborative, seeking less personal glory, being motivated less by self-interest than company interest, being more stable, and being less turf-conscious. (3) Project GLOBE surveyed 17,000 middle managers in 62 countries and determined that visionary and inspirational charismatic leaders who are good team builders do best.

 14.3 Behavioral Approaches: Do Leaders Show Distinctive Patterns of Behavior?

Behavioral leadership approaches try to determine the distinctive styles used by effective leaders. Leadership style means the combination of traits, skills, and behaviors that leaders use when interacting with others. We described some important models of leadership behavior.

In the University of Michigan Leadership Model, researchers identified two forms of leadership styles. In job-centered behavior, managers paid more attention to the job and work procedures. In employee-centered behavior, managers paid more attention to employee satisfaction and making work groups cohesive.

In the Ohio State Leadership Model, researchers identified two major dimensions of leader behavior: Initiating structure organizes and defines what group members should be doing. Consideration is leadership behavior that expresses concern for employees by establishing a supportive climate.

One expert concludes from the Michigan and Ohio studies that effective leaders tend to have supportive relationships with employees, use group rather than individual methods of supervision, and set high performance goals.

 14.4 Contingency Approaches: Does Leadership Vary with the Situation?
Proponents of the contingency approach to leadership believe that effective leadership behavior depends on the situation at hand—that as situations change, different styles become effective. Three contingency approaches are described.

The Fiedler contingency leadership model determines if a leader's style is task-oriented or relationship-oriented and if that style is effective for the situation at hand. Once it is determined whether a leader is more oriented toward tasks or toward people, then it's necessary to determine how much control and influence a leader has in the immediate work environment. The three dimensions of situational control are leader–member relations, which reflects the extent to which a leader has the support of the work group; the task structure, which reflects the extent to which tasks are routine and easily understood; and position power, which reflects how much power a leader has to reward and punish and make work assignments. For each dimension, the leader's control may be high or low. A task-oriented style has been found to work best in either high-control or low-control situations; the relationship-oriented style is best in situations of moderate control.

The House path–goal leadership model, in its revised form, holds that the effective leader clarifies paths through which subordinates can achieve goals and provides them with support. Two variables, employee characteristics and environmental factors, cause one or more leadership behaviors—which House expanded to eight from his original four—to be more effective than others.

Hersey's situational leadership® theory suggests that leadership behavior reflects how leaders should adjust their leadership style according to the readiness of the followers. Readiness is defined as the extent to which a follower possesses the ability and willingness to complete a task. The appropriate leadership style is found by cross-referencing follower readiness (low to high) with one of four leadership styles: telling, selling, participating, delegating.

 14.5 The Full-Range Model: Uses of Transactional & Transformational Leadership
Full-range leadership describes leadership along a range of styles, with the most effective being transactional/transformational leaders. Transactional leadership focuses on clarifying employees' roles and task requirements and providing rewards and punishments contingent on performance. Transformational leadership transforms employees to pursue goals over self-interests. Transformational leaders are influenced by two factors: (1) Their personalities tend to be more extroverted, agreeable, and proactive. (2) Organizational cultures are more apt to be adaptive and flexible.

The best leaders are both transactional and transformational. Four key behaviors of transformational leaders in affecting employees are they inspire motivation, inspire trust, encourage excellence, and stimulate them intellectually.

Transformational leadership has three implications. (1) It can improve results for both individuals and groups. (2) It can be used to train employees at any level. (3) It can be used by both ethical or unethical leaders.

14.6 Four Additional Perspectives
Four additional kinds of leadership are (1) leader–membership exchange model, (2) shared leadership, (3) servant leadership, and (4) e-leadership.

The leader–member exchange (LMX) model of leadership emphasizes that leaders have different sorts of relationships with different subordinates.

Shared leadership is a simultaneous, ongoing, mutual influence process in which people share responsibility for leading. It is based on the idea that people need to share information and collaborate to get things done.

Servant leaders focus on providing increased service to others—meeting the goals of both followers and the organization—rather than to themselves.

E-leadership involves leader interactions with others via the Internet and other forms of advanced information technology, which have made possible new ways for interacting within and between organizations (e-business) and with customers and suppliers (e-commerce). E-leadership can involve one-to-one, one-to-many, within-group and between-group and collective interactions via information technology.

Management in Action

Facebook CEO Is Being Pushed to Take the Company Public

Most everyone in Silicon Valley and on Wall Street agrees: The eventual IPO of social-networking site Facebook could make its founder the world's richest twenty-something.

Yet Chief Executive Mark Zuckerberg, now 25, seems intent on deferring that multibillion-dollar payday.

He's huddled with executives like Intel CEO Paul Otellini and Oracle Corp. President Charles Phillips—the goal being to extract wisdom about how to better run his independent company. He set up a dual-class voting structure that would make him less beholden to any public shareholders. . . .

"We're going to go public eventually, because that's the contract that we have with our investors and our employees," Mr. Zuckerberg said during a recent interview. But, he added, "we are definitely in no rush." . . .

Zuck, as he's known to most, lives in a modest house in Palo Alto and often walks to the office. Employees say he's a demanding boss—one who loves to engage in debate but isn't big on lavishing individual praise. According to one engineer, who wrote an internal memo called "Working with Zuck," it is unwise to "expect acknowledgement for your role in moving the discussion forward; getting the product right should be its own reward."

To the young CEO, Facebook, with its 400-million-plus users, is more than just another tech cog in the cultural landscape. The company's promise, he believes, has to do with facilitating people's ability to share almost any and everything with anyone, at any time—via Web sites, mobile phones, even videogames.

In an era of obsessive communication, "this push towards things becoming more open is probably the most powerful and transformative social change" barring an event such as a war, he says. "We may be the company that really leads this movement. . . . It's not clear that anyone else is going to manage it correctly." . . .

A micromanager, Mr. Zuckerberg has cut down on his meeting obligations and now delegates to senior-level staffers so that he can spend more time mulling Facebook's broader, strategic game plan. . . . He still has the final work on most product decisions and readily abandons concepts a year or more in the making.

"A lot of companies can go off course because of corporate pressures," says Mr. Zuckerberg. "I don't know what we are going to be building five years from now. I don't know what we are going to be building three years from now." . . .

In the company's early days, Mr. Zuckerberg had an artist paint a mural evoking children taking over the world with laptops. He ended meetings by pumping his fist in the air and leading employees in a chant of "domination." . . .

More recently, Mr. Zuckerberg—who himself is the subject of a forthcoming feature film—has used movie lines to cue employees that they are engaged in something greater than getting rich.

At a meeting last spring, Mr. Zuckerberg quoted from the movie *Troy* before hundreds of employees. . . . He recounted the scene where a messenger tells Achilles how scared he would be to confront the giant Thessalonia, whom Achilles was preparing to battle. "That's why no one will remember your name!" Zuckerberg shouted.

When potential hires ask why they should join Facebook, Mr. Zuckerberg said, "Tell them: because people will remember your name."

The company has had its fair share of management gaffes. Late last year [2009], Facebook came under fire for redesigning its privacy controls in a way that caused users to make more of their account data public. . . . Last week, the company acknowledged that a "small number of users" had received private messages intended for other members. Facebook executives regularly stress that they are committed to giving users tools to protect their privacy. . . .

Mr. Zuckerberg has passed up several opportunities to sell and make a killing. . . . By early 2008, Mr. Zuckerberg began to take steps to help prepare the company to go public. He expanded his management team, hiring Google executive Sheryl Sandberg as his No. 2 in March of that year. He sought new perspectives by inviting Netscape co-founder Marc Andreessen and Washington Post Co. Chairman Donald Graham to join his board. He kept voting control over their seats, however.

"The company is definitely set up in a way where myself and the other founders have a lot of control over it," he says. . . .

Any IPO timing is squarely in Mr. Zuckerberg's hands. He owns more than a quarter of Facebook's stock and controls votes for three of five board seats, say people familiar with the matter. . . .

To distract employees from the buzz of an IPO, he pressed them to focus on building a bigger company. He led a toga party to celebrate Facebook's 100-million-user mark. He bought a gong for the office, which employees bang when they launch new products.

In late 2007, he and the board changed the types of shares granted to employees, significantly lessening the pressure on the company to go public and giving him more control over the timing of such an event.

The switch, which the board agreed to, was to pay employees in restricted-stock units instead of options. Holders of RSUs generally can't become shareholders until the company goes public. . . . So the move allowed the company to stay under 500 shareholders, the point at which the Securities and Exchange Commission requires companies to disclose more financial information. . . .

The ranks, though, were still anxious for a payday. Some began to seek private buyers of their shares, complicating the company's internal valuation for employee stock options.

Their moves aggravated Mr. Zuckerberg, who often bragged to employees that he had a special capacity for delayed gratification . . . He hammered home this idea to his management team at an offsite meeting, recounting a story about how he was good at waiting for things as a teenager.

By early 2009, he had changed his own boyish look. Mr. Zuckerberg, who once sported sandals to major meetings, traded his daily uniform of a T-shirt and jeans for a button-down shirt and tie.

For Discussion

1. How many of the five sources of power is Mark Zuckerberg using? Explain.

2. Which of the eight influence tactics is Zuckerberg using?

3. Which different leadership traits and styles does Zuckerberg display? Cite examples and discuss.

4. To what extent is Zuckerberg using the full-range model of leadership? Explain.

5. Is Zuckerberg exhibiting any negative leadership traits, styles, or behaviors? Discuss.

Source: Excerpted from Jessica E. Vascellaro, "Facebook CEO in No Rush to 'Friend' Wall Street," *The Wall Street Journal*, March 14, 2010, pp. A1, A8. Copyright © 2010 by Dow Jones & Company, Inc. Reproduced with permission of Dow Jones & Company, Inc. via Copyright Clearance Center.

Self-Assessment

Do You Have What It Takes to Be a Leader?

Objectives

1. To learn more about the skills required for being a leader.

2. To assess your own leadership ability.

Introduction

Managers cope with complexity: They look at what needs to be done (planning and budgeting), pull together the people needed to get the job done together (organizing and staffing), and ensure that people do their jobs (controlling and problem solving). Leaders, however, cope with change: They look at what needs to be done by setting a direction rather than planning and budgeting, pull people together to do the job through alignment rather than organizing and staffing, and ensure people do their jobs through motivation and inspiration instead of controlling and problem solving. The purpose of this exercise is to assess your skills and determine if you have what it takes to be a leader.

Instructions

Read each of the following statements, and circle the number that best represents your self-perceptions, where 1 = strongly disagree, 2 = disagree, 3 = neither agree nor disagree, 4 = agree, 5 = strongly agree. There is no right or wrong answer.

1. I can separate my personal life from work/school.	1 2 3 4 5
2. I'm honest with myself.	1 2 3 4 5
3. I communicate my ideas clearly.	1 2 3 4 5
4. I regularly prioritize what I need to get done.	1 2 3 4 5
5. I am on time for meetings/classes.	1 2 3 4 5
6. I am positive and upbeat.	1 2 3 4 5
7. I am solution oriented rather than problem oriented.	1 2 3 4 5
8. I take responsibility for my actions.	1 2 3 4 5
9. I do not blame others for my mistakes.	1 2 3 4 5
10. When working in a group, I work with members to solve and prevent problems.	1 2 3 4 5
11. I don't have to redo things because my work is thorough and complete.	1 2 3 4 5
12. I do not procrastinate on projects/tasks.	1 2 3 4 5
13. I do not get distracted when working on projects/tasks.	1 2 3 4 5
14. I work well in a group.	1 2 3 4 5
15. I am people oriented, not just results oriented.	1 2 3 4 5
16. I listen to others beyond just the words being spoken.	1 2 3 4 5
17. When working in a group, I am more concerned with the group's success than my own.	1 2 3 4 5
18. I adjust well to different communication styles.	1 2 3 4 5
19. I praise others when they are doing a good job.	1 2 3 4 5
20. I work at getting ahead, but within appropriate boundaries.	1 2 3 4 5

Total _____

Scoring & Interpretation

Compute your score by adding the responses for all 20 items. The questions in this survey were designed to give you feedback on your skills in the following areas: (1) personal stability, (2) productivity, (3) self-management, (4) communication, (5) boundary setting, (6) work quality, (7) teamwork. All of these skills are found in good managers, and they represent necessary skills for leaders.

Arbitrary norms for leadership skills:

Excellent leadership skills (95–100)
Good leadership skills (85–90)
Moderate leadership skills (75–80)
Low leadership skills (65–70)
Poor leadership skills (60 and below)

1. Were you surprised by your results? Why or why not?

2. Look at the five questions where you scored the lowest. What can you do to improve or develop your skills represented by these items? Explain.

3. Does the content in the five lowest areas relate to Table 14.2? If it does, can you identify additional ways you can improve these traits? Describe and explain.

Questions for this survey were adapted from Interlink Training and Coaching, "The Leadership Assessment Tool," www.interlinktc.com/assessment.html. Interlink Training and Coaching, 3655 W. Anthem Way, Box 315, Anthem, AZ 85086.

Ethical Dilemma

Covering for a Laid-Off Friend

You manage a group of software developers for a large organization and several days ago had the difficult task of notifying a friend who works for the company that he is being laid off. Even though he has performed wonderfully in the past and you hate to see him go, your company lost a contract with a major client and thus his position has become obsolete.

The employee wants to build a house, and you're aware that he is 10 days away from closing on a loan for it. He has sold his previous home and now is living with his in-laws. He asks you for a favor: Could you extend his employment just 10 more days so that he can qualify for his new home loan? Unfortunately, you don't have the authority to do so, and you tell him you can't help him.

He then tells you that the mortgage company will be calling sometime soon to get a verbal confirmation of his employment. The confirmation is an essential prerequisite if your friend is to obtain the loan for his new home. Would you, he asks, tell the mortgage company that he is still employed?

Solving the Dilemma

As a manager, what would you do?

1. Tell the mortgage company your friend is still employed by the company. Your friend needs a break, and you're confident that he'll find a job in the near future.

2. Refuse to lie. It is unethical to falsify information regarding employment.

3. Simply avoid the mortgage company's phone call.

4. Invent other options. Discuss.

chapter 15

Interpersonal & Organizational Communication

Mastering the Exchange of Information

Major Questions You Should Be Able to Answer

15.1 The Communication Process: What It Is, How It Works

Major Question: What do I need to know about the communication process to be an effective communicator?

15.2 Barriers to Communication

Major Question: What are the important barriers I need to be aware of, so I can improve my communication skills?

15.3 How Managers Fit into the Communication Process

Major Question: How can I use the different channels and patterns of communication to my advantage?

15.4 Communication in the Information Age

Major Question: How do contemporary managers use information technology to communicate more effectively?

15.5 Improving Communication Effectiveness

Major Question: How can I be a better listener, reader, writer, and speaker?

Communicating by Listening

The reason that people act subversively against their employers is that they can't or are afraid to communicate with their managers. Resistance may take the form of "malicious compliance" (following supervisors' instructions to the letter while ignoring the real goal), withholding crucial data, or sabotaging projects that reflect directly on the manager.

One bookstore employee sabotaged his non-listening, always-angry boss by going through the store and discreetly pocketing any pens, pencils, even crayons, and then hiding them in a backroom cabinet. "My already preternaturally enraged boss," he reported later, "reached glorious heights of apoplexy."[1]

Effective communication begins with listening; paying attention to the words being spoken. "To begin with, listen to people as if you don't know the answer," suggests Meg Price, a Reno, Nevada human resource professsional. "This means that you will ask more questions to try to understand the situation from the other person's perspective. When you think you've got it, make a statement to the speaker summarizing what you believe they have told you. Only when they agree that indeed you do 'get it' should you begin to offer potential solutions or answers."[2]

Of course, sometimes there are true disagreements, and no amount of listening is going to change that fact. Here, according to David Stiebel, author of *When Talking Makes Things Worse! Resolving Problems When Communication Fails,* is how to identify the nature of a dispute:

- If you only listened to the other person, would she feel satisfied and stop opposing you?

- If you succeed in explaining yourself, would you really change the other person's mind?

- If the other person explained himself more, would you change your mind?

When true disagreements occur, one person ultimately must be willing to change so that negotiations can begin.[3]

For Discussion How good are you at listening? How good do you think most other people are? When someone else is talking, are you mainly thinking about your reply?

---

forecast **What's Ahead in This Chapter**

This chapter describes the process of transferring information and understanding from one person to another. It also describes three communication barriers—physical, semantic, and personal. It shows how you can use different channels and patterns of communication, both formal and informal, to your advantage. It discusses how exceptional managers use information technology to communicate more effectively. Finally, we talk about how to be a better listener, reader, writer, and speaker.

major question?

What do I need to know about the communication process to be an effective communicator?

THE BIG PICTURE

Communication is the transfer of information and understanding from one person to another. The process involves sender, message, and receiver; encoding and decoding; the medium; feedback; and dealing with "noise," or interference. Managers need to tailor their communication to the appropriate medium (rich or lean) for the appropriate situation.

Do you have difficulty accepting compliments, especially from close friends and loved ones? When you're ridiculed, as online, do you respond with over-the-top rage? Do you know how to apologize to someone—and do it in person, not by e-mail or text message, the coward's way? Are you so used to using profanity that you assume others are comfortable with it as well?[4]

All these matters show how difficult it is to communicate well.

Problems with communicating are a fact of human existence, as we just described in the Manager's Toolbox. That said, it is essential to develop your communication skills, which 636 human resource professionals rated as the most important factor in advancing their careers.[5]

No wonder faulty communication has become such a problem in the workplace. According to one survey, executives say 14% of each 40-hour workweek is wasted because of poor communication between staff and managers.[6] That's the equivalent of 7 workweeks of lost productivity a year. Thus, there's a hardheaded argument for better communication: It can save money.

Communication Defined: The Transfer of Information & Understanding

Communication—**the transfer of information and understanding from one person to another**—is an activity that you as a manager will have to do a lot of. Indeed, one study found that 81% of a manager's time in a typical workday is spent communicating.[7]

Everything's clicking. Today some people can work almost anywhere, even more so as laptops, iPads, and cell phones have become such versatile instruments permitting Internet and e-mail access, text messaging, and access to huge databases. Do you think our ability to work outside traditional offices because of today's technology will negatively affect the communication process and employee camaraderie?

The fact that managers do a lot of communicating doesn't mean they're necessarily good at it—that is, that they are efficient or effective. You are an *efficient communicator* when you can transmit your message accurately in the least time. You are an *effective communicator* when your intended message is accurately understood by the other person. Thus, you may well be efficient in sending a group of people a reprimand by e-mail. But it may not be effective if it makes them angry so that they can't absorb its meaning.

From this, you can see why it's important to have an understanding of the communication process.

How the Communication Process Works

Communication has been said to be a process consisting of "a sender transmitting a message through a medium to a receiver who responds."[8] Let's look at these and other parts of the process.

Sender, Message, & Receiver The *sender* **is the person wanting to share information—called a** *message***—and the** *receiver* **is the person for whom the message is intended,** as follows.

Sender → Message → Receiver

Encoding & Decoding Of course, the process isn't as simple as just sender/message/receiver. If you were an old-fashioned telegraph operator using Morse code to send a message over a telegraph line, you would first have to encode the message, and the receiver would have to decode it. But the same is true if you are sending the message by voice to another person in the same room, when you have to decide what language to speak in and what terms to use.

Encoding **is translating a message into understandable symbols or language.** *Decoding* **is interpreting and trying to make sense of the message.** Thus, the communication process is now

Sender **[Encoding]** → Message → **[Decoding]** Receiver

The Medium The means by which you as a communicator send a message is important, whether it is by typing an e-mail traveling over the Internet, by voice over a telephone line, or by hand-scrawled note. This is the *medium,* **the pathway by which a message travels:**

Sender [Encoding] → Message **[Medium]** Message → [Decoding] Receiver

Feedback "Flight 123, do you copy?" In the movies, that's what you hear the flight controller say when radioing the pilot of a troubled aircraft to see if he or she received ("copied") the previous message. And the pilot may radio back, "Roger, Houston, I copy." This is an example of *feedback*—**the receiver expresses his or her reaction to the sender's message.**

Noise Unfortunately, the entire communication process can be disrupted at several different points by what is called *noise*—**any disturbance that interferes with the transmission of a message.** The noise can occur in the medium, of course, as

when you have static in a radio transmission or fadeout on a cell phone or when there's loud music when you're trying to talk in a noisy restaurant. Or it can occur in the encoding or decoding, as when a pharmacist can't read a prescription because of a doctor's poor handwriting.[9]

Noise also occurs in *nonverbal communication* (discussed later in this chapter), as when our physical movements send a message that is different from the one we are speaking, or in *cross-cultural communication* (discussed in Chapter 4), as when we make assumptions about other people's messages based on our own culture instead of theirs. We discuss noise further in the next section.

The communication process is shown below. *(See Figure 15.1.)*

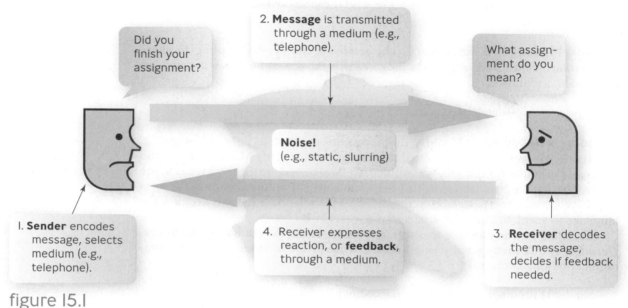

2. **Message** is transmitted through a medium (e.g., telephone).

Did you finish your assignment?

What assignment do you mean?

Noise!
(e.g., static, slurring)

l. **Sender** encodes message, selects medium (e.g., telephone).

4. Receiver expresses reaction, or **feedback**, through a medium.

3. **Receiver** decodes the message, decides if feedback needed.

figure 15.1

THE COMMUNICATION PROCESS

"Noise" is not just noise or loud background sounds but any disturbance that interferes with transmission—static, fadeout, distracting facial expressions, uncomfortable meeting site, competing voices, and so on.

Selecting the Right Medium for Effective Communication

All kinds of communications tools are available to managers, ranging from one-to-one face-to-face conversation all the way to use of the mass media. However, managers need to know how to use the right tool for the right condition—when to use e-mail, when to meet face-to-face, for example. Should you praise an employee by voicing a compliment, sending an e-mail, posting an announcement near the office coffee machine—or all three? How about when carrying out a reprimand?

Is a Medium Rich or Lean in Information?   As a manager, you will have many media to choose from: conversations, meetings, speeches, the telephone, e-mail, memos, letters, bulletin boards, PowerPoint presentations, videoconferencing, printed publications, videos, and so on. Beyond these are the sophisticated communications possibilities of the mass media: public relations; advertising; news reports via print, radio, TV, the Internet.

Media richness indicates how well a particular medium conveys information and promotes learning. That is, the "richer" a medium is, the better it is at conveying information. The term *media richness* was proposed by respected organizational theorists Richard Daft and Robert Lengel as part of their contingency model for media selection.[10]

Ranging from high media richness to low media richness, types of media may be positioned along a continuum as follows:

High media richness
(Best for nonroutine, ambiguous situations)

Low media richness
(Best for routine, clear situations)

| Face-to-face presence | Video-conferencing | Telephone | Personal written media (e-mail, memos, letters) | Impersonal written media (newsletters, fliers, general reports) |

Face-to-face communication, also the most personal form of communication, is the richest. It allows the receiver of the message to observe multiple cues, such as body language and tone of voice. It allows the sender to get immediate feedback, to see how well the receiver comprehended the message. At the other end of the media richness scale, impersonal written media is just the reverse—only one cue and no feedback—making it low in richness.

Matching the Appropriate Medium to the Appropriate Situation In general, follow these guidelines:

- **Rich medium—best for nonroutine situations and to avoid oversimplification.** A *rich* medium is more effective with nonroutine situations.

  Examples: In what way would you like to learn the facts from your boss of a nonroutine situation such as a major company reorganization, which might affect your job? Via a memo tacked on the bulletin board (a lean medium)? Or via face-to-face meeting or phone call (rich medium)?

  The danger of using a rich medium for routine matters (such as monthly sales reports) is that it results in information *overloading*—more information than necessary.

- **Lean medium—best for routine situations and to avoid overloading.** A *lean* medium is more effective with routine situations.

  Examples: In what manner would you as a sales manager like to get routine monthly sales reports from your 50 sales reps? Via time-consuming phone calls (somewhat rich medium)? Or via e-mails or written memos (somewhat lean medium)? The danger of using a lean medium for nonroutine matters (such as a company reorganization) is that it results in information *oversimplification*—it doesn't provide enough of the information the receiver needs and wants. ●

✳ 15.2 BARRIERS TO COMMUNICATION

major question ? What are the important barriers I need to be aware of, so I can improve my communication skills?

THE BIG PICTURE

We describe three barriers to communication. Physical barriers include sound, time, and space. Semantic barriers include unclear use of words and jargon. Personal barriers include variations in communication skills, trustworthiness and credibility, stereotypes and prejudices, and faulty listening skills.

Stand up and give a speech to a group of co-workers? Connecticut businessman Robert Suhoza would prefer to be trampled by elephants, says a news story. "Make small talk at a cocktail party?" it goes on. "Just go ahead and shoot him. Introduce himself to a room full of strangers? Maybe he'll just come back some other time. . . . Even answering the phone seemed at times an insurmountable task: He knew he should pick up the receiver, but he was paralyzed by not knowing who was on the other end, or what the caller wanted."[11]

Suhoza is 53 years old, but all his life he has suffered from social phobia or social anxiety disorder. In this he has plenty of company: One in every eight Americans apparently meets the diagnostic criteria for social anxiety disorder at some point in their lives, making it the third most common psychiatric condition. More women suffer from it than men, although men are more likely to seek treatment.[12]

Social anxiety disorder is an example (though an extreme one) of a communication *barrier*—a barrier being anything interfering with accurate communication between two people. Some barriers may be thought of as happening within the communication process itself, as the table on the opposite page shows. *(See Table 15.1.)* It's more practical, however, to think of barriers as being of three types: (1) *physical barriers,* (2) *semantic barriers,* and (3) *personal barriers.*

Without walls. Supposedly businesses that have open floor plans with cubicles instead of private offices function better because people can more easily talk across the shoulder-high partitions. But do you think the absence of floor-to-ceiling physical barriers might, in fact, lead to other kinds of barriers—such as others' talking making it hard to hear while you're on the phone?

table 15.1 SOME BARRIERS THAT HAPPEN WITHIN THE COMMUNICATION PROCESS

All it takes is one blocked step in the communication process described in the text for communication to fail. Consider the following.

- **Sender barrier—no message gets sent.** Example: If a manager has an idea but is afraid to voice it because (like Robert Suhoza) he or she fears criticism, then obviously no message gets sent.

- **Encoding barrier—the message is not expressed correctly.** Example: If your vocabulary is lacking or English is not your first language, you may have difficulty expressing to a supervisor, co-worker, or subordinate what it is you mean to say.

- **Medium barrier—the communication channel is blocked.** Example: When someone's phone always has a busy signal or a computer network is down, these are instances of the communication medium being blocked.

- **Decoding barrier—the recipient doesn't understand the message.** Example: Perhaps you're afraid to show your ignorance when someone is throwing computer terms at you and says that your computer connection has "a bandwidth problem."

- **Receiver barrier—no message gets received.** Example: Because you were talking to a co-worker, you weren't listening when your supervisor announced today's work assignments.

- **Feedback barrier—the recipient doesn't respond enough.** Example: You give some people someone street directions, but since they only nod their heads and don't repeat the directions back to you, you don't really know whether you were understood.

1. Physical Barriers: Sound, Time, Space, & So On

Try shouting at someone on the far side of a construction site—at a distance of many yards over the roar of earth-moving machinery—and you know what physical barriers are. Other such barriers are time-zone differences, telephone-line static, and crashed computers. Office walls can be physical barriers, too, which is one reason for the trend toward open floor plans with cubicles instead of offices in many workplace settings.

2. Semantic Barriers: When Words Matter

When a supervisor tells you, "We need to get this done right away," what does it mean? Does "We" mean just you? You and your co-workers? Or you, your co-workers, and the boss? Does "right away" mean today, tomorrow, or next week? These are examples of semantic barriers. ***Semantics* is the study of the meaning of words.**

As global communications have become so important, so have semantic difficulties, which we may often encounter when dealing with other cultures (as we discussed in Chapter 4). When talking on the phone with Indians working in call centers in India, for example, we may find their pronunciation unusual. Perhaps that is because, according to one Indian speech-voice consultant, whereas "Americans think in English, we think in our mother tongue and translate it while speaking."[13]

In addition, as our society becomes more technically oriented, semantic meaning becomes a problem because jargon develops. ***Jargon* is terminology specific to a particular profession or group.** (Example: "The HR VP wants the RFP to go out ASAP." Translation: "The Vice President of Human Resources wants the Request For Proposal to go out as soon as possible.") As a manager in a specialized field, you need to remember that what are ordinary terms for you may be mysteries to outsiders.[14]

3. Personal Barriers: Individual Attributes That Hinder Communication

"Is it them or is it me?"

How often have you wondered, when someone has shown a surprising response to something you said, how the miscommunication happened? Let's examine nine personal barriers that contribute to miscommunication.[15]

Variable Skills in Communicating Effectively   As we all know, some people are simply better communicators than others. They have the speaking skills, the vocabulary, the facial expressions, the eye contact, the dramatic ability, the "gift of gab" to express themselves in a superior way. Conversely, other people don't have this quality. But better communication skills can be learned. [16]

Variations in How Information Is Processed & Interpreted   Zheng Yu, a young woman from China teaching her native language to students in Lawton, Oklahoma, was explaining a vocabulary quiz when a student interrupted: "Sorry, I was zoning out. What are we supposed to be doing?" Zheng repeated the instructions, but she was taken aback. "In China," she said afterward, "if you teach the students and they don't get it, that's their problem. Here if you don't get it, you teach it again."[17]

Are you from a working-class or privileged background? Are you from a particular ethnic group? Are you better at math or at language? Are you from a chaotic household filled with alcoholism and fighting, which distracts you at work? Because people use different frames of reference and experiences to interpret the world around them, they are selective about what things have meaning to them and what things don't. All told, these differences affect what we say and what we think we hear.

Variations in Trustworthiness & Credibility   Without trust between you and the other person, communication is apt to be flawed. Instead of communicating, both of you will be concentrating on defensive tactics, not the meaning of the message being exchanged.[18] How will subordinates react to you as a manager if your predecessors in your job lied to them? They may give you the benefit of a doubt, but they may be waiting for the first opportunity to be confirmed in the belief that you will break their trust.

Oversized Egos   Our egos—our pride, our self-esteem, even arrogance—are a fourth barrier. Egos can cause political battles, turf wars, and the passionate pursuit of power, credit, and resources. Egos influence how we treat each other as well as how receptive we are to being influenced by others. Ever had someone take credit for an idea that was yours? Then you know how powerful ego feelings can be.

Faulty Listening Skills   When you go to a party, do people ever ask questions of you and about who you are and what you're doing? Or are they too ready to talk about themselves? And do they seem to be waiting for you to finish talking so that they can then resume saying what they want to say? (But here's a test: Do you actually *listen* when they're talking?)

Tendency to Judge Others' Messages   Suppose another student in this class sees you reading this text and says, "I like the book we're reading." You might say, "I agree." Or you might say, "I disagree—it's boring." The point is that we all have a natural tendency, according to psychologist Carl Rogers, to judge others' statements from our own point of view (especially if we have strong feelings about the issue).[19]

Inability to Listen with Understanding   To really listen with understanding, you have to imagine yourself in the other person's shoes. Or, as Rogers and his coauthor put it, you have to "see the expressed idea and attitude from the other person's point of view, to sense how it feels to him, to achieve his frame of reference in regard to the thing he is talking about."[20] When you listen with understanding, it makes you feel less defensive (even if the message is criticism) and improves your accuracy in perceiving the message.

Stereotypes & Prejudices   A *stereotype* **consists of oversimplified beliefs about a certain group of people.** There are, for instance, common stereotypes about old people, young people, males, and females. Wouldn't you hate to be categorized according to just a couple of exaggerated attributes—by your age and gender, for example? ("Young men are reckless." "Old women are scolds." Yes, *some* young men and *some* old women are this way, but it's unrealistic and unfair to tar every individual in these groups with the same brush.)

We consider matters of gender communication later in this chapter.

Nonverbal Communication   Do your gestures and facial expressions contradict your words? This is the sort of nonverbal communication that you may not even be aware of. We discuss this subject in more detail next.

Nonverbal Communication

Nonverbal communication **consists of messages sent outside of the written or spoken word.** Says one writer, it includes such factors as "use of time and space, distance between persons when conversing, use of color dress, walking behavior, standing, positioning, seating arrangement, office locations, and furnishings."[21] Nonverbal communication is responsible for perhaps as much as 60% of a message being communicated, according to some researchers.[22] Others estimate it as high as 90%.[23] Given the prevalence of nonverbal communication and its impact on organizational behavior (such as hiring decisions, perceptions of others, and getting one's ideas accepted by others), it is important that you become familiar with the various sources of nonverbal communication.[24] Indeed, this is particularly so when you are dealing with people of other cultures around the world, as we saw back in Chapter 4 (Section 4.5) in our discussion of cultural differences.

Body language. If you were this speaker, you would have to be pretty dull-witted not to notice that you've managed to bore *every* listener in the room. In a real-life situation, if you noticed even one person exhibiting this kind of body language, would you continue to speak to those who seem attentive? Or would you try to adjust your remarks—and your own body language—to try to reach the individual who is tuning you out?

Six ways in which nonverbal communication is expressed are through (1) *eye contact,* (2) *facial expressions,* (3) *body movements and gestures,* (4) *touch,* (5) *setting,* and (6) *time.* (Some lists add interpersonal space, which we discussed in Chapter 4.)

I. Eye Contact   Eye contact serves four functions in communication: (1) It signals the beginning and end of a conversation; there is a tendency to look *away* from others when beginning to speak and to look *at* them when done. (2) It expresses emotion; for instance, most people tend to avoid eye contact when conveying bad news or negative feedback. (3) Gazing monitors feedback because it reflects interest and attention. (4) Depending on the culture, gazing also expresses the type of relationship between the people communicating. For instance, Westerners are taught at an early age to look at their parents when spoken to. However, Asians are taught to avoid eye contact with a parent or superior in order to show obedience and subservience.[25]

2. Facial Expressions   Probably you're accustomed to thinking that smiling represents warmth, happiness, or friendship whereas frowning represents dissatisfaction or anger. But these interpretations of facial expressions don't apply across all cultures.[26] A smile, for example, doesn't convey the same emotions in different countries.

3. Body Movements & Gestures   An example of a body movement is leaning forward; an example of a gesture is pointing. Open body positions, such as leaning backward, express openness, warmth, closeness, and availability for communication. Closed body positions, such as folding one's arms or crossing one's legs, represent defensiveness. Body movements can be extremely subtle; for instance, when we say, "I'm looking forward to . . . ," guess which direction we tend to lean (if only very slightly)?[27]

Some body movements and gestures are associated more with one sex than the other, according to communication researcher Judith Hall. For instance, women nod their heads and move their hands more than men do. Men exhibit large body shifts and foot and leg movements more than women do.[28]

We need to point out, however, that interpretations of body language are subjective, hence easily misinterpreted, and highly dependent on the context and cross-cultural differences.[29] You'll need to be careful when trying to interpret body movements, especially when you're operating in a different culture.

4. Touch   Norms for touching vary significantly around the world. For example, as we noted in Chapter 4, in the Middle East it is normal for two males who are friends to walk together holding hands—not commonplace behavior in the United States.

Men and women interpret touching differently, with women tending to do more touching during conversations than men do.[30] If women touch men, it is viewed as sexual; the same interpretation is made when men touch other men.[31] Yet even handshakes and embracing seem to be changing, with the male handshake now evolving into a range of more intimate gestures—"the one-armed hug, the manly shoulder bump, the A-frame clasp with handshake in the middle, the mutual back-slap," as one article puts it.[32] Good teams tend to use touch more than bad teams do, according to some research.[33]

5. Setting   How do you feel when you visit someone who sits behind a big desk and is backlit by a window so her face is obscured? What does it say when someone comes out from behind his desk and invites you to sit with him on his office couch? The location of an office (such as corner office with window versus interior office with no window), its size, and the choice of furniture often expresses the accessibility of the person in it.

6. Time   When your boss keeps you waiting 45 minutes for an appointment with him, how do you feel? When she simply grunts or makes one-syllable responses to your comments, what does this say about her interest in your concerns? As a manager yourself, you should always give the people who work for you adequate time. You should also talk with them frequently during your meetings with them so they will understand your interest.

The table at the top of the next page gives some suggestions for better nonverbal communication skills. *(See Table 15.2.)*

Gender-Related Communication Differences

Men are eight times as likely as women to bargain over starting pay. Indeed, says one account, "Women often are less adroit at winning better salaries, assignments, and jobs—either because they don't ask or because they cave in when they do."[34] In other words, women need to hone their negotiation skills, or else they will fall behind.

Some possible general differences in communication between genders are summarized in the second table on the next page. *(See Table 15.3.)* Note, however, that these don't apply in all cases, which would constitute stereotyping.

table l5.2

TOWARD BETTER NONVERBAL COMMUNICATION SKILLS

You can practice these skills by watching TV with the sound off and interpreting people's emotions and interactions.

Do	Don't
Maintain eye contact	Look away from the speaker
Lean toward the speaker	Turn away from the speaker
Speak at a moderate rate	Speak too quickly or slowly
Speak in a quiet, reassuring tone	Speak in an unpleasant tone
Smile and show animation	Yawn excessively
Occasionally nod head in agreement	Close your eyes

Source: Adapted from W. D. St. John, "You Are What You Communicate," *Personnel Journal,* October 1985, p. 43.

How useful do you think these specific styles are in a managerial context? (Recall the discussion of men and women with reference to leadership in Chapter 14.)

Author Judith Tingley suggests that women and men should learn to "genderflex"—temporarily use communication behaviors typical of the other gender to increase the potential for influence.[35] For example, a female manager might use sports analogies to motivate a group of males.

Deborah Tannen, by contrast, recommends that everyone become aware of how differing linguistic styles affect our perceptions and judgments. For example, in a meeting, regardless of gender, "those who are comfortable speaking up in groups, who need little or no silence before raising their hands, or who speak out easily without waiting to be recognized are more apt to be heard," she says. "Those who refrain from talking until it's clear that the previous speaker is finished, who wait to be recognized,

Linguistic Characteristic	Men	Women
Taking credit	Greater use of "I" statements (e.g., "I did this" and "I did that"); more likely to boast about their achievements	Greater use of "We" statements (e.g., "We did this" and "We did that"); less likely to boast about their achievements
Displaying confidence	Less likely to indicate that they are uncertain about an issue	More likely to indicate a lack of certainty about an issue
Asking questions	Less likely to ask questions (e.g., asking for directions)	More likely to ask questions
Conversation rituals	Avoid making apologies because it puts them in a one-down position	More frequently say "I'm sorry"
Giving feedback	More direct and blunt	More tactful; tend to temper criticism with praise
Giving compliments	Stingy with praise	Pay more compliments than men do
Indirectness	Indirect when it comes to admitting fault or when they don't know something	Indirect when telling others what to do

Source: Derived from D. Tannen, "The Power of Talk: Who Gets Heard and Why," *Harvard Business Review,* September–October 1995; and D. Tannen, *You Just Don't Understand: Women and Men in Conversation* (New York: Ballantine Books, 1990).

and who are inclined to link their comments to those of others will do fine at a meeting where everyone else is following the same rules but will have a hard time getting heard in a meeting with people whose styles are more like the first pattern."[36]

Example

Do Female Executives Have an Edge in Business? Women & Communication

Women in business have the edge in two ways, says Chris Clarke, head of an executive search firm with offices in more than 40 countries. "There is increasing evidence," he says, "that women are superior at multi-tasking, which is needed to handle business complexities, and that they are better at relationships, which is important in developing effective teams."[37]

Overcommunicating. There is another way that women also have an edge, suggests a *BusinessWeek* article: Instead of tightly controlling information, they are more willing to share it.[38] A representative of this viewpoint is Anu Shukla, who sold her Internet marketing company for $390 million and made 65 of her 85 employees millionaires. "It's better to overcommunicate," she says. As an example, she made it her policy to share information with all her employees rather than to impart it to selected employees on a need-to-know basis.

The "CEO Lunch." In addition, Shukla created what she called the "CEO lunch," in which she invited six to eight employees at a time to discuss the business with her.

YOUR CALL

Anne Cummings, professor of business administration at the University of Minnesota at Duluth, suggests there are "masculine" and "feminine" styles in business, in which men tend to be more task oriented and assertive and to take greater intellectual risks whereas women tend to be more relationship oriented and "democratic" and to be more efficient at solving problems.[39] (Of course, all this behavior operates on a continuum, and most people have a multitude of styles.)

Do you think a woman can be successful by taking on the "masculine" style? Can a man be successful taking on the "feminine" style?

Learning "Soft Skills"   By now most male students and managers know they should avoid the use of masculine wording for jobs or roles that are occupied by both genders, using *police officer* instead of *policeman; supervisor* rather than *foreman.* (Conversely, secretaries, nurses, and babysitters should no longer be referred to as "she.") If you stay alert, it's fairly easy to avoid sentence constructions that are demeaning to women. (Instead of saying "he is," say "he or she is" or "they are.")

But, of course, there's more to effective managerial communication than that. Indeed, there are executive-training programs designed to teach men the value of emotion in relationships—the use of "soft skills" to communicate, build teams, and develop flexibility. "The nature of modern business requires what's more typical to the female mold of building consensus as opposed to the top-down male military model," says Millington F. McCoy, managing director of a New York executive search firm. One program given by London-based James R. Traeger helps participants break down the stereotype of the aggressive, controlling man who always wants to take charge and solve problems and to learn to listen and work in harmony.

Women as Executive Coaches   Interestingly, although men hold 82% of the top corporate jobs, when they want the advice of an executive coach—a trained listener to help them with their goals and personal problems—they usually turn to a woman. And, in fact, females always want another female as a coach. As a result, 7 out of 10 graduates of Coach U, the largest training school for executive coaches, are women. Because good coaches, says Coach U's CEO Sandy Vilas (who is male), are intuitive communicators and have done a lot of personal development work, "that profile tends to fit women better." Says Susan Bloch, who heads an executive coaching practice, "When a man is asked to coach another, they have a tendency to compete. Man to man, they have to show each other how great they are."[40] ●

Practical Action

How to Streamline Meetings

Meetings certainly have their uses. Two examples:

- **Meetings help keep everybody clued in:** Apple's Steve Jobs is renowned for holding marathon Monday meetings. The reason they take so much time, he says, is that Apple hires really good people, and "I want [them] making good or better decisions than I would. So the way to do that is have them know everything, not just in their part of the business but in every part of the business. So what we do every Monday is we review the whole business."[41]

- **Meetings help people take ownership of decisions made:** Economics professor Tyler Cowen points out that meetings can help people develop a sense of ownership in the decisions made in them, which can motivate them to turn those decisions into action.[42]

What to Do as a Meeting Participant

It is frustrating to have to be a victim of a poorly run meeting. Problem meetings can result from a lack of focus, nobody watching the clock, and no leader to keep the meeting on track.[43] In one survey, 50% of workers at big companies said they had attended a meeting where at least one participant fell asleep.[44] (At smaller companies, where it is harder to hide, the figure was 26%.) Patrick Lencioni, author of *Death by Meeting,* believes one reason meetings are so ineffective is that top executives discourage conflict.[45] But that tactic backfires, he says, because it makes meetings boring and ignores crucial issues.[46]

What can you do as a participant to make meetings run better?

- **Pull discussions back on point:** As a participant, you can always pull an off-track conversation back by saying, for example, "We were discussing the 2011 budget, but now we seem to be discussing the shortfalls of last year." Or you can try making a summary of a series of comments to prevent others from covering the same ground again.

- **Help the leader create the agenda:** If you're constantly exposed to ineffective meetings, you can also offer your assistance to the meeting leader in creating an agenda, with time frames attached for each item, suggests productivity specialist Odette Pollar. She adds: "Your approach, timing, and tone of voice are important. You must avoid appearing to tell the person what to do."[47]

What to Do as a Meeting Leader

If you're leading meetings, here are some good ways to streamline them:[48]

- **Eliminate unnecessary meetings and meeting attendance:** Don't call a meeting if the same result can be accomplished in some other way: phone call, e-mail, memo, one-on-one visit, and so on. Invite only people who need to attend, and let them know they need stay for only those parts of the meeting that concern them. Hold the meeting in a place where distractions will be minimal. Consider using telephone conferencing or videoconferencing.

- **Distribute meeting agenda in advance:** Do your homework about the issues. Prepare a list of meeting objectives, topics to be covered and the number of minutes allowed for discussion, and information participants should bring. Organize the topics with the most important ones first. Distribute this agenda a day or more in advance, if possible. For informal meetings, phone conversations, and one-on-one appointments, make a list of items to cover.

- **Stay in control of the meeting:** Start on time and stay within the time frame of the agenda items. (Coffee breaks, lunchtime, or quitting time provide built-in limits.) Announce politely at the start of the meeting that you value everyone's time and so you will intervene if discussion becomes off-point, rambling, or unintelligible. Reserve judgments and conclusions until after discussion so that everyone will feel free to give their input.

   Don't allow a few members to monopolize the discussion. Encourage silent members to participate. Try to reach a decision or make an assignment for every item. Use two notepads or pieces of paper, one for general notes, the other for tasks and assignments. Summarize the highlights at the end of the meeting. Map out a timetable for actions to be taken.

- **Do follow-up:** After the meeting, type up tasks and assignments for distribution. Set a date for a follow-up meeting to assess progress.

Your Call

What can you add to these suggestions to make meetings run better? (For more about running meetings, go to EffectiveMeetings.com (www.effectivemeetings.com).

How can I use the different channels and patterns of communication to my advantage?

THE BIG PICTURE

Formal communication channels follow the chain of command, which is of three types—vertical, horizontal, and external. Informal communication channels develop outside the organization's formal structure. One type is gossip and rumor. Another is management by wandering around, in which a manager talks to people across all lines of authority.

If you've ever had a low-level job in nearly any kind of organization, you know that there is generally a hierarchy of management between you and the organization's president, director, or CEO. If you had a suggestion that you wanted him or her to hear, you doubtless had to go up through management channels. That's formal communication. However, you may have run into that top manager in the elevator. Or in the restroom. Or in a line at the bank. You could have voiced your suggestion casually then. That's informal communication.

Formal Communication Channels: Up, Down, Sideways, & Outward

Formal communication channels **follow the chain of command and are recognized as official.** The organizational chart we described in Chapter 8 (page 247) indicates how official communications—memos, letters, reports, announcements—are supposed to be routed.

Formal communication is of three types: (1) *vertical*—meaning upward and downward, (2) *horizontal*—meaning laterally (sideways), and (3) *external*—meaning outside the organization.

Upward bound. How do you communicate with a manager two or three levels above you in the organization's hierarchy? You can send a memo through channels. Or you can watch for when that manager goes to the watercooler or the coffeepot.

I. Vertical Communication: Up & Down the Chain of Command

Vertical communication is the flow of messages up and down the hierarchy within the organization: bosses communicating with subordinates, subordinates communicating with bosses. As you might expect, the more management levels through which a message passes, the more it is prone to some distortion.

- **Downward communication—from top to bottom.** *Downward communication flows from a higher level to a lower level (or levels).* In small organizations, top-down communication may be delivered face-to-face. In larger organizations, it's delivered via meetings, e-mail, official memos, and company publications.

- **Upward communication—from bottom to top.** *Upward communication flows from a lower level to a higher level(s).* Often this type of communication is from a subordinate to his or her immediate manager, who in turn will relay it up to the next level, if necessary. Effective upward communication depends on an atmosphere of trust. No subordinate is going to want to be the bearer of bad news to a manager who is always negative and bad-tempered.

Types of downward and upward communication are shown below. *(See Table 15.4.)*

table 15.4   TYPES OF DOWNWARD AND UPWARD COMMUNICATION

Downward communication

Most downward communication involves one of the following kinds of information:

- Instructions related to particular job tasks. Example (supervisor to subordinate): "The store will close Monday for inventory. All employees are expected to participate."

- Explanations about the relationship between two or more tasks. Example: "While taking inventory, employees need to see what things are missing. Most of that might be attributable to shoplifting."

- Explanations of the organization's procedures and practices. Example: "Start counting things on the high shelves and work your way down."

- A manager's feedback about a subordinate's performance. Example: "It's best not to try to count too fast."

- Attempts to encourage a sense of mission and dedication to the organization's goals. Example: "By keeping tabs on our inventory, we can keep our prices down and maintain our reputation of giving good value."

Upward communication

Most upward communication involves the following kinds of information:

- Reports of progress on current projects. Example: "We shut down the store yesterday to take inventory."

- Reports of unsolved problems requiring help from people higher up. Example: "We can't make our merchandise count jibe with the stock reports."

- New developments affecting the work unit. Example: "Getting help from the other stores really speeded things up this year."

- Suggestions for improvements. Example: "The stores should loan each other staff every time they take inventory."

- Reports on employee attitudes and efficiency. Example: "The staff likes it when they go to another store and sometimes they pick up some new ways of doing things."

Sources: D. Katz and R. Kahn, *The Social Psychology of Organizations* (New York: Wiley, 1966); and E. Planty and W. Machaver, "Upward Communications: A Project in Executive Development," *Personnel* 28 (1952), pp. 304–318.

2. Horizontal Communication: Within & Between Work Units   *Horizontal communication flows within and between work units; its main purpose is coordination.* As a manager, you will spend perhaps as much as a third of your time in this form of communication—consulting with colleagues and co-workers at the same level as you within the organization. In this kind of sideways communication, you will be sharing information, coordinating tasks, solving problems, resolving conflicts, and getting the support of your peers. Horizontal communication is encouraged through the use of committees, task forces, and matrix structures.

Horizontal communication can be impeded in three ways: (1) by specialization that makes people focus just on their jobs alone; (2) by rivalry between workers or work units, which prevents sharing of information; and (3) by lack of encouragement from management.[49]

3. External Communication: Outside the Organization *External communication* **flows between people inside and outside the organization.** These are other stakeholders: customers, suppliers, shareholders or other owners, and so on. Companies have given this kind of communication heightened importance, especially with customers or clients, who are the lifeblood of any company.

Informal Communication Channels

Informal communication channels **develop outside the formal structure and do not follow the chain of command**—they skip management levels and cut across lines of authority.

Two types of informal channels are (1) the *grapevine* and (2) *management by wandering around.*

The Grapevine The *grapevine* **is the unofficial communication system of the informal organization,** a network of gossip and rumor of what is called "employee language." Research shows that the grapevine is faster than formal channels, is about 75% accurate, and is used by employees to acquire the majority of their on-the-job information.[50] Of course, employee language—otherwise known as "gossip"—can be notoriously misleading and a great reducer of morale in a dysfunctional company.[51]

Management by Wandering Around *Management by wandering around (MBWA)* **is the term used to describe a manager's literally wandering around his or her organization and talking with people across all lines of authority.**[52] Management by wandering around helps to reduce the problems of distortion that inevitably occur with formal communication flowing up a hierarchy. MBWA allows managers to listen to employees and learn about their problems as well as to express to employees what values and goals are important. ●

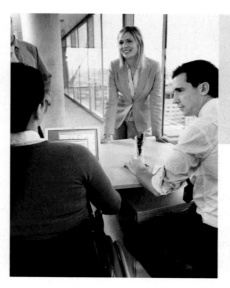

MBWA. Management by wandering around is sort of the reverse of employees exchanging informal views with top managers at the watercooler. That is, by wandering around the organization, top managers can stop and talk to nearly anyone—and thus perhaps learn things that might be screened out by the formal up-the-organization reporting process. If top managers can do MBWA, do you think midlevel managers can as well?

How do contemporary managers use information technology to communicate more effectively?

major question?

THE BIG PICTURE

We discuss digital communication technology and workplace behavior, including the characteristics of the "Always On" (Millennial or Internet) generation. We also describe three technologies that are altering the communication process: videoconferencing, telecommuting, and teleworking. Finally, we discuss some difficulties of the digital age: security problems, privacy concerns, e-mail overload, and cell-phone abuse.

The use of computers and information technology, which has so dramatically affected many aspects of the workplace, has taken us beyond communicating into multicommunicating. ***Multicommunicating* represents "the use of technology to participate in several interactions at the same time,"** in one explanation.[53] Examples would be answering e-mail messages during a lecture, and texting during a dinner conversation or while participating in a group conference call. Although multi-communicating sometimes enables us to get more things done in a shorter amount of time, there are times and places when it also can create *miscommunication* and lead to stress and hurt feelings.[54] For example, texting and checking your e-mail while working with colleagues can be seen as not only annoying but insulting.[55]

Digital Communication Technology & Workplace Behavior[56]

Multicommunicating is an example of how the worldwide digital communication revolution affects how we act and interact in workplace settings—both positively and negatively. The universal digital language of 1s and 0s gives us immediate access to unprecedented amounts of information and globe-spanning opportunities.

However, the very act of using technologies such as e-mail, texting, Facebook, and Twitter may influence the content of our communications. For example, researchers found that peers rate each other differently depending on the medium they use, with people being "far more likely to trash their colleagues via e-mail than when filling out a paper form," according to a *Fortune* writer.[57] Moreover, faster, far-flung digital communication doesn't necessarily mean better communication. In one organization, for example, employees with the most extensive personal digital networks were found to be 7% more productive than their colleagues, but those with the most cohesive face-to-face networks were even more productive—30% more, in fact.[58]

The "Always On" Generation

With the rise of the Internet has also come the rise of the "Always On" generation—or the Net Generation, Gen Y, the Millennials—88 million people born 1977–1997, the largest such cohort in U.S. history. The Always On generation is accustomed to spending 8 hours a day or more looking at various screens—on cell phones, on computers, on TVs—constantly busy with text messaging, e-mail, and the Internet.[59] This generation is much more likely (83%) to sleep with their cell phone next to their bed compared with Gen X (born 1965–1980) at 68% and Baby Boomers (born 1945–1964) at 50%.[60]

Hard on the heels of the Millennials is today's young "iGeneration," for whom technology is "simply a part of their DNA," as one child psychologist observed.[61] Indeed, if you are an 18- to 24-year-old, you generally watch the smallest amount of live TV (3½ hours a day) compared with any other age group, but you spend the most time text messaging (19 minutes a day) and watch the most online video (5½ minutes a day).[62]

table 15.5

EIGHT NORMS OF THE MILLENNIAL OR INTERNET GENERATION

In a couple of years, Millennials (Net Gen, Gen Y) will account for nearly half the employees in the world, and in some companies they already constitute a majority.[63] Their outlook, therefore, is having a profound impact on the workplace, "bringing new approaches to collaboration, knowledge sharing, and innovation in businesses and governments," says University of Toronto professor Don Tapscott, author of *Grown Up Digital*.[64] Tapscott and his fellow researchers have identified eight norms for this generation. *(See Table 15.5.)*

1. **Freedom—the desire to experience new and different things.** This norm, which takes precedence over long-term commitments, is expressed in a desire for flexible work hours and locations, to have a say in how things are done, and for freedom of choice.

2. **Customization—the desire to have personalized products and choices.** Customization covers everything from ringtone choices to Facebook layouts to lifestyle choices.

3. **Scrutiny—not taking "facts" and authority figures at face value.** Knowing that there is both treasure and trash on the Internet, this generation has leaned to be skeptical, to check things out, to ask probing questions. Candor and straight talk are favored.

4. **Integrity—trust in people, products, and employers is important.** This generation cares about honesty, transparency, and keeping commitments—although they are elastic when it comes to pirating music and plagiarism.

5. **Collaboration—relationships are of key importance.** Members of this generation value volunteering, know how to work and play with others, and are eager to offer opinions and suggestions.

6. **Entertainment—keep things moving and interesting.** A job should be both challenging and fun, not a life sentence. For this multitasking generation, the Internet is not only a productivity tool and information source but also a personal communication device and "fun tool of choice."

7. **Speed—instant feedback is expected.** Used to instant-feedback video games and nanosecond answers from Google, Millennials prefer rapid-fire texting, instant messaging, and Tweeting to the slower e-mail. This leads them to urge faster decision making and feedback on job performance.

8. **Innovation—impatience for new and different user experiences.** In the workplace, the traditional hierarchy is rejected in favor of work processes that encourage collaboration and creativity.

Source: Adapted from discussion in D. Tapscott, *Grown Up Digital: How the Net Generation Is Changing Your World* (New York: McGraw-Hill, 2009), pp. 73–96, and from A. Kreitner and A. Kinicki, *Organizational Behavior,* 9th ed. (New York: McGraw-Hill/Irwin, 2010), p. 426.

What kind of attitudes, preferences, and expectations do Millennials have that employers have to take into account in managing them? Millennials "place a strong emphasis on finding work that's personally fulfilling," says one article. "They want work to afford them the opportunity to make new friends, learn new skills, and connect to a larger purpose."[65] The average 26-year-old craves stimulation so much that he or she has "changed jobs an astounding seven times from age 18," says one report.[66] At least as important as compensation are six types of rewards, expressed in order as high-quality colleagues, flexible work arrangements, prospects for advancement, recognition from one's company or boss, a steady rate of advancement and promotion, and access to new experiences and challenges.[67] To deal with this cohort of employees, IBM advises managers giving feedback to be clear, keep it loose, promote a dialogue, and keep notes to make feedback sessions more constructive.[68]

Digital Communication & the New Workplace: Videoconferencing, Telecommuting, & Teleworking

Digital communication has significantly altered the traditional linkages between work, place, and time. Let's consider videoconferencing, telecommuting, and telework.

Videoconferencing As the 2008 recession took hold, companies slashed their travel budgets, but, of course, the need to maintain relationships with far-flung clients and co-workers never went away. As air travel stalled, corporations turned to *videoconferencing,* also known as *teleconferencing,* using video and audio links along with computers to allow people in different locations to see, hear, and talk with one another.[69]

Videoconferencing does not beat face-to-face meetings for opening a relationship with a prospective client or closing a decision. Indeed, one study found that when a company reduces its travel budget for personal meetings, it loses both revenue and profits. In fact, if a company completely eliminated business travel, corporate profits could drop 17% in the first year, the study found, and it would take more than 3 years for profits to reach the same level as before.[70] Still, during tough economic times, meetings via videoconferencing certainly are better than no meetings at all.

Many organizations set up special videoconferencing rooms or booths with specially equipped television cameras. Some of the more sophisticated equipment is known as *telepresence technology,* **high-definition videoconference systems that simulate face-to-face meetings between users.** Whereas traditional videoconferencing systems can be set up in a conventional conference room, telepresence systems require a specially designed room with multiple cameras and high-definition video screens, simulating "the sensation of two groups of people at identical tables facing each other through windows," according to one report.[71]

Clearly, telepresence technology can be quite expensive. Other equipment enables people to attach small cameras and microphones to their desks or computer monitors. This enables employees to conduct long-distance meetings and training classes without leaving their office or cubicle.[72]

Videoconferencing. In this arrangement, people in different locations can interact while viewing each other on a large screen. Videoconferencing offers considerable savings in time and money over the cost of travel. Do you think you would feel inhibited working with people in this way?

Telecommuting   *Telecommuting* involves doing work that is generally performed in the office away from the office, using a variety of information technologies. Employees typically receive and send work from home via phone and fax or by using a modem to link a home computer to an office computer. Among the benefits are (1) reduction of capital costs, because employees work at home; (2) increased flexibility and autonomy for workers; (3) competitive edge in recruiting hard-to-get employees; (4) increased job satisfaction and lower turnover; (5) increased productivity; and (6) ability to tap nontraditional labor pools (such as prison inmates and homebound disabled people).[73]

Telecommuting is more common for jobs that involve computer work, writing, and phone or brain work that requires concentration and limited interruptions. Among U.S. companies with at least 500 employees, 28% have some full-time telecommuters and 40% have some part-time telecommuters.[74] The number of Americans who telecommuted at least one day per month increased from about 12.4 million in 2006 to 17.2 million in 2008.[75]

Although telecommuting represents an attempt to accommodate employee needs and desires, it requires adjustments and is not for everybody.[76] People who enjoy the social camaraderie of the office setting, for instance, probably won't like it. Others lack the self-motivation needed to work at home.[77] However, people like Sylvia Marino of Mill Valley, California, who for 10 years has been telecommuting 350 miles away with Santa Monica–based Edmunds.com, which provides information to car buyers, find it a great way to sustain a career and still be with their children.[78]

Teleworking   Recently, the term *telework* (or *virtual office*) has been adopted to replace the term "telecommuting" because it encompasses not just working from home but working from anywhere: "a client's office, a coffee shop, an airport lounge, a commuter train," in one description. "With cell phones, broadband at home, Wi-Fi, virtual private networks, and instant messaging becoming ubiquitous, telework has become easier than ever."[79] Some of those who lack a conventional office may sign up for shared, or "co-working," spaces, where they socialize around a coffeepot.[80] Whatever the arrangement, employees in different locations and time zones can work simultaneously (called synchronous communication) and team members can work on the same project at different times (asynchronous communication).

The Downside of the Digital Age

It's fair to say that the digital age has introduced almost as many difficulties as efficiencies into people's lives. Describing them all would fill a book in itself, but here let us concentrate on just a few that managers have to struggle with. Some we mentioned earlier, such as the lack of focus brought on by the constant distraction of available electronic gadgets. Other problems are with security, privacy, e-mail overkill, and cell-phone abuse.

Security: Guarding Against Cyberthreats   *Security* **is defined as a system of safeguards for protecting information technology against disasters, system failures, and unauthorized access that result in damage or loss.** Security is a continuing challenge, with computer and cell-phone users constantly having to deal with threats ranging from malicious software (malware) that tries to trick people into yielding passwords, social security numbers, and financial information to deviant programs (viruses) that can destroy or corrupt data. According to the FBI Internet Crime Complaint Center, in 2009 there were 336,655 complaints of online fraud involving $559.7 million, an increase of 22.3% from 2008.[81]

The key to protecting digital communication systems against fraud, hackers, identity theft, and other threats is prevention. The table below presents some ways to protect yourself. *(See Table 15.6.)*

table I5.6

PROTECTING AGAINST SECURITY & PRIVACY BREACHES ON THE INTERNET

- **Pick strong passwords.** Use a mix of letters, symbols, and numbers, following the guidelines on www.microsoft.com/protect/yourself/password/create.mspx.

- **Use different passwords** for different Web services. And never use your Web passwords for PIN codes on credit, debit, or ATM cards.

- **Don't reveal sensitive information**—not even in "private" areas of services such as Facebook or Flickr that offer public access to most material.

- **Don't share files** on services that offer optional sharing, such as Google Docs, unless there is a real need.

- **Keep data** whose disclosure would create legal liability or embarrassment on your personal hard drives and storage devices.

- **Avoid file-sharing services** such as Lime Wire that distribute pirated files. Both the services and the downloads can open your computer to prying eyes.

- **Apply the latest security updates** to all your software, including operating systems, browsers, and antivirus programs.

Source: Reprinted from S. H. Wildstrom, "Security Smarts," April 6, 2009, *BusinessWeek*. Reprinted with permission.

Privacy: Keeping Things to Yourself   *Privacy* **is the right of people not to reveal information about themselves.** Threats to privacy can range from name migration, as when a company sells its customer list to another company, to online snooping, to government prying and spying. A particularly aggravating violation of privacy is *identity theft,* **in which thieves hijack your name and identity and use your good credit rating to get cash or buy things.**

In some cases, Internet users are their own worst enemies, posting compromising information about themselves on social networking sites that may be available to, say, potential employers. Supposedly such Web sites have various options whereby users can choose who is and is not allowed access to their personal information, but Facebook, for one, came in for a good deal of criticism because it altered its privacy controls in such a way as to expose many of its members' personal information online.[82]

Interestingly, however, 18- to 29-year-olds have been found to be more likely than older users of social networks to keep a keen eye on their online profiles and who can access them—just the opposite of what many people expected.[83]

E-Mail: Productivity Enhancer or Time Waster? People tend to have a love-hate relationship with e-mail. We love that we can send and receive e-mail 24/7 from practically anywhere. But we hate the fact the average worker receives 200 e-mails a day, according to some research.[84] Some other disadvantages of e-mail are that (1) there has been a decrease in all other forms of communication among co-workers—including greetings and informal conversations; (2) emotions often are poorly communicated or miscommunicated via e-mail messages; and (3) the greater the use of e-mail, the less connected co-workers reportedly feel.[85]

The table below provides some practical tips for handling e-mail. *(See Table 15.7.)*

table 15.7

TIPS FOR BETTER E-MAIL HANDLING

- *Treat all e-mail as confidential.* Pretend every message is a postcard that can be read by anyone. (Supervisors may legally read employee e-mail.)

- *Be careful with jokes and informality.* Nonverbal language and other subtleties are lost, so jokes may be taken as insults or criticism.

- *Avoid sloppiness, but avoid criticizing others' sloppiness.* Avoid spelling and grammatical errors, but don't criticize errors in others' messages.

- *When replying, quote only the relevant portion.* Edit long e-mail messages you've received down to the relevant paragraph and put your response immediately following.

- *Not every topic belongs on e-mail.* Complicated topics may be better discussed on the phone or in person to avoid misunderstandings.

Sources: J. Yaukey, "E-Mail Out of Control for Many," *Reno Gazette-Journal,* May 7, 2001, p. IE; D. Halpern, "Dr. Manners on E-Mail Dos and Don'ts," *Monitor of Psychology,* April 2004, p. 5; and B. K. Williams and S. C. Sawyer, *Using Information Technology,* 7th ed. (New York: McGraw-Hill/Irwin, 2007), p. 91; and P. R. Brown, "Same Office, Different Planets," *The New York Times,* January, 26, 2008, p. 135.

Cell Phones: Use & Abuse

Cell phones—which are now mostly smartphones that can text, access e-mail and Web pages, view TV programs, and so on—are so widespread that the majority of respondents in one survey said they would sooner give up their land-line phones, TVs, the Internet, and e-mail than surrender their mobile phones.[86] And as smartphones develop more features and make available more applications ("apps"), their importance will only increase.

Cell-phone problems range from merely annoying (loud ring tones and conversations in public places) to unethical and illegal (sending pornographic photos and photographing restricted areas of materials) to deadly (distracting drivers from the road). One survey found that 78% of those interviewed said that people are less polite, courteous, and respectful in cell-phone manners than they were 5 years earlier.[87] Phone use by car drivers makes even young people drive erratically, moving and reacting more slowly and increasing their risk of accidents.[88]

Some tips for handling cell phones (smartphones) are shown in the table at right. *(See Table 15.8.)* ●

table 15.8

FIVE RULES FOR USING CELL PHONES

1. Keep the volume of your voice down while on the phone; no need to SHOUT.

2. Don't force defenseless others on buses, in restaurants, and so on to have to listen to your phone conversations.

3. Shut off your ringer during meetings and public performances; set the phone on "vibrate," and return calls at a discreet distance.

4. Don't text during meetings or other conversations.

5. Don't dial/text while driving.

major question?

How can I be a better listener, reader, writer, and speaker?

THE BIG PICTURE

We describe how you can be a more effective listener, as in learning to concentrate on the content of a message. We also describe how to be an effective reader. We offer four tips for becoming a more effective writer. Finally, we discuss how to be an effective speaker, through three steps.

The principal activities the typical manager performs have to do with communication—listening, 40%; talking, 35%; reading, 16%; and writing, 9%.[89] Listening and speaking often take place in meetings (see the Practical Action box "How to Streamline Meetings" on p. 485 in this chapter), although they are not the only occasions. Human resource managers consider interpersonal communication skills the most important factor in advancing their careers, according to one survey.[90] Let's see how you can be more effective at the essential communication skills.

Being an Effective Listener

Understand me. What's the recipe for effective listening—for really finding out what someone has to say? Probably it is *listen, watch, write, think, question.* What do you do to fight flagging concentration if you're tired or bored? You suppress negative thoughts, ignore distractions about the speaker's style of delivery or body language, and encourage the speaker with eye contact, an interested expression, and an attentive posture. This will make you more involved and interested in the subject matter.

Is listening something you're good at? Then you're the exception. Generally, people comprehend only about 35% of a typical verbal message, experts say.[91] Two-thirds of all employees feel management isn't listening to them.[92] Interestingly, the average speaker communicates 125 words per minute, while we can process 500 words per minute. Poor listeners use this information-processing gap to daydream. They think about other things, thus missing the important parts of what's being communicated.[93] Good listeners know how to use these gaps effectively, mentally summarizing the speaker's remarks, weighing the evidence, and listening between the lines. Listening skills, incidentally, are particularly important when you're communicating in the global culture.

How do you become the kind of manager who others say is a good listener? Following are some suggestions (you can practice them in your college lectures and seminars).[94]

Concentrate on the Content of the Message Don't think about what you're going to say until the other person has finished talking.

- **Judge content, not delivery.** Don't tune out someone because of his or her accent, clothing, mannerisms, personality, or speaking style.

- **Ask questions, summarize remarks.** Good listening is hard work. Ask questions to make sure you understand. Recap what the speaker said.

- **Listen for ideas.** Don't get diverted by the details; try to concentrate on the main ideas.

- **Resist distractions, show interest.** Don't get distracted by things other people are doing, paperwork on your desk, things happening outside the window, television or radio, and the like. Show the speaker you're listening, periodically restating in your own words what you've heard.

- **Give a fair hearing.** Don't shut out unfavorable information just because you hear a term—"Republican," "Democrat," "union," "big business," "affirmative action," "corporate welfare"—that suggests ideas you're not comfortable with. Try to correct for your biases.

Being an Effective Reader

Reading shares many of the same skills as listening. You need to concentrate on the content of the message, judge the content and not the delivery, and concentrate on the main ideas. But because managers usually have to do so much reading, you also need to learn to apply some other strategies.

Realize That Speed Reading Doesn't Work   Perhaps you've thought that somewhere along the line you could take a course on speed reading. By and large, however, speed reading isn't effective. Psychologists have found that speed reading or skimming may work well with easy or familiar reading material, but it can lead to problems with dense or unfamiliar material. For instance, in one study, when questioned about their reading of difficult material, average readers got half the questions right, while speed readers got only one in three.[95]

Learn to Streamline Reading   Management consultant and UCLA professor Kathryn Alesandrini offers a number of suggestions for streamlining your reading.[96]

- **Be savvy about periodicals and books.** Review your magazine and newspaper subscriptions and eliminate as many as possible. You can subscribe to just a few industry publications, scan and mark interesting material, later read what's marked, and pitch the rest. Read summaries and reviews that condense business books and articles.

- **Transfer your reading load.** With some material you can ask some of your employees to screen or scan it first, then post an action note on each item that needs additional reading by you. You can also ask your staff to read important books and summarize them in four or five pages.

- **Make internal memos and e-mail more efficient.** Ask others to tell you up front in their e-mails, memos, and reports what they want you to do. Instruct them to include a one-page executive summary of a long report. When you communicate with them, give them specific questions you want answered.

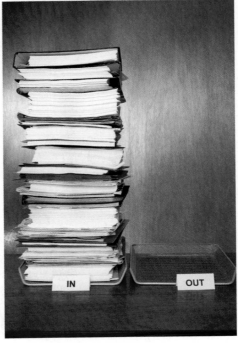

Speed-read this? Maybe you could—if it's easy or familiar material. But lots of things managers are required to read take patient study. How are you going to manage such reading day after day?

Do Top-Down Reading—SQ3R   "The key to better reading is to be a productive rather than a passive reader," writes Alesandrini. "You'll get more out of what you read if you literally produce meaningful connections between what you already know and what you're reading."[97] This leads to what she calls a "top-down" strategy for reading, a variant on the SQ3R (Survey, Question, Read, Recite, Review) method we discussed in the box at the end of Chapter 1.

The top-down system has five steps:

- **Rate reasons to read.** Rate your reasons for reading ("Why should I read this? Will reading it contribute to my goals?").

- **Question and predict answers.** Formulate specific questions you want the reading to answer. This will give you reasons for reading—to get answers to your questions.

- **Survey the big picture.** Survey the material to be read so you can get a sense of the whole. Take a few minutes to get an overview so that you'll be better able to read with purpose.

- **Skim for main ideas.** Skimming the material is similar to surveying, except it's on a smaller scale. You look for the essence of each subsection or paragraph.

- **Summarize.** Summarize as you skim. Verbally restate or write notes of the main points, using your own words. Visualize or sketch the main points. Answer your initial questions as you skim the material.

Being an Effective Writer

Writing is an essential management skill, all the more so because e-mail and texting has replaced the telephone in so much of business communication. In addition, downsizing has eliminated the administrative assistants who used to edit and correct business correspondence, so even upper-level executives often do their own correspondence now.[98] A lot of students, however, don't get enough practice in writing, which puts them at a career disadvantage. Most will have to be able to write standout job-seeking cover letters to accompany their résumés and later to write winning business proposals.[99] Taking a business writing class can be a real advantage. (Indeed, as a manager, you may have to identify employees who need writing training.)

Following are some tips for writing more effectively. These apply particularly to memos and reports but are also applicable to e-mail messages.

Don't Show Your Ignorance E-mail correspondence and texting have made people more relaxed about spelling and grammar rules. Although this is fine among friends, as a manager you'll need to create a more favorable impression in your writing. Besides using the spelling checkers and grammar checkers built in to most word processing programs, you should reread, indeed proofread, your writing before sending it on.

Understand Your Strategy before You Write Following are three strategies for laying out your ideas in writing.

- **Most important to least important.** This is a good strategy when the action you want your reader to take is logical and not highly political.

- **Least controversial to most controversial.** This builds support gradually and is best used when the decision is controversial or your reader is attached to a particular solution other than the one you're proposing.

- **Negative to positive.** This strategy establishes a common ground with your reader and puts the positive argument last, which makes it stronger.[100]

Start with Your Purpose Often people organize their messages backward, putting their real purpose last, points out Alesandrini. You should *start* your writing by telling your purpose and what you expect of the reader.

Write Simply, Concisely, & Directly Keep your words simple and use short words, sentences, and phrases. Be direct instead of vague, and use the active voice rather than the passive. (Directness, active voice: "Please call a meeting for Wednesday." Vagueness, passive voice: "It is suggested that a meeting be called for Wednesday.")

Telegraph Your Writing with a Powerful Layout Make your writing as easy to read as possible, using the tools of highlighting and white space.

- **Highlighting.** Highlighting consists of using **boldface** and *italics* to emphasize key concepts and introduce new concepts, and bullets—small circles or squares like the ones in the list you're reading—to emphasize list items. (Don't overuse any of these devices, or they'll lose their effect. And particularly don't use ALL CAPITAL LETTERS for emphasis, except rarely.)
- **White space.** White space, which consists of wide margins and a break between paragraphs, produces a page that is clean and attractive.[101]

Being an Effective Speaker

Speaking or talking covers a range of activities, from one-on-one conversations, to participating in meetings, to giving formal presentations. In terms of personal oral communication, most of the best advice comes under the heading of listening, since effective listening will dictate the appropriate talking you need to do.

However, the ability to talk to a room full of people—to make an oral presentation—is one of the greatest skills you can have. A study conducted by AT&T and Stanford University found that the top predictor of success and professional upward mobility is how much you enjoy public speaking and how effective you are at it.[102]

The biggest problem most people have with public speaking is controlling their nerves, since 46% of adults say the activity they dread most (exceeding housecleaning, 43%, and visiting the dentist, 41%) is public speaking.[103] Author and lecturer Gael Lindenfield suggests that you can prepare your nerves by practicing your speech until it's near perfect, visualizing yourself performing with brilliance, getting reassurance from a friend, and getting to the speaking site early and releasing physical tension by doing deep breathing. (And staying away from alcohol and caffeine pick-me-ups before your speech.)[104]

As for the content of the speech, some brief and valuable advice is offered by speechwriter Phil Theibert, who says a speech comprises just three simple rules: (1) Tell them what you're going to say. (2) Say it. (3) Tell them what you said.[105]

I. Tell Them What You're Going to Say The introduction should take 5%–15% of your speaking time, and it should prepare the audience for the rest of the speech. Avoid jokes and such phrases as "I'm honored to be with you here today . . ." Because everything in your speech should be relevant, try to go right to the point. For example:

> *"Good afternoon. The subject of identity theft may seem far removed from the concerns of most employees. But I intend to describe how our supposedly private credit, health, employment, and other records are vulnerable to theft by so-called identity thieves and how you can protect yourself."*

2. Say It The main body of the speech takes up 75%–90% of your time. The most important thing to realize is that your audience won't remember more than a few points anyway. Thus, you need to decide which three or four points must be remembered.[106] Then cover them as succinctly as possible.

Be particularly attentive to transitions during the main body of the speech. Listening differs from reading in that the listener has only one chance to get your meaning. Thus, be sure you constantly provide your listeners with guidelines and transitional phrases so they can see where you're going. Example:

> *"There are five ways the security of your supposedly private files can be compromised. The first way is . . ."*

Predictor for success. Enjoying public speaking and being good at it are the top predictors of success and upward mobility. Do you think you could develop these skills?

3. Tell Them What You Said   The end might take 5%–10% of your time. Many professional speakers consider the conclusion to be as important as the introduction, so don't drop the ball here. You need a solid, strong, persuasive wrap-up.

Use some sort of signal phrase that cues your listeners that you are heading into your wind-up. Examples:

"Let's review the main points . . ."
"In conclusion, what CAN you do to protect against unauthorized invasion of your private files? I point out five main steps. One . . ."

Give some thought to the last thing you will say. It should be strongly upbeat, a call to action, a thought for the day, a little story, a quotation. Examples:

"I want to leave you with one last thought . . ."
"Finally, let me close by sharing something that happened to me . . ."
"As Albert Einstein said, 'Imagination is more important than knowledge.'"

Then say "Thank you" and stop talking.   ●

Key Terms Used in This Chapter

Summary

15.1 The Communication Process: What It Is, How It Works

Communication is the transfer of information and understanding from one person to another. The process involves sender, message, and receiver; encoding and decoding; the medium; feedback; and dealing with "noise." The sender is the person wanting to share information. The information is called a message. The receiver is the person for whom the message is intended. Encoding is translating a message into understandable symbols or language. Decoding is interpreting and trying to make sense of the message. The medium is the pathway by which a message travels. Feedback is the process in which a receiver expresses his or her reaction to the sender's message. The entire communication process can be disrupted at any point by noise, defined as any disturbance that interferes with the transmission of a message.

For effective communication, a manager must select the right medium. Media richness indicates how well a particular medium conveys information and promotes learning. The richer a medium is, the better it is at conveying information. Face-to-face presence is the richest; an advertising flyer would be one of the lowest. A rich medium is best for nonroutine situations and to avoid oversimplification. A lean medium is best for routine situations and to avoid overloading.

 15.2 Barriers to Communication
Barriers to communication are of three types: (1) Physical barriers are exemplified by walls, background noise, and time-zone differences. (2) Semantics is the study of the meaning of words. Jargon, terminology specific to a particular profession or group, can be a semantic barrier. (3) Personal barriers are individual attributes that hinder communication. Nine such barriers are (a) variable skills in communicating effectively, (b) variations in frames of reference and experiences that affect how information is interpreted, (c) variations in trustworthiness and credibility, (d) oversized egos, (e) faulty listening skills, (f) tendency to judge others' messages, (g) inability to listen with understanding, (h) stereotypes (oversimplified beliefs about a certain group of people) and prejudices, and (i) nonverbal communication (messages sent outside of the written or spoken word, including body language).

Six ways in which nonverbal communication is expressed are through (1) eye contact, (2) facial expressions, (3) body movements and gestures, (4) touch, (5) setting, and (6) time.

 15.3 How Managers Fit into the Communication Process
Communication channels may be formal or informal.

Formal communication channels follow the chain of command and are recognized as official. Formal communication is of three types: (1) Vertical communication is the flow of messages up and down the organizational hierarchy. (2) Horizontal communication flows within and between work units; its main purpose is coordination. (3) External communication flows between people inside and outside the organization.

Informal communication channels develop outside the formal structure and do not follow the chain of command. Two aspects of informal channels are the grapevine and management by wandering around. (1) The grapevine is the unofficial communication system of the informal organization. The grapevine is faster than formal channels, is about 75% accurate, and is used by employees to acquire most on-the-job information. (2) In management by wandering around (MBWA), a manager literally wanders around his or her organization and talks with people across all lines of authority; this reduces distortion caused by formal communication.

 15.4 Communication in the Information Age
A modern-day trend is multicom-municating, the use of technology to participate in several interactions at the same time. The universal language of 1s and 0s gives us immediate access to unprecedented amounts of information; however, faster, far-flung digital communication does not necessarily mean better communication.

With the rise of the Internet has come the rise of the "Always On" generation (Net Generation, Gen Y, the Millennials), 88 million people born 1977–1997, who are accustomed to digital communication and who in a few years will account for nearly half the employees in the world. Their outlook is having a profound impact on the workplace, bringing new approaches to collaboration, knowledge sharing, and innovation. This generation puts a strong emphasis on finding work that's personally fulfilling, craves stimulation, and seeks high-quality colleagues and flexible work arrangements.

Digital communication has altered traditional links between work, place, and time, as seen in videoconferencing (teleconferencing) and telepresence technology (high-definition videoconferencing systems that simulate face-to-face meetings between users); telecommuting, involving performing office work at home; and teleworking, involving performing office work nearly anywhere.

The downside of the digital age involves problems with security, safeguards for protecting information technology against disasters, system failures, and unauthorized access; privacy, the right of people not to reveal information about themselves, particularly identify theft, in which thieves highjack a person's name and identity and use his or her good credit rating to get cash or buy things; e-mail productivity problems; and cell-phone use and abuse.

✳ 15.5 Improving Communication Effectiveness

To become a good listener, you should concentrate on the content of the message. You should judge content, not delivery; ask questions and summarize the speaker's remarks; listen for ideas; resist distractions and show interest; and give the speaker a fair hearing.

To become a good reader, you need to first realize that speed reading usually doesn't work. You should also be savvy about how you handle periodicals and books, transfer your reading load to some of your employees, and ask others to use e-mails and reports to tell you what they want you to do. A top-down reading system that's a variant on the SQ3R system (survey, question, read, recite, review) is also helpful.

To become an effective writer, you can follow several suggestions. Use spelling and grammar checkers in word processing software. Use three strategies for laying out your ideas in writing: go from most important topic to least important; go from least controversial topic to most controversial; and go from negative to positive. When organizing your message, start with your purpose. Write simply, concisely, and directly. Telegraph your writing through use of highlighting and white space.

To become an effective speaker, follow three simple rules. Tell people what you're going to say. Say it. Tell them what you said.

Management in Action

Effective Communication Takes Work

Executives know success in business depends on identifying and fixing problems before they become crises. It is the most basic rule in management: No matter how smart your strategies seem on paper, if you don't know how they're being executed and whether there are urgent problems, you won't be successful.

The higher executives climb, the less likely they are to know what is and isn't working at their companies. Many are surrounded by yes people who filter information; others dismiss or ignore bearers of bad news.

"I've heard so many executives tell employees to be candid and then jump down their throats if they bring up a problem or ask a critical question," says Yogesh Gupta, president and CEO of Fatwire, a software company that helps businesses manage their Web sites.

Mr. Gupta was determined not to do that when he was recruited to Fatwire from CA in August [2007]. Since then, he has spent hours talking with his 200 employees and seeking the advice of his nine senior managers—all but one of whom are veterans of the company. He has frequent private meetings with each member of the management team so they will feel freer to be candid with him. In that way, he can ask the important questions: What am I doing wrong? What would you do differently if you were running the company? What's the biggest thing getting in the way of you doing your job well?

Already, he learned from these talks that Fatwire should beef up its staff in marketing and in product development. Others have counseled him to improve Fatwire's customer-support processes. Every time he has gotten good advice privately, he has found a way to publicly praise the manager so others will come forward with suggestions.

"I know I have to say, 'You did the right thing to speak up' again and again, because employees fear they'll get blamed if they say anything negative," says Mr. Gupta. . . .

Executives at big companies who have many layers of management between themselves and front-line employees face the biggest challenge finding out how their strategies are actually working. Those who want accurate information must commit to spending time in the field—often and on their own—where they are away from handlers and can coax employees to be forthcoming about problems.

Kathleen Murphy, CEO of ING's U.S. Wealth Management unit, which sells a variety of products, from annuities to financial-planning services, oversees 3,000 employees. She holds town-hall meetings with large groups of employees but admits the sessions "are mostly for me to push my message out because people are less candid at big meetings." So, she also meets regularly with smaller groups of managers at all levels of her division. Once, when an operations group complained about a convoluted work process, she agreed the change they proposed was more efficient.

But she says she doesn't always act on what she hears, believing that executives have to filter out the inevitable complaints from the crucial information and ideas that create a productive and congenial workplace.

An upbeat executive, Ms. Murphy has teamwork in her DNA. She grew up negotiating with her five siblings for elbow room at the dinner table and played lots of sports. She says she has a "low tolerance" for people who are complainers. "There's a big difference between candor that stems from caring about doing things better and negative energy, which can be toxic," she says.

After reorganizing her division recently, Ms. Murphy sat through several meetings at which managers made suggestions and expressed their concerns. She encouraged everyone to voice their objections, but made her case that the changes would help them expand the business and better serve their customers.

They went through "a few rough sessions," she admits. But in the end, they found common ground. Her listening made all the difference. Now moving to a new building, she'll be next door to her customer-service staff.

For Discussion

1. What are Yogesh Gupta and Kathleen Murphy doing to reduce the "noise" in their communications? Discuss.

2. Which of the nine personal barriers to communication are being addressed by Gupta and Murphy? Explain your rationale.

3. How might Gupta and Murphy use the tools of information technology to enhance their communication effectiveness? Discuss.

4. What does this case teach you about effective communication? Explain.

Source: Excerpted from Carol Hymowitz, "Sometimes, Moving Up Makes It Harder to See What Goes on Below," *The Wall Street Journal*, October 15, 2007, p. B1. Copyright © 2007 by Dow Jones & Company, Inc. Reproduced with permission of Dow Jones & Company, Inc. via Copyright Clearance Center.

Self-Assessment

What Is Your Most Comfortable Learning Style?

Objectives

1. To learn about your visual, auditory, and kinesthetic learning/communication style.

2. To consider how knowledge about learning/communication styles can be used to enhance your communication effectiveness.

Introduction

The purpose of this exercise is to find out what your most prominent learning style is—that is, what forms of communication can you best learn from. You should find the information of value for understanding not only your own style but those of others. Knowing your own style should also allow you to be a much more effective learner.

Instructions

Read the following 36 statements and indicate the extent to which each statement is consistent with your behavior by using the following rating scale: 1 = almost never applies; 2 = applies once in a while; 3 = sometimes applies; 4 = often applies; 5 = almost always applies.

1. I take lots of notes.	1 2 3 4 5
2. When talking to others, I have the hardest time handling those who do not maintain good eye contact with me.	1 2 3 4 5
3. I make lists and notes because I remember things better when I write them down.	1 2 3 4 5
4. When reading a novel, I pay a lot of attention to passages picturing the clothing, scenery, setting, etc.	1 2 3 4 5
5. I need to write down directions so that I can remember them.	1 2 3 4 5
6. I need to see the person I am talking to in order to keep my attention focused on the subject.	1 2 3 4 5
7. When meeting a person for the first time, I initially notice the style of dress, visual characteristics, and neatness.	1 2 3 4 5
8. When I am at a party, one of the things I love to do is stand back and "people watch."	1 2 3 4 5
9. When recalling information, I can see it in my mind and remember where I saw it.	1 2 3 4 5
10. If I had to explain a new procedure or technique, I would prefer to write it out.	1 2 3 4 5
11. With free time I am most likely to watch television or read.	1 2 3 4 5
12. If my boss has a message for me, I am most comfortable when he or she sends a memo.	1 2 3 4 5
Total A (the minimum is 12 and the maximum is 60)	_____

1. When I read, I read out loud or move my lips to hear the words in my head.	1 2 3 4 5
2. When talking to someone else, I have the hardest time handling those who do not talk back with me.	1 2 3 4 5
3. I do not take a lot of notes, but I still remember what was said. Taking notes distracts me from the speaker.	1 2 3 4 5
4. When reading a novel, I pay a lot of attention to passages involving conversations.	1 2 3 4 5
5. I like to talk to myself when solving a problem or writing.	1 2 3 4 5

6. I can understand what a speaker says, even if I am not
   focused on the speaker.　　　　　　　　　　1　2　3　4　5

7. I remember things easier by repeating them again and again.　　1　2　3　4　5

8. When I am at a party, one of the things I love to do is
   have in-depth conversations about a subject that
   is important to me.　　　　　　　　　　　1　2　3　4　5

9. I would rather receive information from the radio
   than a newspaper.　　　　　　　　　　　1　2　3　4　5

10. If I had to explain a new procedure or technique,
    I would prefer telling about it.　　　　　　　1　2　3　4　5

11. With free time I am most likely to listen to music.　　1　2　3　4　5

12. If my boss has a message for me, I am most comfortable
    when he or she calls on the phone.　　　　　1　2　3　4　5

Total B (the minimum is 12 and the maximum is 60)　　_____

1. I am not good at reading or listening to directions.　　1　2　3　4　5

2. When talking to someone else, I have the hardest time handling
   those who do not show any kind of emotional support.　1　2　3　4　5

3. I take notes and doodle, but I rarely go back and look at them.　1　2　3　4　5

4. When reading a novel, I pay a lot of attention to passages
   revealing feelings, moods, action, drama, etc.　　　1　2　3　4　5

5. When I am reading, I move my lips.　　　　　　1　2　3　4　5

6. I will exchange words and places and use my hands a lot when
   I can't remember the right thing to say.　　　　1　2　3　4　5

7. My desk appears disorganized.　　　　　　　1　2　3　4　5

8. When I am at a party, one of the things I love to do is enjoy
   activities, such as dancing, games, and totally losing myself.　1　2　3　4　5

9. I like to move around. I feel trapped when seated at
   a meeting or desk.　　　　　　　　　　　1　2　3　4　5

10. If I had to explain a new procedure or technique, I would prefer
    actually demonstrating it.　　　　　　　　　1　2　3　4　5

11. With free time, I am most likely to exercise.　　　1　2　3　4　5

12. If my boss has a message for me, I am most comfortable when
    he or she talks to me in person.　　　　　　　1　2　3　4　5

Total C (the minimum is 12 and the maximum is 60)　　_____

Scoring & Interpretation

Total A is your Visual Score _____; Total B is your Auditory Score _____; and Total C is your Kinesthetic Score _____. The area in which you have your highest score represents your "dominant" learning style. You can learn from all three, but typically you learn best using one style. Communication effectiveness is increased when your dominant style is consistent with the communication style used by others. For example, if you are primarily kinesthetic and your boss gives you directions orally, you may have trouble communicating because you do not learn or process communication well by just being told something. You must consider not only how you communicate but also how the people you work with communicate.

Questions for Discussion

1. Do you agree with the assessment? Why or why not? Explain.

2. How valuable is it to know your learning style? Does it help explain why you did well in some learning situations and poorly in others? Describe and explain.

3. How important is it to know the learning style of those you work with? Explain.

Source: www.nwlink.com/~donclark/hrd/vak.html. Used by permission.

Ethical Dilemma

Should People Making False Statements in Blogs Be Prosecuted?

It bills itself as the world's "most prestigious college discussion board," giving a glimpse into law school admissions policies, post-graduate social networking, and the hiring practices of major law firms.

But the AutoAdmit site, widely used by law students for information on schools and firms, is also known as a venue for racist and sexist remarks and career-damaging rumors.

Now it's at the heart of a defamation lawsuit that legal experts say could test the anonymity of the Internet.

After facing lewd comments and threats by posters, two women at Yale Law School filed a suit on June 8 [2007] in U.S. District Court in New Haven, Connecticut, that includes subpoenas for 28 anonymous users of the site, which has generated more than 7 million posts since 2004.

According to court documents, a user on the site named "STANFORDtrol" began a thread in 2005 seeking to warn Yale students about one of the women in the suit, entitled "Stupid Bitch to Enter Yale Law." Another threatened to rape and sodomize her, the documents said.

The plaintiff, a respected Stanford University graduate identified only as "Doe I" in the lawsuit, learned of the Internet attack in the summer of 2005 before moving to Yale in Connecticut. The posts gradually became more menacing.

Some posts made false claims about her academic record and urged users to warn law firms, or accused her of bribing Yale officials to gain admission and of forming a lesbian relationship with a Yale administrator, the court papers said.

The plaintiff said she believes the harassing remarks, which lasted nearly two years, cost her an important summer internship. After interviewing with 16 firms, she received only four call-backs and ultimately had zero offers—a result considered unusual given her qualifications.

Another woman, identified as Doe II, endured similar attacks. The two, who say they suffered substantial "psychological and economic injury," also sued a former manager of the site because he refused to remove disparaging messages. The manager had cited free-speech protections.

Solving the Dilemma

What is your opinion about the issue of false, negative blogs?

1. The U.S. Constitution allows free speech, and people should be allowed to say whatever they want. Further, it is normal for people to have different perceptions about others. As such, it does not seem fair to prosecute someone who has a unique, negative perception about someone else.

2. The reputations of these two women were damaged by malicious, negative statements that were untrue. The individuals posting these statements should be punished, but not the AutoAdmit site. The site cannot police the accuracy of posted blogs.

3. Both the individuals making the malicious, negative statements and the blog site—AutoAdmit—should be punished. AutoAdmit should be held accountable because the women asked management of the site to remove untrue posts.

4. Invent other options.

chapter 16

Control & Quality Control Improvement

Techniques for Enhancing Organizational Effectiveness

Improving Productivity: Going Beyond Control Techniques to Get the Best Results

How, as a manager, can you increase productivity—get better results with what you have to work with?

In this chapter we discuss control techniques for achieving better results. What are other ways for improving productivity? Following are some suggestions:[1]

- **Establish base points, set goals, and measure results.** To be able to tell whether your work unit is becoming more productive, you need to establish systems of measurement. You can start by establishing the base point, such as the number of customers served per day, quantity of products produced per hour, and the like. You can then set goals to establish new levels that you wish to attain, and institute systems of measurement with which to ascertain progress. Finally, you can measure the results and modify the goals or work processes as necessary.

- **Use new technology.** Clearly, this is a favorite way to enhance productivity. With a word processor, you can produce more typed pages than you can with a typewriter. With a computerized database, you can store and manipulate information better than you can using a box of file cards. Still, computerization is not a panacea; information technology also offers plenty of opportunities for simply wasting time.

- **Improve match between employees and jobs.** You can take steps to ensure the best fit between employees and their jobs, including improving employee selection, paying attention to training, redesigning jobs, and providing financial incentives that are tied to performance.

- **Encourage employee involvement and innovation.** Companies improve productivity by funding research and development (R&D) departments. As a manager, you can encourage your employees, who are closest to the work process, to come up with suggestions for improving their own operations. And, of course, you can give workers a bigger say in doing their jobs, allow employee flextime, and reward people for learning new skills and taking on additional responsibility.

- **Encourage employee diversity.** By hiring people who are diverse in gender, age, race, and ethnicity, you're more likely to have a workforce with different experience, outlooks, values, and skills. By melding their differences, a team can achieve results that exceed the previous standards.

- **Redesign the work process.** Some managers think productivity can be enhanced through cost cutting, but this is not always the case. It may be that the work process can be redesigned to eliminate inessential steps.

For Discussion Some observers think the pressure on managers to perform will be even more intense than before, because the world is undergoing a transformation on the scale of the industrial revolution 200 years ago as we move farther into an information-based economy.[2] In what ways do you think you'll have to become a champion of adaptation?

---

forecast **What's Ahead in This Chapter**

This final chapter explores the final management function—control. Controlling is monitoring performance, comparing it with goals, and taking corrective action as needed. In the first section, we discuss managing for *productivity*, defining what it is and explaining why it's important. We then discuss *controlling*, identify six reasons it's needed, explain the steps in the control process, and describe three types of control managers use. Next we discuss levels and areas of control. In the fifth section, we discuss financial tools for control—budgets, financial statements, ratio analysis, and audits. We then discuss total quality management (TQM), identifying its core philosophies and showing some TQM techniques. We conclude the chapter by describing the four keys to successful control and five barriers to successful control.

major question?

How do managers influence productivity?

THE BIG PICTURE

The purpose of a manager is to make decisions about the four management functions—planning, organizing, leading, and controlling—to get people to achieve productivity and realize results. Productivity is defined by the formula of outputs divided by inputs for a specified period of time. Productivity is important because it determines whether the organization will make a profit or even survive.

In Chapter 1, we pointed out that as a manager in the 21st century you will operate in a complex environment in which you will need to deal with seven challenges—managing for (1) competitive advantage, (2) diversity, (3) globalization, (4) information technology, (5) ethical standards, (6) sustainability, and (7) your own happiness and life goals.

Within this dynamic world, you will draw on the practical and theoretical knowledge described in this book to make decisions about the four management functions of planning, organizing, leading, and controlling.

The purpose is to get the people reporting to you *to achieve productivity and realize results*.

This process is diagrammed below, pulling together the main topics of this book. *(See Figure 16.1.)*

figure 16.1

MANAGING FOR PRODUCTIVITY AND RESULTS

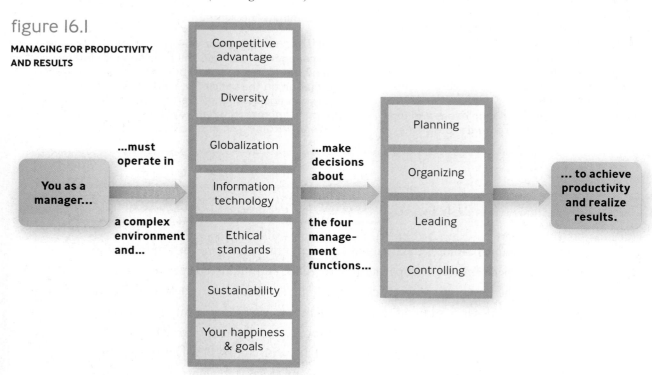

What Is Productivity?

Productivity can be applied at any level, whether for you as an individual, for the work unit you're managing, or for the organization you work for. Productivity is defined by the formula of *outputs divided by inputs* for a specified period of time.

Outputs are all the goods and services produced. Inputs are not only labor but also capital, materials, and energy. That is,

$$\text{productivity} = \frac{\text{outputs}}{\text{inputs}} \quad \text{or} \quad \frac{\text{goods + services}}{\text{labor + capital + materials + energy}}$$

What does this mean to you as a manager? It means that you can increase overall productivity by making substitutions or increasing the efficiency of any one element: labor, capital, materials, energy. For instance, you can increase the efficiency of labor by substituting capital in the form of equipment or machinery, as in employing a backhoe instead of laborers with shovels to dig a hole.[3] Or you can increase the efficiency of materials inputs by expanding their uses, as when lumber mills discovered they could sell not only boards but also sawdust and wood chips for use in gardens. Or you can increase the efficiency of energy by putting solar panels on a factory roof so the organization won't have to buy so much electrical power from utility companies.

Why Increasing Productivity Is Important

"For a company and for a nation," said former General Electric CEO Jack Welch, "productivity is a matter of survival."[4]

Productivity is important to companies because ultimately it determines whether the organization will make a profit or even survive. But the productivity of the nation is important to us individually and collectively. The more goods and services that are produced and made easily available to us and for export, the higher our standard of living.

The U.S. Productivity Track Record During the 1960s, productivity in the United States averaged a hefty 2.9% a year, then sank to a disappointing 1.5% right up until 1995. Because the decline in productivity no longer allowed the improvement in wages and living standards that had benefited so many Americans in the 1960s, millions of people took second jobs or worked longer hours to keep from falling behind. From 1995 to 2000, however, during the longest economic boom in American history, the productivity rate jumped to 2.5% annually, as the total output of goods and services rose faster than the total hours needed to produce them. From the business cycle peak in the first quarter of 2001 to the end of 2007, productivity grew at an annual rate of 2.7%.[5] Then came the recession year 2008, when it fell to 2%. The next year, however, it rose to a spectacular 3.7%—the fastest annual increase in seven years.[6] (A problem in calculating productivity is that only worker hours in the United States are counted, even though many American-owned enterprises have moved overseas, and foreign workers have contributed significantly to final products.)[7]

The Role of Information Technology Most economists seem to think the recent productivity growth is the result of organizations' huge investment in information technology—computers, the Internet, other telecommunications advances, and computer-guided production line improvements.[8] From 1995 to 2001, for example, labor productivity in services grew at a 2.6% rate (outpacing the 2.3% for goods-producing sectors), the result, economists think, of information technology.[9] In particular, many companies have implemented *enterprise resource planning (ERP)* **software systems, information systems for integrating virtually all aspects of a business,** helping managers stay on top of the latest developments.

Maintaining productivity depends on *control.* Let's look at this. ●

Competing internationally for productivity. This oil tanker represents the continual competition among companies and among nations to achieve productivity—"a matter of survival," as GE's Jack Welch put it. Is the United States doing everything it could to be more productive? What about taking measures to reduce dependence on foreign oil?

major question Why is control such an important managerial function?

THE BIG PICTURE
Controlling is monitoring performance, comparing it with goals, and taking corrective action. This section describes six reasons why control is needed and four steps in the control process.

Control is making something happen the way it was planned to happen. ***Controlling*** **is defined as monitoring performance, comparing it with goals, and taking corrective action as needed.** Controlling is the fourth management function, along with planning, organizing, and leading, and its purpose is plain: to make sure that performance meets objectives.

- **Planning** is setting goals and deciding how to achieve them.
- **Organizing** is arranging tasks, people, and other resources to accomplish the work.
- **Leading** is motivating people to work hard to achieve the organization's goals.
- **Controlling** is concerned with seeing that the right things happen at the right time in the right way.

All these functions affect one another and in turn affect an organization's productivity. *(See Figure 16.2.)*

figure 16.2

CONTROLLING FOR PRODUCTIVITY

What you as a manager do to get things done, with controlling shown in relation to the three other management functions. (These are not lockstep; all four functions happen concurrently.)

Why Is Control Needed?

There are six reasons why control is needed.

I. To Adapt to Change & Uncertainty Markets shift. Consumer tastes change. New competitors appear. Technologies are reborn. New materials are invented. Government regulations are altered. All organizations must deal with these kinds of environmental changes and uncertainties. Control systems can help managers anticipate, monitor, and react to these changes.[10]

Example: As is certainly apparent by now, the issue of global warming has created a lot of change and uncertainty for many industries. The restaurant industry in particular is feeling the pressure to become "greener," since restaurants are the retail world's largest energy users, with a restaurant using five times more energy per square foot than any other type of commercial building, according to Pacific Gas & Electric's Food Service Technology Center.[11] Nearly 80% of what commercial food service spends annually for energy use is lost in inefficient food cooking, holding, and storage. In addition, a typical restaurant generates 100,000 pounds of garbage per location per year. Thus, restaurants are being asked to reduce their "carbon footprints" by instituting tighter controls on energy use.

2. To Discover Irregularities & Errors

Small problems can mushroom into big ones. Cost overruns, manufacturing defects, employee turnover, bookkeeping errors, and customer dissatisfaction are all matters that may be tolerable in the short run. But in the long run, they can bring about even the downfall of an organization.

Example: You might not even miss a dollar a month looted from your credit card account. But an Internet hacker who does this with thousands of customers can undermine the confidence of consumers using their credit cards to charge online purchases at Amazon.com, Priceline.com, and other Web retailers. Thus, a computer program that monitors Internet charge accounts for small, unexplained deductions can be a valuable control strategy.

3. To Reduce Costs, Increase Productivity, or Add Value

Control systems can reduce labor costs, eliminate waste, increase output, and increase product delivery cycles. In addition, controls can help add value to a product so that customers will be more inclined to choose them over rival products.

Example: As we have discussed early in the book (and will again in this chapter), the use of quality controls among Japanese car manufacturers resulted in cars being produced that were perceived as being better built than American cars.

4. To Detect Opportunities

Hot-selling products. Competitive prices on materials. Changing population trends. New overseas markets. Controls can help alert managers to opportunities that might have otherwise gone unnoticed.

Example: A markdown on certain grocery-store items may result in a rush of customer demand for those products, signaling store management that similar items might also sell faster if they were reduced in price.

5. To Deal with Complexity

Does the right hand know what the left hand is doing? When a company becomes larger or when it merges with another company, it may find it has several product lines, materials-purchasing policies, customer bases, even workers from different cultures. Controls help managers coordinate these various elements.

Example: In recent years, Macy's Inc. has twice had to deal with complexity. In 2006, it pulled together several chains with different names—Marshall Field's, Robinsons-May, Kaufmann's, and other local stores—into one chain with one name, Macy's, and a much-promoted national strategy. But after losing money in 2007, CEO Terry Lundgren began altering course from a one-size-fits-all nationwide approach to a strategy that tailors the merchandise in local stores to cater to local tastes.[12]

6. To Decentralize Decision Making & Facilitate Teamwork

Controls allow top management to decentralize decision making at lower levels within the organization and to encourage employees to work together in teams.

Example: At General Motors, former chairman Alfred Sloan set the level of return on investment he expected his divisions to achieve, enabling him to push decision-making authority down to lower levels while still maintaining authority over the sprawling GM organization.[13] Later GM used controls to facilitate the team approach in its joint venture with Toyota at its California plant.

The six reasons are summarized below. *(See Figure 16.3.)*

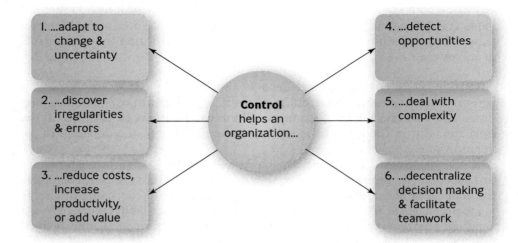

figure 16.3

SIX REASONS WHY CONTROL IS NEEDED

1. ...adapt to change & uncertainty

2. ...discover irregularities & errors

3. ...reduce costs, increase productivity, or add value

Control helps an organization...

4. ...detect opportunities

5. ...deal with complexity

6. ...decentralize decision making & facilitate teamwork

Steps in the Control Process

Control systems may be altered to fit specific situations, but generally they follow the same steps. The four *control process steps* **are (1) establish standards; (2) measure performance; (3) compare performance to standards; and (4) take corrective action, if necessary.** *(See Figure 16.4.)*

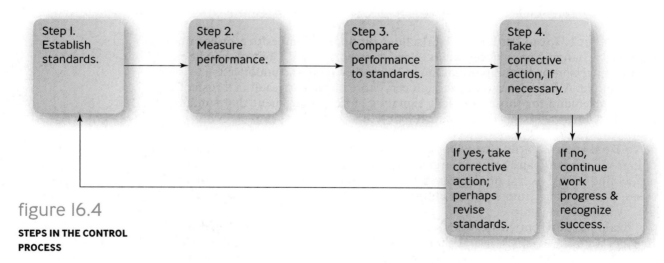

Step 1. Establish standards.

Step 2. Measure performance.

Step 3. Compare performance to standards.

Step 4. Take corrective action, if necessary.

If yes, take corrective action; perhaps revise standards.

If no, continue work progress & recognize success.

figure 16.4

STEPS IN THE CONTROL PROCESS

Let's consider these four steps.

1. Establish Standards: "What Is the Outcome We Want?" A *control standard,* or *performance standard* or simply *standard,* **is the desired performance level for a given goal.** Standards may be narrow or broad, and they can be set for almost anything, although they are best measured when they can be made quantifiable.

Nonprofit institutions might have standards for level of charitable contributions, number of students retained, or degree of legal compliance. For-profit organizations might have standards of financial performance, employee hiring, manufacturing defects, percentage increase in market share, percentage reduction in costs, number of customer complaints, and return on investment. More subjective standards, such as level of employee morale, can also be set, although they may have to be expressed more quantifiably as reduced absenteeism and sick days and increased job applications.

One technique for establishing standards is to use *the balanced scorecard,* as we explain later in this chapter.

2. Measure Performance: "What Is the Actual Outcome We Got?" The second step in the control process is to measure performance, such as by number of products sold, units produced, or cost per item sold. For example, Hyundai has a quality goal signified by GQ 3-3-5-5. The goal represents the company's desire to finish in the top three in quality ratings provided by J.D. Power's dependability survey within three years, and to be among the top five quality automakers within five years.[14]

Performance measures are usually obtained from three sources: (1) written reports, including computerized printouts; (2) oral reports, as in a salesperson's weekly recitation of accomplishments to the sales manager; and (3) personal observation, as when a manager takes a stroll of the factory floor to see what employees are doing.

As we've hinted, measurement techniques can vary for different industries, as for manufacturing industries versus service industries. We discuss this further later in the chapter.

3. Compare Performance to Standards: "How Do the Desired & Actual Outcomes Differ?" The third step in the control process is to compare measured performance against the standards established. Most managers are delighted with performance that exceeds standards, which becomes an occasion for handing out bonuses, promotions, and perhaps offices with a view. For performance that is below standards, they need to ask: Is the deviation from performance significant? The greater the difference between desired and actual performance, the greater the need for action.

How much deviation is acceptable? That depends on *the range of variation* built in to the standards in step 1. In voting for political candidates, for instance, there is supposed to be no range of variation; as the expression goes, "every vote counts" (although the 2000 U.S. presidential election was an eye-opener for many people in this regard). In political polling, however, a range of 3%–4% error is considered an acceptable range of variation. In machining parts for the spacecraft *Orion* (NASA's scheduled 2015 successor to the space shuttle), the range of variation may be a good deal less tolerant than when machining parts for a power lawnmower.

The range of variation is often incorporated in computer systems into a principle called management by exception. **Management by exception is a control principle that states that managers should be informed of a situation only if data show a significant deviation from standards.**

4. Take Corrective Action, If Necessary: "What Changes Should We Make to Obtain Desirable Outcomes?" There are three possibilities here: (1) Make no changes. (2) Recognize and reinforce positive performance. (3) Take action to correct negative performance.

When performance meets or exceeds the standards set, managers should give rewards, ranging from giving a verbal "Job well done" to more substantial payoffs such as raises, bonuses, and promotions to reinforce good behavior.

When performance falls significantly short of the standard, managers should carefully examine the reasons why and take the appropriate action. Sometimes it may turn out the standards themselves were unrealistic, owing to changing conditions, in which case the standards need to be altered. Sometimes it may become apparent that employees haven't been given the resources for achieving the standards. And sometimes the employees may need more attention from management as a way of signaling that they have been insufficient in fulfilling their part of the job bargain. ●

Example

Steps in the Control Process: What's Expected of UPS Drivers?

UPS, which employs 99,000 U.S. drivers, has established Integrad, an 11,500-square-foot training center 10 miles outside Washington, D.C. There trainees practice UPS-prescribed "340 Methods" shown to save seconds and improve safety. Graduates of the training, who are generally former package sorters, are eligible to do a job that pays an average of $74,000 annually.[15]

Establishing Standards. UPS establishes certain standards for its drivers that set projections for the number of miles driven, deliveries, and pickups. For instance, drivers are taught to walk at a "brisk pace" of 2.5 paces per second, except under icy or other unsafe conditions. However, because conditions vary depending on whether routes are urban, suburban, or rural, standards vary for different routes.[16]

Measuring Performance. Every day, UPS managers look at a computer printout showing the miles, deliveries, and pickups a driver attained during his or her shift the previous day. In general, drivers are expected to make five deliveries in 19 minutes.

Comparing Performance to Standards. UPS managers compare the printout of a driver's performance (miles driven and number of pickups and deliveries) with the standards that were set for his or her particular route. For instance, the printout will show whether drivers took longer than the 15.5 seconds allowed to park a truck and retrieve one package from the cargo. A range of variation may be allowed to take into account such matters as winter or summer driving or traffic conditions that slow productivity.

Taking Corrective Action. When a UPS driver fails to perform according to the standards set for him or her, a supervisor then rides along and gives suggestions for improvement. If drivers are unable to improve, they are warned, then suspended, and then dismissed.

YOUR CALL

The UPS controls were devised by industrial engineers based on experience. Do you think the same kinds of controls could be established for, say, filling out tax forms for H&R Block?

Small business. How important is it for small businesses to implement all four steps of the control process? Do you think that employees in small companies—such as a restaurant—typically have more or less independence from managerial control than those in large companies do?

16.3 LEVELS & AREAS OF CONTROL

How do successful companies implement controls?

THE BIG PICTURE

This section describes three levels of control—strategic, tactical, and operational—and six areas of control: physical, human, informational, financial, structural (bureaucratic and decentralized), and cultural.

How are you going to apply the steps of control to your own management area? Let's look at this in three ways: First, you need to consider the *level* of management at which you operate—top, middle, or first level. Second, you need to consider the *areas* that you draw on for resources—physical, human, information, and/or financial. Finally, you need to consider the *style* or control philosophy—bureaucratic, market, or clan, as we will explain.

Levels of Control: Strategic, Tactical, & Operational

There are three levels of control, which correspond to the three principal managerial levels: *strategic* planning by top managers, *tactical* planning by middle managers, and *operational* planning by first-line (supervisory) managers.

I. Strategic Control by Top Managers   *Strategic control* **is monitoring performance to ensure that strategic plans are being implemented and taking corrective action as needed.** Strategic control is mainly performed by top managers, those at the CEO and VP levels, who have an organization-wide perspective. Monitoring is accomplished by reports issued every 3, 6, 12, or more months, although more frequent reports may be requested if the organization is operating in an uncertain environment.

2. Tactical Control by Middle Managers   *Tactical control* **is monitoring performance to ensure that tactical plans—those at the divisional or departmental level—are being implemented and taking corrective action as needed.** Tactical control is done mainly by middle managers, those with such titles as "division head," "plant manager," and "branch sales manager." Reporting is done on a weekly or monthly basis.

3. Operational Control by First-Level Managers   *Operational control* **is monitoring performance to ensure that operational plans—day-to-day goals—are being implemented and taking corrective action as needed.** Operational control is done mainly by first-level managers, those with titles such as "department head," "team leader," or "supervisor." Reporting is done on a daily basis.

Considerable interaction occurs among the three levels, with lower-level managers providing information upward and upper-level managers checking on some of the more critical aspects of plan implementation below them.

Six Areas of Control

The six areas of organizational control are *physical, human, informational, financial, structural,* and *cultural.*

I. Physical Area   The physical area includes buildings, equipment, and tangible products. Examples: There are equipment controls to monitor the use of computers, cars, and other machinery. There are inventory-management controls to keep track of how many products are in stock, how many will be needed, and what their delivery dates are from suppliers. There are quality controls to make sure that products are being built according to certain acceptable standards.

2. Human Resources Area The controls used to monitor employees include personality tests and drug testing for hiring, performance tests during training, performance evaluations to measure work productivity, and employee surveys to assess job satisfaction and leadership.

3. Informational Area Production schedules. Sales forecasts. Environmental impact statements. Analyses of competition. Public relations briefings. All these are controls on an organization's various information resources.

4. Financial Area Are bills being paid on time? How much money is owed by customers? How much money is owed to suppliers? Is there enough cash on hand to meet payroll obligations? What are the debt-repayment schedules? What is the advertising budget? Clearly, the organization's financial controls are important because they can affect the preceding three areas.

5. Structural Area How is the organization arranged from a hierarchical or structural standpoint?[17] Two examples are *bureaucratic control* and *decentralized control*.

- *Bureaucratic control* **is an approach to organizational control that is characterized by use of rules, regulations, and formal authority to guide performance.** This form of control attempts to elicit employee compliance, using strict rules, a rigid hierarchy, well-defined job descriptions, and administrative mechanisms such as budgets, performance appraisals, and compensation schemes (external rewards to get results). The foremost example of use of bureaucratic control is perhaps the traditional military organization.

  Bureaucratic control works well in organizations in which the tasks are explicit and certain. While rigid, it can be an effective means of ensuring that performance standards are being met. However, it may not be effective if people are looking for ways to stay out of trouble by simply following the rules, or if they try to beat the system by manipulating performance reports, or if they try to actively resist bureaucratic constraints.

- *Decentralized control* **is an approach to organizational control that is characterized by informal and organic structural arrangements,** the opposite of bureaucratic control. This form of control aims to get increased employee commitment, using the corporate culture, group norms, and workers taking responsibility for their performance. Decentralized control is found in companies with a relatively flat organization.

Bureaucratic control. In businesses such as large railroads, tasks are explicit and certain, and employees are expected to perform them the same way each time. However, a small railroad, such as one line serving tourists, need not be bureaucratic.

6. Cultural Area The cultural area is an informal method of control. It influences the work process and levels of performance through the set of norms that develop as a result of the values and beliefs that constitute an organization's culture. If an organization's culture values innovation and collaboration, then employees are likely to be evaluated on the basis of how much they engage in collaborative activities and enhance or create new products.

Example: The biotechnology company Genentech, which appears every year on *Fortune's* list of "100 Best Companies to Work For" (no. 16 in 2010, no. 5 in 2008, no. 1 in 2006), is a good example of an organization that promotes, measures, and rewards employee motivation. For instance, all scientists and engineers are encouraged to spend 20% of their workweek on pet projects. Genentech's tremendous revenue growth over the last decade is clearly driven by a set of cultural values, norms, and internal processes that reinforce creativity.[18] ●

16.4 THE BALANCED SCORECARD, STRATEGY MAPS, & MEASUREMENT MANAGEMENT

major question?

How can three techniques—balanced scorecard, strategy maps, and measurement management—help me establish standards and measure performance?

THE BIG PICTURE
To establish standards, managers often use the balanced scorecard, which provides four indicators for progress. A visual representation of the balanced scorecard is the strategy map. Measurement management techniques help managers make evidence-based judgments about performance.

Wouldn't you, as a top manager, like to have displayed in easy-to-read graphics all the information on sales, orders, and the like assembled from data pulled in real-time from corporate software? The technology exists and it has a name: a *dashboard,* like the instrument panel in a car.

"The dashboard puts me and more and more of our executives in real-time touch with the business," says Ivan Seidenberg, CEO at Verizon Communications. "The more eyes that see the results we're obtaining every day, the higher the quality of the decisions we can make."[19]

Throughout this book we have stressed the importance of *evidence-based management*—the use of real-world data rather than fads and hunches in making management decisions. When properly done, the dashboard is an example of the important tools that make this kind of management possible. Others are the *balanced scorecard, strategy maps,* and *measurement management,* techniques that even new managers will find useful.

The Balanced Scorecard: A Dashboard-like View of the Organization

Robert Kaplan is a professor of accounting at the Harvard Business School. David Norton is founder and president of Renaissance Strategy Group, a Massachusetts consulting firm. Kaplan and Norton developed what they call the **balanced scorecard, which gives top managers a fast but comprehensive view of the organization via four indicators: (1) customer satisfaction, (2) internal processes, (3) innovation and improvement activities, and (4) financial measures.**

"Think of the balanced scorecard as the dials and indicators in an airplane cockpit," write Kaplan and Norton. For a pilot, "reliance on one instrument can be fatal. Similarly, the complexity of managing an organization today requires that managers be able to view performance in several areas simultaneously."[20] It is not enough, say Kaplan and Norton, to simply measure financial performance, such as sales figures and return on investment. Operational matters, such as customer satisfaction, are equally important.[21]

The Balanced Scorecard: Four "Perspectives" The balanced scorecard establishes (a) *goals* and (b) *performance measures* according to four "perspectives" or areas—*financial, customer, internal business,* and *innovation and learning.* (See Figure 16.5, next page.)

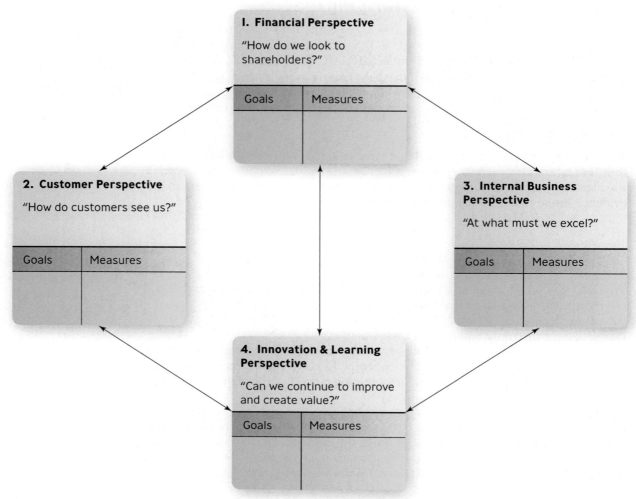

figure 16.5

THE BALANCED SCORECARD: FOUR PERSPECTIVES

1. Financial Perspective: "How Do We Look to Shareholders?" Typical financial goals have to do with profitability, growth, and shareholder values. Financial measures such as quarterly sales have been criticized as being short-sighted and not reflecting contemporary value-creating activities. Moreover, critics say that traditional financial measures don't improve customer satisfaction, quality, or employee motivation.

However, making improvements in just the other three operational "perspectives" we will discuss won't *necessarily* translate into financial success. Kaplan and Norton mention the case of an electronics company that made considerable improvements in manufacturing capabilities that did not result in increased profitability.

The hard truth is that "if improved [operational] performance fails to be reflected in the bottom line, executives should reexamine the basic assumptions of their strategy and mission," say Kaplan and Norton. "Not all long-term strategies are profitable strategies. . . . A failure to convert improved operational performance, as measured in the scorecard, into improved financial performance should send executives back to their drawing boards to rethink the company's strategy or its implementation plans."[22]

2. Customer Perspective: "How Do Customers See Us?" Many organizations make taking care of the customer a high priority. The balanced scorecard translates the mission of customer service into specific measures of concerns that really matter to customers—time between placing an order and taking delivery, quality in terms of defect level, satisfaction with products and service, and cost.

Quiznos is a good example. The company uses a speed-dining approach to develop new products and test out different pricing strategies. The company invites groups of 25 people to a location in which they move from station to station and try out new menu options. This technique has reduced the time from test kitchen to market to six months, as opposed to the one year needed by a key competitor.[23]

3. Internal Business Perspective: "At What Must We Excel?" This part translates what the company must do internally to meet its customers' expectations. These are business processes such as quality, employee skills, and productivity.

Top management's judgment about key internal processes must be linked to measures of employee actions at the lower levels, such as time to process customer orders, get materials from suppliers, produce products, and deliver them to customers. Computer information systems can help, for example, in identifying late deliveries, tracing the problem to a particular plant. (ERP systems, mentioned earlier, can aid this technological boost.)

4. Innovation & Learning Perspective: "Can We Continue to Improve & Create Value?" Learning and growth of employees is the foundation for innovation and creativity. Thus, the organization must create a culture that encourages rank-and-file employees to make suggestions and question the status quo and it must provide employees with the environment and resources needed to do their jobs. The company can use employee surveys and analysis of training data to measure the degree of learning and growth.

Strategy Map: Visual Representation of a Balanced Scorecard

Since they devised the balanced scorecard, Kaplan and Norton have come up with an improvement called the strategy map.[24] A **strategy map is a visual representation of the four perspectives of the balanced scorecard that enables managers to communicate their goals so that everyone in the company can understand how their jobs are linked to the overall objectives of the organization.** As Kaplan and Norton state, "Strategy maps show the cause-and-effect links by which specific improvements create desired outcomes," such as objectives for revenue growth, targeted customer markets, the role of excellence and innovation in products, and so on.

An example of a strategy map for a company such as Target is shown on the next page, with the goal of creating long-term value for the firm by increasing productivity growth and revenue growth. *(See Figure 16.6, next page.)* Measures and standards can be developed in each of the four operational areas—financial goals, customer goals, internal goals, and learning and growth goals—for the strategy.

Measurement Management: "Forget Magic"

"You simply can't manage anything you can't measure," said Richard Quinn, former–vice president of quality at the Sears Merchandising Group.[25]

Is this really true? Concepts such as the balanced scorecard seem like good ideas, but how well do they actually work? John Lingle and William Schiemann, principals in a New Jersey consulting firm specializing in strategic assessment, decided to find out.[26]

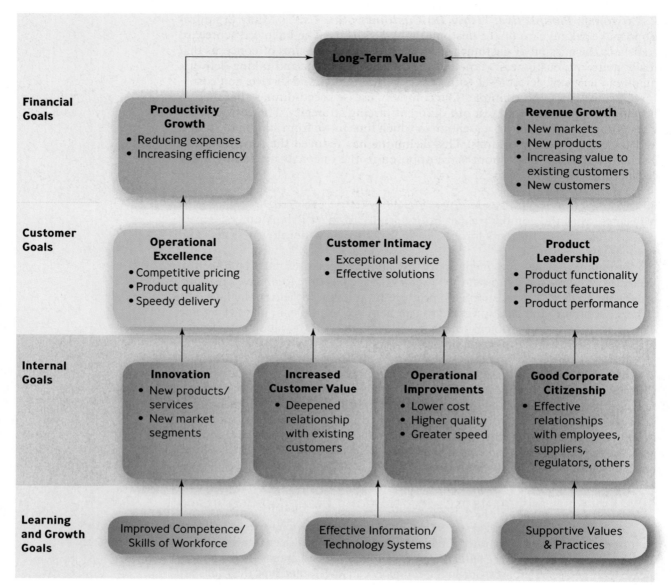

figure 16.6

THE STRATEGY MAP

This example might be used for a retail chain such as Target or Walmart.

Source: T. S. Bateman and S. A. Snell, *Management: Leading & Collaborating in a Competitive World,* 7th ed. (Burr Ridge. IL: McGraw-Hill/Irwin, 2007), Fig. 4.3, p. 124. Adapted from R. Kaplan and D. Norton, "Plotting Success with Strategy Maps," *Optimize,* February 2004, http://www.optimizemag.com/article/showArticle.jhtml?articleId=18200733 (accessed May 31, 2010); and R. S. Kaplan and D. P. Norton, "Having Trouble with Your Strategy? Then Map It," *Harvard Business Review,* September–October 2000, pp. 167–176.

In a survey of 203 executives in companies of varying size, they identified the organizations as being of two types: *measurement-managed* and *non-measurement-managed.* The measurement-managed companies were those in which senior management reportedly agreed on measurable criteria for determining strategic success, and management updated and reviewed semiannual performance measures in three or more of six primary performance areas. The six areas were financial performance, operating efficiency, customer satisfaction, employee performance, innovation/change, and community/environment.

The results: "A higher percentage of measurement-managed companies were identified as industry leaders," concluded Lingle and Schiemann, "as being financially in the top third of their industry, and as successfully managing their change effort." (The last indicator suggests that measurement-managed companies tend to anticipate the future and are likely to remain in a leadership position in a rapidly changing environment.) "Forget magic," they say. "Industry leaders we surveyed simply have a greater handle on the world around them."

Why Measurement-Managed Firms Succeed: Four Mechanisms of Success Why do measurement-managed companies outperform those that are less disciplined? The study's data point to four mechanisms that contribute to these companies' success:[27]

- **Top executives agree on strategy.** Most top executives in management-managed companies agreed on business strategy, whereas most of those in non-measurement-managed companies reported disagreement. Translating strategy into measurable objectives helps make them specific.

- **Communication is clear.** The clear message in turn is translated into good communication, which was characteristic of measurement-managed organizations and not of non-measurement-managed ones.

- **There is better focus and alignment.** Measurement-managed companies reported more frequently that unit (division or department) performance measures were linked to strategic company measures and that individual performance measures were linked to unit measures.

- **The organizational culture emphasizes teamwork and allows risk taking.** Managers in measurement-managed companies more frequently reported strong teamwork and cooperation among the management team and more willingness to take risks.

Four Barriers to Effective Measurement The four most frequent barriers to effective measurement, according to Lingle and Schiemann, are as follows:

- **Objectives are fuzzy.** Company objectives are often precise in the financial and operational areas but not in areas of customer satisfaction, employee performance, and rate of change. Managers need to work at making "soft" objectives measurable.

- **Managers put too much trust in informal feedback systems.** Managers tend to overrate feedback mechanisms such as customer complaints or sales-force criticisms about products. But these mechanisms aren't necessarily accurate.

- **Employees resist new measurement systems.** Employees want to see how well measures work before they are willing to tie their financial futures to them. Measurement-managed companies tend to involve the workforce in developing measures.

- **Companies focus too much on measuring activities instead of results.** Too much concern with measurement that is not tied to fine-tuning the organization or spurring it on to achieve results is wasted effort.

Are There Areas That Can't Be Measured? It's clear that some areas are easier to measure than others—manufacturing, for example, as opposed to services. We can understand how it is easier to measure the output of, say, a worker in a steel mill than that of a bellhop in a hotel or a professor in a classroom. Nevertheless, human resource professionals are trying to have a greater focus on employee productivity "metrics."[28] In establishing quantifiable goals for "hard to measure" jobs, managers should seek input from the employees involved, who are usually more familiar with the details of the jobs. ●

major question?

Financial performance is important to most organizations. What are the financial tools I need to know about?

THE BIG PICTURE

Financial controls are especially important. These include budgets, financial statements, ratio analysis, and audits.

Do you check your credit card statement line by line when it comes in? Or do you just look at the bottom-line amount owed and write a check?

Just as you should monitor your personal finances to ensure your survival and avoid catastrophe, so managers need to do likewise with an organization's finances. Whether your organization is for-profit or nonprofit, you need to be sure that revenues are covering costs.

There are a great many kinds of financial controls, but here let us look at the following: *budgets, financial statements, ratio analysis,* and *audits.* (Necessarily this is merely an overview of this topic. Financial controls are covered in detail in other business courses.)

Budgets: Formal Financial Projections

A *budget* **is a formal financial projection.** It states an organization's planned activities for a given period of time in quantitative terms, such as dollars, hours, or number of products. Budgets are prepared not only for the organization as a whole but also for the divisions and departments within it. The point of a budget is to provide a yardstick against which managers can measure performance and make comparisons (as with other departments or previous years).

Incremental Budgeting Managers can take essentially two budget-planning approaches. One of them, *zero-based budgeting (ZBB),* which forces each department to start from zero in projecting funding needs, is no longer favored. The other approach, the traditional form of budget, which is mainly used now, is incremental budgeting.

Incremental budgeting **allocates increased or decreased funds to a department by using the last budget period as a reference point; only incremental changes in the budget request are reviewed.** One difficulty is that incremental budgets tend

Passing fancy. The truck fleet represents a huge part of a beer distributor's capital expenditures budget. What types of data would be needed to justify expansion of this delivery system?

to lock departments into stable spending arrangements; they are not flexible in meeting environmental demands. Another difficulty is that a department may engage in many activities—some more important than others—but it's not easy to sort out how well managers performed at the various activities. Thus, the department activities and the yearly budget increases take on lives of their own.

Fixed versus Variable Budgets There are numerous kinds of budgets, and some examples are listed below. *(See Table 16.1.)* In general, however, budgets may be categorized as two types: *fixed* and *variable*.

table 16.1   EXAMPLES OF TYPES OF BUDGETS

Type of budget	Description
Cash or cashflow budget	Forecasts all sources of cash income and cash expenditures for daily, weekly, or monthly period.
Capital expenditures budget	Anticipates investments in major assets such as land, buildings, and major equipment.
Sales or revenue budget	Projects future sales, often by month, sales area, or product.
Expense budget	Projects expenses (costs) for given activity for given period.
Financial budget	Projects organization's source of cash and how it plans to spend it in the forthcoming period.
Operating budget	Projects what an organization will create in goods or services, what financial resources are needed, and what income is expected.
Nonmonetary budget	Deals with units other than dollars, such as hours of labor or office square footage.

- **Fixed budgets—where resources are allocated on a single estimate of costs.** Also known as a *static budget,* a ***fixed budget* allocates resources on the basis of a single estimate of costs.** That is, there is only one set of expenses; the budget does not allow for adjustment over time. For example, you might have a budget of $50,000 for buying equipment in a given year—no matter how much you may need equipment exceeding that amount.

- **Variable budgets—where resources are varied in proportion with various levels of activity.** Also known as a *flexible budget,* a ***variable budget* allows the allocation of resources to vary in proportion with various levels of activity.** That is, the budget can be adjusted over time to accommodate pertinent changes in the environment. For example, you might have a budget that allows you to hire temporary workers or lease temporary equipment if production exceeds certain levels.

Financial Statements: Summarizing the Organization's Financial Status

A *financial statement* **is a summary of some aspect of an organization's financial status.** The information contained in such a statement is essential in helping managers maintain financial control over the organization.

There are two basic types of financial statements: the *balance sheet* and the *income statement.*

The Balance Sheet: Picture of an Organization's Financial Worth for a Specific Point in Time
A *balance sheet* **summarizes an organization's overall financial worth—that is, assets and liabilities—at a specific point in time.**

Assets are the resources that an organization controls; they consist of current assets and fixed assets. *Current assets* are cash and other assets that are readily convertible to cash within 1 year's time. Examples are inventory, sales for which payment has not been received (accounts receivable), and U.S. Treasury bills or money market mutual funds. *Fixed assets* are property, buildings, equipment, and the like that have a useful life that exceeds 1 year but that are usually harder to convert to cash. *Liabilities* are claims, or debts, by suppliers, lenders, and other nonowners of the organization against a company's assets.

The Income Statement: Picture of an Organization's Financial Results for a Specified Period of Time
The balance sheet depicts the organization's overall financial worth at a specific point in time. By contrast, the *income statement* **summarizes an organization's financial results—revenues and expenses—over a specified period of time,** such as a quarter or a year.

Revenues are assets resulting from the sale of goods and services. *Expenses* are the costs required to produce those goods and services. The difference between revenues and expenses, called the *bottom line,* represents the profits or losses incurred over the specified period of time.

Ratio Analysis: Indicators of an Organization's Financial Health

The bottom line may be the most important indicator of an organization's financial health, but it isn't the only one. Managers often use *ratio analysis*—**the practice of evaluating financial ratios**—to determine an organization's financial health.

Among the types of financial ratios are those used to calculate liquidity, debt management, asset management, and return. *Liquidity ratios* indicate how easily an organization's assets can be converted into cash (made liquid). *Debt management* ratios indicate the degree to which an organization can meet its long-term financial obligations.

Asset management ratios indicate how effectively an organization is managing its assets, such as whether it has obsolete or excess inventory on hand. *Return ratios*—often called return on investment (ROI) or return on assets (ROA)—indicate how effective management is in generating a return, or profits, on its assets.

Audits: External versus Internal

When you think of auditors, do you think of grim-faced accountants looking through a company's books to catch embezzlers and other cheats? That's one function of auditing, but besides verifying the accuracy and fairness of financial

Accountants at the Academy Awards? No, these are the 2010 Oscar winners. Sandra Bullock was voted Best Actress for her role in *The Blind Side,* and Jeff Bridges was voted Best Actor for his role in *Crazy Heart.* But every year since 1929 the secret ballots for Oscar nominees voted on by members of the Academy of Motion Picture Arts and Sciences have been tabulated by accountants from the firm now known as PricewaterhouseCoopers. The accounting firm takes this event very seriously; secrecy is tight, and there is no loose gossip around the office water cooler. Two accountants tally the votes, stuff the winners' names in the envelopes—the ones that will be handed to award presenters during the Academy Awards—and then memorize the winners' names, just in case the envelopes don't make it to the show. Accounting is an important business because investors depend on independent auditors to verify that a company's finances are what they are purported to be.

statements it also is intended to be a tool for management decision making. *Audits* **are formal verifications of an organization's financial and operational systems.**

Audits are of two types—*external* and *internal.*

External Audits—Financial Appraisals by Outside Financial Experts

An *external audit* **is a formal verification of an organization's financial accounts and statements by outside experts.** The auditors are certified public accountants (CPAs) who work for an accounting firm (such as PricewaterhouseCoopers) that is independent of the organization being audited. Their task is to verify that the organization, in preparing its financial statements and in determining its assets and liabilities, followed generally accepted accounting principles.

Internal Audits—Financial Appraisals by Inside Financial Experts

An *internal audit* **is a verification of an organization's financial accounts and statements by the organization's own professional staff.** Their jobs are the same as those of outside experts—to verify the accuracy of the organization's records and operating activities. Internal audits also help uncover inefficiencies and thus help managers evaluate the performance of their control systems. ●

major question ?

How do top companies improve the quality of their products or services?

THE BIG PICTURE

Total quality management (TQM) is dedicated to continuous quality improvement, training, and customer satisfaction. Two core principles are people orientation and improvement orientation. Some techniques for improving quality are employee involvement, benchmarking, outsourcing, reduced cycle time, and statistical process control.

The Ritz-Carlton Hotel Co., LLC, a luxury chain of 70 hotels worldwide that is an independently operated division of Marriott International, puts a premium on doing things right. First-year managers and employees receive 250–310 hours of training. The president meets each employee at a new hotel to ensure he or she understands the Ritz-Carlton standards for service. The chain has also developed a database that records the preferences of more than 1 million customers, so that each hotel can anticipate guests' needs.[29]

Because of this diligence, the Ritz-Carlton has twice been the recipient (in 1992 and in 1999) of the Malcolm Baldrige National Quality Award. The award was created by Congress in 1987 to be the most prestigious recognition of quality in the United States and is given annually to U.S. organizations in manufacturing, service, small business, health care, education, and nonprofit fields.[30]

The Baldrige award is an outgrowth of the realization among U.S. managers in the early 1980s that three-fourths of Americans were telling survey takers that the label "Made in America" no longer represented excellence—that they considered products made overseas, especially Japan, equal or superior in quality to U.S.-made products. As we saw in Chapter 2, much of the impetus for quality improvements in Japanese products came from American consultants W. Edwards Deming and Joseph M. Juran, whose work led to the strategic commitment to quality known as total quality management.

Deming Management: The Contributions of W. Edwards Deming to Improved Quality

Prior to the 1950s, Frederick Taylor's scientific management philosophy, designed to maximize worker productivity, had been widely instituted. But by the 1950s, scientific management had led to organizations that were rigid and unresponsive to both employees and customers.

W. Edwards Deming's challenge, known as **Deming management,** proposed **ideas for making organizations more responsive, more democratic, and less wasteful.** These included the following principles:

I. Quality Should Be Aimed at the Needs of the Consumer "The consumer is the most important part of the production line," Deming wrote.[31] Thus, the efforts of individual workers in providing the product or service should be directed toward meeting the needs and expectations of the ultimate user.

2. Companies Should Aim at Improving the System, Not Blaming Workers Deming suggested that U.S. managers were more concerned with blaming problems on individual workers rather than on the organization's structure, culture, technology, work rules, and management—that is, "the system." By treating employees well, listening to their views and suggestions, Deming felt, managers could bring about improvements in products and services.

3. Improved Quality Leads to Increased Market Share, Increased Company Prospects, & Increased Employment When companies work to improve the quality of goods and services, they produce less waste, fewer delays, and are more efficient. Lower prices and superior quality lead to greater market share, which in turn leads to improved business prospects and consequently increased employment.

4. Quality Can Be Improved on the Basis of Hard Data, Using the PDCA Cycle Deming suggested that quality could be improved by acting on the basis of hard data. The process for doing this came to be known as the *PDCA cycle,* **a plan-do-check-act cycle using observed data for continuous improvement of operations.** *(See Figure 16.7.)*

figure 16.7

THE PDCA CYCLE: PLAN-DO-CHECK-ACT

The four steps continuously follow each other, resulting in continuous improvement.

① **PLAN** desired and important changes, based on observed data. Make pilot test, if necessary.

② **DO** implement the change or make a small-scale test.

③ **CHECK** or observe what happened after the change or during the test.

④ **ACT** on lessons learned, after study of results. Determine if predictions can be made as basis for new methods.

Source: From W. Edwards Deming, *Out of the Crisis,* figure, page 88; "Plan Do Check Act Cycle." Copyright © 2000 Massachusetts Institute of Technology, by permission of MIT Press.

Initiating a Quality Fix: Crown Audio Redesigns Its Production Line to Eliminate Defective Products

Crown Audio, maker of high-tech audio equipment, found that the market requirements for more complex products were clashing with the need to produce those products cheaply, putting pressure on manufacturing operations. Indeed, the number of defective products requiring rework had become a $4 million headache.

The solution: Crown Audio completely shut down its production so as not to generate any more rework, and then analyzed and tested all the flawed products. Components were apportioned into groups based on their common problems, and then examined for defect reduction strategies before being put back through the production process.

This exercise, says operations vice president Larry Coburn, also gave the company a pretty good handle on the parts of the process that needed changing. "When we started, we had months and sometimes close to a year of backlog that needed to be fixed and repaired," he says. "Now we are talking in terms of hours of rework in front of us."[32]

YOUR CALL

A major part of the quality-improvement process at Crown Audio was dealing with "employee engagement," empowering production employees by providing them with real-time data on which to base their decisions. Now different lines and shifts brag about their first-pass production successes to each other. "Morale is everything in quality," Coburn says. "People want to do a good job, and we have to enable that."

Do you think it's possible to raise employee morale and improve manufacturing quality without taking the drastic step of completely shutting down production lines to analyze every operation?

Core TQM Principles: Deliver Customer Value & Strive for Continuous Improvement

Total quality management (TQM) **is defined as a comprehensive approach—led by top management and supported throughout the organization—dedicated to continuous quality improvement, training, and customer satisfaction.**

In Chapter 2 we said there are four components to TQM:

1. Make continuous improvement a priority.
2. Get every employee involved.
3. Listen to and learn from customers and employees.
4. Use accurate standards to identify and eliminate problems.

These may be summarized as *two core principles of TQM*—namely, (1) *people orientation*—everyone involved with the organization should focus on delivering value to customers—and (2) *improvement orientation*—everyone should work on continuously improving the work processes.[33] Let's look at these further.

I. People Orientation—Focusing Everyone on Delivering Customer Value
Organizations adopting TQM value people as their most important resource—both those who create a product or service and those who receive it. Thus, not only are employees given more decision-making power, so are suppliers and customers.

This people orientation operates under the following assumptions.

- **Delivering customer value is most important.** The purpose of TQM is to focus people, resources, and work processes to deliver products or services that create value for customers.

- **People will focus on quality if given empowerment.** TQM assumes that employees (and often suppliers and customers) will concentrate on making quality improvements if given the decision-making power to do so. The reasoning here is that the people actually involved with the product or service are in the best position to detect opportunities for quality improvements.

- **TQM requires training, teamwork, and cross-functional efforts.** Employees and suppliers need to be well trained, and they must work in teams. Teamwork is considered important because many quality problems are spread across functional areas. For example, if cell-phone design specialists conferred with marketing specialists (as well as customers and suppliers), they would find the real challenge of using a cell phone for older people is pushing 11 tiny buttons to call a phone number.

Teams may be *self-managed teams,* as described in Chapter 13, with groups of workers given administrative oversight of activities such as planning, scheduling, monitoring, and staffing for their task domains. Sometimes, however, an organization needs a ***special-purpose team* to meet to solve a special or onetime problem.** The team then disbands after the problem is solved. These teams are often cross-functional, drawing on members from different departments. American medicine, for instance, is moving toward a team-based approach for certain applications, involving multiple doctors as well as nurse practitioners and physician assistants.[34]

2. Improvement Orientation—Focusing Everyone on Continuously Improving Work Processes Americans seem to like big schemes, grand designs, and crash programs. Although these approaches certainly have their place, the lesson of the quality movement from overseas is that the way to success is through continuous small improvements. ***Continuous improvement* is defined as ongoing small, incremental improvements in all parts of an organization**—all products, services, functional areas, and work processes.[35]

This improvement orientation has the following assumptions.

- **It's less expensive to do it right the first time.** TQM assumes that it's better to do things right the first time than to do costly reworking. To be sure, there are many costs involved in creating quality products and services—training, equipment, and tools, for example. But they are less than the costs of dealing with poor quality—those stemming from lost customers, junked materials, time spent reworking, and frequent inspection, for example.[36]

- **It's better to do small improvements all the time.** This is the assumption that continuous improvement must be an everyday matter, that no improvement is too small, that there must be an ongoing effort to make things better a little bit at a time, all the time.

- **Accurate standards must be followed to eliminate small variations.** TQM emphasizes the collection of accurate data throughout every stage of the work process. It also stresses the use of accurate standards (such as benchmarking, as we discuss) to evaluate progress and eliminate small variations, which are the source of many quality defects.

- **There must be strong commitment from top management.** Employees and suppliers won't focus on making small incremental improvements unless managers go beyond lip service to support high-quality work, as do the top managers at Ritz-Carlton, Amazon.com, and Ace Hardware.

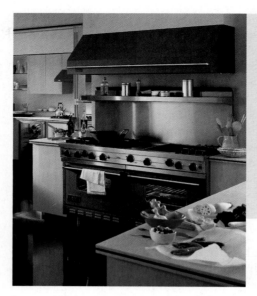

Continuous improvement. In the 1980s, building contractor Fred Carl found restaurant-style commercial stoves impractical for his own home kitchen, so he designed his own, then opened a manufacturing plant in Greenwood, Mississippi, under the name Viking Range Corporation. From Toyota, Viking borrowed Japanese manufacturing techniques grouped under the word *kaizen,* which translates into *continuous improvement.* Production is set up so that if there is a problem everyone on the line is instantly aware of it, and the problem is solved right on the plant floor—so that customers are continuously supplied with elegant yet dependable stoves like the one shown here.

Applying TQM to Services

Manufacturing industries provide tangible products (think jars of baby food), service industries provide intangible products (think child care services). Manufactured products can be stored (such as dental floss in a warehouse); services generally need to be consumed immediately (such as dental hygiene services). Services tend to involve a good deal of people effort (although there is some automation, as with bank automated teller machines). Finally, services are generally provided at locations and times convenient for customers; that is, customers are much more involved in the delivery of services than they are in the delivery of manufactured products.

Customer Satisfaction: A Matter of Perception? Perhaps you're beginning to see how judging the quality of services is a different animal from judging the quality of manufactured goods, because it comes down to meeting the customer's *satisfaction,* which may be a matter of *perception.* (After all, some hotel guests, restaurant diners, and supermarket patrons, for example, are more easily satisfied than others.)

The RATER Scale How, then, can we measure the quality of a delivered service? For one, we can use the *RATER scale,* **which enables customers to rate the quality of a service along five dimensions—***reliability, assurance, tangibles, empathy,* **and** *responsiveness* **(abbreviated** *RATER***)—each on a scale from 1 (for very poor) to 10 (for very good).**[37] The meanings of the RATER dimensions are as follows:

- Reliability—ability to perform the desired service dependably, accurately, and consistently.
- Assurance—employees' knowledge, courtesy, and ability to convey trust and confidence.
- Tangibles—physical facilities, equipment, appearance of personnel.
- Empathy—provision of caring, individualized attention to customers.
- Responsiveness—willingness to provide prompt service and help customers.

What Makes a Service Company Successful? Four Core Elements

With services now employing more than 75% of American workers, universities are bringing more research attention to what is being called "services science." This is a field that uses management, technology, mathematics, and engineering expertise to improve the performance of service businesses, such as retailing and health care.[38]

Harvard Business School scholar Frances X. Frei has determined that a successful service business must make the right decisions about four core elements and balance them effectively:[39]

- **The offering—which features are given top-quality treatment?** Which service attributes, as informed by the needs of customers, does the company target for excellence and which does it target for inferior performance? Does a bank, for example, offer more convenient hours and friendlier tellers (excellence) but pay less attractive interest rates (inferior performance)?

- **The funding mechanism—who pays for the service?** How should the company fund its services? Should it have the customer pay for them? This can be done either in a palatable way, as when Starbucks funds its stuffed-chair ambience by charging more for coffee, or in making savings in service features, as when Progressive Casualty Insurance cuts down on frauds and lawsuits by deploying its own representatives to the scene of an auto accident. Or should the company cover the cost of excellence with operational savings, as by spending now to save later or having the customer do the work? Call centers usually charge for customer support, but Intuit offers free support and has product-development people, as well as customer-service people, field calls so that subsequent developments in Intuit software are informed by direct knowledge of customer problems. Other companies, such as gas stations, save money by having customers pump their own gas.

- **The employee management system—how are workers trained and motivated?** Service companies need to think about what makes their employees *able* to achieve excellence and what makes them reasonably *motivated* to achieve excellence. For instance, bank customers may expect employees to meet a lot of complex needs, but the employees aren't *able* to meet these needs because they haven't been trained. Or they aren't *motivated* to achieve excellence because the bank hasn't figured out how to screen in its hiring, as in hiring people for attitude first and training them later versus paying more to attract highly motivated people.

- **The customer management system—how are customers "trained"?** Like employees, customers in a service business must also be "trained" as well, as the airlines have done with check-in. At Zipcar, the popular car-sharing service, the company keeps its costs low by depending on customers to clean, refuel, and return cars in time for the next user. In training customers, service companies need to determine which customers they're focusing on, what behaviors they want, and which techniques will most effectively influence customer behavior.

Your Call

Pick a services company you're familiar with, such as Domino's Pizza, Starbucks, Amazon, REI, or the college bookstore. In integrating the four core features just discussed, a service company needs to determine whether the decisions it makes in one area are supported by those made in the other areas; whether the service model creates long-term value for customers, employees, and shareholders; and whether the company is trying to be all things to all people or specific things to specific people. How do you think the company you picked rates?

Some TQM Tools & Techniques

Several tools and techniques are available for improving quality. Here we describe *benchmarking, outsourcing, reduced cycle time, ISO 9000* and *ISO 14000, statistical process control,* and *Six Sigma.*

Benchmarking: Learning from the Best Performers   We discussed benchmarking briefly in Chapter 10. As we stated there, *benchmarking* is a process by which a company compares its performance with the best practices of high-performing organizations. For example, at Xerox Corp., generally thought to be the first American company to use benchmarking, it is defined as, in one description, "the continuous process of measuring products, services, and practices against the toughest competitors or those companies recognized as industry leaders."[40]

Example

Searching for "Best Practices": What Kind of Newspaper Ads Work Best?

Benchmarking is a search for "best practices" that can be applied to one's own business. Southwest Airlines, for instance, studied auto-racing pit crews to learn how to reduce the turnaround time of its aircraft at each scheduled stop. Toyota managers got the idea for just-in-time inventory deliveries by looking at how U.S. supermarkets replenish their shelves.

Looking Far Afield. Sometimes companies go far afield in their search for best practices that might benefit them. QualPro Inc. of Knoxville, Tennessee, was able to use multivariable testing (MVT), a statistical technique that originated during World War II when the British were seeking ways to shoot down German bombers more effectively, to help AutoNation, a conglomeration of car dealers, test what combination of up to 30 factors made for more effective newspaper ads. Typically scientific experiments try to test one variable at a time while keeping all other factors constant. But one-at-a-time experiments can take a long time and miss instances involving multiple factors.

Testing Numerous Variables. QualPro tested numerous variables at the same time—for example, half-page versus full-page ads, or color ads versus black and white—to see the effect on dealer sales. "Some surprises popped out," says an account of the experiment. "A full-page ad was no more effective than a half-page one. The addition of color—a considerable expense—did not generate any extra sales."[41]

YOUR CALL

Jeffrey Pfeffer and Robert Sutton, authors of a book on evidence-based management, worry that managers use benchmarking too casually ("GE does it? We should too!").[42] Are you aware of any instances in which a company simply picked up or copied a practice that turned out not to be useful?

Outsourcing: Let Outsiders Handle It   *Outsourcing* (discussed in detail in Chapter 4) is the subcontracting of services and operations to an outside vendor. Usually this is done because the subcontractor vendor can do the job better or cheaper. Or, stated another way, when the services and operations are done in-house, they are not done as efficiently or are keeping personnel from doing more important things.

For example, despite its former (2004–2009) well-known advertising campaign, "An American Revolution," Chevrolet outsources the engine for its Chevrolet Equinox to China, where it found it could get high-quality engines built at lower cost.[43] And when IBM and other companies outsource components inexpensively for new integrated software systems, says one researcher, offshore programmers make information technology affordable to small and medium-size businesses and others who haven't yet joined the productivity boom.[44]

Outsourcing is also being done by many state and local governments, which, under the banner known as privatization, have subcontracted traditional government services such as fire protection, correctional services, and medical services.

Reduced Cycle Time: Increasing the Speed of Work Processes Another TQM technique is the emphasis on increasing the speed with which an organization's operations and processes can be performed. This is known as *reduced cycle time,* **or reduction in steps in a work process,** such as fewer authorization steps required to grant a contract to a supplier. The point is to improve the organization's performance by eliminating wasteful motions, barriers between departments, unnecessary procedural steps, and the like.

ISO 9000 & ISO 14000: Meeting Standards of Independent Auditors If you're a sales representative for DuPont, the American chemical company, how will your overseas clients know that your products have the quality they are expecting? If you're a purchasing agent for an Ohio-based tire company, how can you tell if the synthetic rubber you're buying overseas is adequate?

At one time, buyers and sellers simply had to rely on a supplier's past reputation or personal assurances. In 1979, the International Organization for Standardization (ISO), based in Geneva, Switzerland, created a set of quality standards known as the 9000 series—"a kind of *Good Housekeeping* seal of approval for global business," in one description.[45] There are two such standards:

- **ISO 9000. The *ISO 9000 series* consists of quality-control procedures companies must install—from purchasing to manufacturing to inventory to shipping—that can be audited by independent quality-control experts, or "registrars."** The goal is to reduce flaws in manufacturing and improve productivity. Companies must document the procedures and train their employees to use them. For instance, DocBase Direct is a Web-delivered document and forms-management system that helps companies comply with key ISO management standards, such as traceable changes and easy reporting.

   The ISO 9000 designation is now recognized by more than 100 countries around the world, and a quarter of the corporations around the globe insist that suppliers have ISO 9000 certification. "You close some expensive doors if you're not certified," says Bill Ekeler, general manager of Overland Products, a Nebraska tool-and-die-stamping firm.[46] In addition, because the ISO process forced him to analyze his company from the top down, Ekeler found ways to streamline manufacturing processes that improved his bottom line.

- **ISO 14000. The *ISO 14000 series* extends the concept, identifying standards for environmental performance.** ISO 14000 dictates standards for documenting a company's management of pollution, efficient use of raw materials, and reduction of the firm's impact on the environment.

Statistical Process Control: Taking Periodic Random Samples As the pages of this book were being printed, every now and then a press person would pull a few pages out of the press run and inspect them (under a bright light) to see that the consistency of the color and quality of the ink were holding up. This is an ongoing human visual check for quality control.

All kinds of products require periodic inspection during their manufacture: hamburger meat, breakfast cereal, flashlight batteries, wine, and so on. The tool often used for this is *statistical process control,* **a statistical technique that uses periodic random samples from production runs to see if quality is being maintained within a standard range of acceptability.** If quality is not acceptable, production is stopped to allow corrective measures.

Statistical process control is the technique that McDonald's uses, for example, to make sure that the quality of its burgers is always the same, no matter where in the world they are served. Companies such as Intel and Motorola use statistical process control to ensure the reliability and quality of their products.

Six Sigma & Lean Six Sigma: Data-Driven Ways to Eliminate Defects "The biggest problem with the management technique known as Six Sigma is this: It sounds too good to be true," says a *Fortune* writer. "How would your company like a 20% increase in profit margins within one year, followed by profitability over the long-term that is *ten times* what you're seeing now? How about a 4% (or greater) annual gain in market share?"[47]

What is this name, Six Sigma (which is probably Greek to you), and is it a path to management paradise? The name comes from *sigma,* the Greek letter that statisticians use to define a standard deviation. The higher the sigma, the fewer the deviations from the norm—that is, the fewer the defects. Developed by Motorola in 1985, Six Sigma has since been embraced by General Electric, Allied Signal, American Express, and other companies. There are two variations, *Six Sigma* and *lean Six Sigma.*

- **Six Sigma.** *Six Sigma* **is a rigorous statistical analysis process that reduces defects in manufacturing and service-related processes.** By testing thousands of variables and eliminating guesswork, a company using the technique attempts to improve quality and reduce waste to the point where errors nearly vanish. In everything from product design to manufacturing to billing, the attainment of Six Sigma means there are no more than 3.4 defects per million products or procedures.

  "Six Sigma gets people away from thinking that 96% is good, to thinking that 40,000 failures per million is bad," says a vice president of consulting firm A. T. Kearney.[48] Six Sigma means being 99.9997% perfect. By contrast, Three Sigma or Four Sigma means settling for 99% perfect—the equivalent of no electricity for 7 hours each month, two short or long landings per day at each major airport, or 5,000 incorrect surgical operations per week.[49]

  Six Sigma may also be thought of as a philosophy—to reduce variation in your company's business and make customer-focused, data-driven decisions. The method preaches the use of Define, Measure, Analyze, Improve, and Control (DMAIC). Team leaders may be awarded a Six Sigma "black belt" for applying DMAIC.

- **Lean Six Sigma.** More recently, companies are using an approach known as *lean Six Sigma,* **which focuses on problem solving and performance improvement—speed with excellence—of a well-defined project.**[50]

  Xerox Corp., for example, has focused on getting new products to customers faster, which has meant taking steps out of the design process without loss of quality. A high-end, $200,000 machine that can print 100 pages a minute traditionally has taken three to five cycles of design; removing just one of those cycles can shave up to a year off time to market.[51] The grocery chain Albertsons Inc. announced in 2004 that it was going to launch Six Sigma training to reduce customer dissatisfaction and waste to the lowest level possible.[52]

Six Sigma and lean Six Sigma may not be perfect, since they cannot compensate for human error or control events outside a company. Still, they let managers approach problems with the assumption that there's a data-oriented, tangible way to approach problem solving.[53] ●

What are the keys to successful control, and what are the barriers to control success?

THE BIG PICTURE

This section describes four keys to successful control and five barriers to successful control.

How do you as a manager make a control system successful, and how do you identify and deal with barriers to control? We consider these topics next.[54]

The Keys to Successful Control Systems

Successful control systems have a number of common characteristics: (1) They are strategic and results-oriented. (2) They are timely, accurate, and objective. (3) They are realistic, positive, and understandable and they encourage self-control. (4) They are flexible.[55]

1. They Are Strategic & Results-Oriented   Control systems support strategic plans and are concentrated on significant activities that will make a real difference to the organization. Thus, when managers are developing strategic plans for achieving strategic goals, that is the point at which they should pay attention to developing control standards that will measure how well the plans are being achieved.

Example: Global warming is now shifting the climate on a continental scale, changing the life cycle of animals and plants, scientists say, and surveys show more Americans feel guilty for not living greener.[56] A growing number of companies are discovering that embracing environmental safe practices is paying off in savings of hundreds of millions of dollars. Thus, Sun Microsystems, the technology company, is aiming to reduce its greenhouse gas emissions by 20% by 2012 through a range of practices, such as using energy-saving technology in its computer chips or allowing thousands of its 18,000 employees to work at home.[57]

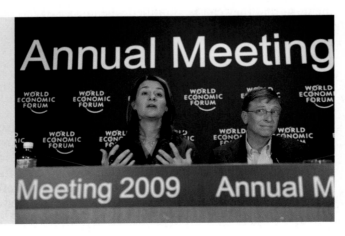

Doing good. Created by Microsoft founder Bill Gates and his wife, the Bill & Melinda Gates Foundation of Seattle is the largest private foundation in the world. It aims to reduce poverty and enhance health care throughout the world and to expand educational opportunities in the United States. The way it seeks to apply business techniques to giving makes it a leader in global philanthropy.

2. They Are Timely, Accurate, & Objective

Good control systems—like good information of any kind—should . . .

- **Be timely—meaning when needed.** The information should not necessarily be delivered quickly, but it should be delivered at an appropriate or specific time, such as every week or every month. And it certainly should be often enough to allow employees and managers to take corrective action for any deviations.

- **Be accurate—meaning correct.** Accuracy is paramount, if decision mistakes are to be avoided. Inaccurate sales figures may lead managers to mistakenly cut or increase sales promotion budgets. Inaccurate production costs may lead to faulty pricing of a product.

- **Be objective—meaning impartial.** Objectivity means control systems are impartial and fair. Although information can be inaccurate for all kinds of reasons (faulty communication, unknown data, and so on), information that is not objective is inaccurate for a special reason: It is biased or prejudiced. Control systems need to be considered unbiased for everyone involved so that they will be respected for their fundamental purpose—enhancing performance.

3. They Are Realistic, Positive, & Understandable & Encourage Self-Control

Control systems have to focus on working for the people who will have to live with them. Thus, they operate best when they are made acceptable to the organization's members who are guided by them. Thus, they should . . .

- **Be realistic.** They should incorporate realistic expectations. If employees feel performance results are too difficult, they are apt to ignore or sabotage the performance system.

- **Be positive.** They should emphasize development and improvement. They should avoid emphasizing punishment and reprimand.

- **Be understandable.** They should fit the people involved, be kept as simple as possible, and present data in understandable terms. They should avoid complicated computer printouts and statistics.

- **Encourage self-control.** They should encourage good communication and mutual participation. They should not be the basis for creating distrust between employees and managers.

4. They Are Flexible

Control systems must leave room for individual judgment, so that they can be modified when necessary to meet new requirements.

Barriers to Control Success

Among the several barriers to a successful control system are the following:[58]

I. Too Much Control

Some organizations, particularly bureaucratic ones, try to exert too much control. They may try to regulate employee behavior in everything from dress code to timing of coffee breaks. Allowing employees too little discretion for analysis and interpretation may lead to employee frustration—particularly among professionals, such as college professors and medical doctors. Their frustration may lead them to ignore or try to sabotage the control process.

2. Too Little Employee Participation   As highlighted by W. Edwards Deming, discussed elsewhere in the book (Chapter 2), employee participation can enhance productivity. Involving employees in both the planning and execution of control systems can bring legitimacy to the process and heighten employee morale.

3. Overemphasis on Means Instead of Ends   We said that control activities should be strategic and results-oriented. They are not ends in themselves but the means to eliminating problems. Too much emphasis on accountability for weekly production quotas, for example, can lead production supervisors to push their workers and equipment too hard, resulting in absenteeism and machine breakdowns. Or it can lead to game playing—"beating the system"—as managers and employees manipulate data to seem to fulfill short-run goals instead of the organization's strategic plan.

4. Overemphasis on Paperwork   A specific kind of misdirection of effort is management emphasis on getting reports done, to the exclusion of other performance activity. Reports are not the be-all and end-all. Undue emphasis on reports can lead to too much focus on quantification of results and even to falsification of data.

   Example: A research laboratory decided to use the number of patents the lab obtained as a measure of its effectiveness. The result was an increase in patents filed but a decrease in the number of successful research projects.[59]

5. Overemphasis on One Instead of Multiple Approaches   One control may not be enough. By having multiple control activities and information systems, an organization can have multiple performance indicators, thereby increasing accuracy and objectivity.

   Example: An obvious strategic goal for gambling casinos is to prevent employee theft of the cash flowing through their hands. Thus, casinos control card dealers by three means. First, they require they have a dealer's license before they are hired. Second, they put them under constant scrutiny, using direct supervision by on-site pit bosses as well as observation by closed-circuit TV cameras and through overhead one-way mirrors. Third, they require detailed reports at the end of each shift so that transfer of cash and cash equivalents (such as gambling chips) can be audited.[60] ●

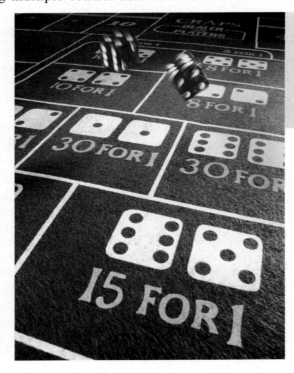

Temptation. Because legal gambling is a heavy cash business, casinos need to institute special controls against employee theft. One of them is the "eye in the sky" over card and craps tables.

Major Question

What are eight keys to personal managerial success?

THE BIG PICTURE

As we end the book, this section describes some life lessons to take away.

We have come to the end of the book, our last chance to offer some suggestions to take with you that we hope will benefit you in the coming years. Following are some life lessons pulled from various sources that can make you a "keeper" in an organization and help you be successful.

- **Find your passion and follow it.** "The mission matters," writes Gary Hamel, cofounder of the Management Innovation Lab. "People change for what they care about." Employees aren't motivated much by the notion of "increasing shareholder value" (or if they are, the result may be an environment in which greed overwhelms higher-minded goals). Says Hamel, "A company must forever be on the way to *becoming* something more than it is right now."[61] And the same should apply to you. Find something you love to do, and do it vigorously.

- **Encourage self-discovery, and be realistic.** To stay ahead of the pack, you need to develop self-awareness, have an active mind, and be willing to grow and change. Here's a life lesson: "Be brutally honest with yourself about what you know, and ask what skills you need to take the next step." This includes not just the tools of your trade—finance, technology, and so on—but most importantly, people skills.

- **Every situation is different, so be flexible.** No principle, no theory will apply under all circumstances. Industries, cultures, supervisors, customers will vary. If you're the new kid in a new job, for instance, you should know that "culture is critical," suggests Angeli R. Rasbury in *Black Enterprise*. A life lesson: "Before you can begin to set goals, know the organization in which you're working. Learn how employees conduct business and view success, and how the company rewards achievement. An organization's culture defines its management and business guidelines."[62] Another life lesson: "Remove 'It's not my job' from your vocabulary."

- **Fine-tune your people skills.** The workplace is not an area where lone individuals make their silent contributions. Today we live and work in a team universe. If, as is the case with Whole Foods Market, getting and keeping a job depends on the reviews of your peers, with teammates voting on your fate, you can see that communication skills become ever more important. Recommendation: Get feedback on your interpersonal skills and develop a plan for improvement.

- **Learn how to develop leadership skills.** Every company should invest in the leadership development of its managers if it is to improve the quality of its future leaders. But you can also work to develop your own leadership skills. An example and a life lesson: "Leaders who wait for bad news to come to them are taking a major risk, so learn to seek it out—as by encouraging employees to bring you news of potential problems and thanking them for it, not punishing them for their candor."[63] You can also pick up news about problems, potential and actual, by practicing "management by wandering around." Another life lesson: "If you set the bar high, even if you don't reach it, you end up in a pretty good place—that is, achieving a pretty high mark."

- **Treat people as if they matter, because they do.** If you treat employees and customers with dignity, they respond accordingly. The highly successful online shoe retailer Zappos, for instance, "is fanatical about great service," says the writer of a *Harvard Business Publishing* online blog, "not just satisfying customers, but amazing them," as in promising delivery in 4 days and delivering in 1. How? It's all in the hiring, which Zappos does with great intensity. After four weeks' training, new call-center employees are offered $1,000 on top of what they have earned to that point if they want to quit—the theory being that people who take the money "obviously don't have the commitment" that Zappos requires of its employees. (About 10% of the trainees take the offer.)[64] The life lesson: "Companies don't engage emotionally with their customers—people do. If you want to create a memorable company, you have to fill your company with memorable people."

- **Draw employees and peers into your management process.** The old top-down, command-and-control model of organization is moving toward a flattened, networked kind of structure. Managers now work more often with peers, where lines of authority aren't always clear or don't exist, so that one's persuasive powers become key. Power has devolved to front-line employees who are closest to the customer and to small, focused, self-managed teams that have latitude to pursue new ideas. The life lesson: "The best organizations will be those whose employees have the power to innovate, not just follow orders from on high."

- **Be flexible, keep your cool, and take yourself lightly.** Things aren't always going to work out your way, so flexibility is important. In addition, the more unflappable you appear in difficult circumstances, the more you'll be admired by your bosses and co-workers. Having a sense of humor helps, since there are enough people spreading gloom and doom in the workplace. Life lesson: "When you're less emotional, you're better able to assess a crisis and develop a workable solution."

We wish you the very best of luck. And we mean it!

Angelo Kinicki
Brian K. Williams

Key Terms Used in This Chapter

audits 525
balance sheet 524
balanced scorecard 517
budget 522
bureaucratic control 516
continuous improvement 529
control process steps 512
control standard 512
controlling 510
decentralized control 516
Deming management 526
enterprise resource planning (ERP) 509

external audit 525
financial statement 524
fixed budget 523
income statement 524
incremental budgeting 522
internal audit 525
ISO 9000 series 533
ISO 14000 series 533
lean Six Sigma 534
management by exception 513
operational control 515
PDCA cycle 527
RATER scale 530

ratio analysis 524
reduced cycle time 533
Six Sigma 534
special-purpose team 529
statistical process control 533
strategic control 515
strategy map 519
tactical control 515
total quality management (TQM) 528
two core principles of TQM 528
variable budget 523

16.1 Managing for Productivity

A manager has to deal with seven challenges—managing for competitive advantage, diversity, globalization, information technology, ethical standards, sustainability, and his or her own happiness and life goals. The manager must make decisions about the four management functions—planning, organizing, leading, and controlling—to get people to achieve productivity and realize results.

Productivity is defined by the formula of outputs divided by inputs for a specified period of time. Productivity is important because it determines whether the organization will make a profit or even survive. Much of productivity growth is thought to result from the implementation of information technology, including enterprise resource planning (ERP) systems. Productivity depends on control.

16.2 Control: When Managers Monitor Performance

Controlling is defined as monitoring performance, comparing it with goals, and taking corrective action as needed. There are six reasons why control is needed: (1) to adapt to change and uncertainty; (2) to discover irregularities and errors; (3) to reduce costs, increase productivity, or add value; (4) to detect opportunities; (5) to deal with complexity; and (6) to decentralize decision making and facilitate teamwork.

There are four control process steps. (1) The first step is to set standards. A control standard is the desired performance level for a given goal. (2) The second step is to measure performance, based on written reports, oral reports, and personal observation. (3) The third step is to compare measured performance against the standards established. (4) The fourth step is to take corrective action, if necessary, if there is negative performance.

16.3 Levels & Areas of Control

In applying the steps and types of control, managers need to consider (1) the level of management at which they operate, (2) the areas they can draw on for resources, and (3) the style of control philosophy.

There are three levels of control, corresponding to the three principal managerial levels. (1) Strategic control, done by top managers, is monitoring performance to ensure that strategic plans are being implemented. (2) Tactical control, done by middle managers, is monitoring performance to ensure that tactical plans are being implemented. (3) Operational control, done by first-level or supervisory managers, is monitoring performance to ensure that day-to-day goals are being implemented.

Most organizations have six areas that they can draw on for resources. (1) The physical area includes buildings, equipment, and tangible products; these use equipment control, inventory-management control, and quality controls. (2) The human resources area uses personality tests, drug tests, performance tests, employee surveys, and the like as controls to monitor people. (3) The informational area uses production schedules, sales forecasts, environmental impact statements, and the like to monitor the organization's various resources. (4) The financial area uses various kinds of financial controls, as we discuss in Section 16.5. (5) The structural area uses hierarchical or other arrangements such as bureaucratic control, which is characterized by use of rules, regulations, and formal authority to guide performance, or decentralized control, which is characterized by informal and organic structural arrangements. (6) The cultural area influences the work process and levels of performance through the set of norms that develop as a result of the values and beliefs that constitute an organization's culture.

16.4 The Balanced Scorecard, Strategy Maps, & Measurement Management

To establish standards, managers often use the balanced scorecard, which provides a fast but comprehensive view of the organization via four indicators:

(1) financial measures, (2) customer satisfaction, (3) internal processes, and (4) innovation and improvement activities.

The strategy map, a visual representation of the four perspectives of the balanced scorecard—financial, customer, internal business, and innovation and learning—enables managers to communicate their goals so that everyone in the company can understand how their jobs are linked to the overall objectives of the organization.

Measurement-managed companies use measurable criteria for determining strategic success, and management updates and reviews three or more of six primary performance areas: financial performance, operating efficiency, customer satisfaction, employee performance, innovation/change, and community/environment. Four mechanisms that contribute to the success of such companies are top executives agree on strategy, communication is clear, there is better focus and alignment, and the organizational culture emphasizes teamwork and allows risk taking. Four barriers to effective measurement are objectives are fuzzy, managers put too much trust in informal feedback systems, employees resist new management systems, and companies focus too much on measuring activities instead of results.

Some areas are difficult to measure, such as those in service industries.

16.5 Some Financial Tools for Control
Financial controls include (1) budgets, (2) financial statements, (3) ratio analysis, and (4) audits.

A budget is a formal financial projection. The most important budget-planning approach is incremental budgeting, which allocates increased or decreased funds to a department by using the last budget period as a reference point; only incremental changes in the budget request are reviewed. Budgets are either fixed, which allocate resources on the basis of a single estimate of costs, or variable, which allow resource allocation to vary in proportion with various levels of activity.

A financial statement is a summary of some aspect of an organization's financial status. One type, the balance sheet, summarizes an organization's overall financial worth—assets and liabilities—at a specific point in time. The other type, the income statement, summarizes an organization's financial results—revenues and expenses—over a specified period of time.

Ratio analysis is the practice of evaluating financial ratios. Managers may use this tool to determine an organization's financial health, such as liquidity ratios, debt management ratios, or return ratios.

Audits are formal verifications of an organization's financial and operational systems. Audits are of two types. An external audit is formal verification of an organization's financial accounts and statements by outside experts. An internal audit is a verification of an organization's financial accounts and statements by the organization's own professional staff.

16.6 Total Quality Management
Much of the impetus for quality improvement came from W. Edwards Deming, whose philosophy, known as Deming management, proposed ideas for making organizations more responsive, more democratic, and less wasteful. Among the principles of Deming management are (1) quality should be aimed at the needs of the consumer; (2) companies should aim at improving the system, not blaming workers; (3) improved quality leads to increased market share, increased company prospects, and increased employment; and (4) quality can be improved on the basis of hard data, using the PDCA, or plan-do-check-act, cycle.

Total quality management (TQM) is defined as a comprehensive approach—led by top management and supported throughout the organization—dedicated to continuous quality improvement, training, and customer satisfaction. The two core principles of TQM are people orientation and improvement orientation.

In the people orientation, everyone involved with the organization is asked to focus on delivering value to customers, focusing on quality. TQM requires training, teamwork, and cross-functional efforts.

In the improvement orientation, everyone involved with the organization is supposed to make ongoing small, incremental improvements in all parts of the organization. This orientation assumes that it's less expensive to do things right the first time, to do small improvements all the time, and to follow accurate standards to eliminate small variations.

TQM can be applied to services using the RATER scale, which stands for reliability, assurance, tangibles, empathy, and responsiveness.

Several techniques are available for improving quality. (1) Employee involvement can be implemented through quality circles, self-managed teams, and special-purpose teams—teams that meet to solve a special or one-time problem. (2) Benchmarking is a process by which a company compares its performance with that of high-performing organizations. (3) Outsourcing is the subcontracting of services and operations to an outside vendor. (4) Reduced cycle time consists of reducing the number of steps in a work process. (5) Statistical process control is a statistical technique that uses periodic random samples from production runs to see if quality is being maintained within a standard range of acceptability.

 16.7 Managing Control Effectively
Successful control systems have four common characteristics: (1) They are strategic and results oriented. (2) They are timely, accurate, and objective. (3) They are realistic, positive, and understandable and they encourage self-control. (4) They are flexible.

Among the barriers to a successful control system are the following: (1) Organizations may exert too much control. (2) There may be too little employee participation. (3) The organization may overemphasize means instead of ends. (4) There may be an overemphasis on paperwork. (5) There may be an overemphasis on one approach instead of multiple approaches.

Management in Action

The Success of Process Improvement Projects Is Harder Than It Seems

What do weight loss plans and process-improvement programs such as Six Sigma and "lean manufacturing" have in common?

They typically start off well, generating excitement and great progress, but all too often fail to have a lasting impact as participants gradually lose motivation and fall back into old habits. . . . Recent studies, for example, suggest that nearly 60% of all corporate Six Sigma initiatives fail to yield the desired results.

We studied process-improvement programs at large companies over a five-year period to gain insight into how and why so many of them fail. We found that when confronted with increasing stress over time, these programs react in much the same way a metal spring does when it is pulled with increasing force—that is, they progress through "stretching" and "yielding" phases before failing entirely. In engineering, this is known as the "stress-strain curve," and the length of each stage varies widely by material. . . .

The discussion that follows is based on what happened at one aerospace company that implemented more than 100 improvement projects, only to determine less than two years later that more than half had failed to generate lasting gains.

Stretching Phase

When a metal spring is pulled initially, the material stretches to accommodate the increase in pressure. In much the same way, the people involved in a process-improvement project generally find themselves stretching and willing to tackle all necessary tasks in the early going.

At the aerospace company, an improvement project typically began with the formation of a team consisting of 10 to 18 members from different departments. A Six Sigma or other improvement expert was assigned to the team to guide and train them. At this stage, teams were excited to learn and apply what they were being taught.

Team members collected data on their current working environment and, with the help of the Six Sigma expert, identified the changes they most needed to make to achieve their stated goal—say, a reduction in the rate of defects in manufactured parts or fewer mistakes in order writing and billing. The expert developed a "to do" list that included action items, responsibilities and deadlines and made sure needed resources were available. . . . While daily production slipped initially when the team transitioned to the new way of working, it improved when the group grew accustomed to the new process. When the team reached its goal—say it reduced billing errors by a certain percentage—the improvement project was declared a success.

The director who was spearheading the company's Six Sigma initiatives shared the teams' achievements with others in the company. Team members were given rewards such as gift certificates to restaurants, and their pictures appeared in the company newsletter. . . .

Yielding Phase

Unfortunately, the story doesn't end there. . . .

In the middle stage of an improvement project—when the Six Sigma expert moves on to another project and top management turns its focus to another group of workers—implementation starts to wobble, and teams may find themselves struggling to maintain the gains they achieved early on.

With the departure of the Six Sigma expert, the teams at the aerospace company lost their objective voice and the person who performed the sophisticated statistical analysis that allowed them to prioritize that tasks that most affected performance, thus needed fixing the most. Without the expert to rein them in, some team members began pushing agendas that benefitted themselves and their departments, making it harder for the team to agree on new goals.

While teams at this stage continued to look for the flaws in their current working environments, they got bogged down trying to perform the statistical analysis previously handled by the expert. Some teams started spending too much time on the improvement project, which affected their ability to meet production quotas and other daily responsibilities.

Amid the confusion and facing pressure from managers to keep up with day-to-day duties, some team members started reverting to old habits in much the same way a person who recently lost weight might start skipping gym sessions when work and daily demands heat up. The team's performance stopped improving and, in some cases, started to regress.

When reporting on the status of their projects, teams tried to make themselves look better by highlighting what they hoped to accomplish in the future, instead of what they were accomplishing now. Team members became discouraged and started to doubt the benefits of the improvement strategies. . . .

Failing Stage

In the final stages of a process-improvement project, team members find themselves unable or unwilling to tackle improvement tasks, and the effort ultimately collapses.

With the improvement expert long gone and no additional training in Six Sigma or other improvement strategies provided by the aerospace company, team members became increasingly discouraged by their failure to build on earlier success. They eventually stopped caring about the improvement project, partly because it wasn't tied to their performance reviews.

As morale sagged, no one stepped forward to assume leadership of the improvement project, so the team lost interest in looking for ways to improve their current work environment. The company allowed newly formed improvement teams to poach people and resources from older teams, so the only improvements that were made were those related to safety—and even then, only the bare minimum was done. Members steadily regressed to their old ways of working, and the group's performance returned to what it had been before the project began.

With projects failing miserably, many teams reported achievements incorrectly, giving a false sense of success. Because the director continued to communicate only about projects that were showing excellent results, it took several months for the division vice president to become aware of the widespread failures and reluctantly inform the company's top executives.

Lessons Learned

Four lessons from our research stand out.

First, the extended involvement of a Six Sigma or other improvement expert is required if teams are to remain motivated, continue learning and maintain gains. If the cost of assigning an improvement expert to each team on a full-time basis is prohibitive, one improvement expert could be assigned on a part-time basis to several teams for an extended period of one to two years. Later, managers could be trained to take over that role.

Second, performance appraisals need to be tied to successful implementation of improvement projects. . . .

Third, improvement teams should have no more than six to nine members, and the timeline for launching a project should be no longer than six to eight weeks. . . .

Fourth, executives need to directly participate in improvement projects not just "support" them. . . . By observing the successes and failures of improvement programs firsthand, rather than relying on someone else's interpretation, executives can make more accurate assessments as to which ones are worth continuing.

For Discussion

1. What are the key reasons the Six Sigma initiatives failed at this aerospace firm? Explain.

2. How can the balanced scorecard and strategy mapping process be used to increase the success of Six Sigma initiatives? Discuss.

3. Which of the three levels of control were missing from these process-improvement initiatives? Provide examples to support your conclusions.

4. Thinking back to what you learned about teams (Chapter 13) and organizational change (Chapter 10), what would you have done differently if you were leading these process-improvement initiatives? Explain.

5. What are the most important takeaways from this case? Explain your rationale.

Source: Excerpted from Satya S. Chakravorty, "Where Process-Improvement Projects Go Wrong," *The Wall Street Journal*, January 25, 2010, p. R6.

Self-Assessment

Do You Have Good Time-Management Skills?

Objectives
1. To determine how productive you are.
2. To discuss what time-management skills need developing.

Introduction
As we learned in this chapter, productivity is important to companies because it determines their profitability. For managers, productivity depends on effective time management, a skill involving planning and self-discipline that should be perfected in college. The purpose of this exercise is to evaluate your time-management skills.

Instructions
Read each question, and answer each one "Yes" or "No." Answer not as you feel you *should* but rather as you feel you *would* if you were being completely truthful.

1. I have a hard time saying "no."

2. I sometimes postpone a task so long that I'm embarrassed to do it.

3. I feel like I'm always in a hurry.

4. I feel guilty when I play or goof off instead of studying.

5. I tend to make excuses when I don't finish my work.

6. I often feel like I have too much to do.

7. I work better under pressure.

8. I feel resentful when someone reminds me I haven't finished my work.

9. I have difficulty deciding how to use my time.

10. I generally put off semester projects until the week before they're due.

Interpretation
Count the number of "No" responses. Your time-management skills may be characterized as follows:

9–10: Excellent

8–9: Good, but they could be improved in minor ways

6–8: Somewhat inadequate; you could benefit from training

4–6: Poor; you definitely need training.

4 or less: Emergency! You know little about time management and need to pay immediate attention here

Questions for Discussion
1. Were you surprised by the results? Why or why not?

2. Many statements in the assessment represent procrastination, with good intentions being eclipsed by excuses and bad time management. Do you frequently procrastinate?

3. What are some ways you could improve your time-management skills? Discuss.

Source: www.ecu.edu/aretsci/cas/advising/TimeManagement .com © Thomas Harriot College of Arts & Sciences, Advising Center, East Carolina University, Greenville, NC.

Is Corporate Monitoring of Employee Behavior Outside of Work Going Too Far?

Attempting to cut health care costs and increase productivity, companies are increasingly trying to get employees to lose weight, stop smoking, and exercise. For example, Incentive Logic Inc. in Arizona "keeps track of points employees earn for everything from walking to passing health screenings and it lets employees redeem their points for iPods, plasma TVs or other items they want from its 3 million-item catalog."

Further, some companies claim that health care costs are higher for smokers and overweight employees than they are for nonsmokers and nonoverweight people. "In response to these higher costs, more employers are instituting bans on hiring smokers, even if they only smoke during off-duty hours, and/or are charging more for health insurance to smokers, overweight workers, and other categories of employees."

Right now, organizations are targeting and monitoring smokers and overweight employees, but other groups might be next. "Other groups that may be subject to such 'lifestyle' regulations include people with hypertension or high serum cholesterol levels, social drinkers, and sports enthusiasts."

What types of employee behavior outside of work should organizations monitor and reward/punish?

Solving the Dilemma

1. Organizations should stay out of our personal lives. If we want to overeat or smoke, that is our choice. Organizations should not be allowed to monitor weight and smoking behavior.

2. Organizations should monitor employees' weight and smoking behavior and reward/punish accordingly. After all, overweight people and smokers cost employers more in terms of health insurance and it's only fair that people pay for these increased costs in one way or another.

3. I'm okay with rewarding/punishing people who are overweight and smoke, but that is it. Organizations have no business tracking how much I drink and what type of sports or social activities I enjoy. If I want to go skydiving, it's my business, not the company's.

4. Invent other options.

Sources: Jane Larson, "Firm's Reward Program Gets Employees Moving," *The Arizona Republic,* May 24, 2008, p. D5; and "Off-Duty but on Your Mind," *Training,* April 2008, p. 11.

The Project Planner's Toolkit
Flowcharts, Gantt Charts, & Break-Even Analysis

How can you use planning tools to enhance your performance and achieve utmost success?

THE BIG PICTURE

Three tools used in project planning, which was covered in Chapter 5, are flowcharts, Gantt charts, and break-even analysis.

Project planning may begin (in the definition stage) as a back-of-the-envelope kind of process, but the client will expect a good deal more for the time and money being invested. Fortunately, there are various planning and monitoring tools that give the planning and execution of projects more precision. Three tools in the planner's tool-kit are (1) flowcharts, (2) Gantt charts, and break-even analysis.

Tool #1: Flowcharts—for Showing Event Sequences & Alternate Decision Scenarios

A *flowchart* **is a useful graphical tool for representing the sequence of events required to complete a project and for laying out "what-if" scenarios.** Flowcharts have been used for decades by computer programmers and systems analysts to make a graphical "road map," as it were, of the flow of tasks required. These professionals use their own special symbols (indicating "input/output," "magnetic disk," and the like), but there is no need for you to make the process complicated. Generally, only three symbols are needed: (1) an oval for the beginning and end, (2) a box for a major activity, and (3) a diamond for a yes or no decision. (*See Figure A.1, next page.*)

Computer programs such as Micrographix's ABC Flow Charter are available for constructing flowcharts. You can also use the drawing program in word processing programs such as Microsoft Word.

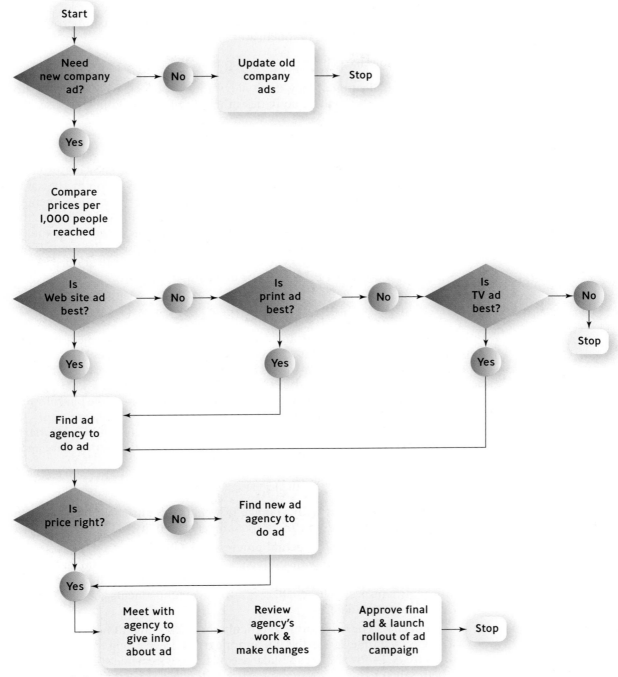

figure A.1

FLOWCHART: WEB SITE, PRINT, OR TELEVISION?

Example of a flowchart for improving a company's advertising

Benefits   Flowcharts have two benefits:

- **Planning straightforward activities.** A flowchart can be quite helpful for planning ordinary activities—figuring out the best way to buy textbooks or a car, for example. It is also a straightforward way of indicating the sequence of events in, say, thinking out a new enterprise that you would then turn into a business plan.

- **Depicting alternate scenarios.** A flowchart is also useful for laying out "what-if" scenarios—as in if you answer "yes" to a decision question you should follow Plan A, if you answer "no" you should follow Plan B.

Limitations Flowcharts have two limitations:

- **No time indication.** They don't show the amounts of time required to accomplish the various activities in a project. In building a house, the foundation might take only a couple of days, but the rough carpentry might take weeks. These time differences can't be represented graphically on a flowchart (although you could make a notation).

- **Not good for complex projects.** They aren't useful for showing projects consisting of several activities that must all be worked on at the same time. An example would be getting ready for football season's opening game, by which time the players have to be trained, the field readied, the programs printed, the band rehearsed, the ticket sellers recruited, and so on. These separate activities might each be represented on their own flowcharts, of course. But to try to express them all together all at once would produce a flowchart that would be unwieldy, even unworkable.

Tool #2: Gantt Charts—Visual Time Schedules for Work Tasks

We have mentioned how important deadlines are to making a project happen. Unlike a flowchart, a Gantt chart can graphically indicate deadlines.

The Gantt chart was developed by **Henry L. Gantt,** a member of the school of scientific management (discussed in Chapter 2). **A *Gantt chart* is a kind of time schedule—a specialized bar chart that shows the relationship between the kind of work tasks planned and their scheduled completion dates.** *(See Figure A.2, next page.)*

A number of software packages can help you create and modify Gantt charts on your computer. Examples are CA-SuperProject, Microsoft Project Manager, SureTrak Project Manager, and TurboProject Professional.

Benefits There are three benefits to using a Gantt chart:

- **Express time lines visually.** Unlike flowcharts, Gantt charts allow you to indicate visually the time to be spent on each activity.

- **Compare proposed and actual progress.** A Gantt chart may be used to compare planned time to complete a task with actual time taken to complete it, so that you can see how far ahead or behind schedule you are for the entire project. This enables you to make adjustments so as to hold to the final target dates.

- **Simplicity.** There is nothing difficult about creating a Gantt chart. You express the time across the top and the tasks down along the left side. As Figure A.2 shows, you can make use of this device while still in college to help schedule and monitor the work you need to do to meet course requirements and deadlines (for papers, projects, tests).

Limitations Gantt charts have two limitations:

- **Not useful for large, complex projects.** Although a Gantt chart can express the interrelations among the activities of relatively small projects, it becomes cumbersome and unwieldy when used for large, complex projects. More sophisticated management planning tools may be needed, such as PERT networks.

- **Time assumptions are subjective.** The time assumptions expressed may be purely subjective; there is no range between "optimistic" and "pessimistic" of the time needed to accomplish a given task.

Accomplished: ||||||||||
Planned: \\\\\\\\

Stage of development	Week 1	Week 2	Week 3	Week 4	Week 5
1. Examine competitors' Web sites	|||||||||||||||||||| ||||||||||	||||||||||||			
2. Get information for your Web site	||||||||||||||||||| ||||||||||	||||||||||||||||| ||||||||||			
3. Learn Web-authoring software		|||||||||||||||||| ||||||||||	||||||||||||||||||| ||||||||||		
4. Create (design) your Web site			\\\\\\\\\\	\\\\\\\\\\\\\\\\\\\\\\ \\	\\\\\
5. "Publish" (put) Web site online					\\\\\\\\\\\\\\\\\\

figure A.2

GANTT CHART FOR DESIGNING A WEB SITE.

This shows the tasks accomplished and the time planned for remaining tasks to build a company Web site.

Tool #3: Break-Even Analysis—How Many Items Must You Sell to Turn a Profit?

***Break-even analysis* is a way of identifying how much revenue is needed to cover the total costs of developing and selling a product.** Let's walk through the computation of a break-even analysis, referring to the illustration. *(See Figure A.3.)* We assume

figure A.3

BREAK-EVEN ANALYSIS

you are an apparel manufacturer making shirts or blouses. Start in the lower-right corner of the diagram on the previous page and follow the circled numbers as you read the descriptions above.

Example

Break-Even Analysis: Why Do Airfares Vary So Much?

Why do some airlines charge four times more than others for a flight of the same distance?

There are several reasons, but break-even analysis enters into it.

United Airlines' average cost for flying a passenger 1 mile in a recent year was 11.7 cents, whereas Southwest's was 7.7 cents. Those are the break-even costs. What they charged beyond that was their profit.

Why the difference? One reason, according to a study by the U.S. Department of Transportation, is that Southwest's expenses are lower. United flies more long routes than short ones, so its costs are stretched out over more miles, making its costs for flying shorter routes higher than Southwest's.

Another factor affecting airfares is the type of passengers flying a particular route—whether they are high-fare-paying business travelers or more price-conscious leisure travelers. Business travelers often don't mind paying a lot (they are reimbursed by their companies), and those routes (such as Chicago to Cincinnati) tend to have more first-class seats, which drives up the average price. Flights to vacation spots (such as Las Vegas) usually have more low-price seats because people aren't willing to pay a lot for pleasure travel. Also, nonstop flight fares often cost more than flights with connections.

Benefits Break-even analysis has two benefits:

- **For doing future "what-if" alternate scenarios of costs, prices, and sales.** This tool allows you to vary the different possible costs, prices, and sales quantities to do rough "what-if" scenarios to determine possible pricing and sales goals. Since the numbers are interrelated, if you change one, the others will change also.
- **For analyzing the profitability of past projects.** While break-even analysis is usually used as a tool for future projects, it can also be used retroactively to find out whether the goal of profitability was really achieved, since costs may well have changed during the course of the project. In addition, you can use it to determine the impact of cutting costs once profits flow.

Limitations Break-even analysis is not a cure-all.

- **It oversimplifies.** In the real world, things don't happen as neatly as this model implies. For instance, fixed and variable costs are not always so readily distinguishable. Or fixed costs may change as the number of sales units goes up. And not all customers may pay the same price (some may get discounts).
- **The assumptions may be faulty.** On paper, the formula may work perfectly for identifying a product's profitability. But what if customers find the prices too high? Or what if sales figures are outrageously optimistic? In the marketplace, your price and sales forecasts may really be only good guesses. ●

chapter notes

CHAPTER I

1. M. Shiels, "Carol Bartz: 'The Safe Pick,'" *BBC News,* January 13, 2009, http://news.bbc.co.uk/2/hi/technology/7827546.stm (accessed January 16, 2010); J. Paczkowski, "Carol Bartz: The ALL CAPS CEO," *All Things Digital,* January 14, 2009, http://digitaldaily.allthingsd.com/20090114/carol-bartz-the-all-caps-ceo (accessed January 16, 2010); K. Swisher, "A Question of Management," *The Wall Street Journal,* June 2, 2009, p. R4; and L. Wolfe, "Biography of Carol Bartz—CEO of Yahoo," *About.com Guide,* http://womeninbusiness.about.com/od/successfulbusinesswomen/p/carol-bartz.htm (accessed January 16, 2010); and J. Temple, "Determination Defines Yahoo CEO," *San Francisco Chronicle,* February 28, 2010, pp. A1, A13.
2. C. Bartz, "Just Deal with It," *Fortune,* September 28, 2009, p. 115.
3. Ibid.
4. M. P. Follett, quoted in J. F. Stoner and R. E. Freeman, *Management,* 5th ed. (Englewood Cliffs, NJ: Prentice Hall, 1992), p. 6.
5. B. A. Carpenter, "Customer Service Automated Phone Answerer Irksome," *Reno Gazette-Journal,* September 23, 2009, p. 11A.
6. Harris Interactive for IMShopping, June 12-16, 2009, in "Ability to Get Human Help Clicks with Online Shoppers," *USA Today,* August 25, 2009, p. 1A.
7. Emily Yellin, author of *Your Call Is (Not That) Important to Us,* quoted in B. D. Phillips, "Please, Stay On the Line," *The Wall Street Journal,* March 24, 2009, p. A15.
8. Scott Broetzmann of CustomerCare Measurement Consulting, quoted in D. Oldenburg, Associated Press, "Tired of Automated Phone Menus? Press 1," *Reno Gazette-Journal,* March 15, 2004, p. 3E.
9. Richard Shapiro, quoted in W. C. Taylor, "Your Call Should Be Important to Us, but It's Not," *The New York Times,* February 26, 2006, sec. 3, p. 3; G. J. Carter, "How to Get a Human to Answer the Phone," *USA Weekend,* April 14–16, 2006, p. 4. See also the Get Human Web site at www.gethuman.com.
10. "At Customer Service, Hunt Is On for a Live Voice," *USA Today,* November 27, 2007, p. 11A.
11. Taylor, 2006.
12. G. Colvin, "Catch a Rising Star," *Fortune,* February 6, 2006, pp. 46–50.
13. "Usual Weekly Earnings of Wage and Salary Workers, Fourth Quarter 2009," *Economic News Release,* Bureau of Labor Statistics, January 21, 2010, http://www.bls.gov/news.release/wkyeng.nr0.htm (accessed January 21, 2010).
14. U.S. Census Bureau, *Current Population Survey, 2009 Annual Social and Economic Supplement,* Table PINC-03. Educational Attainment—People 25 Years Old and Over, by Total Money Earnings in 2008, Work Experience in 2008, Age, Race, Hispanic Origin, and Sex: Both Sexes, 25 Years and Over, All Races, September 11, 2009, http://www.census.gov/hhes/www/cpstables/032009/perinc/new03_001.htm (accessed January 21, 2010).
15. D. Jones and B. Hansen, "CEO Pay Dives in a Rough 2008," *USA Today,* May 8, 2009, http://www.usatoday.com/money/companies/management/2009-05-01-ceo-pay-for-2008-falls_N.htm (accessed January 22, 2010).
16. Survey sponsored by the Corporate Library, reported in C. Hinton, "Media CEO Compensation Reached Over \$2 M in 2008," *Marketwatch.com,* October 20, 2008, http://www.marketwatch.com/story/median-ceo-compensation-reached-over-2-mln-in-2008 (accessed Janury 22, 2010).
17. "Salary.com Survey Finds Median Pay for Small-Biz CEOs," *Birmingham Business Journal,* November 29, 2007, http://www.bizjournals.com/birmingham/stories/2007/11/26/daily23.html?ana=from_rss (accessed January 21, 2010).
18. O. Pollar, "Are You Sure You Want to Be a Manager?" *San Francisco Examiner,* October 4, 1998, p. J-3.
19. M. Csikszentmihalyi, *Flow: The Psychology of Optimal Experience* (New York: HarperCollins, 1990), and *Beyond Boredom and Anxiety* (San Francisco: Jossey-Bass, 1975), *Creativity: Flow and the Psychology of Discovery and Invention* (New York: Harper Perennial, 1996), *Finding Flow: The Psychology of Engagement with Everyday Life* (New York: Basic Books, 1998); and *Good Business: Leadership, Flow, and the Making of Meaning* (New York: Penguin Books, 2003).
20. Reports by Nielsen Online for the Newspaper Association, reported in R. Pérez-Peña, "Newspaper Circulation Falls by More Than 10%," *The New York Times,* October 27, 2009, p. B3.
21. P. R. Kann, "Quality Reporting Doesn't Come Cheap," *The Wall Street Journal,* September 25, 2009, p. A15.
22. A. Clark, "New York Times to Charge Readers for Online Content," *guardian.co.uk,* January 20, 2010, http://www.guardian.co.uk/media/2010/jan/20/new-york-times-charging-content-online (access January 22, 2010).
23. D. Carr, "After a Year of Ruin, Some Hope," *The New York Times,* December 21, 2009, pp. B1, B6.
24. R. Pérez-Peña, "Publishers Make Plans for Devices Yet to Come," *The New York Times,* December 9, 2009, p. B3.
25. P. Coy, M. Conlin, and M. Herbst, "The Disposable Worker," *BusinessWeek,* January 18, 2010, pp. 32–39.
26. U.S. Census Bureau analysis, reported in S. Roberts, "Census Finds Increase in Foreign-Born Workers," *The New York Times,* December 8, 2009, p. A21.
27. U.S. Census Bureau, "An Older and More Diverse Nation by Midcentury," *U.S. Census Bureau News,* August 14, 2008, http://www.census.gov/Press-Release/www/releases/archives/population/012496.html (accessed January 22, 2010).
28. See, for instance, S. E. Page, *The Difference: How the Power of Diversity Creates Better Groups, Firms, Schools and Societies* (Princeton, NJ: Princeton University Press, 2007); C. Dreifus, "In Professor's Model, Diversity = Productivity," *The New York Times,* January 8, 2008, p. D2; and M. J. Pearsall, A. Ellis, and J. Evans, "Unlocking the Effects of Gender Faultlines on Team Creativity: Is Activation the Key?" *Journal of Applied Psychology,* January 2008, pp. 225–234.
29. S. McCartney, "Teaching Americans How to Behave Abroad," *The Wall Street Journal,* April 11, 2006, pp. D1, D4. See also J. Clark, "That 'Ugly American' Image Is Getting a Makeover Guide," *USA Today,* April 28, 2006, p. 9D.

30. T. L. Friedman, *The World Is Flat: A Brief History of the Twenty-first Century* (New York: Farrar, Straus and Giroux, 2005).

31. IDC Research, cited in M. Moreau, "Implementing an eCommerce System—Ask Critical Questions," Blog, Bridgeline Software, January 11, 2010, http://blog.bridgelinesw.com/2010/01/ecommerce-system-critical-questions (accessed January 22, 2010).

32. M. J. Mandel and R. D. Hof, "Rethinking the Internet," *BusinessWeek*, March 26, 2001, p. 118. See also B. Powell, "The New World Order," *Fortune*, May 14, 2001, pp. 134, 136.

33. See C. Graham, "In-Box Overload," *The Arizona Republic*, April 16, 2007, p. A14; and J. Vascellaro, "What's a Cellphone For?" *The Wall Street Journal*, March 26, 2007, p. R5.

34. B. Levisohn, "How to Make a Madoff," *BusinessWeek*, December 16, 2008, http://www.businessweek.com/investor/content/dec2008/pi20081215_232943.htm?chan=investing_investing+index+page_top+stories (accessed January 21, 2010). See also D. Gross, "Membership Has Its Penalties," *Newsweek*, January 12, 2009, p. 18; and M. Hosenball, "Made Money with Madoff? Don't Count on Keeping It," *Newsweek*, January 12, 2009, p. 9.

35. D. R. Henriques, "Madoff, Apologizing, Is Given 150 Years," *The New York Times*, June 30, 2009, pp. A1, B4.

36. M. Elias, "Study: Today's Youth Think Quite Highly of Themselves," *USA Today*, November 19, 2008, p. 7D. The study is J. M. Twenge and W. K. Campbell, "Increases in Positive Self-Views among High School Students: Birth-Cohort Changes in in Anticipated Performance, Self-Satisfaction, Self-Liking, and Self-Competence," *Psychological Science*, November 2008, pp. 1082–1086.

37. L. Powers, "Study Finds Teens Believe Lying, Cheating Required to Succeed," *Reno Gazette-Journal*, November 24, 2009, pp. 1A, 4A.

38. *A Study of Values and Behavior Concerning Integrity: The Impact of Age, Cynicism, and High School Character* (Los Angeles: Josephson Institute of Ethics, 2009).

39. D. Seidman, "Building Trust by Trusting," *BusinessWeek*, September 7, 2009, p. 76.

40. A. Gore, *An Inconvenient Truth* (Emmaus, PA: Rodale, 2006). See also A. Gore and D. Blood, "For People and Planet," *The Wall Street Journal*, March 28, 2006, p. A20.

41. This definition of sustainability was developed in 1987 by the World Commission on Environment and Development.

42. J. Saseen, "Who Speaks for Business?" *BusinessWeek*, October 19, 2009, pp. 22–24.

43. A. S. Ross, "Apple Heats Up Climate Battle," *San Francisco Chronicle*, October 6, 2009, pp. D1, D3; and D. R. Baker, "Shifting Alliances in Debate," *San Francisco Chronicle*, October 9, 2009, C1, C2.

44. S. Lohr, "The Cost of an Overheated Planet," *The New York Times*, December 12, 2006, pp. C1, C5; B. Walsh, "How Business Saw the Light," *Time*, January 15, 2007, pp. 56–57; and J. Ball, "In Climate Controversy, Industry Cedes Ground," *The Wall Street Journal*, January 23, 2007, pp. A1, A17.

45. J. Sandberg, "Down Over Moving Up: Some Bosses Find They Hate Their Jobs," *The Wall Street Journal*, July 27, 2005, p. B1. See also D. Jones, "Besides Being Lonely at the Top, It Can Be 'Disengaging' as Well," *USA Today*, June 21, 2005, pp. 1B, 2B.

46. J. Flanigan, "Managing Your Career as a Business," *The New York Times*, October 15, 2009, p. B4.

47. S. Armour, "Who Wants to Be a Middle Manager?" *USA Today*, August 13, 2007, pp. 1B, 2B.

48. Pollar, 1998.

49. For an instructive account of employee happiness and culture, see the example set by the founder of Nick's Pizza & Pub, described in B. Burlingham, "Lessons from a Blue-Collar Millionaire," *Inc.*, February 2010, pp. 56–63.

50. P. Drucker, reported in R. L. Knowdell, "A Model for Managers in the Future Workplace: Symphony Conductor," *The Futurist*, June–July 1998, p. 22.

51. S. E. Needleman, "What's in a Title? Ego Stroking, Chiefly," *The Wall Street Journal*, December 26, 2007, p. B7.

52. A. Thompson, "The Hardest Management Job," *The Costco Connection*, August 2005, pp. 30–33.

53. "5-Year Winners," *Fast Company*, December 2007–January 2008, p. 115.

54. P. M. Blau and W. R. Scott, *Formal Organizations* (San Francisco: Chandler, 1962).

55. H. Mintzberg, *The Nature of Managerial Work* (New York: Harper & Row, 1973).

56. Ibid.

57. Ed Reilly, quoted in W. J. Holstein, "Attention-Juggling in the High-Tech Office," *The New York Times*, June 4, 2006, sec. 3, p. 9.

58. J. P. Kotter, "What Effective General Managers Really Do," *Harvard Business Review*, March–April 1999, pp. 145–159.

59. L. Stroh, quoted in A. Muoio, "Balancing Acts," *Fast Company*, February–March 1999, pp. 83–90.

60. S. MacDermid, Purdue University, and M. D. Lee, McGill University, two-year study cited in R. W. Huppke, Associated Press, "Take This Job, and Love It," *San Francisco Chronicle*, January 28, 1999, p. B2.

61. A. Deutschman, "The CEO's Secret of Managing Time," *Fortune*, June 1, 1992, pp. 135–146.

62. D. G. Lepore, quoted in Muoio, 1999.

63. J. Cooper-Kahn and L. Dietzel, "What Is Executive Functioning?" *LD Online*, 2008, http://www.ldonline.org/article/What_Is_Executive_Functioning%3F (accessed January 21, 2010).

64. *Generation M2: Media in the Lives of 8- to 18-Year-olds* (Menlo Park, CA: Kaiser Family Foundation, 2010).

65. L. Rosen, cited in B. Stone, "Old Fogies by Their Twenties," *The New York Times*, January 10, 2010, Week in Review section, p. 5. Rosen is the author of *Rewired: Understanding the iGeneration and the Way They Learn* (New York: Palgrave Macmillan, 2010).

66. R. E. Bohn and J. E. Short, *How Much Information? 2009 Report on American Consumers* (San Diego: Global Information Industry Center, University of California, San Diego, 2009).

67. W. Gallagher, quoted in book review, D. G. Myers, "Please Pay Attention," *The Wall Street Journal*, April 20, 2009, p. A13. Gallagher is author of *Rapt* (New York: Penguin Press, 2009).

68. J. Tierney, "Ear Plugs to Lasers: The Science of Concentration," *The New York Times*, May 5, 2009, p. D2.

69. Psychiatrist E. M. Hallowell, quoted in A. Tugend, "Multitasking Can Make You Lose . . . Um . . . Focus," *The New York Times*, October 25, 2008, p. B7. Hollowell is the author of *CrazyBusy: Overstretched, Overbooked, and About to Snap!* (New York: Ballantine, 2006).

70. P. Steel, "The Nature of Procrastination: A Meta-Analytic and Theoretical Review of Quintessential Self-Regulatory Failure," *Psychological Bulletin*, January 2007, pp. 65–94. See also S. Borenstein, "Study: More Americans Doing Less," *San Francisco Chronicle*, January 12, 2007, p. A2.

71. M. Chafkin, "You've Been Yelped," *Inc.*, February 2010, pp. 48–55.

72. S. Perman, "The Entrepreneurial Melting Pot," *Business-Week Online,* June 6, 2005; www.businessweek.com/smallbiz/content/jun2006/sb20060606_980_521.htm?chan=smallbiz_smallbiz+index+page_getting+started (accessed January 21, 2010). See also J. Mehring, "The Real Job Engines," *BusinessWeek SmallBiz,* Spring 2006, p. 42; and A. Weintraub, "Hot Growth," *BusinessWeek,* June 5, 2006, pp. 48–52.

73. S. A. Shane, "How Start-Ups Really Create Jobs—and What This Means for Employment Growth," *The New York Times,* October 19, 2009, http://boss.blogs.nytimes.com/2009/10/19/how-start-ups-really-create-jobs-and-what-this-means-for-employment-growth/ (accessed January 23, 2010).

74. Study by The Guardian Life Small Business Research Institute, reported in M. D. Wolf, "Women-Owned Businesses: America's New Job Creation Engine," *Forbes.com,* January 12, 2010, http://www.forbes.com/2010/01/12/smallbusiness-job-market-forbes-women-entrepreneurs-economic-growth.html (accessed January 21, 2010).

75. M. Mayer, quoted in "Leading the Way," *Newsweek,* September 25, 2006, pp. 51–52.

76. P. F. Drucker, *Innovation and Entrepreneurship* (New York: Harper & Row, 1986), pp. 27–28.

77. A. M. Webber, "Danger: Toxic Company," *Fast Company,* November 1998, pp. 152–161.

78. D. C. McClelland, *The Achieving Society* (New York: Van Nostrand, 1961); D. C. McClelland, *Human Motivation* (Glenview, IL: Scott, Foresman, 1985); D. L. Sexton and N. Bowman, "The Entrepreneur: A Capable Executive and More," *Journal of Business Venturing* 1 (1985), pp. 129–140; D. Hisrich, "Entrepreneurship/Intrapreneurship," *American Psychologist,* February 1990, p. 218; T. Begley and D. P. Boyd, "Psychological Characteristics Associated with Performance in Entrepreneurial Firms and Smaller Businesses," *Journal of Business Venturing* 2 (1987), pp. 79–93; and C. R. Kuehl and P. A. Lambing, *Small Business: Planning and Management* (Fort Worth, TX: Dryden Press, 1990).

79. Global Entrepreneurship Monitor, 2002 study by London Business School and Babson College, reported in J. Bailey, "Desire—More Than Need—Builds a Business," *The Wall Street Journal,* May 21, 2002, p. B4.

80. R. L. Katz, "Skills of an Effective Administrator," *Harvard Business Review,* September–October, 1974, p. 94. Also see M. K. De Vries, "The Eight Roles Executives Play," *Organizational Dynamics,* 2007, pp. 28–44.

81. Shiels, 2009.

82. C. Bartz, quoted in O. Kharif, "To Autodesk—and Beyond?" *BusinessWeek.com,* May 12, 2004, http://www.businessweek.com/technology/content/may2004/tc20040512_0416_tcl47.htm (accessed January 16, 2010).

83. M. Lietke, "Tough First Year for Yahoo's Tough-Talking CEO," *MercuryNews.com,* January 12, 2010, http://www.mercurynews.com/ci_14173777?source=rss (accessed January 16, 2010).

84. Bartz, quoted in Wolfe, 2009.

85. L. M. Fisher, "Profile: Carol Bartz; Imposing a Hierarchy on a Gaggle of Techies," *The New York Times,* November 29, 1992, http//www.nytimes.com/1992/11/29/business/profile-carol-bartz-imposing-a-hierarchy-on-a-gaggle-of-techies.html?pagewanted=1 (accessed January 16, 2010).

86. Ibid.

87. Nilofer Merchant, quoted in Shiels, 2009.

88. Rob Enderle, Enderle Group, quoted in Shiels, 2009.

89. CEO recruiter, quoted in Colvin, 2006.

90. Colvin, 2006.

91. This box is reprinted from B. K. Williams and S. C. Sawyer, *Using Information Technology: A Practical Introduction,* 9th ed. (New York: McGraw-Hill, 2011).

92. W. Gallagher, cited in Tierney, 2009. Gallagher is author of *Rapt* (New York: The Penguin Press, 2009).

93. W. Gallagher, quoted in blog by J. Tierney, "Attention Must Be Paid—but How?" *The New York Times–Tierney Lab,* May 4, 2009, http://tierneylab.blogs.nytimes.com/ (accessed January 21, 2010).

94. F. P. Robinson, *Effective Study,* 4th ed. (New York: Harper & Row, 1970).

95. H. C. Lindgren, *The Psychology of College Success: A Dynamic Approach* (New York: Wiley, 1969).

96. R. J. Palkovitz and R. K. Lore, "Note Taking and Note Review: Why Students Fail Questions Based on Lecture Material," *Teaching of Psychology,* 7(1980), pp. 159–161.

CHAPTER 2

1. C. Hymowitz, "Executives Must Stop Jumping Fad to Fad and Learn to Manage," *The Wall Street Journal,* May 15, 2006, p. B1.

2. D. M. Rosseau, "Is There Such a Thing as 'Evidence-Based Management'?" *Academy of Management Review,* April 2006, pp. 256–269. Other debates about evidence-based management may be found in T. Reay, W. Berta, and M. Kazman Kohn, "Where's the Evidence on Evidence-Based Management?" *Academy of Management Perspectives,* November 2009, pp. 5–18; and R. Briner, D. Denyer, and D. M. Rousseau, "Evidence-Based Management: Concept Cleanup Time?" *Academy of Management Perspectives,* November 2009, pp. 19–32.

3. J. Pfeffer and R. I. Sutton, "Profiting from Evidence-Based Management," *Strategy & Leadership* 34, no. 2 (2006), pp. 35–42; and J. Pfeffer and R. I. Sutton, "Evidence-Based Management," *Harvard Business Review,* January 2006, pp. 63–74. Pfeffer and Sutton are authors of *Hard Facts, Dangerous Half-Truths, and Total Nonsense* (Boston: Harvard Business School Press, 2006). For a discussion of this book, see Hymowitz, 2006.

4. R. I. Sutton, interviewed in "Asked & Answered: Prove It," *Stanford Magazine,* May/June 2006, http://www.stanfordalumni.org/news/magazine/2006/mayjun/dept/management.html (accessed January 28, 2010). Discussions about the need for an evidence-based process in medicine may be found in D. Sanghavi, "Plenty of Guidelines, but Where's the Evidence?" *The New York Times,* December 9, 2008, p. D6; and R. Winslow, "Study Questions Evidence behind Heart Therapies," *The Wall Street Journal,* February 25, 2009, p. D1.

5. Tom Peters, quoted in J. A. Byrne, "The Man Who Invented Management," *BusinessWeek,* November 28, 2005, http://www.businessweek.com/magazine/content/05_48/b3961001.htm (accessed January 28, 2010).

6. Byrne, 2005. See also R. Karlgaard, "Peter Drucker on Leadership," *Forbes.com,* November 19, 2004, http://www.forbes.com/2004/11/19/cz_rk_1119drucker.html; B. J. Feder, "Peter F. Drucker, a Pioneer in Social and Management Theory, Is Dead at 95," *The New York Times,* November 12, 2005, http://www.nytimes.com/2005/11/12/business/12drucker.html; and P. Sullivan, "Management Visionary Peter Drucker Dies," *The Washington Post,* November 12, 2005, http://www.washingtonpost.com/wp-dyn/content/article/2005/11/11/AR2005111101938.html (all accessed January 28, 2010).

7. Pfeffer and Sutton, "Profiting from Evidence-Based Management," 2006.

8. C. M. Christensen and M. E. Raynor, "Why Hard-Nosed Executives Should Care about Management Theory," *Harvard Business Review*, September 2003, pp. 67–74.

9. Christensen and Raynor, 2003, p. 68.

10. G. Hamel, *The Future of Management* (Boston: Harvard Business School Press, 2007).

11. John Chambers, quoted in B. Worthen, "Cisco CEO John Chambers's Big Management Experiment," *The Wall Street Journal*, August 5, 2009, http://blogs.wsj.com/digits/2009/08/05/cisco-ceo-jophn-chamberss-big-management-experiment (accessed January 26, 2010).

12. P. Burrows, "Cisco's Extreme Ambitions," *BusinessWeek*, November 30, 2009, pp. 26–27.

13. B. Rice, "The Hawthorne Defect: Persistence of a Flawed Theory," *Psychology Today*, February 1982, pp. 70–74.

14. A. Maslow, "A Theory of Human Motivation," *Psychological Review*, July 1943, pp. 370–396.

15. D. McGregor, *The Human Side of Enterprise* (New York: McGraw-Hill, 1960).

16. See K. G. Smith, S. J. Carroll, and S. J. Ashford, "Intra- and Inter-organizational Cooperation: Toward a Research Agenda," *Academy of Management Journal*, February 1995, pp. 7–23; R. Crow, "Institutionalized Competition and Its Effects on Teamwork," *Journal for Quality and Participation*, June 1995, pp. 46–54; J. T. Delaney, "Workplace Cooperation: Current Problems, New Approaches," *Journal of Labor Research*, Winter 1996, pp. 45–61; H. Mintzberg, D. Dougherty, J. Jorgensen, and F. Westley, "Some Surprising Things About Collaboration—Knowing How People Connect Makes It Work Better," *Organizational Dynamics*, Spring 1996, pp. 60–71; M. E. Haskins, J. Liedtka, and J. Rosenblum, "Beyond Teams: Toward an Ethic of Collaboration," *Organizational Dynamics*, Spring 1998, pp. 34–50; and C. C. Chen, X. P. Chen, and J. R. Meindl, "How Can Cooperation Be Fostered? The Cultural Effects of Individualism-Collectivism," *Academy of Management Review*, April 1998, pp. 285–304.

17. A. Kohn, "How to Succeed without Even Vying," *Psychology Today*, September 1986, pp. 27–28. Sports psychologists discuss "cooperative competition" in S. Sleek, "Competition: Who's the Real Opponent?" *APA Monitor*, July 1996, p. 8.

18. D. W. Johnson, G. Maruyama, R. Johnson, D. Nelson, and L. Skon, "Effects of Cooperative, Competitive, and Individualistic Goal Structures on Achievement: A Meta-Analysis," *Psychological Bulletin*, January 1981, pp. 56–57. An alternative interpretation of the foregoing study that emphasizes the influence of situational factors can be found in J. L. Cotton and M. S. Cook, "Meta-Analysis and the Effects of Various Reward Systems: Some Different Conclusions from Johnson et al.," *Psychological Bulletin*, July 1982, pp. 176–183. Also see A. E. Ortiz, D. W. Johnson, and R. T. Johnson, "The Effect of Positive Goal and Resource Interdependence on Individual Performance," *The Journal of Social Psychology*, April 1996, pp. 243–249; and S. L. Gaertner, J. F. Dovidio, M. C. Rust, J. A. Nier, B. S. Banker, C. M. Ward, G. R. Mottola, and M. Houlette, "Reducing Intergroup Bias: Elements of Intergroup Cooperation," *Journal of Personality and Social Psychology*, March 1999, pp. 388–402.

19. B. Elbel, R. Kersh, V. L. Brescoll, and L. B. Dixon, "Calorie Labeling and Food Choices: A First Look at the Effects on Low-Income People in New York City," *Health Affairs*, published online October 6, 2009, http://content.healthaffairs.org/cgi/content/abstract/hlthaff.28.6.w1110 (accessed January 28, 2010).

20. A. Hartocollis, "Study Finds Calorie Postings in Restaurants Do Not Change Habits," *The New York Times*, October 6, 2009, p. A25.

21. S. F. Brown, "Wresting New Wealth from the Supply Chain," *Fortune*, November 9, 1998, pp. 204[C]–204[Z]. See also M. Maynard, "Toyota Shows Big Three How It's Done," *The New York Times*, January 13, 2006, pp. CI, C4.

22. See P. Davidson, "Lean Manufacturing Helps Companies Survive," *USA Today*, November 2, 2009, pp. 1B, 2B.

23. Y. Takahashi, "Toyota Accelerates Its Cost-Cutting Efforts," *The Wall Street Journal*, December 23, 2009, p. B4; C. Woodyard, "Toyota's Reputation Needs Some TLC," *USA Today*, December 31, 2009, pp. 1B, 2B; M. Maynard and H. Tabuchi, "Rapid Growth Has Its Perils, Toyota Learns," *The New York Times*, January 28, 2010, pp. A1, B4; K. Linebaugh and N. Shirouzu, "Toyota Heir Faces Crisis at the Wheel," *The Wall Street Journal*, January 28, 2010, pp. A1, A8; and M. Dolan, "Supplier Perplexed by Toyota's Action," *The Wall Street Journal*, January 28, 2010, p. A9.

24. J. Bennett and K. Linebaugh, "Acceleration Mishaps Worry Vehicle Owners," *The Wall Street Journal*, January 28, 2010, p. A8.

25. Statistics by Safety Research and Strategies, reported in Dolan, 2010.

26. For a description of Generation X characteristics, see N. A. Hira, "You Raised Them, Now Manage Them," *Fortune*, May 28, 2007, pp. 38–46.

27. E. Neuborne, K. Kerwin, and bureau reports, "Generation Y," *BusinessWeek*, February 15, 1999, pp. 80–88; N. Munk, "How Levi's Trashed a Great American Brand," *Fortune*, April 12, 1999, pp. 83–90; and J. Strasburg, "Shaking the Blues," *San Francisco Chronicle*, February 3, 2002, pp. G1, G3.

28. P. Sarkar, "Stores Boost Sales with Own Labels," *San Francisco Chronicle*, May 5, 2006, pp. D1, D6; and R. Jana, "Riding Hip Jeans into New Luxury Markets," *BusinessWeek*, January 22, 2007, http://www.businessweek.com/print/innovate/content/jan2007/id20070122_366747.htm (accessed January 28, 2010).

29. "US: Denim Jeans Market Fraying at the Edges—Research," *Just-Style.com*, February 9, 2009, http://www.just-style.com/article.aspx?id=103175; and "US Denim Jeans Market Report: 2009 Edition," *Infoshop.com*, November 2009, http://www.the-infoship.com/report/koan104200-us-denim-jean.html (both accessed January 30, 2010).

30. Mark-Evan Blackman, chair, menswear design department, Fashion Institute of Technology, New York, quoted in B. Hughes, "Workwear—Built to Last, Men Are Workin' It," *San Francisco Chronicle*, January 17, 2010, http://www.sfgate.com/cgi-bin/article.cgi?f=/c/a/2010/01/17/LVNMIBDCUH.DTL (accessed January 30, 2010).

31. Survey of 5,000 U.S. households conducted for The Conference Board by L. Barrington, L. Franco, and J. Gibbons, *I Can't Get No . . . Job Satisfaction, That Is: America's Unhappy Workers*, January 2010, http://www.conference-board-org/utilities/pressDetail.cfm?press_ID=3820 (accessed January 30, 2010).

32. D. Mattioli, "Rewards for Extra Work Come Cheap in Lean Times," *The Wall Street Journal*, January 4, 2010, p. B7.

33. "The Top Gurus," *The Wall Street Journal*, May 5, 2008, p. B6.

34. G. Hamel, with B. Breen, *The Future of Management* (Boston: Harvard Business School Press, 2007), p. 6.

35. G. Hamel, "Break Free!" *Fortune*, September 19, 2007, http://money.cnn.com/magazines/fortune/fortune_archive/2007/10/01/100352608/index.htm (accessed May 18, 2010).

36. E. J. Langer, *Mindfulness* (Reading, MA: Addison-Wesley, 1989). See also D. J. Siegel, *The Mindful Brain: Reflection and Attunement in the Cultivation of Well-Being* (New York:

W.W. Norton, 2007); and M. Landau, "When Doctors Negotiate Uncertainty," *Focus Online: News from Harvard Medical, Dental, and Public Health Schools*, May 4, 2007, http://focus .hms.harvard.edu/2007/050407/education.shtml (accessed January 25, 2010).

37. E. J. Langer, *The Power of Mindful Learning* (Reading, MA: Addison-Wesley, 1997), p. 4.
38. Langer, 1989, pp. 12–13.
39. Langer, 1989, p. 69.
40. "Ratings: Sedans," *Consumer Reports,* February 2010, p. 51.
41. A. Garvin, "Building a Learning Organization," *Harvard Business Review*, July/August 1993, pp. 78–91; and R. Hodgetts, F. Luthans, and S. Lee, "New Paradigm Organizations: From Total Quality to Learning to World-Class," *Organizational Dynamics*, Winter 1994, pp. 5–19D.
42. A. S. Miner and S. J. Mezias, "Ugly Duckling No More: Pasts and Futures of Organizational Learning Research," *Organization Science*, January–February 1996, pp. 88–99; and R. P. Mai, *Learning Partnerships: How Leading American Companies Implement Organizational Learning* (Chicago: Irwin, 1996).
43. B. Breen, "How EDS Got Its Groove Back," *Fast Company*, September 2001, p. 106.
44. D. Ulrich, T. Jick, and M. Von Glinow, "High-Impact Learning: Building and Diffusing Learning Capability," *Organizational Dynamics*, Autumn 1993, pp. 52–66; S. F. Slater, "Learning to Change," *Business Horizons,* November–December 1995, pp. 13–20; and D. M. Noer, *Breaking Free: A Prescription for Personal and Organizational Change* (San Francisco: Jossey-Bass, 1996).
45. M. J. Mandel and R. D. Hof, "Rethinking the Internet," *BusinessWeek*, March 26, 2001, p. 118.
46. Adapted from "Virtual Organization," *Whatis.com*; http:// whatis.techtarget.com/definition/0,,sid9_gci213301,00.html (accessed January 25, 2010).
47. Adapted from "Boundaryless," *Encyclopedia of Small Business*, ed. K. Hillstrom and L. C. Hillstrom (Farmington Hills, MI: Thomson Gale, 2002, and Seattle, WA: eNotes. com, 2006), http://business.enotes.com/small-business-encyclopedia/ boundaryless (accessed January 25, 2010). Regarding the impact of Web services on organizational boundaries, see R. D. Hof, "Web 2.0: The New Guy at Work," *BusinessWeek*, June 19, 2006, pp. 58–59.
48. S. Hamm, "Speed Demons," *BusinessWeek*, March 27, 2006, pp. 68–75. See also J. McGregor, "The World's Most Innovative Companies," *BusinessWeek*, April 24, 2006, pp. 63–74.
49. B. E. Becker, M. A. Huselid, and D. Ulrich, *The HR Scorecard: Linking People, Strategy, and Performance* (Boston: Harvard Business School Press, 2001), p. 4; and G. Gohlander, S. Snell, and A. Sherman, *Managing Human Resources*, 13th ed. (Mason, OH: South-Western Publishing, 2004).
50. S. Meisinger, "Taking the Measure of Human Capital," *HR Magazine*, January 2003, p. 10. See also R. J. Grossman, "Blind Investment," *HR Magazine*, January 2005, pp. 40–47; and *Unlocking the DNA of the Adaptable Workforce: The Global Human Capital Study 2008*, IBM Global Services, http://www.935.ibm.com/services/us/gbs/bus/html/ 2008ghcs.html (accessed January 25, 2010).
51. Inspired by P. S. Adler and S. Kwon, "Social Capital: Prospects for New Concept," *Academy of Management Review*, January 2002, pp. 17–40. See also R. A. Baaron and G. D. Markman, "Beyond Social Capital: How Social Skills Can Enhance Entrepreneurs' Success," *Academy of Management Executive*, February 2000, pp. 106–116; and L. Prusak and D. Cohen, "How to Invest in Social Capital," *BusinessWeek Online*, October 23, 2007, http://www.businessweek.com/-managing/ content/oct2007/ca20071023_070114.htm?chan=search (accessed January 25, 2010).
52. Data from "What Makes a Job Okay," *USA Today*, May 15, 2000, p. 1B.
53. J. Pfeffer and R. I. Sutton, "Evidence-Based Management," *Harvard Business Review*, January 2006, pp. 63–74. See also D. M. Rousseau, "Is There Such a Thing as 'Evidence-Based Management'?" *Academy of Management Review*, April 2006, pp. 256–269.
54. J. Pfeffer and R. I. Sutton, "Profiting from Evidence-Based Management," *Strategy & Leadership* 34(2) (2006), pp. 35–42.
55. M. Arndt, "Built for the Long Haul," *BusinessWeek*, January 30, 2006, p. 66.

CHAPTER 3

1. J. Pfeffer, in A. M. Webber, "Danger: Toxic Company," *Fast Company*, November 1998, pp. 152–161.
2. J. Pfeffer, *The Human Equation: Building Profits by Putting People First* (Boston: Harvard Business School Press, 1996).
3. K. Carney, "How to Keep Staff in a Boom Economy," *Inc.*, November 1998, p. 110.
4. S. Shellenbarger, "More Firms Siding with Employees, Bid Bad Clients Farewell," *The Wall Street Journal*, February 16, 2000, p. B1; and P. J. Frost, *Toxic Emotions at Work: How Compassionate Managers Handle Pain and Conflict* (Boston: Harvard Business School Press, 2002), http://books.google .com/books?id=FOrQrRYw4vOC&pg=PA177&lpg=PA177&dq= %22Benjamin+Group%22+clients&source=web&ots=AI3Hh 7ZJrt&sig=_hwZC67n9mMF30XT9zrmFdcML2c (accessed February 2, 2010).
5. J. Case, *Open-Book Management: The Coming Business Revolution* (New York: HarperBusiness, 1996).
6. C. Kleiman, "Companies Embracing 'Open-Book' Management," *San Jose Mercury News*, May 18, 1997, pp. PC1, PC2.
7. G. T. Brown, quoted in Kleiman, 1997.
8. H. Gilman, "Why We Don't Hate Wal-Mart Anymore," *CNNMoney.com,* October 27, 2009, http://money.cnn. com/2009/10/27/news/companies/dont_hate_walmart. fortune/index.htm?postversikon=2009102710 (accessed February 9, 2010).
9. C. Connolly, "At Wal-Mart, a Health-Care Turnaround," *The Washington Post,* February 13, 2009, http://www .washingtonpost.com/wp-dyn/content/story/2009/02/13/ ST2009021300507.html (accessed February 9, 2010).
10. A. Zimmerman, "Costco's Dilemma: Be Kind to Its Workers, or Wall Street?" *The Wall Street Journal*, March 26, 2004, pp. B1, B3; J. Flanigan, "Costco Sees Value in Higher Pay," *Los Angeles Times,* February 15, 2004, www.latimes.com/ business/la-fi-flan15feb15,1,61048 (accessed February 2, 2010); and C. Frey, "Costco's Love of Labor: Employees' Well-being Key to Its Success," *Seattle Post-Intelligencer*, March 29, 2004, http://seattlepi.nwsource.com/business/166680_ costco29.html (accessed February 2, 2010); S. Greenhouse, "How Costco Became the Anti-Wal-Mart," *The New York Times,* July 17, 2005, sec. 7, p. 1; C. Migden, "Wal-Mart Must Pay Its Share," *San Francisco Chronicle*, March 16, 2006, p. B9; and B. Saporito, "Restoring Wal-Mart," *Time*, November 12, 2007, pp. 46–52; Gilman, 2009; and PayScale, http://www.payscale.com/research/US/Employer= Wal-Mart_Stores,_Inc/Hourly_Rate and http://www .payscale.com/research/US/Employer=Costco_Wholesale_ company/Hourly_Rate (accessed February 9, 2010).
11. "Store Wars: When Wal-Mart Comes to Town," PBS, February 24, 2007.

12. D. Leonhardt, "The Economics of Henry Ford May Be Passé," *The New York Times*, April 5, 2006, pp. Cl, Cl2.

13. J. Goodnight, quoted in D. A. Kaplan, "The Best Company to Work For," *Fortune*, February 8, 2010, pp. 56–64.

14. "The Employee Ownership 100: America's Largest Majority Employee-Owned Companies," The National Center for Employee Ownership, May 2009, http://www.nceo.org/main/article.php/id/11 (accessed February 3, 2010).

15. Forester Research reported in P. Korkki, "When Industries Care about Their Customers," *The New York Times*, December 20, 2009, Business section, p. 2. See also B. Temkin, W. Chu, and S. Catino, *The Customer Experience Index, 2010*, Forrester Research, January 11, 2010, http://www.forrester.com/rb/Research/customer_experience_index,_2010/q/id/55833/t/2 (accessed February 3, 2010).

16. J. Nocera, "Put Buyers First? What a Concept," *The New York Times*, January 5, 2008, pp. B1, B9.

17. Jeff Bezos, quoted in Nocera, 2008, p. B9.

18. UTest review by 600 software professionals, reported in B. Acohido, "Study: Amazon Most User Friendly," *USA Today*, December 7, 2009, p. 2B. See also UTest, "Software Testing Leader Holds Competition to Compare E-Tailers Based on Pricing, Usability, Product Search and Other Feature Sets," December 7, 2009, http://www.utest.com/press/utest-%E2%80%9Cbattle-e-tailers%E2%80%9D-uncovers-more-500-bugs-amazoncom-walmartcom-and-targetcom (accessed February 3, 2010).

19. R. Metz, "Amazon 4Q Profit Climbs 71 Percent on Strong Holidays," *ABCNews*, January 29, 2010, http://abcnews.go.com/Technology/wireStory?id=9696042 (accessed February 3, 2010).

20. B. De Lollis and R. Yu, "Indie Hotels Cater to Elite Travelers," *USA Today*, January 29, 2008, p. 4B.

21. Bureau of Labor Statistics, U.S. Department of Labor, "Union Members in 2009," *Union Members Summary*, January 22, 2010, http://www.bls.gov/news.release/union2.nr0.htm (accessed February 2, 2010).

22. Bureau of Labor Statistics, reported in S. Greenhouse, "Most U.S. Union Members Are Working for the Government, New Data Shows," *The New York Times*, January 23, 2010, pp. B1, B5.

23. J. Schmitt and K. Warner, *The Changing Face of Labor, 1983–2008*, Center for Economic Policy Research, November 12, 2009, http://www.cepr.net/index.php/press-releases/press-releases/demographics-of-labor-movement (accessed February 4, 2010). See also S. Greenhouse, "Survey Finds Deep Shift in the Makeup of Unions," *The New York Times*, November 11, 2009, p. B5.

24. D. Barry, "In a Company's Hometown, the Emptiness Echoes," *The New York Times*, January 25, 2010, p. A9.

25. D. Babwin, "Cities Holding Firms to the Deals They Have," *San Francisco Chronicle*, January 3, 2010, p. A13.

26. S. Medintz, "Getting the Loan Officer on Your Side," *The New York Times*, May 28, 2009, p. B8; and S. Brown, as told to M. Zouhali-Worrall, "Tend to Your Lender," *FSB*, September 2009, p. 53. See also P. Davidson, "This Recession Isn't Being Kind to Entrepreneurs," *USA Today*, June 8, 2009, p. 1B; K. Chu and S. Block, "As Lenders Clamp Down, Credit Scores Take a Hit," *USA Today*, September 22, 2009, pp. 1A, 2A; and P. S. Goodman, "Clamps on Credit Tighten," *The New York Times*, October 13, 2009, pp. B1, B4.

27. F. Ma, quoted in M. Lagos, "Faux Fur May Not Be—State Labeling Law in the Works," *San Francisco Chronicle*, January 21, 2010, p. C2.

28. For a discussion of how politically passionate consumers take aim at certain businesses, see R. S. Dunham, "Companies in the Crossfire," *BusinessWeek*, April 17, 2006, pp. 30–33.

29. N. Singer, "In Recall, Role Model Stumbles," *The New York Times*, January 18, 2010, pp. B1, B2.

30. Interview with Gene Grabowski by M. Philips, "Toyota's 'Tylenol Moment,'" *Newsweek*, February 15, 2010, p. 12.

31. Bureau of Labor Statistics, *International Comparisons of Manufacturing Productivity and Unit Labor Cost Trends 2008*, October 22, 2009, http://www.bls.gov/news.release/prod4.nr0.htm (accessed February 2, 2010); and Bureau of Labor Statistics, reported in P. Wiseman, "Productivity Leaps at 6.2% Rate as Firms Wait to Hire," *USA Today*, February 5, 2010, p. 3B.

32. D. St. George, "More Teens Are Choosing to Wait to Get Driver's Licenses," *The Washington Post*, January 25, 2010, p. A1. The article reports on data from the U.S. Department of Transportation, Federal Highway Administration, "Distribution of Licensed Drivers—2008 by Sex and Percentage in Each Age Group and Relation to Population," *Policy Information*, January 2010, Table DL20, http://www.fhwa.dot.gov/policyinformation/statistics/2008/dl20.cfm (accessed February 6, 2010).

33. M. Kabel, "Diet Trends Affect U.S. Meat Glut," *Reno Gazette-Journal*, May 16, 2006, p. 4D.

34. Centers for Disease Control and Prevention, cited in C. Lochhead, "First Lady Leads Fight over Youths' Obesity," *San Francisco Chronicle*, February 3, 2010, pp. A1, A14.

35. Data analyzed by Associated Press from Centers for Disease Control and Prevention and from Population Reference Bureau, reported in M. Stobbe, "More Babies Born in U.S., Unlike Trend in Europe," *San Francisco Chronicle*, January 16, 2008, p. A8.

36. M. Mather, "Four Scenarios for U.S. Population Growth," Population Reference Bureau, December 2009, http://www.prb.org/Articles/2009/uspopulationgrowth.aspx (accessed February 6, 2010).

37. U.S. Census Bureau, reported in S. Roberts, "Census Finds Increase in Foreign-Born Workers," *The New York Times*, December 8, 2009, p. A21.

38. M. Galanter, reported in W. Glaberson, "When the Verdict Is Just a Fantasy," *The New York Times*, June 6, 1999, sec. 4, pp. 1, 6.

39. D. Bass, "Microsoft Makes Changes to Ease EU Competition," Bloomberg.com, February 21, 2008, http://www.bloomberg.com/apps/news?pid=20601087&sid=azE39eAmWCLU&refer=home (accessed February 2, 2010).

40. American Council on Education, reported by P. Wingert, "'F' in Global Competence," *Newsweek*, May 20, 2002, p. 11. See also D. J. Lynch, "U.S. Firms Becoming Tongue-Tied," *USA Today*, February 9, 2006, p. 6B; and "Execs Learning to Speak Second Language," *Reno Gazette-Journal*, May 5, 2006, p. 6D.

41. G. Allred, quoted in S. Armour, "Facing a Tough Choice: Your Ethics or Your Job," *USA Today*, September 21, 1998, p. B1.

42. L. T. Hosmer, *The Ethics of Management* (Homewood, IL: Irwin, 1987). See also S. Welch, "The Uh-Oh Feeling," *O Magazine*, November 2007, pp. 117–120. For more on money-and-ethics matters, see J. Fleming and L. Schwartz, *Isn't It Their Turn to Pick Up the Check?* (New York: Free Press, 2008).

43. Study by LRN, consultant on corporate ethics, cited in "Corporate Ethics Affect Employee Productivity," *HR Magazine*, July 2007, p. 16.

44. S. Saul, "Unease on Industry's Role in Hypertension Debate," *The New York Times*, May 20, 2006, pp. A1, B9; and C. Arnst, "Hey, You Don't Look So Good," *BusinessWeek*, May 8, 2006, pp. 30–32. For the results of a survey concerning doctors' ethics, see E. G. Campbell, S. Regan, R. L. Gruen, T. G. Ferris, S. R. Rao, P. D. Cleary, and D. Blumenthal, "Professionalism

in Medicine: Results of a National Survey of Physicians," *Annals of Internal Medicine,* December 4, 2007, pp. 795–802.

45. B. Kabanoff, "Equity, Equality, Power, and Conflict," *Academy of Management Review,* April 1991, pp. 416–441.

46. D. Fritzsche and H. Baker, "Linking Management Behavior to Ethical Philosophy: An Empirical Investigation," *Academy of Management Journal,* March 1984, pp. 166–175.

47. Associated Press, "Pacific Salmon to Stay on Endangered List," May 28, 2004, http://msnbc.msn.com/id/5085081, and "Chemicals in Our Water Are Affecting Humans and Aquatic Life in Unanticipated Ways," *Science Daily,* February 21, 2008, http://www.sciencedaily.com/-releases/2008/02/080216095740.htm (both accessed February 2, 2010).

48. J. Sandberg, "Monitoring of Workers Is Boss's Right but Why Not Include Top Brass?" *The Wall Street Journal,* May 18, 2005, p. B1.

49. G. Morgenson, "The Big Winner, Again, Is 'Scandalot,'" *The New York Times,* January 1, 2006, sec. 3, pp. 1, 7; C. Said, "From White Collars to Prison Blues," *San Francisco Chronicle,* May 26, 2006, pp. D1, D6; G. Morgenson, "Are Enrons Bustin' Out All Over?" *The New York Times,* May 28, 2006, sec. 3, pp. 1, 8; K. Clark and M. Lavelle, "Guilty as Charged!" *U.S. News & World Report,* June 5, 2006; A. Sloan, "Laying Enron to Rest," *Newsweek,* June 5, 2006, pp. 25–30, pp. 44–45; M. Gimein, "The Skilling Trap," *BusinessWeek,* June 12, 2006, pp. 31–32. See also S. Labaton, "Four Years Later, Enron's Shadow Lingers as Change Comes Slowly," *The New York Times,* January 5, 2006, pp. C1, C4; J. H. Zamansky, "At the Least, Former Enron Chiefs Are Guilty of Moral Bankruptcy," *USA Today,* February 1, 2006, p. 11A; A. Shell, "Enron Verdicts Good for Investors," *USA Today,* May 30, 2006, p. 1B; K. Eichenwald and A. Barrionuevo, "Enron Shows Businesses Face Tough Tactics," *The New York Times,* May 27, 2006, pp. A1, B4; and D. Glovin, "Refco Ex-Finance Chief Trosten Pleads Guilty to Fraud," Bloomberg.com, February 20, 2008, http://www.bloomberg.com/apps/news?pid=20601087&sid=aBl5wsezRDT4&refer=home# (accessed February 2, 2010).

50. "Wall Street's Dirty Little Secret," *The Week,* November 13, 2009, p. 13.

51. B. Levisohn, "How to Make a Madoff," *BusinessWeek,* December 16, 2008, http://www.businessweek.com/investor/content/dec2008/pi20081215_232943.htm?chan=investing_investing+index+page_top+stories (accessed August 8, 2009). See also D. Gross, "Membership Has Its Penalties," *Newsweek,* January 12, 2009, p. 18; and M. Hosenball, "Made Money with Madoff? Don't Count on Keeping It," *Newsweek,* January 12, 2009, p. 9.

52. D. R. Henriques, "Madoff, Apologizing, Is Given 150 Years," *The New York Times,* June 30, 2009, pp. A1, B4.

53. S. Stecklow, "Hard Sell Drove Stanford's Rise and Fall," *The Wall Street Journal,* April 3, 2009, pp. A1, A12; and E. Perez and J. A. Favole, "Stanford, 5 Others Face Ponzi Charges," *The Wall Street Journal,* June 20, 2009, pp. B1, B3.

54. F. Norris, "Goodbye to Reforms of 2002," *The New York Times,* November 6, 2009, pp. B1, B6.

55. See D. R. Dalton and C. M. Dalton, "Sarbanes-Oxley Legislation and the Private Company: If Not a Marriage, Then Certainly an Engagement," *Journal of Business Strategy,* February 2005, pp. 7–8; "SOX: No One-Size-Fits-All Solution to Dishonest Accounting," Knowledge@W.P.Carey, June 7, 2006, http://knowledge.wpcarey.asu.edu/index.cfm?fa=viewArticle&id=1259 (accessed February 2, 2010); "Research Supports Value of IT Consults in Post-SOX Age," Knowledge@W.P. Carey, June 7, 2006, http://knowledge.wpcarey.asu.edu/index.cfm?fa=viewArticle&id=1261 (accessed February 2, 2010); and W. Cienke, "Small Companies Also Can Benefit from Sarbanes-Oxley," *Small Business Times,* February 22, 2008, http://www.biztimes.com/news/2008/2/22/small-companies-also-can-benefit-from-sarbanes-oxley (accessed February 2, 2010).

56. J. Van Derbeken, "Ex-bank Employee Accused of Swindling Elderly Woman," *San Francisco Chronicle,* February 5, 2010, p. C6.

57. F. J. Evans, quoted in C. S. Stewart, "A Question of Ethics: How to Teach Them?" *The New York Times,* March 21, 2004, sec. 3, p. 11.

58. D. A. Kaplan, "MBAs Get Schooled in Ethics," *Fortune,* October 26, 2009, p. 27.

59. Research by the Center for Academic Integrity, Kenan Institute for Ethics, Duke University, cited in H. Oh, "Biz Majors Get an F for Honesty," *BusinessWeek,* February 6, 2006, p. 14.

60. L. Kohlberg, "Moral Stages and Moralization: The Cognitive Developmental Approach," in T. Lickona, ed., *Moral Development and Behavior: Theory, Research, and Social Issues* (New York: Holt, Rinehart and Winston, 1976), pp. 31–53; and J. W. Graham, "Leadership, Moral Development and Citizenship Behavior," *Business Ethics Quarterly,* January 1995, pp. 43–54. See also S. J. Reynolds and T. L. Ceranic, "The Effects of Moral Judgment and Moral Identity on Moral Behavior: An Empirical Examination of the Moral Individual," *Journal of Applied Psychology,* November 2007, pp. 1610–1624.

61. Adapted in part from W. E. Stead, D. L. Worrell, and J. Garner Stead, "An Integrative Model for Understanding and Managing Ethical Behavior in Business Organizations," *Journal of Business Ethics,* March 1990, pp. 233–242.

62. W. M. Welch, "Employee Screenings See Growth," *USA Today,* June 24, 2009, p. 3A.

63. A. Bennett, "Ethics Codes Spread Despite Criticism," *The Wall Street Journal,* July 15, 1988, p. 13.

64. Society for Human Resource Management Weekly Survey, 2005, cited in J. Thilmany, *HR Magazine,* September 2007, pp. 105–112.

65. T. R. Mitchell, D. Daniels, H. Hopper, J. George-Falvy, and G. R. Ferris, "Perceived Correlates of Illegal Behavior in Organizations," *Journal of Business Ethics,* April 1996, pp. 439–455. See also M. W., "Ethics Training Works," *Training,* November 2005, p. 15; L. Paine, R. Deshpandé, J. D. Margolis, and K. E. Bettcher, "Up to Code: Does Your Company's Conduct Meet World-Class Standards?" *Harvard Business Review,* December 1, 2005, pp. 122–135; and J. Brockner, "Why It's So Hard to Be Fair," *Harvard Business Review,* March 1, 2006, p. 122–132.

66. R. Pear, "Whistleblowers Likely to Get Stronger Federal Protections," *The New York Times,* March 15, 1999, pp. A1, A17.

67. T. Herman, "Tipster Rewards Require Patience," *The Wall Street Journal,* December 26, 2007, p. D3.

68. Associated Press, "Whistle-blowers Help U.S. Recoup Billions," *Reno Gazette-Journal,* September 2, 2008, p. 2B.

69. Survey by Cooperative Institutional Research Program, University of California, Los Angeles, reported in K. Zernike, "Annual Poll of Freshmen Shows Effect of Recession," *The New York Times,* January 21, 2010, p. A23.

70. Jed Emerson, quoted in C. Dahle, "60 Seconds with Jed Emerson," *Fast Company,* March 2004, p. 42.

71. This definition of sustainability was developed in 1987 by the World Commission on Environment and Development.

72. Brian Walker, interviewed by J. Akresh-Gonzales, "Herman Miller CEO Brian Walker on Meeting Sustainability Goals—with Customers' Help," *Harvard Business Review,* December 2009, p. 26.

73. M. Friedman, *Capitalism and Freedom* (Chicago: University of Chicago Press, 1962). See also S. Gallagher, "A Strategic Response to Friedman's Critique of Business Ethics," *Journal of Business Strategy,* January 2005, pp. 55–60.

74. P. Samuelson, "Love That Corporation," *Mountain Bell Magazine,* Spring 1971.

75. A. B. Carroll, "Managing Ethically with Global Stakeholders: A Present and Future Challenge," *Academy of Management-Executive,* May 2004, p. 118. Also see B. W. Husted and D. B. Allen, "Corporate Social Responsibility in the Multinational Enterprise: Strategic and Institutional Approaches," *Journal of International Business Studies,* November 2006, pp. 838–849.

76. J. Mincer and S. Banjo, "Insurers Offer Rewards for Going Green," *The Wall Street Journal,* April 22, 2009, p. D5.

77. C. Palmeri, "The Dividends from Green Offices," *Business-Week,* December 7, 2009, p. 15.

78. C. Batchelor, "Hotels: Relax with a Clear Conscience," *Financial Times,* January 25, 2010, http://www.ft.com/cms/s/0/68c23a26-0953-11df-ba88-00144feabdc0,dwp_uuid=68347df0-11df-ba88-00144feabdc0.html (accessed February 9, 2010); and S. Nassauer, "Less Housekeeping, More Perks," *The Wall Street Journal,* February 4, 2010, p. D3.

79. United Nations Intergovernmental Panel on Climate Change, *Fourth Assessment Report,* Climate Change 2007: Synthesis Report, Summary for Policy Makers, November 2007, http://wwwl.ipcc.ch/ipccreports/assessments-reports.htm (accessed February 28, 2010). See also F. Guterl, "Iceberg Ahead," *Newsweek,* March 1, 2010, pp. 34–37.

80. B. J. Creyts, A. Derkach, S. Nyquist, K. Ostrowski, and J. Stephenson, *Reducing U.S. Greenhouse Gas Emissions: How Much at What Cost?* U.S. Greenhouse Gas Abatement Mapping Initiative, Executive Report, December 2007, McKinsey & Company, www.mckinsey.com/clientservice/ccsi/pdf/US_ghg_-final_-report.pdf (accessed February 2, 2010). See also M. L. Wald, "Study Details How U.S. Could Cut 28% of Greenhouse Gases," *The New York Times,* November 30, 2007, p. C5.

81. Center for Small Business and the Environment, reported in E. Iwata, "Small Businesses Take Big Steps into Green Practices," *USA Today,* December 3, 2007, p. 4B.

82. See R. J. Samuelson, "Greenhouse Simplicities," *Newsweek,* August 27, 2007, p. 47. Also see R. Abrams, "Going Green Makes Good Business Sense," *Reno Gazette-Journal,* March 13, 2007, p. 6D; C. H. Deutsch, "For Suppliers, the Pressure Is On," *The New York Times,* November 7, 2007, pp. H1, H11; B. Feder, "Aiding the Environment, a Nanostep at a Time," *The New York Times,* November 7, 2007, p. H6; A. Martin, "If It's Fresh and Local, Is It Always Greener?" *The New York Times,* December 9, 2007, p. BU11; J. Carlton, "Tech Aims to Green Up Its Act," *The Wall Street Journal,* January 7, 2008, p. B6; and M. Judkis, "10 Ways to Save by Going Green," *U.S. News & World Report,* March 2010, pp. 34–36.

83. J. Ramirez, "How to Live a Greener Life," *Newsweek,* April 16, 2007, p. 82.

84. D. Gross, "Edison's Dimming Bulbs," *Newsweek,* October 15, 2007, p. E22.

85. Ramirez, 2007.

86. D. Ransom, "Consider the Source," *The Wall Street Journal,* November 12, 2007, p. R4.

87. American Wind Energy Association, reported in P. Davidson, "Wind Power Growth Gusts Strongly in U.S.A. in 2007," *USA Today,* January 18, 2008, p. 3B.

88. Iwata, 2007.

89. J. Markoff and S. Lohr, "Gates to Reduce Microsoft Role as Era Changes," *The New York Times,* June 16, 2008, pp. A1, C8; and J. Guynn, "He's Opening Windows to Philanthropy," *San Francisco Chronicle,* June 18, 2006, pp. F1, F5.

90. T. L. O'Brien and S. Saul, "Buffet to Give Bulk of Fortune to Gates Charity," *The New York Times,* June 26, 2006, pp. A1, A15; and D. G. McNeil Jr. and R. Lyman, "Buffet's Billions Will Aid Fight Against Disease," *The New York Times,* June 27, 2006, pp. A1, C4.

91. H. Rubin, "Google's Searches Now Include Ways to Make a Better World," *The New York Times,* January 18, 2008, pp. C1, C5; and K. J. Delaney, "Google: From 'Don't Be Evil' to How to Do Good," *The Wall Street Journal,* January 18, 2008, pp. B1, B2.

92. A.-A. Jarvis, "Pulling Off an Impressive Feet," *Newsweek,* July 3–10, 2006, p. 64.

93. A. Fox, "Corporate Social Responsibility Pays Off," *HR Magazine,* August 2007, pp. 43–47. For an example of an advertising agency that profits from developing social-responsibility campaigns, see S. Kang, "Agency's Social Responsibility Focus," *The Wall Street Journal,* August 17, 2007, p. B3.

94. R. Gildea, "Consumer Survey Confirms Corporate Social Action Affects Buying Decisions," *Public Relations Quarterly,* Winter 1994, pp. 20–21.

95. Caravan survey from Opinion Research developed by LRN of 2,037 adults, reported in "Ethics vs. Price," *USA Today,* June 14, 2006, p. 1B.

96. D. H. Pink, *Drive: The Surprising Truth about What Motivates Us* (New York: Riverhead, 2010).

97. N. T. Washburn, "Why Profit Shouldn't Be Your Top Goal," *Havard Business Review,* December 2009, p. 23.

98. Results can be found in "Tarnished Employment Brands-Affect Recruiting," *HR Magazine,* November 2004, pp. 16, 20.

99. 2003 National Business Ethics Survey, cited in *The Hidden Costs of Unethical Behavior* (Los Angeles: Josephson Institute of Ethics, 2004), p. 3, www.josephsoninstitute.org/pdf/workplace-flier_0604.pdf (accessed February 2, 2010). See also D. Turban and G. Greening, "Corporate Social Performance and Organizational Attractiveness to Prospective Employees," *Academy of Management Journal* 40 (1997), pp. 658–672.

100. M. Baucus and D. Baucus, "Paying the Piper: An Empirical Examination of Longer-Term Financial Consequences of Illegal Corporate Behavior," *Academy of Management Journal* 40 (1997), pp. 129–151.

101. 2003 survey by Wirthlin Worldwide, cited in *The Hidden Costs of Unethical Behavior,* p. 2.

102. 2000 National Business Ethics Survey, cited in *The Hidden Costs of Unethical Behavior,* p. 3.

103. "ACFE's Highly-Anticipated Report to the Nation to Be Published in June," preview of *2006 ACFE Report to the Nation on Occupational Fraud & Abuse,* Association of Certified Fraud Examiners http://www.acfe.com/announcement-rttn-preview.asp (accessed February 2, 2010).

104. Ernst & Young survey 2002 and KPMG Fraud Survey 2003, both cited in *The Hidden Costs of Unethical Behavior,* p. 2.

105. 2003 survey by Wirthlin Worldwide, cited in *The Hidden Costs of Unethical Behavior,* p. 2.

106. D. M. Long and S. Rao, "The Wealth Effects of Unethical Business Behavior," *Journal of Economics and Finance,* Summer 1995, pp. 65–73.

107. A discussion of ethics and financial performance is provided by R. M. Fulmer, "The Challenge of Ethical Leadership," *Organizational Dynamics,* August 2004, pp. 307–317.

108. Study by the Migration Policy Institute, Washington, DC, reported in L. Burton, "Illegal Immigration Impact on Economy Small, Group Says," *San Francisco Chronicle,* December 3, 2009, p. A24.

109. Study by David R. Hekman, *The Academy of Management Journal,* reported in "A Customer Bias in Favor of White Men," *The New York Times,* June 23, 2009, p. D6.

110. U.S. Labor Department statistics, reported in D. Mattioli, "With Jobs Scarce, Age Becomes an Issue," *The Wall Street Journal,* May 19, 2009, p. D4.

111. D. Cauchon, "Older White Males See Jobs Fade," *USA Today,* July 30, 2009, pp. 1A, 2B.

112. S. E. Page, *The Difference: How the Power of Diversity Creates Better Groups, Firms, Schools and Societies* (Princeton, NJ: Princeton University Press, 2007).

113. S. E. Page, quoted in C. Dreifus, "In Professor's Model, Diversity = Productivity," *The New York Times,* January 8, 2008, p. D2. See also G. A. Van Kleef and C. KI. W. De Dreu, "Bridging Faultlines by Valuing Diversity: Diversity Beliefs, Information-Elaboration, and Performance in Diverse Work Groups," *Journal of Applied Psychology,* September 2007, pp. 1189–1199.

114. M. Loden, *Implementing Diversity* (Chicago: Irwin, 1996), pp. 14–15.

115. H. Collingwood, "Who Handles a Diverse Work Force Best?" *Working Woman,* February 1996, p. 25.

116. See A. Karr, "Work Week: A Special News Report about Life on the Job—and Trends Taking Shape There," *The Wall Street Journal,* June 1, 1999, p. A1. See also E. Bazar, "Prayer Leads to Disputes in Workplace," *USA Today,* October 16, 2008, p. 3A.

117. B. Schlender, "Peter Drucker Takes the Long View," *Fortune,* September 28, 1998, pp. 162–173.

118. S. Theil, "The Incredible Shrinking Continent," *Newsweek,* March 1, 2010, pp. 38–39.

119. Stobbe, 2008; H. W. French, "As China Ages, a Shortage of Cheap Labor Looms," *The New York Times,* June 30, 2006, pp. A1, A10; and K. Bradsher, "Defying Global Slump, China Has Labor Shortage," *The New York Times,* February 26, 2010, p. A1.

120. M. Toossi, "Labor Force Projections to 2012: The Graying of the U.S. Workforce," *Monthly Labor Review,* February 2004, http://findarticles.com/p/articles/mi_m1153/is_2_127/ai_ll5346590/pg_13 (accessed February 2, 2010). See also R. L. Wiener, "Age Discrimination and Disparate Impact on Employment," *Monitor on Psychology,* May 2007, p. 27; D. R. Avery, P. F. McKay, and D. C. Wilson, "Engaging the Aging Workforce: The Relationship between Perceived Age Similarity, Satisfaction with Coworkers, and Employee Engagement," *Journal of Applied Psychology,* November 2007, pp. 1542–1556; and E. White, "The New Recruits: Older Workers," *The Wall Street Journal,* January 14, 2008, p. B3.

121. E. Porter, "Stretched to Limit, Women Stall March to Work," *The New York Times,* March 2, 2006, pp. A1, C2.

122. U.S. Labor Department statistics, reported in K. Evans, "Recession Drives More Women into the Work Force," *The Wall Street Journal,* November 12, 2009, p. A8. See also M. P. McQueen, "Better Education Shields Women from Worst Job Cuts," *The Wall Street Journal,* February 12, 2010, p. A4.

123. M. Meece, "One in Four Businesses Calls the Owner 'Ma'am,'" *The New York Times,* November 5, 2009, p. B4.

124. A. H. Eagly and L. L. Carli, *Through the Labyrinth* (Boston: Harvard Businss School Press, 2007).

125. "Women CEOs," Fortune 500, *cnn.money.com,* May 4, 2009, http://money.cnn.com/magazines/fortune/fortune500/2009/womenceos (accessed February 28, 2010).

126. Study by Hilary Lips, Radford University, reported in B. Morris, "How Corporate America Is Betraying Women," *Fortune,* January 10, 2005, pp. 64–74. See also C. Buck, "Author's Theory on Why Women Earn Less," *San Francisco Chronicle,* September 27, 2009, pp. D1, D4, reprinted from *Sacramento Bee.*

127. Association of Executive Search Consultants, *BlueSteps 2007 Diversity Report,* cited in J. D. McCool, "Diversity Pledges Ring Hollow," *BusinessWeek.com,* February 5, 2008, http://www.businessweek.com/managing/content/feb2008/ca2008025_080192.htm?chan=search (accessed February 2, 2010).

128. These statistics were obtained from B. Fitzgerald, "Ms. Fortune 500: Less Women Are Corporate Officers," *The Star Ledger,* February 22, 2007, http://www.nj.com/business/ledger/index.ssf?/base/busines-5/1172123103202440.xml&c. . . ; and "Women CEOs for Fortune 500 Companies," *CNNMoney.com,* http://money.cnn.com/magazines/fortune/fortune500/womenceos (both accessed February 2, 2010). Regarding gender stereotypes, see J. A. Segal, "Woman in the Moon," *HR Magazine,* August 2007, pp. 107–114.

129. For further discussion of various aspects of the glass ceiling, see also R. Morris, "To Get Ahead, Own the Store," *The New York Times,* November 18, 2004, p. C10; R. E. Herzlinger, "A Corporate Push—Against Women," *USA Today,* December 7, 2004, p. 13A; C. H. Deutsch, "Are Women Responsible for Their Own Low Pay?" *The New York Times,* February 27, 2005, sec. 3, p. 7; T. L. O'Brien, "Up the Down Staircase," *The New York Times,* March 19, 2006, sec. 3, pp. 1, 4; E. White, "Why Few Women Run Plants," *The Wall Street Journal,* May 1, 2006, pp. B1, B5; and R. Parloff, "The War Over Unconscious Bias," *Fortune,* October 1, 2007, http://money.cnn.com/magazines/fortune/fortune_archive/2007/10/15/100537276/-index.htm (accessed February 2, 2010). See also K. Miner-Rubino and L. M. Cortina, "Beyond Targets: Consequences of Vicarious Exposure to Misogyny at Work," *Journal of Applied Psychology,* September 2007, pp. 1254–1269.

130. B. R. Ragins, B. Townsend, and M. Matttis, "Gender Gap in the Executive Suite: CEOs and Female Executives Report on Breaking the Glass Ceiling," *Academy of Management Review,* February 1998, pp. 28–42.

131. R. Sharpe, "As Leaders, Women Rule," *BusinessWeek,* November 20, 2000, pp. 75–84.

132. K. Wisul, "The Bottom Line on Women at the Top," *BusinessWeek,* January 26, 2004; http://www.businessweek.com/bwdaily/dnflash/jan2004/nf20040126_3378_db035.htm (accessed February 2, 2010).

133. U.S. Census Bureau, "An Older and More Diverse Nation by Midcentury," *U.S. Census Bureau News,* August 14, 2008, http://www.census.gov/Press-Release/www/releases/archives/population/012496.html (accessed January 22, 2010).

134. U.S. Bureau of Labor Statistics, "Employed Persons by Occupation, Sex, Race, and Hispanic or Latino Ethnicity, 2008 Annual Averages," http://www.bls.gov/cps/race_ethnicity_2008_5.htm (accessed February 28, 2010).

135. "Household Income Rises, Poverty Rate Unchanged, Number of Uninsured Down," U.S. Census Bureau, August 16, 2008, http://www.census.gov/Press-Release/www/releases/archives/income_wealth/012528.html (accessed February 2, 2010).

136. See Equal Employment Opportunity Commission, "Race-Based Charges FY 1997–FY 2009," http://www.eeoc.gov/eeoc/statistics/enforcement/race.cfm (accessed February 28, 2010); B. Leonard, "Web, Call Center Fuel Rise in EEOC Claims," *HR Magazine,* June 2008, p. 30; and M. Luo, "In Job Hunt, Even a College Degree Can't Close the Racial Gap," *The New York Times,* December 1, 2009, pp. A1, A4.

137. B. E. Whitley, Jr., and M. E. Kite, "Sex Differences in Attitudes toward Homosexuality: A Comment on Oliver and Hyde (1993)," *Psychological Bulletin,* January 1995, pp. 146–154.

For different studies producing different percentages, see S. M. Rogers and C. F. Turner, "Male-Male Sexual Contact in the U.S.A.: Findings from Five Sample Surveys, 1970–1990," *Journal of Sex Research* 28 (1991), pp. 491–519; L. S. Doll, L. R. Petersen, C. R. White, E. S. Johnson, J. W. Ward, and the Blood Donor Study Group, "Homosexual and Nonhomosexual Identified Men: A Behavioral Comparison, *Journal of Sex Research* 29 (1992), pp. 1–14; J. Lever, D. E. Kanouse, W. H. Rogers, S. Carson, and R. Hertz, "Behavior Patterns and Sexual Identity of Bisexual Males," *Journal of Sex Research* 29 (1992), pp. 141–167; J. Billy, K. Tanfer, W. R. Grady, and D. H. Kiepinger, "The Sexual Behavior of Men in the United States," *Family Planning Perspectives* 25 (1993), pp. 52–60; E. Laumann, R. Michael, S. Michaels, and J. Gagnon, "Thermidor in the Sexual Revolution?" *National Review*, November 7, 1994, p. 18; and W. D. Mosher, A. Chandra, and J. Jones, "Sexual Behavior and Selected Health Measures: Men and Women 15–44 Years of Age, United States, 2002," *Advance Data from Vital and Health Statistics*, no. 362, September 15, 2005 (Hyattsville, MD: National Center for Health Statistics).

138. October 1, 2003, study by Harris Interactive Inc. and Witeck Combs Communications Inc., reported in C. Edwards, "Coming Out in Corporate America," *BusinessWeek*, December 15, 2003; www.businessweek.com:/print/magazine/content/03_50/b3862080.htm?bw (accessed February 2, 2010).

139. J. M. Croteau, "Research on the Work Experiences of Lesbian, Gay, and Bisexual People: An Integrative Review of Methodology and Findings," *Journal of Vocational Behavior*, April 1996, pp. 195–209; and L. Badgett, "The Wage-Effects of Sexual Orientation Discrimination," *Industrial and Labor Relations Review*, July 1995, pp. 726–739. See also B. R. Ragins, R. Singh, and J. M. Cornwell, "Making the Invisible Visible: Fear and Disclosure of Sexual Orientation at Work," *Journal of Applied Psychology*, July 2007, pp. 1103–1118; and "The Rights of Gay Employees," editorial, *The New York Times*, September 13, 2009, Week in Review section, p. 15.

140. Human Rights Campaign survey, reported in I. DeBare, "Gay, Lesbian Workers Gradually Gain Benefits," *San Francisco Chronicle*, June 30, 2006, pp. D1, D2.

141. K. Springen, "A Boost for Braille," *Newsweek*, May 20, 2002, p. 13.

142. Center for Labor Market Studies, Northeastern University, Boston, and the Chicago Alternative Schools Network, *Left Behind in America: The Nation's Dropout Crisis*, May 5, 2009, www.clms.neu.edu/publication/. . ./CLMS_2009_Dropout_Report.pdf (accessed February 28, 2010).

143. M. Schneider, "2003 National Assessment of Adult Literacy Results," National Center for Education Statistics, December 15, 2005, http://nces.ed.gov/whatsnew/commissioner/remarks2005/12_15_2005.asp. See also M. Kutner, E. Greenberg, Y. Jin, B. Boyle, Y.-c. Hsu, and E. Dunleavy, *Literacy in Everyday Life: Results from the 2003 National Assessment of Adult Literacy* (Washington, DC: National Center for Education Statistics, 2007).

144. T. L. Smith, "The Resource Center: Finding Solutions for Literacy," *HRFocus*, February 1995, p. 7. See also A. Bernstein, "The Time Bomb in the Workforce: Illiteracy," *BusinessWeek*, Febraury 25, 2002, p. 122.

145. M. Loden, 1996; E. E. Spragins, "Benchmark: The Diverse Work Force," *Inc.*, January 1993, p. 33; and A. M. Morrison, *The New Leaders: Guidelines on Leadership Diversity in America* (San Francisco: Jossey-Bass, 1992).

146. G. Dell'Orto, "Special Classes Help 3M Workers Learn How to Get Along," *San Francisco Chronicle*, June 2, 2000, p. B4.

147. U.S. Census Bureau, *Current Population Statistics, Families and Living Arrangements*, Table FG1. Married Couple Family Groups, by Labor Force Status of Both Spouses, and Race and Hispanic Origin of the Reference Person: 2008 (2009).

148. S. Shellenbarger, "Please Send Chocolate: Moms Now Face Stress Moving In and Out of Work Force," *The Wall Street Journal*, May 9, 2002, p. D1. See also A. Bernstein, "Too Many Workers? Not for Long," *BusinessWeek*, May 20, 2002, pp. 126–130; C. Benko, "Up the Ladder? How Dated, How Linear," *The New York Times*, November 9, 2008, Business section, p. 2; K. Evans, "In Downturn's Wake, Women Hold Half of U.S. Jobs," *The Wall Street Journal*, November 12, 2009, http://online.wsj.com/article/SB125797318108844061.html (accessed February 28, 2010); and McQueen, 2010.

CHAPTER 4

1. K. Reinhard, quoted in S. McCartney, "Teaching Americans How to Behave Abroad," *The Wall Street Journal*, April 11, 2006, pp. D1, D4. See also R. Yu, "Cultural Training Has Global Appeal," *USA Today*, December 22, 2009, p. 3B.

2. DDB Worldwide survey, cited in J. Clark, "That 'Ugly American' Image Is Getting a Makeover Guide," *USA Today*, April 28, 2006, p. 9D.

3. *World Citizens Guide*, Business for Diplomatic Action, May 2006, http://www.worldcitizensguide.org/index2.html (accessed February 14, 2010).

4. T. Lowry and F. Balfour, "It's All about the Face-to-Face," *BusinessWeek*, January 28, 2008, pp. 48, 50.

5. E. Schmitt, "A Man Does Not Ask a Man about His Wife," *The New York Times*, January 8, 2006, sec. 4, p. 7.

6. T. Rivas, "Name Game Hits a Global Roadblock," *The Wall Street Journal*, May 30, 2006, p. B5.

7. B. Morris, "The Pepsi Challenge: Can This Snack and Soda Giant Go Healthy?" *Fortune*, March 3, 2008, pp. 55–66.

8. L. Nardon and R. M. Steers, "The New Global Manager: Learning Cultures on the Fly," *Organizational Dynamics*, January–March 2008, pp. 47–59.

9. R. Richmond, "Entrepreneurs with Big Dreams Tap Global Market," *The Wall Street Journal*, April 17, 2007, p. B6.

10. See the related discussion in J. McGregor and S. Hamm, "Managing the Global Workforce," *BusinessWeek*, January 28, 2008, p. 34; C. Boles, "Last Call? Gates Pushes Globalism in Remarks," *The Wall Street Journal*, March 13, 2008, p. B3; and M. Herbst, "Guess Who's Getting the Most Work Visas," *BusinessWeek*, March 17, 2008, pp. 62, 64.

11. Cellular Telecommunications Industry Association, cited in A. Dunkin, "Smart, Useful—and They Won't Put a Sag in Your Suit," *BusinessWeek*, May 30, 1994, p. 141.

12. United Nations estimates, reported in "The Revolution Has Gone Mobile," editorial, *The New York Times*, February 20, 2010, p. A14.

13. Internet World Stats, "Internet Usage Statistics," September 30, 2009, http://www.internetworldstats.com/stats.htm (accessed February 17, 2010).

14. See J. Quittner, "Tim Berners-Lee," *Time*, March 29, 1999, pp. 193–194.

15. "Quarterly Retail E-Commerce Sales, 1st Quarter 2010," *U.S. Census Bureau News*, February 15, 2008, http://www.census.gov/retail/mrts/www/data/html/10Q1.html (accessed June 14, 2010).

16. E. Engleman, "Amazon.com Q4 Sales, Profit Surge on Strong Holiday Sales," *TechFlash*, January 28, 2010, http://www.techflash.com/seattle/2010/01/amazon_q4_earnings.html (accessed February 17, 2010).

17. S. Needleman, "When the Shoe Fits, but Needs a Fix," *The Wall Street Journal,* February II, 2010, p. D2.

18. R. M. Kantor, quoted in K. Maney, "Economy Embraces Truly Global Workplace," *USA Today,* December 3I, I998, pp. IB, 2B.

19. Maney, I998.

20. Kris Gopalakrishnan, interviewed in R. M. Smith, "A Titan of Globalism," *Newsweek,* November I9, 2007, p. E26.

21. M. Srivastava and M. Herbst, "The Return of the Outsourced Job," *Bloomberg BusinessWeek,* January II, 2010, pp. I6–I7.

22. J. Rosen, "Foreign Influence Needn't Be a Bad Thing," *USA Today,* November 23, 2009, p. 8B. See also M. Maynard, *The Selling of the American Economy: How Foreign Companies Are Remaking the American Dream* (New York: Broadway Business, 2009).

23. G. Easterbrook, "The Boom Is Nigh," *Newsweek,* February 22, 2010, pp. 48–49. Easterbrook is the author of *Sonic Boom: Globalization at Mach Speed* (New York: Random House, 2009).

24. "Is Global Finance Sector a Force for Good or Ill?" *The Wall Street Journal,* November 28, 2007, p. B9; and P. Krugman, "Don't Cry for Me, America," *The New York Times,* January I8, 2008, p. A23.

25. L. Uchitelle, "Another Shifting Industy," *The New York Times,* January I9, 2010, pp. BI, B5.

26. P. Izzo, "Many Jobs Gone Forever, Economists Say," *The Wall Street Journal,* February I2, 2010, p. A4; and D. Peck, "How a New Jobless Era Will Transform America," *The Atlantic,* March 2010, pp. 42–56. See also M. Whitehouse, "Radical Shifts Take Hold in U.S. Manufacturing," *The Wall Street Journal,* February 3, 2010, pp. BI, B4.

27. Easterbrook, 2010.

28. N. Negroponte, quoted in Maney, I998.

29. W. Boston, "Porsche and VW Agree to a Merger," *Time,* May 7, 2009, http://www.time.com/time/business/article/0,8599,I8967I4,00.html (accessed February I7, 2010).

30. J. Mouawad, "More Deals Expected in Energy," *The New York Times,* February I7, 2010, pp. BI, B6.

31. S. Weimer, "Mannequin Madness," *California Materials—Exchange,* Integrated Waste Management Board, April 23, 2004, http://www.ciwmb.ca.gov/CalMAX/Creative/2003/Winter.htm (accessed February I4, 2010); I. DeBare, "New Lease on Life for Mannequins," *San Francisco Chronicle,* July 29, 2006, p. J2; S. L. Thomas, "Warehouse Visit Spawns Mannequin Madness," *East Bay Business Times,* February 24, 2006, http://eastbay.bizjournals.com/eastbay/stories/2006/02/27/smallbl.html (accessed February I4, 2010).

32. P. McDonald, quoted in M. L. Levin, "Global Experience Makes Candidates More Marketable," *The Wall Street Journal,* September II, 2007, p. B6.

33. D. Mattioli, "With Fewer U.S. Opportunities, Home Looks Appealing to Expats," *The Wall Street Journal,* December I5, 2009, p. D7. See also P. Engardio, "China's Reverse Brain Drain," *BusinessWeek,* November 30, 2009, p. 58; and T. Abate, "U.S. May Be Set for Brain Drain," *San Francisco Chronicle,* February 27, 2010, p. DI, D2.

34. P. Davidson, "U.S. Job Hunters Eye Other Nations' Help Wanted Ads," *USA Today,* November I6, 2009, p. IB.

35. J. Androshick, quoted in H. Chura, "A Year Abroad (or 3) as a Career Move," *The New York Times,* February 25, 2006, p. B5.

36. T. Chea, "Americans Seek Opportunity in Bangalore," *Reno Gazette-Journal,* April 3, 2006, p. 3E.

37. S. Stapleton, quoted in R. Erlich, "Going Far in the East," *San Francisco Chronicle,* June 24, 2006, pp. CI, C2.

38. R. C. Carter, senior vice president for human resources at A&E Television Networks, quoted in Chura, 2006. For more about Americans working overseas, particularly in India, see J. S. Lublin, "Job Hopping Overseas Can Enhance a Career, but It Takes Fortitude," *The Wall Street Journal,* June 7, 2005, p. BI; N. Lakshman, "Subcontinental Drift," *BusinessWeek,* January I6, 2006, pp. 42–43; and R. J. Newman, "Coming and Going," *U.S. News & World Report,* January 23, 2006, pp. 50–52.

39. "The Global 2000," *Forbes.com,* April 8, 2009, http://www.forbes.com/lists/2009/I8/global-09_The-Global-2000_Sales.html (accessed February I9, 2010).

40. Survey by the Zimmerman Agency for Residence Inn by Marriott, in "Things You Love to Miss," *USA Today*, March I, I999, p. IB.

41. Lowry and Balfour, 2008.

42. Paul Calello of Credit Suisse, quoted in Lowry and Balfour, 2008.

43. Don G. Lents, chairman of international law firm Bryan Cave, quoted in J. Sharkey, "E-Mail Saves Time, but Being There Says More," *The New York Times,* January 26, 2010, p. B7.

44. L. Bergson, "A Road Scholar's Bag of Tricks," *BusinessWeek,* September 29, 2003, http://www.businessweek.com/smallbiz/content/sep2003/sb20030929_6259_sb002.htm? chan / search (accessed February I4, 2010).

45. Yu, 2009.

46. Bergson, 2003.

47. G. Stoller, "Doing Business Abroad? Simple Faux Pas Can Sink You," *USA Today,* August 24, 2007, pp. IB, 2B.

48. Britton and McGonegal, 2007, p. I20.

49. D. A. Heenan and H. V. Perlmutter, *Multinational Organization Development* (Reading, MA: Addison-Wesley, I979).

50. D. Jones, "Do Foreign Executives Balk at Sports Jargon?" *USA Today,* March 30, 2007, pp. IB, 2B.

51. R. Kopp, "International Human Resource Policies and Practices in Japanese, European, and United States Multinationals," *Human Resource Management,* Winter I994, pp. 58I–599.

52. H. R. Varian, "An iPod Has Global Value. Ask the (Many) Countries That Make It," *The New York Times,* June 28, 2007, p. C3.

53. W. J. Holstein, "Colonial Roots Have Spread Worldwide," *The New York Times,* June I6, 2007, p. B3.

54. E. Byron, "P&G's Global Target: Shelves of Tiny Stores," *The Wall Street Journal,* July I6, 2007, pp. AI, AI0. See also L. Wayne, "P. & G. Sees the World as Its Client," *The New York Times,* December I2, 2009, pp. BI, B2.

55. W. M. Cox, "An Order of Prosperity, to Go," *The New York Times,* February I7, 2010, p. A23.

56. D. Gross, "China Leaves Its Wallet at Home," *Newsweek,* December 2I, 2009, p. I0.

57. S. McCartney, "Who's Inspecting Your Airplane?" *The Wall Street Journal,* March 3, 2004, pp. DI, DI2.

58. Study of government data by Economic Policy Institute, Washington, DC, cited in R. Keil and L. Arnold, "New Jobs Created at Low End," *San Francisco Chronicle,* April I3, 2004, p. C5; and J. Hernandez, "Manufacturing Shows Signs of Strengthening," *The New York Times,* February 2, 2010, p. B8.

59. Forrester Research, cited in G. Epstein, "Static Disrupts the Bangalore Connection," *Barron's Online*, September I0, 2007, http://online.barrons.com/article/SBII892I2007482212I65.html (accessed February I4, 2010).

60. Forrester Research, "Losing Our Edge? Estimated Number of High-Skilled U.S. Jobs Moving Offshore," reported in K. Madigan, "Yes: This Is No Longer About a Few Low-Wage or Manufacturing Jobs. Now One Out of Three Jobs Is at Risk," *BusinessWeek,* August 25, 2003, pp. 37–38.

61. B. Schlender, "Peter Drucker Sets Us Straight," *Fortune,* January I2, 2004, pp. II5–II8. See also P. Engardio, "The Future

of Outsourcing," *BusinessWeek,* January 30, 2006, pp. 50–58; E. White, "Smaller Companies Join the Outsourcing Trend," *The Wall Street Journal,* May 8, 2006, p. B3; and L. Buchanan, "The Thinking Man's Outsourcing," *Inc. Magazine,* May 2006, pp. 31–33.

62. J. Thottam, "Is Your Job Going Abroad?" *Time,* March 1, 2004, pp. 26–34.

63. F. Levy, quoted in D. Wessel, "The Future of Jobs: New Ones Arise, Wage Gap Widens," *The Wall Street Journal,* April 2, 2004, pp. A1, A5.

64. For some caveats about offshoring, see M. Bolch, "Going Global," *Training,* January 2008, pp. 28–29; M. Weinstein, "On Target Offshore," *Training,* January 2008, pp. 34–36; and M. Bandyk, "Now Even Small Firms Can Go Global," *U.S. News & World Report,* March 10, 2008, p. 52.

65. A. M. Chaker, "Where the Jobs Are," *The Wall Street Journal,* March 18, 2004, pp. D1, D3; J. Shinal, "Which Types of Jobs Will Be in Demand?" *San Francisco Chronicle,* March 25, 2004, pp. C1, C4; and D. Wessel, "The Future of Jobs: New Ones Arise, Wage Gap Widens," *The Wall Street Journal,* April 2, 2004, pp. A1, A5.

66. J. Spohrer, quoted in Shinal, 2004.

67. P. Drucker, quoted in Schlender, 2004.

68. L. Uchitelle, "College Degree Still Pays, but It's Leveling Off," *The New York Times,* January 17, 2005, pp. C1, C2.

69. M. Thorneman, B. Lannes, and N. Palmer, "Resurrecting the China Joint-Venture," *Far Eastern Economic Review,* October 2008, http://www.feer.com/economics/2008/october/ Resurrecting-the-China-Joint-Venture; and J. Gopwani and M. Szczepanski, "Buick Remains Popular with China's Upper-Middle Class," *Detroit Free Press,* August 30, 2009, http:// www.allbusiness.com/automotive/motor-vehicle-models-new-car/12783271-1.html (both accessed February 21, 2010).

70. K. Bradsher, "China Moves to Beat Back a Tire Tariff," *The New York Times,* September 14, 2009, pp. A1, A3; S. Greenhouse, "Tire Tariffs Are Cheered by Labor," *The New York Times,* September 14, 2009, pp. B1, B4; and D. J. Lynch, "China-U.S. Trade Tensions Grow," *USA Today,* September 15, 2009, p. 3B.

71. "China to Cancel Car Import Quota in 2005," *China Daily,* February 13, 2004; www.chinadaily.com.cn/english/ doc/2004-02/13/ content_305954.htm (accessed February 14, 2010).

72. K. Maher and H. J. Pulizzi, "Chinese Slapped in Steel Dispute," *The Wall Street Journal,* December 31, 2009, p. A3.

73. J. Bhagwati, *Protectionism* (Cambridge, MA: MIT Press, 1988).

74. "WTO Telecoms Deal Will Ring in the Changes on 5 February 1998," World Trade Organization, January 26, 1998.

75. M. Landler, "Britain Overtakes U.S. as Top World Bank Donor," *The New York Times,* December 15, 2007, http://www.ny-times.com/2007/12/15/world/15worldbank.html (accessed February 14, 2010).

76. D. Workman, "U.S. Global Trade Debt by Country," Suite101. com, February 1, 2008, http://import-export.suite101.com/ (article.cfm/us_global_trade_debt_by_country (accessed February 14, 2010).

77. See, for example, E. Papaioannou, R. Portes, and G. Siourounis, "Optimal Currency Shares in International Reserves: The Impact of the Euro and the Prospects for the Dollar," *NBER Working Paper* No. 12333, June 2006, National Bureau of Economic Research, http://papers.nber.org/papers/w12333 (accessed February 14, 2010); and Associated Press, "Report: Greenspan Says Euro Could Replace U.S. Dollar as Reserve Currency of Choice," *International Herald Tribune,* September 17, 2007, http://www.iht.com/articles/ap/2007/09/17/

business/EU-FIN-MKT-Germany-Greenspan-Euro.php (accessed February 14, 2010).

78. S. Theil, "The Euro Zone Doesn't Need Greece," *Newsweek,* February 15, 2010, p. 8. See also R. Donadio and N. Kitsantonis, "Greece Struggles to Tame Debt as Its People Grow More Restive," *The New York Times,* December 12, 2009, pp. A4, A9; C. Forelle, M. Walker, and A. Gallioni, "Europe Vows to Save Greece," *The Wall Street Journal,* February 12, 2010, pp. A1, A10; L. Alderman, "So Fine, So Fickle, So Euro," *The New York Times,* February 14, 2010, Week in Review section, p. 3; M. Moore and A. Max, "Euro Currency Union Shows Internal Strains," *Reno Gazette-Journal,* February 14, 2010, p. 7B; P. Krugman, "The Making of a Euromess," *The New York Times,* February 15, 2010, p. A19; and "Greece Inches Back," editorial, *The New York Times,* February 19, 2010, p. A20.

79. D. Roberts and P. Engardio, "China's End Run around the U.S.," *BusinessWeek,* November 23, 2009, pp. 22–24; T. Wright, "Obama Aims to Regain U.S. Heft in Southeast Asia," *The Wall Street Journal,* November 12, 2009, p. A16; and L. Gooch, "Asia Free-Trade Zone Raises Hopes, and Some Fears about China," *The New York Times,* January 1, 2010, p. B3.

80. See M. A. O'Grady, "One Year After CAFTA," *The Wall Street Journal,* February 26, 2007, p. A18.

81. Samir Khalaf, quoted in H. M. Fattah, "Why Arab Men Hold Hands," *The New York Times,* May 1, 2005, sec. 4, p. 2.

82. G. A. Fowler, "In China's Offices, Foreign Colleagues Might Get an Earful," *The Wall Street Journal,* February 13, 2007, p. D1.

83. "How Cultures Collide," *Psychology Today,* July 1976, p. 69.

84. See P. R. Harris and R. T. Moran, *Managing Cultural Differences,* 4th ed. (Houston: Gulf Publishing, 1996), pp. 223–228; and M. Hilling, "Avoid Expatriate Culture Shock," *HR Magazine,* July 1993, pp. 58–63.

85. For complete details, see G. Hofstede, *Culture's Consequences: International Differences in Work-Related Values,* abridged ed. (Newbury Park, CA: Sage, 1984); "The Interaction between National and Organizational Value Systems," *Journal of Management Studies,* July 1985, pp. 347–357; and "Management Scientists Are Human," *Management Science,* January 1994, pp. 4–13.

86. M. Javidan and R. J. House, "Cultural Acumen for the Global Manager: Lessons from Project GLOBE," *Organizational Dynamics,* Spring 2001, pp. 289–305; R. J. House, P. J. Hanges, M. Javidan, P. W. Dorfman, and V. Gupta, eds., *Culture, Leadership, and Organizations: The GLOBE Study of 62 Societies* (Thousand Oaks, CA: Sage, 2004); and M. Javidan, P. W. Dorfman, M. S. de Luque, and R. J. House, "In the Eye of the Beholder: Cross Cultural Lessons in Leadership from Project GLOBE," *Academy of Management Perspectives,* February 2006, pp. 67–90.

87. A discussion of Japanese stereotypes in America can be found in L. Smith, "Fear and Loathing of Japan," *Fortune,* February 26, 1990, pp. 50–57.

88. G. A. Michaelson, "Global Gold," *Success,* March 1996, p. 16. English is increasingly becoming the language of business and more and more is being taught in foreign business universities. See D. Carvajal, "English as Language of Global Education," *The New York Times,* April 11, 2007, p. A21. In U.S. institutions, enrollments in Arabic-language classes are skyrocketing, but there is a great shortage of teachers. See T. Yahalom, "Surge in Students Studying Arabic Outstrips Supply of Teachers," *USA Today,* September 5, 2007, p. 7D.

89. Harris Poll, National Foreign Language Center, reported in "Lingua Franca?" *USA Today,* February 23, 1999, p. 1A.

90. D. J. Lynch, "U.S. Firms Becoming Tongue-Tied," *USA Today,* February 9, 2006, p. 6B.

91. Center for Applied Linguistics 2008 survey, released November 2009, reported in "What Are the Most Common Foreign Languages Taught in U.S. Schools," *USA Today,* February 16, 2010, p. A1.

92. "How Cultures Collide," 1976.

93. Kari Heistad, CEO of Culture Coach International, quoted in E. Maltby, "Expanding Abroad? Avoid Cultural Gaffes," *The Wall Street Journal,* January 19, 2010, p. B5.

94. T. Mohn, "Going Global, Stateside," *The New York Times,* March 9, 2010, p. B8.

95. B. Stone, "What's in a Name? For Apple, iPad Said More Than Intended," *The New York Times,* January 29, 2010, pp. A1, A3.

96. Michael Norman, senior vice president at Sibson Consulting, quoted in H. Seligson, "For American Workers in China, a Culture Clash," *The New York Times,* December 24, 2009, pp. B1, B2.

97. K. Seong-Kon, writing in *The Korea Herald,* summarized in "A Society That Needs No Appointment," *The Week,* May 29, 2009, p. 14.

98. E. T. Hall, *The Hidden Dimension* (New York: Doubleday, 1966).

99. C. Salazar, "Time Is of the Essence in Peru's Punctuality Effort," *San Francisco Chronicle,* March 2, 2007, p. A16.

100. Robert Levine, quoted in R. Vecchio, "Global Psyche: On Their Own Time," *Psychology Today,* July/August 2007, http://psychologytoday.com/articles/pto-20070723-000007.html (accessed February 14, 2010).

101. C. Woodward, "AP Poll Paints Portrait of Impatient American," *Reno Gazette-Journal,* May 29, 2006, pp. 1C, 7C.

102. A. R. Sorkin, "A Financial Mirage in the Desert," *The New York Times,* December 1, 2009, pp. B1, B5.

103. Results adapted from and value definitions quoted from S. R. Safranski and I.-W. Kwon, "Religious Groups and Management Value Systems," in R. N. Farner and E. G. McGoun, eds., *Advances in International Comparative Management,* vol. 3 (Greenwich, CT: JAI Press, 1988), pp. 171–183.

104. Jacqui Hauser, vice president of consulting services for Cendant Mobility, a relocation-services firm, cited in P. Capell, "Employers Seek to Trim Pay for U.S. Expatriates," April 16, 2005, www.careerjournal.com.

105. J. S. Black and H. B. Gregersen, "The Way to Manage Expats," *Harvard Business Review,* March-April 1999, p. 53.

106. See A. Maingault, L. Albright, and V. Neal, "Policy Tips, Repatriation, Safe Harbor Rules," *HRMagazine,* March 2008, pp. 34–35.

107. S. Dallas, "Rule No. 1: Don't Diss the Locals," *BusinessWeek,* May 15, 1995, p. 8. Also see M. A. Shaffer, D. A. Harrison, H. Gregersen, J. S. Black, and L. A. Ferzandi, "You Can Take It with You: Individual Differences and Expatriate Effectiveness," *Journal of Applied Psychology,* January 2006, pp. 109–125.

CHAPTER 5

1. D. Middleton, "Landing a Job of the Future Takes a Two-Track Mind," *The Wall Street Journal,* December 29, 2009, p. D4. See also J. A. Challenger, "Finding a Job in the 21st Century," *The Futurist,* September-October 2009, pp. 29–33; and E. Gordon, "The Global Talent Crisis," *The Futurist,* September–October 2009, pp. 34–39.

2. M. J. Driver, "Careers: A Review of Personnel and Organizational Research," in C. L. Cooper and I. Robertson, eds., *International Review of Industrial and Organizational Psychology* (New York: Wiley, 1988).

3. T. Gutner, "Doubling Up on Careers Suits More Workers," *The Wall Street Journal,* February 5, 2008, p. B4. See also M. Alboher, *One Person/Multiple Careers: A New Model for Work/Life Success* (New York: Warner Books, 2007).

4. E. White, "Profession Changes Take Time but May Be Worth Wait," *The Wall Street Journal,* November 27, 2007, p. B6.

5. R. Kreitner, *Management,* 7th ed. (Boston: Houghton Mifflin, 1998), p. 160.

6. B. Vlasic, "Ford's Bet: It's a Small World After All," *The New York Times,* January 10, 2010, Business section, pp. 1, 6.

7. R. E. Miles and C. C. Snow, *Organizational Strategy, Structure, and Process* (New York: McGraw-Hill, 1978).

8. R. Newman, "The Great Retail Revolution," *U.S. News & World Report,* March 2010, pp. 19–20; and P. Moeller, "Tough Times Are Molding Tough Customers," *U.S. News & World Report,* March 2010, pp. 22–25.

9. E. Holmes, "Gap Looks Abroad for New Sales, Profit Gains," *The Wall Street Journal,* February 26, 2010, p. B5. See also A. Cordeiro, "Goods Makers Look Abroad," *The Wall Street Journal,* February 24, 2010, p. B7.

10. See, for example, D. Brass, "Microsoft's Creative Destruction," *The New York Times,* February 4, 2010, p. A25.

11. See M. Olson, D. van Bever, and S. Verry, "When Growth Stalls," *Harvard Business Review,* March 2008, pp. 51–61.

12. M. Bustillo and G. Fowler, "Sears Scrambles Online for Lifeline," *The Wall Street Journal,* January 15, 2010, pp. A1, A16.

13. D. C. Hambrick, "On the Staying Power of Defenders, Analyzers, and Prospectors," *Academy of Management Executive,* November 2003, pp. 115–118. For more about the four basic strategy types, see also D. J. Ketchen Jr., "Introduction: Raymond E. Miles and Charles C. Snow's *Organizational Strategy, Structure, and Process,*" *Academy of Management Executive,* November 2003, pp. 95–96; D. J. Ketchen Jr., "An Interview with Raymond E. Miles and Charles C. Snow," *Academy of Management Executive,* November 2003, pp. 97–104; S. E. Brunk, "From Theory to Practice: Applying Miles and Snow's Ideas to Understand and Improve Firm Performance," *Academy of Management Executive,* November 2003, pp. 105–108; and S. Ghoshal, "Miles and Snow: Enduring Insights for Managers," *Academy of Management Executive,* November 2003, pp. 109–114.

14. D. Leider, "Purposeful Work," *Utne Reader,* July/August 1988, p. 52; excerpted from *On Purpose: A Journal about New Lifestyles & Workstyles,* Winter 1986.

15. P. F. Drucker, *The Practice of Management* (New York: Harper & Row, 1954), p. 122.

16. T. A. Stewart, "A Refreshing Change: Vision Statements That Make Sense," *Fortune,* September 30, 1996, pp. 195–196.

17. For application of vision to nonprofits, see A. Kilpatrick and L. Silverman, "The Power of Vision," *Strategy & Leadership,* February 2005, pp. 24–26.

18. P. J. Below, G. L. Morrisey, and B. L. Acomb, *The Executive Guide to Strategic Planning* (San Francisco: Jossey-Bass, 1987), p. 2.

19. Survey conducted by the Society for Human Resource Management and the Balance Scorecard Collaborative, reported in J. Mullich, "Get in Line," *Workforce Management,* December 2003, pp. 43–44.

20. M. Esterl, "Southwest Airlines Results Signal Clearer Skies," *The Wall Street Journal,* October 16, 2009, p. B3; D. Reed, "Reshuffled Deck Leaves Low-Cost Carriers King," *USA Today,* November 10, 2009, pp. 1B, 2B; S. Carey and M. Esterl, "Airlines Appear Headed for Recovery," *The Wall Street Journal,* December 8, 2009, p. B2; "Southwest Airlines Fact Sheet," Southwest.com, revised December 31, 2009, http://www.southwest.com/about_swa/press/factsheet.

html#About%20the%20Company (accessed March 7, 2010); and A. Keeton, "Southwest Airlines Hedges Its Bets," *The Wall Street Journal,* January 22, 2010, p. B3.

21. Hoover's, "Southwest Airlines Company Description," Hoovers.com, http://www.hoovers.com/company/Southwest_Airlines_Co/rrykki-l.html (accessed March 7, 2010).

22. Duke, "2009 Airline On-Time Performance Best Since 2003," *CNN,* February 12, 2010, http://www.cnn.com/2010/TRAVEL/02/12/airlines.performance/index.html (accessed March 7, 2010).

23. James Parker, quoted in W. J. Holstein, "At Southwest, the Culture Drives Success," *BusinessWeek.com,* February 21, 2008, http://www.businessweek.com/managing/content/feb2008/ca20080221_179423.htm (accessed March 7, 2010). Parker is author of *Do the Right Thing: How Dedicated Employees Create Loyal Customers and Large Profits* (Philadelphia: Wharton School Publishing, 2008).

24. S. Stellin, "Now Boarding Business Class," *The New York Times,* February 26, 2008, p. C6.

25. Willie Wilson, quoted in J. Bailey, "On Some Flights, Millionaires Serve the Drinks," *The New York Times,* May 15, 2006, pp. A1, A16.

26. Herb Kelleher, quoted in "How Herb Keeps Southwest Hopping," *Money,* June 1999, pp. 61–62.

27. Jones, "Southwest Thrives on Free-Bags Policy," *USA Today,* December 14, 2009, p. 1B; and T. Maxon, "Southwest's Bags Fly Free Is Adding $100s of Millions in Revenue, Kelly Says," *The Dallas Morning News,* February 4, 2010, http://aviationblog.dallasnews.com/archives/2010/02/southwests-bags-fly-free-is-ad.html (accessed March 7, 2010).

28. Reed, 2009.

29. T. Steinmetz, "Tough Times Call for Tough Measures: Southwest Airlines Strategy Gets Pragmatic about Fees," *eTurboNews,* June 2, 2009, http://www.eturbonews.com/9578/tough-times-call-tough-measures-southwest-airlines-strategy-gets- (accessed March 7, 2010).

30. See E. A. Locke and G. P. Latham, "Building a Practically Useful Theory of Goal Setting and Task Motivation," *American Psychologist,* September 2002, pp. 705–717.

31. Drucker, 1954.

32. Lock and Latham, 2002.

33. The performance management process is discussed by H. Aguinis and C. Pierce, "Enhancing the Relevance of Organizational Behavior by Embracing Performance Management Research," *Journal of Organizational Behavior,* January 2008, pp. 139–145.

34. R. Rodgers and J. E. Hunter, "Impact of Management by Objectives on Organizational Productivity," *Journal of Applied Psychology,* April 1991, pp. 322–336.

35. J. Tierney, "The Advantages of Closing a Few Doors," *The New York Times,* February 26, 2008, pp. D1, D6.

36. Ariely, *Predictably Irrational: The Hidden Forces That Shape Our Decisions* (New York: HarperCollins, 2008).

37. M. Barbaro, "Wal-Mart Sets Agenda of Change," *The New York Times,* January 24, 2008, p. C3; and K. Ohannessian, "CEO Lee Scott Speaks About Wal-Mart's New Strategies," *FastCompany.com,* January 24, 2008, http://blog.fastcompany.com/archives/2008/01/24/ceo_lee_scott_speaks_about_walmarts_new_strategies.html (accessed March 7, 2010).

38. S. Ross, "Wal-Mart's Grand Green Alternative," *San Francisco Chronicle,* February 28, 2010, pp. D1, D2.

39. Adapted from N. Wingfield, "At Apple, Secrecy Complicates Life but Maintains Buzz," *The Wall Street Journal,* June 28, 2006, pp. A1, A11. See also A. L. Peneberg, "All Eyes on Apple," *Fast Company,* December 2007/January 2008,

pp. 83–87, 133–136; "The World's 50 Most Innovative Companies," *Fast Company,* March 2008, p. 92; B. Morris, "What Makes Apple Golden," *Fortune,* March 17, 2008, pp. 68–74; P. Ekind, "The Trouble with Steve," *Fortune,* March 17, 2008, pp. 88–98, 156–160; "The World's 50 Most Innovative Companies," *Fast Company,* March 2009, p. 52; and "The World's 50 Most Innovative Companies," *Fast Company,* March 2010, p. 53.

40. N. Wingfield, "Apple Sets April 3 iPad Debut," *The Wall Street Journal,* March 6–7, 2010, p. B5.

CHAPTER 6

1. G. Hamel, "What Is Management's Moonshot?" *Management 2.0,* December 7, 2007, http://discussionleader.hbsp.com/hamel/2007/12/what_is_managements_moonshot.html (accessed March 28, 2010). See also G. Hamel, "Moon Shots for Management," *Harvard Business Review,* February 2009, pp. 91–98.

2. J. Best, *Flavor of the Month: Why Smart People Fall for Fads* (Berkeley: University of California Press, 2006).

3. J. Best, interviewed by A. Manser, "Flavor of the Month," UDaily, University of Delaware Web site, May 22, 2006, http://www.udel.edu/PR/UDaily/2006/may/jbest052206.html (accessed March 28, 2010).

4. D. Rigby and B. Bilodeau, "Management Tools and Trends 2009," http://www.bain.com/management_tools/Management_Tools_and_Trends_2009_Global_Results.pdf (accessed March 28, 2010).

5. G. Colvin, "The Most Valuable Quality in a Manager," *Fortune,* December 29, 1997, pp. 279–280.

6. J. Pfeffer and R. I. Sutton, "Profiting from Evidence-Based Management," *Strategy & Leadership* 34, no. 2 (2006), pp. 35–42.

7. J. Kellner, "17-Year-Old Entrepreneur Writes Own Business Plan," *Reno Gazette-Journal,* January 29, 2007, p. 8E.

8. Study by Amar Bhide, cited in K. K. Spors, "Do Start-Ups Really Need Formal Business Plans?" *The Wall Street Journal,* January 9, 2007, p. B9.

9. Study by S. Shane, cited in Spors, 2007.

10. C. McNamara, "Strategic Planning (in Nonprofit or For-Profit Organizations)," Free Management Library, http://www.managementhelp.org/plan_dec/str_plan/str_plan.htm (accessed March 28, 2010).

11. A. A. Thompson Jr. and A. J. Strickland III, *Strategic Management: Concepts and Cases,* 6th ed. (Homewood, IL: BPI/Irwin, 1992).

12. D. J. Collis and M. G. Rukstad, "Can You Say What Your Strategy Is?" *Harvard Business Review,* April 2008, pp. 82–90.

13. See G. Hamel, with B. Breen, *The Future of Management* (Boston: Harvard Business School Press, 2007), p. 191; and C. Rampell, "How Industries Survive Change. If They Do," *The New York Times,* November 16, 2008, Week in Review section, p. 3. For a discussion of the effect of the Web on newspapers, see E. Alterman, "Out of Print," *The New Yorker,* March 31, 2008, pp. 48–59; P. R. Kann, "Quality Reporting Doesn't Come Cheap," *The Wall Street Journal,* September 26, 2009, p. A15; R. Pérez-Peña, "Newspaper Circulation Falls by More Than 10%," *The New York Times,* October 27, 2009, p. B3; B. Wyman, "What Newspapers Can Learn from Craigslist," *The Wall Street Journal,* February 13, 2010, p. A13; and B. Evangelista, "Internet Seen as Shaping Delivery, Sharing of News," *San Francisco Chronicle,* March 1, 2010, pp. D1, D2.

14. A. Busch III, quoted in interview with G. Hamel, "Turning Your Business Upside Down," *Fortune,* June 23, 1997, pp. 87–88.

See also D. Kesmodel, "Beer Distributors Want More Than One Best Bud," *The Wall Street Journal,* February 6, 2006, pp. Bl, B2.

15. L. G. Hrebiniak, "Obstacles to Effective Strategy Implementation," *Organizational Dynamics,* February 2006, pp. 12–3l.

16. H. Mintzberg, "The Strategy Concept II: Another Look at Why Organizations Need Strategies," *California Management Review,* 30, no. I (1987), pp. 25–32.

17. Hamel and Breen, 2007, p. 33.

18. B. Horovitz, "Starbucks Perks Up with First Dividend," *USA Today,* March 25, 2010, p. lB.

19. P. Hochman, "Ford's Big Revival," *Fast Company,* April 2010, pp. 90–95, 105.

20. For more on aps, see M. R. della Cava, "It's an App World," *USA Today,* March 31, 2010, pp. lA, 2A.

21. Thilo Koslowski, lead automotive analyst for Gartner, quoted in Hochman, 2010.

22. F. Manjoo, "Killer Apps," *Fast Company,* February 2010, p. 38.

23. J. Surowiecki, "The Return of Michael Porter," *Fortune,* February I, 1999, pp. 135–138.

24. M. E. Porter, "What Is Strategy?" *Harvard Business Review,* November–December 1996, pp. 61–78. Porter has updated his 1979 paper on competitive forces in M. E. Porter, "The Five Competitive Forces That Shape Strategy," *Harvard Business Review,* January 2008, pp. 79–93.

25. Porter, 1996.

26. J. A. Byrne, "Going Where the Money Is," *BusinessWeek,* January 26, 1998, p. 14, review of A. J. Slywotzky and D. J. Morrison, with B. Andelman, *The Profit Zone* (New York: Times Business, 1998).

27. N. Shirouzu, "Toyoda Rues Excessive Profit Focus," *The Wall Street Journal,* March 2, 2010, p B3. Also see K. Linebaugh, D. Searcey, and N. Shirouzu, "Secretive Culture Led Toyota Astray," *The Wall Street Journal,* February 10, 2010, pp Al, A6.

28. R. Farzad and M. Arndt, "Stuck with Sears," *Bloomberg BusinessWeek,* April 5, 2010, pp. 41–48.

29. S. Carey and P. Prada, "Course Change: Why JetBlue Shuffled Top Rank," *The Wall Street Journal,* May Il, 2007, pp. Bl, B2.

30. Carey and Prada, 2007.

31. J. Hanna, "HBS Cases: JetBlue's Valentine's Day Crisis," *Harvard Business School Working Knowledge,* March 31, 2008, http://hbswk.hbs.edu/item/5880.html (accessed March 31, 2010).

32. "Winter Storm Rattles JetBlue," *BusinessWeek,* February 20, 2007, http://www.businessweek.com/investor/content/feb2007/pi20070220_742628.htm?chan=search (accessed March 31, 2010).

33. Hanna, 2008.

34. T. Reed, "Is JetBlue Back?" TheStreet.com, February 5, 2008, http://www.thestreet.com/_more/s/is-jetblue-back/newsanalysis/transportation/10401822.html? (accessed March 31, 2010).

35. M. Gunther, "Nothing Blue about JetBlue," *Fortune,* September 3, 2009, http://money.cnn.com/2009/09/03/news/companies/jetblue_airways_airline.fortune/index.htm (accessed April I, 2010).

36. Walt Disney, quoted in B. Nanus, *Visionary Leadership: Creating a Compelling Sense of Direction for Your Organization* (San Francisco: Jossey-Bass, 1992), p. 28; reprinted from B. Thomas, *Walt Disney: An American Tradition* (New York: Simon & Schuster, 1976), p. 247.

37. B. Iyer and T. Davenport, "Reverse Engineering Google's Innovation Machine," *Harvard Business Review,* April 2008, pp. 59–68.

38. Nanus, 1992, pp. 28–29.

39. R. Kreitner, *Management,* 7th ed. (Boston: Houghton Mifflin, 1998), p. 206. Also see S. Kapner, "How Fashion's VF Supercharges Its Brands," *Fortune,* April 14, 2008, pp. 108–110.

40. B. McKay, "PepsiCo Develops 'Designer Salt' to Chip Away at Sodium Intake," *The Wall Street Journal,* March 22, 2010, pp. Bl, B5.

41. M. E. Lloyd and N. Becker, "Best Buy Offers Rosy Outlook for Year," *The Wall Street Journal,* March 26, 2010, p. B3.

42. M. Esterl, "Carnival Poised to Ride a Wave of Recovery," *The Wall Street Journal,* March 24, 2010, p. B8.

43. C. H. Roush Jr. and B. C. Ball Jr., "Controlling the Implementation of Strategy," *Managerial Planning,* November–December 1980, p. 4.

44. B. W. Barry, "A Beginner's Guide to Strategic Planning," *The Futurist,* April 1998, pp. 33–36 from B. W. Barry, *Strategic Planning Workbook for Nonprofit Organizations,* revised and updated (St. Paul, MN: Amherst H. Wilder Foundation, 1997).

45. Toyota Motor president Akio Toyoda, quoted in A. Ohnsman, J. Green, and K. Inoue, "The Humbling of Toyota," *Bloomberg BusinessWeek,* March 22 & 29, 2010, pp. 32–36.

46. T. Krisher, "Toyota's Sales Jump," *Reno Gazette-Journal,* April 2, 2010, pp. 9A, l0A.

47. D. Wakabayashi, "'Toyota Way' Retains Management Followers," *The Wall Street Journal,* February 26, 2010, p. B4.

48. Ohnsman, Green, and Inoue, 2010.

49. Y. Takahashi, "Toyota Accelerates Its Cost-Cutting Efforts," *The Wall Street Journal,* December 23, 2009, p. B4; C. Woodyard, "Toyota's Reputation Needs Some TLC," *USA Today,* December 31, 2009, pp. lB, 2B; M. Maynard and H. Tabuchi, "Rapid Growth Has Its Perils, Toyota Learns," *The New York Times,* January 28, 2010, pp. Al, B4; K. Linebaugh and N. Shirouzu, "Toyota Heir Faces Crisis at the Wheel," *The Wall Street Journal,* January 28, 2010, pp. Al, A8; and M. Dolan, "Supplier Perplexed by Toyota's Action," *The Wall Street Journal,* January 28, 2010, p. A9.

50. J. R. Healey and A. DeBarros, "Toyota Tops Speed Control Complaints," *USA Today,* March 26, 2010, pp. lB, 2B.

51. N. Bunkley, "Toyotal Halts Production of 8 Models," *The New York Times,* January 27, 2010, pp. Bl, B2; J. R. Healey, "Toyota Halts U.S. Sales of 8 Models," *USA Today,* January 27, 2010, p. lA; and C. Said, "Reports on Priuses Add to Toyota's Woes," *San Francisco Chronicle,* February 4, 2010, pp. Dl, D2.

52. James P. Womack, quoted in Maynard and Tabuchi, 2010.

53. K. Linebaugh and D. Searcey, "Cause of Sudden Acceleration Proves Hard to Pinpoint," *The Wall Street Journal,* February 25, 2010, p. A7; and D. Searcey and K. Linebaugh, "Toyota Moves to Discredit Its Critics," *The Wall Street Journal,* March 6–7, 2010, pp. Bl, B5.

54. C. Woodyard, "Toyota PR Blitz Plays Catch-Up," *USA Today,* February 10, 2010, p. 2B.

55. K. Linebaugh, D. Searcey, and N. Shirouzu, "Secretive Culture Led Toyota Astray," *The Wall Street Journal,* February 10, 2010, pp. Al, A6; andJ. O'Donnell, "'Black Boxes' Play a Growing Role Today," *USA Today,* March 29, 2010, p. 3B.

56. D. Welch, K. Naughton, and B. Helm, "Detroit's Big Chance," *Bloomberg BusinessWeek,* February 22, 2010, pp. 38–44.

57. M. DeBord, "Toyota's Blind Spot," *The New York Times,* February 6, 2010, p. Al7.

58. "'Commercial Jet Fuel Supply: Impact & Cost on the U.S. Airline Industry' Hearing Scheduled for Wednesday Morning," press release, U.S. House Committee on Transportation and Infrastructure, Washington, DC, February 14, 2006, http://www.house.gov/transportation/press/press2006/release5.html (accessed March 30, 2010).

59. J. C. Ogg, "Fuel Hedges Aren't Helping Southwest Shares," 14/7 Wall St., February 5, 2008, http://www.247wallst .com/2008/02/fuel-hedges-are.html (accessed March 30, 2010).

60. D. Levin, "Hedging Helps Low-Cost Airlines Hold Down Price of Aviation Fuel," *Detroit News,* March 18, 2004, www.detnews .com/2004/business/0403/18/c01-95805.htm (accessed March 30, 2010).

61. T. Romo, quoted in E. Roston, "Hedging Their Costs," *Time,* June 20, 2005, http://www.time.com/time/globalbusiness/ article/0.9171,1074147,00.html (accessed March 30, 2010).

62. D. Grossman, "Oil Prices Put Business Travelers Over a Barrel," *USA Today,* March 31, 2008, http://www.usatoday.com/ travel/columnist/grossman/2008-03-28-oil-prices-rising_ N.htm (accessed April 2, 2010).

63. M. E. Porter, *Competitive Strategy* (New York: The Free Press, 1980). See also Porter, 2008.

64. Example from Michael J. Silverstein, *Treasure Hunt,* cited in M. Archer, "Author Finds 'Value Calculus' at Work," *USA Today,* June 12, 2006, p. 7B.

65. P. L. Brown, "Surfers in Turmoil with the Loss of a Major Supplier," *The New York Times,* December 30, 2006, p. A12; and M. Overfelt, "Rough Surf," *USA Today,* February 17, 2006, http://money.cnn.com/magazines/fsb/fsb_archive/2006/ 02/01/8368201/index.htm (accessed March 30, 2010).

66. "Amazon Lets Customers Text to Buy," *Reno Gazette-Journal,* April 2, 2008, p. 11A.

67. L. Rohter, "With Big Boost from Sugar Cane, Brazil Is Satisfying Its Fuel Needs," *The New York Times,* April 10, 2006, p. A1. See also R. Cohen, "Is Ethanol for Everybody?" *The New York Times,* January 10, 2008, http://www.nytimes .com/2008/01/10/opinion/10cohen.html (accessed April 2, 2010).

68. J. Greenberg, quoted in B. Horovitz, "Restoring the Golden Arch Shine," *USA Today,* June 16, 1999, p. 3B.

69. C. Said, "Toymaker Takes Being Green a Step Further—Keeps It Local," *San Francisco Chronicle,* April 19, 2010, pp. D1, D4.

70. K. Zezima, "A Push to Eat Local Food Is Hampered by a Shortage," *The New York Times,* March 28, 2010, News section, p. 12.

71. "The End Again for Indian Motorcycle Corporation," *American Motorcycle Network,* September 22, 2003, www .americanmotor.com/news.cfm?newsid=2236 (accessed March 30, 2010); and S. Carpenter, "Indian Chief Motorcycles Rev into State," *San Francisco Chronicle,* December 29, 2009, pp. D1, D2.

72. L. Aguilar, "Auto Suppliers Branch Out to Other Sectors to Survive," *San Francisco Chronicle,* February 16, 2010, p. D2; reprinted from the *Detroit News.*

73. L. Bossidy and Ram Charan, with C. Burck, *Execution: The Discipline of Getting Things Done* (New York: Crown Business, 2002).

74. Results can be found in "Wanted: Employees Who Get Things Done," *HR Magazine,* January 2008, p. 10.

75. Also see R. Kaplan and D. Norton, "Mastering the Management System," *Harvard Business Review,* January 2008, pp. 66–77.

76. Execution is also discussed by C. Montgomery, "Putting Leadership Back into Strategy," *Harvard Business Review,* January 2008, pp. 54–60; and J. Lorsch and R. Clark, "Leading from the Boardroom," *Harvard Business Review,* April 2008, pp. 105–111.

77. Bossidy and Charan, 2002, pp. 27–28.

78. Development Dimension International (DDI) Global Leadership Forecast of 4,561 respondents from 42 countries, reported in "Mentoring Impact," *USA Today,* March 22, 2006, p. 1B.

79. M. Cottle, "Minding Your Mentors," *The New York Times,* March 7, 1999, sec. 3, p. 8; C. Dahle, "HP's Mentor Connection," *Fast Company,* November 1998, pp. 78–80; and I. Abbott, "If You Want to Be an Effective Mentor, Consider These Tips," *San Francisco Examiner,* October 18, 1998, p. J-3; D. A. Thomas, "The Truth about Mentoring Minorities—Race Matters," *Harvard Business Review,* April 2001, pp. 366–391; S. A. Mehta, "Best Companies for Minorities: Why Mentoring Works," *Fortune,* July 9, 2001, www.fortune .com/fortune/-diversity/articles/0,15114,370475,00.html (accessed April 1, 2010); F. Warner, "Inside Intel's Mentoring Movement," *Fast Company,* April 2002, p. 116; B. Raabe and T. A. Beehr, "Formal Mentoring versus Supervisor and Coworker Relationships: Differences in Perceptions and Impact," *Journal of Organizational Behavior* 24(2003), pp. 271–293; and A. Fisher, "A New Kind of Mentor," *Fortune,* July 2004, www.fortune.com/fortune/annie/0,15704, 368863,00.html (accessed April 1, 2010).

80. Anne Hayden, quoted in Cottle, 1999.

CHAPTER 7

1. M. H. Bazerman, *Judgment in Managerial Decision Making,* 7th ed. (New York: Wiley, 2008). See also D. E. Bell, H. Raiffa, and A. Tversky, eds., *Decision Making: Descriptive, Normative, and Prescriptive Interactions* (Cambridge: Cambridge University Press, 1988).

2. M. Easterby-Smith and M. A. Lyles, *The Blackwell Handbook of Organizational Learning and Knowledge Management* (Oxford: Blackwell Publishing, 2003).

3. B. Fischoff, "Hindsight $\pm$ Foresight: The Effect of Outcome Knowledge on Judgment under Uncertainty," *Journal of Experimental Psychology: Human Perception and Performance* 1(1975), pp. 288–299.

4. E. Rosenthal, "Slow and Steady Across the Sea Aids Profit and the Environment," *The New York Times,* February 17, 2010, pp. A1, A3.

5. J. B. White, "Why 70 Miles Per Hour Is the New 55," *The Wall Street Journal,* March 17, 2010, p. D3.

6. C. F. Chabris, "Old Habits Die Hard," *The Wall Street Journal,* February 19, 2010, p. A13. The article is a book review of C. Heath and D. Heath, *Switch: How to Change Things When Change Is Hard* (New York: Broadway, 2010).

7. "Wean Wall Street Off Its Gambling Addictions," editorial, *USA Today,* March 1, 2010, p. 15A.

8. Chip Heath, quoted in J. Rae-Dupree, "Innovative Minds Don't Think Alike," *The New York Times,* December 30, 2007, business section, p. 3. C. Heath and D. Heath are coauthors of *Made to Stick: Why Some Ideas Survive and Others Die* (New York: Random House, 2007). For other writings pertaining to the curse of knowledge, see J. Fox, "Herd on the Street," *Time,* September 17, 2007, p. 59; D. Jones, "Even Good CEOs Pick the Wrong Direction," *USA Today,* November 7, 2007, pp. 1B, 2B; F. Norris, "Bank Profits Had Whiff of Suspicion," *The New York Times,* November 16, 2007, pp. C1, C2; and P. L. Bernstein, "To Botch a Forecast, Rely on Past Experience," *The New York Times,* December 30, 2007, business section, p. 4.

9. L. DiCosmo, "Warren Buffett Invests Like a Girl," *The Motley Fool,* March 20, 2008, http://www.fool.com/investing/ value/2008/03/20/warren-buffett-invests-like-a-girl.aspx (accessed April 9, 2010).

10. A. Markels, "Built to Make Billions?" *U.S. News & World Report,* August 6, 2007, pp. 51–52. See also A. Markels, "How to Make Money the Buffett Way," *U.S. News & World Report,* August 6, 2007, pp. 46–51.

11. D. Mitchell, "At Last, Buffett's Key to Success," *The New York Times,* April 5, 2008, p. B5. See also J. Clements, "He Invests, She Invests: Who Gets the Better Returns?" *The Wall Street Journal,* February 6, 2008, p. DI.

12. B. M. Barber and T. Odean, "Boys Will Be Boys: Gender, Overconfidence, and Common Stock Investment," *The Quarterly Journal of Economics,* February 2001, pp. 261–292, faulty.haas.berkeley.edu/odean/papers/gender/BoysWillBeBoys.pdf (accessed April 9, 2010).

13. G. Fabrikant, "Few Women Betting on Wall Street Careers," *The New York Times,* January 30, 2010, p. B3.

14. Markels, "Built to Make Billions?" 2007.

15. "The World's Billionaires: #3 Warren Buffett," *Forbes.com,* March 10, 2010, http://www.forbes.com/lists/2010/10/billionaires-2010_Warren-Buffett_COR3.html (accessed April 5, 2010).

16. A. Farnham, "Teaching Creativity Tricks to Buttoned-Down Executives," *Fortune,* January 10, 1994, pp. 94–100.

17. I. DeBare, "The Business May Change, but the Values Are the Same," *San Francisco Chronicle,* April 2, 2006, p. G5.

18. C. Hymowitz, "Everyone Likes to Laud Service to the Customer; Doing It Is the Problem," *The Wall Street Journal,* February 27, 2006, p. BI.

19. The Retail Customer Dissatisfaction Study 2006, conducted by the Jay H. Baker Retailing Initiative, Wharton, University of Pennsylvania, and the Verde Group, Toronto, reported in "Beware of Dissatisfied Customers: They Like to Blab," Knowledge@Wharton, http://knowledge.wharton.upenn.edu/index (accessed April 9, 2010).

20. Hymowitz, "Everyone Likes to Laud Service," 2006.

21. B. Kiviat, "The End of Customer Service," *Time,* March 24, 2008, p. 42.

22. S. Holmes, "The 787 Encounters Turbulence," *BusinessWeek,* June 19, 2006, pp. 38–40. See also S. Holmes, "Cleaning Up Boeing," *BusinessWeek,* March 13, 2006, pp. 63–68; and S. Holmes, "Boeing Straightens Up and Flies Right," *BusinessWeek,* May 8, 2006, pp. 69–70.

23. For a discussion of the strategy behind the Dreamliner, see C. Masters, "How Boeing Got Going," *Time,* September 10, 2007, pp. Global 1–Global 6.

24. J. L. Lunsford, "Boeing, in Embarrassing Setback, Says 787 Dreamliner Will Be Delayed," *The Wall Street Journal,* October 11, 2007, pp. AI, AI6.

25. R. Yu, "Boeing Again Delays Dreamliner's Debut," *USA Today,* January 17, 2008, p. 3B.

26. J. L. Lunsford, "Boeing Delays Dreamliner Delivery Again," *The Wall Street Journal,* April 10, 2008, p. B3.

27. C. Drew, "Another Flight Delay for Troubled Dreamliner," *The New York Times,* June 24, 2009, p. B3; P. Sanders, D. Michaels, and A. Cole, "Boeing Delays New Jet Again," *The Wall Street Journal,* June 24, 2009, pp. AI, A6; D. Reed, "Problems Pile Up on Boeing," *USA Today,* August 6, 2009, pp. IB, 2B; P. Sanders, "Boeing Settles in for a Bumpy Ride," *The Wall Street Journal,* October 7, 2009, p. BI; D. Michaels and P. Sanders, "Dreamliner Production Gets Closer Monitoring," *The Wall Street Journal,* October 7, 2009, pp. BI, B2; and P. Sanders, "At Boeing, Dreamliner Fix Turns Up New Issue," *The Wall Street Journal,* November 13, 2009, pp. BI, B2.

28. P. Sanders and D. Michaels, "Boeing Looks Beyond Dreamliner's First Flight," *The Wall Street Journal,* December 16, 2009, pp. BI, B2.

29. P. Sanders, "Boeing's Dreamliner Lags Testing Schedule," *The Wall Street Journal,* March 30, 2010, p. B3.

30. M. Philips, "Boeing's Turbulence," *Newsweek,* November 2, 2009, p. 14.

31. H. A. Simon, *Administrative Behavior,* 3rd ed. (New York: Free Press, 1996); and H. A. Simon, "Making Management Decisions: The Role of Intuition and Emotion," *The Academy of Management Executive,* February 1987, pp. 57–63.

32. E. Sadler-Smith and E. Shefy, "The Intuitive Executive: Understanding and Applying 'Gut Feel' in Decision Making," *Academy of Management Executive,* February 2005, p. 20.

33. See E. Dane and M. G. Pratt, "Exploring Intuition and Its Role in Managerial Decision Making," *Academy of Management Review,* January 2007, pp. 33–54.

34. See D. Begley, "You Might Help a Teen Avoid Dumb Behavior by Nurturing Intuition," *The Wall Street Journal,* November 3, 2006, p. BI.

35. Courage and intuition are discussed by K. K. Reardon, "Courage as a Skill," *Harvard Business Review,* March 2007, pp. 51–56.

36. Masters, 2007.

37. J. Pfeffer and R. I. Sutton, "Profiting from Evidence-Based Management," *Strategy & Leadership,* 34, no. 2(2006), pp. 35–42; and J. Pfeffer and R. I. Sutton, "Evidence-Based Management," *Harvard Business Review,* January 2006, pp. 63–74. Pfeffer and Sutton have also produced a book, *Hard Facts, Dangerous Half-Truths, and Total Nonsense: Profiting from Evidence-Based Management* (Cambridge, MA: Harvard Business School Press, 2006). For a discussion of the book, see C. Hymowitz, "Executives Must Stop Jumping Fad to Fad and Learn to Manage," *The Wall Street Journal,* May 15, 2006, p. BI.

38. Additional discussion of this topic may be found in T. Reay, W. Berta, and M. Kazman Kohn, "What's the Evidence on Evidence-Based Management?" *Academy of Management Perspectives,* November 2009, pp. 5–18; and R. B. Briner, D. Denyer, and D. M. Rousseau, "Evidence-Based Management" Concept Cleanup Time?" *Academy of Management Perspectives,* November 2009, pp. 19–32.

39. Pfeffer and Sutton, "Profiting from Evidence-Based Management," 2006.

40. Pfeffer and Sutton, "Evidence-Based Management," 2006, pp. 66–67.

41. J. Pfeffer, "Lay Off the Layoffs," *Newsweek,* February 15, 2010, pp. 32–37.

42. G. Loveman, "Diamonds in the Data Mine," *Harvard Business Review,* May 2003, pp. 109–113. See also T. Davenport, L. Prusak, and B. Strong, "Putting Ideas to Work," *The Wall Street Journal,* March 10, 2008, p. R11.

43. T. H. Davenport, "Competing on Analytics," *Harvard Business Review,* January 2006, pp. 99–107.

44. S. Baker, "How Much Is That Worker Worth?" *BusinessWeek,* March 23 & 30, 2009, pp. 46–48.

45. M. Lewis, *Moneyball: The Art of Winning an Unfair Game* (New York: W. W. Norton, 2004). For comment on the Oakland A's and *Moneyball,* see J. Manuel, "Majoring in Moneyball," Baseball America Features, December 23, 2003, http://www.baseballamerica.com/today/features/031223collegemoneyball.html; J. Zasky, "Pay for Performance, Stupid," *Failure Magazine,* June 2003, http://failuremag.com/archives_business_sports_money-ball.html; R. Van Zandt, "Billy Beane's Perfect Draft: A Baseball Revolution?" BaseballEvolution.com, April 13, 2006, http://baseballevolution.com/guest/richard/rvzbeanel.html; and "Moneyball: The Art of Winning an Unfair Game," Wikipedia, July 12, 2006, http://en.wikipedia.org/wiki/Moneyball (all accessed April 9, 2010). For more on the use of technology and software in baseball, see A. Schwarz, "Digital Eyes Will Chart Baseball's Unseen Skills," *The New York Times,* July 10, 2009, pp. AI, A3;

and R. Sandomir, "Bloomberg Technology Embraces Baseball," *The New York Times,* December 6, 2009, Sports section, pp. I, 6. For a discussion of the analytics of the Super Bowl–winning NFL team the New England Patriots, see C. Price, *The Blueprint: How the New England Patriots Beat the System to Create the Last Great NFL Superpower* (New York: Thomas Dunne/St. Martin's Press, 2007).

46. Daryl Morley, quoted in M. Lewis, "The No-Stats All-Star," *The New York Times Magazine,* February 15, 2009, pp. 26–33, 56, 63–64.

47. Davenport, 2006.

48. S. Elliott, "Delivering Something Extra," *The New York Times,* September 29, 2009, p. B3.

49. Muriel Niederle, quoted in J. Tierney, "What Women Want," *The New York Times,* May 24, 2005, p. A25.

50. M. Niederle and L. Vesterlund, "Do Women Shy Away from Competition? Do Men Compete Too Much?" *Quarterly Journal of Economics,* August 2007, pp. 1067–1101.

51. The discussion of styles was based on material contained in A. J. Rowe and R. O. Mason, *Managing with Style: A Guide to Understanding, Assessing and Improving Decision Making* (San Francisco: Jossey-Bass, 1987), pp. 1–17.

52. See Rowe and Mason, 1987; and M. J. Dollinger and W. Danis, "Preferred Decision-Making Styles: A Cross-Cultural Comparison," *Psychological Reports,* 1998, pp. 755–761; and K. R. Brousseau, M. J. Driver, G. Hourihan, and R. Larsson, "The Seasoned Executive's Decision-Making Style," *Harvard Business Review,* February 2006, p. III, http://custom.hbsp.com/custom/KORNFRO602F2006012769.pdf;jsessionid=BBCU302NQJFKOAKRGWCB5VQBKEOYIIPS (accessed April 9, 2010).

53. M. B. Zuckerman, "Policing the Corporate Suites," *U.S. News & World Report,* January 19, 2004, p. 72.

54. Bill Gates, quoted in R. A. Guth, "Bill Gates Issues Call for Kinder Capitalism," *The Wall Street Journal,* January 24, 2008, pp. AI, AI5. See also C. Boles, "Last Call? Gates Pushes Globalism in Remarks," *The Wall Street Journal,* March 13, 2008, p. B3.

55. C. McNamara, "Complete Guide to Ethics Management: An Ethics Toolkit for Managers," www.mapnp.org/library/ethics/ethxgde.htm (accessed April 9, 2010).

56. C. E. Bagley, "The Ethical Leader's Decision Tree," *Harvard Business Review,* February 2003, pp. 18–19.

57. Bagley, 2003, p. 19.

58. Ibid.

59. K. Hodgson, *A Rock and a Hard Place: How to Make Ethical Business Decisions When the Choices Are Tough* (New York: AMACOM, 1992), pp. 66–77.

60. C. E. Cryder, J. S. Lerner, J. J. Gross, and R. E. Dahl, "Misery Is Not Miserly: Sad and Self-Focused Individuals Spend More," *Psychological Science,* June 1, 2008, pp. 525–530. See also S. Finkelstein, J. Whitehead, and A. Campbell, "How Inappropriate Attachments Can Drive Good Leaders to Make Bad Decisions," *Organizational Dynamics,* 38(2009), pp. 83–92.

61. D. Gilbert, *Stumbling on Happiness* (New York: Vintage, 2007).

62. D. D. Wheeler and I. L. Janis, *A Practical Guide for Making Decisions* (New York: Free Press, 1980), pp. 34–35; and I. L. Janis and L. Mann, *Decision Making: A Psychological Analysis of Conflict, Choice, and Commitment* (New York: The Free Press, 1977).

63. R. Beck, "The Difference a Year Made in Mortgage Mess," *San Francisco Chronicle,* December 26, 2007, p. D2. See also S. Lohr, "Wall Street's Math Wizards Forgot a Few Variables," *The New York Times,* September 13, 2009, business section, p. 3; D. Leonhardt, "If Fed Missed Bubble, How Will It See the Next One?" *The New York Times,* January 6, 2010, pp. AI, A4; and J. Pressley, "They Did the Math—and Lost Billions," *Bloomberg BusinessWeek,* March I, 2010, p. 70.

64. S. S. Iyengar and M. Lepper, "When Choice Is Demotivating: Can One Desire Too Much of a Good Thing?" *Journal of Personality and Social Psychology* 79(2000), pp. 995–1006. Sheena Iyengar is author of *The Art of Choosing* (New York: Hachette Book Group, 2010).

65. P. Steel, "The Nature of Procrastination: A Meta-Analytic and Theoretical Review of Quintessential Self-Regulatory Failure," *Psychological Bulletin* 133(2007), pp. 65–94.

66. Gurnek Bains, CEO of YSC, London, quoted in C. Hymowitz, "Best Way to Save: Analyze Why Talent Is Going Out the Door," *The Wall Street Journal,* September 24, 2007, p. BI.

67. A. Levin and L. Parker, "Human, Mechanical Flaws Cut Off Path to Survival," *USA Today,* July 12, 1999, pp. IA, 8A, 9A. Sometimes observers speak of a "fog of war," in which too much information or scattered information overwhelms decision-making abilities. See, for example, E. Lipson, "Hurricane Investigators See 'Fog of War' at White House," *The New York Times,* January 28, 2006, p. A8. Decision makers may also often be unable to discriminate between relevant and irrelevant alternatives, including extraneous considerations in their probability judgments. See M. R. Dougherty and A. Sprenger, "The Influence of Improper Sets of Information on Judgment: How Irrelevant Information Can Bias Judged Probability," *Journal of Experimental Psychology: General,* May 2006, pp. 262–281.

68. Wheeler and Janis, 1980.

69. Based on J. L. Roberts, "I Want My (Web) MTV," *Newsweek,* April 14, 2008, pp. E8–E11.

70. D. Kahnemann and A. Tversky, "Judgment under Uncertainty: Heuristics and Biases," *Science* 185(1974), pp. 1124–1131; A. Tversky and D. Kahneman, "Availability: A Heuristic for Judging Frequency and Probability," *Cognitive Psychology* 5(1975), pp. 207–232; A. Tversky and D. Kahneman, "The Belief in the Law of Numbers," *Psychological Bulletin* 76(1971), pp. 105–110; C. R. Schwenk, "Cognitive Simplification Processes in Strategic Decision Making," *Strategic Management Journal* 5(1984), pp. 111–128; K. McKean, "Decisions," *Discover,* June 1985, pp. 22–31; J. Rockner, "The Escalation of Commitment to a Failing Course of Action: Toward Theoretical Progress," *Academy of Management Review* 17(1980), pp. 39–61; D. R. Bobocel and J. P. Meyer, "Escalating Commitment to a Failing Course of Action: Separating the Roles of Choice and Justification," *Journal of Applied Psychology,* June 1994, pp. 360–363; B. M. Shaw, "The Escalation of Commitment to a Course of Action," *Academy of Management Review,* October 1981, pp. 577–587; and M. Useem and J. Useem, "Great Escapes," *Fortune,* June 27, 2005, pp. 97–102; K. Sengupta, T. Abdel-Hamid, and L. Van Wassenhove, "The Experience Trap," *Harvard Business Review,* February 2008, pp. 94–101; and M. Heilman and T. Okimoto, "Motherhood: A Potential Source of Bias in Employment Decisions," *Journal of Applied Psychology,* January 2008, pp. 189–198.

71. W. Goodman, "How Gambling Makes Strange Bedfellows," *The New York Times,* June 10, 1997, p. B3.

72. R. H. Thaler, "Paying a Price for the Thrill of the Hunt," *The New York Times,* November 15, 2009, Business section, p. 5.

73. P. Slovic, "The Construction of a Preference," *American Psychologist* 50(1995), pp. 364–371; K. J. Dunegan, "Framing, Cognitive Roles, and Image Theory: Toward an Understanding of a Glass Half Full," *Journal of Applied Psychology*

78(1993), pp. 491–503; and K. F. E. Wong, M. Yik, and J. Y. Y. Kwong, "Understanding the Emotional Aspects of Escalation of Commitment: The Role of Negative Affect," *Journal of Applied Psychology,* March 2006, pp. 282–297.

74. S. Thurm, "Seldom-Used Executive Power: Reconsidering," *The Wall Street Journal,* February 6, 2006, p. B3.

75. G. W. Hill, "Group versus Individual Performance: Are *n* + 1 Heads Better Than 1?" *Psychological Bulletin,* May 1982, pp. 517–539. Also see W. T. H. Koh, "Heterogeneous Expertise and Collective Decision-Making," *Social Choice and Welfare,* April 2008, pp. 457–473.

76. N. F. R. Maier, "Assets and Liabilities in Group Problem Solving: The Need for Integrative Function," *Psychological Review* 74(1967) pp. 239–249.

77. Maier, 1967.

78. For more about groupthink, see R. J. Shiller, "Challenging the Crowd in Whispers, Not Shouts," *The New York Times,* November 2, 2008, Business section, p. 5; and J. Zweig, "How Group Decisions End Up Wrong-Footed," *The Wall Street Journal,* April 25 & 26, 2009, p. B1.

79. Methods for increasing group consensus were investigated by R. L. Priem, D. A. Harrison, and N. K. Muir, "Structured Conflict and Consensus Outcomes in Group Decision Making," *Journal of Management,* December 22, 1995, pp. 691–710.

80. See D. L. Gladstein and N. P. Reilly, "Group Decision Making under Threat: The Tycoon Game," *Academy of Management Journal,* September 1985, pp. 613–627.

81. These conclusions were based on the following studies: J. H. Davis, "Some Compelling Intuitions about Group Consensus Decisions, Theoretical and Empirical Research, and Interpersonal Aggregation Phenomena: Selected Examples, 1950–1990," *Organizational Behavior and Human Decision Processes,* June 1992, pp. 3–38; and J. A. Sniezek, "Groups Under Uncertainty: An Examination of Confidence in Group Decision Making," *Organizational Behavior and Human Decision Processes,* June 1992, pp. 124–155.

82. Supporting results can be found in J. R. Hollenbeck, D. R. Ilgen, D. J. Sego, J. Hedlund, D. A. Major, and J. Phillips, "Multilevel Theory of Team Decision Making: Decision Performance in Teams Incorporating Distributed Expertise," *Journal of Applied Psychology,* April 1995, pp. 292–316.

83. See D. H. Gruenfeld, E. A. Mannix, K. Y. Williams, and M. A. Neale, "Group Composition and Decision Making: How Member Familiarity and Information Distribution Affect Process and Performance," *Organizational Behavior and Human Decision Processes,* July 1996, pp. 1–15.

84. "Jack Welch's Lessons for Success," *Fortune,* January 25, 1993, p. 86.

85. See D. Pojidaeff, "Human Productivity and Pride in Work: The Core Principles of Participative Management," *Journal for Quality and Participation,* December 1995, pp. 44–47; and N. A. Holland, "A Pathway to Global Competitiveness and Total Quality: Participative Management," *Journal for Quality and Participation,* September 1995, pp. 58–62.

86. Results are presented in J. T. Delaney, "Workplace Cooperation: Current Problems, New Approaches," *Journal of Labor Research,* Winter 1996, pp. 45–61.

87. For an extended discussion, see M. Sashkin, "Participative Management Is an Ethical Imperative," *Organizational Dynamics,* Spring 1984, pp. 4–22. Also see S. Meisinger, "Management Holds Key to Employee Engagement," *HR Magazine,* February 2008, p. 8.

88. Supporting results can be found in C. R. Leana, R. S. Ahlbrandt, and A. J. Murrell, "The Effects of Employee Involvement Programs on Unionized Workers' Attitudes, Perceptions,

and Preferences in Decision Making," *Academy of Management Journal,* October 1992, pp. 861–873; and D. Plunkett, "The Creative Organization: An Empirical Investigation of the Importance of Participation in Decision Making," *Journal of Creative Behavior,* Second Quarter 1990, pp. 140–148. Results pertaining to role conflict and ambiguity can be found in C. S. Smith and M. T. Brannick, "A Role Replication and Theoretical Extension," *Journal of Organizational Behavior,* March 1990, pp. 91–104.

89. See J. A. Wagner III, "Participation's Effects on Performance and Satisfaction: A Reconsideration of Research Evidence," *Academy of Management Review,* April 1994, pp. 312–330.

90. A thorough discussion of this issue is provided by W. A. Randolph, "Navigating the Journey to Empowerment," *Organizational Dynamics,* Spring 1995, pp. 19–32.

91. G. M. Parker, *Team Players and Teamwork: The New Competitive Business Strategy* (San Francisco: Jossey-Bass, 1990).

92. These recommendations were obtained from G. M. Parker, *Team Players and Teamwork.*

93. A. F. Osborn, *Applied Imagination: Principles and Procedures of Creative Thinking,* 3rd ed. (New York: Scribner's, 1979). For an example of how brainstorming works, see P. Croce, "Think Brighter," *FSB,* January 2006, p. 35.

94. W. H. Cooper, R. Brent Gallupe, S. Pollard, and J. Cadsby, "Some Liberating Effects of Anonymous Electronic Brainstorming," *Small Group Research,* April 1998, pp. 147–178.

95. These recommendations and descriptions were derived from B. Nussbaum, "The Power of Design," *BusinessWeek,* May 17, 2004, pp. 86–94.

96. See N. C. Dalkey, D. L. Rourke, R. Lewis, and D. Snyder, *Studies in the Quality of Life: Delphi and Decision Making* (Lexinton, MA: Lexington Books, 1972). An application of the Delphi technique can be found in T. Grisham, "The Delphi Technique: A Method for Testing Complex and Multifaceted Topics," *International Journal of Managing Projects in Business,* 2009, pp. 112–130.

97. A thorough description of computer-aided decision-making systems is provided by M. C. Er and A. C. Ng, "The Anonymity and Proximity Factors in Group Decision Support Systems," *Decision Support Systems,* May 1995, pp. 75–83; and A. LaPlante, "Brainstorming," *Forbes,* October 25, 1993, pp. 45–61.

98. Results can be found in J. S. Valacich and C. Schwenk, "Devils' Advocacy and Dialectical Inquiry Effects on Face-to-Face and Computer-Mediated Group Decision Making," *Organizational Behavior and Human Decision Processes,* August 1995, pp. 158–173; R. B. Gallupe, W. H. Cooper, M. Grise, and L. M. Bastianutti, "Blocking Electronic Brainstorms," *Journal of Applied Psychology,* February 1994, pp. 77–86; and A. R. Dennis and J. S. Valacich, "Computer Brainstorms: More Heads Are Better Than One," *Journal of Applied Psychology,* August 1993, pp. 531–537.

99. Supportive results can be found in S. S. Lam and J. Schaubroeck, "Improving Group Decisions by Better Polling Information: A Comparative Advantage of Group Decision Support Systems," *Journal of Applied Psychology,* August 2000, pp. 565–573; and I. Benbasat and J. Lim, "Information Technology Support for Debiasing Group Judgments: An Empirical Evaluation," *Organizational Behavior and Human Decision Processes,* September 2000, pp. 167–183.

100. B. B. Baltes, M. W. Dickson, M. P. Sherman, C. C. Bauer, and J. S. LaGanke, "Computer-Mediated Communication and Group Decision Making: A Meta-Analysis," *Organizational Behavior and Human Decision Processes,* January 2002, pp. 156–179.

101. David Dorfman, quoted in H. Lancaster, "How Life Lessons Have Helped a Successful Manager," *San Francisco Sunday Examiner & Chronicle,* August 15, 1999, p. CL-33; reprinted from *The Wall Street Journal.*

102. J. S. Hammond, R. L. Keeney, and H. Raiffa, *Smart Choices: A Practical Guide to Making Better Decisions* (Boston: Harvard Business School Press, 1999).

103. O. Pollar, "Six Steps for Making Tough Choices," *San Francisco Examiner & Chronicle,* April 4, 1999, p. J-3.

104. Lorien Pratt and Mark Zangari, reported in "Making Good Decisions," *The Straits Times,* August 6, 2009, p. C26.

CHAPTER 8

1. S. Stecklow, "Management 101," *The Wall Street Journal,* December 9, 1994, p. BI.

2. O. Pollar, "Don't Overlook the Importance of Delegating," *San Francisco Examiner,* August 8, 1999, p. J-3.

3. C. M. Avery, M. A. Walker, and E. O'Toole, *Teamwork Is an Individual Skill: Getting Your Work Done When Sharing Responsibility* (San Francisco: Berrett-Koehler, 2001); S. Gazda, "The Art of Delegating: Effective Delegation Enhances Employee Morale, Manager Productivity, and Organizational Success," *HR Magazine,* January 2002, pp. 75–79; R. Burns, *Making Delegation Happen: A Simple and Effective Guide to Implementing Successful Delegation* (St. Leonards, Australia: Allen & Unwin, 2002); D. M. Genett, *If You Want It Done Right, You Don't Have to Do It Yourself! The Power of Effective Delegation* (Sanger, CA: Quill Driver Books, 2003); R. Charan, "People Acumen," *Fast Company,* December 2007, http://www.fastcompany.com/articles/2007/12/ram-charan-acumen.html (accessed April 13, 2010).

4. E. Raudsepp, "Why Supervisors Don't Delegate," *Supervision,* May 1979, pp. 12–15; D. Anderson, "Supervisors and the Hesitate to Delegate Syndrome," *Supervision,* November 1992, pp. 9–11; O. Pollar, 1999; Avery et al., 2001; Burns, 2002; and Genett, 2003.

5. K. K. Reardon, *The Secret Handshake: Mastering the Politics of the Business Inner Circle* (New York: Doubleday, 2002) and *It's All Politics: Winning in a World Where Hard Work and Talent Aren't Enough* (New York: Currency/Random House, 2005).

6. K. K. Reardon, interviewed by J. Vishnevsky, "Ask the Expert: Kathleen Kelley Reardon," *U.S. News & World Report,* July 25, 2005, p. EE10. See also C. Bush, "Learn How to Work with Others," *Arizona Republic,* August 21, 2005, p. EC1.

7. E. H. Schein, "The Role of the Founder in Creating Organizational Culture," *Organizational Dynamics,* Summer 1983, pp. 13–28; E. H. Schein, *Organizational Culture and Leadership* (San Francisco: Jossey-Bass, 1985); and E. H. Schein, "Organizational Culture," *American Psychologist* 45 (1990), pp. 109–119.

8. Reward systems are discussed in J. Kerr and J. W. Slocum, "Managing Corporate Culture through Reward Systems," *Academy of Management Executive,* November 2005, pp. 83–94.

9. A thorough description of the competing values framework is provided in K. S. Cameron, R. E. Quinn, J. Degraff, and A. V. Thakor, *Creating Values Leadership* (Northhampton, MA: Edward Elgar, 2006); and K. S. Cameron and R. E. Quinn, *Diagnosing and Changing Organizational Culture* (New York: Addison-Wesley, 1999).

10. J. M. O'Brien, "Zappos Knows How to Kick It," *Fortune,* February 2, 2009, pp. 55–60; and C. Palmeri, "Now for Sale, the Zappos Culture," *Bloomberg BusinessWeek,* January 11, 2010, p. 57.

11. K. Auletta, *Googled: The End of the World as We Know It* (New York: Penguin Press, 2009).

12. B. Worthen, "Cisco CEO John Chambers's Big Management Experiment," *The Wall Street Journal,* August 5, 2009, http://blogs.wsj.com/digits/2009/08/05/cisco-ceo-jophn-chamberss-big-management-experiment (accessed January 26, 2010); and J. Swartz, "Cisco Powers through Recession," *USA Today,* January 15, 2010, pp. 1B, 2B.

13. D. Welch, D. Kiley, and M. Ihlwan, "My Way or the Highway at Hyundai," *BusinessWeek,* March 17, 2008, pp. 48–51.

14. L. Robbins, "For Delivery Companies, Welcome Stress," *The New York Times,* December 13, 2009, news section, p. 3.

15. G. Harris, "Pfizer Pays $2.3 Billion to Settle Marketing Case," *The New York Times,* September 3, 2009, http://www.nytimes.com/2009/09/03/business/03health.html?_r=1&scp=1&sq=Pfizer%20Fraud%20September%202009&st=cse (accessed April 15, 2010).

16. J. Kindler, quoted in R. M. Murphy, "Why Doing Good Is Good for Business," *Fortune,* February 8, 2010, pp. 90–95.

17. B. Breen, "The Thrill of Defeat," *Fast Company,* June 2004, pp. 76–81. A comprehensive article about companies that cultivate cultures that embrace failure and learn from it is J. McGregor, "How Failure Breeds Success," *BusinessWeek,* July 10, 2006, pp. 42–52.

18. J. McGregor, "The Chore Goes Offshore," *BusinessWeek,* March 23 & 30, 2009, pp. 50–51.

19. A. Lucchetti and M. Langley, "Amid Turmoil, a Shake-up at Citi: Perform-or-Die Culture Leaves Thin Talent Pool for Top Wall Street Jobs," *The Wall Street Journal,* November 5, 2007, pp. A1, A16.

20. E. Frauenheim, "Lost in the Shuffle," *Workforce Management,* January 14, 2008, pp. 1, 12–17.

21. E. H. Schein, *Organizational Culture and Leadership,* 2nd ed. (San Francisco: Jossey-Bass, 1992).

22. E. Byron, "Call Me Mike!" *The Wall Street Journal,* March 27, 2006, p. BI.

23. P. Babcock, "Is Your Company Two-Faced?" *HR Magazine,* January 2004, p. 43.

24. Anastasia Kelly, former chief lawyer for AIG, quoted in interview with C. Loomis, "Inside the Crisis at AIG," *Fortune,* March 1, 2010, pp. 47–54.

25. D. MacMillan, "Survivor: CEO Edition," *Bloomberg Business-Week,* March 1, 2010, pp. 33–38.

26. T. E. Deal and A. A. Kennedy, *Corporate Cultures: The Rites and Rituals of Corporate Life* (Reading, MA: Addison-Wesley, 1982), p. 22. See also T. E. Deal and A.A. Kennedy, *The New Corporate Cultures: Revitalizing the Workplace After Downsizing, Mergers, and Reengineering* (Cambridge, MA: Perseus, 2000).

27. C. Jarnagin and J. W. Slocum Jr., "Creating Corporate Cultures through Mythopoetic Leadership," *Organizational Dynamics* 36 (2007), pp. 288–302.

28. A. Farnham, "Mary Kay's Lessons in Leadership," *Fortune,* September 20, 1993, pp. 68–77.

29. See C. Hartnell, A. Ou, and A. Kinicki, "Organizational Culture and Organizational Effectiveness: A Meta-Analytic Investigation of the Competing Values Framework's (CVF) Theoretical Suppositions," under review at the *Journal of Applied Psychology.*

30. Adapted from L. Smircich, "Concepts of Culture and Organizational Analysis," *Administrative Science Quarterly,* September 1983, pp. 339–358.

31. S. McCarney, "Airline Industry's Top-Rated Woman Keeps Southwest's Small-Fry Spirit Alive," *The Wall Street Journal,* November 30, 1996, pp. BI, BII.

32. D. Anfuso, "3M's Staffing Strategy Promotes Productivity and Pride," *Personnel Journal,* February 1995, pp. 28–34.

33. The strength perspective was promoted by T. E. Deal and A. A. Kennedy, 1982.

34. The HP Way is thoroughly discussed in J. Dong, "The Rise and Fall of the HP Way," *Palo Alto Weekly Online Edition,* April 10, 2002; http://www.paloaltoonline.com/weekly/morgue/2002/2002_04_10.hpway10.html (accessed April 13, 2010).

35. J. P. Kotter and J. L. Heskett, *Corporate Culture and Performance* (New York: Free Press, 1992).

36. J. Green, "Management Secrets of the Grateful Dead," *The Atlantic,* March 2010, pp. 64–67. See also "What a Long, Strange Business Plan It's Been," *Bloomberg BusinessWeek,* March 8, 2010, p. 8.

37. B. Barnes, quoted in Green, 2010.

38. The mechanisms are based on material contained in E. H. Schein, "The Role of the Founder in Creating Organizational Culture," *Organizational Dynamics,* Summer 1983, pp. 13–28.

39. Walmart's values are stated on its corporate Web site, "About Wal-Mart," http://www.walmart.com/catalog/catalog.gsp?cat=131473#null (accessed April 13, 2010).

40. D. G. McNeil Jr., "Ally for the Poor in an Unlikely Corner," *The New York Times,* February 9, 2010, pp. D1, D6.

41. J. Stossel and G. Silber, "Sexy Sweats without the Sweatshop," ABC News, July 31, 2006; http://abcnews.go.com/2020/Business/story?id=2257111 (accessed April 13, 2010).

42. D. Moss, "Triage: Methodically Developing Its Employees," *HRMagazine,* July 2007, p 45.

43. D. Clark, "Why Silicon Valley Is Rethinking the Cubicle Office," *The Wall Street Journal,* October 15, 2007, http://online.wsj.com/article/SB119240097861658633.html?mod=hps_us_mostpop_viewed (accessed April 13, 2010).

44. Moss, 2007.

45. J. Ball, "Might Profit Maker," *The Wall Street Journal,* April 8, 2005, p. B1.

46. MacMillan, 2010.

47. C. I. Barnard, *The Functions of the Executive* (Cambridge, MA: Harvard University Press, 1938), p. 73.

48. P. M. Blau and W. R. Scott, *Formal Organizations* (San Francisco: Chandler, 1962).

49. M. Stettner, *Skills for New Managers* (New York: McGraw-Hill, 2000); J. H. Grossman and J. R. Parkinson, *Becoming a Successful Manager: How to Make a Smooth Transition from Managing Yourself to Managing Others* (New York: McGraw-Hill, 2001); and L. A. Hill, *Becoming a Manager: How New Managers Master the Challenges of Leadership,* 2nd ed. (Boston: Harvard Business School Press, 2003). For more on becoming a leader, also see B. Kellerman, "What Every Leader Needs to Know about Followers," *Harvard Business Review,* December 2007, pp. 84–91; M. Gottfredson, S. Schaubert, and H. Saenz, "The New Leader's Guide to Diagnosing the Business," *Harvard Business Review,* February 2008, pp. 63–73; "Timeless Leadership: A Conversation with David McCullough," *Harvard Business Review,* March 2008, pp. 45–49; S. D. Friedman, "Be a Better Leader, Have a Richer Life," *Harvard Business Review,* April 2008, pp. 112–118; and B. Reeves, T. W. Malone, and T. O'Driscoll, "Leadership's Online Labs," *Harvard Business Review,* May 2008, pp. 58–66.

50. E. H. Schein, *Organizational Psychology,* 3rd ed. (Englewood Cliffs, NJ: Prentice-Hall, 1980).

51. For an overview of the span of control concept, see D. D. Van Fleet and A. G. Bedeian, "A History of the Span of Management," *Academy of Management Review,* July 1977, pp. 356–372.

52. Research by V. Smeets and F. Warzynski, "Too Many Theories, Too Few Facts? What the Data Tell Us about the Link between Span of Control, Compensation, and Career Dynamics," *Labour Economics,* Special Issue on Firms and Employees, vol. 15 (2008). Reported in G. Anders, "Overseeing More Employees—With Fewer Managers," *The Wall Street Journal,* March 24, 2008, p. B6.

53. T. A. Stewart, "CEOs See Clout Shifting," *Fortune,* November 6, 1989, p. 66.

54. Pollar, 1999.

55. D. Machalaba, "After Crippling Chaos, Union Pacific Can See the Proverbial Light," *The Wall Street Journal,* August 25, 1999, pp. A1, A8.

56. L. Grant, "New Jewel in the Crown," *U.S. News & World Report,* February 28, 1994, pp. 55–57; H. Rothman, "The Power of Empowerment," *Nation's Business,* June 1993, pp. 49–52; and J. Galbraith, *Designing Complex Organizations* (Reading, MA: Addison-Wesley, 1973).

57. "Virtual Organization," Whatis.com, http://whatis.techtarget.com/definition/0,,sid9_gci213301,00.html (accessed June 12, 2006). See also J. A. Byrne, "The Virtual Corporation," *BusinessWeek,* February 8, 1993, pp. 98–102; G. Lorenzoni and C. Baden-Fuller, "Creating a Strategic Center to Manage a Web of Partners," *California Management Review,* Spring 1995, pp. 146–163.

58. A. Lashinsky, "RAZR's Edge," *Fortune,* June 12, 2006, pp. 124–132.

59. N. Anand and R. L. Daft, "What Is the Right Organization Design?" *Organizational Dynamics* 36(2007), pp. 329–344.

60. T. L. Friedman, "Just Doing It," *The New York Times,* April 18, 2010, Week in Review section, p. 10.

61. J. Hyatt, "The Soul of a New Team," *Fortune,* June 12, 2006, pp. 134–143.

62. Anand and Daft, 2007, p. 336.

63. S. Siekman, "The Snap-Together Business Jet," *Fortune,* January 21, 2002, http://money.cnn.com/magazines/fortune/fortune_archive/2002/01/21/316585/index.htm (accessed April 13, 2010); and Anand and Daft, 2007, p. 336.

64. M. Sappington, "When to Go Unvirtual," *Inc.,* April 2010, p. 73.

65. K. Deveny, "Bag Those Fries, Squirt That Ketchup, Fry That Fish," *BusinessWeek,* October 13, 1986, p. 86.

66. T. Burns and G. M. Stalker, *The Management of Innovation* (London: Tavistock, 1961). See also W. D. Sine, H. Mitsuhashi, and D. A. Kirsch, "Revisiting Burns and Stalker: Formal Structure and New Venture Performance in Emerging Economic Sectors," *Academy of Management Journal,* February 2006, pp. 121–132.

67. T. J. Peters and R. H. Waterman, *In Search of Excellence* (New York: Harper & Row, 1982).

68. Inc.com, "Virtual Company Advice," *101 Great Ideas for Managing People from America's Most Innovative Small-Companies,* October 1999, http://www.inc.com/articles/1999/10/19238.html (accessed April 13, 2010); and M. Puente, "Direct Selling Brings It All Home," *USA Today,* October 27, 2003, http://www.usatoday.com/life/2003-10-27-home-shopping_x.htm (accessed April 13, 2010).

69. P. R. Lawrence and J. W. Lorsch, *Organization and Environment* (Homewood, IL: Irwin, 1967).

70. J. R. Kimberly, R. H. Miles, and associates, *The Organizational Life Cycle* (San Francisco: Jossey-Bass, 1980).

71. This section was adapted from R. Kreitner and A. Kinicki, *Organizational Behavior,* 9th ed. (New York: McGraw-Hill/Irwin, 2010), pp. 515–517.

CHAPTER 9

1. J. Welch and S. Welch, "Dear Graduate. . . ," *BusinessWeek,* June 19, 2006, p. 100.

2. E. Holton, S. Naquin, and E. Holton, *So You're New Again: How to Succeed When You Change Jobs* (San Francisco: Berrett-Koehler Publishers, 2001); M. Watkins, *The First 90 Days: Critical Success Strategies for New Leaders at All Levels* (Boston: Harvard Business School Press, 2003); J. S. Lublin, "How to Win Support from Colleagues at Your New Job," *The Wall Street Journal,* November 25, 2003, p. B1; J. Burke, "Dip, Before Diving, into That New Job," *BusinessWeek Online,* June 28, 2004, http://www .businessweek.com/bschools/content/jun2004/ bs20040628_9967_bs001.htm (accessed April 19, 2010); L. Wolgemuth, "Breaking Out of the First-Job Trap," *U.S. News & World Report,* March 24/March 31, 2008, pp. 56, 58; and L. Buhl, "7 Deadly Sins for New Hires," *San Francisco Chronicle,* April 4, 2010, p. E14.

3. Thom Singer, quoted in A. Bruzzese, "You Must Keep Networking Even After You Get in the Door," *Reno Gazette-Journal,* February 25, 2010, p. 5A.

4. M. Sunnafrank and A. Ramirez Jr., "At First Sight: Persistent Relational Effects of Get-Acquainted Conversations," *Journal of Social and Personal Relationships,* June 1, 2004, pp. 361–379. See also J. Zaslow, "First Impressions Get Faster," *The Wall Street Journal,* February 16, 2006, p. D4.

5. R. Ailes, in "Your First Seven Seconds," *Fast Company,* June–July 1998, p. 184.

6. J. Denrell, "Why Most People Disapprove of Me: Experience Sampling in Impression Formation," *Psychological Review,* October 2005, pp. 951–978. See also M. Krakovsky, "Researcher Disputes Notion You Have Only One Chance to Make a Good Impression," *Stanford Report,* August 18, 2004, http://news-service.stanford.edu/news/2004/ august18/impressions-818.html (accessed April 19, 2010).

7. L. P. Frankel, in "Your First Impression," *Fast Company,* June–July 1998, p. 188.

8. M. Moskowitz, R. Levering, and C. Tkaczyk, "The List," *Fortune,* February 8, 2010, pp. 75–88.

9. A. Fisher, "How to Get Hired by a 'Best' Company," *Fortune,* February 4, 2008, p. 96.

10. A. Lashinsky, "The Perks of Being a Googler," *Fortune,* January 8, 2007, http://money.cnn.com/galeries/2007/ fortune/0701/gallery.Google_perks (accessed April 19, 2010).

11. E. Schmidt, quoted in interview by A. Lashinsky, "Back2Back Champs," *Fortune,* February 4, 2008, p. 70.

12. B. Stone, "Google's Profit and Revenue Rise, but Analysts Wanted More," *The New York Times,* April 15, 2010, http:// www.nytimes.com/2010/04/16/technology/16google.html (accessed April 25, 2010).

13. J. Welch, quoted in N. M. Tichy and S. Herman, *Control Your Destiny or Someone Else Will: How Jack Welch Is Making General Electric the World's Most Competitive Corporation* (New York: Doubleday, 1993), p. 251.

14. P. Capelli and A. Crocker-Hefter, "Distinctive Human Resources Are Firms' Core Competencies," *Organizational Dynamics,* Winter 1996, pp. 7–22.

15. G. Bollander, S. Snell, and A. Sherman, *Managing Human Resources,* 12th ed. (Cincinnati, OH: SouthWestern Publishing, 2001), pp. 13–15; and B. E. Becker, M. A. Huselid, and D. Ulrich, *The HR Scorecard: Linking People, Strategy, and Performance* (Boston: Harvard Business School Press, 2001), p. 4. See also D. Stamps, "Measuring Minds," *Training,* May 2000, pp. 76–85; C. A. Bartlett and S. Ghoshal, "Building Competitive Advantage through People," *MIT Sloan Management Review,* Winter 2002, pp. 34–41; and R. Rodriguez, "Meet the New Learning Executive," *HR Magazine,* April 2005, pp. 64–69.

16. B. E. Becker, M. A. Huselid, and D. Ulrich, *The HR Scorecard: Linking People, Strategy, and Performance* (Boston: Harvard Business School Press, 2001), p. 4.

17. Inspired by P. S. Adler and S. Kwon, "Social Capital: Prospects for New Concept," *Academy of Management Review,* January 2002, pp. 17–40. See also D. Lidsky, "Winning the Relationship Game," *Fast Company,* October 2004, pp. 113–115; J. Steinberg, "One Heart at a Time," *Fast Company,* November 2004, p. 49; K. H. Hammonds, "A Lever Long Enough to Move the World," *Fast Company,* January 2005, pp. 60–63; and A. C. Inkpen and E. W. K. Tsang, "Social Capital, Networks, and Knowledge Transfer," *Academy of Management Review,* January 2005, pp. 146–165.

18. R. Levering and M. Moskowitz, "The 100 Best Companies to Work For," *Fortune,* January 12, 2004, p. 68.

19. R. J. Mirabile, "The Power of Job Analysis," *Training,* April 1990, pp. 70–74; and S. F. Mona, "The Job Description," *Association Management,* February 1991, pp. 33–37.

20. S. Lau, J. Sweeney, and R. Halvorsen, "Minimum Wage, Record Retention, Major Change," *HR Magazine,* September 2007, p. 35.

21. S. G. Stolberg and R. Pear, "Obama Signs Health Care Overhaul Bill, with a Flourish," *The New York Times,* March 23, 2010, http://www.nytimes.com/2010/03/24/health/ policy/24health.html (accessed April 25, 2010).

22. See S. E. Needleman, "More Programs to Halt Bias Against Gays," *The Wall Street Journal,* November 26, 2007, p. B3. A countertrend to age discrimination may be the result of baby boomers retiring, bringing an overall shortfall in workers. See E. White, "The New Recruits: Older Workers," *The Wall Street Journal,* January 14, 2008, p. B3.

23. J. Coffman, O. Gadiesh, and W. Miller, *The Great Disappearing Act: Gender Parity Up the Corporate Ladder,* World Economic Forum White Paper, survey by Bain & Co. and Harvard Business Review, January 30, 2010, http://www .bain.com/bainweb/publications/publications_detail .asp?id=27564&menu_url=publications%5Fresults%2Easp (accessed April 25, 2010).

24. B. Knowlton, "U.S. Job Site Bans Bias over Gender Identity," *The New York Times,* January 6, 2010, p. A15.

25. Equal Employment Opportunity Commission, cited in S. Hananel, "Job Bias Claims Based on Disability, Religion Rise," *ABC News/Money,* January 6, 2010, http://abcnews .go.com/print?id=9490631 (accessed April 25, 2010).

26. M. Bello, "Racial Harassment Cases Rise Sharply," *USA Today,* February 6, 2008, p. 3A.

27. J. Levitz and P. Shishkin, "More Workers Cite Age Bias After Layoffs," *The Wall Street Journal,* March 11, 2009, pp. D1, D2. See also E. M. Brank, and L. E. Wylie, "The Next 'Ism': Ageism and Employment Discrimination," *Monitor on Psychology,* April 2009, p. 22; and L. Wolgemuth, "When Age Bias Hinders the Job Hunt," *U.S. News & World Report,* October 2009, p. 72.

28. S. Shellenbarger, "More Women Pursue Claims of Pregnancy Discrimination," *The Wall Street Journal,* March 27, 2008, p. D1.

29. Government Accountability Office, reported in R. Mantell, "Gender Pay Discrepancy Down; Gap Remains," *MarketWatch,* April 28, 2009, http://www.marketwatch.com/ story/gender-pay-discrepancy-down-but-gap-remains (accessed April 27, 2010).

30. For a thorough discussion of affirmative action, see F. J. Crosby, A. Iyer, S. Clayton, and R. A. Downing, "Affirmative Action," *American Psychologist,* February 2003, pp. 93–115.

31. See H. J. Walker, H. S. Feild, W. F. Giles, J. B. Bernerth, and L. A. Jones-Farmer, "An Assessment of Attraction Toward Affirmative Action Organizations: Investigating the Role of Individual Differences," *Journal of Organizational Behavior,* May 2007, pp. 455–507.

32. E. H. James, A. P. Brief, J. Dietz, and R. R. Cohen, "Prejudice Matters: Understanding the Reactions of Whites to Affirmative Action Programs Targeted to Benefit Blacks," *Journal of Applied Psychology,* December 2001, pp. 1120–1128.

33. For a thorough review of relevant research, see M. E. Heilman, "Affirmative Action: Some Unintended Consequences for Working Women," in B. M. Staw and L. L. Cummings, eds., *Research in Organizational Behavior,* vol. 16 (Greenwich, CT: JAI Press, 1994), pp. 125–169.

34. M. Rotundo, D.-H. Nguyen, and P. R. Sackett, "A Meta-Analytic Review of Gender Differences in Perceptions of Sexual Harassment," *Journal of Applied Psychology,* October 2001, pp. 914–922.

35. Most research on sexual harassment has focused on harassment inside organizations. For a discussion of harassment beyond the boundaries of the organization, see H. J. Gettman and J. J. Gelfand, "When the Customer Shouldn't Be King: Antecedents and Consequences of Sexual Harassment by Clients and Customers," *Journal of Applied Psychology,* May 2007, pp. 757–770.

36. M. Maremont, "A Case Puts a Value on Touching and Fondling," *The Wall Street Journal,* May 25, 1999, pp. B1, B4; S. Armour, "More Men Say They Are Sexually Harassed at Work," *USA Today,* September 17, 2004, p. 1B; C. A. Pierce and H. Aguinis, "Legal Standards, Ethical Standards, and Responses to Social–Sexual Conduct at Work," *Journal of Organizational Behavior* 26 (2005), pp. 727–732; L. A. Baar, "Harassment Case Proceeds Despite Failure to Report," *HR Magazine,* June 2005, p. 159; and S. Shellenbarger, "Supreme Court Takes on How Employers Handle Worker Harassment Complaints," *The Wall Street Journal,* April 13, 2006, p. D1.

37. Equal Employment Opportunity Commission, reported in S. Hananel, "More Men File Claims of Sexual Harassment," *Reno Gazette-Journal,* March 5, 2010, p. 2C; and D. Mattioli, "More Men Make Harassment Claims," *The Wall Street Journal,* March 23, 2010, p. D4. See also C. M. Blow, "Don't Tickle Me, Bro!" *The New York Times,* March 13, 2010, p. A17.

38. Survey in 2007 by Novations Group, Boston, reported in D. Stead, "Is the Workplace Getting Raunchier?" *BusinessWeek,* March 17, 2008, p. 19.

39. Survey in 2007 by Zogby International, reported in T. Parker-Pope, "When the Bully Sits in the Next Cubicle," *The New York Times,* March 25, 2008, p. D5. See also J. A. Segal, "'I Did It, but. . . ,'" *HR Magazine,* March 2008, pp. 91–93.

40. J. Welch and S. Welch, "Hiring Wrong—and Right," *BusinessWeek,* January 29, 2007, p. 102.

41. Dave Lefkow, CEO of TalentSpark, quoted in C. Winkler, "Quality Check," *HR Magazine,* May 2007, pp. 93–98.

42. R. Zeidner, "People Promoted to the Top Jobs Measure Up," *HR Magazine,* April 2010, p. 20. The article reports on a study by Y. Zhang and N. Rajagopalan, "Once an Outsider, Always an Outsider? CEO Origin, Strategic Change, and Firm Performance," *Strategic Management Journal* (forthcoming).

43. S. E. Needleman, "Lifting the Curtain on the Hiring Process," *The Wall Street Journal,* January 26, 2010, p. D5.

44. G. McWilliams, "The Best Way to Find a Job," *The Wall Street Journal,* December 6, 1999, pp. R16, R22. Respondents to the Society for Human Resource Management's *2007 E-Recruiting Survey* also reported that employee referrals generated the highest quality of job candidates and best return on investment for their organization. See T. Minton-Eversole, "E-Recruitment Comes of Age, Survey Says," *HR Magazine,* August 2007, p. 34. Also see D. G. Allen and R. V. Mahto, "Web-Based Recruitment: Effects of Information, Organizational Brand, and Attitudes Toward a Web Site on Applicant Attraction," *Journal of Applied Psychology,* November 2007, pp. 1696–1708.

45. Minton-Eversole, 2007. Also see D. Kirkpatrick, "Web 2.0 Gets Over Its Goofing-Off Phase," *Fortune,* March 31, 2008, pp. 32–34; J. De Avila,"Beyond Job Boards: Targeting the Source," *The Wall Street Journal,* July 2, 2009, pp. D1, D5; M. Weinstein, "Virtual Handshake," *Training,* September 2009, pp. 18–22; D. Koeppel, "HR by Twitter," *FSB,* September 23, 2009, p. 57; and J. Greer, "The Art of Self-Marketing Online," *U.S. News & World Report,* May 2010, p. 30.

46. B. M. Meglino, A. S. DeNisi, S. A. Youngblood, and K. J. Williams, "Effects of Realistic Job Previews: A Comparison Using an Enhancement and a Reduction Preview," *Journal of Applied Psychology* 73 (1981), pp. 259–266.

47. Survey by InfoLink Screen Services, reported in H. B. Herring, "On Our Résumés, Couldn't We All Have Gone to Yale?" *The New York Times,* March 12, 2006, sec. 3, p. 2.

48. Survey by ResumeDoctor.com, reported in C. Soltis, "Eagle-Eyed Employers Scour Résumés for Little White Lies," *The Wall Street Journal,* March 21, 2006, p. B7.

49. Survey by Society of Human Resource Management, reported in M. Villano, "Served as King of England, Said the Résumé," *The New York Times,* March 19, 2006, sec. 3, p. 9.

50. Survey by Background Information Services, reported in Villano, 2006.

51. C. W. Nevius, "If You Like Fiction, Read the Job Résumés," *San Francisco Chronicle,* February 28, 2006, pp. B1, B2. See also D. Koeppel, "That Padded Résumé Won't Help Break Your Fall," *San Francisco Chronicle,* April 23, 2006, p. F5; reprinted from *The New York Times.*

52. Report by Automatic Data Processing, Roseland, NJ, cited in J. L. Seglin, "Lies Can Have a (Long) Life of Their Own," *The New York Times,* June 16, 2002, sec. 3, p. 4. See also S. Armour, "Security Checks Worry Workers," *USA Today,* June 19, 2004, p. 1B.

53. J. S. Lublin, "Job Hunters with Gaps in Their Résumés Need to Write Around Them," *The Wall Street Journal,* May 6, 2003, p. B1.

54. M. Conlin, "Don't Hedge Your Age," *BusinessWeek,* October 6, 2003, p. 14. See also C. Dahle, "A Nip and Tuck for the Résumé," *The New York Times,* April 17, 2005, sec. 3, p. 10.

55. S. McManis, "Little White-Collar Lies," *San Francisco Chronicle,* October 1, 1999, pp. B1, B3.

56. B. Bergstein, "Ex-Wiki Exec's Criminal History," *San Francisco Chronicle,* December 27, 2007, pp. C1, C2.

57. D. Belkin, "More Job Seekers Scramble to Erase Their Criminal Past," *The Wall Street Journal,* November 11, 2009, pp. A1, A16.

58. See E. Krell, "Unmasking Illegal Workers," *HR Magazine,* December 2007, pp. 49–52; and S. Berfield, "Illegals and Business: A Glimpse of the Future?" *BusinessWeek,* January 14, 2008, pp. 52–54.

59. W. M. Welch, "Employee Screenings See Growth," *USA Today,* June 24, 2009, p. 3A.

60. L. Radnofsky and M. Jordan, "Illegal Workers Slip by System," *The Wall Street Journal,* February 25, 2010, p. A6.

61. See K. Gurchiek, "Video Résumés Spark Curiosity, Questions," *HR Magazine,* May 2007, pp. 28, 30–31; and J. McGregor, "Beware of That Video Résumé," *BusinessWeek,* June 11, 2007, p. 12. Recently "facial coding" experts have examined videos of CEOs such as Nike's Phil Knight and Oracle's Larry Ellison for clues about lying; see D. Jones, "It's Written All Over Their Faces," *USA Today,* February 25, 2008, pp. 1B, 2B.

62. References are even a problem in faculty hiring in universities. See D. M. Barden, "The Unreliability of References," *The Chronicle of Higher Education,* January 11, 2008, pp. C1, C4.

63. A. Martin, "As a Hiring Filter, Credit Checks Draw Questions," *The New York Times,* April 10, 2010, pp. B1, B4.

64. C. Choi, "Credit Reports: Who's Looking at Yours, and Why?" *Reno Gazette-Journal,* April 12, 2010, p. 8A.

65. Based on P. Bathurst, "How to Avoid Those Fatal Interview Mistakes," *The Arizona Republic,* March 9, 2008, p. EC1; "Preparation Key to Snaring Job," *The Arizona Republic,* April 15, 2009, p. EC1; T. Musbach, "Common Interview Surprise: Inappropriate Questions," *San Francisco Chronicle,* January 3, 2010, p. D1; J. S. Lublin, "The New Job Is in the Details," *The Wall Street Journal,* January 5, 2010, p. D5; and "4 Keys to Interview Success," *The Arizona Republic,* April 4, 2010, p. EC1.

66. Survey by Society for Human Resource Management, reported in J. Schramm, "Background Checking," *HR Magazine,* January 2005, p. 128.w3

67. A. Finder, "When a Risqué Online Persona Undermines a Chance for a Job," *The New York Times,* June 11, 2006, pp. A1, A24; and S. E. Needleman, "Job Hunters, Beware," *The Wall Street Journal,* February 2, 2010, p. D4.

68. M. Conlin, "You Are What You Post," *BusinessWeek,* March 27, 2006, pp. 52–53; and L. Nicita, "Fired Before You're Hired," *The Arizona Republic,* July 28, 2007, pp. E1, E5.

69. D. Stamps, "Cyberinterviews Combat Turnover," *Training,* August 1995, p. 16.

70. S. E. Needleman, "The New Trouble on the Line," *The Wall Street Journal,* June 2, 2009, pp. B7, B10.

71. D. S. Chapman, K. L. Uggerslev, and J. Webster, "Applicant Reactions Face-to-Face and Technology-Mediated Interviews: A Field Investigation," *Journal of Applied Psychology* 88 (2003), pp. 944–953.

72. See J. Levashina and M. A. Campion, "Measuring Faking in the Employment Interview: Development and Validation of an Interview Faking Behavior Scale," *Journal of Applied Psychology,* November 2007, pp. 1638–1656.

73. E. D. Pursell, M. A. Campion, and S. R. Gaylord, "Structured Interviewing: Avoiding Selection Problems," *Personnel Journal,* November 1980.

74. M. C. Blackman, "Personality Judgment and the Utility of the Unstructured Employment Interview," *Basic and Applied Social Psychology* 24 (2002), pp. 241–250.

75. "Biggest Interviewing Mistakes," *USA Today,* November 19, 2001, p. 1B; D. Murphy, "Interviewers Just Don't Get the Importance of Failure," *San Francisco Chronicle,* May 19, 2002, pp. J1, J3B; Rosner, "Turning Your Job Interview into a Circus Isn't Always Bad," *San Francisco Chronicle,* June 2, 2002, p. J2; L. Adler, *Hire with Your Head: Using POWER Hiring to Build Great Teams,* 2nd ed. (New York: John Wiley, 2002); R. W. Wendover, *Smart Hiring: The Complete Guide to Finding and Hiring the Best Employees,* 3rd ed. (Naperville, IL: Sourcebooks, 2002); A. Arredondo, "Prepare Yourself for the Behavioral Interview," *The Arizona Republic,* March 2, 2008, p. EC1; K. Weirick, "The Perfect Interview," *HR Magazine,* April 2008, pp. 85–88; and AllBusiness.com, "Interviewing Skills Will Help Land the Right Employee for Your Firm," *San Francisco Chronicle,* April 9, 2008, p. C4. Some other articles useful for interviewees are C. Cadwell, "Making the Cover Letter Better," *San Francisco Chronicle,* January 13, 2008, p. H1, which describes how the introductory note accompanying your résumé can help lead to an interview; C. Binkley, "Tassels, Pantsuits, and Other Interview Don'ts," *The Wall Street Journal,* January 17, 2008, p. D8; and J. S. Lublin, "Notes to Interviewers Should Go Beyond a Simple Thank You," *The Wall Street Journal,* February 15, 2008, p. B1.

76. H. Lancaster, "Making a Good Hire Takes a Little Instinct and a Lot of Research," *The Wall Street Journal,* March 3, 1998, p. B1.

77. L. G. Otting, "Don't Rush to Judgment," *HR Magazine,* January 2004, pp. 95–98.

78. M. P. Cronin, "This Is a Test," *Inc.,* August 1993, pp. 64–68.

79. J. S. Lublin, "What Won't You Do for a Job?" *The Wall Street Journal,* June 2, 2009, pp. B7, B11.

80. M. J. Frase, "Smart Selections," *HR Magazine,* December 2007, pp. 63–67.

81. T. Gutner, "Applicants' Personalities Put to the Test," *The Wall Street Journal,* August 26, 2008, p. D4.

82. For more about skills testing, see J. T. Arnold, "Getting Facts Fast," *HR Magazine,* February 2008, pp. 57–62.

83. J. Hodges, "a) Doctor b) Builder c) Cop d) HELP!" *The Wall Street Journal,* April 22, 2010, p. D2.

84. D. P. Shuit, "At 60, Myers-Briggs Is Still Sorting Out and Identifying People's Types," *Workforce Management,* December 2003, pp. 72–74.

85. S. Adler, "Personality Tests for Salesforce Selection: Worth a Fresh Look," *Review of Business,* Summer/Fall 1994, pp. 27–31.

86. Scott Erker of Development Dimensions International, reported in Gutner, 2008.

87. "Personality Assessment Soars at Southwest," *Training,* January 2008, p. 14.

88. "Out of Sight, Yes. Out of Mind, No," *BusinessWeek,* February 18, 2008, p. 60.

89. Senior vice president of human resources Linda Matzigkeit, quoted in M. Bolch, "Nice Work," *HR Magazine,* February 2008, pp. 78–81.

90. B. Rose, "Critics Wary as More Jobs Hinge on Personality Tests," *Chicago Tribune,* October 31, 2004, p. 15.

91. S. Clifford, "The Science of Hiring," *Inc. Magazine,* August 2006, pp. 90–98.

92. V. Knight, "More Employers Are Using Personality Tests as Hiring Tools," *CareerJournal.com,* March 21, 2006; http://www.careerjournal.com/jobhunting/interviewing/20060321-knight.html (accessed April 19, 2010).

93. For a discussion of some of these tests, see P. Bathurst, "Pre-Job Tests Weed Out Imperfect Fits," *The Arizona Republic,* January 28, 2007, p. EC1.

94. D. Cadrain, "Are Your Employee Drug Tests *Accurate?*" *HR Magazine,* January 2003, pp. 41–45.

95. P. Korkki, "Workers May Lie about Drug Use, but Hair Doesn't," *The New York Times,* December 13, 2009, Business section, p. 2.

96. S. Shellenbarger, "Companies Are Finding It Really Pays to Be Nice to Employees," *The Wall Street Journal,* July 22, 1998, p. B1. For more about *The Jungle,* see C. Phelps, "How Should We Teach 'The Jungle'?" *The Chronicle of Higher Education,* March 3, 2006, pp. B10–B11.

97. R. Rigby, "Balloons and Buddies That Help New Recruits Fit In," *Financial Times,* March 17, 2008, http://us.ft.com/ftgateway/superpage.ft?news_id=fto0317200815500343I0 (accessed April 19, 2010).

98. Brookings Institution, cited in Shellenbarger, 1998.

99. MCI Communications surveys, reported in Shellenbarger, 1998.

100. G. R. Jones, "Organizational Socialization as Information Processing Activity: A Life History Analysis," *Human Organization* 42, no. 4 (1983), pp. 314–320.

101. The *Global Workforce Study,* by consultancy Towers Perrin, found that only 21% of employees surveyed around the world are engaged in their work, meaning they are willing to go the extra mile to help their companies succeed. See Towers Perrin, *2007 Global Workforce Study: Key Facts and Figures,* www.towersperrin.com/tp/getwebcachedoc7 .webc=HRS/USA/2007/200710/GWS_Fact_Sheet_ draft_109_07_v5.pdf (accessed April 19, 2010). Also see S. Meisinger, "Management Holds Key to Employee Engagement," *HR Magazine,* February 2008, p. 8.

102. C. McNamara, "Employee Training and Development: Reasons and Benefits," Free Management Library, 1999; http://www.managementhelp.org/trng_dev/basics/ reasons.htm (accessed April 19, 2010). See also "Training Top 125 2008," *Training,* February 2008, pp. 76–111.

103. See "Training: 2007 Industry Report," *Training,* November/ December 2007, pp. 8–24; and I. Bakir and S. Carliner, "Training Spending Stuck in Neutral," *Training,* February 2010, pp. 16–20.

104. R. Van Liew, quoted in "E-Learning's Dirty Little Secret," *Training,* February 2006, p. 6. See also J. Gordon, "Seven Revelations about E-Learning," *Training,* April 2006, pp. 28–31.

105. B. Muirhead, "Looking at Net Colleges" [letter], *USA Today,* November 12, 1999, p. 14A.

106. For a discussion from a training standpoint of how the brain learns, see A. Fox, "The Brain at Work," *HR Magazine,* March 2008, pp. 37–42.

107. M. W. "What If You Held a Training Session and No One Showed Up?" *Training,* January 2006, p. 10.

108. Survey of workers at Ernst & Young, reported in B. Hite, "Employers Rethink How They Give Feedback," *The Wall Street Journal,* October 13, 2008, p. B5.

109. S. A. Culbert and L. Rout, *Get Rid of Performance Reviews! How Companies Can Stop Intimidating, Start Managing— and Focus on What Really Matters* (New York: Business Plus, 2010).

110. S. A. Culbert, "Yes, Everyone Really Does Hate Performance Reviews," *The Wall Street Journal,* April 19, 2010, http://finance.yahoo.com/career-work/article/109343/ yes-everyone-really-does-hate-performance-reviews (accessed April 27, 2010).

111. J. Pfeffer, "Low Grades for Performance Reviews," *BusinessWeek,* August 3, 2009, p. 68.

112. D. J. Cohen, "HR Metrics: A Must," *HR Magazine,* February 2003, p. 136.

113. The term "Munchausen at work" was created by Georgia Institute of Technology business professor Nathan Bennett. See N. Bennett, "Munchausen at Work," *Harvard Business Review,* November 16, 2007, pp. 24–25

114. J. McGregor, "Job Review in 140 Keystrokes," *Business-Week,* March 23 & 30, 2009, p. 58.

115. A meta-analysis of 24 360-degree feedback studies appears in J. W. Smither, M. London, and R. R. Reilly, "Does Performance Improve Following Multisource Feedback? A Theoretical Model, Meta-Analysis, and Review of Empirical Findings," *Personnel Psychology,* Spring 2005, p. 33.

116. D. E. Coates, "Don't Tie 360 Feedback to Pay," *Training,* September 1998, pp. 68–78. See also A. S. Wellner, "Everyone's a Critic," *Inc.,* July 2004, pp. 38, 41; and W. C. Byham, "Fixing the Instrument," *Training,* July 2004, p. 50.

117. "Dell: Home Schooled by the Brass," *BusinessWeek Online,* October 10, 2005; http://www.businessweek.com/ magazine/content/05_41/b3954007.htm (accessed April 19, 2010).

118. C. S. Peck, "360-Degree Feedback: How to Avoid a Disaster," Workinfo.com, http://www.workinfo.com/free/downloads/ 71.htm (accessed April 19, 2010).

119. M. Boyle, "Performance Reviews: Perilous Curves Ahead," *Fortune,* May 15, 2001, www.fortune.com/fortune/subs/ print/0,15935,374010,00.html (accessed April 19, 2010); C. M. Ellis, G. B. Moore, and A. M. Saunier, "Forced Ranking: Not So Fast," *Perspectives,* June 30, 2003, www.imakenews .com/eletra/mod_print_view.cfm?this_id=162170&u= sibson&issue_id=000034313 (accessed April 19, 2010); and A. Meisler, "Dead Man's Curve," *Workforce Manage-ment,* July 2003, pp. 45–49.

120. S. Scherreik, "Your Performance Review: Make It Perform," *BusinessWeek Online,* December 17, 2001, http://www .businessweek.com/magazine/content/01_51/b3762136 .htm?chan=search (accessed April 19, 2010); and J. McGregor, "The Struggle to Measure Performance," *BusinessWeek Online,* January 9, 2006, http://www .businessweek.com/magazine/content/06_02/ b3966060.htm?chan=search (accessed April 19, 2010). See also criticism of forced ranking in J. Pfeffer and R. I. Sutton, *Hard Facts, Dangerous Half-Truths & Total Nonsense: Profiting from Evidence-Based Management* (Boston: Harvard Business School Press, 2006).

121. L. A. Bossidy, "What Your Leader Expects of You," *Harvard Business Review,* April 3, 2007, pp. 58–65.

122. Data from Bureau of Labor Statistics, reported in D. Cauchon, "It Pays to Work for Uncle Sam, Data Show," *USA Today,* March 5, 2010, p. 1A.

123. Adapted from D. L. McClain, "Tricks for Motivating the Pay to Motivate the Ranks," *The New York Times,* November 15, 1998, sec. 3, p. 5.

124. *Employee Benefits Study, 2007* (Washington, DC: U.S. Chamber of Commerce, 2008).

125. Data from the Bureau of Economic Analysis, reported in Cauchon, 2010.

126. W. Kirn, "More Than a Numbers Game," *The New York Times Magazine,* May 10, 2009, pp. 13–14.

127. For a discussion of workplace discipline, see L. E. Atwater, J. F. Brett, and A. C. Charles, "The Delivery of Workplace Discipline: Lessons Learned," *Organizational Dynamics* 36 (2007), pp. 392–403.

128. A. Sherman, "Do You Feel Like You've Hit a Brick Wall at Work?" *The Arizona Republic,* March 21, 2010, p. C1.

129. M. Conlin, "When the Laid-Off Are Better Off," *Business-Week,* November 2, 2009, p. 65.

130. D. Mattioli, "Layoff Sign: Boss's Cold Shoulder," *The Wall Street Journal,* October 23, 2008, p. D6.

131. A. Fisher, "Dumping Troublemakers, and Exiting Gracefully," *Fortune,* February 15, 1999, p. 174.

132. C. Hymowitz, "Why Managers Take Too Long to Fire Employees," *San Francisco Examiner,* February 21, 1999, p. J-2; reprinted from *The Wall Street Journal.*

133. For a discussion of the threat of litigation attending dismissals, see M. Orey, "Fear of Firing," *BusinessWeek,* April 23, 2007, pp. 52–62.

134. R. Moss Kanter, "Show Humanity When You Show Employees the Door," *The Wall Street Journal,* September 21, 1997, p. A22.

135. Moss Kanter, 1997.

CHAPTER 10

1. T. J. Fadem, quoted in O. Port and J. Carey, "Getting to 'Eureka!'" *BusinessWeek*, November 10, 1997, pp. 72–75.

2. C. Hymowitz, "Task of Managing in Workplace Takes a Careful Hand," *The Wall Street Journal*, July 1, 1997, p. B1.

3. T. Peters, "A Brawl with No Rules," *Forbes ASAP*, February 21, 2000, p. 155.

4. M. McGuinn, quoted in Hymowitz, 1997.

5. M. Weinstein, "Innovate or Die Trying," *Training Magazine*, May 2006, pp. 38–44; D. Hall, "The Customer Is Clueless," *BusinessWeek SmallBiz*, Spring 2006, p. 20; D. Brady, "Ideas That Bloom," *BusinessWeek SmallBiz*, Spring 2006, pp. 46–53; and P. Loewe and J. Dominiquini, "Overcoming the Barriers to Effective Innovation," *Strategy & Leadership* 34, no. 1 (2006), pp. 24–31.

6. Anthony Creed, quoted in D. Kirkpatrick, "Throw It at the Wall and See If It Sticks," *Fortune*, December 12, 2005, pp. 142–150.

7. Bruce Judson, quoted in J. M. Pethokoukis, "Bootstrapping Your Way into Business," *U.S. News & World Report*, March 27, 2006, p. 58. See also M. Bandyk, "Launching a Start-Up? Here's What Really Works," *U.S. News & World Report*, February 18, 2008, p. 58.

8. K. Stebbins, "Take a Risk," *Northern Nevada Healthy Living*, February 2008, p. 1.

9. E. Hoffer, *Ordeal of Change* (New York: Harper & Row, 1963).

10. P. Drucker, "The Future That Has Already Happened," *The Futurist*, November 1998, pp. 16–18.

11. Drucker, ibid.; J. C. Glenn, "Scanning the Global Situation and Prospects for the Future," *The Futurist*, January–February 2008, pp. 41–46; M. J. Cetron and O. Davies, "Trends Shaping Tomorrow's World: Forecasts and Implications for Business, Government, and Consumers (Part One), *The Futurist*, March–April 2008, pp. 35–52; M. J. Cetron and O. Davies, "Trends Shaping Tomorrow's World: Forecasts and Implications for Business, Government, and Consumers (Part Two), *The Futurist*, May–June 2008, pp. 35–50; and M. Richarme, "Ten Forces Driving Business Futures," *The Futurist*, July–August 2009, pp. 40–43.

12. Some of these trends are based on K. Albrecht, "Eight Supertrends Shaping the Future of Business," *The Futurist*, September–October 2006, pp. 25–29.

13. C. Anderson, quoted in A. T. Saracevic, "Economic Theories in 'The Long Tail' Don't Deserve Short Shrift," *San Francisco Chronicle*, July 16, 2006, pp. F1, F5. See also C. Anderson, *The Long Tail: Why the Future of Business Is Selling Less of More* (New York: Hyperion, 2006).

14. S. Hamm, "Speed Demons," *BusinessWeek*, March 27, 2006, pp. 68–75.

15. C. M. Christensen, *The Innovator's Dilemma: When New Technologies Cause Great Firms to Fail* (Boston, MA: Harvard Business School Press, 1997). See also F. Arner and R. Tiplady, "'No Excuse Not to Succeed,'" *BusinessWeek*, May 10, 2004, pp. 96–98.

16. W. M. Bulkeley, "Kodak's Move to Digital Shows Progress," *The Wall Street Journal*, November 2, 2007, p. B5; B. Dobbins, "Kodak's Restructuring Clicks," *San Francisco Chronicle*, January 31, 2008, p. C5; and D. Mattioli, "At Kodak, Patents Hold the Key to the Future," *The Wall Street Journal*, April 20, 2010, p. B8.

17. P. Engardio, "The Future of Outsourcing," *BusinessWeek*, January 30, 2006, pp. 50–58.

18. C. Hawley, "Mexico Takes on More Aircraft Construction," *USA Today*, April 7, 2008, p. 11A.

19. M. Bandyk, "Now Even Small Firms Can Go Global," *U.S. News & World Report*, March 10, 2008, p. 52.

20. S. Lohr, "Global Strategy Stabilized IBM During Downturn," *The New York Times*, April 20, 2010, p. B2.

21. K. Bradsher, "China Drawing High-Tech Research from U.S.," *The New York Times*, March 18, 2010, pp. A1, A14.

22. Albrecht, 2006. See also T. O'Driscoll, "Join the Webvolution," *Training*, February 2008, p. 24.

23. A. Toffler and H. Toffler, *Revolutionary Wealth* (New York: Alfred A. Knopf, 2006). Also see T. H. Davenport, L. Prusak, and B. Strong, "Putting Ideas to Work," *The Wall Street Journal*, March 10, 2008, p. R11.

24. R. Gold, B. Casselman, and G. Chazan, "Oil Well Lacked Safeguard Device," *The Wall Street Journal*, April 29, 2010, pp. A1, A8; S. Power and J. R. Emshwiller, "Investigators Focus on Failed Device," *The Wall Street Journal*, May 6, 2010, p. A5; and D. Vergano, "New Equipment Headed to Battle Oil Spill," *USA Today*, May 6, 2010, p. 5A.

25. Kenneth Arnold of K. Arnold Consulting, quoted in Vergano, "New Equipment Headed to Battle Oil Spill," 2010.

26. P. Robertson, D. Roberts, and J. Porras, "Dynamics of Planned Organizational Change: Assessing Empirical Support for a Theoretical Model," *Academy of Management Journal* 36, no. 3 (1993), pp. 619–634.

27. S. Moran, "The Range Gets Crowded for Natural Beef," *The New York Times*, June 10, 2006, pp. B1, B4.

28. M. Warner, "When It Comes to Meat, 'Natural' Is a Vague Term," *The New York Times*, June 10, 2006, p. B4.

29. Andy Grove of Intel, quoted in L. Berlin, "A Look at Apple through the Years: Never Afraid to Change Its Direction," *San Francisco Chronicle*, January 15, 2008, pp. C1, C2.

30. Pew Research Center, reported in S. Jayon, "A Detailed Look at Millennials," *USA Today*, February 24, 2010, p. 10B.

31. K. Talley, "Wal-Mart Ramps Up Online Efforts Globally," *The Wall Street Journal*, April 7, 2010, p. B6.

32. W. M. Welch, "Secondhand Shops at Forefront of Economic Pinch," *USA Today*, April 22, 2010, p. 3A.

33. J. Brinkley, "West Needs to Stand Up to China, End Counterfeiting," *San Francisco Chronicle*, April 25, 2010, p. E8.

34. T. Aeppel, "Show Stopper: How Plastic Cork Popped the Cork Monopoly," *The Wall Street Journal*, May 1–2, 2010, pp. A1, A10.

35. For just one of many articles on this subject, see M. Ambinder, "Beating Obesity," *The Atlantic*, May 2010, pp. 72–83.

36. B. Walsh, "Eco-Buyer Beware," *Time*, September 22, 2008, pp. 71–72; T. Watson, "Eco-Friendly Claims Go Unchecked," *USA Today*, June 22, 2009, p. 1A; K. Galbraith, "Shorted: Paying for Green Power, and Getting Ads Instead," *USA Today*, November 17, 2009, pp. B1, B8; J. Diamond, "Will Big Business Save the Earth?" *The New York Times*, December 5, 2009, http://www.nytimes.com/2009/12/06/opinion/06diamond.html (accessed May 2, 2010); L. Petrecca and C. Dugas, "Going Truly Green Might Require Detective Work," *USA Today*, April 22, 2010, pp. 1B, 2B; and V. O'Connell, "'Green' Goods, Red Flags," *The Wall Street Journal*, April 24–25, 2010, p. A3.

37. S. E. Needleman, "Business Owners Try to Motivate Employees," *The Wall Street Journal*, January 14, 2010, p. B5.

38. V. Foley, director of Lee Hecht Harrison, quoted in E. Zimmerman, "As a New Manager, Get to Know Your Team," *The New York Times*, December 20, 2009, Business section, p. 9.

39. R. D. Hof, "Online Extra: Trading in a Cloud of Electrons," *BusinessWeek Online*, May 20, 2004, www.businessweek.com/@@TUSaZYUQTmOUSw0A/magazine/content/04_19/b3882621.htm (accessed April 28, 2010).

40. The term "Web 2.0" was popularized by Tim O'Reilly, CEO of O'Reilly Media Inc. See T. O'Reilly, "What Is Web 2.0," O'Reilly, September 30, 2005; http://www.oreillynet.com/pub/a/oreilly/tim/news/2005/09/30/what-is-web-20.html (accessed April 28, 2010).

41. See W. E. Halal, "Technology's Promise: Highlights from the TechCast Project," *The Futurist*, November–December 2007, pp. 41 50; B. Charney, "Technological Gadgets Smarten Up," *The Wall Street Journal*, December 31, 2007, p. B3; L. Cauley, "Race Is On for Mobile Web's Pot of Gold," *USA Today*, January 10, 2008, pp. 1B, 2B; M. Mangalindan, "How We Shop," *The Wall Street Journal*, January 28, 2008, p. R3; E. Steel, "Target-Marketing Becomes More Communal," *The Wall Street Journal*, November 5, 2009, p. B10; B. Evangelista, "Retailers Use Social Media to Dangle Deals," *San Francisco Chronicle*, November 25, 2009, pp. D1, D3; S. Rosenbloom and K. A. Cullotta, "Buying, Selling, and Twittering All the Way," *The New York Times*, November 28, 2009, pp. B1, B4; K. Hannon, "How Viral Business Takes Off," *USA Today*, November 30, 2009, p. 4B; A. P. McAfee, interviewed by A. P. Raman, "How a Connected Workforce Innovates," *The Harvard Business Review*, December 2009, p. 80; S. E. Needleman, "Services Combine Social Media, Marketing," *The Wall Street Journal*, February 23, 2010, p. B7; and A. Levy and J. Galante, "Who Wants to Buy a Digital Elephant?" *Bloomberg BusinessWeek*, March 8, 2010, pp. 64–65.

42. R. D. Hof, "Web 2.0: The New Guy at Work," *BusinessWeek*, June 19, 2006, pp. 58–59.

43. See S. Baker, "Beware Social Media Snake Oil," *Bloomberg BusinessWeek*, December 15, 2009, pp. 49–51.

44. M. McArdle, "The Freeloaders," *The Atlantic*, May 2010, pp. 34–36.

45. R. J. Baron, "What's Keeping Us So Busy in Primary Care? A Snapshot from One Practice," *New England Journal of Medicine*, April 29, 2010, pp. 1632–1636. See also S. Lohr, "Study Shows Extent of 'Invisible Work' by Family Doctors," *The New York Times*, April 29, 2010, p. B3.

46. M. Fugate, A. Kinicki, and C. L. Scheck, "Coping with an Organizational Merger over Four Stages," *Personnel Psychology*, Winter 2002, pp. 905–928.

47. D. Reed, "United, Continental Plan Merger," *USA Today*, May 3, 2010, p. 1B.

48. Based on A. Walker, "Measuring Footprints," *Fast Company*, April 2008, pp. 59–60.

49. See "Change Management: The HR Strategic Imperative as a Business Partner," *Research Quarterly*, Fourth Quarter 2007, pp. 1–9; and D. A. Garvin, A. C. Edmondson, and F. Gino, "Is Yours a Learning Organization?" *Harvard Business Review*, March 2008, pp. 109–116.

50. W. G. Dyer, *Team Building: Current Issues and New Alternatives*, 3rd ed. (Reading, MA: Addison-Wesley, 1995).

51. See R. Rodgers, J. E. Hunter, and D. L. Rogers, "Influence of Top Management Commitment on Management Program Success," *Journal of Applied Psychology*, February 1993, pp. 151–155.

52. R. J. Schaffer and H. A. Thomson, "Successful Change Programs Begin with Results" *Harvard Business Review*, January–February 1992, pp. 80–89.

53. P. J. Robertson, D. R. Roberts, and J. I. Porras, "Dynamics of Planned Organizational Change: Assess Empirical Support for a Theoretical Model," *Academy of Management Journal*, June 1993, pp. 619–634.

54. C.-M. Lau and H.-Y. Ngo, "Organization Development and Firm Performance: A Comparison of Multinational and Local Firms," *Journal of International Business Studies*, First Quarter 2001, pp. 95–114.

55. A. G. Lafley, interviewed by R. O. Crockett in "How P&G Plans to Clean Up," *BusinessWeek*, April 13, 2009, p. 44.

56. Survey by Development Dimensions International Inc., 2005, reported in "The Big Picture: All Talk? Despite Management's Focus on Innovation, U.S. Executives Say Their Companies Give It Short Shrift," *BusinessWeek*, March 6, 2006, p. 13.

57. Intel Global Innovation Survey, 2009, conducted by Penn, Schoen, & Berland Associates, reported in D. McGinn, "The Decline of Western Innovation," *Newsweek*, November 23, 2009, pp. 34–37.

58. M. Arndt and B. Einhorn, "The 50 Most Innovative Companies," *Bloomberg BusinessWeek*, April 26, 2010, http://www.businessweek.com/magazine/content/10_17/b4175034779697.htm (accessed May 2, 2010).

59. L. Selden and I. C. MacMillan, "Manage Customer-Centric Innovation—Systematically," *Harvard Business Review*, April 2006, pp. 108–116.

60. C. B. Rabe, *The Innovation Killer: How What We Know Limits What We Can Imagine—and What Smart Companies Are Doing about It* (New York: Amacom, 2006).

61. See J. Rae-Dupree, "Innovative Minds Don't Think Alike," *The New York Times*, December 30, 2007, business section, p. 3.

62. J. Bessant, K. Möslein, and B. von Stamm, "In Search of Innovation," *The Wall Street Journal*, June 22, 2009, p. R4.

63. J. Welch and S. Welch, "Finding Innovation Where It Lives," *BusinessWeek*, April 21, 2008, p. 84.

64. This discussion was adapted from R. Kreitner and A. Kinicki, *Organizational Behavior*, 9th ed. (New York: McGraw-Hill/Irwin, 2010), p. 526, which is based on S. Berkun, *The Myths of Innovation* (Sebastapol, CA: O'Reilly Media, Inc., 2007).

65. See D. Kiley and C. Matlack, "Fiat: On the Road Back to America," *BusinessWeek*, April 20k, 2009, p. 28.

66. R. Jana, "Inspiration from Emerging Economies," *BusinessWeek*, May 12, 2008, pp. 54–55.

67. J. McGregor, "The World's Most Innovative Companies," *BusinessWeek*, April 24, 2006, pp. 63–74.

68. Analysis by Kauffman Foundation, reported by D. Archer, "Learn to Innovate by Thinking Like an Entrepreneur," *Reno Gazette-Journal*, November 8, 2009, p. 13A.

69. A. V. Bhidé, quoted in G. Gendron, "The Origin of the Entrepreneurial Species," *Inc.*, February 2000, pp. 105–114.

70. B. Evangelista, "Movies by Mail: Netflix.com Makes Renting DVDs Easy," *San Francisco Chronicle*, January 26, 2002, p. B1; V. Kopytoff, "Successful Netflix Faces Competition," *San Francisco Chronicle*, March 8, 2004, pp. E1, E4; and M. Boyle, "Reed Hastings," *Fortune*, May 28, 2007, pp. 30–31.

71. S. A. Shane, *The Illusions of Entrepreneurship: The Costly Myths That Entrepreneurs, Investors, and Policy Makers Live By* (New Haven, CT: Yale University Press, 2008).

72. Scott Shane, interviewed by J. Tozzi, "The Entrepreneurship Myth," *BusinessWeek*, January 23, 2008, http://www.businessweek.com/smallbiz/content/jan2008/sb20080123_809271.htm?chan=search (accessed April 29, 2010).

73. V. Wadhwa, R. Freeman, and B. Rissing, *Education and Tech Entrepreneurship*, May 2008, Ewing Marion Kauffman Foundation, http://www.kauffman.org/research-and-policy/education-and-tech-entrepreneurship.aspx (accessed May 3, 2010). See also S. Berfield, "The Truth about Tech Startups," *BusinessWeek*, May 19, 2008, p. 16.

74. R. Cohen, "Vive La Dolce Vita," *The New York Times*, April 16, 2006, sec. 4, pp. 1, 4.

75. A. G. Lafley, in Crockett, 2009.

76. "The 50 Most Innovative Companies 2010," *Bloomberg BusinessWeek,* April 26, 2010, http://bwnt.businessweek.com/interactive_reports/innovative_companies_2010/?chan=magazine+channel_special+report (accessed May 2, 2010).

77. C. Wilson, "Post-it Notes Have Stuck Around for a Reason," *USA Today*, April 21, 2010, p. ID.

78. J. C. Collins and J. I. Porris, *Built to Last: Successful Habits of Visionary Companies* (New York: HarperBusiness, 1994). See also T. J. Martin, "Ten Commandments for Managing Creative People," *Fortune,* January 16, 1995, pp. 135–136.

79. B. Hindo, "At 3M, a Struggle between Efficiency and Creativity," *BusinessWeek*, June 2007, pp. 8IN–14IN.

80. D. Mattioli and K. Maher, "At 3M, Innovation Comes in Tweaks and Snips," *The Wall Street Journal*, March 1, 2010, pp. BI, B4.

81. "America's Most Admired Companies: The 50 All-Stars," *Fortune*, March 22, 2010, pp. 121–126.

82. J. Denrell, "Vicarious Learning, Undersampling of Failure, and the Myths of Management," *Organizational Science,* May–June 2003, pp. 227–243.

83. J. Freese, "Magical Misery Tour," *Fortune Small Business,* May 2008, p. 29.

84. T. J. Allen and S. I. Cohen, "Information Flow in Research and Development Laboratories," *Administrative Science Quarterly*, March 1969, pp. 12–19.

85. L. A. Bettencourt, "The Customer-Centered Innovation Map," *Harvard Business Review,* May 2008, p. 109.

86. L. Bossidy and Ram Charan, with C. Burck, *Execution: The Discipline of Getting Things Done* (New York: Crown Business, 2002).

87. "The 50 Most Innovative Companies 2010," *Bloomberg BusinessWeek,* April 26, 2010, http://bwnt.businessweek.com/interactive_reports/innovative_companies_2010/?chan=magazine+channel_special+report (accessed May 2, 2010).

88. Adapted from R. Kreitner and A. Kinicki, *Organizational Behavior*, 9th ed. (McGraw-Hill/Irwin, 2010), pp. 549–551.

89. This three-way typology of change was adapted from discussion in P. C. Nutt, "Tactics of Implementation," *Academy of Management Journal*, June 1986, pp. 230–261.

90. Radical organizational change is discussed by T. E. Vollmann, *The Transformational Imperative* (Boston: Harvard Business School Press, 1996); and J. A. Neal and C. L. Tromley, "From Incremental Change to Retrofit: Creating High-Performance Work Systems," *Academy of Management Executive*, February 1995, pp. 42–53.

91. Adapted in part from J. D. Ford, L. W. Ford, and A. D'Amelio, "Resistance to Change: The Rest of the Story," *Academy of Management Review,* April 2008, pp. 362–377.

92. See "Vulnerability and Resilience," *American Psychologist,* January 1996, pp. 22–28. See also T. Kiefer, "Feeling Bad: Antecedents and Consequences of Negative Emotions in Ongoing Change," *Journal of Organizational Behavior,* December 2005, pp. 875–897.

93. See R. Moss Kanter, "Managing Traumatic Change: Avoiding the 'Unlucky 13,'" *Management Review,* May 1987, pp. 23–24.

94. Details of this example are provided by B. Schlender, "Inside the Shakeup at Sony," *Fortune,* April 4, 2005, pp. 94–104.

95. K. Lewin, *Field Theory in Social Science* (New York: Harper & Row, 1951).

96. The role of learning within organizational change is discussed by C. Hendry, "Understanding and Creating Whole Organizational Change through Learning Theory," *Human Relations,* May 1996, pp. 621–641; and D. Ready, "Mastering Leverage, Leading Change," *Executive Excellence,* March 1995, pp. 18–19.

97. C. Goldwasser, "Benchmarking: People Make the Process," *Management Review*, June 1995, p. 40; and *Cambridge Advanced Learner's Dictionary* (Cambridge: Cambridge University Press, 2004), http://dictionary.cambridge.org/define.asp?key=94109&dict=CALD (accessed April 28, 2010).

98. R. Kreitner and A. Kinicki, *Organizational Behavior*, 4th ed. (Burr Ridge, IL: Irwin/McGraw-Hill, 1998), p. 619.

99. These errors are discussed by J. P. Kotter, "Leading Change: The Eight Steps to Transformation," in J. A. Conger, G. M. Spreitzer, and E. E. Lawler III, eds., *The Leader's Change Handbook* (San Francisco: Jossey-Bass, 1999), pp. 87–99.

100. The type of leadership needed during organizational change is discussed by S. Furst and D. M. Cable, "Employee Resistance to Organizational Change: Managerial Influence Tactics and Leader-Member Exchange," *Journal of Applied Psychology,* March 2008, pp. 453–462; and D. M. Herold, D. B. Fedor, S. Caldwell, and Y. Liu, "The Effects of Transformational and Change Leadership on Employees' Commitment to a Change: A Multilevel Study," *Journal of Applied Psychology,* March 2008, pp. 346–357.

CHAPTER II

1. "Generation Y: The Millennials—Ready or Not, Here They Come," *NAS Insights,* 2006, http://72.14.253.104/search?q=cache:__bxYtpqItoJ:www.nasrecruitment.com/TalentTips/NASinsights/GenerationY.pdf1%E2%80%9CGeneration+Y:ITheIMillennials,%E2%80%9DINASIInsights,I2006&hl=en&ct=clnk&cd=I&gl=us (accessed May 3, 2010); J. Zaslow, "The Most-Praised Generation Goes to Work," *The Wall Street Journal,* April 20, 2007, pp. WI, W7; H. Dolezalek, "Boomer Reality," *Training,* May 2007, pp. 16–21; N. A. Hira, "You Raised Them, Now Manage Them," *Fortune,* May 28, 2007, pp. 38–46; K. Tyler, "Generation Gaps," *HR Magazine,* January 2008, pp. 69–72; S. Kapuria, "Millennial Workforce: IT Risk or Benefit," posted March 19, 2008, http://www.symantec.com/enterprise/security_response/weblog/2008/03/millennial_workforce_it_risk_o.html (accessed May 3, 2010); P. Bathurst, "Boomers, Younger Employees Give and Take to Find Common Ground," *The Arizona Republic,* April 20, 2008, p. ECI; P. Bathurst, "Millennials at Work," *The Arizona Republic,* May 4, 2008, p. ECI; B. Hite, "Employers Rethink How They Give Feedback," *The Wall Street Journal,* October 13, 2008, p. B5; *The Millennials: Confident. Connected. Open to Change,* Pew Research Center Publications, February 2010, www.pewresearch.org/millennials (accessed May 6, 2010); A. Lenhart, K. Purcell, A. Smith, and K. Zickuhr, *Social Media & Mobile Internet Use among Teens and Young Adults,* Pew Internet & AmericanLife Project, February 3, 2010, http://www.pewinternet.org/Reports/2010/Social-Media-and-Young-Adults.aspx?r=I (accessed May 6, 2010); S. Jayson, "'iGeneration' Has No Off Switch," *USA Today,* February 10, 2010, pp. ID, 2D; K. Palmer, "Talking to Gen Y about the New Culture of Thrift," *U.S. News & World Report,* March 2010, pp. 29–32; *Survey of Young Americans' Attitudes Toward Politics and Public Service,* 17th ed., March 9, 2010, Institute of Politics, Harvard University, http://www.iop.harvard.edu/Research-Publications/Polling/Spring-2010-Survey (accessed May 6, 2010); and C. Dugas, "'Generation Y' Faces Some Steep Financial Hurdles," *USA Today,* April 23–25, 2010, pp. IA, 2A.

2. For a thorough discussion of personality psychology, see D. P. McAdams and J. L. Pals, "A New Big Five: Fundamental

Principles for an Integrative Science of Personality," *American Psychologist,* April 2006, pp. 204–217.

3. The landmark report is J. M. Digman, "Personality Structure: Emergence of the Five-Factor Model," *Annual Review of Psychology* 41 (1990), pp. 417–440. Also see M. R. Barrick and M. K. Mount, "Autonomy as a Moderator of the Relationships between the Big Five Personality Dimensions and Job Performance," *Journal of Applied Psychology,* February 1993, pp. 111–118; C. Viswesvaran and D. S. Ones, "Measurement Error in 'Big Five Factors' Personality Assessment: Reliability Generalization across Studies and Measures," *Education and Psychological Measurement,* April 2000, pp. 224–235; and P. Sackett and F. Lievens, "Personnel Selection," *Annual Review of Psychology,* 2008, pp. 419–450.

4. M. R. Barrick and M. K. Mount, "The Big Five Personality Dimensions and Job Performance: A Meta-Analysis," *Personnel Psychology,* Spring 1991, pp. 1–26.

5. Barrick and Mount, 1991, p. 18; also see H. Moon, "The Two Faces of Conscientiousness: Duty and Achievement Striving in Escalation of Commitment Dilemmas," *Journal of Applied Psychology,* June 2001, pp. 533–540; and M. R. Barrick, G. L. Stewart, and M. Piotrowski, "Personality and Job Performance: Test of the Mediating Effects of Motivation among Sales Representatives," *Journal of Applied Psychology,* February 2002, pp. 43–51.

6. See F. P. Morgeson, M. A. Campion, R. L. Dipboye, J. R. Hollenbeck, K. Murphy, and N. Schmitt, "Reconsidering the Use of Personality Tests in Personnel Selection," *Personnel Psychology*, Autumn 2007, pp. 683–729; and D. Armstrong, "Malingerer Test Roils Personal-Injury Law," *The Wall Street Journal,* March 5, 2008, pp. A1, A13.

7. J. M. Crant, "Proactive Behavior in Organizations," *Journal of Management,* no. 3, 2000, pp. 439–441; and J. M. Crant, "The Proactive Personality Scale as a Predictor of Entrepreneurial Intentions," *Journal of Small Business Management,* July 1996, pp. 42–49.

8. For an overall view of research on locus of control, see P. E. Spector, "Behavior in Organizations as a Function of Employee's Locus of Control," *Psychological Bulletin,* May 1982, pp. 482–497; the relationship between locus of control and other dimensions of personality is examined by R. E. Johnson, C. C. Rosen, and P. E. Levy, "Getting to the Core of Core Self-Evaluation: A Review and Recommendations," *Journal of Organizational Behavior,* April 2008, pp. 391–413.

9. D. Sacks, "60 Seconds with Erik Weihenmayer," *Fast Company,* May 2004, p. 40.

10. See, for example, V. Gecas, "The Social Psychology of Self-Efficacy," in W. R. Scott and J. Blake, eds., *Annual Review of Sociology,* vol. 15 (Palo Alto, CA: Annual Reviews, 1989), pp. 291–316; and C. K. Stevens, A. G. Bavetta, and M. E. Gist, "Gender Differences in the Acquisition of Salary Negotiation Skills: The Role of Goals, Self-Efficacy, and Perceived Control," *Journal of Applied Psychology,* October 1993, pp. 723–735; and D. Eden and Y. Zuk, "Seasickness as a Self Fulfilling Prophecy: Raising Self-Efficacy to Boost Performance at Sea," *Journal of Applied Psychology,* October 1995, pp. 628–635.

11. J. Barling and R. Beattle, "Self-Efficacy Beliefs and Sales Performance," *Journal of Organizational Behavior Management,* Spring 1983, pp. 41–51.

12. A. D. Stajkovic and F. Luthans, "Self-Efficacy and Work-Related Performance: A Meta-Analysis," *Psychological Bulletin,* September 1998, pp. 240–261.

13. For more on learned helplessness, see M. J. Martinko and W. L. Gardner, "Learned Helplessness: An Alternative Explanation for Performance Deficits," *Academy of Management Review,* April 1982, pp. 195–204; and C. R. Campbell and M. J. Martinko, "An Integrative Attributional Perspective of Employment and Learned Helplessness: A Multimethod Field Study," *Journal of Management,* no. 2, 1998, pp. 173–200.

14. W. S. Silver, T. R. Mitchell, and M. E. Gist, "Response to Successful and Unsuccessful Performance: The Moderating Effect of Self-Efficacy on the Relationship between Training and Newcomer Adjustment," *Journal of Applied Psychology,* April 1995, pp. 211–225.

15. See J. V. Vancouver, K. M. More, and R. J. Yoder, "Self-Efficacy and Resource Allocation: Support for a Nonmonotonic, Discontinuous Model," *Journal of Applied Psychology,* January 2008, pp. 35–47.

16. The positive relationship between self-efficacy and readiness for retraining is documented in L. A. Hill and J. Elias, "Retraining Midcareer Managers: Career History and Self-Efficacy Beliefs," *Human Resource Management,* Summer 1990, pp. 197–217.

17. V. Gecas, "The Self-Concept," in R. H. Turner and J. F. Short Jr. eds., *Annual Review of Sociology,* vol. 8 (Palo Alto, CA: Annual Reviews, 1982); also see N. Branden, *Self-Esteem at Work: How Confident People Make Powerful Companies* (San Francisco: Jossey-Bass, 1998).

18. P. G. Dodgson and J. V. Wood, "Self-Esteem and the Cognitive Accessibility of Strengths and Weaknesses after Failure," *Journal of Personality and Social Psychology,* July 1998, pp. 178–197; and D. B. Fedor, J. M. Maslyn, W. D. Davis, and K. Mathieson, "Performance Improvement Efforts in Response to Negative Feedback: The Roles of Source Power and Recipient Self-Esteem," *Journal of Management,* January–February 2001, pp. 79–97.

19. B. R. Schlenker, M. F. Weigold, and J. R. Hallam, "Self-Serving Attributions in Social Context: Effects of Self-Esteem and Social Pressure," *Journal of Personality and Social Psychology,* May 1990, pp. 855–863; and P. Sellers, "Get Over Yourself," *Fortune,* April 2001, pp. 76–88.

20. D. A. Stinson, C. Logel, M. P. Zanna, J. G. Holmes, J. V. Wood, and S. J. Spencer, "The Cost of Lower Self-Esteem: Testing a Self- and Social-Bonds Model of Health," *Journal of Personality and Social Psychology,* March 2008, pp. 412–428.

21. J. W. McGuire and C. V. McGuire, "Enhancing Self-Esteem by Directed-Thinking Tasks: Cognitive and Affective Positivity Asymmetries," *Journal of Personality and Social Psychology,* June 1996, p. 1124.

22. M. Snyder and S. Gangestad, "On the Nature of Self-Monitoring: Matters of Assessment, Matters of Validity," *Journal of Personality and Social Psychology,* July 1986, p. 125.

23. Data from M. Kilduff and D. V. Day, "Do Chameleons Get Ahead? The Effects of Self-Monitoring on Managerial Careers," *Academy of Management Journal,* August 1994, pp. 1047–1060.

24. See F. Luthans, "Successful vs. Effective Managers," *Academy of Management Executive,* May 1988, pp. 127–132; also see W. H. Turnley and M. C. Bolino, "Achieving Desired Images While Avoiding Undesired Images: Exploring the Role of Self-Monitoring in Impression Management," *Journal of Applied Psychology,* April 2001, pp. 351–360.

25. J. D. Mayer, R. D. Roberts, and S. G. Barsade, "Human Abilities: Emotional Intelligence," *Annual Review of Psychology,* January 2008, http://ssrn.com/abstract=1082096 (accessed May 15, 2010).

26. D. Goleman, "What Makes a Leader," *Harvard Business Review,* November–December 1998, pp. 93–102.

27. The Personal Profile Analysis (PPA), by Thomas International, is described in M. Weinstein, "Emotional Evaluation," *Training,* July/August 2009, pp. 20–23.

28. See A. Chapman, "Empathy, Trust, Diffusing Conflict and Handling Complaints," *Businessballs.com*, http://www.businessballs.com/empathy.htm (accessed May 8, 2010).

29. S. Fox and P. E. Spector, "Relations of Emotional Intelligence, Practical Intelligence, General Intelligence, and Trait Affectivity with Interview Outcomes: It's Not All Just 'G,'" *Journal of Organizational Behavior,* March 2000, pp. 203–220.

30. See J. C. Rode, C. H. Mooney, M. L. Arthaud-Day, J. P. Near, T. T. Baldwin, R. S. Busin, and W. H. Bommer, "Emotional Intelligence and Individual Performance: Evidence of Direct and Moderated Effects," *Journal of Organizational Behavior,* May 2007, pp. 399–421; J. Mayer, R. Roberts, and S. Barsade, "Human Abilities: Emotional Intelligence," *Annual Review of Psychology,* January 2008, pp. 507–536; D. Eilerman, "The Significance of Emotional Engagement in Conflict Management," *Mediate.com*, January 2008, http://www.mediate.com/articles/eilermanD10.Cfm (accessed May 8, 2010).

31. See M. Rokeach, *Beliefs, Attitudes, and Values* (San Francisco: Jossey-Bass, 1968), p. 168.

32. M. Rokeach, *The Nature of Human Values* (New York: Free Press, 1973).

33. Survey by Society for Human Resource Management, reported in J. Herzlich, "Work/Life Balance Tops List," *The Arizona Republic,* January 6, 2008, p. EC1.

34. Pew Research Center, cited in K. Palmer, "The New Mommy Track," *U.S. News & World Report,* September 3, 2007, pp. 40–45.

35. Bureau of Labor Statistics, reported in C. Rampell, "Women Now a Majority in American Workplaces," *The New York Times,* February 6, 2010, p. A10.

36. M. Fishbein and I. Ajzen, *Belief, Attitude, Intention and Behavior: An Introduction to Theory and Research* (Reading, MA: Addison-Wesley Publishing, 1975), p. 6.

37. See M. Reid and A. Wood, "An Investigation into Blood Donation Intentions Among Non-Donors," *International Journal of Nonprofit and Voluntary Sector Marketing,* February 2008, pp. 31–43; and J. Ramsey, B. J. Punnett, and D. Greenidge, "A Social Psychological Account of Absenteeism in Barbados," *Human Resource Management Journal,* April 2008, pp. 97–117.

38. B. M. Shaw and J. Ross, "Stability in the Midst of Change: A Dispositional Approach to Job Attitudes," *Journal of Applied Psychology,* August 1985, pp. 469–480; see also J. Schaubroeck, D. C. Ganster, and B. Kemmerer, "Does Trait Affect Promote Job Attitude Stability?" *Journal of Organizational Behavior,* March 1996, pp. 191–196.

39. J. S. Becker, "Empirical Validation of Affect, Behavior, and Cognition as Distinct Components of Attitude," *Journal of Personality and Social Psychology,* May 1984, pp. 1191–1205; the components or structure of attitudes is thoroughly discussed by A. P. Brief, *Attitudes in and around Organizations* (Thousand Oaks, CA: Sage, 1998), pp. 49–84.

40. L. Festinger, *A Theory of Cognitive Dissonance* (Stanford, CA: Stanford University Press, 1957).

41. J. Hempel, "Big Blue Brainstorm," *BusinessWeek Online,* July 28, 2006, p. 70.

42. IBM Jam Events page, https://www.collaborationjam.com (accessed May 5, 2010).

43. S. LeVine, "IBM Piles Up Patents, but Quantity Isn't King," *Bloomberg Businessweek,* January 25, 2010, p. 53.

44. "Students See into the Future During IBM Jam; Faculty and Students from 40 Countries Collaborate with IBM to Build a Smarter Planet," IBM press release, July 29, 2009, http//www-03.ibm.com/press/us/en/pressrelease/28096.wss (accessed May 7, 2010).

45. D. Aberle, quoted in L. Yerkes, *Fun Works: Creating Places Where People Love to Work* (San Francisco: Berrett-Koehler, 2001), p. 126.

46. S. P. Brown, "A Meta-Analysis and Review of Orgnaizational Research on Job Involvement," *Psychological Bulletin,* September 1996, pp. 235–255.

47. See G. Dutton, "Yes! It's Monday," *Training,* July/August 2009, pp. 30–32; "Engaged Employee = Business Pride," *Training,* March/April 2010, p. 14; and R. Silverblatt, "In Search of Workplace Happiness," *U.S. News & World Report,* May 2010, pp. 32–34.

48. R. Flandez, "Vegetable Gardens Help Morale Grow," *The Wall Street Journal,* August 18, 2009, p. B5.

49. See J. K. Harter, F. L. Schmidt, and T. L. Hayes, "Business-Unit-Level Relationship between Employee Satisfaction, Employee Engagement, and Business Outcomes: A Meta-Analysis," *Journal of Applied Psychology,* April 2002, pp. 268–279.

50. See W. H. Macey and B. Schneider, "The Nature of Employee Engagement," *Industrial and Organizational Psychology: Perspectives on Science and Practice,* 2008, pp. 3–30; and A. J. Wefald and R. G. Downey, "Job Engagement in Organizations: Fad, Fashion, or Folderol?" *Journal of Organizational Behavior,* January 2009, pp. 141–145. A proprietary measure of employee engagement is provided by Development Dimensions International, Inc.; see M. Phelps, "Is It Time to Rethink Employee Engagement?" *DDI White Paper,* http://www.ddiworld.com/products_services/e3.asp (accessed May 7, 2010).

51. See *5 Rules for Talent Management in the New Economy,* Watson Wyatt Worldwide, 2009, http://www.towerswatson.com/research/1354 (accessed May 7, 2010).

52. Results based on survey sent by the Hay Group and Bloomberg BusinessWeek.com to 1,863 global respondents in 1,109 organizations, reported in R. Lash and C. Huber, "2009 Best Companies for Leadership," Hay Group Webinar, February 18, 2010.

53. These five job dimensions are developed by researchers at Cornell University as part of the Job Descriptive Index. For a review of the development of the JDI, see P. C. Smith, L. M. Kendall, and C. L. Hulin, *The Measurement of Satisfaction in Work and Retirement* (Skokie, IL: Rand McNally, 1969).

54. See A. J. Kinicki, F. M. McKee-Ryan, C. A. Schriesheim, and K. P. Carson, "Assessing the Construct Validity of the Job Descriptive Index: A Review and Meta-Analysis," *Journal of Applied Psychology,* February 2002, pp. 14–32.

55. These figures come from the annual employee satisfaction survey by the Conference Board, reported in S. Shellenbarger, "Thinking Happy Thoughts at Work," *The Wall Street Journal,* January 27, 2010, p. D2.

56. The various models are discussed in T. A. Judge, C. J. Thoresen, J. E. Bono, and G. K. Patton, "The Job Satisfaction–Job Performance Relationship: A Qualitative and Quantitative Review," *Psychological Bulletin,* May 2001, pp. 376–407.

57. Ibid. Also see M. Riketta, "The Causal Relation between Job Attitudes and Performance: A Meta-Analysis of Panel Studies," *Journal of Applied Psychology,* March 2008, pp. 472–481.

58. Survey of adults conducted for Adecco Staffing North America, reported in K. Gurchiek, "Good News for Moms Reconsidering Work," *HR Magazine,* July 2006, p. 30.

59. See N. Podsakoff, J. A. LePine, and M. A. LePine, "Differential Challenge Stressor-Hindrance Stressor Relationships

with Job Attitudes, Turnover Intentions, Turnover, and Withdrawal Behavior: A Meta-Analysis," *Journal of Applied Psychology,* March 2007, pp. 438–454; M. Riketta, "Attitudinal Organizational Commitment and Job Performance: A Meta-Analysis," *Journal of Organizational Behavior,* March 2002, pp. 257–266.

60. See J. E. Mathieu and D. Zajac, "A Review and Meta-Analysis of the Antecedents, Correlates, and Consequences of Organizational Commitment," *Psychological Bulletin,* September 1990, pp. 171–194; see also M. Riketta, "Attitudinal Organizational Commitment and Job Performance: A Meta-Analysis," *Journal of Organizational Behavior,* March 2002, pp. 257–266.

61. See R. D. Hackett, "Work Attitudes and Employee Absenteeism: A Synthesis of the Literature," *Journal of Occupational Psychology,* 1989, pp. 235–248.

62. Results can be found in M. R. Barrick and R. D. Zimmerman, "Reducing Voluntary Turnover through Selection," *Journal of Applied Psychology,* January 2005, pp. 159–166.

63. Costs of turnover are discussed by R. W. Griffeth and P. W. Hom, *Retaining Valued Employees* (Thousand Oaks, CA: Sage, 2001).

64. M. Littman, "Best Bosses Tell All," *Working Woman,* October 2000, pp. 48–56.

65. Y. Lermusiaux, "Calculating the High Cost of Employee Turnover," www.ilogos.com/en/expertviews/articles/strategic/2003320007_YL.htm (accessed May 6, 2010). An automated program for calculating the cost of turnover can be found at "Calculate Your Turnover Costs," www.keepemployees.com/turnovercalc.htm (accessed May 6, 2010).

66. D. W. Organ, "The Motivational Basis of Organizational Citizenship Behavior," in B. M. Staw and L. L. Cummings, eds., *Research in Organizational Behavior* (Greenwich, CT: JAI Press, 1990), p. 46.

67. See N. P. Podsakoff, S. W. Whiting, P. M. Podsakoff, and B. D. Blume, "Individual-and Organizational-Level Consequences of Organizational Citizenship Behaviors: A Meta-Analysis," *Journal of Applied Psychology,* January 2009, pp. 122–141; and B. J. Hoffman, C. A. Blair, J. P. Meriac, and D. J. Woehr, "Expanding the Criterion Domain? A Quantitative Review of the OCB Literature," *Journal of Applied Psychology,* March 2007, pp. 555–566.

68. D. S. Ones, "Introduction to the Special Issue on Counterproductive Behaviors at Work," *International Journal of Selection and Assessment* 10, no. 1–2 (2002), pp. 1–4.

69. J. Janove, "Jerks at Work," *HR Magazine,* May 2007, pp. 111–117.

70. S. Dilchert, D. S. Ones, R. D. Davis, and C. D. Rostow, "Cognitive Ability Predicts Objectively Measured Counterproductive Work Behaviors," *Journal of Applied Psychology,* May 2007, pp. 616–627.

71. J. R. Detert, L. K. Treviño, E. R. Burris, and M. Andiappan, "Managerial Modes of Influence and Counterproductivity in Organizations: A Longitudinal Business-Unit-Level Investigation," *Journal of Applied Psychology,* July 2007, pp. 993–1005.

72. B. Leonard, "Study: Bully Bosses Prevalent in U.S.," *HR Magazine,* May 2007, pp. 22, 28.

73. See M. Sandy Hershcovis and J. Barling, "Toward a Multi-Foci Approach to Workplace Aggression: A Meta-Analytic Review of Outcomes from Different Perpetrators," *Journal of Organizational Behavior,* January 2010, pp. 24–44; and J. Chamberlin, A. Novotney, E. Packard, and M. Price, "Enhancing Worker Well-Being," *Monitor on Psychology,* May 2008, pp. 26–29.

74. C. Kavanaugh, "'Murder by Proxy,'" *Royal Oak (Michigan) Daily Tribune,* April 19, 2010, http://www.dailytribune.com/articles/2010/04/19/news/doc4bc8dc24905c3220900250.txt (accessed May 7, 2010).

75. R. Brunswick, quoted in C. Hymowitz, "Bosses Have to Learn How to Confront Troubled Employees," *The Wall Street Journal,* April 23, 2007, p. B1.

76. Hymowitz, "Bosses Have to Learn How to Confront Troubled Employees," 2007.

77. Canadian Cancer Society 2002 study, cited in J. Gillum, "Strong Words, Images Target Smoking," *USA Today,* July 13, 2004, p. 10D.

78. D. Dearborn and H. Simon, "Selection Perception: A Note on the Departmental Identification of Executives," *Sociometry* 21 (1958), pp. 140–144.

79. Definition adapted from C. M. Judd and B. Park, "Definition and Assessment of Accuracy in Social Stereotypes," *Psychological Review,* January 1993, p. 110. See also D. T. Wegener, J. K. Clark, and R. E. Petty, "Not All Stereotyping Is Created Equal: Differential Consequences of Thoughtful Versus Nonthoughtful Stereotyping," *Journal of Personality and Social Psychology,* January 2006, pp. 42–59.

80. Results are presented in E. Tahmincioglu, "Men Rule—At Least in Workplace Attitudes," *MSNBC,* http://www.msnbc.msn.com/id/1734508 (accessed May 6, 2010).

81. B. P. Allen, "Gender Stereotypes Are Not Accurate: A Replication of Martin (1987) Using Diagnostic vs. Self-Report and Behavioral Criteria," *Sex Roles,* May 1995, pp. 583–600.

82. J. Landau, "The Relationship of Race and Gender to Managers' Ratings of Promotion Potential," *Journal of Organizational Behavior,* July 1995, pp. 391–400. See also I. H. Lang, "Have Women Shattered Corporate Glass Ceiling? No," *USA Today,* April 15, 2010, p. 11A.

83. J. Levitz and P. Shishkin, "More Workers Cite Age Bias after Layoffs," *The Wall Street Journal,* March 11, 1009, pp. D1, D2; and L. Wolgemuth, "When Age Bias Hinders the Job Hunt," *U.S. News & World Report,* October 2009, p. 72.

84. S. R. Rhodes, "Age-Related Differences in Work Attitudes and Behavior: A Review and Conceptual Analysis," *Psychological Bulletin,* March 1983, p. 38.

85. See T.W.H. Ng and D. C. Feldman, "The Relationship of Age to Ten Dimensions of Job Performance," *Journal of Applied Psychology,* March 2008, pp. 392–423; and R. J. Grossman, "Keep Pace with Older Workers," *HR Magazine,* May 2008, pp. 39–46.

86. J. J. Martocchio, "Age-Related Differences in Employee Absenteeism: A Meta-Analysis," *Psychology and Aging,* December 1989, pp. 409–414; and M. C. Healy, M. Lehman, and M. A. McDaniel, "Age and Voluntary Turnover: A Quantitative Review," *Personnel Psychology,* Summer 1995, pp. 335–345.

87. Central Intelligence Agency, *The World Factbook, 2010,* https://www.cia.gov/library/publications/the-world-factbook/geos/us.html (accessed May 5, 2010).

88. See H. Dolezalek, "Boomer Reality," *Training,* May 2007, pp. 16–21.

89. K. Helliker, "The Doctor Is Still In: Secrets of Health from a Famed 96-Year-Old Physician," *The Wall Street Journal,* March 8, 2005, p. D1.

90. Statistics are reported in "Job Types by Race in the U.S.," *MSN Encarta,* http://encarta.msn.com/media_461546975/Job_Type_by_Race_in_the_U._S.html (accessed May 5, 2010).

91. Data analysis by D. D. Kallick, Fiscal Policy Institute, reported in J. Preston, "Immigrants in Work Force: Study Belies Image," *The New York Times,* April 16, 2010, pp. A1, A3.

92. J. C. Brigham, "Limiting Conditions of the 'Physical Attractiveness Stereotype': Attributions about Divorce," *Journal*

of Research and Personality 14 (1980), pp. 365–375; H. Hatfield and S. Sprecher, *Mirror, Mirror . . . The Importance of Looks in Everyday Life* (Albany, NY: State University of New York Press, 1986).

93. M. M. Mobius and T. S. Rosenblat, "Why Beauty Matters," *American Economic Review,* March 2006, pp. 222–235.

94. Ibid.

95. M. M. Clifford and E. H. Walster, "The Effect of Physical Attractiveness on Teacher Expectation," *Sociology of Education* 46 (1973), pp. 248–258.

96. T. Cash and L. H. Janda, "The Eye of the Beholder," *Psychology Today,* December 1984, pp. 46–52.

97. H. R. Varian, "Beauty and the Fattened Wallet," *The New York Times,* April 6, 2006, http://www.nytimes.com/2006/04/06/business/06scene.html?ex=1301976000&en=a5f0aa1131668f77&ei=5090&partner=rssuserland&emc=rss (accessed August 26, 2010).

98. S. J. Linton and L. E. Warg, "Attributions (Beliefs) and Job Satisfaction Associated with Back Pain in an Industrial Setting," *Perceptual and Motor Skills,* February 1993, pp. 51–62.

99. W. S. Silver, T. R. Mitchell, and M. E. Gist, "Responses to Successful and Unsuccessful Performance: The Moderating Effect of Self-Efficacy on the Relationship between Performance and Attributions," *Organizational Behavior and Human Decision Processes,* June 1995, pp. 286–299; and D. Dunning, A. Leuenberger, and D. A. Sherman, "A New Look at Motivated Inference: Are Self-Serving Theories of Success a Product of Motivational Forces?" *Journal of Personality and Social Psychology,* July 1995, pp. 58–68.

100. C. Forelle and S. Fidler, "Europe's Original Sin," *The Wall Street Journal,* March 3, 2010, p. A1.

101. See D. Eden and Y. Zuk, "Seasickness as a Self-Fulfilling Prophecy: Raising Self-Efficacy to Boost Performance at Sea," *Journal of Applied Psychology,* October 1995, pp. 628–635. For a thorough review of research on the Pygmalion effect, see D. Eden, *Pygmalion in Management: Productivity as a Self-Fulfilling Prophecy* (Lexington, MA: Lexington Books, 1990), ch. 2.

102. L. Iorio, quoted in Dutton, "Yes! It's Monday," 2009, p. 32.

103. D. B. McNatt, "Ancient Pygmalion Joins Contemporary Management: A Meta-Analysis of the Result," *Journal of Applied Psychology,* April 2000, pp. 314–322.

104. These recommendations were adapted from J. Keller, "Have Faith—in You," *Selling Power,* June 1996, pp. 84, 86; and R. W. Goddard, "The Pygmalion Effect," *Personnel Journal,* June 1985, p. 10.

105. R. S. Lazarus, *Psychological Stress and Coping Processes* (New York: McGraw-Hill, 1966); and R. S. Schuler, "Definition and Conceptualization of Stress in Organizations," *Organizational Behavior and Human Performance,* April 1980, p. 1980.

106. American Psychological Association *Stress in America* survey, April 2009, reported in M. Price, "The Recession Is Stressing Men More Than Women," *Monitor on Psychology,* July/August 2009, p. 10.

107. American Institute of Stress, cited in J. W. Upson, D. J. Ketchen Jr., and R. D. Ireland, "Managing Employee Stress: A Key to the Effectiveness of Strategic Supply Chain Management," *Organizational Dynamics* 36 (2007), pp. 78–92.

108. See E. Zimmerman, "When Stress Flirts with Burnout," *The New York Times,* January 17, 2010, Business section, p. 7.

109. Study in *Circulation,* March 1998, reported in "Managers at Risk from Work Stress," *San Jose Mercury News,* April 12, 1998, p. 5E; reprinted from *The New York Times.*

110. S. Shellenbarger, "'Desk Rage': To Vent or Not to Vent," *The Wall Street Journal,* January 26, 2010, p. D3.

111. Supportive results can be found in F. M. McKee-Ryan, Z. Song, C. R. Wanberg, and A. J. Kinicki, "Psychological and Physical Well-Being during Unemployment: A Meta-Analytic Study," *Journal of Applied Psychology,* January 2005, pp. 53–76; and F. M. McKee-Ryan, M. Virick, G. E. Prussia, J. Harvey, and J. D. Lilly, "Life after the Layoff: Getting a Job Worth Keeping," *Journal of Organizational Behavior,* May 2009, pp. 561–580.

112. M. Luo, "For Workers at Closing Plant, Ordeal Included Heart Attacks," *The New York Times,* February 25, 2010, pp. A1, A17.

113. See M. A. Cavanaugh, W. R. Boswell, M. V. Roehling, and J. W. Boudreau, "An Empirical Examination of Self-Reported Work Stress among U.S. Managers," *Journal of Applied Psychology,* February 2000, pp. 65–74; A. J. Kinicki, F. M. McKee-Ryan, C. A. Schriesheim, and K. P. Carson, "Assessing the Construct Validity of the Job Descriptive Index: A Review and Meta-Analysis," *Journal of Applied Psychology,* February 2002, pp. 14–32; A. Weintraub, "Inside Drugmakers' War on Fat," *BusinessWeek,,* March 17, 2008, pp. 41–46; and M. R. Frone, "Are Work Stressors Related to Employee Substance Use? The Importance of Temporal Context in Assessments of Alcohol and Illicit Drug Use," *Journal of Applied Psychology,* January 2008, pp. 199–206.

114. H. Selye, *Stress without Distress* (New York: Lippincott, 1974), p. 27.

115. R. S. Lazarus and S. Folkman, "Coping and Adaptation," in W. D. Gentry, ed., *Handbook of Behavioral Medicine* (New York: Guilford, 1982).

116. R. S. Lazarus, "Little Hassles Can Be Hazardous to Health," *Psychology Today,* July 1981, p. 61.

117. Selye, 1974, pp. 28–29.

118. M. Beck, "When Fretting Is in Your DNA: Overcoming the Worry Gene," *The Wall Street Journal,* January 15, 2008, p. D1. See also L. M. Hilt, L. C. Sander, S. Nolen-Hoeksema, and A. A. Simen, "The BDNF Val66Met Polymorphism Predicts Rumination and Depression Differently in Young Adolescent Girls and Their Mothers," *Neuroscience Letters,* December 2007, pp. 12–16.

119. M. Friedman and R. H. Rosenman, *Type A Behavior and Your Heart* (Greenwich, CT: Fawcett Publications, 1974), p. 84.

120. See M. S. Taylor, E. A. Locke, C. Lee, and M. E. Gist, "Type A Behavior and Faculty Research Productivity: What Are the Mechanisms?" *Organizational Behavior and Human Performance,* December 1984, pp. 402–418; S. D. Bluen, J. Barling, and W. Burns, "Predicting Sales Performance, Job Satisfaction, and Depression by Using the Achievement Strivings and Impatience–Irritability Dimensions of Type A Behavior," *Journal of Applied Psychology,* April 1990, pp. 212–216.

121. S. Booth-Kewley and H. S. Friedman, "Psychological Predictors of Heart Disease: A Quantitative Review," *Psychological Bulletin,* May 1987, pp. 343–362; S. A. Lyness, "Predictors of Differences between Type A and B Individuals in Heart Rate and Blood Pressure Reactivity," *Psychological Bulletin,* September 1993, pp. 266–295; and T. Q. Miller, T. W. Smith, C. W. Turner, M. L. Guijarro, and A. J. Hallet, "A Meta-Analytic Review of Research on Hostility and Physical Health," *Psychological Bulletin,* March 1996, pp. 322–348.

122. J. O'Donnell, "Wanted: Retail Managers," *USA Today,* December 24, 2007, pp. 1B, 3B.

123. M. Richtel, "In Web World of 24/7 Stress, Writers Blog Till They Drop," *The New York Times,* April 6, 2008, News section, pp. 1, 23.

124. T. D. Schellhardt, "Company Memo to Stressed-Out Employees: 'Deal with It,'" *The Wall Street Journal,*

October 2, 1996, pp. B1, B4; see also L. A. Wah, "An Executive's No. 1 Fear," *American Management Association International,* January 1998, p. 87.

125. J. A. Davy, A. J. Kinicki, and C. L. Scheck, "A Test of Job Security's Direct and Mediated Effects on Withdrawal Cognitions," *Journal of Organizational Behavior,* July 1, 1997, p. 323.

126. G. Graen, "Role-Making Processes within Complex Organizations," in M. D. Dunnette, ed., *Handbook of Industrial and Organizational Psychology* (Chicago: Rand McNally, 1976), p. 1201.

127. M. Culp, "Coping When Co-Worker Is Under Stress," *The Hartford Courant,* February 25, 2008, courant.com/business/hc-midred0225.artfeb25,0,4210457.story.com (accessed February 25, 2008).

128. T. D. Wall, P. R. Jackson, S. Mullarkey, and S. K. Parker, "The Demands-Control Model of Job Strain: A More Specific Test," *Journal of Occupational and Organizational Psychology,* June 1996, pp. 153–166; and R. C. Barnett and R. T. Brennan, "The Relationship between Job Experiences and Psychological Distress: A Structural Equation Approach," *Journal of Organizational Behavior,* May 1995, pp. 250–276.

129. "Lousiest Bosses," *The Wall Street Journal,* April 4, 1995, p. A1. For more about bad managers, see J. Sandberg, "Had It Up to HERE? Despite Risk, Some Say Quitting Is Way to Go," *The Wall Street Journal,* August 14, 2007, p. B1; G. G. Scott, *A Survival Guide for Working with Bad Bosses: Dealing with Bullies, Idiots, Back-Stabbers, and Other Managers from Hell* (New York: AMACOM, 2005); and A. Dobson, "Working It Out: Fixing a Strained Relationship with Your Boss," *San Francisco Chronicle,* March 2, 2008, p. H1.

130. J. Schaubroeck and D. C. Ganster, "Chronic Demands and Responsivity to Challenge," *Journal of Applied Psychology,* February 1993, pp. 73–85; E. Demerouti, A. B. Bakker, F. Nachreiner, and W. B. Schaufeli, "The Job Demands Resources Model of Burnout," *Journal of Applied Psychology,* June 2001, pp. 499–512.

131. J. M. Plas, *Person-Centered Leadership: An American Approach to Participatory Management* (Thousand Oaks, CA: Sage, 1996).

132. M. Patsalos-Fox, quoted in W. J. Holstein, "Tension Headaches in the Corner Office," *The New York Times,* March 12, 2006, sec. 3, p. 1.

133. N. E. Adler, T. Boyce, M. A. Chesney, S. Cohen, S. Folkman, R. L. Kahn, and S. L. Syme, "Socioeconomic Status and Health: The Challenge of the Gradient," *American Psychologist,* January 1994, pp. 15–24.

134. The link between stress and depression is discussed by P. Freiberg, "Work and Well-Being: Experts Urge Changes in Work, Not the Work," *The APA Monthly,* January 1991, p. 23.

135. M. Staver, quoted in C. H. Deutsch, "Winning the Battle Against Burnout," *The New York Times,* August 27, 2006, sec. 3, p. 5.

136. See C. H. Deutsch, "Winning the Battle Against Burnout," *The New York Times,* August 27, 2006, sec. 3, p. 5.

137. Absenteeism and stress are discussed by S. Shellenbarger, "Work & Family: Was That 24-Hour Flu That Kept You Home Really Just the Blahs?" *The Wall Street Journal,* July 24, 1996, p. B1.

138. M. Ferri, L. Amato, and M. Davoli, "Alcoholics Anonymous and Other 12-Step Programmes for Alcohol Dependence (Review)," *Cochrane Database of Scientific Reviews,* 2006, Issue 3. See also report in N. Bakalar, "Review Sees No Advantage in 12-Step Programs," *The New York Times,* July 25, 2006, p. D6.

139. Recommendations for reducing burnout are discussed by M. Wylie, "Preventing Worker Burnout while Supporting the Users," *MacWeek,* October 4, 1993, pp. 12–14; and "How to Avoid Burnout," *Training,* February 1993, pp. 15, 16, 70.

140. These examples and techniques are discussed by L. Landon, "Pump Up Your Employees," *HR Magazine,* May 1990, pp. 34–37; and R. L. Rose, "Time Out: At the Menninger Clinic, Executives Learn More About Themselves—and Why They're So Unhappy," *The Wall Street Journal,* February 26, 1996, p. R5.

141. See R. Kreitner and A. Kinicki, *Organizational Behavior*, 8th ed. (Burr Ridge, IL: McGraw-Hill, 2008); and A. Novotney, "The Happiness Diet," *Monitor on Psychology,* April 2008, pp. 24–25.

142. R. Kreitner, "Personal Wellness: It's Just Good Business," *Business Horizons,* May–June 1982, p. 28.

143. See J. J. Medina, "The Science of Thinking Smarter," *Harvard Business Review,* May 2008, pp. 51–54; R. Riney, "Heal Leadership Disorders," *HR Magazine,* May 2008, pp. 62–66; and M. Fugate, A. J. Kinicki, and G. E. Prussia, "Employee Coping with Organizational Change: An Examination of Alternative Theoretical Perspectives and Models," *Personnel Psychology,* Spring 2008, pp. 1–36.

CHAPTER 12

1. Kleiman, "Work-Life Rewards Grow," *San Francisco Examiner,* January 16, 2000, p. J-2; reprinted from *Chicago Tribune.*

2. M. Buckingham and C. Coffman, *First, Break All the Rules: What the World's Greatest Managers Do Differently* (New York: Simon & Schuster, 1999).

3. Kimberly Scott, project leader for Hewitt Associates, which helps compile the *Fortune* list, reported in D. Murphy, "Can Morale Contribute to Safer Skies?" *San Francisco Examiner,* February 11, 2000, p. J-1.

4. S. Shellenbarger, "Work & Family Mailbox," *The Wall Street Journal,* August 5, 2009, p. D3; and C. Tkaczyk, "Offer Affordable (Awesome) Day Care," *Fortune,* August 17, 2009, p. 26.

5. S. Shellenbarger, "Targeting 'Feel-Good' Benefits," *The Wall Street Journal,* July 8, 2009, pp. D1, D2. See also J. Walker, "Even with a Recovery, Job Perks May Not Return," *The Wall Street Journal,* April 5, 2010, http://online.wsj.com/article/SB10001424052702304017404575165854181296256.html; and N. Wallter, "Some Benefits You May Never Get Back," *The Wall Street Journal,* April 11, 2010, http://online.wsj.com/article/SB10001424052702304017404575165854181296256.html (both accessed May 12, 2010).

6. R. Flandez, "Rewards Help Soothe Hard Times," *The Wall Street Journal,* July 17, 2009, p. B4.

7. Jeff Weiss, quoted in S. Shellenbarger, "Perking Up: Some Companies Offer Surprising New Benefits," *The Wall Street Journal,* March 18, 2009, http://online.wsj.com/article/SB123733195850463165.html (accessed May 12, 2010).

8. Bryan Simpson, New Belgium Brewery, quoted in C. Bergfeld and P. Calabrese, for BNET.com, "Recession-Friendly Employee Perks," *Portfolio.com,* February 1, 2009, http://www.portfolio.com/resources/insight-center/2009/02/01/Recession-Friendly-Employee-Perks (accessed May 12, 2010).

9. Adapted from definition in T. R. Mitchell, "Motivation: New Directions for Theory, Research, and Practice," *Academy of Management Review,* January 1982, p. 81.

10. See R. M. Ryan and E. L. Deci, "Intrinsic and Extrinsic Motivations: Classic Definitions and New Directions," *Contemporary Educational Psychology,* January 2000, pp. 54–67.

11. K. G. Volpp, A. B. Troxel, M. V. Pauly, H. A. Glick, et al., "A Randomized, Controlled Trial of Financial Incentives for Smoking Cessation," *New England Journal of Medicine,* February 12, 2009, pp. 699–709.

12. See A. Kohn, "Cash Incentives Won't Make Us Healthier," *USA Today,* May 21, 2009, p. IIA.

13. S. E. Needleman, "The Latest Office Perk: Getting Paid to Volunteer," *The Wall Street Journal,* April 29, 2008, p. DI.

14. See P. W. Hom, L. Roberson, and A. D. Ellis, "Challenging Conventional Wisdom about Who Quits: Revelations from Corporate America," *Journal of Applied Psychology,* January 2008, pp. I–34; J. B. Olson-Buchanan and W. R. Boswell, "An Integrative Model of Experiencing and Responding to Mistreatment at Work," *Academy of Management Review,* January 2008, pp. 76–96; and M. Riketta, "The Causal Relation Between Job Attitudes and Performance: A Meta-Analysis of Panel Studies," *Journal of Applied Psychology,* March 2008, pp. 472–481.

15. K. Down and L. Liedtka, "What Corporations Seek in MBA Hires: A Survey," *Selections,* Winter 1994, pp. 34–39; see also S. Armour, "Companies Get Tough on Absent Employees," *The Arizona Republic,* February 7, 2003, p. A2; reprinted from *USA Today.*

16. A. Maslow, "A Theory of Human Motivation," *Psychological Review,* July 1943, pp. 370–396. A more recent expression of Maslow's theory can be found in C. Conley, *Peak: How Great Companies Get Their Mojo from Maslow* (San Francisco: Jossey-Bass, 2007).

17. H. Benson, "In an Era of High Technology, Low Commitment, One Man Says He's Found a Way to Measure Integrity," *San Francisco Chronicle,* June 21, 2006, pp. EI, E3.

18. P. H. Ray and S. R. Anderson, *The Cultural Creatives: How 50 Million People Are Changing the World* (New York: Harmony Books, 2000).

19. D. E. Meyerson, *Tempered Radicals: How Everyday Leaders Inspire Change at Work* (Boston: Harvard Business School Press, 2003). For examples of the need for achievement, see M. R. della Cava, "Answering Their Calling," *USA Today,* March 13, 2006, pp. ID, 2D.

20. Conley, *How Great Companies Get Their Mojo from Maslow,* 2007.

21. For a complete review of ERG theory, see C. P. Alderfer, *Existence, Relatedness, and Growth: Human Needs in Organizational Settings* (New York: Free Press, 1972).

22. D. C. McClelland, *Human Motivation* (Glenview, IL: Scott, Foresman, 1985).

23. D. McClelland and H. Burnham, "Power Is the Great Motivator," *Harvard Business Review,* March/April 1976, pp. 100–110.

24. S. W. Spreier, M. H. Fontaine, and R. L. Malloy, "Leadership Run Amok," *Harvard Business Review,* June 2006, pp. 72–82.

25. Recent studies of achievement motivation can be found in H. Grant and C. S. Dweck, "A Goal Analysis of Personality and Personality Coherence," in D. Cervone and Y. Shoda, eds., *The Coherence of Personality* (New York: Guilford Press, 1999), pp. 345–371.

26. S. A. Flaum and J. A. Flaum, with M. Flaum, *The 100-Mile Walk: A Father and Son on a Quest to Find the Essence of Leadership* (New York: Amacom, 2006). See also J. C. Mead, "How to Succeed in Business: Walk," *The New York Times,* January 29, 2006, sec. 14LI, p. 6; and S. Berfield, "Walk 100 Miles in My Shoes," *BusinessWeek,* June 26, 2006, pp. 80–81.

27. F. Herzberg, B. Mausner, and B. B. Snyderman, *The Motivation to Work* (New York: Wiley, 1959); and F. Herzberg, "One More Time: How Do You Motivate Employees?" *Harvard Business Review,* January–February 1968, pp. 53–62.

28. Survey by the Conference Board, reported in P. Korkki, "With Jobs Few, Most Workers Aren't Satisfied," *The New York Times,* January 10, 2009, Business section, p. 2. See also P. Coy, "Are Your Employees Just Biding Their Time?" *BusinessWeek,* November 16, 2009, p. 27.

29. J. S. Adams, "Toward an Understanding of Inequity," *Journal of Abnormal and Social Psychology,* November 1963, pp. 422–436; and J. S. Adams, "Injustice in Social Exchange," in L. Berkowitz, ed., *Advances in Experimental Social Psychology,* 2nd ed. (New York: Academic Press, 1965), pp. 267–300.

30. See B. Baird, "Don't Get Mad: Get Even," *The Arizona Republic,* April 20, 2008, pp. DI, D5; C. Hymowitz, "In the Lead: Pay Gap Fuels Worker Woes," *The Wall Street Journal,* April 28, 2008, p. B8; and G. Colvin, "Rewarding Failure," *Fortune,* April 28, 2008, p. 22.

31. U.S. Department of Commerce, cited in A. Salkever, "An Easy Antidote to Employee Theft," *BusinessWeek online,* May 20, 2003, www.businessweek.com/smallbiz/content/may2003/sb20030520_9328_sb018.htm (accessed May 11, 2010). See also J. Greenberg, "Employee Theft as a Reaction to Underpayment Inequity: The Hidden Cost of Pay Cuts," *Journal of Applied Psychology* 75 (1990), pp. 561–568.

32. L. Abboud and M. Colchester, "French Bosses Come Under Siege as Worker Anger Rises," *The Wall Street Journal,* April 1, 2009, p. BI; and D. Gauthier-Villars and L. Abboud, "In France, CEOs Can Become Hostages," *The Wall Street Journal,* April 3, 2009, pp. BI, B5.

33. See D. J. Holman, C. M. Axtell, C. A Sprigg, P. Totterdell, and T. D. Wall, "The Mediating Role of Job Characteristics in Job Redesign Interventions: A Serendipitous Quasi-Experiment," *Journal of Organizational Behavior,* January 2010, pp. 84–105. Also see S. W. Whiting, P. M. Podsakoff, and J. R. Pierce, "Effects of Task Performance, Helping, Voice, and Organizational Loyalty on Performance Appraisal Ratings," *Journal of Applied Psychology,* January 2008, pp. 125–139.

34. See R. A. Posthuma, C. P. Maertz Jr., and J. B. Dworkin, "Procedural Justice's Relationship with Turnover: Explaining Past Inconsistent Findings," *Journal of Organizational Behavior,* May 2007, pp. 381–398; Y. Cohen-Charash and J. S. Mueller, "Does Perceived Unfairness Exacerbate or Mitigate Interpersonal Counterproductive Work Behaviors Related to Envy?" *Journal of Applied Psychology,* May 2007, pp. 666–680; and H. Moon, D. Kamdar, D. M. Mayer, and R. Takeuchi, "Me or We? The Role of Personality and Justice as Other-Centered Antecedents to Innovative Citizenship Behaviors within Organizations," *Journal of Applied Psychology,* January 2008, pp. 84–94.

35. V. H. Vroom, *Work and Motivation* (New York: Wiley, 1964).

36. C. Wallis, "How to Make Great Teachers," *Time,* February 25, 2008, pp. 28–34; and N. Zuckerbrod, "Tenure, Evaluation Process Get Poor Grades in Teacher Survey," *The Arizona Republic,* May 7, 2008, p. A10; and "Teacher Bonus Systems Tested," *Reno Gazette-Journal,* October 22, 2008, p. ID.

37. A Hudson survey of 10,000 employees March 20–26, 2006, found that 48% of managers but only 31% of nonmanagers agreed with the statement "Employees who do a better job get paid more"; 46% of managers but only 29% of nonmanagers agreed with the statement "My last raise was based on performance." Information cited in "Reasons for Raises," *BusinessWeek,* May 29, 2006, p. II.

38. See M. J. Pearsall, M. S. Christian, and A. P. J. Ellis, "Motivating Interdependent Teams: Individual Rewards, Shared Rewards, or Something in Between?" *Journal of Applied Psychology,* January 2010, pp. 183–191.

39. See D. Ariely, "What's the Value of a Big Bonus?" *The New York Times,* November 20, 2008, http://www.nytimes.com/2008/11/20/opinion/20ariely.html (accessed May 13, 2010). Also see letters to the editor, "Getting the Bonus You Deserve," *The New York Times,* November 28, 2008, p. A30.

40. J. S. Lublin, "Valeant CEO's Pay Package Draws Praise as a Model," *The Wall Street Journal,* August 24, 2009, p. B4.

41. J. Bosman, "New York to End Program Giving Cash to the Poor for Desired Behavior," *The New York Times,* March 31, 2010, p. A18.

42. For a thorough discussion of goal-setting theory and application, see E. A. Locke and G. P. Latham, "Building a Practically Useful Theory of Goal Setting and Task Motivation," *American Psychologist,* September 2002, pp. 705–717.

43. See D. Morisano, J. B. Hirsh, J. B. Peterson, R. O. Phil, and B. M. Shore, "Setting, Elaborating, and Reflecting on Personal Goals Improves Academic Performance," *Journal of Applied Psychology,* March 2010, pp. 255–264.

44. DDI Pulse of the Workforce Survey of 1,000 employees, reported in "Stagnating on the Job," *USA Today,* September 21, 2009, p. 1B.

45. See G. R. Oldham and J. R. Hackman, "Not What It Was and Not What It Will Be: The Future of Job Design," *Journal of Organizational Behavior,* February 2010, pp. 463–479.

46. S. Melamed, I. Ben-Avi, J. Luz, and M. S. Green, "Objective and Subjective Work Monotony: Effects on Job Satisfaction, Psychological Distress, and Absenteeism in Blue-Collar Workers," *Journal of Applied Psychology,* February 1995, pp. 29–42; and B. Melin, U. Lundberg, J. Söderlund, and M. Granqvist, "Psychological and Physiological Stress Reactions of Male and Female Assembly Workers: A Comparison between Two Different Forms of Work Organization," *Journal of Organizational Behavior,* January 1999, pp. 47–61.

47. M. A. Campion and C. L. McClelland, "Follow-Up and Extension of the Interdisciplinary Costs and Benefits of Enlarged Jobs," *Journal of Applied Psychology,* June 1993, pp. 339–351.

48. Herzberg et al., *The Motivation to Work,* 1959.

49. J. R. Hackman and G. R. Oldham, *Work Redesign* (Reading, MA: Addison-Wesley, 1980).

50. See S. E. Humphrey, J. D. Nahrgang, and F. P. Morgeson, "Integrating Motivational, Social, and Contextual Work Design Features: A Meta-Analytic Summary and Theoretical Extension of the Work Design Literature," *Journal of Applied Psychology,* September 2007, pp. 1332–1356. Also see A. M. Grant, "The Significance of Task Significance: Job Performance Effects, Relational Mechanisms, and Boundary Conditions," *Journal of Applied Psychology,* January 2008, pp. 108–124; and F. W. Bond, P. E. Flaxman, and D. Bunce, "The Influence of Psychological Flexibility on Work Redesign: Mediated Moderation of a Work Reorganization Intervention," *Journal of Applied Psychology,* May 2008, pp. 645–654.

51. Dr. Paul H. Grundy, IBM's director of health care technology and strategic initiatives, quoted in M. Freudenheim, "A Model for Health Care That Pays for Quality," *The New York Times,* November 7, 2007, p. C3. See also C. Lochhead, "Lessons on Health Care from Europe," *San Francisco Chronicle,* January 29, 2009, pp. A1, A18.

52. See E. L. Thorndike, *Educational Psychology: The Psychology of Learning, Vol. II* (New York: Columbia University Teachers College, 1913); B. F. Skinner, *Walden Two* (New York: Macmillan, 1948); *Science and Human Behavior* (New York: Macmillan, 1953); and *Contingencies of Reinforcement* (New York: Appleton-Century-Crofts, 1969).

53. J. Sandberg, "A Modern Conundrum: When Work's Invisible, So Are Its Satisfactions," *The Wall Street Journal,* February 19, 2008, p. B1.

54. Taisdeal, quoted in Benson, "In an Era of High Technology, Low Commitment, One Man Says He's Found a Way to Measure Integrity," 2006. For an article about the importance of congeniality, see D. Brady, "Charm Offensive," *BusinessWeek,* June 26, 2006, pp. 76–80.

55. A. Zipkin, "The Wisdom of Thoughtfulness," *The New York Times,* May 31, 2000, pp. C1, C10.

56. Gallup Organization study, reported in Zipkin, "The Wisdom of Thoughtfulness," 2000. This differs from a survey by the Society for Human Resource Management, *2007 Job Satisfaction Survey Report,* in which employees said the top five "very important" aspects of job satisfaction were compensation, benefits, job security, work/life balance, and communication between employees and senior management. See S. Miller, "HR, Employees Vary on Job Satisfaction," *HR Magazine,* August 2007, pp. 32, 34. The magazine *Workspace* reported that employees said benefits were more important, followed by compensation and then by "growth and earning potential," as reported in P. B. Brown, "Same Office, Different Planets," *The New York Times,* January 26, 2008, p. B5.

57. E. White, "The Best vs. the Rest," *The Wall Street Journal,* January 30, 2006, pp. B1, B3; and J. Pfeffer, "Stopping the Talent Drain," *Business 2.0,* July 2006, p. 80.

58. See, for example, J. Anderson, "Tying One's Pay to Performance: What a Concept," *The New York Times,* July 15, 2005, p. C7; and G. Farrell and B. Hansen, "Stocks May Fall, but Pay Doesn't," *USA Today,* April 10, 2008, pp. 1B, 2B. See also M. J. Canyon, "Executive Compensation and Incentives," *Academy of Management Perspectives,* February 2006, pp. 25–44.

59. P. Hodson, *2008 Proxy Season Foresights #2—Performance Targets Targeted,* February 15, 2008, Corporate Library, http://www.thecorporatelibrary.com/info.php?id=88 (accessed May 9, 2010). This study by Corporate Library, an independent governance research organization for the Securities and Exchange Commission, is reported in E. Simon, "How Execs Get Bonus Not Clear," *San Francisco Chronicle,* February 21, 2008, p. C3.

60. See S. Bernard, "No Bonuses for Top Goldman Execs," *San Francisco Chronicle,* December 11, 2009, p. A12.

61. B. E. Graham-Moore and T. L. Ross, *Productivity Gainsharing* (Englewood Cliffs, NJ: Prentice-Hall, 1983).

62. "Take Stock of Stock Options," *Human Resource Executive Magazine,* June 3, 2004, workindex.com; www.workindex.com/editorial/hre/hre0406-03.asp (accessed May 11, 2010).

63. K. Clark, "Too Safe a Bet?" *U.S. News & World Report,* June 19, 2006, pp. 37–38. For more on backdating of stock options, see J. Ledbetter, "Backdating: It Ain't Over," *Fortune,* March 20, 2008, http://dailybriefing.blogs.fortune.cnn.com/2008/03/20/backdating-it-aint-over (accessed May 9, 2010); and H. W. Jenkins Jr., "One Last Backdating Whipping Boy?" *The Wall Street Journal,* April 30, 2008, http://online.wsj.com/article/SB120951511131354625.html (accessed May 9, 2010).

64. PricewaterhouseCoopers survey, reported in S. Shellenbarger, "What Job Candidates Really Want to Know: Will I Have a Life?" *The Wall Street Journal,* November 17, 1999, p. B1. See also S. F. Premeaux, C. L. Adkins, and K. W. Mossholder, "Balancing Work and Family: A Field Study of Multi-Dimensional, Multi-Role Work-Family Conflict," *Journal of Organizational Behavior,* August 2007, pp. 705–727; S. Cummins, "Life, Liberty, and the Pursuit of Balance," *BusinessWeek,* October 23, 2007, http://www.businessweek.com/managing/content/oct2007/ca20071023_799034.htm?campaign_id=rss_daily (accessed May 11, 2010); J. Herzlich, "Work/Life Balance Tops List," *The Arizona Republic,* January 6, 2008, p. EC1.

65. K. W. Smola and C. D. Sutton, "Generational Differences: Revisiting Generational Work Values for the New Millennium," *Journal of Organizational Behavior,* June 2002, p. 379.

66. *The Millennials: Confident. Connected. Open to Change,* Pew Research Center Publications, February 2010, www.pewresearch.org/millennials (accessed May 6, 2010).

67. See J. Turano, "Two Workers, Wearing One Hat," *The New York Times,* October 4, 2009, Business section, p. 8; "Half a

Job's Better Than One," *The Week,* November 6, 2009, p. 42; T. Pugh, "'Work Sharing' Helps Limit Layoffs' Impact," *San Francisco Chronicle,* November 15, 2009, p. D3; S. A. Hewlett, "Making Flex Time a Win-Win," *The New York Times,* December 13, 2009, Business section, p. 13; and S. Brown, "Line between Home, Work Will Blur More," *USA Today,* February 8, 2010, p. 11B.

68. See I. J. Dugan, "Working Two Jobs and Still Underemployed," *The Wall Street Journal,* December 1, 2009, p. A15; and S. Shellenbarger, "Recession Tactic: The Mini-Shift," *The Wall Street Journal,* February 24, 2010, p. D4.

69. Walker Information Global Network and Hudson Institute, *2000 Global Employee Relationship Report,* in "Global Workforce Study Highlights Alarming Trends," September 19, 2000, http://www.hudson.org/index.cfm?fuseaction= public-ation_details&id=697 (accessed May 11, 2010).

70. Spherion and Louis Harris Associates 1999 survey, reported in Zipkin, "The Wisdom of Thoughtfulness," 2000.

71. See P. Falcone, "Doing More with Less: How to Motivate and Reward Your Overworked Staff During Lean Times," *HR Magazine,* February 2003, pp. 101–103; D. Kehrer, "Here Are Some Keys to Keeping Good Employees," *Reno Gazette Journal,* March 30, 2004, p. 4D; and J. Noveck, "Do Bosses Need to Be Mean to Get Work Done?" *Nevada Appeal,* July 9, 2006, pp. D1, D2.

72. B. L. Ware, quoted in Zipkin, "The Wisdom of Thoughtfulness," 2000.

73. K. Lingle, quoted in C. Kleiman, "Work-Life Rewards Grow," *San Francisco Examiner,* January 16, 2000, p. J-2; reprinted from *Chicago Tribune.*

74. S. Shellenberger, "Companies Retool Time-Off Policies to Prevent Burnout, Reward Performance," *The Wall Street Journal,* January 5, 2006, p. D1.

75. See A. Fisher, "The Rebalancing Act," *Fortune,* October 6, 2003, pp. 110–113; D. Cadrain, "Cash vs. Non-cash Rewards," *HR Magazine,* April 2003, pp. 81–87; C. Hymowitz, "While Some Women Choose to Stay Home, Others Gain Flexibility," *The Wall Street Journal,* March 30, 2004, p. B1; J. Shramm, "Fuel Economy," *HR Magazine,* December 2005, p. 120; S. Armour, "Cost-Effective 'Homesourcing' Grows," *USA Today,* March 13, 2006, p. 1B; S. E. Needleman, "Pick Worker Rewards Carefully," *The Wall Street Journal,* March 28, 2006, p. B8; M. P. McQueen, "Employers Expand Elder-Care Benefits," *The Wall Street Journal,* July 27, 2006, pp. D1, D6; A. Pomeroy, "The Future Is Now," *HR Magazine,* September 2007, pp. 46–51; S. Shellenbarger, "Good News for Professionals Who Want to Work at Home," *The Wall Street Journal,* November 15, 2007, p. D1; S. Armour, "As Dads Push for Family Time, Tensions Rise in Workplace," *USA Today,* December 11, 2007, pp. 1A, 2A; K. R. Lewis, "Getting Time Off and Getting Work Done a Balancing Act," *San Francisco Chronicle,* December 16, 2007, p. E6; and D. Hudepohl, "Working from Home: Mapping Out Your First 90 Days," *The Wall Street Journal,* February 19, 2008, p. B8.

76. J. Vatner, "Changing a Culture by Removing Walls," *The New York Times,* February 10, 2010, p. B7.

77. A. Hedge, quoted in P. Wen, "Drab Cubicles Can Block Workers' Creativity, Productivity," *San Francisco Chronicle,* March 10, 2000, pp. B1, B3; reprinted from *Boston Globe.*

78. See A. Johnson, "It's True: A Nicer Office Can Boost Morale," *The Arizona Republic,* September 3, 2007, http://www .azcentral.com/arizonarepublic/business/articles/0903biz-workenvironment0903.html (accessed May 20, 2010), which describes a study by Harvard Medical School psychologist Nancy Etcoff that reinforces the idea that a person's physical environment has a big impact on his or her mood at work. Also see I. DeBare, "Shared Work Spaces a Sign of the Times," *San Francisco Chronicle,* February 19, 2008, pp. A1, A7.

79. J. Sturges, N. Conway, D. Guest, and A. Liefooghe, "Managing the Career Deal: The Psychological Contract as a Framework for Understanding Career Management, Organizational Commitment, and Work Behavior," *Journal of Organizational Behavior,* November 2005, pp. 821–838; and J. Badal, "'Career Path' Programs Help Retain Workers," *The Wall Street Journal,* July 24, 2006, pp. B1, B4.

80. J. P. Smith, "Sabbaticals Pervade Business Sector," *Reno Gazette-Journal,* February 22, 2004, p. H1; M. Arndt, "Nice Work If You Can Get It," *BusinessWeek,* January 9, 2006, pp. 56–57; and L. Chao, "Sabbaticals Can Offer Dividends for Employers," *The Wall Street Journal,* July 17, 2006, p. B5.

CHAPTER 13

1. D. L. Duarte and N. T. Snyder, *Mastering Virtual Teams: Strategies, Tools, and Techniques That Succeed,* 3rd ed. (San Francisco: Jossey-Bass, 2006).

2. C. Sandlund, "Remote Control," *Business Week Frontier,* March 27, 2000, pp. F.14–F.20; A. Salkever, "Home Truths about Meetings," *BusinessWeek,* April 24, 2003, http:// www.businessweek.com/smallbiz/content/apr2003/ sb20030424_0977_sb010.htm?chan=search (accessed May 12, 2010); B. J. Alge, C. Wiethoff, and H. J. Klein, "When Does the Medium Matter? Knowledge-Building Experiences and Opportunities in Decision-Making Teams," *Organizational Behavior and Human Decision Processes* 91 (2003), pp. 26–37; B. Snyder, "Teams That Span Time Zones Face New Work Rules," *Stanford Business Magazine,* May 2003, http://www.gsb.stanford.edu/news/bmag/sbsm0305/ feature_virtual_teams.shtml (accessed May 12, 2010); M. K. Brown, B. Huettner, and C. James-Tanny, *Managing Virtual Teams: Getting the Most from Wikis, Blogs, and Other Collaborative Tools* (Plano, TX: Wordware Publishing, 2007); M. Goldsmith, "Crossing the Cultural Chasm," *BusinessWeek,* May 30, 2007, http://www.businessweek.com/careers/ content/may2007/ca20070530_521679.htm?chan=search (accessed May 12, 2010); and L. Noeth, "Supervising a Virtual Team Is Still All about Basics," *Rochester Democrat & Chronicle,* April 27, 2008, http://www.democratandchronicle.com/ apps/pbcs.dll/article?AID=/20080427/BUSINESS01/ 804270332/-1/COLUMNS (accessed May 12, 2010).

3. P. F. Drucker, "The Coming of the New Organization," *Harvard Business Review,* January–February 1988, pp. 45–53.

4. "Top 10 Leadership Tips from Jeff Immelt," *Fast Company,* April 2004, p. 96.

5. T. Kelley, quoted in P. Sinton, "Teamwork the Name of the Game for Ideo," *San Francisco Chronicle,* February 23, 2000, pp. D1, D3. Kelley is coauthor, with J. Littman, of *The Art of Innovation: Lessons in Creativity from IDEO, America's Leading Design Firm* (New York: Random House, 2001) and of *The Ten Faces of Innovation: IDEO's Strategies for Defeating the Devil's Advocate and Driving Creativity Throughout Your Organization* (New York: Currency/Doubleday, 2005).

6. S. E. Page, quoted in C. Dreifus, "In Professor's Model, Diversity = Productivity," *The New York Times,* January 8, 2008, p. D2.

7. This definition is based in part on one found in D. Horton Smith, "A Parsimonious Definition of 'Group': Toward Conceptual Clarity and Scientific Utility," *Sociological Inquiry,* Spring 1967, pp. 141–167.

8. E. H. Schein, *Organizational Psychology,* 3rd ed. (Englewood Cliffs, NJ: Prentice-Hall, 1980), p. 145.

9. J. R. Katzenbach and D. K. Smith, *The Wisdom of Teams: Creating the High-Performance Organization* (Boston: Harvard Business School Press, 1993), p. 45.

10. J. R. Katzenbach and D. K. Smith, "The Discipline of Teams," *Harvard Business Review,* March–April 1995, p. 112.

11. D. Krackhardt and J. R. Hanson, "Informal Networks: The Company Behind the Chart," *Harvard Business Review,* July–August 1993, p. 104.

12. Study by Center for Workforce Development, Newton, MA, reported in M. Jackson, "It's Not Chitchat, It's Training," *San Francisco Chronicle,* January 7, 1998, p. D2.

13. Center for Workforce Development, *The Teaching Firm: Where Productive Work and Learning Converge* (Newton, MA: Education Development Center, 1998). For more on informal learning, see D. W. Livingstone and R. Roth, "Workers' Knowledge: An Untapped Resource in the Labour Movement," paper presented at the International Conference on Union Growth, Toronto, April 30–May 1, 2001, http://www.oise.utoronto.ca/depts/sese/csew/nall/res/31workers.htm (accessed May 12, 2010); V. J. Marsick and K. E. Watkins, "Informal and Incidental Learning," *New Directions for Adult and Continuing Education,* February 26, 2002, pp. 25–34; M. B. Twidale, "Over the Shoulder Learning: Supporting Brief Informal Learning," *Computer Supported Cooperative Work,* December 2005, pp. 505–547; and L. Dublin, "Formalizing Informal Learning," *Chief Learning Officer,* March 2010, http://www.clomedia.com/features/2010/March/2870/index.php (accessed May 17, 2010).

14. T. Elkeles, "Storytelling Drives Knowledge and Information Sharing Across Qualcomm," *Chief Learning Officer,* http://www.clomedia.com/talent.php?pt=s&sid=2871&mode=preview (accessed May 17, 2010).

15. K. K. Spors, "Getting Workers to Share Their Know-How with Peers," *The Wall Street Journal,* April 3, 2008, p. B6. For more on virtual knowledge sharing, see B. Rosen, S. Furst, and R. Blackburn, "Overcoming Barriers to Knowledge Sharing in Virtual Teams," *Organizational Dynamics* 36 (2007), pp. 259–273.

16. See E. Krell, "HR Challenges in Virtual Worlds," *HR Magazine,* November 2007, pp. 85–88; and R. King, "The (Virtual) Global Office," *BusinessWeek,* May 2, 2008, http://msnbci.businessweek.com/technology/content/may2008/tc2008052_842516_page_2.htm (accessed May 12, 2010). See also M. Peckham, "Study: Can Games Improve Workplace Collaboration?" *PC World,* February 10, 2009, http://www.pcworld.com/article/159247/study_can_games_improve_workplace_collaboration.html (accessed May 17, 2010).

17. E. Sundstrom, K. P. DeMeuse, and D. Futrell, "Work Teams," *American Psychologist,* February 1990, pp. 120–133.

18. See K. Buch and R. Spangler, "The Effects of Quality Circles on Performance and Promotions," *Human Relations,* June 1990, pp. 573–582; and E. E. Lawler III, "Total Quality Management and Employee Involvement: Are They Compatible?" *Academy of Management Executive,* February 1994, pp. 68–76.

19. G. L. Stewart and M. R. Barrick, "Team Structure and Performance: Assessing the Mediating Role of Intrateam Process and the Moderating Role of Task," *Academy of Management Journal,* April 2000, p. 135. See also S. E. Humphrey, J. R. Hollenbeck, C. J. Meyer, and D. R. Ilgen, "Trait Configurations in Self-Managed Teams: A Conceptual Examination of the Use of Seeding for Maximizing and Minimizing Trait Variance in Teams," *Journal of Applied Psychology,* May 2007, pp. 885–892.

20. Good background discussions can be found in P. S. Goodman, R. Devadas, and T. L. Griffith Hughson, "Groups and Productivity: Analyzing the Effectiveness of Self-Managing Teams," in J. P. Campbell, R. J. Campbell, and Associates, eds., *Productivity in Organizations* (San Francisco: Jossey-Bass, 1988), pp. 295–327; E. G. Rogers, W. Metlay, I. T. Kaplan, and T. Shapiro, "Self-Managing Work Teams: Do They Really Work?" *Human Resource Planning,* no. 2, 1995, pp. 53–57; and R. Rico, M. Sánchez-Manzanares, F. Gil, and C. Gibson, "Team Implicit Coordination Processes: A Team Knowledge-Based Approach," *Academy of Management Review,* January 2008, pp. 163–184.

21. See K. Kraiger, "Perspectives on Training and Development," in W. C. Borman, D. R. Ilgen, and R. J. Klimoski, eds., *Handbook of Psychology,* vol. 12 (New York: John Wiley, 2003), pp. 176–177; and C. Douglas and W. L. Gardner, "Transition to Self-Directed Work Teams: Implications of Transition Time and Self-Monitoring for Managers' Use of Influence Tactics," *Journal of Organizational Behavior* 25 (2004), pp. 47–65.

22. C. Douglas and W. L. Gardner, "Transition to Self-Directed Work Teams: Implications of Transition Time and Self-Monitoring for Managers' Use of Influence Tactics," *Journal of Organizational Behavior* 25 (2004), pp. 47–65.

23. See B. W. Tuckman, "Developmental Sequence in Small Groups," *Psychological Bulletin,* June 1965, pp. 384–399; and B. W. Tuckman and M.A.C. Jensen, "Stages of Small-Group Development Revisited," *Group & Organization Studies,* December 1977, pp. 419–427. An instructive adaptation of the Tuckman model can be found in L. Holpp, "If Empowerment Is So Good, Why Does It Hurt?" *Training,* March 1995, p. 56. See also C. Gersick, "Marking Time: Predictable Transitions in Task Groups," *Academy of Management Journal,* June 1989, pp. 274–309; and S. Wait, "Team Building Is Critical for Successful Growth," *Reno Gazette-Journal,* August 5, 2006, p. 5E.

24. See F. P. Morgeson, M. H. Reider, and M. A. Campion, "Selecting Individuals in Team Settings: The Importance of Social Skills, Personality Characteristics, and Teamwork Knowledge," *Personnel Psychology,* Autumn 2005, pp. 583–611.

25. Practical advice on handling a dominating group member can be found in M. Finley, "Belling the Bully," *HR Magazine,* March 1992, pp. 82–86; see also B. Carey, "Fear in the Workplace: The Bullying Boss," *The New York Times,* June 22, 2004, pp. D1, D6. A description of three unhelpful co-workers you should try to sidestep (the chronic complainer, the shoulder rubber, and the chatterbox) are described in C. Potter, "Steer Clear: Three Coworkers to Avoid," *San Francisco Chronicle,* January 10, 2010, p. D1. The problem of overcommunication among co-workers appears in J. Spolsky, "A Little Less Conversation," *Inc.,* February 2010, pp. 28–29.

26. Techniques for team building are discussed by P. Falcone, "On the Brink of Failure," *HR Magazine,* February 2008, pp. 82–84; and "Sound of Teambuilding," *Training,* February 2008, p. 16.

27. J. Schaubroeck, S. S. K. Lam, and S. E. Cha, "Embracing Transformational Leadership: Team Values and the Impact of Leader Behavior on Team Performance," *Journal of Applied Psychology,* July 2007, pp. 1020–1030.

28. "Is Your Team Too Big? Too Small? What's the Right Number?" *Knowledge@Wharton,* June 14, 2006, Wharton School, University of Pennsylvania, http://knowledge.wharton.upenn.edu/article.cfm?articleid-1501&CFID-1653072&CFTOKEN-14318984 (accessed May 12, 2010).

29. "A Team's-Eye View of Teams," *Training,* November 1995, p. 16. For more discussion of team size, see V. Hazrati, "Is Five the Optimal Team Size?" *InfoQ,* April 14, 2009, http://www.infoq.com/news/2009/04/agile-optimal-team-size (accessed May 17, 2010).

30. M. E. Shaw, *Group Dynamics,* 3rd ed. (New York: McGraw-Hill, 1981); G. Manners, "Another Look at Group Size, Group Problem-Solving and Member Consensus," *Academy of Management Journal* 18 (1975), pp. 715–724.

31. H. S. Hwang and J. Guynes, "The Effect of Group Size on Group Performance in Computer-Supported Decision Making," *Information & Management,* April 1994, pp. 189–198.

32. S. J. Karau and K. D. Williams, "Social Loafing: Research Findings, Implications, and Future Directions," *Current Directions in Psychological Science,* October 1995, pp. 134–140; S. J. Zacarro, "Social Loafing: The Role of Task Attractiveness," *Personality and Social Psychology Bulletin* 10 (1984), pp. 99–106; P. W. Mulvey, L. Bowes-Sperry, and K. J. Klein, "The Effects of Perceived Loafing and Defensive Impression Management on Group Effectiveness," *Small Group Research,* June 1998, pp. 394–415; and L. Karakowsky and K. McBey, "Do My Contributions Matter? The Influence of Imputed Expertise on Member Involvement and Self-Evaluations in the Work Group," *Group & Organization Management,* March 2001, pp. 70–92.

33. J. Welch and S. Welch, "When a Star Slacks Off," *BusinessWeek,* March 17, 2008, p. 88.

34. B. C. Lim and K. J. Klein, "Team Mental Models and Team Performance: A Field Study of the Effects of Team Mental Model Similarity and Accuracy," *Journal of Organizational Behavior,* January 2006, pp. 403–418.

35. J. L. Yang, "The Power of Number 4.6," *Fortune,* June 12, 2006, p. 122.

36. Deutschman, "The Managing Wisdom of High-Tech Superstars," *Fortune,* October 17, 1994, pp. 197–206.

37. J. R. Hackman, *Leading Teams: Setting the Stage for Great Performances* (Boston: Harvard Business School Press, 2002).

38. J. R. Hackman and N. J. Vidmar, "Effects of Size and Task Type on Group Performance and Member Reactions," *Sociometry* 33 (1970), pp. 37–54.

39. K. J. Klein, cited in "Is Your Team Too Big? Too Small? What's the Right Number?" *Knowledge@Wharton,* June 14, 2006.

40. K. D. Benne and P. Sheats, "Functional Roles of Group Members," *Journal of Social Issues,* Spring 1948, pp. 41–49. See also E. C. Dierdorff and F. P. Morgeson, "Consensus in Work Role Requirements: The Influence of Discrete Occupational Contests on Role Expectations," *Journal of Applied Psychology,* September 2007, pp. 1228–1241; and D. J. McAllister, D. Kamdar, E. W. Morrison, and D. B. Turban, "Disentangling Role Perceptions: How Perceived Role Breadth, Discretion, Instrumentality, and Efficacy Relate to Helping and Taking Charge," *Journal of Applied Psychology,* September 2007, pp. 1200–1211.

41. D. C. Feldman, "The Development and Enforcement of Group Norms," *Academy of Management Review,* January 1984, pp. 47–53.

42. D. Kahneman, "Reference Points, Anchors, Norms, and Mixed Feelings," *Organizational Behavior and Human Decision Processes,* March 1992, pp. 296–312.

43. N. Byrnes, "The Art of Motivation," *BusinessWeek,* May 1, 2006, pp. 57–62.

44. N. Byrnes, "Pain, but No Layoffs at Nucor," *BusinessWeek,* March 26, 2009, http://www.businessweek.com/print/ magazine/content/09_14/b4125054802295.htm (accessed May 17, 2010).

45. "Nucor Named Top U.S. Steel Manufacturer," *Charlotte Business Journal,* April 24, 2008, http://www.bizjournals .com/charlotte/stories/2008/04/21/daily34.html?q= Nucor%20Corp. (accessed May 12, 2010).

46. D. Foust, "The BusinessWeek 50," *BusinessWeek,* March 26, 2009, http://www.businessweek.com/magazine/content/ 09_14/b4125040198774.htm?chan=magazine+channel_ in+depth (accessed May 17, 2010).

47. Feldman, "The Development and Enforcement of Group Norms," 1984.

48. A big part of cohesiveness is building trust. See D. De Cremer and T. R. Tyler, "The Effects of Trust in Authority and Procedural Fairness on Cooperation," *Journal of Applied Psychology,* May 2007, pp. 639–649; J. A. Colquitt, B. A. Scott, and J. A. Lepine, "Trust, Trustworthiness, and Trust Propensity: A Meta-Analytic Test of Their Unique Relationships with Risk Taking and Job Performance," *Journal of Applied Psychology,* July 2007, pp. 909–927; and R. Ilies, D. T. Wagner, and F. P. Morgeson, "Explaining Affective Linkages in Teams: Individual Differences in Susceptibility to Contagion and Individualism–Collectivism," *Journal of Applied Psychology,* July 2007, pp. 1140–1148.

49. See, for example, P. Jin, "Work Motivation and Productivity in Voluntarily Formed Work Teams: A Field Study in China," *Organizational Behavior and Human Decision Processes* 54, no. 1 (1993), pp. 133–155.

50. J. B. Harvey, "The Abilene Paradox: The Management of Agreement," *Organizational Dynamics,* Summer 1988, pp. 17–43.

51. I. Janis, *Groupthink,* 2nd ed. (Boston: Houghton Mifflin, 1982), p. 9. See also K. D. Lassila, "A Brief History of Groupthink," *Yale Alumni Magazine,* January–February 2008, pp. 59–61, www.philosophy-religion.org/handouts/pdfs/ BRIEF-HISTORY_GROUPTHINK.pdf (accessed May 12, 2010).

52. V. Kemper, "Senate Intelligence Report: Groupthink Viewed as Culprit in Move to War," *Los Angeles Times,* July 10, 2004, p. A.17.

53. J. Surowiecki, quoted in J. Freeman, "Books," *The Christian Science Monitor,* May 25, 2004; www.csmonitor.com/2004/ 0525/p15s01-bogn.html (accessed May 12, 2010). Also see J. Surowiecki, *The Wisdom of Crowds: Why the Many Are Smarter Than the Few and How Collective Wisdom Shapes Business, Economies, Societies, and Nations* (New York: Doubleday, 2004).

54. V. H. Palmieri, quoted in L. Baum, "The Job Nobody Wants," *BusinessWeek,* September 8, 1986, p. 60.

55. Surowiecki, quoted in Kemper, "Senate Intelligence Report: Groupthink Viewed as Culprit in Move to War," 2004. See also J. A. LePine, "Adaptation of Teams in Response to Unforeseen Change: Effects of Goal Difficulty and Team Composition in Terms of Cognitive Ability and Goal Orientation," *Journal of Applied Psychology* 90 (2005), pp. 1153–1167.

56. M. R. Callway and J. K. Desser, "Groupthink: Effects of Cohesiveness and Problem-Solving Procedures on Group Decision Making," *Social Behavior and Personality,* no. 2, 1984, pp. 157–164.

57. R. Cyran, "Shifting Fortunes of Cellphones," *The New York Times,* May 12, 2010, p. B2. See also J. Wortham, "Everyone Is Using Cellphones, but Not So Many Are Talking," *The New York Times,* May 14, 2010, pp. A1, B4.

58. B. Stelter, "It's the Show, Not the Screen," *The New York Times,* May 3, 2010, pp. B1, B3; R. Kim, "Time Is Right for Mobile Video Chat," *San Francisco Chronicle,* May 3, 2010, pp. D1, D5; N. Bilton, "Phones Cut the Need to Carry Cash," *The New York Times,* May 3, 2010, p. B10; and J. Temple, "Shoot First, Then Ask the Questions Online," *San Francisco Chronicle,* May 16, 2010, pp. D1, D7.

59. Motorola's handsets have fallen behind Apple's iPhone and Research In Motion's BlackBerry in global unit sales in the first quarter of 2010. See "Motorola Falls Behind Rivals," *San Francisco Chronicle,* May 18, 2010, p. D3.

60. For more on these strategies, see J. Surowiecki, "Soft in the Middle," *The New Yorker,* March 29, 2010, p. 45.

61. G. Sandstrom, "Nokia Tries to Recharge," *The Wall Street Journal,* May 12, 2010, p. B5.

62. Some discussions of sources of conflict appear in E. Bernstein, "When a Co-Worker Is Stressed Out," *The Wall Street*

Journal, August 26, 2008, pp. DI, D2; M. Steen, "Apologizing on the Job," *San Francisco Chronicle,* February 28, 2010, p. DI; E. Zimmerman, "The Office Skirmish: How to Avoid Round 2," *The New York Times,* March 14, 2010, Business section, p. 9; and D. Nishi, "What to Do If Your Boss Is the Problem," *The Wall Street Journal,* April 20, 2010, p. D4.

63. J. A. Wall Jr. and R. Robert Callister, "Conflict and Its Management," *Journal of Management,* no. 3 (1995), p. 517.

64. C. Alter, "An Exploratory Study of Conflict and Coordination in Interorganizational Service Delivery Systems," *Academy of Management Journal,* September 1990, pp. 478–502; S. P. Robbins, "'Conflict Management' and 'Conflict Resolution' Are Not Synonymous Terms," *California Management Review,* Winter 1978, p. 70.

65. Cooperative conflict is discussed in D. Tjosvold, *Learning to Manage Conflict: Getting People to Work Together Productively* (New York: Lexington, 1993); and D. Tjosvold and D. W. Johnson, *Productive Conflict Management Perspectives for Organizations* (New York: Irvington, 1983). See also A. C. Amason, K. R. Thompson, W. A. Hochwarter, and A. W. Harrison, "Conflict: An Important Dimension in Successful Management Teams," *Organizational Dynamics,* Autumn 1995, pp. 20–35; and A. C. Amason, "Distinguishing the Effects of Functional and Dysfunctional Conflict on Strategic Decision Making: Resolving a Paradox for Top Management Teams," *Academy of Management Journal,* February 1996, pp. 123–148.

66. L. Lange, quoted in J. Noveck, "Do Bosses Need to Be Mean to Get Work Done?" *Nevada Appeal,* July 9, 2006, pp. DI, D2. See also D. Brady, "Charm Offensive," *BusinessWeek,* June 26, 2006, pp. 76–80; and A. Dobson and R. Berman, "Building a Better Boss," *San Francisco Chronicle,* September 23, 2007, p. H-I.

67. G. Namie, *U.S. Workplace Bullying Survey,* September 2007, conducted by Workplace Bullying Institute and Zogby International, using 7,740 online interviews, for Waitt Institute for Violence Prevention, www.healthyworkplacebill.org/pdf/WBIsurvey2007.pdf (accessed May 12, 2010).

68. K. L. Zellars, B. J. Tepper, and M. K. Duffy, "Abusive Supervision and Subordinates' Organizational Citizenship Behavior," *Journal of Applied Psychology,* December 2002, pp. 1068–1076.

69. B. J. Tepper and E. C. Taylor, "Relationships Among Supervisors' and Subordinates' Procedural Justice Perceptions and Organizational Citizenship Behaviors," *Academy of Management Journal,* February 2003, pp. 97–105; B. J. Tepper, M. K. Duffy, J. Hoobler, and M. D. Ensley, "Moderators of the Relationship between Coworkers' Organizational Citizenship Behavior and Fellow Employees' Attitudes," *Journal of Applied Psychology,* June 2005, pp. 455–465; B. J. Tepper, M. Uhl-Bien, G. F. Kohut, S. G. Rogelberg, D. E. Lockhart, and M. D. Ensley, "Subordinates' Resistance and Managers' Evaluations of Subordinates' Performance," *Journal of Management,* April 1, 2006, pp. 185–209; B. J. Tepper, M. K. Duffy, C. A. Henle, and L. S. Lambert, "Procedural Injustice, Victim Precipitation, and Abusive Supervision," *Personnel Psychology,* March 2006, pp. 101–123; B. J. Tepper, S. E. Moss, D. E. Lockhart, and J. C. Carr, "Abusive Supervision, Upward Maintenance Supervision, and Subordinates' Psychological Distress," *Academy of Management Journal* 50 (2007), pp. 1169–1180; and B. J. Tepper, "Abusive Supervision in Formal Organizations: Review, Synthesis, and Research Agenda," *Journal of Management,* June 1, 2007, pp. 261–289.

70. R. I. Sutton in "Breakthrough Ideas for 2004: The HBR List," *Harvard Business Review,* February 2004, pp. 13–24, 32–37. Sutton's topic was headed "More Trouble Than They Are Worth." His book based on these ideas is *The No Asshole Rule: Building a Civilized Workplace and Surviving One That Isn't* (New York: Warner, 2007).

71. R. I. Sutton, "R. I. Sutton: Nasty People," *CIO Insight,* May 1, 2004, http://www.cioinsight.com/c/a/Past-Opinions/Robert-I-Sutton-Nasty-People (accessed May 12, 2010).

72. A. M. O'Leary-Kelly, R. W. Griffin, and D. J. Glew, "Organization-Motivated Aggression: A Research Framework," *Academy of Management Review,* January 1996, pp. 225–253. See also G. A. Van Kleef and S. Côté, "Expressing Anger in Conflict: When It Helps and When It Hurts," *Journal of Applied Psychology,* November 2007, pp. 1557–1569.

73. L. R. Pondy, "Organizational Conflict: Concepts and Models," *Administrative Science Quarterly* 2 (1967), pp. 296–320.

74. P. Burrows, "Carly's Last Stand?" *BusinessWeek,* December 24, 2001, pp. 63–70. See B. Pimentel, "Heftier HP Is Ready to Forge Ahead," *San Francisco Chronicle,* May 5, 2002, pp. GI, G4.

75. "Japan: Toyota Falls Victim to a Clash of Cultures," *The Week,* March 12, 2010, p. 18.

76. K. W. Thomas, "Conflict and Conflict Management," in *Handbook of Industrial and Organizational Psychology,* M. Dunnette, ed. (Chicago: Rand McNally, 1976), pp. 889–935; K. W. Thomas "Toward Multiple Dimensional Values in Teaching: The Example of Conflict Behaviors," *Academy of Management Review,* July 1977, pp. 484–490; and M. A Rahim, "A Strategy for Managing Conflict in Complex Organizations," *Human Relations,* January 1985, p. 84.

77. Rahim, "A Strategy for Managing Conflict in Complex Organizations," 1985.

78. R. A. Cosier and C. R. Schwenk, "Agreement and Thinking Alike: Ingredients for Poor Decisions," *Academy of Management Executive,* February 1990, p. 71. Also see J. P. Kotter, "Kill Complacency," *Fortune,* August 5, 1996, pp. 168–170.

79. See "Facilitators as Devil's Advocates," *Training,* September 1993, p. 10; and C. R. Schwenk, "Devil's Advocacy in Managerial Decision Making," *Journal of Management Studies,* April 1984, pp. 153–168.

80. S. G. Katzenstein, "The Debate on Structured Debate: Toward a Unified Theory," *Organizational Behavior and Human Decision Processes,* June 1996, pp. 316–332.

81. W. Kiechel III, "How to Escape the Echo Chamber," *Fortune,* June 18, 1990, p. 130.

CHAPTER 14

1. H. Lancaster, "If Your Career Needs More Attention, Maybe You Should Get an Agent," *The Wall Street Journal,* October 20, 1998, p. BI. See also L. K. Hardie, "Joelle K. Jay: Leadership Coach Inspires Businesspeople to Succeed," *Reno Gazette-Journal,* January 15, 2006, pp. IE, I3E; R. Berman, "Coached Toward Brighter Management," *San Francisco Chronicle,* March 5, 2006, pp. GI, G6; A. S. Wellner, "Do You Need a Coach?" *Inc. Magazine,* April 2006, pp. 85–93; and N. Brozan, "Top Brokers Hire Coaches to Climb Higher," *The New York Times,* May 7, 2006, sec. 4, p. 9.

2. R. L. Knowdell, "The 10 New Rules for Strategizing Your Career," *The Futurist,* June–July 1998, pp. 19–24.

3. C. A. Schriesheim, J. M. Tolliver, and O. C. Behling, "Leadership Theory: Some Implications for Managers," *MSU Business Topics,* Summer 1978, p. 35. See also G. Yukl, "Managerial Leadership: A Review of Theory and Research," *Journal of Management* 15 (1989), pp. 251–289.

4. T. Peters and N. Austin, *A Passion for Excellence* (New York: Random House, 1985), pp. 5–6; but see also B. Kellerman, "Leadership—Warts and All," *Harvard Business Review,* January 1, 2004, pp. 40–45.

5. B. M. Bass, *Bass & Stogdill's Handbook of Leadership: Theory, Research, and Managerial Applications,* 3rd ed. (New York: Free Press, 1990), p. 383.

6. J. P. Kotter, "What Leaders Really Do," *Harvard Business Review,* December 2001, pp. 85–96; the role of leadership within organizational change is discussed in J. P. Kotter, *Leading Change* (Boston: Harvard Business School Press, 1996).

7. F. Smith, quoted in "All in a Day's Work," *Harvard Business Review,* December 2001, pp. 54–66.

8. L. H. Chusmir, "Personalized versus Socialized Power Needs among Working Women and Men," *Human Relations,* February 1986, p. 149.

9. A. Wong, quoted in "My Journey to the Top," *Newsweek,* October 15, 2007, pp. 49–65.

10. R. M. Kramer, "The Great Intimidators," *Harvard Business Review,* February 2006, pp. 88–96.

11. M. Helft and A. Vance, "Apple Passes Microsoft as No. 1 in Tech," *The New York Times,* May 26, 2010, http://www.nytimes.com/2010/05/27/technology/27apple.html (accessed June 5, 2010).

12. Ibid.

13. A. Lashinsky, "The Decade of Steve," *Fortune,* November 5, 2009, http://tech.fortune.cnn.com/2009/11/05/the-decade-of-steve (accessed June 5, 2010).

14. P. Sellers, "Steve Jobs on Building a Startup," *CNNMoney.com,* June 2, 2010, http://postcards.blog.fotune.cnn.com/2010/06/02/steve-job-on-building-a-startup (accessed June 5, 2010).

15. S. Harrison, "Deliberate Acts of Decency," *HR Magazine,* July 2007, pp. 97–99.

16. Based on Table 1 in G. Yukl, C. M. Falbe, and J. Y. Youn, "Patterns of Influence Behavior for Managers," *Group & Organization Management,* March 1993, pp. 5–28.

17. G. Yukl, H. Kim, and C. M. Falbe, "Antecedents of Influence Outcomes," *Journal of Applied Psychology,* June 1996, pp. 309–317.

18. B. Schlender, "A Conversation with the Lords of Wintel," *Fortune,* July 8, 1996, p. 44.

19. R. M. Stogdill, "Personal Factors Associated with Leadership: A Survey of the Literature," *Journal of Psychology* 25 (1948), pp. 35–71; and R. M. Stogdill, *Handbook of Leadership* (New York: Free Press, 1974).

20. B. Bass, *Stogdill's Handbook of Leadership,* rev. ed. (New York: Free Press, 1981).

21. See S. J. Zaccaro, "Trait-Based Perspectives of Leadership," *American Psychologist,* January 2007, pp. 6–16; and R. Sternberg, "A Systems Model of Leadership," *American Psychologist,* January 2007, pp. 34–42. Recent discussions of the trait approach are provided by D. B. Peterson, "High Potential, High Risk," *HR Magazine,* March 2008, pp. 85–88; and "Timeless Leadership: The Great Leadership Lessons Don't Change," *Harvard Business Review,* March 2008, pp. 45–49.

22. Executive coaching is discussed by S. Labadessa, "Now Go Out and Lead!" *BusinessWeek,* January 8, 2007, pp. 72–73.

23. Leadership development programs are discussed in G. M. Spreitzer, "Leading to Grow and Growing to Lead: Leadership Development Lessons from Positive Organizational Studies," *Organizational Dynamics,* November 2006, pp. 305–315; and E. White, "Manager Shortage Spurs Small Firms to Grow Their Own," *The Wall Street Journal,* February 15, 2007, pp. B1, B4.

24. J. M. Kouzes and B. Z. Posner, "The Credibility Factor: What Followers Expect from Their Leaders," *Business Credit,* July–August 1990, pp. 24–28; J. M. Kouzes and B. Z. Posner, *Credibility* (San Francisco: Jossey-Bass, 1993); and J. M. Kouzes and B. Z. Posner, *The Leadership Challenge: How to Get Extraordinary Things Done in Organizations* (San Francisco: Jossey-Bass, 1995).

25. Study by Catalyst, New York, reported in J. S. Lublin, "Women Aspire to Be Chief as Much as Men Do," *The Wall Street Journal,* June 28, 2004, p. D2.

26. Supportive findings are contained in J. M. Twenge, "Changes in Women's Assertiveness in Response to Status and Roles: A Cross-Temporal Meta-Analysis, 1931–1993," *Journal of Personality and Social Psychology,* July 2001, pp. 133–145.

27. R. Sharpe, "As Leaders, Women Rule," *BusinessWeek,* November 20, 2000, pp. 75–84.

28. Study by Hagberg Consulting Group, Foster City, California, reported in Sharpe, 2000, p. 75.

29. For a summary of this research, see H. Ibarra and O. Obodaru, "Women and Vision Thing," *Harvard Business Review,* January 2009, pp. 62–70.

30. See A. H. Eagly, S. J. Karau, and B. T. Johnson, "Gender and Leadership Style among School Principals: A Meta-Analysis," *Educational Administration Quarterly,* February 1992, pp. 76–102.

31. Gender and the emergence of leaders was examined by A. H. Eagly and S. J. Karau, "Gender and the Emergence of Leaders: A Meta-Analysis," *Journal of Personality and Social Psychology,* May 1991, pp. 685–710; and J. L. Prime, N. M. Carter, and T. M. Welbourne, "Women 'Take Care,' Men 'Take Charge': Managers' Stereotypic Perceptions of Women and Men Leaders," *The Psychologist-Manager Journal,* January 2009, pp. 25–49.

32. B. R. Ragins, B. Townsend, and M. Mattis, "Gender Gap in the Executive Suite: CEOs and Female Executives Report on Breaking the Glass Ceiling," *Academy of Management Executive,* February 1, 1998, pp. 28–42.

33. L. Tischler, "Where Are the Women?" *Fast Company,* February 2004, pp. 52–60.

34. P. Sellers, "Power: Do Women Really Want It?" *Fortune,* October 13, 2003, p. 88.

35. See M. Conlin, "Self-Deprecating Women," *BusinessWeek,* June 14, 2004, p. 26. For more on this subject, see also "The 'Masculine' and 'Feminine' Sides of Leadership and Culture: Perception vs. Reality," *Knowledge@Wharton,* http://knowledge.wharton.upenn.edu/index.cfm?fa=printArticle & ID (accessed May 23, 2010); "Guiding Aspiring Female Execs Up the Ladder," *HR Magazine,* January 2006, p. 14; T. G. Habbershon," "It's a Man's World," *BusinessWeek SmallBiz,* Spring 2006, p.16; Q. M. Roberson and C. K. Stevens, "Making Sense of Diversity in the Workplace: Organizational Justice and Language Abstraction in Employees' Accounts of Diversity-Related Incidents," *Journal of Applied Psychology,* March 2006, pp. 379–391; E. Porter, "Women in Workplace—Trend Is Reversing," *San Francisco Chronicle,* March 2, 2006, p. A2, reprinted from *The New York Times;* T. L. O'Brien, "Up the Down Staircase: Why Do So Few Women Reach the Top of Big Law Firms?" *The New York Times,* March 19, 2006, sec. 3, pp. 1, 4; "Breaking into the Boardroom," *The Wall Street Journal,* March 27, 2006, p. B3; E. White, "Why Few Women Run Plants," *The Wall Street Journal,* May 1, 2006, pp. B1, B5; J. Zaslow, "A New Generation Gap: Differences Emerge Among Women in the Workplace," *The Wall Street Journal,* May 4, 2006, p. D1; W. A. Holsetin, "Glass Ceiling? Get a Hammer," *The New York Times,* June 18, 2006, sec. 3, p. 12; C. Hymowitz, "Women Swell Ranks as Middle Managers, but Are Scarce at Top," *The Wall Street Journal,* July 24, 2006, p. B1; S. Vedantam, "Glass Ceiling Breaks When Women Are in Charge, Study Says," *San Francisco Chronicle,* August 13, 2006, p. A17, reprinted from *Washington Post.*

36. B. Groysberg, "How Star Women Build Portable Skills," *Harvard Business Review,* February 2008, pp. 74–81. See also R. D. Arvey, Z. Zhang, B. J. Avolio, and R. F. Krueger, "Developmental and Genetic Determinants of Leadership Role Occupancy among Women," *Journal of Applied Psychology,* May 2007, pp. 693–706. Some popular treatments on the subject of women and leadership are C. V. Flett, *What Men Don't Tell Women about Business: Opening Up the Heavily Guarded Alpha Male Playbook* (New York: Wiley, 2008) and N. DiSesa, *Seducing the Boys Club: Uncensored Tactics from a Woman at the Top* (New York: Ballantine Books, 2008).

37. See research by N. M. Carter and C. Silva, "Women in Management: Delusions of Progress," *Harvard Business Review,* March 2010, pp. 19–21.

38. Data compiled by Bloomberg News from proxy filings, reported in A. Leondis, "CEOs Crack Glass Ceiling," *San Francisco Chronicle,* May 14, 2010, pp. D1, D4.

39. R. Foroohar and S. H. Breenberg, "Working Women Are Poised to Become the Biggest Economic Engine the World Has Ever Known," *Newsweek,* November 2, 2009, pp. B3–B5. See also C. Rampell, "Women Now a Majority in American Workplaces," *The New York Times,* February 6, 2010, p. A10.

40. R. House, M. Javidan, P. Hanges, and P. Dorfman, "Understanding Cultures and Implicit Leadership Theories Across the Globe: An Introduction to Project GLOBE," *Journal of World Business,* Spring 2004, p. 4.

41. R. Likert, *New Patterns of Management* (New York: McGraw-Hill, 1961); and R. Likert, *The Human Organization* (New York: McGraw-Hill, 1967).

42. C. A. Schriesman and B. J. Bird, "Contributions of the Ohio State Studies to the Field of Leadership," *Journal of Management Studies* 5 (1979), pp. 135–145; and C. L. Shartle, "Early Years of the Ohio State University Leadership Studies," *Journal of Management* 5 (1979), pp. 126–134.

43. V. H. Vroom, "Leadership," in M. D. Dunnette, ed., *Handbook of Industrial and Organizational Psychology* (Chicago: Rand McNally, 1976).

44. F. E. Fiedler, "Assumed Similarity Measures as Predictors of Team Effectiveness," *Journal of Abnormal and Social Psychology* 49 (1954), pp. 381–388; F. E. Fiedler, *Leader Attitudes and Group Effectiveness* (Urbana, IL: University of Illinois Press, 1958); and F. E. Fiedler, *A Theory of Leadership Effectiveness* (New York: McGraw-Hill, 1967).

45. A review of the contingency theory and suggestions for future theoretical development is provided by R. Ayman, M. M. Chemers, and F. Fiedler, "The Contingency Model of Leadership Effectiveness: Its Levels of Analysis," in F. Dansereau and F. J. Yamminrino, eds., *Leadership: The Multiple-Level Approaches* (Stamford, CT: JAI Press, 1998), pp. 73–94. Also see M. V. Vugt, R. Hogan, and R. B. Kaiser, "Leadership, Followership, and Evolution," *American Psychologist,* April 2008, pp. 182–196.

46. R. J. House, "A Path-Goal Theory of Leader Effectiveness," *Administrative Science Quarterly,* September 1971, pp. 321–338; and R. J. House and T. R. Mitchell, "Path-Goal Theory of Leadership," *Journal of Contemporary Business,* Autumn 1974, pp. 81–97. The most recent version of the theory is found in R. J. House, "Path-Goal Theory of Leadership: Lessons, Legacy, and a Reformulated Theory," *Leadership Quarterly,* Autumn 1996, pp. 323–352.

47. These studies are summarized in House, "Path-Goal Theory of Leadership: Lessons, Legacy, and a Reformulated Theory," 1996.

48. Supportive results can be found in D. Charbonneau, J. Barling, and E. K. Kelloway, "Transformational Leadership and Sports Performance: The Mediating Role of Intrinsic Motivation," *Journal of Applied Social Psychology,* July 2001, pp. 1521–1534.

49. Results can be found in P. M. Podsakoff, S. B. MacKenzie, M. Ahearne, and W. H. Bommer, "Searching for a Needle in a Haystack: Trying to Identify the Illusive Moderators of Leadership Behaviors," *Journal of Management,* 1995, pp. 422–470.

50. A thorough discussion is provided by P. Hersey and K. H. Blanchard, *Management of Organizational Behavior: Utilizing Human Resources,* 5th ed. (Englewood Cliffs, NJ: Prentice-Hall, 1988).

51. Results can be found in J. R. Goodson, G. W. McGee, and J. F. Cashman, "Situational Leadership Theory," *Group & Organization Studies,* December 1989, pp. 446–461.

52. C. Adams, "Leadership Behavior of Chief Nurse Executives," *Nursing Management,* August 1990, pp. 36–39.

53. See D. C. Lueder, "Don't Be Misled by LEAD," *Journal of Applied Behavioral Science,* May 1985, pp. 143–154; and C. L. Graeff, "The Situational Leadership Theory: A Critical View," *Academy of Management Review,* April 1983, pp. 285–291.

54. The steps were developed by H. P. Sims Jr., S. Faraj, and S. Yun, "When Should a Leader Be Directive or Empowering? How to Develop Your Own Situational Theory of Leadership," *Business Horizons,* March-April 2009, pp. 149–158.

55. For a complete description of the full-range leadership theory, see B. J. Bass and B. J. Avolio, *Revised Manual for the Multi-Factor Leadership Questionnaire* (Palo Alto, CA: Mindgarden, 1997).

56. A definition and description of transactional leadership is provided by J. Antonakis and R. J. House, "The Full-Range Leadership Theory: The Way Forward," in B. J. Avolio and F. J. Yammarino, eds., *Transformational and Charismatic Leadership: The Road Ahead* (New York: JAI Press, 2002), pp. 3–34.

57. "Most Powerful Women in Business," *Fortune,* January 10, 2010, http://money.cnn.com/galleries/2009/fortune/0909/gallery.most_powerful_women.fortune/index.html (accessed May 21, 2010). See also E. MacDonald and C. R. Schoenberger, "The World's Most Powerful Women: The Top 10," *Forbes,* September 17, 2007, pp. 126–127, on which Nooyi was ranked No. 5.

58. B. Morris, "What Makes Pepsi Great?" *Fortune,* March 3, 2008, pp. 54–66.

59. U. R. Dundum, K. B. Lowe, and B. J. Avolio, "A Meta-Analysis of Transformational and Transactional Leadership Correlates of Effectiveness and Satisfaction: An Update and Extension," in B. J. Avolio and F. J. Yammarino, eds., *Transformational and Charismatic Leadership: The Road Ahead* (New York: JAI Press, 2002), p. 38.

60. Supportive results can be found in T. A. Judge and J. E. Bono, "Five-Factor Model of Personality and Transformational Leadership," *Journal of Applied Psychology,* October 2000, pp. 751–765.

61. Supportive research is summarized by Antonakis and House, "The Full-Range Leadership Theory: The Way Forward," 2002.

62. Morris, "What Makes Pepsi Great?" 2008.

63. J. P. Mangalindan, "PepsiCo CEO: 'If All Consumers Exercised . . . Obesity Wouldn't Exist,'" *Fortune,* April 27, 2010, http://money.cnn.com/2010/04/27/news/companies/indra_nooyi_pepsico.fortune/index.htm (accessed May 21, 2010).

64. H. Schultz, "Indra Nooyi," *Time,* April 30, 2008, http://www.time.com/time/specials/2007/article/0,28804,1733748_1733758,00.html (accessed May 23, 2010). See also D. Brady, "Keeping Cool in Hot Water," *BusinessWeek,* June 11, 2007, p. 49.

65. These definitions are derived from R. Kark, B. Shamir, and C. Chen, "The Two Faces of Transformational Leadership:

Empowerment and Dependency," *Journal of Applied Psychology,* April 2003, pp. 246–255. See also R. T. Keller, "Transformational Leadership, Initiating Structure, and Substitutes for Leadership: A Longitudinal Study of Research and Development Project Team Performance," *Journal of Applied Psychology,* January 2006, pp. 202–210; J. Schaubroeck and S. S. K. Lam, "Embracing Transformational Leadership: Team Values and the Impact of Leader Behavior on Team Performance," *Journal of Applied Psychology,* July 2007, pp. 1020–1030; H. Liao and A. Chuang, "Transforming Service Employees and Climate: A Multilevel, Multisource Examination of Transformational Leadership in Building Long-Term Service Relationships," *Journal of Applied Psychology,* July 2007, pp. 1006–1019; S. J. Shin and J. Zhou, "When Is Educational Specialization Heterogeneity Related to Creativity in Research and Development Teams? Transformational Leadership as a Moderator," *Journal of Applied Psychology,* November 2007, pp. 1709–1721; and A. E. Colbert, A. L. Kristof-Brown, B. H. Bradley, and M. R. Barrick, "CEO Transformational Leadership: The Role of Goal Importance Congruence in Top Management Teams," *Academy of Management Journal,* February 2008, pp. 81–96.

66. See A. Erez, V. F. Misangyi, D. E. Johnson, M. A. LePine, and K. C. Halverson, "Stirring the Hearts of Followers: Charismatic Leadership as the Transferral of Affect," *Journal of Applied Psychology* 93 (2008), pp. 602–615; and M. E. Brown and L. K. Treviño, "Leader-Follower Values Congruence: Are Socialized Charismatic Leaders Better Able to Achieve It?" *Journal of Applied Psychology* 94 (2009), pp. 478–490.

67. B. Nanus, *Visionary Leadership* (San Francisco: Jossey-Bass, 1992), p. 8. See also J. Murphy, "Ghosn Hedges Bets on Emissions," *The Wall Street Journal,* May 15, 2008, p. B2: and D. Enrich, "Citigroup Pandit Faces Test as Pressure on Bank Grows," *The Wall Street Journal,* May 6, 2008, pp. A1, A20.

68. See C. Rauwald, "Volkswagen Takes Aim at Rival's Top Perch," *The Wall Street Journal,* February 3, 2010, p. B2.

69. See R. E. Quinn, "Moments of Greatness: Entering the Fundamental State of Leadership," *Harvard Business Review,* July–August 2005, pp. 75–83.

70. D. MacMillan, "Survivor: CEO Edition," *Bloomberg Businessweek,* March 1, 2010, p. 35.

71. Morris, "What Makes Pepsi Great?" 2008.

72. See H. Lui, and A. Chuang, "Transforming Service Employees and Climate: A Multilevel, Multisource Examination of Transformational Leadership in Building Long-Term Service Relationships," *Journal of Applied Psychology,* July 2007, pp. 1006–1019; and J. Schaubroeck, S.S.K. Lam, and S. E. Cha, "Embracing Transformational Leadership: Team Values and the Impact of Leader Behavior on Team Performance," *Journal of Applied Psychology,* July 2007, pp. 1020–1030.

73. Results can be found in Dundum, Lowe, and Avolio, 2002; and A. Erez, V. F. Misangyi, D. E. Johnson, M. A. LePine, and K. C. Halverson, "Stirring the Hearts of Followers: Charismatic Leadership as the Transferal of Affect," *Journal of Applied Psychology,* May 2008, pp. 602–615.

74. See Kark, Shamir, and Chen, "The Two Faces of Transformational Leadership: Empowerment and Dependency," 2003.

75. Supportive results and can be found in B. M. Bass, B. J. Avolio, D. I. Jung, and Y. Berson, "Predicting Unit Performance by Assessing Transformational and Transactional Leadership," *Journal of Applied Psychology,* April 2003, pp. 207–218; P. Wang, and F. O. Walumbwa, "Family-Friendly Programs, Organizational Commitment, and Work Withdrawal: The Moderating Role of Transformational Leadership," *Personnel Psychology,* Summer 2007, pp. 397–427; and D. M. Herold, D. B. Fedor, S. Caldwell, and Y. Liu, "The Effects of Transfor-

mational and Change Leadership on Employees' Commitment to Change: A Multilevel Study," *Journal of Applied Psychology,* March 2008, pp. 346–357.

76. See A. J. Towler, "Effects of Charismatic Influence Training on Attitudes, Behavior, and Performance," *Personnel Psychology,* Summer 2003, pp. 363–381; M. Weinstein, "Leadership Leader," *Training,* February 2008, pp. 41–46; and B. J. Avolio, R. J. Reichard, S. T. Hannah, F. O Walumbwa, and A. Chan, "A Meta-Analytic Review of Leadership Impact Research: Experimental and Quasi-Experimental Studies," *Leadership Quarterly* 20 (2009), pp. 764–784.

77. See J. E. Stiglitz, "Who Do These Bankers Think They Are?" *Harvard Business Review,* March 2010, p. 36.

78. For a discussion of ethics and transformational leadership, see B. M. Bass and P. Steidlmeier, "Ethics, Character, and Authentic Transformational Leadership," revised September 24, 1998, http://docs.google.com/viewer?a=v&q=cache: iGz-TMCbrfJAJ:www.vanguard.edu/uploadedFiles/Faculty/ RHeuser/ETHICS,%2520MORAL%2520CHARACTER% 2520AND%2520AUTHENTIC%2520TRANSFORMATIONAL% 2520LEADERSHIP.pdf+%E2%80%9CEthics,+Character,+ and+Authentic+Transformational+Leadership%E2%80% 9D&hl=en&gl=us&pid=bl&srcid=ADGEEShyjv4cw76QLAtF44- QPFxmiCRijF6orVQ-RQ29QRIcE5thuPQmvlFRbHG2ulWB- OclUOZIpDFu6QAFw7b6otaUXqfi7KQBDZXm8cOQUZg3X a2iVmPXWZdnP_Bzz58IZD3VDvo3jP&sig=AHIEtbR_ jn6e2CyVpR_ixOUlbRNGfThmMA (accessed May 23, 2010).

79. G. Graen and J. F. Cashman, "A Role-Making Model of Leadership in Formal Organizations: A Developmental Approach," in J. G. Hunt and L. L. Larson, eds., *Leadership Frontiers* (Kent, OH: Kent State University Press, 1975), pp. 143–165; F. Dansereau Jr., G. Graen, and W. J. Haga, "A Vertical Dyad Linkage Approach to Leadership Within Formal Organizations: A Longitudinal Investigation of the Role-Making Process," *Organizational Behavior and Human Performance,* February 1975, pp. 46–78; and R. M. Dienesch and R. C. Liden, "Leader-Member Exchange Model of Leadership: A Critique and Further Development," *Academy of Management Review,* July 1986, pp. 618–634.

80. See D. Duchon, S. G. Green, and T. D. Taber, "Vertical Dyad Linkage: A Longitudinal Assessment of Antecedents, Measures, and Consequences," *Journal of Applied Psychology,* February 1986, pp. 56–60.

81. See B. Erdogan, M. I. Kraimer, and R. C. Liden, "Work Value Congruence and Intrinsic Career Success: The Compensatory Roles of Leader-Member Exchange and Perceived Organizational Support," *Personnel Psychology,* Summer 2004, pp. 305–332; and T. N. Bauer, B. Erdogan, R. C. Liden, and S. J. Wayne, "A Longitudinal Study of the Moderating Role of Extraversion: Leader-Member Exchange, Performance, and Turnover During New Executive Development," *Journal of Applied Psychology,* March 2006, pp. 298–310; O. Epitropaki and R. Martin, "From Ideal to Real: A Longitudinal Study of the Role of Implicit Leadership Theories on Leader-Member Exchanges and Employee Outcomes," *Journal of Applied Psychology,* July 2005, pp. 659–676; W. Lam, X. Huang, and E. Snape, "Feedback-Seeking Behavior and Leader-Member Exchange: Do Supervisor-Attributed Motives Matter?" *Academy of Management Journal,* April 2007, pp. 348–363; and S. A. Furst and D. M. Cable, "Employee Resistance to Organizational Change: Managerial Influence Tactics and Leader-Member Exchange," *Journal of Applied Psychology,* March 2008, pp. 453–462.

82. A turnover study was conducted by G. B. Graen, R. C. Liden, and W. Hoel, "Role of Leadership in the Employee Withdrawal Process," *Journal of Applied Psychology,* December

1982, pp. 868–872. The career progress study was conducted by M. Wakabayashi and G. B. Braen, "The Japanese Career Progress Study: A 7-Year Follow-Up," *Journal of Applied Psychology,* November 1984, pp. 603–614.

83. R. J. House and R. N. Aditya, "The Social Scientific Study of Leadership: Quo Vadis?" *Journal of Management* 23 (1997), pp. 409–473.

84. A thorough discussion of shared leadership is provided by C. L. Pearce, "The Future of Leadership: Combining Vertical and Shared Leadership to Transform Knowledge Work." *Academy of Management Executive,* February 2004, pp. 47–57.

85. This research is summarized in B. J. Avolio, J. J. Soskik, D. I. Jung, and Y. Benson, "Leadership Models, Methods, and Applications," in W. C. Borman, D. R. Ilgen, and R. J. Klimoski, eds. *Handbook of Psychology,* vol. 12 (Hoboken, NJ: John Wiley & Sons, 2003) pp. 277–307.

86. L. L. Berry, "The Collaborative Organization: Leadership Lessons from Mayo Clinic," *Organizational Dynamics,* August 2004, pp. 230–231.

87. A. Taylor III, "Bill's Brand-New Ford," *Fortune,* June 28, 2004, p. 74.

88. A. Ignatius, "Meet the Google Guys," *Time,* February 12, 2006, http://www.time.com/time/magazine/article/0,9171,1158956,00.html (accessed May 23, 2010); and Google Corporate Information, "Google Management," http://www.google.com/corporate/execs.html (accessed May 23, 2010).

89. P. Sellers, "MySpace Cowboys," *Fortune,* September 4, 2006, pp. 66–74. See also B. Stelter, "From MySpace to Your Space," *The New York Times,* January 21, 2008, http://www.nytimes.com/2008/01/21/technology/21myspace.html (accessed May 23, 2010).

90. An overall summary of servant leadership is provided by L. C. Spears, *Reflections on Leadership: How Robert K. Greenleaf's Theory of Servant-Leadership Influenced Today's Top Management Thinkers* (New York: Wiley, 1995).

91. D. MacMillan, "Survivor: CEO Edition," 2010.

92. D. Gergen, "Bad News for Bullies," *U.S. News & World Report,* June 19, 2006, p. 54.

93. M. De Pree, quoted in Gergen, "Bad News for Bullies," 2006. The quote is from M. De Pree, *Leadership Is an Art* (New York: Dell, 1989).

94. See B. J. Avolio, J. J. Sosik, D. I. Jung, and Yair Berson, "Stirring the Hearts of Followers: Charismatic Leadership as the Transferal of Affect," 2003, pp. 295–298.

95. L. Capotosto, "Millennial Management," *Darwin,* www2.darwinmag.com/connect/books/book.cfm?ID-188 (accessed May 23, 2010).

96. D. MacRae, "Six Secrets of Successful E-Leaders," *Business Week online,* September 6, 2001; www.businessweek.com/technology/content/sep2001/tc2001096_619.htm (accessed May 23, 2010).

97. D. Q. Mills, *E-Leadership: Guiding Your Business to Success in the New Economy* (Paramus, NJ: Prentice Hall Press, 2001). See also R. Hargrove, *E-Leader: Reinventing Leadership in a Connected Economy* (Boulder, CO: Perseus Books Group, 2001); T. M. Siebel, *Taking Care of eBusiness: How Today's Market Leaders Are Increasing Revenue, Productivity, and Customer Satisfaction* (New York: Doubleday, 2001); S. Annunzio, *eLeadership: Bold Solutions for the New Economy* (New York: Free Press, 2002); and B. J. Avolio and S. S. Kahai, "Adding the "E" to E-leadership: How It May Impact Your Leadership," *Organizational Dynamics* 31 (2003), pp. 325–338.

98. Adapted from D. McCarthy, "10 Tips on How to Lead a Global Virtual Team," *Great Leadership,* February 12, 2009, http://www.greatleadershipbydan.com/2009/02/10-tips-on-how-to-lead-global-virtual.html (accessed May 23, 2010).

CHAPTER 15

1. C. Vinzant, "Messing with the Boss' Head," *Fortune,* May 1, 2000, pp. 329–331.

2. M. Price, "Effective Communication Begins with Listening," *Reno Gazette-Journal,* November 27, 2000, p. 1F.

3. D. Stiebel, *When Talking Makes Things Worse! Resolving Problems When Communication Fails* (Dallas, TX: Whitehall & Nolton, 1997). Reported in O. Pollar, "Talk Is Cheap If You Have Big Disagreements," *San Francisco Examiner & Chronicle,* February 21, 1999, p. J-3.

4. For more on these matters, see E. Bernstein, "Why Do Compliments Cause So Much Grief?" *The Wall Street Journal,* May 4, 2010, pp. D1, D6; J. Zaslow, "Surviving the Age of Humiliation," *The Wall Street Journal,* May 5, 2010, pp. D1,D3; A. Tugend, "An Attempt to Revive the Lost Art of Apology," *The New York Times,* January 30, 2010, p. B5; L. Garcia, "Curses, Roiled Again," *The Arizona Republic,* June 21, 2009, p. EC1, reprinted from *Washington Post;* and S. Elliott, "Bleep or No Bleep, Bolder Words Blow In," *The New York Times,* May 14, 2010, pp. B1, B4.

5. See K. Gurchiek, "Survey: 'Key Skills Advance HR Career," *HRMagazine,* April 2008, p. 38.

6. September 1998 survey by Office Team, reported in S. Armour, "Failure to Communicate Costly for Companies," *USA Today,* September 30, 1998, p. B1.

7. J. R. Hinrichs, "Communications Activity of Industrial Research Personnel," *Personnel Psychology,* Summer 1964, pp. 193–204.

8. J. Kotter, "Power, Dependence, and Effective Management," *Harvard Business Review* 55 (1977), pp. 125–136.

9. J. Sandberg, "From Crib to Cubicle, a Familiar Voice—Our Own—Reassures," *The Wall Street Journal,* March 25, 2008, p. B1.

10. R. L. Daft, and R. H. Lengel, "Information Richness: A New Approach to Managerial Behavior and Organizational Design," in B. M. Staw and L. L. Cummings, eds., *Research in Organizational Behavior* (Greenwich, CT: JAI Press, 1984), p. 196; and R. H. Lengel and R. L. Daft, "The Selection of Communication Media as an Executive Skill," *Academy of Management Executive,* August 1988, pp. 225–232.

11. E. Goode, "Old as Society, Social Anxiety Is Yielding Its Secrets," *The New York Times,* October 20, 1998, pp. D7, D11.

12. See T. J. Bruce and S. A. Saeed, "Social Anxiety Disorder: A Common, Underrecognized Mental Disorder," *American Family Physician,* November 15, 1999, pp. 2311–2320, 2322; and S. Reinberg, "15 Million Americans Suffer from Social Anxiety Disorder," *BusinessWeek,* April 9, 2008, http://www.businessweek.com/lifestyle/content/healthday/614405.html?chan=top+news_top+news+index_lifestyle (accessed May 20, 2010).

13. S. Merchant, quoted in S. Srivastava, "Why India Worries about Outsourcing," *San Francisco Chronicle,* March 21, 2004, p. E3.

14. The role of jargon in communication is discussed by R. Spragins, "Don't Talk to Me That Way," *Fortune Small Business,* February 2002, p. 26; and C. Hymowitz, "Mind Your Language: To Do Business Today, Consider Delayering," *The Wall Street Journal,* March 27, 2006, p. B1.

15. Some of these barriers are discussed in J. P. Scully, "People: The Imperfect Communicators," *Quality Progress,* April 1995, pp. 37–39.

16. See A. Stein, "Straight Talk," *FSB,* December 2009/January 2010, p. 23.

17. S. Dillon, "Guest-Teaching Chinese, and Learning America," *The New York Times,* May 10, 2010, pp. A1, A14. For more about what a difference culture makes, see S. Begley, "West Brain, East Brain," *Newsweek,* March 1, 2010, p. 22.

18. A. Farnham, "Trust Gap," *Fortune,* December 4, 1989, p. 70.

19. C. R. Rogers and F. J. Roethlisberger, "Barriers and Gateways to Communication," *Harvard Business Review,* July–August 1952, pp. 46–52.

20. Ibid., p. 47.

21. W. D. St. John, "You Are What You Communicate," *Personnel Journal,* October 1985, p. 40.

22. The importance of nonverbal communication is discussed by D. Arthur, "The Importance of Body Language," *HRFocus,* June 1995, pp. 22–23; and N. M. Grant, "The Silent Shroud: Build Bridges, Not Barriers," *HRFocus,* April 1995, p. 16. Problems with interpreting nonverbal communication are discussed by A. Pihulyk, "Communicate with Clarity: The Key to Understanding and Influencing Others," *The Canadian Manager,* Summer 2003, pp. 12–13.

23. This statistic was provided by A. Fisher, "How Can I Survive a Phone Interview?" *Fortune,* April 10, 2004, p. 54.

24. See N. Morgan, "The Kinesthetic Speaker: Putting Action into Words," *Harvard Business Review,* April 2001, pp. 113–120. Also see A. Bruzzese, "Communication Is Critical to Coping with Workplace Stress," *Reno Gazette-Journal,* September 4, 2008, p. 6A; and Alex Pentland, interviewed by M. E. Mangelsdorf, "The Power of Nonverbal Communication," *The Wall Street Journal,* October 20, 2008, p. R2.

25. Norms for cross-cultural eye contact are discussed by C. Engholm, *When Business East Meets Business West: The Guide to Practice and Protocol in the Pacific Rim* (New York: John Wiley & Sons, 1991).

26. See J. A. Russell, "Facial Expressions of Emotion: What Lies Beyond Minimal Universality?" *Psychological Bulletin,* November 1995, pp. 379–391.

27. See N. Angier, "Abstract Thoughts? The Body Takes Them Literally," *The New York Times,* February 2, 2010, p. D2.

28. Related research is summarized by J. A. Hall, "Male and Female Nonverbal Behavior," in A. W. Siegman and S. Feldstein, eds., *Multichannel Integrations of Nonverbal Behavior* (Hillsdale, NJ: Lawrence Erlbaum, 1985), pp. 195–226.

29. A thorough discussion of cross-cultural differences is provided by R. E. Axtell, *Gestures: The Do's and Taboos of Body Language Around the World* (New York: John Wiley & Sons, 1998). Problems with body language analysis also are discussed by C. L. Karrass, "Body Language: Beware the Hype," *Traffic Management,* January 1992, p. 27; and M. Everett and B. Wiesendanger, "What Does Body Language Really Say?" *Sales & Marketing Management,* April 1992, p. 40.

30. Results can be found in Hall, "Male and Female Nonverbal Behavior," 1985.

31. J. N. Cleveland, M. Stockdale, and K. R. Murphy, *Women and Men in Organizations: Sex and Gender Issues at Work* (Mahwah, NJ: Lawrence Erlbaum, 2002), p. 108.

32. P. Leo, "Thorny Etiquette Problem for Men: Hug, Kiss, or Handshake?" *Pittsburgh Post-Gazette,* March 23, 2006, http://www.post-gazette.com/pg/06082/675002-294.stm (accessed May 24, 2010). See also R. Marin, "Hug-Hug, Kiss-Kiss: It's a Jungle Out There," *The New York Times,* September 19, 1999, http://query.nytimes.com/gst/fullpage.html?res=9906E0D8123CF93AA2575AC0A96F958260 (accessed May 24, 2010); J. W. Lee and L. K. Guerrero, "Types of Touch in Cross-Sex Relationships between Coworkers: Perceptions of Relational and Emotional Messages, Inappropriateness, and Sexual Harassment," *Journal of Applied Communication Research* 29 (2001), pp. 197–220; D. Jones, "Female Bosses Can Touch More Freely," *USA Today,* February 19, 2002, p. 9B; and D. Brown, "Men Are Hugging Men More, but Rules Aren't Always Clearly Defined," *Seattle Post-Intelligencer,* July 11, 2005, http://seattlepi.nwsource.com/lifestyle/231855_guyhugs.html (accessed May 24, 2008).

33. See B. Carey, "Evidence That Little Touches Do Mean So Much," *The New York Times,* February 23, 2010, p. D5.

34. See J. S. Lublin, "Women Fall Behind When They Don't Hone Negotiation Skills," *The Wall Street Journal,* November 4, 2003, p. B1. See also "Do Women Shy Away from Competition, Even When They Can Win?" *Knowledge@Wharton,* November 16, 2005, http://knowledge.wharton.upenn.edu/article.cfm?articleid=1308 (accessed May 24, 2010); and J. R. Curhan and A. Pentland, "Thin Slices of Negotiation: Predicting Outcomes from Conversational Dynamics within the First 5 Minutes," *Journal of Applied Psychology,* May 2007, pp. 802–811.

35. J. C. Tingley, *Genderflex: Men & Women Speaking Each Other's Language at Work* (New York: American Management Association, 1994), p. 16.

36. D. Tannen, "The Power of Talk: Who Gets Heard and Why," in *Negotiation: Readings, Exercises, and Cases,* 3rd ed., R. J. Lewicki and D. M. Saunders, eds. (Burr Ridge, IL: Irwin/McGraw-Hill, 1999), pp. 147–148. Research on gender differences in communication can be found in V. N. Giri and H. O. Sharma, "Brain Wiring and Communication Style," *Psychological Studies* 48 (2003), pp. 59–64; and E. L. MacGeorge, A. R. Graves, B. Feng, S. J. Gillihan, and B. R. Burleson, "The Myth of Gender Cultures: Similarities Outweigh Differences in Men's and Women's Provision of Responses to Supportive Communication," *Sex Roles* 50 (2004), pp. 143–175.

37. C. Clarke, quoted in A. Pomeroy, "Female Executives May Have a Business Edge," *HR Magazine,* August 2005, p. 16. See also C. Clarke, "A (Necessary) End to Male Dominance," *post-gazette.com,* March 21, 2006, http://www.post-gazette.com/pg/06080/673640-334.stm (accessed May 24, 2010).

38. R. Sharpe, "As Leaders, Women Rule," *BusinessWeek,* November 20, 2000, pp. 75–84.

39. A. Cummings, reported in "The 'Masculine' and 'Feminine' Sides of Leadership and Culture: Perception vs. Reality," *Knowledge@Wharton,* October 5, 2005, knowledge.wharton.upenn.edu/article.cfm?articleide=1287 (accessed May 24, 2010).

40. D. Jones, "Male Execs Like Female Coaches," *USA Today,* October 24, 2001, p. 3B.

41. Steve Jobs, interviewed by B. Morris, "What Makes Apple Golden," *Fortune,* March 17, 2008, pp. 72, 74.

42. T. Cowan, "In Favor of Face Time," *Forbes,* October 1, 2007, p. 30.

43. C. L. Romero, "Tedious Meetings Top Time-Wasters," *Arizona Republic,* April 22, 2003, p. D2.

44. K. Maher, "Running Meetings," *The Wall Street Journal,* January 13, 2004, p. B6.

45. P. M. Lencioni, *Death by Meeting: A Leadership Fable . . . About Solving the Most Painful Problem in Business* (San Francisco: Jossey-Bass, 2004).

46. P. Lencioni, reported in D. Murphy, "Making Sense of Meetings," *San Francisco Chronicle,* April 3, 2004, p. 1C.

47. O. Pollar, "Questions on Peers, Time, and Meetings," *San Francisco Examiner,* June 27, 1999, p. J-3.

48. G. English, "How About a Good Word for Meetings?" *Management Review,* June 1990, pp. 58-60; L. G. McDougle, "Conducting a Successful Meeting," *Personnel Journal,* January 1981; D. Batstone, "Right Reality: Most Meetings Stink . . . 5 Tips for Making Yours Useful," *The Wag,* December 21, 2005, http://www.rightreality.com/wag_items/issues/051221wag.html (accessed May 24, 2010); S. G. Rogelberg, D. J. Leach, P. B. Warr, and J. L. Burnfield, "'Not Another Meeting!' Are Meeting Time Demands Related to Employee Well-Being?" *Journal of Applied Psychology,* January 2006, pp. 86-96; and M. Linksky, "The Morning Meeting Ritual," *Harvard Management Communication Letter,* June 19, 2006, http://hbswk.hbs.edu/archive/5388.html (accessed May 24, 2010).

49. G. M. Goldhaber, *Organizational Communication,* 4th ed. (Dubuque, IA: W. C. Brown, 1986).

50. Early research is discussed by K. Davis, "Management Communication and the Grapevine," *Harvard Business Review,* September–October 1953, pp. 43-49; and R. Rowan, "Where Did That Rumor Come From?" *Fortune,* August 13, 1979, pp. 130-137. The most recent research is discussed in "Pruning the Company Grapevine," *Supervision,* September 1986, p. 11; and R. Half, "Managing Your Career: 'How Can I Stop the Gossip?'" *Management Accounting,* September 1987, p. 27.

51. See S. McKnight, "Workplace Gossip? Keep It to Yourself," *The New York Times,* November 15, 2009, Business section, p. 9.

52. T. J. Peters and R. H. Waterman Jr., *In Search of Excellence* (New York: Harper & Row, 1982); and T. Peters and N. Austin, *A Passion for Excellence: The Leadership Difference* (New York: Random House, 1985).

53. N. L. Reinsch Jr., J. W. Turner, and C. H. Tinsley, "Multicommunicating: A Practice Whose Time Has Come?" *Academy of Management Review,* April 2008, p. 391.

54. See ibid., pp. 391-403, for a complete discussion of multicommunicating.

55. C. Pearson, "Sending a Message That You Don't Care," *The New York Times,* May 16, 2010, Business section, p. 9.

56. Portions of the material that follows were adapted from R. Kreitner and A. Kinicki, *Organizational Behavior,* 9th ed. (New York: McGraw-Hill/Irwin, 2010), pp. 423-430.

57. A. Fisher, "E-Mail Is for Liars," *Fortune,* November 24, 2008, p. 57.

58. Studies at Massachusetts Institute of Technology, reported in A. Pentland, "How Social Networks Network Best," *Harvard Business Review,* February 2009, p. 37.

59. Study by Council for Research Excellence, reported in B. Stelter, "8 Hours a Day Spent on Screens, Study Finds," *The New York Times,* March 27, 2009, p. B6. See also J. Wortham, "Everyone Is Using Cellphones, but Not So Many Are Talking," *The New York Times,* May 14, 2010, pp. A1, B4.

60. Pew Research Center, "The Millennials: Confident. Connected. Open to Change," February 24, 2010, reported in S. Jayson, "A Detailed Look at Millennials," *USA Today,* February 24, 2010, p. 10B.

61. David Verhaagen, quoted in S. Jayson, "'iGeneration' Has No Off Switch," *USA Today,* February 10, 2010, pp. 1D, 2D.

62. "Ground-Breaking Study of Video Viewing Finds Younger Boomers Consume More Video Media Than Any Other Group," press release, March 27, 2009, on study conducted on behalf of Council for Research Excellence by Ball State University's Center for Media Design, www.researchexcellence.com/news/032609_vcm.php (accessed May 25, 2010). See also Stelter, "8 Hours a Day Spent on Screens, Study Finds," 2009.

63. J. C. Meister and K. Willyerd, "Mentoring Millennials," *Harvard Business Review,* May 2010, pp. 68-72.

64. D. Tapscott, *Grown Up Digital: How the Net Generation Is Changing Your World* (New York: McGraw-Hill, 2009), p. 36.

65. Meister and Willyerd, "Mentoring Millennials," 2010, p. 69.

66. T. Abate, "Survey Reveals Attitudes of Millennials Toward Work," *San Francisco Chronicle,* May 30, 2010, p. D3, reporting on survey titled "Millennial Inc.," conducted by marketing firm Mr. Youth and market research firm Intrepid.

67. S. A. Hewlett, L. Sherbin, and K. Sumberg, "How Gen Y & Boomers Will Reshape Your Agenda," *Harvard Business Review,* July–August 2009, pp. 71-76.

68. B. Yite, "Employers Rethink How They Give Feedback," *The Wall Street Journal,* October 13, 2008, p. B5. See also T. J. Erickson, "Gen Y in the Workforce," *Harvard Business Review,* February 2009, pp. 43-49.

69. M. Esterl, "More Lucrative Business Travelers Now Teleconference, Fly Coach," *The Wall Street Journal,* February 18, 2010, pp. B1, B2; C. Jones, "What Helps You Decide When to Travel?" *USA Today,* April 15, 2010, 1B, 2B; and J. Sharkey, "Turning to Teleconferencing as Air Travel Stalls," *The New York Times,* April 20, 2010, p. B6.

70. *The Return on Investment on U.S. Business Travel,* study by Oxford Economics USA, reported in J. Mullich, "The New Face of Face-to-Face Meetings," *The Wall Street Journal,* September 22, 2009, pp. A17, A18.

71. J. Scheck and B. White, "'Telepresence' Is Taking Hold," *The Wall Street Journal,* May 6, 2008, http://online.wsj.com/article/SB12100331805436925S.html (accessed May 23, 2010).

72. J. S. Lublin, "Some Dos and Don'ts to Help You Hone Videoconference Skills," *The Wall Street Journal,* February 7, 2006, p. B1.

73. D. E. Baily and N. B. Kurland, "A Review of Telework Research: Findings, New Directions, and Lessons for the Study of Modern Work," *Journal of Organizational Behavior,* June 2002, pp. 383-400.

74. Data from E. Reed, "Telecommuting by the Numbers," *HR Magazine,* September 2008, p. 61.

75. Survey by WorldatWork, reported in M. Steen, "5 Tips for Successful Telecommuting," *San Francisco Chronicle,* April 11, 2010, p. D1.

76. See E. Garone, "How to Make Working at Home Work for You," *The Wall Street Journal,* April 29, 2008, p. D4; and R. S. Gajendran and D. A. Harrison, "The Good, the Bad, and the Unknown about Telecommuting: Meta-Analysis of Psychological Mediators and Individual Consequences," *Journal of Applied Psychology,* November 2007, pp. 1524-1541.

77. See S. Shellenbarger, "Some Companies Rethink the Telecommuting Trend," *The Wall Street Journal,* February 28, 2008, p. D1.

78. S. Marino, "Debunking the Myths of the Telecommute," *The New York Times,* April 18, 2010, Business section, p. 9. See also M. Conlin, "Home Offices: The New Math," *BusinessWeek,* March 9, 2009, pp. 66-68; A. Bruzzese, "Telecommuters Need Outreach to Stay Connected," *Reno Gazette-Journal,* October 15, 2009, p. 7A.

79. C. Said, "Work Is Where You Hang Your Coat," *San Francisco Chronicle,* July 18, 2005, p. E5.

80. J. Hodges, "Office (and Beanbag) Sharing among Strangers," *The Wall Street Journal,* December 31, 2009, p. D3.

81. FBI National White Collar Crime Center, "IC3 2009 Annual Report on Internet Crime Released," press release, March 12, 2010, http://www.ic3.gov/media/2010/100312.aspx (accessed May 29, 2010).

82. E. Steel and J. A. Vascellaro, "Sites Confront Privacy Loop-hole," *The Wall Street Journal,* May 21, 2010, pp. B1, B2; J. E. Vascellaro, "Facebook CEO Pledges New Privacy Controls," *The Wall Street Journal,* May 25, 2010, p. B1; C. J. Hoofnagle, "The Privacy Machiavellis," *San Francisco Chronicle,* May 25, 2010, p. A12; and B. Worthen, "Face-book Alters Privacy Controls, but Critics Say It's Not Enough," *The Wall Street Journal,* May 27, 2010, pp. B1, B2. See also A. Bruzzese, "Nuture Your Reputation to Avoid Career Trouble Now, in the Future," *Reno Gazette-Journal,* March 4, 2010, p. 5A; and J. Temple, "It's Tough to Keep Online Rep Intact," *San Francisco Chronicle,* May 30, 2010, pp. D1, D6.

83. Study by Pew Internet & American Life Project, reported in L. M. Holson, "The Tell-All Generation Learns to Keep Some Things Offline," *The New York Times,* May 9, 2010, News section, pp. 1, 4. See also D. MacMillan, "Younger Adults Vigilant about Online Identities," *San Francisco Chronicle,* May 27, 2010, p. D2.

84. Research firm Basex, reported in R. Scoble, "Reengineering Your Inbox," *Fast Company,* February 2009, p. 50.

85. Based on K. Byron, "Carrying Too Heavy a Load? The Com-munication and Miscommunication of Emotion by Email," *Academy of Management Review,* April 2008, pp. 309–327.

86. Pew survey, reported in "Americans More Dependent on Cellphones Than Landlines," *The Arizona Republic,* March 8, 2008, p. D3; J. Kornblum, "Text Messaging Taps Out a Family-Friendly Result," *USA Today,* October 20, 2008, p. 7D; and A. R. Carey and J. Snider," Replacing Land-Line Phones with Cellphones," *USA Today,* April 7, 209, p. 1A.

87. 2004 Sprint Wireless Courtesy Report, cited in S. Winn, "The Cell Phone Warning Has a Familiar Ring. Who's Listening?" *San Francisco Chronicle,* December 16, 2004, pp. E1, E4.

88. "Phone Use Slows Driver Reaction," *The Wall Street Journal,* February 3, 2005, p. D5.

89. See M. Burley-Allen, "Listen Up," *HR Magazine,* November 2001, pp. 115–120.

90. Online Survey conducted July 2007 by Society for Human Resource Management, reported in Gurchiek, "Survey: 'Key Skills Advance HR Career,'" 2008.

91. Burley-Allen, 2001; see also C. G. Pearce, "How Effective Are We as Listeners?" *Training & Development,* April 1993, pp. 79–80; and R. A. Luke Jr., "Improving Your Listening Ability," *Supervisory Management,* June 1992, p. 7.

92. Research by The Discovery Group, reported in "Hey, I'm Talking Here," *Training,* December 2005, p. 9.

93. See the discussion on listening in G. Manning, K. Curtis, and S. McMillen, *Building Community: The Human Side of Work* (Cincinnati, OH: Thomson Executive Press, 1996), pp. 127–154.

94. Derived from J. R. Goldon, *A Diagnostic Approach to Orga-nizational Behavior,* 2nd ed. (Boston: Allyn and Bacon, 1987), p. 230; P. Slizewski, "Tips for Active Listening," *HRFocus,* May 1995, p. 7; G. Manning, K. Curtis, and S. McMillen, *Building the Human Side of Work Community* (Cincinnati, OH: Thomson Executive Press, 1996), pp. 127–154; and J. Sandberg, "What Exactly Was It That the Boss Said? You Can Only Imagine," *The Wall Street Journal,* September 19, 2006, p. B1.

95. M. Just, P. A. Carpenter, and M. Masson, reported in J. Meer, "Reading More, Understanding Less," *Psychology Today,* March 1987, p. 12.

96. K. Alesandrini, *Survive Information Overload* (Homewood, IL: Irwin, 1992), pp. 191–202.

97. Ibid., p. 197.

98. K. Tyler, "Toning Up Communications," *HR Magazine,* March 2003, pp. 87–89.

99. See S. E. Needleman, "Standout Letters to Cover Your Bases," *The Wall Street Journal,* March 9, 2010, p. D4; and R. Abrams, "Writing Winning Business Proposals Is Critical to Your Success," *Reno Gazette-Journal,* September 9, 2008, p. 6A.

100. T. Alessandra and P. Hunsaker, *Communicating at Work* (New York: Fireside, 1993), p. 231.

101. Ibid., p. 241.

102. Cited in Ibid., p. 169.

103. TNS for LG Spring Cleaning Survey of 1,000 adults, March 2010, reported in "Activities Adults Say They Dread," *USA Today,* May 14, 2010, p. A1.

104. G. Lindenfield, "Don't Be Nervous," *Management Today,* June 2003, p. 81.

105. P. Theibert, "Speechwriters of the World, Get Lost!" *The Wall Street Journal,* August 2, 1993, p. A16. This section adapted from C. Wahlstrom and B. Williams, *Learning Suc-cess: Being Your Best at College & Life,* 3rd ed. (Belmont, CA: Wadsworth, 2002), pp. 243–245.

106. L. Waters, *Secrets of Successful Speakers: How You Can Motivate, Captivate, and Persuade* (New York: McGraw-Hill, 1993), p. 203.

CHAPTER 16

1. Some new ideas are found in J. Quittner, "How Jeff Bezos Rules the Retail Space," *Fortune,* May 5, 2008, pp. 127–134; A. Taylor III, "Can This Car Save Ford?" *Fortune,* May 5, 2008, pp. 170–178; M. V. Copeland, "Boeing's Big Dream," *Fortune,* May 5, 2008, pp. 180–191; and R. J. Grossman, "Keep Pace with Older Workers," *HR Magazine,* May 2008, pp. 39–46.

2. See, for example, G. Colvin, "Who Wants to Be the Boss?" *Fortune,* February 20, 2006, pp. 76–78.

3. When labor costs rise, productivity slows down, unless other variables are changed. See M. Crutsinger, "Growth of Productivity Slows Down," *San Francisco Chronicle,* August 9, 2006, p. C3.

4. J. Welch, quoted in T. A. Stewart, "U.S. Productivity: First but Fading," *Fortune,* October 1992, p. 54.

5. Office of Macroeconomic Analysis, U.S. Treasury, "Profile of the Economy," March 2008, www.fms.treas.gov/bulletin/b2008-1poe.doc (accessed May 26, 2010). See also "Productivity Rises More Than Expected," CNN Money.com, May 7, 2008, http://money.cnn.com/2008/05/07/news/economy/productivity_ap.ap (accessed May 26, 2010).

6. "U.S. Productivity Growth in Quarter Tops Forecast," *The New York Times,* May 6, 2010, http://www.nytimes.com/2010/05/07/business/economy/07econ.html?src=busIn&scp=1&sq=2009%20productivity%20rate&st=cse (accessed May 31, 2010). See also J. Lahart, "Moment of Truth for Productivity Boom," *The Wall Street Journal,* May 6, 2010, pp. A1, A16.

7. See discussion by A. Tonelson and K. L. Kearns, "Trading Away Productivity," *The New York Times,* March 6, 2010, p. A19.

8. L. Uchitelle, "Productivity Finally Shows the Impact of Com-puters," *The New York Times,* March 12, 2000, sec. 3, p. 4; J. Reingold, M. Stepanek, and D. Brady, "Why the Productivity Revolution Will Spread," *BusinessWeek,* February 14, 2000, p. 112–118; G. S. Becker, "How the Skeptics Missed the Power of Productivity," *BusinessWeek,* January 1, 2004, p. 26; and J. Aversa, "Bernanke Bullish on Productivity Gains," *Business-Week Online,* August 31, 2006, http://www.businessweek.com/ap/financialnews/D8JRJTJO0.htm?chan=search (accessed May 31, 2010).

9. See study by B. P. Bosworth and J. E. Triplett, "Productivity Measurement Issues in Services Industries: 'Baumol's Disease' Has Been Cured," *The Brookings Institution,* September 1, 2003, www.brookings.org/views/articles/bosworth/200309.htm (accessed May 31, 2010). Also see H. R. Varian, "Information Technology May Have Been What Cured Low Service-Sector Productivity," *The New York Times,* February 12, 2004, p. C2.

10. W. Taylor, "Control in an Age of Chaos," *Harvard Business Review,* November–December 1994, pp. 64–70.

11. B. Horovitz, "Can Eateries Go Green, Earn Green?" *USA Today,* May 16, 2008, pp. 1B, 2B.

12. V. O'Connell, "Reversing Field, Macy's Goes Local," *The Wall Street Journal,* March 6, 2008, pp. B1, B8.

13. A. P. Sloan Jr., *My Years with General Motors* (New York: Doubleday, 1964).

14. A. Taylor III, "Hyundai Smokes the Competition," *Fortune,* January 5, 2010, http://money.cnn.com/2010/01/04/autos/hyundai_competition.fortune/index.htm (accessed June 8, 2010).

15. J. Levitz, "UPS Thinks Outside the Box on Driver Training," *The Wall Street Journal,* April 6, 2010, http://online.wsj.com/article/SB2000142405270230391210457516457382341 8844.html (accessed June 1, 2010).

16. D. Foust, "Big Brown's New Bag," *BusinessWeek,* July 19, 2004, pp. 54–56. See also M. Brewster and F. Dalzell, *Driving Change: The UPS Approach to Business* (New York: Hyperion, 2007).

17. W. G. Ouchi, "The Transmission of Control Through Organizational Hierarchy," *Academy of Management Journal,* June 1978, pp. 173–192; and R. E. Walton, "From Control to Commitment in the Workplace," *Harvard Business Review,* March–April 1985, pp. 76–84.

18. A description of Genentech's culture is provided by B. Morris, "The Best Place to Work Now," *Fortune,* January 23, 2006, pp. 79–86.

19. I. G. Seidenberg, quoted in S. E. Ante, "Giving the Boss the Big Picture," *BusinessWeek,* February 13, 2006, pp. 48–51.

20. R. S. Kaplan and D. P. Norton, "The Balanced Scorecard—Measures That Drive Performance," *Harvard Business Review,* January–February 1992, pp. 71–79.

21. For more on the uses of the balanced scorecard, see K. R. Thompson and N. J. Mathys, "The Aligned Balanced Scorecard: An Improved Tool for Building High Performance Organizations," *Organizational Dynamics,* October–December 2008, pp. 378–393; S. C. Voelpel and C. K. Streb, "A Balanced Scorecard for Managing the Aging Workforce," *Organizational Dynamics* 39 (2009), pp. 84–90; and R. S. Kaplan, D. P. Norton, and B. Rugelsjoen, "Managing Alliances with the Balanced Scorecard," *Harvard Business Review,* January–February 2010, pp. 114–120.

22. Kaplan and Norton, "The Balanced Scorecard—Measures That Drive Performance," 1992.

23. See M. Arndt, "Damn! Torpedoes Get Quiznos Back on Track," *Bloomberg Businessweek,* January 25, 2010, pp. 54–55.

24. R. S. Kaplan and D. P. Norton, "Having Trouble with Your Strategy? Then Map It," *Harvard Business Review,* September–October 2000, pp. 167–176. See also R. Kaplan and D. Norton, "Plotting Success with 'Strategy Maps,'" *Optimize,* February 2004, http://www.optimizemag.com/article/show-Article.jhtml?articleId=18200733 (accessed May 31, 2010).

25. R. Quinn, quoted in J. H. Lingle and W. A. Schiemann, "From Balanced Scorecard to Strategic Gauges: Is Measurement Worth It?" *American Management Association,* March 1996, pp. 56–61.

26. Ibid., 1996.

27. See G. L. Neilson, K. L. Martin, and E. Powers, "The Secrets to Successful Strategy Execution," *Harvard Business Review,* June 2008, pp. 61–70.

28. For discussions of how to measure services and intangible assets, see R. S. Kaplan and D. P. Norton, "Measuring the Strategic Readiness of Intangible Assets," *Harvard Business Review,* February 2004, pp. 52–63; K. M. Kroll, "Repurposing Metrics for HR," *HR Magazine,* July 2006, pp. 65–69; and B. Hindo, "Satisfaction Not Guaranteed," *BusinessWeek,* June 19, 2006, pp. 32–36.

29. For more about Ritz-Carlton, see C. Gallo, "How Ritz-Carlton Maintains Its Mystique," *BusinessWeek,* February 13, 2007, http://www.businessweek.com/smallbiz/content/feb2007/sb20070213_171606.htm?chan=search; and C. Gallo, "Employee Motivation the Ritz-Carlton Way," *BusinessWeek,* February 29, 2008, http://www.businessweek.com/smallbiz/content/feb2008/sb20080229_347490.htm?chan=search (both accessed May 26, 2010).

30. D. Jones, "Baldrige Winners Named," *USA Today,* November 24, 1999, p. 3B. See also D. Jones, "Baldrige Award Honors Record 7 Quality Winners," *USA Today,* November 26, 2003, p. B6; and R. O. Crockett, "Keeping Ritz Carlton at the Top of Its Game," *BusinessWeek Online,* May 29, 2006, http://www.businessweek.com/magazine/content/06_22/b3986130.htm?chan=search (accessed May 31, 2010). For more about the Baldrige awards, go to the Baldrige National Quality Program Web site at http://www.quality.nist.gov.

31. W. E. Deming, *Out of the Crisis* (Cambridge, MA: MIT Press, 1986), p. 5.

32. Larry Coburn, quoted in B. Kenney, "Whatever Happened to Quality?" *IndustryWeek,* April 2008, pp. 42–47.

33. R. N. Lussier, *Management: Concepts, Applications, Skill Development* (Cincinnati, OH: South-Western College Publishing, 1997), p. 260.

34. J. Goldstein, "As Doctors Get a Life, Strains Show," *The Wall Street Journal,* April 29, 2008, pp. A1, A14.

35. The Japanese have taken efficiency to a high level. See the example of Matsushita Electric Industrial Co., described in K. Hall, "No One Does Lean Like the Japanese," *BusinessWeek,* July 10, 2006, pp. 40–41.

36. O. Port, "The Push for Quality," *BusinessWeek,* June 8, 1987, pp. 130–136.

37. See H. Liao and M. Subramony, "Employee Customer Orientation in Manufacturing Organizations: Joint Influences of Customer Proximity and the Senior Leadership Team," *Journal of Applied Psychology,* March 2008, pp. 317–328. Also see P. Hellman, "Rating Your Dentist," *Management Review,* July–August 1998, p. 64.

38. S. Lohr, "Academia Dissects the Service Sector, but Is It a Science?" *The New York Times,* April 18, 2008, http://www.nytimes.com/2006/04/18/business/18services.html (accessed May 31, 2010).

39. F. X. Frei, "The Four Things a Service Business Must Get Right," *Harvard Business Review,* April 2008, pp. 70–80.

40. H. Rothman, "You Need Not Be Big to Benchmark," *Nation's Business,* December 1992, pp. 64–65.

41. K. Chang, "Enlisting Science's Lessons to Entice More Shoppers to Spend More," *The New York Times,* September 19, 2006, p. D3.

42. J. Pfeffer and R. I. Sutton, *Hard Facts, Dangerous Half Truths & Total Nonsense: Profiting from Evidence-Based Management* (Boston: Harvard Business School Press, 2006).

43. I. Austen, "In a Chevy, Engine from China and Transmission from Japan," *The New York Times,* March 26, 2008, pp. C1, C8.

44. C. L. Mann, "Globalization of I.T. Services and White-Collar Jobs: The Next Wave of Productivity Growth," December 2003, International Economics Policy Briefs, No. PB03-11, www.iie.com/publications/pb/pb03-11.pdf (accessed May 31, 2010). See also V. Postrel, "A Researcher Sees an Upside in the Outsourcing of Programming Jobs," *The New York Times,* January 29, 2004, p. C2.

45. H. Menzies, "Quality Counts When Wooing Overseas Clients," *Fortune,* June 1, 1997, www.fortune.com/fortune/subs/article/0,15114,378797,00.html (accessed May 31, 2010).

46. B. Ekeler, quoted in Menzies, 1997. See also M. V. Uzumeri, "ISO 9000 and Other Metastandards: Principles for Management Practice?" *Academy of Management Executive* 11, no 1. (1997), pp. 21–28; and T. B. Schoenrock, "ISO 9000: 2000 Gives Competitive Edge," *Quality Progress,* May 2002, p. 107.

47. A. Fisher, "Rules for Joining the Cult of Perfectability," *Fortune,* February 7, 2000, p. 206.

48. J. E. Morehouse, quoted in C. H. Deutsch, "Six Sigma Enlightenment," *The New York Times,* December 7, 1998, pp. C1, C7. For more on Six Sigma, see M. S. Sodhi and N. S. Sodhi, "Six Sigma Pricing," *Harvard Business Review,* May 2005, pp. 135–142; and J. Gordon, "Take *That* to the Bank," *Training,* June 2006, p. 41.

49. D. Jones, "Firms Aim for Six Sigma Efficiency," *USA Today,* July 21, 1998, pp. 1B, 2B.

50. See M. Poppendieck, "Why the Lean in Lean Six Sigma?" *The Project Management Best Practices Report,* June 2004, www.poppendieck.com/pdfs/Lean_Six_Sigma.pdf (accessed May 31, 2010).

51. Arner and Aston, 2004; and A. Aston, J. Carey, and O. Kharif, "Online Extra: The New Factory Floor, and Tomorrow's," *BusinessWeek Online,* May 3, 2004; www.businessweek.com/=@@vr3DfocQkImUSwOA/magazine/content/04_18/b3881601.htm (accessed May 31, 2010).

52. K. Day and J. Howard, "Albertsons Officials to Implement New Efficiency Program," *Reno Gazette-Journal,* February 25, 2004, pp. 1D, 3D.

53. Six Sigma has come under fire for hurting creativity, yet it was adopted as a major initiative by the conglomerate Textron in 2002, and since then the stock has soared. See B. Hindo and B. Grow, "Six Sigma: So Yesterday?" *Business-Week,* June 11, 2007, http://www.businessweek.com/-magazine/content/07_24/b4038409.htm (accessed May 31, 2010); and D. Jones, "CEO Expects Good Things as Textron Does Six Sigma Right," *USA Today,* January 21, 2008, p. 3B.

54. See R. J. Aldag and T. M. Stearns, Management (Cincinnati, OH: South-Western Publishing, 1987), pp. 653–654; D. Robertson and E. Anderson, "Control System and Task Environment Effects on Ethical Judgment: An Exploratory Study of Industrial Salespeople," *Organizational Science,* November 1993, pp. 617–629.

55. K. A. Merchant, *Control in Business Organizations* (Boston: Pitman, 1985), pp. 10–11; K. M. Bartol and D. C. Martin, *Management,* 3rd ed. (Burr Ridge, IL: Irwin/McGraw-Hill, 1998), pp. 533–534; and J. R. Schermerhorn Jr., *Management for Productivity,* 3rd ed. (New York: John Wiley & Sons, 1993), p. 592.

56. See D. Rice, "Climate Now Shifting on a Continental Scale," *USA Today,* May 15, 2008, p. 4D; and annual Rechargeable Recycling Corporation green guilt survey, reported in J. Kornblum, "Survey: More Americans Feel Guilty for Not Living Greener," *USA Today,* May 8, 2008, p. 5D.

57. E. Iwata, "Companies Discover Going Green Pays Off," *USA Today,* May 21, 2008, p. 4B. See also M. Weinstein, "It's Not Easy Being Green," *Training,* April 2008, pp. 20–25; M. Lavelle, "Three Ways That Firms Can Save," *U.S. News & World Report,* April 28, 2008, pp. 46–47; C. Laszlo, "Sustainability for Competitive Advantage," *San Francisco Chronicle,* May 14, 2008, p. B9; and I. DeBare, "Firms Honored for Green Ingenuity and Commitment," *San Francisco Chronicle,* May 21, 2008, pp. C1, C4.

58. Bartol and Martin, *Management,* 1998, pp. 532–533; and S. C. Certo, *Modern Management,* 8th ed. (Upper Saddle River, NJ: Prentice Hall, 2000), pp. 435–436.

59. J. P. Kotter, L. A. Schlesinger, and V. Sathe, *Organization: Text, Cases, and Readings on the Management of Organizational Design and Change* (Homewood, IL: Irwin, 1979).

60. Merchant, *Control in Business Organizations,* 1985.

61. G. Hamel, with B. Breen, *The Future of Management* (Boston: Harvard Business School Press, 2007), p. 6.

62. A. R. Rasbury, "New Kid on the Job: How to Get Off to a Good Start," *Black Enterprise,* May 1, 2008, http//www.thefreelibrary.com/New+kid+on+the+job:+{how+to+get+off+to+a+good+start.-a0178674810 (accessed June 6, 2010).

63. K. Holland, "For the Chief, a Little Skepticism Can Go a Long Way," *The New York Times,* May 25, 2008, business section, p. 14.

64. B. Taylor, "Why Zappos Pays New Employees to Quit—and You Should Too," *Harvard Business Publishing,* May 19, 2008, http://discussionleader.hbsp.com/taylor/2008/05/wy_zappos_pays_new_employees_t.html (accessed July 27, 2010).

credits

CHAPTER 14

Photos: p. 439: David Brabyn/Corbis; p. 441: Ryan Anson/AFP/Getty Images; p. 448: PhotoLink/Getty Images; p. 450: Enigma/Alamy; p. 454: AP Photo/Elaine Thompson; p. 458: Getty Images; p. 460: Virgin America/Bob Riha, Jr./AP Images.

CHAPTER 15

Photos: p. 474: Tom Pennington/Getty Images; p. 478: Photodisc/Getty Images; p. 481: Big Cheese Photo/Jupiter Images; p. 486: Image Source/Getty Images; p. 488: Image Source/PunchStock; p. 491: B Busco/Getty Images; p. 494: Image Source/PunchStock; p. 495: © Comstock/CORBIS; p. 497: © moodboard/CORBIS.

CHAPTER 16

Photos: p. 509: Getty Images; p. 514: © image100/CORBIS; p. 516: Royalty-free/Corbis; p. 522: Bloomberg via Getty Images; p. 525L: GABRIEL BOUYS/AFP/Getty Images; p. 525R: Michael Caulfield/Getty Images; p. 530: Courtesy of Viking Corporation; p. 535: LAURENT GILLIERON/epa/Corbis; p. 537: Brand X Pictures.

name index

A locator with an *n* indicates a note.

Gantt, Henry L., A2
Garcia, Alan, 128–129
Garcia, Ann, 13
Garcia, Jerry, 243
Gardenswartz, Lee, 90–91
Gates, Bill, 88, 212, 444
Gates, Melinda, 88
Gayda, Tim, 230
Gellos, Lou, 402
Gianopoulos, Jim, 366
Gilbert, Daniel, 215
Gilbreth, Frank, 40–42, 45, 53
Gilbreth, Lillian, 40–42, 45, 53
Goizueta, Robert, 113
Golden, Daniel, 336n
Goleman, Daniel, 344, 367n
Gonen, Ron, 133
Goodnight, Jim, 72, 265–266
Gore, Al, 13
Gorelick, Jamie, 446
Graen, George, 462
Graham, Donald, 469
Gratton, L., 420n
Green, Joshua, 243
Greenleaf, Robert, 463
Griffith, John D., 368
Grossman, Robert J., 303n
Grove, Andy, 206, 444
Grover, R., 366n
Gruber, Jeremy, 193
Gudzowsky, Terry, 230
Gupta, V., 126n, 447n
Gupta, Yogesh, 500–501
Gurgel, Udo, 230

H

Hackman, J. Richard, 388–390, 417
Hall, Edward T., 122, 127–128
Hall, Judith, 482
Halpern, D., 493n
Hamel, Gary, 39, 54, 163, 166, 538
Handy, Charles, 191
Hanges, P. J., 126n, 447n
Harrelson, Woody, 95
Harrison, Steve, 441–442
Hartman, Laura P., 100n
Harvey, James, 420
Hastings, Reed, 301–302, 320
Hatfield, J. D., 404n
Hayden, Anne, 187
Hedge, Alan, 398
Heistad, Kari, 133
Henderson, Fritz, 332
Henderson-Townsand, Judi, 107
Herbst, Moria, 403n
Hersey, Paul, 454–456
Herzberg, Frederick, 379–380, 388
Hewlett, Walter, 426
Hewlett, William, 239

Hills, Roderick, 136
Hodgson, Kent, 214n
Hoffer, Eric, 308
Hofstede, Geert, 123
Hogg, Bevil, 257
Holmes, Stanley, 201
Hopkins, Allison, 301–302
House, Robert J., 124, 125n, 126n, 447n, 452–454, 457
Howell, J. M., 461n
Huber, George P., 222n
Hughes, Howard, 365
Hunter, J. E., 223n
Hurd, Mark, 224
Huse, E. G., 316n
Huseman, R. C., 404n
Hymowitz, Carol, 37, 199, 501n

I

Idei, Nobuyuki, 327
Immelt, Jeffrey R., 17, 19, 408
Iorio, Luke, 357
Iverson, F. Kenneth, 418

J

Jackson, Peter, 366
Jacoby, Stefan, 159
Janis, Irvin, 420
Javidan, M., 125n, 126n, 447n
Jellicoe, Roger, 257
Jenkins, Holman W., Jr., 66n
Jobs, Steve, 15, 26, 156, 261–262, 440–441, 460, 485
Johnson, D. E., 455n
Johnson, Ian, 230n
Johnson, Lyndon, 219
Juran, Joseph M., 50, 56–57, 526

K

Kahan, Jim, 332
Kahn, R., 487n
Kanter, Rosabeth Moss, 105, 298, 327
Kaplan, David, 266n
Kaplan, Robert, 517–520
Katz, D., 487n
Katz, Robert, 28
Katzenbach, Jon R., 409
Katzenberg, Jeffrey, 365
Kelleher, Herb, 149, 210
Kelley, Gary, 210
Kelley, J., 232n
Kelley, Tom, 408
Kennedy, James A. C., 460
Kets de Vries, Manfred, 298
Kindler, Jeffrey, 238
King, B., 451n
King, Martin Luther, Jr., 460
Kinicki, A., 224n, 237n, 325n, 444n, 451n, 490n
Kirn, Walter, 296

company index

glossary/subject index

A page number with an *f* indicates a figure; an *n* a note; a *t,* a table

A

Abilene paradox, 420

Ability tests, 285

Absenteeism *When an employee doesn't show up for work,* 351

The Abyss (movie), 365

Accommodating, 427–428

Accountability *Describes expectation that managers must report and justify work results to the managers above them,* 250

Achievement-oriented style of leadership, 453

Acquired needs theory *Theory that states that there are three needs—achievement, affiliation, and power—that are the major motives determining people's behavior in the workplace,* 377–378

Acquisitions and mergers, 106–107, 315

Action plan *Course of action needed to achieve a stated goal,* 148

Action teams, 411

Adaptive change *Reintroduction of a familiar practice, the kind of change that has already been experienced within the same organization,* 326

Adaptive cycle, 143

Adaptive perspective *Perspective of organizational culture that assumes that the most effective cultures help organizations anticipate and adapt to environmental change,* 243

Adhocracy culture *Type of organizational culture that has an external focus and values flexibility,* 238

Adjourning *One of five stages of forming a team; the stage in which members of an organization prepare for disbandment,* 414

Administrative management *Management concerned with managing the total organization,* 40, 42–43

Administrative problems, 143

Advice teams, 411

Affective component of an attitude *The feelings or emotions one has about a situation,* 346

Affirmative action *The focus on achieving equality of opportunity,* 278–279

Age and diversity, 92–93

Age stereotypes, 354

Alcoholism, 361

Alignment, 521

"Always On" generation, 489–490

American Council on Education, 79

American Federation of Teachers, 75

American Management Association, 20, 298

American Metal Market, 418

American Psychological Association, 368

Americans with Disabilities Act *Passed by the U.S. Congress in 1992, act that prohibits discrimination against the disabled,* 94

Analytical style, 211

Analytics (business analytics) *Term used for sophisticated forms of business data analysis, such as portfolio analysis or time-series forecast,* 207–208

Analyzers *Organizations that allow other organizations to take the risks of product development and marketing and then imitate (or perhaps slightly improve on) what seems to work best,* 143

Anchoring and adjustment bias *The tendency to make decisions based on an initial figure,* 218–219

ASEAN; *see* Association of Southeast Asian Nations

Asia-Pacific Economic Cooperation (APEC) *Group of 21 Pacific Rim countries whose purpose is to improve economic and political ties,* 121

Assertiveness, 124–125

Assessment center *Company department where management candidates participate in activities for a few days while being assessed by evaluators,* 285

Asset management, 524

Assets, 524

Association of Certified Fraud Examiners, 89

Association of Executive Search Consultants, 93

Association of Southeast Asian Nations (ASEAN) *A trading bloc consisting of 11 countries in Asia: Brunei, Cambodia, China, Indonesia, Laos, Malaysia, Myanmar (Burma), the Philippines, Singapore, Thailand, and Vietnam,* 121

The Atlantic, 243

Attainable goals, 147–148

Attitude *A learned predisposition toward a given object; a mental position with regard to a fact, state, or person,* 346, 348–350

Attitude of wisdom, 37

Audits *Formal verifications of an organization's financial and operational systems,* 524–525

Authority *The right to perform or command; also, the rights inherent in a managerial position to make decisions, give orders, and utilize resources,* 250, 439

Automated experience, 203

Autonomy, 388–389

Availability bias *Tendency of managers to use information readily available from memory to make judgments; they tend to give more weight to recent events,* 218

Avatar (movie), 112, 364–366

Avoiding, 427

B

Background information, 281–282

Balance sheet *A summary of an organization's overall financial worth—assets and liabilities—at a specific point in time,* 524

Balanced scorecard *Gives top managers a fast but comprehensive view of the organization via four indicators: (1) customer satisfaction, (2) internal processes, (3) the organization's innovation and improvement activities, and (4) financial measures,* 513, 517–519

BARS; *see* Behaviorally anchored rating scale

Base pay *Consists of the basic wage or salary paid employees in exchange for doing their jobs,* 294

Basic assumptions, 239–240

BCG matrix *A means of evaluating strategic business units on the basis of their business growth rates and their share of the market,* 183

Behavior *Actions and judgments,* 347–348; *see also* Individual differences and behavior

Behavior modification, 391

Behavioral component of an attitude *Also known as intentional component, this refers to how one intends or expects to behave toward a situation,* 346

Behavioral-description interview *Type of structured interview in which the interviewer explores what applicants have done in the past,* 284

Behavioral leadership approaches *Attempts to determine the distinctive styles used by effective leaders,* 448–449

Behavioral science *Relies on scientific research for developing theories about human behavior that can be used to provide practical tools for managers,* 47

Behavioral style, 211

Behavioral viewpoint *Emphasizes the importance of understanding human behavior and of motivating employees toward achievement,* 44–47

Behaviorally anchored rating scale (BARS) *Employee gradations in performance rated according to scales of specific behaviors,* 291

Benchmarking *A process by which a company compares its performance with that of high-performing organizations,* 328, 532

Benefits (fringe benefits) *Additional nonmonetary forms of compensation,* 295

Bias in decision making, 195, 217–219

Big Five personality dimensions *They are (1) extroversion, (2) agreeableness, (3) conscientiousness, (4) emotional stability, and (5) openness to experience,* 340

Birth stage The *nonbureaucratic stage, the stage in which the organization is created,* 261

Black Enterprise, 538

The Blind Side (movie), 525

Bloomberg BusinessWeek magazine, 318, 321, 333

Board of directors, 72

Board of regents, 72

Board of trustees, 72

Body movements and gestures, 482

Bonuses *Cash awards given to employees who achieve specific performance objectives,* 245, 395

Bottom line, 524

Boundaryless organization *A fluid, highly adaptive organization whose members, linked by information technology, come together to collaborate on common tasks; the collaborators may include competitors, suppliers, and customers,* 59, 257–258

Bounded rationality *One type of nonrational decision making; the ability of decision makers to be rational is limited by numerous constraints,* 201–202

Boycotts, 76–77

Brainstorming *Technique used to help groups generate multiple ideas and alternatives for solving problems; individuals in a group meet and review a problem to be solved, then silently generate ideas, which are collected and later analyzed,* 223–224

Brainwriting, 224

Brands, 181

Brazil, 190–191

Break-even analysis *A way of identifying how much revenue is needed to cover the total costs of developing and selling a product,* A3–A4

Budget *A formal financial projection,* 522–523

Buffers *Administrative changes that managers can make to reduce the stressors that lead to employee burnout,* 362

Bureau of Labor Statistics, 114

Bureaucracy, 43

Bureaucratic control *The use of rules, regulations, and formal authority to guide performance,* 516

Burnout *State of emotional, mental, and even physical exhaustion,* 361

Business analytics, 207–208

Business plan *Document that outlines a proposed firm's goals, the strategy for achieving them, and the standards for measuring success,* 164

BusinessWeek magazine, 19, 59, 109, 259, 271, 280, 314, 318, 321, 333, 417–418, 445, 484

C

CAFTA-DR; *see* Central American Free Trade Agreement

CAI; *see* Computer-assisted instruction

Career paths, 139

Cascading *Objectives are structured in a unified hierarchy, becoming more specific at lower levels of the organization,* 153

Catalyst, 93

Causal attribution *The activity of inferring causes for observed behavior,* 356

Cell phones, 493

Central American Free Trade Agreement (CAFTA-DR) *Trade agreement involving the United States and Costa Rica, the Dominican Republic, El Salvador, Guatemala, Honduras, and Nicaragua and which is aimed at reducing tariffs and other barriers to free trade,* 121

Centralized authority *Organizational structure in which important decisions are made by upper managers— power is concentrated at the top,* 251

Chain of command, 249

Change, 439; *see also* Organizational change

Change agent *A person inside or outside the organization who can be a catalyst in helping deal with old problems in new ways,* 315

Changing stage, 328

Charisma *Form of personal attraction that inspires acceptance and support,* 460

Charismatic leadership *Once assumed to be an individual inspirational and motivational characteristic of particular leaders, now considered part of transformational leadership,* 460

Chauffeur-driven computer-aided decision-making systems, 225

Cheaper by the Dozen (Gilbreth), 42

China, 98–99, 309–310, 318

Clan culture *Type of organizational culture that has an internal focus and values flexibility rather than stability and control,* 237–238

Classical viewpoint *In the historical perspective, the viewpoint that emphasizes finding ways to manage work more efficiently; it has two branches—scientific and administrative,* 40–43, 197–200

Clawbacks *A term used to refer to a community's rescinding tax breaks when firms don't deliver promised jobs,* 75

Closed system *A system that has little interaction with its environment,* 52

Coaching, 244

Coalition tactics, 442

Code of ethics *A formal, written set of ethical standards that guide an organization's actions,* 84

Coercive power *One of five sources of a leader's power that results from the authority to punish subordinates,* 440

Cognitive component of an attitude *The beliefs and knowledge one has about a situation,* 346

Cognitive dissonance *Term coined by social psychologist Leon Festinger to describe the psychological discomfort a person experiences between what he or she already knows and new information or contradictory behavior, or by inconsistency among a person's beliefs, attitudes, and/or actions,* 347–348

Cohesiveness *The tendency of a group or team to stick together,* 414, 419–420

Collaborating, 428

Collaborative behavior, 420

Collaborative computing *Using state-of-the-art computer software and hardware to help people work together,* 11

Collective bargaining *Negotiations between management and employees regarding disputes over compensation, benefits, working conditions, and job security,* 276

Commission, 395

Common purpose *A goal that unifies employees or members and gives everyone an understanding of the organization's reason for being,* 249

Communication The transfer of information and understanding from one person to another, 474–475
  barriers to, 478–484
  conflict and, 426
  cultural differences, 127–128, 476, 481–482
  digital, 489–493
  effectiveness improvement, 494–498
  ethical dilemma, 504–505

  formal channels, 486–488
  gender differences, 482–484
  globalization and, 104–105, 127–128
  informal channels, 488
  innovation and, 324
  managers and, 20, 486–488
  in measurement-managed firms, 521
  media for, 476–477
  meetings, 485
  nonverbal, 481–483
  process of, 475–476

Comparison, 382

Compensation *Payment comprising three parts: wages or salaries, incentives, and benefits,* 6, 276–277, 294, 394–399

Competitive advantage *The ability of an organization to produce goods or services more effectively than its competitors do, thereby outperforming them,* 8–9, 167, 310, 508

Competitive intelligence *Gaining information about competitors' activities so that one can anticipate their moves and react appropriately,* 174

Competitors *People or organizations that compete for customers or resources,* 73, 309

Complexity, 438

Compressed workweek, 397

Compromising, 428

Computer-aided decision making, 224–225

Computer-assisted instruction (CAI) *Training in which computers are used to provide additional help or to reduce instructional time,* 289

Conceptual *skills* *Skills that consist of the ability to think analytically, to visualize an organization as a whole and understand how the parts work together,* 28–29

Conceptual style, 211

Concurrent engineering, 257

Confirmation bias *Biased way of thinking in which people seek information to support their point of view and discount data that does not,* 218

Conflict *Process in which one party perceives that its interests are being opposed or negatively affected by another party,* 423–429

Conflict resolution, 315

Conscientiousness, 340–341

Consensus *General agreement; group solidarity,* 222–223

Consideration, 449

Constructive conflict *Functional conflict that benefits the main purposes of the organization and serves its interest,* 423–424, 428–429

Consultation, 442

Contemporary perspective *In contrast to the historical perspective, the business approach that includes three viewpoints—systems, contingency, and quality-management,* 39, 50
  contingency viewpoint, 53–55, 259
  quality-management viewpoint, 56–57
  systems viewpoint, 51–52

Content perspectives *Also known as need-based perspectives; theories that emphasize the needs that motivate people,* 374
　acquired needs theory, 377–378
　ERG theory, 376–377
　hierarchy of needs theory, 374–376
　Theory X/Theory Y, 46, 374
　two-factor theory, 379–380
Contingency approach *The belief that the effectiveness of leadership behavior depends on the situation at hand,* 450–457
Contingency design *The process of fitting the organization to its environment,* 259–262
Contingency factors, 388, 390
Contingency leadership model *Fiedler's theory (1951) that leader effectiveness is determined by both the personal characteristics of leaders and by the situations in which leaders find themselves; the leader's style is either task-oriented or relationship-oriented, and it must be determined which style fits the situation at hand,* 450–452
Contingency planning *Also known as scenario planning and scenario analysis; the creation of alternative hypothetical but equally likely future conditions,* 177–178
Contingency viewpoint *In opposition to the classical viewpoint; a manager's approach should vary according to—that is, be contingent on—the individual and the environmental situation,* 53–55, 259
Continuous improvement *Ongoing, small, incremental improvements in all parts of an organization,* 529–530
Continuous improvement teams *Small groups of volunteers or workers and supervisors who meet intermittently to discuss workplace- and quality-related problems,* 411–412
Control
　areas of, 515–516
　balanced scorecard, 513, 517–519
　ethical dilemma, 545
　financial tools for, 522–525
　levels of, 515
　measurement management, 519–521
　need for, 510–512
　performance management, 510–514
　productivity management, 507–509
　strategy maps, 519–520
　system barriers, 536–537
　system success, 535–536
　total quality management
　　core principles, 56–57, 528–530
　　Deming management, 526–527
　　RATER scale, 530
　　tools and techniques, 531–534
Control process steps *The four steps in the process of controlling: (1) establish standards; (2) measure performance; (3) compare performance to standards; and (4) take corrective action, if necessary,* 512–514

Control standard *The first step in the control process; the performance standard (or just standard) is the desired performance level for a given goal,* 512–513
Control systems, 535–537
Controlling *Monitoring performance, comparing goals, and taking corrective action as needed,* 15, 439, 508, 510
Cooperative conflict, 423
Coordinated effort *The coordination of individual efforts into a group or organization-wide effort,* 249
Corporate culture; *see* Organizational culture
Corporate social responsibility (CSR) *The notion that corporations are expected to go above and beyond following the law and making a profit, to take actions that will benefit the interests of society as well as of the organization,* 85–89
Cost-focus strategy *One of Porter's four competitive strategies; to keep the costs, and hence prices, of a product or service below those of competitors and to target a narrow market,* 181
Cost-leadership strategy *One of Porter's four competitive strategies; keeping the costs, and hence prices, of a product or service below those of competitors and targeting the wider market,* 180
Counterproductive work behaviors (CWB) *Types of behavior that harm employees and the organization as a whole,* 352
Countertrading *Bartering goods for goods,* 116
Crazy Heart (movie), 525
Creativity *The process of developing something new or unique,* 318
Crisis management, 359
Cross-functional team *A team that is staffed with specialists pursuing a common objective,* 411
CSR; *see* Corporate social responsibility
Cultural adaptability, 130
Cultural differences
　communication, 127–128, 476, 481–482
　conflict management, 427
　Hofstede & GLOBE models, 123–126
　innovation, 321
　interpersonal space, 127
　language, 127
　national culture, 122–123
　religion, 129
　time orientation, 128–129
Culture *A shared set of beliefs, values, knowledge, and patterns of behavior common to a group of people,* 122–123, 516; *see also* Organizational culture
Current assets, 524
Customer divisions *Divisional structures in which activities are grouped around common customers or clients,* 253–254
Customer perspective, 519, 520f
Customers *Those who pay to use an organization's goods or services,* 8, 73–74, 528–529
CWB; *see* Counterproductive work behaviors

D

The Daily Show, 217
Dashboard, 517

Databases *Computerized collections of interrelated files*, 11

Deadlines, 154

Death by Meeting (Lencioni), 485

Debt management ratios, 524

Decentralized authority *Organizational structure in which important decisions are made by middle-level and supervisory-level managers—power is delegated throughout the organization*, 251

Decentralized control *An approach to organizational control that is characterized by informal and organic structural arrangements, the opposite of bureaucratic control*, 516

Deciding to decide *A manager agrees that he or she must decide what to do about a problem or opportunity and take effective decision-making steps*, 216–217

Decision *A choice made from among available alternatives*, 196

Decision making *The process of identifying and choosing alternative courses of action*, 196
  barriers to, 215–219
  bias in, 195, 217–219
  ethical, 212–214, 232
  evidence-based, 204–208
  group, 220–225
  nonrational, 201–203
  rational, 197–200
  styles, 209–211

Decision-making style *A style that reflects the combination of how an individual perceives and responds to information*, 209–211

Decision tree *Graph of decisions and their possible consequences, used to create a plan to reach a goal*, 212–214

Decisional roles *One of three types of managerial roles: managers use information to make decisions to solve problems or take advantage of opportunities. The four decision-making roles are entrepreneur, disturbance handler, resource allocator, and negotiator*, 20, 22–23

Declining careers, 139

Decoding *Interpreting and trying to make sense of a message*, 475

Defenders *Experts at producing and selling narrowly defined products or services*, 142

Defensive avoidance *When a manager cannot find a good solution and follows by (a) procrastinating, (b) passing the buck, or (c) denying the risk of any negative consequences*, 216

Defensive strategy *Also called retrenchment strategy; one of three grand strategies, this strategy involves reduction in the organization's efforts*, 172

Delegation *The process of assigning managerial authority and responsibility to managers and employees lower in the hierarchy*, 235, 251, 456

Delphi technique *A group process that uses physically dispersed experts who fill out questionnaires to anonymously generate ideas; the judgments are combined and in effect averaged to achieve a consensus of expert opinion*, 224

Deming management *Ideas proposed by W. Edwards Deming for making organizations more responsive, more democratic, and less wasteful*, 526–527

Demographic forces *Influences on an organization arising from changes in the characteristics of a population, such as age, gender, ethnic origin, and so on*, 79, 312

Demotion, 297

Departmental objectives, 153

Development *The education of professionals and managers in the skills they will need to do their jobs*, 288–289

The Devil Wears Prada (movie), 424

Devil's advocacy *Taking the side of an unpopular point of view for the sake of argument*, 429

Diagnosis *Analysis of underlying causes*, 198, 315–317

Dialectic method *The process of having two people or groups play opposing roles in a debate in order to better understand a proposal*, 429

Diamonds in the Data Mine (Loveman), 207

Differential rate system, 41

Differentiation *The tendency of the parts of an organization to disperse and fragment*, 260–261

Differentiation strategy *One of Porter's four competitive strategies; offer products or services that are of a unique and superior value compared to those of competitors and to target a wide market*, 181

Digital communication, 489–493

Directive style, 210, 453

Disabled people, 94

Disciplining and demotion, 297

Discrimination *Prejudicial outlook; when people are hired or promoted—or denied hiring or promotion—for reasons not relevant to the job*, 95, 278

Dismissals, 297–298

Disseminator roles, 22–23

Distributor *A person or an organization that helps another organization sell its goods and services to customers*, 74

Disturbance handler roles, 22–23

Diversification *Strategy by which a company operates several businesses in order to spread the risk*, 182–183

Diversity *All the ways people are unlike and alike—the differences and similarities in age, gender, race, religion, ethnicity, sexual orientation, capabilities, and socioeconomic background*, 10, 90–95, 508

Division of labor *Also known as work specialization; arrangement of having discrete parts of a task done by different people. The work is divided into particular tasks assigned to particular workers*, 249, 416

Divisional objectives, 153

Divisional structure *The third type of organizational structure, whereby people with diverse occupational specialties are put together in formal groups according to products and/or services, customers and/or clients, or geographic regions*, 253–254

Downsizing, 297

Downward communication *Communication that flows from a higher level to a lower level*, 487

Drucker's tips for leadership effectiveness, 449t

Drug abuse, 361

Dumping *A foreign company's practice of exporting products abroad at a price lower than the home-market price, or even below the costs of production, in order to drive down the price of the domestic product,* 118

Dysfunctional conflict, 423

E

E-business *Using the Internet to facilitate every aspect of running a business,* 11

E-commerce *Electronic commerce; the buying and selling of goods and services over computer networks,* 10, 105

E-Leadership (Mills), 465

E-leadership *Leadership that involves one-to-one, one-to-many, and within and between-group and collective interactions via information technology,* 464–465

E-mail *Electronic mail; text messages and documents transmitted over a computer network,* 11, 493

E-Verify, 84, 282

EAPs; *see* Employee assistance programs

Early behaviorism, 44–46

Economic communities, 119–121

Economic forces *General economic conditions and trends—unemployment, inflation, interest rates, economic growth—that may affect an organization's performance,* 77–78

Economic performance, 80

Education, 94, 398

Effectiveness *To achieve results, to make the right decisions, and to successfully carry them out so that they achieve the organization's goals,* 5, 198–199

Efficiency *Using resources—people, money, raw materials, and the like—wisely and cost-effectively,* 5, 9–10

Electronic brainstorming (brainwriting) *Technique in which members of a group come together over a computer network to generate ideas and alternatives,* 224

Embargo *A complete ban on the import and/or export of certain products,* 118

Emotional intelligence *The ability to cope, to empathize with others, and to be self-motivated,* 344

Employee assistance programs (EAPs) *Host of programs aimed at helping employees to cope with stress, burnout, substance abuse, health-related problems, family and marital issues, and any general problems that negatively influence job performance,* 362

Employee-centered behavior, 448

Employee characteristics, 453

Employee engagement *An individual's involvement, satisfaction, and enthusiasm for work,* 349–350

Employee motivation
compensation and other rewards, 394–399
content perspectives, 374–380
ethical dilemma, 404–405
job design perspectives, 387–390
for performance, 372–373

process perspectives, 381–386
reinforcement perspectives, 391–393

Employee organizations, 75

Employee replacement, 296–298

Employee stock ownership plan (ESOP), 72

Employees; *see also* Human resource management; Individual differences and behavior
ethics promotion among, 84–85
as internal stakeholders, 72
organizational change and, 313
people process and, 184–185
resistance from, 324–328, 327–328

Employment tests *Tests legally considered to consist of any procedure used in the employment selection process,* 285–286

Enacted values *Values and norms actually exhibited in the organization,* 239

Encoding *Translating a message into understandable symbols or language,* 475

Engineering problems, 143

Enterprise resource planning (ERP) *Software information systems for integrating virtually all aspects of a business,* 509, 519

Entrepreneur *Someone who sees a new opportunity for a product or service and launches a business to try to realize it,* 22–23, 25–27, 164, 320–321

Entrepreneurial problems, 143

Entrepreneurship *The process of taking risks to try to create a new enterprise,* 24–27

Environmental factors, 453

Environmental scanning *Careful monitoring of an organization's internal and external environments to detect early signs of opportunities and threats that may influence the firm's plans,* 174

Equal Employment Opportunity (EEO) Commission *U.S. panel whose job it is to enforce antidiscrimination and other employment related laws,* 92, 276–279

Equity theory *In the area of employee motivation, the focus on how employees perceive how fairly they think they are being treated compared with others,* 381–383

ERG theory *Theory proposed by Clayton Alderfer that assumes that three basic needs influence behavior—existence, relatedness, and growth—represented by the letters E, R, and G,* 376–377

ERP; *see* Enterprise resource planning

Escalation of commitment bias *When decision makers increase their commitment to a project despite negative information about it,* 219

ESOP (employee stock ownership plan), 72

Espoused values *Explicitly stated values and norms preferred by an organization,* 239

Esteem needs, 374–375

Ethical behavior *Behavior accepted as "right" as opposed to "wrong" according to recognized ethical standards,* 80–81

Ethical climate *A term that refers to employees' perceptions about the extent to which work environments support ethical behavior,* 84

Ethical dilemma *A situation in which you have to decide whether to pursue a course of action that may benefit you or your organization but that is unethical or even illegal,* 80

  atrial fibrillation treatment, 161

  auto industry liability, 65–66

  charitable donations, 305

  covering for a laid-off friend, 471

  decision making, 232

  employee-customer confrontations, 404–405

  employee monitoring, 545

  Fake Bad Scale, 367–368

  false statements on blogs, 504–505

  for-profit college recruiting of homeless, 335–336

  global management, 136

  health history, 100, 193

  management decisions, 35

  marijuana smoking, 435

  organizational culture, 268

Ethical leaders, 461

Ethical responsibilities

  approaches to, 81–82

  in decision making, 198, 212–214

  defining ethics and values, 80–81

  Kohlberg's theories, 83

  as management challenge, 11–12, 508

  of organizations, 84–85

  Sarbanes-Oxley, 83

  social responsibility and, 85–89

  white-collar crime, 82–83

Ethics *Generally accepted standards of right and wrong that influence behavior; these standards may vary among countries and cultures,* 80–81

Ethics officer *A person trained about matters of ethics in the workplace, particularly about resolving ethical dilemmas,* 212

Ethnicity and race, 93–94, 354–355

Ethnocentric managers *Managers who believe that their native country, culture, language, and/or behavior are superior to others,* 111

Ethnocentrism *The belief that one's native country, culture, language, abilities, and/or behavior are superior to those of another culture,* 95

European Union (EU) *Union of 25 trading partners in Europe,* 79, 120

Evaluation, 200, 315–317

Evidence-based decision making, 204–208

Evidence-based management *Form of management that believes in translating principles based on best evidence into organizational practice, bringing rationality to the decision-making process,* 37–38, 163, 204–208, 517

Evolving management theories, 38–39

Exchange rate *The rate at which one country's currency is exchanged for another country's currency,* 119

Exchange tactics, 442

Execution (Bossidy and Charan), 184–186

Execution *As proposed by Larry Bossidy and Ram Charan, execution is not simply tactics, it is a central part of any company's strategy; it consists of using questioning, analysis, and follow-through in order to mesh strategy with reality, align people with goals, and achieve results promised,* 184–187, 199, 324

Executive functioning, 22

Existence needs, 377

Expatriates *People living or working in a foreign country,* 130

Expectancy *The belief that a particular level of effort will lead to a particular level of performance,* 383–384

Expectancy theory *Theory that suggests that people are motivated by two things: (1) how much they want something and (2) how likely they think they are to get it,* 383–385

Expenses, 524

Expert power *One of five sources of a leader's power, resulting from specialized information or expertise,* 440

Expertise, 203

Exporting *Producing goods domestically and selling them outside the country,* 115

External audit *Formal verification by outside experts of an organization's financial accounts and statements,* 525

External communication *Communication between people inside and outside an organization,* 488

External dimensions of diversity *Human differences that have an element of choice; they consist of the personal characteristics that people acquire, discard, or modify throughout their lives,* 92

External locus of control, 342

External recruiting *Attracting job applicants from outside the organization,* 280–281

External stakeholders *People or groups in the organization's external environment that are affected by it. This environment includes the task environment and the general environment,* 73–79

Extinction *The withholding or withdrawal of positive rewards for desirable behavior, so that the behavior is less likely to occur in the future,* 392

Extrinsic reward *The payoff, such as money, that a person receives from others for performing a particular task,* 373

Extroversion, 340–341

Exxon Valdez, 311

Eye contact, 481

F

FAA (Federal Aviation Administration), 76

Facial expressions, 481–482

Fads, 163

Failure, celebrating, 321–323

Fair Labor Standards Act *Legislation passed in 1938 that established minimum living standards for workers engaged in interstate commerce, including provision of a federal minimum wage,* 276

Fairness, 82

Fast Company magazine, 19, 26
Feasibility, 198
Federal Aviation Administration (FAA), 76
Federal Railroad Administration (FRA), 252
Federal Reserve Bank, 216, 253
Feedback *The receiver's expression of his or her reaction to the sender's message. Also, the information about the reaction of the environment to the outputs that affect the inputs; one of four parts of a system, along with inputs, outputs, and transformational processes,* 51, 372–373, 388, 390, 475–476
Femininity, 124–125
Figurehead roles, 22–23
Financial area of control, 516
Financial institutions, 76
Financial perspective, 518, 520f
Financial statement *Summary of some aspect of an organization's financial status,* 524
Finding Nemo (movie), 26
Firings, 297
First-line managers *One of three managerial levels; also called supervisory managers; they make the short-term operating decisions, directing the daily tasks of nonmanagerial personnel,* 18
Fit perspective *Perspective of organizational culture that assumes that an organization's culture must align, or fit, with its business or strategic context,* 168, 242, 262, 387–390
Fixed assets, 524
Fixed budget *Allocation of resources on the basis of a single estimate of costs,* 523
Flavor of the Month (Best), 163
Flexible budgets, 523
Flexible workplace, 396–397
Flow of work, 49
Flowchart *A useful graphical tool for representing the sequence of events required to complete a project and for laying out "what-if" scenarios,* A–A2
Focused-differentiation strategy *One of Porter's four competitive strategies; to offer products or services that are of unique and superior value compared with those of competitors and to target a narrow market,* 181
For-profit organizations, 19, 246
Forbes magazine, 16, 19
Forced ranking performance review systems *Performance review systems whereby all employees within a business unit are ranked against one another, and grades are distributed along some sort of bell curve, like students being graded in a college course,* 293
Forcing, 428
Forecast *A projection of the future,* 177
Foreign firms; *see* Global management
Formal appraisals *Appraisals conducted at specific times throughout the year and based on performance measures that have been established in advance,* 293
Formal aspects of a company, 345
Formal communication channels *Communications that follow the chain of command and are recognized as official,* 486–488

Formal group *A group, headed by a leader, that is established to do something productive for the organization,* 409–410
Formal statements, 243–244
Forming *The first of the five stages of forming a team, in which people get oriented and get acquainted,* 413
Fortune magazine, 6, 16, 19, 72, 145, 149, 156, 167, 198, 257, 265, 272–273, 323, 371, 412, 441, 444, 458, 463, 489, 516
Four generic strategies; *see* Porter's four competitive strategies
Four management functions *The management process that "gets things done": planning, organizing, leading, and controlling,* 14–15, 140
FRA (Federal Railroad Administration), 252
Franchising *A form of licensing in which a company allows a foreign company to pay it a fee and a share of the profit in return for using the first company's brand name and a package of materials and services,* 116
Free trade *The movement of goods and services among nations without political or economic obstruction,* 117
Fringe benefits, 295
Frustration-regression component, 377
Full-range leadership *Approach that suggests that leadership behavior varies along a full range of leadership styles, from take-no-responsibility (laissez-faire) "leadership" at one extreme through transactional leadership, to transformational leadership at the other extreme,* 458–461
Functional conflict, 423
Functional managers *Manager who is responsible for just one organizational activity,* 16, 19
Functional structure *The second type of organizational structure, whereby people with similar occupational specialties are put together in formal groups,* 252–253
Fundamental attribution bias *Tendency whereby people attribute another person's behavior to his or her personal characteristics rather than to situational factors,* 356
Future orientation, 124–125

G

Gainsharing *The distribution of savings or "gains" to groups of employees who reduce costs and increase measurable productivity,* 396
Gantt chart *A kind of time schedule—a specialized bar chart that shows the relationship between the kind of work tasks planned and their scheduled completion dates,* A2–A3
GATT (General Agreement on Tariffs and Trade), 119
Gen Yers, 52, 290, 339, 396, 489–490
Gender, 93, 198, 482–484
Gender egalitarianism, 124–125
Gender studies, 445–446
General Agreement on Tariffs and Trade (GATT), 119
General and Industrial Management (Fayol), 42

General environment *Also called macroenvironment; in contrast to the task environment, it includes six forces: economic, technological, sociocultural, demographic, political-legal, and international,* 77–79

General manager *Manager who is responsible for several organizational activities,* 16, 19

Geocentric managers *Managers who accept that there are differences and similarities between home and foreign personnel and practices and that they should use whatever techniques are most effective,* 111

Geographic divisions *Divisional structures in which activities are grouped around defined regional locations,* 253–254

A Geography of Time (Levine), 129

Get Rid of the Performance Review! (Culbert), 290

Glass ceiling *The metaphor for an invisible barrier preventing women and minorities from being promoted to top executive jobs,* 93

Global economy *The increasing tendency of the economies of the world to interact with one another as one market instead of as many national markets,* 105–106

Global management
  careers in, 108–111
  cultural differences
    blunder avoidance, 133–134
    communication, 127–128
    GLOBE model, 124–126
    Hofstede model, 123–124
    interpersonal space, 127
    language, 127
    national culture, 122–123
    religion, 129
    time orientation, 128–129
  ethical dilemma, 136
  expatriate managers, 130
  free trade and regional economic cooperation, 117–121
  globalization, 104–107
  multinational company expansion, 112–116
  national culture, 133–134

Global outsourcing *Using suppliers outside the United States to provide labor, goods, and/or services,* 114

Global village *The "shrinking" of time and space as air travel and electronic media make it easier for the people of the globe to communicate with one another,* 104–105

Global warming, 87–88

Globalization *The trend of the world economy toward becoming a more interdependent system,* 10, 104, 309–310, 508

GLOBE project *Massive, ongoing cross-cultural investigation of nine cultural dimensions involved in leadership and organizational processes. Started by Robert J. House, GLOBE stands for Global Leadership and Organizational Behavior Effectiveness,* 124–126, 446–447

Goal *Also known as objective; a specific commitment to achieve a measurable result within a stated period of time,* 147–149

Goal displacement *The primary goal is subsumed to a secondary goal,* 221

Goal-setting theory *Employee-motivation approach that employees can be motivated by goals that are specific and challenging but achievable,* 386

Government Accountability Office, 403

Government regulators *Regulatory agencies that establish ground rules under which organizations may operate,* 76

Grand strategy *Second step of the strategic-management process; it explains how the organization's mission is to be accomplished. Three grand strategies are growth, stability, and defensive,* 171–173

Grapevine *The unofficial communication system of the informal organization,* 488

Greece, 356–357

Greenfield ventures *A wholly-owned foreign subsidiary that the owning organization has built from scratch,* 116

Greenwashing, 313

Grey's Anatomy (TV show), 424

Group decision making, 220–225

Group demands, 360

Group-driven computer-aided decision-making systems, 225

Group *Two or more freely interacting individuals who share collective norms, share collective goals, and have a common identity,* 409; *see also* Team
  conflict management, 423–429
  development stages, 413–414
  ethical dilemma, 435
  team versus, 408–412

Group cohesiveness *A "we" feeling that binds group members together,* 414

Groupthink *A cohesive group's blind unwillingness to consider alternatives. This occurs when group members strive for agreement among themselves for the sake of unanimity and avoid accurately assessing the decision situation,* 221, 420–422

Grown Up Digital (Tapscott), 490

Growth needs, 377

Growth strategy *One of three grand strategies, this strategy involves expansion—as in sales revenues, market share, number of employees, or number of customers or (for nonprofits) clients served,* 172

H

Halo effect *An effect in which we form a positive impression of an individual based on a single trait,* 355–356

Happiness and life goals, 13, 508

Harvard Business Publishing, 539

Harvard Business Review, 439

Hassles, 359

Hawthorne studies, 45–46

Health and safety laws, 276–277

Hero *A person whose accomplishments embody the values of the organization,* 240

Heuristics *Strategies that simplify the process of making decisions,* 217–219

Hierarchy culture *Type of organizational culture that has an internal focus and values stability and control over flexibility,* 238

Hierarchy of authority *Also known as chain of command; a control mechanism for making sure the right people do the right things at the right time,* 249

Hierarchy of needs theory *Psychological structure proposed by Maslow whereby people are motivated by five levels of needs: (1) physiological, (2) safety, (3) love, (4) esteem, and (5) self-actualization,* 46, 374–376

High-context culture *Culture in which people rely heavily on situational cues for meaning when communicating with others,* 123

High power distance, 123

High uncertainty avoidance, 123

Historical perspective *In contrast to the contemporary perspective, the view of management that includes the classical, behavioral, and quantitative viewpoints,* 39

   behavioral viewpoint, 44–47

   classical viewpoint, 40–43

   quantitative viewpoint, 48–49

Hofstede model of four cultural dimensions *Model proposed by Geert Hofstede that identified four dimensions along which national cultures can be placed: individualism/collectivism, power distance, uncertainty avoidance, and masculinity/femininity,* 123–124

Holistic hunch, 203

Holistic wellness program *Program that goes beyond stress reduction by encouraging employees to strive for a harmonious and productive balance of physical, mental, and social well-being brought about by the acceptance of one's personal responsibility for developing and adhering to a health promotion program,* 362

Hollow corporation, 255–257

Hollow organization, 255–257

Horizontal communication *Communication that flows within and between work units; its main purpose is coordination,* 487–488

Horizontal loading, 388

Horizontal specialization, 248

Horn-and-halo effect, 355–356

Hostile environment, 279

Hours worked, 20–21

Human capital *Economic or productive potential of employee knowledge, experience, and actions,* 59, 273

Human relations movement *The movement that proposed that better human relations could increase worker productivity,* 46

Human resource inventory *A report listing an organization's employees by name, education, training, languages, and other important information,* 275

Human resource (HR) management *The activities managers perform to plan for, attract, develop, and retain a workforce,* 272

   compensation and benefits, 294–295

   ethical dilemma, 305

   legal requirements, 276–279

   performance appraisal, 290–293

   promotions, transfers, discipline, and dismissals, 296–298

   recruitment and selection, 280–286

   strategic planning and, 272–275

Human resources area of control, 516

Human skills *The ability to work well in cooperation with other people in order to get things done,* 29

Humane orientation, 124–125

Humane Society of the United States, 76

Hygiene factors *Factors associated with job dissatisfaction— such as salary, working conditions, interpersonal relationships, and company policy—all of which affect the job context or environment in which people work,* 379–380

I

Idealized influence, 460

Identity theft *A violation of privacy in which thieves hijack one's name and identity and use one's good credit rating to get cash or buy things,* 492

Ignoring-randomness bias, 195

The Illusions of Entrepreneurship (Shane), 321

IMF; *see* International Monetary Fund

Implementation, 184–187, 199

Import quota *A trade barrier in the form of a limit on the numbers of a product that can be imported,* 118

Importing *Buying goods outside the country and reselling them domestically,* 114

In-group collectivism, 124–125

In-group exchange, 462

In Search of Excellence (Peters), 38

Inc. magazine, 19, 69, 164, 259

Incentives, 294–295

Income statement *Summary of an organization's financial results—revenues and expenses—over a specified period of time,* 524

An Inconvenient Truth (Gore), 13

Incremental budgeting *Allocating increased or decreased funds to a department by using the last budget period as a reference point; only incremental changes in the budget request are reviewed,* 522–523

Incremental innovations *The creation of products, services, or technologies that modify existing ones,* 320

Incremental model *One type of nonrational model of decision making; managers take small, short-term steps to alleviate a problem,* 202

India, 309–310

Individual approach *One of four approaches to solving ethical dilemmas; ethical behavior is guided by what will result in the individual's best long-term interests, which ultimately is in everyone's self-interest,* 81

Individual behavior, 345

Individual differences and behavior

   demographics and, 339

   ethical dilemma, 367–368

   perception and individual behaviors, 353–357

   personality and individual behavior, 340–344

   stress and individual behavior, 358–362

   values, attitudes, and behavior, 345–348

   work-related attitudes and behaviors, 349–352

Individual objectives, 153

Individualism/collectivism, 123–125

Individualized consideration, 460

Indolence, 425

Industrial engineering, 42

Informal appraisals *Appraisals conducted on an unscheduled basis and consisting of less rigorous indications of employee performance than those used in formal appraisals,* 293

Informal aspects of a company, 345

Informal communication channels *Communication that develops outside the formal structure and does not follow the chain of command,* 488

Informal group *A group formed by people seeking friendship that has no officially appointed leader, although a leader may emerge from the membership,* 409–410

Informal learning, 410

Information overload *An overload that occurs when the amount of information received exceeds a person's ability to handle or process it,* 477

Information technology, 10–11, 508–509

Informational area of control, 516

Informational roles *One of three types of managerial roles: managers receive and communicate information with other people inside and outside the organization as monitors, disseminators, and spokespersons,* 20, 22–23

Ingratiating tactics, 442

Initiating structure, 449

Innovation *Introduction of something new or better, as in goods or services,* 8

    in American companies, 318

    culture and, 321

    failure celebration, 321–323

    fostering, 323–324

    learning perspective and, 519, 520f

    myths about, 319

    resources and, 322

    rewards and, 322

    seeds of, 319

    types of, 320

Innovation Jam, 348

Innovative change *The introduction of a practice that is new to the organization,* 326

Innovative entrepreneurs, 320

The Innovator's Dilemma (Christensen), 309

Inputs *The people, money, information, equipment, and materials required to produce an organization's goods or services; one of four parts of a system, along with outputs, transformation processes, and feedback,* 51, 381–382, 508–509

Insider trading *The illegal trading of a company's stock by people using confidential company information,* 82

Inspirational appeals, 442

Inspirational motivation, 460

Institutional collectivism, 124–125

Institutional power, 377

Instrumentality *The expectation that successful performance of the task will lead to the outcome desired,* 383–384

Integrated product development, 257

Integration *The tendency of the parts of an organization to draw together to achieve a common purpose,* 45, 261

Intellectual stimulation, 460–461

Intergroup conflicts, 426–427

Internal audit *A verification of an organization's financial accounts and statements by the organization's own professional staff,* 525

Internal business perspective, 519, 520f

Internal dimensions of diversity *The human differences that exert a powerful, sustained effect throughout every stage of people's lives (gender, age, ethnicity, race, sexual orientation, physical abilities),* 91–92

Internal locus of control *The belief that one controls one's own destiny,* 27, 342

Internal recruiting *Hiring from the inside, or making people already employed by the organization aware of job openings,* 280–281

Internal Revenue Service (IRS), 84, 253

Internal stakeholders *Employees, owners, and the board of directors, if any,* 70–72

International forces *Changes in the economic, political, legal, and technological global system that may affect an organization,* 79

International Monetary Fund (IMF) *One of three principal organizations designed to facilitate international trade; its purpose is to assist in smoothing the flow of money between nations,* 119

Internet generation, 489–490

Internet *Global network of independently operating but interconnected computers, linking hundreds of thousands of smaller networks around the world,* 10, 105

Interpersonal roles *Of the three types of managerial roles, the roles in which managers interact with people inside and outside of their work units. The three interpersonal roles include figurehead, leader, and liaison activities,* 20, 22–23

Interpersonal space, 127

Intervention *Interference in an attempt to correct a problem,* 316–317

Interviews, 283–285

Intrapreneur *Someone who works inside an existing organization who sees an opportunity for a product or a service and mobilizes the organization's resources to try to realize it,* 25

Intrinsic rewards *The satisfaction, such as a feeling of accomplishment, a person receives from performing a task,* 373

Intuition *Making a choice without the use of conscious thought or logical inference,* 202–203

Invention, 318

Iowa Policy Project, 402

IRS (Internal Revenue Service), 84, 253

ISO 9000 series *Set of company quality-control procedures, developed by the International Organization for Standardization in Geneva, Switzerland, that deals with all activities—from purchasing to manufacturing to inventory to shipping—that can be audited by independent quality-control experts, or "registrars,"* 533

ISO 14000 series *Set of quality-control procedures that extends the concept of the ISO 9000 series, identifying standards for environmental performance,* 533

It's All Politics (Reardon), 236

J

Jargon *Terminology specific to a particular profession or group*, 479–480

Job analysis *The determination of the basic elements of a job*, 274

Job-centered behavior, 448

Job characteristics model The job design model that consists of five core job characteristics that affect three critical psychological states of an employee that in turn affect work outcomes—the employee's motivation, performance, and satisfaction, 388–390

Job description *A summary of what the holder of the job does and how and why he or she does it*, 274

Job design *The division of an organization's work among its employees and the application of motivational theories to jobs to increase satisfaction and performance*, 387

Job diagnostic survey, 390

Job enlargement *Increasing the number of tasks in a job to increase variety and motivation*, 387–388

Job enrichment *Building into a job such motivating factors as responsibility, achievement, recognition, stimulating work, and advancement*, 388

Job involvement *The extent to which one is personally involved with one's job*, 349

Job mapping, 324

Job posting *Placing information about job vacancies and qualifications on bulletin boards, in newsletters, and on the organization's intranet*, 280

Job satisfaction *The extent to which one feels positive or negative about various aspects of one's work*, 350

Job sharing, 397

Job simplification *The process of reducing the number of tasks a worker performs*, 387

Job specification *Description of the minimum qualifications a person must have to perform the job successfully*, 274

Joint ventures *An organization that joins forces with another organization to realize strategic advantages that neither could have achieved alone; a U.S. firm may form a joint venture, also known as a strategic alliance, with a foreign company to share the risks and rewards of starting a new enterprise together in a foreign country*, 116

The Jungle (Sinclair), 287

Just-in-time inventory management, 49

Justice approach *One of four approaches to solving ethical dilemmas; ethical behavior is guided by respect for impartial standards of fairness and equity*, 82

K

Kaizen, 530

Knowledge as competitive advantage, 310

Knowledge management *Implementation of systems and practices to increase the sharing of knowledge and information throughout an organization; also, the development of an organizational structure—and the tools, processes, systems, and structures—that encourages continuous learning and sharing of knowledge and information among employees, for the purpose of making better decisions*, 11

Knowledge workers *Someone whose occupation is principally concerned with generating or interpreting information, as opposed to manual labor*, 59

Kohlberg's theories of ethics, 83

Kotter's model for leading change, 328–329

Kouzes and Posner's leadership traits, 445

L

Labor relations, 276–277

Labor unions, 75

Laissez-faire leadership, 458

Language, 127

Large teams, 416–417

Law of effect, 391

Layoff survivor sickness, 298

Layoffs, 297

Leader-member exchange (LMX) model of leadership *Model proposed by George Graen and Fred Dansereau that emphasizes that leaders have different sorts of relationships with different subordinates*, 462

Leader-member relations, 450

Leaders, 22–23, 126t, 244, 438–439

Leadership *The ability to influence employees to voluntarily pursue organizational goals*, 438

  approaches summary, 443t

  behavioral approaches, 448–449

  contingency approaches, 450–457

  e-leadership, 464–465

  ethical dilemma, 471

  full-range model, 458–461

  leader-member exchange, 462

  nature of, 438–443

  servant, 463–464

  shared, 463

  trait approaches, 444–447

Leading *Motivating, directing, and otherwise influencing people to work hard to achieve the organization's goals*, 15, 413–414, 508, 510; *see also* Communication; Employee motivation; Group; Leadership; Team; Individual differences and behavior

Lean Six Sigma *Quality-control approach that focuses on problem solving and performance improvement—speed with excellence—of a well-defined project*, 534; *see also* Six Sigma

Learned helplessness *The debilitating lack of faith in one's ability to control one's environment*, 342

Learning, 289, 410

Learning organizations *An organization that actively creates, acquires, and transfers knowledge within itself and is able to modify its behavior to reflect new knowledge*, 58–60

Learning perspective, 519, 520f

Legal requirements of human resources, 276–279

Legitimate power *One of five sources of a leader's power that results from formal positions with the organization*, 440

Legitimating tactics, 442

Lewin's change model, 328

Liabilities, 524

Liaison roles, 22–23

Licensing *Company X allows a foreign company to pay it a fee to make or distribute X's product or service,* 116

Life cycle of organizations, 261–262

Life goals and happiness, 13, 508

Line managers *Managers who have the authority to make decisions and usually have people reporting to them,* 251

Linear careers, 139

Liquidity ratios, 524

Listening skills, 31, 494–495

LMX model of leadership; *see* Leader-member exchange model of leadership

Local communities as stakeholders, 75

Locus of control *Measure of how much people believe they control their fate through their own efforts,* 342

The Long Tail (Anderson), 308

Lord of the Rings (movie), 366

Love needs, 374–375

Low-context culture *Culture in which shared meanings are primarily derived from written and spoken words,* 123

Low power distance, 123

Low uncertainty avoidance, 123

M

Macroenvironment *Also called general environment; includes six forces: economic, technological, sociocultural, demographic, political-legal, and international,* 77–79

"Magnificent seven" moral principles, 214

Maintenance role *Relationship-related role consisting of behavior that fosters constructive relationships among team members,* 418

Malcolm Baldrige National Quality Award, 526

Management *The pursuit of organizational goals efficiently and effectively by integrating the work of people through planning, organizing, leading, and controlling the organization's resources,* 4–7, 16–19, 438–439, 538–539; *see also* Global management; Management theories

Management by exception *Control principle that states that managers should be informed of a situation only if data show a significant deviation from standards,* 513

Management by objectives (MBO) *Four-step process in which (1) managers and employees jointly set objectives for the employee, (2) managers develop action plans, (3) managers and employees periodically review the employee's performance, and (4) the manager makes a performance appraisal and rewards the employee according to results,* 151–154, 291

Management by wandering around (MBWA) *Style of management whereby a manager literally wanders around the organization and talks with people across all lines of authority,* 488

Management process *Performing the planning, organizing, leading, and controlling necessary to get things done,* 14

Management pyramid, 16–19, 39

Management science *Sometimes called operations research; branch of quantitative management; method of solving management problems by using mathematics to aid in problem solving and decision making,* 48–49

"Management Secrets of the Grateful Dead" (Green), 243

Management theories

    behavioral viewpoints, 44–47

    classical viewpoints, 40–43

    contingency viewpoint, 53–55

    evolving viewpoints, 38–39

    learning organizations and, 58–60

    quality-management viewpoint, 56–57

    quantitative viewpoints, 48–49

    systems viewpoint, 51–52

Managers

    behavior and change, 313

    challenges to, 8–13

    entrepreneurs compared with, 25–27

    ethnocentric, 111

    functions of, 14–15

    geocentric, 111

    leaders contrasted with, 438–439

    leadership attributes, 126t

    polycentric, 111

    rewards, 4–7

    roles, 20–23, 60

    skill requirements, 28–29

Maquiladoras *U.S. manufacturing plants allowed to operate in Mexico with special privileges in return for employing Mexican citizens,* 113

Market changes, 312

Market culture *Type of organizational culture that has a strong external focus and values stability and control,* 238

Market segmentation, 308–309

Masculinity, 123–125

Mass media, 77

Matrix structure *Fourth type of organizational structure, which combines functional and divisional chains of command in a grid so that there are two command structures—vertical and horizontal,* 254–255

Maturity stage *A stage when the organization becomes very bureaucratic, large, and mechanistic. Also the third stage in the product life cycle; period in which the product starts to fall out of favor, and sales and profits fall off,* 261–262

MBO; *see* Management by objectives

MBWA; *see* Management by wandering around

Means-end chain *A hierarchy of goals; in the chain of management (operational, tactical, strategic), the accomplishment of low-level goals are the means leading to the accomplishment of high-level goals or ends,* 147

Measurable and controllable activities, 245

Measurable goals, 147

Measurement management, 519–521

Mechanistic organization *Organization in which authority is centralized, tasks and rules are clearly specified, and employees are closely supervised,* 260

Media richness *Indication of how well a particular medium conveys information and promotes learning,* 477

Medium *The pathway by which a message travels,* 475

Meetings, 485

Megamergers, 106–107

Mentoring, 187

Mercosur *The largest trade bloc in Latin America, with four core members: Argentina, Brazil, Paraguay, Uruguay,* 121

Mergers and acquisitions, 106–107, 315

Message *The information to be shared,* 475–476

Mexico, 113, 309–310

Middle managers *One of three managerial levels; they implement the policies and plans of the top managers above them and supervise and coordinate the activities of the first-line managers below them,* 17–18

Midlife stage *A period of growth evolving into stability when the organization becomes bureaucratic,* 261

Migration Policy Institute, 90

Millennials, 312, 339

Mindfulness, 55

Mindguards, 421

Mindlessness, 55

Minifirms, 106–107

Minnesota Multiphasic Personality Inventory, 368

Miscommunication, 489

Mission *An organization's purpose or reason for being,* 145, 170

Mission statement *Statement that expresses the purpose of the organization,* 145, 163, 170–171

Mistake proofing, 49

Moderate control, 451

Modular structure *Seventh type of organizational structure, in which a firm assembles product chunks, or modules, provided by outside contractors,* 258

Moneyball (Lewis), 207

Monitor roles, 22–23

Monochronic time *The standard kind of time orientation in U.S. business; preference for doing one thing at a time,* 128

Moral-rights approach *One of four approaches to solving ethical dilemmas; ethical behavior is guided by respect for the fundamental rights of human beings,* 81–82

Most favored nation *This trading status describes a condition in which a country grants other countries favorable trading treatment such as the reduction of import duties,* 121

Motion studies, 41

Motivating factors *Factors associated with job satisfaction—such as achievement, recognition, responsibility, and advancement—all of which affect the job content or the rewards of work performance,* 379–380

Motivation *Psychological processes that arouse and direct goal-directed behavior,* 372–373

compensation and, 394–396

nonmonetary compensation and, 396–399

through mutual accountability, 415

Multicommunicating *The use of technology to participate in several interactions at the same time,* 489

Multicultural conflicts, 427

Multinational corporations *Business firm with operations in several countries,* 109

Multinational organizations *Nonprofit organization with operations in several countries,* 109

Multiplier effect, 6

Multitasking, 21–22

Murder by Proxy (Chiaberi), 352

Mutual-benefit organizations, 19, 246

Myers-Briggs Type Indicator, 285–286

Myths, stories, and legends, 244

The Myths of Innovation (Berkun), 319

N

NAFTA; *see* North American Free Trade Agreement

National Business Ethics survey, 89

National Education Association, 75

National Highway Traffic and Safety Administration, 176

National Labor Relations Board *Legislated in 1935, U.S. commission that enforces procedures whereby employees may vote to have a union and for collective bargaining,* 276

Needs *Physiological or psychological deficiencies that arouse behavior,* 374–378

Negative conflict *Conflict that hinders the organization's performance or threatens its interests,* 423–425

Negative reinforcement *Removal of unpleasant consequences following a desired behavior,* 391

Negative stressors, 359

Negotiator roles, 22–23

Network structure *Sixth type of organizational structure, whereby a central core is linked to outside independent firms by computer connections, which are used to operate as if all were a single organization,* 255–257

New York Stock Exchange, 72

The New York Times, 9–10, 74–75, 196, 214, 257, 305, 311, 441

Newspaper Guild, 75

Newspapers and competitive advantage, 9

Newsweek magazine, 156, 201, 206, 217

Niche products, 308–309, 320

Noise *Any disturbance that interferes with the transmission of a message,* 475–476

Nonprofit organizations, 19, 246

Nonrational models of decision making *Models of decision-making style that explain how managers make decisions; they assume that decision making is nearly always uncertain and risky, making it difficult for managers to make optimum decisions,* 201–203

Nonverbal communication *Messages in a form other than the written or the spoken word,* 476, 481–483

Nonwork demands, 360

Norming *One of five stages of forming a team; stage three, in which conflicts are resolved, close relationships develop, and unity and harmony emerge,* 414

Norms *General guidelines or rules of behavior that most group or team members follow,* 418–419

North American Free Trade Agreement (NAFTA) *Formed in 1994, the trading bloc consisting of the United States, Canada, and Mexico,* 120

O

OB; *see* Organizational behavior

Objective *Also known as goal; a specific commitment to achieve a measurable result within a stated period of time,* 147–149, 151–154

Policy *A standing plan that outlines the general response to a designated problem or situation,* 150

Political-legal forces *Changes in the way politics shape laws and laws shape the opportunities for and threats to an organization,* 79

Political pressures, 312–313

Polycentric managers *Managers who take the view that native managers in foreign offices best understand native personnel and practices, and so the home office should leave them alone,* 111

Polychronic time *Kind of time orientation common in Mediterranean, Latin American, and Arab cultures; preference for doing more than one thing at a time,* 128

Ponzi scheme *A scheme is which cash is used from newer investors to pay off older ones,* 12, 83

Porter's four competitive strategies (four generic strategies) *(1) Cost-leadership, (2) differentiation, (3) cost-focus, (4) focused differentiation. The first two strategies focus on wide markets, the last two on narrow markets,* 173, 180–181

Porter's model for industry analysis *Model proposed by Michael Porter for determining competitiveness within a particular industry; suggests that business-level strategies originate in five primary competitive forces in a firm's environment: (1) threats of new entrants, (2) bargaining power of suppliers, (3) bargaining power of buyers, (4) threats of substitute products or services, and (5) rivalry among competitors,* 179–180

Position power, 451

Positive reinforcement *The use of positive consequences to encourage desirable behavior,* 391, 393

Positive stressors, 359

Power, 439–440

Power distance, 123–125, 250

The Practice of Management (Drucker), 38

Predictably Irrational (Ariely), 153

Predictive modeling *Data-mining technique used to predict future behavior and anticipate the consequences of change,* 208

Preferential treatment, 278

Pressure tactics, 442

Primary dimensions of diversity, 91–92

The Principles of Scientific Management (Taylor), 41

Prior-hypothesis bias, 195

Privacy *The right of people not to reveal information about themselves,* 492–493

Proactive change *Planned change; making carefully thought-out changes in anticipation of possible or expected problems or opportunities; opposite of reactive change,* 311

Proactive personality *Someone who is apt to take initiative and persevere to influence the environment,* 341

Problem solving, 439

Problems *Difficulties that inhibit the achievement of goals,* 197, 323

Procedure *Also known as standard operating procedure; a standing plan that outlines the response to particular problems or circumstances,* 159

Process innovation *A change in the way a product or service is conceived, manufactured, or disseminated,* 320

Process perspectives *Theories of employee motivation concerned with the thought processes by which people decide how to act: expectancy theory, equity theory, and goal-setting theory,* 381

equity theory, 381–383
expectancy theory, 383–385
goal-setting theory, 386

Process, 54

Product divisions *Divisional structures in which activities are grouped around similar products or services,* 253–254

Product innovation *A change in the appearance or the performance of a product or a service or the creation of a new one,* 320

Production teams, 411

Productivity, 507–509

Profit sharing *The distribution to employees of a percentage of the company's profits,* 395–396

Program *A single-use plan encompassing a range of projects or activities,* 150

Programmed conflict *Conflict designed to elicit different opinions without inciting people's personal feelings,* 429

Project *A single-use plan of less scope and complexity than a program,* 150

Project management software *Programs for planning and scheduling the people, costs, and resources to complete a project on time,* 11

Project planning tools, A–A4

Project teams, 411

Promotion, 245, 296

Prospect theory, 219

Prospectors *Managers who develop new products or services and seek out new markets, rather than waiting for things to happen,* 142–143

Punishment *The application of negative consequences to stop or change undesirable behavior,* 392–393

Pygmalion effect, 357

Pyramid hierarchy, 16–19, 39

Q

Quality *The total ability of a product or service to meet customer needs,* 8–9, 56

Quality assurance *A means of ensuring quality that focuses on the performance of workers, urging employees to strive for "zero defects,"* 56

Quality control *A means of ensuring quality whereby errors are minimized by managing each state of production,* 56

Quality-management viewpoint *Perspective that focuses on quality control, quality assurance, and total quality management,* 56–57; *see also* Total quality management

Quantitative management *An evolutionary form of operations research whereby quantitative techniques, such as statistics and computer simulations, are applied to management. Two branches of quantitative management are management science and operations management,* 48–49

Quid pro quo, 279

R

Race and ethnicity, 93–94, 354–355

Radical innovations *New products, services, or technologies that replace existing ones,* 320

Radically innovative change *Change involving a practice that is new to the industry,* 326

Rapt (Gallagher), 22

RATER scale *Scale enabling customers to rate the quality of a service along five dimensions—reliability, assurance, tangibles, empathy, and responsiveness—each on a scale from 1 (for very poor) to 10 (for very good),* 530

Ratio analysis *The evaluation of financial ratios (the relationship of two or more things); includes liquidity ratios, debt management ratios, asset management ratios, and return ratios,* 524

Rational model of decision making *Also called the classical model; the style of decision making that explains how managers should make decisions; it assumes that managers will make logical decisions that will be the optimum in furthering the organization's best interests,* 197–200

Rational persuasion, 442

Reactive change *Change made in response to problems or opportunities as they arise. Compare proactive change,* 310–311

Reactors *Managers who make adjustments only when finally forced to by environmental pressures, 143*

Readiness *The extent to which a follower possesses the ability and willingness to complete a task,* 455

Reading skills, 31, 495–496

Realistic job preview *A picture of both positive and negative features of the job and organization given to a job candidate before he or she is hired,* 281

Receiver *The person for whom a message is intended,* 475–476

Recruiting *The process of locating and attracting qualified applicants for jobs open in the organization,* 280–281
background information, 281–283
interviews, 283–285
methods, 280–281
tests, 285–286

Reduced cycle time *The reduction of steps in the work process,* 533

Referent power *One of five sources of a leader's power deriving from personal attraction,* 440

Refreezing stage, 328

Reinforcement *Anything that causes a given behavior to be repeated or inhibited; the four types are positive, negative, extinction, and punishment,* 391

Reinforcement theory *The belief that behavior reinforced by positive consequences tends to be repeated, whereas behavior reinforced by negative consequences tends not to be repeated,* 391–393

Related diversification *Strategy by which an organization under one ownership operates separate businesses that are related to one another,* 182–183

Relatedness needs, 377

Relationship behavior, 456

Relationship-oriented style, 450–452

Relaxed avoidance *The situation in which a manager decides to take no action in the belief that there will be no great negative consequences,* 215–216

Relaxed change *The situation in which a manager realizes that complete inaction will have negative consequences but opts for the first available alternative that involves low risk,* 216

Reliability *Degree to which a test measures the same thing consistently, so that an individual's score remains about the same over time, assuming the characteristics being measured also remain the same,* 286

Religion, 129

Replicative entrepreneurs, 320

Representative bias *The tendency to generalize from a small sample or a single event,* 218

Resistance to change *An emotional/behavioral response to real or imagined threats to an established work routine,* 325–328

Resource allocator roles, 22–23

Resources and innovation, 322

Responsibility *The obligation one has to perform the assigned tasks,* 250

Responsible Restructuring (Cascio), 206

Results appraisals, 290–291

Results-oriented goals, 148, 508

Résumés, 281–282

Retrenchment strategy, 172

Return on assets (ROA), 524

Return on investment (ROI), 524

Return ratios, 524

Revenues, 524

Reward power *One of five sources of a leader's power that results from the authority to reward subordinates,* 440

Rewards, 245, 322, 372–373, 381–382

Risk propensity *Willingness to gamble or to undertake risk for the possibility of gaining an increased payoff,* 209

Rites and rituals *The activities and ceremonies, planned and unplanned, that celebrate important occasions and accomplishments in an organization's life,* 240

ROA (return on assets), 524

ROI (return on investment), 524

Role modeling, 244

Roles *Socially determined expectations of how an individual should behave in a specific position; sets of behaviors that people expect of occupants of a position,* 359–360, 417–418

Root-cause analysis, 49

Rule *A standing plan that designates specific required action,* 150

S

Sabbaticals, 399

Safety needs, 374–375

Salaries or wages, 6, 294

Sales commission *The percentage of a company's earnings as the result of a salesperson's sales that is paid to that salesperson,* 395

Sarbanes–Oxley Act of 2002 *Often shortened to SarbOx or SOX; act establishing requirements for proper financial record keeping for public companies and penalties for noncompliance,* 83

Satisficing model *One type of nonrational decision-making model; managers seek alternatives until they find one that is satisfactory, not optimal,* 202, 221

Scanlon plan, 396

Scenario analysis or planning, 177–178

Scientific management *Management approach that emphasizes the scientific study of work methods to improve the productivity of individual workers,* 40–42

The Secret Handshake (Reardon), 236

Securities and Exchange Commission (SEC), 83, 174, 395, 469

Security *A system of safeguards for protecting information technology against disasters, system failures, and unauthorized access that result in damage or loss,* 492

Seeds of innovation *The starting point for organizational innovation,* 319

Selection process *The screening of job applicants to hire the best candidate,* 281–284

Selective perception *The tendency to filter out information that is discomforting, that seems irrelevant, or that contradicts one's beliefs,* 353–354

Self-actualization needs, 374–375

Self-centered leaders, 447

Self-efficacy *Personal ability to do a task,* 342

Self-esteem *Self-respect; the extent to which people like or dislike themselves,* 342–343

Self-fulfilling prophecy *Also known as the Pygmalion effect; the phenomenon in which people's expectations of themselves or others leads them to behave in ways that make those expectations come true,* 46, 357

Self-managed teams *Groups of workers who are given administrative oversight for their task domains,* 411–412, 529

Self-monitoring *Observing one's own behavior and adapting it to external situations,* 343

Self-serving bias *The attributional tendency to take more personal responsibility for success than for failure,* 356–357

Selling, 456

Semantics *The study of the meaning of words,* 479–480

Senate Intelligence Committee, 421

Sender *The person wanting to share information,* 475–476

Servant leaders *Leaders who focus on providing increased service to others—meeting the goals of both followers and the organization—rather than on themselves,* 463–464

Service Employees International Union, 75

Services, 530–531

Setting and communication, 482

Sex-role stereotypes, 354

Sexual harassment *Unwanted sexual attention that creates an adverse work environment,* 279

Sexual orientation, 94

Shared leadership *Simultaneous, ongoing, mutual influence process in which people share responsibility for leading,* 463

Simple structure *The first type of organizational structure, whereby an organization has authority centralized in a single person, as well as a flat hierarchy, few rules, and low work specialization,* 252

Single-product strategy *Strategy by which a company makes and sells only one product within its market,* 181–182

Single-use plans *Plans developed for activities that are not likely to be repeated in the future; such plans can be either programs or projects,* 150

Situational analysis, 174

Situational control, 450–451

Situational interview *A structured interview in which the interviewer focuses on hypothetical situations,* 284

Situational leadership theory *Leadership model that holds that leaders should adjust their leadership style according to the readiness of the followers,* 454–457

Six Sigma *A rigorous statistical analysis process that reduces defects in manufacturing and service-related industries,* 322, 534, 542–544

Skill-based pay, 396

Skill-building, 398

Skill variety, 388–389

Skills tests, 285

"Skunkworks," 257

Sliders, 417

Slogans and sayings, 244

Small Business Administration, 25

Small teams, 416

SMART goal *A goal that is Specific, Measurable, Attainable, Results oriented, and has Target dates,* 147–148, 386

Social anxiety disorder, 478

Social capital *Economic or productive potential of strong, trusting, and cooperative relationships,* 60, 273

Social loafing *The tendency of people to exert less effort when working in groups than when working alone,* 417

Social performance, 80

Social pressures, 312–313

Social responsibility *Manager's duty to take action that will benefit society's interests as well as the organization's,* 85–89

Socialized power *Power directed at helping others,* 440

Society for Human Resource Management, 84

Sociocultural forces *Influences and trends originating in a country, society, or culture; human relationships and values that may affect an organization,* 78–79

Soldiering, 40

Sonic Boom (Easterbrook), 106

Span of control *The number of people reporting directly to a given manager,* 250

Span of management, 250

Speaking skills, 497–498

Special-interest groups *Groups whose members try to influence specific issues,* 76

Special-purpose teams *A team that meets to solve a special or onetime problem,* 529

Specific goals, 147

Speed to market, 309

Spiral careers, 139

Spokesperson roles, 22–23

SQ3R Method, 31, 495–496

Stability strategy *One of three grand strategies, this strategy involves little or no significant change,* 172

Staff personnel *Staff with advisory functions; they provide advice, recommendations, and research to line managers,* 251

Stakeholders *People whose interests are affected by an organization's activities,* 71
external, 71, 73–79
internal, 70–72

Standard operating procedure *Also known as procedure; a standing plan that outlines the response to particular problems or circumstances,* 150

Standards, 512–513

Standing plans *Plans developed for activities that occur repeatedly over a period of time; such plans consist of policies, procedures, or rules,* 150

Start-ups, 320–321

Static budgets, 523

Statistical process control *A statistical technique that uses periodic random samples from production runs to see if quality is being maintained within a standard range of acceptability,* 533–534

Steady-state careers, 139

Stereotype *A standardized mental picture resulting from oversimplified beliefs about a certain group of people,* 481

Stereotyping *The tendency to attribute to an individual the characteristics one believes are typical of the group to which that individual belongs,* 354–355

Stock options *The right to buy a company's stock at a future date for a discounted price; often a benefit given to key employees,* 294, 396

Stories *A narrative based on true events, which is repeated—and sometimes embellished upon—to emphasize a particular value,* 240, 244

Storming *The second of five stages of forming a team in which individual personalities, roles, and conflicts within the group emerge,* 413–414

Strategic allies *Describes the relationship of two organizations that join forces to achieve advantages that neither can perform as well alone,* 74, 116

Strategic control *Monitoring performance to ensure that strategic plans are being implemented and taking corrective action as needed,* 173, 515

Strategic goals *Goals that are set by and for top management and focus on objectives for the organization as a whole,* 147, 149

Strategic human resource planning *The development of a systematic, comprehensive strategy for (1) understanding current employee needs and (2) predicting future employee needs,* 274

Strategic management *A five-step process that involves managers from all parts of the organization in the formulation and implementation of strategies and strategic goals: establish the mission and the vision; establish the grand strategy; formulate the strategic plans; carry out the strategic plans; maintain strategic control,* 165–167
competitive analysis, 174
dynamics of, 164–168

ethical dilemma, 193
execution, 184–187
forecasting, 177–178
planning and, 140
process, 169–173
strategy formulation, 179–183
SWOT analysis, 174–177

Strategic Management Society, 167

Strategic planning *Determining what an organization's long-term goals should be for the next 1–10 years with the resources it expects to have available; done by top management,* 146, 165–167, 173

Strategic positioning *Strategy that, according to Michael Porter, attempts to achieve sustainable competitive advantage by preserving what is distinctive about a company,* 168

Strategy *A large-scale action plan that sets the direction for an organization,* 165, 167–168, 184–185, 521

Strategy formulation *The process of choosing among different strategies and altering them to best fit the organization's needs,* 173

Strategy implementation *The execution of strategic plans,* 173

Strategy map *A visual representation of the four perspectives of the balanced scorecard that enables managers to communicate their goals so that everyone in the company can understand how their jobs are linked to the overall objectives of the organization,* 519–520

The Straw Bale House, 181

Strength perspective *Perspective of organizational culture that assumes that the strength of a corporate culture is related to a firm's long-term financial performance,* 242

Stress *The tension people feel when they are facing or enduring extraordinary demands, constraints, or opportunities and are uncertain about their ability to handle them effectively,* 358–362

Stressor *The source of stress,* 358

Strong stressors, 359

Structural area of control, 516

Structured interview *Interview in which the interviewer asks each applicant the same questions and then compares the responses to a standardized set of answers,* 284

Study habits, 30–31

Subjective appraisals *Performance evaluations based on a manager's perceptions of an employee's traits or behaviors,* 291

Subsystems *The collection of parts that make up the whole system,* 51

Sunk-cost bias (sunk-cost fallacy) *Biased way of thinking in which managers add up all the money already spent on a project and conclude it is too costly to simply abandon it,* 218

Supervisors, 18

Supplier *A person or organization that provides supplies—raw materials, services, equipment, labor, or energy—to other organizations,* 73

Supportive style of leadership, 453

Surroundings, 398

Sustainability *Economic development that meets the needs of the present without compromising the ability of future generations to meet their own needs,* 13, 508

Touch and communication, 482

Toy Story (movie), 26, 441

TQM; *see* Total quality management

Trade protectionism *The use of government regulations to limit the import of goods and services,* 117–118

Trading bloc *Also known as an economic community; a group of nations within a geographical region that have agreed to remove trade barriers with one another,* 119

Training *Educating technical and operational employees in how to better do their current jobs,* 244, 288–289

Trait approaches to leadership *Attempts to identify distinctive characteristics that account for the effectiveness of leaders,* 444–447

Transactional leader *One who focuses on the interpersonal transactions between managers and employees,* 458–459

Transactional leadership *Leadership style that focuses on clarifying employees' roles and task requirements and providing rewards and punishments contingent on performance,* 458–459

Transfers, 297

Transformation processes *The organization's capabilities in management and technology that are applied to converting inputs into outputs; one of four parts of a system, along with inputs, outputs, and feedback,* 51

Transformational leadership *Leadership style that transforms employees to pursue organizational goals over self-interests,* 459–461

Transitory careers, 139

Transportation, 104–105

Traveling overseas, 103, 109–110, 133–134

Trend analysis *A hypothetical extension of a past series of events into the future,* 177

Troy (movie), 468

TRPA (Tahoe Regional Planning Authority), 76

Turnover *The movement of employees in and out of an organization when they obtain and then leave their jobs,* 351

20-20 hindsight bias, 195

Two core principles of TQM *(1) People orientation—everyone involved with the organization should focus on delivering value to customers; and (2) improvement orientation—everyone should work on continuously improving the work processes,* 528

Two-factor theory *Herzberg's theory that proposes that work satisfaction and dissatisfaction arise from two different work factors—work satisfaction from so-called motivating factors and work dissatisfaction from so-called hygiene factors,* 379–380

Type A behavior pattern *Behavior describing people involved in a chronic, determined struggle to accomplish more in less time,* 359

U

Uncertainty avoidance, 123–125

Underemployed *Working at a job that requires less education than one has,* 94

Unfreezing stage, 328

Unified hierarchy, 153

Unions and associations, 75

United Auto Workers, 75

U.S. Bureau of Labor Statistics, 6, 275

U.S. Census Bureau, 275

U.S. Chamber of Commerce, 295

U.S. Department of Justice, 161

U.S. Department of Labor, 368, 403

U.S. Department of Transportation, A4

U.S. Food and Drug Administration, 161

U.S. International Trade Commission, 118

U.S. Postal Service, 352

U.S. Supreme Court, 100

Unity of command *Principle that stresses an employee should report to no more than one manager in order to avoid conflicting priorities and demands,* 249

University of Michigan Leadership Model, 448

Unrelated diversification *Operating several businesses that are not related to one another under one ownership,* 182

Unrepresentative sample bias, 195

Unstructured interview *Interview in which the interviewer asks probing questions to find out what the applicant is like,* 283–284

Upward communication *Communication that flows from lower levels to higher levels,* 487

U.S. News and World Report, 212

USA Today, 106, 127

Utilitarian approach *One of four approaches to solving ethical dilemmas; ethical behavior is guided by what will result in the greatest good for the greatest number of people,* 81

V

Valence *The value or the importance a worker assigns to a possible outcome or reward,* 383–384

Validity *Extent to which a test measures what it purports to measure and extent to which it is free of bias,* 286

Value orientation, 209–210

Value stream mapping, 49

Value system *The pattern of values within an organization,* 81

Values *Abstract ideals that guide one's thinking and behavior across all situations; the relatively permanent and deeply held underlying beliefs and attitudes that help determine a person's behavior,* 81, 345, 348

Vancouver Sun, 230

Variable budget *Allowing the allocation of resources to vary in proportion with various levels of activity,* 523

Vertical communication, 486–487

Vertical hierarchy of authority, 247

Vertical loading, 388

Videoconferencing *Using video and audio links along with computers to enable people located at different locations to see, hear, and talk with one another,* 11, 490–491

Virtual corporations, 255

Virtual learning, 289

Virtual offices, 491

Virtual organizations *Organization whose members are geographically apart, usually working with e-mail, collaborative computing, and other computer connections, while often appearing to customers and others to be a single, unified organization with a real physical location,* 59, 255, 257–258

Virtual teams, 407

Vision *A long-term goal describing what an organization wants to become; it is a clear sense of the future and the actions needed to get there,* 460

Vision statement *Statement that expresses what the organization should become and where it wants to go strategically,* 145, 163, 171

W

Wages or salaries, 6, 294

The Wall Street Journal, 9, 37, 54, 66, 105, 156, 193, 199, 356, 385, 394, 445

Warfare, 425

Web 2.0, 314

When Talking Makes Things Worse! (Stiebel), 473

Whistle-blower *An employee who reports organizational misconduct to the public,* 84

White Men Can't Jump (movie), 95

Who Wants to Be a Millionaire (TV show), 225

Wholly-owned subsidiary *A foreign subsidiary, or subordinate section of an organization, that is totally owned and controlled by the organization,* 116

Wisdom, attitude of, 37

The Wisdom of Crowds (Surowiecki), 421

Women as executives, 445–446, 484

Work environment; *see also* Global management diversity, 90–95

ethical dilemma, 100

ethical responsibilities, 80–84

external stakeholders, 71, 73–79

internal stakeholders, 70–72

social responsibilities, 85–89

Work-life benefits, 398

Work-related attitudes, 349–350

Work specialization, 249

Workplace behaviors, 351–352

Workplace stress, 358–362

World Bank *One of three principal organizations designed to facilitate international trade; its purpose is to provide low-interest loans to developing nations for improving transportation, education, health, and telecommunications,* 119

World Trade Organization *One of three principal organizations designed to facilitate international trade; it is designed to monitor and enforce trade agreements,* 119

Writing skills, 496–497

Y

Youth stage *The stage in which the organization is in a pre-bureaucratic phase, one of growth and expansion,* 261

Z

Zero-based budgeting (ZBB), 522